P_0	Put value at date 0
P	Price of security
P_i	Probability of state i
rf	Continuously compound risk-free rate
RF	Discrete compound risk-free rate
r_{ij}	Correlation coefficient between security i and j
R_t	Return in period t
$\overline{R}$	Arithmetic average return
ROE	Return on Equity
RP_M	Risk premium on the Market Portfolio
S_0	Spot asset value at date 0
$\sigma 2$	Variance of security returns
σ	Standard deviation of returns
S_p	Sharpe performance measure
$S_t^{d/f}$	Spot exchange rate domestic per foreign at date t
T_p	Treynor performance measure
UV_T	Unit value at date T
X	Option exercise price
X_i	Percentage invested in security i

INVESTMENT

INVESTMENT

CONCEPTS
·
ANALYSIS
·
STRATEGY

FOURTH EDITION

ROBERT C. RADCLIFFE
University of Florida

HarperCollinsCollegePublishers

Acquisitions Editor: Kirsten D. Sandberg
Director of Development: Lisa Pinto
Project Coordination, Text and Cover Design: Ruttle, Shaw & Wetherill, Inc.
Cover Illustration: Tracy Baldwin
Production Manager: Willie Lane
Compositor: Ruttle, Shaw & Wetherill, Inc.
Printer and Binder: R. R. Donnelley & Sons Company
Cover Printer: The Lehigh Press, Inc.

Investment: Concepts, Analysis, Strategy, Fourth Edition

Copyright © 1994 by HarperCollins College Publishers

Library of Congress Cataloging-in-Publication Data
Radcliffe, Robert C.
    Investment : concepts, analysis, strategy / Robert C. Radcliffe.
    —4th ed.
        p.   cm.
    Includes bibliographical references and index.
    ISBN 0-673-46657-4
    1. Investments.   2. Investment analysis.   3. Securities.
    4. Speculation.   I. Title.
    HG4521.R26   1994   93-44888
                                                        CIP

93 94 95 96 9 8 6 5 4 3 2 1

To my family with love and appreciation

CONTENTS

PART 3   ANALYSES   357

CHAPTER 11

Bond Valuation   358

CHAPTER 12

Bond Trading   394

C H A P T E R **15**

C H A P T E R **16**

Instructors and students who seek moderately advanced coverage of the material, yet highly interactive pedagogy and presentation to facilitate the learning process, will no doubt appreciate the fourth edition of *Investment: Concepts . Analysis . Strategy*. This revision renews the educational objectives of preceding editions. Principal among these goals are:

- To integrate theoretical concepts with practical investment applications,
- To stress the economic rationale for various investment concepts, and
- To cultivate the reader's appreciation for well-functioning security markets in today's world economy.

Market feedback confirms that the approach and the content of this new edition indeed support these objectives more effectively than did previous versions of the text. However, this revision entails more than a straightfoward update of content to reflect recent developments in academic theory and security markets; I have taken to heart—and to the printed page—a great many suggestions from instructors and students alike. In most cases, these recommendations persuaded me to refine already well-received aspects of my book. However, in other instances, reviewers demanded that I focus on improving the overall presentation. Among these improvements, readers will note the following:

- A reduction in the number of equations, because even the best students get so caught up in math (the details) that they miss the economic underpinnings (the framework). While texts like this require vigorous use of statistics and equations, I use them only when a student absolutely needs to know.
- A reorganization that enabled me to streamline coverage by some 100 pages without compromising detail and depth of analysis. As reviewers advised, I deleted a number of topics, shortened a few others, and consolidated coverage. For example, I left the intricacies of defined benefit pension asset allocation to more advanced courses, abbreviated the analysis of the determinants of risk-free interest rates, and covered equity valuation in a single chapter.

The fourth edition continues to concentrate on asset allocation with software support by considering the very relevant decisions that investors must make, such as: "How should assets be allocated?" "How should assets be managed?" and "Who should manage them?" Ideal for upper-level investments courses and courses (or two-course sequences) on security analysis and portfolio management, the text moves from more descriptive characteristics of individual markets and instruments and their technical analysis to overall portfolio strategies and techniques of portfolio risk management.

MAJOR CONTENT CHANGES IN THE FOURTH EDITION

Anyone who reads the daily financial press knows how dramatically security markets have changed over the past quarter-century, especially in the late 1980s and early 1990s if not within the last half hour. Innovation is the norm. Technological advances and drastic political reform are upheaving once-fettered security markets to the point where I found myself grappling with what to add and what to delete. After contemplating global market needs, I focused on the following significant improvements to this new edition:

1. *International Component.* Chapter 17, "International Investments," continues to cover topics unique to international investing, such as exchange rates and how to take international security positions. Also, to the extent appropriate in each chapter, I have integrated global coverage in two ways: (1) as a matter of style, where my examples feature non-U.S. companies, and (2) as a matter of explanation. For instance, Chapter 3 on security markets discusses how to conduct security transactions in the United Kingdom and Japan. Chapter 4 on market indexes includes non-U.S. security indexes as well. And Chapter 13 on equity valuation looks at the problems of differences in accounting principles among countries. Furthermore, the text examines who owns what securities and who manages them globally, and it covers international market value and how to determine dollar value of securities outstanding in foreign and domestic markets.

2. *Reorganization.* I reorganized content to merge similar topics in one section and to avoid unnecessary repetition. For an obvious example, readers should look for yield curve theory in Chapter 11, "Bond Valuation," with other bond concepts rather than in the general concepts section. In addition, CAPM-based performance measures are now discussed exclusively in the performance measurement chapter and only referenced in the CAPM chapter. I have also abridged or deleted material from the third edition. Specifically, I abbreviated considerably the analysis of the determinants of risk-free interest rates, presented equity valuation techniques in a single chapter (Chapter 13), and combined option valuation and trading in one chapter (Chapter 16). Finally, I eliminated much of the material on defined benefit pension fund asset allocation.

3. *Derivative Concepts.* Due to the increasing use of futures and options, the concepts section of this edition features a new stand-alone chapter on the fundamentals of derivative valuation and how to use them in hedging risk. Most examples use spot assets that do not currently exist, because the major goal of the chapter is to relate options and futures valuation and trading applications rather than to concentrate on any one contract. For more extensive treatment, instructors can use Chapter 9 on derivatives as an introduction to Chapter 15, "Financial Futures," and Chapter 16, "Financial Options."

4. *New Practical Material.* This edition includes a great number of practical applications, often not found in competing investment texts. Topics include:

   - Evaluation of who owns and who manages financial asset classes
   - An entire chapter (Chapter 20) on how to select professional investment managers
   - Detailed examination of the normal density distribution and how to interpret return standard deviations

- Demonstration of how to express expected returns and standard deviations in terms of percentile return distributions
- Analysis of how to extrapolate single period expected returns and risks to investment horizons longer than a single period
- Discussion of AIMR Performance Presentation Standards
- List of major types of investment computer software and data
- Timely chapter-long case (Chapter 14) on the recent decline of IBM to bring real-world business challenges, decisions, and outcomes into the classroom for analysis

5. *Expanded Assignment Materials.* There are more *Chartered Financial Analyst Exam Questions* at the end of virtually every chapter which are marked by icon for quick reference. Formatted like those found in the CFA certification examination, these give students extra practice for sitting for the exam. There are also more *Datafile Analysis* problems marked by computer icon at the end of every chapter and supported by software described below under Supplements. These short research projects allow students to examine concepts using a large dataset of actual security market information and to practice with such decision-making tools as personal computers and investments software.

6. *Improved Pedagogy and Design.* For more active involvement in the learning process, readers will find *new boxes on special investments topics* pulled from the popular business press. Scattered throughout text, these excerpts heighten human interest in more theoretical content. This edition retains the popular end-of-chapter *Review Problems,* with complete solutions worked out step by step so that students have at least one or two demonstrations of problem-solving methodology used in each chapter. These appear ahead of assignment material at the end of every chapter. Finally, for greater student accessibility, the text sports a new two-color design, re-rendered and rejuvenated art, and more effective, pedagogical use of color with key equations and other features highlighted for quick reference.

Text Organization

Major sections of the book are identical to previous editions. Chapter content within each section, however, is somewhat different.

In Part 1, four chapters provide an *overview* to why security markets exist (Chapter 1), types of securities traded (Chapter 2), market transactions (Chapter 3), and security market indexes (Chapter 4).

Major *concepts* are presented in Part 2. A new Chapter 5 presents various principles of security returns as well as how portfolio risk can be measured using return standard deviations. My experience suggests that students need to know more about what standard deviations are intended to measure than they get from simply knowing a formula. Thus, I have developed an extensive review of how one should interpret return standard deviations. This includes a discussion of percentile return distributions, a device that practitioners use to communicate investment risk to individual investors. The chapter concludes by examining historical average returns and standard deviations on major asset classes.

Portfolio theory is presented in Chapter 6. In addition to the standard treatment of naive and efficient diversification, a detailed example is presented to show how one might calculate an efficient frontier of various asset classes. An appendix to the chapter shows how single period returns and risks can be extrapolated to longer investment horizons. Chapter 7 is devoted to a discussion of the classic Capital Asset Pricing Model (CAPM). Chapter 8 expands on the CAPM by discussing multi-beta versions and Arbitrage Pricing Theory.

Chapter 9 is new to this edition and treats basic concepts of derivative valuation. I believe that the theory of derivative valuation (the Black-Scholes model in particular) has become so important a part of finance theory that it deserves a major place in any review of investment concepts.

This section concludes with a discussion of efficient markets in Chapter 10. In this edition, I have chosen to define levels of market efficiency consistent with Fama's 1991 approach in his review article *Efficient Capital Markets II.*

Part 3, *Security Analysis,* includes seven chapters dealing with individual security types. Two chapters each are given to bonds, equities, and derivatives. Special characteristics of international investing are discussed in Chapter 17.

Investment *strategy* is presented in Part 4. Much of this material comes from my personal experience consulting for sponsors of defined benefit and defined contribution pension plans. Although the material is expressed in the context of an institutional investor, it applies equally well to individual investors. I have chosen to focus on institutional investors since this is the environment in which most students who pursue an investment career will work. In addition, by focusing on large portfolios, all aspects of portfolio management can be addressed. The section begins with an overview of portfolio management discussed in Chapter 18. This includes a discussion of the ''Portfolio Investment Process,'' the creation of a ''Strategic Asset Allocation,'' and a written ''Statement of Investment Policy.'' More time is spent on these topics than is typical for an investment text because of the importance they play in developing a rational investment strategy. Practical aspects of developing a strategic and/or tactical asset allocation are discussed in Chapter 19. Chapter 20 follows with a discussion of how investors should go about finding one or more professional investment managers. Manager selection is a critical topic to most institutional investors and of growing importance to individual investors who invest through mutual funds. The section concludes with a discussion of performance monitoring. An important part of this chapter is the review of the *Performance Presentation Standards* recently developed by the Association for Investment Management and Research.

ASSIGNMENTS AND SUPPLEMENTS TO THE FOURTH EDITION

Datafile Analyses

When students themselves analyze actual market data, they can more readily connect investment concepts to realistic applications and can promote these analytical skills in the job market. In these Datafile Analysis assignments, students use personal computers to examine various datasets of historical security market information. Such analysis provides several pedagogical advantages over the typical end-of-chapter problems. Abstract investment ideas take shape and meaning in the real world. Students increase their awareness of types and uses of data available and enrich their knowledge of the techniques used by professional investment managers and consultants. Students improve their critical-thinking and computer skills. Perhaps most important, students exploit their own creativity by pursuing their own research interests. Datafile Analyses, found at the end of most chapters, include the following:

- risk management using both naive stock diversification and asset allocation
- calculation of mean-variance efficient frontiers
- examination of the January Effect on large and small stocks
- test of the predictability of future security returns using past returns
- cross-country return correlations and global diversification
- financial statement analysis
- selection of actively managed U.S. equity mutual funds
- CAPM-based performance of U.S. equity mutual funds

   Important note: Many of these analyses are abbreviated versions of actual studies conducted by investment consultants for institutional and individual investors. Instructors can use each Datafile Analysis as a separate homework assignment, as part of an extensive term project, or as an in-class demonstration if the classroom is equipped with a computer, a liquid crystal display, and an overhead projector.

Datasets Available for Use in Datafile Analysis
Compiled by Robert C. Radcliffe, University of Florida
Stored in Lotus 1-2-3 WK1 format and available on IBM-compatible diskettes, these datasets contain extensive historical information on security prices, dividends, returns, yield curves, and so forth. Types of data include the following:

INTRATES.WK1: Year-end 1970–1992.
Yields to maturity on; U.S. Treasuries (1, 2, 3, 5, 7, 10, 39 year maturity), Tbills (3, 6, 12 mo.), Fed Funds, Com'l Paper, Bankers Accept., CD's, Euro$, Muni Aaa & Baa, Corp A & Baa.

INDXDATA.WK1: Year-end 1929-1992.
CPI, Per share Prices, Earnings, Dividends & Book Value (SP500, SP400, & DJIA), Per share Balance Sheet & Income Statement Data (SP400) and U.S. Population and GNP.

MFEQUITY.WK1: Approximately 200 U.S. mutual funds which invest in domestic equities. Quarterly Rates of Return: 1st Quarter 1981 to recent quarter. Other data includes (as of March 1993): Name, Style, Assets ($ million), Expense Ratio, Min $ Purchase, Max Sales Charge, 12b-1 fee, Deferred Sales Charge, Portfolio

Turnover, Manager Tenure, Price to Earnings Ratio, Price to Book Ratio, Earnings Growth, Market Cap., Asset Allocation, Industry Allocation (by ten industry types)

RTNSMNLY.WK1, RTNSQTYLY.WK1 and RTNSYRLY.WK1: Monthly, quarterly, and annual returns. Start of 1926 or as available.

CPI, 30-day Tbills, Com'l Paper, CDs, 1-Year Fixed (DFA), Govt Bonds (20-yr and IT), Corp Bonds (20-yr and IT), 5-Year Fixed, U.S. Agencies, Pref. Stock, Lehman: Govt/Corp (Total, LT & IT), Govt (Total, LT & IT), Corp (Total, LT & IT), Lehman Mortgage Backed

S&P 500, 400, 100 & Midcap
Wilshire 5000 Equal and Value Weighted
Russell 3000, 2000, 1000, 2500
Dow Jones Industrial Average & Equity Index
NYSE, AMEX, NASDAQ, Value Line
DFA 6-10, 6-8, 9-10 (Small Stock Portfolios)
EAFE, Europe, Europe XUK, PacRim, PacRim XJPN,
Finl Times ($ & £), UK Small Stock ($ & £), Pounds to Dollar Returns
Japan Large Stock ($ & Yen), Japan Small Stock ($ & Yen), Yen to Dollar
    Returns
Frankfurt, London & Tokyo

STOCKS.WK1: Year-end 1988 through 1992.
Balance sheet and income statement information on the 30 DJIA companies. Data is presented using a template identical to the format used in the PC-PLUS product of Standard & Poors Corp.

Other datasets include detailed information on bond mutual funds, international equity mutual funds, non-U.S. country stock returns, and ten years of quarterly prices and dividends of stock included in the Dow Jones Industrial Average.

ASSETALL
Created by Robert C. Radcliffe, University of Florida
The ASSETALL computer package calculates mean-variance efficient frontiers for up to 50 securities based on their expected returns, standard deviations of returns, and correlation coefficients. The menu-driven program allows for three basic options. Students can: (a) create or revise an input file, (b) calculate an efficient frontier where short sales are *not* allowed, and (c) calculate an efficient frontier where short sales *are* permissible. The program automatically saves the output efficient frontiers according to the dataset name specified by the user. Students can print output files through the program itself or through the DOS print command. Although the menu commands should be sufficient, as most students can figure out how to run the program on their own, a user's manual is stored in ASCII format on the program disks for students to print and use as reference.

A number of preprogrammed spreadsheet packages are provided that allow the student to perform a number of complex investment calculations. These include Black-Scholes option valuations (with continuous or discrete dividends), portfolio expected returns, and standard deviations for a large number of securities and forecasts of percentile terminal wealth distributions for periods of between two and sixty years.

Important note on software: Instructors should ask their HarperCollins representative for the IBM-compatible master disks containing the datasets and ASSETALL, *both of which are free only to adopters for students to copy and use.*

Instructor's Manual with Test Bank

Prepared by Robert C. Radcliffe, University of Florida, and Steven P. Bouchard, Goldey Beacom College

To save instructors valuable lecture preparation time, the new Instructor's Manual includes a thoroughly revised and expanded Test Bank, documentation for dataset and ASSETALL software, supplemental handouts, and detailed solutions to end-of-chapter questions and problems. Instructors who need the Test Bank in electronic form should contact their publisher's representative for more information.

Study Guide

Created by R. Stevenson Hawkey, Golden Gate University

Important note: Sample pages from this new *Study Guide* immediately follow the preface. More accessible to students, this guide features a section on the CFA designation and on how to use a financial calculator—unique for an investment supplement! To build student confidence, each chapter features the following sections: an Overview, a Summary of Key Concepts, a Summary of Key Equations, review questions, review problems (with calculator keystrokes), and objective item test bank. Answers and solutions appear either at the end of the chapter or in end-of-guide appendices. Instructors should ask their HarperCollins representative for a copy, because bookstores will no doubt want to make it available for students who need help.

ACKNOWLEDGMENTS

Truly engaging educational products are never concocted in some obscure laboratory far removed from both classroom and the investments business. Users of previous editions, professional and academic colleagues, manuscript reviewers, supplements authors, and students have all contributed to my writing and teaching efforts in the field of investments.

In addition I would like to acknowledge the help of the following people:
Gilbert Bickum, University of Western Kentucky
Steven P. Bouchard, Goldey Beacom College
Eugene F. Brigham, University of Florida

Robert Brooks, University of Alabama
Young Hoon Byun, Daeyu Securities, Co., Ltd.
Alyce Campbell, University of Oregon
Anne Christ, BenchMark Portfolios, Inc.
Maureen Connors, Dimensional Fund Advisors, Inc.
Vinay Datar, University of Florida
Anand Desai, University of Florida
Gautum Dhingra, Hewitt Associates, Inc.
David Distad, University of California, Berkeley
Dale Domian, Michigan State University
Frank Elston, Eastern New Mexico University
Thomas Eyssell, University of Missouri, St. Louis
James Feller, Middle Tennessee State University
John Gallo, University of Southern Maine
Louis C. Gapenski, University of Florida
Jerry Gramig, PI Analytics, Inc.
R. Stevenson Hawkey, Golden Gate University
Shalom Hochman, University of Houston
Joel Houston, University of Florida
Roger Huang, Vanderbilt University
Bill Jerkovsky, California State University, Northridge
David Kushner, TK Capital Management
Richard LaNear, Missouri Southern State University
Haim Levy, University of Florida
Miles Livingston, University of Florida
Christopher Ma, Texas Tech University
Timothy Manuel, University of Montana
Adolfo Marzol, Chase Home Mortgage
Lalatendu Misra, University of Texas, San Antonio
Robert Mooradian, University of Florida
M.P. Narayanan, University of Michigan
M. Nimalandran, University of Florida
David Nye, University of Florida
Thomas O'Brien, University of Connecticut
Richard Ogden, PI Analytics, Inc.
Robert Pari, Bentley College
Robert Penter, Hewitt Associates, Inc.
John Pickett, Principal/EGT Inc.
Michael Ryngaert, University of Florida
Ed Saunders, Northeastern University
Kevin Scanlon, University of Notre Dame
Louis Scott, University of Illinois at Urbana-Champaign
John Settle, Portland State University
Pat Smith, University of New Hampshire
Paul Swanson, University of Cincinnati
Brian Thompson, Principal/EGT Inc.

Weston Tompkins, Principal/EGT Inc.
Robert Webb, University of Virginia
Robert Wood, Bridgewater College
Robert Wood, Pension Consultant
Soushan Wu, National Chiao-Tung University, Taiwan
Thomas Zwirlein, University of Colorado, Colorado Springs

Special thanks are due Sandra Tompkins, who efficiently typed the manuscript under tight time constraints. A number of other individuals added significant value to the book, especially Steven Hawkey and Steve Bouchard, who increased the quality and utility of the supplements package. The book team at HarperCollins deserves a nod for its efforts on this project: my sponsor Kirsten Sandberg; Kate Steinbacher in sales and marketing; Lisa Pinto, Arianne Weber, and Lynn Brown in development; and Paula Soloway in production. Finally, the person who deserves my deepest thanks is my wife, Irene. Without her patience and support, this revision could not have been completed.

R.C.R.

CHAPTER 6: *Portfolio Theory*

A. OVERVIEW

Common sense and economic theory both suggest that investors (1) prefer more wealth to less, and (2) are risk-averse. Therefore, as the uncertainty increases about a security's future value, investors will demand higher rates of return as inducement to invest; and, in evaluating securities and portfolios, the two critical measures will be expected return (**"mean"**) and variability of return (**"variance"** or standard deviation). Measuring expected return is reasonably straightforward, but measuring risk—particularly *portfolio* risk—is more complex.

Investors minimize portfolio risk by diversifying, that is, by taking advantage of the tendency of securities's returns to offset one another to some extent. Much of the diversifiable risk is eliminated with portfolios containing as few as 20 randomly-selected securities. But portfolio risk cannot be eliminated completely through diversification; and so even a fully-diversified portfolio retains **systematic** or **market risk.**

The investor's ability to reduce portfolio risk through diversification depends on the **correlation** among pairs of securities in the portfolio. If the investor can estimate expected returns, standard deviations, and correlations for pairs of securities, then one can determine the security combinations that provide the minimum risk for any specified level of return. The combination is an **efficient portfolio**; viewed together, these portfolios define the **efficient frontier**. By overlaying an individual's **indifference curves** onto the efficient frontier, the investor can select the portfolio providing the lowest risk consistent with the desired rate of return.

When a risk-free asset is introduced, the efficient frontier can then be described in terms of combinations of the risk-free asset and a *single*, fully diversified **market portfolio**. All investors will buy some combination of these two assets. This implies that the risk of a *single security* can be described in terms of its variability *relative to* the market portfolio, since it is only as part of the market portfolio that the security will be held. This relative risk measure is called **beta.**

B. SUMMARY OF KEY CONCEPTS

1. Most people exhibit positive utility of wealth, but diminishing *marginal* utility of wealth. That is, investors prefer more wealth to less! Moreover, the loss of utility associated with the loss of one unit of wealth is greater than the increase in utility associated with the gain of one unit of wealth. Consequently, investors are risk-averse and demand **risk premiums** to induce them to buy risky securities.

2. Investors care mostly about the risk and return of their portfolios (i.e., of their *total* wealth), and individual securities are considered risky only to the extent that they add risk to the portfolio. The most widely-used measure of portfolio risk is standard deviation.

Sample page: Each Overview reintroduces the reader to key chapter points. Summary of Key Concepts captures each critical concept in one or two sentences for quick review.

7. If investors can borrow or lend at the risk-free rate, in addition to investing in efficient portfolios of risky assets, the efficient frontier changes. It becomes a straight line joining the risk-free asset with a single, optimal risky portfolio, and points on that straight line **dominate** all other investment possibilities.

8. *All* investors will select varying combinations of the risk-free asset and the optimal risky portfolio; that is, selection of the optimal risky portfolio to hold no longer depends on the individual risk preferences of the investor.

9. Since no investor will wish to hold risky securities that are not in the optimal portfolio (they would not be *efficient*), that portfolio *will be the market*, and it is therefore referred to as **the market portfolio.**

10. The risk of a single security can now be defined in terms of the contribution it makes to the risk (standard deviation) of the market portfolio. This risk measure is called **beta**. It is the ratio of the standard deviation of the security to the standard deviation of the market, multiplied by the correlation coefficient between the security and the market.

C. SUMMARY OF KEY EQUATIONS

1. Average returns, variances, and standard deviations of historical returns are calculated as follows:

$$\overline{R} = \frac{\sum_{t=1}^{N} (R_t)}{N}$$

$$s^2 = \frac{\sum_{i=1}^{N} [R_i - \overline{R}]^2}{N-1}$$

2. The covariance between two securities' returns is shown by the following equation:

$$COV_{i,j} = \frac{\sum_{t=1}^{N} (R_{i,t} - \overline{R}_i)(R_{j,t} - \overline{R}_j)}{N-1}$$

3. The correlation coefficient is derived from the covariance:

$$r_{i,j} = \frac{COV_{i,j}}{\sigma_i \sigma_j}$$

Sample page: Summary of Key Equations enumerates the most important numerical tools, with a quick note on application. (Equations shown in these sample pages are for demonstration purposes only and have not been proofread for accuracy.)

8.   We can now define the return on the combined portfolio in terms of the risk-free rate plus a risk premium, where the risk premium depends on the return *per unit of risk* multiplied by the level of risk (portfolio standard deviation):

$$E(R_c) = RF + \sigma_c [\frac{E(R_p) - RF}{\sigma_p}]$$

9.   Finally, the risk that a security contributes to the market portfolio is calculated:

$$B_i = \frac{COV_{i,m}}{\sigma^2_m}$$

or

$$B_i = [\frac{\sigma_i}{\sigma_m}] r_{i,m}$$

D. REVIEW QUESTIONS (Answers are found at the end of this section.)

1.   How can the concept of the marginal utility of wealth be used to distinguish between a gambler and an investor?

2.   Why are securities considered risky "only to the extent that they add risk to the portfolio"? Isn't the risk of the security itself important?

3.   What is "naive" diversification?

4.   If random diversification is extended to include many securities, can portfolio risk be eliminated entirely?

5.   What factor determines the amount of a security's risk that can be diversified away when it is added to a portfolio?

6.   What is the conceptual and mathematical relationship between covariance and correlation?

7.   What is *efficient* diversification?

8.   What is the *efficient frontier*?

9.   What is the risk-free asset? Does it actually exist?

10.   Why do combinations of the risk-free asset and any risky portfolio plot as straight lines?

Sample page: Review Questions reinforce issues highlighted by the Summary of Key Concepts, with answers at the end of the section for self-testing.

Answers to Review Questions (continued)

13.   Since all securities will be held as part of the market portfolio, their relevant risk is the risk that they contribute to the market portfolio (i.e., the portion of their risk that is not diversified away). This depends, in turn, on the correlation between the security and the market portfolio. If we examine the *relative* risk of the security (that is, the ratio of the standard deviations of the security to the market), and adjust that ratio for the correlation between the security and the market, we have *beta,* the measure of the systematic risk that a security contributes to the market portfolio.

E. REVIEW PROBLEMS   (Answers are found at the end of this section.)

1.   Here are 10 years of returns for Mavic, Inc. and the market portfolio:

Year	Mavic	Market
1	8.1%	8.0%
2	3.0	0.0
3	5.3	14.9
4	1.0	5.0
5	-3.1	-4.1
6	-3.0	-8.9
7	5.0	10.1
8	3.2	5.0
9	1.2	1.5
10	1.3	2.4

a.   Calculate the yearly returns of a portfolio created by allocating your money equally between Mavic and the market. Determine the expected return and the standard deviation of Mavic, the market, and your new portfolio.

b.   By comparing the standard deviation of your new portfolio with a weighted average of the standard deviations of Mavic and the market, what can you conclude about the correlation between these two assets? (It is not necessary to calculate the correlation coefficient at this point).

c.   Now calculate the covariance and correlation coefficient between Mavic and the market and determine Mavic's beta.

2.   The expected return on Security A is 5.0% and the standard deviation is 4.0%; for Security B, the values of 8.0% and 10.0%, respectively. The correlation coefficient between A and B is zero.

a.   Determine the weights of the minimum variance portfolio of A and B.

b.   Calculate mean-variance portfolio opportunity set for $X_A = 1.00, .75, .50, .25, .00$.

Sample page: Review Problems ask students to apply the major analytical techniques. Fully worked-out solutions, with references to key equations, appear at the end of the section.

Answers to Review Problems (continued)

5. a.

Year	Mavic	Market	Portfolio
1	8.1%	8.0%	8.05%
2	3.0	0.0	1.5
3	5.3	14.9	10.1
4	1.0	5.0	3.0
5	-3.1	-4.1	-3.6
6	-3.0	-8.9	-5.95
7	5.0	10.1	7.55
8	3.2	5.0	4.1
9	1.2	1.5	1.35
10	1.3	2.4	1.85
Average Return	2.20%	3.39%	2.795%
Std. Deviation	3.53%	6.89%	5.026%

b. A weighted average of the standard deviations of Mavic and the market is [3.53% (.50) + 6.89 (.50)] = 5.21%. As seen above, however, the calculated standard deviation of the portfolio is only 5.026%. The portfolio standard deviation has been reduced by diversification. The risk reduction has been relatively small, however, so it is reasonable to assume that, while Mavic and the market are not perfectly positively correlated, the correlation coefficient is fairly high.

c. $COV_{m,m} = [(8.1 - 2.2)(8.0 - 2.795) + (3.0 - 2.2)(0.0 - 2.795) + ...$
    $+ (1.3 - 2.2)(2.4 - 2.795)] / 10 - 1$
    $COV_{m,m} = 20.552$

   $r_{m,m} = 20.552 / (3.53)(6.89)$
   $r_{m,m} = .845$ (as expected, fairly high positive correlation.)

   Beta = (3.53 / 6.89)(.845)
   Beta = .4329

F. PRACTICE TEST BANK (Answers are found in Appendix A)

True-False Questions

1. Investors demand risk premiums because they prefer more wealth to less wealth.

2. A security with high variability of returns must offer a substantial risk premium, regardless of whether it is held as part of a portfolio or held as the investor's only asset.

3. Investers evaluate portfolio risk and return, rather than risk and return of individual assets.

l portfolio diversification (and risk reduction) by selecting 20 stocks

n efficient and naive diversification has to do with the investor's ication.

ction that is possible through diversification depends on the sets.

isky assets, it is correct to say that one efficient portfolio is as good

ets (including the risk-free asset), it is correct to say that there is ssets that is preferred to all others.

he efficient frontier dominate all other portfolios.

10. Investors who wish to earn a higher return than that offered by the optimal risky portfolio (i.e., the market portfolio) must look for other investments than combinations of the risk-free asset and the market portfolio.

Multiple Choice Questions

The following information applies to Questions 1 - 3:

You have estimated the following returns on stocks 1, 2, and 3:

Economy	Prob.	R_1	R_2	R_3
Good	.40	15.0%	30.0%	18.0%
Fair	.20	10.0	10.0	16.0
Poor	.40	5.0	-10.0	10.0

1. The expected return and standard deviation of each stock are
    a. 10.0%, 4.47%; 10.0%, 17.89%; 14.4%, 3.67%.
    b. 10.0%, 5.23%; 10.0%, 10.0%; 14.4%, 4.47%
    c. 15.0%, 5.0%; 10.0%, 20.0%; 16.0%, 5.0%
    d. None of the above.

2. $COV_{1,2}$, $COV_{1,3}$, and $COV_{2,3}$ are
    a. 40, 16, 80
    b. 80, 16, 40
    c. 80, 16, 64
    d. None of the above.

Sample page: The Test Bank of self-testing items consists of true-false and multiple choice problems similar to those found in the actual test bank, with answers in Appendix A to the Study Guide.

INVESTMENT

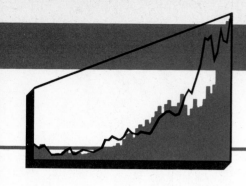

PART 1

Introduction

"What security-selection strategy should I follow in order to achieve the highest possible returns without bearing unacceptable risk?" This is the essential question faced by all investors and speculators.

The goal of any investments text should be to help the reader develop a clear idea of the pros and cons of potential selection strategies. But such strategies can be clearly understood only after one has a sound foundation in the basic concepts and analytic techniques that apply to all securities. Consequently, this text is organized into three broad areas—concepts, analysis, and strategies.

Concepts are discussed in Part 2. The major concepts examined include (1) why financial markets and interest rates exist, (2) what security risk is and how it can be measured, and (3) how expected security returns are related to their risks. In Part 3, we analyze the critical features of specific security instruments, including (1) bonds, (2) stocks, (3) futures, (4) options and (5) international investments. Finally, Part 4 examines various strategies of portfolio management.

But before we can begin to address any of this material, there are certain institutional aspects that need to be reviewed. This is the purpose of the four chapters that make up Part 1.

In Chapter 1, we look at the size of world security markets and discuss why such markets exist. In addition, an overview is presented of the security selection process and important investment concepts. In Chapter 2, the legal and economic characteristics of major types of security instruments are summarized. Next, the way in which security transactions take place in major U.S. markets is discussed in Chapter 3 Finally, Chapter 4 examines a variety of security indexes that are used as benchmarks to evaluate the success of a given investment strategy.

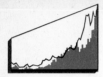

An Overview

Security markets hold a particular fascination for many people. A folklore has developed around past financiers, such as Cornelius Vanderbilt and the Morgans, as well as contemporary financiers, such as Warren Buffet and John Templeton. Market traders have developed their own unique language (index arbitrage, fully hedged, straddled options, technical corrections, etc.). Many people believe that, with a little knowledge and good luck, they too can earn substantial returns.

Yet for all the psychic pleasures and possible monetary rewards that people receive from security trading, the game is played in earnest. The future welfare of individuals and families depends upon the strategies they use to select securities.

Consider the following story. In the 1980s, the U.S. banking system was on the threshold of significant restructuring. The financial transactions in which banks could legally engage were broadened. New types of financial instruments were constantly being developed and tested. And traditional bank customers increasingly bypassed the banking system to borrow or lend directly in public security markets. Perhaps the dominant force driving changes in the banking system was expanding world trade and technological advances, which created a truly global financial market. Given such profound changes, it is only natural that some banks would thrive in such an environment whereas others would fail.

In Figure 1-1, the market values of three major U.S. banks are shown for the decade of the 1980s. In 1980, NationsBank did virtually all of its business in North Carolina (it was known then as the North Carolina National Bank), and its common stock was valued at $246 million. Republic of Texas and InterFirst were domiciled in Texas and valued at $485 million and $760 million, respectively (five times the value of NationsBank). During the early 1980s, each firm was profitable and increased in economic value.

During the mid-1980s, however, the Texas economy experienced a major decline, which took both Texas banks with it. In 1987, the two Texas banks were forced to merge in an attempt to remain economically viable. At the time of the merger, the two banks' combined value had fallen to $150 million. The merger was unsuccessful and, by 1988, the banks' value had declined to a meager $22 million. Finally, they were acquired in 1989 by NationsBank. By the end of 1990, the equity value of NationsBank was $2.3 billion.

Why? And what could have been done? What were the forces that could cause

FIGURE 1-1 *Market Values of Three U.S. Banks*

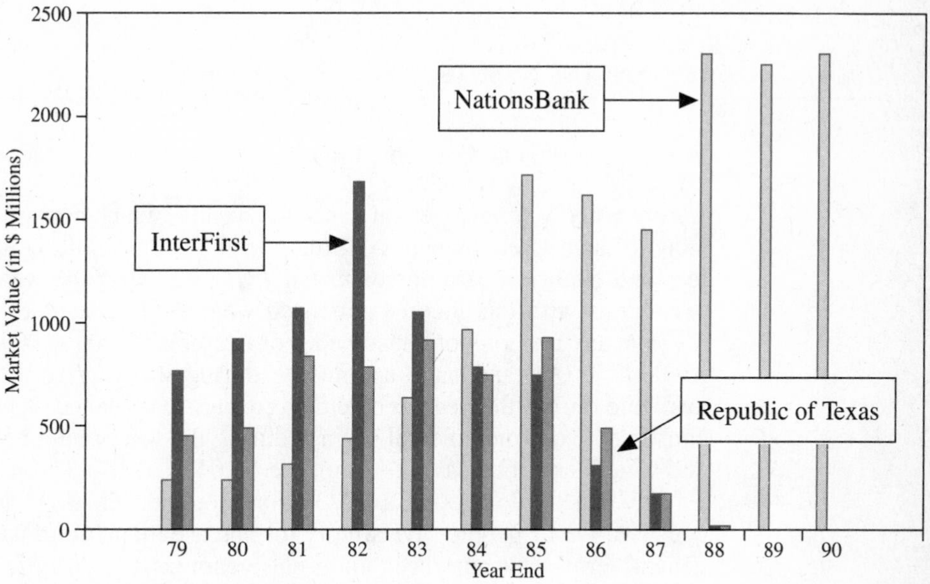

such price changes in each firm? Might a well-trained investor have been able to foresee the future, avoiding the decline in the Texas bank stocks and gaining from a NationsBank increase? Was there a way for a less knowledgeable person to minimize or avoid the risks of owning the stocks of the Texas banks? This book examines these two basic questions about security selection: "Why?" and "What should be done?" Our goal is to gain some insights into questions such as the following:

Why:

- do various types of securities exist?
- do securities trade at a particular price?
- do these prices change over time?

What should be done:

- to reduce risk but still provide a reasonable expected return?
- to compensate for potential inflation?
- to reduce transaction costs and taxes?

   The purpose of this chapter is to provide an overview of three topics: the size and growth of world financial markets, the economic benefits created by financial markets, and basic concepts of security pricing and portfolio management. The value of such an overview is that it helps the reader place details of future chapters into proper perspective and serves as a sort of itinerary of a coming tour. Because this chapter is an overview, readers are not expected to develop a full understanding of all the ideas presented.

INVESTMENT IN FINANCIAL ASSETS

Wealth Is Saved or Consumed

At any point in time, a person has some wealth, which consists of the total market value of any assets owned. As time goes by, this wealth is increased by *income* received from job earnings or *productive returns* on the wealth. People will do two things with this income-enhanced wealth: (1) consume part or all of it and (2) save any portion not consumed. For example, if you start year 1 with a wealth level of $1,000 and have an income during the year of $200, then $1,200 is available during the year to be either consumed or saved. Assuming that $150 is consumed, your incremental savings during the year would be $50 and your year-end wealth and total savings would be $1,050.

Why exactly do people save? On first thought, this might appear to be a trivial question. Don't people save simply to increase their future wealth? While true in general terms, this answer is not precise enough to convey fully the true motivations for saving. The economic benefits that arise from saving are twofold:

1. To achieve *future consumption levels* higher than would be available if one were not to save but instead were to consume *future income levels as received*. For example, a salesperson whose income is erratic from year to year will save in years of above-average earnings in order to obtain a desired consumption level in years of depressed earnings. Similarly, we all save during our working years in order to have resources to consume in our retirement years. Saving thus allows us to obtain consumption when we want it, independent of when income is received. *This "consumption-smoothing" motive for saving is usually associated with what we will define to be an "investment" strategy.*

2. To take advantage of unusually *profitable opportunities*. Occasionally, an opportunity will provide potential returns that are larger than the returns available on other saving opportunities of similar risk. Undertaking such opportunities immediately increases a person's wealth. *This "opportunity" motive is associated with what we will define as "speculative" or "arbitrage" strategies.*

In sum, the ability to save provides people with two distinct benefits: the ability to separate their consumption pattern from their earnings pattern, and the ability to immediately increase their wealth by finding unusually profitable ventures.

Investment Versus Speculation

A distinction has traditionally been drawn between investment and speculation on the following grounds:

- Speculators accept fairly large risks, whereas investors accept only moderate-to-low risks.
- Speculators have a large portfolio turnover, whereas investors have low turnover.

Given these guidelines, there is a gray area, in which it is difficult to identify a particular strategy as being by its nature either speculative or an investment. Individuals might continually switch from one approach to the other.

While there is nothing wrong with this traditional distinction, we will use the terms *investment* and *speculation* in a more precise manner. Throughout the text, the term *investment* refers to the purchase of an asset with the belief that its current market price is fair. The investor expects to earn only a *fair rate of return* commensurate with the asset's risk. An investment can be in assets of high, low, or moderate risk, depending upon the investor's risk tolerance and desired return. The only time investors trade is when they have excess cash, need cash for current consumption, or want tax savings.

In contrast, the term *speculation* refers to the purchase of an asset if it is believed to be *undervalued* and the sale of an asset if it is believed to be *overvalued*. The speculator expects to earn an *abnormal return*, a return above that which is fair, given the asset's risk. This abnormal return represents gains earned from buying undervalued assets before their prices rise to fair value or selling overvalued assets before prices fall. Speculations can occur in securities of any risk level. The speculator will trade actively if a large number of mispriced assets can be found or inactively if few mispriced assets are available.

The key difference between a speculative trade and an investment is information. Speculators believe they have information about an asset that other market participants will soon also learn and that will cause the less-well-informed people to reevaluate the asset's worth. In contrast, investors believe that all currently available information is fully impounded in the asset's price. A speculative trade is an information trade.

This distinction is important because the speculator is effectively making a bet with the other security market participants that states, "My information is better than yours." Before entering into such a bet, the speculator should recognize that there are a large number of sophisticated and intelligent people with access to considerable capital who are also looking for such information. What makes the speculator's information any better than that of others? Is the information truly unique?

Consider the following example. You have just completed a thorough analysis of UK Chem Ltd. and believe they will soon file for a patent on a new chemical process that should dramatically improve the company's long-run profits and dividends. Should you buy stock in anticipation of a price increase once the earnings actually start to improve? If knowledge of the potential patent is widespread, you don't hold any unique information. Market speculators will have already "discounted" the likely profit improvement into current prices. But if you believe the profit potential is not fully reflected in the stock's current price, a speculative buy would be appropriate. Before trading, the wise speculator asks, "Do I really have enough information that others don't, or is there something others know that I don't?"

Another term that we will use extensively in this book is *arbitrage.* In an arbitrage transaction, a person attempts to profit from a security price distortion. For example, assume AT&T common stock is traded on both the New York Stock Exchange and the American Stock Exchange. You own a seat on each exchange, so you pay no transaction costs (that is, broker fees) to trade at either place. If AT&T is currently trading at $40 on the American and $41 on the New York Exchange, you could arbitrage by simultaneously buying at $40 and selling at $41. You could earn a $1 profit per share at no risk and with no capital commitment. Arbitrage transactions can, of course, involve much more complex trades. But their keynotes are that they (1) *entail no risk,* (2) *require no capital commitment,* and (3) *profits are gained by trading on market price imbalances.*

Arbitrageurs play an important role in the operations of the security markets. By attempting to maximize their own profits, they identify and eliminate security price imbalances. The rapid trading by a large number of arbitrageurs guarantees that prices in all markets are closely interrelated and determined by similar economic factors. There is an underlying economic rationality in the markets. Speculators perform similar functions as do arbitrageurs. The principal distinction between the two is that speculation can involve more risk than a pure arbitrage transaction. Arbitrageurs tend to ''cover themselves'' by taking equal but opposite sides of a trade.

Saving in Real Versus Financial Assets

Savings can be placed into two broad categories of assets: real assets or financial assets. Real assets are often tangible resources such as land, buildings, durable goods (tractors, automobiles, personal computers, etc.) and commodities (gold, wheat, lumber, etc.). Real assets can also be intangible resources such as technology and human knowledge. For example, savings used to purchase a home or to pay for college tuition are both savings placed into real assets.

Financial assets are legal claims to a specified portion of the ownership and returns on a real asset. For example, the land, building, and technology owned by the IBM Corporation are real assets. However, to acquire these real assets, company management has issued financial assets that provide specified claims to the ownership and returns of the real assets. In return for these legal claims, claimholders provided IBM management with the cash necessary to acquire the firm's real assets.

Earlier in the chapter, we saw that the ability to save in real or financial assets is valuable to people because it allows them the opportunity to smooth consumption over their lifetime. Financial markets provide an additional advantage. Individuals with profitable ideas but without ownership of sufficient real assets to implement the idea can obtain the necessary financing by issuing financial assets to other people. In doing so, the wealth of each party to the trade can be increased. For example, assume that June Lee needs $100,000 to start a regional business that she expects will have a market value of $150,000 in one year once investors realize the firm's true prospects. She could issue financial claims that provide for partial ownership of the business in return for the required $100,000. She would also retain an ownership interest. If her prediction is true, everyone benefits. She has taken real assets that cost $100,000 and created an incremental value of $50,000. This increase in value is shared between the outside owners of the financial assets and herself.

Financial assets are classified into two broad groups: direct security claims and indirect security claims, as follows:

Security Type	Basic Description
Direct Claims:	
Debt	Promises to pay a stated series of cash flows. If the promise is broken, holders have a specified claim to assets of the issuer.
Equity	Has rights to ownership of assets and profits on assets after all promised debt claims have been satisfied.
Indirect Claims:	
Forward and Futures	Contracts entered into today that *obligate* the buyer (seller) to purchase (sell) a specified asset at a stated price on a stated future date.
Options to buy or sell	Contracts entered into today that provide the owner the *right* to buy (a call option) or to sell (a put option) a specified asset on a stated future date.

Debt and equity securities have been traded in public markets for more than three centuries. Active public markets in forwards, futures, and options are a more recent innovation. The first active market in options was formed in the mid-1970s, and futures contracts on financial assets were not offered until the mid-1980s. Futures and option markets, however, have become an important part of trading in financial assets. For example, in the early 1990s, the outstanding value of futures and option claims to U.S. equity securities was often more than three times the daily trading value of all stocks in the United States. Futures and options are often referred to as *derivative securities,* since their values are derived from the values of the underlying debt and equity securities on which they have a claim.

Value and Growth of Real and Financial World Assets

In the rest of this section, we will examine the value and growth of world asset values, who the owners are of financial assets and who controls the management of financial assets. The conclusions might surprise you!

Estimates of the value of real assets and financial assets are shown in Table 1-1 for the period spanning 1960 through 1991. Before we examine this data, a few caveats must be made.

First, values of real assets are *estimates* based on information from economically well-developed countries. They exclude underdeveloped countries, exclude many forms of real assets and are rough approximations in some cases. Yet, these numbers represent the best estimates presently available. Second, the values shown for financial assets consist of estimates of world debt and equity market values.

TABLE 1-1 *Estimates of Global Assets: Real and Financial*
(in Billions of U.S. Dollars)

	1960	1970	1980	1991
Real Asset Estimates				
U.S.	$677.3	$1,250.0	$5,219.9	$6,377.0
Non-U.S.	NA	NA	$8,646.3	$16,341.0
Total	$677.3	$1,250.0	$13,866.2	$22,718.0
Financial Asset Estimates				
U.S.	$621.2	$1,151.7	$2,552.5	$10,603.0
Non-U.S.	$590.4	$722.7	$3,046.5	$13,229.0
Total	$1,211.6	$1,874.4	$5,599.0	$23,832.0
Total World Wealth Estimate	$1,888.9	$3,124.4	$19,465.2	$46,550.0

SOURCES: *Federal Reserve Bulletins, Morgan Stanley Capital International Perspectives,* Roger Ibbotson and Laurence Siegal, "The World Market Wealth Portfolio," *The Journal of Portfolio Management,* Winter 1983, 5–17., and Ibbotson Associates, Inc. *Wealth of the World,* 1991.

Finally, the financial asset values shown include only countries with well-developed financial markets. For example, financial assets in Mexico, South America, Taiwan, and Thailand are not included.

At the end of 1991, the estimated value of global real and financial assets was about $46 trillion dollars. This was split about equally between the value of real assets and the value of financial assets. Asset values outside the United States have grown more rapidly than asset values within the United States. To some degree, this is due to more complete information about the value of non-U.S. assets in more recent years. Yet, there is little doubt that the value of non-U.S. financial assets have grown more rapidly than those within the United States. Finally, in 1991, the value of non-U.S. financial assets ($13.2 trillion) exceeded the value of U.S. financial assets ($10.6 trillion).

The investment implication is obvious. We live in a world in which real and financial asset decisions need to be made in a global context.

Who Owns U.S. Financial Assets?

Although investment decisions should be made with a global perspective, information about the ownership of non-U.S. financial assets is sparse. Thus, any analysis of who owns financial assets must be restricted to securities traded in the United States.

Estimates of who owned U.S. financial assets at the end of 1991 are shown in Table 1-2. Information is displayed for equities, nonequities (money market securities plus fixed income), and a total. Investor categories consist of institutional investors, depository institutions (commercial banks, savings and loans, etc.), and other. The "other" category consists largely of individual households.

Consider the ownership of *equities.* Approximately one-half was owned by

TABLE 1-2 *Who Owns Marketable U.S. Financial Assets?*
(Billions of U.S. Dollars; December 1991)

	Percent of Total Dollars		
	Equity	*Nonequity*	*Total*
Institutional Investors			
Pension Funds	25.0%	15.9%	19.6%
Insurance Firms	5.2%	27.4%	18.3%
Mutual Funds	9.2%	7.3%	8.0%
Broker Dealers	0.3%	4.4%	2.7%
Foreign Investors	6.7%	15.4%	11.8%
Corporations	NA	2.4%	1.4%
Total	46.4%	72.7%	61.9%
Depository Institutions	NA	7.5%	4.4%
Other	53.6%	19.8%	33.7%
Total	100.0%	100.0%	100.0%
Total Dollars (Billions)	$4,352.5	$6,250.5	$10,603.0

NA = not available.

SOURCES: *Federal Reserve Bulletins, Treasury Bulletins.*

institutional owners. Pension funds alone owned 25% of equity values and mutual funds owned 9%. The growing importance of institutional ownership of the U.S. equity market, mainly by pension funds and mutual funds, has dramatically affected the manner in which equity securities are traded. Individual pension funds and mutual funds manage assets that often exceed a billion dollars. A $100 million portfolio is common. Due to their size, institutional investors trade in large quantities. For example, the standard trade quantity on the New York Stock Exchange is 100 shares and is referred to as a "round lot." In contrast, "large block" trades consist of trades in 10,000 shares or more. During the early 1990s, large block transactions represented more than 50% of all equity trading volume (compared with only 15% in 1960).

The dramatic growth of institutional ownership during the past two decades is shown in Figure 1-2. At the end of 1970, institutional investors owned about 20% of the market value of U.S. equities. By the end of 1991, their ownership position had approached 50%. Most of this growth arose from pension funds and mutual funds.

Pension funds represent the investment portfolios of *pension plans.* A pension plan is a contractual agreement between an employer and employee in which the employer agrees to provide retirement benefits to the employee. If the pension plan requires specified yearly contributions to the pension fund (the word *fund* implies a pool of assets), then the pension plan is called a *defined contribution plan.* If the pension plan requires specified benefits during an employee's retirement, then the pension plan is called a *defined benefit plan.* Employees bear the investment risk of defined contribution plans. Employers bear the investment risk of defined benefit plans. Regardless of the type of plan, fund assets of the pension

FIGURE 1-2 *Institutional Ownership of U.S. Equity*

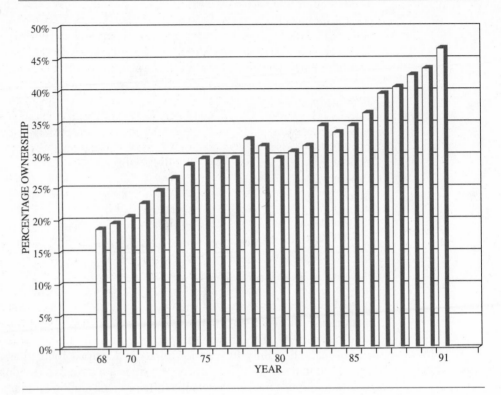

SOURCE: *Federal Reserve Flow of Funds*

will be overseen by a committee of pension trustees. The trustees control how pension-fund assets are invested. Typically, they will invest fund assets across various investment classes (U.S. fixed income, U.S. equity, non-U.S. equity, real estate, etc.). In addition, trustees usually employ a number of investment management organizations that are responsible for determining the specific securities to be held. Trustees invest in a variety of investment classes and employ multiple managers in order to provide diversification of investment risk.

Mutual funds are different from pension funds. A mutual fund is initially created by an investment advisory firm. The advisor defines the fund's objective, any investment constraints, and investment strategies in a registration document that is filed with the Securities and Exchange Commission (SEC). Once the registration statement is approved for completeness and accuracy by the SEC, shares in the mutual fund are offered to the public. Investors in the fund become the equity owners of the fund (hence the term *mutual*). The mutual fund advisor uses the money provided by fund owners to acquire assets of the fund that fulfill the objective and constraints of the registration statement. Usually the advisor specializes in the types of securities held by the fund. For example, the advisor might purchase only U.S. government bonds, shares of large U.S. companies, or shares of companies that do business in the Pacific Rim. Investors in a mutual fund have pooled their capital to purchase a single *commingled portfolio*. There are three potential advantages of investing in mutual funds. First, operating costs are low due to economies of scale inherent in managing large portfolios. For example, the cost of managing a single $100 million portfolio is less than the cost of managing 4,000 portfolios, each worth $25,000. Second, mutual fund advisors are trained investment professionals. Hopefully, the advisor's knowledge can provide greater investment returns (net of costs) than the individual would have obtained by personal management. Finally, and perhaps most importantly, pooling resources into a single commingled portfolio can provide greater diversification for fund owners than if they had invested individually.

Who Manages U.S. Financial Assets?

In the preceding section, we discussed trends in the ownership of U.S. financial assets. But the owners of financial assets need not be the same as the managers of financial assets. For example, while a pension fund might be owned by the employees of a company, fund assets are typically managed by professional investment advisors. Estimates of who managed U.S. financial assets at the end of 1991 are shown in Table 1-3. Our discussion focuses on the management of equity securities.

TABLE 1-3 *Who Manages Marketable U.S. Financial Assets?*

	At December 31, 1991		
	Equity	*Nonequity*	*Total*
Households	29.1%	24.7%	25.9%
Internal Actively Managed			
Depository institutions	0.0%	3.5%	2.1%
Insurance companies	3.6%	27.4%	18.3%
State and local governments	0.0%	5.3%	3.1%
Corporate and foreign	6.7%	17.8%	13.2%
Total	10.3%	53.9%	36.7%
External Actively Managed			
Bank trust departments	14.9%	5.4%	9.3%
Insurance companies	13.8%	5.0%	8.6%
Investment counselors	26.5%	9.6%	16.5%
Total	55.2%	20.0%	34.4%
Passively Indexed	5.3%	1.4%	3.0%
Total			
Total Percent	100.0%	100.0%	100.0%
Total Dollars	$4,352.5	$6,250.5	$10,603.0
(in Billions)			

SOURCES: *Federal Reserve Bulletins, Federal Reserve Flow of Funds, Pension and Investment,* May 18, 1992.

The most striking fact in Table 1-3 is that more than 70% of the value of U.S. equities was professionally managed. Individuals (shown as Households) controlled less than 30%!

Professionally managed assets are separated into three broad groups. *Internal actively managed* assets refers to cases in which the owner of the asset personally manages the assets using an investment strategy that actively identifies stocks to buy or sell. For example, an insurance company will hold U.S. equities as a part of the firm's asset investments. These are purchased using insurance premiums received from customer policies. Management of the insurance company decides which stocks to trade. *External actively managed* assets refers to cases in which the asset owner employs a professional manager to actively buy and sell securities. Professional external management is provided by trust departments of commercial banks, commingled investment pools offered by insurance companies, and investment counseling firms. Mutual funds represent a part of the funds managed by both insurance companies and investment counseling companies. (Until recently the Glass-Stegall Act precluded banks from offering equity mutual funds.) *Passively indexed* assets are also professionally managed portfolios, but they are not actively managed in an attempt to find stocks that are over- or under-valued. Instead, they invest in a specified index of stocks and promise a return very close to that of the index. In 1991, about 5% of U.S. equities were passively managed.

Importance of Institutions: Why and So What?

The major participants in the U.S. equity markets during the 1990s are institutional investors who actively manage the capital of other people. Pension funds and mutual funds are the dominant institutional equity owners, in that they own more than one-third of all equities. Investment counseling companies, bank trust departments, and insurance companies are the dominant institutional equity managers; they control more than one-half of U.S. equity.

The small individual investor has played a diminishing role in equity trading in the United States. If we look beyond the United States, the story is mixed. In the United Kingdom, approximately 80% of all equity value is controlled by the equivalent of U.S. mutual funds. Although accurate statistics are not available for Japan, a large amount of Japanese trading is conducted by investment managers within corporations. However, in less developed countries such as Taiwan and Brazil, institutional asset management is much less important.

It is easy to understand *why* institutional ownership and management has become so dominant in the United States. The advantages are identical to those mentioned for mutual fund ownership: (a) cost reduction, (b) professional management and (c) improved diversification opportunities.

Much of the answer to the question "so what?" is also easy to see. The growth of institutional investing has driven commission rates down, been a force behind the introduction of new types of securities, and led to changes in the manner in which security trades are executed.

BENEFITS OF FINANCIAL MARKETS

Financial markets play a vital role in modern societies. They increase the investment opportunities available and the standard of living, provide an improvement in diversification opportunities, and allow for easy shifts in investment risk levels. It is for these reasons that society has created financial securities—not as a game for the sophisticated to extract wealth from the naive.

The Primary Market

The term *primary market* refers to the initial sale of a security to the public. Someone in need of capital to acquire real assets issues a security claim on the real assets. The initial purchaser of the security pays the issuer money, which is then used to acquire the desired real assets. In return for the capital, the security issuer provides the purchaser with a legal claim to some portion of the ownership and returns on the real assets. This may sound abstract. But it is precisely what occurs at the time of a security's initial issue. There are two ways in which society can benefit from such transactions.

First, *the wealth of society can be increased.* Consider such individuals as Thomas Edison, Henry Ford, and Stephan Jobs. Each had a unique idea that resulted in value to society. But none had (initially) enough personal capital to implement the idea. By selling financial securities, these people were able to obtain the capital necessary to implement their ideas. Society benefitted by improved productivity, and the individuals benefitted by increased wealth and the purchasers of the securities shared in the wealth increase.

The story of these inventors is an obvious extreme. But the concept also relates to everyday life. For example, how many college readers of this text would be able to personally afford their education costs if they had to rely solely on personal assets? Students who borrow to finance their education are doing so to make an investment in their personal human capital. The ability to borrow improves their future wealth as well as their value to society.

Second, the presence of financial markets *increases consumption flexibility.* Without the presence of financial markets, people could consume no more than the market value of any real assets that they owned. Automobiles or houses could not be purchased until people had sufficient real assets to do so. On the opposite side of the problem, people accumulating savings for retirement would be forced to save by acquiring real assets, which they might not have the skill or time to manage and which are riskier than they would prefer. Financial assets provide such savers with an easy and inexpensive way to accumulate wealth.

Secondary Markets: Brokers, Dealers, and Financial Intermediaries

The development of primary markets brings together those who want to make real investments with those who have real savings. It is an important step in the financial development of any society. But the *direct* placement of one's real savings with someone wishing to invest in real assets can be an inefficient process. Improvements are provided by brokers and dealers and the ability to trade in secondary markets. These include:

1. Costs of transactions
2. Differences in desired investment and financing maturities
3. Diversification
4. Liquidity

A broker acts as an agent for someone—typically, in arranging a security purchase or sale. A dealer acts as a principal by taking a long (ownership) or short (owe) position in a security trade.

Costs of Transacting. The transaction costs of directly placing securities between lenders of funds and borrowers of funds can be large. For example, the costs to an electric power company in York, England of directly finding buyers for a $200 million bond offering would be substantial. To float such an issue by itself, the firm would have to seek investors throughout the European Community (E. C.) (at least). Conversely, the costs to an oil sheik of directly investing $200 million over a diversified group of securities would also be large. However, there are significant economies of scale to transaction costs that security brokers and dealers can obtain and that aren't available to one-time (or infrequent) borrowers and lenders.

These economies of scale arise in at least two ways. First, the average out-of-pocket cost declines as the number of transactions increases. The largest part of the cost of finding a borrower or lender is a set-up cost—a fixed cost of initially developing a network of potential traders. After one pays this set-up cost, the marginal cost of any transaction is quite small. For example, the biggest cost to Merrill Lynch (the largest security broker in the United States) of providing brokerage services is the cost of finding customers and developing an efficient communications and clearing network. Once these are in place, Merrill Lynch can execute and clear an order quite inexpensively. Therefore, it makes sense that a permanent brokerage system would be set up to bring potential borrowers and lenders of real assets together. It is a way to improve the efficiency of the primary market.

Second, there are information economies of scale. Infrequent borrowers and lenders simply don't have the knowledge of financial conditions which full-time brokers are able to provide inexpensively. For example, the York power firm might have little knowledge of what impact a change in bond covenants would have on required yields, when the issue should be brought to market to avoid competing with other large primary offerings, whether the sale should be delayed in anticipation of credit loosening within the E. C., etc. Again, efficiency is best served by the creation of a brokerage system that is able to give financial advice.

Brokerage services are offered by a large variety of institutions, some of which aren't usually thought of as brokers. The most apparent are the large retail brokerage firms like Merrill Lynch, Prudential-Bache, Shearson Lehman Hutton in the United States; Daiwa, Namura, and Sanyo in Japan; and Kleinwort, Fleming, and James Capel in the United Kingdom.

Investment bankers also serve a brokerage function when they distribute primary offerings, and commercial banks, as well as savings and loans, offer a form of brokerage service by bringing together borrowers and lenders.

Economies of scale in transaction costs are also a reason for the existence of *dealers.* For example, the system of market makers, specialists, and block-trading houses arose because it is cheaper for society to have particular individuals carry inventories of securities to trade with the public than it would be to find the end buyer and seller in each transaction. Similarly, security underwriters are better able to absorb the risks of a new security offering than is the issuer, since a purchase group can be formed to diversify risks over many offerings. Commercial banks can carry large demand and saving deposits and reinvest them less expensively than could an individual small saver.

Maturity Differences. Dealers are often able to resolve differences in the needs of lenders and the needs of borrowers. One major difference between the two is desired investment maturity. A large number of savers prefer to lend for short time periods. For example, the large volume of demand deposits and savings accounts held in commercial banks and savings and loans are short-term investments. Borrowers, however, often prefer to enter into long-term agreements to finance the acquisition of long-term real assets. A single direct market connecting short-term lenders and long-term borrowers would work to neither party's advantage. However, dealers can step in as *financial intermediaries* to aid both sides. Although, from the depositors' viewpoint, deposits with a financial intermediary would be short-term investments, the intermediary can count on a continual turnover of deposits. One withdrawal would be offset by another deposit. In total, the deposits could be treated as long-term deposits and invested in long-term loans and bonds. Such services are a major function of the commercial banking and savings and loan systems.

Diversification. While primary markets do allow one to diversify by purchasing small claims on a large real asset, dealers are able to improve on this even further. For example, assume you have $50,000 to invest. You could buy only five $10,000 U.S. T-bills, one round lot in each of 10 different stocks selling at $50 per share, etc. The amount of diversification available on such a sum of money is small. Alternatively, you could place your money with a financial intermediary (a dealer) such as a bank or a mutual fund, have it commingled with other financial investors' balances, and as a result obtain greater diversification.

Liquidity. Liquidity refers to the ability to sell (or purchase) a security rapidly and at low cost. Security liquidity is valuable to investors if there is any chance that they will unexpectedly have to dispose of (or acquire) securities. For example, consider the actual case of a large U.S. foundation. In 1992, the value of its investment portfolio was close to $50 billion. Unfortunately, about one-half of its portfolio consisted of unproductive land, *which it could not sell.* Given that the land was unproductive and could not be sold in order to acquire other more productive (and liquid) assets, of what true value was the asset to the foundation? Clearly, very little at the time. When a security is purchased that can be cheaply and easily sold, the purchaser actually acquires two assets. The first represents a claim to the ownership and profits of the underlying real asset. The second is the ability to sell the asset at a low cost of time and money. The ability to trade, liquidity, can have a significant value provided by active trading in security markets.

BASIC FINANCIAL INVESTMENT CONCEPTS

In this section, we review how single-period security returns are calculated, how uncertainty about security returns varies between various asset classes, and how investment risk can be partially controlled by diversification. Basic concepts of security valuation are also discussed.

Single-Period Investment Returns

Rate-of-return calculations can become complex when measured over a series of many time periods. These complexities are examined in Chapter 21. But central to any rate-of-return calculation is the notion of a *single-period rate of return.* The single-period rate of return is defined as the percentage price appreciation plus the percentage cash return (often referred to as the *current yield* on a debt security or *dividend yield* on an equity security) during a given period. Usually, rates of return are expressed in terms of an annualized value, although quarterly, monthly, and even daily returns are used. The single-period rate of return is equal to:

$$\text{Single-Period Rate of Return} =$$

$$\frac{\text{Ending Investment Value} - \text{Beginning Investment Value} + \text{Cash Inflow}}{\text{Beginning Investment Value}}$$

$$R_t = [P_t - P_{t-1} + C_t] / P_{t-1} \tag{1.1}$$

In Equation (1.1) R_t refers to the rate of return in period t, P_t and P_{t-1} refer to the price of a security (or market value of a portfolio) at dates t and $t-1$, and C_t refers to any cash flows received at date t.

Consider the following examples which are related to returns on individual securities. At the start of a year, the market value of a corporate bond issue was $1,020. At year-end, the bond's value is equal to $1,010 and interest equal to $120 is received. The one-year return on the bond is 10.78%.

$$0.1078 = \frac{\$1,010 - \$1,020 + \$120}{\$1,020}$$

During the same year, per-share prices of the company's common stock increase in value from 20 to $25, and a $1.00 dividend is received at year-end. The stock's return is 30% for the year:

$$0.30 = \frac{\$25 - \$20 + \$1}{\$20}$$

Now consider single-period return examples involving security portfolios as opposed to single securities. Our hypothetical portfolio is owned by the McMann Foundation and managed by TK Capital Management. At the start of the year, the portfolio is worth $150 million. During the year, the McMann Foundation placed no additional money with TK Capital. At year-end, dividend and interest on security holdings totaling $4 million are collected by TK Capital. Trustees of the McMann Foundation decide to withdraw $2.5 million of the cash income to cover future expenses of the foundation. The remaining $1.5 million is reinvested. After this reinvestment is made, the portfolio's market value is $170 million. Therefore, the portfolio return is equal to 15%.

$$0.15 = \frac{\$170 - \$150 + 2.5}{\$150}$$

Notice that the portfolio's return is unaffected by any year-end withdrawals by McMann Foundation. For example, if trustees had reinvested the full $4 million at year-end, the ending portfolio's value would have been $172.5 million, resulting in the same 15% return:

$$0.15 = \frac{\$172.5 - \$150 + 0}{\$150}$$

Investment Returns and Risk

Now that you know how single-period returns are calculated, we can turn to the historical record and examine past returns on various classes of financial investments. Although no two securities are exactly alike, it is useful to categorize them into various security classes. Classes that are commonly examined include:

Type of Security	Proxied By
U.S. Money Market	T-bills of the United States government
U.S. Fixed Income	T-bonds (long-term) of the U.S. government
U.S. Large Stocks	Standard & Poors Composite Stock Index
U.S. Small Stocks	Indexes of stocks whose total equity value is in the bottom quintile of listed stocks in the United States
Non-U.S. Stocks	Index of stocks traded in Europe, Australia, and the Far East

Clearly, there are many other security classes that we could define and examine. But these classes have a long history of accurate returns and are sufficient to make an important point: *To receive greater average yearly returns, one must accept greater variability in yearly returns.*

Average yearly returns for these asset classes are shown in Table 1-4. Accurate returns on non-U.S. stocks are available only for the period of 1969–1991. Two averages are shown. The "nominal return" average is based on the actual market return. The "real return" average reflects the average increase in spending power; i.e., subtracting inflation from nominal returns.

Between 1926 and 1991, the average annual nominal return on U.S. T-bills was 3.74%. After subtracting losses in value due to inflation, the average real return on T-bills was a meager 0.5%. In contrast, the nominal and real returns on common stocks of large U.S. companies were 12.43% and 9.19%, respectively. Clearly, stocks of large companies performed better on average than T-bills. The clear winners during this period, however, were stocks of small U.S. companies that provided average nominal and real returns of 19.03% and 15.79%.

A visual comparison of the relative returns on these asset classes is shown in Figure 1-3. One dollar is assumed to be invested at the end of 1925 in each asset class. The future wealth level created by such an investment is determined by compounding the prior year's wealth by the return in a given year. These wealth indices do not consider the affects of taxes or transaction costs. By the end of 1991, an initial $1 investment in each asset class would have grown to:

Investment	1991 Nominal Value from a $1 Investment in 1926
CPI	$ 8
T-bills	11
Government Bonds	22
Large Stocks	676
Small Stocks	2,534

Turning to the shorter history of 1969–1991, non-U.S. equities were the most impressive, providing an average yearly nominal return of 15.68%.

TABLE 1-4 *Average Yearly Returns on Security Classes*

	U.S. T-Bills	U.S. Government Bonds	U.S. Large Stocks	U.S. Small Stocks	Non-U.S. Stocks
1926–1991					
Average Nominal Return	3.74%	5.12%	12.43%	19.03%	NA
Less Average CPI	3.24%	3.24%	3.24%	3.24%	NA
Average Real Return	0.50%	1.88%	9.19%	15.79%	NA
1969–1991					
Average Nominal Return	7.48%	9.25%	11.99%	14.04%	15.68%
Less Average CPI	6.12%	6.12%	6.12%	6.12%	6.12%
Average Real Return	1.36%	3.13%	5.87%	7.92%	9.56%

Notes: All returns are stated in U.S. dollars. Returns to non-U.S. residents will differ. CPI refers to the rates of changes in the Consumer Price Index. NA means not available.

FIGURE 1-3 *Wealth Indices of U.S. Security Classes 1925–1991*

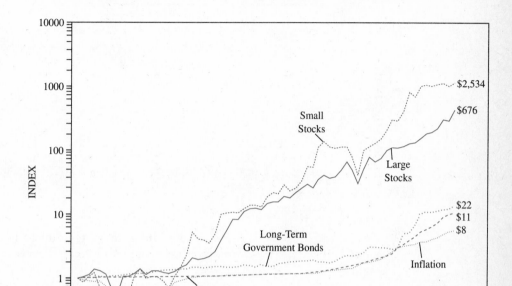

In short, the highest average long-term returns have been earned by investing in equity claims of productive enterprises. But there is a catch. Larger average returns come at the cost of greater return variability. There are many ways in which this can be demonstrated. For example, consider the information plotted in Figure 1-3. By the end of 1972, a $1 investment made in 1926 in large U.S. company stock had grown to $85. Two years later, this value had dropped to $53.34; a negative two-year loss in wealth equal to −37.25%. Adding to the problem, inflation was unusually high during these two years. After inflation reductions, the decline in the real value of an investment in U.S. large stocks during 1973 and 1974 was −53%. Half of one's real investment in common stock was gone in two years! During this same two-year period, the real value of a portfolio invested in T-bills declined by only 5.4%.

A dramatic way of displaying differences in return variability is in a plot of the time series of single-period returns. An example is shown in Figure 1-4. In this case, time series of monthly returns are plotted as opposed to annual returns. Monthly common stock returns are shown in panel A and monthly bond returns are shown in panel B. Clearly, the time series return variability of U.S. common stocks has been greater than that for U.S. long-term government bonds. (If the time series of T-bill returns had been plotted using the same vertical axis as in Figure 1-4, the series would have been virtually indistinguishable from the hori-

FIGURE 1-4 *Monthly Returns On U.S. Stocks and Bonds 1926–1991*

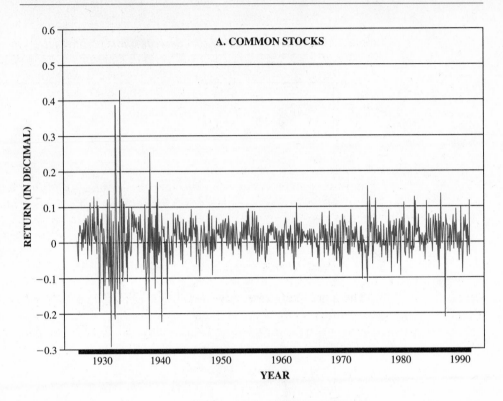

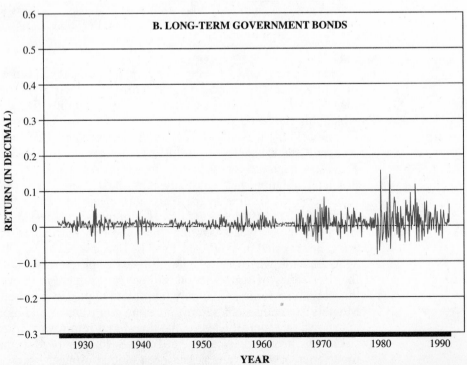

zontal axis.) Notice that Figure 1-4 suggests that common stock returns were more volatile prior to 1945 than after 1945. Also, government bond returns were much more volatile after 1970 than prior to 1970. Not only does the variability of returns differ between asset classes, but the variability of a given asset class seems to change over time.

Investment Risk and Diversification

In most investment strategies, investment risk cannot be eliminated. But it can be controlled by diversification. For example, assume you are considering an investment in one or both of two stocks. Both stocks are unusual in that they will provide a yearly return of either +20% or −10%. If you *knew* that Stock 1 would provide the 20% positive return and that Stock 2 would incur the 10% loss, there would be no need to diversify by purchasing both securities; you would invest solely in Stock 1.

The more likely case, however, is that you would not know which security will have which return. For simplicity, assume that the returns on each stock are not related. If Stock 1 incurs a 10% loss, this has no affect on the return of Stock 2. In Figure 1-5, the return and associated probabilities from two investment strat-

FIGURE 1-5 *Illustration of Two-Stock Diversification*

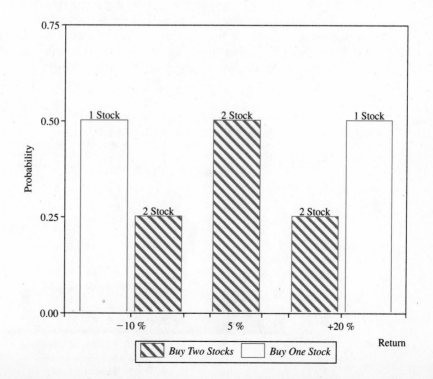

egies are shown. The first strategy consists of an investment in only one of the stocks. The second strategy consists of an equal investment in each stock.

The strategy in which you diversify across both securities, of course, is the less risky. Although the diversification strategy also has a chance that you will lose 10%, the probability that this will occur decreases from $\frac{1}{2}$ to $\frac{1}{4}$.

Why does diversification reduce your risk in this example? Because the two security returns are assumed to be unrelated. In statistical terms, the correlation between the security return is zero. If the returns on the two stocks had been perfectly correlated (the returns on each are identical), there would be no benefits to be gained from diversification.

Strategies of diversification can be grouped into two categories, commonly referred to as *random (or naive) diversification strategies* and *efficient diversification strategies.* Random diversification refers to the ability to reduce portfolio risk by increasing the number of (randomly selected) securities held in a portfolio. Scholars have demonstrated that increasing the number of securities held using a random-selection process will substantially reduce portfolio risk but have no effect upon average portfolio returns. That portion of a portfolio's risk that can be reduced by means of random diversification is known as *diversifiable risk* and is shown in Figure 1-6 as the lightly shaded area. The darker shaded area represents nondiversifiable risk. In practice, the principle of random diversification is followed by requiring diversification over a broad range of industrial classifications, forms of instruments, etcetera, instead of using strict random selection.

Efficient diversification relies upon mathematical programming procedures to calculate portfolios that provide the *largest expected return for a specified risk level.* For example, the shaded area in Figure 1-7 represents the *feasible set* of risks and returns available from a given group of securities being evaluated. The solid curve along the upper boundary of the feasible set is known as the *efficient frontier* and can be calculated using a mathematical programming model. At this

FIGURE 1-6 *Illustration of Random (or Naive) Diversification*

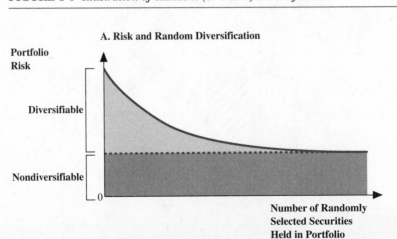

A. Risk and Random Diversification

Portfolio Risk

Diversifiable

Nondiversifiable

0

Number of Randomly Selected Securities Held in Portfolio

FIGURE 1-7 *Illustration of Efficient Diversification*

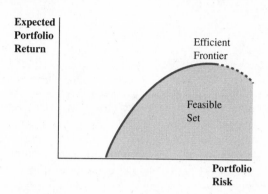

point, we needn't get into the details of how the efficient frontier is developed. The important point is that procedures exist that allow the investor to calculate an efficient frontier, once expected returns and security risks are identified. Given the investor's personal preferences for expected returns and risk, a single portfolio along the efficient frontier is selected.

Required Investment Returns

Financial scholars have extended the principles of portfolio diversification to develop models that examine *equilibrium* relationships between expected security returns and security risk. The term *equilibrium* implies that security prices are fair, in the sense that they fully reflect the investor's risk of owning the security.

The most widely used model to date relating expected returns to security risks is known as the Capital Asset Pricing Model (CAPM). The CAPM asserts that (1) the only risk of a security that is meaningful to rational investors is its nondiversifiable risk; (2) this nondiversifiable risk is measured by a variable known as beta (β); and (3) the beta of a security and the security's expected return are related in a linear fashion.

The CAPM can be written symbolically as:

Capital Asset Pricing Model
$$E(R_i) = RF + \beta_i(RP) \tag{1.2}$$

where $E(R_i)$ = the expected single-period return on security i; RF = the risk free rate of interest; β_i = the beta of security i, reflecting the extent of its nondiversifiable risk; and RP = the risk premium demanded on a security with a beta equal to 1.0. For example, if the annual risk-free rate of interest is now 7%, the beta on the stock of ABC Corporation is 1.5, and the risk premium is 6%, then ABC stock should be priced in the markets to yield an expected single-period return of 16%:

$$16\% = 7\% + 1.5(6\%)$$

Three Steps to Becoming a Successful Investor

This article summarizes a number of important investment concepts that we will examine in detail throughout the book. First, investment returns are determined mainly by the investment risk of a portfolio. Thus, the first decision that all investors should make is how much portfolio risk they are willing to accept. This is known as the asset allocation decision. Second, investment risk can be reduced by proper diversification, both across different asset classes (stocks versus bonds, for example) and within individual asset classes. Finally, investors must decide how the securities held in the portfolio will be selected. For example, should investors personally decide which individual stocks and bonds to own or should they entrust such decisions to professional investment managers such as mutual funds?

Investing can be as simple as 1, 2, 3.

First, you decide how you're going to divvy up your portfolio among broad categories like stocks, bonds, and money market instruments. Second, you decide how you want to diversify within each of these categories. When it comes to picking bond market investments, for instance, you might choose to buy a mix of corporate bonds, government bonds and foreign bonds. Finally, having settled on target percentages for these various investments, you pick the best mutual funds or the best individual securities to build your desired portfolio.

The first decision—how to divide your portfolio among stocks, bonds and money market instruments—is the most critical. "Your asset allocation is the fuel in the return engine," says John Cammack, a vice president with Baltimore's T. Rowe Price Associates mutual fund company.

How should you divide your money among the three major assets? . . . in general, how you should allocate your investment money depends on your time horizon.

If you are going to need your money in the near future, then money market instruments like certificates of deposit, savings accounts and money funds make a lot of sense. These investments will never make you rich, but there's also little or no chance you will lose money.

But if you plan to invest for anything more than a couple of years, sticking with CDs and savings accounts can be a terrible mistake. While these supersafe investments may eliminate the risk that you'll lose money over the short term, they leave you wide open to a potentially more dangerous risk—the risk that the real value of your money will be gradually eaten away by inflation.

Because of the threat from inflation, investment advisers typically favor a hefty dose of stocks or stock mutual funds, providing you plan to invest for at least five years. If you think of risk as the chance that you'll lose money in the short term, then stocks are indeed extremely risky. But if you have the tenacity to stick with your stock investments over five years or longer, then the chance of losing money is slim.

Just consider this: Since the end of 1925, there have been 63 rolling five-year periods. . . . Out of those 63 five-year periods, there have been only seven occasions when stocks lost money, according to data compiled by Ibbotson Associates Inc., a Chicago consulting firm. Five of those seven periods occurred before 1942, four of them during the Great Depression. Since then, there have been only two five-year stretches when stocks have lost money.

Not only are stocks unlikely to lose money over long time periods, they also do a dandy job of outpacing inflation. According to Ibbotson Associates, stocks have returned 10.3% a year since the end of 1925. That compares with 5.2% a year for intermediate-term government bonds and 3.7% annually for Treasury bills. Inflation, meanwhile, has run at a 3.1% annual rate over the same period.

Stocks have thus earned 7.2 percentage points a year more than inflation since 1925, compared with an annual 2.1 percentage points above inflation for intermediate-term government bonds. . . .

Because stocks perform handsomely over long periods, financial advisers usually suggest putting a large chunk of a retirement portfolio into the stock market. The more years you have to go until retirement, the bigger that chunk should be.

Bonds and money market instruments add some downside protection to a portfolio. As a result, they can be particularly appropriate for older investors who don't have decades to recoup their losses from any big stock market drop. . . .

Investment adviser John Blankinship Jr. believes mutual funds are the best way to tap into the securities markets, because they allow small investors to buy diversified portfolios run by professional money managers. Funds are especially useful for buying into exotic areas like foreign stocks and high-yield junk bonds, which are difficult for investors to tap into directly.

"Unless your portfolio is worth $2 million or more, it's difficult to get proper diversification by buying individual securities," argues Mr. Blankinship of Blankinship & Foster, a Del Mar, Calif., investment firm. . . .

Investors may also want to skip mutual funds when it comes to buying U.S. stocks, says John Markese, president of Chicago's American Association of Individual Investors. He thinks diligent investors may be able to add to their returns by picking individual

stocks, especially if they bargain hunt among smaller-company stocks that are less closely followed by Wall Street analysts and thus are more likely to be undervalued. . . .

Of course, the world of investment options doesn't end with mutual funds and individual stocks. What about all those other investments, like limited partnerships, commodity pools, penny stocks, options and futures?

"Most of those things are either very difficult to understand or impossible to understand for individual investors," says Mr. Markese. "Don't invest in anything that you don't fully understand. There's a whole laundry list of things to avoid, from penny stocks to exotic derivatives."

SOURCE: Jonathan Clements, "Three Steps to Becoming a Successful Investor," *Wall Street Journal*, 11 June 1993.

If the current market price of ABC stock actually implies an annual return of 20%, the stock is undervalued and should be bought. For example, the stock might now be trading at $50 per share, be expected to pay a $1 dividend during the next year, and be expected to sell for $59 one year hence. Then the expected single-period return actually implied by today's price is 20%:

$$0.20 = \frac{\$59 - \$50 + \$1}{\$50}$$

The stock would be a bargain at $50, and investors would actively purchase the stock until its current price increases to $51.72 (the price necessary to provide a fair return of 16%).

Security Valuation

Security pricing models are based upon the present values of future cash flows that the security is expected to pay to its owners. In the case of a common stock, these cash flows represent yearly cash dividends (plus an eventual liquidating dividend if the corporation is expected to cease operations at some future date). In the case of a bond, cash flows represent yearly coupon payments plus the face value of the bond at maturity. Symbolically, the basic valuation model is written:

Basic Valuation $$P_0 = \frac{CF_1}{(1 + k)} + \frac{CF_2}{(1 + k)^2} + \frac{CF_3}{(1 + k)^3} + \dots + \frac{CF_N}{(1 + k)^N} \qquad (1.3)$$

where P_0 = today's fair value of the security, CF_t = the expected cash flow in period t, k = the required periodic return given the security's risk, and N = the last date at which a cash flow is received.

Conceptually, security valuation is straightforward: one need only estimate expected future cash flows plus a fair discount rate and then plug them into Equation 1.3 to obtain a value estimate. Pragmatically, however, these values can be difficult to estimate. Expected dividend flows on common stock, for example, require forecasts of future product developments, sales, inflation, cost control, debt policy, taxes, etcetera. The list can be almost endless.

Association for Investment Management and Research

In attempts to find mispriced securities, considerable effort is spent on forecasting a security's expected future cash flows and the proper rate of return at which cash flows should be discounted. Most people who perform such financial analyses belong to a professional organization known as the *Association for Investment Management and Research* (AIMR). The AIMR sponsors publications, professional meetings, and research studies. The association also develops ethical guidelines and has developed a professional designation known as a Chartered Financial Analyst (CFA). To become CFA, the candidate must work in an area directly related to security investment and pass three exams that test the candidate's knowledge of portfolio management, security analysis, accounting, economics, and ethics. Many end-of-chapter problems and questions used in this text are drawn from past CFA exams.

Efficient Investment Markets

When financial analysts discover something about a security that is not reflected in its current price, they will make a purchase or sale recommendation. As investors trade on this information, the security's price will change until the price fully "discounts" the information. In the extreme, the current price of the security will fully reflect all information that might be available about the security at present. And as new information eventually becomes available, security prices will change rapidly to reflect the new information.

A security market is said to be *efficiently priced* if security prices fully reflect all known information. Clearly, the notion of an efficient market is an extreme concept. To fully reflect *all* known information demands a great deal. For the past 25 years, scholars and practitioners have been investigating the extent to which security markets can be characterized as price efficient. We know that they can not be perfectly efficient. If so, there would be no incentives to attract financial analysts to watch for and develop new information. Only the extent of market inefficiency is a question.

Most research has been addressed to well-developed markets such as those in the United States, United Kingdom, Continental Europe, Japan, and Australia.

And, while chinks have been found in this *efficient market hypothesis,* security markets are surprisingly more efficient than many people believe.

SUMMARY

This text deals with the major types of financial securities that are actively traded in world security markets. We began in this chapter by reviewing the growth and size of such markets, who owns the securities, and who controls the management of security portfolios.

At the end of 1991, the value of world financial markets was $23.8 trillion, up from $5.6 trillion in 1980, approximately one-half. Approximately one-half of this equity value was in countries other than the United States. Clearly, investment decisions must be made with a global perspective.

Accurate data on the ownership and control of financial assets is available principally for the United States. When this data is examined, the basic conclusion is that the ownership position of institutional investors has grown to the point that institutions own almost 50% of U.S. equities. Institutional investors include organizations such as pension funds and mutual funds. The growing importance of institutional trading has had significant impacts on the types of securities traded and the manner in which they are traded. Data about who controls (manages) financial assets confirms the importance of institutional investors. At the end of 1991, more than 70% of U.S. equity value was professionally managed.

Given the size of financial markets, it is clear that they must provide important benefits to society. One benefit is the ability to capitalize on a valuable new idea, even if one does not personally have the personal resources to do so. Another is flexibility in consumption. People have the ability to borrow in order to consume when they do not currently have real assets necessary for their consumption needs. Similarly, they can lend in financial markets when they have excess real assets. Financial markets also improve one's ability to diversify and improve the liquidity of securities held.

In the last section of the chapter, we reviewed various investment concepts. The two most important ideas were that higher returns come with increased return variability and that return variability can be reduced (but not eliminated) by proper diversification strategies.

CHAPTER QUESTIONS AND PROBLEMS

At the end of each chapter, a variety of questions and problems are presented to aid you in understanding the concepts and techniques discussed. One or more extended *Review Problems,* together with detailed Solutions, are presented first. These are followed by a number of *Questions and Problems,* which vary in difficulty. Some of the questions do not have well-defined right and wrong responses but instead are designed to provoke thought and discussion. Selected answers to many of these problems are provided in an Appendix at the back of the book. Many of the Questions and Problems are drawn from past CFA Examinations. These are identified by a ⬤CFA symbol.

End-of-chapter problems also include one or more *Datafile Analyses*. These are computer-based projects that use actual security market data to illustrate various concepts covered in the chapter. These Datafile Analyses require access to desktop computers and involve a greater time commitment than standard end-of-chapter problems. But the payoff can be worth much more than the cost. For example, many of the analyses are close to the studies performed by professional investment consultants when they evaluate alternative asset allocations, conduct an investment manager search, or evaluate investment manager performance.

The datafiles used in these problems can be read using any common spreadsheet package. Details about the contents of each file can be obtained by printing the file labeled README.DOC. The following are examples of the type of data included:

1. Yearly, quarterly, and monthly returns on major stock and bond indexes. Both U.S. and non-U.S. indexes are included.
2. Quarter-end prices and dividends on stocks included in the Dow Jones Industrial Average.
3. Quarterly returns on many mutual funds. These include U.S. equity, U.S. bond, and international equity funds. Data on each fund's total assets, investment objective, load, expense ratio, etc. are also provided.
4. Year-end prices, dividends, and earnings of the Dow Jones Industrial and Standard & Poors Indexes.

In addition to these datafiles, a computer program that calculates efficient frontiers is used in a number of the Datafile Analysis problems. This package is referred to as ASSETALL (for asset allocation). Information about this package can be obtained by printing the file labeled ASSETALL.DOC.

REVIEW PROBLEM

Shown below is a data set that consists of the price per share of two securities at various quarter-ends and total dividends paid on each security during the quarter.

	IBM		AMF	
YEAR/QTR	Price	DPS	Price	DPS
91/4	$89.000	$1.21	$21.05	$1.10
91/3	$103.625	$1.21	$20.91	$0.22
91/2	$97.125	$1.21	$20.29	$0.22
91/1	$113.875	$1.21	$20.18	$0.00
90/4	$105.375	$1.21	$18.67	$0.77
90/3	$106.375	$1.21	$18.20	$0.21
90/2	$117.500	$1.21	$20.14	$0.21
90/1	$106.125	$1.21	$19.91	$0.00

YEAR/QTR	IBM		AMF	
	Price	DPS	Price	DPS
89/4	$94.125	$1.21	$20.20	$1.36
89/3	$109.250	$1.21	$21.06	$0.21
89/2	$111.875	$1.21	$19.80	$0.20
89/1	$109.125	$1.10	$18.61	$0.00

IBM is International Business Machines, the well-known computer manufacturer. AMF is American Mutual Fund, a mutual fund that usually invests in the common shares of about 60 U.S. companies.

a. Calculate the quarterly returns on each security.

b. Why are the returns of IBM more volatile than those of AMF?

Solution

a.

YEAR/QTR	RATES OF RETURN	
	IBM	AMF
91/4	− 12.95%	5.93%
91/3	7.94%	4.14%
91/2	− 13.65%	1.64%
91/1	9.21%	8.09%
90/4	0.20%	6.81%
90/3	− 8.44%	− 8.59%
90/2	11.86%	2.21%
90/1	14.03%	− 1.44%
89/4	− 12.74%	2.37%
89/3	− 1.26%	7.42%
89/2	3.63%	7.47%
89/1	NA	NA

b. AMF is a well-diversified mutual fund that holds shares in many firms. Therefore, the return series of AMF will be less volatile.

QUESTIONS AND PROBLEMS

1. What are the two economic motives for saving a portion of one's wealth?
2. Distinguish between investment, speculation, and arbitrage.
3. You are considering a one-year investment in security A or security B. You are *certain* that the one-year return on A will be 12% and that the return on B will be 8%. Is there any reason for you to diversify by purchasing some of each security?
4. What is the difference between naive and efficient diversification? Give an example of naive diversification.
5. You are considering a one-year investment in security C and security D. You expect a one-year return of 12% on each but are uncertain that it will be earned. However, knowing the securities, you are certain that if one security has a return less than 12%, this will have no affect on the return of the other. Is there any reason for you to diversify by purchasing some of each security?
6. The trustees of a pension portfolio hire professional investment managers to manage the equity securities of the portfolio. At present, three managers are employed. One manager in particular has been very successful and has earned returns higher than the

others. This has resulted in a situation in which this manager now controls 60% of all equity assets. The types of equities purchased by this manager are of very small companies engaged in high technology. There are two factions among the trustees. One group is thankful for the manager's past performance but wishes to transfer assets from the manager to the other two managers in an attempt to better diversify the portfolio. The other group believes the manager should retain her current assets and perhaps be given additional assets to manage as compensation for her past good performance. What thoughts do you have on this issue?

7. The federal government of the German Democratic Republic has issued debt securities that will pay 100 marks at the end of years 1–3 plus 1,100 marks at the end of year 4. Expected returns on equivalent securities are 10% per year. What should be the market value of these securities?

8. What is meant by the notion of an efficiently priced security market?

9. If security markets are *not* efficiently priced, who wins?

10. Leslie Mostly inherited $100,000 last year and decided to use the money to begin a long-term investment plan. Her initial decision was to split the $100,000 into equal dollar holdings of common stocks and bonds. One year after this initial investment, her stock holdings had a market value of $55,000 and her bonds were worth $51,000. Leslie received total cash dividends on the stocks of $2,500 and total coupons on the bonds of $4,000. (This cash was *not* reinvested in the portfolio.)
    a. What was Leslie's actual return on her stocks and bonds during the past year?
    b. What was the dividend yield on the stocks and the current yield on the bonds?
    c. Why does the total return on each investment differ from its dividend yield or current yield? Which do you believe is a better measure of each investment's return during the year—the answer in part a or the answer in part b?
    d. What was Leslie's total return on her full $100,000 investment?

11. How does society benefit if security markets are efficiently priced?

12. How might individuals and corporations be harmed if security markets are not efficiently priced?

13. The chapter began with a discussion of the history of three banks. Two failed and one was quite successful. How could investors have reduced their risk exposure inherent in owning these stocks (without prior knowledge of who would succeed and who would fail)?

14. Briefly review the past nominal and real return history of U.S. Treasury Bonds and large U.S. common stocks. What important conclusions should be drawn?

DATAFILE ANALYSIS

1. *Introduction.* Obtain the computer diskette from your instructor that contains the datafiles provided with this text. Associated with these files is an ASCII data set called README.DOC. This file provides an overview of information provided in each datafile. Print this file and keep the output for future reference. Each file can be accessed by a standard spreadsheet package.

2. *Calculate Stock Returns.* Access the QTLYSTK.WK1 data files and review its contents. For each quarter (starting with June 30, 1976), calculate the quarterly rates of return for Aluminum Co. and American Brands.
    a. Find the minimum and maximum quarterly return for each company.
    b. Calculate the quarterly returns on a portfolio of these two stocks in which an equal investment in each stock is made at the *start* of each quarter.

   c. Find the minimum and maximum quarterly returns for this portfolio.

   d. Why is the portfolio's minimum and maximum less variable than is true for the individual stocks?

3. *Asset Class Returns.* Access the RTNSYRLY.WK1 datafile and review its contents. Calculate the average yearly returns for U. S Treasury Bills, 20-year Treasury Bonds, and the S&P 500 index (an index of large U.S. stocks) for the period of 1926–1991. Why are these averages so different?

SELECTED REFERENCES

An entertaining discussion of investment theory and its practical implications for security selection can be found in:

MALKIEL, BURTON, *A Random Walk Down Wall Street,* New York: W. W. Norton, 1981.

A more detailed, but still understandable, review of investment theory is presented in:

BREALEY, RICHARD A., *An Introduction to Risk and Return from Common Stocks,* Cambridge, MA: MIT Press, 1983.

Each year, the business magazine *Fortune* has a special issue entitled ''Investors' Guide.'' These publications provide timely discussion of financial markets and advice on the creation of investment portfolios. A thorough study of historical security returns is presented in:

ROGER G. IBBOTSON and GARY P. BRINSON, *Investment Markets,* New York: McGraw-Hill, 1987.

These results are updated yearly by Ibbotson Associates in the following publication:

Stocks, Bonds, Bills and Inflation, Ibbotson-Associates, Inc. Chicago, updated yearly.

A thorough discussion of portfolio management designed for investment consultants is presented in:

MAGINN, JOHN L. and DONALD L. TUTTLE, Eds. *Managing Investment Portfolios,* Boston: Warren, Gorham and Lamont, 1990.

Finally, if you are interested in journals that have articles aimed at individual investors or practicing investment analysts, you should become familiar with:

The Journal of Portfolio Management, published quarterly by the Institutional Investor, New York.
The Financial Analysts Journal, published bimonthly by the Association for Investment Management and Research, Charlottesville, VA.
AAII Journal, published bimonthly by the American Association of Individual Investors, Chicago.

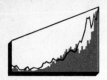

Security Types

In this chapter, we review the major types of marketable securities that trade in world markets. Due to the size and complexity of the U.S. security markets, most of our discussion relates to securities traded in the United States. Similar securities are also traded in other financially developed countries, although with varying degrees of activity. But even if a particular type of security might not be traded actively in another country today, it is most likely that an active trading market will arise to support economic growth.

Our discussion in this chapter is introductory. Just enough is said to provide a basic understanding of the institutional characteristics of each security class so that the conceptual material presented in Part 2 of the text can be better appreciated. Detailed analyses of each security class are presented in Part 3, in which one or more chapters are devoted to each security type.

Although every security is different in some respect from other securities, it is useful to categorize them into various classes based on their type and amount of investment risk. Direct security claims are assigned to one of three asset classes: (1) debt securities with a maturity of less than one to three years referred to as *money market* instruments, debt securities with a maturity of more than three years referred to as *capital market* fixed income securities, and (3) *equity* securities. Indirect claims are classified as either derivatives or commingled portfolios. An estimate of the 1991 U.S. dollar value of direct security claims is shown below.

Security Type	Estimated 1991 Market Value ($ trillion)		
	U.S.	*Non-U.S.*	*Total*
Debt Securities			
Money Market	$1.8	$0.5	$2.3
Fixed Income	4.4	6.8	11.2
Total	$6.2	$7.3	$13.5
Equity	4.4	6.0	10.4

After reading this chapter, you will be amazed at the wide variety of securities that are traded and, perhaps, even wish that the security markets were less complex. But there is a reason for this complexity that should be understood and appreciated. Each security form meets the needs of a segment of the investing public and provides an economic benefit to both purchasers and issuers of the security! This statement should not be taken lightly. Unless these securities provided a unique economic value to both their issuers and their owners, they would not continue to be traded. They are vital to the economic operations of modern society.

MONEY MARKET SECURITIES

Money market securities are debt obligations that usually have low risk of default, short maturities (one year or less), and are actively traded in financial markets. Estimates of the market value of U.S. money market securities at the end of 1991 are shown in Table 2-1. The total value of $1.8 trillion represented about 30% of the value of all publicly traded debt securities in the United States. Non-U.S. money market instruments had a U.S. dollar value equal to about 30% that of U.S. money market securities.

Organizations with temporary needs for cash sell money market securities to individuals and organizations with temporary excess cash. Transactions are large ($100 million is not uncommon) and span short intervals (overnight to one year). Large organizations participate in the money market by direct ownership of instruments. Individuals with smaller sums of money to invest typically participate indirectly through *money market funds;* mutual funds that pool shareholder resources to buy money market instruments.

U.S. Treasury Bills

At the end of 1991, U.S. Treasury bills (or T-bills) had a market value of about $590 billion. This represented about one-third the value of all money market securities in the United States. T-bills are obligations sold by the U.S. Treasury to help finance federal expenditures. At the time of the initial sale, an auction procedure is used in which money market banks, dealers, and other institutional investors submit competitive bids for a given dollar amount. Prices are quoted as a percentage of the T-bill's face value. For example, a bank might submit a bid of $98.275 on a $100 million issue, which, if accepted, means $98.275 million will be paid for bills having a face value of $100 million. Noncompetitive bids may also be made. When the new issue is awarded, the total face value of all noncompetitive bids is subtracted from the face value amount of bills being sold, and the remainder is distributed to competitive bidders offering the highest prices. Competitive bidders pay the price they bid, and noncompetitive bidders pay a price equal to the weighted average price of the competitive sales.

T-bills are referred to as *pure discount bonds* because they do not pay a coupon; the return to the owner comes totally from any price appreciation. As noted above, T-bill prices and discounts are stated as a percentage of face value. Discounts and

TABLE 2-1 *Estimates of the Market Value of U.S. Money Market Securities (End of 1991 in $Billions)*

Security Type	Estimated Value of Securities Outstanding
T-bills	$590.4
Commercial paper	530.3
Negotiable certificates of deposit	435.6
Repurchase agreements	205.2
Bankers acceptances	43.7
Short-term municipals	NA
Eurodollars	NA
Total	$1,804.5

SOURCE: "Estimates of the Market Value of United States Money Market Securities" derived from the FEDERAL RESERVE BULLETIN, March 1992. Reprinted by permission.

percentage prices are determined using a procedure known as the *bank discount method,* assuming there are 360 days per year, according to the following formula:

Bank Discount Method

$$D = Fd\left(\frac{t}{360}\right)$$ (2.1)

$$P = F - D$$

where D = the dollar discount on the $100 face value, F = the $100 face value, d = the quoted yearly discount rate, t = the number of days to maturity, and P = the price per $100 of face value.

For example, if a new three-month (91-day) bill is bought at a quoted discount of 8.55%, the price paid would be 97.83875% of face value (or $97.83875 per $100 of face value):

$$D = \$100 \times 0.0855 \times \left(\frac{91}{360}\right) = \$2.16125$$

$$P = \$100 - \$2.16125 = \$97.83875$$

It is important to recognize that the quoted discount on a T-bill is *not* the true yield to the owner. This discount represents a percentage below face value, whereas the true yield represents the percentage return on the price paid.

There are two general ways of expressing the rate of return on a T-bill. The first is based on *simple* interest and the second is based on *compound* interest. To convert from quoted discounts to effective simple interest yield to maturity, the following formula is often used:

Simple Interest T-Bill Return

r = effective simple interest yield

$$r = \frac{365 \times d}{360 - dt}$$ (2.2)

Using the formula, an 8.55% discount on a 91-day bill results in an *effective simple interest* annualized yield of 8.86%:

$$r = \frac{365 \times 0.0855}{360 - (0.0855 \times 91)} = 0.0886$$

To understand more clearly what this annualized simple interest yield of 8.86% is, consider the following. First, the bill is purchased for $97.83875 and pays back $100 91 days later. This represents a 2.209% 91-day return:

$$91\text{-day return} = \frac{\$100 - \$97.83875}{\$97.83875} = 0.02209$$

To annualize this 91-day return, it is *multiplied* by the number of 91-day periods there are in a 365-day year. This result is 8.86%, identical to that obtained with Equation 2.2 above:

$$0.02209 \times \frac{365}{91} = 0.0886$$

To calculate the *effective compound interest* yield, Equation 2.3 would be used where r' = effective compound interest yield:

**Compound Interest
T-Bill Return** $\qquad r' = \left(\frac{F}{P}\right)^{365/t} - 1.0 \qquad\qquad$ **(2.3)**

Using the data above, the effective annual compound yield would be 9.159%:

$$r' = \left(\frac{\$100}{\$97.83875}\right)^{365/91} - 1.0 = (1.02209)^{365/91} - 1.0 = 0.09159$$

The reason the two annualized yields vary is easy to see. During the 91-day holding period, the rate of return is clearly 2.209%. To annualize this 91-day return, the simple interest approach *multiplies* by 4.01 (the number of 91-day periods in a year), whereas the compound interest approach *compounds* this return for 4.01 periods. But which approach is the better one to use? The answer depends upon whether this is a one-time purchase or other 91-day bills will be consistently purchased in the future. If this is a one-time purchase, the simple interest approach is a realistic estimate of the equivalent annual return. However, if a policy of "rolling over" a sequence of such 91-day bills is expected to be used, then the compound interest approach should be used.

Bills may be bought with either a competitive or a noncompetitive bid at the time of initial offering by the Treasury or after the initial offering from banks and brokers who are qualified to act as government security dealers. Government security dealers provide an active secondary market in all U.S. government securities. Prices at which they are willing to buy or sell are quoted daily in the financial press. An illustration of how these quotes appear is shown below. The quotes are for June 3, 1992;

Sample T-Bill Quotations for Close of Trading June 3, 1992

Maturity	Days to Maturity	Discount		Ask Yield
		Bid	Ask	
June 11, 1992	6	3.65	3.55	3.61
Sept 3, 1992	90	3.71	3.69	3.78
Dec 3, 1992	181	3.86	3.84	3.97
June 3, 1993	363	4.08	4.06	4.25

Quotes are stated in terms of discounts. The *bid discount* is the highest price at which a dealer was willing to buy at the close of trading on June 3, 1992. The *asked discount* is the lowest price at which a dealer would sell. The number of days to actual maturity are two less than the actual number of calendar days. This allows for a two-day period between the date of a trade and the actual date at which cash is paid and the security is registered with the new owner. This is referred to as *skip day* delivery.[1] For example, bills maturing on September 3 were quoted to have 90 days to maturity whereas there were actually 92 days between June 3 and September 3. This T-bill could have been bought from a dealer at $99.0775 or sold to a dealer at $99.0725.

Dealer's Selling Price $= 100 - 0.0369 (100) (90/360)$

$$= 99.0775$$

Dealer's Purchase Price $= 100 - 0.0371 (100) (90/360)$

$$= 99.0725$$

The effective annual yield of 3.78% is calculated using Equation 2.2 as follows:

$$0.0378 = \frac{365 \times 0.0369}{360 - 0.0369 (90)}$$

U.S. T-bills have par values as small as $10,000. State and local taxes are not paid on T-bill income. Owners are registered in Federal Reserve Board computers.

Other Treasury instruments similar to T-bills are also issued occasionally. Tax anticipation notes mature about a week after tax payments are due but may be tendered (turned in) on the tax date and credited against the tax bill *at par*. Since their face value maturity can be hastened by one week, the effective annualized return increases. The U.S. government sells many other debt obligations through either the Treasury or various federal agencies. Since most of these securities are

---

[1] Most bill trades are actually settled the following day (i.e., have a one-day delivery). Prices quoted in the financial press, however, are assumed to have a two-day delivery. This *skip day* delivery quote is used because individuals view the quote in the financial press one day after the quote occurred. For example, bills maturing on September 3 were quoted to have 90 days to maturity whereas there were actually 92 days between June 3 and September 3. This T-bill could have been bought from a dealer at $99.0775 or sold to a dealer at $99.0725 for delivery of cash and securities two days later.

commonly thought of as capital market instruments, they are reviewed later in the chapter. However, because of their low default risk, their high marketability, and the fact that, as time passes, many such issues have short-term maturities, they can often qualify as money market securities. For example, the Federal Home Loan Bank and other agencies sell short-term discount securities which resemble T-bills. Because of their somewhat poorer marketability and slightly greater default risk, these securities sell at yields greater than those of T-bills. Spreads of 5 to 100 basis points are common. A *basis point* represents one-hundredth of a percentage point. For example, if yields rise from 8.55% to 8.90%, they have risen 35 basis points.

Commercial Paper

Commercial paper is an *unsecured promissory note* issued by financially strong finance companies and manufacturing firms. In recent years, it has been the second largest type of money market instrument outstanding in the United States. Commercial paper issuers use this form of financing as an alternative to short-term bank loans. In fact, the growth of the commercial paper market is traced to the mid-1960s when banks had restrictions on the interest rates they could pay depositors in order to attract capital. Since market interest rates had risen above the bank interest limit, banks were unable to obtain sufficient capital to meet the borrowing demands of corporations. As a result, corporations began to obtain financing directly from the national securities market.

Commercial paper is generally issued on a discount basis with maturities of 270 days or less. To reduce the risk of default, commercial paper is backed with lines of credit from banks that guarantee that the issuer will have the cash necessary at maturity. Commercial paper is initially sold both directly by the issuer and through commercial paper dealers. Denominations are in amounts of $100,000 and up. While a relatively active trading market exists, many purchasers hold the paper until maturity. Commercial paper rates are close to those available on certificates of deposit and bankers' acceptances with similar maturity. Income is not exempt from state and local tax, and the securities have more default risk and less liquidity than T-bills.

Certificates of Deposit

At the end of 1991, negotiable certificates of deposit available in the United States had a market value of about $435 billion and constituted the third largest type of money market security. Negotiable certificates of deposit (CDs) are *large deposits* ($100,000 or more) *placed in commercial banks at a stated rate of interest.* Unlike other bank CDs, negotiable CDs may be bought and sold in the open market. They qualify as money market instruments since they have short maturities, have low default risk (although they are insured in part by the Federal Deposit Insurance Corporation, their risk features depend upon the issuing bank), and are reasonably marketable because of their salability in the open market. Their yields are slightly higher than those of equivalent maturity T-bills (25 to 100 basis points) because of their greater risk and poorer marketability.

Repurchase Agreements

Repurchase agreements (repos, or RPs) are not physical securities issued by one party to another. Instead, they are *contractual agreements* between two parties to buy and sell U.S. government securities at particular points in time. Consider the hypothetical example of First Income Securities Corporation, a dealer in U.S. government obligations. First Income Securities generates profits in three ways: by acting as a wholesaler of government securities (standing ready to buy at bid and sell at asked prices), by speculating on future changes in interest rates (buying bonds when rates are expected to fall and selling when rates are expected to rise), and by a variety of arbitrage transactions. In the course of business, the firm is likely to own government securities in amounts considerably in excess of the company's equity capital. The firm can finance this security inventory using either a bank loan or a repurchase agreement. Since repos are often cheaper, they are extensively used.

To enter into a repurchase agreement, First Income will sell a portion of the firm's government securities to, say, a city government which has temporary excess cash *and will agree to repurchase the securities at a stated price on a stated date.* Although the repo is written in a way suggesting that securities are actually sold and are later to be repurchased, in substance the municipality has given the dealer a short-term loan collateralized by U.S. government securities. The effective interest rate on the loan (return to the repo buyer) is simply the percentage difference between the sale price and the purchase price. Such a trade is often profitable to the repo seller (First Income Securities) since the interest rate paid to the repo buyer is often less than the yield on the government securities owned. For example, 181-day T-bills yielding 8.50% might be RP'd for three months at 8.40% and RP'd again for another three months at 8.40%. The repo seller would take the 10-basis-point ''carry'' as profit. The repo buyer would be willing to accept such a low yield because alternative investments with similar risk and scheduled maturity are unavailable. This is especially true for *overnight repos*—situations in which the lender wishes to invest for one day but can find no alternatives available other than a repurchase agreement. Dealers can thus finance large holdings of U.S. governments by continuously reentering into a sequence of many overnight repos.

The term *reverse RP,* which refers to the mirror image of an RP in which securities are acquired with a simultaneous agreement to resell, is sometimes used.

Bankers' Acceptances

A bankers' acceptance is a *time draft* that the accepting bank has agreed to pay at a specified future date. Historically, most bankers' acceptances have arisen in the course of international trade. For example, a U.S. firm might wish to import shoes from a Japanese exporter. The U.S. firm will have its U.S. banker write a *letter of credit* to the Japanese exporter guaranteeing that the goods will be paid for. After receiving the letter of credit, the exporter will ship the goods and simultaneously prepare a draft on the domestic bank. This draft is taken to a Japanese bank together with supporting documentation, such as the letter of credit and shipping documents, and the Japanese bank pays the exporter. The draft is then sent to the U.S. bank, where it is "accepted." At this point, a *bankers' acceptance* has been created which may be returned to the Japanese bank (if it wishes to hold the acceptance as an investment), kept by the domestic bank (if the Japanese bank wants immediate cash and the domestic bank wishes to hold it as an investment), or sold in the open market.

In effect, a bankers' acceptance is a *promissory note* which stipulates a payment amount and a date at which it will be paid. Final payment is made by the U.S. importer or by the accepting bank if the importer defaults. Acceptances are traded on a discount basis with the return to the owner consisting of the difference between the price paid and the acceptance's face value. Denominations of $100,000 or more are normal. Since both the importer and the accepting bank have agreed to pay, default risk is minimal. This low risk and a fairly active trading market allow bankers' acceptances to trade at yields only 25 to 100 basis points greater than those for T-bills with similar maturity.

Bankers' acceptances are used by borrowers who are either too small or too risky to use commercial paper. As a result, the rates are slightly above commercial paper rates. In recent years acceptances have been increasingly used to finance domestic as well as international transactions.

Short-Term Municipal Obligations

The term *municipal* is used to refer to any politically incorporated body other than the federal government and its agencies. Examples are state, county, and city governments, school districts, and turnpike and port authorities. Municipal securities are sold with maturities ranging anywhere from a month to 30 years. The shorter-term, high-quality obligations often qualify as money market instruments.

Eurodollars

Eurodollars are simply deposits in foreign banks *denominated in U.S. dollars.* The market initially developed in Europe, hence the term *Eurodollars.* Today the name is a misnomer since U.S. dollar-denominated deposits can be made in almost any country. Deposits are usually made for a stated time interval (six months or less) and pay a stated rate of interest. Banks receiving Eurodollar deposits use them to make loans also denominated in dollars. The Eurodollar market is a relatively recent phenomenon, growing to major international importance since the early 1960s. Today it represents a major source of financing and investment to large international organizations. Eurodollar deposits are relatively free of default risk, can be easily bought or sold, and are not subject to many of the regulations imposed by the U.S. government on deposits made in domestic U.S. banks. Because of the activities of domestic banks in the market, interest rates tend to track very closely the rates charged on domestic Fed funds.

Federal Funds

The only traders in the Federal funds market are commercial banks that are members of the Federal Reserve System. These banks are required to maintain a specified portion of their total deposits in cash, either as cash in their vaults or as cash deposited with the Federal Reserve System. Since rates of return are not paid on any required reserves maintained with the Federal Reserve, member banks attempt to maintain the smallest possible reserve position. However, since deposit increases and withdrawals cannot be predicted with complete accuracy, some banks find themselves with temporary excess reserves while others are temporarily deficient. As a result, a market has arisen that allows banks with excess reserves to lend to those with deficiencies. This market is known as the Fed funds market.

The Fed funds market is extremely active and deals with huge sums of money. Most borrowing and lending is done on an *overnight* (one-day) basis, although some *term* Fed funds are traded. Many banks rely upon brokers to bring together buyers and sellers, although some banks rely upon correspondent banks or personal knowledge. While the market is not available to non-bank borrowers or lenders, many traders believe that the overnight Fed funds rate is the base on which other money market rates rest.

Trends in Money Market Rates

In Figure 2-1, annualized yields are shown for various money market securities. Their individual rates move together over time with U.S. T-bills consistently among the lowest. During the late 1970s and early 1980s, annualized yields rose dramatically in response to previous unexpected inflation. After inflation was reduced in the mid-1980s, money market rates fell but did not decline as much as did the inflation rate. Thus the real return on these securities increased. However, in 1992, interest rates fell dramatically as the Federal Reserve Board took actions to stimulate U.S. economic growth.

FIXED-INCOME CAPITAL MARKET

Capital market securities differ from money market securities in one or more of the following ways: (1) their maturity is greater than one year, (2) their default risk is greater, and (3) their marketability is poorer. However, a clear distinction between capital market and money market instruments doesn't always exist. For example, Treasury notes and bonds which are about to mature might well be

FIGURE 2-1 *Annual Returns*

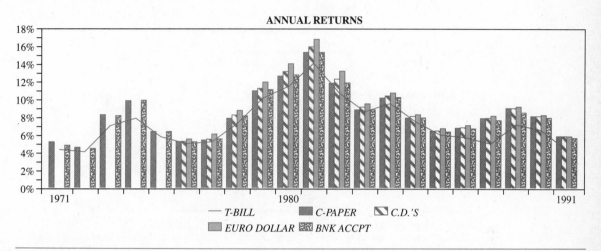

SOURCE: *Federal Reserve Bulletins.*

considered money market securities. The distinction between these two markets is made to add some (slightly artificial) clarity and organization to what is indeed a complex realm of securities.

We will examine only publicly traded fixed income securities. It is important to realize, however, that substantial amounts of debt are privately owned. This private debt market ranges from World Bank loans to countries to credit card loans to individuals. In addition, we will continue to treat only publicly traded debt in the United States. Equivalent securities are traded in many markets world-wide.

Estimates of the size of the major U.S. debt markets as of 1991 are shown in Table 2-2. Governmental obligations accounted for more than one-half the value of all publicly traded fixed income securities. Securities collateralized by home mortgage pools represented about one-quarter of traded fixed income securities. These two types of debt issues grew rapidly during the 1980s and accounted for virtually all the expansion of publicly traded U.S. debt during the 1980s. Surprisingly, corporate debt comprised only 13% of the total.

U.S. Treasury Issues

The U.S. Treasury offers two types of fixed-income securities with maturities greater than one year: Treasury notes and Treasury bonds. These are essentially identical except that *notes* have an initial maturity of ten years or less, whereas *bonds* have a maturity in excess of ten years. Both pay coupons semiannually. They are initially offered by the Treasury in competitive auctions similar to T-bill auctions except that bidders submit desired yields to maturity, as opposed to

TABLE 2-2 *Estimates of the Market Value of Publicly Traded U.S. Fixed Income Securities (End of 1991 in $Billions)*

Security Type	Estimated Value of Securities Outstanding
U.S. Treasuries	$1,606.8
U.S. Agencies	256.9
Total Federal Government	$1,863.7
State and Local Governments	850.0
Total Governmental	$2,713.7
Corporate	605.4
Mortgage Backed	1,043.1
Asset Backed	73.1
Total	$4,435.3

SOURCE: "Estimates of the Market Value of Publicly Traded United States Fixed Income Securities" derived from the FEDERAL RESERVE BULLETIN, March 1992. Reprinted by permission.

discounts, for bills. The average winning bid is then used to determine the issue's coupon (stated in eighths of a dollar) so that the securities can be sold at close to total face value.

Once issued by the Treasury, notes and bonds can be bought or sold in the same manner as T-bills—through large government security dealers. Buyers pay the dealer an asked price and sellers receive the bid price. An illustration of how note and bond quotes appear in the financial pages is shown below.

Sample T-bond and Note Quotations for the Close of Trading on June 3, 1992

Coupon Rate	Maturity	Bid	Ask	Ask Yield
9⅛	Dec 92n	102:27	102:29	3.91%
7⅝	Dec 93n	104:06	104:08	4.78
7⅞	Feb 95-00	103:05	103:09	6.53
7⅝	Feb 02-07	100:15	100:19	7.54
8	Nov 21	101:13	101:15	7.78

The *coupon rate* represents the annual coupon paid on the bond, though coupons are actually paid semi-annually. For example, the 8's pay $40 each six months (in May and November in this case) for a $1,000 face value. Maturities with the symbol "n" refer to Treasury notes. All others are T-bonds. Bid and ask prices are shown with a colon. For example, the 8% coupon bond due in November of 2021 has a quoted bid price of 101:13. The :13 means $13/32$. This issue could have been sold to a representative government bond dealer at a price equal to 101.4063 percent of par. Many Treasuries are callable prior to maturity, which means that the Treasury can repurchase such bonds at a date before the scheduled maturity.

These issues are those with two maturity dates listed. For example, the 7⅝ T-bond can be retired any time between February 2002 and 2007. Finally, the ask yield column represents the *yield to maturity* of each issue. Basically, the yield to maturity is the best estimate of the annual return available to purchasers of the issue who intend to hold the bond to its maturity. In future chapters, we discuss why this yield to maturity is only an estimate. (When callable bonds are selling at prices above face value, the yield shown is the yield to the first possible call data.)

Treasury notes and bonds have the lowest default risk and greatest marketability possible on securities of their maturity. As such, they represent the foundation on which yields of other bonds having similar maturity but different risk and marketability are based.

In 1985, the U.S. Treasury announced the *Separate Trading of Registered Interest and Principal of Securities*—STRIPS. Under the STRIPS program, "selected Treasury Securities may be maintained in the book entry system operated by the Federal Reserve banks in a manner that permits separate trading and ownership of the interest and principal payments." The Treasury does not actually auction zero-coupon bonds. All sales of new bonds are conducted exactly as they have been in the past—with coupon-bearing bonds. However, once the bond is outstanding, the Federal Reserve facilitates the purchase or sale of specified coupons or principal cash flows. Many of the new Treasury bonds are noncallable. Thus, a truly long-term default-free and noncallable zero-coupon bond is available.

Illustrative quoted prices for U.S. Treasury strips are shown below. The same pricing convention used with bonds and notes is also used with strips (37:03 = 37³/₃₂% of par).

Sample U.S. Treasury Strip Quotations for the Close of Trading on June 3, 1992

Maturity	Bid	Ask	Ask Yield
Nov 04	37:03	37:07	8.10%
Nov 09	24:00	24:04	8.32
Nov 21	10:04	10:07	7.90

Consider the zero-coupon issue due November, 2021. The issue could be purchased at a price equal to 10.2188% of par. No cash flows would be received until November of 2021 when par (face value) would be paid.

The quotes shown above refer to the stripping of principal payments on T-bonds. Coupon payments are also available. In this case, the investor receives a dollar annuity equal to the coupons paid by the Treasury security over the bond's life.

U.S. Agency Issues

Agency issues are not direct obligations of the Treasury. Instead, they are sold by various governmental agencies to support their financial activities. A few are backed by the full faith and credit of the United States, and many are guaranteed or supported by the Treasury. But even though agency issues don't have a direct guarantee of payment, they are considered to have top investment quality because governmental backing is implied. Due to the moderately greater risk inherent in agency obligations and their lower liquidity, they provide slightly greater promised yields than equivalent maturity Treasuries. Examples of federal agencies that issue publicly traded debt are the Federal Home Loan Bank, the Farm Credit Assistance Corporation, Federal Land Bank, Student Loan Marketing, and the Resolution Funding Corporation. The Resolution Funding Corporation is the government agency responsible for resolving liabilities of savings and loan firms that went bankrupt in the late 1980s and early 1990s.

State and Local Government Obligations

Municipal issues are bonds sold by states, counties, cities, and other political corporations. The most important feature of municipal bonds is their special tax treatment. Coupon income is totally excluded from federal income tax and is excluded from state income tax in the bond's state of origin. For example, an investor residing in Ohio would pay no income tax on coupon income received from Ohio Turnpike Authority bonds and would pay only state income tax on West Virginia Turnpike Authority bonds. Capital gains on municipal obligations are fully taxed at appropriate capital gains tax rates.

Municipal bonds are of two basic types: general obligations and revenue obligations. *General obligations* (*G.O.*'s) are backed by the full faith and credit of the issuer and repaid from taxes received by the issuing body. *Revenue obligations* are sold to finance a particular project and are repaid from the income earned on the project. Revenue issues do not have a claim to the tax receipts of the issuer, but instead are repaid from the revenue generated by the particular project. For example, municipal electric systems, turnpike and airport authorities, and sewage systems all issue revenue bonds.

Risk, maturity, and marketability of municipal obligations vary considerably. Usually, G.O.'s are less risky than revenues, but risks vary widely among different issuers. Maturities range from the very short-term tax anticipation notes mentioned earlier to 25-year debentures. Typically, long-term municipal issues are sold as serial bonds, as opposed to term bonds. *Serial bonds* have a predetermined series of bonds maturing each year until final maturity. *Term bonds* are repaid in full at one terminal maturity date. For example, if the city of San Francisco sells a 20-year, $50 million serial issue, it might retire $2½ million of specified bonds each year during the next 20 years. As a result, the average life of this 20-year obligation is about 10 years.

Serial bonds are used for two reasons. First, when a portion of principal is retired each year, the default risk might be lower. The municipality is forced to have capital available each year instead of waiting until maturity to come up with a large lump sum. Second, major buyers of municipals are financial institutions that like to stagger the maturity distribution of their bond portfolios over a number of years. When marketing the issue, the municipality can sell a piece of the issue with a given maturity to an institution that needs more bonds of that particular maturity. Thus, the issuer hopes that serialization will aid in the initial marketing of the bonds.

Corporate Issues

Long-term corporate debt obligations are usually term bonds with maturities of five years or more. The financial obligations of the corporate issuer are set forth in a security agreement known as an *indenture*. Indenture agreements usually specify the bond's repayment schedule, restrictions on dividend payments and liquidity, types of collateral, etc. It is the job of the *trustee* (usually a commercial bank) to ascertain that all indenture covenants are compiled with. Types of information provided in the indenture include the following:

1. *Call provisions.* A call provision allows the issuer to redeem the bond by purchasing it from the holder at a specified price. Most corporate bonds are sold with a deferred call provision. Deferred call bars the issuer from calling the bond for a stipulated period (commonly five to ten years), after which time the bond is callable at stipulated prices. Call prices are initially set above face value and decline, in steps, to face value prior to maturity. Initial *call premiums* (the difference between the call price and the face value) are normally equal to one year's coupon payment. In Chapter 11 we will see that a call provision increases an investor's uncertainty about future realized yields since the investor has no way of knowing whether or when the issue will be called. As a result, promised yields on callable bonds exceed those on noncallable issues.

2. *Sinking funds.* Sinking funds are annual payments made to a trustee to ensure eventual repayment of the bonds. Sinking funds may be left to accumulate as a deposit with the trustee or used to immediately retire a portion of the outstanding issue through purchase in the open market.

3. *Collateral provisions.* Bonds that have a legal claim to specific assets of the firm in the event of liquidation or reorganization are *secured bonds*. A *mortgage bond* is secured by a lien on real property, such as plants and buildings. Typically, mortgage bonds will be backed by a lien on a specified set of real assets, but occasionally a *blanket mortgage* is used which provides a lien on all assets of the firm. First, second, third, etc., mortgages can be placed on property with respective claims to assets during liquidation. Mortgage bonds may also be open-end, limited open-end, or closed-end. *Open-end mortgages* allow the issuer to sell additional bonds having equal claim to the mortgaged assets. Such open-end agreements will usually include an *after-acquired property clause* which requires that all future real assets purchased be added to the initial mortgage. *Limited open-end mortgages* allow new bond sales to have a lien on the same property up to a limit. This limit is normally stated as a percentage of the mortgaged debt to property cost, say 30%. Finally, a *closed-end mortgage* prohibits future debt sales with equivalent claim to the assets.

Unsecured bonds are known as *debentures*. Debenture holders are general creditors of the firm and have no legal claim to specified assets. In the event of liquidation they will be paid only after all mortgage bondholders have been reimbursed. Holders of *subordinated debentures* have a lower claim to assets than do general creditors, such as trade creditors (accounts payable).

Income bonds are repaid from the income earned on asset investments. Unlike other bonds, for which the issuer is contractually obligated to repay principal and interest regardless of current income, an income bond has no contractual commitment to pay interest and principal unless income is sufficient to do so. Revenue bonds sold by municipalities are income bonds.

Corporate bonds are often given special features which act as inducements to

Japanese Companies Need to Raise Cash, But First a Bond Market Must Be Built

Financial trading markets are well developed in most countries. This is only natural since they provide a cheap and fast way for people who have the desire to trade to do so. Surprisingly, however, a number of markets still remain undeveloped. This article discusses how the lack of a well-functioning security market can impede a firm's profitability and growth.

TOKYO—With the stock market sagging and banks hip-deep in bad real estate loans, Japanese companies need a corporate bond market to help them raise cash.

It's too bad they don't really have one.

Surprising as it is, the world's second-largest economy and financial system has only the most fledgling of corporate bond markets, an oversight by Japan's finance bureaucrats that has come back to haunt this economically troubled country. Fearing an emerging credit crunch, some regulators, with the urging of foreign and Japanese securities firms, are trying to change all this—however haltingly.

In 1991, regular corporate bonds accounted for 31% of U.S. corporate debt. Compare that with Japan, where as of March just 57 of the 2,500 publicly listed companies had any domestic corporate bonds outstanding.

Japan's corporate bond market is severely limited by government regulations that let only the biggest blue-chip corporations issue bonds, and that force companies

to get their banks to guarantee their bonds. The banks, which don't want the competition from a corporate bond market, have naturally jacked up commissions to make issuing bonds prohibitively expensive for many companies.

That has sent firms abroad to raise funds. For example, Alps Electric Co., a top Japanese maker of electronics parts, needs to redeem $400 million of debt in July. Like hundreds of Japanese corporations in the past few years, Alps originally raised money in Europe by selling bonds with warrants attached—equity-linked bonds that pay low interest but give a buyer stock-purchase rights. . . .

"We never even thought of using the [Japanese] domestic market," an Alps financial officer says. "It's impossible; in effect, it doesn't exist."

If Japan had an active domestic bond market, Alps would have access to new investors, like Japanese regional banks and small companies, which still have cash and are looking for relatively stable investments. And with interest rates in Japan on the decline since mid-1991, Alps likely could have paid less to issue the same amount of debt.

SOURCE: Quentin Hardy, "Japanese Companies Need to Raise Cash, But First a Bond Market Must Be Built," *Wall Street Journal*, 20 October 1992.

potential purchasers as well as cost-saving devices to the corporation in arranging future financing. Examples of such inducements are convertibility and warrants. A *convertible bond* is a debt obligation which allows the owner to tender the bond to the corporation and convert it into a given number of shares of stock. The attraction of convertibility to the bondholder is the guaranteed fixed income plus the ability to share in rapid stock price rises if they should occur. Cost savings to the issuing corporation are largely in lower yields required by investors because of the convertibility.

Bonds are often sold with warrants attached. Like a convertible provision, a bond with a warrant provides the owner with a fixed income plus the ability to share in future stock price increases. The issuing corporation hopes to save through lower required bond yields and automatic future equity sales at the exercise date. A *warrant* is a legal claim that allows the owner to buy a certain number of common shares at a specified *exercise price* any time before a specified *exercise date*. Exercise prices are initially set at levels that are expected to give the owner an eventual price break in buying the stock. For example, assume that a firm will need new equity capital two years hence. Management expects its stock price to be $70 at that time but cannot be sure of this. The firm could issue warrants with an exercise price of $60 and a maximum exercise date of two years. The $60 exercise price is set lower than the expected stock price to allow for management's uncertainty about the $70 value and to provide a potential inducement to exercise the warrant in two years. If the stock does sell for more than $60 two years hence, all warrants will be exercised. Warrant owners will get a favorable stock price and management will get the new equity financing needed.

Asset Backed and Passthroughs

One of the more interesting phenomena of the 1980s was the increased *securitization* of the financial markets. Securitization refers to publicly traded security issues that are collateralized by a collection of many small loans to consumers. For example, credit card purchases of a large number of individuals are collected into a total pool and used as collateral for an *asset backed* bond issue.

The most common form of an asset backed security are those collateralized by home mortgages. For example, the Federal National Mortgage Association issues both short- and long-term bonds referred to as *FNMA issues* (pronounced Fannie Mae). Proceeds are used to purchase mortgages held by savings and loans, mortgage companies, banks, etc. In addition, the Government National Mortgage Association guarantees pools of qualified mortgages that act as collateral for *GNMA* (Ginnie Mae) issues. GNMA issues were the first major type of passthrough securities. As payments of interest and principal are made by mortgagees, they are "passed through" to the GNMA owner. Whereas most other fixed income securities receive all principal payments at the bond's stated maturity, GNMA issues receive both principal and interest throughout the bond's stated life. As such, the average life of a Ginnie Mae passthrough is much shorter than their stated maturity.

Fannie Mae and Ginnie Mae issues have become popular enough with the investing public that private investment firms have started to offer their own version of mortgage-backed securities. These are referred to as *Collateralized Mortgage Obligations* or CMO's. CMO's are also backed by a pool of mortgages but they differ from GNMA and FNMA obligations in that investors purchase the cash flow associated with a given date. This is done by breaking the CMO into various *tranches* (or repayment periods). Owners of the earliest tranche receive all payments made by the mortgage pool until they are fully repaid. After the first tranche is fully repaid, investors in the second tranche begin to receive payments until they are fully repaid. The process continues until all tranches are repaid.

Eurobonds and Yankee Bonds

Eurobonds are bond issues sold in Europe (typically London) that are denominated in a currency other than that of the issuer's domicile country. Eurodollar bonds (denominated in U.S. dollars) are most common although Euro-yen (Japanese currency), Euro-deutschemark (German currency), and Euro-sterling (U. K. currency) bonds are also issued. The motives for issuing a Eurodollar bond are two. First, since they do not have to be registered with the U.S. Securities and Exchange Commission, they can be sold quickly and at a lower cost than if issued in the United States. Second, they are denominated in U.S. dollars and require future payments of U.S. dollars by the issuer. This is exactly what issuers would wish if they have an immediate need for U.S. dollars (to purchase U.S. products) and will have future profits denominated in U.S. dollars.

Yankee bonds are sold in the United States by organizations domiciled outside the United States. These provide a convenient way for U.S. investors who wish to purchase bonds of organizations located outside the United States but receive all payments in U.S. dollars. Similar but smaller markets exist in the United Kingdom (called Bulldog bonds) and Japan (called Samuri bonds).

Guaranteed Investment Contracts

Referred to as GICs, these are intermediate maturity obligations sold by insurance firms primarily to pension funds, endowment plans, and foundations. Their principal benefit is an above-average "guaranteed" (actually only promised) rate of return. Returns are either guaranteed for the next calendar year or for a fixed number of years (typically five-years or less). GICs are not marketable, and the investor can withdraw funds from the insurance company prior to maturity only at substantial penalties. Their attraction is an above-average fixed interest return. (Some people believe that another attraction is the unknown GIC market value. Owners report their values based on an accrued cost accounting basis, which is less variable than actual market values.) The guarantee underlying a GIC is only as good as the assets of the insurance issuer. High GIC rates can be offered to purchasers only if the insurance company uses the proceeds to purchase other securities that provide high returns. Higher returns come with greater risk of loss.

EQUITY SECURITIES

Equity securities provide a residual claim on asset returns once all fixed-income claims have been paid. There are two forms of equities. In the United States, they are called preferred and common stock. Outside the United States, they are typically called preference and ordinary shares.

Accurate estimates of the aggregate value of preferred stock are not available. However, trends in the global value of equity securities are available and they tell a dramatic story. Consider the data displayed in Figure 2-2. Between 1960 and 1991, the value of world equity markets grew from $0.5 trillion to $10.4 trillion.

FIGURE 2-2 *Growth of International Equity Values*

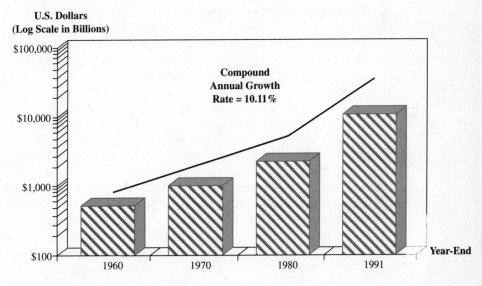

Dollar Value by Region (in billions):

	1960	1970	1980	1991	Compound Annual Growth
U.S.	$345.0	$700.9	$1,380.6	$4,352.5	8.52%
Europe	135.0	194.4	457.0	2,614.3	10.03%
Asia	17.7	50.6	419.3	3,163.5	18.21%
Other	27.4	64.2	173.0	271.2	7.67%
Total	$525.2	$1,010.2	$2,429.9	$10,401.5	10.11%

Percentage by Region:

	1960	1970	1980	1991
U.S.	65.7%	69.4%	56.8%	41.8%
Europe	25.6	19.2	18.8	25.1
Asia	3.4	5.0	17.3	30.4
Other	5.3	6.4	7.1	2.7
Total	100.0%	100.0%	100.0%	100.0%

This represents a compound annual growth rate of more than 10%. The greatest share of this growth occurred between 1980–1991. While equity value growth occurred throughout the financially developed world, Japanese equity values grew the fastest. At the end of 1991, the value of Japanese equities was $3.2 trillion; close to the U.S. equity value of $4.3 trillion. Clearly, equity investment strategies need to be made with a global perspective.

But there is more to the story than is displayed in Figure 2-2. Recall our discussion in Chapter 1 when it was shown that higher rates of return come at the cost of greater variability. Although the market values in Figure 2-2 are not based on security rates of return earned in various equity markets, a significant part of past growth has been due to security return, particularly for Japan. *Not shown in the figure is the fact that, in the first three months of 1992, the rate of return on Japanese stocks was a negative 27%!* Again, greater returns come at the cost of greater return variability.

Preferred (or Preference) Stock

Preferred stock is actually a hybrid security with features of both a fixed-income obligation and a pure equity security. Similar to income bonds, preferred stocks pay a stipulated yearly cash payment only if corporate income is sufficient to do so. Preferred dividends are usually expressed as a percentage of the preferred's par value. For example, a $100 par, 6% preferred issue would pay a $6 dividend each year. If the issue is *cumulative,* any unpaid past dividends (dividends in arrears) accumulate and must eventually be paid before any dividends can be distributed to owners of common stock. Unpaid dividends on *noncumulative* preferred shares do not have to be paid. Some preferred issues are *participating,* which allows the preferred dividend to increase in a stipulated fashion as common stock dividends increase. Owners of preferred stock are usually given the right to vote for directors of the firm (and thus exert some true equity control) only if dividends have not been paid for a year or more. Preferreds also receive preferential (''preferred'') treatment if the firm's assets must be liquidated, in that they have a par value claim to assets before any liquidating dividends are distributed to owners of common stock.

These features are not unique to preferred stock. They are also available on many income bonds. While an indenture agreement does not secure the preferred stock issue, such issues commonly have callability, convertibility, sinking fund, and other features found on income bonds. Because of this, many people consider preferred stock to be the economic equivalent of income bonds.

Common (or Ordinary) Stock

The common stockholders of a corporation represent the firm's ownership. Shares of common stock sold to investors give their owners a claim to any asset returns after all debt and preferred stock obligations are fully satisfied. Common stockholders have a nonguaranteed, residual claim to asset returns. If the firm is successful, common stockholders will share in its success, and debt holders receive only their promised fixed returns. If the firm should fail, common stockholders receive liquidating dividends only after all debt holders and preferred holders have been repaid the face value of their securities.

Because of the ownership risk position that common shareholders bear, they are given two basic rights: the right to managerial control and the right to retain an initial percentage ownership. The *right to control* is provided by allowing common shareholders to vote for members of the board of directors. Normally, ownership of one share will allow one vote for each director to be elected. If you own 100 shares in a firm which is selecting three directors, you can cast 100 votes for each of the three separate positions. This procedure is referred to as *noncumulative voting*. Occasionally, *cumulative voting* is allowed to assure minority groups a voice in management. When cumulative voting is used, a vote can be cast for any one directorship equal to the number of shares owned times the number of positions available. For example, if 100 shares are owned and three directors are to be elected, 300 votes could be cast for one director's position and none for the other two. Shareholder voting occurs at annual meetings of the corporation. If a shareholder is unable to attend this meeting, a *proxy* vote can be given to another party.

An illustration of how common stock price quotations are shown in the U.S. financial press is shown below:

Sample Common Stock Price Quotations for the Close of Trading on June 3, 1992

| 52-Week | | | | Dividend | | | Vol | | | |
High	Low	Stock	Symbol	$	Yield	PE	100's	High	Low	Close
107⅜	81⅝	Intl Business	IBM	4.84	5.4	13	11,291	90¾	89¾	89¾
46	29½	Scott Paper	SPP	0.80	2.0	64	11,422	41	39⅜	37⅞

The first quote is for shares of International Business Machines, whose trading symbol is IBM. During the previous 52 weeks, IBM had sold for as high as $107⅜ per share and as low as $81⅝. (Notice that stocks trade in units of one-eighth dollar.) The dollar dividend shown is an annualized approximation based on the last dividend declaration. The dividend yield is simply the dollar dividend divided by the current stock price. IBM traded for as high as $90.75 and as low as $89.75 during the day. The Price to Earnings ratio (PE) is equal to the stock's current price divided by earnings over the most recent four quarters. It is a measure of the true cost of one share. Volume represents the number of shares traded in units of one hundred shares.

COMMINGLED PORTFOLIOS

The securities discussed above all provide a *direct claim* on the assets of an organization. In contrast, commingled portfolios provide an *indirect claim* to the assets.

A commingled portfolio is a group of securities owned in common by a large number of investors. For example, the Prudential Retirement Income Separate Account (PRISA) portfolio consists of geographically diversified commercial properties in the United States that are managed by an investment team working for Prudential Life Insurance. Owners of the PRISA portfolio are numerous pension funds, endowments, and foundations. They all own the same set of assets.

Commingled portfolios provide three potential advantages: (1) portfolio management costs are reduced due to the economies present in large portfolios, (2) greater diversification can be achieved when investors pool their capital to acquire a single portfolio, and (3) the portfolio is professionally managed. Commingled portfolios are offered by bank trust companies, insurance companies, and investment counsel firms.

Mutual Funds

A special type of commingled portfolio is known as a *mutual fund* (in many other countries, they are called *unit trusts*). Mutual funds sell shares to any individual wishing to own them and stand ready to buy (redeem) any shares that individuals wish to sell; hence, they are often called *open-end* funds. Since the assets owned by a mutual fund are actively traded in public markets, the total market value of the fund can be determined at the end of each day's trading. Dividing this total market value (less any usually small liabilities of the fund) by the number of shares outstanding yields the *net asset value* per share (NAV). All purchases and sales are made at NAV.

Mutual funds follow a specified investment policy so that potential investors can pick a fund which matches their own investment objectives. Some funds, for example, hold broadly diversified portfolios of all traded stocks and bonds and trade as little as possible. These funds are referred to as *index funds*. Index funds are a phenomenon of the efficient markets hypothesis, which states that the best way to select securities is to buy a broadly diversified portfolio of securities which matches one's desired risk level and then trade only for tax reasons or if cash is needed. Other funds restrict themselves to particular types of securities: high growth, high current income, energy-related, municipal bonds, etc. *Money market funds* which invest solely in money market instruments are particularly popular during periods of high interest rates.

The most recent development within this industry is the *family of funds*. In this case, an investment advisory organization forms a number of mutual funds, each having rather narrow objectives. For example, one fund might restrict its holdings to computer technology stocks, another to electric utility stocks, another to medical technology, and another to money market instruments. Once people buy into such a family of funds, they can move their investments between the funds as they choose for a minimal transaction cost. These families of funds provide investors and speculators with improved flexibility at relatively low cost.

Mutual funds can be purchased in one of two ways: (1) directly from a securities broker, in which case a *load* (commission) is paid, or (2) directly from the mutual fund itself, in which case *no load* is paid (though there is sometimes a small transaction cost). The management of a mutual fund will decide how it wishes to market its shares, through a broker network as a load fund or directly to the public as a no-load fund. Load charges are *front-end* loads, meaning that a charge is made when the shares are initially purchased but no charge is made when they are sold. Load fees of between 3% and 6% of the fund's net asset value are normal.

The example below shows how mutual fund prices are shown in the financial press.

Sample Mutual Fund Price Quotations for the Close of Trading on June 3, 1992

Fund Name	NAV	Offer Price
Alliance Balanced	13.00	13.76
Boston Company International	10.83	NL
American Mutual Fund	21.40	22.71
Pioneer Equity Income	13.96	14.81

We can tell by the differences in fund names that they hold different types of securities. Alliance Balanced is a fund that owns both stocks and bonds. The Boston Company fund purchases international (meaning non-U.S.) securities. And the Pioneer mutual fund seeks high dividend income stocks. The only no-load fund shown is Boston Company International. Loads on the other funds cost investors about 6% of the money invested in the funds.

DERIVATIVE SECURITIES

Derivative securities also do not have a direct claim on a real asset. Instead, they have a claim on another security such as a common stock or a bond. As implied by their name, their market value is *derived* from the market value of an underlying direct security. The two broad types of derivative securities are (1) futures and (2) options. There are many types of futures and option securities traded in world markets. We will examine such instruments on financial securities in later chapters. For now, however, it is best to focus on how these securities differ from the underlying assets to which they have a claim.

Our example is based on the common stock of ABC Corporation. These shares have a market value today, but we are mainly interested in their market value at some specified future date T. This is because futures and options give claims to the underlying asset only at a specified future date. For example, a *futures will require* that the owner buy a security in 180 days and an *option will allow* the owner to buy in 180 days.

Think of a graph. In our example, the horizontal axis of this graph will always be the market value of one share of ABC stock at future date T. This market value could be as low as $0.00. However, we will examine cases when the stock is worth $50, $100, and $150. On the vertical axis, we will plot the value of some security at date T (whose value is dependent on the stock price at that time). Four asset positions will be plotted on the vertical axis: (a) own the stock, (b) own a futures contract on the stock, (c) own a call option on the stock, and (d) own a put option on the stock. The derivatives are defined as follows:

-future: The owner is *obligated to purchase* the asset from the seller at an agreed-on price at future date T.

  -call: The owner has the *right to purchase* the asset from the call seller at an agreed-on price at future date T.

  -put: The owner has the *right to sell* the asset to the put seller at an agreed-on price at future date T.

We will use $100 as the date T price at which the futures owner *must buy,* the call owner *may buy,* and the put owner *may sell.*

Consider A–D panels in Figure 2-3. Panel A is the easiest since it reflects a direct ownership of the stock. If the stock is worth $100 at T, the position is also worth $100.

The long futures position in Panel B (long means ownership, short means you owe) moves in the same direction as the direct stock ownership but is always $100 lower. This $100 spread between the stock ownership and the futures ownership is due to the *obligation* to pay $100 at date T. If the stock is worth $150, the futures is worth $50. If the stock is worth $50, the futures is worth $-$50. At date T, the *futures contract is the same as underlying stock minus the obligated purchase price.* This simple fact is the basis on which all futures contracts are valued at dates prior to T.

The ownership of the call at date T is shown in panel C and will have a positive value if the stock is worth more than the stated purchase price at which the owner has a *right to buy.* If the stock is worth $150, the call is worth $50. It is important, though, to realize that the call owner has a right to buy but not an obligation. Thus, if the stock is worth $50, the call's value is $0.0, not $-$50.

The ownership of the put at date T is shown in panel D and will have a positive value if the stock is worth less than the $100 stated price at which the owner may sell. If the stock is worth $50 at date T, then the right to sell at $100 (the put) is worth $50. Because the put provides a right and not an obligation, its value will never be negative.

Notice that the lines in each panel move across the page at 45-degree angles. The importance of this is that one of the securities can be emulated by combinations of the others. For example, what is the date T outcome if you owned both one future and one put? Since the put pays off when the futures loses, the net of this combination is the same as a call option. This observation is the key to how derivative securities are priced in financial markets.

Why do complex securities such as these derivatives exist? The answer is simple; they provide cost-efficient means of hedging security price risk. For example, assume you now own a share of ABC stock and intend to sell it in 180

FIGURE 2-3 *Analysis of Derivatives*

Value of Direct Security Claim

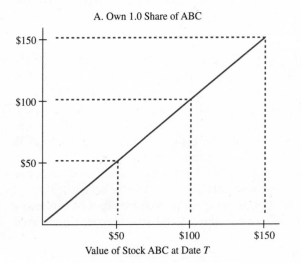

Value of Call Option

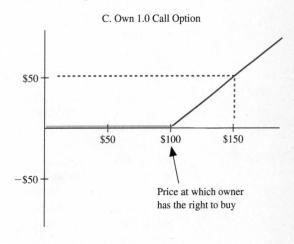

Value of Future Contract

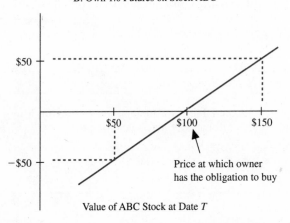

Value of Put Option

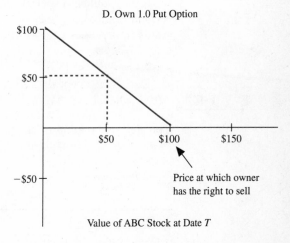

days since you need cash at that time. By selling a 100-day future on the share, you have guaranteed the price you will receive. Alternatively, if you wish to continue to own the share but want to limit your losses if its value should decline, you could buy a long put. This put would guarantee a minimum selling price over the life of the put.

One difference between futures and options is that the futures is a *legal obligation* whereas the option is a *legal right.* There is an another important difference between them. Future buyers pay nothing to a futures seller until a stated future date. Call option and put option buyers, however, pay a price to the seller when the trade takes place. The reason for this is discussed in Chapter 9.

SUMMARY

This chapter has provided an introductory overview of the types of marketable securities available for investment or speculation. Most of these are discussed in more depth in later chapters.

Securities are usually classified as *money market* or *capital market* instruments. Money market securities are short-term, highly marketable, low-risk debt issues that are bought and sold as temporary cash substitutes. The money market is principally a wholesale market in which huge sums of money are traded for very short periods of time. Capital market securities have maturities greater than one year and vary considerably in risk and marketability. Capital market securities are rarely used as short-term cash substitutes. Instead, they are bought by investors for their long-run expected returns or by speculators searching for mispriced securities.

The array of security forms is extensive, ranging from some debt instruments that provide a single future known cash repayment to derivatives that have a claim to the future value of another security. Each type of security provides one or more economic values to society. These include reducing the costs of bringing borrowers and lenders together, providing improved control over investment risk, and reducing the costs of portfolio management.

REVIEW PROBLEM

You are given the following price quotations on a T-bill for the close of trading on May 31 and June 30. (Note that as of June 30, this bill has a 90-day remaining life.)

T-Bill Information

	On May 31		On June 30	
Maturity	*Bid*	*Asked*	*Bid*	*Asked*
Sept 28	9.10%	9.00%	9.30%	9.25%

You are also given price quotations for the same dates on a 90-day T-bill futures contract that has a delivery date of June 30.

T-Bill Futures Contract Information

	Discount Settle Prices on	
Delivery Date	*May 31*	*June 30*
June 30	9.40%	9.25%

a. On May 31, the T-bill had a 120-day remaining life. On that day, what percentage of par value would you pay to purchase the T-bill?

b. On that day, what were the effective simple interest and compound interest yields?

c. Assume you purchased the bill on May 31 and later sold it on June 30. What rate of return did you earn during this one-month period? If you were to express this return on an annualized basis, what would the return be?

d. Is there any reason why, on *June 30,* the futures contract should trade at a discount identical to the T-bill's asked discount?

e. On May 31, why would the future's discount be different from the T-bill's discount on the same date?

f. On May 31, at what price is the futures contract selling? (Use $1 million par for each contract.)

Solution

a. $P = F - Fd\dfrac{t}{360}$

$$= 100 - (100)(0.09)\left(\frac{120}{360}\right)$$

$$= 97.00$$

b. Simple interest:

$$\frac{(365)(0.09)}{360 - (0.09)(120)} = 0.09407, \text{ or } \left(\frac{100 - 97}{97}\right)\left(\frac{365}{120}\right) = 0.09407$$

Compound interest:

$$\left(\frac{100}{97}\right)^{365/120} - 1 = 0.09707$$

c. Purchase price = 97.00 from part a above.

$$\text{Selling price } = 100 - 100(0.093)\left(\frac{90}{360}\right)$$

$$= 97.675$$

$$\text{One-month percentage gain} = \frac{97.675}{97.00} - 1.0$$

$$= 0.00696$$

$$= 0.696\%$$

To annualize, the simple interest should be used if this is an isolated trade.

$$(0.696\%)\left(\frac{365}{30}\right) = 8.468\%$$

If this is only one of many ongoing trades, compound interest is more reflective of the annualized return.

$$(1.00696)^{365/30} - 1.0 = 8.805\%$$

d. June 30 is the delivery date of the futures contract—the date on which the buyer has a claim to an actual 90-day bill. Thus, the future and the actual bill should trade at identical prices. If this were not the case, an investor could trade in each market and make a riskless arbitrage profit.

e. On May 31, the future has 30 days remaining before its buyer will have a claim to an actual 90-day T-bill. Thus, the futures price on May 31 is the market's consensus forecast of what a 90-day bill will trade for on June 30. This forecast of 9.40% turns out to be wrong. Nonetheless, it is the forecast as of May 31.

f. $\$1,000,000 - \$1,000,000\ (0.094)\left(\dfrac{90}{360}\right) = \$976,500,000$

QUESTIONS AND PROBLEMS

1. Sample quotes on U.S. T-bills are shown below for two dates—January 1 and January 15. Assume the quotes represent *end-of-day* transactions and that trades could actually be made at these prices.

As of January 1

Maturity	Discount Bid	Asked	Yield
Jan. 15	9.00	8.70	8.851
Feb. 15	9.10	8.75	8.970
March 15	9.12	8.79	—

As of January 15

Maturity	Discount Bid	Asked	Yield
Feb. 15	8.80	8.70	—
March 15	8.85	8.75	9.000

a. As of January 1, at what price (percentage of par value) could you buy the January 15 bill (assume a full 14-day period)? At what price could you sell?

b. As of January 1, at what price could you buy the March 15 bill? Sell?

c. Find the missing yield values.

d. What would your dollar profit be if you buy $10 million face value of the March bill on January 1 and sell it on January 15?

e. Assume that on January 1 you buy $100 million of February bills at the 8.75% discount. This amount considerably exceeds the equity capital of your firm, and you must finance the inventory in some way. Explain how financing might be arranged and why the financing cost might be less than the 8.75% discount.

2. Two competitive bidders submit bids on $1 million of 91-day bills being offered by the U.S. Treasury. The bids differ by 1 basis point. What is the total dollar difference between each bid?

3. You are given the following T-bill quotations as of the close of trading on June 1 and June 10:

	June 1		June 10	
T-Bill Maturity	Bid	Asked	Bid	Asked
June 30	9.00%	8.80%	9.50%	9.45%

   a. At the end of June 1, how much would you have to pay to purchase $1 million in par vaue of the bills?

   b. Note that only discount quotations are shown. What would be the price quotations for June 1 as they would appear in the financial press?

   c. If you purchased some bills on June 1, what would be the simple interest and compound interest annualized yields? Why do they differ?

   d. Assume you purchased the T-bill on June 1 and later sold it on June 10. What was your nine-day profit (or loss) in percentage terms? What was the cause of this profit (or loss)? What is the annualized equivalent yield?

4. The U.S. Treasury offers $2 billion in 91-day new T-bills and receives the following bids:

Discount	Competitive Bid
8.50%	$200 million
8.55	400 million
8.56	600 million
8.58	1,000 million
8.59	1,500 million
8.60	1,000 million

Discount	Noncompetitive Bid
NA	$500 million

What yield will the noncompetitive bidders receive?

5. An importer must finance various planned purchases of goods. Commercial paper rates are now 7.53%, and bankers' acceptance rates are 7.68%. Why might the importer utilize the bankers' acceptance instead of commercial paper?

6. Price quotations on two mutual funds are shown below:

Fund	NAV	Offering Price
Fidelity Magellan	33.37	34.40
Price New Horizons	12.88	N.L.

   a. If you invest $1,000 in each fund, how many shares would you receive of each?

   b. What is the percentage front-end load on each? Explain what this is.

   c. Interpret what NAV means.

7. You are given the following information on First Street Growth Fund, a mutual fund that invests mainly in high-growth stocks.

Total market value of assets   = $500 million

Accounts payable   =   10 million

Number of shares outstanding =   7 million

    a. What is the net asset value per share?

    b. If this is a no-load fund, how many shares could be acquired with $10,000?

8. Brenda Avey is the investment officer for a large life insurance company that has a marginal tax bracket of 45%. Which of the following two securities provides her with a greater promised yield to maturity?

    a. Preferred stock selling at par with a promised yield of 9.2%.

    b. Corporate bonds selling at par with a promised yield of 11.0%.

9. Assume that a municipal bond and a corporate bond have identical marketability, default risk, and maturity. The municipal is selling at a 5% yield to maturity; the corporate is selling for an 8% yield to maturity.

    a. Should a person in a 30% tax bracket buy the municipal or the corporate security? (Assume the full 8% yield on the corporate is taxable at 30%.)

    b. What is the break-even tax bracket at which an investor is indifferent between the two issues?

10. Define what a Eurobond and a Yankee bond are. Why would someone wish to issue such securities?

11. The chapter summary states that financial securities provide economic values to society. Three possible advantages are:

    a. reduce the cost of bringing borrowers and lenders together.

    b. improve control over investment risk.

    c. reduce costs of portfolio management.

For each advantage, select two securities and discuss how the security provides this advantage.

12. The U.S. government issues T-bonds. For many such issues, investors are allowed to purchase either the series of coupon payments or the final principal payment. On June 3, 1992, a U.S. T-bond was quoted in the financial press as follows:

Coupon Rate	Maturity	Bid	Ask
8	Nov 2021	101:13	101:15

    a. If you were to purchase this bond, what price would you pay?

    b. What cash flows would be available to owners of this bond if they hold the bond to maturity? (Assume a $100 face value.)

    c. The principal value of this bond could have been purchased at a price equal to 10.2188% of face value. Identify the cash flows and dates of such flows associated with this STRIP.

    d. What is the annualized return associated with purchasing the principal strip for $10.2188 and receiving $100 in 29½ years? (Although not discussed in the chapter, this is a basic question about time value of money.)

    e. Given the data above, what should be the value of the bond's stripped coupon payments? Why do you say this? (Neglect any possible tax effects.)

    f. What would you do if the market price of the stripped interest payments was

85:00? (This was not discussed in the chapter, but it illustrates an important financial concept, *arbitrage.*)

13. Price quotations were provided in the chapter for a number of securities as of June 3. These included:

    a. a one-year T-bill trading at a 365-day discount of 4.06%.

    b. shares of IBM stock trading at $89.75 with a forecast annual dividend equal to $4.84.

    In addition, consider a call option on IBM stock that allows the owner to purchase shares of IBM in one year at a price of $90 per share. The options presently cost $5.00.

    a. Calculate the one-year return on the T-bills. (You may assume that 363 days represents a full year.)

    b. If IBM shares sell for $100 in exactly one year, what would be the return on these shares over the year?

    c. If IBM shares sell for $100 in exactly one year, what would be the return on the ownership of one call option?

    d. Repeat parts b and c for a price of IBM equal to $80 in one year.

    e. Given these results, what do you conclude?

14. What is a commingled portfolio?

15. What are the potential advantages of purchasing a commingled portfolio?

16. Futures and options are available on shares of XYZ common stock. The futures require that buyers pay $50 per share in exactly one year. In return, they will receive one share of XYZ. Call options allow buyers to purchase the shares for $50 in one year and put options allow buyers to sell at $50 in one year. Parts a through e of this question require graphs. In each case, the horizontal axis will represent the value of XYZ shares in one year. Its scale should have a minimum value of $0.0 and a maximum value of $75.

    a. On the vertical axis, plot the value in one year of owning one futures contract on XYZ shares.

    b. On the vertical axis, plot the value in one year of owning one call on XYZ shares.

    c. On the vertical axis, plot the value in one year of owning one put on XYZ shares.

    d. How does the ownership of one future on XYZ shares differ from the ownership of one XYZ share (in a year from now)?

    e. Assume you purchase one future on XYZ and one put. Plot the one year payoff of this position.

17. A futures contract exists that allows traders to purchase (or sell) bushels of corn at $3 per bushel in exactly one year. Why might people wish to trade this contract today? Focus on how trades could reduce future uncertainty, not on speculative motives.

18. In what two fundamental ways do options and futures differ?

19. Investment Dealer A purchases 91-day U.S. T-bills from Investment Dealer B. At the same time, A agrees to sell the bills back to B for delivery three weeks later at a predetermined price. Investment Dealer A is transacting a:

    a. repurchase agreement.

    b. reverse repurchase agreement.

    c. call loan.

    d. put loan.

20. A revenue bond is distinguished from a general obligation bond in that revenue bonds:

    a. are issued by counties, special districts, cities, towns, and state-controlled authorities, whereas general obligation bonds are only issued by the states themselves.

    b. are typically secured by limited taxing power, whereas general obligation bonds are secured by unlimited taxing power.

c. are issued to finance specific projects and are secured by the revenues of the project being financed.

d. have first claim to any revenue increase of the tax authority issuing the bonds.

 21. Yankee dollar bonds are U.S.-pay bonds that are:

a. issued by foreign domiciled issuers who register with the SEC.

b. traded principally in London, but to a growing degree in New York as well.

c. free of withholding tax to non-U.S. investors.

d. all of the above.

 22. Income bonds differ from ordinary bonds in that the income bond's coupon:

a. can vary up or down according to changes in the net income of the issuer.

b. varies, but can only move up according to changes in the income of the issuer.

c. is fixed, but payment of interest may be deferred.

d. is fixed, but payment of interest is contingent upon the income of the issuer being sufficient for that purpose.

 23. The dollar value of a U.S. T-bond quoted at 92.24 is:

a. $922.75

b. $922.40

c. $927.50

d. cannot be determined

 24. Eurodollar bonds are:

I.   denominated in U.S. dollars.

II.   underwritten by an international syndicate.

III.   sold at issue to U.S. investors.

a. I, II and III

b. I and II only

c. II only

d. III only

 25. Serial obligation bonds differ from *most* other bonds because:

a. they are secured by the assets and taxing power of the issuer.

b. their par value is usually well below $1,000.

c. their term-to-maturity is usually very long (30 years or more).

d. they possess multiple maturity dates.

DATAFILE ANALYSIS

The purpose of the datafile analyses in this chapter are to review historical changes in annualized promised yields on a variety of U.S. money market instruments as well as yield spreads between these securities.

1. *Money Market Rates.* Access the datafile called ''INTRATES.WK1'' and locate the series for three-month commercial paper, bankers acceptances, negotiable certificates of deposit, Eurodollars, and U.S. T-bills. Each yield is stated on an annualized basis and was calculated at the end of each year shown.

   Plot these yields with time on the horizontal axis. Examine their levels and changes in levels over time. Why they change is an important topic in Chapter 5. As a student of finance, you should be knowledgeable of the level and variability past yields, particularly the high levels of the late 1970s and early 1980s.

2. *Yield Spreads.* Calculate yield spreads between each money market instrument and three-month U.S. T-bills. The yield spread is the difference between an instrument's annualized yield and that of the three-month U.S. T-bill. Explain why these yield spreads exist.

APPENDIX 2A: SOURCES OF BASIC FINANCIAL INFORMATION

This appendix lists and briefly describes the major sources of security information that the *nonprofessional investor or speculator* might find useful. In addition to the listings shown, most brokerage houses distribute market letters and recommendations to customers which can be quite informative. The listing does not include sources of information that professionals would use (such as computerized databases and academic journals). The outline first lists major newspapers, journals, and periodicals. After this, guides to industry and company data are listed. Finally, sources for particular types of securities are shown.

I. The General Financial Press
  A. Newspapers
    1. *The Wall Street Journal:* daily; review articles on current business topics and extensive market price data.
    2. *The European Wall Street Journal:* similar to *WSJ* in the United States but covers European markets.
    3. *The Asian Wall Street Journal:* similar to *WSJ* in the United States but covers Asian markets.
    4. *Financial Times* (London, Paris, Frankfurt, New York, Tokyo): daily; extensive coverage of international news and security markets.
    5. *The New York Times:* daily; review articles on current business topics and extensive market price data.
    6. *Commercial and Financial Chronicle:* weekly; contains daily prices on New York, American, and Toronto exchanges plus weekly prices on regional exchanges and the OTC market.
    7. *Barron's:* weekly; articles on investment topics and extensive weekly price data.
    8. *M/G Financial Weekly:* weekly; prices, charts, and basic financial information on most actively traded securities.
    9. *Wall Street Transcript:* twice weekly; reproduces selected brokerage house reports and interviews with security analysts on a specific industry.
  B. Journals and Periodicals
    1. *Business Week:* weekly; articles on a variety of general business topics.
    2. *Financial World:* biweekly; articles on investment topics.
    3. *Forbes:* biweekly; articles on investment topics and opinions.
    4. *Finance:* monthly; review articles on current events in the financial market.
    5. *Financial Executive:* monthly; news of the Financial Executives Institute.
    6. *Fortune:* biweekly; articles on general business trends for corporate managers.
    7. *Institutional Investor:* monthly; articles of interest to managers of large institutional portfolios.
    8. *Financial Analysts Journal:* bimonthly; articles of interest to practicing financial analysts.
    9. *OTC Review:* monthly; analysis and discussion of stocks traded in the over-the-counter market, plus financial data.
    10. *Journal of Portfolio Management:* quarterly; articles of interest to the professional portfolio manager.
II. Industry and Company Information
  A. Industry Data: General Statistics
    1. *Statistical Abstract of the U.S.:* industrial, social, political, and economic statistics.
    2. *Business Statistics:* historical data for the U.S., updated monthly by the *Survey of Current Business.*
    3. *Standard & Poor's Statistical Service:* statistics in nine major industrial groups, plus stock price averages.
    4. *Basebook:* historical data by Standard Industrial Classification (SIC) number.
    5. *Predicasts:* forecasts by SIC number.
    6. *U.S. Industrial Outlook:* brief analysis of 200 industries.
    7. *F & S Index to Corporations and Industries:* list of articles dealing with industries classified by SIC code.
    8. *American Statistics Index:* guide to statistical publications of the U.S. government.
    9. U.S. government publications:
       ▪ *Census of Mineral Industries*
       ▪ *Census of Selected Services*

- *Census of Construction Industry*
- *Census of Transportation*
- *Census of Retail Trade*
- *Census of Wholesale Trade*
- *Annual Survey of Manufacturers*

B. Industry Data: General Information
1. *Dun & Bradstreet Key Business Ratios:* financial ratios for 125 industries.
2. *Robert Morris Associates Annual Studies:* ratios for a variety of industries.
3. *Standard & Poor's:* reports including the *Investment Advisory Service, Industry Surveys,* and *Outlook,* which provide summaries of financial data and current events.
4. *Value Line Investment Surveys:* summaries of financial data and current events.
5. *Moody's Manuals:* basic industry information and financial data.

C. Company Data
1. Corporate reports: quarterly and annual reports to shareholders by corporate management.
2. Security Prospectus: registration statement filed with the Securities and Exchange Commission (SEC) on any new security offering.
3. Required SEC Reports: monthly statement 8-K, semiannual statement 9-K, and annual statement 10-K provide information that is often more current or thorough than that reported to shareholders.
4. *Standard & Poor's Corporation Record:* historical and financial data.
5. *Standard & Poor's Analysts Handbook:* basic financial information.
6. *Standard & Poor's Stock Reports:* short reviews of financial data and forecasts.
7. *Standard & Poor's Stock Guide:* compact summary of financial information on actively traded stocks.
8. *Moody's Manuals:* historical and financial data; separate volumes deal with industrial, OTC industrial, utility, transportation, and bank-finance stocks.
9. *Value Line Investment Service:* basic financial data and projections on over 1,700 actively traded stocks.

III. Information by Type of Security
A. Money Market Instruments and Bonds
1. *Money Manager:* weekly events occurring in the short- and long-term bond markets.
2. *Weekly Bond Buyer:* weekly events occurring in the short- and long-term bond markets.
3. *Bankers Trust Credit and Capital Markets:* survey of current trends in interest rates.
4. *Moody's Bond Survey:* weekly review of events and financial data.
5. *Value Line Options and Convertibles:* financial data on convertible bonds.
6. *Moody's Bond Record:* financial data on major corporate bonds outstanding.
7. *Moody's Municipal and Government Manual:* data on U.S. government and municipal obligations.
8. *Standard & Poor's Bond Guide:* compact review of major financial data.
9. *Standard & Poor's Convertible Bond Reports:* basic information about actively traded convertible bonds.

B. Stocks: see information listed in parts IA, IB, and IIC.

C. Other Instruments
1. *Value Line Options and Convertibles:* basic information about options.
2. *Vickers Guide to Investment Company Portfolios:* general information on investment companies.
3. *Weisenberger Investment Companies:* annual background, management policy, and financial records for all U.S. and Canadian investment companies.
4. *Investment Dealers Digest Mutual Fund Directory:* semiannual statistics for mutual funds.
5. *Johnson Investment Company Charts:* data on market and various types of funds.
6. Investment Company Institute's *Mutual Fund Fact Book:* basic statistics for the industry.
7. *Commodity Yearbook:* production, prices, etc., for 100 commodities.
8. *Guide to World Commodity Markets:* information and statistics on commodity markets.
9. *Morningstar Mutual Fund:* detailed information on mutual funds.

APPENDIX 2B: PERSONAL COMPUTER DATA SOURCES

This appendix lists and briefly describes the major sources of security information available for personal computer users. Computer data used by academic researchers is not listed due to its cost and the need for mainframe computer facilities.

1. *Dow Jones News / Retrieval.* Online service connecting to more than 40 databases providing current business and general news, company and industry information, stock quotations, and other business and financial services. U.S. prices only.

2. *Compact Disclosure.* Database containing financial and management information extracted from SEC filinfs and annual reports for more than 12,000 U.S. public companies. Includes five years annual financial data.

3. *CIRR Index.* Computer index with abstracts of U.S. brokerage house reports.

4. *Compustat PC Plus.* Financial data on more than 2,000 U.S. corporations stored on CD-ROM. Program allows search for firms with per user-defined criteria.

5. *Value Screen.* Financial data on firms covered in *Value Line.* Program allows search for firms with user-defined criteria.

6. *Morningstar Mutual Funds OnDisc.* Financial information and returns on 1,500 U.S. mutual funds. CD-ROM.

REFERENCES

A thorough examination of money market instruments can be found in:

Cook, Timothy Q., and Timothy D. Rowe, *Instruments of the Money Market,* Richmond, VA: Federal Reserve Bank of Richmond, 1986.

Kidwell, David S., M. Wayne Mann, and G. Rodney Thompson, "Eurodollar Bonds: Alternative Financing for U.S. Companies," *Financial Management,* Winter 1985.

Stigum, Marcia, *The Money Market,* Homewood, IL: Dow Jones-Irwin, 1983.

A detailed discussion of U.S. federal debt issues is:

Handbook of Securities of the United States Government and Federal Agencies, Boston: First Boston Corporation, published biannually.

Detailed statistics of security offerings can be found in:

United States Federal Reserve Bulletins, published monthly.
Treasury Bulletin, Department of Treasury, Washington, D. C., published monthly.
Mutual Fund Fact Book, Investment Company Institute, Washington, D. C., published annually.
Nasdaq Fact Book & Company Directory, National Association of Security Dealers, Washington, D. C., published annually.

Extensive Mutual Fund data is available in:

Investment Companies, New York: CDA/Weisenberger, published annually.
Morningstar Mutual Funds, Chicago, IL: Morningstar, Inc.

Survey articles of recent developments in security markets include:

Goldberg, Craig J., and Karen Rogers, "An Introduction to Asset Backed Securities," *Journal of Applied Corporate Finance,* 1, No. 3, pp. 20–31.

MILLER, MARTIN A., "Financial Innovation: The Last Twenty Years and the Next," *Journal of Financial and Quantitative Management,* 21, December 1986, pp. 459–471.

OCAMPO, JUAN M., and JAMES A. ROSENTHAL, "The Future of Securitization and the Financial Services Industry," *Journal of Applied Corporate Finance,* 1, No. 3., pp. 90–101.

Detailed analyses of option and futures instruments can be found in:

GOSS, B. A. and B. S. YAMEY, Eds. *The Economics of Future Trading,* London: Macmillan, 1976.

STOLL, HANS R. and ROBERT E. WHALEY, *Futures and Options: Theory and Applications,* Cincinnati, OH: Southwestern Publishing Co., 1993.

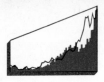

C H A P T E R 3

Security Markets

In this chapter, we review the institutional procedures used to trade equities and fixed income obligations in major world markets. After discussing in some depth the trading procedures used in U.S. markets, contrasting features in the U. K. and Japanese markets are examined.

Procedures unique to options, futures, and investment companies are discussed in later chapters devoted to each. This chapter is largely descriptive in nature, addressing trading procedures as they actually exist, as opposed to asking why they exist.

Security transactions occur in either the *primary market* or the *secondary market.* In a primary market transaction, a buyer gives the original issuer of the security cash in exchange for ownership of the security. For example, weekly T-bill offerings by the U.S. Treasury, municipal bond sales by the state of Ohio, and stock sales by British Airways are all primary market transactions. The key to a primary market transaction is that the original security issuer receives cash, and the public then holds a security that previously didn't exist. Subsequent to the primary offering, the security is traded between members of the public in what are referred to as secondary markets. These secondary markets include both formal exchange markets (such as the New York Stock Exchange and International Stock Exchange in London) and less formal markets (referred to as over-the-counter [OTC] transactions). The issuer of a security is unaffected by secondary market transactions.[1] The sale of a T-bill by a dealer in bills to a commercial bank, the sale of a municipal bond by a New York bond house to a California savings and loan association, and the sale of British Airways ordinary shares by Ms. A to Mr. B are all secondary market transactions.

---

[1] Secondary market transactions can have an indirect effect upon the original security issuer, however, because of information provided by secondary market prices. For example, the price of IBM common stock and debt can be used by IBM management to evaluate their past performance and determine the financing costs necessary to float new security offerings.

PRIMARY MARKET

The Investment Banker

As noted above, a primary market transaction represents the initial sale of a security by an issuer to the public. The issuer receives cash (to invest in productive assets or realign its capital structure), and the public receives securities (for personal investment or speculative purposes).

Figure 3-1 illustrates various decisions that a security issuer faces. First, the legal character of the issue must be determined. Second, issuers must decide whether they are willing to assume the risks of price declines during the distribution period or would rather shift these risks to some other party. Third, a formal marketing strategy must be developed. At any stage of the security offering, the issuer may decide to rely upon internal expertise or call upon the services of an investment banking firm. Investment bankers are organizations that specialize in the creation and placement of securities in the primary market and provide three basic services: (1) advice, (2) underwriting, and (3) distribution.

Advice. Many security issuers do not have the internal expertise or knowledge of market conditions necessary to put together a security issue. In such cases, investment bankers can provide advice about the following:

1. *Type of security offering.* Given the issuer's financial structure and security market conditions, the investment banker can advise the issuer on what type of security—equity or debt—should be sold.
2. *Timing of the offering.* Given current and expected market conditions, the investment banker can suggest whether the offering should be sold immediately or delayed in hopes of a better price.
3. *Legal characteristics of the issue.* For example, if a debt issue is contemplated, the investment banker can provide advice about coupon rate, maturity, protective covenants, convertibility, call prices, etc.
4. *Price of the security.* Given suggestions about each of the above, the investment banker will suggest a price at which the security can be sold.

Issuers may elect to use only the advice services of investment bankers without using their underwriting and distribution services. In such cases, a consulting fee is paid. Many issuers, of course, have the internal financial expertise to make all necessary decisions. For example, national treasuries and many large corporations do not use investment bankers for their advice services.

Underwriting. Once the type of security, date of issue, and security price have been decided upon, the issuer can proceed to sell to the public. However, if the price at which the markets would be willing to absorb the issue is set too high or if the market as a whole declines, the issuer might not receive the total dollar

FIGURE 3-1 *Creation and Sale of a New Security Issue*

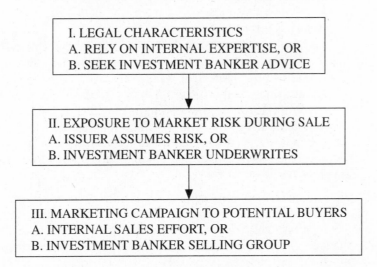

amount desired. For example, assume that Georgia Pacific wishes to raise $100 million in a common stock offering to support new-product expansion. Based upon a secondary market price of $27 for their existing common stock and discussions with their investment banker, management decides to sell 4 million shares at $25 per share. (The $2 price difference is used as an inducement to attract buyers and encourage fast sale.) Unfortunately, soon after the securities are offered, the price at which they are able to sell the shares actually falls to $22. This could occur either because management misjudged the price inducement necessary to attract large numbers of buyers or because all stock prices fell as a result of bad economic news. Regardless of the reason, Georgia Pacific would receive only $88 million of the desired $100 million in cash.

Investment bankers stand ready to absorb any part of the price risk that an issuer would rather not accept. This is referred to as *underwriting* an issue. Three basic degrees of underwriting are used:

1. In a *firm commitment,* the banker purchases the full amount of the issue from the seller at an agreed-upon price. All market risk is shifted from the issuer to the investment banker. The banker will reoffer the securities to the general public at a higher price than that paid to the issuer. In the Georgia Pacific example, the issue might be underwritten at $24 (for 4.17 million shares to assure $100 million in cash) and reoffered at $25 to the general public. The $1 difference between what the issuer receives and what the public pays is known as the *underwriter's spread* and represents the underwriter's compensation for assuming market risks, searching for buyers, and providing financial advice.

2. In a *stand-by agreement,* the underwriter agrees to help sell the new issue for some stated time interval (usually 30 days) but will not "position the security at risk." Once the interval is passed, the underwriter purchases any unsold securities at a predetermined price. Stand-by agreements are commonly used for stock sales that are being distributed through a rights offering.

3. In a *best-efforts basis* sale, the investment banker has no obligation to purchase any of the security issue. The banker acts solely as a broker and returns any unsold securities to the issuer. A best-efforts sale is used for two types of issuers. In the first case, the issuing firm demands a best-efforts sale because it is confident that the securities will be fully sold (because of the firm's size, the risk, and the market's interest in the new securities). In the second case, the investment banker requires a best-efforts sale because the issuing firm is small, unestablished, and risky.

When a firm commitment is used, a *purchase group* of many investment bankers will be formed. The *lead underwriter* (or managing underwriter) conducts all negotiations with the issuer, oversees registration with the Securities and Exchange Commission (SEC), maintains accounting records, and selects other members of the purchase group. However, all members of the purchase group purchase (or "position") a part of the issue. By positioning a portion of many new issues, as opposed to positioning all of one issue, the underwriter obtains greater diversification and lower risk.

Distribution. Some issuers have the ability to market new issues directly to the general public and don't need the distribution services of an investment banker. The largest direct issuer is, of course, the U.S. government, which uses periodic competitive bid sales for Treasury and agency obligations. In addition, common stock sales using rights offerings to existing shareholders have been used increasingly by large corporations that prefer to bypass investment bankers.[2] However, most issuers don't have the extensive contacts with potential buyers that investment bankers are able to develop.

In fact, the buying syndicate itself may not have any direct contact with potential buyers. Security firms have found it profitable to specialize over the years. Some firms have concentrated on providing financial advice and underwriting services to issuers, while others have concentrated on the development of large networks of retail offices. As a result, members of the purchase group often do not have direct contact with potential buyers. To develop an effective distribution team, a *selling group* is usually created that consists of members of both the purchase group and selected retail brokerage houses.

---

[2] One interesting technique of direct placement was used by large utilities in the midwestern United States during the 1920s. Whenever these firms wanted to sell new stock or debt issues, they would have their meter readers sell them door-to-door as they went on their rounds. This novel approach disappeared when the firms were forced into bankruptcy and reorganization during the 1930s.

The operation of the selling group is controlled by the *selling group agreement,* which (1) defines the duration of the agreement (usually 30 days), (2) specifies the split of the underwriter spread among the manager, the purchase group, and the selling group, (3) indicates accounting procedures, and (4) states that no member will sell below the offering price.

Once the underwriting syndicate has been formed, market conditions seem favorable, and all legal requirements have been met, the securities can be actively sold to the public. Prior to that time, potential buyers will have investigated the issue and perhaps even expressed interest to members of the selling group. However, actual purchase orders can't be taken until a formal ''opening of the books.'' Some issues will have an active demand and be sold out within hours, or may even be oversubscribed. Other issues require a longer time to be distributed. During this interval, the managing underwriter is allowed to *stabilize the market* by placing orders to buy the security at a fixed price. This is the only form of security price manipulation legally allowed in the United States. Underwriters claim that market stabilization is necessary to ensure an orderly sale and offset temporary price declines. They claim that the use of price stabilizing reduces their risk exposure and thus reduces the costs to issuing firms.

Negotiated Versus Competitive Selection. When the selling efforts of an investment banker are used, the issuer must decide whether the banker is to be selected on a *competitive* or a *negotiated* basis. In a competitive underwriting, all details of the security offering (type, timing, and legal characteristics) except price are specified, and the investment banker offering the best bid price is selected. A specific time and place are set at which competitive bids are opened. Competitive bid offerings are common in municipal bond sales as well as in debt and equity sales by regulated companies. Competitive bid offerings provide the issuer the potential advantage of receiving the highest possible price because of active competition for the issue. They have the disadvantage of inflexibility because the investment banker is obligated to a firm price and is exposed to considerable market risk.

In a negotiated underwriting, the issuer selects the underwriter it believes is best able to provide the unique advice, underwriting, and selling efforts necessary to the success of the particular offering. The investment banker's compensation is negotiated, as opposed to being set in a formal competitive bid. Statistical tests conducted to date suggest that competitive offerings do provide some cost advantages over negotiated underwritings. However, the cost of issuing a security is difficult to measure, and these results might well be due to inadequate cost data.[3]

---

[3] For example, negotiated fees will include reimbursement to the investment banker for the consulting services usually provided in such offerings. Competitive fees will not include consulting costs even though the issuer has to incur such expenses, either as internal management time or as fees paid to advising bankers. This imprecise cost measurement will make competitive fees appear lower.

Private Versus Public Placement

Private Placement. A *privately placed security* is one that is sold to fewer than 25 buyers and, as a result, needn't be registered with the SEC. While some stock issues are privately placed (often with venture capital firms), bond issues are the more predominant. In recent years, more than 25% of all bond issues have been privately placed.

The major advantages of private placements stem from the fact that such issues aren't registered with the SEC. As a result, a new issue can be placed quickly and without incurring the large costs of preparing a registration statement. Investment bankers might be used to find buyers, for which they are paid a finder's fee of ¼% to 1½% of the issue. But their underwriting services aren't required, thus eliminating any compensation for these services. In addition, loan covenants on privately placed bonds can be less restrictive than if the issue were sold to the general public. The issuer and buyer can "tailor fit" any required covenants, whereas a public sale might require a large number of additional covenants to attract a sufficient number of buyers.

The major disadvantage of a private placement is its lack of marketability. Because the issue is not registered with the SEC, buyers are limited in their ability to subsequently sell the issue, resulting in greater required yields.

Public Placement. With the few exemptions noted below, any new security issue that is sold to more than 25 buyers must be registered with the SEC. The purpose of a registration statement is to ensure that investors receive full and accurate disclosure of any information relevant to the issue. While statutes set a twenty-day waiting period between the time the registration statement is filed and the time securities may be sold to the public, in practice the SEC can shorten or lengthen the period as necessary to enable the SEC staff to review the statement for any omissions or apparent misrepresentations of fact. During periods of heavy activity, six months or more may pass before the registration is acceptable to the SEC staff. Table 3-1 provides a partial listing of the types of information required.

Before individuals are allowed to purchase a new issue, they must be given a *prospectus.* The prospectus is essentially the same as the registration statement, with certain technical information deleted.[4] SEC approval of the registration statement and prospectus does not constitute an opinion about the risks or investment merits of the security. Approval by the SEC simply means that the issuer has disclosed all facts required by law. Certain securities are exempt from registration. Major types include (1) U.S. government obligations, (2) municipal obligations, (3) commercial bank and savings and loan issues, (4) issues sold intrastate, and (5) issues sold to 25 or fewer buyers. Figure 3-2 shows the cover page of a prospectus.

---

[4] Prior to approval by the SEC, a tentative version of the prospectus, known as a *red herring,* is distributed. The red herring differs from the prospectus in two minor ways. First, stamped on the front page in red (hence the term) is a statement indicating that the prospectus and registration statement have not yet received SEC approval. Second, an issue price is not shown.

TABLE 3-1 *Typical Information Required in an SEC Registration Statement*

1. General information on the issuer—location, products, and so forth
2. Purposes of issue
3. Price at which offered to the public
4. Price at which offered to any special group
5. Promoters' fees
6. Underwriting fees
7. Net proceeds to the company
8. Remuneration of any officers receiving over $25,000 annually
9. Disclosure of any unusual contracts, such as managerial profit sharing
10. Detailed capitalization statement
11. Detailed balance sheet
12. Detailed earnings statement for three preceding years
13. Names and addresses of officers, directors, and underwriters
14. Names and addresses of stockholders owning more than 10% of any class of stock
15. Pending litigation
16. Copy of underwriting agreement
17. Copy of legal opinions
18. Copy of articles of incorporation or association
19. Copies of indentures affecting new issues

Shelf Registration

In 1982, the Securities and Exchange Commission (SEC) instituted Rule 415, which has had profound implications for the way transactions take place in the primary market. Rule 415 allows issuers to preregister a security sale. The issuing firm announces its intention to sell a security, files necessary information with the SEC, and accepts competitive bids from investment bankers for the issue. Once the issue is approved by the SEC, the firm can either accept the best competitive bid or delay sale indefinitely. Generally the registration will be delayed until the issuer truly needs capital or prices are viewed to be favorable. When the sale does take place, there is no delay associated with SEC filing and approval. Thus the sale can be executed rapidly.

Issuing Costs

The costs of issuing securities consist of three components:

1. *Out-of-pocket costs* associated with internal clerical costs, management time spent putting the issue together, payments to legal counsel, payments to certified public accountants, etc.
2. The *underwriter spread,* which is the difference between the price received by the issuer and the price at which the underwriter offers it to the public.
3. A *price concession,* which is an inducement offered to the first buyer. The price concession is theoretically equal to the difference between the equilibrium price of the security and the price at which the security is offered to the public.

FIGURE 3-2 *Sample Entries in a Specialist Book*

750,000 Shares

SPAGHETTI WAREHOUSE, INC.

Common Stock

The Company's Common Stock is traded on the American Stock Exchange under the symbol "SWH." On May 22, 1991, the last reported sale price of the Common Stock was $26.75 per share. See "Price Range of Common Stock."

THESE SECURITIES HAVE NOT BEEN APPROVED OR DISAPPROVED BY THE SECURITIES AND EXCHANGE COMMISSION OR ANY STATE SECURITIES COMMISSION NOR HAS THE SECURITIES AND EXCHANGE COMMISSION OR ANY STATE SECURITIES COMMISSION PASSED UPON THE ACCURACY OR ADEQUACY OF THIS PROSPECTUS. ANY REPRESENTATION TO THE CONTRARY IS A CRIMINAL OFFENSE.

	Price to Public	Underwriting Discount(1)	Proceeds to Company(2)
Per Share	$26.75	$1.40	$25.35
Total(3)	$20,062,500	$1,050,000	$19,012,500

(1) *See "Underwriting" for information concerning indemnification of the Underwriters and other matters.*
(2) *Before deducting expenses of the offering estimated at $270,000.*
(3) *The Company has granted the Underwriters an option, exercisable within 30 days of the date hereof, to purchase up to 112,500 additional shares of Common Stock at the Price to Public less Underwriting Discount for the purpose of covering over-allotments, if any. If the Underwriters exercise this option in full, the Price to Public will total $23,071,875, the Underwriting Discount will total $1,207,500, and the Proceeds to Company will total $21,864,375. See "Underwriting."*

The shares are offered by the several Underwriters named herein when, as and if delivered to and accepted by the Underwriters and subject to the right to reject any order in whole or in part. It is expected that delivery of the certificates representing the shares will be made against payment therefor at the office of Montgomery Securities on or about May 30, 1991.

MONTGOMERY SECURITIES   *THE PRINCIPAL/EPPLER, GUERIN & TURNER, INC.*

May 22, 1991

For example, assume ABC Corp. sells 100,000 new common shares at a time when its currently outstanding shares are selling in the secondary market for $50. To attract a large number of buyers for the new issue and to encourage quick distribution, the underwriter suggests an offering price of $48. In addition, the underwriter sets a $2 underwriter spread to compensate for the market risks of positioning the issue, to cover the costs of finding buyers, and to provide a fair profit. Net of the underwriting spread, ABC Corp. receives $46 per share. Finally, total out-of-pocket costs associated with the sale are $100,000.

Issuing costs would be as follows:

Nature of Cost	Cost per Share	Details
Out-of-Pocket Costs	$1	($100,000 ÷ 100,000 shares)
Underwriter Spread	$2	(Specified)
Price Concession	$2	($50 equilibrium − $48 offer)
Total	$5	

Little is known about the size of out-of-pocket costs since accurate data have never been compiled. Underwriter spreads range anywhere from ½% to 15% or more of the issue's offering price. The size of such spreads depends on the risks and distribution efforts faced by underwriters. For example, firm commitments on large municipal bond issues require spreads of only 1% or so during normal market conditions since underwriters are exposed to little market risk and there is an easy-to-identify and active buying market for such issues. However, small preferred stock issues from high-risk corporations can require spreads of 15% or more. Such a large spread would be due to the potential difficulty in finding buyers, the small size of the issue (most authorities believe there are clear economies of scale to underwriting), and the large price risks incurred while the securities remain in the underwriter's inventory. The split of the underwriter spread varies, but a typical split of a $2 spread on a $50 common stock would be $0.40 to the managing underwriter, $0.40 to each member of the purchase group, and the remaining $1.20 to the broker of the stock.

The costs of price concessions are difficult to measure since equilibrium security prices are difficult to estimate. These equilibrium prices represent the price at which the security would sell (under current market conditions) if it were not part of a new offering.

There do appear to be clear price concessions on *new* common stock offerings. These new offerings are referred to as *initial public offerings,* or IPOs. Ibbotson found that an average return of 11.4% could have been earned in the month following a new IPO if (1) one had purchased a broad sample of new offerings between 1960 and 1969, (2) the stocks were acquired at the offering price, and (3) the stocks were sold at the bid price at the end of the month. This 11.4% was statistically significant and represents a rather healthy one-month return. Individual security results were quite variable, however. Some IPOs provided a 70% monthly gain while others yielded a 60% loss. To receive the 11.4% average return, one would have had to participate in virtually every new offering.

Ibbotson's results confirm statistically what has been called the "new issues fad." Requests to buy into new stock offerings often exceeded the size of the offerings by a multiple of 5 to 1.[5] And Ibbotson's results have been confirmed by many other research studies. The true economic causes for price concessions on IPOs are not yet fully understood.

SECONDARY MARKETS

The New York Stock Exchange

The New York Stock Exchange (NYSE) is the largest and oldest organized security market in the United States. Formed in 1792 by a group of merchants to trade federal notes and bonds, the exchange has seen its volume grow from a few bond trades over morning coffee to more than 200 million common stock shares per day in the 1990s. Interestingly, this supposed bastion of free enterprise was formed under a constitution which had all the characteristics of a cartel. Members of the NYSE agreed to trade only among themselves and to charge identical commission rates. These two agreements remained virtually unchanged for more than 150 years and were the fundamental cause of many changes in trading practices during the 1970s and 1980s.

Membership. The NYSE is a corporate association of about 1,500 members, each of whom has bought a *seat* (membership) and has been approved by other members. The cost of a seat is determined by the prevailing demand and supply of memberships, which are in turn a function of the future prospects for the NYSE. In the post-World War II era, seats have sold for as much as $515,000 and for as little as $35,000. Membership prices during the past 20 years dropped dramatically below the "go-go" days of the 1960s as the NYSE encountered increased competition from other markets and the likely elimination of many monopolistic rates. In addition to regular members who own a seat on the exchange, the NYSE allows various firms access to the trading floor by paying an annual fee.

Members are assigned particular roles, as follows:[6]

---

[5] Oversubscribed issues are often allocated by brokers to favored customers. Clearly it pays to be on a broker's favored list. But perhaps one pays to be on the list by incurring large brokerage fees. In addition, underwriters offer price concessions because they don't wish to be exposed to the price risks of carrying the securities in inventory. They shift the risk to an initial buyer and in return offer what appears to be an abnormal return. These risks can be substantial. Perhaps the initial buyer receives a large return only to compensate for risks incurred.

[6] In the recent past some members acted as *odd-lot dealers*. The normal unit of trading on the NYSE is a round lot, or 100 shares. When buyers or sellers of an odd lot (a fraction of 100 shares) wished to trade, their orders were historically taken to an odd-lot dealer. The odd-lot dealer would buy (or sell) at a price equal to the next round-lot transaction on the exchange floor plus (or minus) $1/8$ or $1/4$ dollar. Today odd-lot dealers are an extinct species. Large brokerage houses and many specialists perform the same function of assembling several odd lots into round lots, but do so at substantially reduced costs to traders.

TABLE 3-2 *New York Stock Exchange Listing Requirements*

To be listed on the New York Stock Exchange, a firm must have:
1. Earnings before taxes of at least $2.5 million in the most recent year
2. Earnings before taxes of at least $2.0 million during the two preceding years
3. Net tangible assets of at least $18 million
4. Total market value of common stock of at least $18 million
5. At least 1.1 million shares publicly held
6. More than 2,000 holders of 100 shares or more

1. *Commission brokers* are partners in a brokerage firm and execute orders for their firm's clients on the floor of the exchange. Large brokerage houses will have more than one commission broker on the floor to ensure that customers' orders are rapidly executed.
2. *Floor brokers* are freelance commission brokers. They do not have direct contact with the public, but handle order overflows which the commission brokers are unable to handle. A portion of the commission broker's fee is paid to the floor broker.
3. *Registered traders* buy and sell solely for their own account. They do not handle public orders. Often called floor traders, they are speculators who attempt to buy securities experiencing a temporary influx of sell orders (which are forcing prices down) and sell securities experiencing a temporary influx of buy orders (which are forcing prices up). As a result, floor-trading operations are said to reduce price volatility and add to the market's liquidity. In recent years, floor-trading memberships have been few and their trading activity negligible.
4. *Specialists* stand in the middle of every trade, both figuratively and literally. Their essential role in completing a transaction is discussed below.

Listing Requirements. Only listed securities may be traded on the NYSE floor, and until recently, members were not allowed to trade listed stocks in any market other than the NYSE.[7] In 1991, there were approximately 2,300 stocks and 3,000 bonds listed, which represented a major portion of publicly traded U.S. corporate securities. The original issuer of the security makes the decision to list or not. The major advantage claimed for listing is an improvement in security marketability. Minimum *initial listing* requirements must be satisfied, and, to remain listed, the firm must fill various *continued listing* requirements. In selecting securities to be listed, exchange officials seek firms which are national in scope and have a major standing in a growing industry. The more important listing requirements are shown in Table 3-2.

Specialist Operations. About 25% of all NYSE members act as specialists. Usually, they form partnerships or corporations with other specialists to diversify risk

---

[7] Rule 390 prevented member firms from trading listed stocks in a market other than the NYSE.

exposure and spread administrative costs. These organizations are referred to as *specialist units,* and each unit is assigned a number of stocks in which it acts as specialist. For illustrative purposes, however, it is easiest to think in terms of one specialist assigned to one stock. Specialists perform two functions. First, they act as *brokers* by maintaning the *limit book.* Second, they act as *dealers* by selling and buying shares in which they are specialists.

A *limit order* is a request to buy or sell a security at a given price or better. For example, a limit order to *buy* XYZ Corp. at $75 must be transacted at $75 or less. Since limit orders are usually placed at prices "away from the market" (different from current price levels), the commission broker will leave limit orders with the specialist. The specialist records limit orders in a limit book similar to that shown in Figure 3-3.[8] The figure shows a variety of orders to buy at prices of $30.375 or less and offers to sell at prices of $30.625 or more.[9] Requests to buy are referred to as *bid prices,* and offers to sell are called *asked prices.* None of these limit orders will trade now since the actual market price lies somewhere between the highest bid and the lowest ask. Over time, however, the price of the stock will undoubtedly increase or decrease as favorable or unfavorable news is reported. And when a price change occurs, the specialist will execute any limit orders at that price. For this service, the specialist is given a part of the commission broker's fee.

The more complex and important role of the specialist is to serve as a dealer in the stock. The NYSE uses the specialist's dealer function in an attempt to provide continuous and liquid markets. To fully understand how the specialist can provide these services, a short digression is helpful.

There are any number of ways to mechanically structure security trading activity. One method is known as a *call auction,* in which the name of each security is periodically called off (say, twice a day). At such times, buyers and sellers state the price and number of shares at which they are willing to trade. The resulting trade price is that which allows the greatest number of trades. A system similar to this was used in the early history of the NYSE and is still used on various foreign exchanges. Today's procedures, however, are closer to what we might term a *continuous auction.* Buyers and sellers continuously place orders on the exchange and seek to buy at the lowest price and sell at the highest price.

Return to Figure 3-3 and assume that two commission brokers arrive simultaneously at the specialist's post. Commission broker A has a customer order to buy 300 shares at the best price then possible, and commission broker B has an order to sell 300 shares. They ask the specialist, "How's the market?" And, *if the specialist decides not to trade for his own account,* he will reply, "30⅜ to ⅝." This means that the best price to sell (the bid price) is $30.375, and that the best price to buy (the asked price) is $30.625. Commission brokers A and B will recognize that they can better these prices for their customers if they trade with

---

[8] In the past, the specialist limit book was physically a book. Today, computer technology displays limit orders on a computer screen.

[9] Stock prices are quoted in eighths of $1.

FIGURE 3-3 *Illustration of a Prospectus*

Lot	Buy	Price	Sell	Lot
3	Escher	30		
6 1	Zohail Andress	1/8		
4	Williams	1/4		
5	Jacobson	3/8		
		1/2		
		5/8	Nelson Myers	3 4
		3/4	Chance	4
		7/8	Brown Goedel Bach	8 2 1

each other, so A will offer to buy 300 at $30.50 and B will agree to sell. But this favorable result occurred simply because the brokers were lucky enough to arrive at the specialist's post at the same moment with identical-size orders. If broker A had arrived moments earlier, the customer would have had to buy at $30.625 and broker B's customer would have had to sell at $30.375. It is exactly such situations that the specialist is designed to aid.

Acting as a *dealer* in the stock, the specialist trades at prices between the limit book's high bid and low offer. *In this role, the specialist will absorb temporary imbalances in buy and sell orders.* As compensation, the specialist hopes to earn a *jobber's turn* over time by selling at prices higher, on average, than paid.

If specialists perform their duties as the exchange desires, the public gains in three ways. First, average bid-ask spreads are narrowed by the specialist's quoting prices between the limit book prices. Second, market participants can be assured that prices will not swing erratically over short time periods, as would be the case if all orders were matched against the limit book. Finally, market participants can expect only small price changes for larger than normal orders since the specialist is supposed to stand ready to take on or dispose of larger amounts of stock. (In fact, specialists will occasionally *short sell*—a term discussed later—to meet buy orders.)

To properly fulfill their duties of providing continuous and liquid markets, specialists will often have to "go against the market" for extended periods, and their profits can be quite variable over time. The specialist has no idea whether a particular order is motivated by someone's need for (or excess of) liquidity or by special information. Against the liquidity trader, specialists profit. Against the information trader, they lose. In fact, specialist partnerships are formed in an attempt to diversify away some of the risk of dealing in single stocks. To ensure that specialists are able to provide sufficient depth of liquidity, the NYSE places minimum capital requirements on specialist units. As the volume of trading has increased over time, the minimum capital requirements have also increased.

But specialist operations have received considerable criticism. For example, a special study by the SEC suggested that the gross income per average dollar invested for an average specialist unit was about 100% per year.[10] While the NYSE has no rules barring competition between specialist units for the same stock, until the late 1970s it was a standard practice to assign only one unit per stock. The exchange rationalized the practice by stating that assigning more than one unit would fragment trading activity and cause a decline in liquidity. However, this policy was reversed in the late 1970s, and units were allowed to compete with one another. As a result, a few units did begin to compete.

But even though NYSE specialists have little direct competition on the floor of the exchange, they do face considerable competition from specialists trading similar stocks on other exchanges. As a result, in 1984 NYSE specialists substantially reduced their fees, to approximately $1.50 per round lot. More alarming, however, was the near breakdown of the specialist system and the potential bankruptcy of many specialist units which occurred in the stock market crash of October 19, 1987—"Black Monday."

Recent Automation of NYSE Trading

To efficiently handle the volume of trading activity on the NYSE, the exchange has computerized much of the trading process. They refer to this process as Super DOT (designated order turnaround). In 1991, Super DOT had the capacity to handle 600 million share trades on a given day. At that time, average daily volume was approximately 100 million shares. At the opening of each day, Super DOT accepts up to 30,099 market orders from a given member firm, pairs requests to buy or sell, and notifies the specialist of the net imbalance. This assists the specialist in deciding at what price a stock should open. After trading begins, Super DOT accepts market orders of up to 2,099 shares and typically executes them within one minute. Limit orders as large as 99,999 shares are recorded in the specialist's electronic book and stored until cancelled or executed. The *specialist's electronic book* is a computer display terminal that replaces the old hand-held specialist's book of limit orders. Computerization of limit orders has reduced human errors associated with maintenance of paper records and improved the ability to trace the cause for any errors that do occur.

---

[10] United States House Committee on Interstate and Foreign Commerce, Subcommittee on Commerce and Finance, *Securities Industry Study: Report and Hearings,* 92d Congress, 1st and 2d sessions, chap. 12.

Other Exchanges

The American Stock Exchange. The American Stock Exchange (AMEX) is often referred to as the ''Curb Exchange'' because its earliest brokers traded outdoors on the curb of Wall and Broad Streets in New York City. Clerks would accept requests to trade by telephone and lean outside the office window to pass the order information on to the broker, who was standing on the street. Brokers wore bright multicolored hats so they could be recognized by the clerk, and trade information was passed by means of complex hand signals. The AMEX moved indoors in 1921 and adopted its present name in 1953. The hats are gone, but the hand signals remain. For many years there were no formal listing requirements, but today all securities traded must meet certain financial tests (similar to, but less stringent than, NYSE listing requirements).

Regional Exchanges. A number of regional exchanges exist that provide two basic services. First, they list securities of smaller companies of only regional interest. Second, they dually list popular NYSE stocks and charge lower commissions. This second factor was a major impetus to their growth. Brokers who could not afford a seat on the NYSE could purchase a less expensive seat on a regional exchange and be able to trade the more popular NYSE stocks. Without the regional exchanges, such brokers would have had to feed their orders to NYSE member firms and give up a portion of their commissions. In addition, institutions wishing to trade large blocks of stock could trade at lower commission rates on regional exchanges than on the NYSE. Now that commission rates are no longer fixed by the NYSE, and with the growth of dual listings on the AMEX, the future of the regionals is less bright than it once was. As of 1991, the major regional stock exchanges included the Boston Stock Exchange, the Cincinnati Stock Exchange, the Midwest Stock Exchange, the Pacific Stock Exchange, and the Philadelphia Stock Exchange.

The Over-the-Counter Market. Transactions not handled on one of the organized exchanges are called *over-the-counter (OTC) transactions.* The OTC has no central location at which all trading occurs. Instead, it is a diffuse network of brokers and dealers connected by either telephone or computer terminals. The term *over-the-counter* refers to the trading practices in the 1800s, when buyers and sellers of unlisted stocks would physically present cash or securities at a commercial bank. The bank and trader would actually trade over the counter. With the advent of telephones, the market became a telephone network between brokers and dealers. Cathode ray tubes have now been introduced in trading most OTC stocks, and the market is among the most technologically advanced in the country. Many experts believe the modern OTC market is a picture of what the future will be once organized exchanges are integrated with OTC stocks to create a single central market.

The securities traded in the OTC market differ considerably in size of issuer, legal nature, risk, marketability, etc. Mutual fund shares, most bank and finance stocks, most corporate bonds, and a large portion of U.S. government and municipal obligations are traded OTC. In addition, securities that are too small or unprofitable to meet the listing requirements of an organized exchange are traded OTC. (Many firms that could be listed choose not to be.) The actual size of the market is hard to determine, since any corporate issue is a candidate. All that is needed is a *market maker* in the stock who will buy or sell the stock to interested traders.

The market maker plays essentially the same dealer role for an OTC stock that the specialist does for an exchange-listed stock. (Market makers do not maintain limit books, however.) The market maker carries a trading inventory of a particular security and is willing to buy and sell with members of the general public. Market makers serve a useful purpose since the public buyer needn't spend time trying to find a public seller. The market maker is known and continuously stands ready to buy or sell. In return for this service, a bid-ask spread is required. Buyers acquire securities at the higher asked price, and sellers dispose of securities at the lower bid price. Actively traded OTC securities will have as many as fifteen to twenty market makers competing for public orders. Investment bankers often make a market in the securities they underwrite, and regional brokerage houses typically make markets in local securities. However, many of the large brokerage firms enter the business simply to increase the services available to customers and increase their profits.

Brokers and dealers in OTC securities have formed a self-regulating body known as the National Association of Security Dealers (NASD), which licenses brokers and oversees trading practices. In 1971 the NASD instituted a computerized trading network known as the *NASD Automated Quotation System* (NASDAQ; pronounced NAZ-dak). To be included in the NASDAQ, a security must have at least two market makers, have a minimum number of publicly held shares, and meet certain asset and equity capital requirements. NASDAQ is simply a "real time" information system. Current bid and ask quotations of all market makers on a security are continuously maintained through a telecommunication network. Prior to NASDAQ, a broker could obtain bid-ask quotes only by calling various dealers who made a market in the security. The best bid or ask price could take so long to find that the quote could change before the broker had time to place an order. In fact, there was no guarantee that the *best* quote had been found, since the broker often wouldn't call all market makers. So the advantages of NASDAQ are twofold: (1) it provides *current* quotations, and (2) it brings together quotes from *all* important market makers. At present there are about 5,400 stocks carried on NASDAQ.

Dealers may subscribe to one of three levels of NASDAQ services. At Level I, the broker can view on a computer terminal the highest bid and the lowest ask that market makers are currently offering on each NASDAQ stock. At Level II, *all* bid and ask quotations currently offered are shown with an identification of the market maker providing each quote. At Level III, the user has the ability to actually enter bid and ask quotes into the NASDAQ system. When a bid or ask quote has been entered into the system it is shown to all users of Levels II and III, and the dealer must be willing to trade at least one round lot (100 shares) at these prices until the dealer changes the quotations. It is important to point out, however, that NASDAQ is currently only a reporting system. Actual trades are not made through the NASDAQ computer system but by direct contact between dealers and brokers. However, the system could be easily modified to allow for the actual "crosses" between two parties directly on the system.

OTC stocks with relatively active trading volume are designated by the NASD as *National Market Issues*. All transactions in NASDAQ National Market Issues are immediately reported on the NASDAQ system. For less active issues, dealers report only total transactions at the end of a day.

In addition to OTC stocks traditionally carried on NASDAQ, there are thousands of small, thinly trade stocks whose prices had been reported only once a day on what are referred to as *Pink Sheets*. The Pink Sheets include 11,000 or more inactively traded stocks, including many "penny" stocks and stocks having only a narrow geographic interest. Beginning in 1988, the current quotes for such stocks were also made available on NASDAQ through what is called the OTC Bulletin Board. Because of the extreme thinness of trading in such stocks, prices shown on the OTC Bulletin Board should be viewed with caution.

Prior to the 1980s, trading volume in the OTC market had historically been much smaller than that on formal exchange markets such as the NYSE, AMEX, or regionals. During the 1980s, however, NASDAQ made trading of OTC stocks so much easier that OTC trading volume has increased dramatically. In recent years, shares traded on NASDAQ have been approximately the same as or greater than the volume of shares traded on the NYSE.

Third and Fourth Markets. The *third market* refers to an OTC transaction in a security that is also traded on an organized exchange. The growth of the third market in the 1960s and early 1970s was due to two factors: the growth of institutional trading in large blocks of stock and minimum commission fees charged at the time by exchange members.

Throughout the 1960s large financial institutions (trust companies, pension funds, mutual funds, insurance firms, etc.) managed increasingly larger amounts of marketable securities and tended to trade more actively than they had previously. Large-block trades (transactions of 10,000 shares or more) became quite common. In the 1960s and early 1970s, all members of the NYSE *had to* transact any NYSE listed stock on the exchange floor *at a minimum commission.* But the marginal cost of putting a block together is substantially lower than the minimum commission which was charged, so nonexchange members started to act as block traders. They could perform the same services as member firms but were not bound by exchange rules to charge abnormally high commissions. Exchange member firms attempted to overcome the excessive commissions by offering other services below cost, taking losses on the prices of securities positioned, etc. But all of these attempts were burdensome at the least and often unsuccessful. As a result, the third market flourished. By 1972 third-market trading represented about 8½% of the volume of all NYSE transactions. Since then, activity in the third market has declined significantly because the SEC decided to eliminate fixed commissions. Between 1971 and 1975, negotiated fees were slowly phased in on large-block transactions. Since May 1, 1975 (*May Day*), all commissions have been negotiated and open to full competition.

The *fourth market* refers to transactions made directly between a buyer and a seller of a large block. Brokers and dealers are totally eliminated. The *Instinet* system is a wire network somewhat similar to NASDAQ which provides current information on the number of shares subscribers are willing to buy or sell at specified prices. Transactions in the fourth market are negligible at present.

Security Orders

Basic Types. The standard unit of trading in stocks is a *round lot,* or 100 shares. Any fraction of 100 shares is referred to as an *odd lot.* Because odd-lot transactions require special servicing (assembly of many odd lots into round lots is performed either by one's broker or by the specialist), they require a larger commission per share than do round lots. The most common type of order is a *market order,* in which a customer instructs a broker to either buy or sell at the best price then available. The exact transaction price will not be known with complete certainty when the order is placed, although the eventual trade price will be quite close to prices at the moment the order is placed. The advantage of a market order is that there is no doubt that it will be executed.

A *limit order* is a request to buy or sell at a specified price or better. For example, a limit order to sell at $40 obligates the broker to sell at a price of $40 or more. As we noted earlier, most limit orders are placed at prices somewhat away from prevailing market prices and will be left with the specialist to be entered in the limit book. The disadvantage of a limit order is that the investor is not sure that the security will indeed be bought or sold. For example, assume Lois Lane believes the prospects of SMI Corp. are strong. The stock is selling at $30 per share, but, in an attempt to pick up a point or two, she places a limit order to buy at $29. If the shares of SMI Corp. immediately soar to $50, Lois will never have bought.

Finally, a *stop order* is an order that specifies a given price at which point it becomes a market order. For example, a stop order to sell at $70 will become a market order to sell the moment to stock trades at $70. There is no assurance the stop order will be filled at the stop price, but it is likely to be transacted at a price reasonably close. Stop orders to sell are commonly used to protect profits or minimize losses when one owns the related stock. Stop orders to buy are used to protect profits or minimize losses when one has previously sold the stock short (discussed later). For example, assume Lois Lane had initially placed a market order to buy a round lot of SMI and had been able to buy at $30. If the stock subsequently increased to $50, she would have an unrealized, paper profit of $20. To guard this profit, she could place a *stop-loss order* (an order to sell) at, say, $47. If the stock falls below $47, she automatically sells at about $47 and takes a realized profit of $17. If the stock continues to rise or stays at $50, the stop order is not executed.

Unless stated otherwise, all orders are assumed to be *day orders.* They must be transacted that day or they are terminated. Since market orders are almost always executed on the same day the order is placed, specification of a time period during which the order is valid is used mainly with limit and stop orders. A *good-till-canceled (GTC)* order is, of course, valid until the trader cancels it.

Commissions. When the NYSE was formed in 1792, the founders agreed to two important practices which affected the structure of U.S. security markets for the next two centuries. First, they agreed to *fixed minimum commissions;* second, they agreed that they would not trade any security that was listed on the NYSE in any market other than the NYSE. The second practice eventually became known as Rule 390 and is discussed later. In the early 1970s, the Securities and Exchange Commission (SEC) decided that all commissions should be negotiated between the broker and the customer—that is, they were to be subject to competition. Between 1971 and 1975 negotiated fees were slowly phased in on large-block transactions. And Since May 1, 1975 (*May Day*), all security commissions have been negotiated rates. In practice, most brokerage firms try to set firm-wide rates that apply to particular types of transactions and customers. Thus, the customer and the broker might not actually negotiate a commission every time a trade is made. This is particularly true for a small trade. Commissions for large-block trades, however, are actively negotiated, and the customer who engages in a large block will actively shop around for the cheapest rate.

Three levels of commission rates exist: (1) full-service rates, (2) discount broker rates, and (3) rates for very large block trades.

Execution and Clearing. At this point in our discussion, it might be useful to trace through the various steps of a normal stock trade. There are any number of execution and clearing paths possible. We will follow a fairly common one.

Early Monday morning Clara Voigent calls her broker, Sam Lynch, and indicates that she wants to place a market order for five round lots of SMI Corp. common stock. The stock has recently been selling for about $30, and, based on an article she read in the Sunday financial press about a new patent received by SMI, Clara believes the stock is undervalued and should soon increase in value. Broker Sam will first obtain current price quotes on SMI Corp. by using a computer terminal which is tied into various exchange markets. Assume that the best quotes are available on the NYSE and are $32 bid and $32¼ ask. (Obviously, Clara wasn't the only one who read the favorable news about SMI.) This means that the highest price at which one could sell is $32 (the specialist's or limit book's highest bid) and the lowest price at which one could buy is $32¼ (the specialist's or limit book's lowest ask). Since the best prices are available on the NYSE, Sam decides to route the order to that exchange.

Next Sam needs to decide whether the order will be routed to the NYSE through the exchange's Super DOT system or through the brokerage firm's commission broker on the floor of the exchange.

Assume that Sam chooses the second alternative, since it allows us to look more closely at the mechanics of a trade. Broker Sam prepares a trade ticket describing the details of the trade and transmits the ticket to his firm's trading department. The trading department then communicates the order to the floor of the exchange, where the commission broker is notified. The commission broker walks to the specialist's post where SMI is traded and asks, "How's the market?" The specialist replies, "32 to ¼." Seeing no other brokers in the crowd, the commission broker indicates to the specialist "500 bought," and they exchange cards with information about the trade. The specialist's card is optically scanned by machines at the NYSE, and notice of the trade is printed on a ticker tape throughout the country. The commission broker's information card is returned to employees of the firm's trading department. They notify broker Sam and send Clara a *confirmation* of the trade in the mail. Sam calls Clara to notify her personally and everyone is happy (at least for a while).

Since Clara didn't indicate otherwise, this was a *regular way* contract, meaning that the *settlement date* will be five business days after the *trade date*. On the settlement date, the brokerage firm and the customer exchange cash and securities, and the customer becomes the legal owner of the securities (or no longer the owner if securities had been sold). If Clara had desired, she could have requested a *cash contract,* which requires settlement and passing of title on the trade date. Another form of contract is a *seller's option,* which allows the seller to choose the settlement date.[11] Nonetheless, on the following Monday Clara is required to *deliver* to the brokerage firm $16,125 (500 × $32.25) plus commissions and taxes and, in return, be the legal owner of the stock. That same Monday, the brokerage firm will settle with the other side of the trade—in this case, the specialist.

In any trade there is a buyer who promises to deliver cash for securities and a seller who promises to deliver securities for cash. *Clearing* refers to how this process actually takes place.

Clearing consists of two steps. First, brokers to each side of the trade agree upon the number of shares traded and the price. If a disagreement occurs, it must be reconciled. Second, cash and securities are delivered to the respective sellers and buyers on the settlement date.

Clearing between firms is accomplished in one of four ways. First, the securities and cash can be physically delivered between the two firms representing the buyer and the seller. This is a time-consuming, costly, and error-prone procedure, although it is commonly used between firms in the same city. Second, small firms can use the services of larger brokerage houses to net out their purchases and sales and deliver only the required net cash and securities. Carried one step further, the services of the National Securities Clearing Corporation can be used. This organization handles trades made on the NYSE, AMEX, and OTC. Each member delivers only the net amount of securities or cash necessary to settle its accounts with the clearing corporation. Finally, the Depository Trust Company (DTC) has been organized, at which brokers and dealers may deposit large quantities of "street name" certificates on most actively traded securities. Street name refers to securities registered in the name of a brokerage firm. Customer orders are

---

[11] Cash contracts and seller's options are normally used for tax purposes when title must be passed on a particular date.

cleared simply by computer debits and credits to each firm's accounts at DTC. This reduces to a minimum the flow of paperwork required to physically move stock certificates.

The stock certificates evidencing Clara's ownership of 500 shares of SMI may be physically transferred to her name and either delivered to her or maintained by the brokerage firm in *safekeeping.* Alternatively, Clara may allow the firm to keep the securities for her in *street name.* In that case, her evidence of ownership is a monthly statement from the broker indicating that she owns the shares. Clara will probably not want to be bothered with physical possession of the securities and will keep them in safekeeping or in street name. Because of the large clerical costs associated with keeping customer certificates in safekeeping, most brokerage firms will request that the certificates be held in street name. This allows the broker, for example, to maintain only one certificate in the amount of 30,000 shares for 30 customers who each own 1,000 shares. Each customer's ownership is reflected in the accounting records of the brokerage firm.[12]

In recent years, there has been a movement to eliminate all certificates of stock ownership. Computer records and periodic statements would provide evidence of ownership. In fact, a certificate-less market is virtually the case in the United States since institutions rely solely on computer-registered ownership. Many individuals, however, wish to possess a physical document. As a result, stock certificates are likely to still be available but less common.

Institutional investors are typically managing money for another party. For example, mutual fund assets are managed for the shareholders of the fund. Similarly, investment counsel firms manage the assets of pension plans and wealth of individuals. To protect the true asset owner from possible theft, all securities owned by the institutional investor will be held in *custody.* Securities will still be registered in the institution's name, but their physical control and all accounting is performed by a security *custodian* (typically, a commercial bank).

Margin and Short Sales

Margin Trades. When an account is opened at a brokerage house, it will be specified as either a *cash* or a *margin* account. In a cash account, the customer must fully pay for all securities bought. In a margin account, a portion of the securities bought may be paid for with a loan obtained from the broker. The customer will sign a *hypothecation agreement,* which allows the broker to use the securities bought as collateral on a bank loan given to the broker. Thus, the broker obtains money from a bank and lends it to the customer by using a personal broker loan collateralized by the customer's securities. For this service the broker typically charges an interest rate approximately 1% higher than the rate charged by the bank.

---

[12] Dividends, proxy statements, and any other literature distributed by the corporation on securities registered in street name are sent to the brokerage firm, which in turn forwards them to the customer.

The advantage provided by a margin account is clearly the increased leverage. For a given dollar equity capital, a larger quantity of securities can be bought. This increased leverage raises both the expected returns on an equity investment and the uncertainty about returns.

Federal law states that the Federal Reserve System may specify the *initial margin.* Regulation T allows the Federal Reserve to limit initial loans by brokers and dealers, whereas Regulation U allows it to limit security loans by commercial banks. The initial margin rate is periodically changed by the Federal Reserve as one of its policy tools for controlling economic expansions and recessions. Initial margin is usually higher for stocks than for corporate bonds. Since initial margin requirements were first set in 1934, rates have ranged between 40% and 100% for common stocks. Exchanges and brokerage firms may also specify more rigid initial margin requirements. In fact, some brokerage firms allow cash accounts only. In addition, all exchanges and brokerage firms specify a *maintenance margin* below which either more cash must be placed in the account or some securities must be sold until the account's actual margin is greater than the required maintenance margin.

Assume that in our previous example with Clara V., her broker has specified an initial margin of 60% and a maintenance margin of 35%. If Clara wishes to fully margin her purchase of SMI, she would pay broker Sam $9,675 (60% $\times$ $16,125) and borrow the remaining $6,450 from her brokerage firm. As of that date, her actual margin would exactly equal the required initial margin:[13]

$$\text{Actual Margin} = \frac{\text{Equity}}{\text{Market Value of Securities}}$$

$$= \frac{\text{Market Value of Securities} - \text{Loan Balance}}{\text{Market Value of Securities}}$$

$$= \frac{\$9,675}{\$16,125} = 60\%$$

If Clara guesses right and the price of her SMI stock increases, her actual margin will rise above the required initial margin. For example, if the stock rose to $40:

$$\text{Actual Margin} = \frac{(\$40 \times 500) - \$6,450}{\$40 \times 500}$$

$$= \frac{\$13,550}{\$20,000}$$

$$= 67.75\%$$

---

[13] For illustrative purposes, we will assume Clara has only one stock in her account with broker Sam. In practice, margin is calculated by summing the value of all loans and securities held in a given account.

Clara could either withdraw the excess margin from the account or purchase more stock on margin without contributing more cash. If more shares are acquired with the excess margin, the process is referred to as *pyramiding.*

If Clara guesses wrong and the price of SMI declines, her margin will also decline. As long as the actual margin is between the required initial and maintenance margins, her account is referred to as a *restricted account,* and she would be unable to purchase new stock on margin without restoring the account to the initial margin requirement. However, as long as she doesn't purchase more stock on margin, she needn't place more equity cash into the account. If the actual margin declines below the maintenance margin, she will have to make up the deficiency (and perhaps more) by either selling securities or placing more cash into the account. If the maintenance margin is 35%, her stock value can decline to $19.85 per share before it hits the maintenance limit:

$$0.35 = \frac{(P \times 500) - \$6,450}{P \times 500}$$

$$P = \$19.85$$

At the end of each day, brokerage firms will *mark to market* their margin accounts. That is, they will calculate the actual margin in an account using closing trade prices to determine whether a margin call is needed.

To illustrate how margin might be restored if the stock falls below $19.85, assume that it falls to $15 and that broker Sam's firm requires that any margin deficiency be restored to the maintenance margin of 35%. (This will vary from firm to firm—but restoration to maintenance margin is a minimum.) In this case, Clara could bring the account into balance in a number of ways. These include the following:

1. Add new cash to the account and leave it in the form of cash.
2. Add new cash to the account and purchase more shares of SMI at $15 per share.
3. Sell shares and repay a portion of the loan.

Alternatives 1 and 2 both require a cash deposit of $2,423.08, which is used to increase her equity position—whether the equity is held in cash or securities. To illustrate the cash deposit calculation in the first alternative, we know that:

$$\frac{\text{Original Equity} + \text{New Equity}}{\text{Total Portfolio Value}} = 0.35$$

or

$$\frac{(\$15 \times 500 - \$6,450) + \text{Cash}}{\$15 \times 500 + \text{Cash}} = 0.35$$

This incremental equity of $2,423.08 could be held either as cash or as new shares of SMI Corp. (If new shares are acquired, slightly more than $2,423.08 would be required because $2,423.08 would purchase only 161.5 shares.)

If the third alternative is chosen, Clara sells shares and uses the proceeds to reduce her loan balance. In total, 300 shares would have to be sold. This is shown below, where N refers to the number of shares sold:

$$\frac{\$15(500 - N) - (\$6,450 - \$15N)}{\$15(500 - N)} = 0.35$$

$$N = 300 \text{ shares}$$

Most investors own a number of different securities. When this is true, margin calculations are not made on each security owned but on the aggregate portfolio value and aggregate debt balance. Thus if Clara owned two stocks, she might not have to post margin when SMI Corp. shares fall to $15 if the other stock has increased sufficiently in value.

Short Sales. When people buy securities, it is referred to as going *long,* and they do so in the hopes of future price increases. When people sell securities they own, it is referred to as going *short,* and they do so with the expectation prices will soon drop. When people sell a security which they *don't* own, it is referred to as *short selling,* and they do so in the hopes of buying the stock in the future at a lower price.

The mechanical process of short selling, which is actually quite simple, is displayed in Figure 3-4. Initially, the short seller places an order to short sell, say, 100 shares of a stock which he or she believes is overvalued. The broker will find a willing buyer at, say, $30 per share and execute the sale. Five business days later, the broker will have to borrow shares from a *lender of shares* in order to deliver to the buyer. The lender of shares may be anyone willing to do so, but normally the broker will act as the lender by delivering securities held in "street name" for customers. The buyer receives the 100 shares, pays the $3,000 purchase price, and goes merrily on his or her way. The lender, however, will demand collateral for the shares lent, the most likely collateral being the $3,000 cash received from the buyer. Typically, the cash collateral is provided "flat," that is, without any interest fee paid. If this is the case, it's quite easy to see why lenders (usually brokers) are willing to lend shares. They still have an ownership claim to the shares (through the short seller) but now have additional cash which can be invested to provide a short-term risk-free return. The share loan is a "call" loan, cancelable at any time by either party. If the lender wants the shares returned, the short seller can either find another lender or buy in the open market.

Continuing with this example, assume the share's price actually does fall to, say, $20. The short seller will cover the short by asking the broker to buy 100 shares. The new seller will receive $2,000 and give up 100 shares, which are returned to the lender of shares. In turn the lender gives the $3,000 collateral value back to the broker, who returns a $1,000 profit to the short seller.

With that basic review of short selling, we can mention a few intricacies. First, SEC rules require that all short sale transactions be specified as such. Each month the volume of short sales in various stocks is compiled and reported in the financial press. Second, the SEC requires that a short sale be made on either an "up tick"

FIGURE 3-4 *Short Selling*

A. Origination of Short Sale

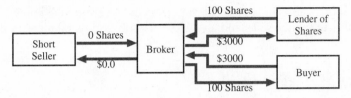

B. Covering of Short Sale

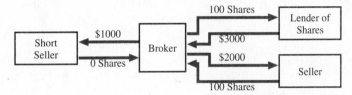

or a "zero tick" if the previously different stock price was lower. For example, assume the sequence of market transactions in a stock is:

$$20 \qquad 18 \qquad 18\frac{1}{8} \qquad 18\frac{1}{8} \qquad 18\frac{1}{8} \qquad 18\frac{1}{4} \qquad 17\frac{7}{8}$$

The first move from 20 to 18 is a down tick. The next move from 18 to $18\frac{1}{8}$ is an up tick, and the next two moves are zero ticks. A short sale could have been transacted at $18\frac{1}{8}$ or $18\frac{1}{4}$. The up-tick rule was created because of a concern that short sellers might start a price decline which the public would continue to feed. As the public continued to sell and further depress prices, the short sellers would cover at artificially low prices.[14]

Next, what happens to cash dividend payments? The new buyer will be carried as a shareholder of record on the corporation's books and receive payments directly from the corporation. The lender of shares (who is also an owner of the stock and deserves dividends) will be paid the dividends by the short seller. The short seller is indifferent to the dividend payment since the dividend payment loss is offset by the profit obtained by share price declines when dividends are paid. In addition, short sellers must post margin in the same amount as if they had gone long. In the example above, if the initial margin had been 50%, the short seller would have had to place equity values with the broker totaling $1,500. This is

---

[14] Such an operation is known as a *bear raid*. *Bull raids* involve creating an initial heavy buying demand to force prices up. As the general public sees the price rise, it begins buying, thus forcing prices even higher as the bull raiders quietly sell out. Bear and bull raids are impossible in an efficient market. However, during the 1800s and early 1900s they were accepted as fact. Whether they are possible today in actively traded securities is doubtful.

probably not a burden to the short seller because any unrestricted long securities can be used as margin. Finally, since the shares will be registered in the new buyer's name, he or she will receive all voting rights. The lender of shares will not retain any voting rights.

Short sales are a tool for sophisticated traders who know how to place stop orders to reduce risks and are able to closely follow changes in market conditions.

PERSPECTIVE ON GLOBAL MARKETS

At present, the major world financial centers are in the United States, Japan, and the United Kingdom. Not only do they have the three largest security markets but they are geographically positioned to provide virtually 24-hour trading of financial assets. In Figure 3-5, dollar volume of equity trading is shown for various markets across the world. Because of their growing importance, we will review the London and Tokyo exchanges.

British Security Market

The London Stock Exchange (LSE) was incorporated in 1773. Like the NYSE, it was a product of an informal market developed around the coffee houses in the city of London. Although the London exchange was overwhelmingly the largest in the United Kingdom (it was the world's largest until World War I), local share markets were also established. These local markets peaked at thirty but now include only six exchange floors. The British exchanges were merged on 1973 into an organization that is currently known as the *International Stock Exchange* (ISE).

All security transactions take place on the ISE. These include ordinary shares (common stocks), preference shares (preferred stock), regional government issues, treasury (gilt-edge) bonds, and shares of investment management firms. A large number of non-British securities are traded in the ISE. As its name implies, the International Stock Exchange is attempting to become the preeminent securities exchange after the formation of the European Community (EC) in 1992.

An equivalent to the U.S. over-the-counter market does not exist. The 3,000 or so stocks on the exchange are now quoted in *normal market size* (NMS). This replaced a prior stock classification scheme in which stocks were designated in an alpha, beta, and gamma system.

Security trading on the ISE is fully computerized under the Stock Exchange Automated Quotations (SEAQ) system. Competitive market makers place bid and ask prices into the computer system against which market orders are matched.

Prior to 1986, there were two features of the U. K. markets that made them fundamentally different from the U.S. market. First, security firms engaged in only one of two activities. They either acted as an agent (broker) for individuals and organizations or as a *dealer* (market maker in the United States and jobber in

FIGURE 3-5 *Dollar Volume of Equity Trading in Major World Markets: 1991*

Value (US $ in Billions)

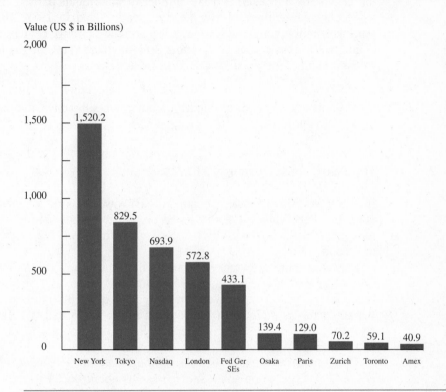

SOURCE: *"Dollar Volume of Equity Trading in Major World Markets: 1991" from 1992 NASDAQ FACT BOOK & COMPANY DIRECTORY, p. 13. Reprinted with permission.*

the United Kingdom). Second, fixed minimum commission rates were charged. Following a court decision on fixed commissions, major changes were triggered by an agreement between the British government and the stock exchange. Fixed commissions were abolished. Security firms were allowed to act as both security agent and a dealer. And foreign companies could own British security firms. This event was so dramatic that it has come to be known as the *Big Bang*.

In anticipation of the Big Bang, the majority of U. K. security firms were purchased by large domestic and foreign firms (often banks). Since the Big Bang, many of these firms have been forced to leave the London market due to low profitability created by intense competition.

The International Stock Exchange has a set of stocks that are traded in the *Unlisted Securities Market*. This set included smaller firms and those with a limited history of financial data, similar to the securities traded on the OTC in the United States. Larger, more established firms are members of the *Official List*. Requirements for both designations were reduced in 1990 in an attempt to be compatible with exchange requirements on the European continent.

Individual share ownership by British citizens increased dramatically during the late 1980s. For example, the number of individuals participating in the stock market increased threefold in the five years ended in 1988. However, a large portion of individual purchases are placed in the shares of professional investment companies. At the end of 1988, about 20% of stocks traded in the ISE were owned by individuals. The remaining 80% consisted of:

1. 65% owned by pension funds, insurance companies, and investment trusts.
2. 15% owned by charities, banks, commercial companies, the public sector, and overseas holders.

The Tokyo Stock Exchange

In 1989, the Tokyo Stock Exchange (TSE) was the world's largest equity market in terms of the value of shares listed on the exchange. Due to a 40% decline in its value in 1990 followed by a 25% decline in early 1992, however, it returned to second place.

Although there are stock exchanges in eight cities, Tokyo accounts for over 80% of total trading. Osaka and Nagoga handle about 13% and 1%, respectively. Stock exchanges in Japan were first established in 1878, but the structure of the markets today is a product of legislation following World War II. The Securities Exchange Law is patterned on the U.S. Securities Act of 1933 and the Securities and Exchange Act of 1934.

There are three defined sections on the Japanese exchanges. The *First Section* consists of larger companies and represents about 96% of total market capitalization. The *Second Section* handles younger, newly quoted firms that would otherwise be traded in the over-the-counter market. The *Third Section* is the over-the-counter market. Trading in First Section securities is handled on the exchange floor through Saitori members, who are similar to U.S. specialists. Second Section trades are handled by computers, similarly to the U.S. NASDAQ and British SEAQ systems.

Interest in the stock market is a public pastime, evidenced by the fact that 70% of all trades are for 5,000 shares or less. However, institutional ownership accounts for about 78% of all shares. Much of this institutional ownership is in *tokkin* accounts. These are share trading accounts of Japanese corporations, whose main business activity is not share trading.

CHANGING MARKET STRUCTURE

A fundamental change in the manner in which U.S. security orders are processed, which can best be described as revolutionary, began during the 1970s. For nearly two centuries, the economic structure of the U.S. security markets had been dominated by various monopolistic rules of the NYSE—in particular, (1) fixed minimum commissions, (2) an increasingly monopolistic specialist system, (3) agreements between the NYSE and AMEX not to dually list securities, and (4) member agreements to trade listed stocks only on the NYSE. Surely there was competition to NYSE trading by regional exchanges, the AMEX, and the OTC. But as long as the largest and most actively traded securities were traded on an exchange that limited membership and fixed the price of its services, such competition was ineffectual.

The factors that allowed a change in the status quo are difficult to identify fully. However, three important and interactive forces were (1) increased institutionalization of the markets, (2) an improved communication and trade execution network, and (3) the introduction and dramatic growth of stock index options and futures.

Increased Institutionalization

The term *financial institution* is applied to organizations such as commercial banks, insurance companies, mutual funds, and pension funds. The critical factor associated with such organizations is the size of the portfolios they control and thus the size of the trades in which they engage. Although each of these organizations trades in common stocks (commercial banks only through their trust operations), pension fund trades are clearly the most important. Pension funds represent the assets that corporations have invested in order to meet future retirement-benefit obligations to their employees. For large corporations, pension assets often exceed $1 billion and are heavily invested in stocks and bonds. With portfolios of this size, it is easy to understand the impacts their trades might have on security markets.

Perhaps the most visible effect of institutional trading is in the increased number of large-block trades. A large block is a trade in excess of 10,000 shares. Block trades in excess of 5 million shares are not uncommon, and in 1986 a 48.8-million-share block trade of Navistar International Corp. was completed.

During the early 1970s total block trading actually grew more rapidly than shown for the NYSE because many blocks went to the third market to avoid having to pay fixed minimum commissions on the NYSE. However, once negotiated commissions came into effect, block trading on the NYSE grew to the extent that it represented 50% or more of all NYSE trading volume by the late 1980s.

Some of the changes in the security markets that the growth of institutional trading contributed to include the following:

1. *Elimination of fixed commissions.* In order to increase transactions of block traders on the listed exchanges and reduce the growth of the third market, the exchanges had a strong motivation to eliminate fixed minimum commissions. Even if the SEC had not ruled minimum commissions illegal, the rapid growth of block trading would probably have led the exchanges to discontinue their use.

2. *Desire for block liquidity.* Many block trades are negotiated in what is known as the "upstairs" dealer market in a manner discussed earlier. Essentially, all parties interested in being a part of the block are contacted by a block trader over the telephone, and a price is negotiated. Often price commissions must be given by the active side of the block to induce other organizations to take the opposite side to the trade. Institutions that are motivated by information not currently discounted in the stock's price might be willing to provide such price inducements for the sake of immediate liquidity. However, institutions whose trades are not motivated by information prefer to find other means of trading that do not require such price inducements.

   Instinet as well as a computer system developed by Jefferies & Company provide a means by which such price inducements can be minimized. Institutions with a block to sell or buy submit their request to the computer system, which matches desires to trade. A subscriber to Instinet can enter a limit order in "the book" (computer), which is then available to other subscribers. The Jefferies system works more like a call market in which buyers and sellers are periodically brought together and a price is set that will trade the largest quantity of shares.

3. *Growth of futures and options.* Futures and options on aggregate stock and bond indexes were developed in the early 1980s. Positions in these instruments allow one to trade an aggregate portfolio instead of single stocks or bonds. This feature has been particularly desired by large institutions, which are often less interested in trading individual security issues than in trading aggregate portfolio positions. The use of such futures and options provides institutional investors with an inexpensive and rapid way to change their portfolio asset allocation.

4. *Globalization of financial markets.* In an attempt to broaden their diversification, pension funds have begun to purchase non-U.S. securities. To aid in this movement, the exchanges have begun to explore ways in which securities on their exchanges can be traded around the world—24 hours a day. In 1988, financial futures on U.S. T-bonds were the first to be traded on a 24-hour basis across various exchanges throughout the world. And in 1989, the National Association of Security Dealers began trading in 300 OTC stocks at 4 A.M. Eastern time. The 1990s will continue to strengthen trading ties between U.S., Japanese, Hong Kong, and British markets.

Communication and Trade Execution

Many of the developments within the past decade were possible only because of improvements in telecommunication and computer processing. All have led to increased integration of security markets and toward the concept of a *Central Market.*

In the *Securities Acts Amendments of 1975,* Congress stated that the SEC should take actions that would rapidly move toward a Central Securities Market. Exactly how this market would work is not yet clear, but its basic functions are. Any Central Market should:

1. Allow for free entry to any individual wishing to act as a dealer in securities (that is, perform the functions now done by OTC market makers and exchange specialists).
2. Provide free access to all bid-ask quotes offered by security dealers.
3. Provide for a single source of trade quotations.

In 1975, a *Consolidated Tape* was developed to print all transactions in NYSE-listed stocks that take place on seven of the largest listed exchanges, NASDAQ, and Instinet. This information is used to publish the daily *composite stock prices* in newspapers.

In addition, listed stock exchanges make current bid and ask stock price quotations available to subscribers through the *Consolidated Quotations Services.* By using it, subscribers can quickly identify the market in which the best price is available and route a trade accordingly. This saves the time that used to be required to explore prices in each market (''shopping around'') and ensures proper price execution.

Dealers now also have the ability to submit bid and ask prices through the *Intermarket Trading System (ITS).* This is an electronic communication network that links seven listed exchanges and the NASD. Brokers representing customers as well as specialists and market makers may submit bid and ask prices and trade through the system. As of 1986, 1,278 stocks were eligible for trading on ITS, and total trades were about 5% of total NYSE stock volume.

The final step toward a true Central Market would be the creation of a single *centralized limit order book* (CLOB) that would link all markets. This has yet to be done, because many questions remain about how it should be implemented in light of the vested interests the larger exchanges have in maintaining their importance.

None of the changes in order processing instituted so far would have been possible without significant improvements in telecommunications and micro-computers.

Options and Futures Growth

The introduction and growth of trading in futures and options on aggregate stock indexes have also had profound impacts on security markets during the past decade. Stock indexes are discussed in depth in Chapter 4. These indexes can be thought of as the average price of the group of stocks included in the index. A portfolio of stocks that is *identical* to the index cannot be bought, but many portfolios are reasonably similar in makeup. Thus, when futures and options were created whose values depended on the stock indexes, investors (particularly large institutional investors) had the opportunity to take positions in both ''spot'' stock portfolios and similar options and futures. This opened the way for trades across the three markets (physically and legally separate stock markets, option markets, and futures markets). These trades could be used to arbitrage price differentials between the markets or to alter portfolio asset allocation.

The impacts of option and futures markets cannot be overstated. They allow individuals and institutional investors an opportunity to quickly and cheaply trade aggregate portfolios of securities. On many days, the value of trading in the option and futures markets exceeds the value of trading in the ''spot'' stock and bond markets.

SUMMARY

Transactions in the securities markets can arise in either the primary market, when an issue is first sold to the general public, or in the secondary markets, where members of the public trade between themselves. The major participant in placing securities in the primary market is the investment banker. Investment bankers specialize in primary offerings and are able to provide advice, underwriting, and placement services to security issuers. A consulting fee is paid when the investment banker provides only advice. But when underwriting and distribution services are also provided, the investment banker's return comes in the form of an underwriter's spread. Securities may be privately or publicly placed. Private placement can be cheaper and quicker, but public placement offers increased marketability. Most publicly placed issues must be registered with the Securities and Exchange Commission (SEC) to ensure full disclosure of information about the issue.

Secondary-market transactions can occur on formal, organized exchanges or in the over-the-counter market. By far the dominant formal exchange market is the New York Stock Exchange (NYSE). It lists the largest and most actively traded stocks in the United States, and their market values exceed the market values of all stocks traded OTC or on other exchanges. Transactions on the NYSE are handled on the exchange floor by a commission broker who contacts the specialist in a stock to determine existing bid-ask prices. The specialist maintains a book of limit orders (from which a commission is earned if a limit order is traded), but, more importantly, acts as a dealer in the stock. As a dealer, the specialist absorbs temporary imbalances in the flow of buy and sell orders with the objective of providing continuity in prices over time and depth of liquidity. In the process, the specialist earns a profit from buying at lower bid prices and selling at higher asked prices. Market makers perform an equivalent role in the OTC market.

During the 1980s, major changes occurred in both the procedures used to trade securities and the profits available to exchange members. Most of these changes seem to be the result of increased institutional activity, improved communication facilities, and the introduction of options and futures.

REVIEW PROBLEM

On Monday, July 3, you ask your broker to buy 200 shares of IBM at market, using the 50% allowed initial margin. The broker charges a commission of 2% and the brokerage firm has a 30% maintenance margin. The broker later calls you and says that the trade was executed at $70 per share. (Note that July 4 is not a business day.)

a. Why might you use a market order as opposed to a limit or stop order?

b. On what date must you pay the brokerage firm? How much must be paid?

c. Since the stock was bought on margin, below what stock price will a margin call be required?

d. If the stock falls to $40 and you intend to deposit more cash into the account to bring it back to the maintenance margin by repaying part of the loan, how much cash must you deposit?

e. If the stock falls to $40 and you intend to sell stock to repay some of the debt to bring it back to the maintenance margin, how many shares must you sell?

Solution

a. A market order assures that a trade takes place at the existing best price. A limit order would be transacted only if prices are at the limit price or better. A stop order specifies a price at which the trade becomes a market order.

b. The settlement day on which cash is paid and securities received is five *business* days after the trade date. Since July 4 is a business holiday, settlement will take place on Tuesday, July 11. At that time you will pay:

Value of securities bought
$$200 \times \$70 = \$14,000$$

Plus commission
$$\$14,000 \times 0.02 \qquad \underline{280}$$
Total $\qquad \$14,280$

Less margin loan
$$0.50 \times \$14,000 \qquad \underline{7,000}$$
Net due $\qquad \$\ 7,280$

c. Maintenance margin $= \dfrac{\text{Security Value} - \text{Loan}}{\text{Security Value}}$

$$0.30 = \frac{(P \times 200) - \$7,000}{P \times 200}$$

$$P = \$50$$

d. Maintenance margin $= \dfrac{\text{Security Value} - \text{Loan} + \text{Cash}}{\text{Security Value}}$

$$0.30 = \frac{(\$40 \times 200) - \$7,000 + \text{Cash}}{(\$40 \times 200)}$$

$$\text{Cash} = \$1,400$$

e. Maintenance margin $= \dfrac{\text{New Security Value} - \text{New Loan}}{\text{New Security Value}}$

$$0.30 = \frac{\$40 \times (200 - N) - (\$7,000 - \$40 \times N)}{\$40(200 - N)}$$

$$N = 116.23 \text{ shares (117 actually)}$$

QUESTIONS AND PROBLEMS

1. What are the relative advantages and disadvantages associated with negotiated and competitive underwritings?
2. How does the specialist make a profit?
3. What is an ADR?
4. Discuss the advantages and disadvantages of:
   a. Market orders
   b. Limit orders
   c. Stop orders
5. Carolina Carpets has just sold 50,000 new common shares to the public at an offering price of $70 per share. The underwriter's spread was $2.50, and management has estimated the internal management costs of selling the issue were $37,500. Immediately after the issue, the price of the stock rose in the secondary markets to $72, where it has remained for the last week.
   a. Identify the various costs involved in this sale.
   b. These are costs to Carolina Carpets. Who are the recipients?
   c. If management had forced the underwriter to offer the issue at $71 per share, what would the underwriter's response likely have been?
   d. If management had used a competitive bid selection instead of a negotiated selection, would its cost have been lower?
6. Short sellers can theoretically lose an infinite amount of money but, at most, earn 100%.
   a. True or false? Explain.
   b. How might stop orders be used to reduce the risks of short selling?
7. Lawrence Carver has just opened a margin account with a local brokerage firm. The firm has a policy of 60% initial margin and 40% maintenance margin. Mr. Carver initially buys 500 shares of a stock at $40 per share on margin.
   a. What are his initial equity and loan balances?
   b. To what price may the security decline before a margin call is required?
   c. If the stock suddenly falls to $20 per share and the broker requires that the maintenance requirement be restored, how much cash must Lawrence add to his position?
   d. If the stock suddenly falls to $20 per share while Lawrence is on an annual vacation to the Middle East, how many shares must be sold to restore the maintenance margin?
8. The manager in an underwriting syndicate will often stabilize the market for the issue by pegging prices at the offering price.
   a. Physically, how might this be done?

    b. What might be the underwriter's rationale for market stabilization?

    c. Will the underwriter always be successful in pegging prices?

    d. Various studies have shown that the market prices of new security offerings rise more in the month or two after initial public sale than would be expected given the security's risk. What does this suggest about the original selling price set by underwriters and the underwriters' ability to stabilize prices?

9. Jennifer and Jason both purchased 100 shares of Little Mint Inc. at the start of the year at a price equal to $50 per share. Jennifer paid the full cost of $5,000 and Jason used 50% margin. His borrowings had an interest rate of 8% per annum.

    a. Calculate that rate of return to each investor if shares of Little Mint Inc. are $69 at year end and a $1 dividend is received at that time.

    b. Repeat part a but assume that the end of year share price is $39.

    c. What conclusion should be drawn from this example about the use of margin in acquiring a stock position?

10. Gerry sold short 100 shares of Little Mint Inc. and borrowed the shares from her broker.

    a. Why would the broker be willing to lend her the shares?

    b. During the year, Little Mint Inc. pays a $1 dividend per share to registered owners of the stock. At that time, Gerry must also pay her broker (the lender of shares) $1 per share. Why would she not be loosing any money when she pays the broker these dividends?

11. Since the introduction of negotiated rates on both large and small stock transactions in 1975, commissions on large blocks have declined the most. Why?

12. During the late 1980s, memberships on the NYSE were trading at prices in excess of $500,000. Why would a brokerage firm pay such a large price?

13. You wish to sell short 100 shares of XYZ common stock. If the last two transactions were at $34\frac{1}{8}$ followed by $34\frac{1}{4}$, you can sell short on the next transaction only at price of:

    a. $34\frac{1}{8}$ or higher.

    b. $34\frac{1}{4}$ or higher.

    c. $34\frac{1}{4}$ or lower.

    d. $34\frac{1}{8}$ or lower.

DATAFILE ANALYSIS

Global Stock Returns

The purpose of this exercise is to compare the returns of stocks on large corporations in the United States, United Kingdom, and Japan since 1970. Knowledge of past international returns is crucial to developing a global perspective of investing. We will use this type of data in future chapters to aid in calculating optimal portfolio investment strategies.

    Review the RTNSYRLY.WK1 datafile and locate the return series for the S&P 500, U. K. Financial Times (in dollars) and Japan Large Company (in dollars). These returns represent portfolio returns that U.S. investors would have earned if they had held portfolios of the largest corporations in each country. Calculate the average annual returns, minimums, and maximums of each return series. Why do you believe they differ?

REFERENCES

An overview of world security markets is presented in:

SOLNIK, BRUNO. *International Investments,* Reading, MA: Addison-Wesley Publishing Co., 1988.
G. T. Guide to World Equity Markets, London: Euromoney Publications, updated annually.

Surveys of current investment banking issues are presented in:

IBBOTSON ROGER G. and JODY L. SINDELAR, "Initial Public Offerings," *Journal of Applied Corporate Finances,* 1, No. 2, Summer 1988.
SILBER, WILLIAM L., "Discounts on Restricted Stock: The Impact of Illiquidity on Stock Prices," *Financial Analysts Journal,* July–August 1991.
SMITH, CLIFFORD W., "Investment Banking and the Capital Acquisition Process," *Journal of Financial Economics,* 15, January–February 1986.
WAGNER, WAYNE H., *The Complete Guide to Securities Transactions,* New York: John Wiley & Sons, 1989.

Review articles of the events surrounding Black Monday include:

MALKIEL, BURTON, "The Brady Commission Report: A Critique," *Journal of Portfolio Management,* Summer 1988.
ROLL, RICHARD, "The International Crash of 1987," *Financial Analysts Journal,* September–October 1988.
RUBINSTEIN, MARK, "Portfolio Insurance and the Market Crash," *Financial Analysts Journal,* January–February 1988.

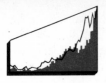

Security Market Indexes

With this chapter, we conclude Part 1, which has provided an overview of security types and security markets. The purpose of this chapter is to examine various security market indexes that track historical prices and rates of return. Knowledge of how these indexes are calculated is important, since underlying each index calculation is an implied portfolio strategy.

MARKET INDEXES

"How's the market today?" This is probably the question that brokers are most often asked by their customers. But why? Why should people be so concerned about moves in aggregate security prices? One reason, of course, is that aggregate market moves have a major impact on the returns of individual securities. Although the realized return on an individual security can be caused by a large number of economic events, numerous studies have shown that somewhere on the order of 30% to 50% of the return variability on an individual common stock is due to aggregate stock market effects. In broadly diversified portfolios, market effects are even more dominant, accounting for 90% or more of the variability of portfolio returns. Second, the prices of many derivatives depend upon various market indexes. Examples include stock index futures and options on stock index values. Third, many people (called technicians) believe that the market tends to move in identifiable patterns. They believe the size and direction of current moves can be related to historical movements and used to determine whether today is a good time to buy or sell. Although considerable statistical data refute the notion that prices move in identifiable patterns, the belief remains widely accepted.

A final and more substantive reason for knowing past levels of aggregate security prices is for use as a performance criterion. How well did an actively managed portfolio perform when compared with a broadly diversified, unmanaged portfolio? As we will see in later chapters, many people suggest that *the best* portfolio of risky securities is the *market portfolio,* a portfolio that includes every risky security in the marketplace, with each security held in proportion to the percentage its total market value represents of the total market value of all securities. For example, if IBM common shares represent 1% of the market value of all risky stocks and bonds in the United States, then one percent of one's investments in United States risky securities should be in IBM. Other people argue that differences in tax rates, in how people are affected by inflation, in earnings expectations, in the types of real assets owned, etc., cause investors to have different optimal investment portfolios. Regardless of who is correct, some *baseline investment portfolio* that meets the needs of a particular investor can be identified. Ideally, we would like to measure the performance of an actively managed portfolio against an individual's baseline investment portfolio, not against some aggregate market index that could be quite different in investment characteristics. But to do so we would have to identify the person's individual baseline investment portfolio and track it over time—certainly a difficult, time-consuming, and costly process.

The advantages of using aggregate market indexes to measure performance are twofold. First, they are convenient. One needn't spend the time and cost required to identify and track specialized baseline investment portfolios. Instead, a published index which is reasonably close in composition to that of the baseline portfolio can be used. For example, if one's baseline portfolio consists mainly of stocks in the oldest and largest U.S. corporations, the Dow Jones Industrial Average might be used to evaluate performance. Similarly, if a portion of the portfolio is invested broadly in stocks of non-U.S. countries, the Europe, Australian, and Far East (EAFE) security index could be used. Alternatively, if the baseline portfolio consists mainly of stocks in numerous small, regional firms, the NASDAQ Price Index could be used. The baseline portfolio and the market index would not perfectly match each other. However, they might be close enough to develop some judgment about how well the actively managed portfolio performed relative to a proxy for the baseline investment portfolio. Second, a *properly constructed* market index can indicate how the "average" investor and speculator did during, say, the past year. If the returns on such an index are 15% in a given year, then we could think in terms of one half of all investors and speculators earning 15% or more, and one half earning 15% or less. To do this, however, we must have a well-constructed index that covers a large number of stocks. For example, the Dow Jones Industrial Average covers only 30 so-called blue-chip stocks and certainly wouldn't reflect average market results.

Overview of Index Types

A large variety of security indexes are published in the financial press. Later in the chapter, we will examine the more important ones. But before doing so, it is important that we have a basic understanding of the principles underlying their calculations.

When most people think of, say, a stock index, they think of a price level since price levels are commonly shown in the financial press. However, each index also has an associated *rate of return* series. Although the return series of a given index is given less attention than the index's price level by the financial press, return series provide more important information about the securities included in an index because return series explicitly account for cash distributions to investors in the form of dividends or interest.

At the most fundamental level, security indexes can be classified into two broad groups: (1) those that measure the market value and returns on a population of securities and (2) those that measure market value and returns on a *sample of securities* in an asset class. For example, the Wilshire 5000 Index is designed to track virtually all stocks that are actively traded in the United States whereas the Dow Jones Industrial Index tracks the stocks of only 30 very large U.S. companies. Each index type has its unique advantages. Aggregate asset class indexes, such as the Wilshire 5000, can be used to determine how the "average" investor in U.S. traded stocks fared during, say, the past year. Indexes of a sample of securities within an asset class, such as the Dow Jones Industrial, might be used as a benchmark for investors who restrict their investments to a similar subset of large capitalization securities.

Two characteristics of aggregate asset class indexes distinguish them from indexes based on a sample of securities. First, aggregate asset class indexes usually report the *total market value* of all securities in the asset class. As noted before, the Wilshire 5000 market value index is equal to the sum of the market capitalization (price times shares outstanding) of virtually all stocks traded in the United States. In contrast, indexes based on a subset of securities in the asset class are usually scaled to some base index value. For example, the base index of the Standard & Poors Stock Index is equal to 10 and that of the NYSE is equal to 50.

The second difference is more important. Indexes that treat a sample of securities use a variety of ways to weight the relative importance of each security. Three weighting schemes are currently used.

1. Price per share, in which case a stock trading at $100 per share has 10 times the impact of a $10 stock.
2. Market capitalization, in which case a stock with a market capitalization of $100 million has ten times the impact of a stock with a $10 million market capitalization.
3. Security return, in which case a stock with a return of 50% has five times the impact of a stock with a 10% return.

Market capitalization weighting is, by far, the most widely used method since it best reflects the return earned by an average investor in the securities tracked by the index.

Illustration of How Indexes Are Calculated

In this section, we review how various index types are calculated for common stocks.[1] For illustrative purposes we will use the hypothetical data shown in Table

---

[1] Although the discussion in this section refers to stock indexes, it could also be applied to fixed income indexes.

4-1. Information is shown for five quarter-ends. Quarter 0 represents the first of the year and Quarter 4 represents the end of the year. Per-share prices, shares outstanding and market capitalization (per-share price times number of outstanding shares) are shown for five stocks, A through E. These five stocks will be used when indexes based on a sample of securities are calculated. In addition, the total capitalization of all stocks other than A through E is shown. Finally, total dividends of stocks A through E as well as all other stocks are shown. These will be used in rate-of-return calculations.

Aggregate Asset Class Indexes. We begin by discussing security indexes that examine the market value and returns of all securities in an asset class. The market value of such an index is simply the sum of the market capitalization of all securities in the index. Symbolically,

Aggregate Market Value of Asset Class

$$AMV_t = \sum_{i=1}^{N} (\text{Market Capitalization})_{it} \quad \quad (4.1)$$

$$= \sum_{i=1}^{N} (P_{it} \, Shs_{it})$$

where AMV_t = aggregate market value of all securities in the index at date t.
 P_{it} = price per share of security i at date t.
 Shs_{it} = number of outstanding shares of i at date t.
 N = number of securities being considered.

For example, the aggregate market value at each quarter-end of the stocks displayed in Table 4-1 is:

Aggregate Market Value of Securities in Table 4-1 by Quarter

0	1	2	3	4
$30,000	$31,000	$41,700	$47,900	$51,500

The rate of return on such an aggregate index is equal to the dollar value change in the index plus all dividend distributions, divided by the beginning index value. For example, the rate of return series on our hypothetical index would be:

Return Series for Aggregate Asset Class by Quarter

	1	2	3	4
Ending Value	$31,000	$41,700	$47,900	$51,500
minus Beginning	30,000	31,000	41,700	47,900
Capital Gain ‹Loss›	1,000	10,700	6,200	3,600
plus Dividends	240	275	320	365
Dollar Gain ‹Loss›	1,240	10,975	6,520	3,965
divided by Beginning	30,000	31,000	41,750	47,900
Return	0.0413	0.3540	0.1562	0.0828

TABLE 4-1 *Hypothetical Stock Index Data*

	Quarter-End				
	0	*1*	*2*	*3*	*4*
Price per Share					
A*	$50	$25	$35	$21	$25
B	50	50	60	65	70
C	50	50	55	60	57
D	50	50	80	100	95
E	50	50	80	100	95
Shares Outstanding					
A*	100	200	200	400	400
B	100	100	100	100	100
C	100	100	100	100	100
D	20	20	20	20	20
E	20	20	20	20	20
Market Capitalization					
A	$5000	$5,000	$7,000	$8,400	$10,000
B	5,000	5,000	6,000	6,500	7,000
C	5,000	5,000	5,500	6,000	5,700
D	1,000	1,000	1,600	2,000	1,900
E	1,000	1,000	1,600	2,000	1,900
Total sample	17,000	17,000	21,700	24,900	26,500
All other stocks	13,000	14,000	20,000	23,000	25,000
Total all stocks	$30,000	$31,000	$41,700	$47,900	$51,500
Dividend Distributions					
Total *A–E*	NA	$170	$185	$210	$240
All other stocks	NA	70	90	110	125
Total all stocks	NA	$240	$275	$320	$365

* Two for one split at end of quarters 1 and 3.

Sample Indices: When Weighted by Market Capitalization. The aggregate asset class index shown above is a market capitalization weighted index based *on all securities in an asset class.* Such indexes were introduced in the mid-1970s, when accurate data could be obtained on virtually all traded securities via computer networks. Prior to the 1970s, however, it was difficult to gather accurate data on over-the-counter stocks and many listed stocks in a timely manner. As a result, indexes were based on a *sample* of actively traded stocks. Also, instead of reporting the total market value of the sample, a base index value was typically assigned to a given point in time. For example, the S&P 500 index has a base value of 10 in 1940–1941. The best known indexes of this type are those prepared by Standard & Poors, the New York Stock Exchange (NYSE), and the National Association of Security Dealers.

Assume that stocks *A* through *E* represent the sample chosen and that the base market value index is set to be 100 at quarter 0. Then the market capitalization weighted index based on this sample at any date *t* would be:

Sample Market Capitalization Weighted Index

$$SMV_t = \left[\frac{\text{Value of Sample's Market Capitalization at date } t}{\text{Value of Sample's Market Capitalization at date } 0} \right] 100 \quad \textbf{(4.2)}$$

$$= \frac{\sum_{i=1}^{N} P_{it} \, Shs_{it}}{\sum_{i=1}^{N} P_{i0} \, Shs_{i0}} * 100$$

For example, the illustrative index value at quarters 0 through 4 would be:

Date	Market Capitalization Index Calculation
0	($17,000/$17,000) * 100 = 100
1	($17,000/$17,000) * 100 = 100
2	($21,700/$17,000) * 100 = 127.65
3	($24,900/$17,000) * 100 = 146.47
4	($26,500/$17,000) * 100 = 155.88

The rate-of-return series for such an index would be calculated in the same manner as aggregate asset class returns, except only stocks in the same index would be used. Using the data in Table 4-1, these returns would be;

Return Series for Sample Market Capitalization Weighted Index

	1	2	3	4
Ending Value	$17,000	$21,700	$24,900	$26,500
minus Beginning	17,000	17,000	21,700	24,900
Capital Gain ‹Loss›	0	4,700	3,200	1,600
plus Dividends	170	185	210	240
Dollar Gain ‹Loss›	170	4,885	3,410	1,840
divided by Beginning	17,000	17,000	21,700	24,900
Return	0.0100	0.2874	0.1571	0.0739

Two comments should be made about market-capitalization-based sample indexes. First, their return series typically have lower average returns and less volatility than return series based on the aggregate asset class from which the sample is drawn. This is because the aggregate class usually includes smaller, more risky firms than the sample index. Second, no adjustments need be made for stock dividends or stock splits since this type of index is based on a firm's total market capitalization. The total market capitalization of a firm is unaffected by stock splits and stock dividends. For example, in Table 4-1 stock *A* is worth $50 and has 100 shares for a market capitalization of $5,000 at date 0. At the end of quarter 1, a 2-for-1 split occurs, after which the stock is trading for $25 with 200 outstanding shares: the market capitalization remains at $5,000. Clearly, there has been no price return on the stock since its total market capitalization has not changed. The important point is that *one does not have to explicitly account for stock splits or stock dividends in calculating market capitalization weighted indexes.* This is not the case for indexes weighted by per-share prices.

Sample Indexes When Weighted by Per-Share Price. Indexes of this type were first developed and published in the early 1900s. They differ from market capitalization indexes in two respects: (1) they usually include fewer securities and (2) the weight given to a security is based on its per-share price as opposed to total market capitalization. The best known indexes of this type are the Dow-Jones Industrial Index and the Nikkei Dow.

In concept, this type of index is supposed to reflect the average price of stocks in the index. For example, assume stocks *A, B,* and *C* in Table 4-1 are to be used in calculating a price weighted index. At date 0, the average price of three stocks is $50:

$$\$50 = (\$50 + \$50 + \$50)/3$$

However, a problem arises whenever there is a stock split or stock dividend. For example, in quarter 1, stock *A* has a 2-for-1 stock split, and its market price per share drops to $25. It would be silly to simply sum quarter 1 prices and divided by 3; the index would exhibit an artificial decline caused solely by the split.

There are two ways in which one could account for such splits or stock dividends. One way is to explicitly adjust the numerator by multiplying stock *A*'s price by a *split-adjustment factor.* Following stock *A*'s 2-for-1 split in quarter 1, this factor would be 2.0, and the revised index would be calculated as follows:

$$\frac{(\$25 \times 2) + \$50 + 50}{3} = \$50$$

The second way is to adjust the denominator so that when an *adjusted divisor* is divided into the post-split sum of stock prices, the index doesn't change. In our example this new divisor would be 2.5 instead of the original 3.0:

$$\text{Old Index Value Prior to Split} = \frac{\text{Sum of Prices After the Split}}{\text{New Divisor}}$$

$$\$50 = \frac{\$25 + \$50 + \$50}{\text{New Divisor}}$$

$$\text{New Divisor} = \frac{\$125}{\$50} = 2.5$$

The method used to adjust for splits has an affect on the relative importance placed on each share in the index. Since this is a problem for the well known Dow-Jones indexes, we will discuss the nature of this bias when we examine the Dow-Jones indexes. Rate-of-return series are rarely reported for this type of index. In concept, however, return series can be calculated in the same manner as with other indexes; price change plus dividend payments during a period are divided by beginning price.

Sample Index Based on Geometric Averages of Price Relatives. Indexes of this type are the least commonly used, perhaps because of the difficulty that investors have in understanding exactly what they mean and because they do not relate to trading strategies which investors could easily employ. The Value Line indexes and Financial Times Industrial Ordinary Share Index are two indexes of this type.

These indexes are based on the geometric mean of relative price movements. Assume you have observed the levels of three variables: X, Y, and Z. The arithmetic mean is simply: $(X + Y + Z) \div 3$. In contrast, the geometric mean is: $(X * Y * Z)^{1/3}$. Arithmetic means are based on addition and division. Geometric means are based on multiplication and roots.

To find the geometric mean of price relatives, the following steps are used. First, the closing price of each stock is expressed as a ratio of the preceding day's price. These *price relatives* are then multiplied together and the Nth root of the product is found, where N refers to the number of stocks being considered. Finally, this *geometric average price relative* is multiplied by the prior day's index value to obtain today's index. Stock splits and stock dividends are handled by making an appropriate adjustment to the security's price from the prior day.

To illustrate these calculations, consider a geometric index based on stocks A through E in Table 4-1. The base date will again be quarter 0 and an index base of 100 will be used. At the end of quarter 1, the price relative for each stock would be 1.0. For example, adjusting for stock A's 2:1 split, its price relative would be:

$$\text{Price Relative}_A = \frac{\text{Price at Year 2}}{\text{Adjusted Price at Year 1}} = \frac{\$25}{\$25} = 1.0$$

Multiplying the five price relatives and taking the 5th root results in a geometric average price relative equal to 1.0:

$$\text{Geometric Average} = \sqrt[5]{(\text{Price Relative}_A)(\text{Price Relative}_B) \ldots (\text{Price Relative}_E)}$$
Price Relative

$$= \sqrt[5]{(1.0)(1.0)(1.0)(1.0)(1.0)} = 1.0$$

As a result, the geometric price relative index at the end of quarter 1 would remain at 100.

$$\begin{array}{ccccc} \text{Geometric} & = & \text{Geometric Average} & \text{Geometric} & \textbf{(4.3)} \\ \text{Index at } t & & \text{Price Relative at } t & \text{*Index at } t-1 \\ 100 & = & 1.0 & \times\ 100 \end{array}$$

Quarter 2 provides a more typical situation. In that case, the Geometric Index would increase to 136.45:

$$\sqrt[5]{\left(\frac{35}{25} \times \frac{60}{50} \times \frac{55}{50} \times \frac{80}{50} \times \frac{80}{50}\right)} \times 100 = (1.3645)(100) = 136.45$$

WORLD STOCK INDEXES

In this section, we review the major common stock indexes that are widely reported in financial newspapers such as *The Wall Street Journal, Barrons,* and *London Financial Times.* A summary is displayed in Table 4-2.

Aggregate Market Value Indices

Recall that these indices estimate the total market value of an aggregate asset class. Such indices are common for bond markets. They are less so for equities.[2] However, three aggregate stock value indices are available.

Ibbotson Associates World Wealth. In an article that appeared in *The Journal of Portfolio Management* during the Winter 1983 issue, Roger Ibbotson and Laurence Siegel provided estimates of the value of world wealth. Since then, Ibbotson Associates has provided year-end updates. Estimates are made by adding security values in various markets across the world.

Wilshire 5000. This is an estimate of the aggregate dollar value of publicly traded stocks in the United States and includes virtually all stocks traded on the NYSE, AMEX, and NASDAQ markets. The number of issues tracked will vary over time but the current total is close to 6,000. At December 31, 1980, its capitalization was $1.4 trillion. By the end of 1991, its capitalization was $4.0 trillion. This is close to the $4.3 trillion estimate of U.S. stock value shown in Chapter 1. In addition to an aggregate value index, Wilshire Associates calculates two returns series; one weighted by market capitalization and the other equally weighted.

CRSP Indexes. The Center for Research in Security Prices (CRSP) at the University of Chicago prepares computer tapes of the daily returns, market prices, shares outstanding, etc. of stocks traded on the NYSE, AMEX, and NASDAQ markets. The tapes are widely used in scholarly studies and are an accurate source of historical aggregate daily stock values.

Market Capitalization Weighted Samples

There are considerably more market indexes that do not report aggregate values but that are still driven by the relative market capitalization of the securities in the sample. These include the following.

---

[2] Total market values are periodically reported for all security indices. However, most stock indices reported on a daily basis are based on a base index value and do not represent aggregate market value.

TABLE 4-2 *Major World Stock Indexes*

Aggregate Stock Value Indexes	*Approximate Number of Stocks*
Ibbotson Associates World Wealth	Variable
Wilshire 5000	6,000
Center for Research in Security Prices	Variable
Market Capitalization Weighted Samples	
World and Regional Market Indexes	
Dow Jones World Stock Indexes	2,200
Financial Times Actuaries World Indexes	2,260
Financial Times Actuaries Eurotrack 100	100
Financial Times Actuaries Eurotrack 200	200
Morgan Stanley Capital International	1,487
Indexes of U.S. Equities	
Dow Jones Equity Market Index	700
NASDAQ Indexes	4,000
New York Stock Exchange Index	3,000
Frank Russell Company Indexes	3,000
Standard & Poors, Inc. Indexes	500
Non-U.S. Equity Markets	
Financial Times Actuaries Share Index	750
Financial Times 500 Share Index	500
Financial Times Stock Exchange 100	100
Tokyo Stock Price Index	1,500
Toronto Stock Exchange Index	300
Price Weighted Samples	
Dow Jones Indexes	65
Nikkei Stock Average	250
Geometric Return Weighted Samples	
Value Line Indexes	1,700
Financial Times Ordinary Share Index	30

Dow Jones World Stock Index. At the start of 1993, Dow Jones & Co. began the publication of an index that tracks the performance of 2,200 companies in ten countries. The coverage represents about 80% of the value of equities traded in these countries. The composite index is called the World Stock Index and has a base value of 100 as of December 31, 1991. In addition, indexes are provided on each of the ten countries surveyed, more than 100 industries and nine economic sectors. The U.S. component of these indexes are available back to June 30, 1982. Non-U.S. indexes begin in 1991.

These new indexes created by Dow Jones & Co. are weighted by each security's market capitalization, unlike previous indexes that were published by Dow Jones since the 1930s.

MSCI Indices. Morgan Stanley Capital International (MSCI) provides index and return data on a variety of world markets. Their data is available in either hardcopy or on-line form through subscriptions with the firm. This data is widely used by professional investors and is one of the best sources of data about world equity markets. Summary data are reported in the financial press.

An example of the data that is available from MSCI is shown in Figure 4-1. The top of the page provides returns for various regions of the world. The bottom of the page shows market capitalization of the countries that they track. The MSCI *World Index* is based on the twenty-one countries shown at the bottom of the page. When the word Free is next to a country, it refers to stocks in the country in which foreigners may invest. MSCI attempts to sample stocks in each country that represent approximately 60% of the value of a country's stock value. They also provide data on 38 different industry classifications. Notice that these are all well-developed financial markets. Recently, MSCI has started to provide data on *Emerging Markets.* These include stocks of countries such as Indonesia, Korea, Taiwan, Brazil, and Greece.

The most widely cited MSCI index is the *EAFE* (pronounced Eefa) index. This index includes all stocks they follow in *Europe, Australia and the Far East,* that is, basically stocks of well-developed countries other than the United States. The EAFE index is widely used to assess the performance of international stock managers.[3] The EAFE index is to non-U.S. stock markets what the Standard and Poors (S & P) 500 index is to U.S. markets. In fact, many stock portfolios are passively managed with the objective of earning the same return as the EAFE index.

FT Actuaries World Indices. For many years, the *Financial Times* has provided daily price indices of world equity markets. Approximately 2,300 stocks are followed in twenty-four countries. Several geographic regions are also compiled. Index values are shown in local currencies as well as in U.S. dollars, U. K. pounds, yen, and deutschemarks.

The *Financial Times* has recently created two additional indices based on the values of European stocks. The FT-Eurotrack 100 includes 100 stocks traded in continental Europe and Ireland. The FT-Eurotrack 200 includes 200 pan-European stocks traded on the London ISE. These are designed to track stocks not of single countries but of the European Community (EC).

S & P Indices. Stock indices calculated by the Standard and Poors (S & P) Corporation treat only U.S.-domiciled corporations. Although the S & P indices might not be well known by the general public, they are clearly the most widely used by professional investors in the United States.

S & P indexes have a base index value equal to 10. This is intended to reflect the average index value between 1941–1943. The S & P 500 consists mainly of large capitalization companies traded on the NYSE that account for approximately 70% of the aggregate value of NYSE stocks. A few NASDAQ securities are also included in order to provide fair representation to financial corporations. Although the Wilshire 5000 is a broader-based index of U.S. stocks, the S & P 500 has

---

[3] In the United States, the term *international* refers to securities other than those domiciled in the United States. The term *global* refers to both U.S. and non-U.S. securities.

FIGURE 4-1 *Recent and Long-Term Performances Up to 31 December 1992*

RECENT AND LONG TERM PERFORMANCES UP TO 31 December 1992

% change		% change	compound annual growth rates in %		
3 months		12 months	2 years	5 years	10 years
	THE WORLD INDEX				
-0.8	THE WORLD INDEX	-7.1	3.8	4.0	12.3
4.7	THE WORLD INDEX IN LOCAL CURRENCIES	-3.3	5.0	5.2	10.2
-0.1	THE WORLD INDEX WITH GROSS DIVIDENDS (1)	-4.7	6.5	6.6	15.5
-0.3	THE WORLD INDEX WITH NET DIVIDENDS (1)(2)	-5.2	5.9	6.0	14.7
-0.8	THE WORLD INDEX FREE (3)	-7.1	3.9	4.0	NA
-1.2	WORLD GDP WEIGHTED	-6.7	3.7	5.5	13.7
	EAFE				
-4.3	EAFE	-13.9	-2.6	-0.2	14.7
5.2	EAFE IN LOCAL CURRENCIES	-8.0	-0.9	1.4	10.8
-3.8	EAFE WITH GROSS DIVIDENDS (1)	-11.8	-0.4	1.6	17.1
-3.9	EAFE WITH NET DIVIDENDS (1) (2)	-12.2	-0.8	1.3	16.7
-4.4	EAFE FREE (3)	-13.9	-2.6	-0.3	NA
-4.1	EAFE GDP WEIGHTED	-11.4	-1.9	2.9	16.0
	NORTH AMERICA				
4.1	NORTH AMERICA	3.0	13.8	11.4	11.3
4.2	NORTH AMERICA IN LOCAL CURRENCIES	3.6	14.1	11.3	11.3
4.9	NORTH AMERICA WITH GROSS DIVIDENDS (1)	6.1	17.4	15.2	15.5
4.6	NORTH AMERICA WITH NET DIVIDENDS (1) (2)	5.2	16.3	14.1	14.2
	PACIFIC				
-3.1	PACIFIC	-19.3	-5.7	-4.6	14.9
0.5	PACIFIC IN LOCAL CURRENCIES	-18.7	-8.8	-3.9	9.0
-2.8	PACIFIC WITH GROSS DIVIDENDS (1)	-18.2	-4.5	-3.6	16.3
-2.8	PACIFIC WITH NET DIVIDENDS (1) (2)	-18.4	-4.7	-3.8	16.0
	EUROPE 13				
-5.5	EUROPE 13	-7.4	0.9	6.1	14.3
10.4	EUROPE 13 IN LOCAL CURRENCIES	6.4	9.6	8.7	12.5
-4.8	EUROPE 13 WITH GROSS DIVIDENDS (1)	-4.2	4.3	9.6	18.1
-4.9	EUROPE 13 WITH NET DIVIDENDS (1) (2)	-4.7	3.8	9.1	17.5
-5.6	EUROPE 13 FREE (3)	-7.0	1.2	6.3	NA
	EUROPE 13 EX THE UK				
-6.7	EUROPE 13 EX THE UK	-7.5	0.4	6.4	14.9
8.9	EUROPE 13 EX THE UK IN LOCAL CURRENCIES	1.5	6.2	7.9	11.9
-6.0	EUROPE 13 EX THE UK WITH GROSS DIVIDENDS (1)	-4.7	3.4	9.5	18.4
-6.2	EUROPE 13 EX THE UK WITH NET DIVIDENDS (1)(2)	-5.4	2.6	8.7	17.5
7.1	**EMERGING MARKETS FREE INDEX**	9.0	30.4	25.8	NA

(1) With dividends reinvested monthly (2) net, after withholding taxes for foreigners not benefitting from any double taxation treaty (such as Luxemburg investment companies) (3) excludes non free shares in Finland, Norway, Sweden and, before 16 July 1992, registered shares, when not available to foreigners, in Switzerland. Based on the Morgan Stanley Capital International dollar denominated indices except when otherwise specified.

traditionally been the benchmark used to measure performance of professional equity managers. "Beating the market" means that a manager's return was greater than the S & P 500 return.

S & P also provides indexes on over 90 industry groups. In 1991, they began reporting a *Mid-Cap Index,* which includes 400 companies not included in the S & P 500. It is designed to mirror the sector and industry weightings of the U.S. economy as measured by Gross National Product (GNP) and to track medium-capitalization securities with market values ranging from $200 million to $5 billion. Adding the aggregate value of securities in the mid-cap index to the S & P 500 captures nearly 90% of the U.S. equity market value.

FIGURE 4-1 (continued)

WEIGHTS IN MSCI INDICES – 31 December 1992

GDP WEIGHT (1)

relative weights

MARKET CAPITALIZATION INDICES

weight as a percentage of index

EAFE	World		COS in index	USD billion	Europe 13 Ex-UK	Europe 13 free	Europe 13	EAFE free	EAFE	Kokusai	World
1.4	0.9	AUSTRIA	21	14.8	1.6	1.0	1.0	0.5	0.5	0.4	0.3
1.9	1.2	BELGIUM	20	38.6	4.3	2.6	2.6	1.3	1.3	0.9	0.7
1.0	0.6	DENMARK	24	20.9	2.3	1.4	1.4	0.7	0.7	0.5	0.4
1.1	0.7	FINLAND	31	8.1	0.9	--	0.5	--	0.3	0.2	0.1
--	--	FINLAND FREE	14	1.3	0.1	0.1	0.1	0.0	0.0	0.0	0.0
11.2	7.0	FRANCE	68	205.9	22.7	13.8	13.7	6.8	6.7	4.9	3.7
13.1	8.2	GERMANY	66	203.8	22.5	13.7	13.5	6.7	6.7	4.8	3.7
9.2	5.8	ITALY	66	59.1	6.5	4.0	3.9	1.9	1.9	1.4	1.1
2.7	1.7	NETHERLANDS	22	100.9	11.1	6.8	6.7	3.3	3.3	2.4	1.8
0.8	0.5	NORWAY	24	11.0	1.2	--	0.7	--	0.4	0.3	0.2
--	--	NORWAY FREE	18	8.7	1.0	0.6	0.6	0.3	0.3	0.2	0.2
4.0	2.5	SPAIN	37	59.5	6.6	4.0	3.9	2.0	1.9	1.4	1.1
2.0	1.3	SWEDEN	31	45.5	5.0	--	3.0	--	1.5	1.1	0.8
--	--	SWEDEN FREE	25	39.2	4.3	2.6	2.6	1.3	1.3	0.9	0.7
2.4	1.5	SWITZERLAND	65	137.8	15.2	--	9.1	--	4.5	3.3	2.5
--	--	SWITZERLAND FREE	65	137.8	15.2	9.2	9.1	4.5	4.5	3.3	2.5
8.9	5.6	UNITED KINGDOM	144	601.2	--	40.3	39.9	19.8	19.7	14.3	10.9
--	--	EUROPE 13 FREE	590	1491.5	--	100.0	99.0	49.0	48.8	35.4	26.9
59.6	37.4	EUROPE 13	619	1507.0	--	--	100.0	--	49.3	35.7	27.2
2.4	1.5	AUSTRALIA	53	86.7	--	--	--	2.9	2.8	2.1	1.6
0.7	0.4	HONGKONG	35	91.7	--	--	--	3.0	3.0	2.2	1.7
36.5	22.9	JAPAN	266	1318.3	--	--	--	43.3	43.1	--	23.8
0.3	0.2	NEW ZEALAND	8	9.8	--	--	--	0.3	0.3	0.2	0.2
0.4	0.3	SINGAPORE/MALAYSIA	54	45.3	--	--	--	1.5	1.5	1.1	0.8
40.4	25.3	PACIFIC	416	1551.8	--	--	--	51.0	50.7	--	28.0
--	--	**EAFE (FREE)**	1006	3043.4	--	--	--	100.0	99.5	--	55.0
100.0	62.6	**EAFE**	1035	3058.8	--	--	--	--	100.0	--	55.3
--	3.1	CANADA	83	134.1	--	--	--	--	--	3.2	2.4
--	34.2	USA	334	2338.4	--	--	--	--	--	55.4	42.2
--	--	STH AFRICAN GOLD MINES	20	4.5	--	--	--	--	--	0.1	0.1
--	--	**THE WORLD INDEX (FREE)**	1443	5520.3	--	--	--	--	--	--	99.7
--	100.0	**THE WORLD INDEX**	1472	5535.8	--	--	--	--	--	--	100.0
--	--	NORDIC COUNTRIES FREE	81	70.0	7.7	4.7	4.6	2.3	2.3	1.7	1.3
4.9	3.1	NORDIC COUNTRIES	110	85.5	9.4	--	5.7	--	2.8	2.0	1.5
50.7	31.8	EUROPE 13 EX THE UK	475	905.8	100.0	--	60.1	--	29.6	21.5	16.4
37.6	23.6	FAR EAST	355	1455.3	--	--	--	47.8	47.6	--	26.3
63.5	39.8	EASEA (EAFE EX JAPAN)	769	1740.5	--	--	--	--	56.9	41.3	31.4
--	37.4	NORTH AMERICA	417	2472.5	--	--	--	--	--	58.6	44.7
--	77.1	KOKUSAI (WORLD EX JAPAN)	1206	4217.4	--	--	--	--	--	100.0	76.2

(1) GDP weight figures represent the initial weights applicable for the next month. They are used exclusively in MSCI "GDP weighted" indices.

Morgan Stanley Capital International Perspective 1'93 Geneva Switzerland

SOURCE: *Excerpt from MORGAN STANLEY CAPITAL INTERNATIONAL PERSPECTIVES. Reprinted with permission.*

NYSE Indices. The New York Stock Exchange (NYSE) calculates five market capitalization weighted indices based on stocks traded on the exchange. These include a composite index plus industrial, utility transportation, and utility sub-indices. Its base value is set at 50 as of December 31, 1965. The base value of 50 was chosen to be close to the average stock value at that time.

Russell Indexes. The Frank Russell company calculates four indexes of U.S. equities:

Index	Capitalization Purpose	Average Number of Stocks	Approximate Market Value (May 1991)
Russell 3000	Broad coverage	3000	$1.0 billion
Russell 1000	Large capitalization	1000	$2.8 billion
Russell 2000	Small capitalization	2000	$100.0 million
Russell 2500	Mid-capitalization	2500	$203 million

The basic index is the Russell 3000, which represented about 98% of investable U.S. equity at the end of 1991. At that time the largest firm (Exxon) had a market capitalization of $72.5 billion and the smallest (Innovex) of $22.0 million. The 1000 Index consists of the 1,000 largest firms in the 3000 Index. Russell refers to this as the Market-Oriented Index since it represents the universe of stocks from which most active equity managers typically select. The 2000 Index consists of the smallest 2,000 stocks in the 3000 Index. This small stock index represented approximately 7% of the Russell 3000 total market value at the end of 1991. Finally, the 2500 Index consists of the smallest 500 companies in the Russell 1000 Index and all of the 2000 Index stocks.

NASDAQ Indices. The National Association of Security Dealers (NASDAQ) maintains the following indices on stocks traded in the NASDAQ system:

Index	Approximate Number of Stocks
Composite	4,000
Industrial	2,770
Other finance	650
Bank	200
Insurance	120
Utility	160
Transportation	60

Since the number of stocks will vary over time, the numbers shown above are approximations. The National Market System (NMS) indices began in July 1984 and were set at a base index of 100. The NASDAQ-100 and NASDAQ-Financial began in February 1985 and were based at 250. The market value of stocks traded in the NASDAQ composite at the end of 1991 was $508 billion, or approximately 10% of the value of U.S. equities.

Non-U.S. Indices. The Tokyo Stock Price Index is known as the TOPIX Index. A Topix index is available for securities trading in both the first section and the second section. Their base values are 100 as of 1968. Coverage is all stocks on the Tokyo Stock Exchange. The principal indices of United Kingdom share prices are published by the *Financial Times* and commonly referred to as FT-SE (*Financial Times*-Stock Exchange or ''foot-see''). The most important such index is probably the FT-SE 100 because it is the base of options and futures contracts.

Other Stock Indices

Price Weighted Samples. The Dow Jones Industrial Average (DJIA) is probably the most widely quoted market index and certainly the oldest. It was first published in 1884 by Charles Dow in an attempt to gauge movements in aggregate stock prices, although it was based on the prices of only 11 stocks. Over time, additional stocks were added until there were 30 by 1928. Since then, a number of substitutions have been made in the stocks included in order to improve the representativeness of the index. But the total number of firms covered has remained at 30. Dow Jones also publishes a transportation index of 20 stocks, a utility index of 15 stocks, and a composite index consisting of the total 65 stocks.

Each index is calculated in the same manner—by adding the prices of the constituent stocks and dividing by a divisor equal to the number of index stocks *adjusted for past splits and stock dividends.* Any time a stock splits or issues a stock dividend of 10% or more, the divisor is recalculated. Stock dividends of less than 10% are ignored in the index calculation and treated instead as additions to reported cash dividends. These policies can have major effects upon the DJIA series, and many commentators believe they have tended to impose a downward bias on the growth of the Dow indexes. The impact of not adjusting for small stock dividend distributions is easy to see. The value decline in a share associated with small stock dividends is lost forever in the price index. For example, if an 8% stock dividend is paid on a share selling for $100 prior to the split, the resulting stock price of $92.59 ($100 ÷ 1.08) would be interpreted as a decline in the DJIA. Perhaps more important is a bias associated with adjusting the denominator. This adjustment scheme has the net effect of reducing the investment in the split shares and increasing the investment in the nonsplit shares. To see this, consider year 1 for stocks *A, B,* and *C.* The index value of $50 is composed of $16⅔ of each stock *A, B,* and *C:*

$$\$50 = \frac{\$50 + \$50 + \$50}{3}$$

$$= \$16\tfrac{2}{3} + \$16\tfrac{2}{3} + \$16\tfrac{2}{3}$$

A given percentage change in the per-share price of any security has an equal impact on the index. *Any* of the shares could fall by 10%, and the index value would decline to $48⅓. However, after the split, stock *A*'s dollar representation drops to $10, while stock *B*'s and stock *C*'s dollar representation increase to $20:

$$\$50 = \frac{\$25 + \$50 + \$50}{2.5}$$

$$= \$10 + \$20 + \$20$$

Now a given *percentage* change in the price of stock *A* has a smaller impact on the index than that of stocks *B* and *C. Any time a stock splits, its relative importance in the DJIA decreases and the relative importance of nonsplit stocks increases.* This is akin to an assumption that the new shares obtained in a split were sold and the proceeds were used to buy additional shares of the nonsplit stocks. If shares that undergo splits are those whose prices increase the most over time, this would result in a policy of continually selling shares of high-priced growth stocks and buying shares of low-priced growth stocks. The DJIA would be biased downward from the value which would have been obtained if the numerator-adjustment approach had been used instead.

Another criticism of the DJIA has to do with its representativeness. Thirty large, mature (so-called blue-chip) stocks are included. Critics argue that the sample of 30 stocks cannot reasonably measure market value changes of the typical stock. In fact, studies of past price movements show that the DJIA has not been as variable as other price indexes, nor has it shown as high a growth rate.

The *Nikkei Stock Average* is often called the Nikkei Dow because it is calculated in the same manner. The Nikkei Dow, however, includes 250 stocks and is thus more representative of the Japanese markets than the DJIA is of U.S. markets.

Geometric Security Return Weighted Samples. These indices are rare. In the United States, the *Value Line Index* is based on geometric averages of share returns on about 1,700 stocks. The index value is set equal to 100 at June 30, 1961. The *Financial Times* Ordinary Share Index is similar but is based on 30 large stocks traded in London.

Implicit Portfolio Strategies

As noted earlier in the chapter, ideally one would wish to identify and track the return performance of some baseline investment portfolio in order to determine how well or how poorly an actively managed portfolio compares. Market indexes represent potential proxies for such baseline portfolios. In addition, if properly constructed, they can provide information about the average returns earned by all speculators and investors.

Each index corresponds to a particular type of investment strategy.

1. Returns earned on the DJIA are associated with the following buy-hold strategy:
   a. Restrict your holdings to 30 blue-chip stocks.
   b. Initially buy one share of each stock.
   c. When cash dividends are received, allocate the total receipts across all stocks in proportion to the *per-share* value of each stock.
   d. When stock dividends or splits are received, sell the new shares and allocate the proceeds across all stocks in proportion to the (post-split) *per-share* value of each stock.

A number of problems are associated with actually following such a policy. First, it makes little sense to weight one's holdings ten times heavier in a $100 stock than in a $10 stock, particularly if the *total* market values of the firms are similar. Second, the policy is not *macroconsistent;* that is, not every investor could follow such a policy. Share supplies and share demands simply wouldn't balance. In addition, many people question the policy of continually switching out of stocks that split and into stocks that haven't split. Finally, not many people have a baseline stock investment portfolio that consists of only 30 blue-chip firms. Even though the DJIA is a widely followed series, it is a poor index on which to judge performance.

2. Returns on the S & P Composite are associated with the following strategy:
   a. Purchase shares in 500 of the largest domestic U.S. corporations.
   b. Weight your holdings of each based upon the total market value of each.
   c. Allocate cash dividends in the same manner, based on each firm's total market value.
   d. When stock dividends or splits are received, keep the new shares.

There are two problems associated with this type of baseline portfolio. First, it is restricted to the 500 largest domestic U.S. firms. Smaller domestic firms and all firms based outside the United States are excluded. Second, some investors may not want to weight security holdings based upon total market value. For example, IBM employees might wish to underweight IBM shares, and people in high tax brackets might wish to underweight stocks with high-dividend yields such as those of public utilities. Nonetheless, the S & P Composite is a much better performance guideline than the DJIA. The sample is more representative and splits are more reasonably handled. Most important, the S & P is macroconsistent. Every investor could follow such a policy, and shares supplied would equal shares demanded.

The NYSE, Russell, and NASDAQ indexes follow investment guidelines identical to those of the S & P and differ only in the types of equity shares considered.

3. The Value Line Index is associated with a much different investment strategy. In particular:
   a. Select about 1,700 actively traded stocks.
   b. Initially purchase an *equal dollar amount* of each security.
   c. Each day sell off the portfolio and repurchase an equal dollar amount of shares at then-existing prices.

This policy is rather implausible. The *initial* equal dollar investment in each stock is fine (although it does make the policy macroinconsistent). The problem arises with the assumed daily rebalancing. Transaction costs would be exorbitant. Notice also that this policy requires that one sell off stocks with price increases and buy those with price decreases. While nothing is wrong with this in theory, it does mean that if the market continues to rise for a long time, the shares that rise the most are sold and those that rise the least are bought. The opposite is true in a falling market. Shares that fall the most are bought and those that fall the least are sold.

The portfolio rebalancing assumed by the Value Line Index is clearly a theoretical construct, not one that could actually be followed in practice.

BOND INDEXES

The financial press has focused mainly on stock indices in the past. But given the rapid growth of the value of bonds outstanding throughout the world, more attention will be given to bond indices in the future. Bond indices tend to focus more on aggregate market value and returns than do most stock indexes. This is probably due to their more recent creation, a product of the computer generation.

The most widely used bond indices are prepared by major U.S. brokerage firms; JP Morgan, Lehman Brothers, Merrill Lynch, and Salomon Brothers. Each firm calculates monthly market values and returns on aggregate bond returns as well as various subcategories. Subcategories typically are determined by the type of issuer and the maturity of the bond.

JP Morgan Indices. These indices focus on government bonds issued in various countries. Returns are presented in both local currencies and after conversion to U.S. dollars. Twelve different country indices are calculated. At the end of 1991, the U.S. dollar value of bonds included in these indices was about $4 trillion.

Lehman Brothers Indices. These indices focus on returns, aggregate market values, and security characteristics of publicly traded debt in the United States. To be included in the indices, a security issue must: (1) be rated investment grade or higher by a bond rating firm, (2) have at least one year to maturity, and (3) have a par value of $50 million or more ($100 million for governments).

The detailed indices, their 1991 end-of-year market values, and average 1991 maturities are shown in Table 4-3. Take a few moments to look at the table. It looks a little imposing, but there *are* some valuable lessons to be learned. There are a lot of publicly traded bonds in the markets. The Lehman Index tracks $3.5 trillion of bonds versus about $4.0 trillion in equities for the Wilshire 5000. The size of this market requires that reasonable indices of bond returns be available to security investors. Notice also the largest types of bond issues: U.S. Governments and Mortgage-Backed. Together, they represented over 75% of fixed-income securities in the United States at the end of 1991. Corporate bonds represented only slightly more than 15% of bond issues at that time. Both of these points are magnified when it is noted that these Lehman Indices do not include money market securities nor debt obligations of state and local governmental bodies.

Lehman Brothers also prepares more than 25 nontaxable Municipal Bond Indices. Approximately 8,000 state and local bond issues are included and grouped into four main sectors: (a) general obligations, (b) uninsured revenue bonds, (c) insured bonds, and (d) prerefunded bonds.

Merrill Lynch Indices. Merrill Lynch maintains three bond index series: taxable U.S. bonds, global issues, and convertible issues. The U.S. bond indices are similar in number and type to the Lehman Brothers Indices. In contrast to Lehman Brothers, Merrill Lynch also reports on T-bill returns and returns for more detailed maturities (2 year, 3 year, 4 year, 5 year, etc.).

TABLE 4-3 *Lehman Brothers U.S. Taxable Bond Indices*

Index	December 31, 1991 U.S. Dollar Value (in Billions)	Average Maturity (in Years)
Aggregate bond index	$3,585.4	9.24
Government/corporate	2,469.2	10.09
Intermediate	1,695.8	4.26
Long-term	773.4	22.88
Government index	1,863.7	9.19
1–3 Year	614.6	1.88
Intermediate	1,365.5	3.97
Long-term	498.3	23.49
Treasury	1,606.8	9.09
Intermediate	1,166.7	3.92
Long-term	440.0	22.82
20 + Treasury	324.1	25.84
Agency	256.9	9.81
Intermediate	198.7	4.31
Long-term	58.2	28.58
Corporate index	605.4	12.86
Intermediate	330.3	5.43
Long-term	275.1	21.77
Industrial	221.3	12.45
Intermediate	126.0	5.75
Long-term	95.3	21.31
Utility	161.2	18.3
Finance	145.2	6.91
Yankee	77.8	13.82
AAA corporate	62.1	11.77
AA corporate	129.3	16.17
A corporate	273.2	11.70
BAA corporate	140.8	12.55
Asset-backed	73.1	2.71
Credit card	46.8	3.25
Auto	19.5	1.53
Home equity	6.8	2.34
Mortgage-backed	1,043.1	7.68
GNMA	415.7	8.83
FHLC	316.0	6.73
FNMA	311.4	7.11

SOURCE: Lehman Brothers Bond Indexes.

Merrill Lynch global bond indices are based on more than 10,000 issues traded in the United States and eight other countries. Eurodollar bonds are included. Their Convertible Securities Index provides returns on both U.S. and non-U.S. convertible bonds and preferred stocks. This is a newly formed series with returns beginning in January, 1987.

Salomon Brothers Indexes. Salomon Brothers provides bond return indices for both U.S. and non-U.S. bond issues. The U.S. bond indices are similar in form to those discussed above. Monthly data begins in 1980. The international series covers eight countries. For each, the series provides U.S. dollar and local currency returns on governmental obligations of a country, Eurodollar issues sold by corporations domiciled in the country and local money market instruments.

Pricing Fixed Income Securities. Although world bond markets are larger in value than world equity markets, there are many bond issues for which an end-of-month market price (based on an actual trade) might not be available. Various pricing services are used to price such issues. Firms that offer such pricing services develop proprietary ''matrix models'' that relate the prices of bonds actually trading at month-end to underlying characteristics of the issue. These characteristics include default rating, maturity, coupon, sinking fund provisions, etc. After a model has been developed that accurately prices bonds for which actual end-of-month trade prices exist, the model is used to price nontraded issues. No pricing model, however, is perfectly reliable, and different models often provide prices for illiquid bonds that are quite different.

SUMMARY

Security market indexes are widely used barometers of the direction of security price levels and the historical returns that could have been earned for various types of portfolios. A knowledge of how the indexes are prepared is important, because underlying the calculation of each is an implicit portfolio strategy. The DJIA, for example, reflects a portfolio of 30 large-company stocks, with each stock weighted according to its price per share (a $100 stock is weighted 10 times more than a $10 stock). In comparison, the S & P 500 reflects a portfolio of 500 large-company stocks, with each stock weighted according to its *total* market value.

REVIEW PROBLEM

1. Assume that you are given the following data on three stocks (none of the stocks paid dividends):

Date	Price			Shares Outstanding		
	A	B	C	A	B	C
0	$40	$50	$30	100	200	300
1	22*	50	28	200	200	300
2	25	55	32	200	200	300

* Two-for-one stock split on the first day of the period.

a. Use the approach followed by Dow Jones to calculate a price index on the three stocks for each period.
b. Now calculate a market-value-weighted index modeled after the S & P 500 Composite Index.
c. Estimate the rate of return on each index for periods 1 and 2.

Solution

1. a. DJIA at period 0: $\dfrac{40 + 50 + 30}{3} = 40$

DJIA at period 1: First find a new denominator:

$$\frac{20 + 50 + 30}{D} = 40$$

$$D = 2.5$$

Next find the index value:

$$\frac{22 + 50 + 28}{2.5} = 40$$

DJIA at period 2: $\dfrac{25 + 55 + 32}{2.5} = 44.80$

b. First find the base date market value:

$$40(100) + 50(200) + 30(300) = 23{,}000$$

The base date index is:

$$10\left(\frac{23{,}000}{23{,}000}\right) = 10$$

S & P 500 at period 1:

$$10\left(\frac{22(200) + 50(200) + 28(300)}{23{,}000}\right) = 9.913$$

S & P 500 at period 2:

$$10\left(\frac{25(200) + 55(200) + 32(300)}{23{,}000}\right) = 11.130$$

c. Since no dividends were paid, returns on each are simply the percentage price change of each index.

Period	DJIA	S & P 500
1	0.	−0.87%
2	12.00%	12.28%

QUESTIONS AND PROBLEMS

1. Security market indexes have a number of possible uses. Describe these uses.
2. Returns on various security indexes are often used to judge the performance of an actively managed portfolio. What potential problems do you see in such comparisons?
3. Underlying each of the following equity indexes is an implied portfolio strategy. Identify the strategy for each.
   a. DJIA
   b. S & P 500
   c. NYSE Composite
   d. Value Line Composite
4. Each of the various indexes reports not only an index price but also a dividend-per-share figure that is consistent with the way in which the index is calculated. For example, we assume that we saw that the S & P 500 at a year-end was $247.08 and that dividends paid on the index were $2.2025 during that quarter-end. Using your knowledge of how the S & P 500 is calculated, how do you suppose the $2.2025 figure was arrived at?
5. Scan a recent financial newspaper in order to gain a clear understanding of the securities traded. Identify security types or investment strategies that are not suitably captured by current market indices. Design such an index.
6. What is meant by the term *macro consistent?*
7. The value of NASDAQ Composite Index was 586.34 at the end of 1991 and 373.84 at the end of 1990. Why was the rate of return on an investment in the aggregate index not NASDAQ equal to 56.87%?
8. In the chapter, we saw no market index that tracks the performance of preferred stocks traded in the United States. Discuss how you could create such an index. What problems might you encounter in creating this index, and how might you attempt to solve such problems?
9. A professional investment manager at Mitchell Hutchins restricts her stock investments to small capitalization U.S. firms engaged in biomedical technology. Which, if any, indices discussed in the chapter might be a reasonable benchmark on which the manager's performance could be judged? If you were to develop a specialized index for this manager, how would you do so?
10. Wilshire provides two return indexes. One is a simple average of the returns on stocks in the Wilshire 5000 (equally weighted). In the other, each stock's return is weighted by companies' market capitalization (value weighted). Which index is macro consistent? Which index do you expect to have the greater return volatility? Which index do you expect to have the greater average yearly return?

11. A plan sponsor with a portfolio manager who invests in small capitalization, high growth stocks should have the plan sponsor's performance measured against which *one* of the following?
   a. S & P 500 Index
   b. Wilshire 5000 Index
   c. Dow Jones Industrial Average
   d. S & P 400 Index

CFA

12. Which *one* of the following statements regarding the Dow Jones Industrial Average (DJIA) is *false?*

    a. The DJIA accounts for approximately 20% of the total market value of all public companies.

    b. The DJIA consists of 30 blue chip stocks.

    c. The DJIA is affected equally by changes in low- and high-priced stocks.

    d. The DJIA divisor needs to be adjusted for stock splits.

13. In calculating the Standard & Poor's stock price indices, the adjustment for stock splits occurs:

    a. by adjusting the divisor.

    b. automatically, due to the manner in which the index is calculated.

    c. by adjusting the numerator.

    d. quarterly, on the last trading day of each quarter.

D A T A F I L E   A N A L Y S I S

In these analyses, you will examine historical returns on a variety of the market indexes discussed in the chapter. The construction of an index has an important effect on the index's return series.

1. *U.S. Stock Index Prices and Dividends.* Access the datafile labeled INDXDATA.WK1 and identify the columns in which prices and dividends are shown for the S & P 500 and DJIA (Dow Jones Industrial Average). Use these end-of-year prices and dividends to calculate the yearly rates of return on both indexes for the period 1930–1992. Calculate the average yearly return on each and comment on why the averages differ. Write the 1991 return on the S & P 500 index on a sheet of paper for use below.

2. *U.S. Stock Index Returns.* Access the datafile labeled RTNSYRLY.WK1 and locate the following U.S. stock indexes:

S & P 500	Wilshire Value Weighted	Russell 3000
S & P Midcap	Wilshire Equal Weighted	Russell 2000
		Russell 1000

Determine the first year for which they all have a return available. Calculate the average yearly return on each index from that year through 1992. Using your knowledge of how each index is calculated, explain why the averages differ.

Now look at the 1991 return on the S & P 500 Index. It is slightly larger than the result obtained in part 1. Why? (Hint: Dividends are paid throughout a year.)

3. *U.S. Bond Index Returns.* In the RTNSYRLY.WK1 datafile are a variety of bond indexes prepared by Lehman Brothers, Inc. Examine those provided. Three U.S. government bond indexes are shown: an aggregate of all U.S. publicly traded government bonds, intermediate-term maturity instruments, and long-term maturity instruments for the period 1973–1992. Calculate the average, minimum, and maximum yearly returns for both the intermediate and long-term issues. Notice that the minimums and maximums are quite different. This is an important bond investment principle discussed in Chapters 11 and 12. The prices and returns of long-term maturity bonds are more valuable than those of shorter-term bonds.

APPENDIX 4 - A

U.S. Fixed Income Returns

First Year	CPI 1926	30-Day T-Bills 1926	Com'l Paper 1947	Cert. Deposit 1947	20-Year T-Bonds 1926	Interm. T-Bonds 1926	20-Year C-Bonds 1926	Lehman Govt. Corp 1973
1926	− 1.49	3.27			7.77	5.38	7.37	
1927	− 2.09	3.13			8.94	4.52	7.44	
1928	− 0.96	3.23			0.08	0.92	2.84	
1929	− 0.21	4.74			3.42	6.01	3.27	
1930	− 6.03	2.43			4.65	6.72	7.98	
1931	− 9.52	1.09			− 5.32	− 2.23	− 1.85	
1932	− 10.30	0.95			16.84	8.81	10.82	
1933	0.51	0.30			− 0.07	1.83	10.38	
1934	2.03	0.18			10.02	9.00	13.84	
1935	3.00	0.14			5.00	7.01	9.61	
1936	1.21	0.19			7.50	3.06	6.74	
1937	3.10	0.29			0.22	1.56	2.75	
1938	− 2.78	− 0.04			5.51	6.23	6.13	
1939	− 0.48	0.01			5.95	4.52	3.97	
1940	0.96	− 0.02			6.09	2.96	3.39	
1941	9.72	0.40			0.93	0.50	2.73	
1942	9.30	0.28			3.22	1.94	2.60	
1943	3.18	0.35			2.07	2.81	2.83	
1944	2.12	0.33			2.82	1.80	4.73	
1945	2.25	0.32			10.73	2.22	4.08	
1946	18.16	0.36			− 0.09	1.00	1.72	
1947	9.01	0.50	1.00	0.89	− 2.63	0.91	− 2.34	
1948	2.71	0.81	1.30	1.14	3.38	1.85	4.14	
1949	− 1.81	1.12	1.50	1.15	6.44	2.32	3.31	
1950	5.79	1.22	1.30	1.27	0.05	0.70	2.12	
1951	5.87	1.49	2.10	1.66	− 3.94	0.36	− 2.69	
1952	0.89	1.65	2.30	1.81	1.16	1.63	3.52	
1953	0.64	1.83	2.50	1.89	3.63	3.23	3.41	
1954	− 0.50	0.86	1.70	1.35	7.18	2.68	5.39	
1955	0.36	1.57	1.80	1.78	− 1.28	− 0.65	0.48	
1956	2.86	2.47	3.10	2.71	− 5.58	− 0.42	− 6.81	
1957	3.02	3.15	3.70	3.51	7.47	7.84	8.71	
1958	1.77	1.53	2.50	2.12	− 6.11	− 1.29	− 2.22	
1959	1.51	2.97	3.60	3.58	− 2.28	− 0.39	− 0.97	
1960	1.48	2.67	4.10	3.55	13.79	11.79	9.07	
1961	0.67	2.12	2.80	2.86	0.96	1.85	4.82	
1962	1.21	2.72	3.30	3.04	6.88	5.56	7.95	
1963	1.66	3.11	3.30	3.39	1.21	1.64	2.19	
1964	1.21	3.53	4.00	3.79	3.51	4.04	4.77	
1965	1.93	3.92	4.30	4.32	0.70	1.02	− 0.46	
1966	3.35	4.75	5.20	5.46	3.64	4.69	0.20	
1967	3.04	4.20	5.40	4.84	− 9.19	1.01	− 4.95	
1968	4.72	5.22	5.90	5.81	− 0.26	4.54	2.57	
1969	6.10	6.57	7.70	7.80	− 5.07	− 0.74	− 8.09	
1970	5.48	6.52	8.70	7.81	12.10	16.86	18.37	
1971	3.36	4.39	5.50	5.00	13.24	8.72	11.01	

U.S. Fixed Income Returns *(continued)*

First Year	CPI 1926	30-Day T-Bills 1926	Com'l Paper 1947	Cert. Deposit 1947	20-Year T-Bonds 1926	Interm. T-Bonds 1926	20-Year C-Bonds 1926	Lehman Govt. Corp 1973
1972	3.42	3.84	4.40	4.49	5.67	5.16	7.26	
1973	8.78	6.93	7.60	8.49	−1.10	4.61	1.14	2.29
1974	12.20	8.01	10.30	10.99	4.35	5.69	−3.06	0.17
1975	7.01	5.80	6.90	6.63	9.19	7.83	14.64	12.29
1976	4.82	5.08	5.70	5.27	16.76	12.87	18.65	15.59
1977	6.77	5.13	5.10	5.55	−0.65	1.41	1.71	2.99
1978	9.03	7.20	7.30	8.14	−1.18	3.49	−0.07	1.18
1979	13.32	10.38	10.51	11.45	−1.21	4.09	−4.19	2.29
1980	12.41	11.26	13.02	13.59	−3.96	3.91	−2.61	3.06
1981	8.94	14.72	15.77	17.27	1.86	9.45	−0.96	7.29
1982	3.87	10.53	13.22	13.05	40.37	29.10	43.79	31.10
1983	3.80	8.80	9.29	9.37	0.69	7.41	4.70	8.00
1984	4.02	9.78	10.55	10.88	15.54	14.02	16.39	15.03
1985	3.77	7.73	8.80	8.30	30.96	20.33	30.90	21.32
1986	1.12	6.15	6.99	6.86	24.45	15.14	19.85	15.63
1987	4.25	5.46	6.88	6.57	−2.70	2.90	−0.27	2.30
1988	4.40	6.36	7.61	7.34	9.68	6.10	10.70	7.58
1989	4.63	8.38	9.60	9.17	18.10	13.29	16.23	14.24
1990	6.11	8.18	8.35	8.16	6.20	9.73	6.78	8.28
1991	3.06	5.60	6.54	5.97	19.26	15.46	19.89	16.13

A P P E N D I X 4 - B

U.S. Stock Index Returns

First Year	S & P 500 1926	Wilshire 5000 1971	Russell Indexes 1000 1979	Russell Indexes 2000 1979	Russell Indexes 3000 1979	DJIA 1930	NYSE W/O Div 1971	AMEX W/O Div 1963	NASDAQ W/O Div 1972	Value Line 1962
1926	11.61									
1927	37.48									
1928	43.61									
1929	−8.41									
1930	−24.90					−29.29				
1931	−43.35					−47.56				
1932	−8.20					−17.14				
1933	53.97					72.37				
1934	−1.43					7.81				
1935	47.66					42.91				
1936	33.92					29.71				
1937	−35.02					−27.94				
1938	31.14					32.18				
1939	−0.42					1.03				
1940	−9.78					−8.02				
1941	−11.58					−9.59				
1942	20.33					13.37				

U.S. Fixed Income Returns *(continued)*

First Year	S & P 500 1926	Wilshire 5000 1971	Russell Indexes 1000 1979	2000 1979	3000 1979	DJIA 1930	NYSE W/O Div 1971	AMEX W/O Div 1963	NASDAQ W/O Div 1972	Value Line 1962
1943	25.91					19.09				
1944	19.73					16.93				
1945	36.41					31.04				
1946	−8.07					−4.26				
1947	5.70					7.43				
1948	5.51					4.22				
1949	18.79					20.09				
1950	31.74					25.69				
1951	24.02					21.31				
1952	18.35					14.15				
1953	−0.98					1.75				
1954	52.62					50.18				
1955	31.54					26.11				
1956	6.56					6.97				
1957	−10.79					−8.44				
1958	43.37					38.55				
1959	11.98					19.95				
1960	0.46					−6.20				
1961	26.89					22.40				
1962	−8.73					−7.62				−16.30
1963	22.78					20.59		14.70		13.60
1964	16.51					18.67		15.00		13.30
1965	12.45					14.16		19.40		19.00
1966	−10.05					−15.65		−5.80		−12.30
1967	23.99					19.04		56.20		29.10
1968	11.08					7.73		33.10		19.80
1969	−8.49					−11.60		−22.50		−28.70
1970	4.03					8.76		−16.00		−20.70
1971	14.32	17.68				9.88	12.34	21.60		9.00
1972	18.98	17.98				18.52	14.27	10.00	23.56	1.00
1973	−14.67	−18.51				−13.30	−19.64	−30.00	−31.06	−35.50
1974	−26.46	−28.38				−23.73	−30.28	−33.22	−35.11	−33.50
1975	37.21	38.40				44.87	31.86	38.39	29.76	44.40
1976	23.85	26.60				22.93	21.50	31.58	26.10	32.20
1977	−7.18	−2.60				−12.86	−9.30	16.43	7.33	0.48
1978	6.57	9.20				2.80	2.15	17.73	12.31	4.31
1979	18.42	25.50	22.31	43.09	24.11	10.67	15.54	64.10	28.11	24.44
1980	32.41	33.66	31.88	38.58	32.51	22.13	25.68	41.25	33.88	18.28
1981	−4.91	−3.70	−5.10	2.03	−4.43	−3.65	−8.68	−8.13	−3.21	−4.43
1982	21.41	18.70	20.30	24.95	20.74	27.16	13.95	6.23	18.67	15.33
1983	22.51	23.40	22.15	29.13	22.74	26.06	17.46	30.95	19.87	22.28
1984	6.27	3.05	4.75	−7.30	3.39	1.35	1.26	−8.41	−11.22	−8.42
1985	32.17	32.56	32.27	31.05	32.16	33.67	26.15	20.50	31.37	20.72
1986	18.47	15.95	17.87	5.68	16.71	27.20	13.98	6.96	7.36	5.01
1987	5.23	2.39	2.94	−8.77	1.94	5.55	−0.25	−1.11	−5.26	−10.64
1988	16.81	17.93	17.23	24.89	17.82	16.21	13.04	17.54	15.41	15.40
1989	31.49	29.19	30.42	16.24	29.32	32.23	24.82	23.53	19.26	11.22
1990	−3.17	−8.10	−4.18	−19.51	−5.06	−0.54	−7.46	−18.49	−17.81	−24.26
1991	30.55	34.20	33.03	48.05	33.66	24.25	27.12	28.22	56.84	NA

A P P E N D I X 4 - C

Selected International Returns (in U.S. Dollars)

	Sol. Bros. World Govt.	MSCI EAFE	London Fin'l Tim	Japan Large
1956			−6.04	
1957			−0.95	
1958			44.66	
1959			57.45	
1960			−5.84	
1961			5.19	
1962			−0.76	
1963			17.89	
1964			−4.45	
1965			12.06	
1966			−4.48	
1967			16.82	
1968			46.83	
1969		2.78	−11.12	
1970		−10.49	−3.77	−15.60
1971		31.19	57.13	61.07
1972		37.65	7.11	114.47
1973		−14.17	−29.34	−15.95
1974		−22.13	−51.14	−13.92
1975		36.83	117.99	17.23
1976		3.78	−13.90	26.37
1977		19.37	67.14	17.22
1978	17.70	34.32	15.50	51.82
1979	−5.98	6.15	20.23	−14.61
1980	17.39	24.45	45.81	29.39
1981	−4.24	−1.04	−9.22	10.41
1982	13.39	0.00	9.23	−0.23
1983	6.28	24.55	16.13	27.79
1984	−1.47	7.88	5.33	17.01
1985	27.60	56.73	50.21	44.13
1986	23.02	69.98	30.54	91.85
1987	18.40	24.93	36.98	41.87
1988	4.37	28.60	7.01	35.34
1989	4.34	10.54	20.14	2.17
1990	11.97	−23.47	8.42	−36.18
1991	15.82	12.14	15.43	8.82

R E F E R E N C E S

For detailed statistics about various secondary markets, including security index levels, you should examine the yearly "fact book" published by each security exchange. In the United States, these include:

NYSE Fact Book, published annually by the New York Stock Exchange.
NASDAQ Fact Book, published annually by the National Association of Security Dealers.
American Stock Exchange Fact Book, also published annually.

Historical returns on many major security indexes can be obtained directly from the brokerage firms that maintain them. In addition, you might find the following more accessible:

Stocks, Bonds, Bills and Inflation, updated annually by Ibbotson Associates, Chicago.
Investment Dimensions, published annually by Dimensional Fund Advisors, Inc., Chicago.

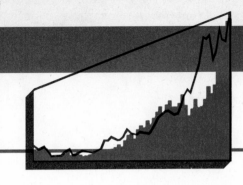

P A R T 2

Investment Concepts

The purpose of Part 1 was to provide an overview of financial markets. We discussed the relative sizes of world debt and equity markets, the variety of instruments traded, how they are traded, and security indexes that can be used to measure investment returns. Using Chapters 1 through 4 as a foundation, we can now move into a thorough treatment of various investment concepts.

We start Part 2 with an overview in Chapter 5 of the concepts treated in Chapters 6 through 10. This overview is followed by a discussion in Chapter 6 of why people are risk averse and what this implies about risk measurement. In Chapter 6, we also examine one of the most important aspects of risk management-diversification—why it works and when it doesn't. We then consider the diversification implications of prior chapters for security markets as a whole. This results in various asset pricing models. The two best known pricing models are the Capital Asset Pricing Model (CAPM) and the Arbitrage Pricing Model (APM). The CAPM is discussed in Chapter 7, and the APM is discussed in Chapter 8. In Chapter 9, we continue to examine how securities are valued but turn to the valuation of derivatives: options and futures. We conclude in Chapter 10 with an examination of the investment and speculative implications of the efficient market hypothesis and the evidence that both supports and refutes it.

The concepts presented in these chapters provide the theoretical background from which various security media can be analyzed and portfolio strategies can be developed, as discussed in later sections of the book.

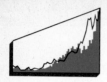

Investment Concepts

The major issue explored in this and the next five chapters is *security pricing*. What factors determine the price at which a security should trade? Do securities actually trade at these prices? And, if not, is there a way to earn speculative profits?

The task of explaining why different securities have different prices is a complex one. Instead of trying to identify all possible variables that surely play a role in security pricing, financial economists focus on simple models in the hope that the more important variables can be identified first and less important identified later. This has led to two well-developed theoretical models: the Capital Asset Pricing Model (CAPM) and the Arbitrage Pricing Model (APM). Although these models are designed to explain differences in security prices, they are actually expressed in an expected rate-of-return form. This means that the models attempt to explain why investors have a specific required return in mind when they evaluate a security. Both models imply:

The Required		A Nominal		Risk Premium(s)
Rate-of-Return	=	Risk-Free	+	for the Risk(s)
for Security *i*		Rate-of-Return		of Security *i*

This chapter serves as an introduction to topics that are discussed in detail in Chapters 6 through 10. We begin by reviewing the economic logic underlying the creation of risk-free rates of interest. The next two sections review the measurement of security returns and risk. Historical returns on a variety of security classes are examined so that you can begin to understand the levels of risk and return that have been experienced in financial markets. The chapter concludes with a discussion of how risk can be managed by asset allocation and diversification.

RISK-FREE INTEREST

Natural Real Rates

Among many past societies, the taking of interest was considered to be unnatural. The ancient Greeks referred to interest as offspring, which led Aristotle to object that the charging of interest was unnatural since money cannot have offspring. Jewish Mosaic laws forbade interest between fellow Jews. Romans were forbidden to charge interest to other Romans, and the Christian religion strongly discouraged interest taking throughout the Middle Ages. Saint Thomas Aquinas stated that interest constituted a payment for time, which he felt should more properly be considered a free gift of the Creator. Even in more recent times, many people considered interest to be an inherent evil, the extortion of income from the have-nots by the haves.

To provide a graphic presentation of the determinants of a natural real risk-free rate of interest, consider a world in which there are only two dates; Date 0 and Date 1. Also assume that there is no risk. Everything is known.

Now consider panel A in Figure 5-1. At Date 0, society is endowed with total resources equal to R_0. These resources may be fully consumed at Date 0 or a

FIGURE 5-1 *Society's Investment Consumption Choice*

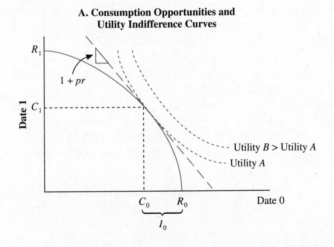

A. Consumption Opportunities and Utility Indifference Curves

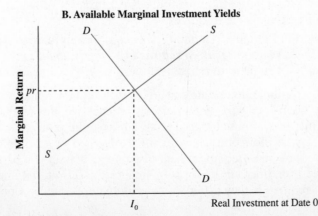

B. Available Marginal Investment Yields

portion could be invested in *real assets*. Note that, as a whole, society cannot be a net owner of financial assets since for each buyer of a financial asset there is a seller. The value of financial assets summed across all people must be zero. In short, investment in real assets is the only alternative to consumption.

If some portion of Date 0 resources are invested in real assets, a productive return *will be* (this is a risk-free world) earned. For example, the first bushel of corn seeded on productive soil, might yield 2 bushels at Date 1. The heavy curve between R_0 and R_1 represents all possible consumption levels at Dates 0 and 1. The slope of this curve at any point represents the increase in Date 1 consumption available if one additional unit of Date 0 resources are invested in real assets. Notice that the slope of the consumption possibility curve decreases as real investment at Date 0 is increased. This reflects a declining marginal return on real asset investment as the amount of investment increases. (The second bushel of corn must be thrown on less productive soil.) In panel B of Figure 5-1 this marginal return is shown as the line *DD*.

Now consider the dotted curves in panel A, called *utility indifference curves*. Any point on a given curve provides the same level of economic utility to society. The higher a curve, the greater the level of economic utility. The slope of an indifference curve at any point represents the increase in Date 1 consumption necessary to provide the same level of current utility if one unit of Date 0 consumption is given up. The fact that the slope of the indifference curves increases as additional consumption at Date 0 decreases means that higher rates of return are demanded. In panel B, this required return is shown as line SS.

So how much real investment will be undertaken at Date 0 and what rate of return will be earned? The answer is clearly at a point *when the marginal return available on investment is equal to the marginal required return*. In panel A, an amount C_0 will be consumed and R_0 minus C_0 will be invested in real assets. And the equilibrium risk-free rate will be the pure rate of interest symbolized as *pr*.

Note that:

1. Interest is indeed a "natural phenomenon." It is the economic force that determines the extent to which real resources will be invested or immediately consumed.

2. The equilibrium real rate of interest is determined by an interaction between (a) the consumption time preferences (thriftiness) of society and (b) the productivity of available resources.

3. In a world of complete certainty, this equilibrium interest rate is set at a level such that investors' *required returns are exactly equal to the productive yields generated* from their investments. Investors will receive the return they require.

The equilibrium interest rate that arises out of classical interest theory is referred to as the *natural*, or *pure, rate*. For convenience we will refer to it symbolically as *pr*. While it is impossible to directly observe the pure rate of interest on riskless real assets, indirect estimates can be obtained by examining financial asset prices. Because risk-free investment in a financial asset is a perfect substitute for a risk-free investment in real assets, financial asset returns must be identical to real asset returns. If they differed, an arbitrage opportunity would exist.

Nominal Risk-Free Rates

One of the most insightful classical economists was Irving Fisher. In 1895, at the request of the American Economic Association, Fisher undertook a detailed examination of the effect of inflation on the rate of interest. These studies were summarized in his text, *The Theory of Interest*. In spite of its age, this is still one of the best discussions of why interest rates exist and what their inherent determinants are.

Fisher's Nominal Risk-Free Return. Fisher's analysis of interest rates is as straightforward and simple as it is important in explaining why interest rates change over time. Fisher begins with the assumption that individuals who lend money realize that what is being lent is not so much pieces of paper (cash) but control of real goods. The rate of return that lenders demand from a loan of capital represents not so much a return on money as it does an increase in their command of real goods. When a sum of money is lent, the lender wishes to receive an increase in *purchasing power* equal to the equilibrium pure rate. If lenders expect an inflation in commodity prices, they will demand a rate of return that provides compensation for both a required real rate of return and the inflation that is expected.

Suppose that both the borrower and lender know with perfect certainty that inflation during the next year will be 5%. If a *real rate* of 3% is required on a loan, the lender will charge a *nominal rate* of 8.15%. For each $1 lent today, $1.05 must be returned next period to keep the lender's purchasing power intact. If the lender requires a 3% increase in next year's purchasing power, he or she will demand a $1.0815 ($1.05 × 1.03) payment in period 2.

The relationship between real and nominal risk-free rates can be expressed symbolically. If *pr* represents the pure rate of interest per annum and $E(I_t)$ represents the annual average inflation expected over the next *t* years, then the *nominal* risk-free rate of interest on a security maturing in year $t(RF_t)$ would be:

Fisher's Nominal Risk-Free Rate Equation

Nominal Risk-Free Rate	=	1.0 plus Risk-Free Pure Rate	×	1.0 plus Expected Inflation	minus 1.0

$$RF_t = [1 + pr][1 + E(I_t)] - 1.0 \qquad (5.1)$$

Assume that Greg Smith is the manager of a money market mutual fund and is attempting to determine what might be an appropriate return to expect on the purchase of U.S. T-bonds of various maturities. He believes that a real return of 2% per year is reasonable and has received the following inflation forecasts:

Year-End	1	2	3	4	5
Average Yearly Inflation	4%	5%	4%	3%	3%

Given these forecasts and using Equation 5.1, Greg should expect the following nominal rates before investing in treasuries.

Bond Maturity	End of Year				
	1	*2*	*3*	*4*	*5*
Expected Return Requirement	6.08%	7.10%	6.08%	5.06	5.06%

Notice that, if inflation rates are expected to change over time, then the required nominal return will depend on a bond's maturity. In the example above, the bond maturing in year 2 has the highest required nominal return because two-year inflation rates are the highest. Anticipated changes in inflation rates over time is a reasonable explanation for the shape of a T-bond yield curve. A yield curve is a plot of the promised nominal return on a bond versus the bonds maturity. Three T-bond yield curves are shown in Figure 5-2.

Alternatively, Mr. Smith might use prevailing nominal returns on risk-free Treasury yields to forecast the market's consensus of future inflation. For example, assume he believes that other people require a real return of 2%. If prevailing yields on Treasury obligations with different maturities are as shown below, he could calculate an estimate of the marketwide consensus of inflation:

FIGURE 5-2 *U.S. Treasury Yield Curves*

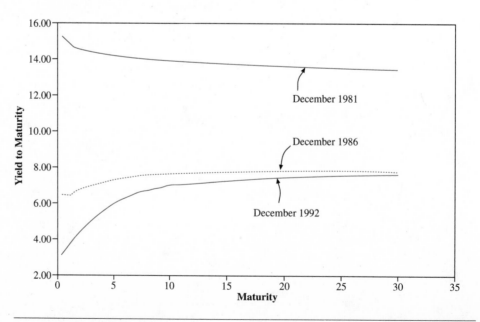

SOURCE: *Federal Reserve Bulletins.*

Maturity Year	Yield on Treasury Bond Maturing in Year	Pure Rate	Implied Average Yearly Inflation
1	7%	2%	4.90%
2	9%	2%	6.86%
3	6%	2%	3.92%
4	5%	2%	2.94%
5	5%	2%	2.94%

Notice that equation 5.1 involves a compounding of the pure real rate and the expected inflation rate. While this compounding is logically necessary, not much accuracy is lost if we simply add the expected inflation rates to the pure real rate. We will refer to this relationship as the Approximate Fisher Equation.

Approximate Fisher Equation				
Nominal Risk-free Rate	equals	Real Risk-free Rate	plus	Expected Inflation
RF_t	$=$	pr	$+$	$E(I_t)$

$$RF_t = pr + E(I_t) \qquad \textbf{(5.2)}$$

Does the Fisher Equation Work? How well does the Fisher equation explain actual rates of return on securities with no risk? There is little doubt that interest rates on securities such as U.S. T-bills are sensitive to potential future inflation. When monetary and governmental authorities set policies that market participants believe will affect inflation, interest rates move exactly as the Fisher equation suggests. And when interest rates across countries are examined, they are directly related to inflationary conditions in the local economies. But accurate tests of the relationship are not possible since market inflation forecasts cannot be observed. In general, there appears to be a strong tie between potential inflation and the level of interest rates.

But interest rates are also affected by policy actions of monetary authorities. During the 1930s and 1940s, the U.S. Federal Reserve Board pegged interest rates at artificially low levels in order to spur economic expansion and reduce government borrowing costs. This policy was discontinued with the Federal Reserve Accord of 1953. More recently, interest rates on U.S. T-bills fell from about 8% in 1990 to about 3% by the middle of 1992. The decline was certainly not due to changes in inflation rates since inflation was stable and at relatively low levels. Instead, the 50% drop in two years was due to expansionary policies of the Federal Reserve Board during a time of prolonged recession.

RETURN MEASUREMENT

Some Definitions

The word *return* can be used in a variety of contexts. To help avoid confusion, it is helpful to review such uses now. These include:

1. Required returns
2. Expected returns
3. Promised returns
4. Realized returns

To keep the example simple, we will consider a commercial paper issue of Magna International Ltd. that promises to pay a single future cash flow equal to $100 in exactly one year from today. After considering Magna's default risk, liquidity of the issue, and returns available on other commercial paper issues, you make two conclusions. First, even though Magna has promised to repay $100, you believe there is a significant chance of default on some amount of the repayment. Specifically, your best expectation of the final repayment is $98. Second, to induce you to purchase the security you would *require* a 12% return. Given this required return and expected future cash flows, you would be willing to pay $87.50 ($98 divided by 1.12). *The required return is the interest rate at which expected future cash flows are discounted.*

It turns out that other investors are more optimistic about the issue than you, and Magna is able to receive an initial issue price equal to $90. If you were to purchase the security for $90 and expect a future inflow of $98, your expected rate of return is 8.9% ($98 divided by $90 minus 1.0). *Your expected return is the interest rate that discounts expected future cash flows to a value equal to the securities current price.* Since your 12% required return is larger than your 8.9% expected return, you should not purchase the issue.

The promised return is the interest rate that discounts promised cash flows back to the security's current price. In this case, Magna International is promising an 11.1% return ($100 divided by $90 minus 1.0). Promised returns exist only for debt securities. Issuers of equities make no (legally binding) promises about future cash flows.

A year passes and you read in the financial press that Magna International has, in fact, declared bankruptcy and will only be able to repay $80 instead of the promised $100. Thus the realized rate of return (earned by investors who initially paid $90) is a negative 11.1%. *The realized return is the interest rate that discounts actual future cash flows back to the original price paid.*

When people speak of security returns, they could have any of these four uses in mind. Be sure you know which is meant.

Return Calculations

The Holding Period Return. In Chapter 1 we defined the rate of return obtained during a given time period to be:

Single-Period Rate of Return	Single-Period Return	=	Percentage Price Appreciation	+	Percentage Cash Return	(5.3)
	R_t	=	$\dfrac{P_t + P_{t-1}}{P_{t-1}}$	+	$\dfrac{C_t}{P_{t-1}}$	

For example, on September 30, 1987, the S&P 500 Index was $321.83. By December 31, 1987, it had declined to $247.08, and $2.2025 in dividends had been paid. Thus, the rate of return for the fourth quarter of 1987 would be calculated to be -22.54%:

$$\frac{\$247.08 - \$321.83}{\$321.83} + \frac{\$2.2025}{\$321.83} = -0.2254$$

However, an important assumption is made when the return is calculated in this fashion. It is assumed that all dividends are paid at the terminal date t. If this is not the case, then Equation 5.3 does not fairly measure the return earned. For example, on December 31, 1982, the S&P 500 was at $140.64. Between then and December 31, 1987, total dividends of $38.86 were paid. Would it then be fair to say that a five-year return of 103% was earned?[1] Clearly not, since the dividend payments were made throughout the five-year interval and, when *reinvested*, would have earned a profit which is not reflected in the 103%. If one is calculating returns for relatively short holding periods (say, one quarter), little harm might be done by assuming all dividends are received at t. But over periods of six months or more, this assumption leads to unacceptable inaccuracies.

The conceptual solution is easy to understand. Simply calculate holding period returns between all dividend-payment periods and then *link* them to find the return for the time period desired. For example, assume that the $2.2025 in dividends paid on the S&P 500 during the fourth quarter of 1987 were paid in three equal installments at the end of each month. Month-end S&P 500 prices, dividends, and monthly rates of return would be as follows:

	9/30/87	*10/30/87*	*11/30/87*	*12/30/87*
S&P 500	$321.83	$251.79	$230.30	$247.08
Dividend	NA	$0.73417	$0.73417	$0.73417
Return to Month	NA	-21.535%	-8.243%	7.605%

To link the returns, we add 1.0 to each return and compound the series. Finally, 1.0 is subtracted to yield the quarter's rate of return:

$$[(0.78465)(0.91757)(1.07605)] - 1.0 = -0.2253, \text{ or } -22.53\%$$

The return of -22.53% is *slightly* different from the original return of -22.54% obtained when we assumed all dividends were paid at quarter-end. But this slight difference will increase when periods greater than a quarter are used and when returns are compounded with other returns over time.

There are two conclusions to draw. First, holding period returns might not be exactly equal to Equation 5.3 *if* dividends (or coupon interest on bonds) are paid at dates other than the terminal date. Second, rates of return that are published by

---

[1] $\dfrac{\$247.08 - 140.64}{\$140.64} + \dfrac{\$38.86}{\$140.64} = 1.03$

various investment advisory firms on indexes such as the S&P 500 will often differ from one another as a result of differing assumptions about when dividends are paid. Some organizations go so far as to calculate daily returns and link them, whereas others assume all dividends are paid at quarter-end.

Unit Value Series. Given that you have a series of holding period returns, it is often useful to create what is known as a *unit value* series. To do so, some base number (say, 1.0) is assigned to the date preceding the first holding period return. This base number is then compounded by each period's return:

$$UV_T = 1.0(1 + R_1)(1 + R_2) \ldots (1 + R_T)$$

Unit Value
$$UV_T = 1.0 \left[\prod_{t=1}^{T} (1 + R_t) \right] \tag{5.4}$$

Later in this chapter, we will examine unit value series on a number of security classes.

Average Versus Geometric Averages. What was the typical yearly return on an investment in, say, the S&P 500 between 1987 and 1991? Yearly returns are shown below. The answer depends on whether we want to know the *arithmetic average* yearly return or the *geometric average* yearly return, since they are not the same.

Year	1987	1988	1989	1990	1991
Nominal S&P 500 Return	5.25%	16.62%	31.59%	−3.09%	30.37%

The arithmetic average was 16.15% and is calculated as follows:

Arithmetic Average Return = (Sum of All Returns) ÷ Number of Years

$$\overline{R} = \left(\sum_{t=1}^{N} R_t \right) \div N \tag{5.5}$$

$$16.15\% = (5.25 + 16.62 + 31.59 - 3.09 + 30.37) \div 5$$

Over this time period, the typical investor who bought a portfolio equivalent to the S&P 500 at the start of a year and sold it at the end of the year would have had an average return of 16.15%. The one-year holding is a critical assumption.

Most investment strategies, however, involve holding periods greater than one year. In that case, the investor is subject to a compounding of the sequence of returns. If there is any variability in the return series, the arithmetic average $\overline{R}$ will not be the same as the average compound return, which we will refer to as $\overline{G}$. When return variability exists, $\overline{R}$ will always be larger than $\overline{G}$, and this difference grows as return variability increases.

The average compound return G is a *geometric* average of the return series and is calculated as follows:

Geometric Average Return = Multiply 1.0 plus the Periodic Returns for all N Periods; Find the Nth Root, Subtract 1.0

(5.6)

$$\overline{G} = \prod_{t=1}^{N} [(1 + R_t)]^{1/N} - 1.0$$

$$0.1533 = [(1.0525)(1.6662)(1.3159)(0.9691)(1.307)]^{1/5} - 1.0$$

To see why $\overline{R}$ and $\overline{G}$ differ, consider the following example. You invest $100 at the start of year 1. During year 1, you experience a positive 20% return. During year 2 you experience a negative 20% return. As shown in the time line below, your $100 initial value declines to $96 at the end of year 2:

	Year 1	Year 2
Return	+20%	-20%
Value $100	$120	$96

The average return, $\overline{R}$, is 0% and suggests you didn't win or lose. But you *know* the initial $100 is now worth $96; you know you lost! In contrast, the average compound return associated with an investment of $100 becoming $96 two periods later is -2.02%:

$$[(1.2)(.8)]^{1/2} - 1.0 = \left(\frac{\$96}{\$100}\right)^{1/2} - 1.0 = -0.0202$$

Why was $\overline{G}$ smaller than $\overline{R}$ in this example? Simply because the 20% decline in value was a 20% decline in both the *initial investment* of $100 and the $20 *profit* you had at the end of year 1. *A given percentage decline in value cannot be offset by an identical percentage increase in value.* This is why $\overline{G}$ will always be smaller than $\overline{R}$ if returns are not constant. $\overline{R}$ treats an $X\%$ decline as identical in impact to an $X\%$ increase. But in fact the two do not have an equal effect upon portfolio values.

Use of the Unit Value Series. The unit value series is particularly useful in calculating $\overline{G}$ values for various time periods. Recall that the unit value at any point in time is the compound growth of 1.00 from the base period to that point in time. If the unit value at date T is divided by the unit value of, (say), $T - 2$, the result is the growth of 1.0 from $T - 2$ to T:

$$\frac{UV_T}{UV_{T-2}} = (1 + R_{T-1})(1 + R_T)$$

To find the compound yearly return over this two-year period, you would take the $T - (T-2)$ root and subtract 1.0. For example, assume you are given the following end-of-year unit values:

	Year-End		
	0	10	20
Unit Value	1.0000	2.3674	8.0623

The geometric average returns over various subperiods are:

Year 0–20:	$(8.0623 \div 1.0)^{1/20} - 1$	= 0.11, or 11%
Year 0–10:	$(2.3674 \div 1.0)^{1/10} - 1$	= 0.09, or 9%
Year 10–20:	$(8.0623 \div 2.3674)^{1/10} - 1$	= 0.13, or 13%

By using a unit value series in this way, geometric average returns can be calculated for any intermediate period.

RISK MEASUREMENT

The concept of investment risk is easy to understand intuitively. You know how much money you put into financial securities today. There is an uncertainty about how much you will take out tomorrow. All quantitative measures of risk as well as strategies to control risk are based on this intuitive notion: *risk is uncertainty about the future value of a portfolio.*

We have three goals in this section. The first is to introduce a widely used measure of investment risk; the *standard deviation.* Naturally, you must have a technical understanding of how standard deviations are calculated. It is more important, however, that you are able to interpret what the term means and apply it to assessing risk. (One can have an intellectual understanding of how an automobile is put together, but unless someone can drive it, knowing how it is made is of little use.) Our second goal is to examine historical returns on a variety of security classes. We do this not with the notion that the past will be repeated in the future but because it is instructive to understand the levels of risk to which investors have been historically exposed. Finally, we introduce two basic ways in which investment risk can be controlled; by changes in the portfolio's asset allocation and by broad diversification.

Discrete Distributions of Future Investment Values

The Scenario. Suppose you are a financial planner. This is a person who provides advice to families on how they might reduce taxes, obtain cost effective insurance and invest in financial securities. Roger and Ying will be meeting with you in an hour to discuss alternative investment strategies. They have savings which they wish to invest for one year. After the year has passed they intend to liquidate the investment portfolio and make a down payment on a house. Their total savings are sufficient today to make the minimum required down payment but no more. They have chosen to delay purchase for one year in order to establish themselves in new jobs.

Roger and Ying have asked you to discuss three investment possibilities: (1) a mutual fund that purchases money market securities, (2) a mutual fund that owns long-term government bonds and (3) a mutual fund that invests in stocks similar to the S&P 500 Index.

TABLE 5-1 *Return Estimates for Three Investment Classes*

		Investment Rate of Return if State Occurs		
State of Economy	*Probability of Occurrence*	*Money Market*	*Government Bonds*	*S&P 500 Stocks*
Deep recession	0.05	6.0%	10.0%	−27.0%
Mild recession	0.20	3.0	6.0	−5.0
Typical economy	0.50	2.0	4.0	9.0
Mild boom	0.20	1.0	2.0	23.0
Strong boom	0.05	−2.0	−2.0	45.0
	1.00			
Expected rate of return =		2.0%	4.0%	9.0%
Variance =		2.0%	5.2%	208.0%
Standard deviation =		1.4%	2.3%	14.4%

You decide that any rate of return that you will show to Roger and Ying should be stated in real return form (after inflation).[2] You also decide that returns on each type of asset will depend on the state of the economy in a year from now. Your best guesses for these returns are shown in Table 5-1.

As a proxy for money market mutual fund returns, you decide to use the one-year return on T-bills. Current nominal returns on one-year U.S. T-bills can be found in the financial press. Assume that a 6.0% nominal return is available with no uncertainty. If someone bought $1.00 worth of such securities, they would pay off $1.06 in one year. After inflation is subtracted from the nominal return, however, the real return on T-bills is uncertain. If economic conditions are typical over the next year, inflation will be 4.0%. Thus, you assign a 2.0% (6.0% − 4.0%) real return on money market securities to the economic state defined as "typical economy." If recessionary conditions arise, the decline in economic activity could cause rates of inflation to decrease, resulting in greater real returns on securities such as T-bills. In contrast, if economic activity accelerated, inflation would increase and real returns on money market securities would be lower.

To proxy a one-year return on government bond mutual funds, you estimate potential one-year returns on long-term Treasury bonds. Promised yields on long-term Treasuries can also be found in the financial press. Assume that the present yield to maturity on U.S. Treasury Bonds that are not callable for 15 years is 8.0%. Inflation during the next year will affect real returns on these securities in the same manner as with money market securities. In addition, the market values of long-term Treasuries in a year from now will depend on interest rate levels that prevail at that time. As a result, the one-year return that investors in such

---

[2] Since house prices are related to inflation rates, Roger's and Ying's required down payment will also be tied to inflation. Thus they will be interested in investment returns after inflation. You should therefore examine real (after inflation) returns. This will not always be the case. An insurance company that promises to pay exactly $100,000 to a policyholder faces no inflation risk and would examine nominal investment returns.

securities will realize depends on future interest rates. The government bond data in Table 5-1 assumes that interest rates will decline if economic activity declines. Decreases in interest rates would cause price increases in long-term bonds, leading to greater realized one-year returns. The opposite results would occur if economic activity accelerates.

Real stock returns are also affected by inflation and changes in interest rates. In addition, stock prices are sensitive to public perceptions of the future profitability of corporations. The one-year stock return data in Table 5-1 assumes that stock prices will decline if economic conditions deteriorate. Conversely, if the economy accelerates, stock prices and one-year returns are assumed to be greater than otherwise.

A *probability distribution* is defined as a set of possible outcomes, with a probability assigned to each outcome. The probability distributions shown in Table 5-1 are referred to as *discrete* distributions, meaning that there are a *finite* number of possible outcomes. We will soon examine *continuous* distributions, but for now it is useful to focus on the discrete distribution in Table 5-1.

The discrete probability distributions in Table 5-1 are displayed graphically in Figure 5-3. Potential returns are shown on the horizontal axis. The probability of a given return is shown on the vertical axis. Notice that the dispersion of returns on stocks is the greatest. It is this dispersion of possible returns that is used as a measure of risk.

Expected Return. If we multiply the probability of a given economic state by the return in that state and then sum these products, we have the weighted average return outcome. This is called the *expected rate of return* or, symbolically, $E(R)$.

$$\begin{matrix} \textbf{Expected} \\ \textbf{Return} \end{matrix} = \begin{matrix} \text{Probability of State} \times \text{Return in State} \\ \text{summed over all states} \end{matrix}$$

$$E(R) = \sum_{i=1}^{N} P_i R_i \qquad (5.7)$$

Here P_i is the probability of state i, R_i is the return in state i, and there are N possible states. For example, the expected real return on the S&P 500 in our example is equal to 9.0%:

$$E(R) = P_1 R_1 + P_2 R_2 + P_3 R_3 + P_4 R_4 + P_5 R_5$$

$$9.0\% = (0.05)(-27.0) + (0.20)(-5.0) + \dots + (0.05)(45.0)$$

Variance and Standard Deviation. The expected return is one measure of the midpoint of a return probability distribution. The statistical measures of variance and standard deviation are measures of the dispersion of potential returns.

To calculate the *variance* of a discrete probability distribution, we use the following procedure:

1. The $E(R)$ is subtracted from each possible return outcome. This difference is then squared.

FIGURE 5-3 *Discrete Probability Distributions*

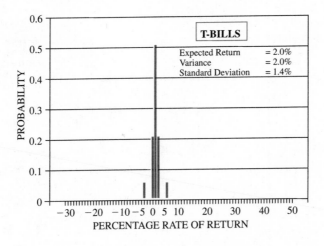

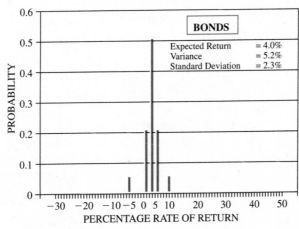

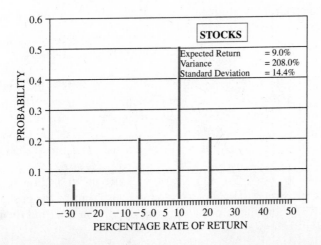

2. Each squared difference is multiplied by the probability of the return outcome.
3. These weighted squared differences are then added.

The variance is simply the weighted average squared deviation from the expected outcome calculated by the following formula:

$$\text{Variance} = \text{Weighted Average Squared Deviation of Returns from the Expected Return}$$

$$\sigma^2 = \sum_{i=1}^{N} [R_i - E(R)]^2 P_i \qquad (5.8)$$

Using the data in Table 5-2 for the S&P 500, its variance is calculated as follows:

$$
\begin{aligned}
208.0\% = \quad & (-27.0 - 9.0)^2\, 0.05 \\
+(& -\ 5.0 - 9.0)^2\, 0.20 \\
+(& \quad 9.0 - 9.0)^2\, 0.50 \\
+(& \quad 23.0 - 9.0)^2\, 0.20 \\
+(& \quad 45.0 - 9.0)^2\, 0.05
\end{aligned}
$$

The measure of variance is stated in the same units as the expected return (in our example, as a percentage). It is a useful statistic that we will refer to often in later chapters. But because it is expressed as a *squared* average deviation from the mean, people have a difficult time mentally interpreting it. Few people are accustomed to thinking in units of squared returns. To express return dispersion in more easily understood units, the square-root of variance is calculated. This is known as the *standard deviation*. The term *standard* can be thought of as standardizing squared return deviations back to a nonsquared value. The standard deviation of a discrete probability return distribution is calculated as follows:

$$\text{Standard Deviation} = \text{Square Root of Variance}$$

$$\sigma = [\sigma^2]^{1/2} \qquad (5.9)$$

Thus, the standard deviation of the S&P 500 returns shown in Table 5-2 would be 14.4%:

$$14.4\% = [208.0\%]^{1/2}$$

Back to the Scenario. There are three important aspects to the investment situation facing Roger and Ying: (1) a short investment horizon, (2) the need for a real dollar return and (3) the fact that their current savings are able to meet a minimum down payment but no more. Each of these distinguishes their investment situation from those of other people and will affect the investment decision they finally make.

In reviewing Table 5-1 and Figure 5-3, Roger and Ying discover that their suspicions are correct. Higher expected returns come at the cost of greater uncertainty. In reviewing the information with them, you interpret the data in a variety of ways. For example:

	Mutual Fund Type		
	Money Market	Govt Bond	S&P 500 Stock
Probability of negative real return	0.05	0.05	0.25
Probability of a real return equal to or greater than 10%	0.00	0.05	0.25
There is a one-in-four chance that the real return will be this or *less*	1.0%	2.0%	−5.0%
There is a one-in-four chance that the real return will be this or *more*	3.0%	6.0%	23.0%
Expected return is	2.0%	4.0%	9.0%
Standard deviation of real return is	1.4%	2.3%	14.4%

After some discussion, they exclude the S&P 500 alternative as being too risky. They also exclude the money market alternative as having insufficient expected return. They feel comfortable with the government bond alternative risk and expected return. As they leave your office they say, "You have been very helpful, but we never did understand that standard deviation thing." You reply, "That's okay. It is used mainly by professionals like myself and is more helpful when we deal with continuous return distributions."

Continuous Return Distributions

The scenario above dealt with a discrete probability distribution with only five possible outcomes. In reality, there are an infinite number of possible return outcomes. To reflect this fact, we use continuous distributions.

A special type of continuous distribution is shown in Figure 5-4. It is known as a *standardized normal distribution.* An understanding of how it is interpreted is critical to understanding investment risk.

First, the distribution is symmetric and centered around a mean (expected value or average) of zero. Second, it is "standardized" such that the value of one standard deviation is equal to 1.0. Finally, the fact that it is a "normal" distribution means that we can find the area between any two points.

Unlike a discrete probability distribution, a specific probability is not attached to specific outcomes. (Given the large number of possible returns, the probability of, say, a 15.000% return is infinitely small.) Instead, we find the probability of an outcome occurring *between two points.* This probability is represented by the area covered between the two points. For example, the probability of an outcome below the mean is 0.5. Similarly, the probability of an outcome (at or) above the mean is also 0.5. And the probability of an outcome between one standard deviation *below* the mean and one standard deviation *above* the mean is 0.68.

The number of standard deviations that an outcome is from the mean is known as a z-score. If you know a given z-score, you can consult a standard normal density table to find the area of the curve between the mean and the outcome. Appendix A to this text is such a table. In addition, a number of commonly used z-scores are shown at the bottom of Figure 5-4. The area from the mean to a

FIGURE 5-4 *Standardized Normal Distribution*

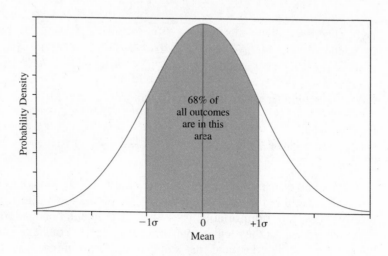

Limits of Variable (Z-Score)		Percentile Distributions Probability of an Outcome Occurring	
Number of Z-scores from the mean	Area from the mean to this point	Below This	At or Above This
$-\infty$	0.50	0.00	1.00
-1.96	0.475	0.025	0.975
-1.64	0.45	0.05	0.95
-1.28	0.40	0.10	0.90
-1.00	0.34	0.16	0.84
-0.67	0.25	0.25	0.75
0.00	0.00	0.50	0.50
$+0.67$	0.25	0.75	0.25
$+1.00$	0.34	0.84	0.16
$+1.28$	0.40	0.90	0.10
$+1.64$	0.45	0.95	0.05
$+1.96$	0.475	0.975	0.025
$+\infty$	0.50	1.00	0.00

negative 1.0 z-score is 0.34. The area from the mean to a positive z-score is also 0.34. Thus, as noted above, the area between -1 z-score and $+1$ z-score is 0.68.

Look at the two columns to the right in Figure 5-4. These provide: (a) the probability of an outcome below this z-score and (b) the probability of an outcome (at or) above this z-score. These columns are often referred to as *percentile distributions*. They are helpful in displaying investment risk to people who do not understand standard deviations.

Estimates for Continuous Return Distributions. There are a number of ways in which expected return and standard deviation estimates of a continuous return distribution might be developed. For example, a scenario analysis used to develop a discrete probability distribution could provide estimates of the continuous distribution's expected return and standard deviation. However, historical returns are more commonly used to develop initial estimates. These historical estimates are then subjectively adjusted by the analyst to reflect current market conditions. For example, the analyst might not believe that the volatility of bond returns during the 1970s and 1980s will be repeated and thus use a smaller standard deviation than the historical value.

Consider the following hypothetical annual rates of return:

Year	1	2	3	4
Return:	10%	−15%	40%	5%

The arithmetic average return is calculated by adding the returns and then dividing by the number of observations.

$$\overline{R} = (\sum_{t=1}^{N} R_t) \div N \tag{5.10}$$

Applied to this data, the average return was 10%:

$$10\% = (10\% - 15\% + 40\% + 5\%) \div 4$$

The variance of the return series is again a weighted average squared deviation from the mean. But now each squared deviation is given an equal weight. To calculate the variance of historical returns, we use the following procedure:

1. The average return is subtracted from each single period return. This difference is then squared.
2. The squared differences are summed.
3. This sum is divided by "the number of periods minus 1.0." (The 1.0 is subtracted for statistical reasons reflecting the loss of one "degree of freedom" in calculating the average.)

Variance of Past Returns = Average Squared Return Deviation

$$\sigma^2 = [\sum_{t=1}^{N} (R_t - \overline{R})^2] \div (N-1) \tag{5.11}$$

Using our hypothetical return data, the variance is

$$= [(10-10)^2 + (-15-10)^2 + (40-10)^2 + (5-10)^2] \div 3$$

$$= 517\%$$

As we saw earlier, squared deviations are difficult to interpret. So the square root of variance is calculated, and the standard deviation:

$$\sigma = [\sigma^2]^{1/2} \tag{5.12}$$

$$22.7\% = [517\%]^{1/2}$$

Applied to Past Real S&P 500 Returns. Between 1926 and 1991, the average annual *real* return on the S&P 500 Index was about 9.0% and the standard deviation was about 20%. The information depicted in Figure 5-5 reflects a continuous distribution based on this data. The shaded area reflects the probability of having a return between 0.0% and the average return of 9.0%. It is found by calculating the number of z-scores that 0.0% is away from the mean and then referring to Appendix A to find the probability associated with such a z-score. The z-score, or number of standard deviations away from the mean, is −0.45 in this example.

$$-0.45 = (0.0 - 9.0) \div 20$$

The probability associated with 0.45 is 0.1736. This means that, in about one out of every three years, $(0.3264 = 0.5 - 0.1736)$ investors in the S&P 500 would incur negative real returns.

Percentile distributions are also shown at the bottom of Figure 5-5. The 0.05 percentile return of −23.8% is calculated as:

$$\text{Percentile Return} = \text{Average} - (z\text{-score}) (\text{Standard Deviation})$$
$$-23.8\% = 9\% - (1.64) (20\%)$$

This implies that there is a 5% chance of a return less than negative 23.8%.

FIGURE 5-5 *Continuous Distribution for Real S&P 500 Annual Returns*

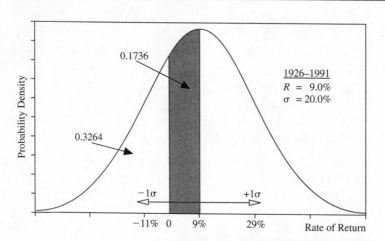

Number of Z - Scores From Average	Associated Real Return	Percentile Distribution	
		Probability Below	Probability At or Above
−1.64	−23.8%	0.05	0.95
−1.28	−16.6	0.10	0.90
−0.67	−4.4	0.25	0.75
0.00	9.0	0.50	0.50
0.67	22.4	0.75	0.25
1.28	34.6	0.90	0.10
1.64	41.8	0.95	0.05

A Review of Past Returns

Unit values for a variety of security classes are shown in Table 5-2. Returns for the EAFE Index are available only since 1969. A unit value series is also shown for the U.S. Consumer Price Index so that real returns can be calculated. All returns are stated in U.S. dollars. Non-U.S. citizens would have experienced different returns due to changes in currency exchange rates. Finally, these unit values assume that all cash received in the form of interest or dividends was reinvested at no cost.

Looking at Table 5-2, a number of points are immediately obvious. For example, U.S. equities had much larger returns than the U.S. bonds. A $1.00 invested in T-bills at the start of 1926 and constantly reinvested in new T-bills would have grown to $11.01 by the end of 1991. A similar investment in the S&P 500 would have grown to $676. Notice also that the unit value of CPI at the end of 1991 was 7.69. A typical good that cost $1.00 at the end of 1925 cost $7.69 by the end of 1991. So the T-bill investor with $11.01 in pocket at the end of 1991 didn't truly fare very well. Such an investor earned an average annual geometric return over this 66-year period of 0.54%.

$$0.0054 = (11.01 \div 7.69)^{1/66} - 1.0$$

But stock investors happy with their $676 experienced some trying times during this 66-year period. For example, look at the declines in S&P 500 unit values between 1927–1932, 1936–1937, and 1972–1974.

Frequency distributions of real returns between 1926–1991 are shown in Figure 5-6 for: (a) U.S. T-bills, (b) U.S. T-bonds, and (c) the S&P 500. A frequency distribution is similar to a discrete probability distribution. Instead of showing specific returns on the horizontal axis, a range of returns is shown. Also, instead of showing a probability of occurrence on the vertical axis, the number of times returns were within a given range are shown. For example, the figure shows that two years had real returns on the S&P 500 between −45% and −50%.

The frequency distributions of T-bill and bond returns do look similar to a normal continuous distribution. The frequency distribution of S&P 500, however, looks less like a continuous normal. Financial economists have debated for years whether stock returns can be characterized by a nonchanging continuous normal distribution. And recent evidence suggests that security return distributions might have constantly changing means and standard deviations. We will discuss this evidence later in the book.

Assuming that past average real returns and standard deviations can be used to describe the continuous distribution of real security returns, percentile distributions of one-year real returns would be as shown in Table 5-3. In one out of every ten years, T-bill real returns would be less than −5.26% compared with a −17.70% for the S&P 500 Index. At the other extreme, in one out of every ten years, T-bill real returns would be greater than 6.26% compared with 36.06% for the S&P 500. The 50th percentile returns would be 0.50% for T-bills and 9.18 for the S&P 500.

The point should be obvious by now. Larger expected returns are available

TABLE 5-2 *Unit Value Series*

Year End	CPI	30-Day T-Bills	20-Year T-Bonds	20-Year C-Bonds	S&P 500	MSCI EAFE
1925	1	1	1	1	1	
1926	0.99	1.03	1.08	1.07	1.12	
1927	0.96	1.07	1.17	1.15	1.53	
1928	0.96	1.10	1.17	1.19	2.20	
1929	0.96	1.15	1.22	1.23	2.02	
1930	0.90	1.18	1.27	1.32	1.52	
1931	0.81	1.19	1.20	1.30	0.86	
1932	0.73	1.20	1.41	1.44	0.79	
1933	0.73	1.21	1.41	1.59	1.21	
1934	0.75	1.21	1.55	1.81	1.20	
1935	0.77	1.21	1.62	1.98	1.77	
1936	0.78	1.21	1.75	2.12	2.37	
1937	0.80	1.22	1.75	2.17	1.54	
1938	0.78	1.22	1.85	2.31	2.02	
1939	0.78	1.22	1.96	2.40	2.01	
1940	0.79	1.22	2.07	2.48	1.81	
1941	0.86	1.22	2.09	2.55	1.60	
1942	0.94	1.22	2.16	2.61	1.93	
1943	0.97	1.22	2.21	2.69	2.43	
1944	0.99	1.23	2.27	2.81	2.90	
1945	1.02	1.23	2.51	2.93	3.96	
1946	1.20	1.24	2.51	2.98	3.64	
1947	1.31	1.24	2.44	2.91	3.85	
1948	1.34	1.25	2.53	3.03	4.06	
1949	1.32	1.27	2.69	3.13	4.83	
1950	1.40	1.28	2.69	3.20	6.36	
1951	1.48	1.30	2.58	3.11	7.88	
1952	1.49	1.32	2.61	3.22	9.33	
1953	1.50	1.35	2.71	3.33	9.24	
1954	1.49	1.36	2.90	3.51	14.10	
1955	1.50	1.38	2.87	3.53	18.55	
1956	1.54	1.41	2.71	3.29	19.77	
1957	1.59	1.46	2.91	3.57	17.63	
1958	1.62	1.48	2.73	3.49	25.28	
1959	1.64	1.53	2.67	3.46	28.31	
1960	1.66	1.57	3.04	3.77	28.44	
1961	1.68	1.60	3.07	3.96	36.09	
1962	1.70	1.64	3.28	4.27	32.94	
1963	1.72	1.69	3.32	4.36	40.44	
1964	1.74	1.75	3.43	4.57	47.12	
1965	1.78	1.82	3.46	4.55	52.98	
1966	1.84	1.91	3.58	4.56	47.66	
1967	1.89	1.99	3.25	4.33	59.09	
1968	1.98	2.09	3.25	4.45	65.64	1
1969	2.10	2.23	3.08	4.09	60.07	1.03
1970	2.22	2.38	3.45	4.84	62.49	0.92
1971	2.29	2.48	3.91	5.37	71.44	1.21
1972	2.37	2.58	4.13	5.76	85.00	1.66
1973	2.58	2.75	4.09	5.82	72.53	1.43
1974	2.90	2.97	4.26	5.65	53.34	1.11
1975	3.10	3.15	4.66	6.47	73.18	1.52

TABLE 5-2 *(continued)*

Year End	CPI	30-Day T-Bills	20-Year T-Bonds	20-Year C-Bonds	S&P 500	MSCI EAFE
1976	3.25	3.31	5.44	7.68	90.64	1.58
1977	3.47	3.48	5.40	7.81	84.13	1.88
1978	3.78	3.73	5.34	7.81	89.66	2.53
1979	4.28	4.11	5.27	7.48	106.17	2.68
1980	4.82	4.58	5.06	7.28	140.58	3.34
1981	5.25	5.25	5.16	7.21	133.68	3.31
1982	5.45	5.80	7.24	10.37	162.30	3.31
1983	5.66	6.31	7.29	10.86	198.83	4.12
1984	5.88	6.93	8.42	12.64	211.30	4.44
1985	6.11	7.47	11.03	16.55	279.28	6.96
1986	6.17	7.93	13.73	19.83	330.86	11.83
1987	6.44	8.36	13.36	19.78	348.16	14.78
1988	6.72	8.89	14.65	21.89	406.69	19.01
1989	7.03	9.64	17.31	25.45	534.75	21.01
1990	7.46	10.43	18.38	27.17	517.80	16.08
1991	7.69	11.01	21.92	32.58	675.99	18.03
Average	3.24%	3.75%	5.11%	5.73%	12.43%	15.68%
Standard Deviation	4.07%	6.55%	8.53%	16.10%	21.28%	22.97%
Geometric Mean	3.14%	3.70%	4.79%	5.42%	10.38%	13.40%

only if one accepts greater return uncertainty. We turn now to two ways in which risk can be controlled.

Risk Management

There are two ways of controlling the risk of an investment portfolio: diversification and asset allocation. Diversification works because the return outcomes on different securities are not perfectly correlated. Unexpected good returns on some securities offset unexpected bad returns on other securities. Consider the following experiment. You have a basket containing 500 sheets of paper. On each sheet is the name of one company in the S&P 500 Index. The average return and standard deviation on each stock are different. But assume that the grand average of the stock's average yearly return is 9.0% and the grand average of their yearly return standard deviation is 40%. You are asked to select *one* sheet at random. Before you select, what average return and standard deviation do you expect to draw? Clearly, 9% and 40%! And if many people had their own baskets and selected one sheet, the average result across all individuals would be: average return = 9% and standard deviation = 40%.

These numbers of 9% and 40% are close to the average annual real return and standard deviation for *individual* stocks in the S&P 500 Index. But we know from work in this chapter that the equivalent data for the aggregate S&P 500 Index

FIGURE 5-6 *Frequency Distribution of Past Returns (One-Year Returns 1926–1991)*

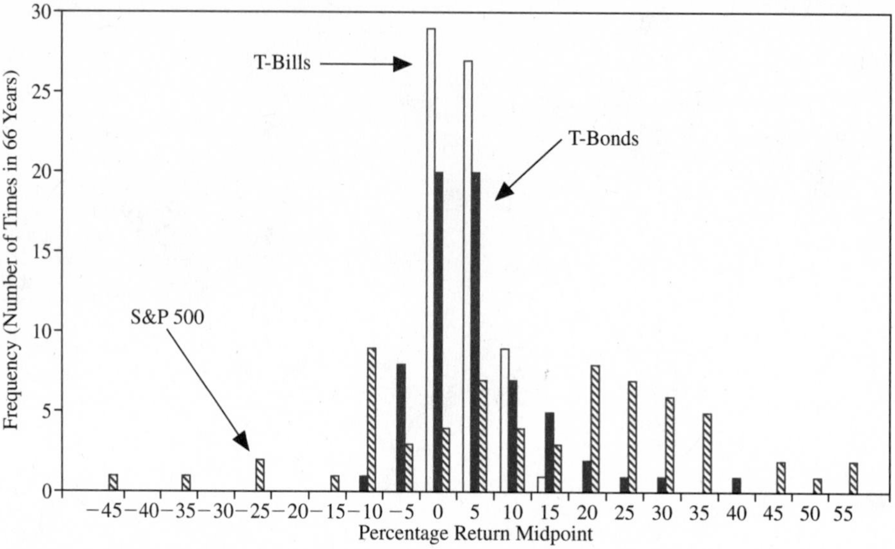

were 9% and 20%. The risk of a single stock was about double the risk of the aggregate portfolio!

The concept of diversification is displayed graphically in panel A of Figure 5-7. Notice, however, that diversification across securities cannot totally eliminate investment risk. This nondiversifiable risk is referred to as *systematic risk* and it plays an important role in asset pricing models such as the Capital Asset Pricing Model (CAPM).

Now consider panel B of Figure 5-7. This panel illustrates how risk can be altered by changing a portfolio's asset allocation.[3] The standard deviation and average of yearly real returns are shown for two asset classes: the S&P 500 and

---

[3] This illustration assumes that T-bill returns are uncorrelated with S&P returns. Correlation is discussed in the next chapter.

TABLE 5-3 *Percentile Real Return Distributions Based on a Continuous Normal Distribution 1926–1991*

	Percentile: Probability of This Return or Less				
	10th	*25th*	*50th*	*75th*	*90th*
U.S. T-bills	−5.26%	−2.52%	0.50%	3.52%	6.26%
U.S. Government Bonds	−11.41	−5.07	1.90	8.87	15.21
S&P 500 Index	−17.70	−4.89	9.18	23.25	36.06

FIGURE 5-7 *Controlling Investment Risk*

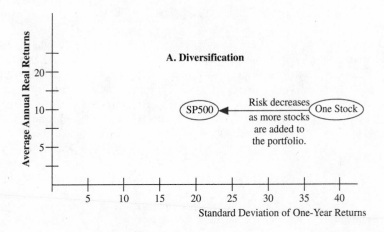

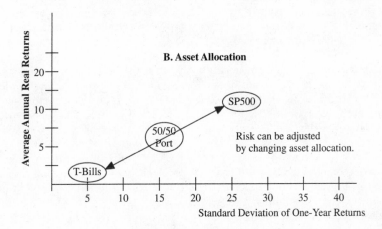

U.S. T-bills. If the S&P is too risky for an investor but the average returns on T-bills too low, a compromise can be achieved by holding some combination of the two. For example, the 50/50 portfolio shown consists of 50% invested in T-bills and 50% invested in the S&P 500. This 50/50 portfolio would have a risk and average return half-way between T-bills and the S&P 500.

Given the complexity of world financial markets, investment texts are forced to cover a large number of topics—so many, in fact, that readers can have difficulties in deciding the fundamental importance of various topics. We are at one of these points. Two of the most important principles of investing are: (1) diversify and (2) asset allocation drives the risk and average returns of the portfolio.

The Worst Disaster

This article from Global Finance *discusses one of the worst stock declines in the international security markets during the five years ended 1992. At the start of that period, investors were unable to foresee the bleak future for Nippon Telegraph and Telephone. In the same fashion, investors were unable to foresee the dramatic growth of other firms. Without perfect foresight, investors should always follow the maxim: "Thou Shalt Diversify!"*

The last five years have seen quite possibly the largest stockholder disaster ever: Between April 1987, when it peaked at 3.18 million yen ($26,281 at the October 1992 exchange rate of 121 yen/$1) per share, and mid-August of this year, when it hit a low of 458,000 yen, Nippon Telegraph and Telephone, Japan's government-owned telecommunications company, lost seven-eigths of its value. With 15.6 million shares outstanding, $351 billion had disappeared from the market value.

Japan privatized its telecommunications monopoly in 1985, and the first offering of NTT shares to the public took place in November 1986, at 1.19 million yen per share, with much fanfare. Fee-hungry securities houses touted the stock to housewives and other novice individual investors as the hottest blue-chip stock ever to be brought to the Tokyo stock market. Even today, individuals comprise the largest proportion of investors in NTT. Additional offerings took place in November 1987, at 2.55 million yen per share, and in October 1988, at 1.9 million yen.

Individual investors who burned their fingers on NTT haven't returned to the stock market, dealing a heavy blow to both the government and the securities houses and contributing to the decline of the Nikkei 225 average, down by more than 50% from its December 1989 peak.

The government still holds 10.2 million, or 65.7%, of NTT's shares and planned to divest an additional 5 million by 1997. But this month, for the third time in a row, the government has had to postpone the issuance of additional shares because of poor market conditions. . . .

Last May, the Diet passed an amendment permitting foreigners to own up to 20% of NTT shares beginning August 1. Some foreign investors did buy NTT in the last two months—and indeed, some foreigners had earlier circumvented the ban through nominee accounts held with Japanese brokerages. But on the whole, foreign investors have been cool to the prospect of buying NTT shares because they're sceptical about the company's fundamentals. They have good reason.

Over the past few years, the company has been spinning off many of its most profitable businesses and is now left with an unprofitable local telephone business. Moreover, the Ministry of Post and Telecommunications continues to meddle heavily in the running of the company. . . .

But analysts say the company also has a more basic problem: It lacks a long-term vision of the type of company it wants to be.

SOURCE: Yoko Shibata, ". . . And Finally, the Worst Stockholder Disaster in the Last Five Years," *Global Finance*, October 1992.

SUMMARY

This chapter provided an introduction to basic investment concepts. We saw that the risk-free interest rate that prevails in financial markets is determined by economic forces in the real goods market. In theory, the risk free rate of interest is determined by the marginal thriftiness of a society and the marginal productivity of real investment. We defined this as the pure real interest rate.

The future payments of most financial securities are not directly tied to future inflation. Thus, investors will adjust the price they are willing to pay for a security to compensate for expected future inflation. The relationship that should exist between nominal interest rates, pure real rates, and inflation expectations is known as the Fisher Equation. It states that the nominal interest rate is equal to the pure real rate compounded by expected inflation. The Fisher Equation is useful in explaining why fixed income securities that differ only in maturities trade at different yields-to-maturity.

We then examined the differences between geometric return averages and arithmetic return averages. For long-term investors, geometric averages communicate better the realized returns that they might expect. Arithmetic averages are more appropriate for shorter-term investors. The concept of a Unit Value series was shown to be a convenient way to display historical security returns.

Investment risk involves the uncertainty of future portfolio values. This uncertainty can be captured by the statistical measure of variance and standard deviation. Variance is the weighted average squared deviation from the mean, and standard deviation is the square root of variance. Assuming that a return distribution can be described as a continuous normal distribution, the mean and standard deviation can be used to calculate the probability that a return will occur within a given return interval. This fact can be used to create percentile return distributions. Percentile return distributions are useful devices in explaining the degree of investment risk to people who do not understand standard deviation.

We concluded the chapter by a short but important discussion on how investment risk can be controlled through diversification and asset allocation. These are major topics in the next few chapters.

REVIEW PROBLEM

You are given the following set of returns.

Year	1	2	3	4
Return	25%	10%	− 30%	15%

   a. Find the average, variance, and standard deviation. (Round to the nearest percent.)
   b. Use these as estimates for a continuous normal distribution to calculate the probability of a return *below* − 10%, 0% and 5%.

Solution:

   a. $\text{Average} = (25 + 10 - 30 + 15) \div 4$

                $= 5\%$

        $\text{Variance} = [(25-5)^2 + (10-5)^2 + (-30-5)^2 + (15-5)^2] \div (4\text{-}1)$

                $= 583\%$

Standard Deviation = [583%]1/2

= 24%

b. Refer to Appendix A for the values of z-scores.

Return	z-score	Probabilty of below
−10%	(−10−5) ÷ 24	0.5−0.2324
	= −0.62	= 0.2676
− 0%	(0−5) ÷ 24	0.5−0.0832
	= −0.21	0.4168
5%	(5−5) ÷ 24	
	=0	0.50

QUESTIONS AND PROBLEMS

1. What are the economic determinants of the real risk-free rate of interest?
2. You wish to earn a real return of 3% per year on various investments. These investments are in default-free zero coupon Treasury bonds that pay $100 at their maturities. Maturities range from end-of-year 1 through end-of-year 4. Your inflation forecast for the next four years are:

Year:	1	2	3	4
Inflation:	4%	6%	8%	5%

   a. Using Equation 5.1, what nominal (annualized) return would you require on each of the four issues?
   b. Using the Approximate Fisher Equation, what nominal (annualized) return would you require on each of the four issues?
   c. Using the answer to part a, what price would you pay for each investment?
3. Why might fixed income securities that are identical except in maturity, trade at different promised returns?
4. You purchase a one-year T-bill at 90% of par. During the year the inflation rate is 5%. What is your real rate of return?
5. What are the differences between required returns, expected returns, promised returns, and realized returns?
6. You are an analyst for Global Equity Mutual Fund. During the past five years, returns on the fund have been:

Year:	1	2	3	4	5
Return:	−20%	+30%	5%	15%	−4%

   a. What was the arithmetic average yearly return?
   b. What was the geometric average yearly return?
   c. Why do the two differ?
   d. Create a unit value series starting at 1.0.
   e. Use this unit value series to calculate the geometric average return between the end of year 2 to the end of year 5.
   f. Calculate the variance and standard deviations of annual returns.
7. You plan to invest for only one year. What types of risks do you face from the following security types:

    a. One-year maturity T-bills?

    b. One-year maturity commercial paper?

    c. Twenty-year maturity Treasury Bonds?

    d. Common stocks?

  8. Why might future inflation not be a concern to some investors?

  9. Sandi Weston is a financial planner. To aid her clients in their investment selections, she has developed the following scenario analysis for returns on various security classes based on potential economic states.

State of Economy in One Year	Probability	*Real Investment Rate of Return if State Occurs*		
		T-Bills	*Corporate Bonds*	*S&P 500 Stocks*
Poor	0.2	5.0%	8.0%	−15.0%
Normal	0.6	3.0%	5.0%	10.0%
Good	0.2	1.0%	0.0%	35.0%

Calculate the expected return, variance, and standard deviation for each investment.

✓ **10.** Between 1969 and 1991, the average annual nominal returns and standard deviations for four asset classes were:

	U.S. T-Bills	*U.S. Govt. Bonds*	*S&P 500*	*EAFE*
Average	7.5%	9.3%	12.0%	15.7%
Standard Deviation	2.5	11.6	16.6	23.0

Assume that these estimates are used to define a continuous normal distribution for each.

    a. What is the probability that each asset class will have a return *below*: −25%, −10%, 0%, 10%?

    b. What is the probability that each asset class will have a return *above*: 0%, 10%, 20%, 30%, 50%?

✓ **11.** Between 1926 and 1991, the average annual nominal return on a U.S. index of small companies was 19.0%. The standard deviation of annual returns was about 40%. Using these values as the mean and standard deviation of a continuous normal distribution, prepare the following percentile distribution.

	Percentile (Probability of Return Below This)						
Percentile	0.05	0.10	0.25	0.50	0.75	0.90	0.95
Return							

  12. What are the important characteristics of a standardized normal density distribution?

CFA ✓ **13.** Assume you invested in an asset for two years. The first year you earned a 15% return, and the second year you earned a *negative* 10% return. What was your annual geometric return?

    a. 1.7%

    b. 2.5%

    c. 3.5%

    d. 5.0%

14. Assume you observe the following nominal yearly returns on two security indexes:

Year:	1	2	3	4	5
T-Bills	4%	4%	5%	6%	4%
Russell 2500	−20%	15%	30%	5%	−10%

Calculate the average return and standard deviation of the following portfolio combination. (Note: A minus sign refers to short selling.)

Portfolio	A	B	C	D	E	F
Percent in T-Bills	100.00%	75.00%	50.00%	25.00%	0.00%	−25.00%
Percent in Russell 2500	0.00%	25.00%	50.00%	75.00%	100.00%	125.00%

DATAFILE ANALYSIS

In previous datafile analyses, you dealt with historical investment risk by calculating minimum and maximum returns. Beginning with this chapter, investment risk will be proxied by the standard deviation of returns. In the analysis below, you will examine two important investment principles: the benefits of asset diversification and risk management by adjusting asset allocation. You will also examine the creation of unit value series and the difference between arithmetic and geometric average returns. You can use any of the following datafiles to conduct these analysis: RTNSYRLY, RTNSQTLY, or RTNSMNLY.

1. *Diversification Across Asset Classes.* Access one of the returns datafiles and identify the return series for the S&P 500 and the EAFE index. EAFE returns begin in 1969. In a blank column of the worksheet, calculate the periodic returns available from a portfolio in which 25% is invested in the EAFE index at the start of each period and 75% is invested in the S&P 500. Find the average and standard deviation of this return series. Repeat this exercise for portfolio mixes of 100/0, 50/50, 25/75, and 0/100. What important investment principles do the results document?

2. *Risk and Asset Allocation.* Repeat the analysis above but this time assume portfolios consist of combinations of U.S. T-bills and the S&P 500. What important investment principle do the results document?

3. *Unit Value and Geometric Means.* Use the U.S. T-bill and S&P 500 return data to calculate unit value series (using a base value of 1.00) starting in 1926 and ending in 1992. Interpret the results (notice how much larger the S&P 500 unit value is in 1992 than is true for T-bills). Calculate the arithmetic and geometric average returns. Why do they differ substantially for the S&P 500 but not as dramatically for T-bills?

REFERENCES

A classic work on the relationship between expected inflation and nominal interest rates is:

FISHER, IRVING, *The Theory of Interest: As Determined by Impatience to Spend Income and Opportunity to Invest It*, New York, Augustus M. Kelley, publishers, 1965 (published originally in 1930).

More recent discussion of interest rates include:

FELDSTEIN, MARTIN and OTTO ECKSTEIN, "The Fundamental Determinants of the Interest Rate," *The Review of Economics and Statistics*, November 1970.

FAMA, EUGENE, "Short-Term Interest Rates as Predictors of Inflation," *American Economic Review*, June 1975.

ROSE, A., "Is the Real Interest Rate Stable?" *Journal of Finance*, December 1988.

Interesting studies of the power of diversification include:

BRENNAN, MICHAEL J., "The Optimal Number of Securities in a Risky Asset Portfolio Where There Are Fixed Costs of Transacting: Theory and Some Empirical Results," *Journal of Financial and Quantitative Analysis*, September 1975.

EVANS, JOHN L. and STEPHEN H. ARCHER, "Diversification and the Reduction of Dispersion: An Empirical Analysis," *Journal of Finance*, March 1978.

STATMAN, MEIR, "How Many Stocks Make a Diversified Portfolio?" *Journal of Financial and Quantitative Analysis*, September 1987.

Portfolio Theory

Without doubt, risk is one of the most striking characteristics of the security markets. An ability to understand, measure, and properly manage investment risk is fundamental to any intelligent investor or speculator. Until the mid-1960s the nature of security risk was poorly understood. Investment texts were only able to loosely define types of risk and to note that demanded returns should be commensurate with the risk inherent in a security. Since then a major revolution has occurred in our understanding of investment risk. Today reasonable approaches to risk measurement and management exist. While some major questions remain unanswered, many of the techniques have gained widespread acceptance in the financial markets.

Our discussion of security risk extends over three chapters. In this chapter we focus on risk to the single *individual*. In the two chapters that follow, we expand the discussion to *all* individuals in the security markets and examine how such risk affects equilibrium security prices. Before we begin, though, a general comment is necessary.

The world is complex. It does not operate according to the strict rules of some mechanical model. Throughout the next three chapters, however, we will attempt to impose some order on the complexities which exist. This often requires that we make what appear to be extreme assumptions at various stages. For example, during most of the discussion we will be dealing with a world in which all investors have identical one-period investment horizons. This is clearly not true to reality. But the models that result from this and other assumptions provide some profound investment implications. Thus, in this chapter, which deals with risk to an individual, we will see:

1. What makes a person risk-averse.
2. Why the risk of a portfolio can be reduced by diversification.
3. How the risk of a portfolio that cannot be reduced by diversification can be managed by asset-allocation changes.
4. Why the risk of a single security should not be calculated in the same way as is the risk of the total portfolio.

SOURCE OF RISK AVERSION

At lunch one day your securities broker, Sam, offers to play the following game with you. Broker Sam will toss a coin in the air and, if heads comes up, he will give you $1. However, if tails comes up you will have to pay him $1. He says the game will be played only once. Would you play? Probably. The game is a reasonable way to pass time, offers a little adventure, and, besides, what is $1 worth these days anyway? But what if Sam offers to replay the game (only *once*, he says) with stakes of $5,000? Would you play? If you are like most people, you wouldn't. *Why?*

Although this simple game might seem rather trivial when compared with the complex decisions that investors and speculators face daily, it really isn't. The beauty of Sam's game and the questions—"Would you play?" and "Why?"— is their simplicity. They reduce to simple terms the nature of the problem faced by all speculators and investors. It turns out that if we can determine the conditions under which people are willing to speculate or invest in risky securities (play Sam's game), we are well on our way to understanding the nature of security risk and developing techniques to measure it quantitatively.

Wealth and Utility of Wealth

To explain why people make the decisions they do, economists rely upon the theory of utility maximization. In this section we examine how utility theory leads to the notion of risk aversion and how the concepts of utility theory can be useful in developing quantitative measures of security risk. Utility theory is a way of describing the relative preferences which an individual has for different wealth levels. For example, if the utility of wealth level 2 is greater than the utility of wealth level 1, we can say that wealth level 2 is preferred to wealth level 1. Utility is often described in terms of the psychological satisfaction or pleasure a person receives from a given wealth level. And economists often talk as if they can somehow calibrate the absolute level of someone's utility as consisting of so many *utils*. But thinking of utility in terms of a number of utils of pleasure and happiness is simply a convenient mental device. We cannot measure utility and say, for example, that level 2 provides twice as many utils as level 1. All we can say is that wealth level 2 is preferred to wealth level 1. In fact, we shouldn't even assign the terms *happiness, satisfaction, pleasure,* etc., to utility. Speaking very strictly, we cannot say for certain that one wealth level is more pleasurable or satisfying than another wealth level. We can say only that one wealth level is preferred to another wealth level. Again, *utility analysis is simply a way of describing the relative preferences that an individual has for different wealth levels.*

In Chapter 1 we saw that real goods markets and financial markets are created because they increase the utility that individuals receive from consumption over time. At that point, we limited the discussion to a one-period, risk-free world. Individuals made choices between known levels of consumption that were available in one period, choosing a particular consumption pattern that would maximize the utility received. But the actual problem faced by individuals is different from this in at least two respects. First, people face more than a one-period world. A decision must be made about the pattern of a future consumption stream. Second, future consumption levels are uncertain. Plan as we may, there is no guarantee that the actual consumption stream will be the one expected.

Conceptually at least, utility theory can handle these difficulties. A series of consumption streams can be introduced. For example, $\tilde{C}_1, \tilde{C}_2, \tilde{C}_3, \ldots, \tilde{C}_E$ can refer to *uncertain* levels of consumption in periods 1, 2, 3, . . . as well as an estate C_E left at death.

Instead of maximizing the utility of a known consumption one period hence, people will maximize the utility of a stream of unknown future consumption levels. Symbolically, this is expressed as:

Utility of Lifetime Consumption   Maximize: $U(\tilde{C}_0, \tilde{C}_1, \tilde{C}_2, \tilde{C}_3, \ldots, \tilde{C}_E)$ **(6.1)**

It is at this point that we make the *first assumption* to keep the analysis tractable—that is, that *a single-period world exists*. Decisions are made today which have an uncertain outcome one period hence. This removes the multiperiod terms ($\tilde{C}_2$, $\tilde{C}_3$, etc.) from Equation 6.1. Now the individual wishes to maximize expected utility of consumption at the end of period 1. Since C_1 will be equal to the person's wealth at that time (W_1), the investor's goal can be stated symbolically as Equation 6.1a.

Utility of Expected-Terminal Wealth   Maximize: $E[U(\tilde{C}_1)] = E[U(\tilde{W}_1)]$ **(6.1a)**

There are any number of ways in which differing wealth levels might be preferred, but most economists assume that more wealth is preferred to less. As one's wealth level increases, so does the utility attached to it. Figure 6-1 illustrates three wealth-preference orderings that all show increasing utility with wealth. The solid line represents a constant, or linear, relationship between wealth and the utility attached to it. If wealth doubles, so does utility. For each unit change in wealth, the change in utility remains constant. An incremental $1,000 provides the same amount of additional utility at an initial wealth level of $10,000 as it does at an initial wealth level of $100,000. In the parlance of economics, the solid line depicts a case of *constant marginal utility* of wealth. The dashed curve also shows an increase in utility as wealth increases but illustrates the case of *decreasing marginal utility*. An incremental $1,000 provides less utility to a person with an initial wealth of $100,000 than it would if the same person's initial wealth were $10,000. Finally, the dotted curve illustrates the case of *increasing marginal utility*. An incremental $1,000 provides more utility to a person with an initial

FIGURE 6-1 *Wealth and Utility*

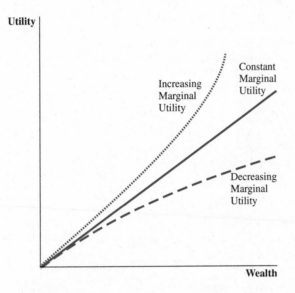

wealth level of $100,000 than it would if the same person's initial wealth were $10,000.[1]

The manner in which people order wealth preferences (the shape of the utility of wealth curve) has profound implications on security pricing and risk measurement. As shown below, people who can be characterized as having constant marginal utility curves are completely indifferent to risk. People with increasing marginal utility curves are risk seekers. And people with decreasing marginal utility curves are risk-averse.

Uncertain Outcomes, Insurance, and Expected Returns

Figure 6-2 plots the utility of wealth curve for Sue Antony. Like most other people, Sue prefers more wealth to less but can be characterized as having decreasing marginal utility. An extra $1 would increase her utility but not by as much as a $1 loss would decrease her utility. Sue is a fairly well-off person with a current wealth (W_0) of $100,000, which provides a corresponding current utility of wealth (U_0).

One day Sue meets with you and your broker for lunch and Sam immediately

---

[1] There is no logical reason for these three curves to be the only possibilities. Friedman-Savage, for example, suggested that over low wealth levels people might exhibit behavior consistent with decreasing marginal utility, but after some point they begin to exhibit behavior consistent with increasing marginal utility. Friedman-Savage used such a curve to explain why people seek particular careers, as well as buy insurance and gamble at the same time.

FIGURE 6-2 *Utility Theory and Risk Aversion*

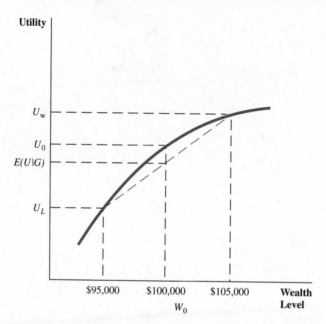

offers to play his usual coin-tossing game. If heads comes up, Sam will pay Sue $5,000. If tails comes up, Sue will pay Sam $5,000. Sue immediately inspects the coin and says: "Nope—this is a fair coin. The odds of winning or losing are identical. Why should I expose myself to a risk without a corresponding return? *My expected utility of wealth if I decide to play the game is lower than my expected utility if I don't play.*"

To see the truth and insight of Sue's statement, refer again to Figure 6-2. Sue has two choices: to play the game or not play the game. If she elects not to play the game, her wealth remains the same and her utility remains at U_0. If she plays the game, her wealth will be either $95,000 or $105,000, with respective utilities of U_L and U_W. Thus, if she decides to play the game with a fair coin, her expected utility would be:

$$E(U|G) = (0.5U_L + 0.5U_W) < U_0$$

Her expected utility from playing the game is less than her current utility, so she won't play.

Given the fair gamble, the reason that expected utility is less than U_0 lies in the fact that Sue has decreasing marginal utility of wealth. The increased satisfaction obtained by a $5,000 increase in her wealth is more than offset by the decreased satisfaction associated with a $5,000 loss. Individuals with decreasing marginal utility are risk-averse.[2]

---

[2] Increasing marginal utility of wealth implies the person is a risk seeker, and constant marginal utility implies risk indifference.

FIGURE 6-3 *Certainty Equivalents and Insurance*

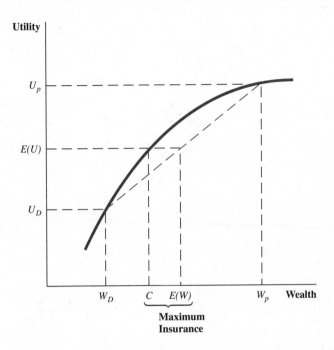

There are some events in life over which we have no control: we aren't given the choice to play the game or not—we are forced to play. For example, assume that most of Sue Antony's wealth is in the form of farm acreage that will either be productive during the next year or suffer little productivity if a drought occurs. Figure 6-3 plots each possibility as either wealth with productivity (W_p) or wealth with a drought (W_D) together with their respective utilities (U_p and U_D). Assume the probability of either is again 50%, so the expected wealth, $E(W)$, lies midway between W_p and W_D. Note that if Sue's wealth level were at point C with no uncertainty at all, her expected utility would be the same as it is now with her uncertain farm acreage. Point C is referred to as the *certainty equivalent* wealth level. Any certain wealth level greater than C would increase her expected utility. As a result, if Sue could *insure* herself against uncertainties (both unfavorable and favorable), the maximum she would be willing to pay is $E(W) - C$. Faced with unavoidable wealth risks, people are willing to buy insurance as long as the cost of the insurance doesn't reduce their expected utility of wealth. This is the basis of the insurance industry as well as of hedging behavior in the securities markets.

When deciding whether to buy or sell securities, however, one consciously accepts risks, and a positive expected return is required in order for the expected utility of wealth not to fall (and, one hopes, to increase). This idea is shown in Figure 6-4. We start by assuming that Sue has fully insured the risks in her wealth, resulting in a current certain wealth of C and corresponding utility of U_C. Now Sam offers to play the game again. If she plays, the outcomes would result in

FIGURE 6-4 *Security Risk and Expected Returns*

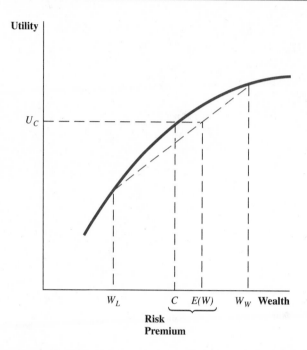

wealth levels W_L and W_W. Clearly, Sue will play only if her expected utility doesn't fall—if her expected wealth is equal to $E(W)$. Sue will demand an expected return to freely take on the chance outcome. Sam can provide this return either by changing the odds of winning and losing or by paying her to play. The form of the return is unimportant. The important fact is that Sue demands a positive expected return simply because she has a decreasing marginal utility of wealth curve.

The return that must be paid to induce people to accept the uncertain outcomes associated with securities is known as the *risk premium*. As can be seen in Figure 6-4, the size of the risk premium will depend upon both the risk aversion of an individual (the slope of his or her utility of wealth curve) and the size of the risk (the distribution of possible wealth levels).

Quadratic Utility

There are many ways of mathematically expressing an individual's utility of wealth. The most widely used approach to date is known as *quadratic utility*. In this case, the utility assigned to a given wealth level is expressed as in Equation 6.2.

**Quadratic
Utility
of Wealth**

$$U(W) = aW - bW^2 \qquad \textbf{(6.2)}$$

Increased wealth leads to increased utility through the aW term. But as wealth becomes larger, these utility increases are dampened by the bW^2 term.

Quadratic utility functions have important portfolio theory implications. Specifically, investors who have quadratic utility of wealth functions will make their portfolio selection based solely on two variables: (1) the expected end-of-period wealth and (2) the standard deviation of end-of-period wealth. If a portfolio's rate of return is defined as end-of-period wealth divided by beginning wealth, then the same can be said about portfolio returns! *Quadratic utility functions imply that investors will base their portfolio selection decisions on the portfolio's expected return and standard deviation of return.* This is the *economic* justification for using return standard deviations as the risk proxy.

MEASURING PORTFOLIO RISK

When analyzing investment risks, we must start with the investor's total portfolio. While risks and returns on individual securities are clearly important, it is the individual's wealth level, or portfolio of *all* holdings, which is of primary concern. For example, assume that you own stock in two beer companies. If one firm improves its market share and earnings at the expense of the other, your total portfolio value might not change. The stock price increase in one firm is exactly offset by the stock price decline in the other. On net, the market value of your portfolio might remain the same.

This is a crucial point. The investor's major concern is with the risk to his or her total wealth. Individual stocks must be considered in relationship to other stocks in the portfolio and are risky only to the extent to which they add risk to the total portfolio. It is from the viewpoint of the portfolio that individual stocks are judged risky. Thus, we start our review of risk at the portfolio level.

Alternative Risk Measures

Returning to Figure 6-4, we can see that the greater the dispersion of possible wealth outcomes, the greater the required risk premium. For example, if another risky venture were to have outcomes more widely dispersed than the W_L and W_W levels, a greater risk premium would be required. So if the investor's utility curve remains fixed, risk must be related to dispersion of possible outcomes.

For illustrative purposes, let us assume we are interested in the risk of a portfolio patterned after the S&P 500. It might or might not be the ''best'' portfolio to own and, in practice, people have a variety of portfolios which differ in relative degrees from the S&P 500 Index. But because it is well known and often emulated, we use it as an illustration. Past yearly real (after inflation) rates of return on the S&P 500 are shown in Table 6-1. We will use real returns as opposed to nominal returns since they are a better measure of changes in people's true wealth levels.

Numerous statistical measures can be used to assess the dispersion of return outcomes and, thus, proxy risk. These include the following:

TABLE 6-1 *Historical Real Returns on the S&P 500 Index: 1962–1991*

Year	Real Return	Year	Real Return
1962	− 9.94%	1977	− 13.95%
1963	21.12%	1978	− 2.46%
1964	15.30%	1979	5.10%
1965	10.52%	1980	20.00%
1966	− 13.40%	1981	− 13.85%
1967	20.95%	1982	17.54%
1968	6.36%	1983	18.71%
1969	− 14.59%	1984	2.25%
1970	− 1.45%	1985	28.40%
1971	10.96%	1986	17.33%
1972	15.56%	1987	0.82%
1973	− 23.45%	1988	12.39%
1974	− 38.66%	1989	26.85%
1975	30.20%	1990	− 9.27%
1976	19.03%	1991	27.31%

1. *Range:* the high outcome less the low outcome. If the maximum possible return on a portfolio is 25% and the lowest possible return is − 10%, the range would be 35%. The difficulties of using range as a risk proxy are that it doesn't consider returns between the extremes and gives no weight to the likelihood of one outcome versus another. The range of returns on the S&P 500 as shown in Table 6-1 was 68.86% and occurred between 1974 and 1975.

2. *Mean absolute deviation:* the average absolute difference between the possible returns on a portfolio and its expected return. Although this might be a reasonable proxy for a portfolio's risk, it is statistically quite difficult to use. In particular, there is no way of easily capturing the effects of correlation among security returns. The mean absolute deviation of S&P 500 returns was 14.2%.

3. *Probability of negative return:* the percentage of the time that returns are less than zero. While intuitively pleasing, this measure doesn't fully address all aspects of risk. For example, returns between 0 and the expected return are neglected. In addition, uncertain returns greater than the expected returns are still uncertain and should be accounted for. Finally, it is difficult to capture the effects of correlations among security returns. Of the 30 years reported in Table 6-1, there were 10 years with less than a zero return. Thus, in 33% of all years, returns on this portfolio were negative.

4. *Semivariance:* the statistical measure of variance of returns below the expected return. Semivariance does not consider uncertainty of returns larger than the expected return and also makes it difficult to capture the effects of correlations between security returns. Semivariance measures are complex equations and, since we will not be using them, we will not illustrate them.

5. *Standard deviation:* the most common measure of portfolio risk. As discussed in the previous chapter, the standard deviation is the square root of variance. Variance is the weighted average squared deviation from the mean. The continuous return distributions for two portfolios, *A* and *B*, are shown in Figure

FIGURE 6-5 *Portfolio Return Distributions*

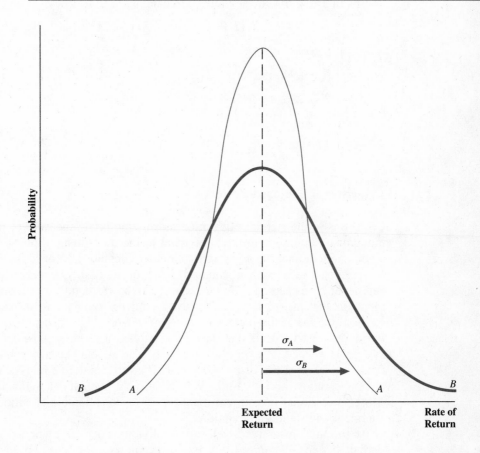

6-5. Both have the same expected return, but the return standard deviation of *B* is larger and thus *B* is more risky. Also, because *A* has the same expected return as *B* but less risk, portfolio *A* is said to *dominate* portfolio *B*.

As shown in Chapter 5, the average returns, variances and standard deviations of *past* returns are calculated as follows:

Average Return
$$\overline{R} = \left(\sum_{t=1}^{N} R_t \right) \div N \tag{6.3}$$

Variance of Returns
$$\sigma^2 = \left[\sum_{t=1}^{N} (R_t - \overline{R})^2 \right] \div (N - 1) \tag{6.4}$$

Standard Deviation
$$\sigma = [\sigma^2]^{1/2} \tag{6.5}$$

where R_t is the return in period t and there are N periods. When applied to the returns in Table 6-1, these values are calculated as follows:

$$\overline{R} = (-9.94 + 21.12 + \ldots + 27.31) \div 30$$

$$= 6.20\%$$

$$\sigma^2 = [(-9.94 - 6.2)^2 + (21.12 - 6.2)^2 + \ldots + (27.31 - 6.2)^2] \div (30 - 1)$$

$$= 296.29\%$$

$$\sigma = (296.29)^{1/2}$$

$$= 17.21\%$$

Criticisms of Standard Deviation

Criticisms of the standard deviation as an appropriate measure of risk have been numerous, ranging from the superficial to the more insightful. At the superficial level, one will hear the argument: "Standard deviation? Nonsense! No one on the Street even knows what a standard deviation is. Risk is a qualitative feel which can never be measured." True, ex ante risk assessment requires subjective judgment on the analyst's part. But this is no reason why it shouldn't be stated explicitly. Seat-of-the-pants decisions may work well in a noncomplex setting, but as alternative decisions become complex, a more sophisticated accounting system is needed. As for the comment that no one knows what the standard deviation is, there was also a time when P/E ratios, internal rates of return, burden coverage ratios, and so forth, were relatively sophisticated financial concepts. Most professional investment managers give considerable attention to risk measurement and standard deviation.

At a more substantive level, some individuals question whether portfolio standard deviations by themselves are adequate measures of risk. These people believe that if rates of return are distributed in a skewed fashion, more statistical information is needed. A skewed distribution is one which is not symmetric; more observations lie in one tail of the distribution than in the other. For example, in Figure 6-6 distribution A is positively skewed, distribution B is symmetric, and distribution C is negatively skewed. Assuming that the expected returns and standard deviations of each distribution are equal, our theory so far says the investor would be indifferent among the three. However, if skewness does matter, then all other things being equal, positive skewness would be preferred.

The importance of skewness remains unresolved. For example, various studies have shown that statistical measures of skewness are quite sensitive to the time period over which data are collected. However, Arditti has presented empirical evidence suggesting that investors prefer positive skewness. In fact, simple logic suggests that future wealth must be positively skewed, since wealth cannot fall below zero but the potential for increase in one's wealth is unlimited. The potential for being at either the lower or upper wealth extremes increases as (1) more-risky securities are purchased and (2) the investment time horizon increases.

A reasonable argument can be made that retains the fundamental importance

FIGURE 6-6 *Illustration of Skewed Return Distributions*

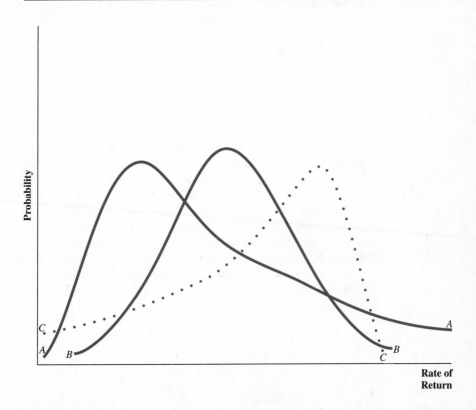

of expected returns and standard deviations, even if the investor faces a long investment horizon and thus significantly skewed terminal portfolio values. If people were forced to hold a single portfolio to some anticipated horizon date, then positive skewness would be large and probably important in the investment decision. But if individuals have the ability to *continuously* rebalance their portfolio holdings, then expected portfolio return and standard deviations dominate any short-term skewness that might exist.

This argument is based on the *ability to continuously rebalance.* If prices move dramatically before a rebalancing trade is possible (such as Black Monday in 1987) or if it takes time before the individual can actually decide whether to rebalance, then skewness may be important.

It is time to make our *second major assumption—the standard deviation of portfolio returns is the proper measure of portfolio risk.*

DIVERSIFICATION

Diversification is the key to effective risk management. Through proper diversification, risk exposure can be minimized without affecting expected portfolio returns. Diversification can be thought of in two ways: *naive diversification* and *efficient diversification*. Naive diversification is appropriate only if one is unable to distinguish between the expected returns and risks of various securities. This is probably not true in reality. Yet, the extent to which risk can be reduced by such a simple rule speaks to the power of diversification.

Naive Diversification

Naive diversification is random diversification, the purchase of a large number of securities without regard to industry classification, expected returns, etcetera. For example, assume you have a list of all stocks contained in the S&P 500 and attach the list to a dart board. One way to select a naively diversified portfolio would be to throw darts at the listing (assuming you are a poor dart player so that selection is indeed random). If you desire a portfolio of 20 stocks, you would throw 20 darts and invest an equal dollar amount in each (unless you're a really bad dart player and some of your tosses totally miss the board).

Figure 6-7 displays the results when such a strategy is applied to stocks contained in the S&P 500. The horizontal axis shows the number of stocks in the randomly selected portfolio and the vertical axis shows the average standard

FIGURE 6-7 *Risk And Naive Diversification Using Real S&P 500 Returns 1926–1991*

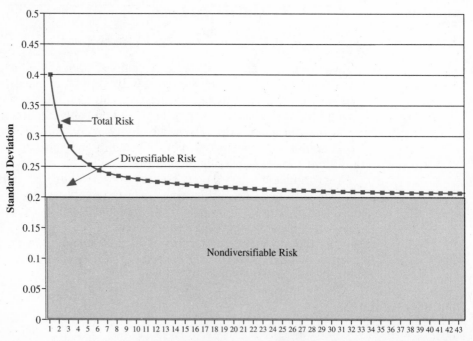

Number of Stocks in Portfolio

deviation (of annualized return) which results from a portfolio of a given size. When only one stock is held, the portfolio standard deviation is identical to the standard deviation of the average stock which was reported above. However, as additional stocks are held, σ_p falls substantially. Reductions in σ_p caused by adding the first few stocks to the portfolio are dramatic, whereas the marginal risk reduction of adding a new stock to a larger portfolio appears to be small. Although the marginal reduction in risk decreases as the portfolio size increases, adding one more stock to any portfolio will (on average) continue to reduce the portfolio risk.

Some care should be given to the interpretation of Figure 6-7. The reductions in risk that are shown to result from randomly increasing the number of securities are the *average* results over many computer simulations. The results are never exactly as shown. The variability is greatest when few securities are held, whereas the outcomes for large portfolios (those with more than 50 stocks) are relatively close to the curve shown. In sum, for the *average* person the results will be as shown in Figure 6-7, but any single person may experience little or no risk reduction until a large number of stocks are held.

Another way to illustrate the risk reduction associated with diversification is depicted in Figure 6-8. The data used to generate the plot was the same as those used in Figure 6-7. The solid line running through the middle of the figure is the average portfolio return earned for each portfolio size. As you can see, average returns are unaffected by the number of securities held. *Diversification, by itself, will not reduce past average returns or future expected returns.* But the two curves surrounding the average return line represent the average plus and minus one

FIGURE 6-8 *Yearly Return and Naive Diversification Using S&P 500 Real Stock Returns*

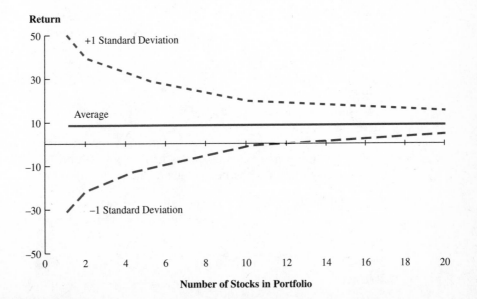

Number of Stocks in Portfolio

standard deviation. Their narrowing as a portfolio grows in size shows, again, the potential risk reduction.

Systematic and Unsystematic Risk. Before we move into the mathematics of why diversification works, it is a good time to point out two concepts that will be important throughout the rest of the book and that can be seen in the results of naive diversification.

1. Some risk cannot be eliminated by diversification. There is an underlying volatility of returns that is *systematic* to all risky securities. Diversification cannot eliminate this *systematic risk*. It can only eliminate return uncertainties that are unique to individual securities—*unsystematic risk*.
2. Individual securities have differing amounts of this nondiversifiable, systematic risk.

Systematic risk is often referred to as *market risk* or nondiversifiable risk—uncertainties about returns that affect all securities. It is created by the sensitivity of a security's return to broad economic forces such as inflation, economic growth, changes in interest rates, and world political conditions. Systematic risk is commonly measured by a variable discussed later in the chapter, Beta.

Unsystematic risk is often referred to as *firm unique risk*—uncertainties about returns on one firm that can be offset by holding securities of other firms in the portfolio. For example, a labor strike at one firm might reduce its profits but lead to higher profits at other firms.

When and Why Diversification Reduces Risk

Why does diversification work? Does it always reduce risk? What effect does it have on expected portfolio returns? To answer these questions, we need to understand how individual securities held in a portfolio determine the expected return and standard deviation of the total portfolio. To minimize needless mathematics so that we can focus on the economic intuition, we will deal with two securities. Call these stocks A and B.

Assume that X_A and X_B are the percentages invested in stocks A and B. Since these are the only investments held, $X_A + X_B = 1.0$.

The expected return for the total portfolio is equal to the *weighted average* of the expected returns of the securities held in a portfolio. The weight applied to each security is simply the percentage of the portfolio invested in the security.

Expected Portfolio Return = Weighted average of expected returns on securities held in the portfolio

Expected Portfolio Return
$$E(R_p) = X_A E(R_A) + X_B E(R_B) \qquad \textbf{(6.6)}$$

Now *suppose* that the standard deviation were also a weighted average of the individual stock standard deviations. *It is not*! But this assumption gets to the heart of the diversification issue. If this were true, then:

Portfolio Standard Deviation $= \sigma_p = X_A \sigma_A + X_B \sigma_B$

and

Portfolio Variance $\qquad = \sigma^2_p = (X_A \sigma_A + X_B \sigma_B)^2$

$$= X^2_A \sigma^2_A + X^2_B \sigma^2_B + 2 X_A X_B \sigma_A \sigma_B$$

Except in a very special case, these equations are *not true*. The error lies in the far right portion of the variance equation where σ_A and σ_B are multiplied. This term is intended to reflect the return interaction between the securities. But to do this correctly, the σ_A and σ_B must be multiplied by the extent to which the security returns are correlated. This is known as the correlation coefficient.

Defining r_{AB} as the correlation coefficient for stocks A and B, the *correct equations* for portfolio variance and standard deviation are:

Variance = Weighted Variances + Weighted Covariances

**Two Security
Portfolio Variance** $\qquad \sigma^2_p = X^2_A \sigma^2_A + X^2_B \sigma^2_B + 2X_A X_B[\sigma_A \sigma_B r_{AB}]$ **(6.7a)**

**Two Security
Portfolio Standard** $\qquad\qquad \sigma_p = [\sigma^2_p]^{1/2}$ **(6.7b)**
Deviation

The term $\sigma_A \sigma_B r_{AB}$ is known as the *covariance* between stock A and B. Notice that it is determined in part by the correlation coefficient. The maximum that two securities can be correlated is $+1.0$ (perfect positive correlation) and the minimum is -1.0 (perfect negative correlation). Portfolio variance and standard deviation are the greatest when $r = +1.0$. Also notice that if $r = +1.0$ the portfolio standard deviation is a weighted average of the individual security standard deviation.

Real securities, however, rarely have returns that are perfectly correlated. *And whenever the correlation coefficient is less than $+1.0$, the portfolio standard deviation is less than the weighted average of the security standard deviations.* Individual security risks are offsetting. The three panels in Figure 6-9 illustrate various degrees of correlation. In panel A, returns on stocks i and j always move in the same direction. Stock i is twice as volatile as stock j and thus has the larger standard deviation. Nonetheless, returns on the stocks are perfectly correlated, $r = +1.0$. In panel B, a relationship between the returns on i and j doesn't exist. Returns on each are totally uncorrelated, $r = 0.0$. In panel C, the returns consistently move counter to each other. They are perfectly inversely correlated, $r = -1.0$.

A Simple Example. Assume two stocks have identical expected returns of 12% and standard deviations of 40%. The portfolio risk of a combination of the two

FIGURE 6-9 *Illustrations of Various Correlation Coefficients*

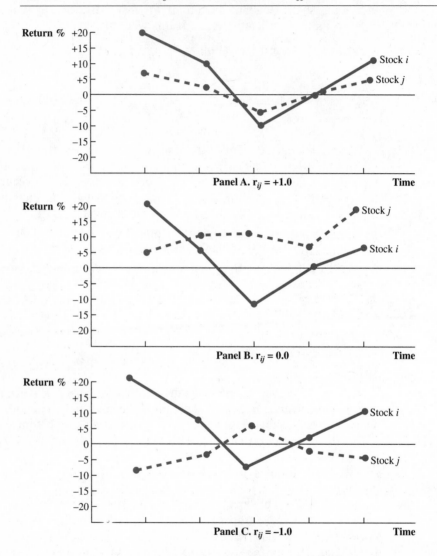

would depend on the percentage invested in each and their return correlation. For example, the data shown in Table 6-2 is based on a correlation coefficient equal to 0.0 and varying combinations of the stocks. The expected portfolio return, of course, is unaffected by the combination chosen. In contrast, portfolio risk is reduced when some amount of both stocks are held. Given the data in this example (zero correlation and identical standard deviations), the minimum risk portfolio consists of an equal investment in each stock.

The minimum risk portfolio given this data is a 50/50 portfolio of the two stocks. Let's examine the minimum portfolio risk for various correlation coeffi-

TABLE 6-2 *Two Stock Portfolio Risk Correlation Coefficient Equal to 0.0*

Percentage Invested in:		Portfolio	
A	B	Expected Return	Standard Deviation
100	0	12%	40.0%
80	20	12	33.0
60	40	12	28.8
50	50	12	28.3
40	60	12	28.8
20	80	12	33.0
0	100	12	40.0

cients. This is shown in panel A of Figure 6-10. As the correlation coefficient declines, so too does the portfolio risk. In fact, *portfolio risk can be eliminated by holding only two assets if their returns are perfectly negatively correlated.* Unfortunately, this simply does not happen with actual securities.

But even if portfolio risk cannot be eliminated by finding two securities with -1.0 correlation, it can be reduced by judicious diversification. In fact, panel A in Figure 6-10 understates the potential for diversification because it deals only with two stocks. What if we had a large number of securities with expected returns and standard deviations identical to stocks A and B. If we invested an equal amount in each security, portfolio risk would *move toward* the points shown in panel B of Figure 6-10. (The points shown are minimum risk limits as the number of securities increase.)

As before, if their returns are all perfectly correlated, diversification does not reduce risk. Notice, however, that risk can theoretically be eliminated if security return correlations are equal to zero. Like a -1.0 correlation, this is not the case for most stocks. Returns on actual stocks typically have correlation coefficients between 0.3 and 0.5.

Another Example. Assume now that the expected returns and standard deviations on stocks A and B differ. Specifically $E(R_A) = 15\%$, $E(R_B) = 10\%$, $\sigma_A = 40\%$, and $\sigma_B = 30\%$. Figure 6-11 shows the risk-return combinations for various correlation coefficients. As the correlation coefficient declines, a lower level of risk is incurred for a given expected return; the risk-return line bends to the left.

Two concepts are illustrated in Figure 6-11. First, to reduce the risk of a portfolio, you should try to identify securities whose returns have a low correlation with the current portfolio. This concept is the motivation for why many investors diversify beyond their traditional holdings of U.S. stocks and bonds into holdings of real estate, non-U.S. stocks, and non-U.S. bonds. Second, as you diversify across additional assets, the expected return might change. For example, assume you start with 100% invested in stock A. As you diversify into B, the expected portfolio return falls. We will see how you can retain the expected return on stock A but still reduce risk by diversifying into B later in the chapter when we add a risk-free security to the portfolio.

FIGURE 6-10 *Effects of Correlation on Portfolio Risk*

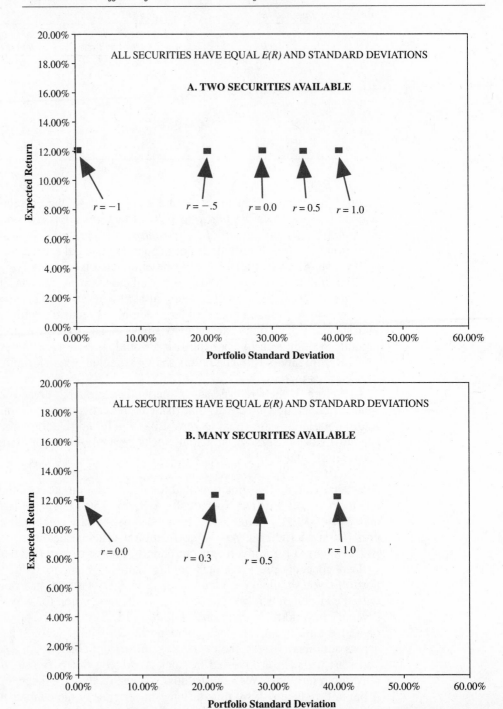

FIGURE 6-11 *Effects of Correlation on Portfolio Risk Different* E(R) *and Standard Deviations*

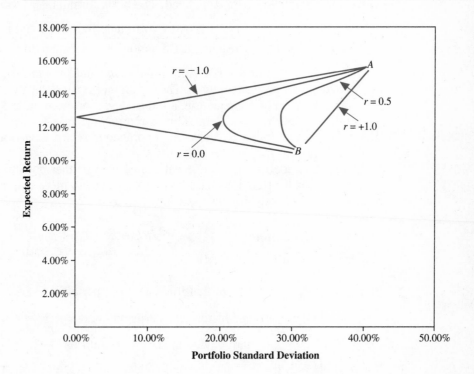

The Minimum Risk Portfolio. When only two securities are being considered, the following formula can be used to find the percentage to invest in the first security, x_A, and the second, x_B, which results in the least risk:

Minimum Risk Portfolio

$$x_A = \frac{\sigma_B^2 - \sigma_A\,\sigma_B\,r_{AB}}{\sigma_A^2 + \sigma_B^2 - 2\,(\sigma_A\sigma_B r_{AB})}$$

(6.8)

$$x_B = 1.0 - x_1$$

For example, if we use the expected returns and standard deviations on stocks *A* and *B* above and assume that the correlation coefficient is 0.5, then the percentage investment in each that will result in minimum risk is calculated as follows:

$$x_A = \frac{[0.3^2 - (0.3)(0.4)(0.5)]}{0.4^2 + 0.3^2 - 2(0.3)(0.4)(0.5)}$$

$$= 0.23$$

$$x_B = 1.0 - 0.23 = 0.77$$

Calculating Correlation Coefficients. Because security correlation determines the extent to which diversification works, it is important that we understand how correlation coefficients are calculated. The basic formula is as follows:

$$\frac{\text{Correlation}}{\text{Between } i \text{ and } j} = \frac{\text{Covariance Between } i \text{ and } j}{(\text{Standard Deviation of } i) * (\text{Standard Deviation of } j)}$$

The standard deviations of securities i and j are calculated in the same manner as we have done for portfolio returns. The covariance is a modification of the variance equation. In the variance equation, a return deviation from the mean is *multiplied by itself*. In the covariance equation, a return deviation for security i from the mean of i is multiplied by the contemporaneous return deviation for security j from the mean of j.

Correlation coefficients can be calculated using either potential future returns or past returns. Correlations based on past returns are more commonly used. The correlation of historical returns is calculated as:

Ex Post Correlation Coefficient
$$r_{ij} = \frac{\sum_{t=1}^{N}(R_{it} - \overline{R}_i)(R_{jt} - \overline{R}_j)/N-1}{\sigma_i \sigma_j} \tag{6.9}$$

where: R_{it}, R_{jt} = returns on securities i and j in period t, where $t = 1$ to N

$\overline{R}_i$, $\overline{R}_j$ = average historical returns on i and j

σ_i, σ_j = standard deviations of i and j returns

In Table 6-3, the correlation coefficient for the hypothetical stocks I and J is calculated. In this case, the ex post correlation coefficient is 0.725, suggesting a positive correlation between the two stocks' returns.

Efficient Diversification

Naive diversification involves the random selection of securities. If N securities are bought, then $1/N$ of the portfolio is invested in each security. *Naive diversification is appropriate only if the investor is unable to distinguish between security expected returns, standard deviations, or correlation coefficients.* This, of course, is rarely the case. For example, it is quite easy to characterize securities by stock versus bond, industry, size of firm, dividend yield, domestic versus foreign, etcetera. So instead of blindly choosing N securities from all that exist, most investors attempt to balance portfolio holding across various security categories.

Efficient diversification improves the process even further by identifying the minimum risk portfolio for any feasible expected return.

The Markowitz Model. The concept of efficient diversification was originally developed by Harry Markowitz in the late 1950s. His insights into defining and managing risk are milestones in the investment literature and he is often referred

TABLE 6-3 *Calculation of the Correlation Coefficient*

	Return on Stock			Return on Stock	
Period	*I*	*J*	*Period*	*I*	*J*
1	10%	12%	5	3%	5%
2	8%	−4%	6	12%	9%
3	−10%	−1%	7	−5%	1%
4	20%	25%	8	2%	−7%

Step 1: Find the average returns:

$\overline{R_i} = [0.10 + 0.08 \ldots - 0.05 + 0.02]/8 = 0.05$

$\overline{R_j} = [0.12 - 0.04 \ldots + 0.01 - 0.07]/8 = 0.05$

Step 2: Find the ex post standard deviations:

$\sigma_i = \sqrt{[(0.10 - 0.05)^2 + (-0.08 - 0.05)^2 \ldots + (0.02 - 0.05)^2]/(8-1)} = 0.0961$

$\sigma_j = \sqrt{[(0.12 - 0.05)^2 + (-0.04 - 0.05)^2 \ldots + (-0.07 - 0.05)^2]/(8-1)} = 0.1029$

Step 3: Find the covariance of returns:

Covariance $= [(0.10 - 0.05)(0.12 - 0.05) + (0.08 - 0.05)(-0.04 - 0.05)$
$+ \ldots + (0.02 - 0.05)(-0.07 - 0.05)]/(8-1) = 0.007171$

Step 4: Find the ex post correlation coefficient:

$r_{ij} = \dfrac{0.007171}{(0.0961)(0.1029)} = 0.725$

to as the father of modern portfolio theory. In fact, the acronym MPT (for modern portfolio theory) is widely used among professional investors. Markowitz received the 1990 Nobel Prize in Economics for his contributions.

Markowitz showed that, if an analyst can develop estimates of expected security returns, standard deviations and correlation coefficients, then the following equations can be solved by a computer program:

Minimize Portfolio Risk

$$\sigma_p = \left[\sum_{i=1}^{N} X_i^2 \sigma_i^2 + \sum_{\substack{i=1 \\ i \neq j}}^{N} \sum_{j=1}^{N} X_i X_j \sigma_i \sigma_j r_{ij} \right]^{1/2} \quad \textbf{(6.10a)}$$

Subject to

A Minimum Stated Expected Return

$$R^* \leq E(R_p) = \sum_{i=1}^{N} X_i E(R_i) \quad \textbf{(6.10b)}$$

The concept of an efficient frontier is shown graphically in panel A of Figure 6-12. The line between stock *A* and stock *B* represents the risk-return combinations for the securities in our previous example (assuming $r_{AB} = 0.5$). The other dots in the figure represent standard deviations and expected returns on other securities. The heavy curve represents the minimum risk portfolio for a given level of risk considering all securities. This is known as the efficient frontier.

There are an infinite number of portfolios that lie on the efficient frontier, simply because there are an infinite number of ways to combine any two portfolios.

FIGURE 6-12 *The Efficient Frontier of Risky Assets*

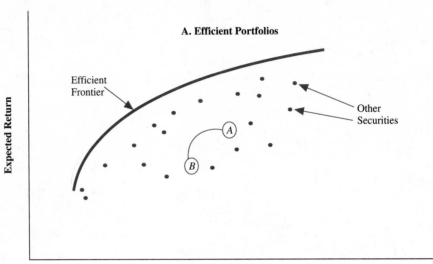

A. Efficient Portfolios

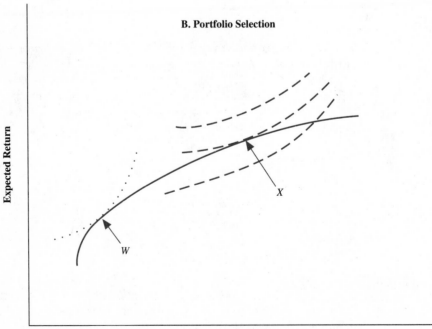

B. Portfolio Selection

The portfolio that an investor selects will depend on his or her risk tolerance. (See panel B.) The dashed curves represent an investor's indifference curves. All points along any one curve provide a given level of utility; the higher the curve, the greater the utility. The slope represents the change in expected return that is required for a small increase in risk. The investor will select the portfolio that is tangent to the highest possible indifference curve. At that point, the risk-return trade-off provided by the indifference portfolio is equal to the trade-off the investor demands. For an individual with the dashed utility curves, this is shown as portfolio X. The dotted curve represents an indifference curve for a more risk-averse investor. We can tell that this investor is more risk-averse because the slope of the curve is steeper than for the other investor. This less-risk-tolerant investor selects portfolio W.

Efficient Asset Class Diversification. When Markowitz first developed the concept of efficient diversification, he expected that it would be applied to the selection of individual securities. However, when this is done, the number of required data inputs are extremely large. As a practical tool, the model is rarely applied to the selection of individual securities. However, it is widely used by sophisticated investors when they are deciding what aggregate asset classes to own and in what proportions. In this section, we review how this is done.

The process starts by identifying various asset classes to be considered. We will use the five classes shown in Table 6-4. These consist of three U.S. security indexes, the European Australian Far East Index, and a U.S. commercial real estate index known as PRISA (Prudential Real Estate Income Separate Account). Also shown in Table 6-4 are average annual *real* returns, standard deviations, and correlation coefficients for each asset class. Although some investors would be interested in nominal returns, most are more concerned about real increases in their wealth. Thus, only real returns are analyzed here. The returns are those that a U.S. investor would have earned. Non-U.S. investors would have experienced different returns due to different currency exchange rates.

TABLE 6-4 *Illustration of Asset Class Selection Historical Real Return Information*

	T-bills	U.S. Govt.	S&P 500	EAFE	PRISA
1926–1990:					
Average Real Return	0.47	1.64	8.90	NA	NA
Standard Deviation	4.49	10.30	21.24	NA	NA
1969–1990:					
Average	1.33	2.52	4.88	9.57	9.03
Standard Deviation	3.03	13.72	17.73	25.06	7.06
Correlation Coefficients (1969–1990):					
T-bills	1.00				
U.S. Govt.	0.67	1.00			
S&P 500	0.40	0.54	1.00		
EAFE	0.27	0.37	0.67	1.00	
PRISA	0.07	0.35	0.12	0.03	1.00

Average annual real returns ranged from as low as 0.47% on U.S. T-bills to 9.57% for the EAFE index. Of course, greater average yearly returns came at the cost of increased yearly return volatility. For example, the standard deviation of yearly real T-bill returns was only 4.49%, whereas the EAFE index had a standard deviation of about 25%. Correlation coefficients ranged from close to 0.0 to almost 0.7.

The next step is to develop expectations of what you believe these variables will be in the future. Historical relationships provide a reasonable basis for such forecasts but often require subjective adjustments. For example, the small real return on T-bills is due in large part to a Federal Reserve policy during the Depression and World War II of ''pegging'' the interest rate at artificially low levels of as well as large unexpected inflation in the United States during the 1970s. Due to economic events such as these, reasonable expectations of future relationships can differ from past results. Table 6-5 shows the assumptions used in this exercise.

A variety of computer programs are available that can use the data in Table 6-5 to calculate an efficient frontier. Usually this allows for various constraints on the portfolio. For example, many institutional portfolios are not allowed to short sell securities. Some investors such as endowment funds might have a minimum desired portfolio dividend yield. And other investors might wish to exclude so-called sin stocks, for example, stocks of firms that manufacture or distribute alcohol or tobacco products. In this example, we do not allow short sales.

The efficient frontier generated from the data of Table 6-5 is shown in Figure 6-13. Optimal percentages to invest in each asset class for a given expected return and risk are shown in Table 6-6. Notice that the lowest-risk portfolio does not consist solely of the lowest-risk class but is a combination of both T-bills and a small account of the S&P 500. This is due to the advantages of diversification.

Clearly, a major problem in creating an efficient frontier is the development of reasonable input assumptions. Such a problem, however, is not unique to efficient portfolio selection. Virtually all major decisions that individuals and organizations make require uncertain inputs. As you gain an understanding of investment concepts and experience with security return distributions, assumptions such as those in Table 6-5 will become less difficult to make.

TABLE 6-5 *Assumed Future Asset Class Relationships*

	T-bills	*U.S. Govt.*	*S&P 500*	*EAFE*	*PRISA*
Expected Real Return	1.0%	2.0%	7.5%	10.0%	4.0%
Standard Deviation	4.0%	8.0%	18.0%	25.0%	12.0%
Correlation Coefficients					
T-bills	1.00				
U.S. Govt.	0.50	1.00			
S&P 500	0.20	0.40	1.00		
EAFE	0.30	0.30	0.70	1.00	
PRISA	0.50	0.10	0.15	0.20	1.00

FIGURE 6-13 *Illustration of Efficient Diversification Across Asset Classes*

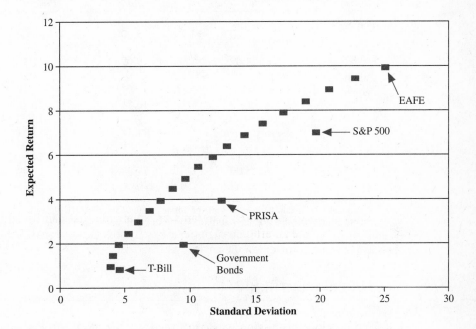

An equally difficult problem is deciding which portfolio on the efficient frontier should be selected. In theory, the answer is easy: select the portfolio that maximizes expected utility. In real life, investors do not specify their utility function or calculate maximum expected utility. Instead, their judgments are more subjective. A device that can help to express potential returns on various portfolios is the percentile distribution. An example, using three portfolios from Table 6-6, is shown in Table 6-7.

TABLE 6-6 *Composition of Selected Optimal Portfolios*

Portfolio	Expected Return	Standard Deviation	Percentage Invested in Asset Classes				
			T-bills	U.S. Govt.	S&P 500	EAFE	PRISA
1	1.03%	4.00%	99.49	—	0.51	—	—
2	2.00	4.69	77.86	3.52	11.21	0.23	7.18
3	3.00	6.11	52.94	9.51	15.40	3.99	18.16
4	4.00	7.82	28.02	15.50	19.58	7.75	29.15
5	5.00	9.67	3.10	21.48	23.77	11.52	40.13
5.5	5.50	10.64	—	15.28	27.40	14.11	43.21
6	6.00	11.68	—	6.03	31.55	16.94	45.58
7	7.00	14.08	—	—	34.94	29.62	35.44
8	8.00	17.18	—	—	35.95	45.69	18.35
9	9.00	20.68	—	—	36.97	61.77	1.26
10	10.00	25.00	—	—	—	100.00	—

TABLE 6-7 *Percentile Return Distributions*

	Portfolio 2	*Portfolio 5*	*Portfolio 8*	
Expected Return	2.00%	5.00%	8.00%	
Standard Deviation	4.69	9.67	17.18	Z-Score Used
Cumulative Percentile				
0.05	− 5.69	− 10.86	− 20.18	− 1.64
0.10	− 4.00	− 7.38	− 13.99	− 1.28
0.25	− 1.14	− 1.48	− 3.51	− 0.67
0.50	2.00	5.00	8.00	0
0.75	5.14	11.48	19.51	0.67
0.90	8.00	17.38	29.99	1.28
0.95	9.69	20.86	36.18	1.64

Returns shown in this table represent the highest return associated with each percentile. For example, there is a 5% chance that the return on Portfolio 2 will be − 5.69% or less.

IMPACTS OF A RISK-FREE RETURN

The previous discussion was concerned solely with portfolios consisting of risky securities. No risk-free securities were considered. We now expand the set of available securities to include such a risk-free asset. When this is done:

1. No longer is there an infinite number of efficient risky portfolios from which one is selected based upon individual risk/return preferences. Instead, a single risky portfolio will dominate all others and will be selected regardless of individual risk/return preferences.
2. The individual achieves a personally suitable combination of risk and return by adjusting the percentage of the portfolio that is invested in risk-free securities.

As a practical matter, many investors do not have access to risk-free securities since they desire real dollar returns. Although nominal risk-free securities are available, their returns after subtracting inflation are uncertain.

As before, the expected return on a portfolio that combines risk-free and risky securities is simply the weighted average of the expected returns on all securities. Assume that you plan to invest 80% of your capital in the S&P 500 and 20% in the risk-free security. If the expected returns on each are $E(R_{SP}) = 12\%$, $RF = 7\%$, then the expected portfolio return is 11.0%:

$$(0.20)\ 7\% + 0.80\ (12\%) = 11\%$$

In general, if $E(R_c)$ represents returns on the *combined* portfolio of risky and risk-free securities, $E(R_p)$ refers to the risky security group, and $X\%$ is invested in the risk-free security, then:

**Expected Return
on Risk-Free and** $\qquad E(R_c) = (X)RF + (1 - X)E(R_p) \qquad$ **(6.11)**
Risky Portfolio

The standard deviation of a combined portfolio is simply the percent invested in risky securities multiplied by the standard deviation of the risky securities. By definition, the variance of returns on RF is zero, and all terms in the standard deviation equation that apply to RF disappear. Using σ_p to represent the risky portfolio's standard deviation, the combined portfolio's risk is:

**Standard Deviation
of Risk-Free and** $\qquad\qquad \sigma_c = (1 - X)\sigma_p \qquad$ **(6.12)**
Risky Portfolio

For example, an 80/20 risky versus risk-free security mix would result in a 16% combined portfolio standard deviation if the risky securities had a 20% standard deviation:

$$0.8 \ (20\%) = 16\%$$

When Equations 6.11 and 6.12 are combined, an interesting result occurs. The relationship between risk and return is linear and equal to:

**Linear Risk/Return
with Risk-Free** $\qquad E(R_c) = RF + \sigma_c \left[\dfrac{E(R_p) - RF}{\sigma_p} \right] \qquad$ **(6.13)**
Securities

Returns expected on portfolios that combine a risk-free security with risky securities come from two sources. First, a risk-free rate is expected to be earned on *both* the risk-free security and the risky set of securities. In addition, a return is earned for bearing risk—a return equal to $[E(R_p) - RF] \div \sigma_p$ for each unit of σ_c. The number of units of σ_c risk incurred depends, of course, on the proportion of funds in the risky securities.

There is no guarantee that the expected return for bearing risk will be positive. That depends totally on the one or more risky securities being evaluated. In a moment we will return to this "risk premium" and see how it might be maximized, but first consider some examples using the following information, which is also plotted in Figure 6-14:

Security	Expected Return	σ
IBM Stock	14%	25%
Risk-Free Security	9%	0

When a 100% investment is made in IBM, the portfolio return is 14%. This 14% comes from two sources: (1) a risk-free return of 9% and (2) a return for bearing risk of 14% − 9% = 5%.

When a 50% investment is made in IBM, risk is half of the 100% investment level and, thus, the return for bearing risk is also half (2.5%):

FIGURE 6-14 *Portfolio Combinations of the Risk-Free Security with a Risky Security*

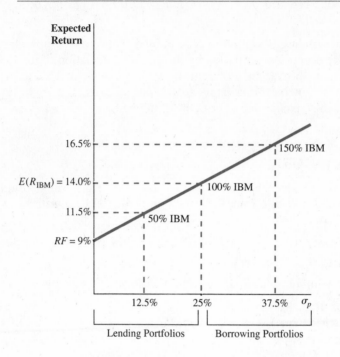

$$E(R_c) = RF + 0.5\,(\sigma_p)\left[\frac{E(R_p) - RF}{\sigma_p}\right]$$

$$= 9.0\% + 12.5\%\,(0.20)$$

$$= 9.0\% + 2.5\% = 11.5\%$$

Portfolios that include some amount of the risk-free security are referred to as *lending portfolios* because a portion of one's money is "lent" to borrowers at the risk-free rate. But in the same way that lending portfolios can be created that reduce expected returns and risk, *borrowing portfolios* can be created that increase risk and expected returns. Borrowing portfolios essentially use *margin* to increase the number of shares that an individual's personal equity can control.

To illustrate, assume you have $10,000 to invest and would prefer a higher return than is expected on IBM in Figure 6-14. You're also willing to accept the higher risk. Consider what would happen if you borrowed $5,000 at the risk-free rate of 9% and used the borrowing plus your personal equity to purchase $15,000 of IBM. Your expected dollar return on IBM shares would be $2,100 ($15,000 × 0.14), and after you pay $450 in interest ($5,000 × 0.09) your net dollar profit would be $1,650. On a $10,000 equity, this is a 16.5% expected return.

The same result can be obtained by using Equation 6.13, if we recognize that borrowing is simply *negative lending:*

$$E(R_c) = RF + \sigma_c \left[\frac{E(R_p) - RF}{\sigma_p} \right]$$

$$= 9\% + 1.5\,(25\%)\,[0.2]$$

$$= 9\% + 7.5\% = 16.5\%$$

On your personal equity, you earn a risk-free 9%. The borrowing also earns 9%, but you must pay that to the people from whom you borrowed, so it is a wash. However, by placing $0.50 in borrowed money into the risky security for each $1.00 of your personal equity, you have magnified your risk exposure by 50%. Thus the expected risk premium increases from 5% to 7.5%. The new expected return is therefore 16.5%. But it comes only with an increase in portfolio standard deviation from 25% to 37.5% (1.5 × 25%).

The Portfolio Separation Theorem. One can combine borrowing and lending with any individual security or portfolio of securities, as displayed in Figure 6-15. In this figure, three lines are shown. The two dashed lines represent risk/return combinations on *RF* combined with IBM and on a portfolio called *O,* which lies on the efficient frontier developed earlier in this chapter. Note that the slope of each line represents the return *expected* to be earned per unit of risk. Clearly, combinations with portfolio *O* are better than combinations with IBM since the slope of the line is greater. However, there is a single portfolio on the efficient frontier that will *maximize* the return earned for bearing risk. This is portfolio *p*,* which lies on the solid line extending from *RF.*

FIGURE 6-15 *Alternative Combinations of Risky Securities with a Risk-Free Security*

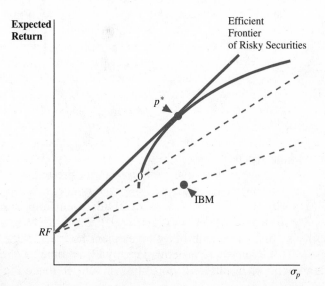

Given the presence of a risk-free rate, two very important implications emerge:

1. *There is a single optimal portfolio of risky securities to own—regardless of the individual's risk preferences.* Different people might disagree on exactly what that optimal portfolio consists of. But for any one individual, there is only one risky portfolio that should be held.

2. *The individual can obtain a desired risk/return profile by combining this optimal risky portfolio with borrowing or lending at RF.* If the risky security portfolio contains more risk than desired, the risk can be reduced by placing a portion of the resources in risk-free securities. If the expected return is too low, the investor should borrow and invest the borrowing in the ideal risky portfolio.

A *separation* now exists between an identification of the ideal risky security portfolio (implication 1) and the selection of an appropriate risk level (implication 2). This is commonly called the *portfolio separation theorem.* The investment decision is now a two-step process: (1) identify the optimal risky security and (2) move along the borrowing-lending line to a personally acceptable risk level.

MEASURING THE RISK OF A SECURITY

Risk and expected return on the *total* portfolio are the two most important features of any investment program. Recognizing this, we have focused almost exclusively on the aggregate portfolio, with no mention of how individual security risk should be defined and measured. Given the benefits of broad diversification, we will assume that the portfolio in which the security is held is well diversified.

The risk of the portfolio can be thought of as a weighted average of the risks of the individual securities in the portfolio. The weights applied to each security are the percentages that the security represents of the total portfolio. Using variance as the measure of risk, this can be stated symbolically as:

Portfolio Variance

$$= \sum_{i=1}^{N} X_i \text{ [Total Risk of Security } i \text{ in Portfolio Now Held]}$$

$$\sigma_p^2 = \sum_{i=1}^{N} X_i \left[X_i \sigma_i^2 + \sum_{\substack{j=1 \\ i \neq j}}^{N} X_j {}^* \text{ Covariance } (i,j) \right]$$

(6.14)

where covariance $(i,j) = \sigma_i \sigma_j r_{ij}$.

Look at the terms in brackets. These represent the risk that security i adds to the portfolio. The first term, $X_i \sigma_i^2$ is very small since, by assuming that this is a diversified portfolio, X_i is small. In a diversified portfolio, a security's standard deviation by itself is relatively unimportant. The next term is a weighted sum of the security's covariance with other investment holdings. This term is not small and represents the ith security's covariance with all other securities held.

Investors who have different portfolios should evaluate the risk of, say, GM differently. For one investor, GM might add significantly to portfolio risk if it were highly correlated with existing portfolio holdings. To another investor, GM might be virtually riskless if it were uncorrelated with existing portfolio holdings. There is no one measure of total security risk that can be used by all investors; it depends upon the particular portfolio held. Only when everyone holds the *same* portfolio will the risk of a given security be identical for everyone.

Relative Security Risk

The measure of *total security risk* (see Equation 6.14) is difficult to interpret. For example, is a total security risk of 0.0058 large or small? To overcome this problem, security risks are often expressed in terms of the risk of the security *relative* to the risk of the total portfolio. Relative security risk is found by dividing total security risk by total portfolio risk:

$$\frac{\text{Relative Risk of}}{\text{Security } i} = \frac{\text{Total Risk of Security } i}{\text{Total Risk of Portfolio}}$$

Symbolically, relative security risk can be expressed as in Equation 6.15:

$$\frac{\text{Relative Risk of}}{\text{Security } i} = \frac{X_i\sigma_i^2}{\sigma_p^2} + \frac{\sum\limits_{j=1}^{N} X_j\sigma_i\sigma_j r_{ij}}{\sigma_p^2} \tag{6.15}$$

In a broadly diversified portfolio, the first term is small. Thus, the risk of security *i* relative to the portfolio in which it is held is calculated as:

**Relative Risk of
Security *i*** $\qquad\qquad = \dfrac{\sigma_i}{\sigma_p} r_{ip}$ $\qquad\qquad$ **(6.16)**
in Portfolio *p*

In a broadly diversified portfolio, the relative risk of a single security is equal to (1) the standard deviation of its returns, (2) divided by the portfolio standard deviation, (3) multiplied by the security's correlation with portfolio returns. This measure of relative security risk is typically referred to as *beta on security i, or* β_i.[3]

Assume that you now own the S&P 500 portfolio we have used throughout the chapter and are considering the addition of a local bank, Fifth Third Bank of Cincinnati. In order to estimate its risk relative to your current portfolio, the following subjective forecasts are made:

---

[3] Beta as calculated in Equation 6.16 depends upon the portfolio of securities now held and will change as the portfolio of securities changes. Betas as reported by investment advisory firms, however, are based upon *one* reference portfolio. While the reference portfolio used varies between advisory services, typically it is some index of aggregate stock market returns, such as the Standard & Poor's Composite Index, the Dow Jones Composite Index, or the NYSE Composite Index.

State of Economy	Probability	Returns on	
		Portfolio	Fifth Third
Good	0.3	20%	14%
Fair	0.4	10%	9%
Poor	0.3	0%	6%

First, the standard deviation of both the S&P 500 portfolio and Fifth Third Bank's potential returns should be found. These will be:

$$\sigma_p = 7.75\% \qquad \sigma_{FT} = 3.13\%$$

Second, the correlation coefficient between the S&P 500 and Fifth Third returns could be found by Equation 6.9:

$$R_{pi} = 0.989$$

Finally, the beta of Fifth Third Bank *relative to your S&P 500 portfolio* can be determined:

$$\beta_{FT} = \frac{3.13}{7.75}(0.989) = 0.40$$

In the context of your portfolio, Fifth Third Bank has much less risk than the average stock now held. For another investor's portfolio this might not be the case. For example, a broadly diversified portfolio of bank stocks may have a beta of 1.0.

SUMMARY

Risk is a dominant characteristic of security investment. Individuals are said to be risk-averse if the pleasure they gain from a $1 increase in wealth is less than the pleasure they lose from a $1 reduction in wealth. By relating the concept of risk aversion to utility theory, we saw that the risk of a security depends upon the possible dispersion of its returns. In turn, the standard deviation was suggested as a reasonable way to quantitatively measure risk.

Risk inherent in the total portfolio is of more direct concern to the investor than are the risks of individual securities. While individual security risks do combine with one another to determine a portfolio's risk level, it is the total portfolio risk that is most crucial. Individual securities should be viewed as bearing a risk to the extent that adding the security to the portfolio changes the portfolio's risk.

The standard deviation of portfolio returns is not simply a weighted average of the standard deviations of the individual securities comprising the portfolio. The effects of differing levels of correlation between security returns must be accounted for. If security returns are perfectly negatively correlated (correlation coefficient = -1.0), diversification with only two securities can totally eliminate portfolio risk. If a large number of uncorrelated securities (correlation coefficient

= 0.0) are available, broad diversification can virtually eliminate portfolio risk. If security returns are perfectly positively correlated (correlation coefficient = +1.0), diversification will provide no risk-reduction advantages. Since security returns generally have a correlation coefficient between 0.0 and +1.0, there are significant advantages to diversification. But in the real world, portfolio risk cannot be totally eliminated. To some extent all security returns are affected by similar events, and this common component of security returns cannot be diversified away.

In a broadly diversified portfolio, the risk of any single security depends upon the standard deviation of the security's returns and the correlation of the security's returns with the returns of the portfolio. Typically, a security's risk *relative* to the risk of the diversified portfolio to which it is added is measured by beta. Beta is calculated as:

$$\beta_i = \frac{\sigma_i}{\sigma_p} r_{ip}$$

where β_i refers to the beta of security i, σ_i and σ_p refer to the standard deviation of returns on the security and the portfolio, respectively, and r_{ip} refers to the correlation coefficient between security i returns and those of the portfolio. Relative risk, or beta, will depend upon the portfolio of securities held. As a result, investors holding different portfolios will evaluate the relative risk of a given stock differently.

Perhaps the best advice that this chapter offers to both investors and speculators is to diversify. Risk-reduction advantages inherent in diversification are significant. That portion of a security's risk that is diversifiable is known as *unsystematic risk,* whereas *systematic risk* refers to the nondiversifiable portion of security risk. Contrasted with naive diversification, efficient diversification models exist that allow one to find a set of different portfolios that minimize portfolio risks for differing levels of expected returns.

REVIEW PROBLEM

Eight quarters of returns are shown below for three securities.

				Percentage Return During Year				
Security	1	2	3	4	5	6	7	8
1	17	7	−4	0	−6	−14	5	11
2	−3	5	11	−3	9	−6	6	5
3	0	11	4	2	3	−1	1	12

a. Find the average return for each.
b. Find the variance of return for each.
c. Find the standard deviation for each.
d. Find the correlation coefficient between 1&2, 1&3, 2&3.
e. At the start of each quarter, you rebalance your portfolio of these three securities to a 1/3 investment in each. What is the expected return, variance and standard deviation of this portfolio?

—Use Equations 6.10a and 6.10b.

—Also do this using the sequence of eight quarterly portfolio returns.

f. What is the average security standard deviation? Why is the portfolio standard deviation smaller?

g. You are considering combinations of the equally weighted portfolio of three risky securities above with a risk-free security which has a known quarterly return equal to 1.0%. Express Equation 6.13.

h. Assume you invest half the portfolio in the risk-free security and the other half in the risky portfolio. What are your expected return and standard deviation?

i. Using Equations 6.14 and 6.16, what is the total risk of security 3 in the portfolio now held and its relative risk?

Solutions

a. $R_1 = (17 + 7 + \ldots + 11) \div 8 = 2$

$R_2 = (-3 + 5 + \ldots + 5) \div 8 = 3$

$R_3 = (0 + 11 + \ldots + 12) \div 8 = 4$

b. $\sigma_1^2 = [(17 - 2)^2 + (7 - 2)^2 + \ldots + (11 - 2)^2] \div (8 - 1) = 100.00$

$\sigma_2^2 = [(-3 - 3)^2 + (5 - 3)^2 + \ldots + (5 - 3)^2] \div (8 - 1) = 38.57$

$\sigma_3^2 = [(0 - 4)^2 + (11 - 4)^2 + \ldots + (12 - 4)^2] \div (8 - 1) = 24.00$

c. $\sigma_1 = (100.00)^{1/2} = 10.0$ $\sigma_2 = (38.57)^{1/2} = 6.21$ $\sigma_3 = (24.00)^{1/2} = 4.90$

d. $r_{12} = \{[(17-2)(-3-3)+(7-2)(5-3)+ \ldots + (11-2)(5-3)] \div (8-1)\} \div (10*6.21) = 0.016$

$r_{13} = \{[(17-2)(0-4) + (7-2)(11-4) + \ldots + (11-2)(12-4)] \div (8-1)\} \div (10*4.90) = 0.379$

$r_{23} = \{[(-3-3)(0-4)+(5-3)(11-4)+ \ldots + (5-3)(12-4)] \div (8-1)\} \div (6.21*4.90) = 0.451$

e. $E(R) = 1/3\,(2) + 1/3\,(3) + 1/3\,(4) = 3$

$\sigma^2 = 1/9(100) + 1/9\,(38.57) + 1/9\,(24)$ sum variances
$+ 2(1/3)(1/3)(10)(6.21)(0.016)$ 2* covariance 1,2
$+ 2(1/3)(1/3)(10)(4.90)(0.379)$ 2* covariance 1,3
$+ 2(1/3)(1/3)(6.21)(4.90)(.451)$ 2* covariance 2,3

$= 25.46$

$\sigma = 5.05$ (say 5)

Using quarterly portfolio returns:

$E(R) = (4.67 + 7.67 + \ldots + 9.33) \div 8 = 3$

$\sigma^2 = [(4.67 - 3)^2 + (7.67 - 3)^2 + \ldots + (9.33 - 3)^2] \div (8 - 1)$

$= 25.46$

$\sigma = 5.05$ (say 5)

f. Average security standard deviation

$$= (10 + 6.21 + 4.9) \div 3$$

$$= 7.04$$

The portfolio standard deviation is lower because security returns were not perfectly correlated.

g. $E(R_c) = 1.0 + \sigma_c [(3 - 1) \div 5]$

h. $\sigma_c = 1/2 (5) = 2.5$

$E(R) = 1.0 + 2.5 (0.4)$

$= 2$

i. Total risk of security 3 in portfolio now held:

$$1/3(24.0) + 1/3(10)(4.9)0.379 + 1/3(6.21)(4.9)0.451$$

$$= 8.0 + 10.765$$

$$= 18.765$$

Relative Risk:
$0.737 = 18.765 \div 25.46$

QUESTIONS AND PROBLEMS

1. Explain why people are willing to purchase insurance and what determines the maximum amount of insurance they will pay for.
2. Why are people risk-averse? How does utility theory suggest that we measure risk?
3. The nominal returns on three international asset classes are shown below for a recent five-year period.

Year	S&P 500	Lehman Govt. Corp	EAFE
1986	18.5%	15.6	69.9
1987	5.2	2.3	24.9
1988	16.8	7.6	28.6
1989	31.5	14.2	10.8
1990	−3.2	8.3	−23.2

   a. Calculate the average return and standard deviation for each.
   b. Calculate the correlation coefficient between each.
   c. What would be the standard deviation of a portfolio that consisted of one-third invested in each (at the start of each year)?
   d. Why is this portfolio standard deviation not equal to the standard deviation of each asset class added together and the sum divided by 3?
4. Jake Leary has managed his own investment portfolio for the past 10 years. He feels he has had reasonable success, but because of the increasing amount of time that he must devote to his business, he is considering placing his funds with an investment

management firm. Being a reasonably intelligent fellow, he calls upon you for advice. Jake initially made a $10,000 investment 10 years ago and has withdrawn all dividends and interest as received. Since then, his yearly performance has been as shown below:

	End of Year									
	1	*2*	*3*	*4*	*5*	*6*	*7*	*8*	*9*	*10*
Portfolio's Value	$11,000	$10,000	$9,000	$11,500	$13,000	$13,000	$14,000	$11,000	$14,000	$15,000
Dividends and Interest	500	500	600	600	400	600	650	600	650	650

a. Calculate the annual rates of return he earned.
b. Calculate the 10-year average return and standard deviation.
c. You gather 10-year data on the following investment management firms:

	10-Year Return	
Firm	*Average*	*Standard Deviation*
A	12%	14%
B	14%	20%
C	8%	20%

Compare Jake's performance with the performance of these three firms.

5. Because ecological problems have recently beset Southeast Phosphorus, Inc., its board of directors have expressed an interest in diversifying the firm's product line through acquisition of another company. Southeast Phosphorus has large mining operations located on the west coast of Florida. After discussions with the firm's investment banking firm, several alternatives seem promising. These include:
   a. Southwest Tin-Mining Corporation, a tin-mining firm located in Texas.
   b. Greenfield Coal Corporation, a coal-mining firm located in Kentucky.
   c. Winn-Dixon Food Marts, a diversified food chain in Florida.
   d. Boston-Mason Foods, a diversified food chain in New England.
   e. Northwest Mining, a major competitor of Southeast Phosphorus, Inc., which mines a substitute product.
   Evaluate the extent to which each of these acquisitions might provide the greatest and least diversification to Southeast Phosphorus. Note: This is a thought question. No *single* correct answer exists; your logic is the important thing.

6. Alan Zaslow holds a well-diversified portfolio of stocks in country A. During the past 10 years, returns on these stocks have averaged +8.0% per year and had a standard deviation of 17.0%. He is unsatisfied with the yearly variability of his portfolio and would like to reduce its risk without affecting overall returns. He approaches you for help in finding an appropriate diversification medium. After a lengthy review of alternatives, you conclude:

   - Future average returns and volatility of returns on his current portfolio will be the same as he has historically experienced.
   - To provide a greater degree of diversification in his portfolio, investments could be made in stocks of the following countries:

Country	Expected Return	Correlation of Returns with Country A	Standard Deviation
B	8%	+1.0	17.0%
C	8%	−1.0	17.0%
D	8%	+0.0	17.0%

a. If Mr. Zaslow invests 50% of his funds in country B and leaves the remainder in country A, would this affect both his expected returns and his risk? Why?

b. If Mr. Zaslow invests 50% of his funds in country C and leaves the remainder in country A, how would this affect both his expected return and his risk? Why?

c. What should he do? Indicate precise portfolio weighting.

✓ 7. Estimates of standard deviations and correlation coefficients for three stocks are:

		Correlation with		
Stock	σ_i	1	2	3
1	8%	1.0		
2	10%	0.5	1.0	
3	12%	0.5	−1.0	1.0

a. If equal investments are made in stocks 1 and 2, what is the standard deviation of the portfolio?

b. If equal investments are made in all three stocks, what is the standard deviation of the portfolio?

c. What percentage of investment in stocks 1 and 3 will minimize portfolio risk? (Hint: See Equation 6.8.)

d. What percentage of investment in stocks 2 and 3 will minimize portfolio risk? Why?

8. Consider a portfolio of three stocks. Calculate the total risk of each stock and the total risk of the portfolio.

	Portfolio		Correlation with		
Stock	Investment	σ_i	A	B	C
A	0.25	10%	1.0	—	—
B	0.40	12%	0.3	1.0	—
C	0.35	15%	0.4	0.6	1.0

Notice that stock C has the largest total risk. Why is this? Do any characteristics of stocks A and B affect the total risk of stock C in this portfolio?

9. Security data follows:

	Expected	Standard	Correlation with		
Security	Return	Deviation	T-bill	Bond	Stock
T-bills	0.04	0.00	1.0		
Bond Fund	0.05	0.08	0.0	1.0	
Stock Fund	0.12	0.15	0.0	0.0	1.0

a. Calculate expected returns and standard deviations on portfolios of the Bond and Stock funds. Consider investments in the Stock fund from 0.0 to 1.0 in increments of 0.1.

b. Does a 100% investment in the Bond fund make sense?

c. What is the optimal portfolio of risky assets given the 4% risk-free rate?

d. Express in an equation the optimal relationship between expected portfolio return and the standard deviation of the portfolio.

e. How would you create a portfolio with an expected return of: 6.6%, 12.32%, or 7.0%?

f. How would you create a portfolio with a standard deviation of 5% or 20%?

10. This chapter deals with naive and efficient diversification.

a. How does efficient diversification compare with naive diversification?

b. What inputs are necessary for efficient diversification?

11. Assume you are considering N stocks. Unfortunately, you are unable to distinguish between them. Your expected return on each is the same. Your standard deviation on each is the same. And you assign the same correlation coefficient for each security pair. What is the optimal percentage to invest in each?

12. Information on three securities follows:

Security	Expected Return	Standard Deviation	Correlation with		
			A	B	C
A	8%	10%	1.0	—	—
B	8%	10%	−1.0	1.0	—
C	15%	20%	0.0	0.0	1.0

Calculate the efficient frontier.

13. It has been mathematically proven that any two portfolios on the efficient frontier can be combined (possibly with negative positions in one portfolio) to create the risk/return values of all other portfolios on the frontier. Why does this make common sense?

Although this is not discussed in the text, it is not too difficult to understand. (Hint: This is true only if the investor is allowed to short sell any asset and use the proceeds to purchase other assets. In that case, a position will always be taken, long or short, in all assets available. No efficient portfolio will exclude an asset.)

14. What is the economic significance of the fact that the optimal portfolio of risky assets is the point on the efficient frontier where the investor's utility curve is exactly tangent?

15. What does the portfolio separation theorem imply about proper investment policy?

16. The risk of a given security is not the same for all investors if they own different security portfolios. Why?

17. Portfolio risk can be measured by the standard deviation of its returns. Why should the risk of an individual security not be measured in the same way?

 18. John Pixel, CFA, has constructed an efficient frontier, shown below, to help him manage his stock portfolio. Pixel's portfolio is indicated by the point P.

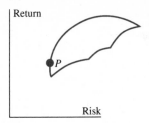

Without lending or borrowing, Pixel could change his portfolio and:
a. both increase returns and reduce risk.
b. increase returns.
c. reduce risk.
d. neither increase returns nor reduce risk.

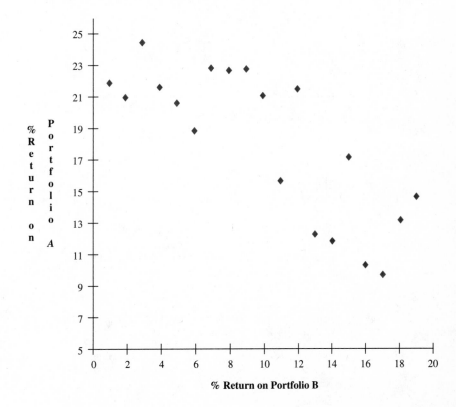

% Return on Portfolio B

19. Based on the scatter plot shown above, the correlation coefficient indicating the relationship between the return on the two portfolios is *closest* to:
  a. +1.0
  b. +0.9
  c. −0.9
  d. −1.0

20. The operating cash flows for ABEX are graphed below.

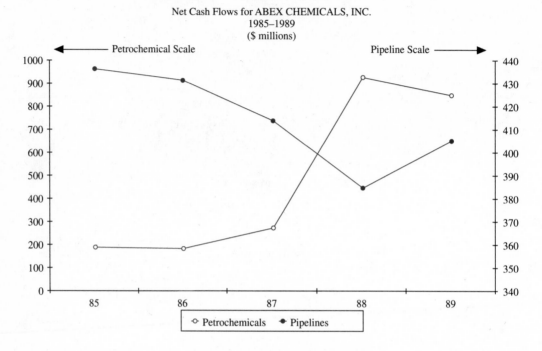

Net Cash Flows for ABEX CHEMICALS, INC.
1985–1989
($ millions)

a. Using *only* the graph, estimate (*without* calculating) the correlation coefficient between petrochemical and pipeline operating cash flows from 1985 through 1989.

b. Using the above graph and the statistics provided below, analyze the impact of ABEX's diversification into petrochemicals on the company's total cash flows from 1985 through 1989. Your analysis should consider measures of central tendency, dispersion, *and* correlation.

Operating Cash Flows Statistics for ABEX Chemicals, Inc.
1985 through 1989 ($ Millions)

Division	Mean	Standard Deviation
Petrochemicals	476.0	368.7
Pipeline	413.6	21.0
Total	889.6	349.8

CFA

21. Which *one* of the following portfolios *cannot* lie on the efficient frontier as described by Markowitz?

	Portfolio	Expected Return	Standard Deviation
a.	W	9%	21%
b.	X	5%	7%
c.	Y	15%	36%
d.	Z	12%	15%

22. Portfolio theory as described by Markowitz is *most* concerned with:
   a. the elimination of systematic risk.
   b. the effect of diversification on portfolio risk.
   c. the identification of unsystematic risk.
   d. active portfolio management to enhance returns.

23. The measure of risk in a Markowitz efficient frontier is:
   a. specific risk.
   b. standard deviation of returns.
   c. reinvestment risk.
   d. beta.

24. Which *one* of the following statements about portfolio diversification is correct?
   a. The risk-reducing benefits of diversification do not occur meaningfully until at least 30–35 individual securities have been purchased.
   b. Typically, as more securities are added to a portfolio, beta would be expected to rise at a decreasing rate.
   c. Because diversification reduces a portfolio's total risk, it necessarily reduces the portfolio's expected return.
   d. Proper diversification can reduce or eliminate nonsystematic risk.

25. Standard deviation and beta both measure risk, but they are different in that beta measures:
   a. only systematic risk, while standard deviation measures only unsystematic risk.
   b. only systematic risk, while standard deviation is a measure of total risk.
   c. only unsystematic risk, while standard deviation is a measure of total risk.
   d. both systematic and unsystematic risk, while standard deviation measures only systematic risk.

DATAFILE   ANALYSIS

In this analysis, you will develop a historical efficient frontier using the data in RTNSYRLY and the efficient frontier program called ASSETALL. Clearly, historical efficient frontiers (based on past realized returns) might not be good estimates of current efficient frontiers that you would develop (based on expectations of future returns). But historical data is easy to obtain, and the results are educational. This is not simply a textbook example, however. What you will do in the analysis is the same that professional investment consultants do for pension funds and endowments when they are trying to determine how millions of dollars will be invested.

1. *Averages and Standard Deviation.* Select five security classes from the RTNSYRLY datafile that you believe differ in average returns and standard deviations. For a period during which they all have returns available, calculate the yearly "real returns" by subtracting CPI (Consumer Pricing Index) returns. Calculate the average and standard deviation of each real return series.

2. *Correlation Coefficients.* To calculate correlation coefficients between each series, it is easiest to use the regression-analysis feature of your spreadsheet. An output of any regression is a statistic called R^2. This is the correlation coefficient squared. Run a regression of each return series against each of the other series and calculate the correlation coefficient as the square root of R^2. The sign (positive or negative) assigned to the correlation coefficient is the sign of the X-coefficient. This will usually be positive, but it is necessary to check the X-coefficient sign. Save your results by writing them down as follows:

Average *Standard Deviation* *Correlations*	*1*	*2*	*3*	*4*	*5*
1	1.0				
2	—	1.0			
3	—	—	1.0		
4	—	—	—	1.0	
5	—	—	—	—	1.0

3. *Input Data.* Obtain the Asset Allocation files from your instructor. One of these files is called AAEDIT.EXE. This program prepares an input data set that is read by the efficient frontier program. To run this program, type "AAEDIT" and follow the menu-driven instructions. You should request a "short-sale-constrained" input data set. This means that short sales are not allowed. The investment in an asset class will either be zero or positive.

4. *Assetall.* The efficient frontier is prepared by a program invoked by typing "ASSE-TALL" (for asset allocation). Follow the menu instructions. You should request a "short-sale-constrained" calculation.

5. *Efficient Portfolios.* Finally, print the output data set created by ASSETALL and interpret the results. When historical efficient frontiers such as this are calculated, one usually finds an asset class in which no investment is ever optimal. Why might this be the case? If security markets are efficient, does it make sense that no investment in a security class would be optimal?

APPENDIX 6A: EXTRAPOLATING INVESTMENT RISK

Portfolio risk is commonly expressed in terms of an annualized basis; that is, as the standard deviation of annual returns. The actual investment horizon of most investors, however, is longer than one year. In this appendix, we examine how potential payoffs inherent over a multiple-year horizon can be calculated and expressed.

The situation that we address is the following. An initial investment of $1.00 is made at the beginning of year 1. This investment is placed in a portfolio that has a *constant* risk and expected return. For example, if the portfolio consists of 60% invested in equities and 40% invested in Treasury bills (T-bills) then the mix is always maintained at

60/40. If the stocks earn a higher return than the T-bills in a given year, then some of the stock is sold and transferred to T-bills in order to keep a constant risk exposure. (This, of course, assumes that the risk of equities and T-bills does not change over time.) In each future year, a return is earned on the portfolio which depends on the portfolio's expected return and standard deviation. For the purposes of this appendix, we will assume that returns drawn in one year are unrelated to any future returns. This is an assumption that could be dropped, but it makes calculations easier and is often characteristic of actual return outcomes.

The question we examine is, "If all profits are reinvested, what is the distribution of terminal wealth after N years?"

To answer this question, we need to use a slightly different measure of rate of return than discussed previously. The rate of return we have used in this and previous chapters assumes that all compounding occurs at the end of the period in which the return is measured. For example, the yearly return has assumed that all cash inflows (dividends and interest) are received at year-end. We will refer to this type of return as a "discrete" return since compounding occurs on a given, discrete date. In contrast, the rate of return that we must use in order to develop reasonable estimates of future terminal wealth requires continuous compounding. This is called the "continuous" return.

Continuously compound returns are used for two reasons. First, it turns out that, if we assume discrete returns are normally distributed, there is the possibility that negative future terminal wealth will be forecast. This, of course, is not logical. But when continuous compound returns are used, terminal wealth can never be below zero. Specifically, if we assume that continuous returns are normally distributed, we are also assuming that terminal wealth is log normally distributed (bounded by a lower value of zero). Second, the use of continuous returns actually makes the calculations easier.

Define $\tilde{R}_t$ as the random discrete return in period t and $\tilde{r}_t$ as the random continuous return in t. Also define TW_N as the terminal wealth after N years from investing \$1 at date 0. The following mathematical relationships exist between these variables:

$$\tilde{r}_t = ln(1 + \tilde{R}_t) \qquad \textbf{(6A.1)}$$

$$(1 + \tilde{R}_t) + exp(\tilde{r}_t) \qquad \textbf{(6A.2)}$$

$$TW_N = (1 + \tilde{R}_1)(1 + \tilde{R}_2) \ldots (1 + \tilde{R}_N) \qquad \textbf{(6A.3)}$$

$$TW_N = exp(\tilde{r}_1 + \tilde{r}_2 \ldots \tilde{r}_N) \qquad \textbf{(6A.4)}$$
$$= exp(\Sigma \tilde{r}_t)$$

Exp(. . .) refers to the transcendental number "e" (2.718) raised to the power of (. . .). For example, consider the sequence of discrete yearly returns of 10%, -20% and 30%. Then:

$$r_1 = ln(1.10) = \quad 0.09531$$

$$r_2 = ln(0.80) = \ -0.22314$$

$$r_3 = ln(1.30) = \quad 0.26236$$

$$TW_3 = (1.10)(0.80)(1.30)$$

$$= 1.144$$

$$= exp(0.09531 - 0.22314 + 0.26236)$$

$$= 1.144$$

The Distribution of Σr_t

	Distribution of summation of r_t				
Cumulative Percentile	0.10	0.25	0.50	0.75	0.90
z-score from Mean	-1.28	-0.67	0.00	0.67	1.28
Summation of r_t	0.19	0.57	1.00	1.42	1.81

The key to forecasting the distribution of future terminal wealth lies in the summation of the r_t values. One uses the assumptions of how individual r_t returns are distributed to infer the distribution of their summation over N years. Once the *distribution of the summation* of r values is known, Equation

6A.4 is used to calculate the distribution of terminal wealth.

Assuming that each r_t is distributed with a constant mean of $\bar{r}$, a standard deviation of s and is uncorrelated with prior returns, then the distribution of the summation of r_t over N periods is normal, with an expected value and standard deviation of:

$$E(\Sigma\bar{r}) = N\bar{r}$$

$$s(\Sigma\bar{r}) = s\sqrt{N}$$

For example, if the expected yearly continuous return is 10% and its standard deviation is 20%, then the expected summation and standard deviation of the summation of r_t values over a 10-year investment horizon would be:

$$E(\Sigma\bar{r}) = 10(0.10) = 1.00$$

$$s(\Sigma\bar{r}) = 0.2\sqrt{10} = 0.6325$$

To calculate the distribution of terminal wealth in year 10, we first need to calculate the distribution of the year-10 summation of r_t values. This summation will be normally distributed since it is based on the addition of variables that are normally distributed. Using the standard normal density z-scores presented in Chapter 5, the cumulative distribution of r_t is shown in the table above.

The Distribution of Terminal Wealth

We can now calculate the percentile distribution of terminal wealth using the percentile distribution of the summation of r_t and Equation 6A.4. Applied to our example, see the table below.

Distribution of Terminal Wealth in Year-10

Cumulative Percentile	0.10	0.25	0.50	0.75	0.90
exp (Σr_t)	exp (0.19)	exp (0.57)	exp (1.00)	exp (1.42)	exp (1.81)
equals	$1.21	$1.77	$2.71	$4.14	$6.11

Distribution of Geometric Annual Returns

Cumulative Percentile	0.10	0.25	0.50	0.75	0.90
1 + (Geometric Return)	$1.21^{1/10}$	$1.77^{1/10}$	$2.71^{1/10}$	$4.14^{1/10}$	$6.11^{1/10}$
equals	1.019	1.059	1.104	1.153	1.198
Annualized Geometric Return	1.9%	5.9%	10.4%	15.3%	19.8%

If $1.00 is invested at the start of year-one in a portfolio that has a constant continuous yearly expected return and standard deviation of 10% and 20% and held for 10 years, then there is a 10% chance that terminal wealth will be $1.21 or less. There is also a 10% chance that terminal wealth will exceed $6.11.

The Distribution of Geometric Returns

Often terminal wealth numbers such as those shown above are converted into annualized geometric return values because investors relate better to annualized returns than future terminal wealth values. Geometric returns were discussed in Chapter 5. Given the year-10 terminal wealths from the initial $1.00 investment in this example, the distribution of annualized geometric returns are shown in the table above.

Investment Implications

So what does it all mean? While the discussion above dealt with technical procedures for extrapolating single-year outcomes to longer investment horizons, the results have important investment implications.

Consider the 10-year annualized geometric returns. A 10-year investor faces only a 10% chance of incurring a positive 1.9% annualized return or less. In contrast, a 1-year investor faces a much larger probability of earning less than 1.9%. This observation makes it appear that long-term investors face lower risk than do shorter-term investors, but this is deceiving.

An annualized geometric return is simply a mathematical calculation. One does not purchase a new car or home with a geometric return. True uncertainty is the uncertainty about future wealth. Since the uncertainty about future wealth increases as the investment horizon increases, long-term investors face greater investment risk than do short-term investors. Investment risk does not decrease as one's investment horizon increases, and time does not provide diversification to one's portfolio.

Long-term investors do not have to, nor should they, accept less risky portfolios. For example, if market returns work against them, long-term investors have considerable freedom to adjust portfolio risk exposure and to offset security investment losses with increased efforts at personal job income.

Finally, notice that the distribution of year-10 terminal wealth is positively skewed. This is logical since wealth is limited by zero on the downside but unlimited on the upside. Over long investment horizons, investment payoffs are positively skewed.

REFERENCES

The classic and first articles dealing with what we now call modern portfolio theory are:

MARKOWITZ, HARRY M. "Portfolio Selection," *Journal of Finance,* March 1952.

MARKOWITZ, HARRY M. *Portfolio Selection: Efficient Diversification of Investment.* Cowles Foundation Monograph 16. New Haven: Yale University Press, 1959.

SHARPE, WILLIAM F. *Portfolio Theory and Capital Markets.* New York: McGraw-Hill, 1970.

If you are interested in the concept of utility theory, a useful paper is:

FRIEDMAN, MILTON and LEONARD SAVAGE, "The Utility Analysis of Choices Involving Risk," *The Journal of Political Economy,* August 1948.

Investment textbooks that provide a good review of utility theory as applied to investment decision making are:

ELTON, EDWIN J. and MARTIN J. GRUBER, *Modern Portfolio Theory and Investment Analysis,* New York: John Wiley & Sons, 1987.

HALEY, CHARLES W. and LAWRENCE D. SCHALL, *The Theory of Financial Decisions,* New York: McGraw-Hill, 1979.

A few recent papers that expand on the principles of portfolio theory include:

BREALEY, RICHARD A. "Portfolio Theory versus Portfolio Practice," *The Journal of Portfolio Management,* Summer 1990.

EZRA, D. DON, "Asset Allocation by Surplus Optimization," *Financial Analysts Journal,* January–February 1991.

LEE, WAYNE Y., "Diversification and Time: Do Investment Horizons Matter?" *The Journal of Portfolio Management,* Spring 1990.

SHARPE, WILLIAM F. and LAWRENCE G. TINT, "Liabilities—A New Approach," *The Journal of Portfolio Management,* Winter 1990.

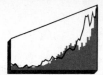

Capital Asset
Pricing Model

In the previous chapter, we concentrated on how individual investors and speculators can determine the single portfolio of risky securities that is optimal to them
and how this portfolio can be combined with lending at the risk-free rate or
borrowing in order to achieve a preferred risk/return trade-off. In this chapter we
extend the discussion to the market in general and examine the following question:
If all investors pursued optimal portfolio selection, how would this affect equilibrium security prices and expected returns?

The equilibrium model discussed in this chapter is known as the *capital asset
pricing model* (CAPM). Embodied in this model are two fundamental relationships. Since there is often confusion between the two, we will state each immediately.

The first relationship, known as the *capital market line,* specifies the return one
should expect to receive on a *portfolio.* If the portfolio provides this expected
return, it is an *efficient portfolio* and should be purchased. If the portfolio provides
a lower return, it should not be held. The capital market line is written symbolically
as:

Capital Market Line $$E(R_p) = RF + \sigma_p\left(\frac{RP_M}{\sigma_M}\right) \qquad (7.1)$$

The return you should expect to receive on any portfolio is equal to a risk-free
rate earned for delaying consumption plus a risk premium earned for bearing risk
inherent in the portfolio. It is important to remember that the capital market line
treats the relationship between expected returns on *efficient portfolios* and the
risks of such portfolios.

The second relationship, known as the *security market line,* is broader and is
able to treat individual securities as well as portfolios. It expresses the return that
should be expected in terms of a risk-free rate and the relative risk of the security
(or portfolio). The security market line is written symbolically as:

Security Market Line $$E(R_i) = RF + \beta_i[RP_M] \qquad (7.2)$$

As with the capital market line, there is a risk-free and a risk component. But the
security market line expresses the risk premium differently and treats *any* security
i, while Equation 7.1 treats efficient portfolios only. As one would expect, the

Three U.S. Economists Win Nobel Prize

Many concepts discussed in Chapter 5 through 8 were originally developed by Harry Markowitz and William Sharpe. In 1990, they were awarded the Nobel Memorial Prize in Economic Science in recognition of the importance of their investment insights. Merton Miller was also a Nobel recipient for his contributions to the theory of corporate finance.

The Nobel Memorial Prize in Economic Science was given to three Americans whose work revolutionized the way that investment portfolios and corporate finances are managed.

The Swedish Academy of Sciences awarded the prestigious $700,000 prize to Harry Markowitz of Baruch College at the City University of New York, William F. Sharpe of Stanford University and Merton Miller of the University of Chicago. All three are financial economists whose work is well-known not only in academia but also among many professionals on Wall Street.

The award came as something of a surprise in the academic economics community. Although the three men are highly respected by their colleagues, their work has been more narrowly focused than that of economists who previously won the award.

In addition, the work by the three men has more direct practical applications than work by previous Nobel economists. "Widows live safer lives because their portfolios are invested according to the diversification principles developed by Markowitz and elaborated by Sharpe," said Harvard economist Lawrence Summers. "Miller's contributions changed what every business school student has learned and the way every corporation thinks about financing itself." . . .

The economics prize was instituted in 1968 by Sweden's Central Bank to complement the five prizes established in the will of dynamite inventor Alfred Nobel. Nobel's original prizes in physics, chemistry, medicine, peace and literature have been awarded since 1901.

HARRY MARKOWITZ

Harry Markowitz was honored for his pathbreaking work in the 1950s developing the theory of "portfolio choice," which analyzed how to consider risk as well as expected return in evaluating investments.

"Markowitz is a pioneer in using formal analysis of portfolio choices involving both risk and return," said Mr. Tobin, the Nobel laureate. He said Mr. Markowitz's work "has practical application for people trying to be rational about portfolio choice, and it also makes a contribution to people's understanding of economics."

In addition, Mr. Markowitz is the creator of SIMSCRIPT, a computer language used to simulate complex economic scenarios.

Mr. Markowitz, who currently is teaching a course at the University of Tokyo, told reporters that he had given up hopes of winning the award nine years ago after it was given to Mr. Tobin, who also did extensive work on portfolio theory.

"I'm obviously surprised by the award, and gratified by the international recognition," Mr. Markowitz said in a statement. "But "I'll also be happy when the attention dies down and I can go back to my students and a blackboard."

Mr. Markowitz earned his doctorate at the University of Chicago in 1954, and is the Marvin Speiser Distinguished Professor of Finance and Economics at Baruch College. In 1989, he received the John Von Neumann Theory Prize. He is 63 years old.

WILLIAM SHARPE

William Sharpe's work is based upon that done by Mr. Markowitz. The two men worked very closely at Rand Corp., a research company, in the late 1950s and early 1960s. "I for all practical purposes did my dissertation with Harry Markowitz," Mr. Sharpe said.

He developed what is now known as the capital asset pricing model, which includes the "beta" measure of risk now in wide use on Wall Street. The model is "almost universally applied in portfolio and investment management," said Mr. Mullins.

Fischer Black, a partner at Goldman Sachs, says the work by Messrs. Sharpe and Markowitz "showed that risk could be measured and that controlling risk was as important as maximizing expected return in managing a portfolio."

Mr. Sharpe, 56 years old, said he had "always fantasized about winning" the Nobel prize, but was nonetheless surprised when informed of the decision yesterday. He currently is Timken Professor Emeritus of Finance at Stanford University's Graduate School of Business, but spends most of his time running a consulting business, William F. Sharpe Associates.

"We work with pension funds, endowments, foundations on how to have their asset allocation match up with their needs," he said. He has written six books on portfolio investment, and is past president of the American Finance Association.

MERTON MILLER

Merton Miller's pioneering work is in the area of corporate finance—specifically, the relationship between a company's capital structure, its dividend policy and its value. Along with Mr. Modigliani, Mr. Miller developed the frequently cited "M&M" theorems of corporate finance.

Although the theory is complex, one conclusion is that a company's value shouldn't be changed simply because it pays out more dividends. Mr. Miller has spent a good deal of time trying to explain why a company's stock price so often rises when an increase in dividends is announced. In an interview, Mr. Miller said the M&M theorems provide a "road map" for understanding the relationship between corporate finance and a company's value. The theorems are widely taught in business schools.

Mr. Miller is the Robert R. McCormick Distinguished Service Professor of Finance at the Graduate School of Business at the University of Chicago. He earned his doctorate from Johns Hopkins University in 1952. He is 67.

Recently, Mr. Miller was chairman of a special panel appointed by the Chicago Mercantile Exchange to examine the role of futures markets in the 1987 stock market crash. He has been a harsh critic of Treasury Secretary Nicholas Brady, who has proposed giving the Securities and Exchange Commission regulatory control over the Chicago futures markets.

"I'm very unhappy about Secretary Brady's behavior on this," said Mr. Miller. "I think he's behaving like a Chicago precinct captain, carrying out this vendetta against the Chicago futures market."

"I think this is a classic case of New York vs. Chicago," he added, "and Secretary Brady has weighed in on the side that he knows—New York."

SOURCE: Excerpt from "Three U.S. Economists Win Nobel Prize" by Alan Murry from THE WALL STREET JOURNAL, October 17, 1990. Reprinted by permission of The Wall Street Journal, copyright © 1990 by Dow Jones & Company, Inc. All Rights Reserved Worldwide.

security market line is the more widely used because of its greater generality. But it can only be understood in the context of the capital market line.

In the standard capital asset pricing model that is developed in this chapter, a single portfolio of risky securities emerges that all investors should hold in combination with borrowing or lending. This portfolio is referred to as the *market portfolio* and consists of *all risky securities in existence, with relative holdings of each dependent on each security's total market value.* The critical role of the market portfolio is, without doubt, the central conclusion of this theory. From the optimality of the market portfolio come both the capital market line and security market line. From it also come a variety of investment and speculative implications that have had major impacts on portfolio strategies within the last decade. The dominance of this market portfolio, however, is simply a logical consequence of the various assumptions made. After reviewing its development, the reader will probably sit back and say, "Of course, it makes perfect sense—if the assumptions are correct." In this chapter these assumptions are treated as abstractions of reality which are needed in order to develop a simple relationship between equilibrium risk and return. Although none of them is strictly true, we will wait until the next chapter to examine the empirical accuracy of the model and the effects of lifting each assumption.

THE CAPITAL MARKET LINE

Assumptions

The intent of this chapter is to develop a model that explains security prices when the security market is at equilibrium. *Equilibrium exists when prices are at levels that provide no incentive for speculative trading.* At equilibrium, the quantity of shares desired for sale by investors (nonspeculators) is equal to the quantity desired for purchase by investors.

If the price of a given security is lower than its equilibrium level, an *excess demand* will arise and speculators will bid up prices until the excess demand is removed. Similarly, if prices are greater than equilibrium, speculators will create an *excess supply* and force prices down by their selling. The point at which price levels attract no information trading is what we consider equilibrium.

If prices are set at equilibrium, trades between buyers and sellers will continue to occur. Individuals (and organizations) who have excess cash and wish to invest come to the market with bids to buy, while individuals (and organizations) who need cash come to the market with offers to sell. However, at equilibrium, no one is offering to buy or sell out of a belief that existing prices are wrong: no one trades with a *speculative* motive, and no one trades because he or she has unique information not yet available to other participants. *For the market to be truly at equilibrium, all buyers and sellers must have the same information.* If they don't, then by definition the market cannot yet be at equilibrium.

Equilibrium prices will change with the passage of time, as world events occur and provide new information about the prospects of the firms that originally issued the securities. And, if events are dramatic, equilibrium price changes will also be dramatic. Hence there is nothing particularly inconsistent about having significant gyrations in security prices over time and a market which is always at equilibrium. The large price movements might simply reflect continuous and occasionally large adjustments to equilibrium levels necessary as new information unfolds. In contrast, many people would argue that actual market prices are never at equilibrium but, instead, are constantly chasing (but never finding) the changing equilibrium levels. Which theory is correct really doesn't matter here. We are interested only in equilibrium pricing, not actual prices. To begin to understand what creates an actual price we must first understand the forces that create an equilibrium price. Only then can we look for differences between actual and equilibrium prices.

At this point we can summarize and state our first assumption: *Equilibrium prices exist only when speculative (information) trading is zero.* For security markets to be at equilibrium we must *assume that all market participants currently have identical information*—they have *homogeneous expectations about the future.*

This assumption of homogeneous expectations is often stated another way: All participants have equal and costless access to information. If new information is released to a select few people, or even released to different groups at different times, prices would be set by the speculative trades of the people or groups who first receive the information. But, again, an equilibrium exists only when all investors have common information.

Next, we will *assume that there are no impediments to achieving exactly the portfolio that one wishes.* In other words, the markets are *frictionless.* Among the principal impediments that might exist are the following:

1. Transaction costs. Brokerage fees and bid-ask spread fees are assumed to be zero, so that all purchases and sales desired will be transacted.
2. Security indivisibility. We will assume that all securities are infinitely divisible. Investors can take any position they wish. If an individual's optimal decision is to own 115.37 shares of AT&T, it is assumed possible.
3. Taxes. We will assume that taxes are zero.[1]
4. Trading price impacts. We will assume that the trading actions of the individual investor do not affect price levels. Your decision, or that of another investor, to trade does not, in isolation from all other trades, affect prices. Only the aggregate of all trades causes prices to move to equilibrium.

Finally, we will carry forward the assumptions of Chapter 6 regarding how the individual chooses an optimal security portfolio:

1. A one-period world exists for all investors.
2. Investors seek to maximize the expected utility of end-of-period wealth, and this utility is determined by expected returns and the standard deviation of returns.
3. People may borrow or lend at a constant risk-free interest rate.

Market Equilibrium

Given these assumptions, we are ready to examine what a state of market equilibrium would imply about the measurement of risk/return trade-off, and security price levels. The analysis is quite easy to understand and is depicted in Figure 7-1.

Consider the situation faced by the individual shown in the figure. The individual first evaluates the expected returns and risks available on various portfolio combinations and, from this, is able to identify the efficient frontier of risky

---

[1] The critical tax impact occurs when capital gains and ordinary tax rates vary. It is simplest to assume away all taxes.

FIGURE 7-1 *Efficient Frontier and Borrowing-Lending Line Available to All Market Participants*

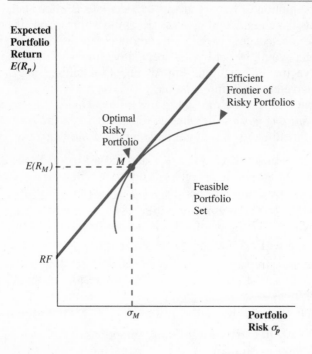

portfolios. Next, the optimal risky portfolio is found by determining which portfolio will provide the largest risk premium when it is held in combination with the risk-free security. This optimal risky portfolio is denoted as portfolio *M*.

Now consider the situation faced by another individual. It is identical. Since investors have homogeneous expectations, each will arrive at the same conclusion—that portfolio *M* is *the* optimal risky portfolio. People will differ in the amount of risk they wish their portfolios to contain, but risk can be adjusted by altering the amount of lending and borrowing. Portfolio *M* is never changed. It is the only portfolio of risky securities that people wish to hold.

Well, what if some security exists which is not in *M*? It won't be owned—not by anyone. Instead, it will be used as wallpaper in family dens, displayed in investment classes to illustrate a great story, etcetera. Conversely, any security that exists and is held in a portfolio is in *M*. Portfolio *M* consists of *all* owned securities.

Portfolio *M* is called the *market portfolio,* and its existence as the optimal efficient portfolio for all investors is the single most important implication of this standard version of the capital asset pricing model. Not surprisingly, this implication has come under attack from academicians and practitioners alike. Much of Chapter 8 will be devoted to such criticisms. But, for now, we will accept this result and see what develops from it.

Optimal X_i Holdings. The investment process consists of two steps: (1) identifying the optimal risky portfolio (the percentage to invest in each available risky security—X_i) and (2) borrowing or lending to achieve the desired risk/return trade-off. The capital asset pricing model states that the market portfolio is the optimal risky portfolio. And since all investors wish to hold this same portfolio, it should be no surprise that the *percentage of a risky portfolio held in security* i *is equal to the total market value of security* i *as a percent of the total market values of all risky securities.*

**Proportion of Risky
Portfolio Held in *i***
$$X_i^* = \frac{P_i N_i}{\sum\limits_{i=1}^{T} P_i N_i}$$
(7.3)

where: $X_i^* =$ optimal percentage of the *risky portfolio* (i.e., excluding borrowing-lending) held in security i.

       $P_i =$ market price of security i.

       $N_i =$ quantity of security i outstanding.

      $T =$ total number of risky securities outstanding.

For example, assume ther are only three risky securities available:

Security	Price	Units Outstanding	Total Value	Percentage of Total
1	$ 30	200	$ 6,000	30%
2	50	200	10,000	50
3	1,000	4	4,000	20
			$20,000	100%

The total market value of these securities is $20,000. Since the securities are held by various market participants, the total wealth of these participants devoted to risky securities is also $20,000. But since they all wish to have the same percentage holdings of each, the percentage which any one person will invest in a given security *must be equal* to the security's percentage of the total value of all risky securities. Thus, everyone will place 30% of their risky portfolio in security 1, 50% in security 2, and 20% in security 3. If this were not the case, the markets would not clear. One or more investors would remain wanting to buy or sell a specific holding.

Why the Market Portfolio? Given our assumptions, it is perfectly reasonable that the market portfolio is optimal. Securities differ only in expected returns and standard deviations of returns. As we saw in Chapter 6, diversification by itself has no effect on expected portfolio returns. For example, if the addition of another security reduces expected returns below the desired level, an investor can borrow to achieve the desired return but still obtain the risk-reduction advantages of the

FIGURE 7-2 *The Market Portfolio of All Risky Assets (Diversifiable and Nondiversifiable)*

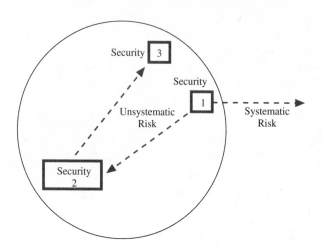

increased diversification. The market portfolio is in essence the most diversified portfolio available. Once it is held, there is no way to further diversify away risk.

Consider Figure 7-2, which schematically shows all risky securities in the world within a large circle. A few of the individual securities are illustrated by the small boxes. Gains or losses in value incurred by particular securities are depicted by arrows showing where the gain or loss came from and went to. Security 1, for example, incurs two losses of value, one that is passed to security 2 and one that is not passed to another asset but simply leaves the system. *Gains and losses to individual securities that are passed on to other securities and remain within the system can be diversified away by holding a portfolio of all securities. These are unsystematic risks. Gains or losses to the total system are nondiversifiable systematic risks.*

Simply stated, the market portfolio is the most broadly diversified portfolio available. Any portfolio with fewer securities or a dissimilar percentage of investments in each security is not adequately diversified.

The CML Equation. The capital market line (CML) states the equilibrium relationship that exists between the returns that should be expected on efficient portfolios of securities and the risks of such portfolios. For reference, look back to Figure 7-1. The CML is the borrowing-lending line extending from *RF* through portfolio *M*.

In equilibrium, the return expected on a *portfolio* of securities must be at least equal to Equation 7.4a or the portfolio is inefficient and will not be held. As you might expect, in equilibrium, the only portfolios which meet the criterion are combinations of *RF* and the market portfolio.

Capital Market Line Equation

$$E(R_p) = RF + \sigma_p \left[\frac{E(R_M) - RF}{\sigma_M} \right]$$

(7.4a)

where: $E(R_M)$ = expected return on the market portfolio.

σ_M = standard deviation of the market portfolio's return.

First, one should expect a risk-free return simply for delaying the consumption of the portfolio's worth. Second, a risk premium should be expected which is determined by two things: (1) the total risk of the portfolio (σ_p) and (2) the best risk-related return per unit of σ available in the market. Since the market portfolio dominates all other risky portfolios in equilibrium, it provides the best risk-related return per unit of σ.

In Equation 7.4a, the term $E(R_M) - RF$ is a measure of the risk premium that is expected to be earned above the risk-free rate for bearing the market portfolio's risk. We refer to it as RP_M. If $E(R_M)$ equals 16% and the risk-free rate is 10%, then $RP_M = 6\%$. You should recognize, however, that the term $E(R_M) - RF$ does not create the percentage risk premium available to market participants. Instead, it is RP_M in combination with RF which creates $E(R_M)$. The term $E(R_M) - RF$ is simply a measurement of RP_M. To avoid any confusion about what is a measurement term and what is a determinant, it is useful to restate the CML as follows:

$$E(R_p) = RF + \sigma_p \left[\frac{RP_M}{\sigma_M} \right] \qquad \textbf{(7.4b)}$$

In Figure 7-3, a plot of the CML is shown.

For illustration, assume that $RF = 10\%$, $RP_M = 6\%$, and $\sigma_M = 20\%$. Then the return on a portfolio which is half as risky as the market portfolio should provide an expected return of 13%:

$$E(R_p) = 10\% + 10\% \left[\frac{6\%}{20\%} \right]$$

$$= 13\%$$

A combination of 50% in the market portfolio and 50% in the risk-free security would provide exactly this 13% expected return. Other portfolios with $\sigma_p = 10\%$ should be judged against the 13%. If the other portfolio has a higher expected return, it should be aggressively purchased. If the other portfolio has a lower expected return, it should not be bought.

If the markets are in equilibrium, however, it would be impossible to find another portfolio with $\sigma = 10\%$ and $E(R_p)$ greater than 13%. The only portfolio capable of both $\sigma_p = 10\%$ and $E(R_p) = 13\%$ is a 50/50 combination of M and RF. All other portfolios are inefficient—dominated by the extensive diversification gains of the market portfolio.

Determinants of the Market Risk Premium. Recall from Chapters 1 and 5 how RF is determined. It is not a number handed to society by a financial dictator. Instead, the risk-free rate is determined by market participants themselves as a function of their time preferences for consumption and the marginal productivity

FIGURE 7-3 *The Capital Market Line (CML)*

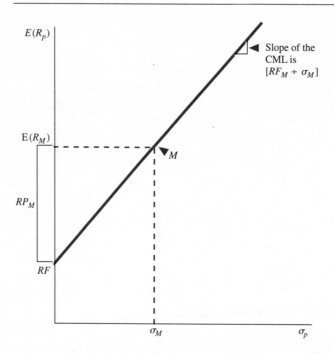

of capital. The risk premium is also determined in the marketplace and is a function of society's risk aversion and the marginal returns available from risky assets. To illustrate the process, consider the three panels of Figure 7-4. In panel A, the risk-free rate is removed. The dashed lines are societal indifference curves reflecting the marginal increases in expected returns for the marginal change in risk that is necessary to maintain a given utility. (Think of these indifference curves as an average across all members of society.) The ideal portfolio is denoted as *M*. Now move to panel B, in which a risk-free rate is introduced. Suddenly, *M* no longer is efficient and M_2 is held in its place. To achieve its desired risk/return level, society will attempt to borrow at *RF* and will place both equity and borrowings in M_2 in order to be at the optimal point *B*. But society cannot borrow from itself. The sum of all individual borrowing and individual lending *must* be zero. It is impossible for society to be at point *B*. However, attempts to purchase M_2 will force the prices of M_2 up and its expected return down. Similarly, lack of demand for *M* will cause its expected returns to rise as its prices fall. Equilibrium will finally result when the optimal risky portfolio *M* is consistent with zero net borrowing and lending, as shown in panel C.

There are two important points to recognize in this illustration. First, the risk premium is not forced on society by risks and expected returns associated with risky assets. Instead, it is the interaction of *available* risk/return trade-offs with society's risk *preferences* that determines the risk premium. Second, any such equilibrium must also be consistent with zero net lending and borrowing.

FIGURE 7-4 *Determination of the Risk Premium*

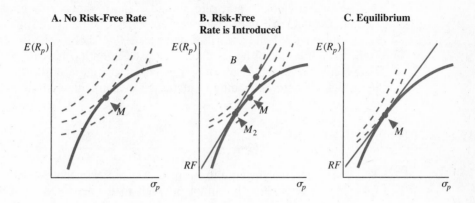

The Market Portfolio

In theory, the market portfolio consists of all risky assets. These would include all risky assets in the world; equities, bonds, real estate, commodities, paintings, etcetera. In practice, the market portfolio cannot actually be held or even identified. And market frictions make trading with certain countries impossible and with others very costly. But the crude data available suggests some interesting implications.

Table 7-1 provides a recent estimate of what the market portfolio might consist of. In the far-right column, the value of non-U.S. assets is estimated to be 64% of the world total. It should be clear that a large part of portfolio M consists of non-U.S. assets—that international diversification is necessary to obtain the broadest diversification possible.

TABLE 7-1 *Market Value of Various Asset Types (1991)*

	Market Value (U.S. $ Trillions)	Percent U.S. Total	Percent World Total
Domestic U.S.:			
Equities	$ 4.4	26%	
Debt	6.2	37	
Real Estate	6.3	37	
Total U.S.	$16.9	100%	36%
Non-U.S.:			
Equities	6.0		
Debt	7.3		
Real Estate	16.3		
Total Non-U.S.	$29.6		64
Total	$46.5		100%

Next, consider only the information shown on domestic U.S. assets. Real estate dominates holdings of either equity or debt. To diversify broadly over only U.S. assets, an individual's portfolio should contain about 37% of its value in real estate.[2] The data in Table 7-1 are very imprecise. But they do suggest the important roles that international securities and real estate should play in the creation of a well-diversified portfolio. In fact, increased attention has recently been focused on exactly these two asset categories, and most large portfolios (pension funds, in particular) have substantially increased investments in each.

THE SECURITY MARKET LINE

The CML specifies the equilibrium relationship between expected return and risk for *efficient portfolios*. It cannot be used to evaluate the equilibrium expected return on a single security because σ_i is not a proper measure of a security's true risk. The risk of a security depends upon the portfolio to which it is added and must reflect the covariability of the security's returns with other assets in the portfolio.

In this section, we examine how the risk of a single security should be measured when the markets are in equilibrium. The analysis is similar to that in Chapter 6, where we evaluated the risk of a single security to one individual. The principal difference here is that we know what the optimal risky asset portfolio is—the market portfolio. The model that is developed is known as the *security market line* (SML).

Beta: A Security's Nondiversifiable Risk

The standard deviation of the market portfolio is:

Market Portfolio Risk
$$\sigma_M = \left[\sum_{i=1}^{N} X_i^2 \sigma_i^2 + \sum_{\substack{i=1 \\ i \neq j}}^{N} \sum_{j=1}^{N} X_i X_j \sigma_i \sigma_j r_{ij} \right]^{1/2} \qquad \textbf{(7.5a)}$$

where there are N different risky assets available. As before, σ_M is a function of each security's variance of returns (σ_i^2) and covariances with other securities ($\sigma_i \sigma_j r_{ij}$). Actually, the variance terms can also be thought of as a covariance term—the covariance of the security with itself. If this is done, Equation 7.5a can be written as

Market Portfolio Risk
$$\sigma_M = \left[\sum_{i=1}^{N} \sum_{j=1}^{N} X_i X_j \sigma_i \sigma_j r_{ij} \right]^{1/2} \qquad \textbf{(7.5b)}$$

---

[2] In fact, a large part of most people's wealth consists of the equity they have in their homes and land. If the value of these are highly correlated with other real assets, this equity ownership in homes and land probably achieves much of the diversification suggested in real estate.

Now, let's pull out of this equation only those terms associated with, say, security 8, so we can look more closely at how it affects σ_M:

Security 8's Terms in σ_M

$$[X_8 X_1 \sigma_8 \sigma_1 r_{8,1} + X_1 X_8 \sigma_1 \sigma_8 r_{1,8} + \ldots$$
$$+ X_8^2 \sigma_8^2 + \ldots$$
$$+ 2 X_8 X_9 \sigma_8 \sigma_9 r_{8,9} + \ldots$$
$$+ 2 X_8 X_N \sigma_8 \sigma_N r_{8N}$$

(7.6)

Look at the first line. Here the weighted covariances between 8 and 1, as well as between 1 and 8, are shown. Since they are equal, all such future covariances are multiplied by 2—for example, on lines 3 and 4. The second line displays the covariance of 8 with itself. The final line treats the covariance of 8 with the last security N.

The equation may look complex, but its economic interpretation is straightforward. Equation 7.6 is simply:[3]

$$2X_8 \text{ [covariance of 8 with the market portfolio]} = 2X_8 [\sigma_8 \sigma_M r_{8M}]$$

The risk of the market portfolio is simply the sum of many such covariance terms for each security. Symbolically:

Market Portfolio Risk

$$\sigma_M = [2X_1(\sigma_1 \sigma_M r_{1M}) + \ldots + 2X_8(\sigma_8 \sigma_M r_{8M})$$
$$+ \ldots + 2X_N(\sigma_N \sigma_M r_{NM})]^{1/2}$$

(7.7)

Finally, we can examine how changes in holdings of security 8 affect the risk of the market portfolio. This is done by taking the derivative of σ_M with respect to X_8:

Changes in σ_M for a Small Change in X_8

$$\frac{\partial \sigma_M}{\partial X_8} = \frac{\sigma_8 \sigma_M r_{8M}}{\sigma_M} = \sigma_8 r_{8M}$$

(7.8)

The risk that security 8 provides to the market portfolio as the percentage invested in security 8 changes slightly is the security's nondiversifiable uncertainty. *Only that portion of its risk that is correlated with the market is important.*

In general, we can say that *the risk of security i is the nondiversifiable risk that it adds to portfolio M* as small changes are made in X_i:

Risk of Security i in Equilibrium

$$= \frac{\text{Nondiversifiable}}{\text{Standard Deviation}} = \sigma_i r_{iM}$$

A more commonly used security-risk measure is the amount of nondiversifiable risk inherent in the security *relative* to the risk of the market portfolio. This relative risk measure is known as *beta* and is equal to:

Beta of Security i

$$\beta_i = \frac{\sigma_i}{\sigma_M}(r_{iM})$$

(7.9)

---

[3] This is not strictly true since only one $X_8^2 \sigma_8^2$ term is shown in Equation 7.6. Given the large number of securities in M, this is a negligible error.

Dividing σ_i by σ_M provides a measure of how volatile the security is in relation to the volatility of the market portfolio. Multiplying by the correlation coefficient determines how much of this relative volatility should be counted. If the security is perfectly correlated with the market portfolio, then all of the relative volatility counts. None of it can be eliminated in M by diversification. If the correlation is zero, then none of the volatility counts. All of it can be eliminated by diversification when combined with M.

The Betas of M and RF. The risk of the market portfolio relative to itself is, of course, 1.0:

Market Portfolio Beta
$$\beta_M = \frac{\sigma_M}{\sigma_M}(r_{MM}) = 1.0 \tag{7.10a}$$

Any security with a beta equal to 1.0 has the same amount of nondiversifiable risk as in the market portfolio. When added to M, risk will not change. So the return which should be expected on a security with a beta of 1.0 should be the same as $E(R_M)$.

The risk of the risk-free rate is by definition equal to zero and it will have a beta of zero:

Risk-Free Beta
$$\beta_{RF} = \frac{0.0}{\sigma_M}(0.0) = 0.0 \tag{7.10b}$$

Similarly, other securities that have a beta of 0.0 should be priced to provide an expected return equal to the risk-free rate. That does not mean that zero-beta securities will *actually* return RF. They may not if they have a positive σ. But as long as they are uncorrelated with M, all such volatility can be diversified away in M. And if all such uncertainty can be eliminated, their *expected* return should be equal to RF.

The Expected Return on Individual Securities (SML)

The capital market line expresses the expected return on an efficient portfolio in terms of the standard deviation of the portfolio:

CML
$$E(R_p) = RF + \sigma_p\left[\frac{RP_M}{\sigma_M}\right] \tag{7.11a}$$

The security market line expresses the expected return on any security or portfolio in terms of the nondiversifiable risk of the asset. That is, for asset i:

The Security Market Line
$$E(R_i) = RF + \sigma_i r_{iM}\left[\frac{RP_M}{\sigma_M}\right]$$
$$= RF + \frac{\sigma_i r_{iM}}{\sigma_M}[RP_M] \tag{7.11b}$$
$$= RF + \beta_i[RP_M]$$

FIGURE 7-5 *The Security Market Line*

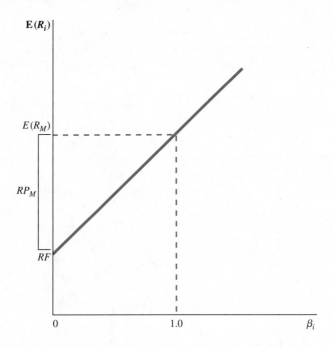

Equation 7.11b is known as the *security market line* and is depicted graphically in Figure 7-5.

Betas of a Portfolio

There are two ways of calculating the beta of a portfolio: (1) at the portfolio level or (2) at the component security level. At the portfolio level, the beta is simply:

Portfolio Beta
$$\beta_p = \frac{\sigma_p}{\sigma_M} \, r_{pM} \tag{7.12}$$

The standard deviation of portfolio returns is divided by the standard deviation of the market portfolio to find the amount of uncertainty in the portfolio relative to M. This value is then multiplied by the correlation between p and M to determine what portion of the relative uncertainty will not be diversified away when p is held together with M. If the correlation coefficient and standard deviations are ex ante measures, this is a proper way of measuring β_p. Such an ex ante beta measures subjective beliefs about the portfolio's relative nondiversifiable risk. However, ex post measures are commonly used as proxies for ex ante data, in which case standard deviations and correlation coefficients of the portfolio's historical returns are used to estimate beta.

There are two possible biases in such a beta estimate:

1. The past can be a poor predictor of the future. Estimates will depend to a large degree on the time period chosen, and all such estimates are often inaccurate predictors.

2. If the composition of the portfolio (the X_i values) has changed over time, the beta associated with current holdings will not be the beta calculated from the past returns of different holdings. The beta measured will not be the beta for the current portfolio.

The beta of a portfolio can also be calculated as a weighted average of the betas on the securities which make up the portfolio:

Portfolio Beta $$\beta_p = \sum_{i=1}^{N} \beta_i X_i \qquad (7.13)$$

For example, the beta of a portfolio consisting of the following securities is 1.0:

Security	X_i	β_i	Product
A	0.25	1.5	0.375
B	0.25	1.0	0.250
C	0.25	1.2	0.300
D	0.25	0.3	0.075
			1.000

The bias in a beta estimate that may arise if a portfolio's composition has changed over time can be easily overcome if the beta on each constituent security is estimated and then averaged.

POTENTIAL USES OF THE CAPITAL ASSET PRICING MODEL

The theory we have been discussing is the classic version of what is known as the theory of capital asset pricing, or the capital asset pricing model (CAPM). In this section we review some of its implications and see how they might be used in practice. Three major topics are examined:

1. Analysis of security *pricing*
2. Development of an ideal investment *strategy*
3. Evaluation of a portfolio's *performance*

Pricing

Our discussion of the capital asset pricing model has said very little so far about prices. The discussion has revolved almost completely around risk and expected returns. It didn't have to—we could have developed an equilibrium model of prices that parallels our model or risk and return. Concentating on risk and expected return was simply a convenient way to approach the problem. Nonetheless, it is a security's price that is transacted in the markets and that determines whether speculative opportunities exist.

The equilibrium price should provide no opportunity for speculative profits. It should be set at such a level that *expected returns from buying the security are identical to those available on an efficient portfolio of equivalent nondiversifiable risk.* For example, if $RF = 10\%$, $RP_M = 6\%$, and the beta of a stock $= 0.7$, then the stock should be priced to provide an expected return of 14.2%:

$$E(R_i) = RF + \beta_i(RP_M)$$

$$14.2\% = 10.0\% + 0.7\,(6.0\%)$$

If this security is trading at a price lower than equilibrium, then a speculative profit is possible and excess demand will exist until the price is forced up to equilibrium. If the security is trading at a higher than equilibrium price, speculators will sell (short sell if there are no restrictions on doing so) until the price is at equilibrium. In short, expected return from owning the security should be:

Equilibrium
Required Return
$$E(R_i) = RF + \beta_i(RP_M) \tag{7.14}$$

The return that will actually be earned consists of any increases (or decreases) in the security's price plus any cash payoff, such as dividends on a stock or coupons on a bond. In the case of a stock:

Actual Security
Return
$$R_{i1} = \frac{P_{i1} - P_{i0} + D_{i1}}{P_{i0}} \tag{7.15}$$

where: P_{i1} = price of security i at the end of period 1.

P_{i0} = price of i at the beginning of period 1.

D_{i1} = dividends received during period 1.

For the security to be priced at equilibrium, the expected outcome of Equation 7.15 should be equal to the fair return expressed in Equation 7.14:

Equilibrium Required Return = Expected Security Return

Equilibrium
Market
Returns
$$RF + \beta_i(RP_M) = \frac{E(P_{i1}) - P_{i0} + E(D_{i1})}{P_{i0}} \tag{7.16}$$

Rearranging this quite logical statement and letting P_{i0}^* represent the equilibrium price of i, we see that this equilibrium price is simply the present value of the expected end-of-period price and dividend discounted at a return appropriate for its level of nondiversifiable risk:

Equilibrium
Security Price
$$P_{i0}^* = \frac{E(P_{i1}) + E(D_{i1})}{1.0 + RF + \beta_i(RP_M)} \tag{7.17}$$

For example, let's compute the equilibrium price of Exxon stock given the following data:

$$RP_M = 6\% \qquad \beta_X = 0.5 \qquad E(P_{X1}) = \$52.70$$

$$RF = 10\% \qquad\qquad\qquad E(D_X) = \$\ 3.80$$

According to the SML, one should expect a 13.0% return on any investment in a security having the amount of nondiversifiable risk present in Exxon shares:

$$10.0\% + 0.5\ (6.0\%) = 13.0\%$$

Since the expected price at the end of the period (say, one year) is $52.70 and the expected dividend is $3.80, the equilibrium price must be $50.00:

$$\frac{\$52.70 + \$3.80}{1.13} = \$50.00$$

The equilibrium pricing formula stated in Equation 7.17 strictly applies to a single-period world that meets all the assumptions made at the start of the chapter. There is no warranty on its validity when it is used in other situations. In practice, however, the principal features of the model are used widely. Security analysts forecast expected future dividends and prices on a stock and discount them to the present using a discount rate generated from the SML. A detailed illustration of how this is done is delayed to Chapter 14, where we have the opportunity to explore the process of security analysis in some depth.

Strategy

The implications for portfolio strategy that arise from the CAPM are quite reasonable and, even if not *strictly* true, they provide clear guidance. At the center of this theory is the market portfolio. It is *the* single optimal portfolio of risky assets—the only portfolio of risky assets that should be held. In theory, this makes sense; in practice, it is impossible to achieve. But even if the market portfolio cannot actually be held, one should not discard the principle of broad diversification. For example, an easy way to own 100 to 200 stocks with a very small equity investment is to purchase three or four mutual funds that hold distinctly different types of stocks. In addition, holdings such as real estate and international securities represent major asset classes which are too often neglected.

The optimal investment in a security depends upon the market value of that security relative to the market value of all securities. For example, if IBM's common stock represents 4.37% of all U.S. equity value, then 4.37% of an individual's U.S. common stock portfolio should be in IBM. Again, this principle is difficult to carry out in practice. However, index funds are designed to be identical to various broad stock indexes (such as the S&P 500). As such, they represent a good way to obtain proper weightings. But even well-run index funds are unable to maintain precisely the same percentages in the fund as in the index. Differences are small, but they do exist. Barring the use of such an index fund, some reasonable relationship between the total value of an issue and its weighting in the portfolio should be maintained. An investor certainly shouldn't place twice as much of his or her money in a small computer firm such as Storage Technology as in a massive firm such as IBM. In such a case, much potential for diversification would be lost.

After a portfolio is broadly diversified (even if not in M), one can adjust the borrowing-lending mix to achieve a preferred risk/return level. Lending portfolios can be created by purchasing U.S. Treasury securities, and borrowing portfolios can be created by using margin. As we will see in Chapters 15 and 16, options and financial futures also provide a number of ways to alter a portfolio's risk level and move along the borrowing-lending line. Finally, we should always remember that greater expected returns come only with greater uncertainty.

Performance Evaluation

Concepts of the CAPM have been increasingly used by investors and speculators to evaluate the performance of one style of management against others. In fact, a number of investment-counseling services offer services that provide comparisons of performance based in large measure on the CAPM. Although these performance measures are typically used to evaluate the risk/return performance of large investment firms, such as mutual funds, bank trust departments, and pension funds, they could also be used by individuals to measure their personal performance, to evaluate the buy-sell selections of security analysts, etcetera. Three basic performance models have been suggested to date: (1) the Sharpe model, (2) the Treynor model, and (3) the Jensen model. These are examined in Chapter 21.

ESTIMATING A SECURITY'S BETA

In theory, beta represents the nondiversifiable, systematic risk of an individual security or portfolio of securities. It reflects a risk for which a return should be expected. Theory treats it as a subjective estimate made by each individual of what the future might hold. It is, indeed, an ex ante opinion of likely systematic risk during the next period of time.

In practice, it is rare that subjective statements of beta are made. Instead, estimates based on historical returns are used. In this section, we examine how these historical estimates of the true beta are prepared. Since the techniques provide only estimates of the true beta, we must be careful to differentiate between the two. Theoretical beta will continue to be represented as β_i. Estimates of β_i will be represented as b_i.

When we move from the theoretical concept of β_i to a real-world estimate, we encounter a variety of serious problems. For example, the world simply does not consist of one period. Should beta be estimated over a time period that consists of the past month, the past five years, or the past twenty years? Should beta be estimated using daily, weekly, monthly, quarterly, etcetera, returns? How should changes in the product line of a firm be factored in? How does one estimate the beta of a bond whose life is continually changing and thus will be less sensitive to systematic economic shocks?

The list of problems associated with estimates of β_i based on historical data is long. And many of these problems remain unresolved. Yet b_i values are commonplace today and the techniques used to develop them should be understood.

The Market Model

The Market Model (MM) is an equation that relates the return on security i during time t to the return on a proxy for the market portfolio during the same time period. The MM is written as:

Market Model $$\tilde{R}_{it} = A_i + b_i\,(\tilde{R}_{Mt}) + \tilde{e}_{it} \tag{7.18}$$

$\tilde{R}_{it}$ represents the volatile return (hence the tilde) on security i during period t. It is equal to the sum of three components. First, a constant return is earned in each period regardless of the return on the market portfolio. This is A_i, referred to as *alpha*. Next, the security is said to have a sensitivity to the market portfolio return denoted by the b_i term. When this beta sensitivity is multiplied by the market return, $\tilde{R}_{Mt}$, we have the security return caused by its market risk exposure. Finally, there is a difference between what the actual return on security i is and what the first two terms suggest the return should have been. This difference is known as the residual error term $\tilde{e}_{it}$.

Due to variability in the nominal risk free rate of interest, the MM is usually estimated in "excess return" form. This simply means that an estimate of the nominal risk-free return is subtracted from both R_{it} and R_{Mt} as follows:

Excess Return
Market Model $$(\tilde{R}_{it} - \tilde{R}F_t) = a_i + b_i(\tilde{R}_{Mt} - \tilde{R}F_t) + \tilde{e}_{it} \tag{7.19}$$

In this form, the constant alpha term, a_i, represents the constant security return in excess of the risk free rate of interest.

Figure 7-6 is a graphical representation of the excess return MM. When the market portfolio proxy has a zero return, the excess security return is expected to have a return of a_i. As the market portfolio has a positive or negative excess return, the extent to which security i tends to share in this return depends on the slope of the line-b_i. During any time period, however, the security's excess return might not be exactly equal to $a_i + b_i(R_{Mt} - RF_t)$. Events that have no effect on the aggregate market portfolio might have an effect on security i. These errors are the e_{it} values.

For example, assume that you are given the following excess return MM data for a mutual fund (AMF):

$$a_{AMF} = 2.0\% \qquad (R_{AMF,t} - RF_t) = 12.0\%$$

$$b_{AMF} = 0.7 \qquad (R_{Mt} - RF_t) = 10.0\%$$

The data are displayed in Figure 7-7. If the excess market portfolio return had been 0.0%, the expected excess return on AMF would have been 2.0%. However, the market portfolio's excess return was 10.0%. The b_{AMF} of 0.7 indicates that AMF would be expected to have a return equal to 7.0% above the alpha of 2.0%.

FIGURE 7-6 *The Market Model*

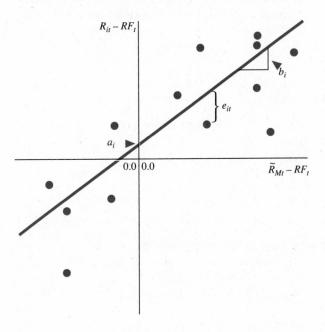

FIGURE 7-7 *Sample Market Model for IBM*

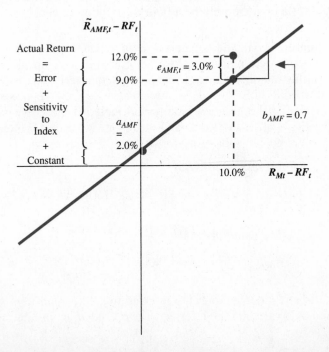

In short, given the 10.0% excess market return, the expected return on AMF would be 9.0%. However, AMF's actual return was 12.0%. The difference of +3.0% is AMF's residual error during this time period. On average, these error terms will be zero because of the way in which the a_i and b_i terms are statistically estimated.

The Market Model Versus the SML. The excess return version of the Market Model (MM) can be expressed in any of the following ways:

$$(\tilde{R}_{it} - \tilde{RF}_t) = a_i + b_i(\tilde{R}_{Mt} - \tilde{RF}_t) + \tilde{e}_{it} \tag{7.20a}$$

Excess Return
Market Model

$$\tilde{R}_{it} = a_i + \tilde{RF}_t + b_i\tilde{R}_{Mt} - b_i\tilde{RF}_t) + \tilde{e}_{it}$$

$$\tilde{R}_{it} = a_i + (1 - b_i)\,\tilde{RF}_t - b_i\tilde{R}_{Mt} + \tilde{e}_{it} \tag{7.20b}$$

Compare Equation 7.20b with the SML equation below:

SML
$$E(R_i) = RF + \beta_i E(R_M)$$

They look suspiciously similar—obviously, this is not a coincidence since b_i is intended to be an estimate of the true β_i. But are they the same? The answer is maybe. There are two principal differences between them: (1) alpha in the MM and (2) a possible difference between the true market portfolio in the SML and the market proxy in the MM.

The average security has a beta of 1.0. Thus, the $(1 - b_i)RF_t$ term will be zero on average. For the MM to be a good representation of the SML, the average a_i term should also be zero. If this is not true: (1) the market might be in a state of disequilibrium, (2) the market proxy used in the MM might be substantially biased, or (3) the SML might simply be a poor description of real security markets.

Beta Estimates. The a_i and b_i parameters in the MM are calculated by regressing a security's historical returns against the returns on a reasonable market portfolio proxy. To illustrate the results of this process, quarterly excess returns (returns in excess of 90 day U.S. T-bills) of two securities were regressed against excess returns on the S&P 500 index. The period included the 10 years ended in 1990. The securities were IBM stock and shares of American Mutual Fund (AMF). Regression results are shown below:

Market Model Regression for IBM

$$(\tilde{R}_{IBM,t} - \tilde{RF}_t) = -0.005 + 0.9147\,(\tilde{R}_{SP,t} - \tilde{RF}_t)$$
$$(0.1675) \qquad\qquad R^2 = 0.439$$

Market Model Regression for AMF

$$(\tilde{R}_{AMF,t} - \tilde{RF}_t) = +0.006 + 0.6849\,(\tilde{R}_{SP,t} - \tilde{RF}_t)$$
$$(0.0332) \qquad\qquad R^2 = 0.917$$

The left-hand-side variables are referred to as the *dependent* variables and the right-hand-side variables are referred to as *independent* variables. Alpha estimates are -0.005 and $+0.006$ respectively. The beta estimates are 0.9147 and 0.6849. Numbers shown in parentheses below the beta estimates are standard deviation estimates of the beta parameters.

The R^2 value measures the proportion of volatility in the dependent variable explained by volatility in the independent variable. R-squared can range from 0.0, in which case, there is no relationship between the variables, to 1.0, in which case, the variables are perfectly correlated.

Notice that the R-square value for the mutual fund AMF is close to 1.0. This is due to the fact that AMF consists of a broadly diversified portfolio of stocks. In contrast, the R-square for IBM is only 0.439 implying a correlation coefficient between IBM returns and S&P 500 returns of 0.66 (the square root of R-square).

The Characteristic Line. The two panels in Figure 7-8 show these results graphically. The line drawn through the scatter diagram is the regression equation shown above. It is commonly known as the characteristic line.

The slope of the characteristic line is our beta estimate and the intercept on the vertical axis is the alpha estimate. The regression procedure used to calculate b_i uses an equation similar to Equation 7.9 that defines the true B value for a security. The only difference is that b_i values are based on past returns and a proxy for the market portfolio. Specifically:

**Regression
Estimate of b_i**
$$b_i = (\sigma_i r_{iM})/\sigma_M$$
(7.21)

where: σ_i = standard deviation of security i's historical excess returns.

σ_M = standard deviation of the market portfolio proxy's historical excess returns.

r_{iM} = historical correlation between excess historical returns on security i and portfolio M.

Beta estimates such as these are available from any number of sources. The major brokerage houses, banks, and investment advisory firms are all very willing to sell their b values. To calculate the regression equation, all one needs is access to historical returns and a regression computer package. The b values obtained from each source will be somewhat different, since each b supplier has its own unique way of calculating the characteristic line. For example, different indexes are used. Some use daily returns, others monthly, etcetera. And many provide "adjusted" b values—something we discuss in a moment. Most of the estimates, however, are reasonably similar.

To illustrate, Table 7-2 presents b values created by the author for various stocks in the S&P 500. The index used to generate these b values was not the S&P 500 but, instead, an index with more than 500 stocks, including many firms smaller than those in the S&P 500. Also shown is the b of the S&P 500. Note that b_{SP500} is slightly less than 1.0, implying that the average stock in the S&P 500 has slightly less systematic risk than the average stock included in this broader index.

FIGURE 7-8 *Characteristic Line for IBM (Panel A)*

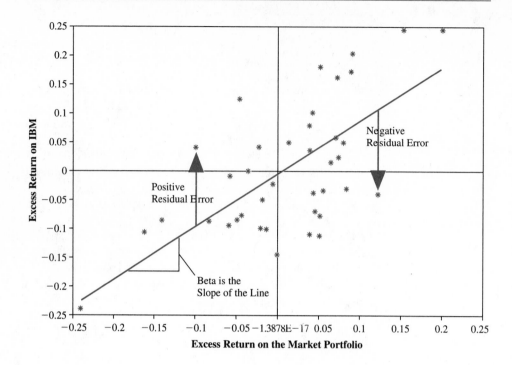

FIGURE 7-8 *Characteristic Line for AMF (Panel B)*

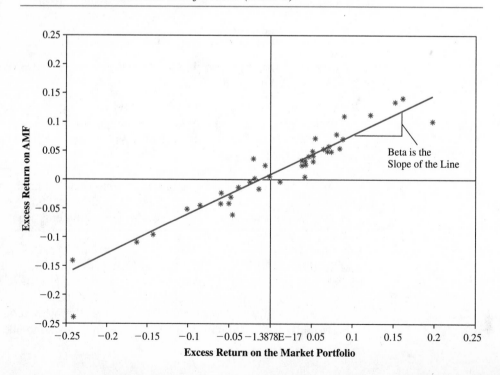

TABLE 7-2 *Illustrative Betas*

Company	Beta
Middle South Utilities	0.299470
Philadelphia Electric Co	0.421063
Chemical New York Corp	0.628447
Goodyear Tire & Rubber Co	0.924434
Niagara Mohawk Power	0.357685
Public Service Elec & Ga	0.334671
Texas Utilities Co	0.241467
Pacific Gas & Electric	0.145618
Southern Co	0.365085
Central & South West Cor	0.282447
Duke Power Co	0.094342
Dana Corp	0.678298
Sears, Roebuck & Co	0.859260
Southern Calif Edison Co	0.253661
Eastman Kodak Co	0.505859
Exxon Corp	0.835662
Beatrice Co	0.438998
Philip Morris Inc	0.587872
Burroughs Corp	0.90162
Georgia-Pacific Corp	1.17036
Honeywell Inc	1.15948
Bankers Trust New York Co	0.92745
Gould Inc	1.21621
Borg-Warner Corp	0.95609
Allied Corp	1.09718
McDonnell Douglas Corp	1.28652
American General Corp	1.02937
American Cyanamid Co	0.89943
Revlon Inc	0.84249
Black & Decker Corp	1.13096
RCA Corp	0.79101
CBS Inc	0.85176
Warner-Lambert Co	0.98033
American Express	0.85300
Kaufman & Broad Inc	2.14235
Federal Paper Board Co	1.06923
National Gypsum Co	1.39210
Grumman Corp	1.48491
Teledyne Inc	1.76380
Wang Laboratories-Cl B	2.22450
Apple Computer Inc	1.50000
General Dynamics Corp	1.30829
Prime Computer	2.40101
Tandy Corp	1.77792
Tonka Corp	1.09149
Lowe's Cos	1.20000
Searle (G. D.) & Co	1.02811
Lockheed Corp	1.57955
Macmillan Inc	1.10984
Wendy's International In	1.05000
Handleman Co	1.03977
Toys R Us Inc	1.20000
Cullinet Software Inc	1.80000
Hasbro Bradley Inds	1.39715
S&P 500	0.94000

Diversifiable Versus Nondiversifiable Risk. The returns plotted in Figure 7-8 can be used to illustrate again the difference between diversifiable and nondiversifiable risk. Notice that rarely does the return plot exactly on the characteristic line. An error almost always exists. It is these error terms that are diversified away. As long as the error for stock i is *not correlated* with the error on all other stocks, the errors will go to zero when all the stocks are combined. If the error terms are correlated, either we have a poor index proxy of the market portfolio or the CAPM is wrong. These are points that are examined more closely in the next chapter.

If security returns are indeed created as Equation 7.20 suggests (a constant + sensitivity to random market returns + a random residual term), then it can be shown that the total risk of a security's return can be decomposed into two parts, as shown in Equation 7.22:

$$\text{Total Risk} = \begin{array}{c}\text{Systematic} \\ \text{Risk}\end{array} + \begin{array}{c}\text{Unsystematic} \\ \text{Risk}\end{array} \tag{7.22}$$

$$\sigma_i^2 = \beta_i^2 \sigma_m^2 + \sigma_{ei}^2$$

where $\sigma_i^2 =$ the variance of returns on security i, $\beta_i =$ the beta of i (or sensitivity of i's returns to market returns), $\sigma_m^2 =$ the variance of returns expected on the market index being used, and $\sigma_{ei}^2 =$ the variance of security i's random residual error return.

The variance of returns on a security is determined by two factors. The first relates to how sensitive a security's returns are to events that affect all securities. This sensitivity is captured by beta. The uncertainty associated with such aggregate economic events is captured by the perceived variance of market returns. This portion of total security risk cannot be diversified since it reflects events that affect all securities. The second factor accounts for uncertainty about a security's returns that are not related in any systematic way to other securities. This part of a security's return is totally independent of returns on other securities. As a result, these residual returns tend to net out across a large number of securities. They offset each other and can be diversified away.

The Accuracy of Beta Estimates

The market model provides estimates of historical b values. How good are these at forecasting future b values? Evidence developed to date suggests two major conclusions:

1. Beta estimates of single stocks are poor predictors of future b values. Predictability improves if beta is estimated for a portfolio, and this predictability increases as the number of securities held in the portfolio increases.
2. Beta estimates tend to move towards 1.0. If b is found to be less than 1.0 during a given time interval, chances are that it will increase in the next time period. Conversely, if b is greater than 1.0, chances are that it will fall.

Predictability

A classic study of how well a past b predicts the future b was conducted by Blume. He used the market model on monthly returns for nonoverlapping seven-year intervals to calculate b on portfolios consisting of from 1 stock to 50 stocks. Then for each portfolio size, he examined the correlation between an initial period's b and the subsequent period's b. Both the correlation coefficient, $r,$ and its squared value, R^2, were calculated. We will discuss only the R^2 measure since its meaning is easiest to understand. In the context of Blume's study, R^2 is the percentage of variability in the subsequent period's b explained by the variability in the initial period's b. If R^2 is 100%, then the subsequent b values are perfectly predicted. If $R^2 = 30\%$, then only 30% of the variability is predicted.

Blume's results are shown in Table 7-3. For single securities, b is a poor predictor. Only 36% of the subsequent period's variability in b is explained by the variability in the initial period. For portfolios, however, the predictability improves markedly. For a 10-stock portfolio, R^2 is 85%, and by the time 50 stocks are held, R^2 is 96%. This is because estimation errors on single-stock b values are uncorrelated with each other and thus disappear in portfolios. The conclusion is obvious. The market model beta for a single stock is a highly questionable estimate of the stock's true systematic risk. Beta estimates of portfolios are more trustworthy.

Betas Tend to Move to 1.0. Studies have also shown that betas estimated in one period tend to be closer to 1.0 in the subsequent period. Again using some of Blume's results, Table 7-4 shows the estimated betas on six portfolios for two time periods. The portfolios are arranged from the smallest beta to the largest. Note that there is a definite trend for low betas in the initial period to have higher betas in the subsequent period, and for high beta portfolios in the initial period to have a smaller b in the subsequent period.

TABLE 7-3 *Predictability of b Values*

Number of Securities in Portfolio	R^2
1	36%
2	53%
4	71%
7	77%
10	85%
20	95%
50	96%

SOURCE: M. Blume, "Betas and Their Regression Tendencies," *Journal of Finance* 10, no. 3 (June 1975): 785–96.
R^2 = Percentage of variability of b in a subsequent period explained by variability of b in the initial period.

TABLE 7-4 *Beta Estimates Move Toward 1.0*

Portfolio	*Initial* 7/54–6/61	*Subsequent* 7/61–6/68
1	0.39	0.62
2	0.61	0.71
3	0.81	0.86
4	0.99	0.91
5	1.14	1.00
7	1.34	1.17

SOURCE: M. Blume, "On the Assessment of Risk," *Journal of Finance* 6, no. 1 (March 1971): 1–10.

The reason why beta estimates tend to more toward 1.0 is not fully understood. Most likely, it is due to measurement errors in the initial period's beta estimate. For example, if the initial beta is greater than 1.0 the chance that beta has been overestimated is greater than the chance that it has been underestimated.

Adjustments to Market Model Betas. Given the small predictive content of Market Model (MM) betas for individual stocks, a variety of methods have been suggested to improve forecasting accuracy. Three of the more popular methods include the following:

1. Arbitrarily adjusting toward 1.0.
2. Adjusting on the basis of Bayesian statistics.
3. Relating betas to fundamental characteristics of the individual stocks.

Recognizing that MM beta estimates in one time interval tend to move towards 1.0 in the next time interval, many organizations adjust calculated market model betas toward 1.0. A variety of methods are used that vary in sophistication. For example, one could use the relatively naive procedure of saying that the predicted beta will be some fraction, say halfway, between the market model estimate and 1.0. For example, an MM estimate of 1.8 would be stated as a predicted beta of 1.4, and an estimate of 0.5 would be predicted as 0.75. In his original study, Blume used a more sophisticated approach and found that his MM betas in a second time period were related to those in a prior time period as follows:

$$b_{i2} = 0.343 + 0.677b_{i1}$$

There is no guarantee, however, that such relationships remain stable over time.

Another approach, first suggested by Vasichek, is based on Bayesian statistics. First, MM estimates are calculated for a large number of stocks. Among the output will be the following statistics:

$$b_i = \text{estimate of beta for stock } i$$

$$\sigma(b_i) = \text{standard deviation of stock } i\text{'s beta}$$

$$\bar{b} = \text{the average of all betas calculated}$$

$$\sigma_{all} = \text{the standard deviation of the sample betas}$$

Vasichek suggested that a revised beta, b_i^*, be calculated for each stock as follows:

Vasichek Beta Adjustment

$$b_i^* = b_i \frac{\sigma_{all}^2}{\sigma_{all}^2 + \sigma(b_i)^2} + \bar{b} \frac{\sigma(b_i)^2}{\sigma_{all}^2 + \sigma(b_i)^2} \qquad (7.23)$$

To illustrate, assume we have just calculated the following for five stock beta estimates:

			Stock		
	1	*2*	*3*	*4*	*5*
b_i	0.8	0.9	1.0	1.1	1.2
$\sigma(b_i)$	0.1	0.1	0.2	0.2	0.4

$\bar{b}$ = average of the betas
   = 1.0
σ_{all} = standard deviation of the sample betas
   = 0.1414

Consider stock 5 with an estimated beta of 1.2. Using Equation 7.23 the Bayesian predicted beta would be 1.02:

$$b_5^* = 1.2 \frac{0.1414^2}{0.1414^2 + 0.4^2} + 1.0 \frac{0.4^2}{0.1414^2 + 0.4^2}$$

$$= 1.2(0.11108) + 1.0(0.88892) = 1.02$$

Note that the two weighting terms add to 1.0. Note also that as $\sigma(b_i)$ becomes larger, the weight given to b_i becomes smaller and the weight given to $\bar{b}$ greater.

Other researchers have suggested that we try to explain future betas not only in terms of past beta estimates but also in terms of fundamental characteristics of the stocks. Such betas, which have come to be known as *fundamental betas,* are widely used. To illustrate, assume that we have calculated market model betas on a large number of stocks in periods 1 and 2. In addition, we have information about certain fundamental characteristics of the stocks. Our data consist of the following for each stock:

b_{i1}, b_{i2} = beta estimate for stock in periods 1 and 2

IND_i = a measure of the firm's industry

LEV_i = a measure of the firm's financial leverage

VOL_i = a measure of past profit volatility

Then the following regression could be run in order to determine the importance of each variable in predicting b_{i2}:

$$b_{i2} = a_0 + a_1(b_{i1}) + a_2(IND_i) + a_3(LEV_i)$$
$$+ a_4(VOL_i) + e_i$$

The estimated regression parameters could then be used to predict betas on stocks not in our sample or to predict future betas, given b_{i2} and a firm's current fundamental characteristics.

There are a variety of statistical procedures that would be better than regression analysis. But the basic concept of what is meant by ''fundamental betas'' should be clear.

SUMMARY

The purpose of this chapter was to examine how securities would be priced under equilibrium risk/return conditions. However, to develop a manageable model of equilibrium, a variety of assumptions had to be made. First, we assumed a *one-period world* in which risk-averse individuals could determine the expected end-of-period utility by knowing the *expected return and standard deviation of portfolio returns.* Next, we assumed a *frictionless market,* a market in which brokerage fees, taxes, etcetera, would not impede trading and all investors had equal costless access to information. Finally, we assumed that all individuals could borrow or lend at a *risk-free rate.*

The model that results from these assumptions is known as the *capital asset pricing model* (CAPM). Embodied in this model are two fundamental economic relationships: (1) the CML, which specifies what the expected return on an *efficient portfolio* should be in terms of the portfolio's standard deviation, and (2) the SML, which specifies what the expected return on any *security or portfolio* should be in terms of its *nondiversifiable risk.* The single efficient portfolio of risky assets that drives the CML and the SML is the *market portfolio,* a portfolio consisting of all risky assets available, with each held in proportion to its total market value.

Under the CAPM's assumptions, this is a perfectly reasonable outcome. The market portfolio is the *most widely diversified portfolio available.* Any other portfolio will suffer in comparison because the risk it contains could be eliminated simply by costless diversification. If the diversification across an additional security reduces the return, the return can be restored by borrowing at *RF.* As first discussed in Chapter 6, the selection of the best risky portfolio is separate from the selection of an appropriate risk/reward level. First, diversify as broadly as possible (buy the market portfolio). Then borrow or lend at *RF* to achieve the risk/return preference of the individual investor.

The CML and SML have gained wide use within the professional investment community. Security analysts use the theory in *pricing* stocks, portfolio managers develop proper portfolio *strategies* around its principles, and consultants use it to evaluate a portfolio's performance. Most such pragmatic applications require estimates of a security's beta.

Beta estimates are usually based on the Market Model (MM) in which historical returns on a security in excess of a risk-free rate are regressed against excess returns on a proxy for the market portfolio. Unfortunately, such beta estimates for individual stocks are often poor predictors of the stock's actual future beta. In contrast, historical beta estimates of diversified stock portfolios are fairly good estimates of the future portfolio beta.

REVIEW PROBLEM # 1

As a financial consultant to a pension fund, you are preparing a presentation on the various aspects of the theory of risk and expected return discussed in this chapter. The following questions review certain major features of this theory.

a. What is meant by market equilibrium and what assumptions are used in its development?

b. Assume there are three major classes of risky securities available, as follows:

Security Class	Total Market	σ	Correlation with			
			RE	E	D	Total
Real Estate	$10,000	20%	1.0			0.65
Equity	6,000	30%	0.3	1.0		0.60
Debt	4,000	15%	0.3	0.3	1.0	0.30

What is the market portfolio? How much of its risky assets should the pension invest in each security type? What is the σ of such a portfolio?

c. If $RF = 8.0\%$ and $RP_M = 5.0\%$, what are the CML and SML equations?

d. One member of the pension fund's board of trustees has stated that their investment portfolio should have a long-run expected return of 12%. In theory, how would this be obtained?

e. An assistant believes that the beta of Textron common stock is 1.2. What should Textron stock be expected to earn to qualify for a purchase?

f. The local representative of a common stock mutual fund has been pressing the pension fund's trustees to invest solely in the fund. One reason that the representative offers is that the fund has a beta of 1.0 and thus its risk is the same as the market portfolio's risk. Comment.

Solution

a. The security market is in equilibrium if prices are at levels that attract no speculative trading. In this case, people have common beliefs about the future. Assumptions used in the model are the following:
(1) We live in a one-period world.
(2) $E(R_p)$ and σ_p are all that matter.
(3) Everyone may borrow or lend at RF.
(4) All investors have homogeneous expectations.
(5) Markets are frictionless.

b. Given these assumptions, and for the markets to clear, the optimal market portfolio is:

Security	X*
Real Estate	0.50
Equity	0.30
Debt	0.20

$$\sigma_p = [(0.5)^2(20)^2 + (0.3)^2(30)^2 + (0.2)^2(15)^2 + 2(0.3)(0.5)(0.3)(20)(30)$$

$$+ 2(0.3)(0.5)(0.2)(20)(15) + 2(0.3)(0.3)(0.2)(30)(15)]^{1/2}$$

$$= 16.7\%$$

c. CML equation:

$$E(R_p) = 8.0\% + \sigma_p\left(\frac{5.0\%}{16.7\%}\right)$$

SML equation:

$$E(R_i) = 8.0\% + \beta_i[5.0\%]$$

d. For each σ_p of an efficient portfolio, a return of 0.3% is earned above the 8% risk-free rate. Thus, to have an expected return of 12.0%, σ_p must be $(12 - 8) \div 0.3$, or 13.33%:

$$8.0\% + 13.33\% [0.30] = 12.0\%$$

Efficient portfolios would be combinations of portfolio M and RF. To get a $\sigma_p = 13.33\%$ when $\sigma_M = 16.7\%$, they should invest 80% of the portfolio in the market portfolio:

$$\frac{13.33}{16.7} = 0.80$$

The remaining 20% would be placed in risk-free securities.

e. $E(R_T) = 8.0\% + 1.2 [5.0\%]$ (the SML)

$$= 14.0\%$$

f. The mutual fund's beta may be 1.0, but this only says that the fund has nondiversifiable (systematic) risk identical to that of the market portfolio. However, unless the mutual fund's percentages of holdings are identical to the percentage weights of the market portfolio, the fund still has some diversifiable (unsystematic) risk and should not be held as the pension's only investment.

R E V I E W   P R O B L E M   # 2

On page 237 is a plot of expected returns and standard deviations of four securities. Point M represents the market portfolio. Points X, Y, and Z can be thought of as individual securities or portfolios of securities.

a. Does a risk/return diagram such as this one imply that the security markets are in equilibrium or disequilibrium according to CAPM?

b. Write the CML and SML equations underlying this diagram.

c. What are the betas of each security?

d. What is the beta of a portfolio consisting of a 1/3 investment in X, Y, and Z? What should be the expected return on this portfolio?

e. Stocks Y and Z are equally risky since they have the same standard deviation. True or false? Why?

f. Another security not shown here is stock A. It has a beta of 0.7 and an expected return of 8.0%. Would you buy or short sell this stock? Is the market in equilibrium? If not, how would equilibrium be achieved?

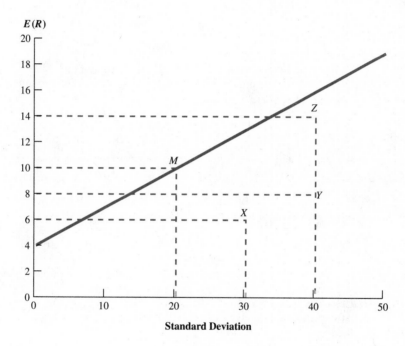

Standard Deviation

Solution

a. The diagram implies a CAPM equilibrium since no security "beats" the market portfolio.

b.
$$\text{CML: } E(R_p) = 4\% + \sigma_p \left(\frac{10\% - 4\%}{20} \right)$$

$$\text{SML: } E(R_i) = 4\% + \beta_i (10\% - 4\%)$$

c.

Security	Beta	Calculation
X	0.3333	$6 = 4 + \beta_X (6)$
Y	0.6666	$8 = 4 + \beta_Y (6)$
Z	1.6666	$14 = 4 + \beta_Z (6)$

   d. $\beta_p = 1/3\ (0.33) + 1/3\ (0.66) + 1/3\ (1.66)$

$$= 0.888$$

$$E(R_p) = 4\% + 0.888\ (6\%).$$

$$= 9.3\%$$

e. False. Z is riskier as evidenced by the higher expected return, which implies a larger beta.

f. The expected return which you should require is 8.2%:

$$E(R_i) = 4\% + 0.7\ (6\%)$$

$$= 8.2\%$$

Since it is priced to return only 8.0%, the stock should be ''underweighted'' or perhaps even sold short. Eventually its price will fall as you and others sell until an 8.2% return is actually expected.

QUESTIONS AND PROBLEMS

1. If the correlation coefficient between the returns on a portfolio and the market portfolio is 1.0, this is an efficient portfolio. True or false? Why?
2. A broadly diversified portfolio of commodities (corn, tin, gold, comic books, etc.) has a zero correlation with the market portfolio. It will therefore provide a return equal to the risk-free rate. True or false? Why?
3. In equilibrium, all investors have homogeneous expectations. What does this mean and why is it a necessary condition for equilibrium?
4. How would an index fund help an investor to purchase the market portfolio?
5. After a thorough analysis of both the aggregate stock market and the stock of XYZ, Inc., you develop the following opinions:

Economic Conditions	Likely Return		Probability
	Aggregate Market	XYZ	
Good	16%	20%	0.4
Fair	12%	13%	0.4
Poor	3%	−5%	0.2

At present the risk-rate is equal to 7%. Would an investment in XYZ be wise?
6. Assume that the risk-free rate of interest is 8%, the market has an estimated risk premium of 6%, and the market's standard deviation of returns is 10%. Calculate the variance (or standard deviation) of returns for each portfolio below.
   Portfolio 1: 30% risk-free bonds, 70% the market
   Portfolio 2: diversified portfolio with beta = 1.5
7. The policy committee of Investor's Diversified Corporation (IDC) recently used reports from various security analysts to develop the following efficient portfolios:

Portfolio	Expected Return	Standard Deviation
1	8%	3%
2	10%	6%
3	13%	8%
4	17%	13%
5	20%	18%

a. If the prevailing risk-free rate is 6%, which portfolio is the best?

b. Assume that the policy committee would like to earn an expected 10% with a standard deviation of 4%. Is this feasible?

c. If a standard deviation of 12% were acceptable, what would the expected portfolio return be and how would IDC achieve it?

8. Consider the following information on three securities. Which has the greatest systematic risk? Which has the smallest?

Security	σ_i	r_{iM}
1	σ_1	r_{1M}
2	$\sigma_2 = \sigma_1$	$r_{2M} > r_{1M}$
3	$\sigma_3 > \sigma_1$	$r_{3M} = r_{1M}$

9. You expect the stock of Firm X to sell for $70 a year from now and to pay a $4 dividend. If the stock's correlation with portfolio M is -0.3, $\sigma_x = 40.0\%$, $\sigma_M = 20.0\%$, $RF = 5\%$, and $RP_M = 5.0\%$, what should the stock be selling for? Explain this result.

10. Using five years of excess monthly returns, the following regression statistics were generated using the market model and a broad common stock index:

Security	A_i	σ_i	r_{il}
Mesa Petroleum	-0.21	14.7%	0.48
Anheuser-Busch	0.15	6.3%	0.25
Teledyne	0.01	11.3%	0.51
XYZ Mutual Fund	0.20	5.2%	0.95
Index	0.00	4.3%	1.00

a. Calculate an estimate of β for each.

b. Do you think the market model betas during the next five-year period will be the same, higher, or lower?

c. Assuming that the index used is the market portfolio, that $RP_M = 7.0\%$, and that the current $RF = 9.0\%$, calculate the equilibrium expected return on each.

d. Assume that each security is the only holding of the portfolio. Calculate required expected returns and explain why these are not the same as the answer to part c.

e. Calculate the beta of a portfolio consisting of an equal investment in each stock.

11. You are given the following estimates of stock i's and stock j's characteristic lines plus estimates of each stock's standard deviation of returns:

$$(\tilde{R}_{it} - \tilde{RF}_t) = 1\% + 1.5\,(\tilde{R}_{Mt} - \tilde{RF}_t)$$

$$(\tilde{R}_{jt} - \tilde{RF}_t) = 4\% + 1.0\,(\tilde{R}_{Mt} - \tilde{RF}_t)$$

$$\sigma\,(\tilde{R}_{it} - \tilde{RF}_t) = 20\%;\ \sigma\,(\tilde{R}_{jt} - \tilde{RF}_t) = 10\%$$

a. One-year T-bills are now yielding 8%. If the market portfolio is *expected* to return 13% during the year, what is the expected return on each stock as of the beginning of the year?

b. The year goes by and the market portfolio *actually* provides a 10% rate of return during the year. Given this, what is your expectation of the return earned on each stock during the year?

c. If stock i actually returned 15% and stock j actually returned 11%, what was the residual error return for each stock?

d. Why might a residual error return arise, and what is its role in diversification?

e. If the standard deviation of stock i's residual error term is 10%, what is your best estimate of the standard deviation of excess returns—that is, $\sigma(\tilde{R}_{Mt} - \tilde{RF}_t)$—on the market portfolio?

12. Management of a mutual fund has considered three alternative strategies:

	% Investment in				
Plan	T-Bonds	Stocks	Beta of T-Bonds	Beta of Stocks	Portfolio
1	0.0	100	0	1.0	?
2	20	80	0	1.0	?
3	30	70	0	1.0	?

a. Which is the most risky strategy?

b. If $RF = 7\%$ and the expected return under plan 1 is 14%, what is the market risk premium?

c. Management believes that this risk premium is too low and that the market will soon adjust it upward. Given this, which plan might management wish to pursue?

d. Would this be a speculative or an investment strategy?

13. Suppose you have gathered quarterly data on the returns of four mutual funds and related them to equivalent market returns (S&P 500) and 90-day T-bill returns via the following regression model:

$$(\tilde{R}_{pt} - \tilde{RF}_t) = \alpha_p + b_p(\tilde{R}_{mt} - \tilde{RF}_t) + \tilde{E}_{pt}$$

	α_p		b_p			Std. Dev.
Fund	Coefficient	Std. Dev.	Coefficient	Std. Dev.	R^2	E_{pt}
1	0.98%	1.00%	0.80	0.05	95%	12%
2	2.18%	1.50%	1.30	0.15	80%	23%
3	2.18%	0.75%	1.20	0.12	90%	18%
4	-0.04%	0.50%	1.02	0.08	97%	14.4%

a. Which fund's returns were the most closely correlated to market returns?

b. Which fund had the most market risk?

c. Which fund had the most total risk?

d. Restate the alpha values in terms of their annualized equivalents.

14. The table below provides two years of excess monthly returns on Campbell Soup, Teledyne, the DFA Small Company Portfolio, and the Wilshire 5000 Common Stock Index. Use the Wilshire 5000 as the market index.

Period	Campbell	Tele	DFA	W5000	Period	Campbell	Tele	DFA	W5000
1	−1.9	14.6	6.3	4.2	13	4.2	1.7	−0.1	−1.6
2	−4.8	4.6	7.1	3.2	14	−6.1	−3.5	−6.5	−3.9
3	4.5	−5.5	5.2	3.6	15	2.7	1.5	1.7	1.4
4	−2.3	−1.3	7.7	7.4	16	0.5	−6.6	−0.1	0.3
5	8.3	4.4	8.7	1.3	17	−7.0	29.7	−5.2	−5.3
6	4.6	7.9	3.5	3.9	18	11.1	19.1	3.0	2.4
7	−1.4	−2.1	−0.9	−3.2	19	−2.5	8.0	−4.2	−1.9
8	8.0	−1.6	−2.0	0.6	20	3.1	6.8	10.0	11.3
9	0.9	2.9	1.3	1.6	21	9.2	2.6	0.3	0.6
10	7.2	0.1	−5.7	−2.6	22	3.4	−3.5	−2.2	0.0
11	2.3	0.8	5.2	2.8	23	−2.5	−4.1	−3.4	−1.1
12	3.4	2.5	−1.4	−1.1	24	2.2	−6.7	1.5	2.4

a. Use the market model to estimate the a_i and b_i terms.

b. Notice that DFA tracks the W5000 much more closely than do the two stocks. Why?

c. Estimate the systematic and unsystematic risk of each.
(Hint: $\sigma_i^2 = \beta_i^2 \sigma_1^2 + \sigma_E^2$.)

d. If $RF = 11\%$ and $RP_m = 6\%$, estimate the equilibrium expected returns on each.

e. Assume that the W5000 is a good estimate of the market portfolio. If each of these securities were to be held as the only risky asset in a portfolio, calculate the return that should be expected. Why does this differ from the estimated returns in part d?

f. Why is the Wilshire 5000 not a good representation of the market portfolio?

15. According to the Capital Asset Pricing Model (CAPM), the risk premium an investor expects to receive on any stock or portfolio increases:

a. directly with alpha.

b. inversely with alpha.

c. directly with beta.

d. inversely with beta.

16. The capital asset pricing model (CAPM) uses _____ as a measure of risk.

a. beta

b. standard deviation of returns

c. variance of returns

d. alpha

17. Capital asset pricing theory asserts that portfolio returns are best explained by:

a. economic factors.

b. specific risk.

c. systematic risk.

d. diversification.

18. The Capital Asset Pricing Model (CAPM) leads to all of the following conclusions *except:*

a. investors will not be paid for risk that can be diversified away.

b. the most important measure of stock risk is beta

c. a well-diversified 30-40 stock portfolio has mostly systematic risk.

d. borrowing and lending do not affect portfolio results.

19. Which *one* of the following is *not* a criticism of beta?
   a. Different calculation methods yield differing beta numbers.
   b. Estimated betas on individual stocks are unstable.
   c. In some periods, low beta stocks outperform high beta stocks.
   d. Wide-scale usage has reduced the effectiveness of the beta measure.

DATAFILE ANALYSIS

In this analysis, you will calculate the Market Model (MM) beta of American Mutual Fund.

1. *Market Model.* Access the datafile labeled MFEQUITY.WK1. Find the return series for American Mutual Fund (AMF), U.S. T-bills, and the S&P 500. Create two columns of excess return by subtracting the T-bill returns from AMF returns and S&P 500 returns. Use the regression option of your spreadsheet to regress AMF excess returns against excess S&P 500 returns. The dependent variable (*Y* variable) will be AMF. The independent variable (*X* variable) will be S&P 500. If you were to create a portfolio consisting of an investment in T-bills and the S&P 500 having a beta equal to that estimated for AMF, how much would you invest in each? Why is the *R*-squared value in this regression large?

Mutual funds such as AMF constantly change the percentage of assets they invest in T-bills and stocks. Given this, will the historical MM beta estimate for AMF be an accurate predictor of future AMF beta risk?

REFERENCES

The Capital Asset Pricing Model (CAPM) is occasionally referred to as the Sharpe-Linter-Mossin model after the following break-through articles:

LINTNER, JOHN, "The Valuation of Risky Assets and the Selection of Risky Investments in Stock Portfolios and Capital Budgets," *Review of Economics and Statistics*, February 1965.

MOSSIN, JAN, "Equilibrium in a Capital Asset Market," *Econometrica*, October 1966.

SHARPE, WILLIAM F., "Capital Asset Prices: A Theory of Market Equilibrium," *Journal of Finance*, September 1964.

A nonmathematical overview of the CAPM and its potential use in security analysis can be found in:

MODIGLIANI, FRANCO and GORDON POGUE, "An Introduction to Risk and Return: Concepts and Evidence," *Financial Analysts Journal*, March–April and May–June 1974.

Papers that examine the estimation of security betas include:

BLUME, MARSHAL. "Betas and Their Regression Tendencies: Some Further Evidence," *Journal of Finance*, March 1979.

HAMADA, ROBERT S., "The Effect of the Firm's Capital Structure on the Systematic Risk of Common Stocks," *Journal of Finance*, May 1971.

ROSENBERG, BARR and JAMES GUY, "Predictions of Beta from Investment Fundamentals," *Financial Analysts Journal*, May–June and July–August 1976.

VASICEK, OLDRICH, "A Note on Using Cross-Sectional Information in Bayesian Estimation of Security Betas," *Journal of Finance*, December 1973.

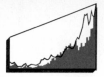

C H A P T E R 8

Capital Asset Pricing Extensions

The capital asset pricing model (CAPM) has two major attractions: (1) its simplicity and (2) its implications. The CAPM is not strictly true, of course. It cannot be given its assumptions. But the extent to which both its simplicity and its implications should be rejected is largely an empirical question. If the model predicts actual security returns in a reasonable fashion, it should not be rejected until a better predictive model is developed. Recent empirical evidence does raise serious questions, however, about the model's validity. As a result, practitioners and scholars are actively studying alternative ways of explaining the determinants of a security's expected and realized return. The principal competition to the CAP at present is a model based on arbitrage theory. Unlike the CAPM, in which a single variable (Beta) determines the expected return on a stock, Arbitrage Pricing Theory (APT) allows for a multiple number of sources of risk. Unfortunately, this theory does not clearly identify what these multiple risks might be.

We begin the chapter with an overview of APT, which leads naturally into a discussion of multifactor CAPM models. Finally, we review some of the more important empirical studies testing variants of each theory.

ARBITRAGE PRICING THEORY

In the early 1970s Stephen Ross offered a model of security pricing known as *arbitrage pricing theory* (APT). In this section we will develop the basic theory and implications. A word of warning is necessary before we begin, however. The final APT model can look deceptively similar to the CAPM. In fact, the two theories *can* lead to the same investment implications. But the theories are based on completely different logical developments and *do not necessarily* result in the same investment implications. As we develop the logic of APT, you will probably understand it better if you put the CAPM out of your thoughts for a while and focus solely on what APT suggests. After this new theory is fully developed, you can then recall your knowledge of CAPM and directly compare the two models. APT is a theory that competes with CAPM—it is not an extension. It is another way to view the world.

Theory of Arbitrage

The Law of One Price. A basic principle of economics is that two goods that are perfect substitutes for each other must be priced identically. If not, arbitrage transactions will occur until the prices of the goods are identical. For example, consider two grocery stores located next to each other and the price of grade A eggs in each. What would happen if store 1 were to sell the eggs for $1.00 a dozen and store 2 were to sell them for $2.00 a dozen? Some enterprising person would stand outside store 2 and take orders to sell eggs for (say) $1.50. Then, each time she received an order, she would immediately buy eggs for $1.00 from store 1. On each order, she would earn a $0.50 arbitrage profit. Of course, the arbitrage would continue until the price of eggs in each store was identical. At that point the arbitrageur would look for other price discrepancies.

We defined arbitrage back in Chapter 1, but it is useful to review the definition in the context of the egg example. First, note that our arbitrageur made no investment. She bought eggs only when she made a sale. True arbitrage involves no capital commitment. Second, note that the arbitrageur had no risk. The purchase and sale prices were known. True arbitrage involves no risk. In short, an arbitrage transaction results in a risk-free profit with no capital commitment. It is the potential for such arbitrage profits between securities which drives the arbitrage pricing theory.

The formal arbitrage pricing theory is a development of the 1970s, but arbitrage transactions have existed since humans developed the most primitive economies. Today arbitrage in the security markets is extensive. A large number of people earn a living by selling gold in one country and simultaneously buying it in another, by purchasing T-bills from one bank and simultaneously selling them to another (remember bid-ask spreads), by purchasing shares of IBM on one stock exchange and simultaneously selling them on another, etcetera. Arbitrage operations are possible as long as prices of perfect substitutes are different. As we will see in Chapter 9, the potential for arbitrage profits is also the force that is responsible for market prices of security options and futures contracts.

The end result of arbitrage is that two perfect substitutes must sell for the same price. This is known as the *law of one price*. Without calling it such, we have, in fact, made use of this principle when developing the standard CAPM. For example, the expected return on securities with the same betas must be identical in equilibrium.

Determinants of Security Returns. Proponents of APT state that returns on securities are due to a variety of events that cause investors to assess what the value of a security should be. For example, inflation rates, food production, and population growth affect the investment worth of all securities to varying degrees. Other events, such as labor strikes in the airline industry or clothing fads, affect a subset of all securities. Finally, certain events have an effect on only a single security. APT expresses this belief as follows:

**APT
Realized
Returns**

$$\tilde{R}_{it} = a_{0t} + b_{i1}\tilde{F}_{1t} + b_{i2}\tilde{F}_{2t} + b_{i3}\tilde{F}_{3t} \ldots b_{iN}\tilde{F}_{Nt} + \tilde{e}_{it}$$

$$= a_{0t} + \sum_{K=1}^{N} b_{iK}\tilde{F}_{Kt} + \tilde{e}_{it} \qquad (8.1)$$

The $\tilde{F}_{Kt}$ terms are referred to as *factors*—events in period t that affect all securities or subsets of securities. For example, $\tilde{F}_{1t}$ might represent real growth of GNP in the United States during year t and thus take on a value of, say, 4.0%. The notion that these factors can influence the returns on either all securities or only particular subsets of securities is important and something we will have more to say about later. The b_{iK} terms represent the return sensitivity of security i to the level of factor K. The a_{0t} term is the return that is expected in period t on all securities when the value of all factors is zero. Finally, the $\tilde{e}_{it}$ term represents the return that is unique to security i in period t.

Two of these variables have symbols similar to CAPM variables (b_{iK} and $\tilde{e}_{it}$), and to a degree they measure somewhat similar forces. But they should not be confused with CAPM betas or residual errors. One of the b_{iK} APT variables *might* represent the sensitivity of a security's returns to returns on the market portfolio, but then again it *might not*. APT is silent as to what the factors are. The factors might be found via statistical tests, but knowledge of the factors is unimportant in the development of this theory. In addition, in APT $\tilde{e}_{it}$ reflects returns unique to security i, whereas in CAPM it is simply a return that is uncorrelated with the market portfolio.

It is important to note that Equation 8.1 is a *linear* equation. None of the terms is raised to an exponent (other than 1.0), and their cumulative effects are summed. This is not done for simplicity—it is a logical consequence of the theory and a major empirical implication. We show why this is so below.

Equation 8.1 can be used to state the *expected return* on a security as follows:

**APT
Expected
Returns**

$$E(R_{it}) = a_{0t} + b_{i1}\overline{F}_{1t} + b_{i2}\overline{F}_{2t} + \ldots + b_{iN}\overline{F}_{N}$$

$$= a_{0t} + \sum_{K=1}^{N} b_{iK}\overline{F}_{Kt} \qquad (8.2)$$

where $\overline{F}_{Kt}$ denotes the expected value of factor K in period t. This relationship is then used to re-express the actual *realized return* in period t as follows:

**APT
Realized
Return**

$$R_{it} = a_{0t} + b_{i1}(\overline{F}_{1t} + \tilde{f}_{1t}) + b_{i2}(\tilde{F}_{2t} + \tilde{f}_{2t}) \ldots$$

$$+ b_{iN}(\overline{F}_{Nt} + \tilde{f}_{Nt}) + \tilde{e}_{it}$$

$$= a_{0t} + b_{i1}\overline{F}_{1t} + b_{i2}\overline{F}_{2t} \ldots + b_{iN}\overline{F}_{Nt} \qquad (8.3)$$

$$+ b_{i1}\tilde{f}_{1t} + b_{i2}\tilde{f}_{2t} \ldots + b_{iN}\tilde{f}_{Nt} + \tilde{e}_{it}$$

$$= E(R_{it}) + (b_{i1}\tilde{f}_{1t} + b_{i2}\tilde{f}_{2t} \ldots + b_{iN}\tilde{f}_{Nt}) + \tilde{e}_{it}$$

where the $\tilde{f}_{Kt}$ terms represent the *unexpected outcome* of a given factor in period t. For example, assume factor 1 reflects real growth in U.S. GNP. If expected

GNP growth is 4.0% but actual growth turns out to be 3.5%, then $\tilde{f}_{1t}$ would be -0.5%.

The last line of Equation 8.3 says that the realized return is composed of two parts: the return that is expected and an unexpected return. The unexpected return is also composed of two parts: return sensitivity to unexpected factor outcomes and to unexpected security-unique events.

Effects of Arbitrage

According to APT, Equation 8.3 is not simply a convenient way to approximate the process by which security returns are generated. The theory of arbitrage pricing implies that Equation 8.3 must be true! If disequilibriums in security market prices are fully arbitraged, then security returns will be generated by exactly such a linear model.

To ensure that all possible arbitrages are in fact conducted, APT makes the following three assumptions:

1. Short selling is unrestricted and short sellers have full use of cash proceeds. If limits are placed on the amount one could short sell or if the cash inflow from short sales cannot be used to finance an offsetting purchase, then complete arbitrage of mispriced securities might not be possible.
2. There are no costs to trading. If transaction costs such as brokerage fees must be paid, the arbitrage of a mispriced security is limited.
3. There are a sufficient number of securities available such that security-unique risk (the uncertainty about e_{it}) can be eliminated by holding a well-diversified portfolio. If the "idiosyncratic" risk can be eliminated, then the only uncertainties that must be dealt with are uncertainties about factor outcomes.

Given these assumptions, Equations 8.1 through 8.3 must be true.

This is best illustrated if we consider a one-factor world. In such a world, APT states that expected and realized returns should be generated by the following relationship:

**One-Factor
Expected Return**
$$E(R_{it}) = a_{0t} + b_{i1}\overline{F}_{1t} \tag{8.4a}$$

**One-Factor
Realized Return**
$$\tilde{R}_{it} = E(R_{it}) + b_{i1}\tilde{f}_{1t} + \tilde{e}_{it} \tag{8.4b}$$

Let's begin the analysis of why this should be so by first assuming that it is not. Consider the three securities shown in Figure 8-1. Clearly their expected returns are *not* linearly related to their factor sensitivities.

Consistent with APT assumptions, we will assume that each security is actually a well-diversified portfolio such that all firm-unique risk is zero. That is, the variance of each e_{it} term is zero.

An arbitrage consists of a transaction guaranteeing a risk-free profit with no capital commitment. Given the data shown in Figure 8-1, there is a clear arbitrage

FIGURE 8-1 *Illustration of One-Factor Expected Returns*

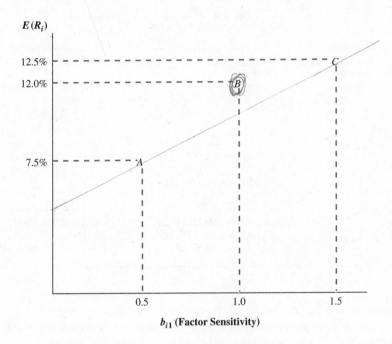

b_{i1} **(Factor Sensitivity)**

available. This consists of buying portfolio B and financing the purchase by short selling a combination of A and C having a factor sensitivity identical to that of B.

Portfolio B has a factor sensitivity of 1.0 and an expected return of 12%. If we were to invest 50% in A and 50% in C, the net factor sensitivity would also be 1.0, but the expected return would only be 10%. In terms of factor pricing we could think of the relationships as follows:

For Portfolios A and C_0:

$$E(R_{it}) = 5\% + b_{i1}\,(5\%)$$

For Portfolio B:

$$E(R_{it}) = 7\% + b_{i1}\,(5\%)$$

It is this extra 2% constant return that will provide the arbitrage profit.

To illustrate the arbitrage, assume we decided to buy $100,000 of portfolio B. To finance the purchase, portfolios A and C would be short sold in an aggregate amount of $100,000. Since we want the factor risk of the A and C portfolios to exactly offset the 1.0 factor risk of B, 50% of the $100,000 would be obtained from A and the remaining 50% from C. Potential outcomes of this transaction are shown in Table 8-1. Three possible unexpected factor outcomes are shown ($f = -5\%$, 0%, and $+5\%$) in order to prove that a known profit is indeed guaranteed. The profit of $2,000 represents the 2.0% greater constant return available on

TABLE 8-1 *One-Factor Arbitrage Outcome*

	Today		End of Period		
	$	Factor Risk	Low $(f_{1t} = -5\%)$	Expected $(f_{1t} = 0)$	High $(f_{1t} = 5\%)$
Buy Portfolio B	−100,000	+1.0	+107,000	+112,000	+117,000
Sell Portfolio A, C					
Portfolio A	+50,000	−0.25	−52,500	−53,750	−55,000
Portfolio C	+50,000	−0.75	−52,500	−56,250	−60,000
Net	0.0	0.0	2,000	2,000	2,000

Low Calculations:

$$100,000 + 100,000 \, [12\% + 1.0 \, (-5\%)] = 107,000$$
$$50,000 + 50,000 \, [7.5\% + 0.5 \, (-5\%)] = 52,500$$
$$50,000 + 50,000 \, [12.5\% + 1.5 \, (-5\%)] = 52,500$$

High Calculations:

$$100,000 + 100,000 \, [12\% + 1.0 \, (5\%)] = 117,000$$
$$50,000 + 50,000 \, [7.5\% + 0.5 \, (5\%)] = 55,000$$
$$50,000 + 50,000 \, [12.5\% + 1.5 \, (5\%)] = 60,000$$

portfolio *B*. Of course, anyone seeing the situation depicted in Figure 8-1 would jump at such an arbitrage. As a result of many such trades, the prices of the securities would adjust until the relationship between each security's expected return and its sensitivity to the factor *is linear*.

This notion is reinforced in Figure 8-2, where expected returns on securities are related to the single common factor by a wavy curve. Clearly, there are a large number of potential arbitrages available in the world depicted in the curve. The important point, however, is that these arbitrage transactions will finally result in a linear relationship between expected returns and factor sensitivities such as that shown by the dashed line.

Factor Portfolios. Let's now consider a world in which there are two factors that affect the returns on all securities. In this case, APT states that expected and realized returns would be generated by the following relationships:

Two-Factor Expected Return
$$E(R_{it}) = a_{0t} + b_{i1}\overline{F}_{1t} + b_{i2}\overline{F}_{2t} \tag{8.5a}$$

Two-Factor Realized Return
$$\tilde{R}_{it} = E(R_{it}) + b_{i1}\tilde{f}_{1t} + b_{i2}\tilde{f}_{2t} + \tilde{e}_{it} \tag{8.5b}$$

In this case, expected returns are related to expected factor outcomes by a hyperplane such as that shown in Figure 8-3. In this case, of course, the expected return on a security (such as *X* shown in the figure) will depend on the security's sensitivity to both factors.

If there are two factors, any arbitrage must result in zero factor sensitivity for both factor 1 and factor 2. This can be done by selecting proper percentage

FIGURE 8-2 *General Illustration of One-Factor Expected Returns*

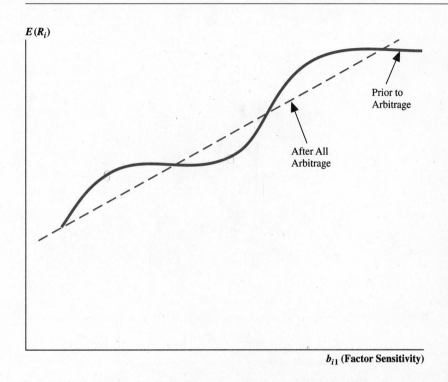

holdings of the various portfolios available. For example, assume that four well-diversified portfolios have factor sensitivities as shown below:

Security Portfolio	Factor Sensitivities		Expected Return
	b_{i1}	b_{i2}	
W	0.80	0.40	7.6%
X	0.40	0.80	7.2%
Y	1.20	0.00	8.0%
Z	0.00	1.20	8.0%

Is there an arbitrage possible in this case?

If expected returns on either factor are not linearly related to factor sensitivity, then an arbitrage is possible. Let's consider factor 1 first. We do this by eliminating all factor 2 risk. Notice that portfolios W and X could be combined in a manner that would result in zero factor 2 sensitivity. This would consist of either:

For a Net Cash Inflow:

Purchase $1 of X
Sell Short $2 of W

For a Net Cash Outflow:

Sell $1 of X
Buy $2 of W

FIGURE 8-3 *Relationship of Expected Returns to Expected Factor Outcomes*

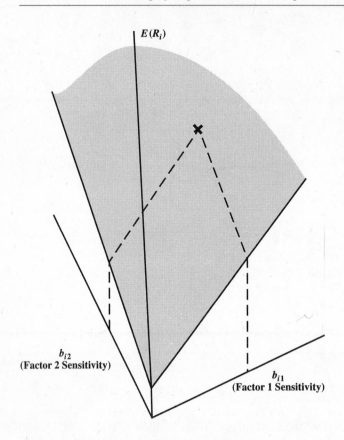

Letting X_i refer to the percentage of your net investment in security i, the resulting factor 1 and factor 2 sensitivities would be:

$$b_{pK} = (X_X \times b_{XK}) + (X_W \times b_{WK})$$

Factor	For a Net Cash Inflow:	For a Net Cash Outflow:

1	$b_{p1} = (1.0 \times 0.40) + (-2.0 \times 0.80)$
	    $= -1.2$
		$b_{p1} = (-1.0 \times 0.40) + (2.0 \times 0.80)$
		    $= +1.2$

2	$b_{p2} = (1.0 \times 0.80) + (-2.0 \times 0.40)$
	    $= 0.0$
		$b_{p2} = (-1.0 \times 0.8) + (2.0 \times 0.40)$
		    $= 0.0$

And the resulting expected returns would be:

$$E(R_{pt}) = X_X \times E(R_{Xt}) + X_W \times E(R_{Wt})$$

For a Net Cash Inflow:	For a Net Cash Outflow:

$E(R_{pt}) = (1.0 \times 7.2) + (-2.0 \times 7.6)$
    $= -8.0\%$
	$E(R_{pt}) = (-1.0 \times 7.2) + (2.0 \times 7.6)$
	    $= +8.0\%$

In short, when W and X are combined to have zero factor 2 sensitivity, they provide an expected return of either $+8.0\%$ or -8.0%, depending on whether there is an initial cash outflow or inflow. Similarly, factor 1 sensitivity of this portfolio is either $+1.2$ or -1.2. Since the expected return and factor sensitivity of portfolio Y are also $+8.0\%$ and $+1.2\%$, it is clear that there is no arbitrage available on factor 1.

In contrast, an arbitrage is available on factor 2. In this case, factor 1 risk is eliminated by trading $2 of X and $1 of W in an opposite position. The results are summarized below:

For a Net Cash Inflow:

Sell $2 X	Plus	Buy $1 W
$b_{p1} = (-2 \times 0.4)$	+	(1×0.8)
$= 0.0$		
$b_{p2} = (-2 \times 0.8)$	+	(1×0.4)
$= -1.2$		
$E(R_{pt}) = (-2 \times 7.2)$	+	(1×7.6)
$= -6.8$		

For a Net Cash Outflow:

Buy $2 X	Plus	Sell $1 W
$b_{p1} = (2 \times 0.4)$	+	(-1×0.08)
$= 0.0$		
$b_{p2} = (2 \times 0.8)$	+	(-1×0.04)
$= +1.2$		
$E(R_{pt}) = (2 \times 7.2)$	+	(-1×7.6)
$= +6.8$		

Since portfolio Z has identical factor 2 risk but a greater expected return, the arbitrage would consist of:

	Cash	Factor 2 Sensitivity
Buy $1 Portfolio Z	$-\$1$	$+1.2$
Sell Portfolio of W and X	$+\ 1$	-1.2
Net	$\$0$	0.0

This example serves to point out three important ideas. First, arbitrageurs can create portfolios that focus on individual factors—portfolios that are insensitive to all other factor outcomes. Therefore, they can arbitrage mispricing within each possible factor and ensure that a linear relationship exists between expected returns and the various factors. Second, investors can create portfolios that have factor sensitivities that meet their unique needs. For example, assume that an oil factor exists and that you are investing pension assets for an oil firm. By proper selection, a portfolio could be created that hedges (to various degrees) the risk to employees of a decline in the oil business. Finally, this example points out the relationship between the factor sensitivity of a total portfolio and the sensitivities of the securities held. The sensitivity of the total portfolio to a given factor is simply a weighted average of the factor sensitivity of each security held.

Symbolically:

Portfolio Sensitivity to Factor K

$$b_{pK} = \sum_{i=1}^{M} X_i b_{iK} \qquad (8.6)$$

where X_i = the percentage invested in security i and b_{iK} = the sensitivity of security i to factor K.

Priced Factors. The proponents of arbitrage pricing theory believe that expected returns on a security are determined by a constant return associated with all securities plus sensitivities to various economic events, or factors. Earlier we expressed this in Equation 8.2 as follows:

APT Expected Returns

$$E(R_{it}) = a_{0t} + b_{i1}\overline{F}_{1t} + b_{i2}\overline{F}_{2t} + \dots + b_{iN}\overline{F}_{Nt}$$

The relationship must be linear and must hold for all securities and portfolios, or arbitrage profits will be available.

Note that the expected return consists of a risk-free return plus a number of terms that could be thought of as risk premiums. A risk-free rate is available since it is (theoretically) possible to create a portfolio that has no net exposure to factor uncertainties and no residual security risk. The risk-free rate might change over time. But within any single period, a known risk-free rate will apply to all securities. The more interesting terms are the factors and security sensitivities.

In our earlier discussion we thought of F_{1t} as being, say, the expected real growth of GNP. The F_{1t} could take on a value of, say, 4%, and b_{i1} might be 3.0. Similarly, F_{2t} might reflect changes in the level of employment with $F_{2t} = 200,000$ and $b_{i2} = 0.00003$. If these are the only two factors used in determining what the expected return on a security should be, they are referred to as *priced factors*. A priced factor is an uncertain economic event that affects the expected return that investors will require.

Earlier we classified the types of events that could affect a security's return into three groups:

1. Events affecting all securities
2. Events affecting a subset of all securities
3. Events affecting only a single security

Clearly, events that affect only a single security can essentially be diversified away. Thus they will not be priced factors—investors will not require compensation for bearing such uncertainties. Similarly, it is clear that events that affect the returns of all securities *will* be priced—investors will demand compensation for bearing their uncertainties. The difficulty arises with events that affect subsets of all securities. APT is mute on whether such factors will be priced. The conceptual answer is probably that it depends on whether such uncertainties can be diversified away. Economic events whose uncertainties can be eliminated through reasonable diversification should not be factors that investors price. The pragmatic answer given by proponents of APT is that they don't know—that only empirical studies can determine what factors are in fact priced.

Let's assume that two factors are priced and that we know the following:

	Factor 1	Factor 2
Type of event	GNP Growth	Employment Change
Expected F_{Kt}	4.0%	200,000
Security A's b_{iK}	3.0	0.00003
Current risk-free rate of interest = 4%		

In this case the expected return on security A would be 22%:

$$= 4.0\% + 3.0\,(4.0\%) + 0.00003\,(200,000)$$

$$= 4.0\% + 12.0\% \qquad + 6.0\%$$

$$= 22.0\%$$

The two values of 12% and 6% associated with the priced factors are thought of as risk premiums. When this is done, the factor sensitivity terms are standardized in a way that makes the average sensitivity $= 1.0$. The b_{iK} values we have discussed are divided by the average b_{iK} values across all securities.

Assume that the average b_{iK} values in the example above are:

$$b_{i1}\ \text{average} = 2.0$$

$$b_{i2}\ \text{average} = 0.00004$$

Then the expected return on security A could be expressed as:

$$E(R_{At}) =\ 4.0\% + \frac{3.0}{2.0}\,(4.0\% \times 2.0) + \frac{0.00003}{0.00004}\,(200,000 \times 0.00004)$$

$$= 4.0\% + 1.5\,(8\%) + 0.75\,(8\%)$$

$$= 22.0\%$$

After this standardization, the APT is usually expressed as:

APT Expected Returns $\qquad E(R_{it}) = a_{0t} + b_{i1}\lambda_{1t} + b_{i2}\lambda_{2t} + \ldots + b_{iN}\lambda_{Nt}$ $\qquad$ **(8.7)**

where the average b_{iK} term is now 1.0 and the λ_{Kt} terms are thought of as the risk premium associated with each priced factor.

APT and the CAPM

You should now recall your knowledge of the CAPM so that we can compare and contrast the two theories.

The theories are similar in a number of respects. Both express the expected return on a security as the sum of a risk-free rate plus a risk premium. Both imply broad diversification. And if there is only one priced factor, b_{i1} of APT is the same as beta$_i$ of the CAPM, and λ_{1t} is the same as the risk premium on the market portfolio.

They differ, however, in their fundamental assumptions. Whereas the CAPM is based on utility theory, APT is based on the economic principle of arbitrage. Although a one-factor model might look suspiciously like the CAPM's security market line, or multifactor models like multibeta CAPM models, they are in fact different species. APT does not assume that investors care only about expected returns and standard deviations of returns. *The theory also says nothing about the optimality of the market portfolio.*

MULTIFACTOR CAPM MODELS

The standard version of the CAPM presented in Chapter 7 implies that: (1) the market portfolio is an efficient portfolio and (2) that expected returns on any security are directly related to the security's beta in the following risk-return relationship:

$$E(R_i) = RF + B_i [RP_M]$$

This model says that there is a *single* variable (or factor) that captures the relevant risk of any security. This result, of course, is a logical consequence of the assumptions on which the model is based. Under differing assumptions, asset pricing theories that have multiple sources of risk can be developed. These are known as multifactor CAPM models. The following is a brief summary of a few of the CAPM based models that have been developed:

1. *Zero-beta model.* One obvious weakness of the basic CAPM is the assumption of a risk-free rate. Although a nominal risk-free rate is available from the purchase of default free, zero coupon Treasury issues, a risk-free real return is not available. Fischer Black has shown that, when a risk-free security does not exist, the lowest-risk security is one that has a zero-beta. We need not go into this model in any depth here. It is sufficient to note that in this model there are two sources of uncertainty: the market portfolio return and the zero-beta portfolio return. This model is commonly called the two-factor CAPM.

2. *Tax models.* If the same tax rate is applied to both capital gains (price changes) and ordinary income (dividends and interest), the existence of taxes does not remove the optimality of the market portfolio nor create other sources of risk. But if the capital gains rate is different from the ordinary tax rate, a security's expected return will be affected by both its beta and its dividend yield. If ordinary tax rates are greater than capital gains rates, securities with larger dividend yields will have to provide larger pre-tax expected returns.

3. *Investor expectations.* The basic CAPM requires that all investors have the same knowledge. From this assumption, it follows logically that they will all wish to own the same portfolio of risky securities. But if there are segments of market participants that have different opinions (say, professional institutional investors versus individual investors), each segment will identify a different optimal risky portfolio. This can result in more than one source of risk affecting security returns. For example, institutional investors might restrict their holdings only to stocks of firms with large market capitalization. This could in turn create a "size effect"—different returns on large capitalization stocks than small capitalization stocks.

4. *Nonmarketable assets.* Not all assets can be publicly traded. The obvious example is human capital, or our personal abilities. Models that account for this fact show that security's covariability with returns on *both* the security market portfolio and human capital returns are important in determining a fair expected return.

5. *Multiperiod models.* The CAPM developed in the last chapter was built on a single investment horizon. When consumption over a series of periods is considered, there are a number of risk faced by investors that are not captured by the standard CAPM beta.

For example, assume that the market portfolio return in a year is positive 10%. This return will be viewed very differently if:

   a. Inflation is 12% versus 2%,

   b. You are unemployed versus employed, or

   c. Interest rates are low versus high.

In addition to knowing what a security's CAPM beta is, you probably would like to know how the security's returns covary with events such as these. That is, when there are future investment periods beyond, say, the next year, you would like to know how a security's return covary with changes in the set of investment opportunities and changes in your personal situation.

In short, asset pricing models based on investors maximizing their personal utility functions can result in equilibrium models in which there is more than one source of risk. The benefit to such utility-based models is that one knows the sources of risk—they can be defined. The disadvantage to utility-based models is that they can always be criticized for certain assumptions that are required to make the model mathematically tractable.

The situation for arbitrage-based models is exactly the opposite. Assumptions used to develop the APT are subject to less criticism. But the number of factors and the nature of the factor risks (i.e., inflation, industrial growth, etc.) are not defined by APT theory.

Using Multifactor Models

The Problem. The basic CAPM is a single-factor model that implies that the *realized* return on a security in excess of the risk-free rate can be expressed as follows:

$$R_{it} - RF_t = a_i + B_i (R_{Mt} - RF_t) + e_{it} \qquad (8.8)$$

The return on security i in period t (R_{it}) in excess of the risk-free return ($-RF_t$) is composed of a constant return (a_i) plus security i's Beta (B_i) times the excess return on the market portfolio ($R_{Mt} - RF_t$) plus a residual error (e_{it}).

This residual error term is important since it represents the risk of owning the security that can be eliminated by diversification. But for this to actually be the case in practice, the error term on any security must be uncorrelated with the error term on all other securities. Although the basic CAPM implies that the error terms will be uncorrelated, considerable evidence shows that this is not true in the real world. For example, as early as 1966 we knew that stock returns were affected not only by broad market movements but also by industry-related events. For example, the results of a study conducted by King are shown in Table 8-2, suggesting that as much as 20% of a stock's return variability can be traced to industry-related events.

TABLE 8-2 *Results of the King Study*

| | Proportion of Return Variability Due to | | | | | |
| | 1952–1960 | | | 1927–1952 | | |
	Market Effects	*Industry Effects*	*Stock Effects*	*Market Effects*	*Industry Effects*	*Stock Effects*
Tobacco Industry	9%	17%	74%	36%	15%	49%
Oil Industry	37	20	43	54	19	27
Metals Industry	46	8	46	63	9	28
Railroad Industry	47	8	45	63	11	26
Utilities Industry	23	14	63	47	13	40
Retail Trade	23	8	69	48	11	41
Overall	31	12	51	52	13	35

SOURCE: *Adapted from B. King, "Market and Industry Factors in Stock Price Behavior," JOURNAL OF BUSINESS 39 (January 1966): 139–90. Reprinted by permission of The University of Chicago Press.*

So what does this mean? Well, if the error terms are uncorrelated across securities, we would be safe in saying:

When error terms are uncorrelated

Expected Excess Stock Return

$$E(R_i - RF) = a_i + b_i E[R_M - RF] \tag{8.9}$$

Stock Variance of Excess Return

$$\sigma_i^2 = B_i^2 \sigma_M^2 + \sigma^2(e_i) \tag{8.10}$$

Expected Excess Portfolio Return

$$E(R_p - RF) = \sum_1^N X_i a_i + \left(\sum_1^N X_i B_i \right) E[R_M - RF] \tag{8.11}$$

Portfolio Variance of Excess Return

$$\sigma_p^2 = \left(\sum_1^N X_i B_i \right)^2 \sigma_M^2 + \sum_1^N X_i^2 \sigma^2(e_i) \tag{8.12}$$

For example, assume we have estimated the single-factor variables for two stocks as shown in Table 8-3. Then the expected excess return, variance, and standard deviation of each stock would be:

Expected Excess Return

$$A = 1.0\% + 1.2\,[10\% - 3\%]$$

$$= 9.4\%$$

$$B = 0.0\% + 0.8\,[10\% - 3\%]$$

$$= 5.6\%$$

Variance of Excess Return

$$A = (1.2)^2 (15\%)^2 + (20\%)^2$$
$$= 724\%$$
$$B = (0.8)^2 (15\%)^2 + (30\%)^2$$
$$= 1044\%$$

Standard Deviation of Excess Return

$$A = (724\%)^{1/2} = 26.9\%$$
$$B = (1044\%)^{1/2} = 32.3\%$$

And if an equal investment were made in each stock, the same variables for the portfolio would be:

Portfolio Expected Excess Return

$$= [0.5(1.0\%) + 0.5(0.0\%)] + [0.5(1.2) + 0.5(0.8)] [10\% - 3\%]$$
$$= \qquad 0.5\% \qquad + [1.0] [7\%]$$
$$= \qquad 7.5\%$$

Portfolio Variance of Excess Return

$$= [0.5(1.2) + 0.5(0.8)]^2 (15\%)^2$$
$$+ (0.5)^2 (20\%)^2 + (0.5)^2 (30\%)^2$$
$$= 225$$
$$+ 325$$
$$= 550\%$$

Portfolio Standard Deviation of Excess Return

$$= [550\%]^{1/2}$$
$$= 23.4\%$$

But when security error terms *are* in fact correlated, calculations based on Equations 8.9 through 8.12 would be wrong. The size of the error made when these equations are used is still being researched. But many practitioners have developed multifactor models that they believe work better than the single-factor model implied by the standard CAPM.

An Illustration. Assume you believe that a two-factor model is necessary to better explain security returns. You believe the first factor is the usual return on some broadly based stock index during period t (R_{Mt}) and the second is the rate of inflation in period t (I_t). Specifically, you hypothesize:

$$R_{it} - RF_t = a_i + B_{i1} (R_{Mt} - RF_t) + B_{i2} (I_t) + e_{it}$$

TABLE 8-3 *Single-Factor Estimates*

	a_i Constant	b_i Beta Estimate	$\sigma(e_i)$ Standard Deviation of Error
Stock A	1.0%	1.2	20%
Stock B	0.0%	0.8	30%

Expected Market Portfolio Returns = 10%.
Risk-Free Rate of Interest = 3%.
Standard Deviation of Market Portfolio Excess Return = 15%.

To estimate the a_i, B_{i1}, and B_{i2} terms, analysts usually rely on multiple regression procedures applied to historical data. For example, assume you have done such a regression analysis for stocks A and B and found the result shown in Table 8-4. In this multifactor model, the expected return and variance of stock i would be calculated as follows:[1]

$$E(R_{it} - RF) = a_i + B_{i1} E(R_{Mt} - RF_t) + B_{i2} E(I_t)$$

$$\sigma^2 = (B_{i1})^2 \sigma_M^2 + (B_{i2})^2 \sigma_I^2 + \sigma^2(e_i)$$

When the data in Table 8-4 is applied to stocks A and B,

Expected Stock Excess Return

$$A = 1.0\% + 1.2 (10\% - 3\%) + 0.5 (2\%)$$
$$= 10.4\%$$
$$B = 0.0 + 0.8 (10\% - 3\%) - 1.2 (2\%)$$
$$= 3.2\%$$

Variance of Stock Excess Return

$$A = (1.2)^2 (15\%)^2 + (0.5)^2 (10\%)^2 + (19.4\%)^2$$
$$= 725\%$$
$$B = (0.8)^2 (15\%)^2 + (-1.2)^2 (10\%)^2 + (27.5\%)^2$$
$$= 1044\%$$

Standard Deviation of Excess Return

$$A = (725\%)^{1/2} = 26.9\%$$
$$B = (1044\%)^{1/2} = 32.3\%$$

Notice that when this version of a multifactor model is used, the total individual stock standard deviation does not change, but the expected individual stock returns do change.

Multifactor models such as this are used for timing and performance evaluation.

---

[1] This assumes that excess market returns and inflation are uncorrelated.

TABLE 8-4 *Multifactor Variable Estimates*

Stock	a_i	B_{i1}	B_{i2}	$\sigma(e_i)$
A	1.0%	1.2	0.5	19.4%
B	0.0%	0.8	-1.2	27.5%

Expected Market Portfolio Return = 10%.
Expected Inflation Rate   = 2%.
Risk-Free Rate of Interest   = 3%.

Standard Deviation of:
Market Portfolio Excess Return = 15%.
Inflation   = 10%.

Consider its use in timing. If you have no special knowledge about returns on a market portfolio of stocks but you believe inflation will be much greater than other people believe, then you might create a portfolio with a B_1 value equal to 1.0 and a B_2 value that is as low as possible. Quantitative portfolio managers actively run portfolios based on such bets.

When used in performance evaluation, analysts are able to attribute the return earned on a portfolio to each of the factors they have decided to examine. For example, BARRA is a quantitative investment consulting firm that uses 13 fundamental stock factors plus 55 industry factors in their multifactor models. These BARRA factors are widely used by portfolio managers to evaluate the source of their portfolio returns. The data shown in Table 8-5 is extracted from a paper that

TABLE 8-5 *Determinants of Portfolio Returns*

Five Factors Contributing to Best Results		
Factor	*Cumulative 91-Month Total*	*Annual**
Size	23.3%	3.07%
Earnings/Price	7.3	0.96
Book/Price	7.2	0.95
Specific Asset Selection	7.1	0.94
Business Machines	1.5	0.20
		6.12%

Five Factors Contributing to Worst Results		
Factor	*Cumulative 91-Month Total*	*Annual**
LOCAP	(7.2)%	(0.95)%
Variability in Market	(7.0)	(0.92)
Drugs, Medicine	(2.3)	(0.30)
Telephone, Telegraph	(1.2)	(0.16)
Transport by Water	(1.1)	(0.15)
		(2.48)%

* Not compounded; cumulative divided by 7.58 years (91 months/12).

SOURCE: Fogler, H. Russell, "Common Stock Management in the 1990s," *Journal of Portfolio Management*, Winter 1990.

The Solomon of Stocks Finds a Better Way To Pick Them

In 1992, a flurry of discussion about the potential "demise of beta" swept both academic halls and corporate boardrooms. The discussion was caused by a paper prepared by Eugene Fama and Kenneth French in which they found little evidence that beta was a good predictor of future stock returns. The following Fortune *article is representative of the public reaction to their paper.*

But the final story has not yet been told. There are numerous papers in progress which are critical of the Fama French tests, suggesting that the results were time sensitive, did not consider changing market risks, etc.

It may be time to throw away your investment books, or at least tear out a few pages. The basic measure of investment risk, which has become an integral part of many stock-picking strategies, is being called into question by the very people who made it famous. Their new findings suggest that you can still beat the market, but doing so may require a new approach.

Simply put, folks had long been led to believe that the more volatile their investments were, the more money they could expect to earn from them over time. The widely accepted measure of volatility that goes along with this belief is something called beta, which compares the price movement of a stock with that of the overall market. A stock that has a beta of 2, for instance, moves 2% in price for every 1% change in the market. A stock that has a beta of 0.5 is only half as volatile as the market. Under the old religion, a stock with a high beta should return more over time than a stock with a low beta.

But now this comforting belief turns out to be no more than a fairy tale. What's more, the big bad wolf turns out to be one of the folks who helped put beta and all its attendant beliefs in the canon of modern finance in the first place—Eugene Fama, a professor of finance at the University of Chicago. Says Fama of his, well, in-Famas findings: "We always knew that the world was more complicated." Beta has long been under attack by other academics, but this turn by one of its most prominent standard bearers promises to finally bring it down.

In a paper that has been circulating recently in preliminary form and will be formally published this summer, Fama and an associate, Kenneth R. French, also at Chicago, studied the performance of more than 2,000 stocks from 1941 to 1990. Says French of their findings: "What we are saying is that over the last 50 years, knowing the volatility of an equity doesn't tell you much about the stock's return." Beta, say the boys from Chicago, is bogus.

Fortunately for investors, the same Fama-French study found other characteristics that did help identify stock market winners. Among the variables that they looked at, the ratio of stock price to book value was consistently the most powerful for explaining the differences in average stock returns. Based on that finding, investors should focus on stocks with low price-to-book multiples. Fama and French also found that low stock-market capitalization proved a valuable indicator of high future returns.

Beyond shaking the investment world, the demise of beta is bringing sweeping change to the executive suite. The capital asset pricing model, a financial cousin of beta, has long been used by managers to determine the attractiveness of new ventures.

SOURCE: Terence P. Paré, "The Solomon of Stocks Finds a Better Way To Pick Them," *Fortune*, 1 June 1992.

appeared in the *Journal of Portfolio Management*. This paper explained how the manager uses BARRA factors to understand why his portfolio had good returns. As displayed in the table, the manager's portfolio did well due to the size, earning, price ratio, and book/price ratio factors of the stocks selected. The manager performed poorly in terms of the LOCAP and variability in market factors.

EMPIRICAL TESTS OF CAPM

The Nature of the Tests

Clearly, the CAPM rests upon a number of assumptions that are not strictly true in the real world. This does not mean, however, that the model is totally without merit. Its validity can be assessed only by examining how well it predicts real-world phenomena. This is an empirical question.

The CAPM is an ex ante model. Individuals develop subjective judgments about (1) the risk-free rate, (2) the beta of a security, and (3) the appropriate market risk premium. While people may not go through such an explicit mental process, perhaps they act as if they do. Tests of the CAPM are always tests of the SML:

Security Market Line	$E(R_i) = RF + \beta_i[RP_M]$	**(8.13)**

This is an ex ante relationship. People develop (common) beliefs about what the systematic risk of security i (β_i) will be in the future and are faced with a future expected risk premium.

Unfortunately, in testing the model we can't look into investors' minds to see whether this is the relationship they use to determine equilibrium expected returns. For example, investors might be totally blind to the importance of security covariance and price a security's standard deviation instead of its covariance to the market. But it is doubtful that serious tests of ex ante pricing could be performed; at least none have been conducted to date. Instead, we rely upon history. Do past security returns tell a story that is consistent with the CAPM? In particular, is the average historical return earned on security i ($\overline{R}_i$) equal to (1) the average historical risk-free rate ($\overline{RF}$) plus (2) a risk premium which is equal to the security's estimated historical beta (b_i) multiplied by the average historical risk premium earned on the market ($\overline{RP}_M$)?

The Historical Test	$\overline{R}_i = \overline{RF} + b_i[\overline{RP}_M]$	**(8.14)**

Compare this statement of how securities should have behaved in the past (if the CAPM is valid) with the ex ante SML in Equation 8.13. They have very similar terms, but the SML terms are *expectations* of the future, whereas the statistical tests rely on *averages* of the past.

Equation 8.14 is justified as the historical equivalent of the SML based on simple logic. Over long intervals, *expectations will be equal to average outcomes*. People are rational enough to recognize when they are consistently over- or underestimating returns or betas. If they find such a bias, they will adjust their expectations until observed outcomes average what they expect them to. If this is true: (1) average historical returns will reflect past expectations of returns, (2) average historical systematic risk will reflect past expectations of systematic risk, and (3) average historical risk premiums will reflect past expectations of risk premiums. Equation 8.14 is the historical counterpart to the SML.

The difficulty of using Equation 8.14 to test the SML is not in its logic; the difficulty lies instead in its implementation. In particular, how are the *b* values estimated and what index is used to measure the market portfolio? Empirical tests that attempt to determine whether Equation 8.14 supports the CAPM are actually testing whether:

1. The *b* values are true estimates of historical betas.
2. The index used to measure historical risk premiums is the market portfolio.
3. The CAPM is correct.

If any of these fails, the test as a whole will fail.

Empirical tests of the SML examine the following regression equation equivalent of Equation 8.14:

Regression Test of SML

$$\overline{R}_i = \alpha_0 + \alpha_1 b_i \qquad (8.15)$$

where the known quantities are:

$\overline{R}_i$ = the average single-period return on security *i* during some past time interval

b_i = the estimated historical beta for security *i*

and the statistically estimated values should be:

α_0 = the average risk-free rate that prevailed during the testing period, $\overline{RF}$

α_1 = the market risk premium earned during the testing period, $\overline{R}_m - \overline{RF}$

Regardless of the means of testing the CAPM, there are a number of implications of the theory that statistical tests should support or question:

1. The intercept term in Equation 8.15 should not be significantly different from the average risk-free rate during the testing period. Occasionally, empirical tests are performed on excess returns, where the risk-free rate that prevailed during a particular period is subtracted from both the left- and right-hand sides of Equation 8.15. In this case, α_0 should not be statistically different from zero.
2. The relationship between $\overline{R}_i$ and b_i should be linear.
3. The term α_1 should be positive and equal to $(\overline{R}_m - \overline{RF})$, the earned risk premium.
4. Beta should be the only factor related to average historic returns. Variables such as a security's diversifiable risk should be statistically insignificant.

Tests on Individual Stocks

Douglas examined the relationship between average security returns and various risk measures on a sample of more than 600 stocks for various time intervals between 1926 and 1960. Using different five-year intervals, he calculated (1) each stock's average quarterly rate of return, (2) the variance of each stock's quarterly rate of return, and (3) the covariance of the stock's return with the quarterly returns of an index of all 600 stocks. Using these values, he then estimated the following regression equation for each five-year period:

Douglas
Single-Stock Test
$$(1 + \overline{R}_i) = \alpha_0 + \alpha_1 (\sigma_i^2) + \alpha_2 (\sigma_{ij}) + e_i \qquad \textbf{(8.16)}$$

where $\overline{R}_i$ = the average quarterly return on stock i during the five-year period, σ_i^2 = the variance of i's quarterly return, σ_{ij} = the covariance between i's return and the index of all the 600 stocks during the five-year period, and e_i = random estimation errors.

His results for each five-year period are displayed in Table 8-6. The α_0 regression coefficient should reflect one plus the quarterly risk-free rate. While his estimates were perhaps slightly higher than quarterly values of $1 + RF$, they weren't the major concern raised by his results. His estimates of α_1 reflect the impact of a security's *total* risk on average returns. Per the CAPM, α_1 values should be zero. But most are positive and statistically significant, with 95% confidence or better, contrary to the CAPM. Estimates of α_2, on the other hand, should reflect the earned price of risk: $(R_m - RF) \div \sigma_m$. Yet most of these values are statistically insignificant. In a related study of individual stock returns and betas, Lintner found similar results.

But both the Douglas and Lintner studies appear to suffer from various statistical weaknesses that *might* explain their anomalous results. In a subsequent study, Miller and Scholes reviewed these statistical problems and concluded that the *empirical* relationship between average security returns and unsystematic risk could be due to (1) measurement errors incurred in estimating individual stock betas, (2) the fact that estimated betas and unsystematic risks are highly correlated, and (3) a skewness that was present in the distribution of observed stock returns. While Miller and Scholes don't reject the implications of the Douglas and Lintner

TABLE 8-6 *Douglas Test of CAPM*

		$(1 + \overline{R}_i) = \alpha_0 + \alpha_1 (\sigma_i^2) + \alpha_2 (\sigma_{ij})$			
	α_0	α_1		α_2	
Period	*Coefficient*	*Coefficient*	*T-Value*	*Coefficient*	*T-Value*
1926–31	0.99	0.15	2.14	0.63	0.72
1931–36	1.03	0.18	6.00	0.17	0.81
1936–41	0.99	0.39	2.60	−0.30	−0.54
1941–46	1.04	0.69	4.93	1.19	1.43
1946–51	1.01	0.08	0.38	0.66	0.53
1951–56	1.02	−0.21	−0.68	−3.51	−1.99
1956–60	1.03	1.13	4.18	−3.21	−2.08

SOURCE: G. Douglas, "Risk in the Equity Markets: An Empirical Appraisal of Market Efficiency," *Yale Economic Essays* 9, no. 1 (1969).

studies, they suggest that the statistical problems encountered when *individual stocks* are used might be the reason for the discouraging results.

Tests on Portfolios

Because of these statistical problems, most tests since then have concentrated upon *portfolios* of securities.

The Black, Jensen, and Scholes Study. Black, Jensen, and Scholes used all NYSE stocks for the period 1931–1965 to form 10 portfolios of different beta levels. Then average monthly "excess returns" on each portfolio were regressed against the portfolio's beta. For example, let's say we have identified 10 different portfolios for each month between 1931 and 1965. During a given month, the return on each portfolio is calculated and the 30-day risk-free rate (which existed at the start of the month) is subtracted. This results in a monthly series of excess returns for each portfolio. The average of each series is then calculated, and this average is regressed against the portfolio betas.

Results of the Black, Jensen, and Scholes study are displayed in Figure 8-4 and shown below:

$$\frac{\text{Monthly}}{\text{Average}} - \frac{\text{Excess}}{\text{Return}} = \alpha_0 \quad + \alpha_1 \text{ (portfolio beta)}$$

$$(\overline{R}_p - \overline{RF}) \quad = 0.359\% + 1.08\% \ (b_p)$$

$$(T\text{-value}) \quad (6.53) \quad (20.77)$$

These results conform with the CAPM in that a clear linear relationship exists between average excess returns and beta. They do not conform with the version of the traditional CAPM in which a known risk-free rate exists. Recall that the portfolio returns are excess returns. If the 30-day T-bill rate had been the risk-free rate, the intercept term should have been zero. However, the intercept term of 0.359% implies that the return on a portfolio with zero systematic risk is not *RF* but something larger. This evidence is contrary to the traditional CAPM. As a result, Black developed a zero-beta CAPM theory, which is discussed earlier.

Black, Jensen, and Scholes also examined the same regression for various time intervals. Results are shown in Figure 8-5. Again, a linear relationship exists, but the intercept term is usually greater than zero and changes in each period. The slope isn't always positive, implying that there are lengthy time intervals during which beta and average returns are negatively related.

Roll's Critique of CAPM Studies

Many other studies of the CAPM have been conducted. But all have been brought into serious doubt due to a critique presented by Richard Roll.

In theory, the market portfolio *M* consists of all risky assets. Since these include

FIGURE 8-4 *Black, Jensen, and Scholes Study*

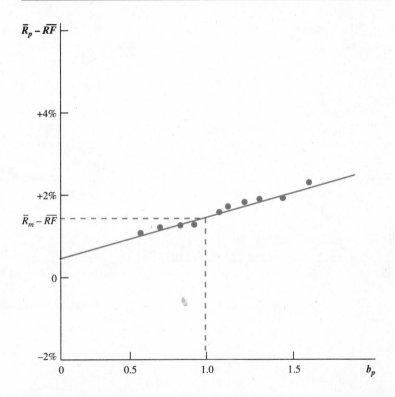

stocks, bonds, futures contracts, real estate, human capital, etcetera, portfolio *M* is impossible to identify. In fact, aggregate common stock returns are difficult enough to determine. While a large number of stocks are included in indexes such as the S&P Composite and the NYSE Composite, literally thousands of OTC stocks are excluded.

Typically, people have compromised by assuming that the returns on the broad stock market indexes are highly correlated with returns on the true portfolio *M*. The appropriateness of this compromise and, in fact, the testability of any version of the CAPM have come under sharp attack, however, in a breakthrough article by Roll. The results of Roll's critique of the CAPM are profound, but they can be summarized as follows:

1. Tests of the CAPM are in reality tests of the market portfolio's mean variance efficiency.
2. The market portfolio consists of all risky assets, which can never be totally observed. Thus, the CAPM (that is, the efficiency of *M*) is untestable.
3. As long as the proxy used for *M* is mean-variance efficient (sits on the efficient frontier) ex post, then the betas calculated against this proxy and average security returns will *mathematically* be linearly related to the proxy portfolio's

FIGURE 8-5 *Black, Jensen, and Scholes Results*

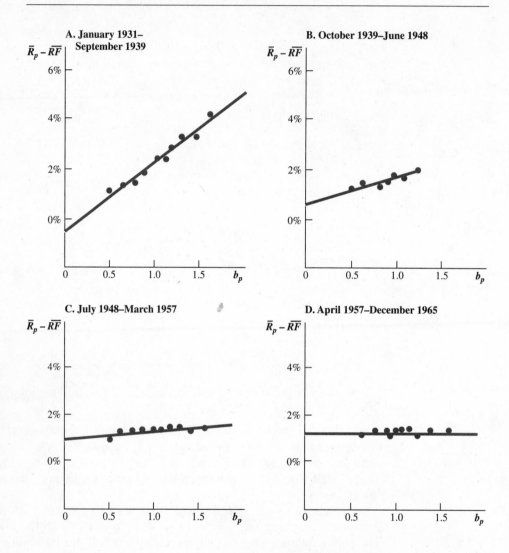

risk and return. The linearity observed in most of the empirical research between security betas and average returns is a mathematical tautology. Its only
economic meaning is that the proxy portfolio was mean-variance efficient. But
this efficiency of the proxy does not prove the efficiency of the market portfolio
or the validity of the CAPM.

4. If the proxy used for M is not ex post mean-variance efficient, the empirical
   results have no meaning whatsoever, and any form of relationship might be
   found between average security returns and beta (approximately linear, curvi-
   linear, residual error risk found to be significant, etc.).

5. Models that attempt to evaluate investment performance via the CAPM are inappropriate.

Roll's critique of the CAPM elegantly expressed what many people had previously stated more informally but without such force and economic rigor. Because of the potential significance of these arguments to existing financial theory, modern investment management techniques, and performance evaluation, we must examine the ideas more thoroughly. The fact that the mean-variance efficiency of the market portfolio is the single testable hypothesis of the CAPM is easy to understand intuitively. For example, in a world in which a risk-free security exists, the CAPM is based upon all individuals electing to hold only one portfolio of *risky assets*. This portfolio must be *M*—the market portfolio of all risky assets. Tests of CAPM are inherently tests of portfolio *M*'s mean-variance efficiency. But it is clear that researchers will never be able to completely identify what portfolio *M* consists of. As a result, the CAPM is untestable.

Roll's third and fourth conclusions are more difficult to understand, and their mathematical proof lies beyond the scope of this book. Nonetheless, we must understand the meaning of the conclusion to appreciate the true status of empirical tests of the CAPM. Assume that there are an unidentifiably large number of risky assets available. To proxy these assets, we examine the historical returns on, say, 1,000 observable common stocks. In calculating individual stock betas, we measure a stock's ex post standard deviation (σ_i), the standard deviation of ex post returns on *some* portfolio (σ_p), and the ex post correlation coefficient between the stock's and the portfolio's return (r_{ip}). Beta is then measured as beta = ($\sigma_i r_{ip}$)/σ_p. An infinite number of reference portfolios could be created using the 1,000 stocks. Of such possible reference portfolios, some will be ex post efficient (in that they provide the lowest variance of returns for a given mean return) and others will not be efficient. If we happen to use *any* of the ex post efficient portfolios, then the following precise mathematical relationship will exist:

Estimated SML $\qquad\qquad \bar{R}_i \doteq RF + \beta_i[\bar{R}_p - RF]$ $\qquad\qquad$ **(8.17)**

While this is the empirical version of the CAPM tested, Roll showed that the relationship is purely mathematical. There is no economic content to it. Studies that have found a linear relationship offer no proof at all that the CAPM is correct. If an empirical test finds a linear relationship, it simply means that the researcher was fortunate enough to have chosen an ex post mean-variance efficient portfolio as a market proxy. If the researcher does not find a linear relationship between historic beta and mean security returns, nothing can be concluded at all. Either the researcher used an inefficient portfolio as the market proxy, or the CAPM is invalid. But it is impossible to distinguish between the explanations.

Roll's fifth conclusion can be illustrated with the use of Figure 8-6. Assume the CAPM is true. The dashed lines represent the actual efficient set of risky real assets and the true capital asset pricing line. However, individuals wishing to evaluate investment performance use a market portfolio proxy, say, the Standard & Poor's Composite Index. If the researchers are lucky, the S&P Composite will represent one of the many available efficient portfolios. Since the composite index

FIGURE 8-6 *Effects of Roll's Comments on Performance Evaluation*

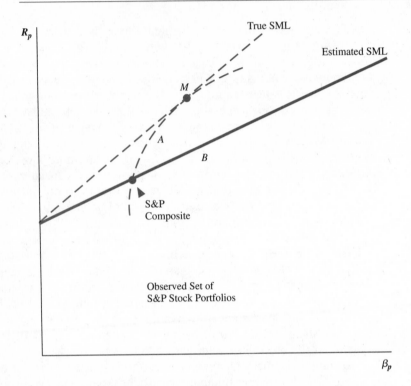

is assumed to be efficient, a linear relationship will exist between return and beta risk, shown as the solid SML line.

With this as background, what is to be concluded about the performance of mutual funds A and B? While A appeared to outperform the market, all it really did was outperform combinations of borrowing and lending portfolios of the S&P. Its apparent good performance is meaningless. Roll's observation is intuitively quite simple. If the market portfolio is *the* best set of risky assets to hold, no other portfolio can ever beat it. If some investment or speculative strategies seem to "beat the market," then either the CAPM is wrong (in which case, it shouldn't be used to evaluate performance), or a poor market proxy was used (in which case, again, it shouldn't be used).

In conclusion, Roll's observations have raised fundamental questions about the CAPM's truth, testability, and use in evaluating investment performance.

Recent Evidence

Recent empirical evidence raises even greater doubts about the validity of the standard CAPM. Fama and French found the stock returns are negatively related to a firm's size and its market price to book value ratio. Firm size was measured by multiplying the number of shares that a firm has outstanding by its market price. Book value represents total firm equity shown in a firm's balance sheet divided by the number of outstanding shares. After controlling for size and market to book, there was no relationship between stock returns and their beta estimates.

Empirical Tests of APT

Because of Roll's suggestion that the CAPM is logically untestable, most recent empirical research has explored the validity of APT. These tests can be classified into two types: (1) tests in which the researcher does not hypothesize any specific type or number of factors but, instead, extracts statistically significant factors from historical returns and (2) tests of whether explicitly defined potential factors are related to security returns. We shall refer to the first class of tests as *unspecified factor* tests and the second class as *specified factor* tests.

Unspecified Factor Tests. In these tests, the researcher begins the study with no preconceived idea as to how many priced factors exist or what any such factors might represent. Instead, a statistical procedure known as factor analysis is used to extract whatever statistically significant factors might be present in a sample of security returns.

Factor analysis is a complex statistical procedure that was developed much before and independent of the development of APT. It takes observations on a large number of variables and tries to identify one or more statistically significant underlying forces which could have created the variables observed. For example, assume that you collect the following observations on a sample of people: height, weight, age, hair color, and hair length. If factor analysis is used, a single important factor related to height, weight, and hair length would emerge. Age and hair color would be unrelated to the factor and unexplained by the model. The factor analysis procedure would not be able to identify what the single factor is a proxy for—even though you could logically deduce that it is a gender factor.

When applied to security returns, a time series of returns on a sample of securities is used. Factor analysis then finds various underlying factors that best explain the covariance of returns within the sample. The number of factors found depends on the statistical significance desired by the researcher and the particular version of factor analysis employed. (There are many.)

In essence, the procedure uses a large number of return observations on many securities to determine whether the returns can be explained by a few common forces. If all security returns are what we have called firm-unique returns, then no common factors would be found. If the CAPM is correct, a number of common factors might be found, but only one priced factor.

After a set of common factors is found, a factor sensitivity is found for each stock and each factor. We will define these as:

$$\hat{b}_{iK} = \text{the sensitivity of security } i \text{ to common factor } K$$

Although these $\hat{b}_{iK}$ values are statistical estimates of our earlier b_{iK} terms, their units can differ considerably.

To examine which of the factors are priced by investors, a cross-sectional regression similar to the following is performed:

Factor Regression

$$\overline{R}_i + a_0 + a_1\hat{b}_{i1} + a_2\hat{b}_{i2} + \ldots + a_N\hat{b}_{iN} + e_i \qquad \textbf{(8.18)}$$

where $\overline{R}_i$ = the average return on security i, b_{iK} = the estimated factor sensitivities, and e_i = an unexplained error term. The regression parameters that are estimated include the constant return term a_0 and the slope coefficients a_1 through a_N.

If a particular factor is priced by investors, the slope term associated with the factor should be statistically significant. For example, if factor 1 is a priced factor, a_1 will be statistically different from 0.0. Alternatively, if a factor is found for which investors do not require compensation in the form of higher (or lower) expected returns, the a_K regression estimate will not be statistically different from zero.

In the earliest version of this test, Roll and Ross used a sample of daily returns on 42 portfolios of 30 stocks each. They suggested that at least three but no more than six common priced factors appeared to exist in their sample. Other studies have found similar results. But these studies are not without critics, as we shall discuss below.

Specified Factor Tests. One of the principal difficulties with the approach above is that the procedure does not suggest what the priced factors represent. Therefore, a number of researchers have hypothesized a variety of possible factors that might be priced and have developed tests to see whether they are. For example, Fogler, John, and Tipton tested a model in which they claim that three factors (returns on a stock market proxy, changes in interest rates, and changes in bond default rates) are related to individual stock returns. In addition, Oldfield and Rogalski investigated aggregate stock returns and T-bill returns as common factors.

The most complete test of a specified factor model to date was conducted by Chen, Roll, and Ross. They suggested that a large portion of the covariances between securities can be explained by unanticipated changes in four variables:

1. The difference between long-term and short-term Treasury yields to maturity
2. Inflation rates
3. The difference between yields to maturity of BB-rated bonds and Treasuries
4. Growth of industrial production

But Is APT Testable?

Serious questions remain, however, whether APT can ever be empirically tested. Studies by Dhrymes, Friend, and Gultekin provided evidence that the number of common factors found in an unspecified factor test increased as: (1) the number of securities in the sample increased, and (2) the length of the time period sampled increased. Roll and Ross responded that this would be expected. As additional securities or returns are collected, additional common factors might emerge. For example, as the sample size increases, firms from a number of new industries might be included that share a common factor. Roll and Ross point out that it is the number of priced factors which is important, not the total number of factors.

Perhaps the most telling criticism of APT was made by Shanken. His argument goes as follows. Assume that APT *does* apply to the underlying economic structure of the economy. There are certain basic economic industries, each of which is sensitive to various factors that are priced by investors. Individual firms then create portfolios of these basic industries. When firms create such asset portfolios, they alter the level of factor risk inherent in their securities. For example, assume that two underlying priced factors exist. Firm A might invest in the underlying economic industries in a way that eliminates all of factor 2. Thus, if APT researchers sample firms similar to firm A, they will conclude that factor 2 doesn't exist. The returns that are examined on securities can mask or exacerbate the underlying factor risks in the economy.

This could be a particular problem if firms are constantly changing the nature of their asset portfolios, as in the case of mutual funds. No one would suggest obtaining empirical estimates of common priced factors from mutual fund returns, since the security holdings of the funds are constantly changing. The problem is less severe at the individual stock level since firms do not shift asset mixes as rapidly as mutual funds do. Nonetheless, the problem remains.

Stationarity of Risk Premiums

Underlying all of the CAPM and APT tests was an unstated assumption: the return-generating process is stationary. By this we mean that the covariances between the returns of any two securities don't change and that the market risk premium doesn't change.

Research into this stationarity assumption is in its infancy, but a number of studies suggest that it is a problem. For example, consider Figure 8-7, in which estimates of monthly standard deviations of the S&P 500 are shown. There is considerable variability in this risk proxy—enough to suggest that investors might change whatever risk premiums they require.

A recent study by French, Schwert, and Stambaugh indicates that this may be the case. When changes in estimates of stock price volatility were related to returns on the S&P 500 during a given month, these researchers found evidence that the expected market risk premium is positively related to the predicted volatility of stock returns.

If investors' perceptions of risk and their required risk premiums are continuously changing over time, tests of various asset pricing models will be difficult. At present, we must be open-minded and continue to explore. We do seem to know two things: (1) return variability and required returns are directly related, and (2) diversification reduces return variability.

FIGURE 8-7 *Estimated Monthly Standard Deviations of the S&P 500*

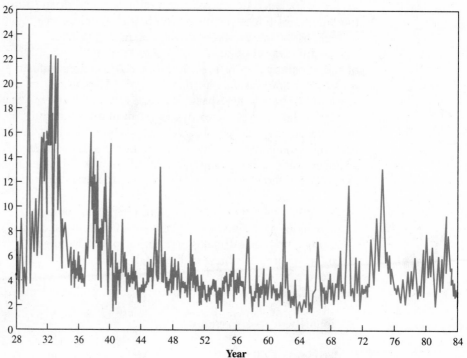

SUMMARY

The CAPM and APT present two ways of viewing how equilibrium security prices might be determined. The basic CAPM presented in the previous chapter implies that there is a single source of risk for which investors must be compensated. This risk is the return uncertainty associated with holding the market portfolio of all risky assets. When various assumptions on which the basic CAPM theory is based are lifted, the models that arise often have multiple sources of risk. It is important to remember, however, that all such asset pricing models are based on investors' attempts to maximize their personal "utility" of lifetime compensation.

APT is not based on utility maximization but instead on the law of one price; two perfect substitutes must trade at identical prices. If perfect substitutes trade at different prices, arbitrage profits are available. A strict definition of arbitrage is the ability to earn risk-free profits at no investment. The APT is appealing in that it says nothing about the optimality of some elusive market portfolios. Its weakness is that the sources of risk are not defined by the theory; they must be empirically identified.

Empirical tests of either theory are difficult to construct since they are based on investor expectations whereas the data available to researchers are realized security returns. In fact, some economists believe that it is conceptually impossible to empirically test either theory using historical data. In the case of the CAPM, one never knows whether the market portfolio proxy being tested is the true market portfolio. In the case of the APT, it is difficult to determine, say, whether factor 2 found in one period of time is the same factor 2 found in another period.

It is also important to realize that tests of these theories are actually *joint tests* of two hypotheses: (1) that the model being tested fairly describes how equilibrium prices are determined and (2) that security prices are at a state of equilibrium according to the model.

Neither pricing theory has yet stood up to rigorous empirical testing. But that does not mean that the models are deceiving ways of thinking about how security prices might be determined. And there is much to be learned from the models about portfolio risk management.

REVIEW PROBLEM

The purposes of the problem are (1) to review how various risk measures are calculated, (2) to review efficient portfolio selection and the CML/SML relationships, and (3) to review Roll's observations about the CAPM.

Assume you have a risk-free rate available equal to 2%. In addition, you have identified two portfolios of stocks that had the following returns over the past five years:

	1	2	3	4	5
Portfolio 1	10.0%	0.0%	10.0%	20.0%	10.0%
Portfolio 2	15.0%	2.5%	15.0%	2.5%	15.0%

a. Calculate the following measures:

$\bar{R}_p$ for $p = 1, 2$

σ_p for $p = 1, 2$ (divide by N = 5 and not N − 1 = 4)

r_{12}

b. What is the minimum variance portfolio and what is its standard deviation?

c. Given a risk-free rate of 2%, what is the *single* ex post efficient portfolio of risky securities?

d. As noted, portfolios 1 and 2 consist of more than one stock. Portfolio 1 is smaller and consists of stocks A and B. The correlation coefficient between A's and B's returns is 0.0. Also $\sigma_B = 2\sigma_A$, $\sigma_A = 7.0711\%$, and $R_A = R_B = 10.0\%$. What then are the optimal X_A and X_B holdings in portfolio 1?

e. Portfolio 1 has a correlation with the single ex post efficient portfolio of about 0.70. Since stocks A and B are uncorrelated with each other, will they also have individual correlations with the efficient portfolio equal to 0.70?

f. What is the beta of portfolio 1?

g. Use the beta of portfolio 1 to calculate the correlation of stocks A and B with the efficient frontier (the single ex post efficient portfolio). Calculate the beta estimate for stocks 1 and 2. (Assume the correlation coefficients are identical.)

h. If you were to calculate market model estimates of the characteristic lines for stocks A and B (using as the index the single ex post efficient portfolio), what would you arrive at?

i. Assume you calculated many such market model beta estimates and called them b_i. You then regress the average return on each stock against these b_i values and get:

$$R_i = 2.0\% + 8.0\% \, b_i \qquad R^2 = 100.0\%$$

Does the linear relationship that perfectly fits the data confirm that the CAPM is correct?

Solution

a. $\bar{R}_1 = (10.0 + 0.0 + 10.0 + 20.0 + 10.0) \div 5 = 10.0\%$

$\bar{R}_2 = (15.0 + 2.5 + 15.0 + 2.5 + 15.0) \div 5 = 10.0\%$

$$\sigma_1 = \left[\frac{(10.0 - 10.0)^2 + \ldots + (10.0 - 10.0)^2}{5} \right]^{1/2} = 6.3246$$

$$\sigma_2 = \left[\frac{(15.0 - 10.0)^2 + \ldots + (15.0 - 10.0)^2}{5} \right]^{1/2} = 6.1237$$

$$r_{12} = \left[\frac{(10.0 - 10.0)(15.0 - 10.0) + \ldots + (10.0 - 10.0)(15.0 - 10.0)}{5} \right]$$

$$\times \frac{1}{(6.32)(6.12)}$$

$$= 0.0$$

b. minimun $X_1 = \dfrac{\sigma_2^2 - \sigma_1 \sigma_2 r_{12}}{\sigma_1^2 + \sigma_2^2 - 2\sigma_1 \sigma_2 r_{12}}$

$$= \frac{6.1237^2 - 0.0}{6.3246^2 + 6.1237^2 - 2(0.0)}$$

$$= 0.484$$

$$X_2 = 1 - X_1 = 0.516$$

$$\sigma_{min} = [(0.484^2)(6.3246^2) + (0.516^2)(6.1237^2)]^{1/2}$$

$$= 4.4\%$$

c. Since portfolios 1 and 2 have the same average return, the minimum variance portfolio from part b above is the *single* ex post efficient portfolio of risky securities.

$$\text{CML: } E(R_p) = 2.0\% + \sigma_p \left(\frac{10.0\% - 2.0\%}{4.4\%} \right)$$

$$\text{SML: } E(R_i) = 2.0\% + B_i (10.0\% - 2.0\%)$$

d. Since $r_{AB} = 0$ and R_A and $\overline{R}_B$, the minimum variance combination of the two is optimal.

$$X_A = \frac{(2 \times 7.0711)^2 - 0.0}{7.0711^2 + (2 \times 7.0711)^2 - 0.0}$$

$$X_A = 0.80$$

$$X_B = 1 - X_A = 0.20$$

e. No. This would be the case only if stocks A and B were perfectly correlated with each other. Otherwise, some of their volatility will be diversified away in the portfolio combination of the two and the portfolio will be more highly correlated with the market portfolio (our ex post single efficient portfolio of risky securities 1 and 2). Portfolios are more correlated with the market portfolio than single stocks.

f.

$$B_1 = \frac{6.3246}{4.4} (0.70) = 1.006$$

g. $B_1 = 1.006 = X_A B_A + X_B B_B$

$$= 0.8 \frac{7.0711}{4.4} r + 0.2 \frac{14.1422}{4.4} r$$

Therefore $r = 0.52$

$$B_A = \frac{7.0711}{4.4} (0.52) = 0.836$$

$$B_B = \frac{14.1422}{4.4} (0.52) = 1.671$$

h. $\tilde{R}_{At} = 1.64\% + 0.836 (\tilde{R}_{mt}) + \tilde{E}_{At}$

$\tilde{R}_{Bt} = -6.71 + 1.671 (\tilde{R}_{mt}) + \tilde{E}_{Bt}$

Beta estimates should be the same as in part g. Alpha estimates are plugged so that average return on the stocks is 10% and average return on the market is also 10%.

i. No. We have here the problem noted by Roll. Whenever an ex post efficient portfolio is used to estimate market model betas, the relationship between the average return on each stock and its market model beta must be linear and perfectly fit the data. The relationship is mathematical only and simply says you used an ex post efficient portfolio. It does not confirm the CAPM.

QUESTIONS AND PROBLEMS

1. In the CAPM, the market portfolio is a mean-standard deviation efficient portfolio. True, false, or uncertain and why?

2. In the chapter, we examined expected excess returns, variance of excess returns, and standard deviation of excess returns for stocks A and B. This was done in the context of both a one-factor and a two-factor model. Consider an equal investment in stock A and stock B.

   a. According to the two-factor model, what would be this portfolio's expected return, variance of return, and standard deviation?

   b. Why are the results in part a different from those found in the chapter when this portfolio was viewed solely from the context of a one-factor model?

3. Briefly, what are the conceptual advantages (disadvantages) of the CAPM and the APT?

4. The SML states that:

$$E(R_i) = RF + \beta_i[RP_M]$$

Empirical tests of this relationship examine a regression of historical average returns on a beta estimate:

$$\overline{R}_i = \alpha_0 + \alpha_1 b_i$$

   a. What is the logic in using the empirical equation as a test of the theory?

   b. How are b_i values obtained? Do you see any potential problems in determining appropriate b_i values?

   c. If the theory is supported, what should α_0 and α_1 turn out to be?

5. A number of researchers have tested non-CAPM versions of historical returns on single stocks, such as:

$$\overline{R}_i = \alpha_0 + \alpha_1(\sigma_i^2) + \alpha_2(b_i)$$

If α_1 turns out to be positive and statistically significant, is this contrary to CAPM? How might the test, when applied to single stocks, be biased? How does a test using portfolios of securities overcome some of these biases?

6. What were the major conclusions of the Black, Jensen, and Scholes study of CAPM?

7. What are the major implications of Roll's critique of the CAPM?

8. Stocks 1 and 2 are affected by three factors, as shown below. Factors 2 and 3 are unique to each stock. Expected values of each are $E(F_1) = 3.0\%$, $E(F_2) = 0.0\%$, and $E(F_3) = 0.0\%$. Neither stock pays a dividend, and they are now selling at prices $P_1 = \$40$ and $P_2 = \$10$. You expect their prices in a year to be $E(P_1) = \$45$ and $E(P_2) = \$10.70$.

$$\tilde{R}_1 = 6.0(\tilde{F}_1) + 0.3(\tilde{F}_2) + 0.0(\tilde{F}_3)$$

$$\tilde{R}_2 = 1.5(\tilde{F}_1) + 0.0(\tilde{F}_2) + 0.4(\tilde{F}_3)$$

   a. What do factors 2 and 3 reflect? In the context of a broadly diversified portfolio, should the 0.3 and 0.4 be positive, as they are shown?

   b. Neglecting F_2 and F_3, create a riskless arbitrage.

   c. Relate the return equations above to the CAPM.

9. In what ways is APT different from the CAPM?

10. Stocks X and Y are affected by three factors, as indicated below:

$$\tilde{R}_X = 3(\tilde{\phi}_1) - 1.0(\tilde{\phi}_2) + 0.0(\tilde{\phi}_3)$$

$$\overline{R}_Y = 1.5(\tilde{\phi}_1) + 0.0(\tilde{\phi}_2) + 0.3(\tilde{\phi}_3)$$

The factors ϕ_2 and ϕ_3 are security-unique factors, and ϕ_1 is a common factor. Stock X is now selling for $50 and stock Y is selling for $25. Neither pays a dividend. You (and other arbitrageurs) expect that stock X will be selling for $58 in one year and stock Y will be selling for $26. Expected ϕ_1 is 4.0.

   a. Create a riskless arbitrage between the two.

   b. Logically, why are ϕ_2 and ϕ_3 unimportant?

c. What price levels of X and Y would no longer provide an arbitrage profit?

d. If actual ϕ_1 is 6.0, ϕ_2 is 2.0, and ϕ_3 is 4.0, what is the realized return on each?

11. You are given the factor sensitivities on four well-diversified stock portfolios. Both factors 1 and 2 are priced factors.

Portfolio	b_{i1}	b_{i2}	$E(R_i)$
A	0.4	0.6	7.8%
B	0.6	0.4	8.2%
C	1.0	0.0	9.0%
D	0.0	1.0	8.0%

a. What is meant by a ''priced'' factor?

b. Find the percentage to invest in A and B such that the combination has:
- zero factor 2 risk
- zero factor 1 risk

c. Is portfolio C correctly valued?

d. What is the relationship between factor 1 and expected returns in the following:

$$E(R_i) = a_0 + b_{i1}\overline{F}_{1t}$$

e. Is portfolio D correctly valued?

f. What is your best estimate of the following relationship:

$$E(R_i) = a_0 + b_{i1}\overline{F}_{1t} + b_{i2}\overline{F}_{2t}$$

g. Create an arbitrage using A, B, and D in which \$100,000 of D is traded. Show the end-of-period value of this arbitrage for the following actual outcomes of factor 2:

$$\text{Low:} \quad F_2 = 0$$

$$\text{Expected:} \quad F_2 = 3$$

$$\text{High:} \quad F_2 = 6$$

h. Why is a risk-free rate available in this model?

i. Why must a fully arbitraged APT model be linear?

12. What are the difficulties associated with testing APT?

13. What is the difference between a specified factor model and an unspecified factor model?

14. Research on the CAPM and beta has concluded that:

    a. short-term results may contradict the CAPM.

    b. estimated betas change over time.

    c. estimated beta depends on the choice of the market index.

    d. all of the above.

15. Compared to CAPM, in the APT:

    a. beta is eliminated as a pricing factor.

    b. inflation is eliminated as a pricing factor.

    c. the risk-free rate loses its significance.

    d. multiple factors are present in the return generation process.

16. The feature of APT that offers the greatest potential advantage over the CAPM is the:

    a. use of several factors instead of a single market index to explain the risk-return relationship.

     b. identification of anticipated changes in production, inflation, and term structure as key factors explaining the risk-return relationship.

     c. superior measurement of the risk-free rate of return over historical time periods.

     d. variability of coefficients of sensitivity to the APT factors for a given asset over time.

17. As the manager of a large, broadly diversified portfolio of stocks and bonds, you realize that changes in certain macroeconomic variables may directly affect the performance of your portfolio. You are considering using an APT approach to strategic portfolio planning, and want to analyze the possible impacts of the following four factors:

- industrial production;
- inflation;
- risk premia or quality spreads; and
- yield curve shifts.

     a. **Indicate** how *each* of these *four* factors influences the cash flows and/or the discount rates in the traditional discounted cash flow valuation model. **Explain** how unanticipated changes in *each* of these *four* factors could affect portfolio returns.

     b. You now use a constant-proportion portfolio allocation strategy of 60% stocks and 40% bonds, which you rebalance monthly.

     Compare and **contrast** an active portfolio approach that incorporates macroeconomic factors, such as the four factors listed above, to the constant-proportion strategy currently in use.

18. You are an investment officer at Pegasus Securities and are preparing for the next meeting of the investment committee. Several committee members are interested in reviewing two asset pricing models—the CAPM and the APT—and their use in portfolio management and stock selection.

     a. **Describe** both the CAPM and APT, and **identify** the factor(s) that determines returns in each.

     b. "The APT model is more general than the CAPM." **Explain** how this observation has meaning in the stock-selection process.

D A T A F I L E   A N A L Y S I S

In these analyses, you will examine changes in the volatility of historical monthly returns on two asset classes. The issue is whether investment risk changes over time.

1. *Bond Volatility.* Access the monthly return series in the RTNSMNLY.WK1 datafile. Identify the return series for 20-year U.S. corporate bonds. Find the standard deviation of monthly returns during the 36-month period 2601–2812 (January, 1926–December, 1928). Copy this cell formula to all future months for which returns on this bond series are available. This will give you a series of standard deviations based on returns during the previous 36 months.

2. *Stock Volatility.* Repeat this exercise for monthly returns on the S&P 500.

3. *Does Risk Change.* Plot the two standard deviation series as a line graph. The *Y*-axis should consist of the two standard deviation series (i.e., have two lines plotted). The *X*-axis should be each month-end. Interpret the results. What implications does this have on tests of asset pricing models?

R E F E R E N C E S

Classic empirical tests of the CAPM include:

BLACK, FISCHER, MICHAEL C. JENSEN, and MYRON SCHOLES. "The Capital Asset Pricing Model: Some Empirical Tests." In Jensen, Michael C. (Ed.) *Studies in the Theory of Capital Markets,* New York: Praeger Publishers, 1972.

FAMA, EUGENE F., and JAMES MACBETH, "Tests of Multiperiod Two-Parameter Model," *Journal of Political Economy,* May 1974.

LEVY, HAIM, "The Capital Asset Pricing Model: Theory and Empiricism," *Economic Journal,* March 1983.

ROLL, RICHARD, "A Critique of the Asset Pricing Theory's Tests: Part I on the Past and Potential Testability of the Theory," *Journal of Financial Economics,* March 1977.

Extensions to the standard CAPM include:

BREEDEN, DOUGLAS T., "An Intertemporal Asset Pricing Model with Stochastic Consumption and Investment Opportunities," *Journal of Financial Economics,* June 1979.

MAYERS, DAVID, "Nonmarketable Assets and the Determination of Capital Asset Prices in the Absence of a Riskless Asset," *Journal of Business,* April 1973.

MERTON, ROBERT, "A Simple Model of Capital Market Equilibrium with Incomplete Information," *Journal of Finance,* July 1987.

One of the original papers to develop the APT is:

ROSS, STEPHEN A., "The Arbitrage Theory of Capital Asset Pricing," *Journal of Economic Theory,* December 1976.

APT tests and reviews include:

CHEN, NAI-FU, RICHARD ROLL, and STEPHEN ROSS, "Economic Forces and the Stock Market," *Journal of Business,* 59, 1986.

ROLL, RICHARD, and STEPHEN ROSS, "An Empirical Investigation of the Arbitrage Pricing Theory," *Journal of Finance,* December 1980.

SHANKEN, JAY, "The Arbitrage Pricing Theory: Is It Testable?" *Journal of Finance,* December 1982.

An illustration of how portfolio managers use multifactor models is discussed in:

FOGLER, H. RUSSELL, "Common Stock Management in the 1990's," *Journal of Portfolio Management,* Winter 1990.

Recent tests of asset pricing models include:

FAMA, EUGENE F., and KENNETH R. FRENCH, "The Cross-Section of Expected Stock Returns," *Journal of Finance,* June 1992.

FRENCH, KENNETH, WILLIAM SCHWERT, and ROBERT STAMBAUGH, "Expected Stock Returns and Volatility," *Journal of Financial Economics,* 19, 1987.

Derivative Securities

The introduction and growth of derivative security markets during the past two decades has been astonishing. Prior to 1973, futures trading was limited to agricultural and natural resource commodities. And options were inactively traded in the over-the-counter market. By the mid-1990s, futures and options were actively traded in world markets on bonds, stocks, currencies, and stock indices as well as many commodities. There is even a well-developed market in options on futures.

In this chapter we examine the economic principles that tie market prices of derivatives to the underlying assets on which they have a claim. The discussion treats derivatives generically, leaving details of specific instruments to later chapters. In fact, most examples in this chapter are based on a hypothetical asset. If you develop an understanding of the economic principles that underlie the valuation of such generic futures and options, it is easy to apply these concepts to futures and options that are currently traded (or that are created in future years).

The interrelationships between five types of securities are examined. The first is a *risky asset.* This could be any asset with an uncertain future value. The hypothetical asset used in our numerical examples is called the World Index Trust (or WIT), an open-end investment company that manages a portfolio of stocks issued throughout the world. WIT fund is the underlying security on which the futures and options in this chapter have a claim. (The underlying asset is often called the ''spot'' asset.) The second security is *risk free* and pays a single future cash flow at date *T.* Other securities are derivatives: a *futures contract, a call option and a put option.* Each derivative has a unique claim to one share of WIT fund which can be made only at date *T.* Derivative securities are created by willing buyers and sellers. Either party to a trade can close out their position prior to date *T* by making an opposite trade. Of course, they can also keep their position open through date *T.* It is this possibility that drives a number of the valuation models that we examine.

In the course of developing valuation models for the derivatives, we will encounter three important ideas.

1. *The values of all five securities are interrelated.* If actual market prices do not properly reflect this interrelationship, arbitrage profits are available. The value of each derivative is based on the possibility of an arbitrage (or, more specifically, the absence of arbitrage in equilibrium).

2. *Returns on any one of the five securities can be emulated exactly by a combination of the other securities.* For example, we will see that a portfolio consisting of a long position in 1.0 unit of the spot and 1.0 put plus a short position in 1.0 call, has the same return as the risk-free security.[1] These emulating portfolios are called *synthetic* portfolios.

3. *The ability to trade in derivatives provides a cheap and fast way to alter the risk of a portfolio.* This is the reason for the astonishing growth of the derivative market.

WHAT IS A DERIVATIVE?

Although derivatives were reviewed in Chapter 2, it is useful to review certain basic ideas here.

Futures Contracts

A futures contract is an agreement made today (date 0) between two parties to trade an asset at a specified price at a stated future date T. The futures buyer agrees to purchase the asset at date T at a mutually agreed price. The futures seller agrees to deliver the asset at date T in return for the agreed price. A futures contract is simply a delayed purchase or sale of a spot asset. Date T is called the *delivery date* of the futures contract.

Although the contract is written as if actual delivery of cash and the underlying spot asset will be made at date T, either party may subsequently reverse his obligation by making an opposite offsetting trade. For example, assume that you buy one futures contract on WIT fund, which obligates you to pay $100 at date T for one share of WIT. You may keep this position through date T, at which time you will pay the $100 and receive (take delivery of) the share. Alternatively, by selling an identical futures contract prior to date T, you offset your original obligation. The difference between your sale and purchase price, of course, is your profit or loss. A large percentage of futures positions are reversed prior to the required delivery date. Most hedgers and speculators do not trade futures in order to physically receive or deliver the underlying spot. Instead, they use the profits and losses on futures trades to manage investment risk.

In Figure 9-1, the *investment value at the delivery date* is shown for both a long and a short futures position. The price which the buyer and seller agreed on date 0 to trade at date T is denoted F_{0T}. In this example, F_{0T} is $100 and the underlying asset is WIT fund. If the underlying asset is trading for $100 *at the delivery date,* then the investment value to both the buyer and seller is zero. However, if the value of WIT fund is $150 at the delivery date, a long futures

---

[1] The term *long* refers to the ownership of an asset. *Short* means sell the asset.

FIGURE 9-1 *Futures Contract Investment Value at Delivery Date*

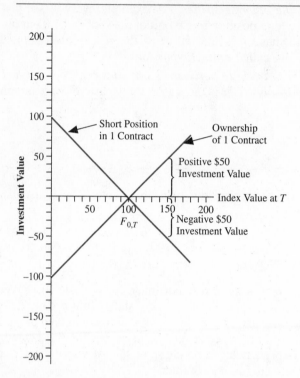

position has an investment value worth $50 and the short position's value is negative $50. Gains to one position are equal losses to the other.

The investment value to a given position (long or short) is simply the difference between the position's selling price and the buying price. Since no other cash flows take place (neglecting transaction costs), the investment value at date T is also the profit or loss from the futures transaction.

Investment value also represents the price you would receive (or have to pay) if you wished to assign your position to someone else. For example, assume you own a contract that allows you to buy WIT fund at $100 on day T. Day T arrives and the market value of a WIT share is $150. Someone else would be happy to pay you up to $50 for your right to buy at $100. However, if you had been a seller of the futures, you would have to pay another party $50 to induce him or her to take your position.

Although these points are straightforward, implicit in them is an important, but less apparent, idea. *At the delivery date, the futures contract investment value will be the same as the underlying spot asset less the required cash payment.*

$$\begin{array}{c} \text{Future Investment Value} \\ \text{at Delivery Date} \end{array} = \begin{array}{c} \text{Underlying Spot} \\ \text{at Delivery Date} \end{array} - \begin{array}{c} \text{Cash Equal to} \\ \text{Contracted Price} \end{array}$$

This can and should be read as a pricing equation. It should also be read as: "The portfolio of securities on the left is the same thing as the portfolio on the right."

The left portfolio can be synthetically created by the securities in the right portfolio.

Another way to think of this relationship is:

$$\frac{\text{Underlying Spot}}{\text{at Delivery Date}} = \frac{\text{Futures Investment Value}}{\text{at Delivery Date}} + \frac{\text{Cash Equal to}}{\text{Contracted Price}}$$

Ownership of the spot asset at the delivery date is the same thing as ownership of the future plus ownership of cash equal to the futures contracted price. With the proper cash in pocket, the future evolves into the underlying spot asset. These relationships exist only at the delivery day, but they are the key to all prior futures prices.

Do not confuse the investment value of a futures position on the delivery date with the price at which the future is trading at that time. The futures price is the amount of money that buyers are willing to pay sellers in order to acquire the underlying asset. *The futures price of a contract that is about to require delivery will be identical to the value of the underlying spot.* For example, back at date zero, futures on WIT traded at $100; $F_{0T} = \$100$. Assume you purchased this contract. If WIT shares are worth $150 on the delivery day *of this contract,* then the contract will also be priced at $150 ($FF_{TT} = \$150$) and the investment value of *your position* will be $50 ($150 − $100). At the day of delivery, the price of the future will equal the value of the spot. If this is not true, then arbitrage profits are available. We will review an arbitrage soon.

There are many important details about futures that are left to Chapter 15 later in the book. One detail that requires mention here is known as mark-to-market. Throughout this chapter, we assume that the only date at which the future requires a cash flow is at the delivery date. In real world trading, *daily profits or losses are paid in cash.* This is known as daily mark-to-market. Its purpose is to reduce the possibility that one side of the trade will default. Neglecting these daily cash flows has a minor impact on the pricing equations developed in this chapter.

Options

An option is an agreement to trade at a stated future date and at a stated price, but *only if the buyer wishes to do so;* it is the buyer's option to trade. An option to buy is a call option. An option to sell is a put option. The stated future date is known as the expiration date. The stated price is known as the exercise price. Many options provide the right to exercise at any time up to and including the expiration date. These are called American options. For simplicity, we will discuss options that may be exercised only at the expiration date—European options.

As with futures contracts, options are created by two willing parties. One party purchases the *option to trade* at a later date and the other sells the option. The seller is called the option writer. Buyers of options will choose to buy (in the case of a call option) or sell (in the case of a put option) only if it is to their benefit to do so. Call owners will buy if the asset's price is greater than the exercise price on the expiration day. Put owners will sell if the asset's price is less than the exercise price on the expiration day. Buyers have a potential gain and no loss

FIGURE 9-2 *Option Investment Values at Expiration Date*

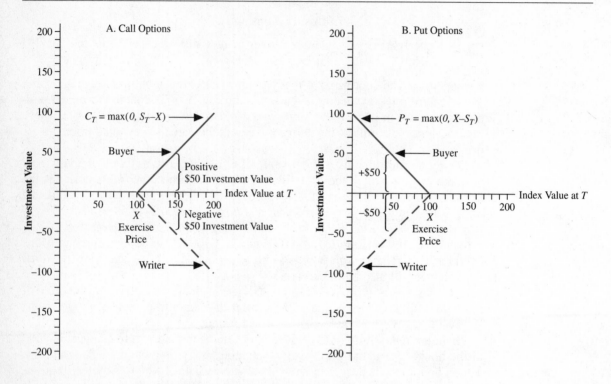

whereas sellers have a corresponding loss but no gain. Therefore, the writer will demand a price to write the option.

The investment values of various option positions at the expiration date are shown in Figure 9-2. Investment value for a call owner is the maximum of either zero or the stock price less the exercise price. If we define C_t as the value of a call at date t, T as the expiration date, X as the exercise price and S_t as the value of the underlying spot asset at date t, then:

Call Price at Expiration Date
$$C_T = \max(0, S_T - X) \tag{9.1}$$

Positive values for call owners are negative for call writers. Investment value for a put owner is the maximum of either zero or the exercise price minus the stock price. Defining P_t as the value of the put at date t, then:

Put Price at Expiration Date
$$P_T = \max(0, X - S_T) \tag{9.2}$$

Profits to option buyers are equal to the option's investment value at the expiration date *less* the initial option premium paid to the writer. For example, if the WIT call had been purchased at a price of $6.54 and the price of a WIT share at T is $104, then the call has an investment value worth $4 and the buyer's net profit will be a negative $2.54. Notice that it is always to the call buyer's advantage to exercise if the stock price exceeds the exercise price at day T, even if a loss is incurred. A $2.54 loss after exercising the call is clearly better than a $6.54 loss if not exercised. Profits to option writers are equal to the investment value of their position at date T *plus* the initial option premium received.

Prior to the expiration date, call and put prices consist of two components. These are illustrated in Figure 9-3 for a call option. The first component is known as the option's *immediate value*. This again is the maximum of zero, or $S_t - X$. The second component is known as the option's *time value*. For example, in Figure 9-3 the call is selling at a $60 price when the underlying asset's price is $150. The immediate value is $50 and the time value is $10. Buyers are willing to pay the $10 time value because time is left before the option expires. During this time, the underlying asset's price can fall by no more the $150 but, theoretically, it could rise in value by much more than $150. Options with positive immediate values are said to be trading *in-the-money*. Options with zero immediate value are *out-of-the-money* (or at-the-money when $S_t = X$).

Option buyers may choose to receive their profits by exercising. As with futures, however, most option positions are closed by offsetting trades.

Using Options to Create Futures Outcomes

Assume calls and puts are available on WIT fund with an exercise price of $100 and an expiration date T. You buy one call and sell one put. What will be the investment value of this portfolio at date T?

The answer is shown graphically in Figure 9-4. If the WIT fund is selling for more than $100 at date T, you will exercise the call (and the put owner will not exercise the put). You will pay $100 and receive one share of WIT fund. If WIT fund is selling for less than $100, the put owner will exercise the right to sell the fund to you at $100 (and your long call position will not be exercised). In this case, you also buy the fund for $100. The portfolio of one long call and one short put provides the same date T outcomes as the long futures position in our earlier

FIGURE 9-3 *Call Option Prices Prior to Expiration*

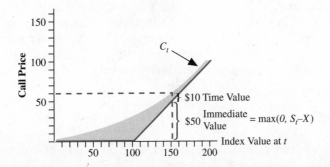

FIGURE 9-4 *Long Call Plus Short Put Equal Long Future*

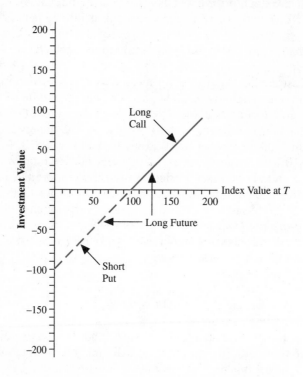

example. This occurs because we assumed that the initial futures price of $100 was equal to the exercise price on the options—$F_{0T} = X$.

The key point to this example is that date T investment values of the future can be synthetically created by a proper position in the options. Prices in the option markets must be interrelated to prices in the futures markets.

WHY DERIVATIVES EXIST

In the 20 years since options and futures on financial assets were first traded on security exchanges, trading volume has grown tremendously. But why? Has the dramatic growth in derivative trading simply been the result of security brokers "pushing" them to customers for brokerage fees? Certainly many option and futures trades are due to broker recommendations. But there must be more to it than this to create such a large and vibrant market.

Controlling Risk

Futures and options provide a fast and cost-efficient way of controlling portfolio risk. For example, assume you are the administrator of a large pension fund and have hired Tuwee, Cheetum Advisors to invest a portion of the portfolio in global (U.S. and non-U.S.) equities. Top management at the advisory firm recently left the organization and you wish to take the money that they currently invest for you and give it to another firm to invest. Unfortunately, it will take a few months (say, until date T) to identify the new manager. Long positions in futures contracts on WIT fund provide a possible way to maintain a global risk exposure and yet retrieve the money from TC Capital. The cash received would be invested in risk-free securities and futures on WIT fund would be bought. At date T, the par value of the risk-free securities plus any profits or losses on the futures would be transferred to your new global manager.

Consider another futures example. Presently, you have 25% of your portfolio invested in global equities that is being managed by four investment-advisory firms. This is greater than your long-term desired allocation of 20%. You could take money from the four firms and allocate it to other asset classes—that is, trade in the spot assets. This could be time-consuming and costly. In addition, you would be constantly taking or giving money to the managers as security prices change over time. An alternative would be to use futures to adjust your asset allocation. In this example, you would sell futures on WIT fund to reduce your global risk exposure.

Options provide a different way to control portfolio risk because their expiration-date investment values are different from the investment values of the spot asset or futures contract. For example, long put options guarantee a minimum selling price. If you own 50 shares of WIT fund and are worried about potential price declines, then a purchase of 50 puts having an exercise price of $100 guarantees a minimum portfolio value of $5,000 (50*$100) at the put's expiration. This is known as an insured portfolio. The cost of the insurance is the price of the puts.

Such an insured portfolio could also be obtained by trading solely in spot assets.[2] In this example, you would constantly monitor the price of WIT fund and if it fell to $100 you would sell your 50 shares and place the $5,000 in risk-free securities having a maturity of date T. Such a strategy entails monitoring and transaction costs. It also means that you will not own shares of WIT fund if its price falls to $100 and then rebounds. In short, the long put position may be preferable to trading in the spot assets.

When trading in spot assets is time-consuming and costly, derivatives offer an alternative way to control portfolio risk.

Improved Borrowing and Lending Rates

We will soon see how mixtures of derivatives and a risky spot asset can create risk-free rates of return. A long position in this mixed portfolio is the same thing as lending money at the risk-free rate. A short position is the same as borrowing

---

[2] This trading strategy is a way to synthetically emulate the purchase of a put. The cost of this synthetic put is the sum of transaction costs and price losses. Since these are unknown when such a trading strategy is begun, the cost of the synthetic put is unknown.

TABLE 9-1   *Hypothetical Returns on a Call Option and the Underlying Asset*

Initial Value of WIT shares		= $ 95.45
Dividend Paid by WIT at Date T		5.00
Initial Value of a Call Option		$ 6.54
Exercise Price of Call Option		$100.00

Price of WIT at Date T	Rate of Return	
	WIT Shares	Calls on WIT
$ 80	−11%	−100%
90	−1%	−100%
100	10%	−100%
110	20%	53%
125	36%	282%
150	62%	664%

money at the risk-free rate. If investors are otherwise unable to lend or borrow at the risk-free rate, they will naturally prefer to use the mixed derivative-spot portfolio to do so. This is not simply theory, but, rather, a technique that is widely used by sophisticated investors.

Increased Leverage

A *covered position* is one in which you have a long or short derivative position and an opposite position in the underlying risky asset. A *naked position* is one in which you have a position only in a derivative. Naked positions are very risky! For example, we will see that the ownership of a call is the same thing as using leverage to acquire the risky asset. It is not unusual to find betas of call options on a stock index to be 10.0 or 20.0 (relative to a beta of 1.0 for the index).

As an example, consider the call options on WIT fund. Assume they are trading for $6.54 at date 0 and that shares in the fund are then worth $95.45. At date T, WIT fund will pay a $5.00 dividend. The rate of return on equal dollar investments in the stock and in the call are shown in Table 9-1. Returns, of course, will depend on the value of WIT shares at date T. If the price falls to $80, an investment in WIT shares suffers an 11% loss versus a 100% loss on the long call option. In contrast, if share prices increase to $150, the return on an investment in WIT shares is 62% versus 664% for the long calls. Naked derivative positions are very slippery poles!

Price Discovery

Some trading in derivatives is not motivated by a desire to manage portfolio risk but instead by new information. Assume you have just discovered that a disaster of international dimensions has just occurred that will cause stock prices to fall around the world. Share values of WIT fund will also fall (they have not yet).[3]

---

[3] This is a far-fetched example since such an event will be reflected very rapidly in security prices.

Which would you rather trade: shares of the fund or options that are leverage positions in the shares? Clearly, you will trade the security that would provide the greatest return—the option.

The point of this example is that the presence of options or futures on a risky asset may increase the number of information traders who follow the asset. If options and futures do increase the number of information traders, they aid in the process of price discovery and increase the spot security's liquidity. Improvements in the process of price discovery will cause a security to trade at prices closer true its to economic worth. Increases in the number of information traders will also decrease the importance of the opinions of a few. Prices will be based on a broader number of informed judgments.

DERIVATIVE VALUATION

Derivative valuation models are based on arbitrage arguments. If the derivative does not trade at prices determined by the valuation equation, then arbitrage profits are available. Recall that an arbitrage is a transaction that: (1) requires no capital investment, (2) has no possibility of a loss and (3) a known profit.

In developing the valuation equations, assumptions are made that are not perfectly true in reality. For example, we assume that transaction costs are zero and that the cash proceeds from any short sale may be used to finance the purchase of other securities. We also assume that fractional units of any security may be traded. These assumptions are clearly inaccurate, but they allow us to focus on the heart of arbitrage valuation. And in most practical situations, they do little damage to the models which arise. For example, only low-cost traders will be attracted to possible arbitrages. Many financial institutions do have the legal ability to short sell a security and use the proceeds to purchase other securities. Finally, the fractional trade problem is not a serious problem in large arbitrage trades.

Another goal to this section is to understand how any one of the securities can be synthetically created by proper mixtures of the other securities. We will see that options and the risk-free security are the building blocks from which any other security can be made. This is a powerful insight.

All examples are based on the information in Table 9-2. The risky asset on which futures and options are traded is the World Index Trust fund. Shares of this mutual fund are now trading at $95.45 and the fund will pay a *known dividend* equal to $5 at date T. In valuation equations, the price of this risky spot asset at date t is written at S_t. The dividend is denoted as D_T. The risk-free security provides a return equal to 10% (over the period from now to T).

Futures with a delivery date at date T are available. The trading price of this future is denoted F_{tT}. Its price now (F_{0T}) is $100. The call and put options are exercisable at date T with identical exercise prices (denoted X) of $100. The value of the call and puts at any date t are C_t and P_t. Current market prices are: $C_0 =$ $6.54 and $P_0 = $2.00.

TABLE 9-2 *Hypothetical Security Price Information*

Data on the WIT Fund		*Symbol*
Current Market Value	$ 95.45	S_0
Expected dividend (paid at T)	5.00	D_T
Data on the risk-free security		
Date T risk-free rate	10%	RF
Data on derivatives		
Futures contract:		
Delivery date	Date T	T
Current price	$100	$F_{0,T}$
Option contracts:		
Expiration date	Date T	T
(both options)		
Expiration price		
(both options)	$100	X
Current call price	6.54	C_0
Current put price	$ 2	P_0

Futures Valuation

Consider the following portfolio that you form today. Buy one share of WIT fund and sell one futures contract at a price of $100. What is this mixed portfolio the equivalent to? Think about the cash flows. Today, you pay $95.45 for the share ($S_0$). This cash flow is known. At the delivery date, you receive a $5.00 dividend ($D_T$) and deliver the share to receive the $100 futures contracted price. Both cash flows are also known! This mixed portfolio is a risk-free security and it should be priced as such! Specifically:

**Relationships
Between Spot Price
and Future Price**

$$S_0(1 + RF) = F_{0T} + D_T \qquad \textbf{(9.3a)}$$

or

$$F_{0T} = S_0(1 + RF) - D_T \qquad \textbf{(9.3b)}$$

Applying Equation (9.3b) to the data in Table 9-2, we find that the current futures price is exactly what it should be: $100.

$$F_{0T} = \$95.45 \,(1.1) - \$5.00$$

$$= \$100$$

The fact that this portfolio is considered risk-free is shown graphically in Figure 9-5. As before, investment value at date T is shown on the vertical axis and date T value of a WIT share (the index) is shown on the horizontal axis. Solid lines represent long positions. Dashed lines represent short positions. The net outcome is shown as the dotted line. The investment value of the long stock position at date T is equal to the stock value plus the $5.00 dividend. Adding the short futures position always results in a net investment value of $105. For example:

	Delivery Date Value of:			
Price of WIT	Long Stock	Dividend	Short Future	Net
$ 0	$ 0	$5	$100	$105
100	100	5	0	105
200	200	5	− 100	105

The example above assumed that the share of WIT was delivered on the futures position to receive the $100. An alternative which results in the same outcome is to simply sell the futures contract on the delivery date. Delivery or sale on the delivery date is the same because *the value of the future must be equal to the value of the underlying spot on the delivery date.* For example, consider the transactions shown below for two delivery date values of the spot. Regardless of the spot price at date T, selling the futures at that time results in the same outcome as if delivery were made.

Numerical Example

	Investment Value		
	$t = 0$	At Date T	
Transactions at $t = 0$		$S_T = \$50$	$S_T = \$150$
Buy Spot Asset	− $95.45		
Sell Future		$100	$100
Transactions at $t = T$			
Receive Dividends		5	5
To Unwind Position:			
Sell Spot		50	150
Buy Future		<50>	<150>
Net	− $95.45	$105	$105

	In General Investment Value	
	$t = 0$	$t = T$
Transactions at $t = 0$		
Buy Spot Asset	− S_o	
Sell Future		F_{0T}
Transactions at $t = T$		
Receive Dividends		D_T
To Unwind Positions:		
Sell Spot		S_T } These are
Buy Future		$-F_{TT}$ } equal
Net	− S_o	$F_{0T} + D_T$

FIGURE 9-5 *Long Spot Plus Short Future Equals Risk-Free Asset*

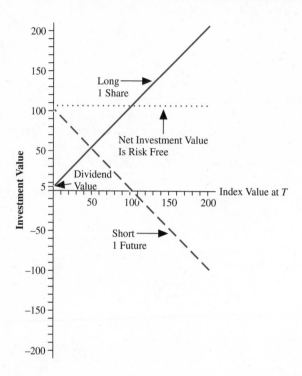

An Arbitrage. What if this future was priced above $100, say, at $105? Arbitrage profits would be available. Notice that we have two ways to obtain risk-free payoffs at date T. One is a portfolio consisting of a long share position in WIT plus a short future position on WIT. If the market value of the future is $105, then this portfolio will cost $95.45 today and pay off $110 ($F_{0T} + D_T = \$105 + \$5$) at date T. This represents a known return of 15.24%. The alternative is simply to purchase the risk-free asset such as T-bills and earn 10%. The arbitrage is quite simple; borrow money at 10% and invest it at 15%.

An example is shown in Table 9-3. The arbitrage starts off with the sale of the future because it is trading at too high a price. A naked short futures position, however, is risky, incurring losses if the price of WIT fund rises and profits if the prices drop. To eliminate this risk, we need a security position that acts exactly the opposite. This would be a long position in spot WIT shares. When the two are combined there is a known cash outflow of $95.45 today and a known inflow of $110 at date T. To complete the arbitrage the outflow is financed by selling $95.45 of T-bills.

Program Trading. In the example above, the arbitrage was unwound at the delivery date by selling spot shares and buying the futures—*both at the same price.*

TABLE 9-3 *Futures Arbitrage Illustration*

	Investment Value			
	$t = 0$	$t = T$		
Transaction at t = 0		$S_T = \$50$	$S_T = \$150$	*Why*
Sell Future		$\overline{\$105}$	$\overline{\$105}$	Future is overvalued
Buy Spot	$-\$95.45$			To create a risk-free position
Sell T-bills	95.45			To finance spot purchase
Transactions at t = T				
Receive Dividends		5	5	
Repay T-bill		-105	-105	95.45 (1.1)
Unwind Position:				
Sell Spot		50	150	
Buy Future		-50	-150	
Net	$\$\quad 0$	$\$\quad 5$	$\$\quad 5$	

Recall that the price of a future that is immediately deliverable will be equal to the underlying spot asset's price: $F_{TT} = S_T$. This must be or easy arbitrage profits are to be had. If a large number of people were unwinding their own arbitrages by selling the spot, it could drive the price of the spot asset down temporarily. The arbitrageurs would be unaffected since they are simultaneously buying the future at the same price. Thus they would be unconcerned that their combined trading behavior has had a temporary depressing effect on spot asset prices.

However, other market participants are affected—particularly, investors who coincidentally wish to sell shares and are forced to trade at temporarily low prices. Arbitrages such as this have had dramatic effects on stock prices at the futures' delivery date. The greatest price impacts have been the result of program trades on stock index futures. Program trading refers to the simultaneous purchase or sale of an entire portfolio of securities. This is particularly easy since the NYSE developed its computerized trading system known as Super-Dot (designated order turn around). Stock index arbitrage is one form of program trading. During 1991, program trading represented 11.0% of total NYSE volume.

During the market crash of 1987, stock index arbitrage and program trading was extensive during the morning. It stopped, however, when arbitrageurs discovered that they were unable to execute trades at current prices. Many observers believe that index arbitrage exacerbated a bad situation. Whether this is true or not is still hotly debated. Nonetheless, NYSE officials have developed procedures that are intended to minimize the affects of program trades. Their "side car" procedure, for example, delays the execution of program trades for 5 minutes if the S&P 500 futures contract declines 12 points below the previous day's close. If orderly trading can not be restored after the 5-minute interval, the imbalance information is publicly disclosed in an attempt to attract offsetting trades. In addition, NYSE Rule 80A states that when the Dow Jones Industrial Average moves 50 points or more from the previous day's close, index arbitrage orders in S&P 500 stocks are subject to a tick test. This means that sell orders may not occur at prices lower than the previous price and buy orders may not be executed at higher prices.

Although futures arbitrageurs are disliked by many individuals because of the price distortions that can be created, arbitrage plays a vital role. A fundamental reason for the existence of futures markets is their potential use in risk management. But they are successful in doing so only if futures prices are properly tied to the value of the underlying spot. In the case of stock futures, this tie is Equation 9.3. If arbitrage does not force futures prices to their theoretically correct values, the ability to use futures to control risk breaks down.

Synthetics. If the payoffs of a long position in a risk-free security such as a T-bill can be replicated by a long position in the risky spot and a short position in the futures, is the same true for the other securities? Yes. Let a positive sign $(+)$ denote a long position and a negative sign $(-)$ denote a short position. In addition, assume that the risk-free security *has a par value equal to S_o $(1 + RF)$ and a maturity at date T.*[4] Then the following relationships are true:

Asset	Synthetic Portfolio to Create Asset
+ Risk-Free Security =	+ Risky Spot − Futures
+ Futures =	+ Risky Spot − Risk-Free Security
+ Risky Spot =	+ Future + Risk-Free Security

The panels in Figure 9-6 illustrate the last two relationships. The risk-free synthetic was displayed previously in Figure 9-5.

In addition to showing us how to synthetically replicate one security with the other two, these relationships provide insights into thinking about each. As a good example, consider how you could replicate the delivery date investment value of owning a futures. You would purchase the spot asset today and fully finance it with a risk-free borrowing (which has a maturity date equal to date T and a current value equal to S_0). The amount borrowed would exactly cover the initial purchase of the spot.

At T, the spot asset has an investment value equal to $S_T + D_T$ and the debt has a par value of $S_0(1 + RF)$. The dividends (D_T) are known and can be used to pay off a portion of the debt, leaving $S_0 (1 + RF) - D_T$ of debt to be repaid. This quantity, of course, is the equivalent to the contracted price of the future at date 0. The conclusion is that *a long futures position is economically the equivalent to a leveraged purchase of the risky spot asset with sufficient leverage to fully pay for the spot's initial cost.*

	$t = 0$	$t = T$
Buy 1 spot	$-S_0$	$S_T + D_T$
Borrow Risk-Free	S_0	$-S_0(1 + RF)$
Net	0	$S_T - [S_0 (1 + RF) - D_T]$
		$= S_T - F_{0T}$

---

[4] The current price of this debt is S_0. Thus one unit of the debt would exactly finance the purchase of the spot risky asset.

FIGURE 9-6 *Futures Synthetics*

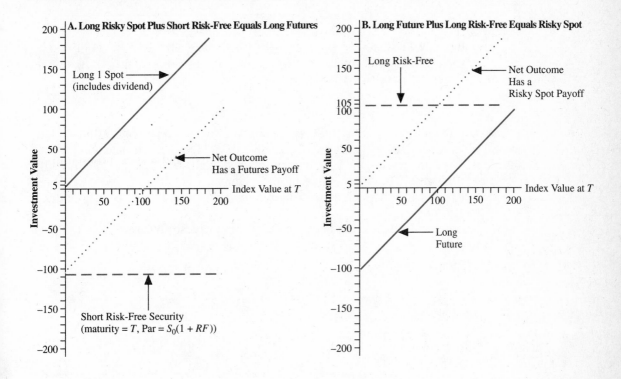

Option Valuation

There are two basic valuation models for options: the Put-Call Parity Model and the Black-Scholes Option Pricing Model. The Put-Call Parity Model focuses on expiration date outcomes whereas the Black-Scholes Option Pricing Model is a continuous-time model. Both are based on arbitrage profits that could be earned if the respective valuation equation does not explain actual market prices. We continue to assume zero transaction costs and European options. For simplicity, we will initially assume that no dividend will be paid on the risky spot asset. Examples are based on calls and puts of WIT fund shares shown in Table 9-2.

Put-Call Parity Model. Put-Call Parity deals with two basic ideas. What should the value of options be? And how can an asset be synthetically created using other assets?

Consider the following portfolio created at $t = 0$. Purchase 1 unit of WIT fund shares, purchase 1 put on the shares, and write 1 call on the shares. The cost of the portfolio and its investment value are shown below. Two possible expiration date values of the shares are shown, $50 and $150.

	Investment Value		
	$t = 0$	$t = T$	
		$S_T = \$50$	$S_T = \$150$
Buy 1 WIT share	$-\$95.45$	$\$ 50$	$\$150$
Buy 1 Put ($x = \$100$)	$-$ 2.00	50	0
Write 1 Call ($x = \$100$)	6.54	0	$-$ 50
Net	$-\$90.91$	$\$100$	$\$100$

Notice that all portfolio cash flows are known. Today we pay $90.91 and at date T we receive $100, regardless of the value of WIT shares on date T. Since the cash flows are certain, the relationship between them should be the 10% risk-free rate of interest. The same is true in this example, since $90.91 times 1.1 equals $100. Thus we can conclude that the *relationship* between the security prices is correct.

The general relationship between the prices of these four securities is shown below.

	Investment Value		
	$t = 0$	$t = T$	
		$S_T < X$	$S_T > X$
Buy 1 Risky Asset	$-S_0$	S_T	S_T
Buy 1 Put	$-P_0$	$X - S_T$	0
Write 1 Call	C_0	0	$-[S_T - X]$
Net	$-[S_0 + P_0 - C_0]$	X	X

Since all net cash flows are known, the initial outflow should be tied to the known terminal inflow as follows:

$$[S_0 + P_0 - C_0] (1 + RF) = X \tag{9.4}$$

Look at this relationship and assume that we know what the value of the risky spot asset (S_0) is and that we also know that the option's exercise price is X. But we do not know what the value of C_0 and P_0 should be. The logic to finding $P_0 - C_0$ follows.

The combination of $[S_0 + P_0 - C_0]$ is risk-free and pays $X = \$100$ at date T. Today ($t = 0$), the value of this combination should be $X \div (1 + RF) = \$100 \div 1.1 = \$90.91$. Observing that the current value of the risky spot is $S_0 = \$95.45$, we conclude that:

$$P_0 - C_0 = \$90.91 - \$95.45 = -\$4.54$$

Since the difference between actual put and call market values is $-\$4.54$, we conclude again that the interrelationship between the security prices is fair.

The logic underlying the above discussion is known as Put-Call Parity. It results in *relative* put and call prices for which there are no arbitrage profits. The basic *Put and Call Parity Model* can be expressed as:[5]

Put-Call
Parity Model $$C_0 - P_0 = S_0 - [X \div (1 + RF)] \tag{9.5}$$

This model does not identify what the value of the call should be or what the value of the put should be. It identifies the value of one option *relative* to the other.

By rearranging Equation 9.5, we can express the value of any one asset as a function of the other assets. These relationships are useful in understanding how replicating synthetic portfolios can be formed. Two of these relationships are shown below:

Alternative Ways
of Expressing $$C_0 = S_0 - [X \div (1 + RF)] + P_0 \tag{9.6a}$$
Put-Call Parity $$S_0 = C_0 + [X \div (1 + RF)] - P_0 \tag{9.6b}$$

Consider Equation 9.6a. A call option's expiration date values can be artificially replicated by purchasing 1 unit of the underlying risky spot, financing part of this cost with risk-free borrowing (having a par equal to X), and purchasing an insurance policy (the put) that guarantees that the loan will be repaid. The expiration date outcomes of such a portfolio are shown in panel A of Figure 9-7. When the risky spot asset trades *below* $X = \$100$ at date T, the spot's value together with the put's value is sufficient to pay off the par value of debt (par = $\$100$). In this case, the investment value of the portfolio is zero, the same as a call's outcome. When the risky spot asset trades *above* $X = \$100$, the value of the portfolio is always the spot's value minus the debt's par $(S_T - X)$—again, the same as a call's outcome.

This synthetic call portfolio shows what a call option is. Economically, *a call option is a leveraged position in the underlying risky spot asset* (plus insurance to guarantee debt repayment).

Now consider Equation 9.6b, which identifies the synthetic risky spot asset. It consists of the purchase of 1 call, the purchase of one unit of risk-free debt, and the sale of 1 put. Expiration date investment values of this portfolio are shown in panel B of Figure 9-7.

A Put-Call Parity Arbitrage. The market prices of the WIT options in our example were equal to their theoretically correct values. This equality is important to people who wish to use options to control portfolio risk exposure. As with futures, market prices of options must equal their theoretical values or the techniques of controlling risk using them break down.

---

[5] When a known dividend equal to D_T is to be paid on the risky spot asset at date T, the Put-Call Parity Model becomes:

$$C_0 - P_0 = S_0 - [(X + D) \div (1 + RF)]$$

FIGURE 9-7 *Option Synthetics*

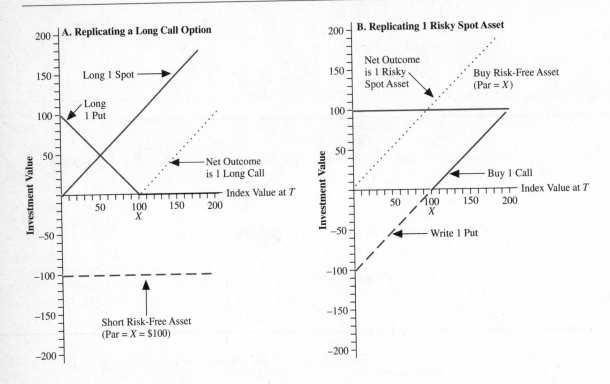

If the relative put-call market values had been different, an arbitrage would be possible. For example, assume that the call was trading for $7.00 and the put was $2.00. Thus the call was overvalued relative to the put and the put undervalued relative to the call. The detailed arbitrage in one unit of the risky spot is shown in Table 9-4.

Black-Scholes Option Pricing Model. The Black-Scholes model is based on the following assumptions:

1. A constant risk-free rate of interest exists at which people can borrow or lend any amount of money.
2. There are no transaction costs.
3. Stock may be short sold without restrictions.
4. The standard deviation of the stock's return is constant.
5. The stock pays no dividends.
6. Stock prices follow a continuous diffusion process.
7. Continuous rates of return are normally distributed.

The last two assumptions deserve some explanation. The Black-Scholes option valuation model is based on continuous time. They were able to demonstrate how the payoffs of a call option can be synthetically replicated by a proper mixture of

TABLE 9-4 *Put-Call Parity Arbitrage*

	Investment Value			
	$t = 0$	$t = T$		
		$S_T = \$50$	$S_T = \$150$	*Why*
Sell 1 Call	\$7.00	\$ 0.00	− \$50.00	Call is overvalued relative to put
Buy 1 Put	− 2.00	50.00		Put is undervalued relative to call
Buy 1 Risky Spot	− 95.45	50.00	150.00	To remove risk
Net	− 90.45	100.00	100.00	
Finance Risk-Free	90.45	− 99.50	− 99.50	90.45 (1.1)
Net	0.00	0.50	0.50	(7.00-6.54) (1.1)

the underlying asset and a risk-free security. Given that this is possible, arbitrage will guarantee that the cost of the call is the same as the cost of creating the synthetic call. Unlike the Put-Call Parity Model, a put option is not required to synthetically create the call. But the put option can be dropped only if the investor *continuously* rebalances the synthetic. This rebalancing is needed due to the passage of time or the change in any other variable in their pricing model. In short, the use of a continuous time model allows us to value the call option separate from the put. The opposite is also true. A put can be valued without knowledge of an equivalent call's value.

The synthetic call portfolio will exactly replicate the actual call payoffs as time passes only if underlying security prices follow a *continuous diffusion process*. This means that transactions can always occur. There is the *continuous* opportunity to trade securities in the synthetic in order to rebalance the position to one that will have a call payoff in the next moment. In addition, to maintain a properly balanced synthetic, security prices must follow a diffusion process. This simply means that, if a stock goes from \$50 to \$55 during a day, the move does not occur in one single jump but instead there is an opportunity to trade at all intermediate prices (\$50.01, \$50.02, etc.). If prices of any asset jump from one level to another without the opportunity to rebalance at every intermediate price, the synthetic will not replicate the actual option outcomes. (This was, in fact, a serious problem for individuals who were trading synthetic put options on Black Monday in 1987.)

The assumption that continuous compound rates of return are normally distributed has two advantages. First, it makes the mathematics of the Black-Scholes continuous time framework more tractable. Second, it means that the lowest market value for any security is zero. In contrast, if we had assumed that discrete compound returns are normally distributed, there is the chance of negative security prices, which is logically impossible.

Black and Scholes demonstrated that under these conditions, the call can be valued as a function of only the stock price and the value of debt. The Black-Scholes Option Pricing Model is:

Black-Scholes Option Pricing Model

$$C_0 = N(d1)S_0 - N(d2)\frac{X}{e^{(rf)(T)}} \qquad (9.7)$$

where $e = 2.7183$, rf is the *continuously* compounded annual risk-free rate, and T is the time remaining to expiration on an annual basis. $N(d1)$ and $N(d2)$ play important roles. Statistically, they are the cumulative value of the standard normal-density function between $-\infty$ and $d1$ or $d2$. The values of $d1$ and $d2$ are calculated as follows:

$$d1 = \{ln\ (S_0 \div X) + T\ [rf + (\sigma^2 \div 2)]\} \div \sigma \sqrt{T}$$
$$d2 = d1 - \sigma \sqrt{T}$$

Here, σ is the annualized standard deviation of the underlying risky spot assets return (expressed as a continuously compound annualized return). For example, assume we collect the following data on the WIT fund call options:

Known Information	New Information
$X = \$100$	$rf = 0.10$ per annum
$S_0 = \$95.45$	$T = 0.75$ years
	$\sigma = 0.16$ per annum

First, $d1$ and $d2$ would be:

$$d1 = \{ln\ (95.45 \div 100) + 0.75\ [0.10 + (0.16^2) \div 2]\} \div 0.16 \sqrt{0.75}$$
$$= 0.27\ \text{(rounded)}$$
$$d2 = 0.27 - 0.16 \sqrt{0.75}$$
$$= 0.13\ \text{(rounded)}$$

Second, the value of $N(d1)$ and $N(d2)$ must be found. This is illustrated in Figure 9-8, which represents a standard normal-density function. The cumulative probability below the zero mean is 50%. The value of $d1$ is *positive* 0.27, meaning that it lies 0.27 standard deviations *above* the zero mean. If we refer to Appendix A, which provides cumulative probabilities for various standard deviations, we find that 0.27 corresponds to a cumulative probability of 0.1064 above the zero mean. In total, $N(d1)$ would be $0.5 + 0.1064 = 0.6064$. Using a similar procedure for a $d2$ equal to 0.13, we find an $N(d2) = 0.5517$. (Note: If $d1$ or $d2$ values are *negative*, they lie *below* the zero mean. In such cases, the table entries in Appendix A are subtracted from 0.5.)

Finally, we can calculate the Black-Scholes value of this call option:

$$C_0 = 0.6064\ (\$95.45) - 0.5517\ [100 \div e^{(0.1)}\ (0.75)]$$
$$= 0.6064\ (\$95.45) - 0.5517\ [\$92.774]$$
$$= \$6.70$$

This is very close to the call's market value of $6.54 but suggests that the market price is slightly undervalued.

$N(d1)$ plays an important role. First, it is the dollar change in the call option's price for a $1.00 change in the stock's price (assuming all other variables remain

FIGURE 9-8 *Normal Density Function, d1 and d2*

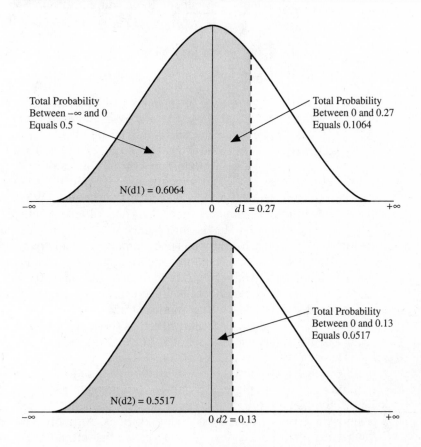

Total Probability
Between −∞ and 0
Equals 0.5

Total Probability
Between 0 and 0.27
Equals 0.1064

N(d1) = 0.6064

−∞   0 $d1 = 0.27$ +∞

Total Probability
Between 0 and 0.13
Equals 0.0517

N(d2) = 0.5517

−∞   0 $d2 = 0.13$ +∞

constant).[6] For the calls on WIT shares, a dollar increase in WIT shares will result in a $0.6064 increase in the call price. Second, it is a hedge ratio between the risky spot asset and the call that will result in an *instantaneously risk-free* combination. If you purchase 0.6064 shares of stock and write 1.0 call, then this portfolio is the same thing as instantaneously holding a risk-free security.

Black-Scholes Synthetics. The Black-Scholes Option Pricing Model can be used to synthetically replicate the *instantaneous outcomes* of any of the three securities. One unit of the risk-free debt security has a current value of $X \div e^{(rf)(T)}$. Define this as TB_0, standing for the price of a T-bill at date 0. Then the following relationships exist. (Positive signs mean purchase, negative signs mean sell.)

---

[6] Strictly speaking, $N(d1)$ should be interpreted only for very small changes in the stock price since its value changes as stock prices change.

Security to Replicate	Synthetic Replicating Portfolio
Call	$= + N(d1) S_0 - N(d2) TB_0$
Risky Spot	$= + [1/N(d1)] C_0 + [N(d2) \div N(d1)] TB_0$
$N(d2)$ T-bills	$= + N(d1) S_0 - 1.0 C_0$

For example, if you wished to replicate instantaneous outcomes of one WIT call, you should purchase 0.6064 shares of WIT and issue 0.5517 units of T-bills each worth TB_0. To replicate one share of WIT, purchase $(1 \div 0.6064)$ WIT calls and purchase $(0.5517 \div 0.6064)$ units of T-bills. Finally, 0.5517 units of T-bills is replicated by purchasing 0.6065 shares of WIT and selling 1.0 call.

This all looks complex, but synthetic security portfolios are actively used by sophisticated investors. Consider two actual examples. When investments are made in securities of countries other than one's home country, the investments face exchange-rate risk—that is, uncertainty about currency exchange rates when the money is returned. To limit this uncertainty, you could purchase currency puts to guarantee a sale price of the foreign currency. But puts are not available on all currencies, and it may be very costly to insure each currency risk in the portfolio. Alternatively, you could synthetically create a put on the exact "basket" of currencies that you own by appropriate trades in the spot currencies and the domestic risk-free asset. Procedures such as these are also called *dynamic strategies*. The term *dynamic* refers to the fact that the synthetic is constantly rebalanced as security prices change or time passes.

An *enhanced portfolio* is the term used for another form of synthetic replication. Assume you wish to place $10 million in nominally risk-free securities such as T-bills. Synthetic T-bill returns could also be obtained by mixed futures/risky spot positions and mixed option/risky spot positions. An individual who manages an "enhanced portfolio" chooses the alternative that provides the greatest return.

OTHER SECURITIES AS OPTIONS

Many securities are better understood when viewed from option theory. In fact, many people consider options and risk-free debt to be the building blocks of all other securities.

Debt instruments that have the potential for default are effectively a position in two securities. The first is risk-free debt that will pay off a known value. The second is a put that debt holders have sold to equity holders. This put allows equity holders the option to legally forgo all promised debt payments if they transfer assets of the firm to bond holders. This means that equity holders are able to sell firm assets to bond holders at a price equal to the promised bond payments. Obviously, equity owners will pay debt holders what they have been promised if assets are worth more than what has been promised to debt holders. But if assets are worth less than debt holders were promised, debt holders are required to take possession of the assets and suffer a loss. We will review this view of risky debt at more length when we examine principles of bond valuation in Chapter 11. But the important point is that option theory is the key to pricing potential bond default risk.

There is another way to view the option position of equity owners. Equity owners own a call option on firm assets that has been written by debt holders. The exercise price of this option is the promised payments to bond holders. If firm assets are worth more than these promised payments, debt holders will be paid and equity holders will claim ownership to the assets.

Bonds that are callable prior to scheduled maturity have an imbedded call option that bond holders have sold to equity holders. Such bonds can be purchased at a stated price by equity holders prior to maturity. Convertible bonds also have imbedded options that allow bond holders the right to buy equity shares at a stated price (the convertible's conversion price).

There are innumerable other examples of how securities can be viewed as options, but the basic point should be clear. A knowledge of option theory expands our understanding of how securities should be valued.

SUMMARY

The existence of active markets in financial futures and options provides a fast and inexpensive way to manage the risk of a portfolio. For example, someone who wishes to increase the equity risk of a portfolio could either purchase futures contracts or buy calls on the desired equity. If a reduction in equity risk is desired, then futures contracts could be sold or put options bought.

The key to the pricing of derivative securities is the fact that their maturity-date investment values can be exactly replicated with spot assets whose prices are known. For example, the ownership of a future on asset Z is the same thing as purchasing asset Z and fully financing its cost by risk-free borrowing. Similarly, the expiration date payoff of owning a call on asset Z plus a risk-free security can be the same as owning asset Z and a put on Z. These replicating portfolios are called synthetics. *It is the opportunity for arbitrage between derivatives and synthetics that causes security prices to be closely interrelated and creates the market value of each derivative.*

REVIEW PROBLEM 1

Use the following information:
Spot Price (S_0) $500
Future Price (F_{01}) $530

Maturity (T) 1 year
Risk-Free Rate (RF) 10% per year
Dividend (D_1) $20 paid at the end of one year

a. Is the future priced correctly?

b. Is it ever possible that futures price (F_{0T}) may be lower than the spot (S_0)? If yes, illustrate using your own assumptions.

c. Combine the spot and the future to synthetically create a T-bill.

d. Combine the spot and a T-bill to create a future.

e. Artificially mimic the spot with a future and a T-bill.

Solution to Review Problem 1

a. $F_{01} = S_0 (1 + RF) - \text{Div}_T = 500(1.1) - 20 = \$530$
Yes

b. Yes. Assume dividend of $60 paid at T $D_T = \$60$
$F_{01} = S_0(1 + RF) - D_T = 500(1.1) - 60 = \$490$

c. Making a T-bill (par = $550, mat = T) from spot and future

At 0	0	T
Buy Spot	<500>	
Sell Future		+530
At T		
Receive Div		+ 20
Close Position		
Sell Spot		net is
Buy Future		zero
Net	<500>	+550
		1 + return = 1.1

d. Making a future with spot and T-bill

A + 0	0	T
Buy Spot	<500>	
Sell T-bill	+500	
At T		
Receive div		+ 20
Sell spot		$+S_{DD}$
Buy T-bill		<550>
Net	0	$S_{DD} - 530$

e. Making a spot with futures and T-bill

A + 0	0	T
Buy T-bill	<500>	
·Buy Future		<530>

At *T*

Sell T-bill		$+550$
Sell Future		$+S_{DD}$
Net	$<500>$	$S_{DD} + \$20$

R E V I E W   P R O B L E M   2

Using the information from problem 1, answer the following:
a. Draw expiration-day payoffs on spot.
b. Draw expiration-day payoffs on long future.
c. Draw expiration-day payoffs on long call with exercise price of $530.
d. Draw expiration-day payoffs on short call with exercise price of $530.
e. Draw expiration-day payoffs on long put with exercise price of $530.
f. Draw, as in e, payoffs on a short put.
g. Draw expiration-day payoffs on a portfolio of long future, short call, and long put.

Solution to Review Problem 2

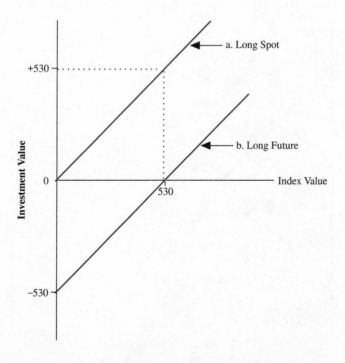

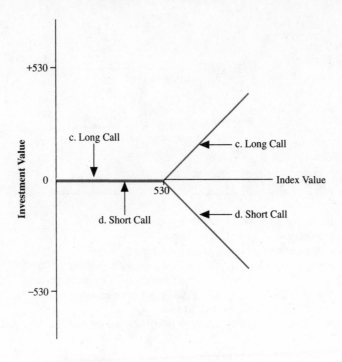

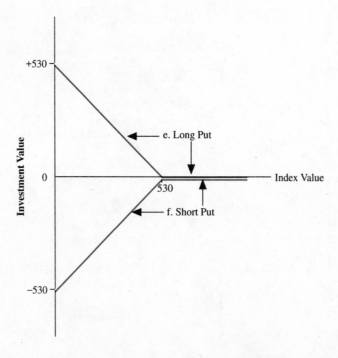

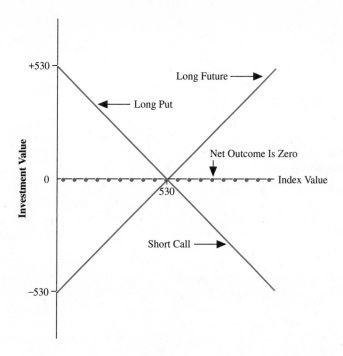

QUESTIONS AND PROBLEMS

1. Define derivatives and name three examples.
2. If derivatives can be created by combining existing securities, then the derivatives seem to be redundant. Explain why such ''redundant'' securities are so popular.
3. Derivatives are very risky. Prudent investors should not trade these under any circumstances. True or false? Discuss why.
4. You write a call. On expiration day, your payoff will be zero at best. You are guaranteed to not get any positive payoff. (This is true.) Why would you get into such a deal?
5. You decide to buy your dream house for $100,000. A local bank lends you 90% of the purchase price. As a condition for the loan, the bank also requires you to purchase ''mortgage guarantee'' insurance from the ''Fearnot Insurance Company.'' Express this investment in the form of the put-call parity model and carefully identify each term. Assume a risk-free rate of 10% per year. For convenience, assume that the mortgage is due in one year and that there are no monthly payments. The insurance costs $1,000.
6. In the Black-Scholes Options Pricing Model a risk-free security is synthetically created by_____. Complete the sentence. Explain carefully how many units of existing securities are needed.
7. Consider the following information:

$$F_{0T} = \$100 \qquad C_0 = \$10 \qquad P_0 = \$8$$

Both puts and calls have maturity T and exercise price of $100. The underlying asset is the same for each derivative. Also, there will be no dividends associated with the future. Do you see an arbitrage opportunity? No additional information is available.

8. You are told the following information about a futures contract on the FT-SE 100, a major U.K. stock index.

Spot Price of FT-SE	300£
Spot Dividend (paid in 1 Year)	12£
Future Price	312£
Delivery Date	1 year
Risk-Free Rate	8% (for 1-year)

a. Simon Benton manages a portfolio of U.K. stocks and T-bills currently worth 90£ million and 50, respectively. The stock is virtually the same as what the FT-SE 100 index measures. He decides to sell 300,000 (90£ million ÷ 300£) of the futures. What *will be* the value of this portfolio when the future's delivery date arrives?

b. Keith Jackson has been given 90£ million to invest in U.K. stocks. Instead, he purchases 90£ million worth of 1-year U.K. T-bills and buys 300,000 of the futures. What will be the value of this portfolio at the future's delivery date if the FT-SE 100 is then worth 350£? Repeat for a FT-SE 100 value of 250£.

c. Lisa Jordan manages a mixed portfolio of U.K. stocks and T-bills. Currently, the value of the stocks is 3£ million more than she wishes. How could she trade in the futures to create the same outcome as actually selling the 3£ million spot stock?

d. Why would the trade in part C not work if Lisa had actually wanted the 3£ million placed in long-term U.K. corporate bonds?

e. Why might people decide to trade futures instead of the actual spot?

9. You are told the following information about options on the FT-SE 100:

Spot price of FT-SE 100	300£
Spot Dividend (paid in 1-year)	0 £
Expiration (both options)	1-year
Risk-Free Rate	8% (for 1-year)
Exercise Price (both options)	300£
Call Price	41.67£
Put Price	15.00£

Standard Deviation of FT-SE 100 Returns 25% per year

a. Is put-call parity working?

b. Illustrate the arbitrage that is possible.

c. Find the Black-Scholes value of the call. (Use 8% as the continuous risk-free rate.)

d. Simon Benton manages 94.5£ million of U.K. stock, which is similar in make-up to the FT-SE 100 index. He sells 4.5£ million of the stock and buys 300,000 puts. What will be the value of this portfolio in 1-year at the following FT-SE levels: 100, 200, 300, 400?

e. Lisa Jordan has 94.5£ million in cash. She buys 83,333,333.33£ worth of U.K. T-bills. (Note that total par is 90£ million.) She invests the rest in 267,978.56 call options (11,166,666.67 ÷ 41.67). What will be the value of this portfolio in 1-year at the following FT-SE 100 levels: 100, 200, 300, 400?

    f. Why are the values in parts d and e different? What is the implication for arbitrage and hedging in the option?

 10. Which of the following variables influence the value of options?

    I. Level of interest rates

    II. Time to expiration of the option

    III. Dividend yield of underlying stock

    IV. Stock price volatility

    a. I and IV only

    b. II and III only

    c. I, III and IV only

    d. I, II, III and IV

 11. To preserve capital in a declining stock market, a portfolio manager should:

    a. buy stock index futures.

    b. sell stock index futures.

    c. buy call options.

    d. sell put options.

 12. Which one of the following would tend to result in a high value of a call option?

    a. Interest rates are low.

    b. The variability of the underlying stock is high.

    c. There is little time remaining until the option expires.

    d. The exercise price is high relative to the stock price.

 13. Which one of the following transactions would be considered a protective strategy?

    a. Sell a call against a stock you sold short.

    b. Buy a call on a stock you own.

    c. Sell a naked put.

    d. Buy a put on a stock you own.

14. It is extremely important to IPC's management that the pension fund's present surplus level be preserved pending completion of buyout financing. For the next three months (until September 1, 1990), management's goal is to sustain *no loss* of value in the pension fund portfolio. Today, June 1, 1990, this value is $300 million. Of this total, $150 million is invested in equities in the form of an S&P 500 Index fund, producing an annual dividend yield of 4%; the balance is invested in a single U.S. government bond issue, having a coupon of 8% and a maturity of 6/1/2005. Since the "no-loss strategy" has only a three-month time horizon, management does not wish to sell any of the present security holdings.

Assume that sufficient cash is available to satisfy margin requirements, transaction costs, and so forth, and that the following market conditions exist as of June 1, 1990:

- the S&P 500 Index is at the 350 level, with a yield of 4.0%;
- the U.S. government 8.0% bonds due 6/1/2005 are selling at 100; and
- U.S. T-bills due on 9/1/90 are priced to yield 1.5% for the three-month period (i.e., 6% annually).

Available investment instruments are the following:

Contract	Expiration	Current Contract Price	Strike Price	Contract Size
S&P 500 Index future	9/1/90	355	—	$175,000
Future on U.S. government 8.0% bonds due 6/1/2005	9/1/90	$101.00	—	$100,000
S&P 500 call option	9/1/90	$ 8.00	350	$ 35,000
S&P 500 put option	9/1/90	$ 7.00	350	$ 35,000
U.S. government 8.0% due 6/1/2005 call option	9/1/90	$ 2.50	100	$100,000
U.S. government 8.0% due 6/1/2005 put option	9/1/90	$ 4.50	100	$100,000

a. Assume that management wishes to protect the portfolio against any losses (ignoring the costs of purchasing options or futures contracts), but wishes also to participate in any stock or bond market advances over the next three months. Also, assume that management does *not* wish to use dynamic hedging.

Using the above instruments, **design** *two* strategies to accomplish this goal, and **calculate** the number of contracts needed to implement each strategy.

b. Using the put-call parity relationship and the fair value formula for futures (both shown below), **recommend** which *one* of the *two* strategies designed in part a should be implemented. **Justify** your choice.

Put Price = Call Price *minus* Security Price *plus* Present Value of (Exercise Price *plus* Income on the Underlying Security)

Futures Price = Underlying Security Price *plus* (T-bill Income *minus* Income on the Underlying Security)

REFERENCES

Recently published textbooks devoted solely to options and futures include:

CHANCE, DONALD M., *An Introduction to Options and Futures*. Orlando, FLA: Dryden Press, 1989.

HULL, JOHN, *Options, Futures and Other Derivative Securities*. Englewood Cliffs, NJ: Prentice-Hall, 1989.

MARSHALL, JOHN F., *Futures and Option Contracting*. Cincinnati, OH: South-Western Publishing Co., 1989.

STOLL, HANS R., and ROBERT E. WHALEY, *Futures and Options: Theory and Applications*. Cincinnati, OH: South-Western Publishing Co., 1993.

The various option and futures exchanges have numerous pamphlets that describe the derivatives traded on their exchange. The following address can be used to obtain literature from the Chicago Board of Trade:

Chicago Board of Trade
Literature Services Department
141 W. Jackson Boulevard
Chicago, IL 60604-2994
(312) 435-3558

Excellent overviews of derivative security uses can be found in:

BLACK, FISCHER, "Fact and Fantasy in the Use of Options," *Financial Analysts Journal,* July–August 1975.

FRENCH, KENNETH R., "Pricing Financial Futures Contracts: An Introduction," *Journal of Applied Corporate Finance,* Winter 1989.

SCHOLES, MYRON, "The Economics of Hedging and Spreading in Futures Markets," *Journal of Futures Markets,* Summer 1981.

Some interesting recent articles treating derivatives are:

CHANCE, DON M., "Option Volume and Stock Market Performance," *The Journal of Portfolio Management,* Summer 1990.

RENDELMAN, RICHARD J., and THOMAS J. O'BRIEN, "The Effects of Volatility Misestimation on Option Replication Portfolio Insurance," *Financial Analysts Journal,* May–June 1990.

Classic studies of derivative valuation can be difficult for students who have weak training in mathematics. But the general arguments can usually be followed. You might examine:

BLACK, FISCHER, "The Pricing of Commodity Contracts," *Journal of Financial Economics,* September 1976.

BLACK, FISCHER, and MYRON SCHOLES, "The Pricing of Options and Corporate Liabilities," *Journal of Political Economy,* May–June 1973.

COX, JOHN C., JONATHAN INGERSOLL, and STEPHEN A. ROSS, "The Relation Between Forward and Futures Prices," *Journal of Financial Economics,* December 1981.

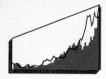

Efficient Market
Theory

Few ideas are more controversial or hold more profound trading implications than the concept of an efficient securities market. No longer is it taken for granted that active security trading can result in higher long-run rates of return than available from a passive investment strategy.

In its strictest interpretation, efficient market theory (EMT) states that security prices will always fully reflect all known information. If a firm announces unexpected positive information about earnings, the investing public rushes to buy the security at previous prices—only to find that they must trade at a higher new price that fully reflects the announcement. When investors buy at the new price, they can expect only a fair return given the security's risk.

Expressed somewhat differently, EMT states that the security market is a *fair game:* the odds of having a future return greater than should be *expected, given a security's present risk,* are the same odds of having a lower return than should be expected—50%. There is no way to use the information available at a given point in time to earn abnormal returns. Positive returns will be expected, of course, because securities contain risk for which premium will be earned. However, long-run abnormal returns will be zero.

Although the EMT has caused a major revolution in investment management, it is highly controversial. While active security selection can be intellectually challenging and emotionally exciting, the "game" is played in deadly earnest. People's careers and savings are at stake. To many technicians and fundamentalists, persons who espouse the efficient market theory are ignorant of the facts of life. They believe that such investment strategies are likely to prevent people from earning all they might from their investments (as well as cause many technicians and fundamentalists to lose their jobs). To many proponents of an efficient market, technicians and fundamentalists are either charlatans or naive optimists whose policies would needlessly drain investors' savings. Because of this controversy and its profound implications, we will review a broad range of empirical studies.

Empirical studies of efficient markets can be thought of as belonging to one of two eras. During the 1960s and 1970s, virtually all tests of EMT were supportive. To the extent that potential inefficiencies were present in the tests, they were not pursued. The concept of an efficient market was a logical and clearly important new theory. And most empirical evidence suggested that it was, indeed, a powerful theory. Beginning in the 1980s, a number of studies began to appear that indicated that either security markets were not as efficient as scholars previously believed or that our understanding of asset pricing models and market efficiency had to be considerably broadened. Empirical tests from both eras are presented here in order to provide a complete taste of the development of EMT.

THREE APPROACHES TO SECURITY SELECTION

Three distinct schools of thought claim to offer the ideal way to select securities; technical selection, fundamental selection, and selection based on the efficient market hypothesis. Both technical and fundamental approaches advocate active trading in the hopes of earning excess risk-adjusted returns. Efficient market strategies call for a passive management approach in order to minimize transaction costs. Because tests of EMT are closely tied to the approaches used by technicians and fundamentalists, it is helpful to review each.

Technical Analysis

Technicians believe that an examination of historical price and volume movements can identify price patterns from which future prices can be forecast. Because of their reliance upon price charting, technicians are also referred to as *chartists*. A pure technician pays no attention to a company's earnings prospects, financial condition, product risk, patent protection, and so forth, believing that historical price movements tell the whole story.

Dow Theory. The classic technical tool is Dow Theory. Originally developed by Charles H. Dow, editor of *The Wall Street Journal* from 1889 to 1902, as a means of describing historical market movements, it was expanded upon by William Hamilton, who suggested that it could be used to predict market moves. Dow theorists believe price movements consist of three types, all of which are occurring at any moment in time. *Primary* moves consist of major trends that usually last between one and four years. Primary moves up are referred to as Bull markets (aggressive and charging). Primary moves down are referred to as Bear markets (defensive and retreating). Within each primary move are a number of *intermediate* or *secondary* moves that interrupt the primary move and retrace a substantial portion of the change in prices since the last intermediate move. Intermediate moves are said to be technical corrections that drain the energy of speculative excesses which might have developed. These corrections usually last less than two months. Finally, *minor* price changes or *ripples* will occur more or less randomly around the basic primary and secondary moves. Dow theorists often describe these price movements in terms of the movement of the ocean. Primary moves are akin to tidal flows, intermediate moves are similar to waves, and minor moves represent ripples.

Figure 10-1 provides hypothetical price and volume data on the DJIA and DJTA. From date 0 to date 2 the market has been at a trough and not moving in any particular direction. Starting around date 2, "smart money" begins to realize that economic conditions are likely to improve and result in higher stock values. A period of "stock accumulation" begins in which shares are acquired by "strong hands" from "weak hands" (by leaders from followers). Slowly trading volume picks up and prices rise until date 3. On date 3 a technical correction begins as individuals who had bought shares at depressed prices sell in order to take their profits. However, prices don't fall far because the smart money continues to buy. Soon prices resume their upward direction in the Bull market. Trading volume and prices continue to increase as additional demand for shares is created by the "followers" who had previously been pessimistic but are now changing their opinion in the face of substantially higher prices. A second intermediate move occurs at date 5, but again prices recover and rise above the date 5 peak. The Bull market continues. Eventually, trading volume reaches an all-time high as extreme optimism and speculation prevail. It is at this time of speculative excess that smart money begins to sell and cause a price decline at date 7. Although prices rebound, the new peak at date 8 is lower than the prior peak. Although this suggests that a Bear market has developed, it must be "confirmed" by the Transportation Index. By date 9 the Transportation Index also has an abortive recovery and confirms that a Bear market indeed is in process. (Unfortunately, by then prices of the industrials have continued to fall.) The scenario of a Bear market is the opposite of a Bull market.

Head and Shoulders. Consider another example of charting. Figure 10-2 illustrates a hypothetical bar chart. Technicians will search such a chart for a "pattern" that can be used to predict future price moves. As drawn in Figure 10-2, the bar chart illustrates what technicians label a "head and shoulders" pattern. The left shoulder is supposed to build upon a strong rally (good volume and price rises). Profit taking on high volume causes prices to fall temporarily and completes the left shoulder. A similar pattern of price increase (rising above the left shoulder) followed by profit taking follows, but this time on more moderate volume. Finally, the right shoulder is formed on light volume, indicating a growing technical weakness (inability of buying support to sustain the general upward trend of the left shoulder and head). At this point it is important to identify the "neckline," which is a straight line connecting low points in the last two technical corrections. If the price on the right should "break through" the neckline on high volume, the technician considers this to be a sell signal. Inverted head-and-shoulder movements are upside-down patterns with a declining neckline.

Support and Resistance Levels. A support level is a price level at which prices are unlikely to fall through; or if they do, the fall will come only on high volume and considerable bad news about the firm. Resistance levels are price levels that are unlikely to be exceeded; but if they are, the rise will come on high volume and considerable good news about the firm. Breakthroughs of support and resistance levels on low volume will soon be reversed. The explanation given for

FIGURE 10-1 *Dow Theory Illustration*

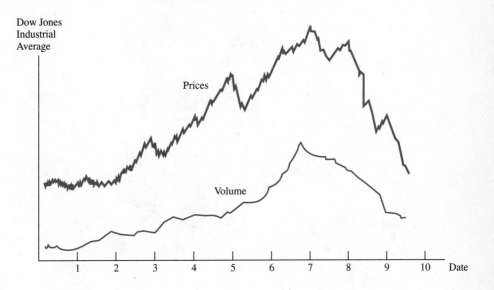

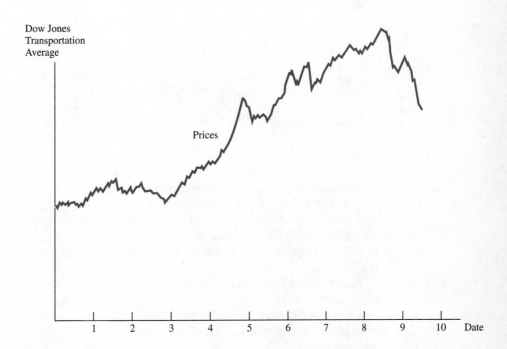

FIGURE 10-2 *Hypothetical Head-and-Shoulder Move*

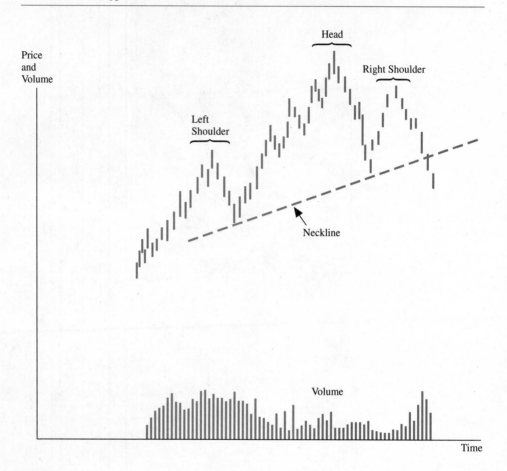

support and resistance levels relates to a perceived market psychology. Most people will know the price band in which the stock has been traded and observe that it hasn't recently broken through the support or resistance levels. Therefore, they stand ready to buy when prices hit the support level (prices are more likely to rise than fall) and sell at the resistance level (prices are more likely to fall than rise).

Figure 10-3 illustrates a hypothetical price band and a break through the resistance level on high volume. The breakthrough would be considered a bullish sign, and some technicians believe that what had been the former resistance level will now be the new support level. The opposite is believed about a breakthrough of the support level.

Other Technical Tools. There could easily be as many ways of employing technical selection techniques as there are technicians. A widely publicized statistic

FIGURE 10-3 *Hypothetical Support and Resistance Levels*

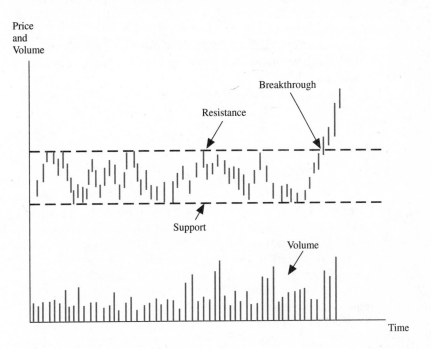

is the *advance-decline* line. Each day the number of stocks that decline are subtracted from the number of advances and the net accumulated overtime. It is intended to be an indicator of the "breadth" of price rises or declines. It is often considered a leading indicator of price movements in DJIA or S&P 500 stocks. *Moving average* price lines represent the average price for, say, the past 200 days. There is no one single trading rule based on moving averages, but they are all based on the level of current prices relative to it. Trading rules are also based on statistics such as the amount of odd-lot trading, the quantity of short sales, and the average mutual fund cash position.

Does It Work? Whether a technical analyst is able to identify securities that will provide future returns in excess of what they should given their risk is an empirical issue. But logically, should such procedures work in a competitive security market in which a large number of people are seeking a road to wealth? If a pattern that continually repeats itself can be identified by one investor, it is likely that the same pattern will be identified by many investors. Soon, their trading activities will alter prices so that the pattern no longer exists.

For example, consider the widely cited "Summer Rally" in which stock prices are supposed to rise during the early Summer months (as the weather improves and vacation season arrives). If you observe that prices rise every June more than in May, what would *you* do? Buy in May and sell after June! Naturally you won't be alone and soon the June rally will move to May, then April until there is no single month in which returns are greater, on average, than any other month. For technical selection to work, it takes either an inattentive market or an individual with an uncanny ability to uncover trends.

If security markets are efficiently priced, then technical selection rules will not work. Technicians will, on average, earn positive returns but only because they invest in risky securities. But any patterns that might have existed in past prices will currently be reflected in current prices. Past prices *are* a part of current information.

Fundamental Selection

Proponents of the second approach are known as fundamentalists. It has been said that a technician is to a fundamentalist as an astrologer is to an astronomer. Fundamental analysts examine basic economic forces affecting a company in an attempt to forecast future earnings, dividends, and security risks. Given projections of potential returns and risks, fundamental analysts estimate what they believe to be the fair market value of a security. This so-called intrinsic value is then compared with the security's current market price and a buy, sell, or hold recommendation is made. Simply put, fundamentalists believe that thorough financial analysis of a security can identify mispriced securities.

The job of a *good* fundamentalist is complex, requiring unique analytic skills and training. In recent years a professional association of financial analysts and portfolio managers (known as the Association for Investment Management and Research) has developed a certification program similar to the Certified Public Accountant designation. A sequence of three day-long tests is taken over a minimum three-year period. Upon successful completion, the participant is granted the designation of *Chartered Financial Analyst (CFA)*. Only individuals actively involved in investment management may take the exams. The purpose of the CFA designation is to ensure high standards of professional training and ethical conduct. While the CFA designation is not a formal requirement for individuals wishing to engage in investment management, it is widely respected and is informally required for advancement in many firms.

The goal of a fundamental analyst is to find information about a security that is not yet reflected in its market price. In a highly competitive market, developing such information from sources other than illegal insider sources is difficult and costly. One must be trained to understand a company's financial statements, have a knowledge of the risks and potentials of a firm's product offering, and spend the time necessary to examine many securities. The time and out-of-pocket cost of only sitting for the CFA exam, for example, is not trivial.

Efficient Market Selection

The efficient market theory (EMT) states that fundamental analysts are so good at their jobs that all mispriced securities have been identified. Therefore, mispriced securities won't exist. The market price of a security will equal its fair intrinsic value. If this were not the case, well-informed and sophisticated fundamentalists would immediately recognize the potential profits and, through buying and selling, instantly drive the market price into equilibrium.

If the notion of an efficient market is correct, security selection turns out to be quite simple. First, define the level of risk that is acceptable for a given portfolio. Then create a combination of broadly diversified holdings of stocks and bonds that provides that risk level. Finally, never trade simply because you believe prices are too high or too low; they aren't—they are always fair. Trade only if you have excess cash, need cash, or want tax advantages.

THE CONCEPT OF AN EFFICIENT MARKET

Why?

Security prices are determined by expectations of future economic profits, risks, and interest rates. In developing such expectations, individuals assess any information that is available at that time. For example, when deciding whether IBM common stock is fairly priced, one would review international economic conditions, competition, the state of computer technology, patents, market saturation, management expertise, antitrust legislation, inflation, and so forth. While the list of relevant information is almost endless, the point is that such information is crucial to making a pricing decision. It is in this sense that we can say that security prices might fully reflect all relevant information. *A securities market in which market prices fully reflect all known information is called efficient.*

Paradoxically, security markets can be efficient only if a large number of people disagree with the EMT and attempt to find ways of earning speculative profits. To make a speculative profit, an individual must hold unique information about a security that other market participants are unaware of. As soon as new information is obtained, speculators who have the information will immediately trade. If the speculators discover favorable information, they will attempt to purchase the security before others become aware of it and bid the price up. If speculators discover unfavorable information, they will immediately sell. As a result, profit-maximizing speculators will attempt to obtain information before other market participants. This results in a race for new information and, *at the extreme*, all information will be reflected in security prices as soon as it becomes available.

The term *price efficient* is used to indicate that security markets are efficient in processing information.[1] Prices will not adjust to new information with a *lag* but, instead, instantaneously. Four conditions will create an efficiently priced market:

---

[1] A *price-efficient* market is different from an *institutionally efficient* market. The latter refers to the ease, speed, and cost with which investors in real goods are able to obtain financial resources from real goods savers.

1. Information is costless and available to all market participants at the same point in time. (People have *homogeneous expectations*.)
2. There are no transaction costs, taxes, or other barriers to trading. (The markets are *frictionless*.)
3. Prices are not affected by the trading of a single person or institution. (People are *price takers*.)
4. All individuals are rational maximizers of expected utility.

Clearly, all four conditions are not *strictly* true. Information is *provided* to some individuals (corporate directors) before others, and some individuals (security analysts) might be more adept at *creating* new information by interrelating a complex set of previously available information. But if this is true, amateur investors (who tend to receive information last and are least able to analyze it) would hire well-informed professionals to provide them with the information and to manage their portfolios. In this way amateur investors would be capable of indirectly trading on information as soon as it becomes known. The second condition is clearly untrue since transaction costs, taxes, and legal investment restrictions do exist. Yet transaction costs are relatively minor and wouldn't lead to the major price distortions that many fundamentalists and technicians believe exist. The effects of taxes and legal restrictions on trading activities (such as margin requirements) are less clear.

Because these criteria aren't strictly true in the "real" world, a distinction is made between a *perfectly efficient* and an *economically efficient* market. A perfectly efficient market is one in which prices *always* reflect all known information, prices adjust instantaneously to new information, and speculative profits are simply a matter of luck. In an economically efficient market, prices might not adjust instantaneously to information, but, over the long run, speculative profits can't be earned after transaction costs such as brokerage commissions and taxes are paid.

This point has been elegantly examined in a paper by Grossman and Stiglitz titled "On the Impossibility of Informationally Efficient Markets." In a world in which information is costly to obtain, security prices must offer a profit incentive to compensate individuals for their costs incurred in searching for new information. If prices are always "correct," no one will have a profit incentive to search for new information. This would, of course, quickly lead to a situation in which new information is not discovered and reflected in prices. In the Grossman and Stiglitz analysis, actual security prices reflect the information of informed traders plus a random "noise term." This noise term is, on average, zero—so security prices do, on average, fully reflect the information held by informed traders. However, there is variability in the noise term, meaning that individual securities might be over- or undervalued. The size of such price distortions depends on a number of factors, including the number of informed traders. Their number will increase until the marginal profits available from being an informed trader are equal to the training and search costs required to become informed. Thus, security price inefficiencies will be large enough to support a profession of informed traders, but informed trader profits should be only large enough to offset their costs of being informed. Again, the security market might not be perfectly efficient but, instead, economically efficient.

So What?

From a philosophic standpoint, an efficient capital market is a crucial component of any capitalistic society. With an efficient capital market, security prices provide accurate signals for capital allocation. Security prices of high-risk industries will be set so that high rates of returns will be both demanded *and* expected. Security prices of low-profit industries will be low and discourage further investment. Conversely, industries that fulfill an important public need will have potentially high profits, resulting in high security prices and an influx of needed capital. Thus, an efficiently priced security market properly assesses the future of particular industries and allocates capital as needed. When firms sell securities, they expect to receive fair prices. When investors purchase securities, they expect to pay fair prices.

Second, in an efficient security market, speculative profits are, *on average*, nonexistent. Because security prices reflect all known information, mispriced securities are impossible to find. Speculators who believe they have identified such a mispriced security are actually missing a crucial bit of information. Over time speculative trading does nothing but reduce the speculator's wealth as transaction costs and taxes are incurred which are not offset by speculative profits. Occasionally, some speculators will ''luck out'' and earn substantial profits. But this is not due to any permanent insight or ability on their part. Instead, such profits are due solely to chance and would be available to passive investors as well. For every lucky speculator there is an equally unlucky speculator. Speculation is a zero-sum game.

An additional implication of an efficient market is that the demand curve for a security should be perfectly elastic. This is illustrated in Figure 10-4.[2] Since all investors hold the same information, they will all agree upon the same fair market price. Investors are said to have homogeneous expectations. In Figure 10-4 the fair market price of the security (given available information) is $50. At prices above $50 an infinite number of shares would be offered, and at prices below $50 no shares would be offered. Thus, $50 would be the only market price in existence until new information entered the market. Since investors have common beliefs, shifts in the supply curve would have no impact upon prices. For example, if a corporation decided to issue additional common shares, stock prices should not be affected. Any additional shares would be absorbed at existing prices. In addition, large block purchases and sales of stock by financial institutions should have no effect on share prices.

---

[2] *Elasticity* is an economic term relating the sensitivity of changes in one variable to changes in another. Typically, it relates the percentage change in quantity (demanded or supplied) to the percentage change in price. A demand elasticity of 1.0 means that a given percentage change, say, in price will lead to the same percentage change in quantity demanded. Perfectly inelastic demand means that any percentage change in price will have no effect on quantity demanded. Perfectly elastic demand means that a small percentage change in price will produce an infinite percentage change in quantity.

FIGURE 10-4 *Demand and Supply of Shares Given Homogeneous Expectations*

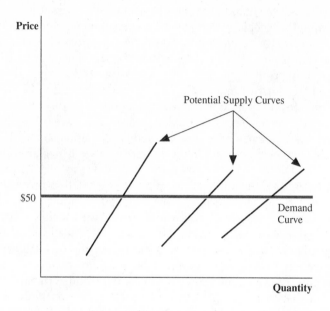

Empirical Implications

Empirical tests of EMT can be assigned to three categories:

1. *Return predictability*. Can past data be used to predict future returns? Original studies that examined this question addressed the value of technical analysis and were referred to as *weak form* tests of efficient markets. However, recent tests have gone beyond technical rules to include predictive powers of fundamental economic variables such as dividend yield, interest rate, and earnings yield levels. These tests also examine whether speculative bubbles arise in security prices.

2. *Event studies*. How rapidly do security prices adjust to unexpected new events? Original studies of this issue were referred to as *semi-strong form* tests of EMT. The issues examined by these tests have not changed. But the power of the methodology has become so important to the study of finance that the studies are now commonly referred to by the name of methodology used. These studies examine the market price reaction to events such as: earnings and dividend announcements, stock splits, management forecasts, and so forth.

3. *Private information*. Are there individuals with private information that they use to earn excess risk-adjusted returns? For example, do security analysts, portfolio managers, or corporate insiders have privileged information on which excess returns are earned? Original tests in this area were called *strong form* tests of EMT.

Each category tests a level to which prices might *fully reflect information*. Return prediction tests examine *past information*. Event studies examined *new information*. And private information tests examine the value of *non-public information*.

While the concept of price efficiency applies to fixed income securities and derivatives, the bulk of past research has focused on common stocks in the United States. In order to provide at least some understanding of the issues, our discussion is limited to studies of the U.S. stock market.

EMT and Asset Pricing Models

The end result of both the capital asset pricing model (CAPM) and arbitrage pricing theory (APT) is a price-efficient securities market—a market in which expected returns are directly related to the risks inherent in a security that cannot be eliminated by diversification. For both the CAPM and APT to be true, security prices must be efficient prices. But the reverse is not necessary. An efficient market could exist without the CAPM or APT as the model underlying security prices. The relationship between the CAPM and EMT (or APT and EMT) runs one way. Both the CAPM and APT imply an efficient market, but an efficient market does not imply either the CAPM or APT.

Empirical tests of EMT often require estimates of expected security returns in order to see whether a particular trading rule or group of investors can consistently earn returns in excess of an expected fair return. For example, are the returns earned by corporate insiders consistently higher than should be expected—that is, are they higher more than 50% of the time? If one were to buy stocks that rise 5% above a previous low price and sell stocks that fall 5% below a previous high price, would the returns be consistently higher than should be expected? If one buys a market index portfolio on Monday and sells it on Friday, would the returns earned be consistently higher than should be expected? There are innumerable questions such as these that require an estimate of expected security returns. In such cases the CAPM is often used. But it has been used because it was the best model of expected returns available at the time. Its use does not mean that an efficiently priced market is also a market in which the CAPM prevails. Arbitrage pricing theory, in fact, has been increasingly used to test various implications of EMT.

Finally, it is important to recognize that whenever the CAPM or APT is used to test for market efficiency, the test is actually a joint test—a test of market efficiency and a test of the pricing model used. In many situations where market inefficiencies are presumably found, it is difficult to tell whether such inefficiencies really exist or whether the risk/return model used is incorrect.

ARE RETURNS PREDICTABLE?

The first tests of market efficiency were actually done before finance scholars had even coined the term *efficient markets*. In fact, the theory of efficient markets arose not only as a logical consequence of having a highly competitive security market but also as a convenient explanation for the empirical results that had been found.

The conclusion reached in virtually all of the original tests of return predictability was that ''security prices have no memory,'' meaning that future prices are unrelated to past prices. And along with this conclusion came the opinion that technical analysis is of no use in identifying the direction of future prices. Most scholars continue to believe that technical analysis does not provide abnormal return. But there is a growing evidence that past and future returns are somehow related. Precisely what this relationship is and why it would occur is hotly debated. Currently, there are two general schools of thought. The first believes that security prices depart from their true fundamental values for lengthy but indeterminable periods of time. Proponents argue that this can be seen in stock prices that are more volatile than they should be as well as in negative return correlations over long intervals. The other school says that market prices are always efficient, or rational. Proponents argue that both the apparent excess volatility and the observed negative correlation are simply the results of changing risks and required returns.

Early Tests

The first tests of market efficiency were conducted in the early 1970s. Most of these tests were of two basic types: random walk and filter trading rule tests.

Random Walk Tests. If security markets are efficient, prices will reflect all known information. As a result, prices will change only as new information arrives. But, by definition, new information must be random. If information flows followed an identifiable trend, this trend would become known and thus be reflected in current prices. Thus, ''new'' information must be random. And since new information enters randomly and prices react instantaneously to the information, *changes in stock prices will be random.*

In an efficient market, security prices follow what is referred to as a *random walk.* By this we mean that price changes over time are random. A price rise on day 0 doesn't increase or decrease the odds of a price rise or fall on day 1, day 2, and so forth. Price changes on any particular day are uncorrelated with historical price changes. If security prices do, indeed, follow a random walk, technical trading rules are useless. When people speak of randomness in security prices, they actually mean randomness in *percentage price changes*. No one argues that *prices* of a stock are not correlated from one day to the next. They are. Nor do people argue that dollar price changes between two days are uncorrelated with previous dollar price changes. They are too. The question is whether relative (or percentage) price changes are related over time. The correlation which exists between price levels or dollar price changes exists solely because of the *level* of a stock's price and is economically meaningless.

The first known test of the random walk hypothesis was performed by a French mathematician, Bachelier, about 1900. Although he successfully showed that stock prices could be characterized as following a random walk, his work lay dormant for more than fifty years. In 1953 Kendall examined the correlation of weekly changes in nineteen British security price indices as well as spot prices for cotton and wheat. In his analysis of the data, Kendall (rather dramatically) suggested:

> The series looks like a wandering one, almost as if once a week the Demon of chance drew a random number from a symmetrical population of fixed dispersion and added it to the current price to determine the next week's price.

Since Kendall, a large number of tests of the random walk hypothesis have been performed. One of the best known was conducted by Fama.

Like others, Fama was interesting in the extent to which the return on a stock in a given time period is correlated with its return in a subsequent time period. This type of correlation is referred to as either *autocorrelation* or *serial correlation*. If the autocorrelation is sufficiently large enough, then one can make trading decisions based on past returns. For example, if a time series of daily returns has a negative autocorrelation equal to, say -0.8, then one should buy at the start of a day all stocks that had low return the previous day. For example, consider panel A of Figure 10-5. This is a visual example of what a return series with autocorrelation equal to -0.8 would look like. Returns on day t are represented by the horizontal axis and returns on day $t + 1$ are represented on the vertical axis. Clearly, one could take advantage of such a return pattern.

Fama examined daily returns for each of the 30 stocks in the DJIA between the years 1957 and 1962. Returns on day t were correlated with the returns on day t-1, day t-2, through day t-10. He found that the autocorrelation was usually positive. This, of course, is not surprising because stocks are risky and, thus, will on average have positive returns. However, the average autocorrelation was very close to zero. For a 1-day log, the average was 0.026 and 11 out of the 30 stocks were statistically significant. Panel B in Figure 10-5 shows what a return series looks like if it has an autocorrelation of 0.026. It is unlikely that speculative trading profits could be made using such a series.

In addition to the daily return correlations, Fama calculated correlations for returns using time intervals greater than a day. Returns were calculated over four-,nine-, and sixteen-day intervals and then correlated with prior four-, nine-, and sixteen-day returns. Again, few correlations were statistically different from zero and, in such cases, the correlation was small enough to be of no probable use to traders who rely upon clear trends.

Many other studies similar to Fama's were conducted during the 1960s and 1970s. On the whole, these studies indicated that:

1. Short-term security returns are generally unrelated to prior returns. This is true not only for the United States but also for many other countries.

2. In those cases where a significant correlation does exist between past and present returns, the size of the correlation is so slight that it is doubtful that profitable trading rules could be developed.

3. A minor tendency seems to exist toward positive correlation. But this can be explained by realizing that stocks contain risk and will, on average, yield positive returns. The slight positive correlation in returns simply reflects long-

FIGURE 10-5 *Illustrative Autocorrelations*

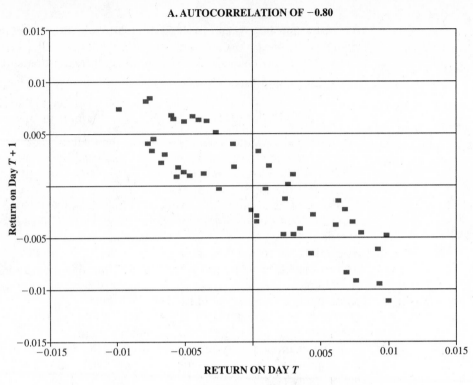

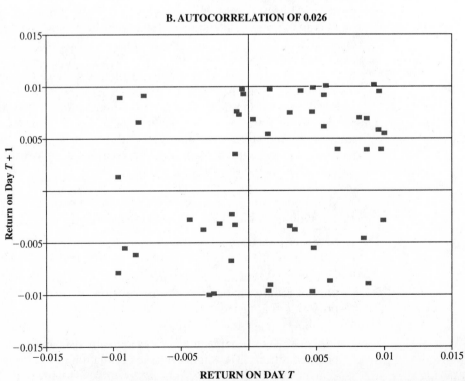

run positive returns on stocks. When returns are adjusted for such a risk impact, they show no correlation.

4. A "large return" day tends to be followed by another "large return" day. But there is no relationship with the *direction* of the subsequent return. That is, given a large price drop on day 0, the price change on day 1 is also likely to be large—but the direction unknown.
5. Tests on T-bill and futures prices suggest they, too, follow a random walk.

Filter Trading Rule Tests. A trading rule is exactly what its name implies: a rule that specifies when a given security will be bought or sold. In practice, a large number of trading rules have been developed, and many are widely used today. A great deal of research has gone into testing the usefulness of such rules. On the whole, this research suggests that trading rules that practitioners have used in the past do not work. However, many of the studies performed during the past decade have uncovered price anomalies that might provide excess trading-rule profits. Some of these are discussed below.

There are four criteria that any trading rule must meet before it can be declared a winner:

1. It must be based only on information known at the date that the rule is implemented.
2. Returns must be calculated after all transaction costs and taxes.
3. Returns must be compared against an equivalent-risk passive buy-hold strategy.
4. Excess risk-adjusted returns must be earned consistently over a long time period.

A filter trading rule consists of the following decision criteria:

If the security price moves up by $X\%$ above a prior low, buy and hold until the price falls by $Y\%$ below a previous high, at which time simultaneously sell and go short.

Such a rule is close to the spirit of many chartist policies and is easily testable. Alexander, as well as Fama and Blume, has examined the profitability of such a rule. In a 1961 study, Alexander concluded:

In fact, at this point I should advise any reader who is interested only in practical results, and who is not a floor trader and so must pay commissions, to turn to other sources on how to beat buy and hold.

Since the Fama and Blume study included several features not present in Alexander's study, we will concentrate upon their results. They tested the profitability of 24 potential filters ranging in size from 0.5% to 50% on each of the 30 Dow Jones industrials. Average results for each of these filters are shown in Table 10-1. Note that:

1. Average security returns *before* commissions (column 1) varied, depending upon the filter. The most profitable filter appears to be the smallest (0.5%). Thus, it seems that some slight positive correlation within security returns did

TABLE 10-1 *Annual Returns for Various Filters Averaged over All Companies*

Filter	Average Return per Security		Breakdown of Average Return per Security Before Commissions		Number of Profitable Securities per Filter (5)	Total Transactions (6)
	Before Commissions (1)	After Commissions (2)	Long (3)	Short (4)		
0.005	0.1152	−1.0359	0.2089	0.0097	27/30	12,514
.010	.0547	−.7494	.1111	−.0518	20/30	8,660
.015	.0277	−.5614	.1143	−.0813	17/30	6,270
.020	.0023	−.4515	.0872	−.1131	16/30	4,784
.025	−.0156	−.3732	.0702	−.1378	13/30	3,750
.030	−.0169	−.3049	.0683	−.1413	14/30	2,994
.035	−.0081	−.2438	.0734	−.1317	13/30	2,438
.040	.0008	−.1950	.0779	−.1330	14/30	2,013
.045	−.0117	−.1813	.0635	−.1484	14/30	1,720
.050	−.0188	−.1662	.0567	−.1600	13/30	1,484
.060	.0128	−.0939	.0800	−.1189	18/30	1,071
.070	.0083	−.0744	.0706	−.1338	16/30	828
.080	.0167	−.0495	.0758	−.1267	15/30	653
.090	.0193	−.0358	.0765	−.1155	17/30	539
.100	.0298	−.0143	.0818	−.1002	19/30	435
.120	.0528	.0231	.0958	−.0881	21/30	289
.140	.0391	.0142	.0853	−.1108	19/30	224
.160	.0421	.0230	.0835	−.1709	17/30	172
.180	.0360	.0196	.0725	−.1620	17/30	139
.200	.0428	.0298	.0718	−.1583	20/30	110
.250	.0269	.0171	.0609	−.1955	15/29	73
.300	−.0054	−.0142	.0182	−.2264	12/26	51
.400	−.0273	−.0347	−.0095	−.0965	7/16	21
.500	−.2142	−.2295	−.0466	−.1676	0/4	4

SOURCE: Reprinted from "Filter Rules and Stock-Market Trading," JOURNAL OF BUSINESS, Special Supplement, January 1966, pp. 226–41, by E. Fama and M. Blume, by permission of The University of Chicago Press. Copyright © 1966 by The University of Chicago. All rights reserved.

exist which an extremely small filter could capture to yield positive returns. (Recall the slight positive correlation noted in the early Fama study.)

2. Average security returns *after* commissions were usually negative or quite small. This is consistent with the belief that security markets are not perfectly efficient but are economically efficient.

3. Columns 3 and 4 decompose the before-commission returns into respective long and short positions. Clearly, someone who wishes to use a filter trading rule should think twice about short selling. Returns on short positions were disastrous.

In sum, the slight positive correlation that may exist in short-term security returns did not lead to a profitable filter trading rule. The extremely low filter necessary to capture such correlations required extremely large commission fees. Given this evidence, Fama and Blume saw no point in examining the *consistency* of nonexistent profits or adjusting for *equivalent risk levels*. The only people who might be enriched by using filtering techniques of this sort would be brokers. Speculators would quickly go bankrupt.

Although filter rules are close in spirit to the principles suggested by technicians, they are not widely used in practice. However, the use of moving averages is broadly acclaimed. The moving average rule is:

If the stock's price moves above its moving average by *X*%, buy it and hold until the price moves *Y*% below its moving average and then sell short.

Often 5% filters and a 200-day moving average are suggested by technicians. Such a rule has been tested by various researchers—with mixed but essentially unfavorable news for technicians. For example, in one study by Seelenfreund, Parker, and Van Horne, daily prices were obtained for 30 randomly selected NYSE stocks. Initially, $1,000 was assumed either to be invested via a buy-hold strategy in each of the 30 stocks or to be speculated with by following a moving average rule. Various filters (0%, 2%, 5%, 10%, and 15%) and moving averages (100-day, 150-day, and 200-day) were used.

Rarely did a moving average filter yield larger profits than the buy-hold strategy—before or after commission fees. In fairness to the moving average rule, however, a number of adjustments in the methodology might have yielded better results. First, there is no guarantee that risks inherent in the buy-hold strategy are equivalent to those in the trading strategy. Using the moving average strategy, one is periodically "out of the market" and, thus, will incur no market risk. Using the buy-hold strategy, one is constantly invested in the market and exposed to market risk. Conceptually, buy-hold returns *should* have been higher because of risk exposure. Second, when the moving average strategy requires that one be out of the market, cash is assumed to be held. Superior results might be available if, on such occasions, a diversified portfolio of stocks were held instead of cash. In fact, other studies have suggested moving averages may yield better results. The question remains unresolved, but no one has presented results that are clearly in favor of a moving average rule.

Recent Findings

Early tests of random walk had three common characteristics: (1) they examined individual stocks as opposed to portfolios, (2) they looked at returns over relatively short time horizons (daily and weekly) and (3) they assumed stationarity of risk and expected returns. Each of these could bias the results against finding statistically significant autocorrelations. For example, the large standard deviation associated with individual stocks could mask any autocorrelation that might be present. However, if portfolios of many stocks are formed, much of the single-stock volatility is diversified away and it might be easier to see any autocorrelation. Also, by looking at short time intervals, we are unable to observe any long-term mispricing that might be present. Finally, if expected returns and risks are constantly changing over time, what might appear to be a random series over, say, a five-year period, could be an orderly one within various subsets of the period. Recent studies have taken up such issues.

Random Walk Revised. Recent research shows that future returns are more predictable than early studies suggested.

The first serious challenge to random walk was a study by Lo and McKinley. Forming *portfolios* of stocks based on firm capitalization (shares outstanding times price per share) they found that weekly returns were positively autocorrelated, particularly for the smallest capitalization stock portfolios.

The fact that the smallest capitalization portfolio has the greatest autocorrelation suggested to many researchers a possible bias in the Lo and McKinley study that is referred to as nonsynchronous trading. This simply means that not all stocks in a portfolio trade on the date at which a return is calculated. When this occurs, there is an artificial autocorrelation present in the return series. To resolve the matter, Conrad and Kaul formed a sized-based portfolios of stocks *that traded* at the end of a return period and showed that the Lo and McKinley result was not seriously biased. Conrad and Kaul found autocorrelations of weekly returns of the large capitalization portfolios on the order of 9%. Smaller capitalization portfolios had autocorrelations close to 30%!

But can you profit from such autocorrelation? A recent study by Jegadeesh suggests that it might be possible. Jegadeesh formed ten portfolios at the end of each month between 1934 and 1987 based on the predicted return of a stock. Predicted returns were based on autocorrelation coefficients developed from monthly returns over the previous five years. The Market Model discussed in Chapter 7 was used to measure abnormal returns. Surprisingly, the average *monthly abnormal return* for the portfolio predicted to do the best was 1.87% and the equivalent for the portfolio predicted to do the worst was -0.33%. These are CAPM risk-adjusted excess *monthly* returns.

Long Horizon Results. Even if returns over daily, weekly, or monthly intervals were uncorrelated, this does not mean that the EMT is correct. For example, suppose that the fundamental value of a security is constant over time but its market price departs from the fundamental value for years, such as Figure 10-6 shows. Researchers who examine daily returns over longer intervals are clearly negatively autocorrelated. Differences between market prices and fundamental values are called *bubbles*.

In 1981 Shiller published a paper that caused considerable excitement. The telling part of Shiller's study is captured in Figure 10-7. The line labeled P* is the detrended value of the S&P 500 *if investors had perfectly forecast future real dividend payments of the S&P 500.* Each P* is the present value of *actual* future real (adjusted for inflation) dividends. (Since dividends beyond 1979 were unknown, Shiller made a future growth assumption based on past growth rates.) The P variable represents the detrended value of the *actual* security index (also adjusted for inflation). From the figure, it appears that stock price bubbles have

FIGURE 10-6 *Illustration of Price Bubbles*

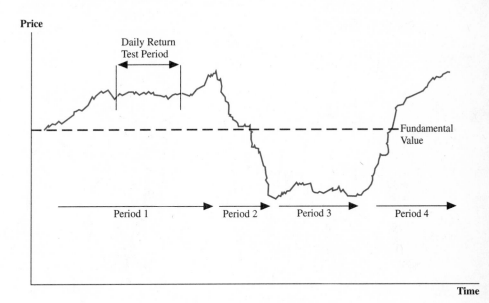

arisen in the past. While departures from the perfect foresight *P** could have been due to dividend uncertainty, the growth of dividends has been remarkably steady over time.

The Shiller paper caused a flurry of new research on the predictability of long-horizon returns. Unfortunately, the number of observations available when long-horizon returns are used is too small to provide a reasonable statistical conclusion.

The Shiller results as well as the results of other studies that claim to find negative correlation in long-horizon returns might not be violations of EMT. Fama and French suggest that such findings can be easily explained by changes in market risk premiums and required returns. Whatever the reason, our understanding of security markets has come a long way from the early statement of random walk.

Debondt and Thaler investigated the notion of bubbles as applied to individual stocks. Research in experimental psychology indicates that most people tend to overreact to unexpected and dramatic news events. Debondt and Thaler created portfolios of past "winner" and "loser" stocks, that is, stocks that had recently had large returns or small returns. Examining the subsequent returns on these portfolios, they found that the "loser" portfolio out performed the previous "winner" portfolio. Their results are shown in Figure 10-8. The vertical axis is a measure of the accumulation of excess returns. Loser portfolios outperformed the equity market by 19.6% 36 months after formation. Winner portfolios underperformed the market by 5%.

Many people believe that this is not actually evidence of market bubbles and

FIGURE 10-7 *Shiller's Detrended Estimates of a Perfect Foresight Stock Index Versus Actual Index (S&P Composite)*

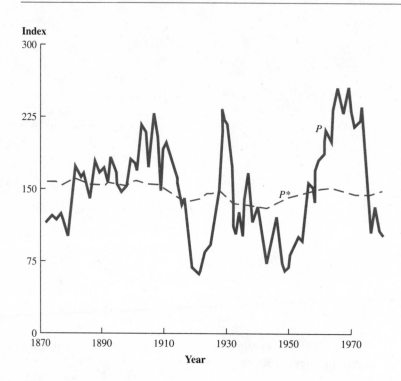

overreaction. Instead, it could be due to the well-known January effect associated with small capitalization stocks. Notice that most of the loser portfolio returns arise in January. Loser stocks are likely, by definition, to have small capitalizations.

Return Patterns. If the random walk hypothesis is valid, there should not be any consistent patterns in security returns. While early tests of random walk did not detect any strong evidence that return patterns exist, more recent studies have found persuasive evidence of systematic patterns in stock returns. These patterns are referred to as:

1. The January Effect
2. The Monthly Effect
3. The Weekly Effect
4. The Daily Effect

The *January Effect* refers to the fact that stock returns in January are greater than returns in other months. This is particularly true for stocks of relatively small firms. In a study conducted by Keim, portfolios of small firms *always* had January returns greater than portfolios of large firms during the period 1963–1979. Pre-

FIGURE 10-8 *The Performance of Past Winner and Loser Portfolios*

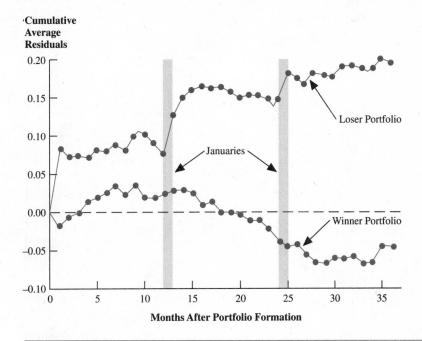

SOURCE: *W. DeBonat and R. Thaler, "Does the Stock Market Overreact?" Journal of Finance 11, no. 3 (July 1985).*

vious to the Keim study, it was well known that portfolios of small stocks tended to have greater yearly returns than portfolios of large stocks, even when adjusted for estimated CAPM betas or APT factors. But the startling evidence of Keim showed that nearly 50% of this excess return comes in the *first five days of January!*

Figure 10-9 is based on the Keim study. Months of the year are shown on the horizontal axis. The vertical axis represents the average difference between excess returns on a portfolio of the smallest 10% of NYSE and AMEX stocks and excess returns on a portfolio of the largest 10% of NYSE and AMEX stocks. During January the average difference was $+0.714\%$. The average difference for all months excluding January was 0.102%. When annualized, these figures translate to yearly returns of about 8.9% and 1.2%, respectively.

Clearly something unusual is happening to small stocks in January. What this might be is still unknown. The major explanation offered to date is known as the *tax selling hypothesis.*

The folklore underlying the tax selling hypothesis is that, late in the year, individuals sell stocks that have declined in value during the year in order to realize a capital loss for tax purposes. Proceeds from the sales are then reinvested in early January, and the buying pressure causes the prices of such stocks to rise.

FIGURE 10-9   *The January Effect, 1963–1979*

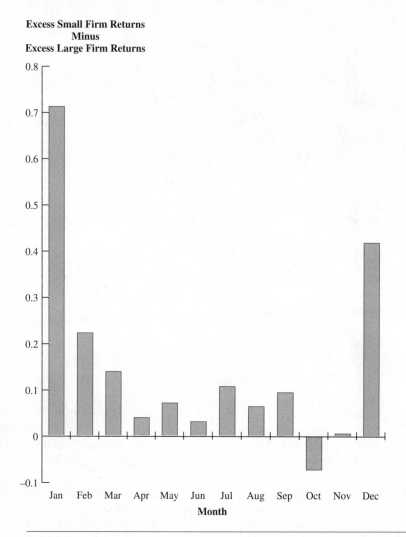

Adapted from D. Klein, "Size-related Anomalies and Stock Return Seasonality: Further Empirical Evidence," Journal of Financial Economics (June 1983).

Since stocks with small capitalization are likely to be heavily weighted in the small stock portfolios, returns on such portfolios would tend to exhibit the greatest returns in January. While some empirical evidence supports this view, much does not. For example, in Keim's study, small firms which hadn't experienced price declines in the previous year still incurred large positive returns in January. In addition, the January Effect is worldwide, observed even in countries in which there are no capital gains taxes and countries in which the taxable year does not end in December. Also, why should people who sell low-priced securities in order to realize a capital loss wait until January of the next year to reinvest?

A difference has also been found in the pattern of returns during any month, which is referred to as the *Monthly Effect*. Ariel found that during the period 1963–1981, returns in the first half of any month (on an equally weighted market index) were much greater than during the second half of the month. During this 19-year period, the annualized return during the first half of any month was 51.1% versus a 0.0% return during the second half of the month. Even when January returns were removed, Ariel found statistically significant average returns in each half of the month. Why this occurs is unexplained.

The *Weekly Effect* refers to the unusual behavior of stock returns on Monday versus other days of the week. Evidence shows that Monday stock returns are lower, on average, than those on other days of the week. Logic would suggest that, if daily stock returns are positive over long sampling periods and if stock returns arise from a continuous accumulation of new information, the Monday returns should be three times as large as on other trading days. This simply isn't the case.

Finally, a *Daily Effect* has also been found: stock prices tend to increase dramatically in the last 15 minutes of trading, regardless of the day of the week. In a study by Harris, which used transactions data for all NYSE stocks during the period between December 1981 and January 1983, he found that stock prices rose in the last 15 minutes of trading 90% of the time.

The Small-Firm–P/E Effect. Prior to the late 1970s a number of studies had suggested that stocks with a low price-to-earnings ratio (P/E) outperformed those with high P/Es. However, a rigorous study of this possibility in the context of the CAPM was not conducted until 1977 when Basu used a standard market model approach to the question. Basu sampled an average of 500 stocks over the years 1956–1969. For each year, the stock's P/E was calculated and then placed in one of five P/E groups. Monthly returns were then calculated on each group (portfolio) assuming an equal investment in each stock in the group. This was done using a buy-and-hold strategy for the next twelve months. Market model estimates were then obtained for each group's monthly returns over the full fourteen-year period.

The results are summarized in Table 10-2. Portfolio *A* was the highest P/E group and portfolio *E* the lowest. Average annual returns were lowest for the high P/E firms and greatest for the low P/E firms. P/E and average returns were inversely related. This could make sense, of course, if the low P/E stocks had the greatest systematic risk. But the table shows that this was not the case. Low P/E stocks had the lowest estimated betas. Strange . . .

In 1981 Reinganum confirmed Basu's finding but suggested that perhaps it really wasn't a low P/E causing the excess returns but instead a "small-firm effect." When Reinganum compared excess daily returns on portfolios of stocks having different total market capitalization (price per share times shares outstanding), he found results similar to Basu's. Low-capitalization stocks outperformed high-capitalization stocks.

TABLE 10-2 *Portfolio Performance by P/E Group*

	Group					
	A	A*	B	C	D	E
Median P/E	35.8	30.5	19.1	15.0	12.8	9.8
Average Annual Rate of Return	9.34%	9.55%	9.28%	11.65%	13.55%	16.30%
Estimated Beta	1.11	1.05	1.04	0.97	0.94	0.99

A* contains the highest P/E quintile stocks in A but excludes those with negative earnings.

SOURCE: "Investment Performance of Common Stocks in Relation to Their Price—Earnings Ratios—A Test of the Efficient Market Hypothesis" by Basu from JOURNAL OF FINANCE 32 (June 1979), p. 667. Reprinted by permission.

EVENT STUDIES

In a perfectly efficient security market, prices adjust instantaneously to new information. For example, if Texas Instruments announces it has a patent on a new transistor which is both cheaper to produce and longer-lived than existing transistors, the price of its stock should increase immediately to a new equilibrium level. If its price adjusts with a lag or overadjusts, speculative profits would be available. This is illustrated in Figure 10-10, where price is plotted against time. Period 1 represents the date of a favorable announcement by the firm. Prior to date 1, investors believe that the company's long-run dividend growth will be a constant 6% per year and that a return on equity of 13% would be fair. Given these beliefs, together with last period's dividend payment of $4.62 per share, the stock sells for $70 per share [$70 = (4.62 × 1.06) ÷ (0.13 − 0.06)]. At date 1 the firm announces that a new product line should increase its long-run growth in dividends to 7% per year without adversely affecting the firm's risk. If the EMT is correct, the stock price should increase to $82.40 at date 1 (immediately after the announcement) and remain there until further new information arrives. The path of EMT prices is shown by the solid line. However, if market participants do not immediately recognize the importance of the firm's announcement, a lag in price adjustment will occur, as illustrated by the dashed line. Clearly, if a lagged response to new information exists, speculative profits would be available and equal to $82.40 − $70.00. Alternatively, prices might consistently overreact to the announcement, as shown by the dotted curve that initially rises above the equilibrium price. In this case speculators could also earn profits on any overreaction.

The Methodology as Applied to Stock Splits

A stock split is simply an increase (or a decrease for a reverse split) in the number of shares that a corporation has outstanding. In a 2-for-1 split, shareholders would receive two new shares for each old share. Stock dividends are small stock splits, typically cases where one-quarter or fewer new shares are received for each initial

FIGURE 10-10 *Immediate vs. Lagged Price Adjustment*

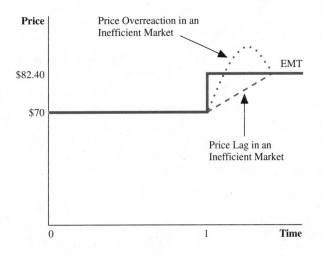

Information		
Time	0	1
Last Dividend	$4.62	$4.62
Expected Growth	6%	7%
Required Return	13%	13%

share held. Because a split has no effect on a firm's investments or financial structure, it should also have no effect upon the firm's total market value. Individual share prices would decline, of course, but total firm value would remain unchanged. Stock splits represent a fairly easy event on which to test the semistrong-form EMT because the announcement of data can be reasonably determined and because we know what the effect of the announcement should be. Moreover, they provide a good introduction to how one might conduct a semistrong-form test.

In the best-known test of stock splits, Fama, Fisher, Jensen, and Roll (FFJR) examined 940 splits on the NYSE between 1927 and 1959. Virtually all splits greater than 5:4 were examined. FFJR hypothesized that splits themselves provide no new information about a firm. Price movements to levels other than those suggested by the split should be related to more fundamental information, such as cash dividend announcements. For example, an $80 stock which undergoes a 2:1 split should provide the investor with a zero return on the split date; that is:

$$R = \frac{P_t - P_{t-1} + D_t}{P_{t-1}} = \frac{(\$40 \times 2) - \$80 + \$0}{\$80} = 0.0$$

Note that the split price ($40) is adjusted for the total number of shares owned after the split date. If a positive (or negative) return were found on the split date that was not associated with more fundamental company news, then security prices would be reacting to the split, and evidence of market inefficiency would be found.

According to the CAPM, stock returns are affected by both aggregate-market and company-unique information. Thus, if one is attempting to identify the impact of a firm-unique event, the market-related part of returns must be controlled for. Unadjusted, raw stock returns at the date of a split should not be used. For example, if a security's return on a split date were +5.0%, this could be due to favorable market information affecting all stocks, favorable company information, or both. In an attempt to isolate that part of a security's return that was unique to company events alone, FFJR examined "residual errors" from the market model; that is:

$$
\underbrace{\frac{\text{Raw Return}}{\text{on Day } t}}_{\tilde{R}_t} = \underbrace{\frac{\text{Constant Average}}{\text{Daily Return}}}_{a} + \underbrace{\frac{\text{Return Due}}{\text{to Market Moves}}}_{b(\widetilde{RM_t})} + \underbrace{\frac{\text{Return Due}}{\text{to Firm News}}}_{\tilde{e}_t} \quad \textbf{(10.1)}
$$

where $\tilde{R}_t$ = the return on stock in period t, a = the constant average return, b = the beta estimate of the stock, $\widetilde{RM}_t$ = the return on the aggregate market portfolio during period t, and $\tilde{e}_t$ = the residual error in period t, the portion of the raw return due to firm-unique events. Estimates of a and b can be developed using a regression equation relating a stock's historical returns to historical market returns. Using regression estimates of the a's and b's, FFJR calculated the e_t values for each stock split during the 29 months prior to and 30 months following each split.

Two additional steps were taken before the data were analyzed. First, an *average firm-unique return* (*AR*) was found for each month surrounding the split, as follows:

Average Market Model Residual in Month *t*
$$
AR_t = \frac{\sum\limits_{i=1}^{N} e_{i,t}}{N} \quad \textbf{(10.2)}
$$

where AR_t = average firm-unique return for month t (any of the 29 months before or 30 months after the split), $e_{i,t}$ = firm-unique return on stock i during month t, and N = number of splits examined in a given month.

Second, a *cumulative average firm-unique return* (*CAR*) was found for each month by summing all average firm-unique returns through a particular month. Mathematically:

Cumulative Market Model Residual in Month *t*
$$
CAR_t = \sum\limits_{K=-29}^{t} AR_K \quad \textbf{(10.3)}
$$

To empirically evaluate the price impact of a split, either the AR_t or the CAR_t values may be examined. Conventionally, the cumulative average return is discussed the most.

FIGURE 10-11 *Stock Price Movement Around Stock Splits*

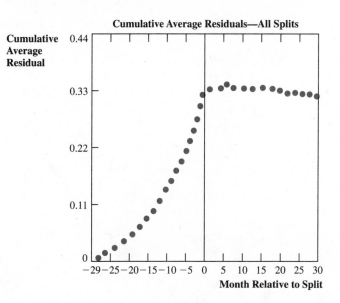

Figure 10-11 presents a plot of *CAR* for each of the 60 months surrounding a split. Month 0 represents the month in which the split occurred. An examination of the figure suggests that:

1. Stocks that split appear to have had a dramatic increase in price during the 29 months prior to the split. This is reflected in the substantial growth in *CAR* prior to the split date. However, these price increases cannot be attributed to the eventual split, since rarely was a split announced more than four months prior to the effective date of the split.
2. After the split date, the *CAR* is remarkably stable. This implies that from the split date forward, firm-unique returns were zero. The split had no immediate or long-run impact on security prices.

Results displayed in Figure 10-11 suggest the market is efficient in that splits, by themselves, had no observable effect on security prices. In addition, FFJR examined how more fundamental economic news provided at the date of the split would affect stock prices. To do this, they segregated the split stocks into two groups: one in which cash dividends were reduced and the other in which cash dividends were increased. They hypothesized that a change in cash dividend payments would provide indirect information about the firm's future prospects and that market prices would adjust rapidly to the new information.

Results for each of these groups are displayed in Figure 10-12. When *CAR*s are grouped according to this more fundamental economic news, the series behaves differently. Companies that increased cash dividends had a positive growth in *CAR* after the split (prices continued to rise with the favorable news). For stocks

FIGURE 10-12 *Stock Price Movement Around Stock Splits Incurring Divided Policy Changes*

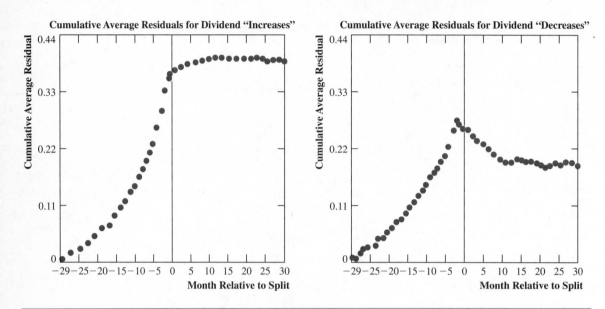

SOURCE: *E. Fama, L. Fisher, M. Jensen, and R. Roll, "The Adjustment of Stock Prices to New Information,"* International Economic Review *(February 1969). Copyright © 1969.*

in the "decreases" group, security prices fell. In sum, splits by themselves appear to have had no impact upon stock prices. But when real information is provided coincident with the split, prices adjust in the direction expected.

The FFJR study was the first in a series of studies that relied upon a methodology suggested by the capital asset pricing model (CAPM). Refinements have been made to the procedure, but the basic methodology remains unchanged. Even if you believe that empirical tests of the CAPM and Roll's comments have cast doubts on the model's validity, there is little disagreement that aggregate market returns must be controlled for when firm-unique events are being examined. For example, a market factor can play a dominant role in the arbitrage pricing model (APM)—the major alternative to the CAPM. Examination of average and cumulative firm-unique returns derived from a market model similar to Equation 10.2 is one of the best techniques we have at present to evaluate the price effects that are firm-unique.

Earnings Announcements. Early studies examining the behavior of stock prices during the weeks surrounding an earnings announcement all indicated that the announcements possessed informational content and that the value of the information was rapidly reflected in share prices. The real question, however, is not whether earnings announcements do or don't have an informational value but, instead, what impacts *expected versus unexpected* earnings announcements have on stock prices. Corporate earnings announcements may or may not represent new information to investors. To the extent that announced earnings are what investors expect, stock prices should have already discounted the announced earnings level. However, to the extent that announced earnings are unexpected, a price adjustment would be necessary. If markets are efficient, the adjustment would be virtually instantaneous. If they are inefficient, a lag would exist and signal the possibility of speculative profits.

Rendleman, Jones, and Latane categorized the size of unexpected earnings into ten groups. To do this, they calculated a measure of standardized unexpected earnings (*SUE*), as follows:

Standardized Unexpected Earnings
$$SUE = \frac{EPS - E(EPS)}{SEE} \qquad (10.4)$$

where *EPS* represents the earnings per share announced for a given quarter, *E(EPS)* is their estimate of *EPS* based on a regression analysis of the firm's historical earnings, and *SEE* is the standard error of the estimate (the standard deviation of the error term in the regression). Data were obtained from quarterly earnings announcements made by approximately 1,000 firms during the period 1972–1980. *SUE* was calculated for each firm for a given quarter and, based on its value, the firm was placed into one of ten groups. This was done for all quarters. Finally, *CAR* was calculated for each group starting 20 days before the announcement through 90 days after the announcement.

Average results are shown in Figure 10-13. Note that immediately prior to the announcement day, security returns moved exactly in the direction one would expect. Firms with positive values of *SUE* had positive returns in excess of what the market model would suggest and firms with negative values of *SUE* had returns lower than expected. This is consistent with the rapid price adjustment that EMT implies. The results are not consistent with EMT, however, if the announcement was "leaked" to some individuals, as the slight preannouncement moves in *CAR* tend to suggest. More important, however, are the continued movements in *CAR* over the 90 days after the announcement. For EMT to be strictly true, all price adjustments should occur at the date of the announcement. Yet the *CAR* values after the announcement date are large enough to cover transaction costs and leave a tidy speculative profit. Either the market model did not adequately capture the expected returns on these securities or we have a violation of semistrong-form efficiency.

In sum, prices do appear to adjust to unexpected announcements. But the speed of this adjustment process is questionable. There is evidence that a lag exists that might provide speculative profits—particularly if the speculator doesn't have to pay large brokerage fees.

Initial Public Offerings

According to the efficient market theory (EMT), the prices at which new security offerings are sold to the public should, on average, be equal to their equilibrium levels. There should not be a persistent undervaluing of new shares, since cor-

FIGURE 10-13 *Recent Evidence on Unexpected Earnings*

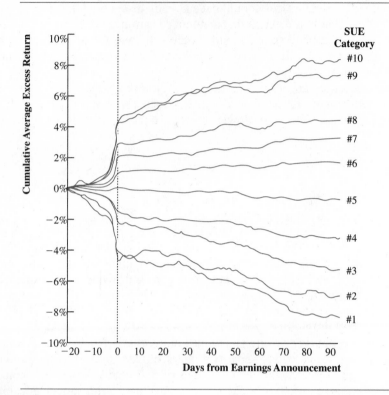

SOURCE: *"Empirical Anomalies Based on Unexpected Earnings and Importance of the Risk Adjustments" by R. Rendleman, C. Jones and H. Latane from* JOURNAL OF FINANCIAL ECONOMICS, *Volume 10, Number 3 (November 1982), p. 285, Figure 1.*

porate issuers will insist that their underwriters obtain the best price possible. Similarly, a persistent overvaluation shouldn't exist, as buyers wish to pay the lowest price possible. If investors have homogeneous beliefs, new issue prices should be equal to their equilibrium values. Ibbotson has investigated the historical price behavior of new issues during the first 60 months of a new issue's life and found mixed results. Based upon Ibbotson's data, initial purchasers of new issues appear to receive approximately an 11–12% abnormal return during the first month the security is held. However, by the third month new issue prices appear to have reached equilibrium levels.

The statistically significant abnormal returns during the first couple of months of a new issue's life have to be disturbing to strict proponents of the EMT. Initial purchasers appear to be given a price inducement to accept the new offering. Yet when viewed from the perspective of a technician or of many fundamentalists, who believe that gross inequities remain in the markets for lengthy periods of time, the results must be even more disturbing. From their viewpoint, the apparent inefficiency found by Ibbotson isn't nearly as large as other inefficiencies they believe are commonplace, and it is eliminated within a couple of months. We should also note that Ibbotson's results were based upon the CAPM and might not adequately reflect the total risk taken on by first-time purchasers of new issues. In fact, Ibbotson's results suggest continuing decreases in beta risk during the first 60 months of an issue's life. There may well have been a large, unmeasurable risk associated with the first couple of months that could reasonably explain the apparent 11–12% abnormal performance. But until we gain a better understanding of such risks, the results are contrary to semistrong-form efficiency.

Other Studies. Many other studies of semistrong-form efficiency have been conducted. Some of the more representative are the following:

1. *Money supply growth.* Studies by Rozeff and by Rogalski and Vinso all suggest that money supply growth directly affects stock prices. However, anticipated changes in the growth rates are reflected in prices before the change, and unexpected changes are almost instantaneously reflected in prices.
2. *Dividend change.* Both Watts and Pettit have modeled dividend changes and shown that prices tend to anticipate such changes.
3. *Management forecasts.* Various studies have found the unexpected forecasts of earnings by a firm's management are fully reflected in stock prices within two days.
4. *Accounting changes.* Changes in accounting techniques that have a *real* effect on share values such as the tax effects of switching from FIFO to LIFO inventory accounting have immediate impacts on stock prices. Cosmetic accounting changes refer to changes in accounting policies that change financial statements of a firm but have no effect on future cash flows of a firm. *Cosmetic* changes do not seem to cause share prices to change.

TESTS FOR PRIVATE INFORMATION

Efficient market theory (EMT) states that *all* information is reflected in security prices. This means that no individual has private information that would influence prices if revealed. Tests for the value of private information have focused on three groups: (1) Corporate insiders, (2) security analysts, and (3) portfolio managers.

The results have been mixed. The value of insider information is well documented. Insiders have private information on which they earn abnormal returns. But outsiders are unable to profit from insider trading once the information is made available to the general public. Some security analysts also seem to be able to develop information about security values that is not reflected in prices until released to the public. But the ability of active portfolio managers to earn abnormal returns remains an open question. Studies of mutual fund performance have yielded both positive and negative conclusions, depending on the indices against which the fund managers are evaluated.

Corporate Insiders

Corporate insiders are defined as directors, officers, and major shareholders. If anyone has access to privileged information, it should be such insiders. Studies by Jaffee, Seyhun, and Givoly-Palmon all show that corporate insiders do earn abnormal profits from their trading. Jaffee's study showed that two months after a period of intensive insider trading in a state, cumulative average excess returns on the stock were 2.09%.

In an attempt to provide full public disclosure, the Securities Exchange Commission (SEC) reports insider trades in its *Official Summary of Insider Trading*. Once published, the information is available to the general public. Could public investors use this data, which is typically available two months after an insider trade, to earn speculative profits? Jaffee's study found that abnormal public returns of about 2.5% were possible after transaction costs. But in a follow-up study, Seyhan showed that most of this return was due to the performance of small-capitalization stocks—that is, the small firm effect.

Security Analysts

Security analysts are the epitome of market professionals. Trained in sophisticated analytic techniques and devoting full-time efforts to evaluating the investment worth of a narrow list of stocks, they should be capable of identifying mispriced securities. However, this doesn't always seem to be the case.

Diefenbach examined the usefulness of research recommendations made by security analysts to institutional clients. (Generally, such reports are not available to the public at large.) His results showed that buy recommendations outnumbered sell recommendations by a 26:1 margin. On average, the buy recommendations *fell* in price by -3.0% and only 47% of the recommendations had a price rise greater than the S&P Industrials. Clearly, an analyst's buy recommendations did not, on aggregate, beat a passive strategy of buy-hold. A few analysts were able to considerably outperform the S&P Index. But when Diefenbach examined the consistency with which such analysts were able to provide superior performance, he concluded that chance alone could have done as well. There was no obvious consistency in superior performance.

Sell recommendations yielded a different story. While there were very few sell recommendations, they were more accurate. In total, 74% of the sell recommendations fell in price by more than the S&P industrials. Only one analyst suffered the indignity of having the majority of his sell recommendations *outperform* the S&P during the next year.

A large number of studies have examined the stock recommendations of *Value Line*. The *Value Line Investment Survey* publishes rankings on approximately 1,700 stocks. A ranking of 1 represents a strong buy recommendation. A ranking of 5 is the most negative recommendation. Numerous studies have shown that stocks ranked 1 statistically outperformed those with a 5 ranking over the next year. When a stock's ranking was changed, market prices of the stock reflected the change within a few days.

But some of these results may be unique to a specific time period and not available to a real portfolio strategy. For example, in a review of recent EMT studies, Fama stated:[3]

> Over the 6.5 years from 1984 to mid-1990, group 1 stocks earned 16.9% per year compared with 15.2% for the Wilshire 5000 Index. During the same period, Value Line's Centurion Fund which specializes in group 1 stocks, earned 12.7% per year—live testimony to the fact that there can be large gaps between simulated profits from private information and what is available in practice.

Portfolio Managers

The ability of portfolio managers to earn excess risk-adjusted returns has been studied extensively, but no firm conclusions have emerged. The basic problem is that we are unable to properly measure portfolio risk. For example, if risk is proxied by a portfolio's beta, three problems are encountered. First, what index should be used as a proxy for the market portfolio? The abnormal performance of equity mutual funds can (and does) depend on the index used. Second, the betas of many funds are constantly changing as portfolio managers actively trade securities. Time-series portfolio betas, such as market model betas, are *single estimates* of the portfolio's average beta. Finally, we know that small capitalization and low price-to-earnings stocks provide returns that are not explained by market model betas. If the Capital Asset Pricing Model (CAPM) is used to evaluate manager performance, managers who hold such stocks will appear to perform better than other managers.

A good example of these concerns can be seen in a recent study of equity mutual fund performance. Ippolito examined a twenty-year return history for 143 funds (1965–1985). Fund returns were measured after all mutual fund expenses but before any load fees. Using the following market model regression equation, he found that the average fund had a alpha of $+0.83\%$ per year:

Market Model Regression

$$R_{Ft} - RF_t = \text{alpha}_F + \text{Beta}_F (R_{SP500,t} - RF_t) + e_{Ft}$$

Given that the average fund outperformed passive combinations of T-bills and the S&P 500 *after* expenses, Ippolito concluded that before expense returns had to be even higher; that is, the managers were truly informed traders.

In follow-up study, Elton, Gruber, Das, and Hklarka (EGD&H) examined the effect of relying on 1-year T-bills and the S&P 500 index as proxies of the passive risk-free and risky security portfolios. Many funds own debt instruments other than T-bills as well as stocks not in the S&P 500 Index. EGD&H replaced T-bills with a return series of government and corporate bonds. They also added a third

---

[3] This statement comes from: Fama, Eugene, ''Efficient Capital Markets: II,'' *Journal of Finance,* 46, 1991. This paper is an excellent overview of recent empirical studies of efficient market theory (EMT).

passive portfolio consisting of returns on non-S&P 500 stocks. When these three passive portfolios are used to evaluate manager performance, the average excess return dropped to -1.1% per year.

Much research remains to be done on the value of actively managed portfolios. Because we have been unable to develop reliable risk benchmarks, we cannot say whether active management does or does not provide greater risk-adjusted returns than does passive management.

STRATEGY IN AN EFFICIENT MARKET

The evidence presented in this chapter indicates that the markets are certainly *not perfectly efficient*. However, for many people with little knowledge, high search costs, and large transaction costs, the markets are probably close to being economically efficient. Such people might be wise to consider themselves as operating in an efficient market and to follow reasonable investment strategies. If they wish to speculate, it should be with a limited portion of their portfolio.

Reasonable trading strategies in an efficient market include the following:

1. *Diversify.* Purchase shares in a number of no-load stock and bond mutual funds that have a policy of minimal trading activity. Consider holding some amount of international and real estate funds. An ideal fund would be a passive index fund.
2. *Select a suitable asset allocation.* Examine the historical volatility of the aggregate security indices to subjectively determine an acceptable asset allocation.
3. *Don't try to time security price moves.* Simply buy and hold. Rebalance asset allocation as security price rise and fall to the desired allocation. Trade when cash is needed or available. Don't try to find mispriced securities or asset classes.
4. *Keep tax considerations in mind.* For example, zero-tax pension funds should be placed in high-coupon bonds because such bonds have higher before-tax yields. Although the stock evidence is less clear, it does seem that high-dividend-yield stocks also sell at high before-tax expected yields. Some care should be taken, however, that these tax considerations don't reduce portfolio diversification.
5. *Consider marketability.* The portfolio should provide the degree of marketability that might be needed to meet unexpected cash needs.

SUMMARY

An efficient securities market is the consequence of intense competition for information. Individuals seeking speculative profits will search out any information that will aid in identifying mispriced securities. And, at the extreme, all such information will be reflected in existing prices.

A perfectly efficient market is one in which market prices are exactly equal to current intrinsic values. The conditions necessary for a perfectly efficient market are the following: (1) information must be provided freely and instantaneously to all market participants, (2) there must be no costs associated with trading, (3) actions taken by a single individual cannot affect prices, and (4) people maximize expected utility. Since the first two requirements are not strictly true, we differentiate between a perfectly efficient market and an economically efficient market. In an economically efficient market, prices may vary from true intrinsic worth, but long-run speculative profits are not available after transaction costs. In such a market a passive strategy of *investing* will yield larger long-run returns than will a speculative strategy.

The extent to which security markets can be characterized as being economically efficient can be tested only by examining empirical data. To date, such empirical evidence indicates the following:

1. Short-term returns do not follow a pure random walk. However, the autocorrelation in returns of individual stocks is quite small. Trading rules that rely on historical price charts are useless after transaction costs are paid.

2. Long-term returns may be negatively correlated. This could be due to market inefficiencies (bubbles) or changes in market risk premiums over time.

3. A number of "anomalies" have been found that remain unexplained. These include the small firm (or price-to-earnings) and January effects.

4. New information is reflected in security prices with little time lag. In fact, market prices often adjust before an actual announcement. There is some evidence, however, that the postannouncement price adjustment can extend over a month or more and that speculative profits may be available if one pays small transaction costs.

5. Some individuals appear to have private information that is not reflected in prices until after they trade. Corporate insiders clearly gain from their trading activities. Security analysts might also be able to develop information about a stock's value that is not reflected in its price. But the value of such private information is usually quite small, and it is difficult for the public to gain from the information after transaction costs.

6. Professional equity managers provide returns that are very close to the returns of passive portfolios. We are unable to determine whether active management beats passive management because proper risk benchmarks have not been developed.

It appears that markets are *not strictly efficient*. But for all practical purposes, it is wiser to approach security selection from the viewpoint of EMT than to assume that gross mispricing exists.

REVIEW PROBLEM

In this problem you will use market model estimates of residual returns on two stocks to determine whether the announcement of an unexpected cash dividend had any impact on security values and whether a lag occurred in any such adjustment.

Market returns are shown below for 12 periods before the announcement ($T = -12$

to -1), the date of the announcement ($T = 0$), and 12 periods after the announcement ($T = 1$ to 12).

	Before Announcement				After Announcement		
			Rates of Return				
T	Stock 1	Stock 2	Market	T	Stock 1	Stock 2	Market
−12	3	5	2	0	−11.776	−21.12	−15
−11	2	4	2	1	6.41	10.338	6
−10	14	15	11	2	2.08	2.848	1
−9	−20	−35	−24	3	6.41	10.338	6
−8	9	16	10	4	−2.25	−4.642	−4
−7	6	9	6	5	−5.714	−10.634	−8
−6	5	11	6	6	0.714	1.05	0
−5	0	6	3	7	−1.884	−3.444	−3
−4	10	14	8	8	5.044	8.54	5
−3	17	32	21	9	−6.214	−10.934	−8
−2	0	−4	−1	10	−1.884	−3.444	−3
−1	5	13	5	11	11.106	19.026	12
				12	11.972	20.524	13

a. Estimate the following market model regressions for each stock using the returns for $T = -12$ to $T = -1$:

$$\tilde{R}_t = a + b(\widetilde{RM_t}) + \tilde{e}_t$$

b. The results of step a should yield the following:

$$R_1 = 0.714 + 0.866 \ (RM)$$

$$R_2 = 1.050 + 1.498 \ (RM)$$

Use these two models to estimate residual errors for days $T = 0$ to $T = +12$.

c. Compute the average residual for each day in the postannouncement period as well as the cumulative average residual.

d. Comment on whether these results are consistent with EMT.

Solution

a. The market model regressions are shown in step b above.
b. through d.

T	Stock 1	Stock 2	AR	CAR
0	0.5	0.3	0.4	0.4
1	0.5	0.3	0.4	0.8
2	0.5	0.3	0.4	1.2
3	0.5	0.3	0.4	1.6
4	0.5	0.3	0.4	2
5	0.5	0.3	0.4	2.4
6	0	0	0	2.4
7	0	0	0	2.4
8	0	0	0	2.4
9	0	0	0	2.4
10	0	0	0	2.4
11	0	0	0	2.4
12	0	0	0	2.4

This is inconsistent with EMT in that a lag occurs in the adjustment of stock prices. By the end of day $T = 5$ a 2.4% cumulative excess return is earned.

QUESTIONS AND PROBLEMS

1. What are the four conditions that would lead to a perfectly efficient market?
2. What is the difference between a perfectly efficient and economically efficient security market?
3. If the security markets are in fact efficient, should anyone decide to become a security analyst or active portfolio manager? What would the impact of such a decision be on efficiency?
4. "For the CAPM to be correct, the security markets must be efficient." "For the security markets to be efficient, the CAPM must be correct." Evaluate these statements.
5. "The concept of a random walk in stock prices is bizarre and implies totally irrational behavior by the investing public. Nothing could be further from the truth than random walk. Prices are related to fundamental economic worth." Comment.
6. Technicians often say that trading conditions change in the market such that a rule that works during one period might not work during another period. They believe trading rules shouldn't be inflexible but, instead, should be adjusted as new market conditions arise. Comment.
7. a. "Speculation is a zero-sum game across the market at any point in time as well as for any single speculator over time." How is this statement related to EMT?
   b. For the markets to be efficient, speculators must trade on any price disequilibriums. If speculators earn profits from doing so, is this inconsistent with market efficiency?
8. Consider the following situations and indicate in each case whether the concept of market efficiency is violated:
   a. A friend tells you that the concept of market efficiency is clearly invalid, offering as proof the fact that during the past three years she has considerably beaten the market averages. Returns on her portfolio in each year were 15%, 18%, and 25%, whereas the market returns were only 12%, 15%, and 18%.
   b. A financial consulting firm has just announced a newly designed complex computer program that would have generated consistent (risk-adjusted) excess returns after all transaction costs and taxes if it had been used during the last ten years.
   c. Ten years ago a financial consulting firm began to use a complex computer program to analyze financial reports. Since the introduction of this technique, the firm has consistently earned (risk-adjusted) excess returns after all transaction costs and taxes.
   d. During the past five years most people have earned positive average returns. However, some people have earned considerably more than others.
   e. You have correlated the percentage change in gold prices from day 0 to day 1 (as of 9:00 A.M. each day) with the percentage change in the NYSE Composite Index during day 1 (percentage change from 10:00 A.M. to 4:00 P.M.). You find a statistically significant correlation coefficient of negative 0.45.
   f. A research study finds that firms switching from expensing R&D expenditures to capitalizing them have positive and statistically significant *CAR* levels that increase steadily for five months. Beyond five months the *CAR* steadily returns to zero.
   g. Trading activity by corporate insiders results in permanent and statistically significant *CAR* levels.

9. A large portion of the empirical studies rely upon a methodology suggested by the capital asset pricing model. Do you find any logical inconsistency in using the CAPM to test for inefficiencies in the market? How is this concern at least partially resolved by the arbitrage pricing model?

CFA

10. The efficient market theory (EMT) has major implications for the practice of portfolio management. One obvious implication is the determination of superior analysts. Another is how to carry out the management of portfolios, assuming no access to superior analysts. Assume that none of the analysts to whom you have access is superior. List and discuss five of the specific investment practices you should implement for your clients.

CFA

11. In recent years several major financial institutions have developed index funds and offered these to pension accounts and others.
    a. Give the justification used for investing in these index funds, which simply attempt to replicate the market.
    b. Indicate whether this justification is consistent with the EMT.

12. Recent empirical tests of the EMT have uncovered a number of results suggesting that inefficiencies may exist.
    a. List and briefly discuss those presented in the chapter.
    b. Assume that you wish to defend EMT in light of these apparent inconsistencies. How would you do so?

13. Recent empirical evidence suggests that expected stock returns change over time—that risk premiums are inversely related to the business cycle.
    a. Why might risk premiums change in such a manner?
    b. How does this partly explain the larger than expected volatility in aggregate stock prices (such as the S&P Composite) that Shiller found?
    c. If market risk premiums do change over time, should an investor's asset allocation (where the assets are on, say, the CAPM borrowing-lending line) be constant?

14. Suppose you have found that returns on the S&P 500 Index are negative on Mondays more than 70% of the time. What trading strategy would you pursue? Would you tell others? As others find the same fact, what will happen?

15. What is the January Effect? What trading strategy does it suggest?

16. In a recent year, stock prices in Taiwan increased 500%. What implication might this have on the efficient market hypothesis? Take both the pro and con side.

17. On October 19, 1987 (Black Monday), stock prices fell by 22%; erasing more than $500 billion in investor wealth. What implication does this have on the efficient market theory (EMT)?

18. Shiller has suggested that stock prices might depart from their fundamental values causing bubbles in prices. How might changes in market risk premiums explain Shiller's charge that stock prices are too volatile?

CFA

19. As vice president for quantitative research for a large investment firm, your recent studies have provided strong empirical evidence of the following:

    • The stocks of small-capitalization firms tend to outperform the stocks of large-capitalization firms over the long term.
    • The stocks with a low price-to-earnings ratio tend to outperform the stocks of large-capitalization firms over the long term.
    • The companies that had the largest unexpected year-to-year increases in earnings also provided the best same-year price appreciation.

    a. Comment on the practical limitations of managing a portfolio based on these findings.

     b. Comment on the adjustments that would be appropriate in an equity portfolio that incorporates the findings above given an anticipated change from a bear market to a bull market environment.

20. In an efficient market:

     a. security prices react quickly to new information.

     b. security prices are seldom far above or below their justified levels.

     c. security analysis will not enable investors to realize consistently superior returns on their investments.

     d. all of the above.

21. The weak form of the efficient market hypothesis asserts that:

     a. stock prices do not rapidly adjust to new information.

     b. future changes in stock prices cannot be predicted from past prices.

     c. corporate insiders should have no better investment performance than other investors do.

     d. arbitrage between futures and cash markets should not produce extraordinary profits.

DATAFILE ANALYSIS

1. *Autocorrelation of Stock Returns.* One implication of the efficient market theory (EMT) is that past returns will be uncorrelated with future returns. Here, you will analyze whether this is true for returns on the S&P 500. Access the RTNSYRLY.WK1 datafile. Insert a blank column next to the S&P 500 returns. In this new column, copy the S&P 500, but offset by 1 year. That means that the return in 1926 in one column will be next to the return in 1927, and so forth. Calculate the correlation between returns in one year $t + 1$ by regressing one series against the other. The correlation coefficient is the square-root of the output variable labeled *R*-square. Is this correlation coefficient large enough to suggest that EMH is incorrect? (No statistical test is necessary.)

2. *January Effect.* Using the datafile RTNSMNLY.WK1, eliminate all return series except DFA 9-10. This is a series of returns on the ninth and tenth market capitalization deciles of stocks traded on the NYSE (the smallest 20 percent of firms traded). Next, eliminate all returns between 1926–1949. Using the remaining returns (1950–1992 small-firm returns), calculate the average return earned *by month*. Notice that the average return in January is much larger than the average for other months. Repeat this exercise using monthly S&P 500 returns over the same time interval. Contrast the results.

REFERENCES

Two classic reviews of the notion of efficient markets and empirical tests of the theory were written by Fama:

FAMA, EUGENE F., "Efficient Capital Markets: A Review of Theory and Empirical Work," *Journal of Finance,* May 1970.

FAMA, EUGENE F., "Efficient Capital Markets II," *Journal of Finance,* December 1991.

Other papers cited in the chapter that are not referenced in tables or figures are:

DIEFENBACH, R. "How Good is Institutional Research?" *Financial Analysts Journal,* January–February 1972.

FAMA, EUGENE F., "The Behavior of Stock Prices," *Journal of Business,* January 1965.

GROSSMAN, STANLEY, and JOSEPH STIGLITZ, "On the Impossibility of Informationally Efficient Markets," *American Economic Review,* June 1980.

JAFFE, JEFFREY, "Special Information and Insider Trading," *Journal of Business,* July 1974.

LO, ANDREW W, and A. CRAIG MACKINLEY, "Stock Prices Do Not Follow Random Walks: Evidence from a Simple Specification Test," *Review of Financial Studies,* Spring 1988.

ROZEFF, MICHAEL, "Money and Stock Prices: Market Efficiency and the Lag Effect of Monetary Policy," *Journal of Financial Economics,* September 1974.

An interesting recent paper on security market efficiency is:

BROWN, KEITH C., W. V. HARLOW, and SEHA M. TINIC, "How Rational Investors Deal with Uncertainty (or, Reports of the Death of Efficient Market Theory Are Greatly Exaggerated)," *Journal of Applied Corporate Finance,* Fall 1989.

To help explain security price movement in general and the market crash of 1987 in particular, some people advocate the concept of "chaos theory." A well-written book that surveys chaos theory is:

PETERS, EDGAR, *Chaos and Order in the Capital Markets: A New View of Cycles, Prices, and Market Volatility.* New York: John Wiley & Sons, 1991.

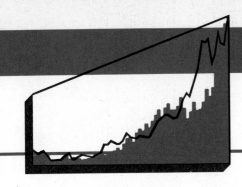

P A R T 3

Security Analyses

Our purpose in Part 3 is to analyze in depth each major type of security class. Fixed income securities and equities are treated in two chapters: the first chapter examines important *valuation* principles and the second examines various *trading* strategies. This is followed by two chapters devoted to derivative securities. In the first, futures valuation and trading strategies are discussed. In the second, the valuation and trading of listed options are discussed. The section concludes with important aspects of investing internationally that are not encountered when investment is limited to one's domestic country.

Our discussion of security analyses in this part of the text comes between general investment concepts of Part 2 and portfolio strategy in Part 4. This organization was not idly chosen. The organization is, in fact, quite natural. It is virtually impossible to develop a good understanding of how various security types should be valued and traded without a reasonable grasp of investment concepts such as diversification, determinants of required returns, portfolio theory, and theories of security pricing. In the same fashion, it is equally difficult to develop effective portfolio strategies without a solid knowledge of each major type of security class.

Bond Valuation

The international bond markets are large, representing about one-half of the value of all publicly traded financial securities in the world. The variety of instruments is diverse, ranging from default-free U.S. government bonds to high-risk corporate obligations having various imbedded options.

Estimates of the value of securities traded in major bond markets are shown in Table 11-1. (The table does not include money market instruments.) Three conclusions are clearly apparent. The value of securities traded in world bond markets underwent dramatic growth in the decade of the 1980s. As an example, the total market value of U.S. bonds increased at a compound annual growth rate of more than 12%! In addition, more than 75% of all bonds traded in the United States are obligations of governmental units or mortgage-backed securities. Finally, the U.S. bond market is clearly the largest fixed income market in the world.

Chapter 2 discussed various institutional features of bonds. Here and in the next chapter, we develop a more complete analysis of bond investment and speculation. In this chapter, we discuss bond valuation. In the next chapter, we examine bond trading strategies.

The price at which a bond trades is the present value of future promised cash flows discounted at a required rate of return. This required return is called the bond's *yield to maturity* (*YTM*). The yield to maturity of any bond consists of four elements:

1. A nominal return required to induce people to save (commonly measured as the yield to maturity on a U.S. T-bond).
2. Compensation for default risk.
3. Compensation for various options imbedded in the bond such as the right to call the bond prior to its stated maturity.
4. Tax features.

Bond prices are inversely related with required yields to maturity. If YTMs increase, the market value of bonds fall; if YTMs decline, bond market values rise. And these price changes can be dramatic! In 1982 the return on long-term U.S. T-bonds was 40%—twice that year's return on U.S. common stocks. And this bond return was due solely to the fact that the yields to maturities on these bonds had declined from 13.4% at the start of the year to 10.5% by year-end.

TABLE 11-1 *Estimates of World Bond Values 1991 and 1981*

Bond Category (a)	1991 U.S. Dollar Value of Publicly Traded Bonds (In $ Trillion)				
	U.S.	Japan	Germany	Other	Total
Central Government	$1.8	$ 1.3	$ 0.3	$ 2.1	$ 5.5
State and Local	0.9	0.06	0.03	0.11	1.1
Mortgage-Backed	1.1	NA	NA	NA	1.1
Subtotal	$3.8	$1.36	$0.33	$2.21	$ 7.7
Corporate	0.6	0.2	0	0.2	1
Other (b)	0.5	0.6	0.6	0.2	1.9
Total	$4.9	$2.16	$0.93	$2.61	$10.6
1981 Estimate	$1.5	$ 0.6	$ 0.3	NA	$ 2.4

(a) Money Market securities are not included.
(b) Foreign bonds and Eurobonds.
SOURCES: *Various issues of Lehman Brothers Bond Market Reports and Salomon Brothers International Bond Market Analysis, 1992.*

Clearly, a good understanding of bond yields to maturity is necessary for proper bond selection and management.

SOME BASIC CONCEPTS

Yields to Maturity on Coupon Bonds

The *yield to maturity* (*YTM*) on a coupon bond is that interest rate that will discount future cash flows to the bond's current price. Since yields to maturity might be different for various maturities, we associate each yield with a given maturity as follows:

YTM_M = yield to maturity on a bond having a maturity of M years

For a bond that pays coupons at the end of each year, the YTM_M is found by solving the following equation:

**Definition
of Yield
to Maturity**

$$P_0 = \frac{C}{(1 + YTM_M)^1} + \frac{C}{(1 + YTM_M)^2} + \cdots$$
$$+ \frac{C}{(1 + YTM_M)^M} + \frac{F}{(1 + YTM_M)^M}$$

(11.1)

where P_0 = the current market price of the bond, C = the coupon payment received at each year-end, M = the number of years to maturity, and F = the par value of the bond.

To illustrate the formula's use, consider a five-year, noncallable bond that pays a 9% coupon at the end of each year and has a $1,000 face value. If the bond is currently selling at a price of $962.10, its yield to maturity is 10%:

$$\$962.10 = \frac{\$90}{(1 + YTM_5)^1} + \frac{\$90}{(1 + YTM_5)^2} + \frac{\$90}{(1 + YTM_5)^3} + \frac{\$90}{(1 + YTM_5)^4}$$

$$+ \frac{\$1,090}{(1 + YTM_5)^5}$$

$$= \frac{\$90}{1.1^1} + \frac{\$90}{1.1^2} + \frac{\$90}{1.1^3} + \frac{\$90}{1.1^4} + \frac{\$1,090}{1.1^5}$$

$$= \$81.82 + \$74.38 + \$67.62 + \$61.47 + \$676.81$$

Many readers will recognize the yield to maturity to be the same concept as the *internal rate of return* used in capital budgeting. It is a useful measure to help evaluate both historical rates of return and expected rates of return. But there are dangers in its indiscriminant use.

Bond-Pricing Theorems

Equation 11.1 specifies the relationship between bond price, coupon rate, maturity, and yield to maturity from which the following five bond theorems have been developed. To illustrate each theorem, we examine the price of both 8% coupon bonds and 6% coupon bonds having one of three possible maturity dates: one year, five years, and nine years. Results are displayed in Figure 11-1.

1. *When the annual coupon rate and yield to maturity are identical, a bond will always sell at par.* In Figure 11-1, this is shown as the solid horizontal lines at the par and market values of $1,000. For example, the 8% coupon rate pays $80 each year on $1,000 face value. If investors demand an annual yield of 8%, they would be willing to pay $1,000 since the $80 coupon then represents exactly what they require.

2. *Bond prices move inversely to changes in yields to maturity.* Note in Figure 11-1 that when yields to maturity are greater than the coupon rate, the bonds sell at less than par (at a discount).[1] In such cases investors expect to receive the yield to maturity from both an annual coupon and an annual price appreciation. When the yield to maturity is less than the coupon rate, prices will be greater than par (at a premium). Investors are then expecting a yearly return equal to the coupon payment minus an annual price depreciation.

3. *Long-term bonds are more price sensitive to a given change in the yield to maturity than are shorter-term bonds.* Note in panel A (the 8% coupon issue) that a change in the yield to maturity from 8% to 6% causes the one-year bond to increase in value from $1,000 to $1,018.87. The five-year bond increases from $1,000 to $1,083.96.

---

[1] *Discount bonds* are bonds that sell for less than par value (usually $1,000). *Premium bonds* are those which sell for more than par value. *Deep discount bonds* are bonds selling at sizable discounts, say, for $500 to $600.

FIGURE 11-1 *Relationship Between Bond Price, Coupon Rate, Maturity, and YTM*

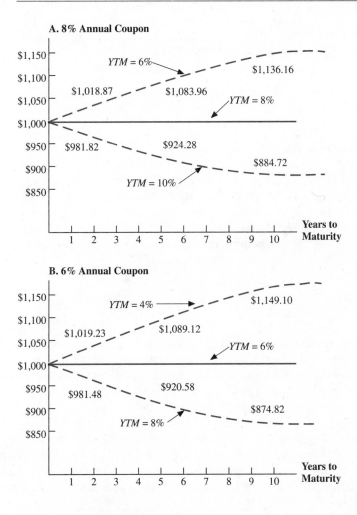

A. 8% Annual Coupon

B. 6% Annual Coupon

4. *While the price sensitivity of a bond increases with its maturity (theorem 3), this sensitivity increases at a decreasing rate.* Again refer to panel A and the shift in yields to maturity from 8% to 6%. Note that the one-year bond increases by $18.87, or 1.89%, whereas the five-year bond increases by $83.96, or 8.40%. The longer-term bond increased by 651 basis points more (840 − 189) than the shorter-term bond. However, the basis-point change is less between the nine-year and five-year issues. While the nine-year obligation increases by $136.16, or 13.62%, this is only a 522-basis-point improvement (1362 − 840) over the five-year bond. The longer a bond's maturity, the greater its price sensitivity. But this sensitivity increases at a decreasing rate.

5. *High-coupon bonds are less price sensitive to a given yield to maturity change than are lower-coupon bonds.* To see this, examine both panels A (8% coupon) and B (6% coupon) for bonds with a nine-year maturity. If yields to maturity

are initially 6%, the 8% coupon issue sells at a premium ($1,136.16), and the 6% issue sells at par. Now assume that the yield to maturity rises to 8%. The high-coupon bond falls in price by $136.16, or 11.98%. The price of the lower-coupon bond falls by $125.18, or 12.52%. The percentage price movement is greater on the low-coupon bond. (In Chapter 12, we will see that this coupon effect is related to the effective maturity of the bond, i.e., its duration.)

These five bond theorems play an important role in the development of the various yield curve theories as well as other concepts of investing and speculating.

Semiannual Interest

Most coupon bonds quote the coupon payments as if they were paid once a year, but interest is actually paid semiannually. For example, a 7% coupon, four-year bond which pays interest semiannually will provide a sequence of eight coupon payments of $35 each six months plus $1,000 at the end of four years. To value such a bond, we must think in terms of *six-month periods* instead of yearly periods. If the stated annual yield to maturity is 8%, the bond's present worth would be $966.33:

$$\frac{\$35}{1.04} + \frac{\$35}{1.04^2} + \frac{\$35}{1.04^3} + \ldots + \frac{\$35}{1.04^8} + \frac{\$1,000}{1.04^8} = \$966.33$$

When semiannual coupon payments are made, (1) the number of periods to maturity is doubled, (2) the coupon payment is half the quoted annual rate, and (3) the discount rate is half the stated annual yield to maturity. If quarterly (or even more frequent) payments are made, adjustments similar to those involved with semiannual interest should be made.

Notice that while a stated annual *YTM* of 8% is used, the *effective YTM* is higher. The investor starts out with, say, a $1 investment on which 4 cents is earned at the end of six months. This balance of $1.04 then earns an additional 4% during the second six months. So by year-end, $1.0816 is available for each $1 invested. The effective yield is 8.16% even though the market-quoted yield is 8%.

Value at Noninterest Dates. Equation 11.1 assumes that we are finding a bond's value immediately after an interest payment date and that a full period (six months or one year, depending on coupon-payment dates) remains until the next cash receipt. Bond trades, of course, are only rarely made at a coupon-payment date. When trades occur at other times, accrued interest must be accounted for. The procedure used to do this consists of the following steps:

1. Calculate the value of the bond at the next interest-payment date, assuming interest has just been paid.
2. Add the next interest payment to this amount. The sum will represent the bond's value immediately prior to the next interest payment.
3. Find the present worth of this amount.

4. Subtract the interest that has accrued on the bond since the last interest-payment date.

Consider a 10% coupon issue that matures in 10 years and 2 months. Interest is paid semiannually and investors require a quoted 8% annual *YTM*.

1. As of the next interest date, the bond will have 10 years of life remaining and should sell at:

$$\sum_{t=1}^{20} \frac{\$50}{1.04^t} + \frac{\$1,000}{1.04^{20}} = \$1,135.92$$

2. Adding the $50 interest payment to be received at that time, the total value of the cash plus the security value will be $1,185.92.
3. Two months prior to this date, this sum will be worth $1,170.52:

$$\frac{\$1,185.92}{1.04^{2/6}} = \$1,170.52$$

4. But a portion of the next interest payment belongs to the owner for the prior four months. This accured interest of $33.33 (50 × 4/6) is subtracted from the above value to find the adjusted true value of the bond today, $1,137.19.

This procedure can be expressed in equation form and solved by computer for either price or *YTM*. Bond traders and brokerage houses use exactly such a procedure when calculating prices or yields.

Yields on Pure Discount Bonds

A pure discount bond is one that does not pay any coupons but pays a single lump sum at its maturity. Since the only source of return on such bonds is price appreciation, they always trade at discounts from the lump sum to be received at maturity. For example, assume that bond 1 and bond 2 are both pure discount bonds and mature in exactly one year and two years, respectively. If the bonds have $1,000 par values and investors desire a 5% return during the next year and a 7.5% annualized return during the next two years, the bonds will trade at the following prices:

$$\text{Bond 1:} \quad \frac{\$1,000}{1.05} = \$952.381$$

$$\text{Bond 2:} \quad \frac{\$1,000}{1.075^2} = \$865.333$$

Pure discount bonds will be of particular use in this chapter, since we will be able to use their market values to calculate a structure of underlying forward rates.

We will refer to the *yield to maturity on a pure discount bond* as I_M. It is calculated by solving the following equation:

**Yield to Maturity
on a Pure
Discount Bond**

$$P_0 = \frac{F}{(1 + I_M)^M}$$

(11.2a)

or

(11.2b)

$$I_M = \left(\frac{F}{P_0}\right)^{1/M} - 1.0$$

where P_0 = the current market price of the pure discount bond, F = the bond's par value, and M = the number of years to the bond's maturity.

For example, assume that we could observe the market prices of bonds 1 and 2 above to be \$952.381 and \$865.333, respectively, but that we did not yet know their respective yields to maturity. Using Equation 11.2b, these yields would be calculated as follows:

$$\text{Bond 1:} \quad I_1 = \left(\frac{\$1,000}{\$952.381}\right)^{1/1} - 1.0 = 0.05, \text{ or } 5\%$$

$$\text{Bond 2:} \quad I_2 = \left(\frac{\$1,000}{\$865.333}\right)^{1/2} - 1.0 = 0.075, \text{ or } 7.5\%$$

Yields to maturity calculated for coupon bonds (YTM_M) will be equal to yields to maturity of discount bonds *only if the yield curve is flat*. This rarely (if ever) occurs. More commonly, both yield structures tend to increase as bond maturities increase. In this case, YTM_M will be somewhat lower than I_M.

Forward Rates

At a given point in time, a set of (pure discount) yields to maturity exist for securities that are identical in all respects but maturity. We have defined this as the term structure of interest. Basically, each I_M reflects the rate of return that buyers are promised if they buy the bond at current prices. The term structure depicts *current*, or *spot*, rates of interest for a given maturity. Underlying any set of yields to maturity, however, is a set of other interest rates that are referred to as implied *forward rates*. These forward rates play an important role in yield curve theory and in advanced investment and speculative strategies. Symbolically, we will denote the forward rate as:

f_{Mt} = the forward rate of interest which will have an M period maturity in t years from today

For simplicity, we will think of periods as being years even though periods could conceivably be of any length. Therefore:

$f_{1,0}$ = the forward rate on one-year investments as of today, that is, today's actual one-year *spot rate*

$f_{1,1}$ = the forward rate on one-year investments as of one year from now (start of year 2)

$f_{1,2}$ = the forward rate on one-year investments as of two years from now (start of year 3)

$f_{5,10}$ = the forward rate on five-year investments as of ten years from now (start of year 11)

Forward rates are calculated using pure discount bond yields to maturity with the following equation:

Forward Rate
$$f_{Mt} = \left(\frac{(1 + I_{t+M})^{t+M}}{(1 + I_t)^t} \right)^{1/M} - 1.0 \qquad \textbf{(11.3)}$$

For example, assume that yields to maturity are now $I_1 = 8\%$ and $I_2 = 9\%$. This implies a forward rate on one-year investments of 10% in exactly one year from now:

$$f_{1,1} = \left(\frac{(1 + I_{1+1})^2}{1 + I_1} \right)^{1/1} - 1.0$$

$$0.10 = \left(\frac{1.09^2}{1.08^1} \right) - 1.0$$

Thus an $I_2 = 9\%$ and an $I_1 = 8\%$ imply that a one-year forward rate of return equal to 10% can be "locked in" (assured) today by trading in the one-year and two-year pure discount bonds.

To illustrate how one could lock in this 10% forward return, consider the market values of discount bonds with one- and two-year maturities. Call these bond A and bond B.

$$\text{Price of } A = \frac{\$1,000}{1.08^1} = \$925.93$$

$$\text{Price of } B = \frac{\$1,000}{1.09^2} = \$841.68$$

To lock in a one-year forward rate starting at the beginning of year 2, investors would sell short the one-year bond and buy some multiple of the two-year bond. They will buy an amount of the two-year bond such that their initial investment in the two-year issue is identical to the cash received on the short sale of the one-year bond.

Details of the trade are shown in Table 11-2 and explained as follows:

1. *At the start of period I* sell short 1.0 of bond A. This provides immediate cash inflow of $925.93, which is used to purchase 1.1 of bond B. The net cash flow at the start of period 1 will be zero.
2. *At the end of period 1* the short sale of Bond A will have to be covered. This requires a $1,000 cash outflow. The long position of 1.1 of bond B is left untouched, so the net cash flow at the end of period 1 will be negative $1,000.
3. *At the end of period 2* the 1.1 of bond B will mature and provide $1,000 cash for each full bond. A net cash inflow of $1,100 will be received.

TABLE 11-2 *Locking In Forward Rates*

| | Cash Flows Received (Disbursed) at End of Period | | |
	0	1	2
1.0 Bond *A*	$ 925.93	($1,000)	—
1.1 Bond *B*	(925.93)	—	$1,100
Net Cash Flow	$0	($1,000)	$1,100
Return in Period 2 =	$\dfrac{\$1,100 - \$1,000}{\$1,000} = 10\%$		

Effectively, this process allows one to be uninvested during period 1 but assured an investment during period 2 on which a 10% yield is locked in.

These examples serve to emphasize two important points. First, when thinking about interest rates we should consider *existing yields* as displayed in current yield curves as well as *implied forward rates*. Interest rates consist of explicitly known spot rates as well as implied forward rates of interest.

Second, the yield to maturity on a pure discount security can be regarded as an average of many shorter-term implied forward rates. In the example above, the 9.0% yield to maturity on the two-year bond *B* is actually an average of an immediate one-year rate of 8.0% and a forward one-year rate of 10.0%. This ''average'' is not an arithmetic average. Instead it is a *geometric average* similar to the geometric average discussed in Chapter 5.

Discount Bond Yield to Maturity

$$I_M = \sqrt[M]{(1 + f_{1,0})(1 + f_{1,1})(1 + f_{1,2}) \ldots (1 + f_{1,M-1})} - 1.0 \qquad (11.4)$$

Using the data for the two-year bond in our example above:

$$\sqrt[2]{(1.08)(1.1)} - 1.0 = 9.0\%$$

Equation 11.4 is the key to understanding the three yield curve theories.

Expected Spot Rates

Earlier we defined the spot rate of interest to be the rate of return promised on a bond if an investment is made in the bond now. Spot rates are the YTM_M and I_M yields to maturity. In addition to current spot rates of interest, speculators will develop estimates of *expected future spot rates*. We will define the expected spot rate of interest as:

$E(I_{Mt})$ = today's expectation of what the spot rate will be on pure discount bonds which will have an *M* period maturity in *t* years from now.

Whenever forward rates implied by the existing yield curve differ from a person's expectation of future spot rates, a speculative trade is called for. Only when forward rates are identical to expected spot rates [f_{Mt} is equal to $E(I_{Mt})$] will there be no speculative trading. We will see later that this is the basis of one yield curve theory known as the unbiased expectations theory (UET).

YIELD CURVE THEORIES

The relationship between yields to maturity and the maturity of a bond is known as the *term structure* of interest rates. An example of the term structure (or yield curve) for U.S. Treasury securities is shown in Figure 11-2. Due to their low default risk, the U.S. Treasury yield curve is commonly thought of as the base on which the YTMs on other securities are based. The curve can be an "eyeballed" best fit line or estimated using a variety of quantitative techniques.

Ideally, yield curves should be plotted for securities that are alike in all respects other than maturity. As a practical matter this is extremely difficult. All any yield curve really controls for is default risk. But securities that have similar risks of default are often substantially different in other respects—for example, in coupon rates, marketability, and callability. Such differences often cause *outliers* on a given yield curve.

Bonds with coupon rates below current rates of interest sell at a discount. Purchasers of such low-coupon bonds expect to earn the current rate of interest by receiving both a yearly coupon payment and a yearly price appreciation as the bond approaches face value at maturity. When this text was last revised, tax rates on ordinary income (coupons) and capital gains (price changes) were equal. For

FIGURE 11-2 *Illustration of a Yield Curve : 6/30/93*

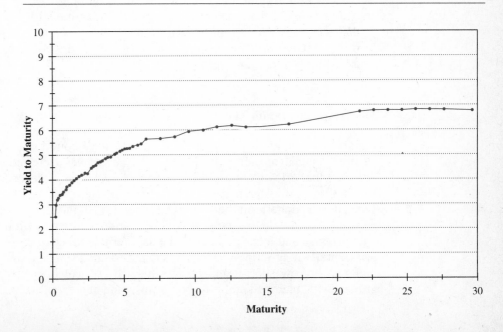

much of U.S. history and in many other countries, however, the capital gains tax rate is lower. When this is the case, the *effective tax rate on low-coupon bonds is lower than the tax rate on high-coupon bonds*. As a result, before-tax yields on low-coupon bonds can be lower than those on high-coupon bonds and still provide an equivalent aftertax yield.

Yield curves vary considerably over time in level and shape. Typically, they are low and upward sloping during periods of slack economic activity. During rapid business growth and full employment, they tend to be high and somewhat downward sloping. Understanding what might cause the yield curve to have a particular shape and why yield curves change over time is the purpose of this section.

There are three basic theories that have been used to explain the yield curve.

1. *Market segmentation theory (MST)* proponents argue that people have strong preferences about the maturity structure of their financial borrowing and lending. These preferences tend to create financial asset demand and supply conditions that are *unique* to each *maturity segment* of the yield curve. Interest rates within each segment are determined largely by *current demand and supply within that segment.*

2. *Unbiased expectation theory (UET)* proponents argue that arbitraguers will seek to profit from any yield distortions between maturity segments. They will buy instruments whose yields are currently high and simultaneously sell instruments whose yields are currently low. Their trading will cause the yield on securities of differing maturities to be related. According to UET, interest rates will be determined by *current as well as expected future supply and demand conditions across all maturities.*

3. *Liquidity preference theory* (LPT) proponents largely accept the conclusions reached by UET but also believe that yields on long-term securities will typically be higher than yields on shorter-term securities. LPT proponents argue that securities with a longer term to maturity are exposed to greater amounts of interest rate risk for which lenders will demand a compensation known as a "liquidity premium."

Market Segmentation Theory

Market segmentation theory (MST) states that economic units that demand or supply financial resources have maturity preferences (referred to as *preferred habitats*) that effectively create a number of *somewhat* independent market segments. Conventionally, these segments are referred to as short-term (less than one year), intermediate-term (one through five years), and long-term (greater than five years). For example, on the supply side, commercial banks prefer to lend short-term, savings and loans prefer intermediate-term lending, and life insurance companies prefer long-term investments. On the demand side, consumer finance firms prefer to borrow short-term, retailers finance cyclical inventory and receivable growth with intermediate-term borrowing, and plant expansion is typically financed with long-term security sales. MST states that the shape and movement of the yield curve are determined by levels of current financial supply and demand within each market segment.

Maturity Preference. Why do economic units have preferred habitats? The answer is simple—to minimize risk. To minimize risk exposure, the average maturities of investments and financing should be equal. In Chapter 12 this statement is modified slightly when the concept of duration is discussed. Duration is simply the average date at which cash flows are received. By matching the duration of assets and liabilities one can minimize interest-rate risk.

Strictly applied, MST suggests that this creates a level of financial supply and demand unique to each particular investment maturity range. Maturity preferences are so strong that participants in any one segment are unlikely to leave that segment for better yields within other market segments. Thus, the yield curve would be determined solely by *current demand and supply conditions within each market segment.*

Few believers in MST apply the concept in such a strict manner. While market participants may have clear maturity preferences, a certain flexibility exists that allows trading between adjacent segments. In addition, a large number of individuals who are indifferent to maturity will arbitrage rates between markets. The operations of these arbitrageurs are discussed below. Rates between various segments will thus be related to some extent. Nonetheless, proponents of MST argue that the dominant force which shifts the yield curve is a change in financial demand and supply within imprecisely defined maturity ranges. But even in this less strict version yield curves are essentially created by *current demand and supply conditions.*

To illustrate the reasoning underlying MST, we will trace its logic in explaining shifts in the yield curve during a period of economic recovery and expansion. Figure 11-3 shows yield curves for three stages of business activity. Starting with the trough of a business recession, the yield curve is reasonably flat for all but the shortest-maturity instruments. Such short-term instruments are what firms rely upon to provide liquidity needs. The low level of economic activity will cause businesses to accumulate large liquidity reserves instead of reinvesting operating fund flows in unneeded inventory, receivables, and plant. The desire for increased liquidity is reinforced by businesses' attempts to guard against short-term insolvency problems that might be brought on by the recession. The net result will be a large supply of funds to the money market, causing very low short-term rates. As business activity begins to pick up, excess liquidity is spent on working capital and plant additions. In addition, total demand for credit increases across all maturity segments. This causes short-term money market rates to rise substantially while there are less dramatic rate increases across all maturity segments. Finally, as business activity moves toward the peak of the economic recovery, rates are the highest in the intermediate-maturity range in response to large demands for credit needed to support the cyclical expansion in receivable and inventory balances. According to MST, each shift in the yield curve is caused by a change in the *current* supply and demand for credit within a given maturity segment.

FIGURE 11-3 *MST and the Business Cycle*

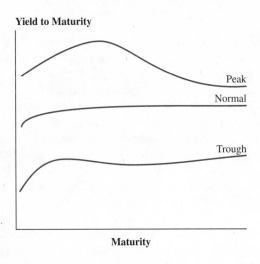

Unbiased Expectations Theory

Arbitrage in a Segmented Market. In a segmented market, yields to maturity are effectively created by current supply and demand conditions within each segment. If one is able to forecast changes in *future* supply and demand, considerable opportunity for arbitrage may exist. In a market setting such as that of MST, this shouldn't be too difficult. Consider the movement of the yield curve over the course of a business cycle. If one believes in a segmented market, a repeated pattern of yield curves will exist coincident with normal business expansion and retraction. If this is so, bonds should be bought at the peak of the economic activity (to obtain large capital gains as yields eventually fall) and sold short at the trough of a recession (to gain from price declines incurred as interest rates rise and the economy expands).

   To understand the possibilities for arbitrage, consider the following example. Three pure discount bonds of different maturities exist: one year, two years, and three years. We are now at date 1, a period of normal business activity. Yields to maturity on each of three bonds can be observed as prevailing market rates at date 1. These known I_M's are shown in Figure 11-4 as the solid line. Date 2 is expected to be the peak of the economic expansion, with rather high interest rates, particularly on bonds that mature two years after the start of date 2. Date 3 represents the trough of a recession with commensurately low interest rates. I_M's expected at dates 2 and 3 are shown in Figure 11-4 as the dashed lines. To complete the example, two added facts are helpful. First, we will assume that the various bonds are discount bonds, that is, they pay no intermediate coupons. The purchaser's sole return will come from capital appreciation. Second, the arbitrageurs are willing to make up to a three-year commitment at date 1. They will *not*

FIGURE 11-4 *Yield Curves to Be Arbitraged*

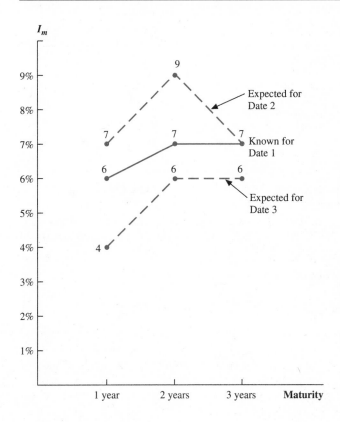

consider the purchase of three-year bonds at date 2 or two-year bonds at date 3. Both of these assumptions ease the analysis considerably but do not change the essence of the conclusions.

If arbitrageurs are willing to place their money at risk for three years, they could follow any one of a number of plans. For example, they could simply buy one three-year bond at date 1. Alternatively, they could mix a sequence of three one-year bonds or a two-year bond plus a subsequent one-year bond, and so forth. Being indifferent to bond maturity, the arbitrageurs will select a policy which is expected to maximize their total three-year return. Table 11-3 lists the various possible strategies together with the third-year expected wealth of placing $1 into a given strategy at date 1. Clearly, a strategy of buying one-year bond at date 1 followed by a two-year bond at date 2 will yield the largest expected profit. The lowest expected total return would be received if a sequence of three one-year bonds were purchased.

Earlier in the chapter we examined how arbitrageurs might lock in a future interest rate. This concept applies directly to this example. Note that of the four strategies in Table 11-3, those that involve purchase of a one-year bond at date 3

TABLE 11-3 *Arbitrage Strategies and Profits*

Strategy	Year 3 Expected Wealth per $1 Investment at Date 1	Rank	Details of Calculation
A. One 3-year bond	$1.225	2	1.07 × 1.07 × 1.07
B. Three 1-year bonds	$1.180	4	1.06 × 1.07 × 1.04
C. One 2-year bond followed by a 1-year bond	$1.190	3	1.07 × 1.07 × 1.04
D. One 1-year bond followed by a 2-year bond	$1.259	1	1.06 × 1.09 × 1.09

are ranked lowest. Arbitrageurs are capable of making larger profits in year 3 than the expected 4% one-year spot yield for that period. For example, the strategy of buying 1.07 three-year bonds at date 1 and short selling 1.0 two-year bond at date 1 will yield a 7% locked-in return during year 3. Details of this calculation are as follows:

Market Value at Start of Year 1

| 2-year bond | $1,000 ÷ 1.07^2 = $873.44 |
| 3-year bond | $1,000 ÷ 1.07^3 = $816.29 |

Strategy	Arbitrage Cash Flows at Year-End			
	0	1	2	3
Short sell 1.0 2-year bond	$873.44	—	($1,000)	—
Buy 1.07 3-year bonds	($873.44)	—		$1,070
Net cash flows	0	0	($1,000)	$1,070

7% yield in year 3

There are a host of ways in which people can arbitrage in a segmented market. But the techniques are less important at this point in our discussion than is the idea. As long as the yield curve is determined by current demand and supply conditions, considerable arbitrage profits are available simply by making reasonable estimates of future demand and supply conditions.

Effects of a Fully Arbitraged Market. What would happen to interest rates if arbitrage were extensive? First, attempts by arbitrageurs to obtain speculative profits would eliminate all such profits. Bonds that provided large yields would be actively bought, driving their prices up and yields down. Bonds that provided insufficient yields would be actively sold, driving their prices down and yields up. Soon all possible profit opportunities would disappear. Second, long-term interest rates would be a geometric average of the current short-term spot rate and the market's consensus estimate of *expected future spot rates*. This theory of a fully arbitraged market, referred to earlier as the *unbiased expectations theory* (UET), was initially discussed by Irving Fisher and later developed by Friedrich Lutz.

According to proponents of UET, the relationship between long- and short-term rates can be written as follows:

Future Value of \$1

$$[1 + I_m]^M = [1 + I_1][1 + E(I_{11})][1 + E(I_{12})] \cdots$$
$$[1 + E(I_{1M-1})]$$

(11.5)

where I_M = the yield to maturity on a pure discount bond maturing in M years, and $E(I_{1t})$ = the market's consensus forecast of expected one-year spot rates t years from today. This means, for example, that the terminal wealth expected from purchasing a 10-year pure discount bond should be the same as the *expected* terminal wealth on a sequence of 10 one-year bonds.

Expected Terminal Wealth on a 10-Year Bond	*Expected Terminal Wealth on a Sequence of 10 One-Year Bonds*
$[1 + I_{10}]^{10}$	$= [1 + I_1][1 + E(I_{11})][1 + E(I_{12})] \ldots [1 + E(I_{19})]$

In addition, there is no particular reason to restrict the explanation to one-year forward rates. For example, the terminal wealth expected on a 10-year bond should be equal to the terminal wealth expected from first buying a six-year bond and then buying a four-year bond.

Expected Terminal Wealth on a 10-Year Bond	*Expected Terminal Wealth on a 6-Year Bond Followed by a 4-Year Bond*	
	6-Year Bond	*4-Year Bond*
$[1 + I_{10}]^{10}$ =	$[1 + I_6]^6$ $\times$	$[1 + E(I_{4,6})]^4$
	$[1 + I_1][1 + E(I_{11})] \ldots [1 + E(I_{15})]$	$[1 + E(I_{16})] \ldots [1 + E(I_{19})]$

Consider the following numerical example. Today, the start of year 1, the yield to maturity on a one-year bond is known to be 6.0%. Somehow a market consensus is developed that the expected one-year spot rate at the start of year 2 will be 6.5% and the one-year spot rate at the start of year 3 will be 7.0%:

Start of Year	*Expected 1-Year Bond Rate at Start of Year*	
1	6.0%	Known—today's 1-year rate
2	6.5%	Expected spot rates
3	7.0%	

By investing \$1 at the start of year 1 in a one-year bond, \$1.06 would be received at the end of the year. Reinvesting this \$1.06 at the start of year 2 would yield \$1.129 by the end of year 2 (1.06×1.065). By the end of year 3, \$1.208 would be available (1.129×1.07). The terminal wealth on a three-year bond would have to equal exactly \$1.208 per dollar invested or arbitrage profits would be available. Thus, $(1 + I_3)^3 = 1.208$. The *annual* yield to maturity on the three-year bond would be the geometric average of the three yearly returns:

$$\sqrt[3]{1.208} - 1.0 = 6.5\%$$

Using the same data:

- the yield to maturity of a two-year bond today would be 6.25% ($\sqrt[2]{(1.06)(1.065)} - 1.0$).

- the expected yield to maturity of a two-year bond starting at the beginning of year 2 would be 6.75% ($\sqrt[2]{(1.065)(1.07)} - 1.0$).

- the expected yield to maturity of a one-year bond starting at the beginning of year 3 would be 7.0% (by definition).

Determinants of Discount Bond Yield to Maturity

$$I_M = \sqrt[M]{[1 + I][1 + E(I_{11})][1 + E(I_{12})] \ldots [1 + E(I_{1,M-1})]} - 1.0 \qquad (11.6)$$

The yield to maturity on a bond maturing at the end of period M is equal to the geometric mean of expected yields on a sequence of shorter-term bonds with equal maturity.[2]

A major implication of UET is that the forward rates that are implied in the yield curve are the same as the market's consensus forecast of expected future spot rates; that is, UET states that:

$$\text{Forward Rates} = \text{Expected Spot Rates}$$

$$f_{Mt} = E(I_{Mt}) \qquad (11.7)$$

For example, if a five-year bond is currently yielding 9% to maturity and a four-year bond has an 8.7% *YTM*, then the implied one-year expected spot rate per UET at the *start* of year 5 would be 10.21%:

$$\frac{1.09^5}{1.087^4} - 1.0 = \frac{1.5386}{1.3961} - 1.0 = .1021$$

Implications of UET. If UET is strictly correct, any speculative profits that might have existed under MST will have been fully arbitraged away. Returns on the *next* speculative transaction will be zero. If UET is not strictly correct, some speculative profits will be available for the first group of speculators who act upon new information. But they must act quickly, before their information is incorporated into existing interest rates. The unbiased expectations theory is the same as the efficient market theory, but it is EMT applied to only a narrow set of securities: debt instruments.

In addition, the return expected for a given holding period does not depend upon the maturity of the instrument purchased. For example, if you intend to invest for a one-year period, the return you can *expect* will be *identical* whether you (1) buy a sequence of one-month instruments, (2) buy a one-year instrument,

---

[2] Again, this equation is strictly true only for pure discount bonds. It is approximate for coupon obligations.

(3) buy a 20-year instrument and sell it a year from now, or (4) choose some other approach. This is true for any desired holding period.

Finally, all that is known about the likely course of future interest rates is already incorporated into present yield curves. The best predictor of future interest rates is today's yield curve. Individuals using sophisticated econometric models or simple intuition will be unable to predict future interest rates any better than individuals who use today's yield curve. This doesn't mean that the yield curve is an accurate predictor of future interest rates. It only means that nothing better is available. *Forward rates of interest implicit in the yield curve are unbiased estimates of expected future spot rates.*[3]

Expected Inflation and Nominal Risk-Free Rates. According to a strict version of the unbiased expectations theory, *a major determinant of a yield curve's shape is expectations of future inflation.* For example, assume that a real rate of 2% is deemed to be fair during all future years. Knowing this together with expected annual future rates of inflation, one can estimate both expected spot rates and yields to maturity on bonds of varying maturities. For example, assume that you have developed the following data:

Start of Year	Desired Real Rate	+	Expected Inflation During Year	=	Expected Spot Rate	Implying a Current I_M of
1	2%		5%		7%	7.00%
2	2%		8%		10%	8.49%
3	2%		6%		8%	8.33%
4	2%		4%		6%	7.74%

The reader may recognize that this relationship is simply Irving Fisher's theory about the determinants of nominal risk-free rates:[4]

Nominal Risk-Free Rate $$RF_t = r^* + E(I_t) \qquad \textbf{(11.8)}$$

RF_t stands for the nominal yield to maturity on a risk-free bond that matures in t years.

Market segmentation theory explains changes in the level and shape of the yield curve during the course of a business cycle as the result of changes in current demand and supply conditions within various market segments. According to UET the overall level of the yield curve shifts as a result of two forces: (1) changes in the *expectations* of future demand and supply conditions across all market

---

[3] Cox, Ingersoll, and Ross have demonstrated that if the risk-free rate is stochastic (uncertain over time), logical inconsistencies exist in UET. In particular, they show that it is impossible for expected holding period returns for various maturities to be identical at the same time that forward rates are unbiased estimates of expected future spot rates. We will bypass a discussion of their argument because of its highly technical nature and because any errors which arise in UET appear to be slight.

[4] Equation 11.8 is a modified version of Equation 5.1. The interaction term between the future inflation rate and the real rate, $I_t r^*$, is dropped since its size is negligible. In addition, an expected inflation term is used instead of a known future inflation rate.

segments and (2) changes in *expected* rates of inflation. During a business up-swing, the yield curve will rise if market participants *revise their expectations* about future demand for and supply of funds or revise their expectations about future inflation.

Liquidity Premiums

In some respects, *liquidity preference theory* (LPT) is a refined version of the market segmentation theory. In its most general form, LPT states that borrowers and lenders have preferred maturity habitats but can be induced to trade in other maturity segments if offered an inducement to do so in the form of a higher rate of return. This yield inducement is referred to as a *liquidity premium.*

When LPT was originally developed, its proponents stated that lenders of funds (who are typically households) prefer to lend short-term, whereas borrowers (who are typically corporations) prefer to borrow long-term. As a result, the original proponents of liquidity preference believed lenders would demand a premium to be enticed to invest their funds long-term. Investors in long-term obligations would earn a higher yield than would investors who insisted upon short-term securities. Borrowers would have to pay a higher interest rate to borrow long-term than if they borrowed short-term.

Proponents of liquidity preference argue that the implied forward rate is actually composed of the expected spot rate plus a liquidity premium. Symbolically:

**Implied
Forward
Rate**
$$f_{Mt} = E(I_{Mt}) + l_{Mt} \tag{11.9}$$

where f_{mt} = the implied forward rate on a pure discount bond with a maturity of M years in t years from now, $E(I_{Mt})$ = the expected spot rate on a bond with a maturity of M years in t years from now, and l_{Mt} = the liquidity premium associated with a bond with a maturity of M years in t years from now.

The only difference between the LPT and UET models is whether a liquidity premium exists. For example, assume that the yields to maturity on (pure discount) bonds maturing at the end of years 5 and 6 are 8.7% and 9.0%, respectively. The implied one-year forward rate at the beginning of year 6 would be 10.5%:

$$\frac{1.09^6}{1.087^5} - 1.0 = 10.5\%$$

According to UET the expected one-year spot rate for year 6 is 10.5%. However, LPT would say that the expected spot rate is slightly lower than 10.5% by the amount of the liquidity premium.

The early developers of liquidity preference (chiefly Hicks) believed lenders preferred to lend short-term whereas borrowers preferred to borrow long-term. As a result, all liquidity premiums would be positive and the yield curve would provide upwardly biased estimates of expected spot rates. Figure 11-5 depicts the difference between the two models for the case of constant expected spot rates.

FIGURE 11-5 *Effects of Liquidity Premiums on Implied Forward Rates*

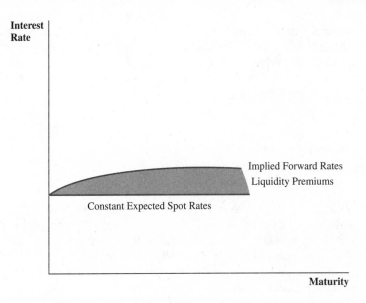

Liquidity premiums are all positive, causing implied forward rates to be greater than expected spot rates. As a result, the actual yield curve observed in the financial press will be upward sloping even though spot rates are not expected to change.

Volatility of Long-Term Interest Rates

Both UET and LPT state that the long-term interest rate is an average of current and rationally expected future short-term rates (plus liquidity premiums in LPT). This has an important empirical implication. Since long-term rates are averages of short-term rates, the series of long-term interest rates that we observe as time passes should be less volatile than the time series of short-term rates. Long moving averages tend to smooth out the series averaged. Thus, if one were to plot the historical time series of short-term and long-term rates, the long-term rates should be much less volatile.

This simply is not the case. Although long-term rates have been somewhat less volatile than short-term rates, long-term rates have been more volatile than naive versions of either theory would imply.

Three explanations have been offered: (1) changes in desired real returns as time passes, (2) varying liquidity premiums as time passes, and (3) investor overreaction to changes in short-term rates. The first two explanations could conceivably explain the large volatility of long-term rates in the context of either UET or LPT models. In fact, even a casual observation of short-term interest rates suggests that desired real returns do change. There have been many periods in which the expected real returns on T-bills have been zero or negative. Similarly, there have been many periods in which large positive real returns could have been easily forecast on T-bills. Changing liquidity premiums are more difficult to measure. But if the large volatility in long-term rates is to be explained by changes in desired real returns and liquidity premiums, the changes in these variables must be much larger than most scholars have thought was true in the past. It is possible that long-term rates are more volatile than rational expectations models such as UET and LPT would allow.

DEFAULT RISK

Two Ways of Viewing Risky Debt

Default risk is the possibility that *promised* coupon and par values of a bond will not be paid. For example, in the early 1980s, the Washington Public Power Supply defaulted on bonds that had been sold to finance nuclear power plants in the state of Washington. Although each WPPS (as in WHOOPS) bond *had promised* very specific coupon and eventual par value payments to owners, it was clear that investors had to expect much less. When the potential for default exists, one's expected return is less than the bond's promised yield to maturity.

Default risk is best understood from the viewpoint of option theory. For example, consider the following simple example, which is graphically depicted in Figure 11-6. The equity owners form a corporation financed in part by the sale of risky debt. The debt holders are promised a single future payment known as par value. When this par value is due to be paid, the equity owners have an *option*. They can either pay the debt par value, or they can turn the assets over to the debt holders and declare bankruptcy.

Essentially the equity position in the firm represents the ownership of two things: the asset of the firm and a put option that allows the equity owner the ability to sell the assets to debt holders at par. This way of viewing default risk is shown in panels A and B of the figure. In panel A, *risky debt represents a portfolio of: a long position in risk-free debt and a short put* (which has been sold to equity owners). Equity has long asset and a long put position.

Panels C and D provide an alternative way of viewing risky debt. In panel C, the debt owner has a portfolio consisting of long assets and a short call on the assets (sold to equity owners). Equity owners shown in panel D have a long call position on the assets of the firm.

Considering debt that faces the possibility of default from the view of option theory is more than an interesting intellectual exercise. Option theory is the key to valuation of risky debt.

Suppose debt having a par value of $50 is due in 1 year. The (continuously compound) risk-free interest rate is 10% per annum. The current value of the assets are $70 and the standard deviation of annualized returns on the assets is 70%. If the debt were risk-free, it would be worth $45.24:

FIGURE 11-6 *Risky Debt Viewed from Option Theory at Maturity*

A. Risky Debt is same as:

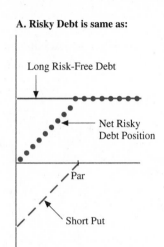

B. Equity is same as:

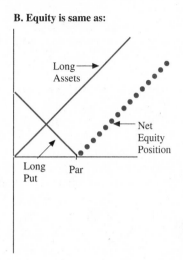

C. Risky Debt is same as:

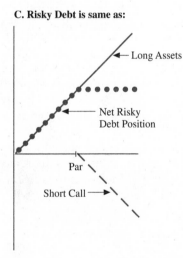

D. Equity is same as:

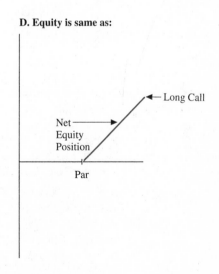

$$\$45.24 = \$50 \div e^{0.1}$$

The $70 asset value today will be shared between the equity and debt holders. Since the equity position is the same as a 1-year call on the firm's assets, we can use the Black-Scholes Option Pricing Model to value the equity and then back into the value of the debt! Based on the data in this example, the call's value would be $28. Thus the bond's value 1 year before maturity would be $42 ($70 − $28).

Notice that this is $3.24 lower than the value of a 1-year risk-free security. Also observe that the yield-to-maturity on the risky debt is 19%.

$$0.19 = (\$50 \div \$42) - 1$$

Thus, the default risk premium in this example is 9 percentage points.[5]

Rating Agencies

The default risks of most actively traded bonds are rated by various independent organizations. Standard & Poor's and Moody's are the largest of these rating agencies, concentrating upon corporate and municipal issues. Fitch's is a smaller organization that concentrates upon institutional issues. These ratings reflect each agency's opinion about an issue's potential default, *not* its relative investment merits. Table 11-4 presents a summary of the ratings used by Moody's and S&P.

Not only do the ratings provide an opinion about the default risk of an issue, but they are often used to define allowable bond purchases for some investors. For example, the Comptroller of the Currency has stated that bank investments must be *investment grade.* Historically, the comptroller has defined investment grade to include bonds rated in the top four rankings. In addition, *legal lists* of approved bonds are used in some states to identify bonds that regulated savings banks, trust companies, and insurance companies may purchase. These legal lists rely upon ratings by Moody's and Standard & Poor's. Rating designations in addition to those shown in Table 11-4 are sometimes used to more accurately reflect an agency's opinion. For example, Standard & Poor's will occasionally indicate a $(+)$ or $(-)$ on ratings between AA and BB. Moody's will apply A1 and Baa1 to the better-quality *municipals* within the A and Baa categories. Non-rated issues are designated NR.

To evaluate a bond's potential for default, rating agencies rely upon a committee analysis of the issuer's *ability* to repay, *willingness* to repay, and *protective provisions* for an issue. Ratings given by Moody's and S&P for a particular issue will usually be identical. When a difference does exist, it will be no larger than one grade and reflects the relative strength or weakness of each agency's opinion.

The Historical Accuracy of Ratings

With rare exceptions, the ratings assigned by S&P and Moody's have closely followed actual historical default rates. In a thorough study of corporate bonds issued between 1900 and 1943, Hickman examined by rating category the proportion of bonds that defaulted. Nine rating categories were used, with the following results:

---

[5] In actual practice, it is difficult to use option theory to price bond default risk because of the complexities of real world bonds that include coupon payments, sinking funds, call provisions, and so forth.

TABLE 11-4 *Corporate Bond Ratings*

Standard & Poor's	Moody's	
AAA	Aaa	highest quality
AA +	Aa1	high quality
AA	Aa2	
AA −	Aa3	
A +	A1	upper medium quality
A	A2	
A −	A3	
BBB +	Baa1	medium quality
BBB	Baa2	
BBB −	Baa3	
BB +	Ba1	speculative
BB	Ba2	
BB −	Ba3	
B +	B1	very speculative
B	B2	
B −	B3	
CCC	Caa	poor quality, may be in default
CC	Ca	highly speculative
C	C	poorest quality
D		in default

Rating Category	Comparable S&P Rating	Percent of Par Value Defaulting Prior to Maturity
I	AAA	6%
II	AA	6
III	A	13
IV	BBB	19
V–IX	Below BBB	42

SOURCE: *W. B. Hickman, Corporate Bond Quality and Investor Experience* (Princeton, NJ: Princeton University Press, 1958).

The two highest-rated categories experienced similar and relatively low default rates. As the ratings decreased, the default rate increased.

Hickman also examined the actual *realized YTM*s on bonds of each rating and compared them with *promised* yields. If investors properly assess future rates of default, the difference between promised and realized yields should reflect the expected default rates. For each bond he calculated a realized annual return based upon buying the bond at its issue price, receiving the sequence of coupons actually paid, and obtaining the terminal value of the bond when it reached maturity, defaulted, or was called. Results of this analysis are shown in Table 11-5. Surprisingly, Hickman found that realized *YTM*s exceeded promised *YTM*s. This occurred because, during the period he studied, interest rates fell, resulting in a

TABLE 11-5 *Realized YTM by Rating*

Rating Category	Average Promised YTM	Realized YTM	
		Hickman	Fraine/Mills
I	4.5%	5.1%	4.3
II	4.6	5.0	4.3
III	4.9	5.0	4.3
IV	5.4	5.7	4.5
V–IX	9.5	8.6	NA

SOURCES: W. B. Hickman, *Corporate Bond Quality and Investor Experience* (Princeton, NJ: Princeton University Press, 1958); H. Fraine and R. Mills, "The Effect of Defaults and Credit Deterioration on Yields of Corporate Bonds," *Journal of Finance* 16, no. 3 (September 1961).

large number of bonds being called as issuers took advantage of lower rates. When the original issues were called, investors received a call premium above par and thus a higher realized return than promised. Consequently, Hickman's realized yields were unduly influenced by interest rate movements during his study period.

To correct for this, Fraine and Mills substituted promised yields for realized yields whenever realized yields were larger. Their results are shown in the right-most column of Table 11-5. When modified by Fraine and Mills, promised yields exceeded realized yields, and the difference increased for the lower default ratings.

Junk Bonds

A junk bond is a high-default risk, high-yield bond. There are two ways a bond can become a junk bond. Many were financially sound when originally issued but became high-risk over time as the financial condition of the issuer deteriorated (fallen angels). Other bonds were quite risky at the time of issue. These bonds are almost always uncollateralized and subordinated to other debt that a firm has outstanding. Junk bonds of this type became popular in the mid-1980s when Drexel Burnham Lambert used them to help finance leveraged buy-outs and mergers.

Junk bonds have always played a role in bond trading but became much more common in the 1980s. For example, the average market value of *newly issued* bonds rated B or CCC during the 1970s was $322 million. This contrasts with total new issue value (B or CCC grade) in 1986 of $25.9 billion!

The attraction of junk bonds was the large promised return. Many studies have attempted to determine whether promised yields on junk bonds are larger than necessary given the actual default experience of the bonds. Researchers have faced two problems. Many of the bonds have not been outstanding long enough to develop a reliable estimate of their default experience. In addition, these bonds are inactively traded, so reliable prices are difficult to develop. A recent study by Cornell and Green suggests that returns on mutual funds that specialize in low-grade corporate bonds are approximately equal to the returns on an index of high-grade bonds. They also found that low-grade bond fund returns are sensitive to stock returns. In short, *realized* yields on diversified portfolios of low-grade bonds are similar to those of investment grade securities in that they do not provide excess returns. And, as the option model suggests, debt securities facing considerable default risk will trade very much like an equity security.

Yield Spreads

Yield spreads are often calculated for bonds of equivalent maturity. For example, if two bonds with 10-year maturities are selling at promised YTMs of 8% and 9.5%, respectively, the yield spread between the two is 150 basis points.

Yield spreads are typically plotted over some historical time period for bonds of similar maturity but differing default risk. For example, promised yields to maturity are shown in Figure 11-7 for U.S. T-bonds as well as Aaa grade and Baa grade corporate bonds. During bad economic times, there is a tendency for yield spreads to widen, more so for Baa than Aaa issues.

CALL AND TAXES

Call Impacts on Yields

Virtually all corporate bonds and a large percentage of municipal bonds may be retired prior to formal maturity by exercise of a call provision. Issuers will call an issue if the present value of future coupon savings associated with refunding the issue offsets the costs of doing so. To the investor the effects of a call are twofold. First, the realized return during the time span for which the bond has been held will be larger than promised because principal repayment occurs earlier than anticipated and because a call premium is typically received. Second, when the bond is called, reinvestment of the call proceeds must be made at a lower rate of return than available on the original issue. On net, the second effect offsets the first, and the realized return over the horizon date is lower than if the issue had not been called.

Assume you bought a 10-year, triple-A, 10% coupon bond in 1985 at a promised *and* expected *YTM* of 10% (no default risk). You anticipate holding the bond for the full 10 years and do not expect a change in the yield curve from 10%. Since coupons are expected to be reinvested at 10%, a 10% realized return is expected. For five years you are correct, but at the start of year 6 the yield curve drops dramatically, and the issuer calls each bond at a price of $1,050. At that date the best yield available on five-year bonds of equivalent risk is 6%.

Your realized return on the initial issue for the five years it was held will be a fine 10.67%:

$$0.1067 = \sqrt[5]{\frac{\$1,660.51}{\$1,000}} - 1.0$$

FIGURE 11-7 *Illustration of Past Yield Spreads*

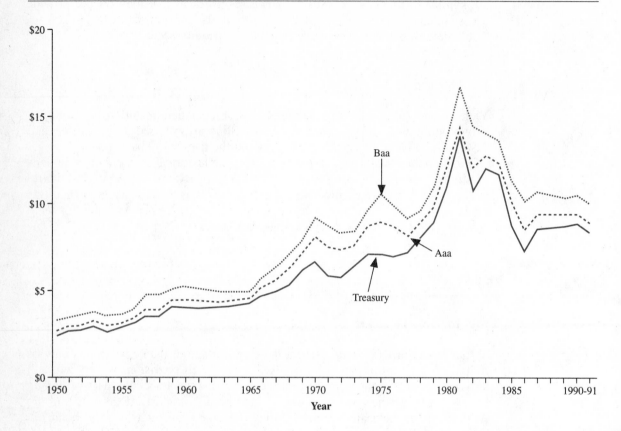

Year

where:

$$\underset{\$1,660.51}{\underset{\text{Investment Value}}{\text{Year 5}}} = \underset{\$1,050}{\text{Call Price}} + \underset{\$500}{\underset{\text{Received}}{\text{Total Coupons}}} + \underset{\$110.51}{\underset{\text{Interest}}{\text{Interest on}}}$$

However, if the yield curve does not change from 6%, your realized return between years 6 and 10 will be 6%. During the full 10 years, your average annual realized return will be about 8.31%:

$$\sqrt[10]{(1.1067^5)(1.06^5)} - 1.0 = 8.31\%$$

The low investment rate available after the call causes your *10-year realized yield* to be less than promised. Naturally, investors do not like the call privilege and will request larger promised yields if call is likely.

The fact that realized yields are often less than promised yields on callable bonds does not mean that such bonds are poor investments. As with their view of default risk, investors recognize that realized yields may be less than promised, and they adjust prices downward so that they expect to receive a fair return. To date, research on callable bonds suggests that:

1. Callable bonds sell at higher promised yields than noncallable issues.
2. Immediately callable bonds sell at higher promised yields than bonds that have a deferred call.
3. The yield spread between callable and noncallable bonds widens during periods of high interest rates.
4. The yield spread between callable and noncallable bonds increases with the bonds' maturities.

When people buy a callable bond, they are in effect placing a bet with the issuer. The issuer will develop expectations of future interest rate decreases and be willing to pay a higher call premium as long as the future interest savings associated with a call are expected to offset the call expense. Investors, on the other hand, are betting that the call premiums are more than adequate to offset a possible call resulting in a reinvestment at a low interest rate. Who's won the game in the past? We don't know.

When buying a callable bond, investors should examine the level to which interest rates must fall before the issue would be called. For example, assume Cadiz Pedro, Inc., sells a 20-year, 9% coupon bond at par. The issue is first callable at the end of five years at a price of $1,100. If Cadiz does call the bond at the end of year 5, it will incur a cash outflow of $1,100 per bond and save $90 per year for 15 years plus $1,000 15 years hence (in year 20). The internal rate of return on this call would be 7.84%:

$$\frac{\$90}{1.0784} + \frac{\$90}{1.0784^2} + \cdots + \frac{\$90}{1.0784^{15}} + \frac{\$1,000}{1.0784^{15}} = \$1,100$$

If interest rates are expected to be 7.84% or lower by the end of year 5, the issue might well be called.

One way to control against call risk would be to purchase low-coupon, deep-discount bonds. Even though interest rates may decline, prices of these issues are unlikely to rise to their stated call prices. However, before-tax yields on deep-discount bonds are often lower than equivalent-risk, high-coupon bonds. This is caused by the different ways in which returns on low- and high-coupon bonds are taxed.

Tax Impacts on Yields

Coupon income on corporate bonds is taxed at the investor's ordinary tax rate. Long-term capital gains and losses are often taxed at lower capital gains rates. To understand the effects which differences in ordinary and long-term capital gains rates can have on before-tax bond yields, consider the following scenario. Investors are attempting to value two bonds of identical risk. Bond L matures in five years and pays a $30 yearly coupon. Bond H matures in five years and pays a $100 yearly coupon. Given the risks of the bond, investors wish to receive an after-tax return of 5% on each. Their average ordinary and capital gains tax rates are 50% and 25%, respectively.

To price each bond, future *after-tax* cash flows should be discounted at the demanded after-tax return of 5%. Prices of bonds L and H would be:

$$P_L = \sum_{t=1}^{5} \frac{30(1 - 0.5)}{1.05^t} + \frac{1,000 - (1,000 - P_L)(0.25)}{1.05^5}$$

$$= \$811.53$$

$$P_H = \sum_{t=1}^{5} \frac{100(1 - 0.5)}{1.05^t} + \frac{1,000 - (1,000 - P_H)(0.25)}{1.05^5}$$

$$= \$1,000$$

The price of L would, of course, be lower since its coupons are lower.

Given these prices, what is the before-tax yield to maturity on each? Using before-tax flows, we would find the before-tax *YTM* on L to be 7.68% and on H to be 10%.[6] The low-coupon issue will sell at a lower before-tax *YTM* since its *effective* tax rate is lower.

To determine whether a person should be in low- or high-coupon bonds that are otherwise identical, the *after-tax* return on each should be calculated. For example, using the data above, individuals with marginal tax rates higher than 50% would prefer the low-coupon bond, and individuals with lower tax rates (or even zero rates, such as endowment funds and charities) would select the higher-coupon issue.

When this text was last revised, the ordinary and capital gains tax rates were identical. However, historically the capital gains rate has been lower than the ordinary rate.

State and Local Bonds. Bond issues of state and local governments in the United States provide tax exemptions from federal income taxes. Thus their pre-tax yields to maturity are usually lower than pre-tax yields of equivalent-risk government and corporate bonds. Specifically, *interest income* paid by municipal issues is not subject to federal taxes (and usually not subject to local taxes in the state of issue). Income due to realized capital gains or losses (the price at which one sells minus the purchase price) is subject to federal taxes.

For state and local bonds trading at close to par value (hence zero expected capital gains or losses), the relationship between after-tax and before-tax yields is shown in Equation 11.10:

6

$$\$811.53 = \sum_{t=1}^{5} \frac{30}{1.0768^t} + \frac{1,000}{1.0768^5}$$

$$\$1.000 = \sum_{t=1}^{5} \frac{100}{1.1^t} + \frac{1,000}{1.1^5}$$

$$\frac{\text{After-Tax}}{\text{Yield}} = \frac{\text{Before-Tax}}{\text{Yield}} \quad \frac{(1\text{-Tax})}{\text{Rate}} \qquad \textbf{(11.10)}$$

For example, if municipals currently provide a yield to maturity of 6.4% and one's federal tax rate is 25%, then the before-tax yield required on corporates of equivalent default risk and maturity would be 8.89%.

$$0.0889 = 0.064 \div (1 - 0.28)$$

If corporate bonds provided a yield to maturity lower than 8.89%, equivalent municipals would be preferred.

SUMMARY

The value of a bond is equal to the present worth of promised future cash flows when discounted at an appropriate yield to maturity. The yield to maturity depends on four basic characteristics of the bond: (1) required yields on default free bonds of similar maturity, (2) default risk inherent in the bond, (3) the ability to call the bond prior to scheduled maturity, and (4) any special tax advantages associated with the bond.

The term structure of interest rates (or yield curve) relates the maturity of a bond to their yield to maturity. Three term structure theories have been developed: market segmentation theory (MST), unbiased expectations theory (UET), and liquidity preference theory (LPT).

Market segmentation theory states that the term structure of interest is dominated by individuals and institutions who attempt to hedge their investment risks. A hedge is created by matching the maturity of an investment with the financing maturity. Such hedging creates desires to buy or sell securities within only a narrow maturity range. As a result, the yield curve is said to be created by current levels of demand and supply in various maturity segments.

The unbiased expectations theory states that if MST is correct, then significant arbitrage profits would be available by forecasting future demand and supply conditions. Believers in UET suggest that such arbitrage will continue until profits from additional arbitrage no longer exist. At this point the yield curve will not reflect current demand and supply conditions within particular maturity segments but, instead, will reflect expectations about future demand and supply over all maturity segments. The shape of the yield curve would reflect expectations about future interest rates.

Liquidity preference theory builds upon UET by adding a liquidity premium to bonds of longer maturity. Since long-term bonds are quite price sensitive to interest rate changes, they have a principal risk that short-term lenders would prefer not to accept. To induce lenders to buy maturities that have such a risk, borrowers will have to offer a yield inducement—a liquidity premium. Liquidity premiums are believed to vary with the overall level of interest rates. However, the direction of this impact is debated.

Owners of bonds that have default risk effectively have a position in two securities. The first is default-free debt. The second is a short put position that provides equity owners the option of either repaying the debt in cash or selling the firm's assets to debt holders at the debt's par value. In principle, option theory can be used to price the incremental YTM required for a given level of default risk. In reality, bonds that are issued are more complex than existing option theory models can handle.

Default risk and call risk can be reduced by selecting instruments with little chance of default or call, as well as by diversifying over a variety of different bonds. But default and call risk cannot be eliminated. The level of default risk is estimated by professional rating agencies such as Standard & Poor's and Moody's, who assign default quality rankings to the more actively traded issues. Historically, default rates have been closely related to the quality ratings these firms assign. Call risk can be judged by estimating the level to which interest rates must fall before the issuer would find it profitable to call the issue.

REVIEW PROBLEMS

1. You are given the following (incomplete) data on U.S. Treasury securities. Assume a $1,000 par value for each and a coupon payment at year-end.

Security	Maturity	Coupon Rate	Price	YTM
A	2 years	10%	$982.87	—
B	4 years	10%	—	12%
C	4 years	12%	—	12%

   a. Without performing any calculations, what will be the price of C?
   b. Without performing any calculations, will the price of B be greater or less than that of C?
   c. Calculate the missing data.
   d. If interest rates rise, in what direction will the bond prices move? Which will move more, A or B? Which will move more, B or C?

2. Throughout this problem, assume that we are dealing with zero-coupon bonds. Yields to maturity on bonds having three different maturities are as follows:

Bond	Maturity	YTM
A	1 year	11.0%
B	2 years	12.0%
C	3 years	11.5%

   a. Calculate the implied one-year forward rates for the starts of years 2 and 3.
   b. Prepare a forecast of what the yield curve is *expected* to be at the start of year 2 according to UET.
   c. Calculate the implied forward rate on two-year bonds for the start of year 2.
   d. Assume you believe that spot rates on one-year bonds will be 8% at the start of year 3. Illustrate the arbitrage you would enter into to take advantage of this.
   e. Assume UET is correct and that a *real* risk-free rate of 3% per annum is required. What inflation forecasts are implicit in the yield curve?
   f. Assume UET is correct. What return would you expect during the next year if you:

- Buy the one-year bond?
- Buy the three-year bond and sell in a year?

Solutions

1. **a.** Bond C will sell for $1,000. Bond theorem 1 states that when the annual coupon rate and yield to maturity are identical, a bond will always sell at par.
   b. Bond B will have a lower price than C because B has a lower coupon.
   c. The *YTM* of bond A is found by trial and error or with a calculator to be 11%:

$$\frac{100}{1.11} + \frac{1,100}{1.11^2} = 982.87$$

   The price of bond B will be $939.25:

$$\frac{100}{1.12} + \frac{100}{1.12^2} + \frac{100}{1.12^3} + \frac{1,100}{1.12^4} = \$939.25$$

   The price of bond C was stated to be $1,000 in part a above.
   d. Bond prices will move down—this is bond theorem 2. Bond B will fall more than bond A, according to bond theorem 3. And bond B will fall more than bond C, per bond theorem 5.

2. **a.**
   $$f_{1,1} = \frac{1.12^2}{1.11} - 1 = \frac{\text{Accumulated wealth of \$1}}{\text{invested in two-year bond at end of year 2}} - 1$$

   Accumulated wealth of \$1
invested in two-year bond at end of year 2
   Accumulated wealth of \$1
invested in one-year bond at end of year 1

   $$= 0.13, \text{ or } 13\%$$

   $$f_{1,2} = \frac{1.115^3}{1.12^2} - 1$$

   $$= 0.1051, \text{ or } 10.51\%$$

   b. In one year, the expected one-year rate is 13%, according to part a. To find the expected two-year rate, we would use Equation 11.4:

$$I_2 = [(1.13)(1.1051)]^{1/2} - 1$$

$$= 0.1175, \text{ or } 11.75\%$$

   c. Investing $1 in a three-year bond will produce a value of $1.115^3 = \$1.3862$ at the end of year 3. Investing $1 in a one-year bond will produce a value of $1.11 at the end of year 1. For $1.11 to grow to $1.3862 two years later, the average compound return (remember $\bar{G}$?) would be

$$\left[\frac{1.3862}{1.11}\right]^{1/2} - 1 = 0.1175, \text{ or } 11.75\%$$

   d. Since the implied forward rate for year 3 is 10.51% (from part a above), you would want to lock in that rate instead of eventually receiving the expected spot of 8% in year 3.

	End-of-Period Cash In (Out)			
Transaction	0	1	2	3
Buy 1.0 three-year bond 1,000/1.115³	(721.40)	—	—	1,000
Sell short 0.9049 two-year bond at				
a price of 797.19 = 1,000/1.12²	721.40	—	(940.90)	
	0	0	(904.90)	1,000
			Net Return =	10.51%

e.

	Nominal	—	Real	=	Average Yearly Inflation
1 year	11.0%	—	3.0%	=	8.0%
2 year	12.0%	—	3.0%	=	9.0%
3 year	11.5%	—	3.0%	=	8.5%

(Note that this calculation does not allow for the interaction term in the Fisher equation (Equation 5.1) in Chapter 5. This is often done because of its small numerical value.)

f. The one-year return from buying a three-year bond and selling in a year is not known with certainty but is expected to be 11.0%. Note that this 11% return expected during the next year on the current three-year bond is identical to the *known* return on current one-year bonds.

	Today	Year 1
Buy at 1,000/(1.115³)	(721.40)	
Sell at 1,000/(1.1175²)		800.76

Return = 11.00%

The 11.75% expected yield on two-year bonds at the start of year 2 comes from part c above.

QUESTIONS AND PROBLEMS

1. High-coupon bonds are less price sensitive to interest rate moves than are lower-coupon bonds. Why is this so?
2. National Aviation has three bond issues of similar risk outstanding:

Issue	Par	Maturity	Coupon	Current Price
A	$1,000	5 years	7%	$ 922.30
B	1,000	10 years	10%	1,210.40
C	1,000	10 years	4%	788.96

   a. What is the yield to maturity on each of these issues?
   b. Note that the yields to maturity for bonds B and C are equal. Is this likely to be the case if capital gains tax rates are lower than ordinary tax rates?
   c. Without calculating prices, which of these three bonds will experience the greatest percentage price appreciation if yields to maturity fall by 100 basis points on each? Why?
   d. Between bonds B and C, which will experience the greatest percentage price appreciation if yields to maturity on each fall by 100 basis points? Why?
   e. Assume yields do drop by 100 basis points. Find the new market price of each

3. Describe the rationale suggested by believers in MST for changes in the level and shape of the yield curve over the course of a classic business cycle.

4. What is an implied forward rate of interest? How can a forward rate be locked in by using existing yields on bonds of various maturities?

5. How does Fisher's theory of nominal interest rates fit into the UET approach to yield curves?

6. *Describe* carefully the *immediate* effects on the money and capital markets of each of the following events. Consider each of the events independently.

   a. An increase in policy loans by life insurance companies.

   b. Revision of federal income tax laws to permit issuers to deduct dividends on preferred stocks in arriving at corporate taxable income. The 85% dividend income exclusion available to corporate investors will be unchanged.

   Note: Answer this question from the viewpoint of both MST and UET.

7. a. Draw a series of yield curves that should be in evidence on each of the following dates:

   Date 1—Relatively stable prices and money supply

   Date 2—Rapidly rising rates of inflation

   Date 3—The bottom of an economic downturn

   Date 4—The top of an expansionary cycle

   b. As an aggressive portfolio manager of a moderate-sized, taxable fund comprised solely of fixed-income securities, discuss the strategies you would employ to optimize rates of return. Assume that quality guidelines must be maintained and that you expect interest rates will:

   - Decline
   - Rise

8. The yield to maturity on a pure discount five-year bond is 8.7%. The yield to maturity on a six-year bond (of equal risk) is 9.0%. Calculate the implied one-year forward rate for the start of year 6.

9. The yield to maturity on a five-year bond is currently 8%, the yield to maturity on a six-year bond is 9%, and the yield to maturity on a seven-year bond is 9.5%.

   a. Calculate the implied forward rate on a *one*-year bond at the start of year 6.

   b. Calculate the implied forward rate on a *two*-year bond at the start of year 6.

10. If 20-year riskless bonds (say, pure discount U.S. T-bonds) are currently yielding 8% to maturity and similar five-year bonds are now yielding 8.5% to maturity, what is the expected rate on a 15-year bond that will *start* at the end of year 5? How might a speculator lock in this rate? Prove with calculations.

11. Assume two pure discount bonds are available. Bond X is selling at $926 and matures in one year. Bond Y is selling at $873 and matures in two years.

   a. Outline a strategy to lock in a forward rate for year 2.

   b. What return is locked in by this strategy?

   c. If you expect that in a year from now, one-year rates will be 8%, should you proceed with this transaction? If not, what should be done?

   d. What does UET say about the transaction in part c—that is, is it valid or not? Why?

12. National Products, Inc., has just issued a 10-year bond at par that pays an annual coupon of 12%. The issue is first callable at $1,120 per bond any time after the first four years of the bond's life. In answering the following questions, assume that neither you nor NPI will incur any transaction costs in future bond transactions.

   a. If NPI does call the bond at the *start* of year 5, what is the internal rate of return earned by the firm?

   b. If you expect that *YTM*s on six-year bonds will be 8% at the *start* of year 5, do you expect NPI to call the issue?

   c. Assume that the yield curve is flat and remains constant at 12% during years 1, 2, 3, and 4. At the start of year 5, however, the yield curve drops to 8%. NPI calls the bond issue and you use the proceeds to reinvest in a new six-year bond at par. Subsequently, yields remain at 8%. What is your 10-year return?

13. Interest rates on Aa Corporate bonds with a 10-year maturity presently trade at an 8% *YTM*. Similar municipal bonds have a 6% *YTM*.

   a. John Sterns's marginal tax bracket is 30%. Should he purchase the corporates or the municipal bonds?

   b. At what tax bracket would a person be indifferent between the two security types?

   c. Endowment funds and pension funds do not pay taxes. Should they ever purchase municipal bonds?

   d. Mutual funds do not pay taxes. Should they ever purchase municipal bonds?

14. Century Savings is a large savings and loan company with one type of debt outstanding—certificates of deposit that promise to pay a total of $100 million in exactly one year. The risk-free interest rate is 8%. (You can assume this is a continuous compound rate.) The current market value of loans owned by Century Savings is equal to $110 million. The expected 1-year return and standard deviation on these assets are 10% and 7%.

   a. Value the equity position as a call option on the firm's assets.

   b. Given this call value, what is the current value of the CDs?

   c. What is the yield to maturity and default risk premium on the CDs?

   d. What would happen to default risk if management sold current assets and purchased new assets with a higher expected return and risk?

   e. If the federal government guarantees par repayment to all owners of the CDs, who bears the default risk?

15. The following are the average yields on U.S. T-bonds at two different points in time:

	Yield-to-Maturity	
Term to Maturity	January 15, 19XX	May 15, 19XX
1 year	7.25%	8.05%
2 years	7.50%	7.90%
5 years	7.90%	7.70%
10 years	8.30%	7.45%
15 years	8.45%	7.30%
20 years	8.55%	7.20%
25 years	8.60%	7.10%

   a. Assuming a pure expectations hypothesis, **define** a forward rate. **Describe** how you would calculate the forward rate for a three-year U.S. T-bond two years from May 15, 19XX using the actual term structure above.

   b. **Discuss** how *each* of the *three* major term structure hypotheses could explain the January 15, 19XX term structure shown above.

   c. **Discuss** what happened to the term structure over the time period and the effect of this change on U.S. T-bonds of 2 years *and* 10 years.

   d. Assume that you invest solely on the basis of yield spreads, and in January 19XX acted upon the expectation that the yield spread between 1-year and 25-year U.S. Treasuries would return to a more typical spread of 170 basis points. **Explain** what you would have done on January 15, 19XX, and **describe** the result of this action based upon what happened between January 15, 19XX and May 15, 19XX.

16. The investment committee of the money management firm of Gentry, Inc. has typically been very conservative and has avoided investing in high-yield (junk) bonds, although they have had major positions in investment-grade corporate bonds. Recently, Pete

Squire, a member of the committee, suggested that they should review their policy regarding junk bonds because they currently constitute over 25% of the total corporate bond market.

As a part of this policy review, you are asked to respond to the following questions.

a. Briefly discuss the liquidity *and* pricing characteristics of junk bonds relative to *each* of the following types of fixed income securities:

- Treasuries;
- high-grade corporate bonds;
- corporate loans; and
- private placements.

Briefly discuss the implications of these differences for Gentry's bond portfolio managers.

The committee has learned that the correlation of rates of return between Treasuries and high-grade corporate bonds is approximately 0.98, while the correlation between Treasury/high-grade corporate bonds and junk bonds is approximately 0.45.

b. Briefly explain the reason for this difference in correlations, and **briefly discuss** its implications for bond portfolios.

DATAFILE ANALYSIS

1. Review the yield curve information that is provided in the datafile labeled "INTRATES.WK1". Plot the yield curves for the end of 1971, 1981, 1991, and the current curve. You will have to refer to the financial section of a newspaper to obtain data about the current yield curve. Explain why these yield curves have been so variable.

REFERENCES

Textbooks that treat yields to maturity in detail include:

LIVINGSTON, MILES. *Money and Capital Markets,* Kolb Publishing. Miami, FL. 1993.

VAN HORNE, JAMES C. *Financial Market Rates and Flows,* Prentice-Hall. Englewood Cliffs, NJ.1984.

Default risk studies include:

FISCHER, LAWRENCE, "Determinants of Risk Premiums on Corporate Bonds," *Journal of Political Economy,* June 1959.

FRAINE, H. G., and R. MILLS, "Effects of Defaults and Credit Deterioration on Yields of Corporate Bonds," *Journal of Finance,* September 1961.

A mathematically difficult but seminal paper on yield curve theory is:

COX, JOHN, JONATHAN INGERSOLL, and STEPHEN ROSS, "A Reexamination of Traditional Hypotheses About the Term Structure of Interest Rates," *Journal of Finance,* September 1981.

There have been numerous recent studies of the junk bond market. Two reviews are:

ALTMAN, EDWARD I., "Setting the Record Straight on Junk Bonds: A Review of the Research on Default Rates and Returns," *Journal of Applied Corporate Finance,* Summer 1990.

CORNELL, BRADFORD and KEVIN GREEN, "The Investment Performance of Low-Grade Bond Funds," *Journal of Finance,* March 1991.

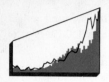

Bond Trading

The value of publicly traded fixed income securities represents about one-half the value of all traded financial assets. In this chapter we examine how individuals and portfolio managers can manage their bond holdings. We look at both active management techniques and passive strategies.

Active bond management involves trading strategies designed to take advantage of mispriced securities. For example, a bond trader might find equivalent risk collateralized mortgage obligations trading at different prices or believe that the yield to maturity spreads between U.S. Treasuries and AAA Corporate bonds will soon narrow. Passive strategies assume that security prices are efficiently priced and that the costs associated with identifying mispriced bonds exceed potential trading gains. Passive strategies look at why bonds should be held in a given portfolio. For example, what portion of the investor's total portfolio should be allocated to fixed income securities, what maturity structure should be held, whether interest rate risk should be immunized, and so forth. Interest rate immunization involves trading strategies in which the investor is unaffected by any changes in interest rates. But before discussing active and passive management, it is important that we understand why realized returns on fixed income securities will likely be different from promised yields to maturity.

REALIZED BOND RETURNS AND RISK

Yield to maturity is a *promised* rate of return that will actually be earned only under very restricted assumptions. In this section we develop the notion of a *realized bond return* and discuss why it differs from the promised yield to maturity.

The Horizon Date and Realized Returns

Securities are bought to be sold. When an investor purchases a security, it is with the hopes of earning a fair rate of return up to some terminal *horizon date,* at which time the security will be sold to provide cash for current consumption. For example, college students may need cash in a few years to support graduate education. A husband and wife may be investing to provide cash during retirement ten to fifteen years away, and insurance firms will invest to provide cash to service expected future insurance claims. All of these investors have a horizon date in mind at which time they expect to sell their securities.[1] Speculators also have a terminal horizon date at which they expect to conclude a given security transaction. The concept of horizon date (*HD*) is crucial to an understanding of bond yields, risks, and trading strategies.

Consider the situation of Continental Casualty Corporation, a medium-sized casualty insurance firm. CCC has just begun to offer a new type of insurance policy which is expected to require cash to meet insured losses three years after each new policy is signed. Thus, *HD* equals three years. All insurance premiums are paid when the policy is signed, and these proceeds are invested in bonds. In a sense, CCC is indifferent to intermediate yearly returns on its bond investments. The important consideration is the amount of net profit available in year 3 after all insurance losses are paid. For example, assume that each policy provides CCC with a $1,000 premium at the start of year 1 which may be invested for three years, at which time the investments will have to be sold to pay expected insurance losses of, say, $1,225. If the investment of $1,000 grows to a value greater than $1,225 by the end of year 3, the firm will have earned a profit. If the $1,000 investment grows to only $1,225 (or less), the firm will just break even (or incur losses). The *sequence* of yearly rates of return on CCC's bond investments is of little importance. Instead, the firm is interested in the terminal worth of its investments at the end of year 3—the horizon date.

Consider the following three alternative sequences of yearly returns:

	Return During Year		
Series	*1*	*2*	*3*
A	6.10%	5.00%	10.00%
B	20.00%	−10.00%	13.40%
C	9.00%	4.00%	8.07%

In each case a $1,000 investment grows to exactly $1,225 by the end of year 3:

Series	Horizon Date *Value*		*Details*
A	$1,225	=	$1,000 (1.061 × 1.05 × 1.1)
B	1,225	=	1,000 (1.20 × 0.9 × 1.134)
C	1,225	=	1,000 (1.09 × 1.04 × 1.0807)

Even though each series has a different *sequence* of yearly returns, CCC should be indifferent among them. Each provides the same terminal wealth. Expressed in the form of a rate of return, each series provides the same average *annual*

---

[1] Clearly, most individuals will have a *number* of horizon dates in mind. For example, a retired couple may intend to sell a portion of their security portfolio at the start of each year to meet that year's consumption needs. For simplicity's sake, however, we will restrict our discussion to a single date.

realized rate of return. The *annual realized return* on a bond investment will be denoted as *ARR* and represents the constant annual discount rate that will discount the horizon date value of a bond investment back to the initial dollar investment made. Mathematically:

$$\text{Initial Investment Value} = \frac{\text{Horizon Date Investment Value}}{(1 + ARR)^{HD}} \qquad \textbf{(12.1a)}$$

or

$$\textbf{Annual Realized} \atop \textbf{Return} \quad ARR = {}^{HD}\!\sqrt{\frac{\text{Horizon Date Investment Value}}{\text{Initial Investment Value}}} - 1.0 \qquad \textbf{(12.1b)}$$

where *HD* represents the number of years to the horizon date. In the CCC example the *ARR* would be 7.0% regardless of which series of yearly returns is earned:

$$\sqrt[3]{\frac{\$1,225}{\$1,000}} - 1.0 = 7.0\%$$

Determinants of *ARR*

The annual realized return on a bond investment is determined by the size of the investment's horizon-date dollar value. Anything that can change the *HD* value will change the *ARR*. Factors that can change this *HD* value include:

1. Changes in the general level of interest rates affecting:
   a. The bond's *HD* market value
   b. Earnings on the reinvestment of coupons
2. Characteristics of the individual bond investment, including:
   a. The bond's coupon rate
   b. The bond's potential default
   c. The bond's potential call

As an illustration, start by assuming that a 9% noncallable, four-year, default-free bond could be bought today for $1,000. Since the bond is selling at par, its promised *YTM* is equal to 9%—the coupon rate. Also assume that the yield curve is flat, the bond is held for three years, and *the level of interest rates remains unchanged at 9%*. What will the *ARR* be? To determine this, we need to know what the year 3 *HD* value will be. This value consists of the following components: the market value of the bond, the receipt of all coupons, and the receipt of interest earned on reinvestment of coupons.

The market value of the bond will be $1,000 at the end of year 3 since interest rates don't change. In total, $270 in coupons will have been received (three years times $90 per year). Finally, $25 in *interest earned on interest* will have been received: two years' interest on the first $90 coupon payment ($90 × 1.09² −

$90) plus one year's interest on the second coupon ($90 $\times$ 1.09 $-$ $90). Thus, the investment value at the end of year 3 will sum to $1,295:

Component	HD Value
Market Value of Bond	$1,000
Receipt of Coupons	270
Interest on Interest	25
Total	$1,295

The *ARR* will equal 9.0%:

$$\sqrt[3]{\frac{\$1,295}{\$1,000}} - 1.0 = 9.0\%$$

In this case the *ARR* does equal the promised *YTM*. But this occurs only because the following conditions are met: (1) *interest rates in the economy don't change* from 9%, resulting in a constant market value of $1,000 and reinvestment of coupons at a rate equal to the promised *YTM*; (2) the bond *does not default*; and (3) the bond *isn't called.*

Now let's change one assumption—the level of interest rates. Assume that immediately after the bond is bought at par, the level of interest rates increases to 10% and remains there. At the end of year 3 the $1,000 investment will be worth $1,288.81:

Component	HD Value	Details
Market Value of Bond	$ 990.91	($1,090 $\div$ 1.1)
Receipt of Coupons	270.00	
Interest on Interest	27.90	[$90(1.10^2) - \$90] + [\$90(1.10) - \$90]$
Total	$1,288.81	

Now the *ARR* will be 8.82%:

$$\sqrt[3]{\frac{\$1,288.81}{\$1,000.00}} - 1.0 = 8.82\%$$

Determinants of Bond Risk

Anything that influences the distribution of realized horizon date returns also affects bond risk.

Default Risk. If the issuer of a bond is unable to make all coupon and principal payments as promised, realized yields will be less than promised. The greater the uncertainty about default, the greater the uncertainty about realized returns that might be available at some horizon date.

Call Risk. Issuers are often allowed to retire a bond issue prior to scheduled maturity. As a result, investors are uncertain that coupon and principal payments will be made as scheduled in the indenture agreement. Call risk is discussed later in the chapter.

Reinvestment Rate Risk. Uncertainty about possible shifts in the yield curve creates an uncertainty about future returns from coupon reinvestment. If future reinvestment rates are different from a bond's promised *YTM*, its realized *YTM* will not equal its promised yield. The same is true for yields to horizon dates. If reinvestment rates between now and a future horizon date are uncertain, realized returns as of that horizon date will also be uncertain.

Price Risk. Bond prices are inversely related to required rates of return. If required returns increase, bond prices fall, and vice versa. The only date at which a bond's price is certain is at maturity (barring default or call). As a result, price risk exists whenever an individual's horizon date and a bond's maturity differ.

How to Reduce Interest Rate Risk

Default and call risks cannot be eliminated, and required bond yields must be adjusted for the relative degrees of each. However, reinvestment rate and price risk *can* be virtually eliminated by selecting appropriate bond lives. Reinvestment rate risk and price risk both arise from uncertainty about future interest rates. In fact, both risks are aspects of a more basic risk: *interest rate risk.* But note that changes in interest rates work in opposite directions on reinvestment and price risks. If interest rates increase, reinvestment income *increases* whereas bond prices *decline.* Conversely, a reduction in interest rates causes reinvestment income to *decline* and bond prices to *increase.* Since the two forces move in opposite directions, it is possible for the favorable impacts of one to exactly offset the unfavorable impacts of the other. This is the basic concept behind strategies that *immunize* a portfolio against interest rate risk. The fact that reinvestment rate risk and price risk can offset each other by proper selection of a bond's maturity has only recently been fully understood. Because of its growing importance in both investment theory and practice, we will spend considerable time with the concept in this chapter.

Consider the following situation. You are the investment adviser for Anne Curat. Anne has just come to you with $100,000 which she wishes to invest for *exactly* 4.24 years. She states that the investment must be in default-free, non-callable bonds. Anne will pay you a commission based upon how close her realized *HD* return is to what you initially promise. After a quick survey you believe the following opportunities are available to her:

Bond	Coupon	Maturity	Promised YTM	Current Price
A	0%	4.24 years	9%	$ 693.92
B	9	2.00	9	1,000.00
C	9	20.00	9	1,000.00
D	9	5.00	9	1,000.00

In addition, the yield curve is now flat and is expected to stay flat.

If interest rates don't change between now and 4.24 years from now, you really don't have a problem; each of the four bonds would provide a 9% realized return. But since interest rates may well change, you are somewhat uncertain about each bond's realized return over the 4.24-year period. Indeed, you foresee the possibility that immediately after the $100,000 is invested, interest rates may rise to 11% or fall to 7%. What should you do? First, promise Anne a 9% realized yield and then consider each bond in turn.

Bond *A* is a zero-coupon bond maturing in exactly 4.24 years. Since all of its yield comes in the form of price appreciation, it is not exposed to price or reinvestment risk. Its realized return will be 9%, regardless of future shifts in the yield curve.[2] Bonds *B*, *C*, and *D* will each be exposed to varying degrees of price and reinvestment rate risk. Bond *B* has a maturity much shorter than the 4.24-year *HD* and will be exposed to considerable reinvestment rate risk. When bond *B* matures in two years, a new bond will have to be bought at a *YTM* which is currently uncertain. Bond *C* matures after the horizon date and will be exposed to considerable price risk since its market value in 4.24 years will depend upon yields at that date, which are currently uncertain. Bond *D* matures slightly after the horizon date and will be exposed about equally to both reinvestment rate and price risks.

This can be seen in Table 12-1, where *HD* cash values are calculated for each bond and for each possible shift in the yield curve. Realized yields for bonds *B*

---

[2] $\text{Year 4.24 Investment Value} = \$100,000 \times \dfrac{\$1,000}{\$693.92} = \$144,108.83$

$$ARR = \sqrt[4.24]{\$144,108.83/\$100,000} - 1.0 = 9.00\%$$

TABLE 12-1 Bond Values in 4.24 Years Considering Reinvestment and Price Risks

Interest Rate	Price at Horizon Date*	+	Total† Coupons	+	Interest on Intermediate Cash Flows	=	Horizon Date Cash Value	Realized Returns
Bond B:								
7%	$1,016	+	$320	+	$44	=	$1,380	7.89%
9%	1,021	+	360	+	60	=	1,441	9.00%
11%	1,025	+	400	+	78	=	1,503	10.09%
Bond C:								
7%	1,208	+	360	+	46	=	1,614	11.95%
9%	1,021	+	360	+	60	=	1,441	9.00%
11%	874	+	360	+	75	=	1,309	6.56%
Bond D:								
7%	1,035	+	360	+	46	=	1,441	9.00%
9%	1,021	+	360	+	60	=	1,441	9.00%
11%	1,006	+	360	+	75	=	1,441	9.00%

* Includes interest accrued in year 5.
† Coupons are paid annually.

and *C* are clearly uncertain. If the yield curve falls to 7%, realized yields on *B* will be less than 9% because of lower investment rates, and they will be higher than 9% for *C* since its price increases more than enough to offset lower reinvestment rates. If the yield curve increases to 11%, the opposite will occur. Bond *B* will have a return greater than 9% because of improved reinvestment rates, and *C* will have a lower return because its price decline more than offsets larger interest on interest.

Notice the curious results for bond *D*. Regardless of shifts in the yield curve, it provides a 9% realized yield. Why? The answer lies in the fact that *D*'s reinvestment rate and price risks exactly *offset* each other. *The coupon rate and maturity of bond* D *were selected so that the "average date" of its cash flows is exactly 4.24 years hence.* While *D* repays principal of $1,000 at the end of five years, cash is received in the form of $90 coupons at each year-end. The average date at which a dollar of cash is received on bond *D* is 4.24 years. Economically, bond *D* is equivalent to a 4.24-year, zero-coupon bond.

Macaulay Duration

Frederick Macaulay was the first to term the "average date" at which cash is received on a bond as *duration*. His estimate of a bond's duration is appropriately called Macaulay Duration. It is calculated as follows:

Macauley Duration
$$D = \sum_{t=1}^{M}\left[\frac{t \times PV_t}{\displaystyle\sum_{t=1}^{M} PV_t}\right]$$
(12.2)

where *D* = the duration of a bond, *t* = a given year number, *M* = the number of years to maturity, PV_t = the present value of cash flows received in year *t*, and ΣPV_t = the present value of all cash flows (the bond's price). Bond *D*'s duration is shown below. First, the present value of each year's cash flows is found using the bond's promised *YTM* as the discount rate. These are then stated as a percentage of the total present value. Finally, these percentages are multiplied by the year number in which the cash flow is received and summed.

Year	Cash Flow	Present Value	Percentage of Total	Year Number	Product
1	$ 90	$ 82.57	8.257%	1	0.0826
2	90	75.75	7.575	2	0.1515
3	90	69.50	6.950	3	0.2085
4	90	63.76	6.376	4	0.2550
5	1,090	708.42	70.842	5	3.5421
		$1,000.00		D =	4.2397 years

A Simple Approach to Calculating D. The calculation of *D* in Equation 12.2 may appear quite imposing. But the logic behind it is really very simple. To illustrate this, consider again the cash flow data on the five-year, 9% coupon bond discussed above. This bond promises to pay $90 at each year-end plus $1,090 at its maturity in five years. Now, consider this to be not one bond, *but a portfolio of five distinctly different bonds.* The first bond in this portfolio matures in one year and pays $90. The second bond matures in two years and has one cash payment equal to $90 at its maturity, and so forth. Finally, the last bond matures in five years and pays a single cash flow of $1,090 at its maturity. In short, our original bond is now considered to be a portfolio of *five different zero-coupon bonds.*

What is the duration of each of these zero-coupon bonds? Since each provides cash at one date only (its maturity), *the duration of each is identical to its maturity.* The duration of the one-year $90 bond is one year, the duration of the two-year $90 bond is two years, and so forth. We are just about ready to calculate the duration of this portfolio of five bonds. But to do so we must know that *the duration of a portfolio is equal to the weighted average duration of the bonds held in the portfolio*; that is:

Duration of a Portfolio
$$D_P = \sum_{i=1}^{N} X_i D_i \qquad (12.3)$$

where D_P represents the portfolio's duration, D_i represents the duration of i, and X_i is the percentage of the portfolio invested in bond i.

Look again at the duration calculation for the original five-year, 9% coupon bond which we are now considering to be a portfolio of five zero-coupon bonds. The dollar investment made in the one-year zero-coupon bond is $82.57—the present value of $90 received in one year. The dollar investment made in the two-year zero-coupon bond is $75.75—the present value of its $90 maturity cash payment in two years, and so forth. The total value of this portfolio is $1,000. Thus, X_1 is equal to 8.26%, X_2 is equal to 7.58%, . . . , and X_5 is equal to 70.84%. We can now use Equation 12.3 to calculate the portfolio's duration:

$$D_P = X_1 D_1 + X_2 D_2 + X_3 D_3 + X_4 D_4 + X_5 D_5$$

$$= 0.08257(1) + 0.07575(2) + 0.06950(3) + 0.06376(4) + 0.70842(5)$$

$$= 4.2397 \text{ years}$$

The number and types of calculations we have just used to find the bond's duration are identical to those in Equation 12.2. But we have employed a convenient mental device that allows us to calculate a bond's duration without having to memorize Equation 12.2. All we have to do is consider a coupon bond to be a portfolio of many zero-coupon securities and recognize that the duration of a portfolio is the weighted average of the duration of the securities held in the portfolio.

Modified Duration. The Macaulay Duration Equation makes two assumptions about yield curves. First, by discounting all future cash flows at a single yield to maturity, we are implicitly assuming that the yield curve is flat—that all cash flows *should be* discounted at the same interest rate. Second, if yield curves are flat, then any change in the level of rates must be identical for all maturities. If one-year rates rise by 100 basis points, *YTM*s of 20-year bonds also rise by 100 basis points. (Conceptually, this means that all forward rates are identical.)

These assumptions, of course, do not reflect the yield curves of actual bonds. A number of modifications have been made to the duration equation suggested by Macaulay in an attempt to provide better duration estimates. But these modifications usually result in duration measures close to Macaulay durations. And no perfect measure of a bond's true duration will be possible until we are able to reliably explain the process underlying shifts in yield curves. In short, Macaulay duration measures are reasonable estimates of a bond's effective maturity.

Reducing Interest Rate Risk. Figure 12-1 illustrates the relationship between a bond portfolio's duration, the investment horizon of the portfolio (HD) and net interest rate risk.

Inherent default and call risks are unaffected by duration or the investor's *HD*. However, reinvestment and price risks are. Whenever a bond's duration is shorter than the *HD*, uncertainty about future reinvestment rates dominates price risks and a *net reinvestment rate risk* exists. Whenever a bond's duration is longer than the *HD*, uncertainty about future price levels dominates reinvestment risks and a *net price risk* exists. However, *these two risks exactly offset each other when the duration equals the HD.*

A bond portfolio that has a duration equal to the investment horizon date faces no interest rate risk and is said to be *immunized.* Bond immunization does work in practice. For example, Fisher and Weil examined the standard deviation of bond returns for three different horizon dates (5 years, 10 years, and 20 years) using two alternative investment strategies. In strategy 1 a bond portfolio with a 20-year maturity was constantly held. At the start of each year, 20-year bonds were bought, and the old bonds (which would then have a 19-year maturity) were

FIGURE 12-1 *Duration, Horizon Date, and Bond Risks*

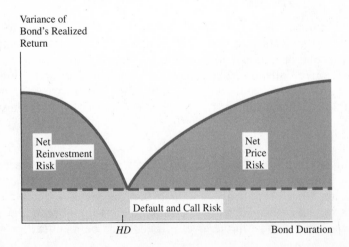

sold. In strategy 2 they constantly held bonds with a maturity equal to the desired *HD*. Their data consisted of yearly returns on long-term, high-grade corporate bonds between 1925 and 1968.[3] If bond immunization works, the standard deviation of actual realized returns from expected realized returns should be lower in strategy 2. Results are shown below.

Length of Horizon Date	Standard Deviation of Differences Between Expected Versus Actual Horizon Date Investment Value	
	Strategy 1	Strategy 2
5 years	0.115	0.0026
10	0.174	0.0120
20	0.182	0.0290

SOURCE: Reprinted from "Coping with the Risk of Interest-Rate Fluctuations: Returns to Bondholders from Naive and Optimal Strategies," *Journal of Business* 44, no. 3 (October 1971) by L. Fisher and R. Weil, by permission of The University of Chicago Press. © 1971 by The University of Chicago. All rights reserved.

The values represent the standard deviation of differences between expected and actual *HD* wealth assuming an initial portfolio value of $1. Clearly, the duration strategy provided the smallest variation in *HD* wealth.

Immunization Does Not Guarantee Real Returns. A portfolio that is immunized against interest rate risk guarantees a *nominal* rate of return over the portfolio's investment horizon. The real return to the portfolio, however, is uncertain. For example, if you wish to purchase a home in one year, then one-year T-bills provide a certain nominal dollar value in a year. But since home prices are affected by inflation during the year the ownership of one-year T-bills does not guarantee that you will have enough money to purchase a home. Immunization can conceptually eliminate interest rate risk. It has nothing to do with inflation uncertainty.

Before you decide to immunize a portfolio from interest rate risk, be clear about its purpose: are real or nominal returns desired? If the answer is nominal returns, then a totally risk-free portfolio (no default, call, or interest rate risk) is possible. If the answer is real returns, then a risk-free portfolio is not possible.

Bond Price Changes. While not exact, the following relationship exists between percentage bond price changes, duration, and changes in a bond's *YTM*:

$$\frac{\% \text{ Change in}}{\text{Bond Prices}} \approx -D \left[\frac{\% \text{ Change in}}{(1 + YTM)} \right] \quad \textbf{(12.4a)}$$

For example, assume that the *YTM* on a bond is expected to decline from 11% to 10% in the near future. If the bond has a four-year duration, the expected price increase is (*about*) 3.6%:

$$-4 \left(\frac{1.10 - 1.11}{1.11} \right) = 3.6\%$$

---

[3] Since a bond's maturity is not the same as its duration (except for zero-coupon bonds), Fisher and Weil's test was only an approximation of the duration strategy.

Speculators needn't examine maturity and coupon effects separately, since both are included in the duration measure. If interest rates are expected to fall across all maturities, buy bonds with a long duration. If yields are expected to change by different amounts in each duration range, buy bonds with a duration which will provide the largest return per Equation 12.4.

Rebalancing. The reason Equation 12.4 is not exact is due to the fact that duration is dependent on the level of interest rates. Any time the level of interest rates changes, a bond's duration will change. For example, the duration of a three-year, 10% coupon bond selling at a *YTM* of 12% would be 2.73 years. If interest rates suddenly fell to 8%, the bond's new *D* value would be 2.74 years. Although the change in *D* in this example appears small, much larger differences would be obtained if a bond with a longer maturity had been used. The important point, however, is that duration is inversely related to the level of interest rates. If *YTM*s rise, *D* falls. If *YTM*s fall, *D* increases.

An investor with a 2.73-year horizon date could immunize against interest rate risks by holding the 10% coupon, three-year issue when rates are 12%. If rates do fall to 8%, the gain in the value of the bond's price (expected 2.73 years hence) will exactly offset the lower returns available from coupon reinvestments. The investor would be immunized against this first shock to interest rate levels. However, once this shock has occurred, the duration of all bonds held will change. The portfolio will have to be *rebalanced*.

Conceptually, every time interest rates increase, the duration of a bond portfolio is shortened. To remain immunized, the portfolio should be rebalanced by purchasing bonds with a longer duration than the portfolio would then have. For example, if the investor's *HD* is 5.0 years, bonds with an initial weighted average duration of 5.0 years would be held. If interest rates were to rise suddenly, the investor would gain enough from higher-coupon reinvestment returns to exactly offset the decrease in bond prices expected at the horizon date. However, after the rate increase there would be a mismatch between the *HD* and the *now* shorter-term *D* value. In order to remain immunized, the investor would have to decrease percentage holdings of shorter-duration securities and increase holdings of longer-duration bonds.

Exactly the opposite situation would occur if interest rates fell. In that case the investor would be immunized against a *single* shock to rates by having price gains offset coupon reinvestment losses. However, unless the portfolio is rebalanced after the change, *D* would be longer than *HD*, and the investor would be exposed to interest rate risk. To remain immunized, the investor should increase holdings of shorter-duration instruments and reduce holdings of long-duration instruments. Of course, it is impractical to continually rebalance the bond portfolio for every change in interest rates; the transaction costs would be phenomenal. In practice, many portfolio managers rebalance yearly. While this doesn't eliminate interest rate risk, it does keep transaction costs to a reasonable level.

The degree to which duration changes as the yield to maturity changes is referred to as bond *convexity*. Large convexity implies large changes in duration

FIGURE 12-2 *Bond Price vs.* **YTM**

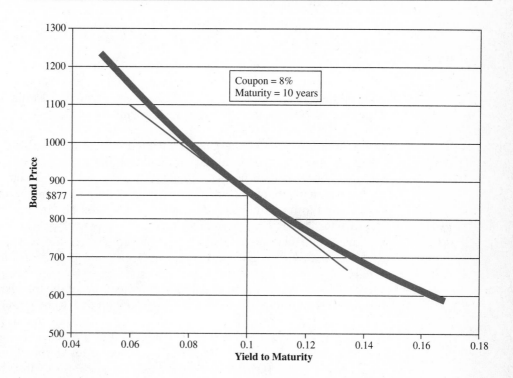

and, in turn, inaccurate forecasts of price changes in Equation (12.4a). Convexity is largest for:

1. low-coupon bonds
2. long-maturity bonds
3. low yields to maturity

Consider the relationship displayed in Figure 12-2. The price of a 10-year, 8% coupon bond is shown on the vertical axis for various yields to maturity on the horizontal axis. As the figure shows, the bond would be worth $877.11 at a *YTM* of 10%. At its present price, the duration of this bond is 7.043946 years.

What would be the bond's change in price if interest rates were to increase to 11%? Equation 12.4a would predict a negative 6.40359% price change, meaning a $56.17 decline:

$$-\$56.17 = -7.043936\,[0.10 \div 1.10]\,\$877.11$$

But if one calculates the new price at a *YTM* of 11%, the new price would be $823.32—an actual price drop of $53.79.

The reason for the difference between the predicted and actual price change is that duration applies to a given current *YTM* level and changes as the *YTM* changes. It involves the slope (or first derivative) of the "price–*YTM*" curve. Using Equation 12.4a, we can calculate this slope as:

$$\frac{\text{Change in}}{\text{Bond Price}} = -D[\% \text{ change in } YTM][\text{Current Price}] \qquad \textbf{(12.4b)}$$

Convexity represents the second derivative of the "price–*YTM*" curve. In the example shown, convexity is negative. As *YTM* increases, the slope of the "price–*YTM*" curve decreases. Active bond managers give considerable thought to the duration and convexity of the bond instruments they trade.

Bullet Immunization Versus Cash Dedicated Portfolios. Assume that you are the administrator of a pension fund. The fund will have payment obligations of two types: (1) future benefit payments to current employees and (2) current and future benefit payments to retired employees ("retired lives"). Immunized portfolios are widely used to fund the pension's retired-life portion but are less used for active employees. This is because retired-life benefit payments can be projected more accurately and because benefits to current employees are real-dollar liabilities (tied to inflation through salary growth). Real-dollar liabilities *cannot* be immunized.

Table 12-2 gives hypothetical actuarial projections of the total benefits that will be paid to retired lives. Instead of a single horizon date to be immunized, a series of many horizon dates exists. Each could be immunized separately, of course, but it would be easier and cheaper if they could all be immunized at one time. This is really very simple to do. Instead of using the series of many horizon dates, a single weighted average horizon date is calculated in exactly the same way that a bond's duration is calculated.

For example, let's assume that interest rates are 10% for all maturities. In order to fund the $5 million due at the end of year 1, $4,545,454.54 in zero-coupon, one-year duration bonds would have to be bought ($5 million ÷ 1.10). Similarly, to fund the $5 million due at the end of year 2, $4,132,231.41 would have to be bought ($5 million ÷ 1.10^2). Continuing with the other liabilities, a total investment of $21.47 million would be required. The duration of these liabilities is calculated below in the same fashion that the duration of a bond is calculated.

Year	Current Funding Requirement	Percentage of Total	Weighted Average Liability Duration
1	$ 4.54 million	21.15%	0.2115
2	4.13	19.24	0.3847
3	3.01	14.02	0.4206
4	2.73	12.72	0.5086
5	2.48	11.55	0.5776
6	1.69	7.87	0.4723
7	1.54	7.17	0.5021
8	0.93	4.33	0.3465
9	0.42	1.96	0.1761
10	0.00	—	—
Total	$21.47 million	100.00%	3.6000 years

TABLE 12.2 *Hypothetical Pension Fund—Total Benefits Paid to Retired Lives*

End of Year	Pension Obligation	End of Year	Pension Obligation
1	$5 million	6	$3 million
2	5	7	3
3	4	8	2
4	4	9	1
5	4	10	0

The weighted average duration of these liabilities is 3.6 years. To immunize this liability series, $21.47 million must be invested in bonds which have a portfolio duration equal to 3.6 years. In theory this could be done by purchasing $21.47 million of one bond with a 3.6-year duration. This is an example of *bullet immunization*. In general, bullet immunization refers to situations in which the average duration of the bond portfolio equals the duration of the portfolio liability stream.

A *cash dedicated* bond investment portfolio is one which will provide coupon payments and maturing principal amounts *exactly* when required to meet liabilities (desired cash receipts). A dedicated portfolio is an immunized portfolio, but a very special type of immunization occurs. Recall from our pension example that a single bond with a 3.6-year duration would be sufficient to immunize the pension's liability stream. If one wished to purchase two bonds, one with a three-year duration and one with a four-year duration, then 40% would be invested in the three-year bond and 60% in the four-year bond. This combination also results in a portfolio duration of 3.6 years. Many other combinations resulting in a 3.6-year duration are possible, of course. A cash dedicated portfolio simply carries these possible combinations to the limit. In a cash dedicated portfolio, rebalancing is theoretically unnecessary. Scheduled coupons and maturing principal amounts exactly match the cash needs.

Dedicated portfolios have a number of advantages over more classic immunization techniques. First, they are easier to understand. Exact cash matching as a means of immunization against interest rate risk is a much easier concept to follow than the reinvestment and price risk offsets associated with normal immunization. Second, a rebalancing is not necessary every time interest rates change, as is necessary with normal immunization. In addition, if a good cash match is in fact possible, a more accurate forecast of future returns is possible. One need not worry about *D*'s assumption of a flat yield curve with parallel shifts over time. Finally, the procedure can result in a larger number of bonds being held and thus a greater amount of diversification than might be obtained by standard immunization.

Dedicated portfolios do have their costs, however. Most of these relate to reduced flexibility. In particular, many bond managers desire to trade bonds in an attempt to pick up abnormal profits through quality swaps and other speculative trades. In a dedicated portfolio, the bond manager faces more constraints on available trading opportunities.

PASSIVE BOND INVESTMENT

By our definition of investment versus speculation, investors accept security prices as fair—that is, priced so that the expected return is commensurate with the risk. Investors rely upon active trading by speculators to seek out and trade in mispriced securities in order to ensure that gross distortions among security prices will not exist. While some speculative profits might exist, they are small and not worth the cost to the investor of finding them.

A passive strategy does not mean that there are no decisions to be made. Passive investors must continually monitor the bond portfolio to ensure that it has an appropriate default risk exposure, will not suffer from bond calls, and has the desired duration.

Asset Allocation

Bonds can expand portfolio risk return opportunities. By including bonds in a portfolio, the investor can gain in two ways. First, bond returns are less than perfectly correlated with other security classes. Thus, when mixed with other asset classes, the increased diversification causes investment risk to decline. In addition, by altering the portfolio's allocation between bonds and other security classes, total portfolio risk can be easily managed.

The risk of owning a diversified set of bonds depends on: (1) whether real returns or nominal returns are desired and (2) the bond investment strategy chosen.

Consider the following case. An insurance company has a five-year investment horizon and is not concerned about future rates of inflation. The company is considering the risks and expected returns for various equity and bond combinations. Different bond investment strategies are being considered, as follows:

1. Buy and hold a five-year duration zero coupon government bond.
2. Purchase a 1-year government bond and roll its maturity value into a sequence of new 1-year government bonds.
3. Buy 10-year duration government bonds and rebalance the duration at the start of each year to maintain a constant 10-year duration.

The *five-year* expected returns and risks of these strategies are shown in Figure 12-3. Clearly the first strategy is the best since it is based on a zero-risk (default, call, and interest rate) portfolio. The second has risk associated with future reinvestment income. The third has uncertainty about the value of 10-year duration bonds in five years from now.

Notice in the example above that short-term instruments such as T-bills are *not* risk-free. Also notice that the risk-free security is a buy-hold bond portfolio with an initial duration of 5 years. It is *not* an actively managed portfolio. For example, if a *constant* 5-year duration portfolio were evaluated it would also have risk attached to the year-five value. In short, bond risk depends on the bond strategy chosen.

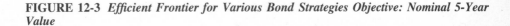

FIGURE 12-3 *Efficient Frontier for Various Bond Strategies Objective: Nominal 5-Year Value*

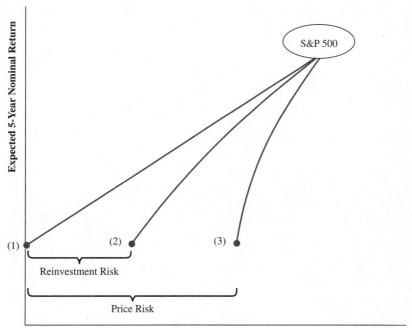

Now consider another example. Janet and Charles are saving to purchase a second home in 5 years. Since housing prices are expected to move perfectly with inflation, their objective is expressed in terms of a real rate of return. They are also considering the same three bond strategies as the insurance company did.

Illustrative efficient frontiers facing Janet and Charles are shown in Figure 12-4. Notice that bonds are no longer risk-free; inflation risk is present. Notice also that strategies 1 and 2 are reversed. This is because unexpected inflation has a greater impact on a 5-year duration bond than it does on 1-year bonds. The yields on the short-term bonds are adjusted at the start of each year for any revised inflation forecasts.

The risk of owning bonds depends on: (1) whether one's objective is a real return or a nominal return and (2) the bond trading strategy chosen.

Bond Diversification. Whenever the returns on securities are not perfectly corre-lated, diversification across the securities will reduce portfolio risk. To illustrate the potential advantages inherent in corporate bond diversification, McEnally and Boardman collected monthly rates of return for 515 corporate bonds rated Baa or better from December 1972 through June 1976. They then simulated the results

FIGURE 12-4 *Efficient Frontier for Various Bond Strategies Objective: Real 5-Year Value*

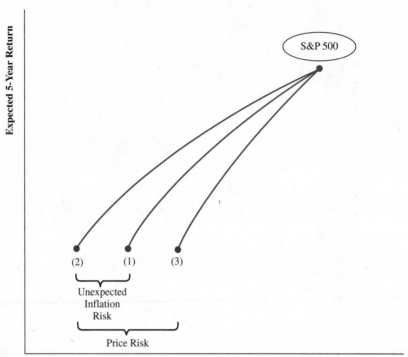

that would have been obtained by holding portfolios with different numbers of bonds. Each portfolio's risk was measured by the variance of that portfolio's monthly return during the full time period examined. Portfolios were constrained to consist of only one quality rating (Aaa, Aa, A, or Baa), and the number of bonds allowed in each portfolio ranged from 1 to 40. Their results are displayed in Figure 12-5.

The reduction in bond portfolio risk made possible by increasing the number of bonds held is dramatic and is achieved quite rapidly. While McEnally and Boardman showed that the benefits associated with common stock diversification are even greater, the reduction in bond risk is still substantial.[4]

Since many bonds have par value of $1000, it is difficult for small investors to diversify by direct ownership. A realistic alternative is to purchase shares in a

---

[4] Notice that the lowest-risk portfolio appears to be in the highest default-risk group. This is most likely due to the fact that higher default-risk bonds have shorter maturities. Thus, they would have lower price sensitivity to shifts in the yield curve.

FIGURE 12-5 *Naive Bond Diversification*

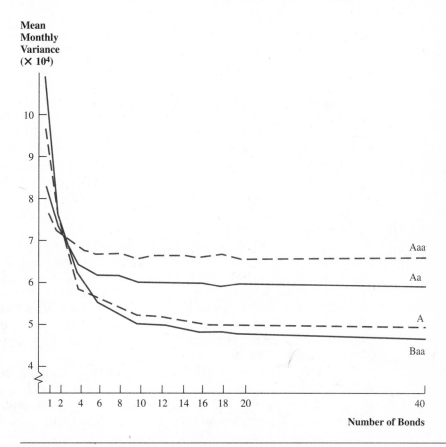

Mean
Monthly
Variance
(× 10^4)

SOURCE: "Aspects of Corporate Bond Portfolio Diversification" *by R. McEnally and C. Boardman from The Journal of Financial Research, Spring 1979. Reprinted by permission.*

commingled mutual fund. During the 1980s and early 1990s, the number of bond mutual funds grew dramatically. By 1991 the aggregate value of bond mutual funds in the United States was greater than the aggregate value of stock funds. Even large investors such as pension and endowment funds invest indirectly in bonds. Often they purchase mutual fund shares. More typically, however, they employ professional investment managers to invest in bonds.

Index bond funds attempt to provide returns that emulate a specific bond index such as the Lehman Brothers Government/Corporate or Salomon Brothers World Bond Index. Many mutual funds and bond managers, however, specialize in particular bond types and particular bond durations. For example, a Short Term Investment Fund (a STIF) will allow high-grade corporates and governments with maturities ranging from 1 to 3 years. When purchasing bond mutual funds that specialize in a particular segment of the bond market, it is best to diversify across a number of fund types.

Effects of Calls

In early 1986, investors became increasingly convinced that rapid inflation had been licked for some years into the future. Federal Reserve monetary policies had been steadily reducing inflation over the prior four years and, in early 1986, oil prices fell dramatically as world demand for oil declined and OPEC unraveled. The result was a dramatic decrease in interest rates across all maturities. By mid-1986, 30-day T-bills were selling at a *YTM* of less than 6.0% and 30-year T-bonds were selling at a *YTM* of 7.2%. Just six months earlier these yields had been 8.5% and 11.5%, respectively. The resulting increases in bond prices were equally dramatic. Many long-term bonds experienced returns during the year prior to March 31, 1986, of 45% or more. But not all was rosy—particularly for people who owned callable bonds.

Many people bought long-term bonds in the early 1980s with the belief that they would be getting high coupon earnings for many years to come. Unfortunately, they had given too little attention to their bonds' call provisions. As interest rates plummeted, large numbers of call announcements appeared in the financial press. One advisory firm estimated that there were more than 330 calls by taxable corporations during 1986. And potential municipal bond calls were impossible to estimate, owing to the large number of bond issues outstanding (about 53,000 different issues in 1986).

As a result, most of the price increases in bonds came in the U.S. Treasury market, because T-bonds are not callable until five years before maturity. Investment portfolios with large holdings of Treasuries increased substantially in value. But portfolios of corporate and municipal bonds had their returns limited by the call provisions on these bonds.

Besides affecting the returns on actively managed bond portfolios, these calls were an embarrassment to many professionals who had supposedly created fully immunized bond portfolios. When bonds held in such portfolios were called, all aspects of immunization were lost. It was foolhardy to try to immunize using callable bonds.

When a bond is likely to be called by the issuer prior to maturity, the *YTM* can be a misleading figure. In such cases the investor should calculate an *expected yield to call date*. Because considerable uncertainty exists about the expected call date, most bond houses calculate and publish a *yield to first call* return. Instead of using an expected date of call, the first possible call date is used.

Yield to Call

$$P_0 = \sum_{t=1}^{C} \frac{COUPON}{(1 + YTM_C)^t} + \frac{CALL}{(1 + YTM_C)^C} \qquad (12.5)$$

where *CALL* is the dollar payment which would be made at the first call date, *C* is the number of periods until call, and YTM_C is the yield to first call.

International Bond Investment

Communication and trading procedures between countries have developed to the point that investors should consider placing a portion of their portfolio assets in fixed income securities issued in foreign countries. While non-U.S. citizens have invested heavily in U.S. bonds (particularly U.S. Treasury issues) for many years, extensive international bond investment by U.S. citizens is more recent.

There are two benefits gained from foreign bond investment. First, foreign bond returns are less than perfectly correlated with U.S. security returns. Thus, they provide an opportunity to further diversify a portfolio.

Second, there are often periods when the yields to maturity available on foreign bonds are greater than available for equivalent risk issues in one's domestic economy. In Chapter 17, the concept of Interest Rate Parity is discussed. *Interest Rate Parity states that in equilibrium, the real rate of interest must be the same in every country.* If real rates (after expected inflation) differ across countries, then arbitrage profits are available from borrowing in the low-interest country and lending in the high-interest country. There are, in fact, extended periods during which interest rates between countries are not in equilibrium. For example, in the early 1990s short-term U.S. Treasury interest rates were close to 3% whereas short-term German government rates were close to 9%!

When one invests in a foreign country, a risk is incurred that is not present in domestic investing—this is called *exchange rate risk*. For example, assume you invest in German money market securities that will return 9% at year-end. Although the return in Germany is certain, the rate at which German marks can be converted into U.S. dollars in a year is unknown today.

To hedge this risk, most international bond managers trade in futures or forward contracts. For example, assume that 1 million dollars is exchanged into German marks at an exchange rate of $0.60 per mark and invested in a one-year German government T-bill paying a return of 9%. At the end of the year, 1,816,660 marks will be available for return to the United States (1,666,666 × 1.09). To eliminate uncertainty about the exchange rate, forward contracts or futures could be traded. In this example, the ideal contract would require that 1,816,666 marks be delivered for a specific number of dollars. Let's assume that the forward or futures rate is $0.59 per mark. Thus, $1,071,833 would be "locked-up" for return to the United States in one year (1,816,666 × 0.59). Accounting for the change in the exchange rate, the net U.S. dollar return would be 7.18%.

Small investors wishing to acquire exchange-rate-hedged positions in foreign bonds should consider mutual funds that specialize in international bonds.

ACTIVE BOND SPECULATION

There are numerous ways to speculate in bonds. But regardless of the techniques used, there are certain keys to successful bond speculation. These include the following:

1. *Fast access to new information.* Speculators must have early access to economic and political news so that they can trade before bond prices change in reaction to the new information.
2. *Liquidity.* Because speculators must be able to trade quickly on new information without affecting market prices, they prefer to trade in bonds with large active markets.
3. *Interest rate sensitivity.* Most bond speculation revolves around forecasts of future interest rates. For this reason, speculators prefer to trade largely in instruments whose prices are influenced by changes in the general level of interest rates, as opposed to those for which default and call risks are important. Most speculation is done in high-quality corporate and municipal bonds or U.S. government issues.

One way to order the process of bond speculation is shown in Figure 12-6. Initially, a set of investment objectives are specified which are used to determine the ideal bond investment portfolio. We will use Leibowitz's term for this ideal investment portfolio and refer to it as the *baseline portfolio*. The baseline portfolio will be fully immunized, having a portfolio duration equal to the planned horizon date. In addition, the baseline portfolio should consist of bonds having appropriate default risk, call protection, tax characteristics, marketability, and other features necessary to fulfill the portfolio's stated objectives. After the baseline portfolio has been determined (but not yet bought), the manager of the portfolio will forecast future levels of the yield curve and alter the portfolio's duration in hopes of improving upon the next period's return. If interest rates are expected to rise, duration will be shortened in order to reduce expected price losses and improve reinvestment income. If interest rates are expected to fall, duration will be lengthened in order to reduce expected losses from lower reinvestment income and improve expected price gains. The portfolio is not fully immunized and thus is subject to interest rate risk. But the manager might judge the risks well worth taking for the extra returns expected. After the portfolio's duration is set, the manager will examine individual bonds and purchase those offering the greatest yields but still meeting the portfolio's long-run objectives. (Later in the chapter we will discuss how this is done when bond swaps are examined.) Finally, the manager will constantly monitor the portfolio's performance, new economic and political news, and prices of bonds that might be substituted (swapped) for those now held.

We will now consider two important steps in analyzing future yield curves and potential bond swaps.

Trading on Yield Curve Shifts

Theoretically, if a fully immunized bond portfolio is maintained, the *ARR* between the time at which the portfolio is acquired and the *HD* at which the portfolio is sold should be equal to the portfolio's promised *YTM* when initially bought. For example, panel A in Figure 12-7 plots as the solid line a hypothetical yield curve

FIGURE 12-6 *The Process of Bond Speculation*

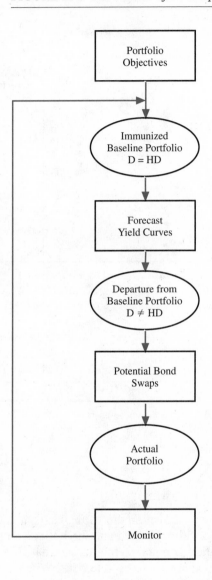

for pure discount bonds that have no call or default risks. If the horizon date is 10 years and a portfolio of bonds with a 10-year duration is initially bought, then the expected *ARR* over the next 10 years is 10%. However, as we just saw, the expected returns during any *single* year are expected to be different from this geometric average *ARR*. For example, during year 1 the expected return would be 8% *if* the yield curve shifts through time as the unbiased expectations theory suggests it should. This first-year expected return is plotted as the solid line in

FIGURE 12-7 *Yields on Discount Bonds with No Default or Call Risk*

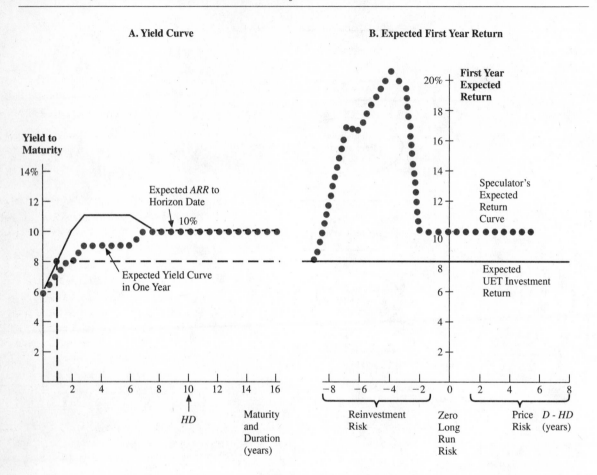

A. Yield Curve

B. Expected First Year Return

panel B. The one-year return is shown on the vertical axis, and the difference between the duration of the portfolio selected and the horizon date is shown on the
horizontal axis. When duration is equal to the horizon date ($D - HD = 0$), the
portfolio is fully immunized against interest rate risks. When duration is less than
the *HD*, the portfolio is exposed to net interest rate reinvestment risk. When duration is greater than the *HD*, the portfolio is exposed to net interest rate price risk.

Assuming the *HD* is 10 years, the baseline portfolio should have a duration of
10 years. However, the speculator will forecast future levels of the yield curve
and temporarily change the portfolio's duration in an attempt to pick up yearly
returns greater than expected from the immunized baseline portfolio. For example,
if the dotted curve in panel A of Figure 12-7 reflects the speculator's estimate of
the yield curve level in exactly one year, this would result in the one-year rates
of return as shown in panel B by the dotted curve.

If the baseline portfolio is held, the speculator expects a 10% one-year return.

However, by shortening the portfolio's duration, the speculator can expect a return as high as 21%. Of course, when the portfolio's duration is set below (or above) that of the baseline portfolio, interest rate risk is incurred. The portfolio manager must decide whether the added expected return is worth the risk.

Bond managers who alter a portfolio's duration based on a forecast of future interest rates are called bond *timers* or, more formally, *interest rate anticipators*. There is little empirical evidence that active bond timing works, although this does not mean that all bond timing doesn't work. There will be many periods in which the interest rate forecast is correct. But studies conducted to date suggest that active bond timing decisions are about as successful as the flip of a coin would be.

Bond portfolio duration can be changed by: (1) trading in "spot" bonds or (2) trading in bond derivatives. For example, assume that a bond manager wants to reduce her portfolio duration from 7 years to 4 years. She could do so by actually selling long-duration bonds and buying bonds with shorter durations. Alternatively, she could leave the spot bond positions alone and reduce duration by *selling* a futures contract on U.S. T-bonds. Detailed calculations of the quantity to trade are complex enough to delay to Chapter 15. But derivative positions are often fast and cheap alternatives to trading in spot assets.

Bond Swaps

Once a weighted portfolio duration has been determined, the speculator can begin to select particular bonds. Although our discussion has been worded to imply that this is the first time the bond portfolio has been set up, in practice speculators make modifications to existing portfolios. For this reason, the techniques used to decide which bonds to purchase or sell are known as *bond swaps*. We will review a few of these bond swaps using the data shown in Table 12-3. The table shows two types of bonds—bonds now owned and potential replacements. Bonds that are now owned are designated by a single letter (Q, R, S, etc.), and potential replacements are designated by double letters (QQ, RR, SS, etc.).

Rate Anticipation Swap. If a speculator believes interest rates will soon fall (and that this has not yet been fully recognized in current prices), bonds should be bought in hopes of capital gains. To maximize price appreciation, *long-term, low-coupon issues* should be acquired. Stated differently, bonds with short durations should be replaced by equivalent-risk, long-duration bonds. For example, consider bond Q, which is now owned, and bond QQ, which might be used to replace it. If promised *YTM*s on both bonds are expected to fall reasonably soon from 12% to 10%, the approximate percentage price increase in each would be:

Bond	Actual Percentage Price Increase	$\approx$	$-D\left[\dfrac{Percentage}{Increase\ in\ (1\ +\ YTM)}\right]$
Q	12.29	$\approx$	$-6.33(-0.0179) = 11.33$
QQ	17.04	$\approx$	$-8.48(-0.0179) = 15.18$

TABLE 12-3 *Bond Swap Data*

Bonds	Default Rating	Years to Maturity	Annual Coupon	Years to Duration*	Current Price	Promised YTM
Now Owned						
Q	AA	10	12%	6.33	$1,000.00	12.0%
R	AA	15	12	7.63	1,000.00	12.0
S	AA	4	10	3.49	1,000.00	10.0
T	BBB	10	13	6.13	1,000.00	13.0
U	BBB	10	13	6.13	1,000.00	13.0
V	AA	10	5	7.57	646.65	11.0
W	AA	5	6	4.41	848.35	10.0
Potential Replacement						
QQ	AA	15	7%	8.48	$ 659.46	12.0%
RR	AA	13	5	8.61	550.35	12.0
SS	AA	4	10	3.49	996.83	10.1
TT	AA	10	14.25	6.13	1,127.07	12.0
UU	AAA	10	11	6.54	1,000.00	11.0
VV	AA	14.67	12	7.57	1,000.00	12.0
WW	AA	5	6	4.41	848.35	10.0

* Calculated as D_i.

Now consider bonds *R* and *RR*. Bond *R* has a longer maturity but a higher coupon than *RR*. What should be done in this case if rates are expected to decline? Select *RR*, since its lower coupon offsets its shorter maturity, resulting in a longer duration than *R* has. If one expects rates to rise but is forced to hold some bond investments, holding bonds with short durations will minimize expected price losses.

Yield Pickup Swap. Occasionally two identical bonds will sell at temporarily different prices and *YTM*s. For example, bonds *S* and *SS* are identical in all respects except that *S* is now selling at $1,000 to yield 10.0% to maturity, while *SS* is selling at $996.83 to yield 10.1% to maturity. A yield pickup swap could involve selling *S* and buying *SS*. Price imbalances like this could be due to temporary abnormal buying or selling in one of the issues. Care should be taken, however, that the two securities are indeed perfect substitutes. Minor yield differences could be due to slight default-risk differentials, differences in call features, or differences in marketability.

Quality Swaps. If the economy is currently at a peak of business expansion and headed into a recession, one might well expect both a decline in all interest rates and a widening in yield spreads between bonds of differing default risk. The trading strategy in this case would be to buy *long-duration, high-quality bonds*, since yields on these issues would decline the most. Yields on lower-quality issues would also fall in sympathy with all rates. But increased default-risk spreads would partially offset such declines. For example, bonds *T* and *TT* have similar long durations, but *TT* is of better quality. If rates are expected to decline and yield spreads to widen, bond *TT* would be preferable.

Quality swaps are possible even if one doesn't expect overall rates to move dramatically. For example, bonds *U* and *UU* have a 2% yield spread that reflects default-quality differences between the two. If the trader believes this spread will widen, bond *U* should be short sold and *UU* bought. Although the speculator might not know which of the two bond prices will adjust, being short in *U* and long in *UU* will cover any possible outcome. In fact, if the short and long positions are based upon each bond's duration, there should be only minimal risk in the transaction. Many bond traders evaluate the appropriateness of current yield spreads by examining trends in historic averages.

Tax Swaps. A variety of tax swaps exist; we will discuss two. The first of these involves trading based upon coupon rates. Consider bonds *V* and *VV*, which are identical except for coupons. (Their maturities differ, but they have equal durations.) Notice that the *YTM* of *V* is lower than that of the equivalent-duration, higher-coupon issue, *VV*. This simply reflects the fact that effective tax rates on low-coupon bonds are lower than on higher-coupon issues; thus their before-tax yields may be lower. Assume, for simplicity, that you are in a 50% tax bracket. Should you swap *VV* for *V*? The answer, of course, depends upon the after-tax Yield to Maturity on each. In fact, the after-tax yield is 6.85% on *V* and 6.00% on *VV*. Clearly, *V* should be held.[5]

A second type of tax swap involves selling a bond now owned at a taxable loss to obtain an immediate tax advantage and reinvesting *both* the sale proceeds and the tax savings. Assume you had originally bought bond *W* at $1,000. Since its current price is $848.35, you could sell it with a *realized* tax loss of $151.65. If your capital gains rate is 30%, taking this loss will allow you to reduce taxes by $45.50 (0.30 × $151.65). You could immediately reinvest the sale proceeds of $848.35 in bond *WW* and be in the same situation except that you *now* have $45.50 in tax savings that can also be reinvested. Of course, you will pay $45.50 in capital gains when bond *WW* matures, but in the meantime, you have had free use of $45.50 to invest for larger total returns. To be allowed this form of tax swap, bonds *W* and *WW* must be legally different issues. For example, bond *V* couldn't be sold to realize a taxable loss and then immediately repurchased. The IRS considers a sale and repurchase of the same security to be a "wash sale" and will disallow the taxable loss.

---

[5] The after-tax *YTM*s are found by calculating the discount rate that will discount all *after-tax* cash flows to the initial bond price. For bond *V*:

$$\$646 = \sum_{t=1}^{10} \frac{\$50(1 - 0.5)}{1.0685^t} + \frac{\$1,000 - (\$1,000 - \$646)(0.25)}{1.0685^{10}}$$

For bond *VV*:

$$\$1,000 = \sum_{t=1}^{14.67} \frac{\$120(1 - 0.5)}{1.06^t} + \frac{\$1,000 - (\$1,000 - \$1,000)(0.25)}{1.06^{10}}$$

This assumes a 25% capital gains tax in the maturity year.

Contingent Immunization

Contingent immunization is really a very simple notion. The owner of a bond portfolio and the manager agree to a *minimum return* that will be earned or exceeded over some future time period (commonly five years). The manager is then free to actively speculate with the portfolio until enough of its value has been lost that the only way to guarantee the minimum return is immediate immunization. Contingent immunization provides downside risk protection on the bond portfolio's return.

As an example, assume that contingent immunization is to be used to manage $10 million starting on January 1, 1995. At that date, the portfolio's owner and the manager agree to two basic objectives:

1. The minimum compound annual return will be 9.55%.
2. This 9.55% will be calculated over the next five years.

Note that the return in any one year could be much less than 9.55% because the agreement calls for an *average* compound return of 9.55% over the next five years. Both parties realize that the minimum portfolio value after five years will be $15.78 million ($10 million $\times$ 1.0955^5).

Also assume that on January 1, 1995, the annual return available on default- and call-free government bonds with a five-year duration is 11.3%. The difference between the 11.3% which could be earned if the $10 million were to be fully immunized and the 9.55% guarantee is a margin of safety given to the portfolio manager to induce active trading. The portfolio owner is willing to accept the 175-basis-point difference in the hope that the manager's active management will result in a compound return greater than the 11.3% return of a passive immunized strategy.

The portfolio manager could conceptually approach active trading in one of two ways. In the first case, he or she could take a portion of the $10 million and immunize it so that it will be worth the guaranteed $15.78 million in five years. In total, $9.24 million would be necessary:

$$\frac{\$10,000,000(1.0955^5)}{1.113^5} = \$9,238,173$$

The remaining $761,827 could then be actively managed and, perhaps, even totally lost. It is unlikely that this procedure would be used, but it does point out again the margin of safety given to the manager.

Alternatively, the manager could begin to actively trade the portfolio. At the end of each day, the new fully immunized return which is then available would be calculated and compared with the portfolio's value at that time. If the portfolio's value compounded at that return is greater than the guaranteed $15.78 million promised for December 31, 1999, the manager continues to have a margin of safety. For example, assume that one year later the return available from immunizing four-year-duration government bonds has risen to 12%. If the portfolio has a value in excess of $10.03 million, a margin of safety still exists:

$$\frac{\$10,000,000(1.0955^5)}{1.12^4} = \$10,027,437$$

If the portfolio has a value equal to $10.03 million, it must be immediately immunized. (If its value is less than $10.03 million, it is time to fire the manager and the firm's computer programmers.)

Contingent immunization is a risk-reduction technique. It places bounds on the risks accepted in an active bond-management program. Given the volatility of interest rates in the 1970s and 1980s and the risks associated with an unencumbered active management strategy, it is a valuable risk-reduction tool. However, there is no magic underlying its procedures. There is no reason to expect contingent immunization to result in greater returns than those available from a truly immunized strategy unless bond managers are, indeed, able to predict future bond prices. And, if they are able to do so, why limit their abilities to generating excess returns? Contingent immunization is a strategy that lies between passive bond selection and unencumbered active bond management.

SUMMARY

This chapter has illustrated how the fundamental concepts of bond pricing and returns as discussed in Chapter 11 can be applied to bond investment management and speculation. Crucial to both styles of trading is the concept of duration and the matching of duration with a planned horizon date to minimize interest rate risk exposure. While immunization might not completely eliminate interest rate risk, it can reduce it substantially.

Investment portfolios in bonds should (1) contain only bonds of an appropriate default risk, (2) be immunized against interest rate risk, (3) be reasonably well protected against unforeseen calls, (4) have good marketability, and (5) include instruments that will increase after-tax yields. Bond diversification can reduce the variability of single-period rates of return.

Bond speculation can be profitable if the speculator is able to consistently predict future bond prices. Bond speculation can be thought of as taking place at two levels. At the first level, yield curves forecast for some future date are used to calculate potential single-period returns on bonds of different durations. These are then evaluated to see whether the returns expected by departing from a fully immunized portfolio are worth the risks incurred. At the second level, individual bonds are examined to see whether a bond swap would be profitable. Swaps examined in this chapter included (1) rate anticipation swaps, (2) yield pickup swaps, (3) quality swaps, and (4) tax swaps.

Historical evidence and logic suggest that active bond management will not, on average, result in larger returns than are available from passive immunization strategies. A market in which there are so many traders with equal access to information should set prices fairly, as efficient market theory suggests.

Contingent immunization is a recent approach to integrating a passive immunization strategy with a more active strategy. It sets limits on the amount of downside risk associated with an actively managed bond portfolio. Whether contingent immunization provides greater value than a fully immunized portfolio depends on whether active bond management works.

APPENDIX 12-A

CONVERTIBLE BONDS

Institutional Features. A convertible security is a bond or preferred stock that may be converted at the owner's discretion into a prescribed number of the firm's common shares. As with put and call options, a terminology has developed around convertibles which must be understood before their investment value can be examined. The *conversion ratio* indicates the number of shares obtained when each bond (or preferred share) is tendered for conversion. A conversion ratio of 20:1 on a bond means 20 shares of common will be received for each bond converted. A conversion ratio of 2:1 on a preferred share will provide two common shares for each preferred. The *conversion price* of a security is the bond's (or preferred's) par value divided by the conversion ratio. For example, a conversion price of $50 per share on a 1,000 par bond implies a conversion ratio of 20:1. Clearly, the extent of the conversion privilege can be stated in terms of either the conversion ratio or the conversion price. Conversion terms of many bonds provide for an increase in the conversion price over time. For example, a bond may not be convertible for the first five years of its life, have a conversion price of $100 during years 6 through 10, $110 for the subsequent five years, and so forth. Conversion prices are usually adjusted for stock splits or stock dividends. They are not protected against cash dividend payments.

Three identifiable values can be attached to convertibles. These are illustrated in panel A of Figure 12A-1. *Conversion value* is the security's value as stock. For example, if a bond is convertible into 20 shares of a stock now selling for $35, its conversion value would currently be $700. If the stock is expected to grow at a constant 8% rate each year, future conversion values would be as shown in the figure. *Straight-debt value* is the security's value as a nonconvertible bond. If the instrument pays a 7% coupon, has a maturity of 10 years, and bonds of identical default risk and maturity are currently selling at promised yields to maturity of 10%, its initial straight-debt value will be $815.62. Assuming that promised yields to maturity on straight debt do not change over the bond's life, the straight-debt value should increase steadily to $1,000 at maturity in year 10.

At any point in time, the *minimum* value of the convertible will be the larger of either its straight-debt or its conversion value. However, actual *convertible bond values* are always greater than straight-debt or conversion values. Panel A of Figure 12A-1 shows an initial convertible bond value of $1,000 which increases over time.

Convertibles invariably sell at premiums over both their straight-debt and con-

FIGURE 12 A-1 *Conversion, Straight-Debt, and Convertible Bond Values*

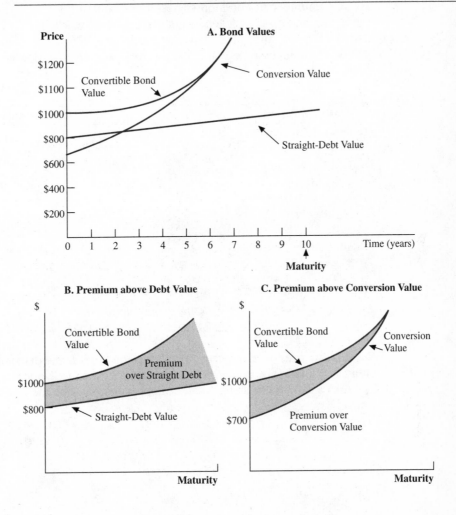

version values. To illustrate, premiums above straight-debt value are shown in panel B of Figure 12A-1, and premiums above conversion value are shown in panel C. Note that the two premiums are inversely related. At low conversion values, the premium over conversion value is large, but the premium over straight-debt value is small. At high conversion values, the premium over conversion value is small, and the premium over debt value is large. The reason for this is clear once we understand why premiums exist.

Convertible Premiums. Purchasers of a convertible security receive two distinct legal rights to the future cash flows of a firm. The first is the right to fixed yearly coupons (or preferred dividends) plus par value when the security matures, is called, or is converted. This legal right has a present worth that represents the straight-debt value. The second right allows the security owner to acquire a specified number of common shares at any time during the convertible's life by tendering the bond. This legal right has a present worth equal to the value of one call on the stock times the conversion ratio.

For example, assume you know the following information about a convertible bond:

Convertible Bond Characteristics

Straight Bond Information		Stock Information	
Yearly Coupon	$70	Current Stock Price	$40
Maturity Date	10 years	Yearly Std. Dev. of Stock Return	50%
Known Call Date	3 years	Conversion Price	$50
Call Price	$1,070		
Quality Rating	Baa		

Market Information

10-Year Risk-Free Rate	8%
3-Year Risk-Free Rate	9%
10-Year Baa Rate	11%
3-year Baa Rate	12%

The value of the bond as straight debt would equal $929.73:

$$\sum_{t=1}^{3} \frac{\$70}{1.12^t} + \frac{\$1,070}{1.12^3} = \$929.73$$

Note that a three-year maturity, a call price of $1,070, and discount rates for three-year Baa bonds are used since the bond *will* be called in three years. Next, the value of a call on one share could be approximated using the Black-Scholes option model as:

$$C = \$40(0.6879) - \frac{\$50}{2.718^{0.09(3)}} (0.3520)$$

$$= \$14.08$$

where:

$$d_1 = \frac{\ln\left[\dfrac{40}{50}\right] + 3\left(0.09 + \dfrac{0.25}{2}\right)}{0.5\sqrt{3}} = 0.49$$

$$d_2 = \frac{\ln\left[\dfrac{40}{50}\right] + 3\left(0.09 + \dfrac{0.25}{2}\right)}{0.5\sqrt{3}} = 0.38$$

$$N_{d1} = 0.6879$$

$$N_{d2} = 0.3520$$

FIGURE 12 A-2 *Conversion Premiums*

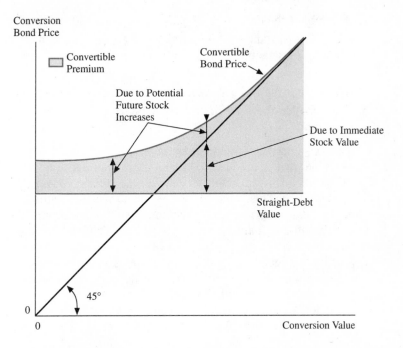

Each call would be worth about $14.08. Since each bond provides 20 calls, the conversion premium of the bond should be worth $281.60 ($14.08 × 20). In total, the convertible bond would be worth its debt value plus its conversion premium value, or $1,211.33 ($929.73 + $281.60).

Figure 12A-2 depicts the theoretical relationship between conversion premiums and conversion values. At very *low* conversion values, the premium will be small since there is only a small likelihood the bond will ever be worth anything other than its straight-debt value. The convertible bond will sell at a slight premium, however, since there is some small probability that conversion value will eventually exceed debt value. At *high* conversion values, the premium will be large. There are two reasons for this. First, the convertible has a clear immediate value as stock (an in-the-money option). Second, if some time remains before the bond is expected to be converted, there is a value associated with potential future stock price increases.

In principle, convertible premiums can be determined by the option pricing model. In practice, this is quite hard to do and may yield inaccurate results. Difficulties are caused mainly by (1) not knowing when the bonds will be converted (the exercise date), (2) not knowing the impact that changes in the firm's capital structure will have on stock prices, and (3) the fact that the Black-Scholes model does not adequately handle stocks that pay cash dividends. To date, a precise model of convertible bond values has not been developed.

Nonetheless, the option pricing model is helpful in explaining the relative size of convertible premiums. Specifically:

1. The higher the current *stock price*, the larger the conversion premium.
2. The more distant the expected *exercise date* (which is the date when the corporation is expected to call the bonds), the larger the conversion premium.
3. The more *variable the stock returns*, the larger the conversion premium.
4. The greater the *risk-free rate*, the larger the conversion premium.
5. The smaller the *cash dividends* paid by a firm, the larger the conversion premium.

The existence of convertible bond premiums is often attributed to the fact that convertible owners are able to share in the potential price growth of the common stock but incur lower downside risk because of the convertible's minimum value as straight debt. This is quite true. As the conversion value of the bond increases, so will its market price. And if the conversion value should decline precipitously, the convertible will always retain its straight-debt characteristics. Thus owners of a convertible bond receive the best of both its stock and bond characteristics but few of its bad features. To obtain these relative advantages, buyers are willing to pay a premium. This premium will be large if stock price growth is favorable, and considerable downside risk protection is achieved by having a bond floor not much below existing prices. As the conversion value moves to levels substantially above the straight-debt floor, downside risk protection diminishes and premiums disappear.

This explanation of convertible premiums is essentially identical to that offered from the option pricing model. The potential to share in stock price growth is equivalent to the option value that arises from what we have labeled potential appreciation value. And the downside risk protection is equivalent to the fact that losses from owning a call option are limited. The choice of which explanation is better is a matter of personal taste and convenience. However, the option pricing model explicitly recognizes convertibles for what they are—complex call options on common stock—and it identifies those factors that affect the size of convertible premiums.

As with put and call options, owners of a convertible bond will typically not convert voluntarily. Instead, they will be *forced* to convert when the corporation calls the bonds at a price substantially below existing conversion values. For example, assume that a corporation has convertible bonds outstanding that are now callable at $1,070 but with a conversion value of $1,200. If the firm wishes to reduce its debt and increase its equity, it would call the bonds. Owners of the convertibles would clearly convert since conversion provides a value of $1,200 where the call provides only $1,070.

Convertible investors would convert *voluntarily* only if dividend yields began to exceed coupon yields. For example, assume the convertible is selling at $1,210 when its conversion value is $1,200. The convertible is *effectively* stock and will rise and fall almost one-for-one with the stock. It is exposed to the same price risk as the stock. If coupon payments are $50, the bond's current yield would be 4.13% ($50 ÷ $1,210). If total dividend receipts received upon conversion would be $80, the dividend yield would be 6.61% ($80 ÷ $1,210). The investor is exposed to identical price risks and *price* returns with either the convertible or the stock. But, since dividend yields are larger, a higher return would be earned if the investor voluntarily converted.

REVIEW PROBLEM

The yield curve on U.S. Treasury obligations is shown below:

Maturity	YTM	Maturity	YTM
1 year	10%	5 year	11%
2 year	10	6 year	10
3 year	11	7 year	10
4 year	12	8 year	10

a. Under what conditions would the maturity of various T-bonds be identical to their duration?

b. Assume that each is a zero-coupon bond. Forecast next year's yield curve based on UET.

c. You are the financial vice-president for a casualty insurance firm and have estimated that the firm will have to pay $7 million in damage claims in exactly one year and $10 million in exactly two years. How could you immunize these liabilities today?

d. If you do immunize as in part c, will you earn 10% with certainty?

e. If you were to place some of your money in one-year and three-year bonds *today*, what percentage should each represent in order to be immunized? And for one-year and two-year bonds?

Your economic staff has forecast the following yield curve for one year hence (other years are not needed):

Maturity in One Year	YTM
1	12%
2	5%

f. According to UET, which strategy will provide the greater expected return during the next year?

- Immunize over one-year and two-year bonds
- Immunize over one-year and three-year bonds

g. According to your economic staff, which strategy provides the greatest expected returns during the next year?

- Immunize over one-year and two-year bonds
- Immunize over one-year and three-year bonds

Solution

a. Maturity and duration would be identical if each security pays no cash prior to its maturity date, that is, if all are zero-coupon bonds.

b. One year from now each *YTM* will be what it is today less the contribution of today's one-year spot rate. *YTM*s for one year hence are:

Maturity in One Year	YTM
1	$(1.10^2 \div 1.1) - 1.0 = 10.00\%$
2	$(1.11^3 \div 1.1)^{1/2} - 1.0 = 11.50$
3	$(1.12^4 \div 1.1)^{1/3} - 1.0 = 12.67$
4	$(1.11^5 \div 1.1)^{1/4} - 1.0 = 11.25$
5	$(1.10^6 \div 1.1)^{1/5} - 1.0 = 10.00$
6	$(1.10^7 \div 1.1)^{1/6} - 1.0 = 10.00$
7	$(1.10^8 \div 1.1)^{1/7} - 1.0 = 10.00$

c.

End of Year	Liability	Present Value at 10%	Percent of Total	Weighted Duration
1	$ 7.00 million	$ 6,363,636	43.50%	0.4350
2	10.00	8,264,463	56.50	1.1300
		$14,628,099	100.00%	1.5650

An investment of $14.63 million will have to be made in a bond portfolio having a duration of 1.565 years. This could be a single bond, multiple bonds, or even a perfect cash-matched dedicated portfolio.

d. Not necessarily. For any immunization other than a cash-matched dedicated portfolio, three things must be true: (1) you must be able to rebalance at zero transaction costs every time interest rates change, (2) the yield curve must be flat, and (3) all shifts in the yield curve must be parallel. In reality only the flat yield curve is present in this example. Such problems will not be present for a cash-matched dedicated portfolio.

e. From part c, *D* must be 1.565 years. Let X_i be the percentage to invest in bonds with duration (maturity in this question) equal to *i*.

For X_1 and X_3:

$$1.565 = X_1(1.0) + (1 - X_1)(3.0)$$

$$X_1 = 71.75\% \text{ and } X_3 = 28.25\%$$

For X_1 and X_2:

$$1.565 = X_1(1.0) + (1 - X_1)(2.0)$$

$$X_1 = 43.5\% \text{ and } X_2 = 56.5\%$$

f. According to UET, expected returns are the same for any maturity strategy. Only risk is affected by differing duration strategies. However, both alternatives in part e have identical durations. Thus, UET would imply that both strategies have the same expected return and the same risk. They are identical.

g. The yield curve that your staff projects is different from what UET implied in part b. Using the forecasts of your staff, the returns on each duration strategy would be:

Strategy $X_1 = 43.5\%$ and $X_2 = 56.54\%$

Return in the next year on a current two-year bond:

$$P_0 = \$1,000 \div 1.10^2 = \$826.45$$

$$E(P_1) = \$1,000 \div 1.12 = \$892.86$$

$$E(R) = \frac{892.86}{826.45} - 1.0 = 8.04\%$$

$$E(R_P) = 0.435 \,(10\%) + 0.5654 \,(8.04\%)$$

$$= 8.89\%$$

Strategy $X_1 = 71.75\%$ and $X_3 = 28.25\%$

Return in the next year on a current three-year bond:

$$P_0 = \$1,000 \div 1.11^3 = \$731.19$$

$$E(P_1) = \$1,000 \div 1.05^2 = \$907.03$$

$$E(R) = \frac{907.03}{731.19} - 1.0 = 24.05\%$$

$$E(R_P) = 0.7175 \,(10\%) + 0.2825 \,(24.05\%)$$

$$= 13.97\%$$

The strategy of immunizing over the one-year and three-year bonds provides the greatest expected return.

QUESTIONS AND PROBLEMS

1. Laurie Marcus is employed as a corporate bond arbitrageur for a large broker-dealer firm. On September 1, she notices two bonds that are quite similar in nature but that are selling at different promised yields to maturity. Each bond has identical call terms, default risk, and maturity. Bond A is a 10-year, 8% coupon (paid $40 each August 30 and February 30), selling at a promised YTM of 8%. Bond B is a 10-year, 8% coupon (also with the same semiannual dates), selling at a promised YTM of 7.8%.
   a. What is the market price of each bond?
   b. Which of the two bonds might she buy, and why? Might she wish to sell short one of the bonds and go long on some of the other? Why?
   c. Assume she buys one bond A and one bond B on September 1. In exactly one year she sells both bonds at par. What is her realized return on each? (Assume coupon reinvestment at 8%.)

2. What is the value of D for a four-year bond that pays a $40 coupon each six months? Assume YTM is a 10% stated annual rate.

3. The duration of a bond portfolio is 7.3 years and the average YTM of bonds held is 12%. Estimate the percentage increase in the portfolio's value if YTMs fall to 11%.

4. The duration measure D makes some very specific assumptions about the nature of yield curves. What are these?

5. The bond investment officer of Pacific Insurance Corp. is evaluating the firm's current portfolio holdings and finds the following:

Bond Category	Total Market Value	Duration (D)	Yields to Maturity Current	Yields to Maturity Expected
A	$ 50 million	1 year	9%	10%
B	$100	3 years	9	10
C	$ 50	5 years	9	10
D	$100	7 years	9	10
E	$200	12 years	9	10

a. What is the bond portfolio's duration?

b. If the expected YTMs are estimates for one month hence, what is the approximate percentage gain or loss in the portfolio's market value during the next month?

c. If the firm has specified a horizon date of 7.4 years, should the bond manager be worried about the expected price losses and shift into the shorter-duration bonds?

d. Assume the manager elects to maintain this immunized position. If interest rates do rise to 10%, what adjustments will have to be made in the portfolio in order for it to remain immunized?

6. The current yield curve for A-quality bonds is flat at a promised YTM of 10%. You buy a 10-year, 9% annual coupon issue. Immediately the yield curve falls to 8% and remains there until you sell at the end of three years. Assuming all coupon receipts are reinvested, what is your ARR? Why is it not equal to the 10% promised YTM? What type of risk was most important in this situation?

7. The yield curve for A-quality bonds is flat at a promised yield to maturity of 10%. You decide to buy a sequence of three one-year bonds (selecting bonds selling at par—that is, with coupon rates equal to the then-existing promised YTM). Immediately after you buy the first one-year bond, the yield curve falls to 8% and remains there. By the end of year 3, what is your ARR? Why is it not equal to 10%? What type of risk was most important in this situation?

CFA

8. a. Assume a $10,000 par value zero-coupon bond with a term-to-maturity at issue of 10 years and a market yield of 8%.
   (1) **Determine** the duration of the bond.
   (2) **Calculate** the initial issue price of the bond at a market yield of 8%, assuming semiannual compounding.
   (3) Twelve months after issue, this bond is selling to yield 12%. **Calculate** its then-current market price. **Calculate** your pretax rate of return, assuming you owned this bond during the 12-month period.
   b. Assume a 10% coupon bond with a duration (D) of eight years, semiannual payments, and a market rate of 8%.
   (1) **Determine** the duration of the bond.
   (2) **Calculate** the percentage change in price for the bond, assuming market rates decline by 2 percentage points (200 basis points).

CFA

9. The trustees of the Farnsworth Pension Fund, which is expected to have a long-term positive net cash flow, are considering the purchase of one of two noncallable bonds. As indicated below, these bonds are identical in every aspect except coupon (and resulting price).

	Bond A	Bond B
Par	$1,000.00	$1,000.00
Coupon	10.00%	5.00%
Market price	100	68⁷/₈
Length to maturity	10 years	10 years
Yield to maturity	10.00%	10.00%
Current yield	10.00%	7.26%
Present value of $1,000 in 10 years	$ 377.00	$ 377.00
Present value of 20 semiannual coupons	$ 623.00	$ 311.00
Present value of bond	$1,000.00	$ 688.00

    a. Discuss the two bonds in terms of the certainty of achieving a specific realized compound yield.

    b. Discuss how your answer to part a would be affected if you expect interest rates to rise.

    c. Discuss how your answer to part a would be affected if you expect interest rates to fall.

10. What happens to the value of D if YTMs rise? If they fall? Assuming your HD is fixed in time and you wish to be fully immunized, will you have to rebalance the bonds held in your portfolio (sell some and buy others) in order to remain immunized against further interest rate changes?

11. You are the manager of a $50 million fixed-income portfolio which is run under a strategy of contingent immunization. The plan calls for a four-year horizon and a minimum return of 10%. Currently, immunized returns available on four-year-duration bonds are 11.5%.

    a. How much could you lose on the first day and still be able to provide the 10% minimum return?

    b. A year goes by and the value of the portfolio is now $60 million. At that time, immunized returns on three-year-duration bonds are 11.0%. Do you need to immunize?

    c. If interest rates rise, this could be favorable or unfavorable to you. Explain why.

    d. At the end of four years the value of the portfolio has grown from $50 million to $87 million. Have you provided any value to the portfolio?

    e. Why do people use contingent immunization instead of simply allowing fixed-income managers full discretion over the portfolio they manage?

12. The ability to immunize is very desirable for bond portfolio managers in some instances.

    a. Discuss the components of interest rate risk—that is, assuming a change in interest rates over time, explain the two risks faced by the holder of a bond.

    b. Define immunization and discuss why a bond manager would immunize his or her portfolio.

    c. Explain why a duration-matching strategy is a superior technique to a maturity-matching strategy for the minimization of interest rate risk.

    d. Explain in specific terms how you would use a zero-coupon bond to immunize a bond portfolio. Discuss why a zero-coupon bond is an ideal instrument in this regard.

    e. Explain how contingent immunization, another bond-portfolio-management technique, differs from classical immunization. Discuss why a bond portfolio manager would engage in contingent immunization.

13. A friend of yours is the administrator of a college endowment fund that is designed to pay the expenses of a unique program at the college. Expenses of the program will be $1 million each year for seven years. After seven years the program will have been outmoded by new technology and will be disbanded. Interest rates on default- and call-free bonds are 12% for all maturities. Present various immunization strategies ranging from the purchase of one bond to the creation of a dedicated portfolio. Provide calculations and a discussion of the pros and cons of each approach.

14. The current yield curve on U.S. Treasury obligations is shown below. Assume all are pure discount bonds. If you wish to maintain an average portfolio duration of six years but are willing to temporarily depart from it, use this information to develop a number of possible speculations.

Maturity	YTM	Maturity	YTM
1 year	8.0%	6 years	8.5%
2	9.0	7	8.0
3	9.5	8	7.0
4	9.0	9	7.0
5	8.5	10	7.0

You have reason to believe that the yield curve by the *end of the coming year will be*:

Maturity	YTM	Maturity	YTM
1 year	7.0%	6 years	8.0%
2	8.0	7	8.0
3	8.0	8	7.0
4	8.0	9	7.0
5	8.0	10	7.0

15. You are given the following current yield curve on U.S. Treasuries. Assume for all calculations that all are pure discount bonds.

Maturity	YTM	Maturity	YTM
1 year	8.0%	6 years	8.5%
2	9.0	7	8.0
3	9.5	8	7.0
4	9.0	9	7.0
5	8.5	10	7.0

a. What is the duration of each of these pure discount bonds?
b. Assume your *HD* is four years and you want to buy only bonds with maturity in years 1 and 6. What percentage investment should be made in each to assure a fully immunized portfolio?
c. Using the notion of UET, calculate next year's expected yield curve.
d. If you bought the five-year bonds and held them to maturity, what is your expected *ARR*? (Assume you believe in UET.)
e. If you bought the five-year bonds and sold them in exactly one year, what is your expected return? Why is this different from the *ARR* found in part d? (Again, assume UET.)

16. You have gathered the following data on a variety of bonds that are candidates for various *investment* portfolios:

Bond	Moody's Quality Rating	D	Annual Coupon	YTM	Call Price	Current Price
1	Aa	3.7 years	9.00	9.00%	$1,090	$1,000
2	Aa	3.5	13.00	9.27	1,100	1,120
3	Baa	10.0	10.00	10.50	1,150	980
4	A	10.0	10.00	9.30	1,150	1,075
5	A	15.0	5.00	9.00	1,050	700
6	Baa	7.0	11.00	10.50	1,200	1,027
7	A	7.0	3.00	7.00	1,050	700

Evaluate the appropriateness of each bond for each of the following investment portfolios:

a. A charitable organization which has yearly contribution campaigns. While the organization would like to use all contributions to fund current research as well as to help families with current difficulties, the directors are somewhat concerned about yearly volatility in total contributions to the fund. As a result, the directors would like to maintain an average investment life of four to five years.

b. A pension fund for employees in a young and growing company. Expected retirement benefits will not begin to any major degree for at least another 20 years.

c. A pension fund for employees of a large midwestern city. A large proportion of the workers will be retiring within the next five years although their benefits are likely to be paid largely between years 5 through 10.

d. A doctor in a high income tax bracket who plans to retire within the next year and live off his extensive investments.

17. Consider the following bond data:

Bond	Default Rating	Years to Maturity	Annual Coupon	D	Current Price	Promised YTM
1	Aa	10	13%	—	$1,000.00	13.0%
2	Baa	13	4	—	415.80	14.0
3	A	8	9	7.3	—	13.2
4	Aa	5	10	4.5	—	13.0
11	Baa	10	10	—	791.31	14.0
12	Baa	15	8	—	631.47	14.0
13	A	10	11	7.1	—	13.2
14	B	7	10	4.5	—	14.5

a. Is the duration of bond 11 shorter or longer than the duration of bond 12?

b. Assume you believe the yield spread between Aa and Baa bonds should be 75 basis points (0.75%), as opposed to the 100 basis points shown between bonds 1 and 2. Develop an arbitrage strategy between the two.

c. You are considering the addition of either bond 2 or bond 12 to the portfolio of a high-tax-bracket client whose investment characteristics include a desire for moderate-to-low default risk and moderate duration. Select either 2 or 12 and justify your choice.

d. The yield curve is now flat and is expected to drop as we begin to enter a recession. Between bonds 3 and 13, which would a speculator buy?

e. The yield curve is now flat and you expect it to drop as we enter a recession. However, yields on high-default-risk bonds won't drop as dramatically as low-default-risk bonds because of an increase in risk premiums. Between bonds 4 and 14, which might you buy?

f. Consider only bond 14. If the *YTM* on this bond were to move downward to 12.0% (tomorrow morning), by about what percentage would its price be expected to rise?

18. As senior investment officer for the Street Insurance Company, you have been asked by the president to justify the increased turnover rate in the debt portfolio over the past year. You have been given the following examples of transactions that were executed by your staff. Describe the bond-portfolio-management methods illustrated by the transactions.

Month	Rating	Issue	Price	Yield
January	Sold: Aaa	Standard Oil of California 7% due 4/1/96	91¼	7.83%
	Bought:	U.S. T-bonds 7% due 5/15/98	92	7.72%
June	Sold:	U.S. T-bonds 7% due 5/15/98	97	7.26%
	Bought: Aaa	Standard Oil of California 7% due 4/1/96	94	7.57%
July	Sold: Aaa/AA	Pacific Telephone & Telegraph 7⅝% due 6/1/09	100	7.625%
	Bought: Aa/AA	Illinois Power 7⅝% due 6/1/03	99¾	7.65%
October	Sold: Aa/AA	Illinois Power 7⅝% due 6/1/03	99	7.71%
	Bought: Aaa/AA	Pacific Telephone & Telegraph 7⅝% due 6/1/09	98¾	7.73%
March	Sold: Aaa	General Electric 7½% due 3/1/96	105	7.07%
	Bought: Aaa	Short-term investments		

19. Active bond management, as contrasted with a passive buy-and-hold strategy, has gained increased acceptance as investors have attempted to maximize the total return on the bond portfolios under their management. The following bond swaps could have been made in recent years as investors attempted to increase the total returns on their portfolios. From the information presented, identify the reason(s) investors may have made each swap.

	Action		Call	Price	YTM
(a)	Sell:	Baa-1 Georgia Pwr. 1st Mtg. 11⅝% due 2000	108.24	75⅝	15.71%
	Buy:	Baa-1 Georgia Pwr. 1st Mtg. 7⅜% due 2001	105.20	51⅛	15.39
(b)	Sell:	Aaa Amer. Tel. & Tel. Notes 13¼% due 1991	101.50	96⅛	14.02
	Buy:	U.S. Treasury Notes 14¼% due 1991	NC	102⅕	13.83
(c)	Sell:	Aa-1 Chase Manhattan Notes Zero Coupon due 1992	NC	25¼	14.37
	Buy:	Aa-1 Chase Manhattan Notes Float Rate due 2009	103.90	90¼	—

	Action		Call	Price	YTM
(d)	Sell:	A-1 Texas Oil & Gas 1st Mtg.			
		$8^{1}/_{4}\%$ due 1997	105.75	60	15.09
	Buy:	U.S. T-bond			
		$8^{1}/_{4}\%$ due 2005	NC	65.60	12.98
(e)	Sell:	A-1 K Mart Convertible Deb			
		6% due 1999	103.90	$62^{3}/_{4}$	10.83
	Buy:	A-2 Lucky Stores S.F. Deb			
		$11^{3}/_{4}\%$ due 2005	109.86	73	16.26

20. Suppose you are advising someone who is planning on investing in either a long-term bond or investing in a sequence of investments in short-term bonds (i.e., rolling over the proceeds of one bond into another short-term bond). The bonds have no credit risk.

    a. The investor is saving to fund a college education. Which of the two strategies would you undertake? Defend your answer.

    b. Now suppose you are told that the long-term bond has a higher yield-to-maturity than the short-term bond. How does this affect your choice? Again, defend your answer.

21. Discuss the concept of convexity.

22. You are an active interest rate anticipator and believe that interest rates are more likely to rise during the next year than they are likely to fall. Your current portfolio duration is 7 years. What change in duration might you make? What type of convexity would you wish to have—that is, positive or negative and large or small?

23. Convexity is more important when rates are:

    a. high.

    b. low.

    c. expected to change very little.

    d. depends upon whether the note is selling at a premium or a discount.

24. Positive convexity implies:

    a. that price increases at a faster rate as yields drop, than price decreases as yields rise.

    b. that price changes are equal for increases in yields and decreases in yields.

    c. that price increases at a slower rate as yields drop, then price decreases as yields rise.

    d. nothing with respect to future price changes.

25. Most U.S. Treasury notes have the following degree of convexity:

    a. negative

    b. positive

    c. zero

    d. additional information is required

DATAFILE ANALYSIS

1. *Bond Mutual Fund Duration.* Review the contents of the MFBOND.WK1 datafile. Regress the returns on Babson TR-Long mutual fund on the returns of the index of 20-year government bonds. Interpret the results.

REFERENCES

Excellent discussions of bond duration can be found in:

BABCOCK, G., "Duration as a Link Between Yield and Value," *Journal of Portfolio Management*, Summer 1984 and Fall 1984.

BIERWAG, GERALD O., and GEORGE KAUFMAN, "Coping with the Risk of Interest Rate Fluctuations: A Note," *Journal of Business*, July 1977.

MCENALLY, RICHARD, "Duration as a Practical Tool in Bond Management," *Journal of Portfolio Management*, Summer 1977.

TRAINER, FRANCIS, JESSE YAWITZ, and WILLIAM MARSHALL, "Holding Period Is the Key to Risk Threshold," *Journal of Portfolio Management*, Winter 1979.

Helpful reviews of bond management techniques can be found in:

HOMER, SYDNEY, and MARTIN L. LIEBOWITZ, *Inside the Yield Book: New Tools for Bond Management*. Englewood Cliffs, NJ: Prentice-Hall, 1972.

LIEBOWITZ, MARTIN L., "Horizon Analysis: A New Analytic Framework for Managed Bond Portfolios," *Journal of Portfolio Management*, Spring 1975.

TUTTLE, DONALD L., Ed., *The Revolution in Techniques for Managing Bond Portfolios*. Charlottesville, VA: Institute of Chartered Financial Analysts, 1983.

Interesting papers in recent practitioner journals include:

BIERWAG, GERALD O., CHARLES J. CORRADO, and GEORGE C. KAUFMAN, "Computing Durations for Bond Portfolios," *Journal of Portfolio Management*, Fall 1990.

LANGETIEG, TERRENCE C., MARTIN L. LEIBOWITZ, and STANLEY KOGELMAN, "Duration Targeting and the Management of Multiperiod Returns," *The Financial Analysts Journal*, September–October 1990.

LEIBOWITZ, MARTIN L., WILLIAM S. KRASKER, and ARDAVAN NOZARI, "Spread Duration: A New Tool for Bond Portfolio Management," *Journal of Portfolio Management*, Spring 1990.

MESSMORE, THOMAS E., "The Duration of Surplus," *Journal of Portfolio Management*, Winter 1990.

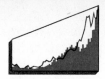

Equity Valuation

The analysis and valuation of equity securities can be an exciting process. It requires a blending of many interesting disciplines including economic theory, business strategy, developments in technology, international competition, and so forth. The equity analyst must look into the heart of a business venture to assess the profit potential of the firm as well as the major nondiversifiable risks of the firm. In this chapter we examine various equity valuation models. In Chapter 14, we illustrate how an active equity analysis as well as passive equity strategies might be conducted.

Most of this chapter is devoted to a discussion of the dividend discount model in which per share equity value is said to be the present value of expected future dividends per share. Since this model is based on expected future dividends, we examine how future dividend growth can be estimated. We also examine what this model says about the economic determinants of two widely used ratios of investment value: price to earnings and price to book value ratios.

There are other reasonable models that can be used to value a stock. Among these are models that focus on the earnings of a firm, the cash flow of a firm, and the investment opportunities of a firm. After presenting each, we will see that each is a variant of the basic dividend discount model. By focusing on different aspects of stock valuation, however, they provide another way of looking at the problem.

But before any of these valuation models can be examined, we should clarify the differences in required, expected, and actual equity returns.

EQUITY RETURNS

When bond selection was discussed in Chapters 11 and 12, a clear distinction was made between expected realized returns, promised yields to maturity, and actual realized returns. The same ideas apply to common stock selection, although the conventional terminology is somewhat different, and common stocks are usually evaluated over a single period (one month, one year, etc.), as opposed to over a planned horizon date.[1] Individuals will *purchase* a stock if their *required return is less than (or equal to) their expected return* on the stock. Conversely, they will *sell* a stock if their *required return exceeds* the stock's *expected return*. Once the buy or sell decision is made, a single-period *actual return* is realized that may be different from that expected or required.

The required rate of return should fairly compensate investors for both delaying immediate consumption and accepting the risk inherent in the security. In terms of the traditional capital asset pricing model (CAPM), this can be expressed as:

Security Market Line (SML)
$$RR_i = RF + \beta_i(RP_m)$$
(13.1)

where RR_i refers to the required single-period return on stock i, RF is the current risk-free rate of interest (compensation for delaying consumption), β_i is the amount of nondiversifiable risk in stock i relative to the aggregate market portfolio, and RP_m is the risk premium required on a stock of average risk. Assume that you have completed an analysis of Achilles Corporation and believe the stock has 20% more nondiversifiable risk than the average stock (implying a beta of 1.2). If the risk-free rate is now 8% and you believe a 5% risk premium on an average stock is fair, your required yearly return will be 14% [8% + 1.2(5%)]. This is shown in Figure 13-1 as point A.

Single-period expected returns on a stock are composed of an expected dividend yield plus an expected capital gains yield. Mathematically:

Single Period Expected Return
$$E(R_t) = \frac{D_t}{P_{t-1}} + \frac{P_t - P_{t-1}}{P_{t-1}}$$
(13.2)

where $E(R_t)$ refers to the expected return during period t, D_t is the expected dividend to be paid at the end of period t, and P_t (or P_{t-1}) is the price of the stock at the end of period t (or $t - 1$). For example, assume that Achilles Corporation is now selling on the NYSE at $40. You expect that a year from now a $2 dividend will be paid and the stock will be selling for $46. As a result, your expected return is composed of a 5% dividend yield plus a 15% capital gain yield, a total expected return of 20%:

$$\frac{\$2}{\$40} + \frac{\$46 - \$40}{\$40} = 0.2$$

This is plotted in Figure 13-1 as point B.

Any difference between expected and required returns is referred to as an expected *excess return*. Excess returns represent *pure* profit, a profit earned above that required to compensate for the stock's risk. According to the efficient market theory, excess returns will not exist. Individuals will buy or sell the stock until

---

[1] Theoretically, the single period can be thought of as the time interval between now and the horizon date. If, for example, the horizon date is two years away, two years would be used as the single period. In practice, however, stock returns are usually evaluated over time intervals shorter than typical horizon dates.

FIGURE 13-1 *Required Versus Expected Returns*

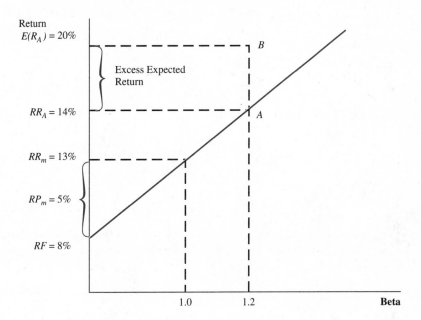

its price is set so that expected returns equal required returns. However, if the markets are not perfectly efficient, excess returns such as the difference between points *A* and *B* in Figure 13-1 might be possible.

Actual returns are calculated in the same manner as expected returns, except that actual dividends and prices are used instead of expected values. For example, if Achilles *actually* pays a dividend of $2.10 and sells for $43 at year-end, the actual return would be 12.75%:

$$\frac{\$2.10}{\$40} + \frac{\$43 - \$40}{\$40} = 0.1275$$

Throughout this chapter and the next we examine various aspects of common stock selection. As with the two bond chapters, this chapter concentrates on fundamental valuation concepts; the next chapter focuses more directly upon stock trading. Two broad topics are discussed in this chapter: (1) stock valuation and (2) stock returns. Because of the pivotal role that stock prices play in determining returns, valuation is taken up first.

MARKET CLEARING PRICES

The market price of a stock, like that of all other economic goods, is a function of supply and demand. At a given point in time, the available supply of the stock

FIGURE 13-2 *Security Price Determination*

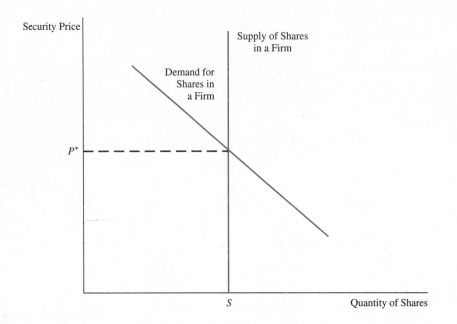

is fixed and equal to the quantity sold by the issuer. This is illustrated by the vertical line *S* in Figure 13-2. Total demand to own the stock depends upon the price at which it could be bought. At high prices only the most optimistic individuals would be willing to hold the security in their portfolios, and demand would be small. At low prices demand would increase. Any time there are differences of opinion about any stock's (or any security's) future prospects, a downward-sloping demand curve, such as that shown in Figure 13-2, would result.

As shown in Figure 13-2, the equilibrium price of the stock is *P**. At *P**, total desire to own the stock equals the outstanding supply. At higher prices investors desire to hold fewer shares than are actually available, and attempts by investors and speculators to sell shares will drive prices down to *P**. At prices lower than *P** attempts to buy shares will drive prices up.

Figure 13-2 is useful in making four points:

1. Investors need not all agree about the proper value of a security. Forecasts of future prospects will differ among investors when they hold different information about the security. This is important to recognize, since the discussion of market value in this chapter is addressed largely to the single investor's assessment of a stock's value within his or her portfolio. Our aim is not so much to establish *P** as it is to determine the price a particular investor would be willing to pay. We will refer to this price as its *intrinsic* or *fair value*.

2. The current market price is *not* a market consensus about the intrinsic value of the security. Instead, it reflects the opinion of the *marginal investor*. This individual would not wish to own the security if its price were slightly higher.

3. The slope of the demand curve is determined by the extent to which investors have similar beliefs about a security's prospects. When a diversity of opinions exists, the demand curve will be downward sloping, and changes in supply will affect prices. When there is complete agreement, the demand curve is horizontal; regardless of supply, only one price will prevail.[2] The extent to which individuals assign similar values to a security depends upon the information they hold. If all investors hold the same information, the demand curve is horizontal. If information is not costless and not available to everyone, a downward-sloping demand curve would result.

4. Equilibrium prices, and thus market trading prices, will change only when (a) new information enters the market to cause a shift in the demand curve or (b) the quantity supplied changes (assuming investors have diverse opinions).

As noted, the focus of this section is on how an individual investor might assign a value to a given stock. This value estimate may differ from existing trading prices if the investor holds either more or less information about the security than does the market average. Wise investors will attempt to determine *why* their value estimates differ from market prices. Is it because they have better information or poorer information?

ALTERNATIVE VALUATION TECHNIQUES

General Approaches to Valuation

Historically, six approaches to assessing the value of a security have been used. These are:

1. Par value
2. Book value
3. Liquidation value
4. Replacement value
5. Substitution value
6. Present value

To help illustrate the meaning and usefulness of each approach, a hypothetical balance sheet of Busch, Inc., is shown in Table 13-1.

Par Value. The par value (or stated value) of stock is specified in the firm's corporate charter. Par value is simply a legal definition that has no economic impact upon the firm. The fact that Busch common stock had a $1 par value is useful to know only because it occasionally aids in calculating the number of common shares outstanding. Dividing Busch's common stock dollar balance of

---

[2] Assumptions of homogeneous expectations and a perfectly elastic demand curve are used in the traditional version of the CAPM.

TABLE 13-1 *Busch, Inc., Consolidated Balance Sheet, December 31, 1995*

Assets	(millions)	Liabilities and Equity	(millions)
Cash and Marketable Securities	$ 69.4	Accounts Payable	$ 491.7
Accounts Receivable	373.0	Wage and Salaries	180.0
Inventories	427.8	Other Current Liabilities	343.9
Other Current Assets	150.4	Total	1,015.6
Total	1,020.6	Long-Term Debt	1,126.8
Gross Plant and Equipment	6,099.3	Deferred Taxes	1,090.8
Accumulated Depreciation	1,671.7	Convertible Preferred	286.9
Net Plant	4,427.6	Shareholder Equity	
		Common Stock ($1 Par)	295.3
Other Assets	385.6	Capital in Excess of Par	6.1
		Retained Earnings	2,472.2
		Foreign Currency Adj.	0.9
		Treasury Stock	(460.8)
		Total	2,313.7
	$5,833.8		$5,833.8

$295.3 million by the $1 par shows the firm had 295.3 million shares outstanding. Many firms issue stock without designating a par or stated value.

Book Value. The total book value of a security is the dollar amount recorded on the firm's balance sheet. For example, the book value of Busch's common equity was $2,313.7 million. To find book value per share, total book value is simply divided by the number of shares outstanding. Busch had 295.3 million common shares outstanding and thus had a book value per share of $7.84 ($2,313.7/295.3).

As a general rule, book value is a poor indicator of the value of a stock for at least three reasons. First, it is historical in nature rather than future-oriented. In the case of Busch, a large percentage of its land, plant, and equipment are recorded in historical, original-cost dollars and may bear little relationship to current, inflated prices. The replacement value of its assets is surely larger than recorded book values. Second, comparability of reported book values between companies is a significant problem. Two companies may be identical in all respects except for their accounting procedures. For example, LIFO versus FIFO inventory valuation, straight-line versus declining balance depreciation, capitalizing versus expensing R&D, and so forth, are all generally accepted accounting principles that can lead to significantly different book values among firms.[3] Finally, book

---

[3] There are situations in which book value is a good estimate of a security's value. For example, public utility commissions in various states follow a policy of increasing (or decreasing) customer rates whenever the market price of the stock is below (or above) book value per share. If commissions actively pursue this policy of setting market value ÷ book value ratios equal to 1.0, market prices should be very close to book values. In addition, for some firms the recorded book value is a reasonable approximation of the asset's replacement value. For example, short-term bank loans and demand deposits are probably recorded at values close to their true values.

value reflects solely the original dollar investment made by a security holder. If this investment earns a return higher (or lower) than investors currently require, the current intrinsic worth should be higher (or lower) than the initial investment.

Liquidation Value. The liquidation value of a security represents the cash a security holder would receive if the firm discontinued operations, sold its assets, and distributed the net proceeds to security holders in order of legal priority. Liquidation is, by definition, the last action a firm would ever take, and thus liquidation value represents the *minimum* value of a security. Because corporate liquidations are rare and asset liquidation values are difficult to assess, liquidation value is typically not calculated. Even if a security's liquidation value were known, the assets of a firm are generally worth more as a going concern than in liquidation. If they are not, the firm should be liquidated.

Replacement Value. Replacement value represents a security's claim to the current reproduction value of the firm's assets. It differs from liquidation value in that liquidation value applies to the net selling value of assets, whereas replacement value applies to the cost required to reproduce existing asset productivity at today's prices. If there were no transaction costs associated with liquidating a firm (attorney fees, selling commissions, disassembly costs, etc.), liquidation and replacement values should be equal. However, such costs do exist, and replacement value exceeds liquidation value.

The problem with using replacement value as a measure of a stock's worth is two-fold and is similar to that of using liquidation value. First, replacment value is difficult to determine. Second, a stock bears an economic value to the extent that future cash flows are expected. These cash flows might be totally unrelated to the asset's replacement value.

Substitution Value. Substitution value reflects the value of a security when compared with that of substitute securities. An example will best illustrate this procedure. Assume that we wish to assign a value to the common stock of ABC Corporation. The company's product line is shown below:

Product	Total Dollar Earnings
A	$10 million
B	7 million
C	3 million
	$20 million

If we could find three different firms each of which, respectively, sells only product A, B, or C, then we should be able to create a portfolio of the three which would exactly duplicate ABC Corporation. The total market value of the portfolio of the three firms would equal the substitution value of ABC Corporation. Assume that we find three such firms, and observe:

Firm	Traded Market Value	÷	Total Dollar Earnings	=	Market Value Per $ Earnings
AAA Corp.	$500 million	÷	$50 million	=	$10
BBB Corp.	$600 million	÷	$40 million	=	$15
CCC Corp.	$ 8 million	÷	$ 1 million	=	$ 8

Knowing this, we could estimate a substitution value for ABC Corporation as follows:

Product	Market Value Per $ Earnings	×	ABC Corp. Total Dollar Earnings	=	Substitution Value
A	$10	×	$10 million	=	$100 million
B	$15	×	7 million	=	$105 million
C	$ 8	×	3 million	=	$ 24 million
					$229 million

The substitution value of ABC would equal $229 million.

There are two problems with using substitution value. First, it neglects any economies (or diseconomies) of scale that might arise when products *A* and *B* are produced together as opposed to separately. Second, and more important, is the practical problem of identifying comparable firms. Management talent, patents and copyrights, geographic areas, and so forth, all cause considerable differences in firms even though their product lines appear identical. Substitution value estimates are imperfect at best.

Present Value. The basis of the present-value approach was discussed in Chapter 11 when the bond valuation model was presented. According to the present-value model, the current worth of a security is equal to the present value of the future economic benefits that the security holder expects to receive. A variety of present-value models exist. We will concentrate upon the most commonly used version, known as the *dividend valuation model.*

To illustrate the dividend valuation model, we will calculate the equity value of Midwest Machinery, Inc. Midwest's current financial statements are shown in Table 13-2.

THE DIVIDEND VALUATION MODEL

The most commonly used approach to valuing common stock is to find the present value of expected future dividends. After an analysis of the future prospects and risks of a firm, the analyst estimates the dividends *per share* expected to be paid in each future year as well as an appropriate rate of return to be earned in each future year. If we define D_t as the dividend per share expected to be received at the end of year t, N as the number of years during which dividends will be paid, and K_t as the required return for year t, then the value of the stock would be:

TABLE 13-2 *Midwest Machinery Financial Statements, End of Year 0*

Assets	*(millions)*	*Liabilities and Equity*		*(millions)*
Current Assets	$ 20	Current Liabilities	(8%)	$ 10
		Long-Term Debt	(8%)	30
		Total Debt		$ 40
Gross Plant	$150	Common Stock ($1 Par)		2
Accumulated Depreciation	⟨70⟩	Paid-in Surplus		10
Net Plant	$ 80	Retained Profits		48
Total Assets	$100	Total Equity		$ 60
		Total Liabilities and Equity		$100

	(millions)
Sales	$200.0
Cost of Goods Sold	120.0
Gross Profit	$ 80.0
Selling, General, and Administration	50.0
Depreciation	10.0
Net Operating Income	20.0
Interest	3.2
Net Income Before Tax	16.8
Taxes (50%)	8.4
Net Income	$ 8.4
Total Dividends Paid	$ 8.4

General Dividend Valuation Model

$$P_0 = \frac{D_1}{1 + K_1} + \frac{D_2}{(1 + K_1)(1 + K_2)}$$
$$+ \ldots + \frac{D_N}{(1 + K_1)(1 + K_2) \ldots (1 + K_N)}$$

(13.3)

Since common stock has an infinite legal life, N could be infinity. However, if investors expect that the firm's assets will eventually be liquidated, N would be equal to the number of periods until expected liquidation.

To demonstrate the application of Equation 13.3, assume that a business venture is formed to harvest timber from a large tract of land. Timber cutting is expected to last three years and to provide dividends per share of $2, $3, and $25 at the end of years 1, 2, and 3, respectively. At the end of year 3 the land is to be sold and the corporation dissolved. After an analysis of expected risk-free rates and risks associated with the project, the investor determines that a return of 9%, 10%, and 12% in each respective year would be necessary. Given this information, the value of each share would be $22.95:

$$\frac{\$2}{1.09} + \frac{\$3}{(1.09)(1.10)} + \frac{\$25}{(1.09)(1.10)(1.12)} = \$22.95$$

How a Fund Picks a Stock

In this article, the portfolio manager for a mutual fund called Strong Discovery Fund discusses the procedures he uses in selecting a stock in which the fund will invest.

You always hear how important it is to diversify, diversify, diversify, and that investing in a mutual fund is an excellent way to do so. But did you ever wonder how fund managers pick the stocks that (in the best-case scenario) bring high returns to personal investors?

Dick Strong, portfolio manager of the **Strong Discovery Fund,** an aggressive growth fund that had a return of 28.91 percent for the 12-month period ending March 31, 1992, shed some light on the subject. Strong and analyst Walter Morris allowed YOUR MONEY to get a bird's-eye view of fund management by sharing each painstaking step in the process of selecting stocks for the Discovery fund.

"To begin with, Strong is a top-down shop," explains Morris. "This means that the principals—Dick, Chip Packley, and myself—first look at the general economic environment and then pick the industry segments that seem poised for profits. We're the opposite of a bottom-up shop, which picks front-runner stocks first and then looks at economic trends. Dick has a knack for spotting major themes that will drive the economy."

Right now Strong has his eye on rising housing starts and the companies that will benefit from them. This is how he spotted Morgan Products, a home door and window manufacturer. . . .

"The first step, after identifying what industry segment we see coming up," explains Morris, "is going into our computer screens and scanning our huge on-line data base of all public companies. Our system is like a more extensive *Value Line,* with all the companies segmented by industry. Average-Joe investors could do this on a much less detailed basis."

"We then look for the cheapest stocks [lowest stock price relative to the value of the company] within the market sector we're going after," he continues. "We do a lot of complicated financial calculations, like discounted cash flow. The main gist is to look backward at the company's history and make future projections based on our analyses."

Morris is quick to point out that although the research process sounds mechanical, the human factor is the driving force behind it. "No matter how many numbers you crunch on the computer, you still have to make sense out of them. Otherwise, it's garbage in, garbage out."

After the analysts have compiled a list of the top 10 or 20 contenders, they request and thoroughly scrutinize these companies' annual reports and other materials. The all-important next step is to meet with management, either by visiting the company or arranging a meeting elsewhere. In the case of Morgan Products, Strong and Morris decided to meet the company's president and CFO at a restaurant halfway between Morgan's Lincolnshire, Ill., headquarters and Strong's Milwaukee offices. During the meeting the Morgan representatives fleshed out the company's financial picture, work environment, distribution channels, and their plans for future profitability.

After meeting with the management of a potential buy, Strong, Morris, and Packley hash it out over the numbers, and give their personal impressions as well. Portfolio manager Strong has the ultimate responsibility of giving the green light to buy, so he gets as much input as he can.

The buying range for a given stock is based on the earlier calculations, "but the actual number can be illusory," Morris says. "If it comes up as $18.95, it actually means a range of $17 to $19."

So what happens when it's time to actually purchase the shares? "If and when we're ready to buy, we work with outside brokers like Goldman Sachs or Merrill Lynch," explains Strong, "I can execute a transaction with a phone call."

Once shares are actually bought, they're not forgotten. The principals monitor the company's activity on a quarterly basis.

"Bottom line, I think it's really important to remember that this business is as much an art as a science," says Morris. "It's the human factor that's crucial—there's no manual you can consult for what we do."

SOURCE: Christine Verdi, "How a Fund Picks a Stock," *Your Money,* July 1992.

Clearly, the dividend model is analogous to bond valuation models. The difference lies solely in the difficulties of specifying the inputs—the uncertainty about future dividends and the appropriate discount rate. Reasonable estimates of the level and timing of future dividends can be made only after the analyst has developed well-informed opinions about future national and international economic events, determinants of industry growth, probable firm market share, cost control, financing policies, and so forth. Developing such opinions can be a major task.

Required returns are also difficult to specify. If the assumptions of the CAPM are reasonably valid, it could be used. On that basis, the required return in year t would be equal to:

$$K_{et} = RF_t + \beta_t(RP_{mt})$$

where K_{et} = required equity return in year t, RF_t = risk-free rate available in year t, β_t = the beta of the stock expected for year t, and RP_{mt} = the market risk premium during year t. Differences in any of these return determinants from year to year would cause differences in individual K_{et}'s. Again, these variables are difficult to estimate with any reasonable confidence.

In practice, professional analysts generally apply a *single discount rate* to all cash flows rather than a rate unique to each year. In this case the dividend model becomes:

Dividend Valuation with a Single Discount Rate
$$P_0 = \frac{D_1}{1 + K_e} + \frac{D_2}{(1 + K_e)^2} + \cdots + \frac{D_N}{(1 + K_e)^N}$$
$$= \sum_{t=1}^{N} \frac{D_t}{(1 + K_e)^t}$$
(13.4)

Security Market Line
and K_e is estimated from:
$$K_e = RF + \beta_e(RP_m)$$
(13.5)

Conceptually the risk-free rate used is the expected yield to maturity on a risk-free security maturing in year N. As a practical matter, yields on long-term governments not subject to default or call risks are used. We use long-term nominal returns because they best reflect the inflation expectations over the life of the stock. Beta and the market risk premiums are assumed to be constant over time. The subscript e is used to designate an equity variable. K_e represents the cost of equity capital and β_e represents the beta of equity capital (as opposed to the cost and beta of debt capital or firm assets).

Capital Gains Versus Dividends. If the average stockholder were asked why a particular stock had been purchased, the answer would most likely be, "For its return—for the dividends and capital gains I expect to receive," and (neglecting risk) the answer is correct. But if capital gains are part of the returns that an investor values, why don't they appear in Equation 13.4? They do, although not explicitly.

Consider the situation in which a shareholder expects to sell shares at the end of year 2. The value of the stock at the end of period 0 would be equal to the present value of any dividends expected during years 1 and 2 plus the present value of the expected stock price at the end of year 2:

$$P_0 = \frac{D_1}{1 + K_e} + \frac{D_2}{(1 + K_e)^2} + \frac{P_2}{(1 + K_e)^2}$$

Yet the expected price at the end of year 2 should be equal to the present value (at the end of year 2) of dividends expected to be paid after year 2:

$$P_2 = \frac{D_3}{1 + K_e} + \frac{D_4}{(1 + K_e)^2} + \cdots$$

Thus, P_0 *is* determined by both future dividends and future selling prices. But since *all future selling prices must reflect future expected dividends,* the base determinant of existing stock prices is expected future dividends.

Constant Growth Model. If the dividends paid by a firm are expected to grow at a *constant growth rate to infinity,* Equation 13.4 can be considerably simplified. Defining G as this expected constant growth rate, Equation 13.4 reduces to:

Constant Dividend Growth Model

$$P_0 = \frac{D_1}{K_e - G}$$

$$= \frac{D_0(1 + G)}{K_e - G}$$

(13.6)

For example, consider the data on Midwest Machinery. Assume that after a thorough analysis of Midwest, an analyst concludes:

1. $RF = 8\%$
2. $RP_m = 5\%$
3. Beta of Midwest $= 1.2$
4. Long-run growth in dividends *per share* $= 5.6\%$
5. Expected dividend next year $= \$2.52$

Given these data, a required return of 14% is necessary [8% + 1.2(5%)], and the analyst would assess the value of Midwest to be $30 per share:

$$\frac{\$2.52}{0.14 - 0.056} = \$30$$

Firms that are expected to pay dividends that will grow at a constant rate to infinity clearly do not exist. Yet some firms do have reasonably stable dividend growths over relatively long time periods. In such cases Equation 13.6 provides a good approximation of the security's worth.

It is instructive to examine the composition of a stock's expected returns when the constant growth model is valid. Investors develop estimations of G and K_e and then determine a market price, P_0, so that the required return is expected to be earned. By rearranging Equation 13.6 we can see that, during each year, this expected return comes in two forms: an expected dividend yield and a growth in stock price. If the investor's required return equals the expected return, then:

Equilibrium Between Required and Expected Returns

$$\frac{\text{Required Yearly Return}}{} = \frac{\text{Expected Dividend Yield}}{} + \frac{\text{Expected Growth in Stock Price}}{} \quad (13.7)$$

$$K_e = \frac{D_1}{P_0} + G$$

For example, a stock that is selling for $25 and last paid a $0.92 dividend that is expected to grow over the long run at a constant rate of 9% per year is providing an expected return of 13%:

$$\frac{\$0.92(1.09)}{\$25} + 0.09 = 0.13$$

Whether the 13% is an appropriate return to expect on such an investment depends upon one's perceptions of the risk-free rate, the stock's beta, and the market risk premium.

In the case of Midwest Machinery, if its shares were now trading at $50, the analyst would not recommend a purchase. At a market price of $50 the expected return is 10.64% when a 14% return should be required:

$$\text{Expected Return} = \frac{D_1}{P_0} + G = \frac{\$2.52}{\$50} + 0.056 = 0.1064$$

As initially presented in Equation 13.6, G was defined as the dividend growth rate, but G also indicates the rate of growth in the stock's price. When a stock is priced via Equation 13.6, the best estimates of what K_e and G will be in the future are current estimates. Certainly they will change. But the best *estimates* of both, say five years hence, are the estimates made now, at period 0. Thus, the best estimation of the denominator in future years is today's denominator. The only term for which an expected change can be forecast is next period's dividend. Each year the numerator is expected to grow at a rate G. As a result, stock price is also *expected* to grow at rate G.

Consider another example. Assume that an analyst believes dividends paid on the Dow Jones Industrial Average (DJIA) will grow at a fairly constant rate over the long run. The analyst also believes the Dows are *properly valued* today at a current market price of $3,500. If the long-term, risk-free rate is 8%, the market risk premium is 6%, the beta of the DJIA is 1.0, and next year's expected dividend yield on the DJIA is 5%, what is the estimated value of the DJIA one year hence? First, a required rate of return of 14% is necessary (14% = 8% + 1.0 × 6%). Next, since the constant growth model applies, 5% of this required return will come in the form of an expected dividend yield, with the remaining 9% coming from yearly price growth. Thus, the DJIA is expected to be 9% higher, or $3,815, one year hence.

The constant growth model is appropriate whenever G is assumed constant to infinity, regardless of whether G is greater than zero, less than zero, or equal to zero. When G is exactly zero, Equation 13.6 reduces to an equation that is used to value a perpetuity:

Value with Zero Growth

$$P_0 = \frac{D}{K_e}$$

(13.8)

When growth is negative, large dividend yields will be required to offset yearly price losses in order to earn required returns.

Nonconstant Growth. Few stocks can reasonably meet the assumption of constant dividend growth. Young, developing firms are likely to pay no dividends early in their lives as all profits are retained in the business to support necessary asset expansion. (An example would be IBM during the early years of computer development.) Once such firms are well established and can institute dividend payments, the payments are likely to grow at a faster yearly rate than the firm is capable of sustaining over the long run. Finally, even mature firms are likely to have erratic dividend growth rates as the profits of the firm respond to normal business cycles.

For most of these situations, a *nonconstant growth* model would be appropriate. When using the nonconstant growth model, a future date is expected to eventually arrive beyond which the constant growth model can be used but before which dividends are expected to grow at yearly rates different from this longer-run constant rate. Working through an example will help make this clearer. Consider the stock of a department store in a city that is experiencing rapid population growth. Last year's dividend was equal to $1. During the next three years this dividend is expected to grow at 12% per year owing to a combination of population growth and lack of competition. Subsequently, growth will equal the population growth of 7% a year for another five years as competition from scheduled new store openings takes hold. Finally, as population growth slows, a long-run constant dividend growth of 3% per year is expected. What is the intrinsic value of this security if the required return is 15%?

The solution is shown in Table 13-3. First, expected yearly dividends are calculated for each of the next eight years (the years of abnormal growth). These are then discounted at a 15% required return to find their respective present values. In total, the present value of the first eight years' dividends is equal to $6.57. Beyond year 8 the constant growth model can be used. The value of a share at the end of year 8 would be equal to year 9's dividend divided by $K_e - G$. This year 8 share value is $16.91. To express this future price in terms of its present value, the $16.91 is discounted at the 15% required return for eight periods to get $5.53. The value today of all dividends expected beyond year 8 is $5.53. Summing the present value of dividends between now and the end of year 8 ($6.57) with the present value of dividends beyond year 8 ($5.53), the value of the share is $12.10.

The general formula applied to nonconstant growth firms is:

Nonconstant Dividend Growth Valuation

$$P_0 = \sum_{t=1}^{T} \frac{D_0(1 + G_1)(1 + G_2)\ldots(1 + G_t)}{(1 + K_e)^t}$$

$$+ \frac{D_T(1 + G)}{K_e - G} \times \frac{1}{(1 + K_e)^T}$$

(13.9)

TABLE 13-3 *Illustration of Nonconstant Growth Model*

Future Year	Yearly Growth	Expected Dividend	Present Value at 15%
1	12%	$1.12	$ 0.97
2	12	1.25	.95
3	12	1.40	.92
4	7	1.50	.86
5	7	1.61	.80
6	7	1.72	.74
7	7	1.84	.69
8	7	1.97	.64
Total of Years 1–8			$ 6.57

Plus present value of price at end of year 8:

a. Price at end of year 8:

$$P_8 = \frac{D_8(1 + G)}{K - G}$$

$$= \frac{\$1.97(1.03)}{0.15 - 0.03}$$

$$= \$16.91$$

b. Present value at period 0:

$$\frac{\$16.91}{1.15^8} = \qquad \$ 5.53$$

Total Value at Period 0 $\qquad$ $12.10

where G_t represents the growth rate in any year of abnormal growth t, T is the last date of abnormal growth, and G is the long-run constant growth rate after year T.

Determinants of G. Sustainable growth in dividends per share, whether constant or not, is directly related to two fundamental factors: the rate of return on equity investments and the percentage of earnings retained in the business. Symbolically:

Sustainable Growth $\qquad$ $G = ROE \times B$ $\qquad$ **(13.10)**

where B is the retention ratio (percentage of net income retained in the business) and ROE is the return on equity invested in the firm.

To illustrate this relationship, consider Midwest Machinery again. Assume that with the existing assets and capital structure, the firm could continue to earn net income equal to $8.4 million. Additions to plant needed to replace deteriorating equipment would be exactly covered by yearly depreciation provisions, and all income would be paid as dividends. Now assume that the board of directors suddenly decides to start retaining 40% of future earnings on which a 14% rate of return can be earned. If this policy is implemented immediately, the $8.4 million net income will be apportioned between $3.36 million in retained equity (0.4 retention × $8.4 income) and $5.04 million in dividends. Since 2 million shares are outstanding, present dividends per share will be $2.52 ($5.04 ÷ 2). Total equity will increase by the $3.36 million to $63.36 million. At a return on equity of 14%, next year's net income will be $8.87 million (0.4 × $63.36), and dividends per share will be $2.66 [$8.87 × 0.6) ÷ 2.0]. As a result of this retention policy, dividends will grow from $2.52 this year to $2.66 next year, a growth rate of 5.6%:

$$G = ROE \times B$$

$$= 14\% \times 0.4 = 5.6\%$$

The return on equity can also be separated into its individual components.[4] Analytically, *ROE* is a function of three factors:

1. *Asset efficiency*—the extent to which management can generate sales from a given asset base. Asset efficiency is measured by the asset-turnover ratio: sales ÷ assets.
2. *Expense control*—the extent to which management can increase net income after taxes from a given sales base. Expense control is measured by the after-tax profit margin: net income ÷ sales.
3. *Debt utilization*—the extent to which management relies upon debt financing to support a given level of assets. Debt utilization is measured by the ratio: total assets ÷ total equity.

When these terms are multiplied, individual terms cancel to yield the return on equity:

Return on Equity $ROE = \dfrac{\text{Asset}}{\text{Efficiency}} \times \dfrac{\text{Expense}}{\text{Control}} \times \dfrac{\text{Debt}}{\text{Utilization}}$ **(13.11)**

Determinants of Return on Equity $\dfrac{\text{Net Income}}{\text{Equity}} = \dfrac{\text{Sales}}{\text{Assets}} \times \dfrac{\text{Net Income}}{\text{Sales}} \times \dfrac{\text{Assets}}{\text{Equity}}$

A decomposition similar to this one is often helpful when analyzing historical or potential changes in equity returns. In the case of Midwest Machinery, the 14% *ROE* is composed of an asset efficiency ratio of 2.0 ($2 in sales generated for each dollar of assets), an expense control ratio of 4.2% ($0.042 of profits per $1 of sales), and a debt utilization measure of 1.67 ($1.67 in assets for each $1 of equity).

Calculating Historical Growth Rates. Past dividend growth rates of individual stocks are often poor predictors of future dividend growth. But past growth is

---

[4] *ROE* is the accounting rate of return on the book value of equity. It is not the market rate of return that the shareholder actually receives. Although market returns and accounting returns are related, many factors influence returns that do not affect accounting returns (at least not immediately). For example, changes in *RF*, *RP_m*, beta, expected dividend growth, etc., all affect stock prices and thus actual market returns but have no direct effect upon *ROE*.

important to know, if for no other reason than to explain why such growth occurred. In contrast, dividend growth rates of aggregate security indices such as the S&P 500 are more predictable.

Two general approaches can be used to calculate the growth rate inherent in any variable (dividends in our case). We will call this growth rate the *compound annual growth rate* (CAGR). The easier approach simply finds the annual rate of growth associated with a beginning and terminal value as follows:

Compound Annual Growth

$$V_T = V_o(1 + CAGR)^T \tag{13.12a}$$
$$CAGR = (V_T \div V_o)^{1/T} - 1.0 \tag{13.12b}$$

where V_T is the terminal value and V_o is the beginning value. For example, the dividends per share on the S&P 500 were $0.69 in 1926 and $12.20 in 1991. This represents a CAGR over this 65-year period of 4.52%:

$$0.0452 = [12.20 \div 0.69]^{1/65} - 1.0$$

The problem with this approach is that it neglects all values between the beginning and terminal values. This can be overcome by using a CAGR calculated from a *log-least-squares* regression equation. In this case, the log-natural of yearly dividends per share (DPS) is calculated and regressed against a year identifier as follows:

Log Least Squares CAGR

$$ln(DPS_t) = a + b\,(Year_t) + e_t \tag{13.13}$$

Here $ln(DPS)$ is the random dependent variable and $Year_t$ could be 1926, 1927, . . . 1991 or 1, 2, 3, . . . , 65. As long as successive values of Year are incremented by 1.0, the absolute scale of Year affects only the intercept term a, which is unimportant. The e_t values are random error terms. The b term is the estimated compound annual growth rate using all years of data.

In Figure 13-3, the natural logs of nominal S&P 500 dividends per share are shown on the vertical axis relative to the associated year on the horizontal axis. Actual values are shown as asterisks. Predicted values obtained from regression Equation (13.3) are shown by the solid line. The slope of this line represents the CAGR based on log-least-squares methodology and the b coefficient in the following regression equation:

$$ln(DPS_t) = -94.1 + 0.0484\,(Year_t) \qquad R^2 = 92.8\%$$

The constant term of -94.1 represents the natural log of dividends when the year number is equal to 0. In a regression of this sort, the term is meaningless. The more important term is the slope coefficient b. This slope represents the unit change in the natural log of dividends for each 1.0 unit change in time-one year. *Because one full unit change in the natural log of dividends (or any number) is 100%*, the 0.0484 value is interpreted as an average annual compound growth rate of 4.84%. The R^2 term is the percentage of variation in the dependent variable (natural log of DPS) associated with variation in the independent variables (time).

FIGURE 13-3 *Growth of S&P 500 Dividends (1926–1991)*

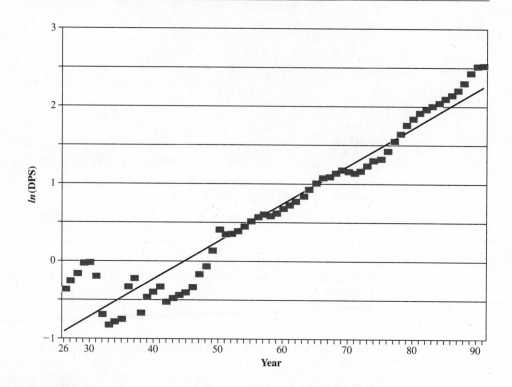

R-squared in a regression with a single independent variable is the correlation coefficient between the dependent variables squared. It can range from 0% to 100%, where 0% indicates no correlation and 100% indicates perfect correlation. The high *R*-squared in the DPS model above indicated that the annual growth rates of nominal dividends per share on the S&P 500 were fairly stable between 1926–1991.

In Table 13-4, CAGRs based on log-least-squares regressions are shown for a variety of periods. Except for the 1920s and early 1930s, nominal growth in S&P 500 dividends has been relatively stable. Compared with the 65-year nominal CAGR of 4.84%, the post-World War II dividend growth has been 5.51%.

Growth Stocks

To most laymen the term *growth stock* simply means a stock whose price is expected to increase at a faster rate than the average. For many years this definition was also common within the professional analyst community. However, as understanding of the determinants of stock values has developed, a more precise definition has arisen. *A growth stock is one for which the available returns on investments are greater than investors' required returns.*

TABLE 13-4 *Log-Least-Squares Compound Annual Growth Rates of S&P 500 Dividends per Share*

Period	CAGR	R^2
1926–1991	4.84%	92.8%
1926–1946	−0.96%	6.5%
1946–1991	5.51%	97.9%
1971–1991	7.14%	98.9%

A true growth situation has major implications for the value of the firm. This can be understood by examining the constant dividend growth model:

$$P_0 = \frac{D_1}{K_e - G} = \frac{D_1}{K_e - (B \times ROE)}$$

Next year's dividend per share will be equal to next year's earnings per share less any earnings retained in the business. Next year's earnings per share will equal per share book value (BV) times the accounting return on equity. Thus the constant dividend growth model can be expressed as follows:

$$P_0 = \frac{(BV \times ROE)(1 - B)}{K_e - (B \times ROE)} = BV \times \left[\frac{ROE(1 - B)}{K_e - (B \times ROE)} \right] \quad \textbf{(13.14)}$$

Note how the relationship between accounting returns on equity (ROE), desired investment return (K_e), and the retention rate (B) affects the value of a stock. Of course, ROE can be greater than, equal to, or less than K_e. This can be expressed symbolically by stating:

$$ROE = K_e + C \quad \textbf{(13.15)}$$

where C is a constant representing some difference between ROE and K_e. Substituting Equation 13.15 into 13.14 results in:

Market Price Versus Book Value
$$P_0 = BV \left[\frac{K_e(1 - B) + C(1 - B)}{K_e(1 - B) - CB} \right] \quad \textbf{(13.16)}$$

If ROE (returns earned) equals K_e (returns demanded), the stock's price is *not* affected by the payout ratio and will be equal to the book value per share. This was the case for Midwest Machinery. While future dividends are expected to grow, the value of the stock was equal to its book value. However, when ROE exceeds K_e (C is positive), the stock price will be larger than its book value and will increase as the retention rate increases. Finally, when ROE is less than K_e (C is negative), stock prices will be less than book value and will decrease as the retention rate increases.[5]

---

[5] This is true only if the firm restricts new investment to equal retained profit plus new debt in an amount that maintains a target capital structure.

TABLE 13-5 *Relationship Between P_0, K_e, ROE, and B*

Firm	Book Value per Share	K_e	ROE	Price of Various B		
				B = 0.3	B = 0.5	B = 0.8
NRML	$50	12%	12%	$50.00	$50.00	$ 50.00
GRTH	50	12	14	62.82	70.00	175.00
NGRT	50	12	10	38.89	35.71	25.00

These relationships are illustrated in Table 13-5 for three firms. Firm NRML represents a normal firm in which competitive pressures have forced *ROE* to equal K_e. Note that regardless of the retention rate, the stock price of NRML is the same as the stock's book value. Firm GRTH represents a typical growth situation in which *ROE* exceeds K_e. In this case the stock price increases as the retention rate increases. Finally, Firm NGRT is a negative-growth situation with K_e greater than *ROE*. As NGRT retains larger portions of income, its price falls.

The simple fact that a stock is a "growth" stock doesn't necessarily mean it is a good buy. Growth stocks may sell at their intrinsic values and should be bought for their investment merits rather than for their speculative potential. If one is searching for mispriced securities, growth stocks should provide no more candidates than normal- or declining-growth stocks. A good analyst will recognize a growth situation for what it is and look closely at why the firm's *ROE* exceeds K_e as well as how long this might persist.

The Price/Earnings Ratio

The price/earnings ratio of a stock is equal to the stock's current market price divided by some measure of earnings per share; that is:

$$\text{P/E Ratio} = \frac{\text{Market Price}}{\text{Earnings per Share}} \qquad (13.17)$$

As such, the P/E ratio indicates the dollar price being paid for each $1 of a firm's earnings. P/E ratios are widely used by professional analysts as a measure of the relative prices of different stocks.

The stock's current market price is easy to determine, since it is probably reported in the financial press. Earnings per share (*EPS*), however, are more difficult to determine. The easiest earnings figure to use would be the latest *ESP* as shown on the company's financial statements. In fact, P/E ratios reported in the financial press are typically calculated using such latest reported *EPS* numbers. However, people buy a stock not for its past earnings but, instead, for its expected future earnings. As a result, many security analysts will report P/E ratios based upon next year's expected *EPS*. Even then a problem can arise when comparing P/E ratios among firms if some of the firms are expected to have abnormally high *EPS* next year whereas others are expected to have an abnormally poor year. To correct for such an unusual situation, many analysts calculate the P/E ratio based upon an estimate of *normalized* earnings per share. Normalized *EPS* can be estimated either by a purely subjective guess or by using sophisticated statistical models. Regardless of how normalized earnings are calculated, they are meant to reflect the normal level of the firm's earnings exclusive of any temporary effects caused by the state of the business cycle, seasonal conditions in the industry, or unusual events affecting the firm.

Conceptually, the P/E ratio is determined by three factors: (1) investors' required returns, (2) expected earnings retention rate, and (3) expected returns on equity. Again, the easiest way to demonstrate this is to use the constant dividend growth model:

$$P_0 = \frac{D_1}{K_e - G}$$

Defining E_1 as next year's expected earnings per share and using other terms as we have previously, the constant growth price model can be rearranged into a P/E ratio model as follows:

Determinants of P/E Ratio

$$P_0 = \frac{E_1 \times (1 - B)}{K - (ROE \times B)}$$

$$P_0/E_1 = \frac{E_1(1 - B) \div E_1}{K - (ROE \times B)} = \frac{1 - B}{K - (ROE \times B)}$$

(13.18)

Equation 13.18 states that if dividends are expected to grow at a constant growth rate, the P/E ratio is theoretically equal to the stock's expected dividend payout ratio $(1 - B)$ divided by the difference between the required return and the expected growth rate $(ROE \times B)$. In the case of Midwest Machinery, we have been assuming an expected payout ratio of 60%, a required return of 14%, and an expected constant ROE of 14%. This would imply a theoretical P/E ratio of 7.14:

$$\frac{0.60}{0.14 - 0.14(0.4)} = 7.1429$$

In other words, we should be willing to pay $7.14 for each $1 of Midwest's earnings per share expected next year. Since we had earlier assumed an earnings per share next year of $4.20 ($8.4 million net income ÷ 2.0 million shares), this implies a stock price of $30.00:

Estimated Current Stock Value		Theoretical P/E Ratio	×	Expected Earnings Next Year
P_0	=	P_0/E_1	×	E_1
$30	=	7.1429	×	$4.20

Figure 13-4 shows the P/E levels for the Standard & Poor's Composite Index. Price/earnings ratios are shown for each year-end from 1926 through 1991. To measure earnings per share, Standard & Poor's used reported earnings during the

FIGURE 13-4 *Price to Earnings Ratio S&P 500 1926–1991*

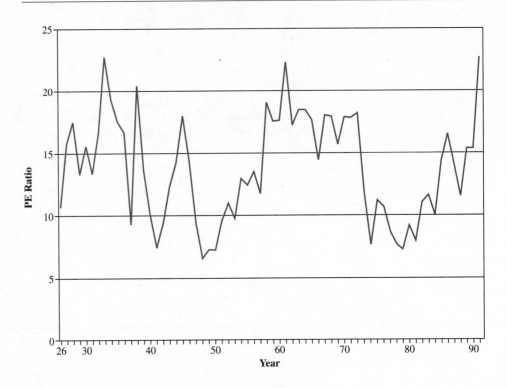

year for which a P/E ratio is shown (E_0 instead of E_1). As can be seen, aggregate market P/E ratios have been quite volatile. Unfortunately, many people simply look at today's P/E ratio, compare it with historical values, and then conclude that the market (or a single stock) is either overvalued or undervalued. For example, at the end of 1979 P/E ratios were at their lowest point for a number of years, and this persuaded many people that the market was undervalued. The market may, or may not, have been undervalued in late 1979, but a simple comparison of historical averages to current P/E ratios isn't adequate information on which to make such a decision. P/E ratios *should* change over time in response to changes in expected payout ratios, expected corporate returns on equity, and required returns.

Abnormal Growth. When a firm's dividends per share are expected to grow for a number of years at a faster (or slower) rate than expected in the long run, variants of Equation 13.18 can be used. We will illustrate only one abnormal growth model in which yearly growth will be G^* through year T and G thereafter. In this case the current price/earnings ratio is a multiple of the expected P/E ratio at the end of year T:

Abnormal Growth P/E Ratio

$$P_0/E_1 = \left(\frac{P_T}{E_{T+1}}\right)\left(\frac{1 + DY + G^*}{1 + K_e}\right)^T$$

$$= \left(\frac{1 - B}{K_e - G}\right)\left(\frac{1 + DY + G^*}{1 + K_e}\right)^T$$

(13.19)

where T = the last year during which abnormal growth occurs, B = the long-run retention ratio expected after year T, DY = the stock's current dividend yield, G^* = the abnormal dividend growth rate through year T, G = the constant dividend growth rate after year T, and K_e = required equity return.

For example, consider a stock on which the required return is 12%. Abnormal dividend growth of 10% per year will continue for 10 years, after which the growth rate will fall to 7%. The retention ratio after year T is expected to be 50%, and the current dividend yield is 5%. Thus, the P/E ratio *at the end of year T* is expected to be:

$$P_T/E_{T+1} = \frac{1.0 - 0.5}{0.12 - 0.07}$$

$$= 10.0$$

The current P/E ratio would be:

$$P_0/E_1 = 10.0 \left(\frac{1.0 + 0.05 + 0.1}{1.12}\right)^{10}$$

$$= 10(1.30)$$

$$= 13.0$$

OTHER VALUATION APPROACHES

The preceding discussion was based on a model that says that a share of stock is worth the present value of future dividends expected to be paid on the share. This makes perfect sense—the only way a share of stock can improve the owner's ability to consume is to pay dividends. A common stock is not like a painting, a record, or a book. It isn't bought for the enjoyment gained from looking at it, listening to it, or reading it on a rainy evening. A stock is bought for the future consumption opportunities it provides. And these can come only from the dividends it provides. Without the potential for future dividends, a stock is worth nothing.

Other valuation models exist in which dividends are not explicitly seen in an equation. We will examine three of these: (1) earnings valuation, (2) cash flow valuation and (3) investment opportunities valuation. However, all of these approaches are simply rearrangements of the basic dividend model. The role of dividends as the source of stock value never disappears.

Earnings Valuation

Underlying any ongoing stream of dividends are the earnings of the firm. These earnings, by definition, belong to the equity shareholders, so why can't we simply express the value of a share of common stock in terms of the earnings per share that the firm is expected to generate? We can. But in doing so an important point must be recognized: *Any earnings that are retained within the firm (not paid as dividends) are additional investments made by shareholders in the firm and should also be valued.*

For example, let's return to the Midwest Machinery example. To review, we are at the start of year 1. During year 0, Midwest earned $8.4 million on 2 million shares, or $4.20 per share. Since none of these earnings were retained in year 0, earnings per share will also be $4.20 in year 1. However, during year 1 Midwest intends to begin retaining 40% of all profits in the firm. This would result in retained profits of $1.68 per share and dividends per share of $2.52 in year 1. Beyond year 1 the retained profits will generate an expected *ROE* of 14% and result in a sustainable growth rate of 5.6%. Finally, investors require a return of 14%. Placing this information into the constant dividend growth model, each share of Midwest is worth $30:

$$P_0 = \frac{D_1}{K - G} = \frac{\$2.52}{0.14 - 0.056} = \$30$$

Now consider the valuation of the expected earnings that each share has a claim to. In particular, consider the $4.20 earnings per share (*EPS*) for year 1. All of this $4.20 belongs to the shareholder even though the firm will retain some of it. So why not simply find its present value? It does belong to the shareholder, so why not value it? And looking beyond year 1, all subsequent *EPS* also belong to the shareholder. So why not find their present values and say that the stock is worth the sum of the present values of all future *EPS*?

The answer is very simple. When a firm's management retains a portion of a shareholder's *EPS*, it is the same as the shareholder's being paid all *EPS* in dividends and then *reinvesting* the earnings retained. When Midwest Machinery pays dividends per share of $2.52 on earnings per share of $4.20, it is the same as paying the full $4.20 in dividends and having the shareholder immediately reinvest $1.68 in the firm. Retention of profits represents new investment by the equity owners.

It is perfectly correct to value the earnings per share of a stock as long as the reinvestment of earnings is also valued. The worth of a share of common stock is equal to the present value of all future expected earnings per share less the present value of all future investments per share:

General Earnings Valuation Model

$$P_0 = \sum_{t=1}^{N} \frac{EPS_t}{(1 + K_e)^t} - \sum_{t=1}^{N} \frac{IPS_t}{(1 + K_e)^t}$$

$$P_0 = \sum_{t=1}^{N} \frac{EPS_t - IPS_t}{(1 + K_e)^t}$$

(13.20)

where: EPS_t = the expected earnings per share in year t

IPS_t = the expected investment per share in year t

This equation values the expected future earnings-per-share stream that legally belongs to the shareholder. But it also values expected future investments made by the shareholder in order to generate the *EPS* stream.

Constant Growth Earnings Valuation. The general earnings valuation model shown in Equation 13.20 can be simplified considerably if future growth is expected to be constant. Again using G as this expected constant growth rate, Equation 13.20 reduces to:

Constant Growth Earnings Model
$$P_0 = \frac{EPS_1 - IPS_1}{K_e - G}$$
(13.21)

Applied to the Midwest Machinery example:

$$P_0 = \frac{\$4.20 - \$1.68}{0.14 - 0.056}$$

$$= \$30$$

Note that the dividend valuation model and the earnings valuation model are identical. The dividend model focuses upon net cash flows received by the investor (dividends), whereas the earnings model explicitly accounts for both the legal ownership of *EPS* and the incremental future reinvestment of earnings.

A Special Case. If the return that investors require (K_e) is identical to the return earned on owners' investments in the firm (ROE), the worth of a stock is simply the capitalized value of next year's earnings per share:

Value When $K_e = ROE$
$$P_0 = \frac{EPS_1}{K_e}$$
(13.22)

In fact, that is exactly the case for Midwest Machinery. Investors require a return of 14% and the firm is expected to generate a 14% *ROE* on any equity investment made in the firm. Thus, Equation 13.22 can be used to value the shares of Midwest:

$$P_0 = \frac{\$4.20}{0.14}$$

$$= \$30$$

When $ROE = K_e$, the retention of profits will have no impact on a stock's value. For example, if Midwest retains $1.00 at period 0, the dollar will grow to $1.14 one year later. But when this $1.14 is discounted back to its period 0 present value at 14%, it is worth exactly $1.00. *When* ROE = K_e, *retained earnings are invested in assets which have a zero net present value.*

Equation 13.22 would usually apply to firms in highly competitive, mature industries, such as food distribution, paper products, and public utilities.[6] It would not apply to developing industries, such as computer technology, or industries in decline, such as typewriter manufacturing. As a practical matter, it is wise to always use Equation 13.20 or Equation 13.21, since they apply to all firms.

Cash Flow Valuation

In principle, the worth of any asset is the present value of all future *cash flows* generated from the asset. In the calculation of accounting earnings per share there are a number of expenses that are no more than accounting entries. Depreciation, amortization of patents, goodwill, bad debt allowances, and many other "accounting expenses" involved no cash outflow during the year in which they are reported. Shouldn't they be added back to reported earnings per share in order to more fairly represent the cash flows generated from business operations?

Many analysts, in fact, do add such noncash expenses to earnings per share and compute the value of cash flows per share generated by the firm. This is referred to as a *cash flow valuation model*. First, expected cash flows from operations for year t (CF_t) are calculated as follows:

Cash Flow per Share
$$CF_t = EPS_t + \frac{NCE_t}{N_t}$$
(13.23)

where NCE_t refers to total noncash expenses expected in year t and N_t refers to the number of shares expected to be outstanding in year t. In addition, the investment per share (IPS_t) used in the earnings valuation model must be adjusted from a *net* investment to a *gross* investment. It was implicit in the earnings model that depreciation (and other noncash expenses) would be reinvested in the firm. However, if we wish to treat such items explicitly as cash available to equity holders, we must also explicitly recognize that such cash flows are in fact reinvested. The expected gross investment per share for year t (GPS_t) is calculated as:

Gross Investment per Share
$$GPS_t = IPS_t + \frac{NCE_t}{N_t}$$
(13.24)

Using these two adjustments, the cash flow valuation model is:

General Cash Flow Valuation Model
$$P_0 = \sum_{t=1}^{N} \frac{CF_t - GPS_t}{(1 + K_e)^t}$$
(13.25)

As you might imagine, a constant growth equivalent model can also be applied to this cash flow approach. We will not formally define it since it should be obvious given the two previous constant growth models. But let's illustrate its application to Midwest Machinery. First, expected cash flow for year 1 is found to be $9.20:

---

[6] Public utilities face indirect competition through regulatory authorities. A principal objective of most regulatory agencies is to set consumer prices at a level where ROE will be equal to K_e.

$$CF_1 = EPS_1 + (NCE_1 \div N_1)$$

$$= \$4.20 + (\$10.0 \div 2.0) = \$9.20$$

Second, expected gross reinvestment is \$6.68:

$$GPS_1 = IPS_1 + (NCE_1 \div N_1)$$

$$= \$1.68 + (\$10.0 \div 2.0) = \$6.68$$

Thus, the stock is worth \$30 using the cash flow valuation model:

$$\frac{\$9.20 - \$6.68}{0.14 - 0.056} = \$30$$

The dividend and cash flow models yield the same price, of course, because they both show the net cash that is received by shareholders—dividends. The only difference is cosmetic, in that the cash flow version explicitly shows cash flows available from operations and cash flows reinvested in the firm.

Investment Opportunities Valuation

The investment opportunities model separates the value of a share into two components: (1) the value of the existing assets and (2) the value of future investment opportunities. As an example, let's consider a competitor of Midwest Machinery—Western Machinery Corporation—that is identical to Midwest in all respects except in the return its equity holders require. Assume that the value of K_e for Western Machinery is 12%. As a result, the per share value of the stock will be:

$$P_0 = \frac{D_1}{K_e - G} = \frac{\$2.52}{0.12 - 0.056} = \$39.375$$

Let's take a close look at why the stock is selling for \$39.375. First, the earnings per share of the firm are \$4.20. To help make the example less complex, we will assume that accounting depreciation is equal to the actual economic depreciation of the firm's assets. Thus, management could pay all earnings of the firm as dividends to shareholders and not deplete the economic productivity of the assets. The existing assets are capable of providing a perpetual stream of dividends equal to current earnings per share. The present value of this perpetual dividend flow available from existing assets is \$35:

$$\frac{EPS}{K_e} = \frac{\$4.20}{0.12} = \$35$$

Without retaining any profits, the existing assets can generate cash flows which have a current worth of \$35 per share.

However, the management of Western Machinery does intend to make future investments in the firm. For example, at the end of the current year each shareholder will be asked to invest an incremental \$1.68 (the retained profits per share). When this \$1.68 is invested at 14%, it will yield an expected perpetual cash flow of $0.2352 ($1.68 $\times$ 0.14). Discounted at 12%, this perpetual cash flow stream will be worth $1.96 (0.2352 ÷ 0.12) at the end of the year. But the shareholder has been asked to pay $1.68 for the new assets, so the end-of-year expected *net present values* of these new investments will be $0.28 ($1.96 − $1.68).

The same type of analysis could be applied to all future years. Management will ask shareholders to invest in new assets which generate positive net present values. These net present values won't be forthcoming until future years, but there is no reason why their current present values should not be added to the stock's price. When the company is expected to maintain a constant retention of profits (*B*) and be able to invest at a constant return on new investment (*ROE**), the stock can be valued as follows:

Constant Growth Investment Opportunities Model

$$\underset{P_0}{\underset{\text{Share}}{\underset{\text{Per}}{\text{Price}}}} = \underset{\dfrac{EPS_0}{K_e}}{\underset{\text{Assets}}{\underset{\text{Existing}}{\text{Value of}}}} + \underset{\dfrac{B(EPS_0)}{K - (ROE^*)B}\left[\dfrac{ROE^* - K}{K}\right]}{\underset{\text{Investment Opportunities}}{\text{Value of Future}}} \quad \textbf{(13.26)}$$

When applied to Western Machinery:

$$P_0 = \frac{\$4.20}{0.12} + \frac{0.4(\$4.20)}{0.12 - 0.056} \times \frac{0.14 - 0.12}{0.12}$$

The current stock value of $39.375 consists of a $35.00 value placed on existing assets plus a $4.375 value associated with today's worth of the expected future profitability of new investments.

Equation 13.26 is the constant growth version of the investment opportunities model. When *ROE** and *B* values are expected to change over time, the more general model shown below should be used.

General Investment Opportunities Model

$$P_0 = \frac{EPS_0}{K_e} + \sum_{t=1}^{\infty} \frac{B_t EPS_t (ROE^* - K_e)}{K_e} \left(\frac{1}{1 + K_e}\right)^t \quad \textbf{(13.27)}$$

Again, the results obtained under each valuation model will be identical. They all value expected dividend flows. However, each focuses on a different approach to dividend valuation, and each approach can provide useful insights. For example, the investment opportunities model separates the value of existing assets from the value of future investment opportunities. If a large part of a stock's worth is associated with future opportunities, the security analyst would certainly wish to place an emphasis on technological developments and potential competition within the industry.

THE OPTION VALUE OF LEVERAGED EQUITY

Whenever equity holders borrow, they have the *option* to either pay all promised cash flows to debt holders or to declare bankruptcy and turn the firm's assets over to debt holders. The equity owner's position in this case is the same as owning the assets plus a *right to sell* the assets to bond holders. This right to sell is clearly a put option with an exercise price equal to the promised payments to debt owners.

$$\begin{matrix} \text{Owning} & \underrightarrow{\quad\text{is the}\quad} & \text{Owning} & & \text{Owning a Put} \\ \text{Equity} & \text{same as} & \text{Firm Assets} & + & \text{on Firm Assets} \end{matrix}$$

An alternative way to view the option position of equity holders is as a call option on firm assets. When promised cash flows are due to debt holders, equity holders will make the payments if the value of assets is greater than the promised payment. The exercise price of this call is clearly the promised payment to the debt holder.

$$\begin{matrix} \text{Owning} & \underrightarrow{\quad\text{is the}\quad} & \text{Owning a Call} \\ \text{Equity} & \text{same as} & \text{on Firm Assets} \end{matrix}$$

The option position of equity holders provides a direct explanation for how shareholders might be able to ''extract wealth'' from debt holders. Think of the value of a firm's assets as being the present value of future cash flows from the assets (A). This value will be apportioned between the value of debt (D) and the value of equity (E). That is $A = D + E$. If equity holders take actions that cause the value of D to fall without affecting asset value, then what is lost in D is gained in E. Since E is the value of a call option on A, anything that increases the value of an equity call option will decrease D.

One of the most important determinants of a call options value in the Black-Scholes Option Pricing Model is the standard deviation of the underlying asset's return. The greater the standard deviation of the asset's returns, the greater the value of the call. This presents equity owners with a motive to increase the riskiness of firm assets. Doing so increases bond default risk. And the reduction in bond values is simply transferred to equity holders.

Potential bond owners, of course, recognize this threat and will not purchase debt unless they are promised very high returns (e.g., junk or high yield bonds) or are protected. Equity holders offer a variety of protections: loan covenants, collateralization with specific low risk assets, yearly financial statement audits, dividend restrictions, and so forth.

Few (if any) security analysts actually apply option theory to the valuation of stocks. Current option models are unable to deal with the complexities of real world financial arrangements. Yet option theory is a useful device to explain the actions of highly leveraged firms in which equity owners have little to lose but the potential for sizeable gains. The *limited liability* aspect of equity is an important part of the value for highly leveraged firms.

PRICE AND EARNINGS GROWTH

Growth of corporate earnings and stock prices are intimately related. Over the *long run* there is a close correspondence between the two. For example, in Figure 13-5 the level of the S&P Composite Index is plotted together with its earnings

FIGURE 13-5 *Price Level and Earnings of the S&P 500 Index*

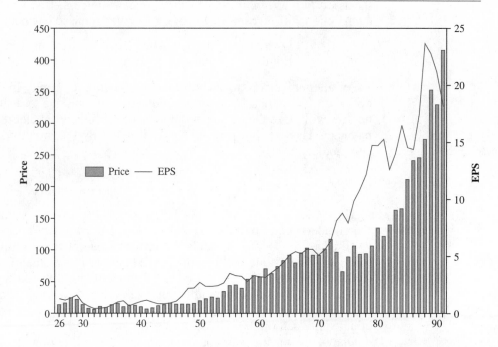

per share between 1927 and 1991. Clearly, over the long run, market price levels increase with earnings. And in the *short run*, unexpected changes in earnings can have dramatic effects on stock prices. Stocks with unexpected favorable earnings announcements show significant price growth. Stocks with unexpected unfavorable announcements decrease in value. Unexpected earnings changes *do* affect stock prices. Most of a stock's price adjustment occurs *before* the announcement date. In order to capture possible gains, you must be able to predict unexpected earnings announcements earlier than the average person.

However, earnings and growth rate predictions are more difficult to develop than one might believe. For example, historical growth rates are very poor predictors of future growth. A large body of research suggests that historical growth rates are only slightly related to future growth. This was first noted by Little in a paper appropriately titled "Higgledy Piggledy Growth." Little reported that successive changes in earnings per share of British firms were statistically uncorrelated. Numerous studies flowed from "Higgledy Piggledy," most confirming the results. For example, Brealey studied 700 U.S. firms and found correlations of earnings changes to be close to zero.

How have security analysts fared in their earnings predictions? The answer is debatable, but some evidence suggests not so well. The best-known study of security analysts' forecasts was conducted by Cragg and Malkiel. Their study was based upon earnings forecasts for 185 corporations made by five financial institutions. They found that over half the variation in forecasted growth was associated with historical growth. Even though historical growth is an extremely poor predictor of the future, a large part of the analysts' forecasts relied upon this past growth.

SUMMARY

The most widely used stock valuation model is known as the dividend valuation model, in which the intrinsic worth of a stock is estimated by discounting all future *expected dividends per share* at a return that depends upon the stock's risk. If dividends are expected to grow at a constant rate for an indefinite period of time, the general dividend model reduces to the constant dividend growth model. This model states that the intrinsic worth of a stock (P_0) is:

$$P_0 = \frac{D_0(1 + G)}{K_e - G}$$

where D_0 refers to the *per share* dividends just paid, G refers to the expected constant growth rate, and K_e refers to the required return on an equity investment. A nonconstant growth variant of this basic model allows for a number of years during which dividends per share grow at different rates but assumes that, after some point in the future, the best estimate of dividend growth is a constant rate.

A growth stock was defined as a stock for which the shareholders' required return is less than the return a company is actually able to provide. Whenever a firm is able to earn a larger rate of return on shareholder investments than shareholders require, shareholders will prefer the firm to retain a larger portion (perhaps all) of the firm's earnings since this will increase the expected future dividend stream as well as the stock's intrinsic worth. Alternatively, if required returns are equal to the marginal returns the firm is able to earn on new shareholder investment, shareholders will be indifferent to the level of profit retention in the firm.

Valuation models that focus upon characteristics other than dividends have been developed. For example, models may be based on earnings per share, cash flow per share, or a firm's investment opportunities. Each of these, however, is no more than a variant of the basic dividend model. Without the prospect of future dividends, a stock is worth nothing.

REVIEW PROBLEM # 1

Here is some financial and stock market information about a hypothetical firm called Data Control.

Data Control, Inc.
Financial Statements for the Year Ended December 1995

Assets	(millions)	Liabilities and Equity	(millions)
Current Assets	$1,300	Debt	$1,200
Net Plant	1,500	Equity	1,600
Total Assets	$2,800		$2,800

	(millions)
Sales	$4,800
Cash Expanses	4,110
Depreciation	150
Net Operating Income	540
Interest	100
New Income Pretax	440
Tax	(200)
Net Income	$ 240
Dividends Paid	$ 144

Market Information as of December 1995

Common Shares Outstanding	40 million
Price Per Share	$47.70
Risk-Free Rate	9%
Expected Return on the Market	14%
Estimated Beta	1.20

a. Calculate what the required return on Data Control should be using the security market line.
b. Calculate the sustainable growth rate (*G*) which would exist if the financial relationships shown in the balance sheet and income statements were to remain constant over time.
c. What is the fair market price of Data Control? (Use the dividend valuation model.)
d. Use the constant earnings and cash flow models to determine the stock's fair value.
e. Would you buy this stock? Why or why not?
f. What would a firm believer in efficient market theory say about your decision in part e?
g. Assume that Data Control's beta is really 1.0. Now what should the stock sell for?

Solution

a. K_e = $RF + B(RP_m)$

   = $9\% + 1.2(14\% - 9\%)$

   = 15%

b. G = $B \times ROE$

   6% = $0.4 \times 15\%$

$$B = \frac{240 - 144}{240} = 0.40$$

$$ROE = \frac{240}{1600} = 0.15$$

c. The constant growth model can be used here since the retention rate and *ROE* are expected to remain constant:

$$P_0 = \frac{D_0(1 + G)}{K_e - G} = \frac{3.60(1.06)}{0.15 - 0.06}$$

$$= 42.40$$

d. Constant earnings valuation model:

$$P_0 = \frac{(EPS_0 - IPS_0)(1 + G)}{K_e - G}$$

$$= \frac{(6.00 - 2.40)(1.06)}{0.15 - 0.06}$$

$$= 42.40$$

$$EPS_0 = 240 \div 40 = 6.00$$

$$IPS_0 = (240 - 144) \div 40 = 2.40$$

Constant cash flow valuation model:

$$P_0 = \frac{(CF_0 - GPS_0)(1 + G)}{K_e - G}$$

$$= \frac{(9.75 - 6.15)(1.06)}{0.15 - 0.06}$$

$$= \$42.40$$

$$CF_0 = EPS_0 + (Deprec. \div 40)$$

$$= 6.00 + (150 \div 40) = 9.75$$

$$GPS_0 = IPS_0 + (Deprec. \div 40)$$

$$= 2.40 + (150 \div 40) = 6.15$$

e. Given this information, the stock is worth $42.40. Since it is selling for $47.70, it is overpriced and you should not purchase it. In fact, if you really believe the $42.40 price, you might short sell it.

f. "You must have missed some important information. The market price of $47.70 totally reflects all information available to the markets on the stock."

g. The required return would be 14%:

$$9\% + 1.0(14\% - 9\%) = 14\%$$

And the fair price would be $47.70:

$$\frac{\$3.60(1.06)}{0.14 - 0.06} = \$47.70$$

If the true beta is 1.0, the stock is fairly priced in the markets.

REVIEW PROBLEM # 2

You have gathered the following data on five stocks that are assumed to have constant dividend growth. In addition, data are given on a sixth stock that is not expected to have constant growth.

Stock	1	2	3	4	5
Price	$111.11	$62.50	$125.00	$31.25	$11.76
D_1	$ 4.00	$ 3.00	$ 5.00	$ 1.00	$ 0.40
G	8%	8%	10%	12%	13%
Beta	6.0	0.8	1.0	1.2	1.4

Stock 6:

Last Dividend = $0.20
(Just Paid)

Growth in Dividends:

Years 1–5   = 20%

Year 6 Plus =   5%

Beta   =   1.6

a. Calculate the expected returns on stocks 1 through 5.
b. Use this information to specify the security market line.
c. What should stock 6 be selling for today?

Solution

a. In the constant growth model:

$$P_0 = D_1/(K - G)$$

Therefore:

$$K = D_1/P_0 + G$$

Using this relationship for stocks 1 through 5:

$$K_1 = 4.00/111.11 + 0.08 = 11.6\%$$

$$K_2 = 3.00/62.50 \ + 0.08 = 12.8\%$$

$$K_3 = 5.00/125.00 + 0.10 = 14.0\%$$

$$K_4 = 1.00/31.25 \ + 0.12 = 15.2\%$$

$$K_5 = 0.40/11.76 \ + 0.13 = 16.4\%$$

b. A graph of the K values above against the betas of each indicates the following SML relationship:

$$K = 8\% + \text{beta } (6\%)$$

c. The price at which stock 6 should trade can be calculated as follows:

$$K_6 = 8\% + 1.6(6\%) = 17.6\%$$

Year	Div.	Price	Present Value at 17.6%
1	0.2400	—	0.2041
2	0.2880	—	0.2082
3	0.3456	—	0.2123
4	0.4147	—	0.2168
5	0.4977	—	0.2213
5	—	4.1475*	1.8439
		Total	2.9066

$$*P_6 = \frac{0.4977(1.05)}{0.176 - 0.05}$$

$$= 4.147$$

Stock 6 should sell for $2.91. If it is trading for more than $2.91, it is not providing a return commensurate with its (CAPM) risk and thus should not be purchased. If it is trading for less than $2.91, it should be bought.

QUESTIONS AND PROBLEMS

1. Discuss the relative pros and cons of using the following approaches to estimate a security's value:
   a. Par value
   b. Book value
   c. Liquidation value
   d. Replacement value
   e. Substitution value
   f. Present value

2. Why is it wrong to say that the worth of a stock is the present value of expected future earnings per share on that stock?

3. A friend of yours has just completed a computer program that estimates the *total* dividends which a firm is expected to pay and finds the present value of these at the discount rate of your choosing. The friend calls the result "Total Equity Value" and divides this by the number of shares now outstanding to calculate today's per-share value. Where is your friend's grand effort in error?

4. You have made a very preliminary analysis of three common stocks with the information set forth below. All three stocks have the same investment grade or quality. Assume that the same important numerical financial ratios and relationships that currently exist (such as price/earnings ratio, payout ratio, dividend yield, etc.) will extend into the future, with small cyclical variations, for as far as you can see. For the investments being considered, you require a rate of return of 10% a year. Based solely on the information given in this problem:

CFA

a. Which, if any, of the stocks meet your requirements? Show your calculations.

b. Which one of the three stocks is most attractive for purchase?

	Stock		
	A	B	C
Return on Total Assets	10%	8%	12%
Return on Stockholders' Equity	14%	12%	15%
Estimated Earnings per Share in Current Year	$2.00	$1.65	$1.45
Estimated Dividend per Share in Current Year	$1.00	$1.00	$1.00
Current Market Price	27	25	23

5. Dividends per share of Jacques's Jackets were $2.54 ten years ago. The latest dividend (just paid) was $5.00. The stock has a beta of 1.5. The risk-free rate is 6%, and the market risk premium is 4%.

   a. If future dividend growth is expected to be identical to historical growth, what should the market value of JJ stock be?

   b. If JJ stock is selling at the price found in part a, what are next year's expected dividend yield and capital appreciation yield?

6. Historically, RR Corporation has retained 60% of its profits in the business. This is expected to continue. Future asset returns (*ROA*) are expected to be 10%, and the debt-to-equity ratio will remain constant at 25%. The risk-free rate is 8%, RP_m can be taken as 5%, and beta is about 1.3. The present dividend (just paid) was $2.50, and the stock is selling at $45. Should you buy or sell the stock?

7. You have been requested to estimate a fair market price for a new stock offering. Long-run growth will be constant, and the following data apply.

Last Year's Dividend per Share	$3
Last Year's Earnings per Share	$4
After-Tax Profit Margin	2%
Debt-to-Equity Ratio	100%
Asset Turnover	4 times
RF	8%
RP_m	6%
Beta	1.5

   a. Estimate the firm's return on equity.

   b. Estimate the firm's expected dividend growth.

   c. Estimate the fair value of the stock.

8. First Arizona Bancgroup dividends are expected to grow with population, personal income, and inflation at about 8% (forever). The stock is selling at $40 and beta is 0.90. *RF* is 8% and RP_m is 5%. What is the implied growth rate in the stock's price if next year's dividend will be $2.00? Would you buy or sell the stock?

9. The common shares of GEB Resources are currently being traded on the OTC at $35 per share. A dividend of $2.00 was just paid. You expect this dividend per share to grow at a constant rate of 6%. What must your required return be if you believe the $35 price is reasonable?

10. Hulu Huup, Inc., has introduced a new line of huups to be used only by consenting adults. In evaluating the company, you believe earnings and dividends will grow at a rate of 20% for the next three years, after which the growth rate will fall to −5%. If the beta of HH is 2.0, the risk-free rate is 6%, and the market risk premium is 6%:

   a. Calculate the current fair value of the stock today if the last dividend (D_0) was $3.

   b. Calculate the value of the stock at the end of year 3 and at the end of year 4.

   c. If your projections hold true, what will the dividend yield be during year 3? Why is it so large compared with the required return?

11. Use the constant growth dividend valuation model to explain the economic forces that determine the price/earnings ratio of a broad stock market index. Obtain estimates of each of these as of the date you work this problem and compare the resulting P/E ratio with the actual P/E of the S&P 500.

12. A ratio that is widely used to gauge the level of the stock market is known as the price-to-book ratio (P/B ratio). It is calculated by dividing the market price of an individual stock (or a market index) by the accounting book value of the stock (or the index).

   a. Use the constant growth model to show what economic forces determine the P/B ratio.

   b. Under what conditions will the ratio be greater than 1.0?

13. Under what conditions will a stock's market value be the same as its accounting book value? Explain why.

14. Consider the following information about stocks A and B:

	Stock A	Stock B
Expected Dividends Next Year	$1.00	$2.33
Expected Constant *ROE*	20%	20%
Expected Retention Rate	70%	30%
Required Return on Securities of Equivalent Risk	20%	20%

   a. Which stock is more sensitive to changes in risk premiums and growth expectations?

   b. Is either a true growth stock?

15. Many portfolio managers claim to be growth-stock managers. When asked what this means, they often respond, "We purchase stocks that are expected to have greater than average price growth over the coming decade."

   a. Is this a fair definition of a true growth stock? Why?

   b. Would you expect true growth-stock managers to have larger portfolio *returns* than managers who purchase more income-oriented stocks?

   c. Would you expect true growth-stock managers to have better *risk/return performance* than managers who purchase more income-oriented stocks?

16. A past issue of Value Line published the following estimates for DuPont:

$$\text{Beta} = 1.15 \qquad b_{1985} = 60\%$$

$$D_{1985} = \$3.10 \qquad ROE_{1985} = 15\%$$

$$D_{1988} = \$4.00$$

   a. The stock was selling for $49. Estimate the expected returns from purchasing at $49 and receiving the dividend stream projected by Value Line.

   b. The risk-free rate (long-term Treasuries) on this date was 11.5%. Using a market risk premium of 6%, what do you conclude about the purchase of DuPont shares?

   c. What would a staunch believer in EMT say about your conclusion in part b?

17. South Central Bank Corporation is a Florida bank holding company with loans and deposits of $500,000,000 which are expected to grow at close to the local population estimates of 4% per year. Because of the continued emphasis the bank wishes to place on both wholesale (business) banking and its traditional retail business, its yield spread is expected to remain around 4%. Last year this yield spread (return on loans less cost of funds) provided a *net* interest income of $20,000,000. Expenses and taxes are expected to be 70% of net interest income. Earnings are now $6,000,000, or $5.00 per share. Dividend payout is, and will remain, about 50%. A fair return on South Central's stock would be 13.5%.

a. What is a share of South Central worth today?

b. If the stock is selling at $30, would you suggest it to either a retired couple or a young surgeon? (Select only one.)

 18. Estimate the sustainable earnings growth rate given the following information:

$$\text{Return on Equity} = 20\%$$

$$\text{Dividend Payout Ratio} = 30\%$$

    a. 6%
    b. 10%
    c. 14%
    d. 20%

19. The constant growth dividend discount model can be used both for the valuation of companies and for the estimation of the long-term total return of a stock.

    Assume: $20 = the price of a stock today

                    8% = the expected growth rate of dividends

              $.60 = the annual dividend one year forward

    A. Using *only* the above data, **compute** the expected long-term total return on the stock using the constant growth dividend discount model. **Show** calculations.

    B. **Briefly discuss** *three* disadvantages of the constant growth dividend discount model in its application to investment analysis.

    C. **Identify** *three* alternative methods to the dividend discount model for the valuation of companies.

20. A firm's earnings per share increased from $10 to $12, its dividends per share increased from $4 to $4.80, and its share price increased from $80 to $90. Given this information, it follows that:

    a. the stock experienced a drop in its P/E ratio.
    b. the company had a decrease in its dividend payout ratio.
    c. the firm increased its number of common shares outstanding.
    d. the required rate of return decreased.

21. Assuming all other factors are constant, which *one* of the following will reduce the P/E ratio?

    a. The dividend payout ratio decreases.
    b. Inflation expectations decline, resulting in a reduction in the nominal risk-free rate.
    c. The beta of the stock declines.
    d. The market risk premium decreases.

 D A T A F I L E   A N A L Y S I S

1. *Nominal Growth Rates.* Access the data set labeled INDXDATA.WK1. In new columns next to the following variables, calculate the natural log of the variable:

Earnings Per Share: SP 500 and DJIA

Dividends Per Share: SP 500 and DJIA

Regress these four new variables against year for the period 1929–1991. (There will be four regressions.) Compare the various CAGRs and discuss why the values might differ.

2. *Real Growth Rates.* Divide the earnings per share and dividends per share by a Unit Value series of the consumer price index. Calculate the CAGRs of these constant dollar values. Compare these constant dollar growth rates with nominal CAGRs. Notice, for example, the lower R-squares.

REFERENCES

The classic text treating fundamental security selection was originally written by Graham and Dodd. Its most recent edition is:

COTTLE, SIDNEY, ROGER F. MURRAY, and FRANK E. BLOCK, *Graham and Dodd's Security Analysis.* 5th ed. New York: McGraw-Hill Book Co., 1988.

Interesting recent articles dealing with stock valuation include:

BRINSON, GARY P., BRIAN D. SINGER, and GILBERT L. BEEBOWER, "Determinants of Portfolio Performance II: An Update," *Financial Analysis Journal,* May–June 1992.

CUTLER, DAVID M., JAMES M. PORTERBA, and LAWRENCE H. SUMMERS, "What Moves Stock Prices," *Journal of Portfolio Management,* Spring 1989.

EDWARDS, MARK, and WAYNE H. WAGNER, "The Five W's and an H," *Journal of Portfolio Management,* Fall 1991.

FERSON, WAYNE E., and CAMPBELL R. HARVEY, "Sources of Predictability in Portfolio Returns," *Financial Analysts Journal,* May–June 1991.

FOGLER, H. RUSSELL, "Common Stock Management in the 1990s," *Journal of Portfolio Management,* Winter 1990.

LEIBOWITZ, MARTIN L., and STANLEY KOGELMAN, "Inside the P/E Ratio: The Franchise Factor," *Financial Analysts Journal,* November–December 1990.

SILBER, WILLIAM L., "Discounts on Restricted Stock: The Impact of Illiquidity on Stock Prices," *Financial Analysts Journal,* July–August 1991.

VANDER WEIDE, JAMES H., and WILLARD T. CARLETON, "Investor Growth Expectations: Analysts vs. History," *Journal of Portfolio Management,* Spring 1988.

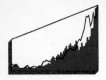

Equity Trading

Judging from popular financial publications, television commentaries, and typical brokerage firm reports, it might seem that the *most important* investment question is, "What stocks should be held?". This impression, of course, would be wrong. Individual stock selection is among the last of the investment decisions that one should make. Portfolio diversification and asset allocation are much more important decisions to proper portfolio management.

Nonetheless, the evaluation of individual stocks can be an exciting venture. Stock analyses involve a blending of economics, marketing, science, technology, international competition, international politics, and so forth.

PASSIVE EQUITY INVESTMENT

The extent to which people should rely on passive or active management of their common stock portfolios depends upon two factors: (1) their opinions about how efficient the stock market is priced and (2) their opinions about their own personal knowledge.

Individuals who believe that market prices can deviate substantially from a stock's intrinsic value will choose active management strategies. How successful they will be is, of course, widely debated. For example, if professional equity mutual fund managers have a difficult time providing consistent risk-adjusted performance in excess of passively managed portfolios, one might ask how non-professionals would be able to do so.

Perhaps more important than one's opinion about the concept of market efficiency is one's knowledge. Without appropriate training or unique skills, identifying stocks that are mispriced is a difficult task. Even if a person believes that security markets are price-inefficient, without unique knowledge and skills investors should probably trade as if they did believe in market efficiency (i.e., passively).

Passive portfolio management is not a boring exercise. It requires all decisions associated with active portfolio management except individual security analysis and selection. For example, many large pension plans are passively managed but require a large number of people to monitor the portfolio's diversification and asset allocation. Such people do not ask *which* Malaysian stocks should be held in the portfolio. Instead, they ask whether Malaysian stocks in general should be held—that is, are the diversification gains greater than the costs of ownership?

Passively managed equity portfolios should be tailored to the aggregate portfolio's stated goal, with particular attention to diversification and asset allocation.

Diversification

One of the most important rules that passive equity investors should follow is to diversify broadly. Broad diversification can be achieved in a number of ways. For example, an investor could buy shares of one or more well-diversified equity mutual funds. Another approach would be to spread stock investments across a large number of different industries. Perhaps the easiest way to assure broad diversification would be to purchase an equity index fund. Ideally, the index fund's assets would mirror an aggregate market portfolio that the investor wishes to emulate. Many investment funds have been created to emulate the returns on various stock market indexes such as the S&P 500, the Wilshire 5000, and the EAFE index.

Two caveats about diversification deserve mention. First, the term *proper diversification* does not always mean that every security in an asset class should be owned and weighted by their relative market capitalizations. Diversification is a way of spreading, or hedging, one's bets. When viewed in this way, proper diversification might consist of underweighting or overweighting specific stocks or industry classes in order to offset nonsecurity risks that the investor faces. For example, consider the pension portfolio of employees who work for a defense contractor. Since a large part of their wealth (job income) is tied to future defense spending, their pension portfolio should underweight securities that might be hurt by defense cutbacks and overweight securities that might benefit from such cutbacks. In short, when nonsecurity risks that an investor faces are considered, market index funds might not be the ideal passive portfolios to own.

Second, many investors mistakenly believe that owning 20 to 30 stocks will eliminate virtually all the diversifiable risk present in common stocks. For investors with a relatively short investment horizon (say, a few years), this is a fair statement. But for investors who have a long investment horizon, greater amounts of diversification are necessary to reduce diversifiable investment risk. A detailed explanation of why the investment horizon impacts the extent to which a portfolio should be diversified is presented in Chapter 20. Only the general conclusions are presented here.

Consider two investors. Ms. Neary intends to invest in stocks for 1 year. Mr. Long intends to invest in stocks for a minimum of 20 years. Each investor faces two different types of risks: (1) volatility of yearly returns around a future average return and (2) uncertainty about the future average yearly return. For Ms. Neary, volatility risk is the more important. For Mr. Long, volatility risk is dominated by uncertainty about the future average yearly return.

As a practical matter, almost all volatility risk can be eliminated by holding 20 to 30 randomly selected stocks. Thus, Ms. Neary could probably obtain virtually all the benefits of equity diversification that are available to her by owning 30 stocks (or a single diversified equity mutual fund). But a much larger number of stocks are needed to eliminate the diversifiable portion of uncertainty about future average security returns. Therefore, Mr. Long would have to diversify more extensively in order to reduce the diversifiable risk to which he is exposed. He could do so by: (1) purchasing an equity index fund (if he wishes to invest passively), (2) purchasing a number of actively managed mutual funds (if he wishes to pursue an active investment strategy by employing professional managers), or (3) invest in a large number of personally select equities if he wishes to personally manage the equity portfolio.

Think about this issue in the context of the Market Model equation:

Market Model

$$R_{it} = a_i + B_i[R_{Mt} - RF_t] + e_{it} \qquad (14.1)$$

where R_{it} is the return on stock i in year t, R_{Mt} and RF_t are the return on the stock market and risk-free rate in year t, a_i and B_i are the Market Model alpha and beta values for stock i, and e_{it} is the residual return on stock i in year t.

If stocks are selected at random, volatility risk arises from uncertainty about the betas that will be drawn plus uncertainty inherent in the yearly residual returns. This type of risk is rapidly diversified. In fact, many empirical studies have shown that 20 to 30 randomly selected stocks will (on average) eliminate virtually all the diversifiable portion of volatility risk.

But diversification does not work as rapidly in reducing the uncertainty inherent in different stock alphas. Although the uncertainty inherent in annualized alpha values might appear small, when compounded over a longer investment horizon, the differences become significant. For example, consider a $1.00 investment for 40 years. If the geometric average annual return is 12%, the terminal value will be $93.05. But, if the average annual return is only two percentage points lower, the terminal value will only be $45.30!

To summarize, long-term investors need to diversify more extensively than do short-term investors. This is because long-term investors are more exposed to uncertainty inherent in the average rate of return at which the portfolio will grow. Although this type of risk is relatively small over short investment horizons, it compounds with the investment horizon.

Asset Allocation

In theory, investors should own a portfolio on the efficient frontier that provides an appropriate risk-return trade-off to them. In practice, most investors are unable to specify the inputs necessary to form such an efficient frontier. But they can examine historical risks and average returns to gain an intuitive grasp of the risk of various asset combinations.

Care should be taken to be sure that the benchmark used to evaluate equity risk is similar to the securities that are actually held. For example, it would be wrong to use the S&P 500 as the equity benchmark, decide to place 50% of the portfolio in stocks of such risk, and then actually place 50% of the portfolio in stocks having a beta (using the S&P as the market proxy) equal to 0.7 or 1.2. The proper average beta in this example should be 1.0.

One way to achieve the desired level of equity risk is to restrict portfolio holdings of stocks to a specific beta level. For example, if one wants to have a portfolio beta of 0.5, the total portfolio could be invested in stocks with a beta of 0.5, or between 0.4 and 0.6. This limits portfolio diversification, however, since only the stocks with a given beta are held and all others are excluded. A better approach would be to place 50% of portfolio assets in risk-free bonds with an appropriate duration and the remaining 50% in broadly diversified groups of stocks.

Closely related to beta rankings are the quality rankings assigned to stocks by various investment advisory services. The best-known rankings are those used by Standard & Poor's. To develop the ratings, Standard & Poor's uses a computerized scoring system based upon a stock's earnings and dividend record for the most recent 10 years and assigns the following quality ratings:

A+	Highest	B+	Average	C	Lowest
A	High	B	Below Average	D	In Reorganization
A−	Above Average	B−	Lower		

There is a high correlation between a stock's quality rating and its beta.

Many investors are sensitive to the interest rate risk exposure of their portfolio but wish to own stocks as opposed to immunized bonds due to greater long-run expected returns on stocks. Although stock portfolios that are immunized against interest rate risk are conceptually feasible, they are difficult to develop in practice. However, a significant amount of interest rate risk can be reduced. The most common measure of a stock's duration is the reciprocal of the "expected stock return minus the expected growth rate." This measure of duration, however, assumes that the Constant Dividend Growth Model applies. Practitioners have also used statistical procedures to find stocks that are relatively insensitive to changes in interest rates and offer portfolios of such stocks as immunized equity investments.

Tax Factors. Returns on common stocks arise from both yearly dividend yields, which are taxed at ordinary tax rates, and capital gains, which are often taxed at the lower capital gains rate. When the capital gains tax rate is lower than the ordinary tax rate, many practitioners tailor a stock portfolio's mix of dividend yield and growth components to the tax characteristics of its owner. The procedure is similar to that used on high-coupon versus low-coupon bonds. For example, consider two stocks that have identical risks and therefore identical after-tax required returns. The before-tax expected returns may vary, however, if the dividend-yield/price-growth mix is different. Returns on the firm with the larger price growth rate would be taxed at an effectively lower rate and therefore would sell at lower before-tax required and expected returns. Individuals in higher-than-average tax brackets would purchase stocks with high growth rates in order to minimize taxes and maximize after-tax returns. Individuals in lower-than-average tax brackets (or zero brackets for charitable organizations and pension funds) would purchase the high-dividend-yield stocks.

To economists who have studied this problem, however, the impact of taxes upon before- and after-tax returns is not quite so clear. It is beyond the scope of this text to get into all the arguments about dividend policy. However, we can note that there is some empirical evidence by Litzenberger and Ramaswamy that suggests that low-dividend-yield stocks do sell at lower before-tax expected returns. This contradicts other evidence by Black and Scholes, which suggested that the dividend-yield effects are negligible or nonexistent. Both theoretically and empirically the question remains unresolved. In practice, stock portfolios can be designed with an eye to reducing tax liabilities, but considerable care should be taken to ensure that this doesn't leave the portfolio with large amounts of potentially diversifiable risk.

Year-end tax swaps can be used in the investment portfolio to delay tax payments in the same way they are used in bond portfolios. For example, assume that you own a portfolio of stocks that is diversified by having one stock from each of the various S&P industry categories. Perhaps one of these stocks is shares in Dow Chemical that were bought at $35 but are now selling at $25. You could sell Dow for a *realized* taxable loss of $10 and immediately reinvest the $25 proceeds in a close substitute for Dow—say, Union Carbide. This swap leaves you with a $25 investment in the chemical industry but allows you to take an immediate tax savings on the $10 realized loss. If your capital gains tax bracket is 25%, you save $2.50 in taxes, which can be invested. Eventually, this $2.50 tax refund will have to be repaid to the goverment when Union Carbide shares are sold. But you receive the interest earnings on the $2.50 until Union Carbide is indeed sold.

Timing. Because, according to EMT, stock prices are always equal to their intrinsic values (or no further away than the size of a buy-sell transaction cost), investment timing is really no problem. Buy when excess cash is temporarily available and sell when cash is needed. Over any investment time horizon this simple buy-hold strategy would be expected to yield larger returns for a given risk level than would attempts to time purchases and sales in anticipation of future price moves. Market prices are presumed to always be fair, and speculative attempts at timing would lead only to the larger transaction costs associated with active trading and the possibly greater risks associated with less than full diversification.

Marketability. Finally, a portfolio's marketability should fit its stated marketability objectives. Normally, this does not present a problem to small- and medium-sized portfolios, since a large number of common stocks exist that can be sold quickly and at low transaction costs in the secondary markets. In addition, the use of money market instruments can increase portfolio marketability. For very large portfolios (say, a $5 billion pension fund) marketability can present a larger problem, however. In such cases the portfolio must be invested in a large number of different stocks, each having a reasonable block trading market.

Warren Buffett Comments on Stock Selection

The following comes from the 1987 Annual Report to Shareholders of Berkshire Hathaway, Inc. It was written by the well-known and highly respected active investor Warren E. Buffett.

Whenever Charlie and I buy common stocks for Berkshire's insurance companies (leaving aside arbitrage purchases, discussed later) we approach the transaction as if we were buying into a private business. We look at the economic prospects of the business, the people in charge of running it, and the price we must pay. We do not have in mind any time or price for sale. Indeed, we are willing to hold a stock indefinitely so long as we expect the business to increase in intrinsic value at a satisfactory rate. When investing, we view ourselves as business analysts—not as market analysts, not as macroeconomic analysts, and not even as security analysts.

Our approach makes an active trading market useful, since it periodically presents us with mouth-watering opportunities. But by no means is it essential: a prolonged suspension of trading in the securities we hold would not bother us any more than does the lack of daily quotations on World Book or Fechheimer. Eventually, our economic fate will be determined by the economic fate of the business we own, whether our ownership is partial or total.

Ben Graham, my friend and teacher, long ago described the mental attitude toward market fluctuations that I believe to be most conducive to investment success. He said that you should imagine market quotations as coming from a remarkably accommodating fellow named Mr. Market who is your partner in a private business. Without fail, Mr. Market appears daily and names a price at which he will either buy your interest or sell you his.

Even though the business that the two of you own may have economic characteristics that are stable, Mr. Market's quotations will be anything but. For, sad to say, the poor fellow has incurable emotional problems. At times he feels euphoric and can see only the favorable factors affecting the business. When in that mood, he names a very high buy-sell price because he fears that you will snap up his interest and rob him of imminent gains. At other times he is depressed and can see nothing but trouble ahead for both the business and the world. On these occasions he will name a very low price, since he is terrified that you will unload your interest on him.

Mr. Market has another endearing characteristic: He doesn't mind being ignored. If his quotation is uninteresting to you today, he will be back with a new one tomorrow. Transactions are strictly at your option. Under these conditions, the more manic-depressive his behavior, the better for you.

But, like Cinderella at the ball, you must heed one warning or everything will turn into pumpkins and mice: Mr. Market is there to serve you, not to guide you. It is his pocketbook, not his wisdom, that you will find useful. If he shows up some day in a particularly foolish mood, you are free to either ignore him or to take advantage of him, but it will be disastrous if you fall under his influence. Indeed, if you aren't certain that you understand and can value your business far better than Mr. Market, you don't belong in the game. As they say in poker, "If you've been in the game 30 minutes and you don't know who the patsy is, *you're* the patsy."

Ben's Mr. Market allegory may seem out-of-date in today's investment world, in which most professionals and academicians talk of efficient markets, dynamic hedging and betas. Their interest in such matters is understandable, since techniques shrouded in mysterly clearly have value to the purveyor of investment advice. After all, what witch doctor has ever achieved fame and fortune by simply advising "Take two aspirins"?

The value of market esoterica to the consumer of investment advice is a different story. In my opinion, investment success will not be produced by arcane formulae, computer programs or signals flashed by the price behavior of stocks and markets. Rather an investor will succeed by coupling good business judgment with an ability to insulate his thoughts and behavior from the super-contagious emotions that swirl about the marketplace. In my own efforts to stay insulated, I have found it highly useful to keep Ben's Mr. Market concept firmly in mind.

ACTIVE EQUITY SPECULATION

The purpose of any security analysis should be to identify mispriced securities so that active management can "add value" to the portfolio. The term *add value* is the way in which investment practitioners speak of excess risk-adjusted returns. Unless active management actually does add value after all transaction costs and management fees have been considered, then a passive management strategy should be followed.

Finding a mispriced security is not the same as finding a company that is well managed, has good prospects for a significant earnings increase, the potential for higher long-run growth in market price, and so forth. A company may indeed be well managed, but this does not mean that securities of the firm are mispriced. The same is true for companies experiencing rapid earnings growth or potential stock price growth. In fact, firms with such characteristics have probably attracted considerable attention by security analysts as well as the general public and will, thus, be the least likely securities to be mispriced.

Approaches Used in Active Management

There are many ways in which professional security analysts and portfolio managers conduct their search for mispriced securities. One is referred to as a *top-down approach.* In this method, analysts start by developing an opinion about future economic conditions of their local country, geographic region, and the world. Such aggregate forecasts are then translated into forecasts of industry sales growth that, in turn, feed into individual firm sales and profit forecasts. An opposite approach is referred to as the *bottom-up approach.* As you might imagine, this approach begins at the individual-firm level. Industry forecasts are based on a sum of the forecasts of firms in an industry, and these, in turn, are summed to develop aggregate economic forecasts.

In recent years, many security analysts and portfolio managers have been labeled "quants," which is short for quantitative. Techniques used by these so-called quants vary a great deal. Some employ simple ranking techniques such as, "Buy all stocks that are in the bottom decile of both price-to-earnings ratio and equity capitalization." Others use sophisticated statistical procedures to identify "factor risk exposures," and use these to form portfolios that have varying risk exposures to each factor.

There is no single way to classify the approaches used by professionals who engage in active stock trading. But regardless of the approach used, it will not provide value added to a portfolio unless information that is not reflected in current prices can be found. The nature of this information can be categorized as information about: (1) aggregate asset classes, (2) specific industries, and (3) individual stocks. Professionals who trade on opinions about aggregate market prices are called "market timers." They alter a portfolio's asset allocation in anticipation of above- or below-average returns on various security classes. The formal name for market timing is Tactical Asset Allocation. Individuals who make decisions based on stock unique information are called ''stock pickers.'' Industry-based decisions form a sort of middle ground; they might be either timing or stock-picking decisions.

Most professional managers specialize in either timing or stock selection. In this chapter, we examine common procedures used in stock selection. Timing is reviewed in Chapter 19, where we examine portfolio asset allocation.

Beginning the Analysis. To help illustrate how individual stock analyses are conducted, we examine the situation of International Business Machines Corporation (IBM) in early 1993. One motive for selecting IBM is the fact that the company is well known. But it is also a good example of a firm that has experienced the effects of dramatic technological change and global competitive pressures.

There is a risk associated with focusing on a single company. All analyses are company-unique because each company has its unique strengths and weaknesses. Thus there are analytic procedures that might be important for, say, a commercial bank, that are unimportant for a computer manufacturer. Each company analysis is different and will require different analytic procedures.

At the start of any stock analysis, one should become familiar with the company's product line and its past financial performance. This is the base for forecasts of future corporate profitability, dividends per share, equity risk exposure, and current intrinsic stock value.

IBM in the Early 1900s. In 1993, IBM was the world's largest manufacturer of information-processing equipment. The firm obtained revenues from the sale of computer hardware, proprietary software systems, maintenance, various special services, and income from the financing of hardware sales. Hardware sales included large mainframe computer processors, midrange computers known as ''minis,'' and personal computers (PCs). About 60% of the firm's revenues were generated from non-U.S. operations.

During the 1980s and early 1990s, IBM experienced profound changes in the nature of its business. This can be seen in the summary financial data below.

	1980	1990	1992
Sales (billions)	$26.2	$69.0	$64.5
Net Income (billions) (before accounting changes)	$ 3.5	$ 6.0	− $ 6.9
Earnings Per Share	$ 6.10	$10.51	− $12.03

During the 1980s, revenues of IBM increased in every year and had an average compound annual growth of 10%. Earnings-per-share grew at a lower, but still respectable, rate of 6.5% per year. This period of sales and profit expansion translated into rising stock prices. As Figure 14-1 shows, IBM's stock price rose from $57 at the end of 1981 to $155 at the end of 1985—almost tripling in value.

In 1986, however, earnings per share fell by 27%. Naturally, this created

FIGURE 14-1 *IBM Stock Prices (Year-End 1981–1992)*

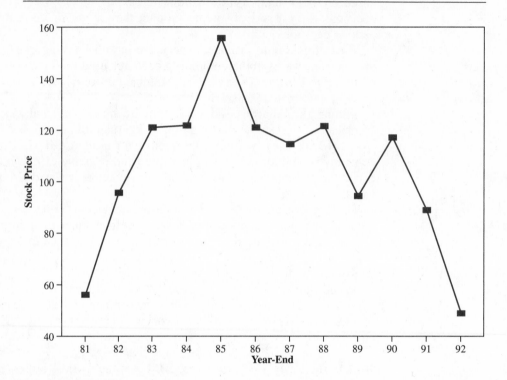

concern about the company's future growth prospects and caused stock prices to decline. By the end of 1990, share prices were less than $100. Management responded in the early 1990s with a significant restructuring of the firm. Various corporate divisions were to be made into semi-autonomous business entities with each enterprise unit operating as an independent firm. There were even suggestions that these units might sell common shares to the public and become independent of the IBM parent. Initially, the stock market responded favorably to the proposed restructuring, and the stock price rose to $120 by the end of 1990.

But it soon became clear that problems facing IBM were larger than anticipated. For the first time in the corporation's history, corporate revenues declined in 1991. And in 1992, the firm's earnings per share fell to a negative $12.03 (compared with a positive $10.51 in 1990). As the stock slid to $50 at the end of 1992, it was clear that dramatic actions had to be taken by the firm if it was to remain a viable force in the computer business. Among these actions was the resignation of many top officers, including the chairman of the board of directors.

The pressure on IBM's earnings can be traced to two forces: (1) the concept of a "product life cycle" and (2) economic conditions.

Product Life Cycles. The concept of a product life cycle, as Figure 14-2 illustrates, can be thought of as consisting of three stages. In the *pioneering stage,* basic

FIGURE 14-2 *The Product Life Cycle*

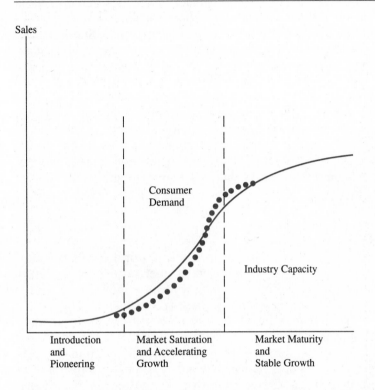

research and development of a new product occur. Customer demand tends to be small due to uncertainties about the product's reliability and hoped-for technological improvements. Mainframe computers were in this stage in the 1940s and 1950s. PCs entered this stage in the early 1980s. In the *market saturation and growth* stage, consumer demand grows more rapidly than producers are able to supply. As a result, sales grow rapidly and profit margins are high because there is little price competition. Computer mainframes were in this stage roughly between 1960–1985. PCs were in this stage in the mid-1980s. In the *mature and stable growth stage,* a product's potential market is largely saturated, resulting in efforts to reduce production costs and intense price competition. By the 1990s the long-term growth potential of mainframe computers had declined substantially from that of the previous 20 years. And the market for PCs had also rapidly moved into its mature stage.

For IBM, product risk is the same as technological risk. During the 1980s, PCs moved through both the growth stage into the early part of the mature stage. Although IBM was among the first companies to produce PCs and obtained about 20% of revenues from such products in 1992, price competition for these products was intense. As a result, profit margins on PCs are much lower than for mainframes.

Economic Risk. Revenue growth for a firm the size of IBM is closely tied to global economic growth. In fact, about two-thirds of 1992 revenues were in countries other than the United States, making firm revenues sensitive to the global economy. The 1990 recession in the United States began to spread to other countries in 1991 and 1992. This economic decline, when added to the maturing of the mainframes business and intense price competition in the PC business, caused revenues to fall in 1991 by 8%.

The situation faced by IBM in the early 1990s was serious. It faced a maturing product line, intense price competition for much of its product line, and economic conditions that, at least temporarily, depressed product sales. In the light of this situation its stock price had declined to a 10-year low of $50. Whether this $50 stock price properly reflected IBM's intrinsic value at the time depended on one's opinion of how IBM would react and how successful they would be.

Accounting Standards

A major source of information about a firm comes from its published financial statements. Although accountants attempt to provide investors with reasonable *estimates* of the true economic value of a firm's assets, liabilities and profits, the techniques they use are imprecise. True economic values are difficult to determine. If they were not, there would be no need for security analysts and active portfolio managers.

Two basic problems exist. The first arises from the difficulty of measuring economic values. For example, many accounting principles are based on historical (actual) costs. Thus, a retail firm that buys a computer for $100 and sells it for $110 shows a gross profit of $10 in its accounting income statement. But, if the firm must pay $110 to replace the old computer due to inflation, true economic profit would be zero.

The second problem arises because corporations use different accounting rules. As a result, financial statements of two firms might not be *comparable*. For example, IBM might account for cost of goods sold by the last-in-first-out (LIFO) rule, whereas a competitor might use a first-in-first-out (FIFO) rule.

In the United States, the *Financial Accounting Standards Board* (FASB) was created by the American Institute of Certified Public Accountants to examine alternative ways of accounting for various business transactions. After thorough study of an issue and public comments on a draft statement, the FASB issues a document called a Statement of Financial Accounting Standards (SFAS). These SFASs provide the basis of current generally accepted accounting principles in the United States. A number of the more significant SFASs are shown in Table 14-1. Although FASB (faz-bee) has dealt with many difficult issues and narrowed the range of acceptable accounting methodologies, considerable latitude remains.

The comparability problem is most serious when comparing firms that are domiciled in different countries. For example, firms in the United States that use long-term lease financing are required to report the cost value of the leased asset as an asset of the firm and the present value of future lease payments as a liability of the firm. This is not required in many other countries.

TABLE 14-1 *Major Statements of Financial Accounting Standards*

SFAS Number	Topic
5	Accounting for contingencies
14	Financial reporting for segments of a business enterprise
28	Accounting for sales with leasebacks
34	Capitalization of interest cost
47	Disclosure of long-term obligations
52	Foreign currency translation
55	Determining whether a convertible security is a common stock equivalent
78	Classification of obligations that are callable by the creditor
80	Accounting for futures contracts
87	Employer's accounting for pensions
95	Statement of cash flows
98	Accounting for leases
106	Employer's accounting for postretirement benefits other than pensions

In short, although financial statements provide much useful data, serious mismeasurement and comparability problems can arise.

A Review of IBM Accounting Statements

As noted above, a major source of historical information about a company is its published financial statements. Although financial statements express the true economic condition of a firm with error, they should be thoroughly read and the accounting principles on which they are based thoroughly understood. Just as an engineer needs to understand calculus, a financial analyst must understand accounting.

Consolidated Balance Sheet. Look at IBM's consolidated balance sheet displayed in Table 14-2. This is a *big* company, with assets of $86.7 billion at the end of 1992. About one-half of its assets are devoted to current assets. The firm has $5.6 billion in highly liquid short-term assets (cash, cash equivalents, and marketable securities). Receivables total $21.6 billion. This includes $7.4 billion in sales type lease receivables. And a review of IBM's 1992 financial statement footnotes would have showed that an additional $13.5 billion would be due on sales leases during the next five years. Finally, inventories were $9.8 billion. A review of the financial statement footnotes showed that the preponderance of inventories was work in process ($6.0 billion). In conclusion, more than $39 billion of IBM's 1992 assets were classified as current assets and, thus, were expected to be converted into cash during the next year. This does not mean that the firm would not have a liquidity problem during the near term, but it is part of the total liquidity picture.

One final comment about the firm's 1992 assets is in order. What type of assets would make up "Sundry Assets" valued at *$21.3 billion*? Again, footnotes to the financial statements provide help; $13.5 billion represent the present value of sales

TABLE 14-2 *Consolidated Statement of Financial Position*
International Business Machines Corporation and Subsidiary Companies

(Dollars in millions) At December 31:	1992	1991*
Assets		
Current Assets:		
Cash	$ 1,090	$ 1,171
Cash equivalents	3,356	2,774
Marketable securities, at cost, which approximates market	1,203	1,206
Notes and accounts receivable—trade, net of allowances	12,829	15,391
Sales-type leases receivable	7,405	7,435
Other accounts receivable	1,370	1,491
Inventories	8,385	9,844
Prepaid expenses and other current assets	4,054	1,657
	39,692	40,969
Plant, Rental Machines and Other Property	52,786	55,678
Less: Accumulated depreciation	31,191	28,100
	21,595	27,578
Investments and Other Assets:		
Software, less accumulated amortization (1992, $8,531; 1991, $6,950)	4,119	4,483
Investments and sundry assets	21,299	19,443
	25,418	23,926
	$ 86,705	$ 92,473
Liabilities and Stockholders' Equity		
Current Liabilities:		
Taxes	$ 979	$ 2,449
Short-term debt	16,467	13,716
Accounts payable	3,147	3,507
Compensation and benefits	3,476	3,241
Deferred income	3,316	3,472
Other accrued expenses and liabilities	9,352	7,566
	36,737	33,951
Long-Term Debt	12,853	13,231
Other Liabilities	7,461	6,685
Deferred Income Taxes	2,030	1,927
Total Liabilities	59,081	55,794
Stockholders' Equity:		
Capital stock, par value $1.25 per share—shares authorized: 750,000,000		
Issued: 1992—571,791,950; 1991—571,349,324	6,563	6,531
Retained earnings	19,124	26,983
Translation adjustments	1,962	3,196
Treasury stock, at cost (shares: 1992—356,222; 1991—331,665)	(25)	(31)
	27,624	36,679
	$ 86,705	$ 92,473

* Restated for the American Institute of Certified Public Accountants Statement of Position, "Software
  Revenue Recognition."
The notes on pages 44 through 65 are an integral part of this statement.
SOURCE: International Business Machines, *1992 Annual Report.*

type lease payments to be made to IBM over the next five years—the $13.5 billion on sales leases noted above.

Now examine the sources of financing from debt and equity. Equity represented about 32% of total assets. Current liabilities were $36.7 billion, but not all of this was due to be paid in the next year since $3.3 billion represented deferred income. Neglecting this item, net working capital (current assets minus current liabilities) was $6.3 billion—down from $7.3 billion in 1991. Long-term debt of $12.8 billion represented only 15% of assets. About one-half of long-term debt was denominated in currencies other than the U.S. dollar. Other liabilities consisted principally of accruals for nonpension postretirement benefits. These last two points come from footnotes to the 1992 financial statements.

Consolidated Statement of Earnings. Turn now to the consolidated income statement shown in Table 14-3. Net earnings for the year were negative $4.9 billion based on revenues of $64.5 billion. There are three basic reasons for this earnings loss. First, although sales growth was essentially flat in 1992, costs of sales rose from $32.1 billion to $35.1 billion, more than a 9% growth.

Second, the firm incurred sizeable costs associated with corporate restructuring during 1992. Due to the increased competition facing the firm, top management had decided that the firm should be restructured into a number of largely autonomous, independent business units (IBUs). At the time of the *1992 Annual Report*, the company had not made clear the exact composition of these IBUs. But management had stated that certain IBUs might even go public. If taken at face value, this meant that the traditional monolithic vertical structure of IBM was to become a horizontal structure of independent businesses. Each unit would be free to produce for, or buy, from any other firm in order to maximize their individual profits. If true, IBM was in the process of becoming a *portfolio of independent businesses* managed by IBM's board of directors and senior management. This could have profound effects on future profitability. In addition to costs associated with the creation of such IBUs, many employees were offered favorable severance benefits if they agreed to terminate their employment with IBM. These restructuring costs totaled about $11.6 billion in 1992!

Finally, a one-time positive addition to earnings equal to $1.9 billion was created by a change in generally accepted accounting principles.

Since two major costs incurred in 1992 were associated with events unique to 1992 and would not be recurring in future years, it is best to exclude them from any analysis of long-term corporate profitability. Adding these costs back to the 1992 income statement results in the following:

	As Reported	After-Tax Adjustments		As Adjusted
		Restructure Costs	Accounting Changes	
Net Earnings	− $4,965	+ $8,857	− $1,900	+ $1,992
Earnings per share	− $8.70	+ $15.52	− $3.33	$3.49

TABLE 14-3 *Consolidated Statement of Earnings*
International Business Machines Corporation and Subsidiary Companies

(Dollars in millions
except per share amounts)   For the year ended December 31:

	1992	1991*†	1990*
Revenue:			
Sales	$ 33,755	$ 37,093	$ 43,959
Software	11,103	10,498	9,865
Maintenance	7,635	7,414	7,198
Services	7,352	5,582	4,124
Rentals and financing	4,678	4,179	3,785
	64,523	64,766	68,931
Cost:			
Sales	19,698	18,571	19,401
Software	3,924	3,865	3,118
Maintenance	3,430	3,379	3,302
Services	6,051	4,531	3,315
Rentals and financing	1,966	1,727	1,579
	35,069	32,073	30,715
Gross Profit	29,454	32,693	38,216
Operating Expenses:			
Selling, general and administrative	19,526	21,375	20,709
Research, development and engineering	6,522	6,644	6,554
Restructuring charges	11,645	3,735	—
	37,693	31,754	27,263
Operating Income	(8,239)	939	10,953
Other Income, principally interest	573	602	495
Interest Expense	1,360	1,423	1,324
Earnings before Income Taxes	(9,026)	118	10,124
Provision for Income Taxes	(2,161)	716	4,157
Net Earnings before Changes in Accounting Principles	(6,865)	(598)	5,967
Effect of Changes in Accounting Principles‡	1,900	(2,263)	—
Net Earnings	$ (4,965)	$ (2,861)	$ 5,967
Per Share Amounts:			
Before Changes in Accounting Principles	$ (12.03)	$ (1.05)	$ 10.42
Effect of Changes in Accounting Principles‡	3.33	(3.96)	—
Net Earnings	$ (8.70)	$ (5.01)	$ 10.42

Average Number of Shares Outstanding:
1992—570,896,489; 1991—572,003,382;
1990—572,647,906

* Restated for the American Institute of Certified Public Accountants Statement of Position, ''Software Revenue Recognition.''
† Reclassified to conform with 1992 presentation.
‡ 1992, cumulative effect of Statement of Financial Accounting Standards (SFAS) 190, ''Accounting for Income Taxes''; and 1991, transition effect of SFAS 106, ''Employers' Accounting for Postretirement Benefits Other Than Pensions.''
The notes on pages 44 and 65 are an integral part of this statement.
SOURCE: International Business Machines, *1992 Annual Report.*

After-tax restructuring costs were calculated as:

After-Tax Cost	equals	Before-Tax times $(1.0 - $ Tax Rate) Cost
$8,857	=	$11,645 * $(1.0 - $ $2,161/$9,026)

In our analysis of IBM profitability, we will use these adjusted 1992 profits.

Consolidated Statement of Cash Flows. The Statement of Cash Flows as shown in Table 14-4 is a relatively recent addition to published financial statements. First adopted in 1987 in *Statement of Financial Accounting Standards No. 95*, it replaces a previous document known as the Source and Use of Funds Statement. The Statement of Cash Flows shows why a firm's cash balance changed from one year to the next. The statement organizes cash flows into three general categories: (1) cash flows arising from operating activities, (2) cash flows applied to long-term investment activities, and (3) cash flows obtained from financing activities.

Cash flows from *operating activities* are inflows (or outflows) of cash to the business due to normal business operations—cash revenues less cash outlays associated obtaining the revenues. Cash flows from operating activities represent the fundamental source of liquidity to a firm. The dominant source of operating cash flows is usually net income adjusted for all expenses that do not involve a current cash flow (such as depreciation). In addition, increases in current liabilities or reductions in current assets contribute to cash flows from operating activities. Conversely, reductions in current liabilities or increases in current assets represent a reduction in cash flows from operating activities.

In 1992, cash flows to IBM from operating activities were $6.3 billion. Part of this was due to $7.7 billion in net income adjusted for noncash expenses:

Net earnings	$-$4,965 (million)
Plus (minus) noncash expenses:	
Accounting adjustment	$-$1,900
Restructuring charges	$8,312
Depreciation	$4,793
Software amortization	$1,466
Total	$7,706

Even though the firm reported a net loss for the year, positive after-tax cash flows were created from revenues after all noncash expenses are added back to net earnings. This $7.7 billion cash increase was supplemented by a $1.76 billion decrease in receivables and inventories and a $0.46 billion decrease in other liabilities. But it was also partially offset by a $3.4 billion increase in other current assets and a $0.3 billion decrease in accounts payable. On net, operating activities provided $6.3 billion in new cash to the firm in 1992.

Of this $6.3 billion, a total of $5.9 billion was used in *investment activities*. Most of this increased investment was accounted for by increases in plant, property, and software investments.

Cash flows provided by *financing activities* were equal to $0.6 billion. These

TABLE 14-4 *Consolidated Statement of Cash Flows*
International Business Machines Corporation and Subsidiary Companies

(Dollars in millions) For the year ended December 31:	1992	1991*†	1990*†
Cash Flow from Operating Activities:			
Net earnings	$ (4,965)	$(2,861)	$ 5,967
Adjustments to reconcile net earnings to cash provided from operating activities:			
Effect of changes in accounting principles	(1,900)	2,263	—
Effect of restructuring changes	8,312	2,793	(843)
Depreciation	4,793	4,772	4,217
Amortization of software	1,466	1,564	1,086
(Gain) loss on disposition of investment assets	54	(94)	32
Other changes that provided (used) cash—			
Receivables	1,052	(886)	(2,077)
Inventories	704	(36)	17
Other assets	(3,396)	5	(3,136)
Accounts payable	(311)	384	293
Other liabilities	465	(1,179)	1,916
Net cash provided from operating activities	6,274	6,725	7,472
Cash Flow from Investing Activities:			
Payments for plant, rental machines and other property	(4,751)	(6,497)	(6,509)
Proceeds from disposition of plant, rental machines and other property	633	645	804
Investment in software	(1,752)	(2,014)	(1,892)
Purchases of marketable securities and other investments	(3,284)	(4,848)	(1,234)
Proceeds from marketable securities and other investments	3,276	5,028	1,687
Net cash used in investing activities	(5,878)	(7,686)	(7,144)
Cash Flow from Financing Activities:			
Proceeds from new debt	10,045	5,776	4,676
Payments to settle debt	(10,735)	(4,184)	(3,683)
Short-term borrowings less than 90 days—net	4,199	2,676	1,966
Proceeds from (payments to) employee stock plans—net	(90)	67	(76)
Payments to purchase and retire capital stock	—	(196)	(415)
Cash dividends paid	(2,765)	(2,771)	(2,774)
Net cash provided from (used in) financing activities	654	1,368	(306)
Effect of Exchange Rate Changes on Cash and Cash Equivalents	(549)	(315)	131
Net Change in Cash and Cash Equivalents	501	92	153
Cash and Cash Equivalents at January 1	3,945	3,853	3,700
Cash and Cash Equivalents at December 31	$ 4,446	$ 3,945	$ 3,853
Supplemental Data:			
Cash paid during the year for:			
Income taxes	$ 1,297	$ 2,292	$ 3,315
Interest	$ 3,132	$ 2,617	$ 2,165

* Restated for the American Institute of Certified Public Accountants Statement of Position, "Software Revenue Recognition."
† Reclassified to conform with 1992 presentation.
SOURCE: International Business Machines, *1992 Annual Report.*

were represented by about \$0.7 billion used to repay long-term debt and \$2.8 billion to pay dividends less \$4.2 billion in new short-term debt obligations.

Finally, IBM's reported cash balance declined by \$0.5 billion because it had sizeable cash balances in countries other than the United States that suffered a decline in value during 1992 due to a decrease in foreign exchange rates. The total of these four sources and uses of cash resulted in a reported increase in 1992 cash equal to \$0.5 billion.

What conclusions can we draw from Table 14-4? Although cash flows from operating activities were basically the same in 1991 and 1992, they were down from 1991. As a result, the firm reduced its investment cash outflows and increased its cash inflows from financing activities in 1991 and 1992. In order to maintain its cash-reserve position, the firm had to reduce capital investment and increase both short- and long-term borrowings. This is not a tenable long-run situation.

Financial Analysis of IBM

Although the financial statements provided by corporations often do not fully reflect the economic profits (or losses) of a firm and present comparability problems when examining more than one firm, they are a major source of data to security analysts. In this section, we illustrate how one can analyze such statements.

When conducting a financial statement analysis, it is usually best to compare trends in one firm against those of other firms that have a similar size and product line. Unfortunately, there are no other firms that are similar enough to IBM to make such comparisons meaningful. For example, although Intel, Microsoft, and Hewlett-Packard are all large firms engaged in computer technology, their product lines are quite different from the product line of IBM. Therefore, we will examine trends in the financial condition of IBM in isolation.

To aid in the analysis of IBM's financial statements, we will use the summary financial statements as shown in Tables 14-5 and 14-6. These summary statements provide information for the year-ends 1981, 1986, 1990, and 1992. As such, we will be able to examine trends over a fairly long interval. The summary income statements in Table 14-5 have been adjusted so that they do not include extraordinary charges or credits unique to a single year.

Leverage and Return on Equity. The intrinsic value of a stock is the present value of expected future per-share dividends discounted at an appropriate risk-adjusted interest rate. This requires two estimates: (1) forecasts of expected future dividends and (2) a risk-adjusted discount rate. We will examine the discount rate that might be applied to expected IBM dividends later in the chapter. In this section, we examine the economic forces underlying the basic sources of a firm's ability to pay dividends—its return on equity.

A major determinant of a firm's future earnings and dividends is the rate of return earned on equity investment (ROE). In Chapter 13, Equation 13.11 expressed ROE as a product of three variables: a measure of asset utilization, a

TABLE 14-5 *IBM Summary Income Statements Adjusted for Extraordinary Transactions*
(In $ Billions)

	1981	1986	1990	1992
Revenue	$29.07	$51.25	$68.93	$64.52
Cost of sales	11.74	22.71	30.71	35.07
Gross profit	$17.33	$28.54	$38.22	$29.45
Operating costs	10.66	19.68	26.78	25.48
Net operating income				
Before taxes	$ 6.67	$ 8.86	$11.44	$ 3.97
Interest expense	0.41	0.47	1.32	1.36
Net income before taxes	$ 6.26	$ 8.39	$10.12	$ 2.61
Taxes	2.65	3.60	4.15	0.62
Net income	$ 3.61	$ 4.79	$ 5.97	$ 1.99

measure of expense control, and a measure of debt utilization. Equation 13.11 provides a reasonable way to establish why a given ROE was earned or why it is changing over time. But it is *technically* inaccurate because it does not properly handle interest expense.

Consider the following example. Each dollar invested in firm assets provides a return on assets before taxes equal to 13%. Let's call this ROA_{BT}. The tax rate is

TABLE 14-6 *IBM Summary Balance Sheets*
(In $ Billions)

	1981	1986	1990	1992
Current assets				
Cash & securities	$ 2.03	$ 7.28	$ 4.55	$ 5.65
Notes & accts. receivable	4.38	9.97	15.31	12.83
Lease receivable	NA	NA	5.68	7.40
Inventory	2.80	8.04	10.11	8.38
Other	1.10	2.46	3.27	5.43
Total	$10.31	$27.75	$38.92	$39.69
Net fixed assets	18.80	30.06	27.24	21.60
			21.24	25.41
Total assets	$29.11	$57.81	$87.57	$86.70
Current Liabilities				
Accts. payable	$ 0.87	$ 1.97	$ 3.37	$ 3.14
Short-term debt	0.77	1.41	7.60	16.47
Other	5.68	9.36	14.31	17.13
Total	$ 7.32	$12.74	$25.28	$36.74
Long-term debt	2.67	4.17	11.94	12.85
Other liabilities	1.44	6.52	18.25	9.49
Total debt	$11.43	$23.43	$55.47	$59.08
Equity	$17.68	$34.37	$37.00	$27.62
Total liabilities and equity	$29.11	$57.80	$92.47	$86.70

called T and is equal to 40%. Thus, the after-tax return on assets (ROA_{AT}) would be 7.8%:

After-Tax
Return on Equity
$$ROA_{AT} = (1-T)\ ROA_{BT}$$
$$7.8\% = (1-0.4)\ 13\%$$
(14.2)

Assume that financing for this firm comes from two sources, equity and debt capital. Specifically, for each $1.00 raised as equity capital (E), $1.00 is also raised in debt capital (D). Thus, the ratio of debt to equity capital is 1.0. Debt owners are promised an interest rate (K_D) equal to $2^2/_3\%$. (This may appear to be a very low cost of debt financing, but there is a reason that we explain later.)

Given this scenario, what will be the after-tax return on equity (ROE_{AT})?

To understand the answer to this question, consider each $1.00 of capital investment separately. First, the $1.00 of equity that is invested in assets earns a 13% return before-tax and a 7.8% return after tax. In addition, the $1.00 of debt invested in assets also earns 13% before tax. After paying debt holders the promised interest of $2^2/_3\%$ on each $1.00 of debt, a residual return equal to $10^1/_3\%$ ($13\% - 2^2/_3\%$) is available before tax for shareholders to claim. After paying taxes at a 40% rate on this residual return, 6.2% ($10^1/_3\%* 0.6$) is available to shareholders.

Symbolically, this relationship is written as:

ROE and
Financial
Leverage

| Return to Equity | = | Asset Investment Return | + | Residual Financing Return | **(14.3)** |

$$ROE_{AT} = (1-T)ROA_{BT} + (1-T)\ (ROA_{BT} - K_D)D/E$$

Using the example above:

$$0.14 = (1-0.4)(0.13) + (1 - 0.4)(0.13 - 0.0266)\ 1/1$$
$$= (0.078) \qquad + (0.062)\ 1/1$$

In words, the return that equity holders earn is equal to the after-tax return on assets of the firm plus the residual after-tax return on assets after debt interest is paid.

To illustrate the effects of debt financing on a firm's ROE, consider the data displayed in Table 14-7. Three economic states are shown together with their respective probabilities of occurring. Returns on assets in the Fair economic state are identical to the ROA_{AT} used above. The *after-tax* return on assets in the other two states are either 9% less or 9% more. For each economic state, four different debt levels are shown ranging from zero debt to $3.00 in debt per $1.00 of equity. There are two important principles illustrated in Table 14-7:

1. When the cost of debt financing is less than the return earned on assets, then leverage increases the rate of return to equity holders.
2. If there is an uncertainty about the return on assets, then leverage increases the uncertainty of returns to equity holders.

TABLE 14-7 *Affects of Leverage on Return on Equity*

Economic State	Probability	Returns on Assets Before-Tax	After-Tax	Debt to Equity Ratio No Debt	1 to 1	2 to 1	3 to 1
Poor	0.2	-2.00%	-1.20%	-1.20%	-4.00%	-6.80%	-9.60%
Fair	0.6	13.00%	7.80%	7.80%	14.00%	20.20%	26.40%
Good	0.2	28.00%	16.80%	16.80%	32.00%	47.20%	62.40%
Expected		13.00%	7.80%	7.80%	14.00%	20.20%	26.40%
Standard Deviation		9.49%	5.69%	5.69%	11.38%	17.08%	22.77%

Assumed tax rate equals 40%.
Before-tax cost of debt financing equals 2 2/3%.

The first principle can be seen in the Fair and Good economic states shown in the table. In these states, the $2\frac{2}{3}\%$ pre-tax cost of debt financing is less than the pre-tax Returns on Assets (13.0% and 28.0%). In both states, the Return on Equity is positively related to the level of debt financing used. In contrast, in the Poor economic state, the cost of debt financing exceeds the Return on Assets. When this is the case, greater debt financing leads to lower returns to equity holders. Finally, notice in the table that, since the *expected* Return on Assets exceeds the cost of debt financing, the *expected* Return on Equity increases with the use of debt.

The second principle can be seen in the variability in Return on Equity as the debt level increases. When no debt is used, the after-tax ROE is the same as the after-tax ROA and ranges from a minimum of -1.2% to a maximum of 16.8%. In contrast, when the debt to equity ratio is 3/1, the minimum and maximum ROE are -9.6% and 62.4%, respectively. This principle can also be observed in the standard deviation of ROE. When no debt is employed, the standard deviation of after-tax ROA and ROE are both 5.69%. When $3.00 in debt are used per $1.00 of equity, the standard deviation of ROE increases to 22.77%![1]

Financial Leverage and Equity Beta. Since the use of debt financing increases the volatility of returns to equity owners, it also increases their nondiversifiable risk. Stated in terms of the Capital Asset Pricing Model (CAPM), debt financing increases the beta of equity investment.

It can be shown that the relationship between the nondiversifiable risk inherent in a firm's assets, the level of debt financing used by the firm, the firm's income tax rate, and the nondiversifiable risk borne by shareholders is:

Equity Beta as a Function of Asset Beta

$$B_E = B_A + B_A (D/E)(1-T)$$
$$= B_A (1 + D/E)(1-T)$$

(14.4)

---

[1] The increase in standard deviation of ROE that comes with an increase in a firm's debt level is a nondiversifiable increase in risk. We return to this later in the chapter when we examine the relationship between the beta of equity and the firm's use of debt financing.

where B_E equals the beta of equity, B_A is the beta associated with the firm's assets, and T is the firm's tax rate. D and E represent the market value of D and equity. We will use this relationship later in the chapter when we estimate IBM's equity beta in early 1993.

An Alternative Analysis of Return on Equity

In Chapter 13, we saw how the return on equity of a firm could be separated into three underlying causes: asset efficiency, expense control, and debt utilization. This type of analysis has come to be known as the *DuPont Model* since the DuPont corporation has used the approach to evaluate the relative performance of its various divisions. As discussed above, the Dupont Model is technically inaccurate since it does not properly account for the effects of debt financing and related interest costs. Nonetheless, the Dupont Model is widely used by security analysts since it provides a quick and logical way to analyze financial trends.

In fact, many analysts prefer to use a more detailed analysis of ROE that also highlights the effects of interest expenses and income tax. Such a model is shown in Equation 14.5 below:

$$ROE_{AT} = \overset{\text{Sales}}{\underset{\text{Turnover}}{\rule{0pt}{0pt}}} \quad \overset{\text{Pre-Tax}}{\underset{\substack{\text{Operating} \\ \text{Income}}}{\rule{0pt}{0pt}}} \quad \overset{\text{Interest}}{\underset{\text{Impacts}}{\rule{0pt}{0pt}}} \quad \overset{\text{Tax}}{\underset{\text{Impacts}}{\rule{0pt}{0pt}}} \quad \overset{\text{Debt}}{\underset{\text{Utilization}}{\rule{0pt}{0pt}}}$$

(14.5)

Detailed Analysis of ROE

$$ROE_{At} = \frac{TS}{TA} \times \frac{NOI_{BT}}{TS} \times \frac{NI_{BT}}{NOI_{BT}} \times (1-T) \times \frac{TA}{E}$$

Here TS refers to total sales, NOI_{BT} and NI_{BT} refer to Net Operating Income (before interest expense) and Net Income (after interest expense) both before taxes, TA and E refer to Total Assets and Equity, and T is the average income tax rate. For example, using the IBM 1992 data shown in Tables 14-5 and 14-6:

$$1992 \text{ IBM ROE} = \frac{\$64.52}{\$86.7} \frac{\$3.97}{\$64.52} \times \frac{\$2.61}{\$3.97} \times (1 - 0.2375) \times \frac{\$86.70}{\$27.62}$$

$$= 0.744 \quad 6.15\% \times 0.6574 \times (0.7625) \quad \times 3.139$$

$$= 7.20\%$$

The asset turnover of 0.744 is best interpreted as follows. For each $1.00 of assets, $0.744 in sales were generated. The 6.15% represents the 1992 before-tax and before-interest profit margin. For each $1.00 of sales, profits before interest and taxes were 6.15 cents. When these two values are multiplied, the result is the pre-tax operating return on assets equal to 4.75%. The 0.6574 reflects the impacts of interest charges on pre-tax income. For each $1.00 of pre-tax Net Operating Income (NOI), interest had the effect of reducing pre-tax Net Income (NI) to $0.6574. The next term reflects the reduction in profits due to corporate income taxes. For each $1.00 in pre-tax income, after-tax income was $0.7625. Finally, the 3.139 reflects the fact that for each $1.00 of equity, IBM had $3.139 in total assets. When multiplied, these five terms yield IBM's 1992 return on equity of 7.2%.

An Analysis of Trends in IBM's ROE. In Table 14-8, two analyses of IBM's Return on Equity are displayed. The data in the top half of the table analyze the firm's ROE in terms of its Return on Assets and residual gain from the use of financial leverage, as shown in Equation 14.3. The bottom half of the table presents an extended Dupont Model, as shown in Equation 14.5.

Using the residual leverage model of Equation 14.3, it is clear that IBM's pre-tax return on assets declined significantly (from 22.91% to 4.58%) during the period 1981–1992. The reason for such a dramatic decline clearly must be explained! Also, during this period, the use of debt financing grew from a debt to equity ratio of 0.65 in 1981 to 2.13 by the end of 1992. This raises two basic questions: (1) Why did the firm rely increasingly on nonequity financing? and (2) Is the current level of debt excessive? A hint at the answer to the first question might lie in the fact that the greatest increase in debt occurred between 1990 and 1992, a period in which asset returns fell substantially. Possibly, management consciously increased debt in an orderly manner during the 1980s but the increase during the early 1990s was required to finance asset expansion at a time when cash flows from operations were declining.

Now consider the expanded *DuPont Model data* at the bottom of Table 14-8. The first two rows suggest why the firm's ROA had declined so dramatically. First, asset turnover (sales divided by assets) showed a continued slippage from 1.0 in 1981 to 0.74 in 1992. During 1981, the firm was able to generate $1.00 in sales for each dollar of assets. By 1992, only $0.74 in sales were being generated

TABLE 14-8 *Analyses of IBM Return on Equity*

	1981	1986	1990	1992
ROE as a Function of ROA and Financial Leverage				
ROA before-tax	22.91%	15.33%	13.06%	4.58%
TIMES 1-t	0.5767	0.5709	0.5899	0.7625
Equals ROA after-tax	13.21%	8.75%	7.71%	3.49%
Debt divided by equity	0.6465	0.6817	1.0445	2.1390
Pre-tax debt cost	3.59%	2.01%	2.95%	2.30%
(1.0-tax rate)	0.5767	0.5709	0.5899	0.7625
After-tax debt cost	2.07%	1.15%	1.74%	1.76%
ROE	20.42%	13.94%	13.94%	7.20%
Detailed Components of ROE				
Asset turnover	0.9986	0.8865	0.7871	0.7442
Pre-tax profit margin	22.94%	17.29%	16.60%	6.15%
Reduction in income due to interest	0.9385	0.9470	0.8846	0.6574
Reduction in income due to taxes	0.5767	0.5709	0.5899	0.7625
Assets to equity ratio	1.6465	1.6817	2.0445	3.1390
ROE	20.42%	13.93%	13.94%	7.20%

per dollar of assets. This could be due to a temporary decline in economic activity. But it is probably more likely to be caused by a fundamental change in the revenue generation power of the product line of the firm since the decline in the asset turnover was steady throughout the period shown. Second, the pre-tax profit margin declined from 22.9% in 1981 to 6.15% in 1992. While the profit margin showed a steady decline throughout the period shown, a sizeable decline occurred between 1990 and 1992. This suggests that two forces might have worked on the pre-tax profit margin: a fundamental shift in product line and competition during the full period plus a temporary decline in the early 1990s due to the recession.

Interest expenses grew as a percent of pre-tax *net operating income* throughout the period with a large increase in the early 1990s. By 1992, $1.00 of pre-tax net operating income was reduced to $0.66 in pre-tax *net income.*[2]

Taxes reduced net income at about the same rate throughout the 1980s. However, in 1992, taxes actually had the effect of increasing profitability relative to 1990. This is probably a temporary effect caused by the firm's poor profitability during 1992. Finally, as we saw in the top half of Table 14-8, the level of debt financing grew steadily during the 1980's and had a major increase in the early 1990s. By 1992, the ratio of assets to equity was 3.139 (1.0 plus the debt to equity ratio of 2.139).

Analyses of Total Capital versus Total Assets. Equations 14.3 and 14.4 as well as the data in Table 14.8 are based on the total assets of a firm. Many of these assets, however, are financed with debt capital that is either costless to the firm or that have costs that are difficult to identify. For example, IBM's 1992 before tax debt cost of 2.3% (shown in Table 14-8) was equal to total interest expense of $1.36 billion divided by total nonequity financing of $59.08 billion. (The $2 2/3\%$ interest cost used in an earlier example is analogous to this 2.3% cost.) However, most of the $1.36 billion of interest expense was associated mainly with the firm's outstanding long-term debt of $12.84 billion. Thus, the cost of long-term debt was $1.36 divided by $12.85 or 10.58%. The lower cost of 2.3% shown in the analyses above was due to costless sources of short-term debt and "other liabilities."

Many analysts believe that a more accurate analysis of a firm's financial position can be obtained if one examines the profitability of total "capital" as opposed to total assets. Capital is usually defined as long-term debt plus common equity (and any preferred stock). When this is done, total assets are replaced with total capital, and total debt is replaced with long-term debt.

Asset Efficiency

Since the return to equity owners is the result of management's ability to efficiently control asset investments, maintain cost controls, and the firm's financing deci-

---

[2] It is important to remember the difference between net operating income and net income. Net operating income represents income from assets *before* the subtraction of interest expense. Net income is net operating income less interest expense.

sions, it is important to examine each in some depth. Usually this should be done by comparing results for the firm in question with other firms having similar product lines as well as with industry averages. IBM so dominates the computer business that such comparisons would be meaningless in its case. Thus we will examine IBM in isolation.

There are many ways of evaluating how efficiently a firm manages its assets. Many of these relate revenue dollars to the dollar value of an asset investment. For example, the total asset efficiency ratio (also called total asset turnover) is simply total sales divided by total assets. However, there are other ways to measure the efficient utilization of assets that you might find more meaningful. There is no simple best way or set of rules to follow when measuring asset efficiency. Use your own judgment, and adapt your analysis to the situation at hand. The ratios discussed below are only illustrative of what can be done.

Various measures of IBM's asset efficiency are shown in Table 14-9. The Total Asset Turnover is equal to total revenues *divided by total sales*. Although it carries the title "turnover," it is probably more easily interpreted as the dollar value of sales generated for each dollar of total assets. The larger the number the better. (This statement is usually true. At very high turnovers, however, the firm might be losing sales due to insufficient assets.) IBM's "asset turn" fell from $1.00 in sales per dollar of assets in 1981 to about $0.74 by the end of 1992.

The second ratio shown in Table 14-9 is the fixed asset turnover. It is equal to total revenues divided by either net or gross (of accumulated depreciation) fixed assets. The numbers shown in the table are based on net fixed assets. Be cautious when using this ratio since it can provide misleading results. For many firms, additions to fixed assets are lumpy, causing short-term moves in the ratio to be erratic. It will also vary between firms due to differences in depreciation methodologies. Neglecting these possible problems, there is a strong suggestion that the growth of IBM's net fixed assets outpaced sales growth between 1981 and 1992. This could be the culprit underlying the decline in total asset turnover. But we need to look further in order to be sure.

Unlike the two previous turnover ratios, inventory turnover is best thought of as a measure of actual turnover. Based on product sales, how many times did the firm use up and then restore inventory? Inventory turn is calculated in two ways: (1) dividing sales by inventory balances and (2) dividing cost of goods sold by inventory. The second approach is better since cost of goods sold and inventories are both stated in dollars before a gross profit margin increase. Also, if one wishes

TABLE 14-9 *IBM Asset Efficiency Ratios*

	1981	*1986*	*1990*	*1992*
Total Asset Turnover	1.00	0.89	0.79	0.74
Fixed Asset Turnover	1.55	1.70	2.53	2.99
Inventory Turnover				
(on Cost of Sales)	4.19	2.82	3.04	4.18
Average Collection Period (days)	54.99	71.01	81.07	72.58

to be strict about the notion of "turnover," it should be calculated only for revenues that involve sales from inventory. For example, in IBM's case, software revenues have little to do with inventory levels.

The inventory turn numbers in Table 14-9 are based on yearly cost of sales divided by inventory. For example, in 1992 the calculation is $35.07 \div \$8.38 = 4.18$. On the whole, there does not appear to be a serious weakening of inventory control. If anything, the inventory turnover in 1992 is the best since 1981.

The average collection period is calculated as 365 days per year divided by the number of times receivables were turned over during the year. For example, the 1992 value was calculated as follows. First, the receivable turnover was calculated as total sales divided by accounts receivable (($64.52 / $12.83 = 5.0288). This receivable turn was then divided into 365 days per year (365 / 5.0288). This resulted in a 1992 collection period of 72.58 days. During the period covered by Table 14-9, the receivable collection period increased between 1981 and 1990. However, since 1990 the collection period has been shortened considerably, suggesting a more aggressive collection policy by IBM management.

Expense Control

Earlier, we saw that a major reason for IBM's decline in ROE was due to decreased profit margins. The easiest way to examine this type of problem is to create a "percentage income statement" in which each element of the income statement is stated as a percentage of total revenue.

A percentage income statement for IBM is shown in Table 14-10. During this period, the net income (after taxes) profit margin decreased from 12.42% in 1981 to 8.66% in 1990 and 3.08% in 1992. Clearly, much of the decline between 1990 and 1992 can be traced to competitive pressures during the economic recession of the early 1990s. But the long-term downward drift prior to that recession is more likely due to increased competition within the PC market and a decrease in the percentage of sales generated by mainframe computers. The decline in IBM's profit margin can be traced to each expense category. Costs of goods sold, oper-

TABLE 14-10 *IBM Percentage Income Statement*

	1981	1986	1990	1992
Revenue	100.00%	100.00%	100.00%	100.00%
Cost of sales	40.39%	44.31%	44.55%	54.36%
Gross profit	59.61%	55.69%	55.45%	45.64%
Operating costs	36.67%	38.40%	38.85%	39.49%
Net operating income before taxes	22.94%	17.29%	16.60%	6.15%
Interest expense	1.41%	0.92%	1.91%	2.11%
Net income before taxes	21.53%	16.37%	14.68%	4.05%
Taxes	9.12%	7.02%	6.02%	0.96%
Net income	12.42%	9.35%	8.66%	3.08%

ating costs, and interest expenses each increased as a percentage of sales. Unless IBM is able to develop new products that other firms cannot effectively compete against, it is difficult to see how their profit margins will increase much above 9%. In fact, it is quite possible that the firm's long-run profit margin could be lower than 9% if the highly competitive PC market continues to grow more rapidly than the mainframe market.

In short, it is unlikely that IBM will be able to restore its profit margin to levels it earned before the growth of the PC market.

Debt Capacity

In Table 14-11, three types of debt utilization are shown: (1) measures of debt levels, (2) measures of debt capacity and (3) liquidity ratios. Measures of debt levels examine the amount of debt outstanding relative to equity financing. Debt capacity measures examine a firm's ability to pay its current financial costs from operating income and cash flow. Liquidity ratios examine the relationship between short-term debt obligations and liquid assets.

The only measure of debt level that might not be self-explanatory is the ratio of long-term debt to capital. As noted above, capital refers to permanent financing provided to the firm and is usually measured as long-term debt plus common equity (and preferred stock, if present). Thus the long-term debt-to-capital ratio for 1992 was 0.32 ($12.85 ÷ $40.67). At the end of 1992, long-term debt represented more than 30% of permanent financing, up from 11% in 1986. All other measures of debt confirm that IBM has relied on increased debt financing. The increased use of debt was clearly a management policy designed to help finance capital asset grow and provide higher returns to equity owners.

Measures of debt capacity are used to evaluate the firm's ability to meet its

TABLE 14-11 *IBM Debt Utilization Ratios*

	1981	1986	1990	1992
Measures of Debt Levels				
Debt to assets	0.39	0.41	0.51	0.68
Debt to equity	0.65	0.68	1.04	2.14
Short-term debt to total debt	0.64	0.54	0.57	0.62
Long-term debt to capital	0.13	0.11	0.22	0.32
Measure of Debt Capacity				
Times interest earned	16.27	18.85	8.67	2.92
Times interest covered				
Earnings plus noncash expenses	NA	NA	12.68	7.52
Liquidity ratios				
Current ratio	1.41	2.18	1.54	1.08
Quick ratio	1.03	1.55	1.14	0.85

promised financial payments. The basic ratio of this type is *Times Interest Earned* (TIE) ratio. Since interest is paid before taxes, the income available to pay interest is also before-tax income. The TIE ratio is calculated as:

Times Interest Earned
$$\frac{\text{Net Income Before Tax \& Interest}}{\text{Interest}} \qquad (14.6)$$

For example in 1992, TIE was:

$$2.92 = (3.97 / 1.36)$$

The higher the TIE ratio, the greater the firm's debt capacity.

Since interest is actually paid in cash, many analysts calculate a *Times Interest Covered* ratio by adding all noncash expenses to the numerator in Equation 14.6. For many firms, the major noncash expense is depreciation. However, any other noncash expenses should also be added back to pre-tax net operating income if such noncash expenses are significant. In the case of IBM, amortization of software costs (shown in Table 14-4) is also a major noncash expense. Adding 1992 depreciation and software amortization to 1992 net operating income before tax (NOI_{BT}) results in cash flows available to meet interest expenses of $10.229 billion:

$$
\begin{array}{cccccc}
\text{Cash available} & & & & & \text{Software} \\
\text{for Interest} & & NOI_{BT} & \text{Depreciation} & & \text{Amortization} \\
\$10.229 & = & \$3.97 & + \quad \$4.793 & + & \$1.466
\end{array}
$$

and an interest coverage ratio of 7.52 times ($10.229 / $1.36).

The level of interest coverage that a firm should have before one should be concerned with the firm's ability to meet its financial obligations varies between firms and depends largely on a firm's inherent business risk (uncertainty about a firm's net operating income). While IBM's coverage ratio in 1992 of 7.52 is down considerably from 12.68 in 1990, profits in 1992 were probably as low as they would be for the foreseeable future. Thus, it appears that the firm was in no serious immediate danger of being unable to meet its interest obligations.

Liquidity ratios are measures of a firm's short-term solvency, the ability to meet immediate debts. Two standard ratios are:

Current Ratio
$$\text{Current Assets} \div \text{Current Liabilities} \qquad (14.7)$$

Quick Ratio
$$(\text{Current Assets} - \text{Inventory}) \div \text{Current Liabilities} \qquad (14.8)$$

For many firms, inventory might not be as liquid as other current assets. Thus inventory is subtracted from current assets in calculating the Quick Ratio.

A review of IBM's liquidity ratios indicates that the firm's liquidity had declined between 1986 and 1992. As we have seen above, improvements in sales volume and profit margins were critical—in this case, to restore the firm's short-term liquidity.

Management Evaluation

In the long run, a firm's profit level and risks are determined by the actions of the firm's management. In the short run, external forces such as governmental policies, international events, weather, and business cycles can have impacts on profits that may not deserve a pat (or slap) on management's back. Although the historical record is an obvious place to begin an evaluation of management, some care should be taken in how the record is evaluated.

Beyond historical ratio analysis, what can the analyst do? This is a difficult question to answer. In fact, there is no reasonably sure procedure. Instead, the analyst is usually forced to develop a general impression based on a variety of creative observations. Some of these are discussed below.

A Few Approaches to Evaluating Management. Some techniques and considerations of management evaluation include the following:

1. *Anticipatory management.* How accurately did management foresee major changes in the industry and position the firm to take full advantage of these changes? In the case of IBM, management seriously misestimated the growth of the PC market, the decline of mainframe computer sales, and pressure on profit margins due to intense international competition.

2. *Extent and reliability of information provided to the public.* Does management provide a thorough review of the firm's financial status and prospects, or is minimal information given, and only begrudgingly? How accurately does the information provided to the public seem to reflect the actual situation? Annual reports and other financial statements presented by IBM are models of Generally Accepted Accounting Principles and management's discussions are usually forthright about the nature of their problems (as management saw them in the early 1990s).

3. *Clarity of goals and corporate strengths.* Has management clearly defined the nature of its comparative advantages and then focused only on ventures in which these advantages can be put to best use? Historically, IBM management had clearly defined its strength to be a research advantage in mainframe computer design and services. The firm did not use temporary excess cash flows to invest in, say, car leasing or hamburger chains. Instead, each of IBM's products made internal economic sense, in that they built on or enhanced other products of the firm. Diversification wasn't undertaken for its own sake. But after the major shift in computer technology that took place in the middle 1980s, the firm appeared to lose an understanding of its role in the future of its industry.

4. *Focus of top management.* Does top management spend its time addressing the issues that can lead to increased economic value, such as asset efficiency, expense control, and capital expenditures? Or is a large part of the time devoted to less important factors, such as accounting techniques, expansion of EPS via mergers, engaging in share sales, and repurchases in response to beliefs that share prices are over- or undervalued?

5. *Management depth.* Are there a number of top managers who could move into the chief executive officer's position, or is the firm dominated by one or two key managers? Similarly, are all levels of management equally strong, or is just the upper level strong, with weak middle or lower levels? Managers at IBM were all well trained and motivated. Their problem, however, seemed to be that middle and senior management levels had a single, common view on the future direction of the firm. Independent opinions were missing.

6. *Employee morale.* Even the best management team can do little unless employees are satisfied with their jobs and eager to help the firm.

7. *Opinions of competitors.* A good key to the abilities of a firm's management is the opinions of other firms. Usually a good management team will distinguish itself in the industry and gain widespread respect.

Much has been written about how to distinguish between good and mediocre management. Unfortunately, most of the conclusions don't hold up under close scrutiny. For example, is decentralized management better than centralized management? We really don't know. It may depend on the firm's product line and the nature of management's comparative advantage. Is a larger R & D budget indicative of good management? Not if it doesn't pay off. Does the fact that management is willing to take greater risks indicate good management? Not really. Does rapid sales growth indicate good management? Not if the growth is obtained simply by retaining a larger portion of profits or if new ventures are undertaken for growth alone, with little attention to profitability. There is no simple technique to evaluate management quality. Rather, the analyst is forced to rely on a blend of personal creativity, logic, and intuition.

Inside Information

An analyst is able to identify an over- or undervalued stock only by having better information than other people. The *sources* of this information can be categorized as follows:

1. *Direct* information provided by *employees* of the firm—for example, the president's projection of *EPS* or a clerk's statement about unfilled orders.

2. *Direct* information provided by *nonemployees*—for example, a government attorney's private statement that the firm is to be indicted for bribery or a public statement that the Department of Defense has placed a $100 million order with the firm.

3. *Inferential information* developed by examining a large amount of data and drawing conclusions about it—for example, concluding that a new law may have dramatic effects on a firm's profits and growth. Or that potential debt structure and foreign competition could seriously increase the firm's default risk.

Under Rule 10-5b of the Securities Exchange Act, transactions based on direct information provided by employees that has not been made available to the general public are illegal, and any profits earned must be returned to the original share-holders. For example, in the 1960s Texas Gulf Sulphur discovered a rich new oil field, and various officers of the firm, plus some outsiders, traded on information about how productive the discovery—which had not yet been made public— would be. Under Rule 10-5b, a large portion of these inside profits was taken away. Similarly, when a security analyst learned from a former employee of Equity Funding that something was amiss within the firm, he discussed the matter with various institutional clients of his firm. They then sold shares before the information became widely known among the general public and before share prices fell dramatically. The analyst was charged with violating Rule 10-5b.

The most recent insider trading scandal erupted when the Securities Exchange Commission (SEC) charged Ivan Boesky with a wide variety of insider trades. The common denominator in most of his trades involved privileged information about potential corporate mergers. Boesky obtained tips from individuals who worked for the investment banking firms that were putting the mergers together. The indictment and conviction of Boesky have made most market participants very sensitive to illegal insider trading.

Trading on direct information provided by nonemployees (that is not yet publicly available) may or may not be illegal. It depends on the situation. However, trades based on inferential information developed by the analyst as a result of analyzing data in a unique manner are not illegal.

Analysts should be wary of suggesting trades on any *material nonpublic* information. If such information is offered by employees of the firm, the analyst (or the firm) should make a public announcement before suggesting trades for specific clients.

Final Valuation of IBM Stock Price

In this section we conclude our analysis of IBM common stock by estimating its intrinsic value in early 1993. At the close of trading in 1992, shares of IBM were trading close to $50. To estimate a fair value, we will use the dividend valuation model. This requires an estimate of an appropriate discount rate as well as forecasts of expected future dividends per share. Because uncertainty existed about future dividends, three price estimates are developed; one based on a *pessimistic* dividend forecast, one based on *expected* dividends, and one based on an *optimistic* forecast.

Do not think of this valuation as *proof* that IBM shares were either properly valued or mispriced. The presentation in this section is only illustrative of the procedures that security analysts would use to evaluate a company's intrinsic value. A more complete analysis of the firm than we have conducted might result in different dividend forecasts and required returns.

Required Returns. Although scholars have yet to find an asset pricing model that stands up to rigorous empirical testing, the standard Capital Asset Pricing Model (CAPM) shown in Equation 14.9 is a common-sense model that is widely used.

<table>
<tr><td></td><td>Expected
Stock Return</td><td>=</td><td>Risk Free
Interest</td><td>+</td><td>Stock's
Beta</td><td>(Market Risk
Premium)</td></tr>
<tr><td>**Capital Asset
Pricing Model**</td><td>$E(R_i)$</td><td>=</td><td>RF</td><td>+</td><td>B_i ×</td><td>(RP_m) **(14.9)**</td></tr>
</table>

As discussed in earlier chapters, the risk-free rate used to evaluate securities with long-term payoffs (such as common stocks) should be a long-term default-free interest rate since such rates include compensation for both a real risk-free return and *expected long-term inflation.* In early 1993, yields to maturity on long-term U.S. Treasuries were close to 7.0%. We will use this as our measure of RF.

The selection of an appropriate market risk premium is more judgmental. The long-run difference between historical returns on a broad market index such as the S&P 500 and risk-free government bonds can provide some direction. But such differences are sensitive to the beginning and ending date chosen. In truth, it is the analyst who must specify the desired risk premium. For illustrative purposes, we will use a market risk premium of 6%.

Betas are usually estimated in a two-step process. First, an estimate of a firm's historical beta is developed by regressing historical past rates of return on the stock against a broad stock market return series. This historical estimate is then adjusted to reflect any recent changes in the security's systematic risk that the analyst believes has occurred.

To estimate IBM's historical beta, the excess return Market Model regression (discussed in Chapter 7) was used. Recall that excess returns are equal to the return on a security minus T-bill returns during the same time period. The S&P 500 index was to be used as a proxy for the aggregate stock market portfolio. Using quarterly excess returns between 1982 and the end of 1992, the following Market Model regression was obtained:

Excess return on
IBM in Quarter t = -0.013 + 0.846 (Excess Return on S&P 500 in Quarter t)

$$R^2 = 34.6\%$$

This equation suggests that a reasonable estimate of IBM's beta during the period 1982–1992 was 0.85. In Figure 14-3 the characteristic line for IBM during this period is shown.

While Market Model regressions such as this may provide reasonable estimates of a firm's *past* beta, they should not be blindly used as an estimate of the firm's current equity beta. This is particularly true when major changes have occurred in a firm's product line and its use of debt financing.

To assess how changes in a firm's product line and financial leverage may have changed its equity beta, Equation 14.4 is particularly helpful. For example, IBM had an average tax rate of about 40% between 1982 and 1992 as well as an average ratio of debt to equity of 1 to 1. Therefore, its historical *asset beta* can be estimated using Equation (14.4) to be about 0.71:

$$B_E = B_A (1 + D/E)(1 - T)$$

$$0.85 = B_A (2.0)(1 - 0.4)$$

$$B_A = 0.85 / 1.2$$

$$= 0.71$$

This estimated asset beta of 0.71 is probably smaller than the firm's asset beta in early 1993 due to recent changes in its product line (a larger weight to PCs and reduced weight on mainframe computers) as well as increased competition. For purposes of illustration, assume that our best estimate of IBM's asset beta in early 1993 was 1.0.

In addition, the firm's use of debt financing in 1993 was considerably larger than during the period used in the Market Model regression. Using a 1.0 asset beta, a debt to equity ratio of 1.0 (somewhat less than year-end 1992 to reflect the firm's desire to reduce debt outstanding at that time) and a future tax rate of 40%, the firm's equity beta in 1993 would have been close to 1.2:

$$B_E = 1.0 \ (1.0 + 1.0) \ (1 - 0.4)$$

$$= 1.2$$

Based on an equity beta of 1.2, a 7.0% risk-free rate and an aggregate market risk premium of 6.0%, a fair rate of return to expect on IBM shares would have been 14.2%:

$$14.2\% = 7.0\% + 1.2 \ (6.0\%)$$

FIGURE 14-3 *IBM Characteristic Line Quarterly Returns 1982–1992*

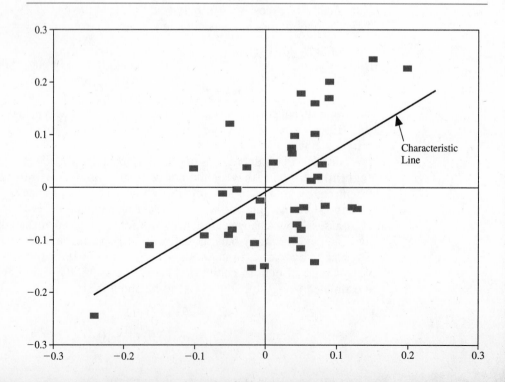

We will use this 14.2% as the risk-adjusted discount rate to find the present value of future dividends per share.

Forecasts of Dividends Per Share. During 1992, IBM paid a per-share dividend of $4.84. If investors had expected this $4.84 dividend to grow at a *constant* growth rate in the future, the task of valuing the shares would have been relatively straightforward. We would only have to estimate a constant future growth rate and use the constant dividend valuation model.

Unfortunately, the situation was more complex. IBM had maintained a constant $4.84 dividend since 1990 and was unlikely to increase its dividend until profit growth had been permanently restored. In fact, there was even some threat (albeit small) that the dividend might be temporarily cut. Thus, the use of a constant growth dividend valuation model is inappropriate. Instead, a nonconstant dividend growth model is required.

In valuing IBM shares in early 1993, three stock price estimates are developed based on expected, pessimistic, and optimistic dividend forecasts. Details and justifications for each are displayed in Table 14-12. A plot of these forecasts together with past dividends is shown in Figure 14.4.

When these dividend forecasts are discounted at the estimated required return of 14.2% (as shown in Table 14-12), the following early 1993 share price values are obtained:

Calculated Share Price Estimates

Pessimistic	Expected	Optimistic
$41.86	$48.99	$64.93

TABLE 14-12 *1993 IBM Stock Price Analysis Dividend Forecast Assumptions*

Details of Assumed Expected Growth (after 1996):

Net Income Profit Margin	0.07	Return to late 1980s values as profits recover
Asset Turnover	0.8	but competition remains intense.
Return on Assets	0.056	
Assets to Equity Ratio	2	Close to inferences that management has stated.
Return on Equity	0.112	
Retention Rate	0.5	Close to management inferences.
Sustainable Internal Growth	0.056	

Year	Dividend Growth Rate			Per Share Dividend Forecasts			Present Value at 14.2%		
	Pessimistic	Expected	Optimistic	Pessimistic	Expected	Optimistic	Pessimistic	Expected	Optimistic
1993	0.00%	0.00%	2.00%	$4.84	$4.84	$4.94	$4.24	$4.24	$4.32
1994	0.00%	0.00%	2.00%	$4.84	$4.84	$5.04	$3.71	$3.71	$3.86
1995	0.00%	0.00%	2.00%	$4.84	$4.84	$5.14	$3.25	$3.25	$3.45
1996	0.00%	0.00%	2.00%	$4.84	$4.84	$5.24	$2.85	$2.85	$3.08
1997 and be- yond	3.60%	5.60%	7.60%	$5.01	$5.11	$5.64	$27.81	$34.94	$50.22
						Total	$41.86	$48.99	$64.93

FIGURE 14-4 *Past and Potential Future IBM DPS*

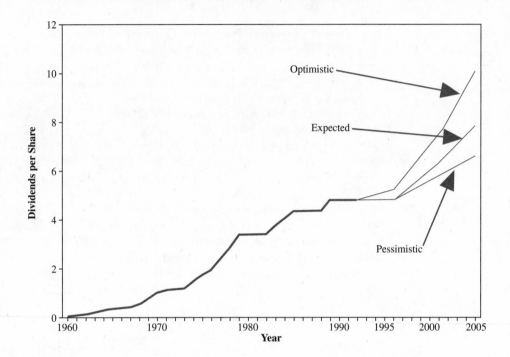

Since share prices were trading for about $50 at that time, it appears that shares of IBM were properly valued in early 1993.

Price Sensitivity to Assumptions. The results one obtains from a stock valuation such as this are totally dependent on the assumptions that are made. To examine

TABLE 14-13 *Sensitivity Analysis of Price to Input Assumptions*

	Stock Intrinsic Values Based on: Expected Dividend Growth Beyond 1996					
Discount Rate	*3.0%*	*4.0%*	*5.0%*	*5.6%*	*7.0%*	*8.0%*
11.0%	$56.06	$62.38	$70.81	$77.36	$100.30	$129.79
12.0%	$49.90	$54.69	$60.84	$66.45	$80.53	$97.75
13.0%	$44.97	$48.70	$53.36	$56.76	$67.33	$78.52
14.2%	$40.21	$43.06	$46.52	$48.99	$56.33	$63.61
15.0%	$37.57	$39.98	$42.87	$44.91	$50.83	$56.51
16.0%	$34.72	$36.71	$39.06	$40.69	$45.32	$49.63

Growth rates until 1997 are the same as in Table 14-12.
Growth rates in 1997 and beyond are shown in the table above.
Discount rate applies to all years.

how sensitive the results might be, it is useful to conduct a *sensitivity analysis* in which various assumptions are changed. An example of a sensitivity analysis is shown in Table 14-13.

Given the situation faced by IBM in 1993, it was unlikely that dividends would increase for a number of years. Therefore, the results shown in Table 14-13 are based on a $4.84 dividend through 1996. After 1996, dividend growth rates are allowed to vary as shown in the table. Discount rates, however, apply to all estimated dividends. All stock prices above the line drawn through the table represent cases in which the stock would have been undervalued in early 1993.

One of these cases is of special interest—when growth is estimated to be 5.6% as above but with a required return of 12%. In this case, the stock's estimated intrinsic value would be $66.45, undervalued relative to prevailing prices at the time. This stock price is close to the value we would have estimated if we had used IBM's historical estimated beta of 0.85. Stated another way, if we had not assumed that IBM shares had more market risk in 1993 than during the previous 10 years, we would have concluded that the shares were undervalued.

SUMMARY

Like all other asset classes, the equity portion of a portfolio may be passively or actively managed. Passive management refers to cases in which no attempts are made to find mispriced securities. A passively managed portfolio should be well diversified and reflect the liquidity and tax situation of the investor. The common way in which a passive equity portfolio is created is by the purchase of a commingled index fund.

Active equity management should be used only if one has special skills and knowledge that can be used to find stocks that are trading at prices other than their intrinsic values. Often, the investor may not personally have such skills but employ someone else who claims to be able to provide value-added. Actively managed equity mutual funds are a good example. Active equity managers engage in *two* basic activities: (1) market timing or (2) stock selection. Market timing is also called Tactical Asset Allocation and involves predictions about which asset classes will have the highest (lowest) rates of return in the near future. Stock selection activities deal with identifying individual stocks that are mispriced. Most of this chapter dealt with techniques used in stock selection. These are often referred to as fundamental analyses.

A good fundamental analyst will become intimately familiar with the history of a company, the economics and technology of its industry, management abilities, and so forth; all with the goal of valuing expected future dividends per share. There is no single right way to conduct a fundamental analysis. In fact, the more creative one can be, the more likely it is that information not reflected in current market prices can be found.

REVIEW PROBLEM

Table 14-A and 14-B present the financial statements of a firm that is similar to IBM, Corp., which we will call KAL.

a. Calculate the interest adjusted Return on Assets for both years.

b. If the firm had used no financial leverage in 1996, what would its ROE have been?

c. Calculate various measures of assets efficiency for each year.

d. Calculate measures of debt level, capacity, and liquidity.

e. Assume the beta of this firm is 0.85 (the same as IBM's historical beta found in this chapter). Also assume a risk-free rate of 8.0% and a market risk premium of 5%. What rate of return should you require according to the Capital Asset Pricing Model (CAPM)?

f. If you expect the 1996 return on equity and dividend retention rates to continue into the future, what do you expect the annual sustainable growth rate of dividends per share will be?

g. Given the answers to parts e and f (i.e., assuming constant dividend growth) what should be the market price of KAL?

h. KAL shares are selling for $122. Is this a buy, hold, or sell candidate?

i. The data in this review problem is actually that of IBM as of 1982 and 1986. Share prices of IBM at the end of 1986 were also $122 and the return on long-term U.S. Treasuries was 8%. No answer is required to this part of the review problem. Simply compare your answer in part h to the subsequent price performance of IBM in Figure 14-1.

Solution

	1992	1996
a.		
Tax Rate	3,521/7,930 = 0.444	3,600/8,389 = 0.429
NOI after tax	4,409 + (1 − 0.444)454 = 4,661	4,789 + (1 − 0.429)475 = 5,060
ROA	4,661/32,541 = 14.32%	5,060/57,814 = 8.75%

TABLE 14-A

KAL, Inc. Balance Sheets (in Thousands)	1992	1996
Cash and Securities	$ 3,300	$ 7,257
Receivable	5,433	10,825
Inventory	3,492	8,039
Other	789	1,628
Total Current Assets	13,014	27,749
Net Fixed Assets	19,527	30,065
Total Assets	$32,541	$57,814
Current Liabilities	$ 8,209	$14,747
Long-Term Debt	2,851	4,169
Deferred Taxes	1,521	4,524
Common Equity	19,960	34,374
Total Liabilities and Equity	$32,541	$57,814

TABLE 14-B

KAL, Inc. Income Statements (in Thousands)	1992	1996
Revenues	$34,364	$51,250
Cost of Sales	− 13,688	− 22,706
Gross Profit	20,676	28,544
Operating Expenses	− 12,620	− 20,685
Operating Income	8,056	7,859
Interest		
Income	328	1,005
Expense	− 454	− 475
Net Interest	− 126	530
Earnings before Taxes	7,930	8,389
Taxes	− 3,521	3,600
Net Income	$4,409	$4,789
Depreciation	$3,143	$3,316
Earnings per Share	$7.39	$7.81
Dividends per Share	$3.44	$4.40

b. 8.75%

c.

Total Asset Turn	34,364/32,541 = 1.056	51,250/57,814 = 0.886
Fixed Asset Turn	34,364/19,527 = 1.760	51,250/30,065 = 1.705
Inventory Turn (CGS)	13,688/3,492 = 3.92	22,706/8,039 = 2.82
Sales per day	34,364/365 = 94.15	51,250/365 = 140.41
Average Collection Period	5,433/94.15 = 57.7 days	10,825/140.4 = 77.1 days

d.

Total Debt	8,209 + 2,851 + 1,521 = 12,581	14,747 + 4,169 + 4,524 = 23,440
Total Capital	22,811	38,543
Debt to Assets	12,581/32,541 = 0.386%	23,440/57,814 = 0.405
Debt to Equity	= 0.630	= 0.682
STD to Total	= 0.652	= 0.629
LTD to Capital	= 0.125	= 0.108
Times Interest Earned	(8,056 + 328)/454 = 18.5 times	(7,859 + 1005)/475 = 18.7 times
Times Interest Covered	(8,384 + 3,143)/454 25.4 times	(8,864 + 3,316)/475 25.6 times
Current Ratio	13,014/8,209 = 1.58	27,749/14,747 = 1.88

Quick Ratio   9,522/8,209   19,710/14,747
                            = 1.16   = 1.34

e. Required Return = 8.0% + 0.85(5.0%) = 12.25%

f.

$$
\begin{aligned}
G &= \quad \text{ROE} \quad \times \text{Retention Rate} \\
&= 4,789/34,374 \times (7.81 - 4.40)/7.81 \\
&= 0.1393 \times 0.4366 = 0.0608
\end{aligned}
$$

g. Price = \$4.40(1.0608) / (0.1225 − 0.0608) = \$75.64

h. Based on the pricing assumptions, this is a sell candidate.

QUESTIONS AND PROBLEMS

1. Evaluate the reasonableness of the following hypothetical statements:
   a. ''Most analysts of the office-equipment industry are forecasting a substantial increase over prior years in the earnings per share of Amdahl Corporation and Burroughs Corporation. As a result, they are suggesting active purchasing of common shares of both firms.''
   b. ''Yesterday's announcement by the management of Tech Labs that back orders are continuing to increase is causing many analysts to revise upward their forecasts of Tech Labs' earnings. Yet the market price of the firm's stock doesn't seem to have fully discounted the likely earnings revision. We suggest active buying of these shares at levels below \$20.''
2. Identify the characteristics of an *equity* investment portfolio for the following accounts:
   a. A \$20.0 million pension fund which will not have to pay large retirement benefits for another 20 years. Employees are factory workers and clerical staff for a young high-technology firm. Most employees own no stocks or bonds of their own.
   b. A 45-year-old lawyer with a successful practice. The lawyer is in a high tax bracket, won't need the funds until retirement, and is willing to accept above-average risk. \$200,000 is to be invested. No other investments are held.
   c. A 60-year-old machinist with a portfolio worth \$80,000, an average tax bracket, and a desire for less-than-average risk. Major retirement income will come from a diversified pension fund.
   d. A young family with two children not yet in school. Both parents have promising careers as CPAs and are willing to accept moderate risk. At present they have \$10,000 to invest and expect that at least that amount will be available for new investment every year.
3. Using five years of monthly returns, you have estimated the historical equity beta of Marine Products Corporation to be 1.0. During this time span the firm's debt structure was reasonably stable, with the total debt-to-total-asset ratio averaging 0.40. The firm's tax rate was 46%.
   a. Estimate the historical asset beta.
   b. If the firm's total debt-to-total-asset ratio is expected to increase to 0.70, what is a reasonable estimate of the future beta?
 4. The Coca-Cola Company (KO) and PepsiCo, Inc. (PEP) are the leading companies in the worldwide market for soft drinks and snack foods.

   KO is the world's largest soft-drink company. Principal products in terms of sales volume are Coca-Cola, Tab, Sprite, Hi-C, and Minute Maid Orange Juice. In 1982, KO acquired Columbia Pictures for \$692 million in cash and stock in order to capitalize on what its management sees as ''enormous opportunities in the passive leisure-time industry.'' In 1983, KO disposed of Wine Spectrum (Taylor Wine Company and the Monterey Vineyard). Soft drinks provide about 72% of KO's annual net sales, food products 16%, and entertainment 12%.

PEP is the world's largest producer of snack foods and the second largest factor in the soft-drink market behind KO. Snack foods (Frito-Lay) and food service (Pizza Hut and Taco Bell) represent about 50% of PEP's annual sales volume, with soft drinks (Pepsi, Diet Pepsi, Teem) accounting for an additional 39%.

Since 1976 the number of gallons of soft drinks sold in the United States has grown at an annual rate of 3.7%. During this period the annual increase in gallons sold in the United States was 4.6% for KO and 6.4% for PEP. Some analysts predict that despite the introduction of soft drinks with greater appeal to an older population, unit growth in the United States will slow as the 13- to 24-year-old age group declines in relative importance.

KO and PEP have diversified their product offerings and have sought out foreign markets where the population is younger on average and the growth is faster than in the United States. The geographical distribution of net operating revenues is approximately as follows:

Estimated 1983 Net Operating Revenues

	KO	*PEP*
U.S. and Puerto Rico	58%	77%
Europe and Africa	18	8
Canada and Pacific	16	4
Latin America	8	11
	100%	100%

Because of the strong U.S. dollar, high inflation rates in Latin markets, and price controls in Mexico, 1983 was a difficult year for KO and PEP. Many analysts believe that earnings for each of these companies will increase considerably in 1984 as price controls are relaxed in Mexico and foreign economies improve.

a. Base your answer to this question solely on the foregoing information and the data in Table 14-C.

   (1) Compare the economy, the food and beverage industry, KO, and PEP in terms of growth and stability for the period 1976–1983. Show comparisons in current dollars and constant dollars, identifying those trends that are useful for making investment decisions.

   (2) List four conclusions you can draw from the comparisons.

   (3) List three problems in using the data to draw useful investment conclusions.

b. Base your answer to this question on the ratios provided in Tables 14-D and 14-E and the company data in Tables 14-G and 14-H. Return on stockholders' equity is a prime measure of management's performance and can be calculated using turnover, leverage, pretax profit margin, and income tax rate. Utilizing these ratios:

   (1) Calculate the net return on average common equity for KO and PEP for the two years 1977 and 1983.

   (2) Identify the ratios that account for the level and trend of return on equity for each company in these two years.

c. When the annual net sales of KO and PEP were regressed against GNP for the years 1973–1983, a high degree of correlation was found to exist. The regression equation, standard error of estimate, and coefficient of correlation for each company are listed below:

TABLE 14-C *The Economy, the Industry, the Companies*

	U.S. GNP			Food and Beverage Industry				Company Sales*			
						Prod. Index (1967 = 100)		KO		PEP	
Year	Current $ (billions)	Constant $ (billions)	GNP Price Index (1972 = 100)	Current $ (billions)	Consumer Price Index (1967 = 100)	Food	Beverage	Current $ (millions)	Constant $ (millions)†	Current $ (millions)	Constant $ (millions)†
1983 (est.)	$3,304	$1,536	215.2	$417	298.6	155.9	199.7	$6,820	$2,284	$7,700	$2,579
1982	3,073	1,485	206.9	397	289.1	151.0	193.7	6,249	2,162	7,499	2,594
1981	2,954	1,514	195.1	376	272.4	152.0	197.1	5,889	2,162	7,027	2,580
1980	2,632	1,475	178.4	345	246.8	149.6	193.4	5,621	2,278	5,975	2,421
1979	2,418	1,479	163.4	312	217.4	147.4	189.5	4,689	2,157	5,089	2,341
1978	2,164	1,439	150.4	276	195.4	142.7	180.1	4,095	2,096	4,300	2,201
1977	1,918	1,370	140.0	250	181.5	138.8	168.1	3,394	1,870	3,649	2,010
1976	1,718	1,298	132.3	231	170.5	132.9	156.9	2,989	1,753	3,109	1,823
Compound Annual Growth Rate (1976–1983)											
	9.8%	2.4%	7.2%	8.8%	8.3%	2.3%	3.5%	12.5%	3.8%	13.8%	5.1%
Standard Deviation (1976–1983)											
	3.2%	2.7%	2.0%	2.8%	3.5%	1.6%	3.2%	6.3%	5.4%	6.5%	4.2%

* Results from continuing operations—no adjustments made for sale of Wine Spectrum by KO in 1983.
† Series represents current dollar sales deflated by the U.S. consumer price index.
SOURCES: *Economic Indicators,* November 1983; corporate annual reports.

	KO	PEP
Coefficient of Correlation	.996	.997
Standard Error of Estimate ($ millions)	$158.1	$166.1
Regression Equation	−966.76 + 2.36 (GNP)	−2053.81 + 3.02 (GNP)
1983 Sales ($ millions)	$6,820	$7,700

TABLE 14-D *Selected Financial Ratios*

	EBIT ÷ Assets		Total Assets ÷ Common Equity		Net Earnings ÷ Pretax Earnings		Net Sales ÷ Total Assets	
Fiscal Year	KO	PEP	KO	PEP	KO	PEP	KO	PEP
1983 (est.)	21.1%	14.7%	1.78×	2.56×	56.0%	58.0%	1.33×	1.75×
1982	23.7	16.9	1.68	2.57	55.0	57.2	1.47	1.82
1981	24.3	17.7	1.60	2.53	55.4	58.5	1.69	1.89
1980	24.3	18.3	1.59	2.39	55.1	56.5	1.77	1.90
1979	26.2	18.5	1.51	2.20	55.4	59.8	1.70	1.92
1978	27.8	19.8	1.46	2.13	54.4	56.1	1.69	1.89
1977	27.9	20.1	1.41	2.31	54.0	55.4	1.59	1.83
1976	28.3	16.9	1.39	2.55	53.4	54.4	1.57	1.77
Averages								
1980–83	23.3%	16.9%	1.66×	2.51×	55.4%	57.5%	1.57×	1.84×
1976–79	27.6	18.8	1.44	2.30	54.3	56.4	1.64	1.85
1976–83	25.4	17.9	1.55	2.41	54.8	57.0	1.60	1.85

Note: Average of beginning- and end-of-year assets and equity used where applicable in computing ratios.

TABLE 14-E *Selected Financial Ratios*

Fiscal Year	Pretax Earnings ÷ Net Sales		Net Earnings ÷ Total Assets		Net Earnings ÷ Common Equity		Dividends ÷ Net Earnings	
	KO	PEP	KO	PEP	KO	PEP	KO	PEP
1983 (est.)	14.8%	6.4%	11.0%	6.5%	19.6%	16.6%	64.6%	53.1%
1982	14.9	7.1	12.1	7.4	20.3	18.9	62.8	48.9
1981	13.7	7.2	12.8	8.0	20.6	20.3	59.5	44.1
1980	13.1	7.7	12.8	8.3	20.3	19.8	63.2	44.1
1979	15.2	8.2	14.3	9.4	21.6	20.8	57.6	40.9
1978	16.2	9.2	14.9	9.8	21.8	20.9	57.4	40.6
1977	17.5	9.7	15.1	9.9	21.3	22.8	57.5	38.6
1976	18.0	9.6	15.1	9.2	21.1	23.4	55.7	35.4
Averages								
1980–83	14.1%	7.1%	12.2%	7.6%	20.2%	18.9%	62.5%	47.6%
1976–79	16.7	9.2	14.9	9.6	21.4	22.0	57.1	38.9
1976–83	15.4	8.1	13.5	8.6	20.8	20.4	59.8	43.2

Note: Average of beginning- and end-of-year assets and equity used where applicable in computing ratios.

Assuming that current dollar GNP increases 8% per annum to $4,850 billion in 1988, calculate the projected sales for each company in that year. Calculate the annual sales growth projected for KO and PEP and compare these projections to the growth of earnings implied by each company's return on equity as calculated in part b.

d. As a portfolio manager for a pension fund with a long time horizon, you are considering either KO or PEP as an addition to the portfolio.

(1) Calculate the implied total return for both KO and PEP.

TABLE 14-F *Market Valuations and Other Common Stock Data*

Fiscal Year	Average Annual Price/ Earnings Ratio		Average Annual Dividend Yield		Earnings per Common Share		Dividends per Common Share	
	KO	PEP	KO	PEP	KO*	PEP†	KO	PEP
1983 (est.)	12.4×	11.9×	5.2%	4.4%	$4.15	$3.05	$2.68	$1.62
1982	9.6	12.1	6.5	4.1	3.95	3.23	2.48	1.58
1981	9.6	9.4	6.7	4.2	3.90	3.22	2.32	1.42
1980	9.7	7.7	6.5	5.1	3.42	2.86	2.16	1.26
1979	11.4	8.8	5.1	4.4	3.40	2.70	1.96	1.11
1978	13.7	11.6	4.2	3.5	3.03	2.40	1.74	0.98
1977	14.3	11.5	4.0	3.3	2.68	2.14	1.54	0.83
1976	17.7	13.9	3.1	2.5	2.38	1.79	1.33	0.63
Averages								
1980–83	10.3×	10.3×	6.2%	4.5%				
1976–79	14.3	11.4	4.1	3.4				
1976–83	12.3	10.9	5.2	3.9	8.3%	7.9%	10.5%	14.4%

* Includes results of Columbia Pictures from June 30, 1982.
† Amounts for 1978–81 restated to reflect overstatement of net income aggregating $92.1 million.
Sources: Corporate annual reports and the Value Line Investment Survey, December 2, 1983.

TABLE 14-G *Selected Financial Statistics for the Coca-Cola Company*

	1983 (est.)	*1982*	*1981*	*1980*	*1979*	*1978*	*1977*	*1976*
				Fiscal Year				
Operations (in $ millions)								
Sales	6,820.0	6,249.0	5,889.0	5,621.0	4,689.0	4,095.0	3,394.0	2,989.0
Depreciation	180.0	148.9	136.9	131.0	110.0	91.0	80.0	70.0
Interest	73.0	74.6	38.3	35.1	10.7	7.8	NA	NA
Income Taxes	444.0	419.8	360.2	330.4	318.0	303.0	273.0	251.0
Net Earnings	565.0	512.2	447.0	406.0	395.0	361.0	321.0	288.0
Financial Position (in $ millions)								
Cash	616.4	311.0	393.0	289.0	209.0	369.0	418.0	403.0
Receivables	831.3	751.8	483.5	523.1	435.1	338.3	279.9	237.3
Current Assets	2,444.2	2,076.6	1,636.2	1,622.3	1,305.6	1,236.6	1,103.5	1,027.3
Total Assets	5,331.0	4,923.3	3,564.8	3,406.0	2,938.0	2,582.8	2,254.5	2,007.0
Current Liabilities	1,702.7	1,326.8	1,006.3	1,061.6	884.2	744.0	596.3	506.4
Long-Term Debt	475.0	462.3	137.3	133.2	31.0	15.2	15.3	11.0
Common Equity	2,990.0	2,778.7	2,270.8	2,074.7	1,918.7	1,739.6	1,578.0	1,434.0

(2) Calculate the SML-based expected return for both KO and PEP using the security market line data shown below.

(3) Discuss the implications of the calculations in parts d(1) and d(2) for choosing either KO or PEP.

(4) Select either KO or PEP for the portfolio. Give three well-supported reasons for your choice.

TABLE 14-H *Selected Financial Statistics for PepsiCo, Inc.**

	1983 (est.)	*1982*	*1981*	*1980*	*1979*	*1978*	*1977*	*1976*
				Fiscal Year				
Operations (in $ millions)								
Sales	7,700.0	7,499.0	7,027.0	5,975.0	5,089.0	4,300.0	3,649.0	3,109.0
Depreciation	260.0	230.4	205.5	172.9	142.1	117.0	93.7	79.1
Interest	156.0	166.2	149.7	114.7	73.1	52.0	46.0	45.0
Income Taxes	206.0	226.8	210.8	200.8	168.2	174.3	158.3	135.3
Net Earnings	285.0	303.7†	297.5	260.7	250.4	223.0	196.7	161.7
Financial Position (in $ millions)								
Cash & Equivalents	397.3	280.3	239.0	232.0	205.0	167.0	256.0	231.0
Receivables	785.7	746.1	741.4	596.7	557.2	433.6	374.4	324.5
Current Assets	1,739.4	1,590.6	1,762.5	1,326.5	1,201.4	1,010.5	997.0	903.7
Total Assets	4,588.9	4,197.5	4,040.0	3,399.9	2,888.9	2,416.8	2,130.3	1,853.6
Current Liabilities	1,440.0	1,345.6	1,430.7	1,005.3	843.6	650.7	574.5	478.9
Long-Term Debt	786.7	864.2	816.1	781.7	619.0	479.1	427.9	278.6
Common Equity	1,786.3	1,650.5	1,556.3	1,381.0	1,247.0	1,165.0	971.9	753.0

* Amounts for 1978–1981 restated to reflect overstatement of net income aggregating $92.1 million.
† Before unusual charge of $79.4 million.

| | Per Common Share | |
	KO	PEP
Stock Price (Jan. 16, 1984)	$51\frac{3}{4}$	$36\frac{7}{8}$
1984 Estimated Earnings	$4.80	$3.55
Indicated Dividend	$2.90	$1.71
Price Range (1983)—High	$57\frac{1}{2}$	$40\frac{1}{4}$
—Low	$45\frac{1}{2}$	$32\frac{5}{8}$
Book Value	$23.85	$20.95
Value Line Beta	.80	.95

	Other Market Data	
Risk-Free Return	9.0%	
Expected Market Return	14.0%	

5. Mulroney continued her examination of Eastover and Southampton by looking at the five components of return on equity (ROE) for each company. For her analysis, Mulroney elected to define equity as total shareholders' equity, including preferred stock. She also elected to use year-end data rather than averages for the balance sheet items.

TABLE 14-I *Eastover Company (EO) ($ millions, except shares outstanding)*

Income Statement Summary

	1986	1987	1988	1989	1990
Sales	$5,652	$6,990	$7,863	$8,281	$7,406
Earnings before interest & taxes (EBIT)	$ 568	$ 901	$1,037	$ 708	$ 795
Interest expense (net)	(147)	(188)	(186)	(194)	(195)
Income before taxes	$ 421	$ 713	$ 851	$ 514	$ 600
Income taxes	(144)	(266)	(286)	(173)	(206)
Tax rate	34%	37%	33%	34%	34%
Net income	$ 277	$ 447	$ 565	$ 341	$ 394
Preferred dividends	(28)	(17)	(17)	(17)	(0)
Net income to common	$ 249	$ 430	$ 548	$ 324	$ 394
Common shares outstanding (millions)	196	204	204	205	201

Balance Sheet Summary

	1986	1987	1988	1989	1990
Current assets	$1,235	$1,491	$1,702	$1,585	$1,367
Timberland assets	649	625	621	612	615
Property, plant, & equipment	4,370	4,571	5,056	5,430	5,854
Other assets	360	555	473	472	429
Total assets	$6,614	$7,242	$7,852	$8,099	$8,265
Current liabilities	$1,226	$1,186	$1,206	$1,606	$1,816
Long-term debt	1,120	1,340	1,585	1,346	1,585
Deferred taxes & other	1,000	1,000	1,016	1,000	1,000
Equity-preferred	364	350	350	400	0
Equity-common	2,905	3,366	3,695	3,747	3,864
Total liabilities & equity	$6,614	$7,242	$7,852	$8,099	$8,265

TABLE 14-J *Southampton Corporation (SHC) ($ millions, except shares outstanding)*

Income Statement Summary

	1986	1987	1988	1989	1990
Sales	$1,306	$1,654	$1,799	$2,010	$1,793
Earnings before interest & taxes (EBIT)	$ 120	$ 230	$ 221	$ 304	$ 145
Interest expense (net)	(13)	(36)	(7)	(12)	(8)
Income before taxes	$ 107	$ 194	$ 214	$ 292	$ 137
Income taxes	(44)	(75)	(79)	(99)	(46)
Tax rate	41%	39%	37%	34%	34%
Net income	$ 63	$ 119	$ 135	$ 193	$ 91
Common shares outstanding (millions)	38	38	38	38	38

Balance Sheet Summary

	1986	1987	1988	1989	1990
Current assets	$ 487	$ 504	$ 536	$ 654	$ 509
Timberland assets	512	513	508	513	518
Property, plant, & equipment	648	681	718	827	1,037
Other assets	141	151	34	38	40
Total assets	$1,788	$1,849	$1,796	$2,032	$2,104
Current liabilities	$ 185	$ 176	$ 162	$ 180	$ 195
Long-term debt	536	493	370	530	589
Deferred taxes & Other	123	136	127	146	153
Equity	944	1,044	1,137	1,176	1,167
Total liabilities & equity	$1,788	$1,849	$1,796	$2,032	$2,104

a. Based on the data shown in Tables 14-I and 14-J, **calculate** *each* of the *five* ROE components for Eastover and Southampton in 1990. Using the *five* components, **calculate** ROE for *both* companies in 1990. **Show** all calculations.

b. Referring to the components calculated in part a, **explain** the difference in ROE for Eastover and Southampton in 1990.

c. Using 1990 data, **calculate** an *internal* (i.e., *sustainable*) growth rate for *both* Eastover and Southampton. **Discuss** the appropriateness of using these calculations as a basis for estimating future growth.

Mulroney recalled from her CFA studies that the constant-growth discounted dividend model (DDM) was one way to arrive at a valuation for a company's common stock. She collected current dividend and stock price data for Eastover and Southampton, shown in Tables 14-K and 14-L.

d. Using 11% as the required rate of return (i.e., discount rate) and a projected growth rate of 8%, **compute** a constant-growth DDM value for Eastover's stock and **compare** the computed value for Eastover to its stock price indicated in Table 14-L. **Show** calculations.

Mulroney's supervisor commented that a two-stage DDM may be more appropriate for companies such as Eastover and Southampton. Mulroney believes that Eastover and

TABLE 14-K *Eastover Company (EO)*

	1986	1987	1988	1989	1990	1991
Earnings per share	$ 1.27	$ 2.12	$ 2.68	$ 1.56	$ 1.87	$ 0.90
Dividends per share	0.87	0.90	1.15	1.20	1.20	1.20
Book value per share	14.82	16.54	18.14	18.55	19.21	17.21
Stock price						
—High	28	40	30	33	28	30
—Low	20	20	23	25	18	20
—Close	25	26	25	28	22	27
Average P/E	18.9×	14.2×	9.9×	18.6×	12.3×	27.8×
Average price/book	1.6×	1.8×	1.5×	1.6×	1.2×	1.5×

Southampton Corporation (SHC)						
	1986	1987	1988	1989	1990	1991
Earnings per share	$ 1.66	$ 3.13	$ 3.55	$ 5.08	$ 2.46	$ 1.75
Dividends per share	0.77	0.79	0.89	0.98	1.04	1.08
Book value per share	24.84	27.47	29.92	30.95	31.54	32.21
Stock price						
—High	34	40	38	43	45	46
—Low	21	22	26	28	20	26
—Close	31	27	28	39	27	44
Average P/E	16.6×	9.9×	9.0×	7.0×	13.2×	20.6×
Average price/book	1.1×	1.1×	1.1×	1.2×	1.0×	1.1×

S&P 500						
	1986	1987	1988	1989	1990	1991	*5-Year Average (1987–1991)*
Average P/E	15.8×	16.0×	11.1×	13.9×	15.6×	19.2×	15.2×
Average price/book	1.8×	2.1×	1.9×	2.2×	2.1×	2.3×	2.1×

Southampton could grow more rapidly over the next three years and then settle in at a lower but sustainable rate of growth beyond 1994. Her estimates are indicated in Table 14-M.

e. Using 11% as the required rate of return, **compute** the two-stage DDM value of Eastover's stock and **compare** that value to its stock price indicated in Table 14-M. **Show** calculations.

f. **Discuss** *two* advantages and *three* disadvantages of using a constant-growth DDM. **Briefly discuss** how the two-stage DDM improves upon the constant-growth DDM.

TABLE 14-L *Current Information*

	Current Share Price	*Current Dividends Per Share*	*1992 EPS Estimate*	*Current Book Value Per Share*
Eastover (EO)	$ 28	$ 1.20	$ 1.60	$ 17.32
Southampton (SHC)	48	1.08	3.00	32.21
S&P 500	415	12.00	20.54	159.83

TABLE 14-M *Projected Growth Rates*

	Next 3 Years (1992, 1993, 1994)	Growth Beyond 1994
Eastover (EO)	12%	8%
Southampton (SHC)	13%	7%

In addition to the discounted dividend model (DDM) approach, Mulroney decided to look at the price/earnings ratio and price/book ratio, relative to the S&P 500, for *both* Eastover and Southampton. Mulroney elected to perform this analysis using 1987–1991 and current data.

g. Using the data in Tables 14-K and 14-L **compute** *both* the current and the 5-year (1987–1991) average relative price/earnings ratios and relative price/book ratios for Eastover and Southampton. **Discuss** *each* company's current relative price/earnings ratio as compared to its 5-year average relative price/earnings ratio and *each* company's current relative price/book ratio as compared to its 5-year average relative price/book ratio.

h. Mulroney previously calculated a valuation for Southampton for both the constant growth and two-stage DDM as shown below:

	Discounted Dividend Model Using	
	Constant Growth Approach	Two-Stage Approach
Southampton	$29	$35.50

Using *only* the information provided and your answers above, **select** the stock (EO or SHC) that Mulroney should recommend as the better value, and **justify** your selection.

6. Based on your knowledge of history, what would you expect were the largest types of firms in the United States at each of the following dates? What happened to such firms during the next 50 years? What conclusion should we reach? 1800, 1850, 1900, and 1950, 1990?

DATAFILE ANALYSIS

1. *Statement Analysis.* Review the financial statement data in the STOCKFS.WK1 data file. Select one or more firms and conduct a financial analysis of each. What types of data or other information would you like to have in order to develop an opinion about the stock's intrinsic value?

REFERENCES

As noted in Chapter 13, a classic text treating fundamental security selection was originally written in 1934 by Benjamin Graham and David Dodd. Its most recent revision is:

COTTLE, SIDNEY, ROGER F. MURRAY, and FRANK E. BLOCK, *Graham and Dodd's Security Analysis.* 5th ed. New York: McGraw-Hill Book Co., 1988.

Thorough reviews of financial statement analysis can be found in:

BERNSTEIN, LEOPOLD A., *Financial Statement Analysis: Theory, Application, and Interpretation,* 4th ed. Homewood, IL: Richard D. Irwin, 1988.

HELFERT, ERICH A., *Techniques of Financial Analysis,* 6th ed. Homewood, IL: Richard D. Irwin, 1987.

Discussions of the determinants of a stock's beta include:

HAMADA, ROBERT S. "The Effect of the Firm's Capital Structure on the Systematic Risk of Common Stocks," *Journal of Finance,* May 1972.

ROSENBERG, BARR, "Prediction of Common Stock Betas," *Journal of Portfolio Management,* Winter 1985.

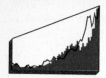

Financial Futures

A revolution in the types of securities traded in financial markets began during the mid-1970s that continues unabated today: the introduction of futures contracts on financial securities. Although markets in futures contracts had existed for centuries, these contracts were traded almost exclusively on commodities such as corn, gold, wood products, oil, and so forth. Trading of commodity futures remains an active market today. But the dominant source of trading in today's futures markets is in financial futures.

Futures contracts on a wide variety of financial assets have been created, and potential new contracts are constantly under review by futures exchanges. Clearly, not all newly offered financial futures contracts have been, or will be, successful in attracting an active public interest. For example, the first futures contract offered in the United States was on Government National Mortgage Association (GNMA) certificates. But due to uncertainties about what type of GNMA certificate was actually being bought through the futures contract, this particular market never developed an active following, and the contract was soon eliminated. Many other financial futures contracts, however, have been well accepted by security traders and are now an integral part of security markets throughout the world.

The most actively traded contracts to date are futures on stock indexes such as the S&P 500 Index and the New York Stock Exchange (NYSE) Index. Although ownership of a stock index futures contract does not provide the futures owner with the immediate ownership of stock, it does give a claim to ownership at the delivery date of the contract. The owner of a stock index future effectively has a delayed ownership claim to stocks in the index. To illustrate the importance of such contracts in today's financial markets, consider the following statistic: On April 23, 1993, the dollar value of stocks traded on the NYSE was about $11.0 billion. On the same day, the dollar value of NYSE stocks traded through stock index futures contracts exceeded $11.3 billion!

There was nothing unusual about the April date. In fact, trading claims to stock values are often larger in futures markets than in the underlying "spot" stock market. On the same date, claims to U.S. dollar-denominated short-term debt instruments had a trading value of $113.8 billion and claims to U.S. dollar long-term debt instruments had a trading value of $10.1 billion. Clearly, such financial futures markets play an important role in today's financial system.

But why? Why would a newly developed market in financial futures have become such an important part of today's financial trading system? The answer is simple. Financial futures provide a cost-efficient and highly liquid market in which investors can rapidly adjust portfolio risk exposure. Financial futures improve the investor's ability to *hedge* portfolio risk. Although many financial futures trades are motivated by *speculative* profit opportunities, the success of this new market is due to its usefulness in managing financial risk. Such hedging activities are the fundamental reason for this market to exist and constitute a major topic throughout this chapter.

This chapter builds on the overview of financial futures presented in Chapter 9. Here we go into more detail about the types of financial futures, their valuation, and how they can be used to hedge portfolio risk or earn speculation profits.

BASIC FUTURES CONCEPTS

A *forward contract* is an agreement made today to trade at a future date. All terms of the trade (the good, price, and future date) are agreed to today whereas the actual trade occurs later. The buyer of the forward contract is legally obligated to deliver money equal to the forward's price, and the seller is legally obligated to deliver the specified good. A *futures contract* is simply a forward contract that is traded on a securities exchange.

Forward contracts, formal or informal, have been part of commerce for thousands of years. The first evidence of futures contracts is traced to negotiable lettres de faire during twelfth-century Europe. Over time, the center of forward and futures trading moved to London. In the United States, futures trading developed in the middle 1800s in various agricultural commodities. Presently, all economically developed countries have active commodity futures markets and many less developed countries are in the process of setting up their own commodity futures markets.

For most of this chapter, we assume that forward and futures contracts are identical, although strictly speaking, this is not correct. Differences between them, which are reviewed later in the chapter, have relatively minor effects on either their prices or their use as risk-management tools.

We will denote the futures price at which buyers and sellers agree to trade as F_{tT}. Date T refers to the date at which the trade is to take place. For a given futures contract, date T never changes and is called the "delivery date" of the contract. Date t refers to the date at which a future with a delivery date of T is priced. Date $t = 0$ refers to the original date at which a futures trade occurs. For example, if F_{0T} is equal to $100, then the buyers and sellers agree on date 0 to trade a good at date T for a price of $100. Tomorrow, the price at which a futures deliverable at date T may change, say, to $102 (in which case, $F_{1T} = $102). But the contracted price between buyers and sellers who traded on date 0 remains $100.

Buyers at date 0 are *obligated* to pay F_{0T} at date T, and sellers are obligated to deliver the good at date T for a price of F_{0T}. *Both parties know the price at which they will trade.* Thus all uncertainty about future trading prices is removed. This is the fundamental reason why futures markets exist. By trading a futures contract, investors are able to eliminate (or, more generally, reduce) uncertainty about the price at which they will eventually buy or sell. If F_{0T} = \$100, both buyer and seller have the opportunity to trade at date T at a price of \$100.

The commodity or financial asset on which a futures contract is written is referred to as the "spot" good. For example, the spot good on T-bill futures are the underlying T-bills on which the future has an eventual claim. Similarly, the spot good on an S&P 500 futures are the stock included in the S&P 500 Index. When the delivery date T arrives, market prices of the spot good will probably be different from the initial contracted futures price of F_{0T}. If spot prices at date T are higher than the contracted price of F_{0T}, then people who bought the future at date 0 have a futures profit (equal to the seller's loss). If spot prices at date T are lower than F_{0T}, then buyers have a futures loss (equal to the seller's profit).

At the date of the futures trade, both parties to the future know the price at which they can trade at date T and, in this sense, they are able to eliminate uncertainty about future price risk. After the spot good and money are exchanged at date T, an opportunity profit or loss equal to the difference between F_{0T} and the spot price on date T is incurred. But regardless of whether the buyer or seller is eventually happy that they entered into the contract, they both guaranteed the price at which they would trade, thus eliminating earlier price risk.

Consider the case in which a producer of oatmeal intends to purchase a bushel of oats at date T and a farmer intends to sell a bushel of oats at the same time. Both individuals can eliminate the uncertainty they have about date T trading prices by trading a futures on a bushel of oats today. Let's say that the futures price at which they agree to trade is F_{0T} = \$1.00. When the delivery date arrives, actual spot prices will most likely not be equal to \$1.00. For example, assume the price of spot oats on date T is \$1.25. The producer of oatmeal will purchase oats through the futures contract at a price of \$1.00 (incurring an opportunity profit of \$0.25), and the farmer will sell oats at \$1.00 through the futures (incurring an opportunity loss of \$0.25). But the price at which each party trades is known at date 0 to be \$1.00.

The difference between the spot price on the delivery date of a futures (S_T) and the initial trade price of the futures (F_{0T}) is the opportunity gain or loss on the futures position. For the buyer, this value will be $S_T - F_{0T}$. For the seller, it will be $F_{0T} - S_T$. This opportunity gain or loss is known as the *futures investment value* at the delivery date T. The relationship between delivery date spot prices and futures investment values is displayed in Figure 15-1. Investment values to the futures owner are shown as the solid line. Investment values for the futures seller are shown as the dashed line. Owning a future is called a "long position," and selling a future is called a "short position."

When the delivery date spot price (S_T) is equal to the price at which the parties agreed to trade (F_{0T}), neither party wins or loses and the future's investment value is zero. At spot prices in excess of F_{0T}, the buyer has a positive investment value in the contract equal to ($S_T - F_{0T}$) and seller has a negative investment value of

FIGURE 15-1 *Delivery Data Futures Contract Investment Values*

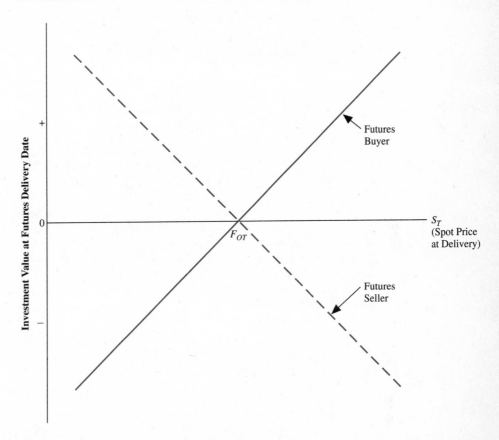

$(F_{0T} - S_{0T})$. At spot prices less than the agreed futures trade price, the buyer incurs a negative investment value and the seller incurs a positive investment value.

Basics of Futures-Spot Pricing

The prices at which buyers and sellers will agree to trade through a futures contract are always closely related to the underlying spot good price at that time. For example, consider the price at which people will agree to trade a spot good through a futures contract on the delivery date of the future. At the date of delivery, ownership of the spot good and ownership of a futures contract will be identical. They both provide immediate ownership of the spot good. Therefore, the price at which investors will agree to trade via the future will be the same as the underlying spot good's price. For example, what would you do if you observed that a spot bushel of oats is trading at $0.90 and a futures on oats *that is now deliverable* is trading for $0.95? Clearly, you would buy in the spot market at $0.90 and sell in the futures market at $0.95.

This type of trade is known as an arbitrage trade. An arbitrage trade is one in which:

1. No risk is incurred (you both *owned* the good in the spot market and *owed* the good in the futures market).
2. No cash investment is required (the $0.95 delivery price on the future will more than finance the $0.90 purchase price of the spot).
3. A known profit is earned ($0.95 − $0.90).

Arbitrage trades such as this are the basis on which futures contracts are priced. In our example, your trading, when added to trades of other arbitragers, would rapidly cause the price of the deliverable futures contract to be identical to the prevailing spot price.

Prior to the delivery date, there is also a relationship between futures prices and the underlying spot good prices that, if violated, creates arbitrage profits. The ownership of a futures contract guarantees that you will own the spot asset at date T and guarantees the price that you will have to pay. There is another way in which you could accomplish the same outcome (that is, ownership at T at a known price). Simply purchase the spot asset today and fully finance its current cost by borrowing at a risk-free interest rate.[1] Specifics of the trade are shown below:

Transactions	Cash Flows	
At date 0	Date 0	Date T
Buy Spot Asset	$-S_0$	
Borrow at *RF* Rate	$+S_0$	
At date T		
Repay Borrowing		$-S_0(1+RF)$
Pay Storage Costs		$-SC$
Net	0	$-[S_0(1+RF)+SC]$

The only net cash flow takes place at date T and is the sum of the borrowing repayment and any storage costs (SC) such as insurance and warehousing fees. For a known cost equal to $S_0(1+RF) + SC$, you are assured ownership of the spot asset at date T. By engaging in a trade such as this, traders are able to *synthetically create* payoffs that are identical to those of a futures contract. This is known as a synthetic futures contract.

A synthetic future can provide exactly the same outcome as a traded future: ownership of the spot good at date T at a known future cost. Thus, the price at which investors will agree to trade the spot good via the futures contract must be the same as that available using the synthetic future. If this were not true, then an arbitrage profit would be available by trading in both the synthetic and the future.

---

[1] It is assumed that you can borrow at a risk-free interest rate because all cash flows in this trade are known with certainty.

The pricing relationship that arbitrage forces between the futures contract and the current price of the underlying spot good is referred to as Futures-Spot Parity:

Futures-Spot Parity Model
$$F_{0T} = S_0 (1 + RF) + SC \qquad \textbf{(15.1)}$$

Other than differing storage costs between differing spot goods, this is the basic model used to value all futures contracts.

Basis and Basis Risk. The *basis* of a futures contract is equal to the current futures price minus the current price of the underlying spot good:

$$\text{Basis} = \text{Futures Price} - \text{Spot Price}$$

Typically, futures prices exceed spot prices, resulting in a positive basis. For example, assume that on December 31, 90-day T-bill futures maturing in March of the next year have a contract value of $97.913 per $100 of par value T-bills. If the purchase price of the underlying spot T-bill (one that will have a 90-day maturity as of the end of March) is $95.975 per $100 of par value T-bills, the basis between the futures and spot is $1.938 ($97.913 − $95.975).

As Equation 15.1 suggests, the basis of a futures contract should consist of interest (S_0*RF) and storage costs. Together, these are referred to as carrying costs. For example, assume you now hold a spot T-bill that matures in *180 days*. The market value of this T-bill is now $95.975 per $100 par. If you intend to hold this T-bill for three months and then sell it, you will require that the expected selling price be sufficient to cover all costs that you incurred while holding the T-bill in inventory. For a T-bill the only carrying cost would be a risk-free return on your investment. (For agricultural and metallurgical commodities, carrying costs such as insurance and storage would be incurred.)

Assume that the three-month risk-free return is now 2.0193%. Compounding the current spot T-bill's value at this rate results in the price at which you should *expect* to sell in three months:

$$\frac{\text{Expected Spot Selling}}{\text{Price in 3 Months}} = \frac{\text{Current}}{\text{Spot Price}} \times \frac{\text{3-Month}}{\text{Carrying Cost}}$$

$$\$97.913 = \$95.975 \times 1.020193$$

But notice that this expected selling price should also be the current market price of a 90-day T-bill future deliverable three months from now. In three months, the future and your (current 180-day) spot T-bill will be perfect substitutes.

If market prices are in equilibrium, the carrying costs associated with owning the spot instrument should be equal to the basis on the futures contract. If the two are different, abnormal profits are available by taking opposite positions in the spot and futures. For example, if the three-month risk-free rate in our example had actually been 1.0% instead of 2.02%, one should buy the 180-day spot T-bill and simultaneously sell the futures. This would lock in a 90-day risk-free return of 2.02% when other 90-day risk-free assets are yielding only 1%. But the net result of many people's doing this would cause prices to change until abnormal profits no longer existed and the basis would be identical to the carrying costs of owning the spot instrument.

Now let's examine the relationship between the basis and the risk inherent in a hedged position. The basic motivation of any hedge is to increase the certainty of a future (not *futures*) trading price. This future trading price can be stated in terms of the *initial basis* when the hedge is first taken and the *cover basis* when the hedge is offset (that is, covered):

$$\frac{\text{Realized Future}}{\text{Trading Price}} = \frac{\text{Initial}}{\text{Spot Price}} + \frac{\text{Initial}}{\text{Basis}} - \frac{\text{Cover}}{\text{Basis}} \quad\quad \textbf{(15.2)}$$

$$P_N \quad = \quad S_O \quad + (F_{0T} - S_O) - (F_{NT} - S_N)$$

In the equation, N refers to the date at which the hedge is *lifted* (covered) by offsetting trades in the futures and spot markets.

When the hedge is created on day 0, everything is known except for the cover basis. If the spot security and futures contract are on *identical instruments* and the hedge is *covered on the delivery date*, then the cover basis will have to be zero and the future trading price to be realized will be known with certainty. A perfect hedge is available. However, if the cover basis is not known with certainty, a perfect hedge will not be possible. The cover basis will be unknown in two cases: (1) if the cover date is different from the futures contract's delivery date, or (2) if the spot security is different from the security underlying the futures contract. Hedged positions are risky to the extent that there is uncertainty about the cover date basis.

In Figure 15-2, the relationship between futures and spot prices over a futures life is shown. Prices of the two securities will be very highly correlated. But they will not be perfectly correlated due to changes in carrying costs that affect only the future. The important point in Figure 15-2, however, is the fact that futures basis goes to zero at the delivery date, $F_{TT} = S_T$.

Futures Versus Forwards

Generally, we will treat futures and forwards as identical instruments throughout this chapter. Doing so allows us to develop simple valuation models and trading strategies. But there are differences between the two types of securities.

Default Risk. The first distinction between futures and forwards is the potential for default under the forward contract. If you are careful in selecting the partner with whom you forward contract, the probability of default may be small, but it does exist. There is no guarantee that the other party will indeed honor the contract. The exchanges on which futures are traded, however, pride themselves on the fact that no customer has lost money through default by the other party to a contract. The exchanges have large insurance reserves to reimburse defaults by buyers or sellers.

Marketability. A standard forward contract is not marketable. The only way to get out of it would be to renegotiate with the other party to the contract, or, if

FIGURE 15-2 *Convergance of Futures Price to Spot*

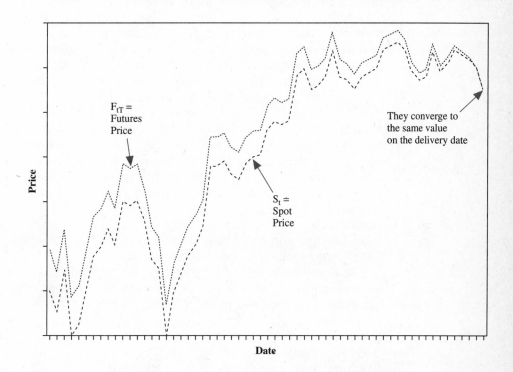

they are unwilling to renegotiate, to enter into an offsetting contract with still another party. In both cases, you are likely to be in the weaker bargaining position. In addition, there could be substantial time and cost associated with renegotiation. Futures contracts, however, are continuously traded on organized exchanges. You can get out of a futures contract simply by calling your broker.

Transaction Costs. Transaction costs include cash expenses as well as the opportunity cost of time spent in finding a party to trade with. Both of these can be substantial when a standard forward contract is used. In comparison, the transaction costs of entering into or closing out a futures contract or an artificial forward contract are considerably less.

Marking to the Market. In a forward contract, the only time that cash is paid is at the maturity date. This is not the case for a futures contract. A futures contract requires both an initial cash margin and subsequent cash inflows or outflows associated with a process called *marking to the market*. Margin is usually very small, and it can be met by cash, letters of credit, or short-term U.S. Treasury instruments. If letters of credit are used, no cash is actually paid. If U.S. Treasuries are used, the owner still has a claim to the earnings on the securities. Thus, margin does not represent an incremental cash outflow to the person who has bought or sold a futures contract. The process of marking to the market, however, will usually result in a series of cash inflows and outflows before the contract's maturity. This is a major difference between futures and forward contracts.

Valuation Effects of Mark-to-Market. Because futures are marked-to-market each day, their prices are theoretically different than equivalent forward contracts. To see why this is true, assume that you own a futures contract on the S&P 500 Index. At the end of each day's trading, you will either receive cash (if the futures price increases) or pay cash (if the future price declines). Also assume that when you receive cash you invest in short-term risk-free securities and when you are required to pay cash you borrow at the short-term risk-free rate. Finally, assume you know that, whenever you receive cash, interest rates are high and, whenever you must borrow, interest rates will be low.

In this case, you expect to earn positive profits from the daily mark-to-market since you will invest when rates are high and borrow when rates are low. Thus, you would be willing to commit to a higher price with the future than for an equivalent forward contract. In contrast, the futures seller expects to incur losses from daily mark-to-market activities and will require that a higher price be paid on the future than for an equivalent forward.

The example above is clearly extreme since no one can predict interest rates so precisely. But the example does show that, if futures prices are positively correlated with the level of interest rates, then the price of a future should be greater than the price of an identical forward. The opposite is also true: if futures prices are negatively correlated with interest rates, then the price of a future should be smaller than the price of an identical forward. As a practical matter, however, this correlation is small enough to be neglected, and it is safe to assume that the price of a future should be the same as a forward.

Contract Specifications. Forward contracts may be created on any security or good. Artificial forward contracts may be created on a variety of securities, depending on the spot instruments that exist. Futures contracts, however, can only be traded on futures instruments listed on an exchange. This can be important. For example, assume you are the treasurer of GTE and know that you will have to borrow on March 15 in order to pay scheduled quarterly income taxes. To help assure a borrowing rate, you might wish to sell a T-bill future maturing on March 15. Unfortunately, such a futures contract does not exist. There are contracts maturing later in March that can guarantee you a late March trading price. But if you were to sell one of these with the intention of offsetting it on March 15, you would not know the March 15 price and would not be able to eliminate your uncertainty. In contrast, you could enter into a standard forward contract with an investment banker or create an artificial forward contract with the terms you desire. Forward contracts have considerably greater flexibility.

HEDGING

There are two basic motives for trading a futures contract. The first is a speculative motive in which the trader believes that the futures price is wrong and attempts to take advantage of current mispricing. For example, the current trading price of a futures contract on 90-day T-bills with a March delivery date might guarantee a 90-day rate of return of 2.5% between the end of March and the end of June. If you believe that 90-day rates will actually be 1.5% in late March, you could enter into a speculative trade in which you purchase the future. If your prediction is accurate, you will become the owner of 90-day T-bills in March that provide a larger rate of return than available on spot T-bills at that time. This is referred to as a *long speculation*, since you take ownership of the future. In contrast, if you expect 90-day T-bill rates to be 2.5% in late March, the speculative trade would consist of selling the futures. If correct, you will receive cash at the futures delivery date that can be invested at 2.5% but only have to deliver a T-bill paying a return of 2.0%. This type of trade is a *short speculation*, since you take a short position in the future.

While a large portion of futures trades are motivated by speculations such as above, the major economic benefit created by futures markets arises from trades based on a *hedging* motive. The following examples illustrate the basics of various hedging trades. Details associated with each financial futures contract are discussed later in the chapter.

1. *Long T-bill Futures Hedge:* Mr. Sims is the treasurer of a building contracting firm. The company is presently constructing a large plant for another firm and is due progress payments of $1.0 million at the end of each calendar quarter. It is now January 15, and Mr. Sims is planning how to invest the progress payment that will be received at the end of March. He knows that, when the payment is received, it will be used to purchase 90-day T-bills since the firm will have the need for more cash at the end of June.

   Mr. Sims could simply wait until the end of March and invest the $1.0 million in 90-day T-bills at that time. The problem with this alternative, of course, is that the return that would be earned is not known today. There is an uncertainty about future T-bill rates. Mr. Sims may have an opinion about what the rate will be, but he recognizes that his skills do not lie in interest-rate prediction. To eliminate this uncertainty, he could purchase a 90-day T-bill futures contract with a delivery date of late March. Once the contract is bought, he will know what the firm will earn between March and June.

2. *Short T-Bond Futures Hedge.* Ms. Myers is the portfolio manager for a college endowment fund. Recently, the investment committee of the fund decided to move $5.0 million from the endowment's investments in U.S. T-bonds to T-bills investments. Although this transfer is sure to receive the approval of the endowment's Trustees, the physical transfer may not take place until formal approval has been given by the Trustees. This approval is expected in one month from now. Ms. Myers, however, has been given full discretion to trade in financial futures.

   If she were to await the Trustees' approval, the price at which the T-bonds would be sold is uncertain. But, if she were to sell T-bond futures with a one-month delivery date, she would ''lock-up'' the price at which they would be sold and remove all price uncertainty.

3. *Long Stock Index Futures Hedge.* Mr. Cusimano is responsible for managing

a portion of the equity holdings of a large state employees' pension fund. His portion of the portfolio is supposed to represent an indexed portfolio with returns similar to those of the S&P 500 Index. It is now early January and Mr. Cusimano is planning for anticipated future state contributions to his portfolio that will be made at the end of each calendar quarter. Each contribution will be approximately $25.0 million.

Again, he could wait until each contribution is received to invest in stocks that are similar to the S&P 500 index. Alternatively, he could guarantee the purchase price at which each contribution will be invested by purchasing $25.0 million of S&P 500 futures contracts with delivery dates of late March, June, September, and December.

Notice that in each of the hedging transactions above, the individuals were not making a trade based on their opinions about future security prices. Instead, their sole motive was to eliminate uncertainty about eventual trade prices. Elimination of price uncertainty is the motive for hedging with futures contracts.[2]

Criteria for a Perfect Hedge

Each of the preceding examples are close to what are called *perfect hedges*. A perfect hedge is one in which all price risk has been eliminated. While perfect hedges are possible to create in practice, they are more the exception than the rule. In order to create a perfect hedge, three things must be true:

1. The *future's maturity* must be identical to the date at which one wishes to trade in the spot market. For example, if money available to the treasurer in our earlier illustration isn't going to be received until April 15, the hedge we created would not totally eliminate interest rate uncertainty. An uncertainty about changes in rates between late March and mid-April would still exist.
2. The *size of the contract* traded must be identical to the amount of cash one wishes to borrow or lend. For example, if you had really planned to borrow only $1,000 for your vacation, the trade on $1 million in T-bills simply wouldn't eliminate your interest rate risk. Uncertainty caused by the mismatching of the size of the futures contract and your needs would still exist.
3. The *spot instrument* on which the future is written must be identical to the security one wishes to eventually trade. For example, it is doubtful that you could borrow at the same rate as the U.S. Treasury. Uncertainty about changes in the spread between your borrowing rate and T-bill yields would still exist.

Perfect hedges are rare. However, the closer the futures contract specifications are to a person's needs, the more the hedge can reduce risk.

---

[2] A general rule to follow when deciding whether one should purchase or sell futures contracts in a hedge is: *do with the futures what you intend to do with the spot.* If you will be a buyer of spot securities, the hedge requires the purchase of futures. If you will be a seller of spot securities, sell the futures. The appropriate number of contracts to trade is discussed below.

Optimal Hedges

When a futures contract's specifications are not identical to the instrument that is being hedged, risk will still remain. However, it can be minimized. Consider a portfolio of two securities: a futures contract and the spot market instrument being hedged. When the hedge is entered into, there is uncertainty about the maturity-date futures price (σ_F) plus uncertainty about the value of the spot instrument (σ_S). In addition, there will be a correlation between the maturity-date prices of the two securities (r_{FS}). If Q_S refers to the quantity of the spot instrument you wish to hedge, we can use the risk concepts discussed in Chapter 7 to find that amount of the futures contract (Q_F^*) that will lead to a minimum variance portfolio. This value of Q_F^* is:

Optimal Hedge $$Q_F^* = Q_S \frac{\sigma_S}{\sigma_F} r_{FS} \qquad (15.3)$$

For example, assume you wish to purchase $15.0 million of 90-day T-bills in mid-April but the nearest futures delivery date is at the end of March. Most likely, the uncertainty about the mid-April spot price will be close, if not identical, to uncertainty about the futures price in late March. So assume that $\sigma_S = \sigma_F$, but the correlation coefficient between the two instruments will not be 1.0. The correlation will be large, however, say, 0.9. As a result, a value of $15.0 million in spot T-bills implies that a total value of $13.5 million in March T-bill futures should be bought:

$$\$13.5 = \$15.0 \ (1.0)(0.9)$$

If each future was selling for $979,125, the 13.79 futures contracts would provide a minimum-risk portfolio. Because fractional futures contracts cannot be bought, either 13 or 14 contracts would be traded. Risk would be reduced but not eliminated.

Equation 15.3, as well as simple logic, suggests that the closer the financial future contract specifications are to the spot instrument being hedged, the better the hedge will be. In general, one should attempt to find contracts that:

1. Provide a security with maturity and risk characteristics similar to those of the spot instrument being hedged.
2. Mature close to the date at which the spot instrument is to be bought or sold.
3. Have a contract value that can closely hedge the total dollar value of spot instruments to be bought or sold.

SHORT-TERM DEBT FUTURES

During the past decade, numerous futures have been offered on short-term, high-grade financial assets. Many of these were unable to develop an active following and are now dormant. The more actively traded contracts (as of early 1993) are

TABLE 15-1 *Active Short-Term Debt Futures in 1993*

Contract	Trading Unit	Exchange
90-Day U.S. T-Bills	$1,000,000	CME
30-Day Federal Funds Rate	$5,000,000	CBT
Eurodollar Time Deposit	$1,000,000	CME, IMM, LIFFE
One-Month LIBOR	$3,000,000	CME, IMM

CBT—Chicago Board of Trade.
CME—Chicago Mercantile Exchange.
IMM—International Monetary Market.
LIFFE—London International Financial Futures Exchange.

shown in Table 15-1. Futures on 90-day U.S. T-bills and Eurodollars are the most active.

T-Bill Futures

All of our previous examples have been on T-bill futures because they are the most easily understood of all financial futures, and they are widely used. The only active T-bill futures contracts are written on 90-day spot bills.

To understand various trading strategies available in T-bill futures, it is important to recall a few T-bill pricing relationships. First, T-bills trade at discounts to par value and receive no coupons; they are pure discount bonds. Second, the percentage discount is not the same as the annualized bond equivalent yield. Instead, the quoted discount rate represents the percentage below par at which the bill is bought, not the percentage return on actual money invested. In addition, when calculating the actual dollar discount at which a bill is traded, the Federal Reserve assumes there are 360 days per year. Assume that at the close of trading on July 30, a T-bill maturing on August 28 could be bought at a quoted discount of 7.13%. Since the bill has a remaining life of 29 days and prices are determined using 360 days per year, the discount would be $0.5744 per $100, giving a purchase price equal to 99.4256% of face value:

$$\frac{\text{Dollar Discount}}{\text{per \$100 Face}} = \text{Face Value} \times \text{Quoted Discount} \times \frac{\text{Days Remaining}}{360}$$

$$\$0.5744 = \$100 \times 0.0713 \times \frac{29}{360}$$

$$\frac{\text{Purchase Price}}{\$100 \text{ Face}} = \text{Face Value} - \text{Dollar Discount}$$

$$\$99.4256 = \$100 - \$0.5744$$

For each $99.4256, one could receive $100 29 days hence. This implies a simple interest bond yield of about 7.27%:

$$\frac{\text{Simple Interest}}{\text{Yield}} = \frac{\text{Face Value}}{\text{Purchase Price}} - 1.0 \times \frac{365}{\text{Days Remaining}}$$

$$= \quad \frac{\$100}{\$99.4256} \quad - 1.0 \times \quad \frac{365}{29}$$

$$7.27\% \quad = \quad 0.5777\% \quad \times \quad \frac{365}{29}$$

Finally, if the bills deliverable under a futures contract are assumed to have a 90-day maturity, a change in the quoted discount of one basis point represents a $25 change in the value of a $1 million face value futures contract:

$$\$1,000,000 \times 0.01\% \times \frac{90}{360} = \$25$$

For example, if a bill contract is purchased at a discount of 5.20%, the delivery price contracted for would be $987,000:

$$\text{Delivery Price} \quad = \quad \frac{\text{Face Value}}{\text{of Contract}} \quad - \left(\begin{array}{c} \text{Discount in} \\ \text{Basis Points} \end{array} \times \begin{array}{c} \text{Amount Change per Basis Point} \\ \text{per \$1 Million Face Value} \end{array} \right)$$

$$= \quad \$1,000,000 \quad - \quad (520 \quad \times \quad \$25)$$

$$\$987,000 \quad = \quad \$1,000,000 \quad - \quad \$13,000$$

If a person buys a 90-day T-bill future at a 5.20% discount and later sells it at a 5.10% discount, a $250 profit would have been earned:

$$\text{Profit} = \$25 \text{ [Interest Basis Points at Purchase} - \text{Interest Basis Points at Sale]}$$

$$\$250 = \$25 \quad (520 \quad - \quad 510)$$

or

$$\text{Profit} = \quad \text{Selling Price} \quad - \quad \text{Purchase Price}$$

$$\$250 = \quad [\$1 \text{ million} - (\$25 \times 510)] \quad - [\$1 \text{ million} - (\$25 \times 520)]$$

Alternatively, if the future had been bought at a 5.20% discount and sold at a 5.30% discount, a $250 loss would have been incurred. This $25 price impact for each 1-basis-point change in a $1 million 90-day T-bill future is quite helpful in quickly pricing T-bill futures contracts and figuring trading gains and losses.

Section A in Table 15-2 shows hypothetical discounts and actual prices for various 90-day bill futures at the close of trading on June 30, 19X1. Section B shows hypothetical discounts and actual prices for cash bills of various maturities on the same day. We will use this information to illustrate a variety of hedging and speculative transactions. While the examples clearly don't exhaust all possible combinations, they do provide a general sense of the types of trades which speculators and hedgers can enter into.

Basic Long Hedge. If an organization's cash flow projections show that in the near future a large sum of excess cash will be temporarily available, T-bill futures can be used to lock in a future interest rate at which the excess cash can be invested. For example, assume it is now June 30, 19X1, and $20 million in cash will be available to invest for a 90-day period as of middle to late September

TABLE 15-2 *90-Day T-Bill Futures and Cash Prices as of June 30, 19X1*

A. 90-Day T-Bill Futures Prices

| | 6/30/X1 | | |
Delivery Date	Actual Price	Discount	Bond Yield
September 19X1	97.87	8.52%	8.82%
December 19X1	97.84	8.64	8.95
March 19X2	97.80	8.80	9.12
June 19X2	97.75	9.02	9.36
September 19X2	97.69	9.22	9.58
December 19X2	97.65	9.42	9.76
March 19X3	97.59	9.64	10.02
June 19X3	97.55	9.82	10.18

B. Spot T-Bill Prices

| | Days After | 6/30/X1 | | |
Maturity	June 30	Actual Price	Discount	Bond Yield
September 23, 19X1	86	97.86	8.97%	9.28%
December 22, 19X1	176	95.78	8.63%	9.13%

19X1. As a long hedge, September T-bill futures contracts would be bought on June 30. When the $20 million cash actually becomes available (say, on September 23), the futures contracts would be sold and spot T-bills bought.

Ideally, the $20 million cash would become available and the futures position would be closed exactly on the futures delivery date. This would mean that spot and futures rates on the bills would be identical (cover basis = $0), resulting in an actual yield on the cash bills equal to the yield at which the initial futures were bought. For example, assume that on June 30, bill futures were bought at an 8.52% discount and that by September 23, 90-day spot bill rates had fallen to discounts of 8.00%. The net transaction would be as follows:

Futures	Discount Rate	Price per $10-Million T-Bills	Bond Yield
Bought 90-Day Futures on 6/30/X1	8.52%	− $9,787,000	8.82%
Sold 90-Day Futures on 9/23/X1	8.00	9,800,000	8.28
Profit	0.52%	13,000	0.54%
Spot			
Buy 90-Day T-Bill on 9/23/X1	8.00	− 9,800,000	8.28%
Net Result	8.52%	− $9,787,000	8.82%

Although discounts available on spot bills fell to 8.00%, the futures hedger was actually able to lock in an 8.52% discount because of the profits earned on the futures transactions. This profit of $13,000 was composed of a 52-basis-point change in 90-day futures rates at $25 per basis point ($1,300 = 52 × $25) times 10 contracts. This allowed the hedger to pay only $9,787,000 in out-of-pocket cash for bills selling for $9,800,000.

This perfect hedge worked because the cover basis was zero. The 90-day futures sold at the same discount as did the spot bill. If the hedge had been placed in futures deliverable at dates different from when cash would become available for spot investment (for example, by buying December futures in the above example), the cover basis would most likely be different from zero.

In this example, there is another way to lock in a 90-day rate on June 30 for money that would become available on September 23. Instead of trading in futures, one could lock in a synthetic *forward rate* in the cash market. Note that the time difference between the September 23 and December 22 spot bills is exactly 90 days. If one were to buy a December 22 bill and short sell some September 23 bills, there would be no cash position until September 23. But once the short sale is closed on September 23, a 90-day long position would be held. Details are shown in Table 15-3. On June 30, December 22 spot bills are bought for $957,800. To come up with the cash, the 0.9787 September 23 bill is sold short. As a result, there is no cash position between June 30 and September 23. However, on September 23 the short position is covered at a cost of $1,000,000, *per bill,* or $978,700 in cash outflow, since the 0.9787 September bill was short. On December 22 the long position matures and provides $1,000,000. In net, $978,700 is invested on September 23 for a $1 million cash return 90 days later. This represents a return of 2.18% for 90 days: a *discount return* of 9.52% or a *bond equivalent* return of 8.82%.

Speculation. According to Table 15-2, a bill future now exists that requires that the buyer pay $978,700 in the third week of September 19X1. In return, the buyer will receive 90-day T-bills with a total face value of $1 million. This future is said to sell at a discount of 8.52%, although the effective annual bond yield is

TABLE 15-3 *Creation of 90-Day Forward Rate as of June 30, 19X1*

	Cash Flows—In (Out)		
	June 30	September 23	December 12
Buy Dec. 22 Spot Bill	$957,800		$1,000,000
Short Sell 0.9787 Sept. 23 Bill*	− 957,800	−$978,700	
	$ 0	−$978,700	$1,000,000

Annualized Return:
Discount = 8.52%[†]
Bond Yield = 8.82%[‡]

* $\dfrac{\text{Dec. Bill Price}}{\text{Sept. Bill Price}} = \dfrac{95.78}{97.86} = 0.9787.$

† $\dfrac{\$1,000,000 - \$978,700}{\$1,000,000} \times \dfrac{360}{90} = 8.52\%.$

‡ $\dfrac{\$1,000,000 - \$978,700}{\$978,700} \times \dfrac{365}{90} = 8.82\%.$

actually about 8.82%. If a speculator expected that 90-day cash bills would *actually* be selling at discounts greater than 8.52% towards the end of September 19X1, the futures contract should be sold. The speculator's belief that bill rates will rise might rest on any one of a number of reasons, for example, a belief that investors will revise upward their expectations of inflation, unexpectedly tight Federal Reserve policy, or unusually large new Treasury sales in late September. But regardless of the reason, the speculator would sell in anticipation of lower cash bill prices in the delivery month than contracted for in the bill future.

Assume that on June 30 the speculator sells one September 19X1 bill contract. At that time, the normal margin associated with futures trading will have to be posted and a brokerage commission paid. In September the speculator may either hold the contract open for delivery or cover the initial sale by purchasing the same contract just prior to the delivery date. Since the futures contract should sell at the same discount as an equivalent cash bill at delivery, the profits or losses from either strategy would be the same. If the speculator had guessed right and 90-day T-bill discounts rise to, say, 9.00%, a profit of $1,200 would have been earned (9.00% − 8.52%, or 48 basis points × $25 per basis point). However, the speculator has gambled that bill discounts won't fall. If they do, the speculator would be stuck with having to deliver an 8.52% discount bill when the cash bill actually available at that time yielded less. For example, if bill discounts actually fell by 48 basis points because of a temporary easing of credit by the Fed, a $1,200 loss would have been incurred.

Arbitrage. Arbitrage transactions can be accomplished by going long and short between both spot bills and futures. For example, we saw above that a 90-day investment return starting on September 23 could be obtained either by buying a 90-day bill future deliverable in September *or* by short selling some spot bills maturing on September 23 and simultaneously buying December 22 spot bills. As the example was originally designed, one would have been indifferent between the two approaches since each was expected to provide the same return. However, if the September future had been selling at 8.30% (with no changes in spot prices), an arbitrage consisting of selling the September future and creating a long September forward position should be entered into. Whenever futures rates are different from implied forward rates in the spot market, a profitable arbitrage opportunity exists (at least before transaction costs).

Consider another potential arbitrage. Suppose 90-day and one-year spot bills are selling at 8.80% and 9.00%, respectively. If the following 90-day futures are also available, what sort of arbitrage opportunity exists?

Delivery Month	90-Day Bill Discount
3 months	8.85%
6 months	8.90%
9 months	8.70%

A one-year investment in bills could be obtained either by buying a one-year spot bill at 9.00% or by purchasing a three-month spot bill plus a *strip* of each of the 90-day futures at an average discount *less* than 9.00%. Clearly, the one-year spot bill would provide the higher expected return. In fact, an arbitrage consisting of going long the one-year spot bill plus short the three-month bill and each future would provide a nearly riskless profit.

The Valuation of T-Bill Futures. Consider the spot T-bills shown in Table 15-2. On June 30, a T-bill maturing on December 22 is selling for 95.78% of par. If you were to buy it and hold it until September 23, it would then have a maturity of 90 days. Thus, its price on September 23 should be identical to the price at delivery of the 90-day futures. But the expected price of this December 22 spot bill is easily calculated. If you are to invest $95.78 on June 30 in a risk-free security and hold the investment until September 23, you would demand a risk-free rate of return. Since the September 23 spot T-bill is selling for $97.86, the risk-free return associated with the June to September period is:

$$\frac{\$100}{\$97.86} - 1 = 2.187\%$$

Thus the expected price of the December 22 spot T-bill should be $97.87 on September 23:

$$\$95.78\,(1.02187) = \$97.87$$

It turns out that the September futures are priced correctly. If they had been trading at a value different from the expected value of the spot instrument, arbitrage profits would have been available. In general, if F_{Tt} refers to the price of a T-bill futures contract with a delivery at date T quoted at date t, and $S_{T+90,t}$ refers to the date t spot price of an instrument which *will be a perfect substitute* for the futures on date T, then:

Futures Price Determined by Current Spot Prices

$$F_{tT} = S_{T+90}(1 + RF_{T-t}) \qquad \textbf{(15.4)}$$

The spot instrument chosen must be a perfect substitute for the futures at date T. In addition, the risk-free rate used should apply to the period from t to T.

Eurodollar Deposit Contracts

Recall that a Eurodollar is a deposit in a non-U.S. bank that is reported in a dollar denomination. Because Eurodollar deposits are not subject to U.S. banking reserve requirements as well as a number of other regulations, the size of this deposit market has increased substantially in recent years. Eurodollar rates are based on the *London Interbank Offer Rate,* known more commonly as the LIBOR rate. At the end of each day, a number of approved London banks are surveyed for the rate they are willing to pay on Eurodollar deposits. The middle 10 interest rates are then averaged and used as the published closing LIBOR rate. This rate is used to settle any Eurodollar futures that are then deliverable. This rate is generally accepted as one of the best indicators of short-term interest rates.

Futures contracts on three-month Eurodollar deposits are the most actively traded short-term debt futures in the world. They are priced on a discount basis similar to T-bill futures. However, settlement occurs in cash based on the spot LIBOR rate; actual security delivery is not allowed.

INTERMEDIATE AND LONG-TERM DEBT FUTURES

The most actively traded futures on intermediate and long-term debt issues are shown in Table 15-4. The most active contract is presently the U.S. T-bond futures.

U.S. Treasury Bond Futures

Each contract is on $100,000 of par value U.S. T-bonds having a maturity (or call, if callable) of at least 15 years and an *assumed* coupon of 8%. Prices are quoted in thirty-seconds of a dollar. Thus a price of 71-02 represents a price quote of $71\frac{2}{32}$, or $71,062.50, on a single $100,000 par contract. Each point ($\frac{1}{32}$) represents a value of $31.25 per contract.

Delivery. The price of any futures contract depends on the price at which the deliverable security is expected to sell on the delivery date. For T-bill contracts the deliverable instrument is easily identified. The deliverable instrument on a T-bond contract is not so easy to identify. Because of its critical importance in determining T-bond futures prices, we must look a little closer at T-bond delivery.

Delivery can take place at any time during the maturity month and is initiated by the short side. Once the short has declared an intention to deliver, the clearing corporation matches the short with the oldest outstanding long position, and securities and cash are exchanged two business days later. This uncertainty about the precise date of delivery causes a risk to the futures purchaser which cannot be hedged.

The second aspect of delivery that creates a risk is that the bonds that are

TABLE 15-4 *Active Long-Term Debt Futures in 1993*

Contract	Trading Unit	Exchange
U.S. T-Bonds	$100,000	CBT, LIFFE
U.S. T-Bonds	$ 50,000	MCE
German Govt. Bond	250,000 marks	LIFFE
U.S. Treasury Notes	$ 40,000	CBT
5-Year U.S. Treasury Notes	$100,000	CBT
2-Year U.S. Treasury Notes	$200,000	CBT
Municipal Bond Index	$ 1,000	CBT
Long Gilt	50,000 pounds	LIFFE

CBT—Chicago Board of Trade.
LIFFE—London International Financial Futures Exchange.
MCE—MidAmerica Commodity Exchange.

deliverable are not precisely defined. Any U.S. T-bond with a maturity in excess of 15 years (or a call date longer than 15 years, if it is callable) will qualify. This means that a wide range of coupons and maturities will qualify for delivery. Recognizing that the value of each bond is affected by its maturity and coupon, the clearing corporation has extensive tables that attempt to adjust for such differences. These tables are used to convert the contractual trade price to an actual invoice price which the purchaser of the future will pay. This adjustment factor is called the *delivery factor.* Yet the tables are unable to precisely price each of the many alternative bonds available for delivery. There will always be a few bonds that are the *cheapest to deliver.* As a result, active participants in the market will constantly evaluate the cheapest bonds to deliver and base the futures price on their expected value in the month of delivery.

Potential Use in Portfolio Management. Throughout this chapter most of the examples of how futures might be used have dealt with the hedging of specific cash flow needs or specific security holdings. Implicit in these are speculative and arbitrage trades which could occur if market prices are not in equilibrium. Many of the same techniques also apply to T-bond futures. However, T-bond futures can also be used to manage aggregate bond portfolio risk. It is this potential role that we will examine.

Assume that you are the manager of a $1 billion pension fund that has a policy of maintaining an asset mix of 50% equities, 40% bonds, and 10% cash. Since the relative performance of each of these security types varies over time, the actual market value mix will often depart from this desired mix. Assume that the bonds currently have a market value of $440 million—$40 million more than desired. There are two ways in which the bond position can be restored to $400 million: (1) sell $40 million in spot bonds and allocate it to stocks and cash as appropriate or (2) sell T-bond futures.

As we saw in Chapter 12, the duration of a bond portfolio (D_p) is a measure of how sensitive the value of the portfolio is to a change in interest rates. Specifically:

$$\begin{matrix} \text{\% Change in} \\ \text{Bond Prices} \end{matrix} = -D_p \times \left[\begin{matrix} \text{\% Change in} \\ (1 + YTM) \end{matrix} \right] \qquad (15.5)$$

An alternative way of expressing this relationship is:

$$\begin{matrix} \text{\% Change in} \\ \text{Bond Prices} \end{matrix} = -D_p \left(\frac{YTM_t - YTM_{t-1}}{1 + YTM_{t-1}} \right) \qquad (15.6)$$

Assume that the duration of your portfolio is four years. Thus, a 100-basis-point increase in, say, an existing YTM of 10% will cause a 3.64% decrease in your bond portfolio's value, or a dollar loss of $16.0 million:

$$- 4\left(\frac{0.11 - 0.10\%}{1.10} \right) = 3.64\%$$

$$-0.0364 \times \$440 \text{ million} = -\$16.0 \text{ million}$$

This $16.0 million is called the *dollar duration* of the portfolio. Since the negative sign on D_P is unnecessary, it will be dropped:

$$\frac{\text{Dollar}}{\text{Duration}} = D_P\left(\frac{YTM_t - YTM_{t-1}}{1 + YTM_{t-1}}\right) \times \frac{\text{Bond}}{\text{Portfolio Value}} \qquad \textbf{(15.7)}$$

Note that if you actually had $400 million invested in bonds, the dollar duration would be $14.55 million (0.0364 × $400). T-bond futures can be sold in an amount that would adjust the actual dollar duration from $16.0 million to $14.55 million—that is, decrease it by $1.45 million.

To calculate the duration of the T-bond future, we must first determine which T-bond is the cheapest to deliver. Assume this cheapest-to-deliver bond has a duration of 6.24 years. Since each contract is a claim on $100,000 worth of an 8% T-bond, the dollar duration of such a T-bond future is:

$$6.24\left(\frac{0.11 - 0.10}{1.10}\right) \times \$100,000 = \$5,672.73$$

Unfortunately, the bond that is cheapest to deliver does not have an 8% coupon. Thus we must adjust this 8% coupon bond's dollar duration into the actual deliverable bond's dollar duration. Mechanically, this is done by dividing the 8% coupon result by a *delivery factor* provided in CBT's tables. Assume the delivery factor for this bond is 0.9883. Thus, the dollar duration of the cheapest to deliver T-bond future is:

$$\frac{\text{Dollar Duration}}{\text{T-Bond Future}} = \frac{\dfrac{\text{Duration of}}{\text{Deliverable Bond}}}{\text{Delivery Factor}} \left(\frac{YTM_t - YTM_{t-1}}{1 + YTM_{t-1}}\right) \times \$100,000$$

$$\$5,739.88 = \frac{6.24}{0.9883}\left(\frac{0.11 - 0.10}{1.10}\right) \times \$100,000$$

So we finally arrive. To reduce the bond portfolio's dollar duration by $1.45 million, you would sell 253 T-bond futures:

$$\frac{\$1,450,000}{\$5,739.88} = 253 \text{ T-bond futures}$$

There is no doubt that this is a tedious calculation. The logic, however, is correct, and the calculations can be easily programmed on any microcomputer and many calculators. The use of T-bonds to alter bond portfolio risk is actually much easier and perhaps cheaper than direct sale or purchase of spot bond instruments.

EQUITY INDEX FUTURES

In 1982, stock index futures began trading. Ten years later, four contracts were actively traded, as shown in Table 15-5.

The S&P 500 Contract

The S&P 500 Index future is quoted in terms of the value of the S&P 500 Composite Index, but the actual dollar value of each contract is 500 times the quoted value. For example, if the contract's settle price is $400, the contract's value is $200,000. Minimum price moves are 0.05, or $25. If you bought the contract at $400 and later sold at $390, your loss would be $5,000.

As with other futures contracts, no cash payment is made at the date of the trade except for a good-faith deposit (margin). The values of daily portfolio positions are marked to market. Contracts are available with settlement dates in March, June, September, and December. Delivery (settlement) occurs on the third Thursday of the maturity month.

A unique feature of stock index futures is that physical delivery of the underlying asset never occurs. Instead, the contract requires that, at maturity, all profits be paid to the customer by the clearing corporation and that all losses be paid to the clearing corporation by the customer. Because of daily marking to market, virtually all of the profits and losses will have already been distributed.

Pricing. Refined valuation models which fully take into account daily marking to market and other risk features of these contracts are not reviewed here. However, a simple arbitrage valuation model is used in practice and provides prices reasonably close to those observed.

Assume that you purchase a stock portfolio at date t that is identical to one "unit" of the S&P 500 Index. The value of this spot portfolio is S_t. You know that you intend to sell the portfolio at date T. Its price at date T (S_T) is, of course, unknown to you today. But the dividends you will receive between t and T (D_T) are reasonably predictable. Let's assume they are known with certainty and will all be paid on date T. Given this information, you could guarantee the price at which you will sell the spot portfolio by selling one futures contract at a price of F_{tT}. The cash inflows and outflows that would result are:

	Date	
	t	T
At Date t:		
Buy Spot Portfolio	$-S_t$	
Sell Future		F_{tT}
At Date T:		
Sell Spot Portfolio		$.\ S_T$
Buy Future		$-F_{TT}$
Collect Dividends		D_T
Net	$-S_t$	$F_{tT} + D_T$

Two things should be recognized. First, at its maturity, the value of the futures contract must be equal to the spot index value at that time ($S_T = F_{TT}$). That is, after all, how the index contract is legally written. As a result, the S_T and F_{TT} cancel each other out. Second, note that once S_T and F_{TT} cancel, every cash flow

TABLE 15-5 *Active Stock Index Futures 1993*

Contract	Trading Unit	Exchange
S&P 500 Index	500 times index	CBT
Nikkei 225 Stock Average	$5 times index	CME
NYSE Composite Index	500 times index	NYFE
Major Market Index	$500 times index	CBT

CBT—Chicago Board of Trade.
CME—Chicago Mercantile Exchange.
NYFE—New York Futures Exchange (part of NYSE).

is known with certainty. S_t is the current spot index value, D_T is the known dividend, and F_{Tt} is the known futures price at which you trade. For an investment of S_t, a *known* payoff of $F_{Tt} + D_T$ is available. To eliminate the potential for arbitrage, a risk-free rate must equate the two cash flows. Letting RF refer to the risk-free rate available over the period t to T:

Arbitrage Spot and Index Future Relationship

$$S_t = \frac{F_{tT} + D_T}{1 + RF}$$ **(15.8)**

Restating this in terms of the futures price:

Arbitraged Stock Index Futures Price

$$F_{tT} = S_t(1 + RF) - D_T$$ **(15.9)**

This arbitrage pricing model says that the value of the future is the certainty equivalent value of owning the spot index less the dividends that will be earned on the spot index that are not available on the futures contract.

To illustrate Equation 15.9, assume that the following current spot information is known:

Spot Price of the S&P 500 Index   = $400

Annual (discrete) Risk-Free Rate   = 9%

Annual Dividend Yield of the S&P 500 Index = 4%

Then a three-month contract on the S&P 500 should trade for $404.71:[3]

$$\$404.71 = \$400(1.09)^{0.25} - (0.01 \times \$400)$$

Hedging Strategies

Futures hedging using stock index futures is designed to alter the systematic risk exposure of a portfolio. If index futures are purchased, systematic market risk is increased. If index futures are sold, systematic market risk decreases. Trading in

---

[3] This assumes that all dividends are paid on the futures' delivery date.

stock index futures has no impact on a portfolio's diversifiable, non-market risk. Thus, for the futures contract to be a good hedging vehicle, it should be on a stock index that is similar in makeup to the spot equities that are owned.

Three of the more common hedging uses of stock index futures are discussed here:

1. Adjusting portfolio betas
2. Creating index portfolios
3. Use in portfolio insurance programs

The examples use the hypothetical data on an S&P 500 future presented above. The spot S&P 500 Index is $400, the annual risk-free rate is 9%, and the spot stock index will pay a $4 dividend in exactly three months. We will assume that a futures contract is available on the S&P 500 that is deliverable in three months and that is now trading in the market for $404.71.[4]

Adjusting Portfolio Betas. Assume that you are the administrator of a $100 million pension fund. An investment committee that sets investment strategy has a desired T-bill/equity mix of 40/60. The investment committee has also stated that the beta of the equity portfolio should be equal to 1.0 (relative to the S&P 500 Index). A number of professional managers have been employed to run portions of the pension fund in the hopes that their unique skills can provide long-run returns in excess of what the fund would earn if it were to fully ''index'' the portfolio.

Because of recent moves in stock prices and purchases by the managers, the present portfolio differs from the investment committee's stated objectives. At present, the equity portfolio represents $70 million of the $100 million portfolio. And the average beta of stocks held by portfolio managers is 1.0. The situation is summarized below:

	Actual		Desired	
Asset	Dollars	Beta	Dollars	Beta
T-bills	$ 30 million	0.00	$ 40 million	0.00
Equity	70 million	1.0	60 million	1.00
Portfolio	$100 million	0.7	$100 million	0.60

You could achieve the desired position by actually trading in the spot securities—by selling $10 million of stock and using the proceeds to purchase T-bills. But this could be costly, confusing, and time-consuming. Alternatively, you could trade in S&P 500 futures to achieve the desired position *without* disturbing the underlying spot portfolio.

The critical question is not whether stock futures can do the job, but how many contracts should be traded.

---

[4] This market price is identical to the futures' theoretically correct value. If actual market prices differ from theoretical values, some of the hedging advantages of the contract are reduced. In practice, arbitrage maintains a close relationship between theoretical and market prices.

Well, consider the present situation. Since the $70 million equity position has a beta of 1.0, it is similar to owning 350 "units" of the S&P 500 Index:

$$\frac{\$70,000,000}{\$400 \times 500} = 350$$

If the beta on the $70 million had been only 0.9, only 315 units of the index would effectively be owned:

$$350 \times 0.9 = 315$$

Stated more formally, the number of effective units of a stock index that is owned can be stated as:

$$\begin{array}{c}\text{Actual Units of} \\ \text{Stock Index Owned}\end{array} = \left(\frac{\$ \text{ Value of Actual Equity Portfolio}}{\$ \text{ Value of the Spot Index Unit}}\right)\left(\begin{array}{c}\text{Beta of} \\ \text{Actual Portfolio}\end{array}\right)$$

$$Q_t = \left(\frac{EMV_t}{S_t \times I}\right)(B_t) \qquad \textbf{(15.10)}$$

where Q_t equals the effective number of index units owned at date t, EMV_t equals the equity market value at date t, S_t equals the quoted spot index at t, I is an adjustment factor unique to each futures contract (for example, 500 for the S&P 500 futures), and B_t is the equity portfolio beta at date t.

$$Q_t = \frac{\$70,000,000}{\$400 \times 500}(1.0)$$

$$= 350$$

We can use the same logic to calculate the *desired* units of the index we wish to own. In this case, let's represent desired values with an asterisk:

$$\begin{array}{c}\text{Desired Units of} \\ \text{Stock Index}\end{array} = \left(\frac{\$ \text{ Value of Desired Equity Portfolio}}{\$ \text{ Value of the Spot Index Unit}}\right)\left(\begin{array}{c}\text{Beta of} \\ \text{Desired Portfolio}\end{array}\right)$$

$$Q_t^* = \left(\frac{EMV_t^*}{S_t \times I}\right)(B_t^*) \qquad \textbf{(15.11)}$$

In our example, the desired number of units of the spot index is 300:

$$\left(\frac{\$60,000,000}{\$400 \times 500}\right)(1.0) = 300$$

Therefore, the quantity of stock index futures to trade (T_t) is simply the difference between the two:

**Optimal Stock Index Futures
to Adjust Systematic Risk**

$$T_t = Q_t^* - Q_t$$

$$= 300 - 350 \qquad \textbf{(15.12)}$$

$$= -50$$

Fifty equity contracts should be traded. The negative sign implies that they should be sold.

Would it work? Would the actual portfolio position together with a short position in 50 S&P 500 futures provide exactly the same future payoffs as (costlessly) adjusting the spot portfolio to the desired position? Probably not, since stock index futures transactions can only adjust systematic risks. Thus, if the spot equity portfolio is not perfectly correlated with the stock index, futures will not provide the same delivery date payoffs. *But if the spot portfolio is perfectly correlated with the stock index, trades in futures will provide exactly the desired outcome.*

Creating Index Portfolios. An index portfolio is a portfolio of securities that will have a return equal to (or close to) the return on a given security index. The underlying index could be a U.S. common stock index such as the S&P 500, a U.S. bond index such as the Shearson Lehman Hutton Government/Corporate Bond Index, or international stocks in the Europe, Australia, Far East Index. Index portfolios are held in order to obtain broad diversification within a given asset class and in the belief that active investment managers cannot provide greater risk-adjusted performance.

Prior to the introduction of stock index futures, index portfolios were created by actual purchases of the spot securities in weights similar to the index. For example, if an S&P 500 Index portfolio were to be formed, long positions in 500 stocks would ideally be taken with each held in proportions similar to their current weightings in the index. In practice, however, returns on spot index portfolios often do not totally emulate the underlying index. Transaction costs and the inability to maintain identical security weightings both cause return differences.

Stock index futures offer a cheap alternative to creating an indexed position in common stocks. This is done by: (1) purchasing T-bills having a maturity date equal to the stock index futures delivery date and (2) purchasing a proper quantity of index futures. If the stock index future is purchased at a price equal to its theoretical value, the net position will provide a return *identical* to the underlying index return.

To demonstrate this idea conceptually, let S_t be the quoted value of the spot stock index at day t, RF the risk-free rate over the life of a given futures contract, D the value of known dividends paid on day T, and T the delivery date of the stock index future. The index portfolio transaction is summarized below:

At day 0, T-bills are purchased in a dollar amount equal to the current spot price of the index $- S_0$. This investment will be worth $S_0(1 + RF)$ at the future delivery date. Also on day 0 a long position in 1.0 future contract is taken. This conceptually obligates you to cash outflow on the delivery date equal to $S_0(1 + RF) - D$, the future's theoretical value. But since the T-bill has a cash inflow at that time equal to $S_0(1 + RF)$, the net of the two cash flows is a positive cash flow equal to the spot index dividend of D. Finally, to obtain a cash inflow equal to the spot index value on day T, you sell the futures contract (initially bought on day 0) at the end of day T. At that time, the value of the future must be identical to the value of the spot index.

	Cash Flows	
Today	*0*	*Futures Delivery*
Buy T-Bills	$-S_0$	$+ S_0 (1 + RF)$
Buy 1.0 Futures		$-F_{0T} = - [S_0(1 + RF) - D]$
Net		$+D$

Delivery Date		
Sell the Future Above		$+F_{TT} = S_T$
Total	$-S_0$	$S_T + D$

The net effect of this transaction is that you spend S_0 on day 0 and receive $S_T + D$ at the delivery date. Your return is identical to the actual returns on the index!

To illustrate, assume you have $10 million in cash and wish to earn a return identical to that of the S&P 500 Index. It is December 31 and the following spot and futures information is available:

Spot S&P 500 Index	$400
Dividend to Be Paid in Three Months	$ 4
Futures Price (Deliverable in Three Months)	$404.71
Three Month Risk-Free Rate	2.17782%

At spot prices of $350 and $450 on the delivery date, the quarterly rate of return on the spot S&P 500 Index would be -11.5% and 13.5%, respectively:

$$-0.115 = (350 - 400 + 4) \div 400$$

$$0.135 \quad (450 - 400 + 4) \div 400$$

The transactions in Table 15-6 show that a mixed futures and T-bill position would achieve the same results.

Use in Portfolio Insurance Programs. In Chapter 16, the concept and application of portfolio insurance is discussed. A minimum portfolio value can be insured by

TABLE 15-6 *Creating an Indexed Portfolio with Futures*

Transaction	Date	Delivery Date	
		$S_T=\$350$	$S_T=\$450$
Today	0		
Purchase T-bills	$-\$10,000,000$	$\$10,217,782$	$\$10,217,782$
Buy 50 Futures		$-10,117,750$	$-10,117,750$
$\$10,000,000 \div (\$400 \times 500)$			
Delivery Date			
Sell 50 Futures		8,750,000	11,250,000
Total	$-\$10,000,000$	$\$ 8,850,032$	$\$11,350,032$
Rate of Return		-11.5%	13.5%

trading listed put and call options or by using a trading strategy that dynamically replicates the payoffs of the options. Dynamic replication requires that stock be sold when its value declines and bought when its value increases. Because of costs associated with actually trading in the spot stock, stock index futures are commonly used. For example, if the trading strategy calls for the sale of $10,000,000 in spot stock, futures with a claim to $10,000,000 of the stock index are sold instead. Clearly, for this procedure to work, the actual stock held must be reasonably similar to the stock index on which the futures are traded.

Speculative Strategies

If the futures contract is traded at values different from those implied by Equation 15.9, speculative profits are possible. The most widely known speculation is an index arbitrage.

Index Arbitrage. In the preceding illustration, the S&P 500 futures had a theoretical value equal to $404.71:

$$\$404.71 = \$400 \, (1.0217782) - \$4$$

If the actual futures price is different, an index arbitrage is possible.

Assume that the actual futures price is $406.71. Then an arbitrage consisting of selling the futures would be profitable, since the market price of $406.71 is greater than the theoretical value of $404.71. Details of an illustrative arbitrage are shown in Table 15-7, in which $10 million of futures are sold. At current prices of $406.71, a total of 49.1751 contracts are sold. (We assume that fractional contract may be traded to increase precision).

$$406.1751 = \$10,000,000 \, / \, (\$406.71 \times 500)$$

This naked futures position, of course, is quite risky (losing if delivery date spot prices are higher than $406.71 and winning at lower spot prices). To remove this risk, 49.1751 units of the spot index are bought at a cost of $9,835,020. To finance the cost of the spot index, $9,835,020 in T-bills are sold short.

At the delivery date, three things happen. First, the short T-bills are repaid. At an interest cost of 2.17782%, this requires a payment of $10,049,209:

$$\$10,049,209 = \$9,835,020 \, (1.0217782)$$

Second, dividends are received on 49.1751 units of the spot index in the amount of $98,350:

$$\$98,350 = \$9,835,020 \times 0.01$$

Finally, the arbitrage is "unwound" by selling 49.1751 units of the spot and buying the 49.1751 futures. Net cash flows of $49,141 are received at the delivery date—regardless of the spot price at that time.

A few comments about this index arbitrage are in order. First, although the transaction appears to be complex, it simply involves the purchase of one risk-

TABLE 15-7 *Illustration of Index Arbitrage*

Fair Futures Value = $404.71		Date T		
Actual Futures Value = $406.71				
At Date 0	Date 0	$S_T = \$350$	$S_T = \$450$	Reason
Sell Futures (1)		+$10,000,000	+$10,000,000	Futures Are Overvalued
Buy Spot (2)	−9,835,020			Remove Risk
Sell T-bills	+9,835,020			Provide Financing
At Date *T*				
Repay T-bills (3)		− 10,049,209	− 10,049,209	
Receive Dividends (4)		98,350	98,350	
Unwind Arbitrage				
Sell Spot (5)		8,605,642	11,064,397	
Buy Futures (5)		− 8,605,642	− 11,064,397	
Net Outcome	0	$49,141	$49,141	

(1) Number of contracts = $10,000,000 ÷ ($406.71×500) = 49.1751.
(2) Value of stock = 49.1751 × ($400×500).
(3) T-bill payment = $9,835,020(1.09)$^{0.25}$ = $10,049,209.
(4) Dividends = 0.01 × $9,835,020 = $98,350.
(5) Value traded = 49.1751 × ($350×500) = $8,605,642
    or   = 49.1751 × ($450×500) = $11,064,397.

free security (buy spot and sell an equivalent number of futures) that provided a three-month return of 2.6775% and financing it with another risk-free security at a cost of 2.1778%:

$$0.026775 = \frac{\$10,000,000 + \$98,350}{\$9,835,020} - 1$$

$$0.021778 = (1.09)^{0.25} - 1$$

Second, real life arbitrages will differ from this example in that fractional contracts cannot be traded and transaction costs are incurred. In practice, there is a low and high price range of index futures for which index arbitrage profits are not available. In the early years of the index contracts, this price range was frequently violated. In recent years, index futures usually lie within this price range, and only low-cost traders are able to take advantage of index arbitrages.

Notice that the arbitrage must be unwound on the delivery date by trading in both the spot and futures market. This is because actual delivery on the futures is not allowed—index futures require cash (profit) delivery. As large arbitrage trades are placed on the delivery date, they can have substantial impacts on market prices. In the example above, shares of the S&P 500 were sold at the delivery date and would depress stock prices. Arbitragers are indifferent to such price-pressure impact since they are simultaneously buying in one market and selling in another at the same price. But other investors who happen to trade at the same time are not indifferent and may find that they have traded at prices very different from what they expected.

Such price pressure impacts are due to a large influx of arbitrage-related trades that might be requests to either buy or sell stocks in the spot index. If the potential quantity of these arbitrage trades as well as whether they would be buy or sell orders could be predicted, a sufficient number of other investors would place offsetting trades in the hopes of taking advantage of expected price pressures. Unfortunately, such predictions are very imprecise. Thus, starting in 1987, the time of delivery was changed from the close of trading on Thursday afternoon to the opening of trading on Friday morning. This meant that the amount and direction of arbitrage trading would be known to the exchanges, allowing them to both delay opening and publicize the amount of arbitrage trades in order to attract offsetting trades.

Finally, even though index arbitrage did have dramatic effects on delivery date spot prices prior to 1987, the economic function of arbitrage is important. The fundamental reason why futures exist is that they allow the control of price risk—rapidly and cheaply. But this risk management can be effective only if futures are properly priced. If futures prices are allowed to vary from their theoretical values, the true economic benefits of having such markets disappear.

OPTIONS ON FINANCIAL FUTURES

A growing number of option contracts on financial futures have been developed in recent years. An option on a financial futures is exactly what its name implies: you buy (or write) a put or call option on a financial futures contract. Actively traded futures options are shown in Table 15-8.

TABLE 15-8 *Actively Traded Options on Financial Futures 1993*

Contract	Trading Units	Exchange
Interest Rate		
U.S. T-Bonds	$100,000	CBT
U.S. T-Notes	$100,000	CBT
Municipal Bond Index	$100,000	CBT
U.S. 5-Year Treasury Notes	$100,000	CBT
Eurodollar	$1,000,000	IMM, LIFFE
LIBOR—1 Month	$3,000,000	IMM
U.S. T-Bills	$1,000,000	IMM
Long Gilt	50,000 pounds	LIFFE
Stock Index:		
S&P 500	$500 times premium	CME
Major Market Index	$500 times premium	CBT
NYSE Composite	$500 times premium	NYFE
Nikkei 225 Stock Average	$ 5 times index	CME

CBT—Chicago Board of Trade.
CME—Chicago Mercantile Exchange.
IMM—International Monetary Market.
LIFFE—London International Financial Futures Exchange.

TABLE 15-9 *Prices of Options on Financial Futures*

Future	Strike Price	Calls		Puts	
		August	*September*	*August*	*September*
U.S. T-bond	100	2-26/64	2-43/64	0-1/64	0-17/64
S&P 500	410	7.90	10.45	3.95	6.55

Consider the T-bond quotations shown in Table 15-9. Among these are call options on a future on $100,000 of 8% coupon U.S. Treasury Bonds. If the call is exercised, the call owner purchases a futures contract on Treasury Bonds. The future which is purchased will be deliverable in one month. Option price quotations on T-Bond futures are shown as a percentage of par. For example the August calls cost 2 26/64 percent of $100,000, or $2,406.25. For this payment, the call buyer may exercise the option to purchase $100,000 of T-bonds at par.

Next consider the call options on the S&P 500 futures contract with a delivery date of August. It has an exercise price of $410 times 500, or $205,000. Its market price is $7.90 × 500, or $3,950.

Why Options on Futures Exist

Option contracts are available on actual spot securities such as the S&P 500 Index, the NYSE Index, and T-bonds. So why create options on futures contracts for each? What is gained by having the underlying security a futures contract instead of the spot security? Three principal reasons have been offered:

1. *Delivery is eased.* Using a futures contract as the security underlying the option eases delivery in two ways. First, the quantity of futures is unlimited. If you are forced to deliver a T-bond future as the writer of a call, for example, you could simply *create* a new T-bond future by purchasing one in the futures market. In contrast, the supply of actual spot T-bonds is limited. Second, there is a greater certainty about what is being delivered when a future is used. (This is true only for T-bonds.) The deliverable instrument is a future on a $100,000 par 8% long-term T-bond. When the spot security is deliverable, one could receive any number of different types of coupons or maturities.

2. *Price accuracy.* Options on futures and the futures themselves are traded almost side by side on the same exchanges. Thus, the option prices can continuously reflect existing futures prices. In contrast, spot securities are traded in other markets and their prices are available with a slight lag.

3. *Flexibility.* The option on a future provides the opportunity to acquire the future without incurring an incremental transaction cost.

The relative importance of each of these reasons depends on the type of securities being traded. For example, ease of delivery is quite important for T-bond contracts. As a result, options on T-bond futures are more widely used than are options on spot T-bonds. However, ease of delivery is less important for stock index option contracts.

Details about option pricing and trading are discussed in the next chapter.

SUMMARY

Futures contracts on financial instruments are a phenomenon of the 1980s and 1990s. At present, active markets exist on:

1. Short-term debt instruments, such as T-bills, CDs, and Eurodollar deposits
2. Long-term debt instruments, such as T-bonds, T-notes, and GNMAs
3. Stock indexes, such as the NYSE and S&P 500

Options on various futures have also been recently offered.

Individuals who go long a financial futures contract are legally obligated to buy the security at a stipulated price in a stipulated month. Individuals who go short a contract are required to deliver the security at the stipulated price in the stipulated month. Physical delivery rarely occurs, however, since long and short positions are usually offset before the contract's maturity date.

The basic purpose of financial futures is to reduce price risk by hedging one's physical security position with an opposite futures position. A perfect hedge that eliminates all risk is difficult to achieve in practice, but risk can be substantially reduced by selecting futures that (1) mature close to when cash is needed or will be available, (2) have a contract value similar to the amount being hedged, and (3) have a deliverable security similar to the security you intend to buy or sell.

Financial futures are one more tool with which the risk and return position of a portfolio can be managed. They open up a variety of new ways to speculate and can easily alter the market risk exposure of a portfolio (the stock/bond mix). However, similar to options, they are complex instruments and should be used only after they are well understood.

REVIEW PROBLEMS

1. You are given the following price quotations on spot T-bills. Assume the futures mature on the last day of the month and ignore marking to market.

T-Bill Spot Price Quotations

Maturity	Life	Discount
March 30	30 days	10.00%
June 30	120 days	11.00%

Futures Price Quotations

Security	Maturity	Contract	Discount
T-Bill Future	March 30	$1 million—90 day spot	11.80%

a. Find the market price for $1,000,000 in par value of each T-bill instrument.
b. Do you think the T-bill future is fairly priced?
c. How can you create a riskless arbitrage?

2. You are the administrator of a portfolio worth $500 million. Over the long run, you would like to maintain a cash/bond/stock mix of 5%/30%/65%. Owing to recent movements in the markets the present mix is 5%/40%/55%. You plan to adjust this mix to that desired by using financial futures. Assume that interest rates are now 10%.

a. Your bonds have a duration equal to what you would like to maintain, $D_1 = 5$ years. The cheapest-to-deliver T-bond has a duration of 8.2 years and a delivery factor of 0.975. How many T-bonds futures should you buy or sell?

b. The beta of your stock portfolio is close to 1.2 and that of the NYSE is close to 1.0. If you wish to maintain the 1.2 beta, how many NYSE futures should you buy or sell? Assume the spot NYSE is trading at $120 and futures on the NYSE are $130.

Solutions

1. a. March 30 Spot T-Bill $= \$1 \text{ million} \left[1 - 1(0.1)\dfrac{30}{360} \right]$

   $= \$991,666.67$

   June 30 Spot T-Bill $= \$1 \text{ million} \left[1 - 1(0.11)\dfrac{120}{360} \right]$

   $= \$963,333.33$

   T-Bill Future $= \$1 \text{ million} \left[1 - 1(0.118)\dfrac{90}{360} \right]$

   $= \$970,500$

   (or $1 million $-$ $25 per basis point $\times$ 1180 basis points)

   b. The return on the 90-day T-bill that could be delivered on the future should be identical to the return on a forward contract created with spot T-bills. Forward contract (90-day) yield:

	Today	March 30	June 30
Buy 1.0 June 30	−$963,333.33	—	$1,000,000
Short Equivalent March 30			
($963,333 ÷ 991,666)	963,333.33	−$971,428.56	—
Net	$ 0.0	$971,428.56	$1,000,000

   90-day return = 2.94%

   Futures contract (90-day) yield:

   $$\frac{\text{Sell}}{\text{Buy}} - 1.0 = \frac{1,000,000}{\$970,500} - 1 = 3.04\%$$

   One or more of the following must be true: (1) the future is underpriced, (2) the June 30 spot is overpriced, (3) the March 30 spot is underpriced.

   c. A riskless arbitrage would be:

	Today	*Today*	*March 30*
Buy 1.0 Future		$ 0.0	− $970,500.00
Sell 1.0 June 30 Spot		$963,333.33	
Buy 0.971428 March 30 Spot		− 963,333.33	971,428.56
On March 30			
Sell Future at Any Price (say, $1)			1.00
Buy June 30 Spot *at the Same Price*			− 1.00
Net Cash Flow		$ 0.0	$ 928.56

2. a. First you intend to *sell* futures that are the equivalent of $50 million in five-year duration bonds. The dollar duration of this would be:

$$5\left(\frac{.11 - .1}{1.1}\right)(\$50 \text{ million}) = \$2.27 \text{ million}$$

Next, the dollar duration of a single T-bond futures contract is:

$$\frac{8.2}{0.975}(\$100,000)\left(\frac{.11 - .1}{1.1}\right) = \$7,645.69$$

The number of T-bond contracts that is equivalent to $2.27 million in dollar duration is:

$$\frac{\$2,270,000}{\$7,645.69} = 297$$

b. You would *buy* stock futures that are the equivalent of $50 million in stock with a beta of 1.2. This would be:

$$\frac{\$50,000,000}{120 \times \$500} \times 1.2 = 1,000 \text{ contracts}$$

QUESTIONS AND PROBLEMS

1. What is the difference between a futures contract and a forward contract?
2. It is January 1, and a 90-day T-bill future maturing in June is trading at an 8.85% (360-day) discount. You buy five contracts.
   a. What are you now legally obligated to do under the contract?
   b. How much margin must you provide if $2,000 margin per contract is required?
   c. At what discount will you be required to provide cash in order to restore the initial margin if maintenance margin is per contract $1,500?
   d. If you sell two weeks later at a discount of 8.95%, what is your dollar profit or loss?
   e. If you are considering holding to maturity and selling five contracts at that time (instead of taking delivery), what is your expected profit if the markets are in equilibrium?
   f. As of January 1, what is the dollar duration of your position?

3. It is now March 1. You buy a September T-bond future selling at $95.25 to yield 8.57%. On June 1 you cover the long future by selling at $99.25 (8.09% yield) and simultaneously buy spot T-bonds at $99.75. What is your net purchase price?

4. Ninety-day and 180-day spot T-bills are now selling for $99.25 and $98.50, respectively. In addition, you observe that the price of a 90-day T-bill future that matures in 90 days is $99. Create an arbitrage that will take advantage of any price imbalances.

5. Spot and futures prices are shown below for the close of trading on January 1:

Spot T-Bill Instruments

Maturity	Quoted Discount
90 days	8.0%
180 days	8.2%
270 days	8.4%
360 days	8.6%

Futures on 90-Day T-Bills

Maturity	Quoted Discount
Current	?
90 days	8.0%
180 days	9.0%
270 days	?

   a. What should the discount be on the futures that are currently maturing?

   b. If the markets are now in equilibrium, what should be the discount on the 270-day futures? (Ignore marking to market.)

   c. Why did part b require that marking to market be ignored?

   d. Again, ignore marking to market. Create an arbitrage on the 90- and 180-day futures.

6. Why should a perfect hedge work?

7. What is the importance of delivery in futures pricing? Contrast the delivery features of futures on T-bills, T-bonds, and stock indexes.

8. On December 30, T-bond futures maturing exactly two years later were quoted at 67-24.

   a. Interpret this price quote.

   b. Why is the price so low? These are, after all, default- and call-free U.S. Treasury obligations.

   c. In deciding what price is actually paid for any T-bonds actually delivered, the clearing corporation divides the price quotation by a delivery factor that is generally less than 1.0. Why do they do this, and why do you suppose it is less than 1.0?

9. It is now January 1, and you hold $5 million par value of corporate bonds with a market value of $4,893,750. You sell 50 T-bond contracts at $1,025 per bond. By March 15, the basis (between the future and the average corporate bond value) has changed from $46.25 to $51.25. If you simultaneously sell spot and buy futures, what is your net selling price? What is your gain or loss on the initial corporate bond value?

10. People hedge in financial futures to reduce price risk. What must happen to the hedge basis during the life of a hedge in order for the hedge to be perfect, that is, to eliminate all price risk? What features of a financial future should one look at in order to reduce price risks as much as possible?

11. The optimal hedge as shown in Equation 15.3 requires estimates of σ_S, σ_F, and r_{FS}. Assume you are hedging with a contract that has a good history available. How might you statistically estimate each term?

12. Assume that you intend to borrow $100 million in mid-February. It is now January 1, and 90-day T-bill futures maturing at the end of arch are quoted at an 8.0% discount. Assume you have statistically estimated the following:

   - Standard deviation of futures prices $= \$2$
   - Standard deviation of your borrowing price $= \$3$
   - Correlation between S and $F = 0.7$

   What is the optimal hedge?

13. Outline a basic trading strategy for each of the cases presented below. You may buy or sell any of the financial futures contracts discussed in the chapter. Be sure to specify the contract's maturity month.

   a. It is January 1, and the treasurer of a life insurance company maintains large holdings of U.S. T-bills, as follows:

1-month maturity	$1.5 million
3-month maturity	0.7 million
6-month maturity	1.0 million
1-year maturity	2.0 million

   The treasurer wishes to hold these bills in order to protect the firm from temporary liquidity needs, but wishes to protect against losses in value if interest rates rise.

   b. The investment adviser to a college endowment fund has been told that in early June a major contribution of $500,000 will be received. Believing that rates are now at a peak, the adviser will be investing the contribution in T-bonds.

   c. In early March a mutual fund manager has a large position in intermediate- and long-term corporate bonds. He is forecasting a rise in interest rates.

   d. The situation is the same as in part c, except the manager is forecasting a decline in interest rates.

   e. A real estate investment trust buys mortgages from local financial institutions and then packages them for resale to the market. It is February 15, and the package should be ready for sale by middle August.

   f. The treasurer of a corporation estimates that on May 15, $10 million in commercial paper will have to be sold to finance seasonal working capital needs. The treasurer believes that by May commercial paper rates will be higher than existing rates on June financial futures.

   g. The situation is the same as in part f, except the treasurer believes June futures rates are higher than will exist in May.

14. What does dollar duration measure?

15. It is January 1. The duration of your bond portfolio as measured by D_1 is 6.0 years, its market value is $700 million, and its yield to maturity is 10%. Assume that D_1 for the cheapest-to-deliver T-bond is 6.5 years and has a delivery factor of 0.90.

   a. How many futures contracts would you buy or sell to increase the effective value of the portfolio to $800 million with $D_1 = 6.0$ years?

   b. How many futures contracts would you buy or sell to leave the market value at $700 million but reduce its duration to four years?

   c. In either case above, what factors might cause the holding you take on to be wrong?

   d. Ignoring part c, what would you do when the futures mature?

16. Hedges of a stock portfolio using stock index futures work best if the portfolio is similar to the underlying futures index. Why is this so?

17. Stock index futures can increase or decrease a portfolio's systematic *market* risk. They cannot hedge unsystematic risks. Why?

18. You are the administrator of a stock portfolio that is now worth $1 billion and has a beta of 1.1. You would like to reduce the beta to 1.0 and reduce the equity claim to $900 million. Futures prices of the NYSE index contract are 115 and the spot value is 113.

   a. How could you accomplish your goal with futures?

   b. Actually, you have many maturity dates to choose from. How might you decide which to use?

   c. What would you do when the futures mature?

   d. Why might this not work out the way you wish?

19. On December 31, six-month T-bills were priced to provide a six-month return of 4.28%. (This is the effective return, not the discount.) At the same time, the S&P 500 Index closed at $400, and the futures contract on the S&P 500 with a June maturity closed at $412. Dividends expected on the S&P 500 between January and June of the next year were $8.00. Was the future priced according to the arbitrage valuation model?

20. A general model for valuing stock index futures is not currently available. However, an arbitrage model is often used to approximate the value of a stock index future.

   a. What is the arbitrage that is conducted?

   b. Is the current futures price equal to the expected value of the index when the contract matures?

   c. What is the role of dividends in this model?

   d. What problems does the model assume away?

21. Today is June 30, and you observe the following market data:

S&P 500 Index:
Current price	$300.00
Dividend to be paid in 3 months	$ 3.00

T-Bills:
Quoted discount on 3-month 90-day bill	8.00%

S&P 500 Index Future
Quoted price of a future with a 3-month (90-day) delivery date	$324.00

   a. Is the future properly priced?

   b. Illustrate the index arbitrage that could be conducted. (Trade in spot stock now worth $100 million and assume you can trade fractional units.)

   c. You manage a $500 million portfolio of equities and T-bills. At present, $250 million of equities with a beta of 1.1 are held. You would prefer that the portfolio effectively have $300 million of equity and that the equity beta be 1.0. How many futures could you trade to achieve this outcome without trading the spot equity?

   d. Will the futures/spot position taken in part c result in the same portfolio values in three months as an adjustment of the spot portfolio to your desired mix? Illustrate for S&P 500 values of $280 and $320. Explain any difference.

REFERENCES

Recent texts with extensive discussion of financial futures are shown below. Each has further detailed listings of references.

CHANCE, DON M. *An Introduction to Options and Futures.* Orlando, FL: Dryden Press, 1989.

FIGLEWSKI, STEPHEN. *Hedging with Financial Futures for Institutional Investors.* Cambridge, MA: Ballinger Publishing, 1986.

HULL, JOHN. *Options, Futures, and Other Derivative Securities.* Englewood Cliffs, NJ: Prentice-Hall, 1989.

MARSHALL, JOHN F. *Futures and Option Contracting: Theory and Practice.* Cincinnati, OH: Southwestern Publishing Co., 1989.

STOLL, HANS R. and ROBERT E. WHALEY, *Futures and Options: Theory and Applications.* Cincinnati, OH: Southwestern Publishing Co., 1993.

Each of the various futures exchanges has extensive literature about their contracts. You should write to the following addresses and request a listing of the publications that are currently available:

Chicago Board of Trade, Literature Services Department, 141 W. Jackson Boulevard, Suite 2210, Chicago, IL 60604-2994.

Chicago Mercantile Exchange, International Monetary Market, 30 South Wacker Drive, Chicago, IL 60606.

Kansas City Board of Trade, Marketing Department, 4800 Main Street, Suite 303, Kansas City, Missouri, 646112.

New York Futures Exchange, Inc., 20 Broad Street, New York, NY, 10005.

FINEX, Four World Trade Center, New York, NY, 10048.

The role of stock index futures in the "Crash of 1987" has been extensively studied. A few of the studies are shown below.

COMMODITY FUTURES TRADING COMMISSION, *Final Report on Stock Index Futures and Cash Market Activity During October, 1987.* 1988.

HARRIS, LAWRENCE. "The October 1987 S&P 500 Stock-Futures Basis." *Journal of Finance,* March 1989.

BLUME, MARSHALL E., A. CRAIG MACKINLAY, and BRUCE TERKER, "Order Imbalances and Stock Price Movements on October 19 and 20, 1987." *Journal of Finance,* September 1989.

STOLL, HANS R., and ROBERT E. WHALEY, "The Dynamics of Stock Index and Stock Index Futures Returns." *Journal of Financial and Quantitative Analysis,* December 1990.

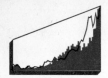

Options

In 1973, call options on a select number of common stocks began trading on a formal securities exchange for the first time in history. This event marked the start of a revolution in security market trading: the introduction of active markets in derivative securities.

When these first call options were introduced, their trading on a listed exchange was considered by many people to be a fairly risky experiment. Options had, in fact, been traded for many years in over-the-counter market, but their trading had never been active. The experiment was an outstanding success! Within a decade, call options were available on all actively traded stocks in the United States, put-option trading had begun, option trading expanded to many U.S. and non-U.S. exchanges, and option contracts had been created on a large number of debt instruments and currencies.

By the early 1980s, the extraordinary success of listed option contracts spurred the futures exchanges to offer a competitive product: futures contracts on financial securities. The futures contracts that were offered on common stocks differed from stock option contracts in what turned out to be a key respect. Stock futures were traded on *portfolios* of stocks such as the S&P 500 Index, whereas stock options were traded on individual stock issues. Trading of futures on stock index portfolios soon became the more popular form of derivative trading, since trading in claims to an aggregate portfolio of stocks was a more efficient way to manage a portfolio's total equity risk exposure. As trading in stock index futures grew, trading in options on individual stocks declined.

As expected, the option exchanges countered by offering option contracts on stock portfolio indexes. Two of these option contracts are now the most actively traded options in the world: options on the S&P 100 Index and the S&P 500 Index. For example, the dollar claim to stocks traded through these two contracts on April 23, 1993 was about $11.8 billion. On the same date, the dollar claim to stocks traded through options on individual stocks was considerably less—only about $4.0 billion. These trading values compare with a trading value of approximately $11.0 billion for individual spot stocks on the New York Stock Exchange (NYSE) on the same day.

In this chapter, we extend our introductory discussion on options presented in Chapter 9. The discussion there is useful for individuals who are interested only in a basic understanding of what option contracts are and how they are valued. Here, we take up topics that must be understood by investors who actually intend to trade options. The chapter is divided into two broad areas. First, we discuss a variety of practical issues associated with valuing calls and puts. Second, we examine how options can be used in portfolio management for hedging and speculative purposes. To help refresh your knowledge, we begin with a review of basic option concepts.

BASIC OPTION CONCEPTS

The owner of a *call* option has the right to *buy* the spot asset that underlies the option from the writer of the option. The owner of a *put* option has the right to *sell* the underlying spot asset to the writer of the option. The price at which owners may buy or sell is referred to as the option's *exercise price,* and the date after which the option may no longer be exercised is the option's *expiration date.* The owner of a *European* option may exercise the option only at the option's stated expiration date. The owner of an *American* option may exercise at any time prior to the options expiration.[1] Unless stated otherwise, all options discussed in the chapter are assumed to be European options.

Option owners will exercise their *right to trade* only if it is beneficial for them to do so. In the case of a call option, the owner will exercise only if the underlying spot asset is trading at a price greater than the option's exercise price. For a put option, the owner will exercise only if the underlying spot asset is trading for less than the option's exercise price. Notice that whatever is a benefit to an option owner is an equal detriment to the writer. To compensate the option writer for accepting this risk, the owner must pay a price to the writer at the date of trade.

In this chapter, we will continue to use the option symbology introduced in Chapter 9. Specifically:

S_t = Market value of underlying spot good at date t. The trade date is designated as $t = 0$. The expiration date is designated as $t = T$.

X = Exercise price of the option.

C_t = Call value at date t.

P_t = Put value at date t.

For example, assume you are considering the purchase of a call option on a stock index known as the Japan Index that would allow you the right to purchase one unit of the index for $170 on August 25. The spot Japan Index is currently quoted as $175, and the price of the call option is $8. In this case:

---

[1] The label applied to American versus European options, of course, traces to the location in which each contract was originally traded. Today, many option contracts traded in the United States are European options; they may be exercised only on the expiration day.

$$S_t = \$175$$
$$X = \$170$$
$$C_o = \$\ \ 8$$
$$T = \text{August 25}$$

The option writer is obligated to provide you with one unit of the index in return for \$170 *if* you decide to trade on August 25. Clearly, you will elect to buy only if the Japan Index is worth more than \$170 on the expiration date. For example, if the index is \$177 on August 25, then you will exercise your call and pay \$170 for something worth \$177. Since your original cost was \$8, you incur a net loss on the transaction. This loss is equal to the option's value on the expiration date of \$7 less the initial price that you paid of \$8. But the net loss of \$1 from exercising is better than a net loss of \$8 if you do not exercise.

Notice that the positive \$7 option investment value on the expiration date to you as the call owner represents a negative \$7 option investment value to the writer. Again, to induce the writer to be placed in such a situation, a reasonable initial cash payment must be given to the writer—the initial option price.

Expiration Date Outcomes

As suggested in the previous discussion, each party to an option trade faces two related but different expiration date outcomes: (1) the option's investment value and (2) the net profit. These are shown graphically in Figure 16-1. Outcomes for long (ownership) positions are shown as solid lines. Short (writer) outcomes are the dashed lines. Consider panel A, in which the *investment value* of the option position is shown. *At the expiration date,* the option's investment value is the same as the price at which the option trades in financial markets. If the market price is different from the investment value of owning the option, then easy arbitrage profits are possible.[2]

At the expiration date of a call option, the option will have a zero investment value if the underlying spot good is worth less than the exercise price. At spot values greater than the exercise price, the call has an investment value equal to the spot's price minus the exercise price. Symbolically:

---

[2] For example, suppose that the expiration date of the Japan Index call option has arrived. You observe that the spot Japan Index is trading for \$175 and the call option is trading for \$6 (greater than its investment value of \$5). The arbitrage would be to purchase the Japan Index for \$175 and sell the option for \$6. Option owners will exercise and pay you \$170 for the Japan Index spot that you deliver to them. Before transaction costs, you will earn a \$1 profit on no investment and at no risk:

$$\$1 = -\$175 + \$6 + \$170$$

In reality, the arbitrage of a stock index option such as the Japan Index is slightly more complex since actual delivery of the spot is not allowed with stock index options. However, the net results would be the same.

FIGURE 16-1 *Expiration Data Outcomes*

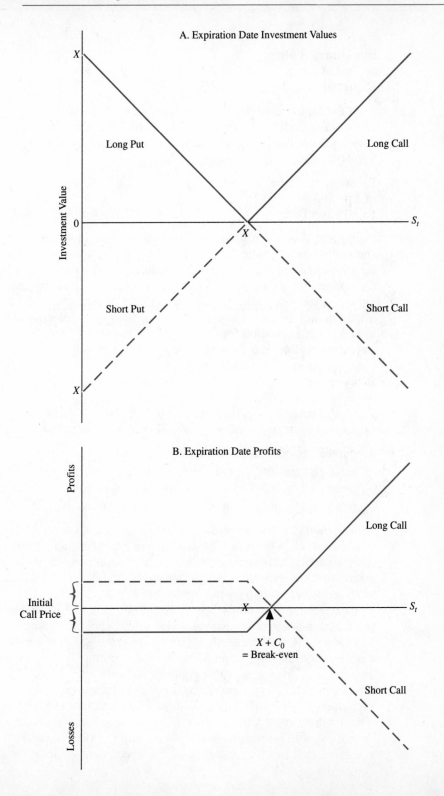

A. Expiration Date Investment Values

B. Expiration Date Profits

Investment Value of Call at Expiration	$C_T = 0$	if $S_T < X$	**(16.1)**
	$= S_T - X$	if $S_T > X$	

At the expiration date of a put option, the option will have a positive investment value if the underlying spot good is worth less than the exericse price. At spot values greater than the exercise price, the put will have a zero investment value. Symbolically:

Investment Value of Put at Expiration Date	$P_T = X - S_T$	if $S_T < X$	**(16.2)**
	$= 0$	if $S_T > X$	

In panel B of Figure 16-1, the *net profits* from a long or short call position are shown for the expiration date. This net profit is simply the investment value of the position minus (for the owner) or plus (for the writer) the initial price paid for the option. For the call owner to break even, the underlying spot good must have an expiration date value of $S_T = X + C_o$. For example, if $8 had been paid for a call having an exercise price of $170, then the spot asset must sell for more than $178 at expiration for the call owner to profit (writer to lose).

Clearly, option traders are primarily interested in their profits and losses. However, option valuation and risk management trades are easier to understand if we focus on option investment values instead of net profits.

Put-Call Parity Prices. Early research on option valuation showed that the expiration date investment values of a call option could be synthetically created by:

1. purchasing one unit of the underlying spot asset.
2. selling a zero-coupon risk-free security (that has a maturity identical to the call option's expiration date and a par value equal to the call's exercise price).
3. purchasing a put option with equivalent terms as the call.

This is illustrated in Figure 16-2, in which the spot good is assumed to be a common stock. The vertical axis displays the investment value of each security. The horizontal axis represents the expiration date value of the spot stock asset. Payoffs on the synthetic call are shown by the darker solid line. Payoffs on the other assets are shown by the lighter lines.

Consider the situation when S_T is equal to the call's expiration price, X. The put option has a zero investment value at this spot price. And, although the stock has value of $+X$, it is exactly offset by the requirement to repay $-X$ on the short debt position. In sum, when S_T equals the expiration price, this portfolio of three assets has an investment value equal to zero—exactly what a long call investment value would be. Now consider spot prices in excess of X. When this happens, the repayment of debt offsets a part of the increased spot stock value but not totally. The net investment value is then $S_T - X$—again, exactly what a long call option would payoff. (You might find it useful to refer to Equation 16-1.) Finally, when the spot stock is worth less than X, the investment value of the long put exactly

FIGURE 16-2 *Creating a Synthetic Call Option*

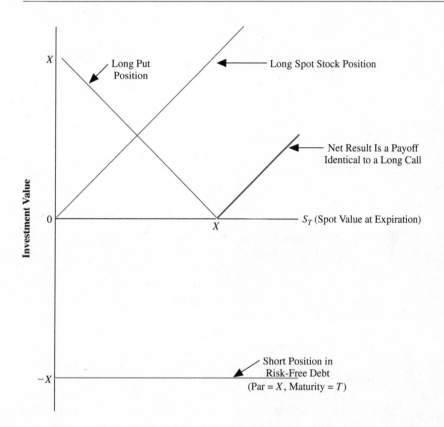

compensates for any decreases in the spot stock's value. The value of the put plus the stock is sufficient to repay the debt. But after the debt is repaid, there is a zero investment value. Again, the result is the same as a long position in a call option.

Since the portfolio of these three assets will have the same expiration date investment value as a call option, the market value of the portfolio should logically be the same as the market value of the call option. If this were not true, then arbitrage profits would be available. The pricing relationship between the actual call and the synthetic call is known as put-call parity and is written symbolically as follows:

Put Call Parity Model
$$C_t = S_t - [X \div (1 + RF)^T] + P_t \qquad (16.3)$$

The risk-free interest rate *RF* represents an annual risk-free rate.

There are two important implications in Equation 16.3. First, the equation demonstrates what a call option actually is: a leveraged ownership of the underlying spot asset plus the ownership of an insurance policy (the put) that guarantees that the debt borrowing will be repaid. Positive signs in the equation represent a purchase, and negative signs represent the sale or issuance of a security. Thus, $+S$ and $+P$ represent the purchase of the spot and the put and $-X$ represents the sale of zero-coupon debt having a par value of X. Second, the equation can be rearranged to show how any one of the four assets can be synthetically replicated by positions in the other three assets. For example, to synthetically create the ownership of a risk-free security, the spot asset and the put would be bought and the call would be written.

Call Option Values Prior to the Expiration Date

Prior to an option's expiration date, its value will be greater than is shown in Equations 16.1 and 16.2. The situation for a call option is displayed in Figure 16.3. The dotted line represents the value of the call if this were the expiration date. Prior to the expiration date, the values shown by the dotted line are referred to as the option's *immediate value*. The solid curve reflects the option's actual market value. The difference between an option's actual value and its immediate value is known as the option's *time value*. For example, an option exercisable at $170 that is trading for $12 when the underlying spot asset is worth $180 has an immediate value of $10 and a time value of $2.

An option has a time value prior to its expiration date because the most that that underlying spot can fall is to zero, but there is (conceptually) no limit to its potential price increase.

Black-Scholes Valuation. Around the time when the first listed option contracts were traded, Fischer Black and Myron Scholes developed the first option valuation equation in which a European call option could be valued without having to know the value of the equivalent put option. This was a seminal event in financial research. Today, the model is extensively used (with refinements) by option hedgers and speculators.

The call valuation model that Black and Scholes developed is shown below:

**Black-Scholes
Call Option
Pricing Model**
$$C_t = S_t N(d1) - [(X) \div e^{(rf)(T)}]N(d2) \qquad (16.4)$$

where $N(d1)$ and $N(d2)$ represent the value of the cumulative normal-density function at $d1$ and $d2$, and rf represents the annual *continuously compound* risk-free rate of interest which is the same as $1n(1 + RF)$. Much of the discussion in this chapter deals with the practical implementation of the model.

Determinants of Call Prices. The Black-Scholes option pricing model can be used in a variety of ways. Most important, perhaps, is its ability to explicitly indicate the various factors that determine call premiums. These are:

1. *Current stock price.* The higher the stock's price, the greater the call premium.
2. *Exercise price.* The higher the exercise price, the lower the call premium.

FIGURE 16-3 *Call Values Prior to Expiration*

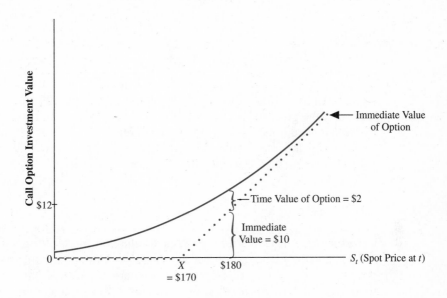

3. *Time to expiration.* The longer the time to expiration, the greater the possibility that the stock will eventually sell above the call's exercise price and thus the greater the call premium.
4. *Variance of stock returns.* The more variable the future returns on a stock, the greater the possibility the stock will eventually sell above the call's exercise price and thus the greater the call premium.
5. *Risk-free rate.* The greater the risk-free rate, the greater the call's value. This relationship is not as intuitively clear as the others. Remember that calls will be priced in accordance with their ability to create a riskless future payoff. When this future certain cash flow is discounted to obtain *present worths* of a mixed stock-and-call portfolio, higher discount rates yield lower present values. Since the mixed portfolio consists of owning stock and writing calls, a lower present worth can be obtained only by higher call premiums.

Note that the value of a call is *not a "direct" function of expected future stock prices*. This point is true for each of the call valuation models developed in this chapter. In none of them is the call price directly affected by possible future stock prices. Only *current stock prices* are needed to value the call. The reason is simple. Calls are valued based on the fact that they can be mixed with stock positions to create a risk-free portfolio. If the value of the long stock position and short call position is not the same as the value of equivalent risk-free debt, arbitrage profits are possible.

The call price is, of course, affected *indirectly* by expected future stock prices in that possible future prices determine today's stock price. The important point, however, is that investors do not need to predict future stock prices in order to value a call.

TOPICS IN OPTION VALUATION

In this section, we examine a variety of topics associated with the practical implementation of the Black-Scholes option pricing model. This includes a discussion of the potential for early exercise of American options, adjustments to the model that need to be made when cash dividends are paid, and how various inputs to the model are estimated. The section concludes with an alternative valuation model known as the Binomial Model.

Early Exercise of American Options

The Black-Scholes equation provides a valuation model for a *European* option, one that can only be exercised at the stated expiration date. In contrast, American options may be exercised at the expiration date *or before*. Logically, an American option must be worth *at least* the same as a European option. If an American option will never be exercised early, then its value will be the same as a European option. If there is a possibility of early exercise, the Black-Scholes option pricing model provides an estimate of the American option's value that is biased downward.

Call Options on Stocks with No Cash Dividend. Consider an American call option that is exercisable at $50 any time during the next three months. The stock is selling for $55 and will not pay any cash dividends during the option's life. The option is trading for $7.

This $7 call price can be thought of as consisting of two components, an immediate in-the-money value and a time value:

Immediate Call Value	$5
Time Value	2
Call's Market Price	$7

Assume that you own the option but would prefer to own the stock. Should you exercise the option today in order to obtain the stock? No! If you are, in fact, foolish enough to exercise, you would pay the exercise price of $50 to be the owner of the stock. Alternatively, you could sell the option for $7 and use the proceeds together with only $48 to buy the stock in the open market. Clearly, the better alternative is to sell the option, since it results in a smaller out-of-pocket cash flow.

If we exercise any call on a non-dividend stock prior to its expiration date, we throw away the time value inherent in the option. The only time that one should exercise a call on a stock that pays no cash dividends is when the call's time value is zero. This will occur only at the call's expiration date.

Since American calls on stocks that will not pay cash dividends should never be prematurely exercised, such American calls will be worth the same as equivalent European calls—that is, the Black-Scholes model can be used to value such American calls.

Call Options on Stocks with Large Cash Dividends. When large cash dividends are to be paid, it is possible that early exercise is optimal. For example, consider the situation of the call option above but now assume that a $15 cash dividend will be paid tomorrow. This is illustrated in Figure 16-4. On the day before the stock goes ex-dividend, the stock is selling for $55 and the call for $7. Assuming that the $7 call price is a proper price according to the Black-Scholes model, the call must trade for this amount or arbitrage profits would be available. Tomorrow, however, the stock will go ex-dividend and drop in value to about $40. As a result, the call's value will also fall—to a new Black-Scholes value of, say, $3.

Should you exercise this call? Yes—but only very late on the day prior to the ex-dividend date. By exercising, you capture the call's immediate value of $5 ($55 − $50). If you do not exercise, you will be left with a call that is worth only $3 tomorrow. In short, if the call's immediate value $(S_t − X)$ is greater than the value of the call once the stock goes ex-dividend, you should exercise immediately before the ex-dividend date.

Note that the exercise takes place just before the ex-dividend date. At any prior time, the call will have a time value (albeit small) which you should not lose through premature exercise.

A revised version of the Black-Scholes model has been developed by Roll as well as Cox, Ross, and Rubinstein that takes into account the potential for early exercise of an American call. A reasonable approximation consists of calculating

FIGURE 16-4 *Call Values Before and After Ex-Dividend Date*

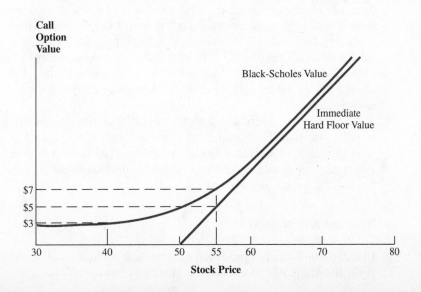

two Black-Scholes call values. The first would use the stated expiration date together with any intermediate cash dividends. The second would use the early exercise date as the option's life. The larger of the two call values should be its fair market price.

Put Options. There are always situations in which early exercise of a put is better than non-exercise, even if the stock does not pay cash dividends. To understand why, we return to the put-call parity model for *European* options:

Put-Call Parity	$$C_t = S_t - [X \div (1 + RF)^T] + P_t$$	**(16.5a)**

Since the price of the call must be less than (or equal to) the stock price, we can say:

$$S_t \geq C_t \tag{16.5b}$$

and

$$S_t \geq S_t - [X \div (1 + RF)^T] + P_t \tag{16.5c}$$

Canceling terms in Equation 16.5d, we can say that the price of a European put will always be equal to or less than the present value of the exercise price:

European Put Price Bound	$$P_t \leq X \div (1 + RF)^T$$	**(16.6)**

Equation 16.6 makes perfect sense. The most that a put option can be worth is its exercise price (when $S_T = \$0$). But since this cannot be collected on a European put until the expiration date, the maximum current put value will be the present value of X.

Now consider this relationship as shown in panel A of Figure 16.5. Three European put value lines are shown representing the option: (1) at its expiration date, (2) one month prior to expiration, and (3) two months prior to expiration. Note that at high stock prices the put is worth more ''alive'' than ''dead''—it has a positive time value. However, at low stock prices the European put can actually have a negative time value. The option owner would prefer to exercise today but cannot, since the option is European. At stock prices to the left of points 1 and 2, the put owner would prefer to own an American put since it could be *immediately* exercised.

Because early exercise of a put might be desirable, American puts must be worth more than European puts. This is illustrated in panel B of Figure 16-5. Unfortunately, models that identify points such as 1 and 2 in panel A and calculate American put values are very complex. Valuation models of American puts are beyond the scope of this book.

Dividend Adjustments

Listed options are not protected against cash dividends. When such dividends are paid, the value of the underlying stock decreases which, in turn, causes the call

FIGURE 16-5 *The Value of American and European Puts*

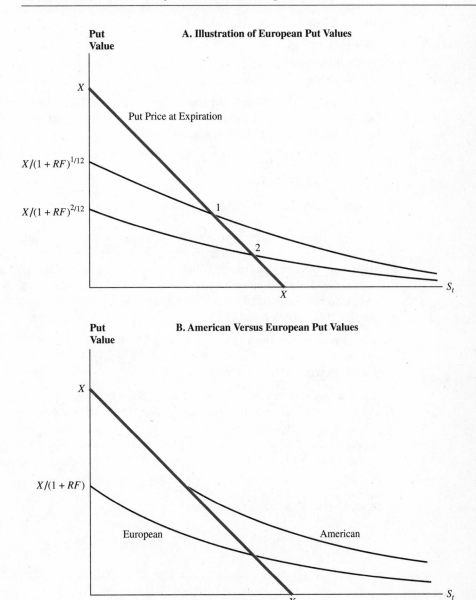

value to fall and the put value to rise. If future dividends are known, there are two ways to incorporate them into current option values. The first treats known discrete future dividends, and the second treats known continuous dividend distributions.

Let D_n represent a known discrete cash dividend to be paid n periods from now. There are N such payments. Define a value of $T = 1$ as representing one year and n as the fraction of one year. In this case, whenever the stock price (S_t) is used in the Black-Scholes model, it should be reduced by the present value of the N discrete dividends.

Discrete Dividend Adjustments to Stock Price

$$S_t = S_t - \sum_{n=1}^{N} [D_n \div e^{(rf)(n)}] \qquad (16.7)$$

For example, assume the current stock price is $68.125 and known dividends of $2.00 will be paid in exactly one and two months from now. If $rf = 10\%$ per year, then the adjusted stock price would be:

$$S_t = \$68.125 - [\$2.00 \div e^{(0.1)(0.08333)}] - [\$2.00 \div e^{(0.1)(0.1666)}]$$

$$= \$64.17$$

Any Black-Scholes calculation that involves S_t would have $64.17 substituted in place of $68.125.

A similar procedure is used when continuous dividends are paid. This is close to what happens with stock indexes. Although individual stocks in the index distribute discrete payments, when they are summed across all securities in the index the dividend stream is better thought of as continuous. If the continuous dividend rate is defined as d, then the following adjusted stock prices are used in the Black-Scholes equation:

Continuous Dividend Adjustment to Stock Price

$$S_t = S_t \div e^{dT} \qquad (16.8)$$

For example, if call options on the S&P 500 expire in one-half year, the spot S&P 500 is now $350 and the spot continuous dividend rate is 4.0% per year, then:

$$S_t = \$350 \div e^{(0.04)(0.5)}$$

$$= \$343.07$$

Calculating Black-Scholes Prices

Assume that you observe the following year-end prices:

Illustrative December 31 Price Quotes

	Options on the S&P 100		Options on IBM Stock		
	Call A	Put A	Call X	Call Y	Put X
Exercise Price	$240	$240	$110	$120	$110
Exercise Date	March	March	April	April	April
Option Price	$13.75	$15.00	$11.25	$6.25	$4.50
Current Price of Underlying Stock	S&P 100 Spot Index = $238.26		IBM Stock Price = $115.625		

Are these values consistent with the Black-Scholes equation?

According to the dividend-adjusted Black-Scholes model, the calls and puts should be a function of six variables:

1. S_t = current stock price

2. X = option exercise price

3. T = time to expiration

4. D_n = cash dividends paid on day n

5. rf = constant, continuously compounded risk-free rate

6. σ = standard deviation of the stock's continuously compounded return

Three of these variables are directly observable: S_t, X, and T. Although T may be expressed in any unit of time you wish, it is commonly thought of as a fraction of one year, since rf and σ are usually expressed as annualized equivalents. The other three variables must be either calculated or estimated.

Cash Dividends. Cash dividends are relatively easy to estimate. In the case of a single stock such as IBM, one can forecast one or more cash dividends during the option's life based on a historical pattern. In many cases, management will have publicly announced any dividends which will be paid during the option's life. For example, assume we can forecast that IBM stock will go ex-dividend in exactly one month and that the cash dividend will be $1.10. Dividends on stock indexes can also be reasonably predicted for short time horizons based on simple extrapolations of the past. Dividends on stock indexes, however, occur in a continuous fashion instead of at identifiable single dates.

Although we could value the index option using Equation 16.8, future examples are easier to understand if we assume discrete dividends for both options. Assume that the dividend yield on the S&P 500 Index (during the stock index option's life) is 0.91%. This suggests that dividends on the March S&P 100 options would be $2.168:

S&P 100 Spot Price	$238.26
Dividend Yield	$\times$ 0.0091
	$2.168166

Risk-Free Interest. The best proxy for the risk-free rate is the return on a T-bill with a maturity equal to the option's expiration.[3] The price at which a T-bill is traded depends on whether one buys at the dealer's *asked discount* or sells at the dealer's *bid discount.* For convenience, we will average the two discounts.

Assume that on December 31, the average of the bid-ask discounts on a T-bill maturing in late March was 5.68%. Thus, the average trade price of one T-bill would be:

---

[3] If the T-bill rate that applies to any intermediate dividend payments is different, then it should be applied to such cash flows.

$$\text{Price} = 100 - 100(0.0568)/(90/360)$$

$$= 98.58\% \text{ of par}$$

The discrete and continuous three-month returns associated with this price are:

$$RF_{\text{discrete}} = (100/98.58) - 1.0$$

$$= 1.44\%$$

$$rf = \ln(1 + RF_{\text{discrete}})$$

$$= \ln(1.0144)$$

$$= 1.43\%$$

This 1.43% three-month continuous rate needs to be expressed as an annualized rate, given that we have chosen to consider a value of $T = 1.0$ to represent one year. This can be done in two ways:

$$rf_{\text{annual}} = \ln[(100/\$98.58)^4]$$

$$= 5.721\%$$

or

$$rf_{\text{annual}} = \ln(100/\$98.58) \times 4$$

$$= 5.721\%$$

The two approaches are mathematically identical.

We will use this 5.721% continuous risk-free rate for all dividends and options in our examples. In practice, however, if discounts vary with different T-bill maturities, then a variety of discount rates should be used.

Standard Deviation. The standard deviation term σ in the Black-Scholes equation represents the standard deviation of continuous compound price returns and is assumed to be constant over the option's life. Since it is not directly observable, it is the toughest variable to estimate. There are two general ways to handle the problem. We illustrate the first using the S&P 100 options and the second using the IBM options.

In the first approach, one looks at the past to estimate what σ might be during the option's life. The choice of the time period chosen will, of course, affect the estimate. If the return-generating process is stationary, statistical theory suggests that the number of return observations should be as large as feasible in order to reduce biases in the results. Unfortunately, there is no reason to believe that the volatility of stocks and stock indexes remains constant over time. The analysis of past standard deviation is, at best, an approximation of what the future holds.

Assume we are examining a sequence of N quarterly returns. For each quarter, we would calculate the continuous compound return as follows:

Discrete Return $$R_t = \frac{\text{Ending Price} + \text{Dividends}}{\text{Beginning Price}} - 1.0 \qquad \textbf{(16.9)}$$

Continuous Return

$$r_t = \ln(1 + R_t) \tag{16.10}$$

It is the standard deviation of the r_t series that we wish to estimate. First, the average continuous return, m, is found. It is then used to find an *unbiased* estimate of σ:

Mean Continuous Return

$$m = \frac{\left(\sum\limits_{t=1}^{N} r_t\right)}{N} \tag{16.11}$$

Unbiased Estimate of σ

$$\sigma = \left[\frac{\sum\limits_{t=1}^{N} (r_t - m)^2}{N - 1}\right]^{1/2} \tag{16.12}$$

Note that $N - 1$ is used in this equation instead of N. In large samples this results in unbiased estimates of σ. Assume that this results in:

$$m = 3.54\% \text{ per quarter}$$

$$\sigma = 8.56\% \text{ per quarter}$$

Since RF and T are being expressed as annualized returns, we need to convert the 8.56% quarterly standard deviation to an annualized equivalent. Although we will not show the mathematical proof here, when one is dealing with a series of continuous returns drawn from a stationary distribution and uncorrelated with each other over time, then:

Multiperiod Standard Deviation of Continuous Returns

$$\sigma \text{ for } T \text{ period} = \sqrt{T} \times \sigma \text{ for 1 period} \tag{16.13}$$

Therefore, the annualized standard deviation based on the historical S&P 500 continuous returns would be 17.12%:

$$\sigma_{\text{annual}} = \sqrt{4} \times 8.56\%$$

$$= 17.12\%$$

Standard deviation estimates obtained in this fashion will depend on the time period chosen and will change over time. The second approach uses the actual call prices to infer the standard deviation that is currently being priced in the call—that is, C_t and all other terms are used to calculate the *implied standard deviation (ISD)* of the call. When this is done for the IBM calls:

$$ISD \text{ for Call } x = 29.55\%$$

$$ISD \text{ for Call } y = 32.85\%$$

Once the *ISD* values are found for each call, a *weighted implied standard deviation* (*WISD*) is calculated. The simplest way to calculate the *WISD* is to treat each *ISD* equally. If there are N calls outstanding and σ_i is the *ISD* for call i, then:

Equally Weighted WISD

$$WISD = \left(\sum_{i=1}^{N} \sigma_i \right) \bigg/ N \qquad \qquad \textbf{(16.14)}$$

Using the two *ISDs* on IBM calls, the *WISD* would be (29.55% + 32.85%)/2 = 31.20%.

A variety of weighting procedures are used in practice. Some underweight options deep in- or out-of-the-money. Others weight by the sensitivity of the option price to changes in the standard deviation. But regardless of the approach taken, *WISD* values appear to be better predictors of actual future price volatility than estimates based on historical price changes.

S&P 100 Call and Put Price Estimates. Using the estimate of σ based on historical data and the dividend-adjusted Black-Scholes model, the theoretical value of the S&P 100 calls would be calculated as follows:

$$T = {}^3/_{12} = 0.25$$

$$S_t = \$238.26 - \frac{\$2.168}{e^{0.05721(0.125)}}$$

$$= \$236.11$$

$$d_1 = \frac{\ln\left(\dfrac{236.11}{240.00}\right) + 0.25(0.05721 + 0.1712^2/2)}{0.1712\sqrt{0.25}}$$

$$= 0.019$$

$$d_2 = d_1 - \sigma\sqrt{t}$$

$$= 0.019 - 0.1712\sqrt{0.25}$$

$$= -0.067$$

$$N(d1) = 0.508 \qquad N(d2) = 0.4721$$

$$C_{SP100} = \$236.11(0.508) - \frac{\$240}{e^{(0.05721)(0.25)}}(0.4721)$$

$$= \$8.25$$

Clearly, one of two things must be true. Either the standard deviation estimate used is too small or the market price of the call is too high.

To value the put we will use the following dividend-adjusted version of put-call parity (again assuming dividends are received halfway through the option's remaining life):[4]

$$\frac{\text{Value of Risk-Free Portfolio Today}}{S_t + P_t - C_t} \qquad \frac{\text{Value of Risk-Free Portfolio at Expiration Date}}{X + (D)e^{rf(T/2)}}$$

implying that:

Dividend Adjusted Put-Call Parity
$$P_t = C_t - S_t + \frac{X + (D)e^{rf(T/2)}}{e^{rfT}} \qquad \textbf{(16.15)}$$

Assume that we wish to know if the put is properly valued *relative* to the call. In this case, we should use the call's actual market price instead of its theoretical price.[5] Substituting in the appropriate values, we find that if the call is $13.75, the put should be selling for $14.23:

$$= \$13.75 - \$238.26 + \frac{\$240 + 2.168e^{0.05721(0.125)}}{e^{0.05721(0.25)}}$$

$$= \$14.23$$

Given that the put's market price is $15, it is *overvalued* relative to the call's price. Later in the chapter we will examine an *index arbitrage* that could be conducted in this case.

IBM Call and Put Price Estimates

Using the *WISD* and the $1.10 dividend to be paid in one month, the theoretical value of the IBM call X should be:

$$T = {}^4/_{12} = {}^1/_3$$

$$S_t = \$115.625 - \frac{\$1.10}{e^{0.0572(1/12)}}$$

$$= \$114.53$$

---

[4] The put-call parity model used here has been adjusted to account for the receipt of the $2.168 dividend halfway through the option's life.

[5] If the theoretical price were used and resulted in a theoretical put price different from the actual market price, we wouldn't know if this was due to an inaccurate theoretical call price or a mispriced put. Because of our uncertainty about the theoretical call price, it is best to ask: Given the call's market price, is the put fairly valued?

$$d_1 = \frac{\ln\left(\frac{114.53}{110}\right) + \frac{1}{3}(0.05721 + 0.312^2/2)}{0.312\sqrt{\frac{1}{3}}}$$

$$= 0.42$$

$$d_2 = d_1 - \sigma\sqrt{T}$$

$$= 0.42 - 0.312\sqrt{\frac{1}{3}}$$

$$= 0.24$$

$$N(d1) = 0.6628 \qquad N(d2) = 0.5948$$

$$C_{\text{IBM}} = \$114.53(0.6628) - \frac{\$110}{e^{(0.05721)(1/3)}}(0.5948)$$

$$= \$11.72$$

Thus the theoretical price is very close to its actual market price of $11.25.

Using call X's actual market price and a dividend-adjusted put-call parity equation, the market price of the put should be $4.64:

$$P_P = P_t = C_t - S_t + \frac{X + D \times e^{(rf \times 3/12)}}{e^{rf \times T}}$$

$$= \$11.25 - \$115.625 + \frac{\$110 + 1.1 \times e^{(0.05721 \times 3/12)}}{e^{(0.05721 \times 1/3)}}$$

$$= \$4.64$$

Like the IBM call, the market price of the put ($4.50) is very close to its theoretical value.

A Formula for $N(d1)$ and $N(d2)$. The values of $N(d1)$ and $N(d2)$ are the value of the cumulative normal-density function between minus infinity and either $d1$ or $d2$. They can be found by reference to a table such as that in Appendix A. There is also an approximate formula that can be easily used on hand-held calculators or personal computers (PCs). The following equation is usually accurate to four decimal places:

$$N(d) = 1 - N^*(d)(a_1 k + a_2 k^2 + a_3 k^3) \text{ for } d \geq 0 \qquad \textbf{(16.16)}$$

$$= 1 - N(d) \qquad\qquad\qquad \text{for } d < 0$$

where:

$$K = 1 \div (1 + 0.33267d)$$

$$a_1 = 0.4361836$$

$$a_2 = -0.1201676$$

$$a_3 = 0.937298$$

$$N*(d) = 1 \div [(\sqrt{2}\pi)\, e^{d2 \div 2}]$$

Put Valuation

The value of a European put option on a stock that pays no dividends can be calculated using a Black-Scholes valuation equation as follows:

European Put Value on a Zero-Dividend Stock
$$P_t = [X \div e^{(rf)(T)}]\, N(-d2) - S_t\, N(-d1) \qquad \textbf{(16.17)}$$

Note that the value of $N(\ )$ is evaluated at the negative of $d1$ and $d2$.

Assume that the underlying stock price on which a put is traded is \$40, the put exercise price is \$40, the expiration date is $1/2$ year, the continuous risk-free rate is 10%, and the standard deviation of stock returns is 20% per year:

$$d1 = \{\ln(40/40) + 0.5\,[0.1 + 0.04 \div 2]\} \div 0.2\,\sqrt{0.5}$$

$$= 0.4243$$

$$d2 = 0.4243 - 0.2\,\sqrt{0.5}$$

$$= 0.2828$$

$$N(-0.4243) = 0.3357\quad N(-0.2828) = 0.3886$$

$$P_t = [\$40 \div e^{(0.1)(0.5)}]\,(0.3886) - \$40\,(0.3357)$$

$$= \$1.36$$

The pricing of American puts is more difficult since they might be exercised early.

The Binomial Model

The Binomial model is used largely to show the logic underlying option valuation, how one security (say, a call) can be replicated by appropriate positions in two other securities (say, the underlying spot and debt). While the model can be computerized and used to value actual options, it is more commonly used for teaching purposes. It is called the binomial model because it assumes that, during the next period of time, the underlying spot price will go to *only of two possible values*.

Although this assumption might seem to be a strange one on which to develop a practical valuation model, it really isn't if we think of a "period of time" as being very short and of the eventual expiration date as being many periods from now. Our discussion of the binomial model proceeds in two stages. In the first, the mechanics of a single-period binomial valuation is discussed. In the second, the single-period approach is extended to multiple periods.

Single-Period Binomial Model. Suppose one-period call options are available on shares of Unique Corporation. Each option is exercisable at $40, and Unique shares are now selling at $50. The firm owes its name to the fact that at the option's expiration date its shares will be selling at one of only two possible prices—either $62.50 or $37.50. What should the call option sell for?

To answer this, remember that if we could form a portfolio of the stock and option that results in a risk-free expiration date outcome, we could value the option. That is, the stock's price and the price of the risk-free portfolio are observable, so we can infer what the call option value must be.

In the put-call parity model, a risk-free position was obtained by trading in 1.0 units of each asset (for example: buy 1.0 stock, buy 1.0 put, write 1.0 call). In the current situation this 1:1 *hedge ratio* is no longer valid.

Note that the stock prices could be either $62.50 or $37.50, a price range of $25. In contrast, the call will be worth either $22.50 ($62.50 − $40) or $0, a price range of $22.50. Since the stock price is more variable, the hedge ratio will be less than 1.0. For our stock position to exactly offset a short position in 1.0 call, we should buy less than 1.0 share. It turns out that the risk-free hedge ratio is simply:

$$\frac{\text{Risk-Free}}{\text{Binomial}} = \frac{\text{End-of-Period Range of Option Prices}}{\text{Expiration Date Range of Stock Prices}} \quad \textbf{(16.18)}$$

In our example, the hedge ratio if 0.90 ($22.50/$25).

The calculations below show that a portfolio of 0.90 shares long and 1.0 call short is indeed risk-free. This portfolio replicates a T-bill having a par value of $33.75:

Using a Call and Stock to Replicate a Risk-Free Position

		Expiration Date	
	Today	$S_T = \$37.50$	$S_T = \$62.50$
Buy 0.90 Stock	−45.00	+$33.75	+$56.25
Write 1.0 Call	+ C	—	−$22.50
	−$45.00 + C	+$33.75	+$33.75

Assuming that the one-period risk-free rate is 10%, the current price of the call should be $14.32:

$$C = 0.90(\$50) - \frac{\$33.75}{1.1}$$

$$= \$14.32$$

Look closely at the equation above and compare it mentally with the put-call parity equation for the value of a call (Equation 16.3). Three things are different. First, the hedge ratio of 0.9 is multiplied by the stock price. Although a hedge ratio is not explicitly shown in the put-call parity equation, a hedge ratio implicitly exists and is equal to 1.0. In this respect, the two models are similar; only the value of the risk-free hedge ratio changes. Next, the second term in the put-call parity model is the discounted present value of X. In the binomial equation above, the second term could be thought of as being the present value of X multiplied by a second type of hedge ratio. In the binomial example above, this second hedge ratio is 0.84375, since $0.84375 \times \$40 = \$33.75$. In the put-call parity approach, this second hedge ratio is implicitly 1.0. Again, the two models are essentially the same, except that they use different values of the hedge ratio. The third difference between them is that no puts are needed in the binomial model. This is the only fundamental difference between the two models.

The fact that a put is not required in the binomial model is due solely to the assumption that only two stock prices would exist at the expiration date. With only two possible outcomes, two assets are sufficient to create a risk-free portfolio. If three or more outcomes are possible, then more than two assets are needed to value the call. In the context of a multiperiod binomial model, however, this problem tends to disappear.

Look again at the binomial call price in our example:

$$C = 0.90(\$50) - \frac{\$33.75}{1.1}$$

What this really says is that you can replicate the outcomes of the call option with a portfolio of stock and cash! In this case, 0.90 shares of stock would initially be purchased and risk-free debt worth $\$33.75/1.1$ would be issued. The fact that such a portfolio is identical to the call is shown below:

Using Stock and Debt to Replicate a Call Position

	Today	$S_T = \$37.50$	$S_T = \$62.50$
		Expiration Date	
Buy 0.90 Stock	−$45.00	+$33.75	+$56.25
Issue Debt	+$30.68	−$33.75	−$33.75
	−$14.32	−$ 0.0	$22.50

Similarly, the stock position could be replicated with a portfolio of the call and T-bills. *Any one asset can be replicated by holding appropriate quantities of the other two.*

Given the logic of the single-period binomial approach, what should a put be worth in our illustration above if it is also exercisable at $40? Since the range of stock prices at the expiration date is $25 and the put's range is $2.50 ($2.50 − 0), the risk-free hedge ratio is 0.10 ($2.50/$25)—that is, 0.1 share of stock should be bought for each 1.0 put bought. This results in the following risk-free portfolio:

<table>
<tr><td colspan="4" align="center">*Using a Put and Stock to Replicate a Risk-Free Position*</td></tr>
<tr><td></td><td></td><td colspan="2" align="center">*Expiration Date*</td></tr>
<tr><td></td><td align="center">*Today*</td><td align="center">$S_T = \$37.50$</td><td align="center">$S_T = \$62.50$</td></tr>
<tr><td>Buy 0.90 Stock</td><td align="center">− $5.00</td><td align="center">+ $3.75</td><td align="center">+ $6.25</td></tr>
<tr><td>Buy 1.0 Put</td><td align="center">− P</td><td align="center">+ $2.50</td><td align="center">—</td></tr>
<tr><td></td><td align="center">− $5.00 − P</td><td align="center">− $6.25</td><td align="center">$6.25</td></tr>
</table>

$$P = \frac{\$6.25}{1.1} - \$5.00$$

$$= \$0.68$$

Mulitperiod Binomial Valuation. The principles underlying the binomial model can be extended to value an option that has an expiration date more than one period from now. Although there is no limit on the number of periods between "now" and the option's expiration, the basic approach can be illustrated with a two-period example.

Consider a stock that is now trading for $50. During any period of time the stock will either increase or decrease by 25%. Thus, over the course of two periods, the stock price will follow one of the branches shown in panel A of Figure 16-6. The assumption of *equal percentage price changes* within a given period and across all time periods is made solely for convenience. The binomial approach does not require it.

Note that this stock is identical to the stock used in the previous example. A call is available on this stock that has an exercise price of $40 and an expiration date at the end of period 2. Again, this is the call used in the single-period example, but it now has two periods to expiration. If the risk-free rate is constant and equal to 10% per period, what should the call trade for today?

Well, let's see what we know about the call. The situation is depicted in panel B of Figure 16-6. We definitely know the expiration date values for each of the three possible expiration date stock prices. For example, if the stock goes up by 25% in both periods, the stock will be worth $78.125 at the end of period 2. Therefore the call will be worth $38.125, given its exercise price of $40. What we don't know (yet) are the potential call values at the end of period 1 or, of course, what the call value should be today. Call values at the end of period 1 will clearly depend on possible expiration date stock prices. These end-of-period-1 call values are denoted as:

C_1^u = price of call given that the stock went up in period 1

C_1^d = price of call given that the stock went down in period 1

FIGURE 16-6 *Prices of Stock and Calls During the Next Two Periods*

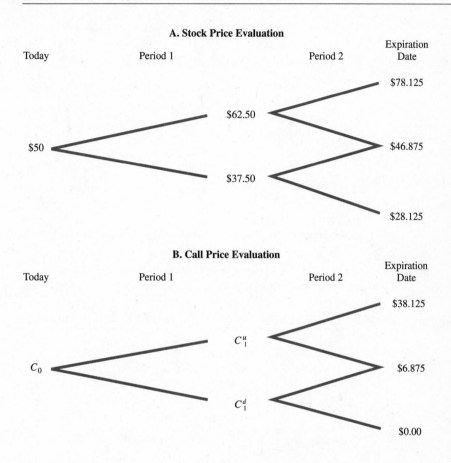

A. Stock Price Evaluation

| Today | Period 1 | Period 2 | Expiration Date |

$50 $62.50 $78.125

$46.875

$37.50 $28.125

B. Call Price Evaluation

| Today | Period 1 | Period 2 | Expiration Date |

C_0 C_1^u $38.125

$6.875

C_1^d $0.00

Can you determine what C_1^u and C_1^d should be? Certainly. In both cases, there is only one period remaining, so the single-period binomial approach can be used. We will calculate C_1^u and C_1^d in a moment. But remember that when this is done, a portfolio of the stock and call is created which replicates a risk-free security. The portfolio is risk-free because a risk-free hedge ratio is calculated as the range of possible end-of-period call prices divided by the range of possible stock prices. This hedge ratio represents the number of stocks to purchase for each 1.0 call written.

If this is true for the last period of the option's life, why shouldn't it be true for all other periods? It is! *In any period, a risk-free portfolio can be created based on that period's end-of-period stock prices and call prices.* Therefore, to calculate what today's option price should be, we value the options when they have only one period remaining in their life and then "roll back" to today.

Results of this process are shown in Table 16-1. Three steps are used. In the first, C_1^u is found using the single-period approach. As shown, the risk-free hedge

TABLE 16-1 *Two-Period Binomial Valuation Example*

1. Find C_1^u:
   a. Hedge ratio = ($38.125 − $6.875)/($78.125 − $46.875)
      = 1.0
   b. Value of call in risk-free replicating portfolio:

	Period 1	End of Period 2	
		$S =$ $46,875	$S =$ $78.125
Buy 1.0 Stock	− $62.50	+ $46.875	+ $78.125
Write 1.0 Call	+ C_1^u	− 6.875	− 38.125
	− $62.50 + C_1^u	$40.00	$40.00

$C_1^u = \$62.50 - \$40/1.1$
$\quad\quad = \$26.136$

2. Find C_1^d:
   a. Hedge ratio = ($6.875 − $0)/($46.874 − $28.125)
      = $0.366^2/_3$
   b. Value of call in risk-free replicating portfolio:

	Period 1	End of Period 2	
		$S =$ $46,875	$S =$ $78.125
Buy $0.366^2/_3$ Stock	− $13.75	+ $10.3125	+ $17.1875
Write 1.0 Call	+ C_1^d	− 0.0	− 6.875
	− $13.75 + C_1^d	$10.3125	$10.3125

$C_1^d = \$13.75 - \$10.3125/1.1$
$\quad\quad = \$4.375$

3. Find C_0:
   a. Hedge ratio = ($26.136 − $4.375)/($62.50 − $37.50)
      = 0.87044
   b. Value of call in risk-free replicating portfolio:

	Period 1	End of Period 1	
		$S = \$37.50$	$S = \$62.50$
Buy 0.87044 Stock	− $43.522	+ $32.6415	+ $54.4025
Write 1.0 Call	+ C_0	− 4.375	− 26.1360
	− $43.522 + C_0	$28.2665	$28.2665

$C_0 = \$43.522 - \$28.2665/1.1$
$\quad\quad = \$17.825$

ratio is 1.0 stock per 1.0 call, and the call price should be $26.136. In the second step, C_1^d is found in a similar manner. Note that the hedge ratio in this case is $0.366^2/_3$ because the call's expiration date values are not as variable as the stock's. Thus, fewer shares are held in order to make the hedged portfolio risk-free.

In the final step, C_0 is calculated. Note that the hedge ratio in this case depends on the *period 1 stock prices and period 1 call prices* found in steps 1 and 2. At the beginning of period 1, the risk-free hedge ratio is 0.87044, and the call should trade for $17.825.

Obviously, when the binomial model is extended to a multiperiod case, the calculations can be tedious. Thus, most people rely on computer programs to solve for proper option prices. But the principle that a risk-free combination of the stock and option can be achieved within each period remains. As the stock's price changes over time, the hedge ratio also changes, so the stock position will have to be rebalanced. But the ability to constantly have a risk-free portfolio means that the option's price can always be solved for.

TRADES BASED ON EXERCISE DATE PAYOFFS

Option payoffs can be evaluated at two points in time: on the expiration date of the option or at the next moment in time. In this section various hedging and speculative strategies that focus on an option's expiration date will be examined. Continuous-time hedging and speculation are discussed in the next section.

Hedging Strategies

To hedge usually means to take a position that offsets some type of risk. When applied to options, this risk is the uncertainty about the value (or rate of return) of the underlying security on which the option is written. A hedge is not conducted in the expectation of abnormal profits. Instead, the hedge simply alters the risk inherent in owning the underlying asset.

Portfolio Insurance. An insured portfolio has a minimum floor value if the underlying asset declines beyond some point but increases in value if the asset increases in value. Based on the put-call parity model an insured portfolio can be created with options in one of two ways:

1. Buy 1.0 put for each 1.0 share owned.
2. Buy T-bills having a par value equal to the desired minimum portfolio value and calls with any remaining funds.

Although the concept of portfolio insurance could be applied to each of the individual stocks in a portfolio, it is usually cheaper to trade in stock index options which are similar to the holdings of the aggregate stock portfolio. Thus, if one owns an equally weighted portfolio of stocks similar to the Dow Jones Industrials, an index option on the American Stock Exchange's Major Market Index might be traded. Similarly, if a value-weighted portfolio of many large capitalization stocks is owned, index options on the S&P 100, S&P 500, or NYSE might be better. Throughout our examples of portfolio insurance, we will use the price quotes shown earlier in the chapter for S&P 100 options. In review:

$$S_t = \$238.26 \qquad C_t = \$13.75 \qquad rf = 5.721\%$$
$$X = \$240.00 \qquad P_t = \$15.00 \qquad T = 3 \text{ months}$$

Portfolio Insurance with Puts. Assume that you have $10 million in cash that you wish to invest in equities similar to those included in the S&P 100 Index. You know that in $1\frac{1}{2}$ months the stocks will pay a 0.91% dividend yield which you intend to reinvest at a risk-free return of 5.721% (continuous annual rate) for another $1\frac{1}{2}$ months. You also believe that the value of the stocks will rise on average during the next three months, but obviously their values could also decline substantially. If you are very sensitive to declines in the value of your portfolio during the next three months, you could either: (1) invest most of the $10 million in risk-free securities such as three-month T-bills with the residual in equities or (2) place the majority of the $10 million in stocks but insure a minimum portfolio value by purchasing puts—in effect, buying insurance.

To guarantee a *fixed* minimum floor, you should purchase 1.0 put for each 1.0 "unit" of the stock index you own. Since S&P 100 puts with a $240 exercise price are *quoted* at $15, the cost of one put is really $1,500. The actual (or spot) S&P 100 Index doesn't really trade in the market, but, if it did, each unit would be quoted at $238.26. Since each put is on 100 units of the index, the cost of buying a unit of the spot S&P 100 Index would be $23,826 (if it actually traded). Since we need a 1:1 relationship between the long put and long stock position, the number of puts and stock would be identical and equal to 394.85:

$$N(\$1,500 + \$23,826) = \$10 \text{ million}$$

$$N = 394.8511411$$

Here N equals the quantity of stock index units and puts purchased. Although fractional shares and puts cannot actually be traded, we will assume that they can be in order to see that a truly insured portfolio is conceptually possible. The initial investment consists of:

$$
\begin{array}{lll}
\text{Stock } (N \times \$23,826) & = & \$\ 9,407,723 \\
\text{Puts }\ \ (N \times \$1,500) & = & \underline{592,277} \\
& & \$10,000,000
\end{array}
$$

The expiration date value of this portfolio for various S&P 100 Index values is shown in Table 16-2. Dividends will be received in $1\frac{1}{2}$ months and be reinvested at the risk-free rate to provide a known value of $86,225 at the expiration date. The long put position will, of course, have a positive value only if the S&P 100 Index is below $X = \$240$ on the expiration date. Note that, if this does occur, the increased put value exactly offsets the decreased stock value. Below $X = \$240$, the put and stock values move in a 1-for-1 inverse relationship (hence the 1.0-for-1.0 hedge ratio!). The minimum value of this insured portfolio is:

Minimum Portfolio Value:

Guaranteed Stock Value	
(394.8511411 units at $24,000/unit)	$9,476,427
Guaranteed Dividend Value	86,225
Total	$9,562,652

TABLE 16-2 *Portfolio Insurance Illustration Long Stock and Long Puts*

S&P 100 Index at Expiration Date (S)	Reinvested Dividends[1]	Put Value[2]	Stock Value[3]	Portfolio Value
$200	$ 86,225	$1,579,404	$ 7,897,023	$ 9,562,652
$220	86,225	789,702	8,686,725	9,562,652
$238.26	86,225	68,704	9,407,723	9,562,652
$240	86,225	0	9,476,427	9,562,652
$260	86,225	0	10,266,130	10,352,355
$280	86,225	0	11,055,832	11,142,056

[1]$(0.91\% \times 9{,}407{,}723)e^{(0.05721 \times 0.125)} = \$86{,}225.$

[2]$((\$240 - S) \times 100) \times 394.8511411$ (or $0.00 if $S > \$240$).

[3]$(S \times \$100) \times 394.8511411.$

Any time the S&P 100 Index closes at less than $240 you are guaranteed that your portfolio's value is $9,562,652. But if the stock index increases in value above $240, your insured portfolio also increases in value.

Naturally, there is a cost—one has to pay $592,277 to buy the puts. This represents almost 6% of the portfolio's initial value. To many investors this would represent a rather sizable outlay to insure the portfolio's minimum value three months from now. And if one were to continuously "roll over" the hedge, there would soon be no portfolio value left to insure! But some investors might be so concerned with short-term losses in the portfolio's worth that they would be willing to pay the cost.

The cost of the portfolio insurance has both direct and opportunity cost components. The direct cost is the $592,277 spent on the puts. The opportunity costs consist of lost dividends and potential lost stock price appreciation on the $592,277. The lost dividend is constant for all spot prices and equal to $5,428:

$$(\$592{,}277 \times 0.91\%)e^{(0.05721 \times 0.125)} = \$5{,}428$$

The opportunity cost due to potential spot price appreciation applies to spot prices greater than $240 and increases directly with spot prices above $240. This price appreciation opportunity cost can be calculated as follows:

Units of Spot That Could Be Purchased at $23,826	
100% Stock Portfolio: $10,000,000/$23,826 =	419.7095610
Insured Portfolio: $ 9,407,723/$23,826 =	−394.8511411
(off slightly because of rounding)	
Increased Spot Units in 100% Stock	24.8584199

Price Appreciation
Opportunity Cost $= (24.8584199 \times 100)(S - \$238.26)$

$\qquad = 2{,}485.84199\,(S - \$238.26)$
$\qquad$ for $s > 240$ at expiration

To illustrate the impact of the put costs, consider the following two expiration date spot prices: $240 and $280.

Value of 100% Stock:	$S_T = \$240$	$S_T = \$280$
Stock: $\$10,000,000 \times S/238.26$	$10,073,029	$11,751,868
Dividends: $(\$10,000,000 \times 0.91\%)e^{(0.05721)(0.125)}$	91,653	91,653
	$10,164,682	$11,843,521
Value of Insured Portfolio:		
From Table 16-2	$-9,562,652$	$-11,142,056$
Excess from 100% Stock	\$ 602,030	\$ 701,465

The components of the portfolio value differences are

	$S_T = \$240$	$S_T = \$280$
Direct Cost of Puts	$592,277	$592,277
Opportunity Costs:		
Dividends	5,428	5,428
Price Appreciation $(24.8584199 \times 100)(S - \$238.26)$	4,325	103,760
	$602,030	$701,465

The expiration date investment values of a 100% stock investment and the insured portfolio are shown in Figure 16-7. The cost of an insured portfolio is visually clear. For the insured portfolio to be worth more than a 100% stock position, the stock must fall by an amount that exceeds the direct cost of the puts ($592,277) and the lost dividends (5,428). This would occur at spot S&P 100 prices of $224.86 or less:

$$\text{Exercise Price} \quad - \quad \frac{\text{Cost Per Unit}}{}$$

$$\$240 \quad - \quad \frac{(\$592,277 + \$5,428)}{(394.8511411 \times 100)} = \$224.86$$

Neglecting dividends, the insured portfolio value is determined by the exercise price of the put options chosen. If a lower exercise price is selected, then the floor value is also lower. (This, of course, results in lower direct and opportunity costs.) Investors have as many minimum portfolio values as there are put exercise prices.

The costs of portfolio insurance can be large, and they increase as spot index value increases above the put's exercise price. During the middle to late 1980s, portfolio insurance was the rage—particularly with corporate pension sponsors facing financial distress. In the 1990's, portfolio insurance is not as widely used.

Portfolio Insurance with Calls. Portfolio insurance can also be obtained by buying calls and T-bills. Again, assume that you have $10 million in cash to invest. In order to directly compare a "call/T-bill" strategy with the "stock/put" results above, assume that you wish to have a minimum portfolio value identical to that in the stock/put example—$9,562,652.

This means that you need to purchase 9.562652 T-bills, each having a par value of $1 million. Since the current price of a three-month T-bill was earlier found to be 98.58% of par, a total of $9,426,861 will have to be spent on the T-bills:

$$0.9858 \times \$9,562,652 = \$9,426,861$$

FIGURE 16-7 *Portfolio Insurance, Long Puts, and Long Stock*

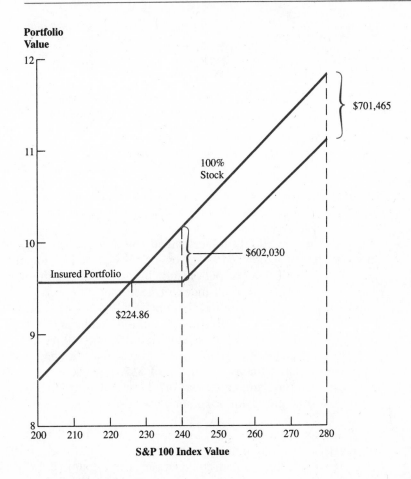

This would leave $573,139 to purchase calls on the S&P 100 Index, or a total of 416.83 calls:

$$\text{Dollar Investment in S\&P 100 Calls} = \$10,000,000 - \$9,426,861$$

$$= \$573,139$$

$$\text{Number of S\&P 100 Calls} = \$573,139/(\$13.75 \times 100)$$

$$= 416.8283636$$

In Table 16-3 the expiration date investment values of this call/T-bill portfolio are shown. The minimum portfolio value is $9,562,652, simply because we bought enough T-bills to achieve this level. And at spot S&P 100 values above $X = \$240$

TABLE 16-3 *Portfolio Insurance Illustration, Long Calls and Long T-Bills*

S&P 100 Index at Expiration Date	T-Bill Value[1]	Call Value[2]	Portfolio Value
$200	$9,562.652	0	$ 9,562,652
$220	$9,562.652	0	$ 9,562,652
$238.26	$9,562,652	0	$ 9,562,652
$240	$9,562,652	0	$ 9,562,652
$260	$9,562,652	$ 833,657	$10,396,308
$280	$9,562,652	$1,667,313	$11,229,964

[1]$9.562651 \times \$1,000,000 = \$9,562,652$.
[2]$416.8283636 \times (S - \$240) \times 100$ if $S > \$240$.

the portfolio increases in value because of investment value payoffs on the long calls. This is a portfolio with a minimum floor value that also participates with increases in the index above $240.

Similar to portfolio insurance gained with a long put-long stock position, this insurance has both direct costs and opportunity costs. But note that in our example the use of calls instead of puts results in lower opportunity costs. For example, Table 16-2 shows that at an index of $280 the total portfolio is worth $11.142 million if puts and the spot index are bought. However, Table 16-3 indicates that the portfolio would be worth $11.229 million if calls and T-bills are bought.

Why? The answer can be traced back to the put-call parity equation examined early in the chapter. At that point, we found that the theoretical put value was $14.23 versus an actual market price of $15. The put was overvalued relative to the call. Therefore, strategies that involve purchasing the calls would dominate equivalent strategies using long put positions.

Portfolio Insurance on Other Assets. Minimum portfolio values can be obtained on any security or commodity on which options are traded. For example, assume you own 10 T-bonds. You could create a minimum future floor value on the portfolio by purchasing 10 puts on T-bonds at the desired exercise price and expiration date. Alternatively, you could emulate the expiration date payoffs of such a portfolio by purchasing calls on T-bonds and T-bills.

Portfolio insurance can even be obtained on assets which do not have traded puts or calls by creating synthetic option positions. This is discussed later in the chapter.

Call Overwriting. A common practice among many investors is a technique known as call overwriting. This is simply writing calls on stocks that are owned in the portfolio. The benefit of call overwriting is that it increases the immediate cash inflow to the portfolio. The cost is that it limits portfolio price appreciation.

Assume you own 100 shares of IBM stock and that the calls are those shown earlier in this chapter:

Stock Price = $115.625	Call Exercise	= $110.00
Call Price = $11.25	Call Expiration Date	= 4 months

TABLE 16-4 *Call Overwriting, Initial and Expiration Date Values*

	At Date of Overwriting Program				
	Stock Value	+$11,562.50			
	Call Premium	+ 1,125.00			
		$12,687.50			

	At Expiration Date (in Four Months)				
	Known Values				
Stock Price	Premium[1]	Dividend[2]	Calls	Stock	Total
$ 90	$1,146.66	$111.58	$ 0	$ 9,000	$10,258.24
$100	$1,146.66	$111.58	$ 0	$10,000	$11,258.24
$110	$1,146.66	$111.58	$ 0	$11,000	$12,258.24
$115.625	$1,146.66	$111.58	−$ 562.5	$11,562.5	$12,258.24
$120	$1,146.66	$111.58	−$1,000	$12,000	$12,258.24
$130	$1,146.66	$111.58	−$2,000	$13,000	$12,258.24
$140	$1,146.66	$111.58	−$3,000	$14,000	$12,258.24

[1]$1,125 × $e^{0.05721 \times 4/12}$ = $1,146.66.

[2](100 × $1.10)$e^{0.05721 \times 3/12}$ = $111.58.

The effects of writing 1.0 call for each 100 shares owned are shown in Table 16-4 and Figure 16-8. Note that the immediate value of the portfolio increases by the amount of the call premium—$1,125. Investing this cash inflow in T-bills also tends to increase the expiration date value of the portfolio. But by writing the calls you have stated your willingness to sell the stock to a call buyer at a fixed price of $110 even if the stock is worth more at the expiration date.

Speculation

Speculative strategies attempt to take advantage of disequilibrium prices (perceived or real). Although a variety of speculations are possible, we focus on index arbitrage.

Index Arbitrage. The term *index arbitrage* is applied to the speculative transaction that can be conducted when the prices of derivative securities are not in line with current prices of a stock index. In a strict arbitrage, there is a zero-risk cash inflow with no required cash outflow.

To illustrate an index arbitrage, we will use the S&P 100 Index calls and puts reviewed earlier. On December 31, the S&P 100 Index closed at $238.26. A call on the index selling for $13.75 was exercisable in three months at $240. An equivalent put sold for $15. Finally, the continuous risk-free interest rate was 5.721% (annualized), and a known dividend of $2.168 was to be paid in $1\frac{1}{2}$ months on the index.

From these data, we concluded that the put is overvalued relative to the call. Since we cannot be sure which of the two options is mispriced (they both could

FIGURE 16-8 *Call Overwriting*

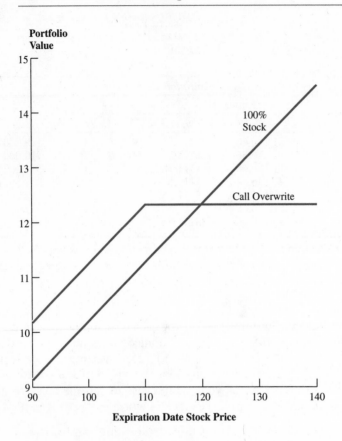

Expiration Date Stock Price

be), we will take offsetting positions in both. Since the put is overvalued relative to the call, the put will be sold and the call purchased.

However, a short put and long call position involves a fair degree of risk. If the stock index falls in value, we lose on the call. If the index rises in value, we win on the put. To offset this risk, a short position in the underlying stock index is taken. We know from put-call parity that if all positions are taken in a 1.0-to-1.0 relationship, the expiration date value of the portfolio is risk-free.

But even though we now have a risk-free portfolio, the transaction is not a pure arbitrage since there is a net cash outflow required at the expiration date. A pure arbitrage will have only one positive and risk-free cash flow. To make the transaction into a true index arbitrage we must buy T-bills today that have an expiration date payoff sufficient to pay the (risk-free) cash required in the put, call, and stock portfolio.

To illustrate such an arbitrage, assume that there are no transaction costs and that we can trade in fractional quantities of the assets. Also, all dividends paid on the short sale of the stock are financed initially with the purchase of T-bills.

In Table 16-5, the results of this transaction are shown for an initial trade in

TABLE 16-5 *Illustration of a Stock Index Arbitrage*

	Today	1½	S&P 100 = $200	S&P 100 = $250
1. Sell 500 Puts	+$ 750,000		− $ 2,000,000	$ 0
2. Buy 500 Calls	− 687,500		0	+ 500,000
Risky Option Portfolio	+$ 62,500		− $ 2,000,000	+$ 500,000
3. Sell 500 Units of S&P 100	+ 11,913,000	− $108,400	− $10,000,000	− $12,500,000
	+$11,975,500	− $108,400	− $12,000,000	− $12,000,000
4. Buy T-Bills				
a. Finance Dividends	− 107,627	+ $108,400		
b. Finance $12 Million	− 11,829,591		+ $12,000,000	+ $12,000,000
Net	+$ 38,282	$ 0	$ 0	$ 0

500 puts and calls. Two possible expiration date values are used for the S&P 100 Index ($200 and $250) in order to show that outcomes from the arbitrage are, in fact, insensitive to eventual index values. First, 500 puts are sold and 500 calls bought to take advantage of the price disequilibrium:

1. Sell 500 puts:

Net Inflow = (500 × 100) × $15 = +$750,000
Expiration Date Value = − (500 × 100) × ($240 − $200) = − $2,000,000

2. Buy 500 calls:

Net Outflow = (500 × 100) × $13.75 = $687,500
Expiration Date Value = (500 × 100) × ($250 − $240) = +$500,000

Stocks are then added in order to make the portfolio risk-free. Note that this will be a short position in stocks requiring the payment of a cash dividend in 1½ months.

3. Sell 500 units of S&P 100 Index:

Net Inflow = (500 × 100) × $238.26 = $11,913,000
Dividend = (500 × 100) × $2.168 = $108,400
Expiration Date Value:
= − (500 × 100) × $200 = − $10,000,000
= − (500 × 100) × $250 = − $12,500,000

Note that all cash flows are known today. The transaction provides an immediate cash inflow of $11,975,500. In return, $108,400 must be paid in 1½ months and $12,000,000 at the option's expiration. This is identical to obtaining a risk-free loan!

To make it a pure arbitrage, T-bills are used to finance all future cash outflows:

4. a. To finance dividends on the short stock position:

$$\$108,400/e^{(0.05721 \times 0.125)} = \$107,627$$

b. To finance expiration date payment:

$$\$12,000,000/e^{(0.05721 \times 0.25)} = \$11,829,591$$

The arbitrage profit from this transaction is $38,282—received today!

Some comments about such arbitrages are necessary. First, the profit is large simply because the trades were large; index arbitrages are usually conducted only by large institutions. Second, transaction costs and the inability to trade in fractional units of the assets will reduce the profit and increase risk exposure. However, many large institutions pay very small commissions and are able to trade in quantities large enough to minimize risk. In addition, all trades must be executed instantaneously at known asset prices. If the price of an asset changes by the time that the trade is expected, all arbitrage profits can disappear. That is why the NYSE's *designated order turnaround* (DOT) system is critical to successful index arbitrage.

Note that large positions in the stock index must be taken—either long or short. But since the index itself is not traded, how is this done? There are three things that could be done. First, one could actually buy or sell all shares in the index in appropriate quantities such that the stock position mirrors the index. This is most easily done with options on the Major Market Index since it consists of only 20 stocks that are equally weighted. Second, one could create a "basket" of stocks that closely track the index. Finally, one could trade in an index equivalent in the financial futures market.

TRADES BASED ON CONTINUOUS TIME

In the previous section, we reviewed a variety of hedging and speculative strategies based on an option's value at its expiration date. Such strategies are usually based on applications of the put-call parity model. In this section, we use the Black-Scholes model to illustrate continuous-time option strategies. A continuous-time strategy is one that is constantly rebalanced so that the stock/option position has the desired short-term return payoffs—usually risk-free. In practice, continuous rebalancing can be quite costly, so investors and speculators will rebalance daily or weekly.

Hedging Strategies

Continuous-time option strategies can be used to alter the risk exposure of a portfolio. Before examples of such strategies are shown, however, we need to review the importance of the N_{d1} term in the Black-Scholes model and see how the (instantaneous) beta of a call can be calculated.

Importance of $N(d1)$. Figure 16-9 plots Black-Scholes call premiums versus stock prices for options exercisable at $50 when the standard deviation of stock returns is 0.5, the risk-free rate is 10%, and three exercise dates are assumed (three, six,

FIGURE 16-9 *Hedging and Option Prices*

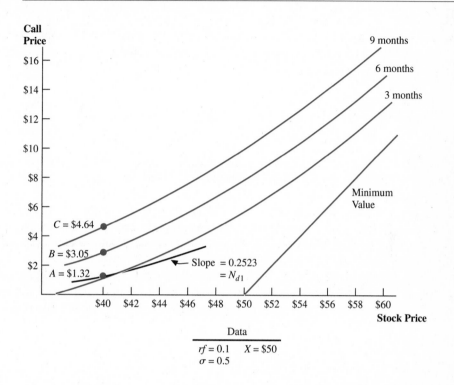

Data

$rf = 0.1$ $X = \$50$
$\sigma = 0.5$

and nine months). As we saw earlier, call premiums increase with the stock's price and expiration date. Assuming that the stock is currently selling at $40, the options would be worth $1.32, $3.05, and $4.64, respectively, as illustrated by points A, B, and C in the figure.

Also shown in Figure 16-9 is a line drawn tangent to point A. The slope of this line is important since it represents the change in the value of the call premium for a very small change in the stock's price. The slope at A is 0.2523, meaning that if the stock price changes from $40 by approximately $0.01, the option premium will move in the same direction by an amount equal to $0.002523.

Another way to view point A is to say that if one share of the stock is bought and one call option is sold, only 74.77% (100% − 25.23%) of the future price variability remains. Alternatively, we could sell 3.96 options (1 ÷ 0.2523) for each share bought and eliminate *all* price uncertainty. The change in the option's price for a small change in the stock's price is known as the *hedge ratio. The hedge ratio indicates the number of shares that should be bought for each call sold in order to eliminate price risk. N(d1) is this hedge ratio.* In the same manner, 1.0 ÷ hedge ratio indicates the number of options that should be sold for each share bought.

The hedge ratio is easily calculated by using the Black-Scholes option model value of $N(d1)$. $N(d1)$ is the hedge ratio that will protect against small price changes. For example, assume you buy one share of the stock in Figure 16-9 for $40 and sell 3.96 of the A options at $1.32 per option. As a result, your investment is $34.77 ($40 − 3.96 × $1.32). If the stock's price immediately falls to $39.50, the option would now sell for approximately $1.19. Your equity investment remains constant:

Value of Stock	$39.50
Value of 3.96 Calls	(4.73) (3.96 × $1.19)
Equity Value	$34.77

While the stock decreased $0.50, you gained $0.50 through reduced call values.

These hedges are appropriate, however, for only short time intervals and small changes in stock prices. Any time $N(d1)$ changes, the hedge ratio should also be revised. The hedge ratio will change with changes in the stock price, risk-free rate, stock return price variance, and time to expiration. Ideally, hedges should be continuously changed. As a practical matter, instantaneous hedges are impossible.

Risk-free positions can also be accomplished using only the options themselves. Assume that a stock has two calls available that differ in either expiration date or striking price. If $N(d1)$ for the first option is 0.4, then 2.5 of this option should be sold for each share bought to create a riskless hedge. If $N(d1)$ for the second option is 0.5, then 2.0 of this option would be sold for each share bought. Alternatively, you could buy 1.25 (0.5/0.4) of the first option for each 1.0 of the second option sold. Or 0.8 of the second should be bought (0.4/0.5) for each 1.0 of the first sold. Options can be combined to yield riskless hedges. But again, such hedges are riskless only for an instant in time.

Call Betas. Continuous time hedges are based on the beta of the underlying portfolio and the beta of the call option. Analytically, if β_c refers to the call option beta and β_s refers to stock beta, then:

Beta of a Call
$$\beta_c = N(d1) \frac{S_t}{C_t} \beta_s \qquad (16.19)$$

The economic intuition underlying the beta of a call is relatively straightforward. For a cost of C, you control an asset that is worth S—that is, you have "leveraged up" your investment by effectively borrowing $(S - C)$. Both your investment of C and your borrowing of $(S - C)$ are invested in the stock. Given that the stock has a beta of β_s, the beta of your leveraged position is equal to the "stock price divided by the call price" times the beta of the stock. But the call's price does not move dollar-for-dollar with the stock. Instead, for each $1 change in the stock price the call price changes by $N(d1)$ dollars (approximately). To reflect this fact, we multiply the leveraged beta position by $N(d1)$.

Adjusting a Portfolio's Systematic Risk. Assume that you own $10 million of stock that is very similar to the S&P 100 Index. Since your spot stock portfolio

FIGURE 16-10 *Dynamic Replication of Portfolio Insurance*

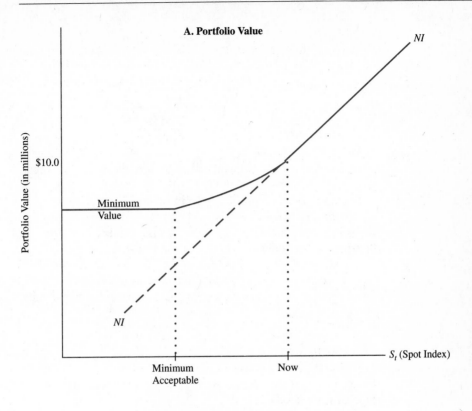

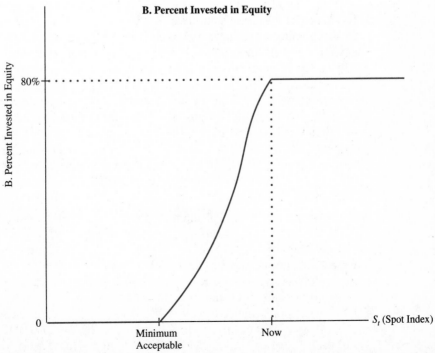

tinues to fall. If the stock index falls to a minimum acceptable index or below, all stock should have been sold and reinvested in T-bills.

The results of such a strategy are shown by the solid lines in each panel.

This dynamic replication of owning put options will work only if one is able to trade at stock index prices specified in the strategy. For example, if the strategy requires that 5% of the equity position be sold when the stock index is down by 5 points to $450, then one must be able to sell when the stock index is $450. The strategy clearly would not work if—when the trade is executed—the spot index is down by another 50 points.

Dynamic replication of portfolio insurance in stock portfolios was the rage in the years just before the 1987 Market Crash. Unfortunately, the strategy did not work in a large number of cases because stock index prices fell so precipitously that insurance trades in equities could not be accomplished at the prices required by the strategy (if at all). Although dynamic replication of portfolio insurance has been used much less actively on common stocks since 1987, the procedure has been expanded to other asset classes such as debt instruments and currencies.

Speculative Strategies

Continuous-time models can also be used in speculative strategies to take advantage of mispriced options.

Incorrect ISD Values. The price of a call will depend on the standard deviation of the underlying stock returns that market participants access. This standard deviation should be identical for calls on a given stock with a given expiration date. If the implied standard deviation is different for two call options that differ only in exercise prices, a speculative profit is possible.

For example, consider the call options on IBM stock examined earlier in the chapter. The standard deviations implied by the market prices of two IBM calls and their $N(d1)$ values were:

IBM Call Option	Implied Std. Dev.	$N(d1)$
Call X	29.55%	0.6628
Call Y	32.85%	0.4761

The options had identical exercise dates and should, therefore, have identical implied standard deviations.

Call Y, however, had a larger implied standard deviation than call X. Although we cannot say which, if either, implied standard deviation is correct, we can say that call Y is overvalued relative to call X since call Y has the greater implied standard deviation. To take advantage of this, call Y should be sold and call X purchased. Given their respective $N(d1)$ values, a risk-free position would consist of 1.5088 (1.0/0.6628) of call X bought per 2.1004 (1.0/0.4751) of call Y sold. For each 1.0 of call X bought, 1.3920 of call Y should be sold.

SUMMARY

The existence of exchange-traded options has multiplied the ways in which investors can alter portfolio risk and engage in speculative strategies. Perhaps the most useful aspect of trading in options is their use in adjusting the systematic (beta) risk of a portfolio. Underlying positions in stocks, bonds, T-bills, and so forth, need not be disturbed. Instead, option positions are taken on top of the spot security positions to temporarily increase or decrease the aggregate portfolio risk. This explains the trading dominance of stock index options such as those on the S&P 100.

Trading in stock index options has caused the spot stock market, T-bill market, and option market to become more interrelated. If prices between the markets are not in equilibrium, large speculative profits can be obtained through index arbitrage.

The key to valuing options is to recognize that they can be replicated by appropriate positions in the underlying spot asset and a risk-free security. The ability to create such synthetic options is the basis of both put-call parity and the Black-Scholes option pricing model.

REVIEW PROBLEM

Consider the following options on a single stock:

	Calls		Put C
	A	B	
Months to Expiration	3	9	3
Continuous Yearly rf	10.00%	10.00%	10.00%
Discrete Yearly RF	10.52%	10.52%	10.52%
Std. Dev. Stock Returns	40%	40%	40%
Exercise Price	$55	$55	$55
Option Price	$2.56	—	$6.20
Stock Price	$50	$50	$50
Cash Dividend	$0	$0	$0

a. Why should call B sell for more than call A?
b. Is the put-call parity model working for options A and C?
c. How would you trade call A, the stock, and T-bills in order to replicate the expiration date outcomes of put C?
d. Calculate the Black-Scholes values of call A and call B.
e. Interpret what $N(d1)$ and $N(d2)$ mean.

Solution

a. Call B has the longer time to expiration. There is a greater chance that the call will be exercised at a positive value.

b. $C_t - P_t = S_t - X/(1 + RF)^T$ in theory

$$= \$50 - \$55/(1.1052^{0.25}) = -\$3.64$$

Actual difference $= \$2.56 - \$6.20 = -\$3.64$

Therefore, put-call parity is working.

c. Buy 1.0 call A, sell short 1.0 stock, buy debt now worth $\$55/(1.1052^{0.25})$.

d. *Call A Data*

$$d_1 = \frac{\ln\left(\frac{50}{55}\right) + 0.25\left(0.10 + \frac{0.4^2}{2}\right)}{0.4\sqrt{0.25}} = -0.25$$

$$d_2 = \frac{\ln\left(\frac{50}{55}\right) + 0.25\left(0.10 + \frac{0.4^2}{2}\right)}{0.4\sqrt{0.25}} = -0.45$$

$N(d1) = 0.5 - 0.0987 = 0.4013$

$N(d2) = 0.5 - 0.1736 = 0.3264$

$$C = \$50(0.4013) - \frac{\$55}{e^{(0.1)(0.25)}}(0.3264)$$

$$= \$2.56$$

Call B Data

$$d_1 = \frac{\ln\left(\frac{50}{55}\right) + 0.75\left(0.1 + \frac{0.4^2}{2}\right)}{0.4\sqrt{0.75}} = -0.11$$

$$d_2 = d_1 - \sigma\sqrt{T} = -0.23$$

$N(d1) = 0.5 + 0.0438 = 0.5438$

$N(d2) = 0.5 - 0.091 = 0.409$

$$C_t = \$50(0.5438) - \frac{\$55}{e^{(0.1)(0.75)}}(0.409)$$

$$= \$6.32$$

e. To replicate the instantaneous payoffs of the call, one should buy $N(d1)$ shares and issue $N(d2)$ units of debt that is now worth $X/e^{rf \times T}$.

QUESTIONS AND PROBLEMS

1. A call and put exist on the same stock. Each is exercisable at $50. They trade now for:

$$S_t = 45 \qquad C_t = \$8 \qquad P_t = \$1$$

Calculate the expiration date investment value, and net profit from:
  a. Buy 1.0 call
  b. Write 1.0 call
  c. Buy 1.0 put
  d. Write 1.0 put
Do this for expiration date stock prices of $40, $45, $50, $55, and $60.

2. What economic reasons have been offered for the existence of options?
3. Assume that call options on Xerox are to expire today. They have an exercise price of $70, the stock is trading at $65, and the option is selling for $8. What is the arbitrage?
4. Consider the following put and call options:

	Call	Put
Market Price	$ 7	$ 2
Exercise Price	$70	$70
Exercise Date	4 mo.	4 mo.
Risk-Free Rate = 10% annualized (discrete compound)		
Stock Price = $75		

  a. Is put-call parity working?
  b. What is the arbitrage based on put-call parity?
5. You are given the following information:

$$S_t = \$74 \qquad P_t = \$5.09 \qquad X = \$65$$

$$rf = 10\% \qquad \text{Expiration} = 1 \text{ year}$$

Assume that the stock pays no dividends and that the risk-free rate will remain constant.
  a. What should be the price of a call also exercisable at $65 with an expiration date of one year?
  b. How could you develop a portfolio of these securities that will have a payoff in one year that is identical to being long the stock? Short the stock? (You may not buy or sell the stock.)
  c. How could you develop a portfolio of these securities that will have a payoff in one year that is identical to writing one put? (Again, you may not trade the put.)
  d. Underlying these calculations is the economic definition of what a call and a put really are. What does a call consist of? What does a put consist of?
6. You wish to purchase a call option on a local warehouse having an expiration date of one year and an exercise price of $1 million. The warehouse owner will not sell you such an option but is willing to sell the warehouse for $1.1 million. The current risk-free interest rate is 9% per year, and insurance on a one-year, $1 million loan would be $10,000. How could you create a synthetic call option on the warehouse?
7. An analysis of Hylough Corporation suggests that in one year the price of its common shares will be either $80 or $50. They currently sell for $60. An option that expires in one year with an exercise price of $60 can be bought for $10.23. What is the one-year risk-free rate?
8. You are considering the sale of a call option with an exercise price of $100 and one year to expiration. The underlying stock pays no dividends, its current price is $100,

CFA

and you believe it has a 50% chance of increasing to $120 and a 50% chance of decreasing to $80. The risk-free rate of interest is 10%.

a. Describe the specific steps involved in applying the binomial option pricing model to calculate the call option's value.

b. Compare the binomial option pricing model to the Black-Scholes option pricing model.

9. The value of a stock index is now $100. At the end of any future period the stock index will be either 20% greater than its beginning price or 16²/₃% lower. A European put is available on the stock index. It is exercisable at $100 and has an expiration date at the end of three periods from now—that is, after the third stock return.

a. Trace out the price pattern of the stock index for three periods.

b. What are the potential expiration date values of the put?

c. Calculate the intermediate values of the put as what the put should be worth today.

d. Assume you buy 1.0 put and 1.0 stock. Trace through the value of this portfolio over future periods.

10. Consider the information provided below:

Options on ABC Stock

	Call Options				*Put Option*
	A	*B*	*C*	*D*	*E*
Current Market of:					
Option	$16.12	$10.62	$ 8.31	$10.50	$ 7.25
Stock	$80	$80	$80	$80	$80
Option Information:					
Exercise Price	$70	$80	$90	$90	$70
Months to Expiration	3	3	3	6	3
Market Information:					
Continuous Yearly *rf*	12%	12%	12%	12%	12%
Expected Cash Dividends	0	0	0	0	0
Std. Dev. of Stock Returns	60%	60%	60%	60%	60%

a. Calculate the Black-Scholes value of each option.

b. Note that call A and put E have identical terms. Use the put-call parity model to value the put, given the Black-Scholes value of call A. Comment on why the put's value is the same as found in part a.

c. Interpret what the terms $N(d1)$ and $N(d2)$ mean for call A and put E.

11. What are the underlying assumptions of the Black-Scholes model, and why are they needed?

12. Assume that you are given the following information on a stock and its calls:

$$S_t = \$65$$
$$X = \$60$$
$$rf = 12\% \text{ (continuous annual)}$$
$$\sigma = 40\% \text{ (annual)}$$

$$\text{Maturity} = 6 \text{ months}$$

You also know with certainty that the stock will pay a $1 dividend in exactly three months, followed by a $1 dividend just before the option's expiration date in six months.

   a. What should be the price of this call?

   b. Without performing any calculations, if you had neglected to consider the dividend payments, would you have estimated the price to be the same, greater, or less than in part a? Why?

13. All other things being equal, a $1 increase in a call option's exercise price will lead to a $1 decrease in the call option's value. True or false? Why?

14. You have been given the following series of monthly returns on a stock. The returns are discrete returns. Calculate the ex post estimate of the Black-Scholes standard deviation.

1	2	3	4	5	6	7	8	9	10	11	12
5%	15	2	−8	1	−4	20	5	−8	10	8	0

15. You have calculated the implied standard deviations on two call options. They differ only in exercise price. (They are on the same stock and have identical expiration dates.) What is the instantaneous risk-free speculation that is possible?

	Call A	Call B
ISD	40%	50%
$N(d1)$	0.8	0.6

16. Assume that a dividend of D dollars will be paid on the expiration date of a put and call option. Derive the put-call parity model for this case.

17. The market value of a portfolio which you manage is $30 million. You have been asked to use either puts or calls in a portfolio insurance program. Since the portfolio is similar to the S&P 100 Index, you intend to use S&P 100 Index options. Relevant data are:

Current Spot Value of S&P 100	= $300
Current (discrete) Risk-Free Rate	10% per year
Dividend Yield on S&P 100	2% per year
(Assume they are paid in exactly six months from now)	

Option Information:	Call	Put
Current Price	$35	$5
Exercise Price	$280	$280
Expiration Date	6 months	6 months
Option Type	Euro	Euro

   a. Is put-call parity working?

   b. Illustrate the expiration date values of an insured portfolio using the puts. Do this for S&P 100 values of $200, $250, $300, and $350.

   c. Use the calls together with T-bills to create an insured portfolio which has the same minimum floor value as in part b. Calculate its values for S&P 100 values of $200, $250, $300, and $350. Compare the results with those obtained for part b and explain why they are different.

   d. Using the puts, at what S&P 100 Index value are you better off with the insured portfolio than with a 100% stock position?

18. Use the data from question 17 to illustrate the outcomes of an index arbitrage. Trade in stock worth $10 million.

19. What are the conditions under which an American call would be exercised early?

20. A local broker has advised the trustees of a charitable organization to sell calls on stocks held in the organization's portfolio in order to increase the portfolio's cash yield. Comment.

21. How does the use of options in a portfolio affect the portfolio's stock/bond mix?

22. EverSafe Insurance Company holds 10,000 shares of Exxon at a cost of $80 per share in the pension account of one of its clients. As portfolio manager for the account you expect the shares to rise gradually over the next six to nine months. The following Exxon call options are quoted on the CBOE:

	Expiration		
Exercise Price	3 months	6 months	9 months
70	12	13	$14^1/_2$
80	$2^1/_2$	$6^1/_2$	8
90	NA	$2^1/_2$	$4^1/_2$

The current price of Exxon shares is 81. State the rationale for and implications of writing call options that expire in nine months with an exercise price of $80.

23. Explain the economic intuition underlying what the beta of a call is:

$$beta_c = beta_s \times (S_t/C_t) \times N(d1)$$

24. You are the manager of a $100 million portfolio which is now invested as follows: $50 million in stock similar to the S&P 100 and $50 million in T-bills. Relevant data on S&P 100 calls include:

$$
\begin{aligned}
\text{Price of S\&P 100 Spot Index} &= \$250 \\
\text{Price of S\&P 100 Call} &= \$15 \\
N(d1) \text{ of Call} &= 0.75 \\
\text{Beta of S\&P 100 Spot Index} &= 1.0
\end{aligned}
$$

How many calls would you trade to change the portfolio's instantaneous beta to:
a. 0.0
b. 1.0
c. 0.6

25. An at-the-money protective put position (comprised of owning the stock and the put):
a. protects against loss at any stock price below the strike price of the put.
b. has limited profit potential when the stock price rises.
c. returns any increase in the stock's value, dollar for dollar, less the cost of the put.
d. provides a pattern of returns similar to a stop-loss order at the current stock price.

26. In the Black-Scholes option valuation formula, an increase in a stock's volatility:
a. increases the associated call option value.
b. decreases the associated put option value.
c. increases or decreases the option value, depending on the level of interest rates.
d. does not change either the put or call option value because put-call parity holds.

27. An American option is more valuable than a European option on the same dividend paying stock with the same terms because the:
a. European option contract is not adjusted for stock splits and stock dividends.
b. American option can be exercised from date of purchase until expiration, but the European option can be exercised only at expiration.
c. European option does not conform to the Black-Scholes model and is often mispriced.

d. American options are traded on U.S. exchanges, which offer much more volume and liquidity.

CFA

28. You have decided to buy protective put options to protect the U.S. stock holdings of one of GAC's portfolios from a potential price decline over the next three months. You have researched the stock index options available in the United States and have assembled the following information:

Stock Index Option	Current Index Value	Underlying Value of One Put	Strike Price of Put	Put Premium	Average Daily Trading Volume of Puts
S&P 100	365.00	$100 times index	365	$10.25	10,000
S&P 500	390.00	$100 times index	390	$11.00	4,000
NYSE	215.00	$100 times index	215	$ 6.25	1,000

(For each stock index option, the total cost of one put is the put premium times 100.)

	Beta vs. S&P 500	Correlation with Portfolio
Portfolio	1.05	1.00
S&P 100	0.95	0.86
S&P 500	1.00	0.95
NYSE	1.03	0.91

a. Using all relevant data from the above table, **calculate** for *each* stock index option *both* the number and cost of puts required to protect a $7,761,700 diversified equity portfolio from loss. **Show** all calculations.

b. **Recommend** and **justify** which stock index option to use to hedge the portfolio, including reference to *two* relevant factors other than cost.

You know that it is very unlikely that the current stock index values will be exactly the same as the put strike prices at the time you make your investment decision.

c. **Explain** the importance of the relationship between the strike price of the puts and the current index values as it affects your investment decision.

d. **Explain** how an option pricing model may help you make an investment decision in this situation.

REFERENCES

Recent texts devoted to financial derivatives are shown below. They each have extended references.

CHANCE, DON M., *An Introduction to Options and Futures*. Orlando, FL: Dryden Press, 1989.

HULL, JOHN, *Options, Futures and other Derivative Securities*. Englewood Cliffs, NJ: Prentice-Hall, 1989.

MARSHALL, JOHN F., *Futures and Option Contracting: Theory and Practice*. Cincinnati, OH: Southwestern Publishing Co., 1989.

STOLL, HANS R., and ROBERT E. WHALEY, *Futures and Options: Theory and Applications*. Cincinnati, OH: Southwestern Publishing Co., 1993.

The security exchanges on which options are traded have many publications that provide up-to-date information on the contracts traded on their respective exchanges. Most of this literature provides an introduction to how the instruments can be used for hedging purposes. You should write to the following addresses and request a listing of the publications currently available:

American Stock Exchange, Options Marketing Department, 86 Trinity Place, New York, NY 10006.

Chicago Board Options Exchange, LaSalle at Van Buren, Chicago IL 60605.

Chicago Mercantile Exchange, 30 South Wacker Drive, Chicago, IL 60606.

New York Stock Exchange, Options and Index Products, 11 Wall Street, New York, NY 10005.

The Options Clearing Corporation, 440 South LaSalle Street, Suite 908, Chicago, IL 60605.

Pacific Stock Exchange, Options Marketing, 115 Sansome Street, 7th Floor, San Francisco, CA 94104.

Philadelphia Stock Exchange, 1900 Market Street, Philadelphia, PA 19103.

The original article in which the Black-Scholes model was developed is:

BLACK, FISCHER, and MYRON SCHOLES, ''The Valuation of Option Contracts and a Test of Market Efficiency,'' *Journal of Finance*, May 1972.

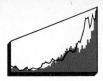

International Investing

Any serious investment strategy should be viewed from a global perspective. In the 1990s, limiting portfolio investments to securities of the United States is akin to limiting portfolio investments in the 1890s to securities of, say, the state of Pennsylvania. It excludes many potentially profitable markets and limits portfolio diversification.

The value of non-U.S. financial markets has always represented a large fraction of world financial assets, as shown in Table 17-1. In 1960, the value of U.S. financial assets was slightly greater than 50% of world financial assets. By the end of 1991, U.S. financial assets were 44% of the world total. If the costs of international diversification are not too large, then a portfolio should probably be globally diversified.

International diversification is not without cost, however. Brokerage fees in most countries are larger than in the United States, security markets are less liquid, and financial data on non-U.S. companies is difficult to obtain. Perhaps the greatest deterrent to international investment is a lack of knowledge—specifically, about exchange rate risks.

Each of these costs has declined substantially during the past 15 years and will continue to decline as global markets become more competitive. Also, as investors continue to learn about the advantages of portfolio diversification and how to deal with exchange-rate risk, the fraction of international securities held in portfolios will grow.

We begin this chapter with a look at how international diversification can reduce portfolio risk. In doing so, we will see that international investing has an element of risk that is not present in domestic investment: exchange rate risk. Because of its importance, we examine various exchange rate theories such as purchasing power parity and interest rate parity. These theories are designed to show why exchange rates change and how exchange rate risk can conceptually be reduced by trading in derivative securities. In the last part of the chapter, we turn to various practical issues of investing internationally.

WHY INVEST GLOBALLY?

Investment professionals place different meanings on the terms *international investment* and *global investment*. International investment refers to investing in

TABLE 17-1 *Market Values of World Financial Markets (in $ Billions)*

Market	1960	1970	1980	1991
Money Market Securities				
U.S.	45.9	128.0	372.8	1,805.2
Non-U.S.	13.9	23.1	90.7	530.0
Total	59.8	151.1	463.5	2,335.2
Fixed Income Securities				
U.S.	230.3	322.8	799.1	4,435.3
Non-U.S.	396.9	390.4	1,906.5	6,650.0
Total	627.2	713.2	2,705.6	11,085.3
Equity Securities				
U.S.	345.0	700.9	1,380.6	4,325.5
Non-U.S.	180.2	309.2	1,049.3	6,049.0
Total	525.2	1,010.1	2,429.9	10,374.5
Total Financial Markets				
U.S.	621.2	1,151.7	2,552.5	10,566.0
Non-U.S.	591.0	722.7	3,046.5	13,229.0
Total	1,212.2	1,874.4	5,599.0	23.795.0

securities beyond the borders of one's own country. Global investment refers to investing in securities throughout the world. The distinction is important because some investment managers consider themselves to be global managers whereas others are solely international managers. Buying a global portfolio is different from buying an international portfolio.

The case for global investment is easy to make. Apart from the costs of doing so, global investment reduces portfolio risk by expanding one's diversification opportunities.

If one takes the standard capital asset pricing model (CAPM) to its limit, the single optimal portfolio of risky assets that all investors should hold consists of all risky assets in the world. This, of course, is absurd. Political restrictions placed on capital flows into and out of many countries, the lack of liquid security markets in all but the most developed countries, substantial differences in the availability of information, differing tax rates, and so forth, all severely damage the CAPM in a world context.

Nonetheless, an examination of the total value of marketable assets within the more developed countries suggests that the principle of diversification may still be valid. Consider Figure 17-1, which shows the composition of world financial markets at the end of 1991. Although the figure is a pie chart, think of it as representing the globe. If one were to restrict portfolio holdings—say, to only U.S. markets—then economic shocks that transfer U.S. wealth to other regions of the world would represent a risk that could be eliminated by international diversification.

This is not simply theory; it works in practice. Recall from Chapter 6 that there are two basic ways of diversifying: naive diversification and efficient diversifi-

FIGURE 17-1 *World Financial Assets (1991)*

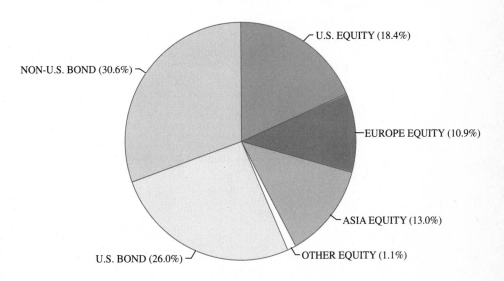

U.S. EQUITY (18.4%)

NON-U.S. BOND (30.6%)

EUROPE EQUITY (10.9%)

ASIA EQUITY (13.0%)

U.S. BOND (26.0%)

OTHER EQUITY (1.1%)

cation. Naive diversification is undertaken when you are unable to differentiate between the expected returns, return standard deviations, and return correlations of differing securities. In such cases, an equal percentage investment is made in any securities held. Efficient diversification is used when you can differentiate between expected returns, and so forth. Both approaches show that international diversification is valuable in reducing portfolio risk.

One of the classic studies examining the potential for international diversification was performed by Solnik in the mid-1970s. Solnik examined the results of the naive diversification strategy that would result if a U.S. investor had randomly selected securities from two different groups. The first group consisted solely of U.S. stocks. The second group consisted of both U.S. and European stocks. Stock returns were calculated weekly for the period 1966–1971.

Results are shown in Figure 17-2. As we saw in Chapter 6, naive diversification does reduce portfolio risk up to some limit that we have referred to as nondiversifiable market risk. This happens whether one is dealing with returns on U.S. domestic stocks or returns on both U.S. and international securities. The important implication of Figure 17-2 is that the nondiversifiable risk of internationally diversified portfolios was considerably lower than that of portfolios restricted to U.S. securities. Solnik's results have been replicated in numerous other studies.

The composition of an efficiently diversified portfolio depends, of course, on one's assumptions. If you are sufficiently pessimistic about returns and risks of foreign investments, your efficient portfolio may not call for any international diversification. But consider the past record as well as a little economic logic.

The Europe, Australia, and Far East (EAFE) index was created in 1969 as an index of equity returns in economically developed countries other than the United States. As such, it represents the returns that could have been earned on a broadly

FIGURE 17-2 *Naive Domestic U.S. Diversification Versus Naive International Diversification*

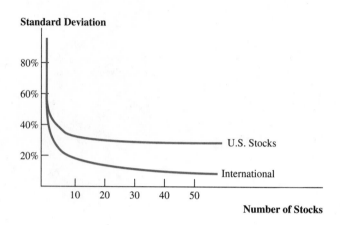

diversified group of international equities. In Table 17-2 the average returns, standard deviations, and correlation coefficients are shown for three U.S. asset classes as well as for the EAFE index. The data are based on nominal annual U.S. dollar returns. Using this historical data, two historical efficient frontiers, shown in Figure 17-3, were calculated. The frontier shown as a dotted curve includes only the three U.S. asset classes. The solid curve adds the EAFE index. Clearly, U.S. investors would have been better off in the past 20-plus years to have been globally diversified.

To see why this was the case, look again at Table 17-2, particularly the information about the EAFE index. Its average return was clearly the largest, but its standard deviation was also the largest. Both reflect the fact that countries included in the EAFE index experienced rapid re-industrialization as they revived from World War II economic collapse. It would be dangerous to extrapolate exceptional events of the past to the future. But even if future EAFE returns and risks are more in line with those of the U.S. economy, the correlation among U.S. securities and international securities suggests that international diversification will reduce portfolio risk in the future.

TABLE 17-2 *Historical Data on U.S. Asset Classes and EAFE Annual Nominal Returns 1969–1991*

Security Class	Average Return	Standard Deviation	Correlation Coefficients			
			TB	GB	SP	EAFE
U.S. T-Bills	7.49%	2.50%	1.00			
U.S. Government Bonds	9.25	11.60	−0.01	1.00		
S&P 500 Index	11.99	16.61	−0.06	0.46	1.00	
EAFE	15.68	22.97	−0.30	0.23	0.58	1.00

FIGURE 17-3 *Historical Efficient Frontiers*

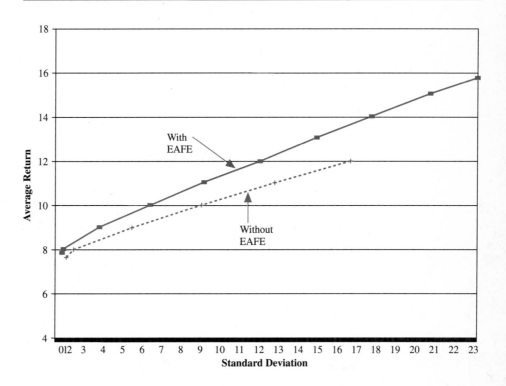

The historical correlation between EAFE returns and returns on the S&P 500 was 0.58. Remember, these are two very diversified portfolios. The S&P 500 index is composed of 500 large U.S. stocks. The EAFE index consists of approximately 1,000 stocks spread across 18 countries. A correlation coefficient of 0.58 between two well-diversified portfolios is quite low. If portfolios of equivalent size consisting solely of U.S. stocks were to be created, their return correlation would likely be greater than 0.9.

Because security returns are not highly correlated across world markets, international diversification reduces portfolio risk.

As further evidence, consider Table 17-3. The table is based on a study by Roll in which he compared correlation coefficients of monthly returns on various equity markets across the world. Since each non-U.S. equity market represents a portfolio that is smaller than the EAFE index, the correlations with U.S. returns are smaller than the 0.58 EAFE correlation.

Look at the bottom line, which shows correlation coefficients of U.S. equity returns with other countries. The highest correlations are with countries such as Canada and the United Kingdom, which have similar economic compositions to the United States. The lowest correlations are with countries such as Hong Kong, Mexico, and New Zealand, which have different economic bases.

TABLE 17-3 *Correlation Coefficients of Monthly Percentage Changes in Major Stock Market Indexes (local currencies, June 1981–September 1987)*

	Australia	Austria	Belgium	Canada	Denmark	France	Germany	Hong Kong	Ireland	Italy	Japan	Malaysia	Mexico	Netherlands	New Zealand	Norway	Singapore	South Africa	Spain	Sweden	Switzerland	United Kingdom
Austria	.219																					
Belgium	.190	.222																				
Canada	.568	.250	.215																			
Denmark	.217	−.062	.219	.301																		
France	.180	.263	.355	.351	.241																	
Germany	.145	.406	.315	.194	.215	.327																
Hong Kong	.321	.174	.129	.236	.120	.201	.304															
Ireland	.349	.202	.361	.490	.387	.374	.067	.320														
Italy	.209	.224	.307	.321	.150	.459	.257	.216	.275													
Japan	.182	−.025	.223	.294	.186	.361	.147	.137	.183	.241												
Malaysia	.329	−.013	.096	.274	.151	−.013	.159	.082	−.119	.114	.109											
Mexico	.220	.018	.104	.114	−.174	−.009	.002	.149	.113	.114	−.021	.231										
Netherlands	.294	.232	.334	.545	.341	.344	.511	.395	.373	.344	.333	.151	.038									
New Zealand	.389	.290	.275	.230	.148	.247	.318	.352	.314	.142	−.111	.136	.231	.230								
Norway	.355	.009	.233	.381	.324	.231	.173	.356	.306	.042	.156	.262	.050	.405	.201							
Singapore	.374	.030	.133	.320	.133	−.085	.037	.219	.102	−.038	.066	.891	.202	.196	.212	.280						
South Africa	.279	.159	.143	.385	−.113	.267	.007	−.095	.024	.093	.225	−.013	.260	.058	.038	.156	−.056					
Spain	.147	.018	.050	.190	.019	.255	.147	.193	.175	.290	.248	−.071	.059	.170	.095	.075	.056	−.088				
Sweden	.327	.161	.158	.376	.131	.159	.227	.196	.122	.330	.115	.103	.000	.324	.136	.237	.180	.070	.181			
Switzerland	.344	.401	.276	.551	.283	.307	.675	.379	.290	.287	.130	.099	.026	.570	.397	.331	.157	.112	.192	.334		
United Kingdom	.377	.073	.381	.590	.218	.332	.263	.431	.354	.328	.354	.193	.068	.534	.014	.313	.250	.168	.209	.339	.435	
United States	.328	.138	.250	.720	.351	.390	.209	.114	.380	.224	.326	.347	.063	.473	.083	.356	.377	.218	.214	.279	.500	.513

SOURCE: R. Roll, "The International Crash of October 1987," *Financial Analysts Journal*, September–October 1988, pp. 20–21.

These correlation coefficients show that international investment reduces risk because the economies of different countries are based on different industries. As long as this is true, global investment will reduce portfolio risk. Not only would global diversification have worked in the past, logically it will work in the future.

Domestic Versus International Returns

A domestic return is the return people receive in their domestic (local) currency. International returns are the returns earned from investing in another country—*after conversion to one's local currency.*

To illustrate, consider two companies that are similar, except for their country of origin: Tuff Truck, Inc. (TT) is a U.S. firm, and Lloyd's Lorry, Ltd. (LL) a British firm. At the beginning of the year, shares of TT trade on the New York Stock Exchange for $50, and shares of LL trade on the London International Stock Exchange for £50. By the end of the year, TT sells for $60 and has paid a $1 dividend; LL sells for £60 and has paid a £1 dividend. Thus the return a U.S. resident earns on TT is 22%, and the return a British resident earns on LL is also 22%. However, the return a U.S. resident would have earned on LL (and the return a British resident would have earned on TT) is not necessarily 22%. When an international investment is made, the return on the investment is composed of a return on the underlying security in the foreign country *and* a currency return. When you buy a foreign security, you buy both the *security and the currency* in which the security is denominated.

To continue with the example, assume that at the start of the year it takes $1.50 to buy one British pound note—the exchange rate is $1.50 per £. To purchase shares in Lloyds Lorry at £50, a U.S. resident would have to pay $1.50 per £, or $75. At the end of the year, the investor would have a claim to £60 in share value and £1 in dividends. Let's say that the exchange rate at that time is $1.20 per £. If the share value and dividends are reclaimed to the United States, the U.S. resident would receive only $73.20 (£61 at $1.20 per £). As a result, the U.S. investor's return on the British security is a negative 2.4%:

$$-0.024 = \frac{\$73.20}{\$75.00} - 1.0$$

The investment in LL provided a positive return, but this was offset by investment losses on the British pound. This -2.4% return is the U.S. investor's international return.

In order to calculate the international return on an investment in security i, the return on security i must be compounded by the return on the foreign currency. In our example, each $1 U.S. investment in LL resulted in a $+22\%$ return, as $1 grew to $1.22. However, each $1 U.S. investment in the foreign currency resulted in a -20% return, as the value of £1 fell from $1.50 to $1.20. Compounding the 1.22 by 0.80 results in an end-of-year value of $0.976 for each $1 investment at the beginning of the year:

$$\$0.976 \ = \ \$1(1.22)(0.80)$$

This, of course, represents a 2.4% loss.

In general, if R_I represents the international return, R_S represents the security return, and R_x represents the return on the exchange of currency:

Return on International Investment
$$1 \ + \ R_I \ = \ (1 \ + \ R_S)(1 \ + \ R_x) \qquad\qquad \textbf{(17.1)}$$

The foreign return is equal to a compounding of the security return (in the foreign country) by the exchange rate return. Applied to the U.S. investor in the example above:

$$(1 \ + \ R_I) \ = \ 0.976 \ = \ (1.22)(0.80)$$

And if we apply this equation to the British resident's return on Tuff Truck, a return of $+52.50\%$ was earned:

$$(1.22)(1.25) \ - \ 1 \ = \ 0.525$$

where

$$R_x \ = \ \frac{\$1.50 \text{ per pound}}{\$1.20 \text{ per pound}} \ - \ 1$$

$$= \ 25\%$$

Exchange rate returns can represent a sizeable part of the return earned on international investment. For example, consider the data in Table 17-4. Average annual returns and standard deviations are shown for U.S. investments in a variety of countries over the period 1970–1980. Both positive and negative average exchange rate return were earned. When the average exchange rate return is positive, it means that the value of the foreign currency increased relative to the dollar. Thus U.S. investors who owned the foreign currency profited.

The first three columns of data show average annual domestic returns, exchange rate returns, and total international returns to U.S. residents. For example, consider the data for Germany. The average annual return on an index of German stocks that a resident of Germany would have earned was 4.14%. U.S. residents purchasing German stocks would also have earned this 4.14%. But in addition, U.S. residents who purchased German stocks had to purchase German currency to do so. The average annual return on this currency investment was 6.65%. When the domestic return is compounded by the exchange rate return, U.S. investors earned an average 11.07% return per year. In contrast, consider a German resident's investment in U.S. stocks. These stocks provided an average annual domestic return of 6.78% to both U.S. and German owners. But the German investor would have suffered a 6.24% exchange rate loss. On net, a German investor in U.S. stocks would have had a 0.12% average annual return.[1]

---

[1] $1.0 \ \div \ 1.0665 \ = \ 0.9376$
$(1.0678)(0.9376) \ = \ 1.0012$

TABLE 17-4 *Ex Post Average Annual Returns and Standard Deviations for U.S. Investors (December 1970–December 1980)*

Stocks of Country	Average Annual Return			Standard Deviation of Returns		
	Domestic	*Exchange*	*Total U.S.*	*Domestic*	*Exchange*	*Total U.S.*
Germany	4.14%	6.65%	11.07%	13.87%	11.87%	18.39%
Belgium	7.12	4.97	12.44	13.28	11.02	18.76
Denmark	11.41	2.49	14.18	15.41	10.28	17.65
France	7.79	2.16	10.12	22.00	10.24	25.81
Italy	6.64	−4.22	2.14	24.21	8.58	26.51
Norway	8.05	3.58	11.92	28.61	8.89	29.92
Netherlands	7.02	5.79	13.22	16.37	10.97	18.91
United Kingdom	12.93	−0.12	12.79	28.94	8.84	31.61
Sweden	8.52	1.84	10.52	15.05	8.89	18.06
Switzerland	2.67	9.63	12.56	16.80	14.67	21.40
Spain	0.76	−1.29	−0.54	16.71	9.10	20.26
Australia	10.86	0.53	11.45	24.62	9.15	27.15
Japan	13.80	6.68	21.40	16.39	10.42	19.55
Hong Kong	26.05	−0.41	25.53	47.95	5.63	45.80
Singapore	22.69	−4.69	16.94	35.82	6.52	36.03
Canada	14.85	−1.88	12.69	18.92	4.16	20.29
United States	6.78	0.00	6.78	16.00	0.00	16.00

SOURCE: B. Solnik and B. Noetzlin, ''Optimal International Asset Allocation,'' *Journal of Portfolio Management* (Fall 1982): 11–21.

The last three columns in Table 17-4 show the annualized standard deviation of domestic returns, exchange rate returns, and total foreign returns to U.S. investors. Note that the standard deviation of total foreign returns is not the sum of domestic and exchange rate standard deviations. This happens because domestic and exchange rate returns are not perfectly correlated.

Two important implications can be drawn from Table 17-4:

1. The *average return* on foreign investment in a given country is often substantially affected by average exchange rate returns.

2. The *volatility of returns* on foreign investment in a given country is also often substantially affected by volatility of exchange rates.

Exchange rates play an important role in the risks and returns on foreign investment.

Table 17-4 is based on a scholarly study ended in 1980. A summary update is shown in Figure 17-4. During this period, exchange rates continued to have positive and negative effects on U.S. dollar foreign returns and contributed as much as $1/3$ the total foreign return.

A Brief History of Currency Exchange Rates. From the days of the Egyptian and Roman empires until the early 1900s, gold was used as the international medium of exchange. Each country would declare the units of gold into which its currency could be converted and then attempt to maintain this par value over time. The growth in a country's currency was limited to the quantity of gold it could acquire.

FIGURE 17-4 *Return Components of Major Stock Markets 1981–1990*

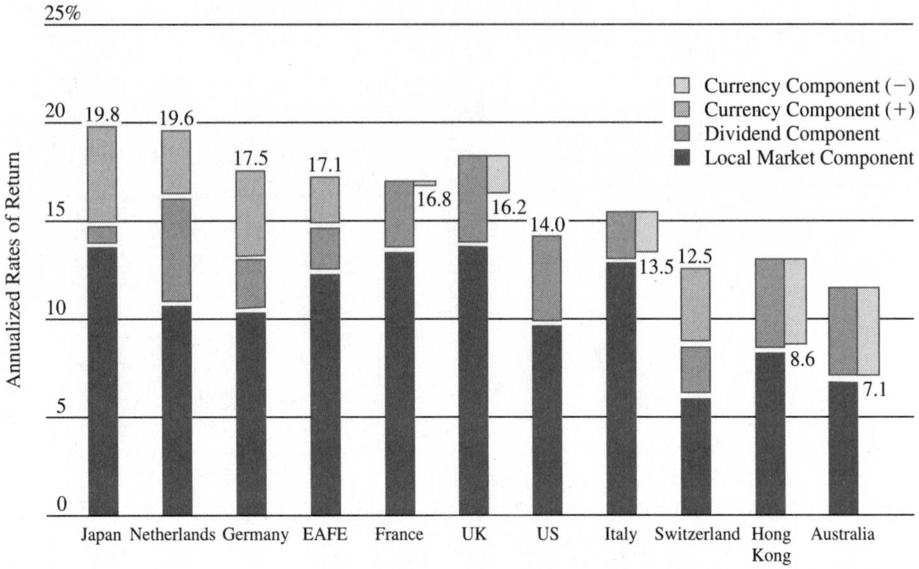

During World War I, shipping activities were interrupted and most countries suspended the gold standard. Between World War I and World War II, currency exchange rates fluctuated over wide ranges. During that time a number of countries, such as the United States, the United Kingdom, and France returned to variants of the gold standard. For example, the United States set its price of gold at $35 per ounce but traded gold only with central banks of foreign countries. Individuals were unable to turn in dollars for physical gold.

The Bretton Woods Agreement of 1944 was adopted by the Allied Powers to aid world economic development in the post-World War II era. This agreement created the International Monetary Fund (IMF) and the International Bank for Reconstruction and Development (World Bank). In addition, all signatory countries fixed the value of their currency in gold but did not have to actually exchange gold for currency. Only the dollar remained convertible, at $35 per ounce. In essence, this meant that the U.S. dollar became the world currency standard.

In subsequent years, use of the U.S. dollar as the world standard for fixed exchange rates became a problem due to growing U.S. trade deficits. In 1971, then-President Nixon suspended all U.S. Treasury purchases or sales of gold when one-third of U.S. gold supplies were sold to non-U.S. central banks during the first half of the year.

In response, the world's leading trading nations (the Group of Ten) signed the Smithsonian Agreement in which currencies were revalued and allowed to depart somewhat from the U.S. dollar. This was the beginning of freely floating exchange rates. In 1976, true flexible exchange rates were allowed in a treaty known as the Jamaica Agreement. Nations were not required to make their exchange rates

FIGURE 17-5 *U.S. Dollar Movement Under Floating Exchange Rates*

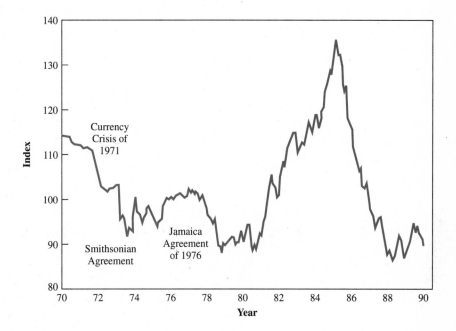

flexible, and many countries continue to maintain fixed rates based on the U.S. dollar.

In Figure 17-5, the history of U.S. dollar exchange rates versus an index of 15 other countries is shown. The exhibit dramatically shows the importance of exchange rate returns to international investors.

Exchange Rate Quotations

Current exchange rates are published daily in most financial newspapers. An example of such exchange rates is displayed in Table 17-5. The values shown in the first column are referred to as *direct quotations*. They represent the number of U.S. dollars required to purchase one unit of the foreign currency. For example, on December 31, 1992, $1.51 would have been needed to purchase one British pound. We will symbolically refer to the direct exchange as $S^{d\backslash f}$; where S refers to the spot exchange rate and the superscript $d\backslash f$ stands for domestic per unit of foreign.

Values shown in the second column are *indirect quotations*. They represent the number of foreign currency units that 1.0 U.S. dollars will purchase. For example, one U.S. dollar would have purchased 0.66 British pounds on December 31, 1992. We will symbolically refer to indirect spot quotations as $S^{f\backslash d}$.

By convention, most financial newspapers show indirect quotations. Only cur-

TABLE 17-5 *Illustrative Exchange Rates, December 31, 1992*

Currency	Direct Quotation $ Required to Buy One Unit of Foreign Currency	Indirect Quotation Number of Units of Foreign Currency per U.S. Dollar
British Pound	1.5115	0.6616
Canadian Dollar	0.7896	1.2665
French Franc	0.1812	5.5175
German Mark	0.6184	1.6170
Greek Drachma	0.0047	214.8500
Italian Lira	0.0007	1478.5000
Japanese Yen	0.0080	124.7500
Swiss Franc	0.6845	1.4610

SOURCE: *The Wall Street Journal,* January 4, 1993.

rencies dominated in pounds are shown as direct quotations. It is also convention on all international currency markets to state exchange rates on a "U.S. dollar basis." For example, to find the exchange rate between Japanese yen and German marks, quotations of the yen per dollar and mark per dollar would have to be examined. This convention reduces confusion when comparing exchange rates on, say, the Frankfurt exchange with those on the Tokyo exchange. Again, the exception is the British pound, in which case a foreign currency quote is shown directly against the pound as opposed to the dollar.

Exchange Rate Theory

A large body of theory and empirical testing has examined various aspects of currency exchange rates. Although much of it lies beyond the scope of this book, we should examine some fundamentals of the classic theory integrating international exchange.

Our concern is with three basic questions about exchange rates. First, what causes the existing (or spot) exchange rate between two countries? Second, what causes this exchange rate to change over time? Third, is there any way in which exchange rate risk can be hedged? The answer to each of these questions is clearly important to anyone considering the diversification of a portfolio using international securities.

Spot Exchange Rates. The equilibrium spot exchange rate between two countries is determined by the quantity of money circulating in each country. For example, consider two countries that produce only one commodity, say, rice. Country A issues money denominated in units called Azz, and country B issues money denominated in units Bzz. The rice production and money units outstanding for each country are:

	Country A	*Country B*
Rice Production	100,000 lbs	200,000 lbs
Money Units in Circulation	100,000 Azz	400,000 Bzz
Local Price of Rice	1 Azz/lb	2 Bzz/lb

The equilibrium exchange rate must be 0.5 Azz per 1.0 Bzz (or 2 Bzz per 1.0 Azz). If this were not the case, arbitrage transactions would be possible. For example, if the current exchange rate were 1.0 Azz per 1.0 Bzz, country A's currency would be overvalued relative to country B's. A person in country B with 10,000 Bzz of currency could buy rice in either country. If the rice were bought in the domestic market, 5,000 pounds could be acquired (10,000 Bzz ÷ 2 Bzz per lb). If the rice were bought in the foreign market from country A, the 10,000 Bzz would first be converted to 10,000 Azz (that is, a 1:1 exchange rate) and then 10,000 pounds of rice would be bought in country A. Knowing this, people in country B would rapidly bid up the number of Bzz units they are willing to pay for an Azz until the exchange rate reached 2 Bzz per 1.0 Azz.

Reality, of course, is considerably more complex. Countries produce a tremendous variety of goods, political restrictions are imposed on the import and export of goods, and so forth. But the basic variable that determines the level of a current exchange rate is the quantity of money circulating in each country.

To express the determinants of the current exchange ratio symbolically, let:

$S_0^{d/f}$ = the spot exchange rate between one unit of domestic currency and one unit of foreign currency at period 0 (e.g., $S_0^{A/B}$ = 0.5 and $S_0^{B/A}$ = 2.0)

P_0^d = the price per unit of output at period 0 of domestic production (e.g., P_0^A = 1 Azz and P_0^B = 2 Bzz)

P_0^f = the price per unit of output at period 0 of foreign production (e.g., P_0^B = 2 Bzz and P_0^A = 0.5 Azz)

The spot exchange rate is:

Spot Exchange Rate
$$S_0^{d/f} = \frac{P_0^d}{P_0^f} \tag{17.2}$$

Changes in Exchange Rates. Changes in exchange rates are caused by relative inflation rates in two countries. To continue with our example, assume that, one year later, rice production in each country is unchanged but that there are now 120,000 units of Azz circulating and 420,000 units of Bzz. The unit price of rice in country A will now be 1.20 Azz (120,000 Azz ÷ 100,000 lbs), and the unit price in country B will be 2.10 Bzz (420,000 Bzz ÷ 200,000 lbs). Thus, the new equilibrium exchange rate will be 0.57 Azz per 1.00 Bzz (or 1.75 Bzz per 1.0 Azz).

The exchange rate changed because the countries experienced differing rates of inflation. Inflation in country A was 20%, and in country B it was 5%. Because inflation was more rapid in country A, the value of its currency fell relative to country B's.

Answers to Commonly Asked Questions about Currency Trading

In early 1992, foreign currency prices moved dramatically in response to uncertainties about the future economic integration of the European Economic Community. This article appeared in The Wall Street Journal *at that time to explain how currency markets operate and the history of major events in the currency markets.*

How big are the world's currency markets?

Huge. According to a 1990 survey by the Bank for International Settlements, $650 billion a day of foreign exchange is traded round the globe. That's more volume than the New York Stock Exchange rings up in two months.

Who does all this trading?

A wide range of players. Major banks are most active, accounting for nearly 80% of trading, according to the New York Federal Reserve Bank. But multinational companies account for billions of dollars of trading as well. Global money managers, individual speculators and tourists also are active.

Where does trading occur?

Most trading is done electronically, via bank-to-bank phone links. There isn't any dominant exchange that handles spot trading—the trading of currency for immediate delivery. Instead, activity during any 24-hour period migrates from one time zone to another, moving from Europe to the U.S., Australia, Japan and then back to Europe.

But about $14 billion a day of currency futures are traded at the Chicago Mercantile Exchange. And the Phildelphia Stock Exchange does a sizable business in currency options.

Can countries control their exchange rates?

Not very well. World exchange rates have been left to float since 1971, though members of the European Economic Community have tried to loosely link their currencies for most of the past two decades. But as certain European currencies become unusually strong or weak, authorities repeatedly have been forced to change the targeted values of those currencies in what is known as a currency realignment.

How does a realignment work?

Policy makers from European nations agree to boost the targeted values of their strongest currencies, while lowering the targeted values of the weakest currencies. Last weekend, for example, the Italian lira was effectively devalued 7% against other European currencies. By abruptly changing exchange rates, these realignments are meant to bring about a new period of currency stability.

Already this week, though, speculation is mounting that the European Community will need to realign rates again. The betting is that the German mark will strengthen, while the lira once again, the Spanish peseta and the British pound will be devalued.

Aside from revaluations, can countries do anything to control their exchange rates?

Each year, countries' central banks make billions of dollars in currency trades designed to stabilize exchange rates. But such central-bank intervention often proves futile, as even the trading might of the U.S. Federal Reserve, the Bank of England or the German Bundesbank proves insufficient to overcome market forces.

Why do currency values fluctuate so much?

Much—but not all of the answer—has to do with economic fundamentals. Traders like to channel money into countries with low inflation rates, trade surpluses and high interest rates. Those currencies, as demonstrated by the mark and the Japanese yen, tend to strengthen over time. By contrast, high inflation rates, big trade or budget deficits and low interest rates often amount to a prescription for a weakening currency.

This week, however, "it would be a mistake to relate what's happening to economic fundamentals," says Will Brown, chief economist at J.P. Morgan & Co.

So what other factors are at work?

Trader sentiment and political pressures. Within Europe's exchange-rate mechanism, traders have been making money lately by betting that the British pound and Italian lira will weaken, and that the mark will strengthen. As huge buy-and-sell orders course through the market, that view has become a self-fulfilling prophecy.

What's more, European economic unity is up for

typically earns about $150 million every quarter before taxes and expenses from its currency-trading operation. Bankers Trust New York Corp., BankAmerica Corp. and J.P. Morgan each are good for about half that amount every quarter. . . .

Who are the losers in this market?

Central banks, for one. Yesterday, the Bank of England bought pounds aggressively early in the day, in an effort to shore up its currency. But that effort was for naught; the pound kept sinking, and the British central bank was left with trading losses.

Small speculators often end up as losers, too. Of the 1,287 seats on the Chicago Merc's International Monetary Mart, about 25% change hands every year. And market players say that most of the people who sell their seats do so because they have incurred unsustainable losses.

Does anyone regulate currency trades?

Central banks such as the Fed provide some degree of oversight. And futures trading, in particular, is watched by the Commodities Futures Trading Commission. But in general, the currency markets are much more lightly regulated than stock or bond trading.

Which of the world's currencies are the most important ones in traders' eyes?

At the top of the list, alongside the dollar, are the mark and the yen. A survey of 300 major traders last year by Greenwich Associates found that 28% of dollar trading in North America is in the mark, 23% in the yen, 13% in the British pound and 9% in the Swiss franc. Rounding out the list of major trading currencies, at 3% to 7% each, are the Canadian dollar, Australian dollar and French franc.

Sometimes, though, less-prominent currencies can take center stage. This week, a lot of attention is turning to the Swedish krone and the Italian lira.

a crucial French vote this weekend. Although the repercussions of that vote are complex, many traders have decided that it presents one more reason to pile money into favored currencies and bet against weak ones.

In all this turmoil, who is getting rich?

If history is any guide, big banks' trading desks should be making a killing. Citicorp, for example,

---

SOURCE: *The Wall Street Journal*, September 17, 1992.

The relationship that exists between past and future exchange rates is referred to as the *purchasing power parity model* and is written symbolically as:

Purchasing Power Parity Model

$$S_1^{d/f} = S_0^{d/f} \left(\frac{1 + I_1^d}{1 + I_1^f} \right)$$

(17.3)

where

$S_1^{d/f}$ = the number of domestic current units necessary to acquire 1.0 unit of foreign currency at date 1

I_1^d = the domestic inflation rate during period 1

I_1^f = the foreign inflation rate during period 1

In practice, the purchasing power parity model often will not explain short-term movements in exchange rates. However, there is little doubt that a major force causing shifts in exchange rates is relative inflation rates between countries.

In short periods, however, exchange rates are also influenced by interest rates and monetary policy differences between countries, political stability, trade balances, and economic growth.

Forward Exchange Rates. Consider the following numerical example. Today, 1-year nominal risk-free interest rates in the United States are 10% (RF_{US} = 10%) and are 12% in the United Kingdom (RF_{UK} = 12%). The spot exchange rate is $2 per £ or £0.5 per dollar. There is also a forward contract that allows the swap of dollars and pounds in exactly one year at $1.90 per £ or 0.5263 £ per dollar. We will define today's contracted price of this forward as $F_0^{d/f}$ = $1.90. As a U.S. resident, what should you do—invest in the United States or the United Kingdom?

Each $1.00 invested in the United States will provide a payoff of $1.10. An investment of $1.00 in the United Kingdom is a little more complex. When the $1.00 is converted to £, you know that it will purchase 0.5 £, which will grow to 0.56 £ by year-end. To guarantee the exchange rate at which these 0.56 £ will be returned to the United States, *today* you would either sell pound futures or buy dollar futures. At the forward exchange rate of $1.90 per £, the 0.56 £ will be worth $1.064 ($1.90*0.56) at year-end.

Since the U.S. investment grows to $1.10 whereas the U.K. investment grows to only $1.064, you should choose to invest in the United States. In fact, you could engage in an arbitrage in which you purchase U.S. risk-free securities financed by short selling U.K. risk-free securities. From the perspective of a U.K. resident, investment in the United States is also preferable. Arbitrage trades will continue to occur in the spot currencies and risk-free interest rate markets as well as the currency futures markets until people are indifferent between investing locally or in foreign markets. Symbolically, this will occur when the:

**Payoff from
Local Investment**   = Payoff from Foreign Investment

$$1 + RF_L = (1 + RF_F)(F_0^{d/f} \div S_0^{d/f}) \qquad (17.4)$$

where RF_L is the risk-free rate in the *local* economy, RF_F is the risk-free rate in the *foreign country*. $F^{d/f}$ refers to the price of the futures contract, the number of domestic currency units per unit of foreign currency. The value of $F_0^{d/f} \div S_0^{d/f}$ is simply the (known) exchange rate return or the price at which you sell pounds divided by the price at which you buy pounds. In this example, you sold pounds at a price of $1.90 per pound, $F_0^{d/f}$. And you bought pounds at price of $2.00 per pound.

$$(1 + R_x) = F_0^{d/f} \div S_0^{d/f}$$

$$0.95 = (\$1.90 \text{ per pound}) \div (\$2.00 \text{ per pound})$$

Equation 17.4 can be solved for the equilibrium forward exchange rate as follows:

Spot
Futures $$F_0^{d/f} = S_0^{d/f} [(1 + RF_L) \div (1 + RF_F)] \qquad \textbf{(17.5)}$$
Parity

This is referred to as *Spot-Futures Parity.*

In our example above, the equilibrium forward rate would be:[2]

$$\$1.96 = \$2.00 [(1.10) \div (1.12)]$$

The nominal risk-free rate (RF) in each country should be equal to a compounding of the real return in each country by the expected rates of inflation in each country.

Expected Inflation and Forward Rates. If the current spot rate is $2 per pound and the equilibrium 1-year forward rate is $1.96 per pound, the value of the pound is forecast to fall relative to the dollar. The ownership of one pound is expected to have a claim to fewer dollars. Why might this be? A similar question could be asked about why the U.K. nominal risk-free rate might be greater than that in the United States?

The answer to both questions, of course, could be due to differences in expected inflation in the two countries. If the Fisher Equation (discussed in Chapter 5) is used, then

Nominal
Risk-Free $$(1 + RF_L) = (1 + r_L) [1 + E(I_L)]$$
Rates $$(1 + RF_F) = (1 + r_F) [1 + E(I_F)]$$

If the real risk-free return in the local economy (r_L) equals the real risk-free return in the foreign economy (r_F), then *Spot Futures Parity* model shown in Equation 17.5 can be re-expressed as:

Spot
Futures $$F_0^{d/f} = S_0^{d/f} \frac{1 + E(I_L)}{1 + E(I_F)} \qquad \textbf{(17.6)}$$
Parity

The true reason why *equilibrium* forward rates differ from current spot rates is due to differences in expected inflation in the local and foreign country.

---

[2] This assumes that spot exchange rates and spot interest rates do not change in adjustment to equilibrium.

For example, assume that the real risk-free return in the United States and United Kingdom is 3%. This implies that expected inflation in the United States is 6.8%, and in the United Kingdom it is 8.7%:

$$1.068 = 1.10 \div 1.03$$

$$1.087 = 1.12 \div 1.03$$

Using Equation 17.6, the equilibrium forward rate is $1.96:

$$\$1.96 = \$2.00 \, (1.068 \div 1.087)$$

Notice that Equation 17.6 states that *today's forward rate is simply equal to today's expectation of the future spot rate.*

Interest Rate Parity. If capital is allowed to flow between countries at zero cost, taxes are identical and currency exchange rates are flexible, then the expected real rate of return for a given risk level should be identical in all countries. If this were not true, then people would borrow in low real-return countries and invest in high real-return countries. This suggests that one should be careful about making an investment decision based solely on quoted *nominal* returns in foreign countries. Exchange rate gains or losses must also be considered.

For example, consider the nominally risk-free 1-year returns in two foreign countries:

	United Kingdom	Germany
Local 1-year risk-free rate	12%	6%
Spot exchange rate	$2 per £	$0.70 per M (mark)
1-year forward rate	$1.9 per £	$0.74 per M

Neglecting the exchange rate information, it would appear that the United Kingdom is a good place in which to invest and Germany a good place to borrow. The opposite conclusion, however, is true. When Equation 17.4 is used to calculate the returns net of currency transactions, we find:

$$
\begin{aligned}
\text{Payoff in Local Currency} &= \text{Payoff from International Investment} \\
&= \$1 \, (1 + RF_F)(1 + R_x) \\
&= \$1 \, (1 + RF_F)(F_0^{d/f} \div S_0^{d/f}) \\
\$1.064 &= \$1 \, (1.12) \, (\$1.9 \div \$2.0) \text{ for UK} \\
\$1.121 &= \$1 \, (1.06) \, (\$0.74 \div \$0.7) \text{ for Germany}
\end{aligned}
$$

A situation in which German risk-free returns are substantially higher than UK risk-free returns (net of currency returns) cannot last long if arbitrage is allowed to occur. If such arbitrage is effective in adjusting exchange rates and risk-free rates between countries, the following interest rate parity model will result:

FIGURE 17-6 *Interest Rate Parity Relationship*

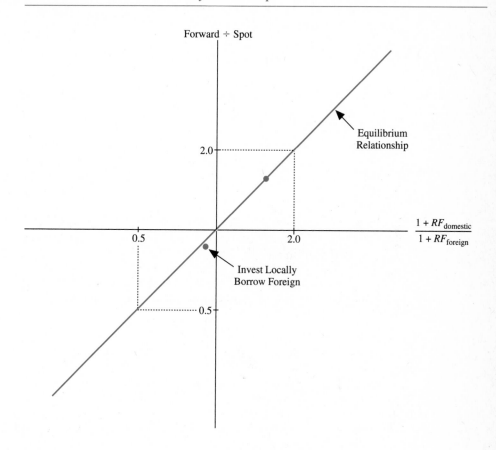

Forward ÷ Spot

2.0

0.5

2.0

Equilibrium
Relationship

$$\frac{1 + RF_{\text{domestic}}}{1 + RF_{\text{foreign}}}$$

Invest Locally
Borrow Foreign

0.5

Interest Rate Parity		

$$\frac{1 + RF_L}{1 + RF_F} = \frac{F_0^{d/f}}{S_0^{d/f}} = \frac{1 + E(I_L)}{1 + E(I_F)} \qquad (17.7)$$

The ratio of forward to spot prices should be equal to the ratio of the risk-free payoff in the domestic economic to the risk-free payoff in the foreign economy. These ratios are all due to differences in expected inflation in the two economies.

This relationship is shown in Figure 17-6. When all markets are in equilibrium, the ratios should plot on a 45-degree line passing through 1.0 on both axis. Recall our first example in this section in which nominal 1-year risk-free rates were 10% in the United States and 12% in the United Kingdom. The spot rate was $2.00 per pound and the future was $1.90 per pound. Given this data, the interest-rate parity ratios are:

Ratio of Risk-Free Rates	Ratio of Forward to Spot
$(1.10) \div (1.12) = 0.982$	$\$1.90 \div \$2.00 = 0.95$

Since the ratios differ, the markets are not in equilibrium and (neglecting transaction costs) an arbitrage trade is possible.

HEDGING EXCHANGE RATE RISK

There are three ways in which the exchange rate risk associated with international investment can be hedged.

The first involves the maintenance of offsetting positions in both the currency and commodities of a foreign country. For example, assume that you are a U.S. investor. You have purchased shares of a British stock index worth $15,000 when the exchange rate is $1.50 per British pound. In addition, you plan to visit Britain in three months and spend the $15,000. If the exchange drops to $1.20, your £10,000 investment will be worth only $12,000 ($1.20 × £10,000). But this investment loss is offset by your commodity gain—the $12,000 still purchases £10,000 of British goods. By being long the currency and short British goods, your risk is eliminated.

In reality, a hedge such as this is usually unreasonable. It is hard to imagine, for example, a pension fund both investing in British pounds and intending to spend dollars on British commodities.

A second approach is more viable and should be followed by anyone who is serious about international investment—diversify over many countries. The exchange rate risk incurred when investments are made in a single foreign country can be substantial. However, if exchange rate returns are uncorrelated, much of the risk (depending on the number of countries available) can be eliminated. For example, Table 17-6 presents the correlation coefficients of exchange rate returns between various countries from the perspective of a U.S. investor. The data apply to the ten-year period ending in 1980. Consider the correlation of 0.94 in exchange

TABLE 17-6 *Correlation Coefficients of Exchange Rate Returns, Various Countries, 1970–1980*

	Aus	Bel	Can	Den	Fra	Ger	Ita	Jap	Net	Spa	Swe	Swi	UK
Austria	1.00												
Belgium	0.94	1.00											
Canada	−0.09	−0.13	1.00										
Denmark	0.83	0.87	−0.09	1.00									
France	0.11	0.03	−0.02	0.05	1.00								
Germany	0.95	0.91	−0.12	0.83	−0.01	1.00							
Italy	0.04	0.10	−0.11	0.06	−0.02	0.11	1.00						
Japan	0.15	0.23	−0.54	0.24	−0.34	0.22	−0.05	1.00					
Netherlands	0.96	0.94	−0.16	0.88	−0.05	0.95	0.10	0.24	1.00				
Spain	0.43	0.38	0.07	0.62	0.36	0.46	0.55	−0.13	0.49	1.00			
Sweden	0.60	0.64	0.29	0.72	0.46	0.53	−0.01	−0.20	0.63	0.00	1.00		
Switzerland	0.90	0.90	−0.30	0.79	0.07	0.84	0.10	0.33	0.88	0.14	0.44	1.00	
United Kingdom	0.21	0.20	−0.29	0.11	−0.01	0.23	0.42	0.28	0.18	0.25	−0.07	0.22	1.0

SOURCE: Calculated from information provided in Ibbotson, Carr, and Robinson, "International Equity and Bond Returns," *Financial Analysts Journal* (July/August 1982): 2–24.

rate returns on investments in Belgium and Austria. Clearly, a U.S. investor would not have obtained much reduction of exchange rate risk by diversifying foreign investments across these two countries. However, diversification of exchange rate risk would have worked if investments had been made in Canada and Austria, because the correlation between their exchange rate returns is -0.09. The economies of many countries are so closely integrated that diversification of foreign investment among them will not reduce exchange rate risk. However, there are many countries for which the correlation is quite small and in which diversification will reduce exchange rate risk. A number of other studies have also shown that exchange rate returns are often close to zero. Much, although not all, exchange rate risk can be eliminated by broad diversification among countries.

The third approach to hedging involves positions in derivatives or synthetic derivatives. Options and futures are traded on currencies of most economically developed countries. In addition, derivatives are also traded on currency baskets.

A basket is an index of the currencies of many countries. Examples of two baskets on which options and futures are available are shown in Figures 17-7 and 17-8. The currency weights shown are as of 1992 but they may change over time.

FIGURE 17-7 *USDX Component Currencies*

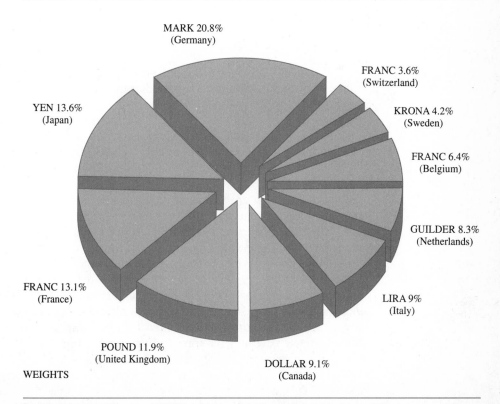

MARK 20.8%
(Germany)

FRANC 3.6%
(Switzerland)

KRONA 4.2%
(Sweden)

FRANC 6.4%
(Belgium)

GUILDER 8.3%
(Netherlands)

LIRA 9%
(Italy)

YEN 13.6%
(Japan)

FRANC 13.1%
(France)

POUND 11.9%
(United Kingdom)

DOLLAR 9.1%
(Canada)

WEIGHTS

SOURCE: *Information Literature of FINEX, A Division of the New York Cotton Exchange, 1992.*

FIGURE 17-8 *ECU Component Currencies*

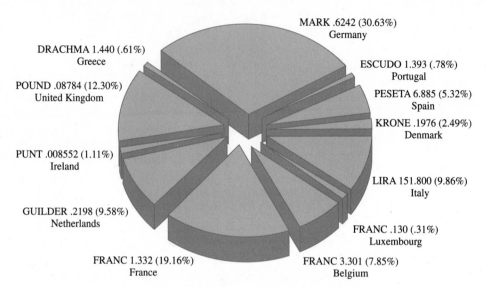

To calculate the ECU value use the amounts, which are constant. The percentages shown are from January 6, 1992.

SOURCE: *Information Literate of FINEX, A Division of the New York Cotton Exchange, 1992.*

The U.S. Dollar Index (USDX) is a broad index of non-U.S. dollar currencies designed to hedge exchange rate risks that U.S. investors face when a portion of their portfolio is international (non-U.S.). The ECU is a basket of European currencies. It is referred to as the ECU since the new currency of the European community is called the European Currency Unit (or ECU). Currency baskets are often used in place of derivative trades on each currency held in the portfolio to save transaction costs. They are analogous to futures and options on aggregate stock indexes.

As a practical matter, hedging with currency futures and options has its problems. The most obvious is cost. Any option and futures position that is to "overlay" a portfolio of currencies requires active oversight and trading if it is to be successful. For large pension portfolios with many active international bond and equity managers, costs of oversight and trading can be large.

There is also the question of how much to hedge. For example, all examples in this chapter have dealt with forward contracts on nominally risk-free securities. Since the security is risk-free, the amount of currency to be hedged at year-end is known: that is, you know exactly how many forwards are needed to eliminate exchange-rate risk. But if the foreign investment is in risky bonds or equities, the quantity of currency units available at year-end is uncertain. If risky assets are held, hedging with derivatives will reduce but not eliminate currency risk.

Finally, currency derivatives have maturities (delivery dates and expiration dates) that are 1 year or less. Rolling over a sequence of short-term hedges does

purchase and sale. Price pressure costs represent price impacts caused by a large trade. These are hard to measure and there have been no thorough studies of price pressure in non-U.S. markets. Based on U.S. studies, though, smaller capitalization stocks tend to have the greatest price pressure impacts. In short, transaction costs vary between countries but are usually larger for countries other than the United States, United Kingdom, Germany, and Japan.

One way to estimate the summation of these costs is to examine *expense ratios* for international mutual funds. The expense ratio is equal to all expenses associated with managing the fund (except transaction costs) divided by the average value of assets during a year. In 1991, the median expense ratio of actively managed international mutual funds was 1.75% compared with a median ratio of 1.10% for domestic U.S. Growth & Income Mutual Funds. For actively managed international bond funds, the median was 1.60% versus 1.07% for U.S. Government Bond Funds.

Passively managed portfolios are not as costly to maintain. A total cost of about 50 basis points is reasonable to expect. In short, if active international management is to beat passive management, it must provide pre-expense returns 1.0%–1.5% more than passive management.

SUMMARY

Given the size of non-U.S. financial markets and improved telecommunications, all investors should give serious consideration to investing globally. The advantage of doing so is the improved diversification that can be gained. Although individual country markets are increasingly interrelated, the economic bases of various countries are sufficiently different that diversification benefits are available.

One way for U.S. residents to gain an international exposure is to purchase American Depository Receipts (ADRs), trust certificates that have a claim to a foreign stock held in safekeeping by a U.S. bank in its foreign branch. A more effective approach is to purchase shares in an international commingled fund such as a mutual fund or closed-end country fund.

When a foreign security is purchased, one actually buys two assets: (1) the security and (2) the currency of the country in which the security is domiciled. As a result, the return earned on foreign investment comes from both the security return (in its local currency) and an exchange-rate return. This creates a new element of risk that investors need to understand and decide how to deal with— exchange-rate risk.

Exchange rates between economically developed countries are flexible and free to adjust to market forces. A few less developed countries still retain fixed exchange rates. The major force underlying changes in exchange rates is differential inflation in two economies. For example, if Country 1 has no inflation but Country 2 experiences a 10% inflation rate, then the equilibrium value of Country 2's currency should decline by 10% relative to Country 1. This is referred to as *purchasing power parity.*

Expectations of future inflation are also priced in forward currency contracts. For example, if expected inflation in Country 1 is 0% and in Country 2 it is 10%, then the forward contract on Country 2's currency will be priced 10% lower then its spot exchange rate. This is referred to as *spot futures parity*.

Investors seek to invest in countries that will provide the greatest risk-adjusted returns. Borrowers seek to borrow in countries that will require the lowest cost. In equilibrium, the real rate of return will be equal for all countries. This concept is known as *interest rate parity*.

These three equilibrium models are based on costless arbitrage. In real world situations, arbitrage is impeded by transaction costs, legal restrictions on the free flow of currencies, and economic policies of central governments.

The benefits of hedging depend on how long one intends to remain invested internationally and the security risk of the portfolio. Exchange-rate risk of a short-term risk-free foreign investment can be eliminated by proper use of forwards, futures, and options. This is because one knows exactly how much currency to hedge and has derivatives with the necessary maturity to engage in a hedge. With risky portfolios, the quantity to be hedged is uncertain. There are currently no long-term derivatives available. Long-term investors in risky securities might best rely on broad country diversification and time.

REVIEW PROBLEM

1. You are a U.S. resident thinking about investing $100,000 in German stocks. The exchange rate is currently $0.30 per mark. You expect that the German stocks will earn 15% for German residents. You also expect that the inflation rate over the next year will be 9% in Germany and 6% in the United States.

   a. If you do not hedge your investment, what is your expected one-year return? What part is due to domestic expected returns and what part is due to exchange rate returns?

   b. Given this information, what do you think the one-year forward rate should be?

   c. Assume the one-year forward rate is exactly what you calculated in part b. What hedge would you make to offset exchange rate risk?

   d. Assume that the German stocks do provide a domestic return of 15%, but that the exchange rate in a year is $0.40 per mark. If you hedged, what is your return?

   e. Why may this hedge not work?

Solution

a. Dollar and deutsche mark (DM) flows are:

Today			One Year Later	
Invest Dollars	$100,000		$111,834	Receive Dollars
Buy DM at $0.30/DM		15%		Sell DM at $0.2917*
Invest DM	333,333 DM	Return	$383,333 DM	Receive DM

$$*\text{Expected Spot Rate} = (\$0.30)\left(\frac{1.06}{1.09}\right) = \$0.2917$$

$$\text{Expected Return on Dollar Investment} = \frac{\$111,834}{\$100,000} - 1.0 = 11.834\%$$

Domestic Return $= 15\%$

$$\text{Exchange Rate Return} = \frac{0.2917}{0.300} - 1.0 = -2.752\%$$

$R_L = (1.15)(0.9725) - 1.0 = 11.834\%$

Note that by not hedging, your *expected* return is equal to the compounding of the 15% domestic return and the -2.75% exchange rate loss. However, since you are uncertain about the exchange rate in one year from now, you are also uncertain about the exchange rate return.

b. The forward rate should be the expected spot rate of $0.2917/DM.

c. Sell futures (or forward) contracts on 383,333 DM at a price of $0.2917/DM. This will lock in the expected return of 11.834%. (This is lower than the 15% domestic German return, but recall that inflation in Germany is expected to be greater by about 3 percentage points. Thus, equilibrium returns on German stocks should be about 3 percentage points higher than the returns on domestic U.S. stocks. Given the lower U.S. inflation rate, the 11.83% might be fair.)

d. You have sold futures contracts on 383,333 DM at $0.2917/DM. If the exchange rate in a year is $0.400/DM, the 383,333 DM received in a year from now can be translated back to $153,333, for a gain of $41,499 more than expected. But this is exactly offset by a $41,499 loss on the futures $[(0.2917 - 0.4) \times 383,333]$. Thus, your return is exactly what was expected—11.83%. Given the hedge there is no uncertainty in your expected return *associated with exchange rates*.

e. The hedge might not work:
   (1) if contracts in 383,333 DM units are unavailable.
   (2) if the contracts mature on dates other than those on which you intend to translate marks into dollars.
   (3) if the domestic German return is not 15%.

QUESTIONS AND PROBLEMS

1. A $1 million investment is made in Canadian stocks when the exchange rate is $0.70/Canadian dollars. At that time, the six-month forward exchange rate is $0.72. The expected six-month domestic return is 9%. The U.S. expected inflation rate for the next six months is 5%.
   a. What is the expected inflation rate in Canada?
   b. What is the expected exchange rate for six months ahead?
   c. Is the value of the dollar expected to increase or decrease? Why?
   d. What is the expected foreign return? Without a hedge, what factors create uncertainty about this return?
   e. Assume that a hedge is used, that the actual exchange rate is $0.68/Canadian dollar in six months, and that the domestic Canadian return is 12%. What foreign return is earned and what were its causes?

2. On January 1 the price of a share of a Japanese stock is 10 yen and the exchange rate is $0.40 per yen. The stock pays no dividends during the year. At the end of the year, the stock is selling for 12 yen and the exchange rate is $0.35 per yen. What was the stock's return to both a Japanese investor and a U.S. investor?

3. The current spot rate between U.S. dollars and British pounds is $1.25/£. The nominal risk-free rate in the U.S. is 8.15%, and the real risk-free rate of interest is 3%.

a. What is the expected U.S. inflation rate?

b. If the one-year forward rate is $1.19/£, what is the expected inflation rate for Britain?

c. If the real risk-free rate is also 3% in Britain, what should be the nominal risk-free rate in Britain?

4. You are given the following spot quotations:

> $1.9 per 1 British pound
> $0.7 per 1 German mark
> 2 German marks per 1 British pound

a. Are these exchange rates in equilibrium?

b. What arbitrage might you engage in with $1,000,000?

5. You are given the following information:

Country	One-Year Risk-Free Rate	Spot Price	One-Year Forward Price
United States	8%		
Japan	6%	$0.008 per 1 Yen	$0.008 per Yen
Germany	8%	$0.007 per 1 Mark	$0.007 per Mark
United Kingdom	10%	$1.900 per pound	$1.95 per pound

a. Use the interest rate parity model to determine which set of prices are inconsistent.

b. Illustrate any potential arbitrage with $1,000,000.

c. Assuming that spot currency prices won't change, what should be the exchange rate between marks and pounds?

6. In reading the financial press, you notice that forward prices of U.K. pounds (dollars per 1.0 pound) are lower than spot prices. What should this tell you about current risk-free rates in the United Kingdom relative to the United States?

7. Yearly returns on a portfolio of small capitalization stocks in Japan are shown in both local currency (Yen) and U.S. dollars below. Calculate the yearly exchange rate returns.

	1986	1987	1988	1989	1990
In dollars	60%	87%	32%	38%	−33%
In Yen	26	43	36	58	−37

8. A U.S. mutual fund purchases $1,000,000 worth of a diversified British stock portfolio at an exchange rate of $2 per pound. No futures or forward currency hedge is used. Complete the table below.

Dollar Based on Portfolio Return

Return in Local Currency	Exchange Rate at Year-End		
	$1.75/£	$2/£	$2.25/£
−15%			
10%			
35%			

9. Repeat Question 8, but assume you sell 550,000 one-year pound futures at a price of $2 per pound.

10. You are considering an investment in stocks of the United Kingdom and France. Information about your expectations is shown below:

	U.K.	France
Domestic Return		
Expected Return	18%	20%
Standard Deviation	30%	35%
Exchange Rate Return		
Expected Return	5%	−4%
Standard Deviation	10%	10%
Correlation with Domestic Return	0.30	0.00

    a. What is the expected return from a foreign investment in each country?

    b. Use the concepts from Chapter 6 to calculate the standard deviation of the foreign return on each country's stocks.

11. The value of the pension portfolio that you manage is $1 billion, and it is all invested in U.S. stocks. Its expected return is 15% and its standard deviation is 25%. Foreign investments are available in other countries; the expected foreign return and the standard deviation of each are 15% and 30%, respectively. The correlation between each foreign return and the U.S. return is 0.30. If you invest the $1 billion equally in the United States and in foreign countries, what are the expected return and standard deviation of your portfolio?

CFA   **12.** Renée Michaels, CFA, plans to invest $1 million in U.S. government cash equivalents for the next 90 days. Michaels's client has authorized her to use non-U.S. government cash equivalents, but only if the currency risk is hedged to U.S. dollars by using forward currency contracts.

    A. **Calculate** the U.S. dollar value of the hedged investment at the end of 90 days for *each* of the two cash equivalents in the table below. **Show** all calculations.

    B. **Briefly explain** the theory that best accounts for your results.

Interest Rates
90-Day Cash Equivalents

Japanese Government	7.6%
German Government	8.6%

Exchange Rates
Currency Units per U.S. Dollar

	Spot	90-Day Forward
Japanese Yen	133.05	133.47
German Deutschemark	1.5260	1.5348

CFA   **13.** You are the treasurer of USDS. One USDS board member has suggested that most of FI's cash be invested in one-year U.S. T-bills to reduce exposure to the pont. The suggested hedge is consistent with the firm's comprehensive strategy addressing foreign exchange exposure.

On January 1, 1990, the yield-to-maturity on one-year U.S. T-bills was 7.1%, while the comparable yield-to-maturity on one-year Lumbarian T-bills was 14.6%; the exchange rate was 4 ponts per one U.S. dollar. FI's cash position was such that 60 million ponts could be invested for one year without concern that this money would be required for operations.

a. Assume your economist's exchange rate forecast of a 5% decline in the value of the pont (vs. the U.S. dollar) by year-end 1990 proves to be correct. **Calculate** the proceeds at maturity, in U.S. dollars, of a 60-million pont investment in U.S. T-bills versus the same investment in Lumbarian T-bills. Assume that the holding period is the 1990 calendar year.

b. Using the T-bill yield information provided above and the four ponts per one U.S. dollar exchange rate at January 1, 1990, **calculate** the one-year forward exchange rate at the beginning of 1990 that would support the interest rate parity relationship.

c. Assuming that the one-year forward exchange rate at the beginning of 1990 was 4.1 ponts per one U.S. dollar, **describe** the transactions that a U.S. arbitrageur could execute to realize riskless profits, and **calculate** the amount of profits per $100 of exposure a U.S. arbitrageur would realize.

DATAFILE ANALYSIS

Access the data set called RTNSWRLD.WK1, and review its contents. For all countries having return data from 1971 and beyond, calculate their correlation with the S&P 500 returns. Interpret the financial significance of the results.

Notice that Norway and New Zealand have low correlations with U.S. returns. Does this mean that a large fraction of a U.S. investor's portfolio should be placed in equities of these two countries? (Hint: Refer to the data in Table 17-7.)

REFERENCES

Statistics on international equities are maintained and published by Morgan Stanley Capital International (MSCI) in their *MSCI Perspective* publications. The data is available at a cost directly from MSCI Geneva Switzerland or in most major libraries.

Overviews of the equity markets in most financially developed economies and many emerging markets are provided in the following publications.

The GT Guide to World Equity Markets, London; Euromoney Publication Plc., updated annually.

For a good text devoted solely to the international investing, see:

SOLNIK, BRUNO, *International Investing*, 2nd ed. Reading, MA: Addison-Wesley Publishing Company, 1991.

Interesting scholarly papers on international investing include:

CUMBY, ROBERT E., and JACK D. GLEN, "Evaluating the Performance of International Mutual Funds," *Journal of Finance*, June 1990.

FRENCH, KENNETH R., and JAMES M. POTERBA, "Were Japanese Stock Prices Too High?" *Journal of Financial Economics,* October 1991.

IBBOTSON, ROGER L., LAWRENCE SIEGEL, and KENNETH LOVE, "World Wealth, Market Values and Returns," *Journal of Portfolio Management*, Fall 1985.

PRINGLE, JOHN J., "Managing Foreign Exchange Exposure," *Journal of Applied Corporate Finance*, Winter 1991.

ROLL, RICHARD, "The International Crash of 1987," *Financial Analysts Journal*, September-October 1988.

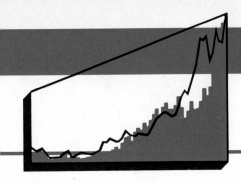

P A R T 4

Strategy

Prior chapters either focused on specific investment concepts or analyzed individual types of securities. We now put it all together in a discussion of the investment process and investment strategies.

The basic decisions that all investors must make are: 1. What security classes will be owned? 2. What portion of the portfolio will be held in each asset class? 3. Will the investment within a given asset class be actively or passively managed? 4. If active management is to be used, will the investor decide which securities are to be held or should professional managers be employed? 5. Is the performance of the portfolio reasonable?

In Chapter 18 we look at the process that should be used in making these decisions and how they should be formally documented in a statement of investment policy.

Chapter 19 follows with a discussion of the asset-allocation decision. Most professional investors believe that the asset-allocation decision is the most important decision that any investor will make since it determines the risks and expected returns of the portfolio.

After the portfolio's asset allocation has been selected, the investor should turn to each asset class and decide whether investment in the class will be passively or actively managed. Both passive and active management considerations have been discussed at some length in prior chapters. But we have not yet discussed the widely used investment practice of employing multiple active managers within an asset class. Types of professional managers and the manager-selection decision are the subjects of Chapter 20.

The concluding chapter, Chapter 21, surveys techniques used to evaluate portfolio performance. This is typically done at the aggregate portfolio level, for each asset class and for each investment manager.

Each chapter presents an interview with a professional investment consultant. These interviews show that the issues discussed here are not mere theories; they are actually applied.

Portfolio Management

The process of portfolio management is conceptually simple, in that it involves a logical set of steps common to any decision: plan, implement, and monitor. Yet applying this process to actual portfolios can be complex, and opinions are divided on how best to do so. Ideally, investment theory and empirical evidence would provide clear guidelines for each stage of the portfolio-management process; but, unfortunately, this isn't the case. Large gaps exist in current theory, and empirical tests often yield contradictory results.

But even though theory and empirical evidence cannot provide definitive answers, they can at least guide the process of portfolio management. Certain basic principles should be applied to all portfolio decisions:

1. *It is the portfolio that matters.* Individual securities are important only to the extent that they affect the aggregate portfolio.

2. *Larger expected portfolio returns come only with larger portfolio risk.* The most important portfolio decision is the amount of risk that is acceptable. That is determined by the asset allocation within the security portfolio.

3. *The risk associated with a security type depends on when the investment will be liquidated.* A person who plans to sell in one year will find future portfolio values to be less risky than a person who plans to sell in 25 years.

4. *Diversification works.* Diversification across various securities will reduce a portfolio's risk. If such broad diversification results in an expected portfolio return or risk level that is lower (or higher) than desired, then borrowing (or lending) can be used to achieve the desired level.

5. *Portfolio decisions should be tailored to the particular needs of its owner.* Contrary to the capital asset pricing model (CAPM), there is not a single "market portfolio" of risky assets that everyone should own. Investors have differing taxes, knowledge, liquidity needs, regulatory requirements, and so forth that need to be considered when designing the investment portfolio.

6. *Competition for abnormal returns is extensive.* Investors are constantly searching for information that is not reflected in current security prices so that they can profit by being the first to discover the information. As a result, the prices of widely followed securities trade very close to their fundamental intrinsic value. In addition, returns from active speculation appear to be similar to passive investment strategies.

THE PORTFOLIO INVESTMENT PROCESS

Overview

The process used to manage a security portfolio is conceptually the same as that used in any managerial decision. One should:

1. Plan.
2. Implement the plan.
3. Monitor the results.

This *portfolio investment process* is displayed schematically in Figure 18-1. Each aspect of the process is discussed in some detail later. For now, however, we will simply give an overview of the complete process.

The aspect of portfolio management most often overlooked is adequate planning, yet this is perhaps the most important element of proper portfolio investment and speculation. In the planning stage, a careful review should be conducted of the investor's financial situation and current capital market conditions. Taken together, these will suggest a set of investment and speculative policies to be followed. These policies should then be formally documented in a written *statement of investment policy* (SIP). The SIP will document: (1) the portfolio objective, (2) strategies that may (or may not) be used, and (3) various investment and speculative constraints. An output of proper planning will be a clearly defined *strategic asset allocation* (SAA). The SAA represents the optimal combination of various asset classes in an efficient market. The SAA is an indexed portfolio that would actually be held if a passive, pure-investment strategy is to be employed. The SAA portfolio might never actually be held, since adjustments in line with various speculative strategies may be made, but it represents the basic pure "investment" portfolio against which actual portfolio returns can be compared in order to determine whether speculative strategies are actually "adding value."

In the *implementation stage*, the investor must first decide who will select the individual securities to be held. If the investor wishes to do so personally, this is referred to as internal management. If the investor decides to employ the services of professional investment managers (such as mutual funds), it is referred to as external management. We saw in Chapter 1 that about 70% of all U.S. financial assets are professionally managed. After the internal/external decision is made, individual securities or managers are identified. Investment-manager searches are discussed in Chapter 20. In addition, a Tactical Asset Allocation (TAA) decision must be made. TAA refers to temporary departures from the SAA in the belief that certain security classes are mispriced. TAA is discussed in Chapter 19.

The last stage in the portfolio investment process consists of monitoring portfolio returns in order to determine which speculative decisions seem to be adding value to the portfolio and to ascertain that the portfolio's objective and constraints are being met and have not changed. Portfolio monitoring is discussed in Chapter 21.

FIGURE 18-1 *The Portfolio Investment Process*

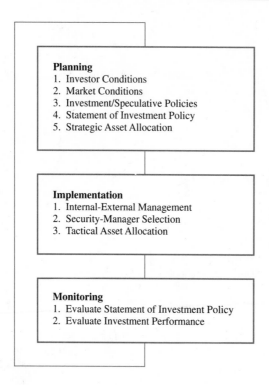

Planning
1. Investor Conditions
2. Market Conditions
3. Investment/Speculative Policies
4. Statement of Investment Policy
5. Strategic Asset Allocation

Implementation
1. Internal-External Management
2. Security-Manager Selection
3. Tactical Asset Allocation

Monitoring
1. Evaluate Statement of Investment Policy
2. Evaluate Investment Performance

Planning

Aspects of the planning stage are shown in Figure 18-2. Investor and capital market conditions are blended in order to determine a set of investment and speculative policies as well as a long-run strategic asset allocation (SAA). These are formally expressed in the statement of investment policy.

Investor Conditions. The first, and perhaps most important, question that must be answered is this: *"What is the purpose of the security portfolio?"* While this question might seem obvious, it is too often overlooked, giving way instead to the excitement of selecting the securities that are to be held. Understanding the purpose for trading in financial securities will help to: (1) define the expected portfolio liquidation date, (2) aid in determining an acceptable level of risk, and (3) indicate whether future consumption needs are to be paid in nominal or real dollars.

For example, a 90-year-old woman with small to moderate savings probably (1) has a short investment horizon, (2) can accept little investment risk, and (3) needs protection against short-term inflation. In contrast, a young couple investing for retirement in 40 years have (1) a very long investment horizon, (2) a willingness to accept moderate to large investment risk, and (3) a need for protection

FIGURE 18-2 *Portfolio Planning Stage*

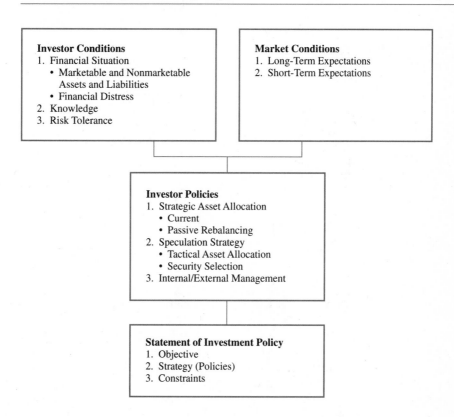

against long-term inflation. This suggests that the 90-year-old woman should invest solely in low-default-risk money market securities. The young couple could invest in many other asset classes for diversification and accept greater investment risks. In short, knowing the eventual purpose of the portfolio investment makes it possible to begin sketching out appropriate investment/speculative policies.

Next, the *complete* financial status of the investor must be understood. For example, consider the augmented balance sheet for a Mr. Paulson, shown in Table 18-1. Two types of assets and liabilities are defined. Marketable assets and liabilities refer to assets that could be sold now and liabilities that could be paid for now. These represent the assets and liabilities that would be reported by standard accounting procedures, only stated at current market value. Mr. Paulson's current marketable net worth is $140.

Nonmarketable assets are of two types. Insurance policies effectively represent long positions in put options that pay off under certain conditions, for example, physical disability or loss of assets through theft or damage. Although they cannot be sold to other individuals, they represent an asset to Mr. Paulson that has a positive (albeit difficult to determine) value. The second type of nonmarketable asset is the present value of expected future pay. This pay comes in three forms:

TABLE 18-1 *Hypothetical Present-Value Balance Sheet for Mr. Paulson*

Marketable Assets		*Marketable Liabilities*	
Security Portfolio	$ 100	Short-Term Debt	$ 50
Home	200	Mortgage	140
Personal Possessions	30		$ 190
	$ 330		
		Nonmarketable Liabilities	
Nonmarketable Assets		Present Value of Minimum	1,500
Insurance Policies	20	Future Consumption	
Present Value of			
Expected Future Pay:		*Net Worth*	140
Employment	1,000	Marketable Equity	520
Social Security	500	Nonmarketable Equity	
Pension Benefits	500		660
	$2,020		$2,350
		Total	
Total	$2,350		

(1) wage income from employment, (2) retirement income from social security, and (3) retirement income from employment-based pension benefits. The total risk of each of these nonmarketable assets and the extent to which they can be diversified or hedged differ considerably. For example, the $1,000 asset value arising from future wage income is closely tied to the talents of Mr. Paulson and the future fortunes of his employer. This asset cannot be diversified. The only way in which its risk can be reduced would be by taking offsetting hedges in other asset and liability positions. For example, if Mr. Paulson is employed as a computer salesman by IBM, he could hedge his risk by underweighting IBM shares and the shares of other computer companies in his security portfolio. In contrast, the risk inherent in the $500 present value of future pension benefits can be reduced by making sure that the employer has fully funded the pension plan and has invested all pension funds in a well-diversified security portfolio.

How should the $100 marketable security portfolio be invested? This is the critical investment question which Mr. Paulson faces. To answer this question, he should *not* focus on the distribution of returns on the $100 security portfolio itself. Instead, *he should focus on the distribution of his future net worth.*[1]

Portfolio investment and speculation decisions are too often based solely on potential security portfolio payoffs with no attention given to interactions between the security portfolio and other economic assets and liabilities of the individual or investment organization. This is the wrong approach. We saw one example above—the underweighting of computer stocks in Mr. Paulson's security portfo-

---

[1] In previous chapters, we focused solely on the returns on the underlying asset investments. This implicitly assumed that there were no other assets and no liabilities. Thus, the assets and net worth were identical.

lio. Consider another example. If the current value of future consumption is directly correlated with unexpected inflation, assets that hedge against this risk should be weighted more heavily than if little inflation risk were present.

The potential for temporary financial distress must also be considered. The economic net worth of Mr. Paulson might always remain positive. But if cash flows from his wage income are variable, he could find himself unable to pay current debts. For example, as a computer salesman, his compensation might be volatile and tied to economic activity. Thus, it is possible that his employment income might be low at the same time that the value of his security portfolio has fallen in value as a result of poor economic conditions. This suggests that a larger position in low-risk liquid securities should be taken.

In short, the total economic position of the individual must be examined. The unique short- and long-term risks inherent in major assets and liabilities must be understood. Although this is difficult to quantify, the problem is important and deserves careful thought.

The investor's knowledge of various securities also has an important impact on the types of security classes that should be held and the speculative strategies employed. The investor must understand that yearly equity returns are quite variable, short-term returns on bonds are sensitive to the bonds' duration, futures require daily mark-to-market, options are leveraged positions, international investment entails considerable exchange rate risk, and so forth. If the investor does not truly understand the nature and extent of a security's short- and long-term risk, the security should not be held.

Finally, the tolerance that the investor has for investment risk must be considered. This is clearly a difficult aspect of developing a proper investment strategy. Investment theories are largely based on a single future date at which the portfolio will be liquidated; theory speaks to the standard deviation of the security portfolio's value at that date. But this neglects a number of very important practical investment considerations. These include the following:

1. The relationship between investment horizon date payoffs from the marketable security portfolio and payoffs from other assets or liabilities of the investor (both marketable and nonmarketable). Two examples of this were presented above.

2. The investor's reaction to portfolio results during periods of time that are shorter than the investor's true investment horizon. For example, even though Mr. Paulson is investing for retirement and should be relatively unconcerned about yearly portfolio returns, a year or two with particularly good or bad returns might cause him to make short-term decisions that are not in his best long-term interest—for example, selling stock after it has fallen in value to buy gold at high prices. Long-term investors must be able to bear up to the despair or euphoria that temporary price swings can cause.

3. Although students of investment theory can interpret what the "standard deviation" of returns or wealth means, most investors cannot. Thus, the nature and extent of security risk must be communicated to investors in a way they can truly understand.

Market Conditions. An assessment of potential future returns on various classes or marketable securities must also be made. This is discussed in the next chapter and will not be treated here. However, two points need to be made. First, short-term (say, one year) expectations might differ considerably from longer-term expectations. If so, the portfolio's tactical asset allocation will differ from the long-term strategic asset allocation. Both short- and long-term market forecasts must be made *if one has any intent of engaging in tactical asset allocation* (*TAA*). The forecasts might turn out to be identical. But if TAA is allowed, both forecasts should be explicitly made. Second, forecasts should be stated in real dollars if future consumption and liabilities are tied to inflation. If consumption and liabilities are unaffected by inflation, then nominal return forecasts are appropriate.

Strategic Asset Allocation. The most important investment decision that the owner of a portfolio must make is the portfolio's asset allocation. Asset allocation refers to the percentage invested in various security classes. Security classes are simply the type of securities discussed earlier in the text:

1. Money market investment
2. Fixed-income obligations
3. Common stock
4. Real estate investment
5. International securities

Futures and options are not unique asset classes since they are effectively positions in another asset class such as common stock or bonds. Thus, futures and options do not provide any significant diversification advantages if they are properly priced. They simply alter the nondiversifiable risk position in the underlying asset.

A number of studies have shown that 90% or more of a portfolio's rate of return is determined by the portfolio's asset allocation. Of much less importance are the actual securities held. The simple fact that $X\%$ is invested in stocks as a class or $Y\%$ in bonds as a class is *the* dominant force that generates portfolio returns.

Strategic asset allocation (SAA) represents the asset allocation that would be optimal for the investor if all security prices trade at their long-term equilibrium values—that is, if the markets are efficiently priced.

Passive Rebalancing. Few investment strategies are static. They require changes as time passes, as the investor's wealth changes, as security prices change, as the investor's knowledge expands, and so on. Thus, the optimal strategic asset allocation will also change. Even if the investor continues to believe that all security prices are fair, the SAA will probably require periodic rebalancing. Such changes are *passive* changes to the portfolio. These are not active changes made in the hopes of earning excess risk-adjusted returns from potential security price disequilibriums. Instead, they represent logical shifts in the investor's strategic asset allocation in response to changes in the investor's condition or (fairly priced) market conditions.

Conceptually, we could think of investors as continuously revising their SAA. Thus, there would be no need to plan for a passive rebalancing strategy. At each moment in time, investors would evaluate their personal investment needs and market expectations to develop a current strategic asset allocation. As a practical matter, however, the costs of doing this are too large. For example, pension funds spend large sums of money and months of effort to develop an SAA. They simply cannot afford to engage in a continuous analysis of what their SAA should be. Individual investors who have much less capital and knowledge face even larger problems. As a result, it makes sense that part of the SAA decision should be a decision about how the SAA is to be changed as certain important economic variables change.

Thus, the SAA decision should actually contain two elements: (1) definition of a current SAA and (2) specification of a rebalancing strategy that passively adjusts the current SAA to changes in the investor's situation and security market conditions.

Speculation Strategy. After the investor has determined a current strategic asset allocation and decided how the allocation should be passively rebalanced as time passes, net worth changes, or stock prices vary, a decision must be made as to the types and amounts of security speculation that will be allowed. Speculative strategies can be classified as either tactical asset allocation (timing) decisions or security selection decisions.

Implementation

In Figure 18-3, the implementation stage is shown schematically. This consists of any active timing between asset classes and the selection of individual managers or securities to be held in each asset class.

Tactical Asset Allocation. If one believes that the price levels of certain asset classes, industries, or economic sectors are temporarily too high or too low, actual portfolio holdings should depart from the asset mix called for in the strategic asset allocation. Such a *timing* decision is referred to as tactical asset allocation (TAA). As noted, TAA decisions could be made across aggregate asset classes (stocks, bonds, and T-bills), industry classifications (steel, airline, food), or various broad economic sectors (basic manufacturing, interest-sensitive, consumer durables).

Security or Manager Selection. Investors must decide whether they intend to make individual security-selection decisions or whether they intend to employ the services of external professional managers. Large investment pools (pension fund, endowments, etc.) are managed by professionals—either as direct employees of the organization or as contracted service companies. Mutual funds are the logical source of external professional management available to smaller investors.

If one intends to follow a passive investment strategy, then one index fund for each asset class is adequate. Each would be very diversified and designed to track

FIGURE 18-3 *Portfolio Implementation Stage*

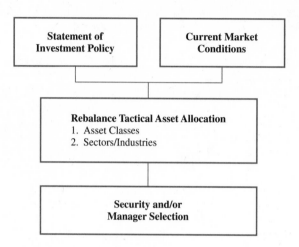

the returns on the aggregate asset class that it emulates. If active external managers are used, then a number of different organizations should be selected in order to obtain reasonable levels of diversification. Active managers tend to specialize and often do not own well-diversified portfolios. Thus, it is important to determine how they differ from each other and invest across managers who are distinctly different.

Portfolio Monitoring

The portfolio monitoring stage is shown schematically in Figure 18-4. There are three aspects to this monitoring. First, the actual portfolio held should be examined to ascertain that it is in compliance with the statement of investment policy and to determine whether any passive rebalancing of the asset mix is required. Second, investment performance should be reviewed. This should consist of a review of returns on (1) the aggregate portfolio, (2) each asset class and investment manager, and (3) the returns from any speculative strategies employed. Finally, adjustments to the SIP and investment managers should be made if necessary. Performance monitoring is the subject of Chapter 21.

THE STATEMENT OF INVESTMENT POLICY

The portfolio objective, constraints, and strategy should always be stated explicitly in a written document. This is not a nicety that only large portfolios need—it is a necessity for all portfolios. This statement of investment policy (or whatever one elects to call it) can be amended periodically as economic conditions or the

FIGURE 18-4 *Portfolio Monitoring Stage*

portfolio owner's needs change. In fact, the statement of policy should probably include the requirement that the statement itself be reviewed at least every two to three years.

There are at least four advantages to having a written statement of policy:

1. Requiring that a written document be prepared forces the investor to make difficult decisions that might otherwise be set aside.
2. A well-thought-out SIP can add discipline and stability to the long-run management of the portfolio, reducing whipsaw reactions to temporary price swings. By acting as documentation and education for why particular decisions were made, it should reduce capricious changes in investment strategies.
3. A well-drafted SIP defines the investor's strategic asset allocation (SAA) and passive rebalancing strategies.
4. Future performance evaluation is simply impossible without a clear benchmark against which a comparison can be made. The strategic asset allocation serves as the benchmark.

In a sense, the statement of investment policy is the constitution under which the investor's assets are to be managed. As such, it should be prepared only after the investor has fully investigated all major aspects of managing an investment portfolio.

The Portfolio Objective

Conceptually, the objective is to maximize expected return for an acceptable risk level. While true in theory, measuring whether the objective is being met in practice is difficult.

TABLE 18-2 *Hypothetical Strategic Asset Allocation*

Asset Class	Strategic Asset Allocation	Total
Short-Term Debt:		10%
U.S.	5%	
Non-U.S.	5%	
Fixed Income:		20
Government and Agency		
U.S. 1–3 Year	1	
U.S. 3–10 Year	3	
U.S. Long-Term	1	
Non-U.S.	5	
U.S. Asset Backed	5	
U.S. Corporate		
5–10 Year AAA	3	
High Yield (Junk)	2	
Equities		55
U.S. Large Capitalization	20	
U.S. Mid Capitalization	10	
U.S. Small Capitalization	5	
Europe	5	
Japan	5	
Pacific Rim	5	
Emerging Markets	5	
U.S. Real Estate		15
	100%	100%

Typically, the portfolio objective is a return objective based on the portfolio's SAA. For example, assume that the desired SAA is the one shown in Table 18-2. This is certainly a complex asset allocation consisting of a wide variety of security classes. But it is representative of the detail considered by large investment pools such as pension funds and foundations. If a passive strategy is used, then the portfolio objective should be to earn a return equal to the weighted average return on appropriate benchmarks for each asset class. The weights would be the percentage investment in each asset class (w_i), and the benchmarks would be a good proxy of returns on the asset class in the period examined (b_{it}). For U.S. large capitalization stocks shown in Table 18-2, the weight should be 0.20 and the benchmarks could be an index return such as the S&P 500 or the Russell 1000. Symbolically:

Passive Portfolio Return Objective in Period t
$$= \sum_{i=1}^{N} w_i b_{it}$$
(18.1)

If an active speculative strategy is being used, then the portfolio objective might be 100–200 basis points above the passive return.

Notice that the objective is not a specific rate of return. Unless the portfolio is invested relatively risk-free, specific return objectives are impractical. Also, the horizon interval over which the objective is measured should be neither too short nor too long. A three- to five-year period is common.

Constraints

Any constraint can, of course, reduce the chances of achieving the portfolio objective. For example, it would be virtually impossible to earn a 4% yearly real return if the portfolio is constrained to holdings of short-term Treasury obligations, since in the past, nominal returns on such securities have barely offset inflation. Common sense dictates that there be a reasonable relationship between the objective and the constraints. Typical constraints included in a statement of policy pertain to:

1. *Portfolio risk level.* If the objective is stated in terms of a desired rate of return, the most important constraint should be the acceptable risk of the portfolio. In theory, the risk level could be expressed as a portfolio beta or the standard deviation of portfolio returns.

     In practice, aggregate portfolio risk is usually defined in terms of the percentage of the portfolio allocated to various security types. For example, a 60/40 equity/fixed-income asset allocation is a common constraint of many large pension portfolios. Actually, such an approach is a fairly good way to identify allowable portfolio risk as long as the types of securities included in each group are well defined.

2. *Allowed securities.* All parties to the management of the portfolio should have a clear understanding of the types of securities that may be purchased. For example, if 40% of all assets are to be invested in fixed-income securities, the intended duration, default risk, callability, tax features, and so forth, should be clearly identified. If an external manager is to be used, such as a mutual fund, the statement of policy should clearly specify the principal investment characteristics of the types of funds that may be purchased—for example, the mutual fund beta, S&P quality, and dividend yield. This is commonly known as a manager assignment statement. (A manager assignment statement is not intended to tell the manager precisely what securities are to be purchased. Instead, it should provide general guidelines as to the types of securities to be purchased. Examples include low dividend yield versus high dividend yield, low beta versus high beta, etc.)

3. *Diversification.* Regardless of whether the portfolio owner, a mutual fund, or some other party will be making purchase and sale decisions, some statement should be made about the extent of diversification desired. This can be done by specifying (1) the minimum number of securities to be held, (2) the maximum percentage of the portfolio that may be held in a given security, (3) the maximum percentage of the portfolio that may be held in a given industry, (4) the R^2 obtained when portfolio returns are regressed against some market index such as the S&P 500, and so on.

     If more than one external manager is to be given money to invest, the diversification restrictions required from each can be less stringent than required for the portfolio as a whole. Nonetheless, the greater the diversification of the aggregate portfolio, the less its risk.

4. *Tax and liquidity.* Consideration should be given to both the tax and liquidity requirements of the portfolio. Investors in a high marginal tax bracket are faced

with complex portfolio decisions that only professional financial consultants trained in taxation can address. If taxes are an important factor, however, the principle that it is the total portfolio of all invested assets that matters is particularly critical. Marketable securities and real asset investments must be considered together in order to increase total after-tax portfolio returns. Investors that do not pay taxes, such as pension funds, may wish to exclude the purchase of securities that are priced in large part for their tax advantages. An example would be low-coupon bonds. Investors with average marginal tax rates may wish to include a statement that the portfolio be reviewed periodically during the course of a year in order to identify possible tax swaps.

Liquidity needs vary considerably among investors. Liquidity can be obtained in two principal ways: (1) by allocating an appropriate percentage of the portfolio to short-term securities or money market managers, or (2) by requiring that the bonds and equities purchased be highly marketable. Which of the two approaches is the more reasonable depends on why liquidity is needed. If quick access to cash is needed in order to make scheduled withdrawals from the portfolio (for bills, vacations, retirement, etc.), the first approach reduces transaction costs. However, if liquidity is desired to enable active speculation, the second approach may be more effective in reducing transaction costs.

5. *Social investing.* A growing concern of the 1980s was the extent to which an investment portfolio should be constrained by social issues. In the mid-1980s, the major issue was investment in U.S. corporations doing business in South Africa. But even prior to that, many portfolios were restricted from purchasing securities of firms engaged in alcohol or tobacco sales. There is no doubt that such restrictions reduce the diversification potential of the portfolio. How much so depends, of course, on the number of securities which are restricted. In the case of South Africa, the author has seen lists of restricted securities ranging from 30 to more than 200. The elimination of 30 securities probably would have minimal impact on diversification (although some of the 30 were large firms such as IBM). In contrast, the elimination of 200 securities could do severe damage to the ability to diversify.

6. *Strategy.* Finally, the statement of policy should discuss the forms of active speculation that will be allowed. In the broadest sense, speculative transactions can be related to either *timing* or *selection.* Based on one's belief in the usefulness of timing and selection speculation, the statement of policy should identify the extent to which they may be used.

PORTFOLIO TYPES AND THEIR NEEDS

Security portfolios are owned by individuals and organizations having dramatically different objectives and constraints. To illustrate how the portfolio investment process applies to different situations, we will briefly examine two different groups: (1) individuals and (2) pension funds.

Individuals

The range of portfolio objectives, constraints, and strategies varies more among individual investors than among any other group of portfolio owners. As a result, we can provide only an overview of the major issues that most individual investors face.

Considerations in Setting the Objective. The most likely objective of a person's security portfolio is to provide a supplement to social security and pension benefits during the individual's retirement. Other needs, such as saving for a house, vacation, child's education, and so forth, are also common, of course. But the pervasive need is to increase income during retirement. As a result, an individual's age has a significant effect on the perceived riskiness of various types of securities. For example, a person who is 25 years from retirement can ride through the inevitable good and bad years of stock returns, whereas someone in retirement will be immediately affected by such movements since portions of the portfolio will have to be liquidated to meet current consumption needs. All other things held equal, the amount of equity risk inherent in a portfolio should decrease as an individual draws closer to retirement.

In addition to the individual's age, his or her other assets should be considered. Particular attention should be given to any real estate holdings and the nature of the person's career. In order to ensure the greatest possible diversification, the individual should probably underweight securities whose returns are highly correlated with returns on such existing assets.

Finally, the individual's level of investment knowledge can affect the portfolio's constraints and strategy. Unfortunately, there is often a big difference between what should be done conceptually and what is done in practice. Because most individual investors lack investment expertise, they should attempt to diversify broadly (say, by purchasing a mutual fund), minimize costs (trade little and only in no-load mutual funds), and avoid active speculation and complex securities (such as options and futures). In practice, however, a major portion of the security information that individuals receive comes from brokers, who are paid only if their customers trade.

Consequently, many individuals own security portfolios that are poorly diversified, invest in load mutual funds, trade actively on broker recommendations, and use complex securities such as options and futures to gain speculative profits. Many brokers and brokerage firms sincerely try to provide general investment counseling. However, as a rule, such efforts are meager in comparison with the efforts devoted to persuading the customer to trade.

In sum, three factors are important in determining the individual investor's portfolio constraints and strategy:

1. A focus on retirement benefits
2. Other assets owned
3. Level of investment knowledge

Constraints. With this as background, various constraints can be considered. Among the most common are the following:

1. *Risk level.* This is a decision that the individual should make after reviewing information about the risks and expected returns from various asset mixes. Later in the chapter, we will examine how this might be done. All other things held equal, the equity portion should decrease as the person approaches retirement.

2. *Strategy.* The investor's knowledge should largely determine what can be held. People with little knowledge should minimize holdings of complex instruments, such as options and futures, and instruments that require close monitoring, such as bonds with above-average default risk.

3. *Diversification.* Consideration should be given to the nature of other assets owned so the securities portfolio can underweight similar investments. No-load mutual funds and bank trust accounts are reasonable ways of achieving a diversified portfolio.

4. *Taxes and liquidity.* Investors in high tax brackets should seek professional advice. In general, they will find that municipal bonds, low-coupon bonds, and low-dividend-yield stocks provide larger after-tax returns. Investors in lower tax brackets should own taxable bonds with high coupons and dividend yields. Liquidity requirements depend on the individual's age and desire to speculate.

5. *Speculation.* In general, individual investors do not have the training and rapid access to new information necessary to successfully engage in speculative trades. They should follow a passive investment approach.

Life Cycle Investment. The major reason why most individuals and families save is to supplement retirement income. In the United States, consumption during retirement is paid from three possible sources: (1) social security, (2) pension benefit payments, and (3) personal investment portfolios. The situation varies across other countries with some relying more on social security and others relying almost exclusively on personal investment saving. The discussion below focuses on a U.S. investor.

Consider the case of Stuart Chu. Stuart is 35 years of age, unmarried, and employed by a food distributor. Stuart intends to retire at age 65 and should expect to live for another 15 years after retiring. Although his current salary is $30,000, it should grow at a real annual rate of 0.5%. Thus his expected salary at retirement (in current dollars) is $34,840 ($30,000 $\times$ 1.005^{30}). (Throughout this example, we neglect taxes and future inflation.)

In retirement, social security benefits should replace about 40% of retirement salary. Pension retirement benefits will provide additional income, say, equal to 30% of final salary. The remaining 30% of final salary will have to be provided by Stuart's personal savings plan. Let's assume that Stuart wishes to develop a personal investment strategy that will add $5,000 per year to the income received from social security and pension benefits.

The amount that Stuart will have to invest to provide an expected $5,000 annuity between 30 years from now and 45 years depends on two things: (1) when he invests and (2) the rate of return he expects to earn on his investment (i.e., the risk of the investment).

Let's assume that he intends to invest risk-free once he reaches retirement and that the best current estimate of what the real risk-free rate will be at that time is 2% per year. Thus, at the start of his retirement (end of year 35), he will need a portfolio worth $64,246 to provide a 15-year $5,000 annuity at a return of 2%.

$$\$64,246 = \sum_{t=1}^{15} [\$5,000 \div (1.02)^t)]$$

If Stuart wished to make a one-time investment today that will grow to $64,246, the size of the investment required will depend on the real return that he expects to earn between today and retirement. This expected real return will, of course, depend on the risk of the portfolio in which he invests. For example, at a 2% risk-free real rate, he would have to invest $35,469 today. At a moderate risk, he would expect to earn higher returns and, thus, have to invest less today. For example, at a 6% expected return, only $11,186 need be invested today to provide the expected portfolio value of $64,246 in 30 years.

$$\$35,469 = \$64,246 \div (1.02)^{30}$$

$$\$11,186 = \$64,246 \div (1.06)^{30}$$

It is unlikely that Stuart would have the resources to make such an investment today. Typically people will save during their working years and spend during retirement years. This is illustrated in Figure 18-5 using the data in this example. Values shown by the dotted lines are associated with a 6% real return. For simplicity, the figure is based on an annuity savings plan. More realistically, people will save a level percentage of income.

In panel A the total value of the portfolio over time is shown. For both assumed pre-retirement returns, the portfolio is expected to be worth $64,246 at retirement. But since investment earnings on the 2% portfolio are expected to be smaller than for the 6% portfolio, the 2% portfolio requires greater contributions throughout the pre-retirement period. The differences in these contributions can be easily seen in panel B.

There are good reasons to believe that individuals with many years until retirement will be more risk-tolerant than the same individuals during retirement. For example, individuals who will not retire for many years have the ability to offset negative security portfolio results by additional efforts at their jobs. In contrast, retired individuals have very limited opportunities to supplement portfolio returns. We will see in the next chapter that longer investment horizons have greater investment risk than shorter horizons. There is no diversification benefit associated with time. But long-term investors are probably more risk-tolerant since they have the ability to recoup security losses by other means. This has led many investment counselors to believe that the greatest investment risk can be taken early in one's career, that investment risk should decrease as one approaches retirement, and that risk should be very small during retirement.

FIGURE 18-5 *Retirement Saving and Spending*

RETIREMENT SAVINGS AND SPENDING

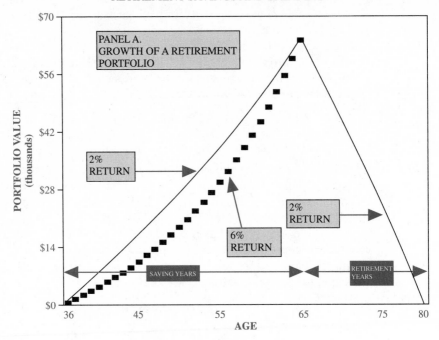

PANEL A.
GROWTH OF A RETIREMENT
PORTFOLIO

2%
RETURN

6%
RETURN

2%
RETURN

SAVING YEARS

RETIREMENT
YEARS

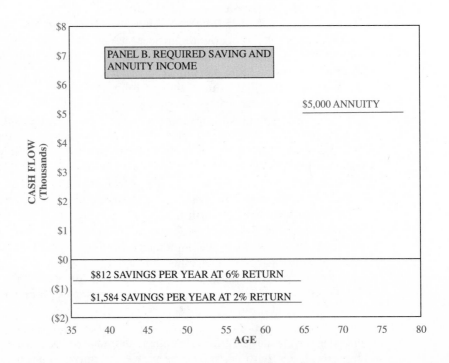

PANEL B. REQUIRED SAVING AND
ANNUITY INCOME

$5,000 ANNUITY

$812 SAVINGS PER YEAR AT 6% RETURN

$1,584 SAVINGS PER YEAR AT 2% RETURN

A Statement of Investment Policy for Stuart Chu

ASSET ALLOCATION

Considerations. The purpose of this investment plan is to supplement my retirement income. Since my retirement will be in the distant future, I am willing to accept greater investment risk today than I will accept as the date of retirement approaches. Also, since one major risk I face is uncertainty about inflation between today and my retirement, the investments that are selected should provide a decent long-term hedge against inflation. A large part of my wealth is presently invested in my home and the land on which it is built. Thus I need little further investment in real estate other than to provide diversification against the fall in local real estate values. Finally, I am not particularly knowledgeable in security investment selection and wish to minimize my costs of investing. Therefore, I will invest solely in index mutual funds.

Conclusions. The initial asset allocation of my portfolio will be:

Type of Index Mutual Fund	Percent of Portfolio
Money Market Funds	10%
Bond Index Funds	15%
Large Capitalization U.S. Stocks	40%

Type of Index Mutual Fund	Percent of Portfolio
Small Capitalization U.S. Stocks	5%
Foreign Bond Funds	0%
Foreign Stock Funds	20%
Real Estate Investment Trusts	10%
	100%

OBJECTIVE

Since these funds are to be invested in passive index mutual funds, I expect my return on each to be their index benchmark less 25 basis points per year to cover operating expenses.

CONSTRAINTS

1. To pay taxes on dividend receipts from the mutual funds, I will retain 30% of all dividends and reinvest the remainder in each fund.
2. At the end of each calendar quarter, I will invest 7% of my net salary in this investment portfolio.
3. Quarterly investments will be made into these funds so that my asset allocation will be approximately the same as stated above.
4. I will engage in no tactical asset allocation (TAA).

Pension Funds

The growth of employee retirement-benefit plans has been one of the dominant forces affecting the security markets since the mid-1900s. Since the early 1960s, of all institutional investors, pension funds have owned the largest amount of common stocks, and their relative importance continues to grow. For example, in 1960 noninsured pension funds owned 5% of the market value of all stocks listed on the NYSE. By 1990, their ownership interest had increased to about 25%.

There are two basic forms of employee benefit plans: (1) *defined contribution plans* and (2) *defined benefit plans.*[2] Defined contribution plans specify the amount that the employer will contribute to an employee's retirement plan. The contribution could be a flat dollar amount, a percentage of the employee's pay, or a

---

[2] We will not discuss Keogh plans or Individual Retirement Accounts (IRAs), which allow employees to place a limited amount of their earnings in a tax-deferred retirement plan.

specified share of corporate profits (a profit-sharing plan). Once the contribution has been made, all investment risk is borne by the employee. If the investment portfolio has performed better than expected, when an employee begins to withdraw pension benefits his or her payments will be larger than expected. If investment performance has been lower than expected, the employee's benefits will also be lower than expected. Again, all the investment risk of a defined contribution plan is borne by the employee. Consequently, employees covered by such a plan should be given considerable say in how their funds are invested.

In contrast, defined benefit plans specify a contractual benefit that will be paid to the employee after retirement. The size of the retirement benefit is calculated in a variety of ways. Examples of benefit formulas include: (1) a percentage of earnings (say, 50% of an employee's average salary during the last three years of employment), (2) an amount per year of service (say, $300 times the number of years of service), and (3) a percentage of earnings per year of service (say, 1% of the sum of all yearly earnings). Regardless of the precise formula used, defined benefit plans provide a contractual retirement benefit to the employee. All investment risk is borne by the employer. As such, the employer should have the strongest say in how plan assets are invested.

Funding a Defined Benefit Plan. Under a defined benefit plan, the employer has a legal obligation to pay employees a contractually agreed-upon retirement benefit. The sole purpose of having a pension investment portfolio is to be able to meet these obligations in the future.

To help understand the various forces that determine the objective, constraints, and strategy of a pension portfolio, it is necessary that we understand the general process by which benefit liabilities are "funded." We will not delve too deeply into the details of pension funding here. However, the general process of pension funding is relatively easy to understand. In fact, the pension-funding decision is no more than an application of time-value-of-money concepts.

Assume that you are the owner of a business which has 100 employees, each of whom now receives compensation of $20,000 a year. You have signed a pension agreement with the employees promising to pay a yearly individual pension benefit equal to 30% of the retiring employee's compensation during his or her last year of employment. This retirement benefit will be paid at year-end during each year of the employee's retirement until the employee dies. A pension investment portfolio has been set up to help pay these future benefits. At present, the portfolio has a market value of $1 million.

You face two questions:

1. What are the *expected benefit payments?*
    a. In what years?
    b. In what dollar amounts?
2. What *contributions* should be made to the pension portfolio to ensure that the expected benefit payments will be met?

In order to calculate the expected benefit payments and required contributions, a number of assumptions need to be made:

1. Salary growth—Merit: 1.0% per year
    Inflation: <u>5.0% per year</u>

    Total: <u>6.0% per year</u>

2. Mortality rate—Preretirement: None
    Postretirement: All employees live 15 years after retirement
3. Termination rate: No one leaves employment until retirement in 25 years
4. Years to retirement: Everyone will retire in 25 years
5. Postretirement benefit increases: None (no cost-of-living adjustment)
6. Investment returns—Real: 4% per year
    Inflation: <u>5% per year</u>

    Total: <u>9% per year</u>

7. Funding method: Annual annuity sufficient to fully fund by retirement

Estimated retirement benefits and required contributions are calculated in Table 18-3. Consider first the estimated benefits. Current salaries total $2 million. Since no employees are expected to leave employment because of death or termination, and since all employees are expected to retire in 25 years from now, the retirement benefit is based on the expected total salary payout in 25 years. Yearly salary growth consists of a merit increase and an inflation component, which sum to 6% per year. Growing at 6%, the current $2 million salary base will be $8.58 million in 25 years. Since employees have a right to yearly benefits equal to 30% of this total and all are expected to live for 15 years after retirement, the retirement benefits will be a 15-year annuity of $2,575,122 (30% × $8.58 million).

Now let's calculate the contributions that are required in order to pay these benefits. The yearly contribution will depend on two things: (1) the return we expect to earn on portfolio investments and (2) the funding method chosen. The expected investment return is 9% per year, consisting of a 4% real return and a 5% inflation component (the same inflation rate used for salary growth). The funding method requires that all benefit liabilities be "fully funded" by the retirement date (end of year 25) and that any contributions necessary to fully fund the portfolio be made in annual annuity installments.[3] The present value at the end of year 25 of the $2.57 million, 15-year-benefit annuity at a 9% investment rate is $20.76 million. Thus, if the pension portfolio has a value of $20.76 million at the end of year 25 and earns 9% each year, it will be able to exactly meet the yearly $2.57 million benefit liability. Unfortunately, the current $1 million portfolio growing at 9% per year will be worth only $8.62 million in 25 years. A deficiency of $12.13 million exists. To meet this deficiency a 25-year contribution annuity of $143,260 is necessary. Given the assumptions we have made, a level $143,260 yearly contribution to the pension portfolio is required. If any of the assumptions were to change, so would the contribution requirement. For example,

---

[3] In practice, contributions are typically not calculated as level-dollar annuities but, instead, as a level percentage of expected future salary.

TABLE 18-3 *Estimated Pension Benefit Payments and Contributions*

Estimated Benefits	*Years of Employment*		*Years of Retirement*			
	0	*25*	*26*	*...*	*39*	*40*
Current Salary	$2,000,000	–				
Salary at Retirement: $2,000,000 × 1.06^{25}	–	$ 8,583,741				
Retirement Benefits: $8,583,741 × 30%	–	–	$2,575,122	...	$2,575,122	$2,575,122
Estimated Level Contributions						
P.V. of Benefits at Retirement: $2,575,122 × $\sum_{t=1}^{15} \dfrac{1}{1.09^t}$	–	$20,757,286				
Future Value of Current Portfolio: $1,000,000 × 1.09^{25}	–	$ 8,623,081	–		–	–
Deficiency		$12,134,205				
Level Annuity Contribution Required to Meet Deficiency: $12,134,205 ÷ $\sum_{t=1}^{25} 1.09^{t-1}$		$143,260 ... $143,260				

what would happen if we increased the assumed inflation rate? First, the yearly benefit liability would rise because the employees' ending salaries would be larger. However, the investment return would also rise and, all other things being equal, cause required contributions to fall. Taking into acccount both effects, contributions would fall since the inflation rate increases the investment return for the full 40-year period of the portfolio's accumulation and liquidation, whereas the salary growth is affected for only the 25-year employment period. Increasing the assumed inflation rate without allowing for cost-of-living adjustments to benefits during the employees' retirement harms the employees and provides a gain to the employer in the form of lower contributions. We will not examine other possible modifications to our assumptions. But two things are clear. First, the analysis can quickly become quite complicated as we move from our simple example to more realistic cases. Second, the assumed investment return is only one of many components that determine a pension fund's contribution requirement.

ERISA. Retirement-benefit plans of corporations are subject to the legal requirements of the Employee Retirement Income Security Act (ERISA). Prior to ERISA, pension sponsors were legally responsible for their actions under a somewhat loose common-law principle known as the *Prudent Man Rule*. Historically, the Prudent Man Rule evaluated the risk of a security in isolation from other securities held in the portfolio and required that professional fiduciaries purchase only securities with low enough risks that a ''prudent man'' would also own them. In

1974 Congress enacted ERISA, the first nationwide statutory law to regulate the management of corporate pension funds. In many ways, the intent of ERISA was similar to the Prudent Man Rule. However, it differs in two important aspects. First, the risk of a security is now considered in the context of the total portfolio. Thus, a very risky security may now be purchased (although it may not have been allowed under the Prudent Man Rule) if its risk is offset by other securities in the portfolio. Second, ERISA explicitly requires that sponsors diversify "the investments of the plan so as to minimize the risk of large losses, unless under the circumstances it is clearly prudent not to do so."[4] In short, ERISA is a legislated version of what modern portfolio theory says the Prudent Man Rule should be.

Only corporate pension funds must follow ERISA requirements. All other professional fiduciaries are still subject to the common-law Prudent Man Rule. However, if logic prevails, legal interpretation of the Prudent Man Rule will move more closely towards the risk and diversification concepts inherent in ERISA.

PBGC. At the same time that Congress enacted ERISA, it created a governmental agency that guarantees certain minimum benefit payments to employees belonging to defined benefit plans. This agency is the Pension Benefit Guarantee Corporation (PBGC). It plays a role analogous to that of the Federal Deposit Insurance Corporation, which guarantees deposits in national banks and savings and loans. PBGC, however, guarantees pension benefits to employees of corporations that default on their pension promises—usually through firm bankruptcy. All firms that fall under ERISA are required to pay a yearly insurance fee to the PBGC for each member of their defined benefit plans. Since governmental pension plans do not fall under ERISA, their future benefits are not guaranteed by the PBGC.

Considerations in Setting Objectives and Constraints. Sponsors of defined benefit plans are interested, of course, in the risk/reward characteristics of their investment portfolios. But this is solely because a portfolio's expected return and risk directly affect both expected contributions and uncertainty about such contributions. *The objective of a defined benefit plan sponsor is to minimize expected contribution costs without accepting undue risk.* Portfolio risk and return must be viewed in this context—as one of a number of factors that influence expected contribution levels and uncertainty.

In view of this, let's examine the constraints we've discussed before:

1. *Risk level.* Again, this depends on the circumstances facing the pension sponsor as well as the sponsor's tolerance for risk. For example, consider a plan that is underfunded, fairly mature, and unable to draw large contributions from the sponsoring corporation or governing body. Such a plan will have to be exposed to larger investment risk in the hopes of greater returns than otherwise. An opposite example would be a plan that is fully funded today.

---

[4] From section 404 (a) (1) (c) of the Employee Retirement Income Security Act of 1974.

Investment Consultant Interview

This interview was conducted with John Pickett and Robert Wood, who are pension consultants with The Principal/Eppler, Guerin & Turner, Inc.

Question: In your capacity as Pension Consultants, what exactly do you do?

JOHN: We assist plan sponsors in formulating an investment game plan. In the case of a Defined Benefit Pension Plan, we help the plan sponsor tie together the actuarial side as well as the investment sides of the plan. Many times we find these components have not been coordinated, thus the investments have not been structured to meet the long-term actuarial needs of the plan.

In the case of a Defined Contribution Plan, we work with the plan sponsor in quantifying their objectives, in structuring an investment plan and, most important, we develop a way to communicate to employees the risks and potential returns associated with various investment opportunities.

BOB: That is right. As a pension and asset consultant, our job is effectively that of a teacher; teaching the client about Capital Market Theory and how different asset classes have different long-term levels of performance, long-term levels of volatility, and, very importantly, short-term levels of volatility.

Question: What's the first step after a client retains you?

BOB: The first step is to get the client to understand their current financial situation. Are they over-funded or under-funded according to their current actuarial study? Are they expanding as a business or contracting? Is their work force made up of mainly older employees making it a mature plan which has less tolerance to risk? Or, is it a company like Dell Computer or Apple Computer, with a very young work force, which can take on more risk as measured by asset class and portfolio volatility?

JOHN: As in any consulting relationship, the first step is to understand the needs and objectives of the client. We often find that clients have never truly focused on their "risk tolerance" or "time horizon." They have never completely understood how much money they are willing to lose over a certain time period.

Once we have gained an understanding of our client's needs, then we assist them in developing an investment program to meet those objectives.

The first step is to draft a written policy. This is known as a Statement of Investment Policy (SIP).

In the case of a Defined Benefit Plan, we'll perform an asset/liability study which simulates the impact that changes in the asset allocation will have on the liability side of the plan. It also shows how changes in demographics might impact the sponsor's liability.

As a result of this study, plan sponsors are able to develop a long-term asset allocation which is also known as the Strategic Asset Allocation.

In the case of the Defined Contribution Plan, we will assist the plan sponsor in focusing on objectives such as:

- The probability of funding a certain level of retirement benefits;
- The probability of losing money over a fixed period of time; and
- The probability of meeting rate of return objectives.

The result of this exercise would also be a Strategic Asset Allocation.

Other integral parts of the policy statement would be:

- Makeup and duties of a retirement committee;
- Frequency of meetings and items to be covered;
- Rate of return objectives of the plan;
- Minimum return expectations and time horizons for managers; and
- Proxy voting.

Question: What is the most important thing to teach a plan sponsor?

BOB: How to manage risk and the importance of diversification as a risk management tool. These are difficult things for untrained investment boards to understand.

Consider asset allocation. If we are dealing with a new asset class, the client needs to be educated about the asset class itself. For example, if they are introducing real estate into their portfolio of global fixed income they need to understand both the characteristics of that asset class and how it relates to other asset classes.

JOHN: There is no free lunch! There is a tradeoff between risk and return. High return only comes from taking high risk. This may not be apparent over short-term time horizons, but over the long term this fundamental economic law always is enforced.

Question: What is the biggest change in investment holdings you have seen in the last five years?

JOHN: In the past five years we have seen a marked increase in the level of investment sophistication on the part of plan sponsors. This has resulted in a high level of acceptance to new asset classes which add diversifying characteristics to a traditional portfolio of domestic stocks and bonds.

BOB: International components of portfolios have increased dramatically. More and more plan sponsors are adding international equities; some are adding international fixed income, others are adding global fixed income.

Question: What's the most important thing you would tell a plan sponsor, whether they hired you or not?

BOB: Diversify!

JOHN: In addition to diversification, they need to focus on a long-term horizon and keep their sights on those goals. Do not deviate from the long-term goals and react to short-term aberrations in the market.

Pension Plan sponsors, as do other investors, become over-euphoric at market highs or pessimistic at market bottoms.

Sponsors of this second plan would probably accept less return (and risk) than they would in other circumstances.[5] In short, the risk level a pension plan selects will depend on both the sponsor's risk tolerance and the financial circumstances facing the plan.

2. *Allowable securities.* Because of their large size, most pension funds have the financial ability and investment sophistication to hold a diverse group of different asset classes. For example, direct and indirect investment in real estate equity, international investment, venture capital pools, and so forth are widely used.

3. *Diversification.* Again, because of their size and investment sophistication, pension plans can purchase a wide variety of asset types in order to increase portfolio diversification. Examples were mentioned above and include real estate, foreign investment, and venture capital projects.

4. *Taxes and liquidity.* Pensions do not pay taxes on investment income. As a result, holdings of securities that provide major tax advantages need to be closely evaluated. For example, municipal bonds and preferred stock are rarely

---

[5] The sponsor of a plan that is more than fully funded might ask another party, such as an insurance company, to assume the pension's liabilities. The sponsor would pay the insurance firm an amount equal to the actuarial value of the liabilities and sell off the assets of the plan. Since the plan is overfunded, excess cash will be received from the sale of assets over the actuarial liability. This excess cash will then be used by the corporation as it wishes—to buy a new plant, retire debt, etc. During the middle 1980s, such pension-plan terminations were common.

purchased. Similarly, much of the return on equity investment in depreciable real estate comes in the form of tax advantages that the pension cannot realize.

With rare exceptions, the benefit liabilities of pension funds are long term in nature. As a result, there is little need for liquidity and immediate cash flow.

5. *Speculation.* Sponsors of pension plans have access to the best information available through myriad investment consultants. As a result, they are usually aware of the arguments in favor of or against active speculation. Many pension funds have, in fact, concluded that the best approach is to index—to purchase money market, bond, and equity index funds as well as to immunize via dedicated portfolios. Most pension funds, however, have not given up the search for speculative profits. Nonetheless, they maintain close control of the risks that their managers are able to accept. Managers are usually assigned specific roles. For example, an equity manager might be told to invest only in high-quality, low-beta securities and a bond manager might be told to guarantee a return via contingent immunization. In short, to the extent speculation is allowed, the sponsor will maintain active control over total portfolio risk.

Defined Contribution Plans. In recent years, most newly formed pension plans are defined contribution plans. Their advantages over defined benefit plans include:

1. *Administrative costs.* Growing regulation of defined benefit plans and yearly insurance payments to the Pension Benefit Guarantee Corporation have caused many employers who are creating new pension plans to select a defined contribution form.
2. *Investment risk.* Employers bear all investment risk of a defined benefit plan. Recognizing that pension assets are essentially retirement savings plans for employees, many plan sponsors have chosen to pass investment risk to the employee by using the defined contribution plan.
3. *Portability.* Portability refers to employees' ability to take their pension assets from one employer to another when they switch employment. While defined benefit plans are not portable, many (not all) defined contribution plans are portable.

Defined contribution plans are basically tax-sheltered retirement savings plans for employees. Since employees bear all investment risk, they should (in theory) decide the way in which their pension assets should be allocated across various asset classes. But assuring that employees make well-informed decisions requires that the employer provide an educational program that details the expected returns and risks of each asset class available to employees. Typically, the employer will select a number of investment managers who manage various security classes—thus providing employees a wide range of choices. Each employee is allowed to decide the proportion of their pension assets that are allocated to each manager. In some situations, however, the employer, believing that the employee is not knowledgeable enough, makes the asset-allocation decision of all employees as a pool.

SUMMARY

The portfolio investment process consists of three logical stages:

1. *Planning.* The needs, knowledge, and risk tolerance of the investor are brought together with long-run capital market expectations to define the investor's long-run strategic asset allocation (SAA). The SAA decision should consist of two subdecisions: (*a*) what the current SAA should be and (*b*) how the SAA should be passively rebalanced as time passes, as the investor's wealth changes, or as stock prices change. The portfolio objective, constraints, and all speculative strategies which are to be allowed should be formally documented in a written statement of investment policy.

2. *Implementation.* Once the strategic asset allocation has been determined, various speculative strategies can be considered. Such strategies fall into two broad approaches: timing and selection. Timing decisions over- and underweight various asset classes, industries, or economic sectors in an attempt to earn excess risk-adjusted returns. Such timing decisions are referred to as tactical asset allocation decisions. Security selection speculation consists of over- or underweighting individual securities within a given asset class. If timing and selection strategies are not used, then the investor's portfolio should consist of index funds that are held in proportions consistent with the SAA. If security prices are efficiently priced, timing and selection decisions will result in a loss of value because of transaction costs.

3. *Monitoring.* The portfolio should be periodically monitored to ensure that all constraints of the statement of investment policy are being met and to monitor returns from asset allocation and speculative strategies.

REVIEW PROBLEM

You are examining the financial condition and investment policies of two defined benefit pension plans, Yung Technology and Auld Land Signs. Information about each is given below:

	Yung	*Auld*
Current Investment Portfolio Value	$5.0 million	$60.0 million
Employee Information		
Number of employees	1,000	1,000
Average current salary	$20,000	$30,000
Benefit payments as % of final salary	25%	25%
Average years to retirement	30	15
Actuarial Assumptions		
Annual salary growth	4%	4%
Mortality rate prior to retirement	0%	0%
Employee termination preretirement	0%	0%
Retirement cost-of-living increases	0%	0%
Average years of retirement	15 years	15 years

Investment Portfolio Assumptions

Desired stock/bond mix	70%–30%	30%–70%
Expected nominal stock return (per year)	10%	10%
Expected nominal bond return (per year)	4%	4%

Funding Policy   Year-end annuity to fully fund requirements by end of last employment year

a. What are the basic differences in the benefit liabilities of each firm?

b. Both Yung and Auld desire that the value of their investment portfolios be sufficient to meet the retirement benefits of their employees. Specifically, their goals are to have portfolio values on the last day of an average person's employment equal to the present value of expected future benefit liabilities. What is this desired portfolio value for each firm?

c. Given the asset allocation chosen by each firm, is the current portfolio value sufficient to meet the needs of part b above?

d. If Yung wishes to make year-end level-dollar (annuity) contributions to its investment portfolio, what must the contribution be?

Solution

a. The plans differ principally in their maturities. The Yung pension plan has an employee base with an average of 30 years to retirement. In contrast, the Auld pension plan's employees will retire on average in 15 years. All other things being equal, Yung can accept greater investment risk.

b. *Present Value of Benefit Liabilities at Average Retirement Date*

Benefit Annuity	Yung	Auld
Current Salary Base	$20.000 million	$30.000 million
Compound Rate of Growth to Average Retirement	1.04^{30}	1.04^{15}
Retirement Salary Base	$64.868 million	$54.028 million
Benefit Payment Rate	0.25	0.25
15-Year Benefit Annuity	$16.217 million	$13.507 million
Actuarial Investment Return		
Stock Return (0.7 × 10%)	7.0%	
(0.3 × 10%)		3.0%
Bond Return (0.3 × 4%)	1.2%	
(0.7 × 4%)		2.8%
Expected Portfolio Return	8.2%	5.8%

Present Value Factor of a 15-Year Annuity

$$\sum_{t=1}^{15} \frac{1}{1.082^t} \qquad\qquad \sum_{t=1}^{15} \frac{1}{1.058^t}$$

$$= \frac{1}{0.082}\left(1 - \frac{1}{1.082^{15}}\right) \qquad = \frac{1}{0.058}\left(1 - \frac{1}{0.058^{15}}\right)$$

$$= 8.4559 \qquad\qquad\qquad\qquad = 9.804$$

Present Value of Annuity
(8.4559 × $16.217) $137.129 million

(9.8404 × $13.507) $132.914 million

c. *Growth of Current Portfolio with No Contributions*

	Yung	*Auld*
Current Portfolio Value	$ 5.0 million	$ 60.0 million
Compound Rate of Growth	1.082^{30}	1.058^{15}
Expected Portfolio Value	$53.18 million	$139.78 million

The Auld pension plan has assets that are expected to grow to more than necessary to meet future benefit liabilities. It is overfunded slightly. Management could either reduce the investment risk exposure by investing less in stocks or withdraw some of the assets from the portfolio. Regardless of any such decisions, future contributions are not expected to be needed.

Since the Yung pension plan does not have sufficient current portfolio assets to meet expected benefit liabilities, Yung will have to provide future contributions and may wish to increase its commitments to stocks in order to increase the expected investment returns.

d. Future value annuity factor with interest = 8.2% and period = 30 years is:

$$\sum_{t=0}^{29} 1.082^t = 117.524$$

Value of Liability at Retirement	=	$137.129 million
Expected Current Portfolio Value	=	53.180 million
Deficiency	=	$ 83.949 million
Required Annual Contribution	=	83.949 ÷ 117.524
	=	$ 0.714 million

QUESTIONS AND PROBLEMS

1. Consider the data given in the Review Problem for Yung Technology. Discuss the interrelationship between (a) the expected contribution level and its uncertainty and (b) the asset-allocation decision.

2. You are being interviewed for a job as a portfolio manager at an investment counseling partnership. As part of the interview, you are asked to demonstrate your ability to develop investment portfolio policy statements for the clients listed below:

    a. A pension fund that is described as a mature defined benefit plan, with the work force having an average age of 54. There are no unfunded pension liabilities, and wage-cost increases are forecast at 9% annually.

    b. A university endowment fund that is described as conservative, with investment returns being utilized along with gifts and donations to meet current expenses. The spending rate is 5% per year and inflation in costs is expected at 8% annually.

    c. A life insurance company that is described as specializing in annuities. Policy premium rates are based on a minimum annual accumulation rate of 14% in the first year of the policy and a 10% minimum annual accumulation rate in the next five years.

List and discuss the objective and constraints that will determine the portfolio policy that you would recommend for each client.

3. John Smalle, an associate in your firm, has asked you to help him establish a financial plan for his family's future. John is 27 years old and has been with your firm for two years. Anne, his 26-year-old wife, is employed as a psychologist for the local school district. They are childless now but may have children in a few years. John and Anne have accumulated $10,000 in savings and recently inherited $50,000 in cash. They believe they can save at least $5,000 yearly. They are currently in a 25% income tax bracket and both have excellent career opportunities. They are eager to develop a financial plan and understand that it will need to be periodically adjusted as their circumstances change. You tell John that you would be happy to meet with Anne and him to discuss their financial plans.

   a. Identify and describe an appropriate investment objective and investment constraints for the Smalles and prepare a comprehensive investment policy statement that is based on the objective and constraints.

   b. State and explain your asset-allocation recommendations for the Smalles based on the policy statement you developed in part a.

4. Jason Robertson is a successful business executive who voluntarily retired at age 63 after 40 years of service with a privately owned firm of which he was a shareholder. He is married and has three adult children who are married and self-supporting. At time of retirement Mr. Robertson owned his own home free and clear of mortgages, held $25,000 in life insurance, and had savings and a miscellaneous list of good-quality bonds and stocks aggregating $50,000 in value. He is also entitled to a yearly pension of $30,000, which is fully funded and has survivor's benefits to his wife of $17,000. Upon retirement, he liquidated the preferred and common shares acquired in his company over a span of 25 years under a stock purchase plan and realized cash of $170,000 (net, after provision for capital gains taxes). As a retirement benefit, Mr. Robertson and his wife are also entitled to the protection of a major medical group health insurance program fully subsidized by his firm.

As he reviews his financial position at retirement, Mr. Robertson considers himself quite well off, but he believes he should obtain some professional advice about the proper management of his capital resources at this stage of his life. Accordingly, he makes an appointment with you as an investment counselor to discuss his financial affairs. During an initial conversation, you learn that he requires an annual pretax income of $45,000 to $50,000 to maintain his present standard of living, and he would like to leave as large an estate as possible for his three children. He is concerned about the effects that inflation and taxation may have on his desired income and asset objectives.

   a. Discuss the general investment policy Mr. Robertson should follow to attain his financial objectives.

   b. Exhibit A indicates various categories of securities available, assumed yields, and three portfolios that have been constructed for the $220,000 Mr. Robertson has available for investment. Select and justify the portfolio that you think is most appropriate for Mr. Robertson to achieve his investment objectives.

5. You are the chief investment officer for your company's pension fund and are preparing for the next meeting of the Investment Committee. Several committee members are interested in reviewing and updating past discussions relating to the use of index funds

EXHIBIT A *Three Portfolio Alternatives*

Category of Security	Recent Market Yield	Portfolio No. 1	Portfolio No. 2	Portfolio No. 3
Money Market Securities	9.50%	$ 10,000	$ 10,000	$ 10,000
Government Bonds				
Short-Term	8.98			20,000
Intermediate-Term	9.57		10,000	30,000
Long-Term	10.06			50,000
Long-Term Corporate Bonds				
AAA Rated	9.26			50,000
AA Rated	9.46			
A Rated	9.62		30,000	
BBB Rated	10.10		20,000	
Tax-Exempt Municipal Bonds	6.30	80,000	20,000	
Preferred Stocks	8.86			20,000
Transportation Common Stocks	4.95			
Utility Common Stocks	8.95	10,000	30,000	20,000
Financial Common Stocks	5.30	10,000	20,000	
Industrial Common Stocks	5.00	110,000	80,000	20,000
Total		$220,000	$220,000	$220,000

for your pension fund, which utilizes both internal management and multiple external managers. Prepare brief answers to the following requests from committee members:

a. Cite and explain four reasons why consideration should be given to using an index fund.

b. Cite two decisions that are part of the investment process and that should have priority over the decision about whether or not to use an index fund.

c. Cite and explain four strategies and/or operating features that could cause an index fund portfolio to have a different return from the index itself.

d. Explain why the following are, or are not, suitable indexes on which to base an index fund:

(1) The Dow Jones Industrial Average

(2) Standard & Poor's 500 Stock Index

6. You are a portfolio manager and Senior Executive Vice President of Advisory Securities Selection, Inc. Your firm has been invited to meet with the trustees of the Wood Museum Endowment Fund. Wood Museum is a privately endowed charitable institution that is dependent on the investment return from a $25 million endowment fund to balance the budget. The treasurer of the museum has recently completed a study that indicates a need for cash flows from the endowment fund of $3.0 million in 1982, $3.2 million in 1983, and $3.5 million in 1984 in order to balance the budget. At the present time, the entire endowment portfolio is invested in T-bills and money market funds because the trustees fear a financial crisis. The trustees do not anticipate any further capital contributions to the fund. The trustees are all successful businessmen, and they have been critical of the fund's previous investment advisers for not following a logical decision-making process. In fact, several previous managers have been dismissed because of their inability to communicate with the trustees and their preoccupation with the fund's relative performance rather than the cash flow needs.

Advisory Securities Selection, Inc., has been contacted by the trustees because of its reputation for understanding and relating to its clients' needs. The trustees have specifically asked to meet with you because of your recent article in a professional journal outlining the decision-making process of your firm. In the letter of invitation addressed to you, the trustees have included the flow chart in Exhibit B and the following quotations from a speech by Professor William F. Sharpe that were included in the article:

> It is important to understand that, even if the market were perfectly efficient with every security plotting right on the plane, the investment management process would still require sophisticated procedures. In particular, it would require the tailoring of portfolios to meet clients' attitudes toward risk and clients' attitudes toward yield vis-à-vis gains.
>
> One important part of this exercise [modern portfolio theory] is finding out what the client is all about—where one client differs from another.

The Trustees have asked you, as a prospective portfolio manager for the Wood Museum Endowment Fund, to prepare a written report in response to the following questions. Your report will be circulated to the trustees prior to the initial interview on June 15.

a. Explain in detail how *each* of the following relates to the determination of either investor objectives or investor constraints that can be used to determine the portfolio policies for this three-year period for the Wood Museum Endowment Fund:

- Liquidity requirements
- Return requirements
- Risk tolerance
- Time horizon
- Tax considerations
- Regulatory and legal considerations
- Unique needs and circumstances

b. Interest rate futures, common stock options, immunization, and international diversification are investment strategies that can be used as modifiers of portfolio risk.
  (1) Explain how *each* of these four investment strategies can be used to modify portfolio risk.
  (2) Identify and explain which one of these four strategies is *most* suitable for the Wood Museum Endowment Fund.

7. You have been named as investment adviser to a foundation established by Dr. Walter Jones with an original contribution consisting entirely of the common stock of Jomedco, Inc. Founded by Dr. Jones, Jomedco manufactures and markets medical devices invented by the doctor and collects royalties on other patented innovations.

All of the shares that made up the initial contribution to the foundation were sold at a public offering of Jomedco common stock and the $5 million proceeds will be delivered to the foundation within the next week. At the same time, Mrs. Jones will receive $5 million in proceeds from the sale of her stock in Jomedco.

Dr. Jones' purpose in establishing the Jones Foundation was to "offset the effect of inflation on medical school tuition for the maximum number of worthy students."

You are preparing for a meeting with the foundation trustees to discuss investment policy and asset allocation.

a. Define and give examples that show the differences between an investment objective, an investment constraint, and an investment policy.

EXHIBIT B *The Portfolio Management Process*

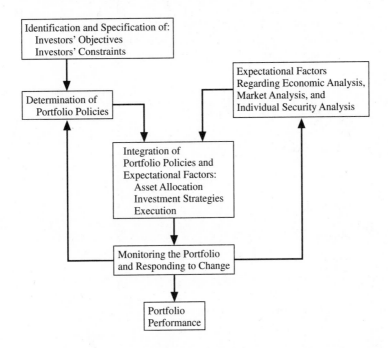

b. Identify and describe an appropriate investment objective and set of investment constraints for the Jones Foundation.

c. Based on the investment objective and constraints identified in part b, prepare a comprehensive investment policy statement for the Jones Foundation to be recommended for adoption by the trustees.

d. Discuss the issues involved in determining whether or not the investment adviser should make the asset-allocation decision for the Jones Foundation investment portfolio.

e. Identify and describe the critical capital market variables required for a two-asset allocation model for the Jones Foundation.

f. Discuss the difficulties associated with using historical information in making estimates of each of the critical variables enumerated in part e.

8. Jack Quick and Heidi Bronson have been discussing the CFA Level I study materials as they relate to the determination of portfolio policies for different types of investors. Quick remembers reading that behind all investment portfolios are investors, each of whom is unique, and that there is literally a different set of portfolio management opportunities, needs, and circumstances for every investor. Because of this diversity of investor situations, Quick has concluded that it is impossible to generalize about portfolio policy determination—everything must be done on a case-by-case basis. Bronson agrees in terms of specific portfolio construction but reminds Quick that there is a *framework* illustrated in the readings through which portfolio policies can be established for even the broadest range of investor types and interests.

a. Outline a broadly applicable *framework* for establishing portfolio policies, incorporating objectives and constraints, such as the one that Bronson has recalled.

b. Bronson is working on a defined benefit retirement portfolio for a sizable and growing corporation with a young work force. Quick is working on a modest personal portfolio now providing essential income to a 70-year-old widow whose assets pass on her death to her children. *Apply* your part a *framework* to each of the above investment situations, taking into account all of the relevant *framework* elements. (You may find it helpful to use a matrix format for this answer.)

DATAFILE ANALYSIS

1. *Communication of Investment Risk.* Access the data set called RTNSYRLY.WK1. How might you communicate the historical risks and returns associated with U.S. money market securities, U.S. fixed income securities, U.S. equities, and foreign equities to individuals who have no formal training in finance or statistics?

REFERENCES

A thorough treatment of the investment process can be found in:

MAGINN, JOHN L., and DONALD L. TUTTLE, *Managing Investment Portfolios.* Sponsored initially by the Chartered Financial Analysts (now the Association for Investment Management and Research). Boston: Warren, Gorham and Lamont, 1983.

Recent articles related to the process of portfolio management include:

BREALEY, RICHARD A., "Portfolio Theory Versus Portfolio Practice," *The Journal of Portfolio Management,* Summer 1990.

LEE, WAYNE Y., "Diversification and Time: Do Investment Horizons Matter?" *The Journal of Portfolio Management,* Spring 1990.

WAGNER, WAYNE H., and MICHAEL BANKS, "Increasing Effectiveness via Transaction Cost Management," *The Journal of Portfolio Management,* Fall 1992.

ZEIKEL, ARTHUR, "Investment Management in the 1990's," *Financial Analysts Journal,* September-October 1990.

An interesting discussion of the investment policy statement was presented in the *Financial Analysts Journal.* The first article in September-October 1990 presented a mock policy statement about which readers were asked to comment. The follow-up article discussed the reactions to the mock policy statement.

GOOD, WALTER R., and DOUGLAS A. LOVE, "Reactions to the Investment Policy Statement," *Financial Analysts Journal,* March-April 1991.

"Investment Policy Statement," *Financial Analysts Journal,* September-October 1990.

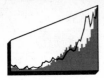

Asset Allocation

The asset allocation that an investor chooses is clearly the most important invest- ment decision that must be made. It is the prime force driving future portfolio returns, both average returns, and return volatility.

This chapter examines three topics. The first is a brief review of a recent study documenting the importance of a portfolio's asset allocation. The following two sections discuss, in turn, strategic asset allocation and tactical asset allocation. Recall from our discussion in Chapter 18 that strategic asset allocation (SAA) represents the asset allocation that investors would choose if they believed that aggregate security asset classes are efficiently priced. Tactical asset allocation (TAA) represents the asset allocation that investors would choose if they believed that certain security asset classes are mispriced.

IMPORTANCE OF ASSET ALLOCATION

Many studies document the importance of asset allocation in well-diversified portfolios. A recent study by Brinson, Singer, and Beebower (BSB) is an inter- esting example. They looked at the quarterly returns of 82 pension funds during the 10 years ending in 1987. Their study is unusual in that it examined returns of actual aggregate portfolios. Most previous studies examined the returns of single investment managers, usually an equity mutual fund. Since ownership of an individual mutual fund often represents only a part of an investor's total portfolio, prior studies looked at only a piece of the total picture.

The BSB study estimated how a pension fund's actual return could be split into returns arising from:

1. The pension fund's strategic asset allocation (SAA).
2. Any tactical asset allocation (TAA) decisions.
3. Security selection decisions of managers employed by the fund.
4. Other effects due to interactions and errors of measurement on their part.

Their basic findings are shown in Tables 19-1 and 19-2. Table 19-1 shows the rate of returns (annualized) associated with each decision. The average actual fund

679

TABLE 19-1 *Determinants of Portfolio Performance (82 Pensions, 1977–1987)*

Return Due to:	Average	Maximum	Minimum
Strategic Asset Allocation	13.49%	14.56	12.43%
Tactical Asset Allocation	−0.26	0.86	−1.81
Security Selection	+0.26	6.12	−3.32
Not Measurable	−0.08	1.33	−3.50
Actual Return	13.41%	NA	NA

NA—Not applicable since minimum or maximum in each category do not apply to the same pension fund.

SOURCE: Based on results in G. Brinson, B. Singer, and G. Beebower, "Determinants of Portfolio Performance II: An Update," *Financial Analysts Journal,* May-June 1991.

return was 13.41%. A passive investment based on each fund's SAA would have earned a return of 13.49%. That means that the average pension fund in the sample: (1) would have earned more if they had passively invested in their SAA and (2) a greater part of the average pension return was due to the SAA it chose.[1] On average, TAA resulted in a negative 0.26% yearly return. Security selection decisions by investment managers contributed an average yearly return of 0.26%. But the security selection returns ranged from −3.50% to 6.12%.

We should not conclude from Table 19-1 that security selection techniques work and timing techniques do not, since the results are based on a sample of only 82 portfolios. In addition, the extent to which these portfolios actually attempted to time the effects of management fees, differences in procedures used to calculate return, and so forth, create an uncertainty about the precision of the results. Any one of these items could swamp a 26-basis-point outcome.

The data in Table 19-2 confirms the importance of a portfolio's SAA. When a pension fund's actual portfolio returns were regressed against the returns that would have been achieved by passive investment in its SAA, the R-square was 91.5%. This means that over 90% of all variation in portfolio returns can be traced to the portfolio's SAA. Other decisions are relatively minor.

When regressions were expanded to include returns from TAA, the average R-squared increased from 91.5% to 93.3%. And when security selection returns were added, the average R-square rose to 96.1%. Again, it is clear that the SAA of a portfolio is the most important determinant of portfolio returns.

STRATEGIC ASSET ALLOCATION

There are a variety of approaches used in practice to establish the desired strategic asset allocation (SAA). Here, we examine four:

---

[1] The effect of transaction costs on passive strategic asset allocation (SAA) and actual portfolio returns was not clarified in this study.

TABLE 19-2 *Percentage of Variation in Returns Caused by Passive and Active Decisions*

Percentage of Return Variation due to:	Average	Maximum	Minimum
Strategic Asset Allocation	91.5%	98.2%	67.7%
Plus			
Tactical Asset Allocation	93.3	98.3	69.4
Plus			
Security Selection	96.1	99.8	76.2

SOURCE: Based on results in G. Brinson, B. Singer, and G. Beebower, ''Determinants of Portfolio Performance II: An Update,'' *Financial Analysts Journal,* May-June 1991.

1. Cash flow requirements.
2. Historical risk/return tables.
3. Asset pricing models.
4. Efficient diversification.

The section concludes with a discussion of a much-misunderstood issue—time diversification.

Cash Flow Requirements

Perhaps the most naive approach attempts to develop an asset mix that will provide interest and dividend cash flow to match the cash needs of the portfolio owner. For example, assume that a $10 million endowment fund has anticipated cash outflows of $600,000 for the next year. Current yields on U.S. T-bonds are 11%, and the Standard & Poor's Composite has a dividend yield of 4%. If interest and dividend receipts are to be equal to $600,000, 71.43% of the portfolio should be invested in stocks and 28.57% invested in bonds:

	Dollar Investment	×	Current Yield	=	Cash Inflow
Stocks	$ 7,143,000	×	4%	=	$285,720
Bonds	2,857,000	×	11%	=	314,270
	$10,000,000				$599,990

The only advantage of this approach is its simplicity. Apart from that, it is wrong. For example, it makes no provision for required future growth in cash outflows. To illustrate, assume that the endowment's cash outflows will grow at a 9% annual rate. If the growth rate associated with the common stocks being evaluated is 11% and the growth rate of bonds is 0%, then the 71.43%/28.57% stock/bond allocation will provide a portfolio growth rate of only 7.8% (11% × 0.7143). The artificial requirement that interest and dividends be the sole source of required cash outflows leads to poor decisions.

But the conceptual fault of this approach is even more fundamental—it ignores the risks associated with portfolios being evaluated. There are numerous stock/bond portfolios that provide expected returns large enough to cover the current and future cash flow needs of this investor. However, they differ considerably in risk. Any asset-allocation decision should explicitly consider both the risks and the expected returns associated with the allocation.

Historical Risk/Return Tables

One commonly used way to communicate the risks and returns associated with various asset mixes is to provide tabled values of historical returns. An example is shown in Table 19.3. Two asset classes are evaluated: (1) a GIC (guaranteed investment contract) that is assumed to provide a guaranteed real return (after inflation) and (2) common stocks as proxied by the annual real returns on the S&P Composite Index between 1926 and 1991. Returns are shown for six portfolios ranging from 100% invested in a GIC to 100% in the S&P Composite. The 50th percentile column shows the portfolio return that should be expected if the future is the same as the past and if the investor holds the portfolio for a one-year period. For example, if the future is the same as the 1926–1991 period, the expected return on a stock portfolio that is held for one year and that is similar to the S&P 500 is 9.2%. Columns to the left and right of the expected return show the rate of return for various probabilities. For example, if 100% is held in stock, there is a 10% chance that the annual return will be less than (or equal to) −16.8%. Similarly, there is a 10% chance that the return will be greater than 43.4%. Since many people find it difficult to interpret standard deviations, historical return tables such as this are used by professional investment counselors to communicate the manner in which asset allocation determines both expected portfolio returns and risks.

Tables can also be used to illustrate how the length of the holding periods affects potential annualized returns. For example, Table 19-4 provides similar data to Table 19-3 but for a 10-year investment horizon. The calculations that are used develop forecasts such as those in Table 19-4 are discussed later in the chapter. To make the data comparable to that of Table 19-3, the returns shown are not 10-year returns but, instead, are *geometric average annualized returns.* Note that the range of potential realized annualized returns is smaller for the 10-year horizon than for the 1-year interval. This observation is important when we discuss the potential for diversification across time later in this section.

TABLE 19-3 *Percentile Return Distribution*
One-Year Holding Period

Portfolio	Asset Mix		Percentile Return				
	GIC	S&P 500	10th	25th	50th	75th	90th
A	100%	0%	1.0%	1.0%	1.0%	1.0%	1.0%
B	80	20	−2.8	−0.2	2.6	5.61	8.4
C	60	40	−6.5	−1.5	4.3	8.5	12.6
D	40	60	−10.0	−2.8	5.9	15.4	24.7
E	20	80	−13.5	−4.1	7.6	20.6	33.7
F	0	100	−16.8	−5.3	9.2	26.0	43.4

TABLE 19-4 *Percentile Return Distribution*
Annualized Geometric Average for a 10-Year Holding Period

Portfolio	Asset Mix		Percentile Return				
	GIC	S&P 500	10th	25th	50th	75th	90th
A	100	0	1.0%	1.0%	1.0%	1.0%	1.0%
B	80	20	0.9	1.7	2.6	3.6	4.4
C	60	40	0.8	2.4	4.3	6.2	7.9
D	40	60	0.6	3.1	5.9	8.8	11.5
E	20	80	0.4	3.7	7.6	11.5	15.2
F	0	100	0.2	4.4	9.2	14.2	19.0

Tables such as the ones just shown are invaluable tools for expressing the returns and risks associated with various asset mixes. They communicate useful information to portfolio owners who are unfamiliar with statistics such as variance and covariance. But they do have weaknesses. These include the following:

1. The data are very sensitive to the time period chosen. It is not unusual that the inclusion or exclusion of a few years of returns will result in figures that differ by more than 150 basis points. As such, the data should not be interpreted too strictly. Instead, they should be viewed as illustrative of the potential return and risk levels.
2. Many asset classes simply do not have a history of returns that can be trusted. Examples include real estate and international assets.
3. When more than two asset classes are being considered, tabled values become unwieldy to use.
4. Many people believe that the distribution of past returns is not a good proxy for potential future returns.
5. This approach illustrates risks and average returns on arbitrarily selected portfolio combinations. There is no attempt to isolate efficient portfolios for various risk levels.

Asset Pricing Models

Two major theories exist that attempt to define risk and explain the market value of any asset: the capital asset pricing model and arbitrage pricing theory. Both have implications for an investor's decision on strategic asset allocation.

The Capital Asset Pricing Model. As discussed in Chapters 7 and 8, the Capital Asset Pricing Model (CAPM) has a great deal to say about the optimal portfolio of risky assets for any investor. In particular, the CAPM implies that people should own *all* risky assets in proportions which depend on the total market values of each asset. For example, if U.S. corporate bonds represent 15% of the value of all risky securities, then 15% of everyone's risky security portfolio should consist of U.S. corporate bonds. Once such a risky portfolio has been acquired, there are no further diversification benefits to be gained. If this portfolio is too risky, it can be held in combination with a risk-free security. If it is not risky enough, then the investor should borrow (at the risk-free rate) and invest the borrowings. In short, the CAPM suggests that the optimal risky asset portfolio is the market portfolio of all risky assets.

Although the CAPM is a profound conceptual tool, its practical implications should not be interpreted too strictly. People have differing investment horizons, tax rates, transaction costs, and so forth—each causing different optimal asset mixes. Investment concepts such as the value of diversification and the importance of systematic risk needn't be abandoned. However, the optimal allocation of different classes of assets must consider the unique needs of each portfolio. The CAPM should be used only as a theoretical starting point from which actual portfolios are created that better fulfill the needs of the portfolio owner.

Arbitrage Pricing Theory. In contrast to the CAPM, arbitrage pricing theory (APT) does not give any special importance to the market portfolio of all risky assets. It suggests that a variety of economic risks might be nondiversifiable. As a result, investors will demand a risk premium to accept such risks. Examples of such "priced" risk factors would include inflation, industrial production, default risk, and the slope of the yield curve. If you subscribe to the notion of APT, the first thing you should do is eliminate the non-priced, diversifiable risks by broad diversification. Next, you should specify the priced factors on which you wish to place your bets or to hedge against. For example, if you wish to hold a portfolio that is neutral to all factors, the portfolio sensitivity to each factor should be 1.0. This would result in a risky security portfolio virtually identical to the market portfolio of CAPM. A fully diversified portfolio would have a beta of 1.0 on each nondiversifiable factor risk.

The potential advantage of APT over CAPM lies in the ability to hedge risks in assets and liabilities that the investor incurs outside the marketable security portfolio. For example, assume that the investor is the sponsor of a defined benefit pension plan whose business is heavily influenced by unexpected changes in inflation. To partially hedge this risk, securities with large sensitivities to an inflation factor would be underweighted.

As with the CAPM, there are substantial problems in basing a strategic asset allocation (SAA) on the principles of APT. Most important, we don't know what the priced APT factors are! Various consulting firms have *assumed* a variety of potential return factors, but there is little evidence that such factors indeed exist. APT remains an important way to think about problems. But its quantitative application is questionable.

Efficient Asset Allocation

If the investor can develop reasonable estimates of expected returns, standard deviations and correlation coefficients between security classes, then Markowitz mean-variance efficient portfolios can be found. The process of finding efficient portfolios consists of the following four steps:

1. Segment portfolio needs.
2. Select asset classes.
3. Develop market expectations.
4. Evaluate the efficient frontier for a desired horizon date.

1. Segment Portfolio Needs. Often the investment portfolio is intended to meet a variety of needs. For example, pension fund portfolios are expected to provide investment returns to help pay benefits to two distinct groups of individuals: (*a*) past employees who are currently receiving pension benefits, and (*b*) present employees who will receive benefits at a distant future date. The nature of the liability to each group can be quite different. In the case of "retired lives," the liability is relatively short-term, virtually known with certainty, and often in the form of nominal dollars. Thus the retired-lives portion of the pension plan is ideal for some form of bond immunization. In contrast, the nonretired-lives portion of a pension's liability stream is long-term, is difficult to predict with precision, and usually varies directly with inflation. As such, it is much less suitable for immunization techniques.

2. Select Asset Classes. When asset classes are defined, they should be as distinctly different from each other as possible in order to provide the greatest potential for diversification. For example, there is little to be gained by adding a "call option group" to a portfolio that otherwise consists of T-bills and common stock. This is because a call option is essentially a long position in a given stock and a short position in T-bills. In the same fashion, returns on Treasury note financial futures are highly correlated with spot Treasury notes and bonds. In short, there is little value associated with including asset classes that are highly correlated.

Many asset classes, however, have returns that are relatively uncorrelated. For example, Table 19-5 presents correlation coefficients on a number of asset classes using annual real returns (after inflation) for the period 1969–1991. Returns prior to 1969 were not available for PRISA and the EAFE indexes.[2]

The number of different asset classes that an investor should consider depends in large part on the size of the portfolio and the knowledge of the investor. Once we move from well-known asset classes such as T-bills, government/corporate bonds, and common equities into less-known asset classes such as real estate, international equities, and venture capital, there is a greater need for professional expertise. Yet there are no hard and fast rules relating portfolio size to classes of assets selected. The trade-off between potential diversification gains and increased formation costs is a decision that is unique to each portfolio.

To illustrate the value gained from diversification, the historical data in Table 19-5 were used in a computer program to find two ex post efficient frontiers. These are displayed in Figure 19-1. The frontier to the right consists of holdings of T-bills, government bonds, the S&P 500 (a proxy for large firms), and small

---

[2] PRISA is a commingled equity real estate portfolio managed by Prudential Insurance. It is used here as a proxy for real estate equity investment returns.

TABLE 19-5 *Correlation Coefficients, Standard Deviation and Average Returns on Selected Asset Classes (Real Returns, 1969–1991)*

	Correlation Coefficients						
Class	*T-bills*	*Bonds*	*Bonds*	*S&P 500*	*Small Company*	*PRISA*	*EAFE*
T-bills	1.00						
Govt	0.67	1.00					
Corp	0.66	0.97	1.00				
S&P 500	0.41	0.56	0.61	1.00			
Small Co.	0.14	0.28	0.36	0.77	1.00		
PRISA	0.22	0.11	−0.23	0.25	0.35	1.00	
EAFE	0.28	0.37	0.36	0.64	0.47	0.30	1.00
	Percentage Yearly Real Returns						
Average	1.37	3.13	3.36	5.87	7.93	2.32	9.56
Standard Deviation	2.96	13.71	14.31	17.94	27.43	6.38	24.51

company stocks. These have traditionally been the security classes used in SAA decisions. Note that the efficient frontier of these five asset classes provides a greater average return for each level of standard deviation than would have been obtained by holding any one of the five asset classes. This is the benefit of diversification.

The higher efficient frontier adds two asset classes to the traditional group: real estate and international equities. Again, the benefits of diversification are clear. Although the composition of ex post efficient frontiers will depend on the time period evaluated, holding many asset classes always dominates holding one asset class.[3] Diversification works!

3. Develop Market Expectations. In order to develop Markowitz efficient frontiers, estimates must be made of the *expected* returns and covariances of returns on each asset class being evaluated. It is at this point that two difficult problems must be faced. First, how can the concept of a single-period efficient frontier be used in the context of a multiperiod decision? Second, how does one develop the expected returns and covariances which are used as inputs to the model?

A reasonable approach to solving the multiperiod problem is to estimate an *average date* at which there will be net cash outflows. This is done in much the same way that we calculate the duration of the cash inflows for a bond. For example, consider the following simplified example.

Assume that a pension plan will have three equal cash outflows of $100 at the end of years 1, 2, and 3. In addition, the U.S. Treasury yield curve is flat at a yield to maturity of 10%. Note that the cash outflows to the pension plan are, in fact, cash inflows to the pension beneficiaries. In essence, the beneficiaries own a

---

[3] The greatest-return portfolio is an exception. It consists of a 100% investment in the asset class with the greatest return.

FIGURE 19-1 *Historical Efficient Frontiers*

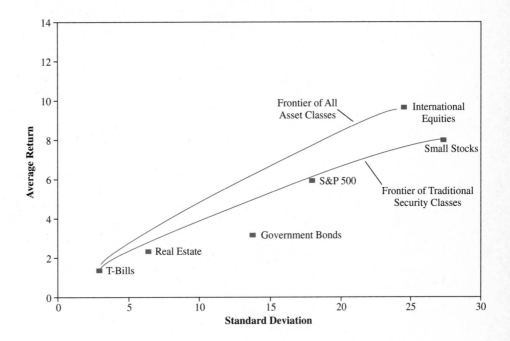

bond that promises to pay $100 at each year-end for three years. The duration of
this bond is 1.9 years:

Year-End	Cash Flow	Present Value at 10%	Percent of Total	Weighted Duration
1	$100	90.91%	36.66%	0.3666
2	100	82.64	33.33	0.6666
3	100	75.13	30.30	0.9090
Total		247.96		1.9422

If beneficiaries are correct in considering their benefits as having a 1.9-year
duration, then the pension sponsors are also correct in considering their future
liability stream as having the same duration.

By using the notion of duration, a multiperiod pension liability stream can be
stated in terms of a single-period cash outflow. And the length of this single-
period cash outflow can then be used as the horizon date in the Markowitz model.
For example, in our example, the pension sponsor would evaluate expected returns
and covariances on various asset groups *assuming that they are to be held for 1.9
years.*

There are difficulties with this technique of reducing a multiperiod problem to
a single-period problem. The liability stream is not known with certainty, the

covariance between future benefits and security returns isn't considered, and the appropriate interest rate for calculating the duration is unclear. But until investment theory can offer something better, the calculation of benefit duration is a reasonable way to restate a multiperiod problem to fit the single-period asset-selection model.

Although the precision of this approach can be questioned, one thing is clear: The risk associated with owning various classes of assets depends upon how long one intends to own the assets. Many investors, particularly pension funds, are long-term investors. As such, it is inappropriate for them to evaluate the risk inherent in, say, common stocks by the volatility of one-year common stock returns. Some attempt must be made to evaluate the risk of a security class over the anticipated holding period.

Let's move now to the difficulties inherent in estimating expected returns and covariances for each asset class. Ideally, these are *informed* opinions held by the *portfolio owner* (pension sponsor) about the likely returns and uncertainty of each asset class. But where do these opinions come from? How can one estimate the required inputs?

In practice, four major approaches are widely used:

1. Historical data
2. Econometric simulations
3. Existing market prices
4. Personal opinion

Historical Data. Historical returns are available on many security classes. A widely used source for such returns is published papers and monographs periodically updated by Roger Ibbotson and various coauthors. They present a series of monthly returns on T-bills, U.S. government and corporate bonds, and the S&P 500 extending back to January 1926. They have also prepared historical estimates of returns on forms of real estate and international investments.

Historical returns are certainly the place to begin. But some care must be taken. For example:

1. Many knowledgeable people believe that the future that investors face in the late twentieth century is fundamentally different from the events that shaped the 1920s through 1980s. If this is true, the past will be a poor predictor of the future.

2. Some asset classes, such as international investments, have a very short history of past returns. And during the time periods for which such data are available, a few major economic events shaped the pattern of returns. For example, the returns on international securities were swamped by the deterioration of the U.S. foreign exchange rate during the 1970s and 1980s.

3. Some historical return estimates are very imprecise. Estimates of real estate returns, in particular, are usually based on appraised market values instead of actual market trading prices. This tends to smooth out returns and make real estate investment appear to be less risky than it is.

The information obtained from historical data can be sensitive to the time period examined. For example, consider the panels in Figure 19-2. In panel A, average yearly real returns are plotted for various 20-year periods. Each point in the panel represents the average return for the 20 years ended at the date of the point. It is obvious that average yearly returns, even over relatively long time spans, are quite volatile. In panel B, standard deviations of yearly returns based on a 20-year return series are shown. Although standard deviations are less sensitive to the time period chosen than are average returns, they are also dependent on the period evaluated. All efficient frontier data estimates that are based on historical data are sensitive to the historical time period evaluated. This, of course, is simply a result of the basic problem that we are trying to deal with—risk.

Econometric Simulations. Econometric simulations are also available from a variety of consulting firms. These simulations are based on empirically tested economic relationships that tie various sectors of the economy together.

Simulations provide at least three principal aids to the analyst. First, developing and understanding the internal structure of the model forces analysts to be explicit in their opinions about the process generating security returns over time. Second, a large variety of alternative strategies can be experimented with to determine the ranges of potential returns during future years. Finally, input variables may be altered in an attempt to determine how sensitive the output is to various input factors. Naturally, the quality of the output is only as good as the quality of the model structure.

Existing Market Prices. Some people use existing market prices to estimate necessary efficient frontier inputs. For example, security analysts at Wells Fargo Bank forecast future dividend growth rates for a large number of stocks and then use these estimates together with each stock's *existing* market price to estimate expected rates of return. And prevailing yields to maturity (or yields to a given duration) can be used to estimate both current and expected future bond returns. In short, many of the needed inputs can be inferred from prevailing market prices.

Unfortunately, this is a very difficult task for many classes of assets, real estate and international equities in particular. In addition, none of these procedures is able to estimate the correlation coefficient between returns on alternative assets.

Personal Opinion. Certainly one can, and should, examine historical data, econometric simulations, and prevailing market prices. But, in the end, it should be the personal opinion of the portfolio owner that determines the expected returns, standard deviations, and correlation coefficients necessary to determine an efficient frontier.

4. Evaluate the Efficient Frontier for the Desired Horizon Date. Once the needed inputs are available, it is a simple matter of finding a computer package that can compute a Markowitz efficient frontier. A number of such programs have been developed and are available at moderate cost.

Assume that after a thorough review of historical returns and expected long-run economic conditions, we develop the return distribution assumptions shown in Table 19.6. These represent our beliefs about the one-year return payoffs that we expect to prevail in the long run. Thus, they are the return distribution data

FIGURE 19-2 *Long Run Historical Outcomes*

Return

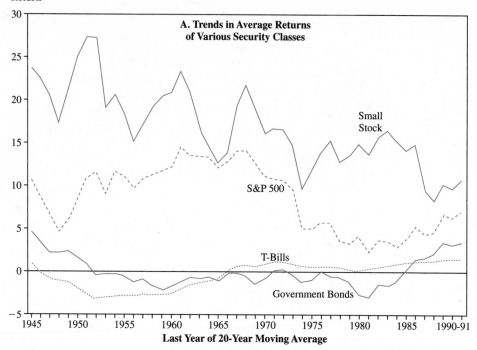

A. Trends in Average Returns
of Various Security Classes

Small
Stock

S&P 500

T-Bills

Government Bonds

Last Year of 20-Year Moving Average

Standard
Deviation

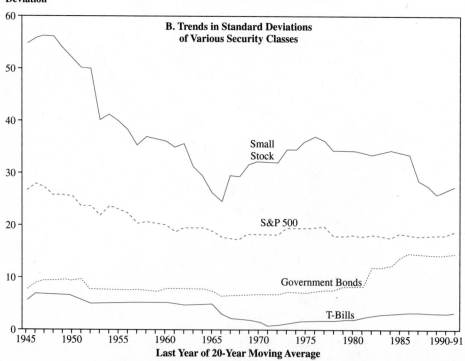

B. Trends in Standard Deviations
of Various Security Classes

Small
Stock

S&P 500

Government Bonds

T-Bills

Last Year of 20-Year Moving Average

TABLE 19-6 *Hypothetical Ex Ante Return Distribution Assumptions about One-Year Returns Expected over the Long Run*

		Govt.	Corp.		Small	Real	Int'l
Class	T-Bills	Bonds	Bonds	S&P 500	Company	Estate	Equity
T-Bills	1.00						
Govt. Bonds	0.60	1.00					
Corp. Bonds	0.60	0.95	1.00				
S&P 500	0.20	0.30	0.30	1.00			
Small Company	0.12	0.20	0.20	0.80	1.00		
PRISA	0.25	0.05	0.05	0.35	0.40	1.00	
EAFE	0.30	0.40	0.40	0.60	0.40	0.30	1.00

Header spanning: *Correlation Coefficients*

			Yearly Real Return				
Average	1.5%	2.5%	3.5%	8.5%	14.0%	5.0%	11.0%
Standard Deviation	4.0	10.0	11.0	20.0	40.0	15.0	30.0

on which the SAA decision should be made. They are not necessarily equal to forecasts we might make for the coming year. Such shorter-term forecasts should be used in developing the TAA.[4]

The efficient frontier which results from these forecasts is shown in Figure 19-3. The composition of five efficient portfolios is shown at the bottom of the figure. Note that portfolio *A* is dominated by holdings of T-bills. But even such low-risk portfolios include small amounts of other asset classes—in this case, the S&P 500 and real estate—in order to obtain the benefits of diversification.

If an investor has a one-year investment horizon, then the one-year return payoffs shown in Figure 19-3 can be used to determine an appropriate SAA. Rarely, however, will the investment horizon be as short as one year. And, if it were, it is doubtful that forecasts of returns on international equities, corporate bonds, stocks, and so forth, would be necessary, since the SAA would probably be obvious: invest primarily in one-year, low-default-risk money market instruments. In most cases, we need to determine the return outcomes of various one-year efficient portfolios over longer investment horizons.

In Table 19-7, the payoffs of portfolio *C* (shown in Figure 19-3) are displayed for various investment horizon dates. We will not review the mathematics underlying the projections since they are relatively complex and are not needed for the purpose of our discussion.[5]

---

[4] You might find it useful to compare the ex ante estimates in Table 20-6 with the ex post values in Table 19-5. Do you agree with the differences between the tables? Why or why not? By answering such questions you are beginning to develop the ability to make ex ante forecasts.

[5] The discrete returns of Figure 19-3 are expressed as continuous returns. For example, portfolio *C's* 6.0% discrete expected return is expressed as a 5.823% continuous return. Normally distributed continuous returns are used since they result in lognormally distributed portfolio values. This assures that the portfolio will never have a negative value. If normally distributed discrete returns are used, there is a probability that the portfolio will have a negative value in the future. But this is clearly impossible!

FIGURE 19-3 *Estimated Efficient Frontier Based on Annual Real Returns*

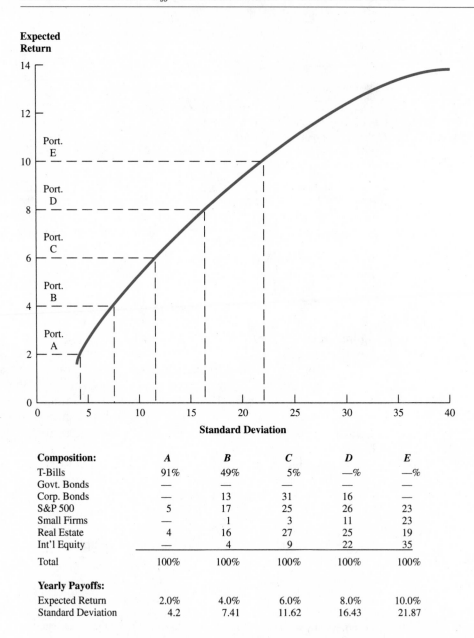

Composition:	A	B	C	D	E
T-Bills	91%	49%	5%	—%	—%
Govt. Bonds	—	—	—	—	—
Corp. Bonds	—	13	31	16	—
S&P 500	5	17	25	26	23
Small Firms	—	1	3	11	23
Real Estate	4	16	27	25	19
Int'l Equity	—	4	9	22	35
Total	100%	100%	100%	100%	100%

Yearly Payoffs:

	A	B	C	D	E
Expected Return	2.0%	4.0%	6.0%	8.0%	10.0%
Standard Deviation	4.2	7.41	11.62	16.43	21.87

Table 19-7 has two parts. In the top part, terminal wealth percentiles from initially investing $1 are shown. For example, if $1 is invested in portfolio *C*, there is a 1% chance that the portfolio will be worth less than $0.81 or more than $1.39 *after one year.* If the investment horizon is one year, there is a significant probability that the portfolio will decline in value! In contrast, consider the 30-

year investment horizon. At that point, there is a 1% chance that the portfolio will be worth less than $1.30 or more than $25.28. With a 30-year investment horizon, there is little chance that the portfolio's value will be less than the initial investment.

Two comments about these terminal wealth forcasts need to be made. First, note that terminal wealth is skewed toward higher wealth levels and that this skewness increases as the investment horizon increases. Consider the 30-year horizon. The 50th percentile is $5.74; that is, there is a 50% chance that wealth will be less than $5.74 or greater than $5.74. At the lower end, there is a 1% chance of the portfolio's value being lower than $1.30, a spread of $4.44 from the 50th percentile. But at the upper end, there is a 1% chance of the portfolio's value being greater than $25.28, a spread of $19.54 from the 50th percentile. Clearly the terminal wealth distribution is skewed "to the right." Second, terminal wealth is displayed in percentile fashion instead of in terms of standard deviations. Because of the skewness of portfolio values, the standard deviation becomes a less meaningful measure of risk. In addition, most investors are able to interpret

TABLE 19-7 *Investment Payoffs of Portfolio* C

Investment Horizon (Years)	Terminal Portfolio Wealth Percentiles								
	.01	*.05*	*.10*	*.25*	*.50*	*.75*	*.90*	*.95*	*.99*
1	0.81	0.88	0.91	0.98	1.06	1.15	1.23	1.28	1.39
2	0.77	0.86	0.91	1.01	1.12	1.26	1.39	1.47	1.65
3	0.75	0.86	0.92	1.04	1.19	1.36	1.54	1.66	1.90
4	0.73	0.86	0.94	1.08	1.26	1.48	1.70	1.85	2.17
5	0.73	0.87	0.96	1.12	1.34	1.59	1.87	2.05	2.45
10	0.76	0.98	1.12	1.40	1.79	2.29	2.87	3.28	4.21
15	0.84	1.14	1.35	1.77	2.40	3.24	4.26	5.02	6.83
20	0.95	1.36	1.65	2.26	3.20	4.55	6.24	7.53	10.76
30	1.30	2.01	2.54	3.74	5.74	8.81	12.97	16.34	25.28
	Geometric Return Percentiles								
	.01	*.05*	*.10*	*.25*	*.50*	*.75*	*.90*	*.95*	*.99*
1	−19.1	−12.45	−8.67	−1.99	6.00	14.63	23.02	28.32	38.95
2	−12.5	−7.40	−4.60	0.28	6.00	12.03	17.77	21.34	28.36
3	−9.3	−5.08	−2.74	1.31	6.00	10.90	15.51	18.36	23.93
4	−7.4	−3.67	−1.61	1.92	6.00	10.23	14.19	16.63	21.36
5	−6.1	−2.69	−0.83	2.35	6.00	9.78	13.30	15.46	19.64
10	−2.7	−0.2	1.1	3.4	6.00	8.7	11.1	12.6	15.5
15	−1.2	−0.55	0.86	3.26	6.00	8.80	11.39	12.97	16.01
20	−0.2	1.6	2.5	4.2	6.00	7.9	9.6	10.6	12.6
30	0.9	2.4	3.2	4.5	6.00	7.5	8.9	9.8	11.4

Input Assumptions: Portfolio C

Mean Continuous Return:	5.823
Standard Deviation:	11.620
Serial Correlation Assumptions:	
Serial Correlation:	0.000
Current Return Level:	3.540

Investment Consultant Interview

This interview was conducted with Brian C. Thompson, Ph.D., Senior Pension Consultant with The Principal/Eppler, Guerin & Turner, Inc.

Question: Can you briefly describe your duties as an investment consultant?

We work with clients to establish game plans based on specific needs. Formally, this includes developing a Statement of Investment Policy and determining a Strategic Asset Allocation. Once this is done, we determine the appropriate manager structure for each asset class targeted. This involves style analysis, defining the desired portfolio characteristics and manager diversification.

After the asset allocation and manager structure are defined, we assist the client in finding managers to meet each required role. After these managers are hired, they are monitored on an ongoing basis both qualitatively and quantitatively.

Question: How important is the development of a Strategic Asset Allocation?

Both academic and consulting studies across the country clearly show it is the primary determinant of investment performance. It has far more importance in generating long-term investment returns than either market timing or security selection. We give a great deal of emphasis to understanding client goals and requirements so that an appropriate Strategic Asset Allocation can be developed.

Question: What approach do you take to determine a Strategic Asset Allocation for clients?

We use optimization software to generate efficient asset mixes from a given set of return assumptions and constraints. After reviewing projected outcomes from each efficient mix with the client, one efficient mix is selected as the Strategic Asset Allocation target mix.

This is a fairly structured approach that is really a blend of art and science. The underlying return characteristics of asset classes such as domestic equities, international equities, domestic fixed income, global fixed income and real estate, all require making judgments about results of historical analysis. And, clients don't provide the utility indifference curves to help us select the best strategic mix. We attempt to quantify the clients' requirements by reviewing the impact of projected outcomes under different mixes.

For example: A Pension Review Board would be sensitive to having projected future liability coverage by assets at a certain level. Clients may also be sensitive to losses or low returns over given time frames. These types of constraints are usually formalized in probability terms.

Question: How extensively are these efficient frontier models used in the investment environment today?

Due to the development of personal computers and the availability of software, these models are widely used by consulting firms and major pension plan sponsors.

Since the tools are widely available, the difference in quality of the study and merit of recommendations is largely determined by the financial, statistical and communication skills of the analyst using the tools.

In recent years, many portfolio managers have seen the benefit of using these models to encourage diversification into the asset classes they manage. These models are often used as marketing tools to show the merits on a risk/reward basis of participating in less traditional asset classes such as international equities, emerging markets, global fixed income or timberland.

Question: What are some of the key problems and shortcomings in using currently available efficient frontier models for determining the Strategic Asset Allocation?

Three main concerns come to mind:
1. Single time period limit;
2. Return distribution assumptions; and
3. Specifying requirements.

First, let us consider the single time period limit.

The currently available optimization models typically generate results for one future time period instead of across time. Since volatility over longer time periods is more important for most investors, it would be beneficial for software to provide distributions for efficient mixes across time and for specified time frames. Quite often movement from a current structure to a target structure is phased in over time and it would be beneficial to show transition targets.

Second, the determination of appropriate return

distribution assumptions for input into these models is really much more complex than most users realize. Almost all software allows return assumption inputs by expected return and standard deviation for a single period. The underlying assumption is that the single period return distribution is normally distributed and is stationary (doesn't change) over time. These assumptions may not be true since returns can have an abnormal or a non-stationary distribution. It can be shown that return distributions are *skewed* or display *kurtosis* or other abnormal characteristics. And, it is well known that parameters such as *mean* and *variance* change over time.

Quite often, because of lack of data, *variance/covariance* input is estimated from time series of different lengths for different asset classes. The return expectations used are also often based on different time series and adjusted by judgment to conform to "reasonable" outlooks. This process tends to be as much art as science.

Third, the determination of client requirements is only partially specified and not directly integrated into the generation of the most efficient mix for the client. Current models need to be more flexible to handle a broader range of constraints and to evaluate the cost of these constraints to the client. Also, acceptance criteria for Strategic Asset Allocation solutions such as liability coverage need to be directly considered in the optimization. The use of *mean-variance* criterion to generate efficient frontiers can also be challenged. Other objective functions and constraints may be more appropriate.

The current state of asset/liability modeling for pension funds or endowment fund cash projection models is to solve problems in a two-phase process. The first phase is to develop an efficient frontier of asset mixes to consider. The second phase usually involves selecting a small number of the likely efficient asset mix candidates to input to a simulation model where projections of future financial measures are evaluated. This approach is cumbersome and is limited to generating acceptable efficient mix alternatives which are not necessarily optimal solutions.

percentile distributions more easily than statistical measures such as standard deviation and skewness.

In the second part of Table 19-7, percentile distributions are shown for the geometric returns underlying each of the terminal wealth levels above. For example, consider the $5.74 terminal wealth at year 30. This translates into a geometric return of 6% per year:

$$\$1.00(1 + G)^{30} = \$5.74$$

$$G = (\$5.74/\$1.00)^{1/30} - 1.0$$

$$G = 6.00\%$$

Geometric return percentiles are often used in SAA studies because investors are able to interpret them more readily than terminal wealth outcomes.

Short Sale Constraints. Most investment portfolios have constraints against short selling any securities. In such cases, the optimal percentage in any asset class is either zero or a positive number. The lowest-risk portfolio typically consists of a large investment in T-bills, a small investment in another asset class (due to diversification gains), and zero investment in other assets. The highest return portfolio is a 100% investment in one asset class and a zero investment in all others.

Many asset pricing models, however, assume that one can short sell and make use of the sale proceeds to purchase other assets. When short sales are allowed, a positive or negative investment is made in every asset class. Roll's critique of empirical tests of the Capital Asset Pricing Model (CAPM), for example, requires that one be able to short sell any asset class and make use of the proceeds.

Because short sales are rarely allowed (particularly for aggregate asset classes), all examples in this chapter have a short sale constraint.

Can Investors Diversify Over Many Time Periods?

The concept of time diversification is often misunderstood. To see the source of this misunderstanding, look at the geometric mean return outcomes in Table 19-7 for a 1-year holding period and a 30-year holding period. The lowest and highest 1-year returns shown are −19.1% and −38.95%. In contrast, the lowest and highest 30-year geometric annualized returns are 0.9% and 11.4%. It would *seem* that the longer one's investment horizon, the lower one's investment risk. If true, this would have profound implications on practical portfolio decisions.

This notion that investment risk might decline as the investment horizon increases is shown graphically in Figure 19-4, which is based on percentile geometric returns shown in Table 19-7.

FIGURE 19-4 *Dispersion of Geometric Mean Decreases for Longer Investment Horizons*

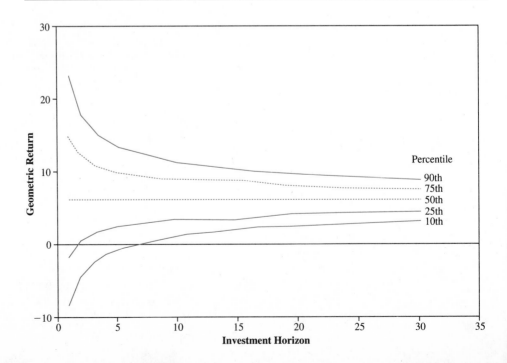

The explanation often given for the narrowing of differences in percentile returns is that good years supposedly offset bad years. Unfortunately, this conclusion is wrong. The longer one's investment horizon, the greater the investment uncertainty. The narrowing of percentile return differences is simply a mathematical result.

One invests in a portfolio with the intent of future consumption. But one consumes future wealth, not geometric annualized returns. And, the longer one's investment horizon, the greater the uncertainty about future wealth. Time does not reduce uncertainty. Instead, *risk compounds over time*! This can be easily seen in Figure 19-5, in which various terminal wealth percentiles are shown.

To help understand the intuition of time diversification and see why investing for a longer number of time periods does not reduce risk, let's consider a roulette wheel analogy. If you bet $1.00 and spin the wheel once, there is an uncertainty about the payoff. This is analogous to investing $1.00 in a single stock. Now assume that you are allowed to spin the wheel 10 times and average the results to determine your payoff. This is analogous to making an equal investment in 10 stocks (each with identical risk and zero correlation between their return outcomes). Clearly, averaging 10 spins is less risky than taking the payoff from a single spin just as investing in 10 stocks is less risky than investing in a single stock. By owning many securities, you spread your risks, and good payoffs on one offset poor payoffs on another.

FIGURE 19-5 *Dispersion of Terminal Wealth Increases for Longer Investment Horizons*

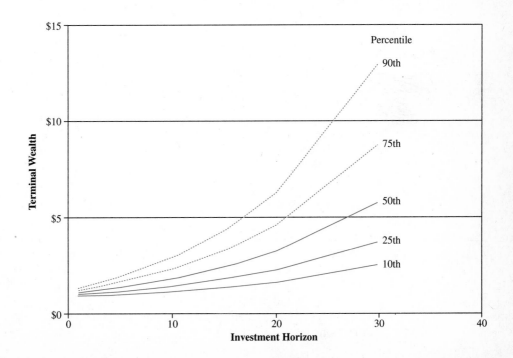

In contrast, investing for many periods is similar to having a payoff after each spin, *accumulating* the outcomes of many spins as opposed to *averaging* the outcomes. In short, investing for many time periods compounds the investment risk of any single period.

Risk Tolerance and the Investment Horizon. Investment risk increases as the investment time horizon increases. But this does not mean that long-term investors should select less risky portfolios than short-term investors do. There are a number of perfectly logical reasons why investors with long investment horizons might accept greater risks.

For example, consider the problem from the perspective of a young couple with a financially sound labor income versus a newly retired couple. Both couples invest with the goal of supplementing their pension retirement benefits. Assume that neither couple is wealthy and that each couple expects they will have to liquidate a sizeable portion (if not all) of their investment portfolio during retirement. There are significant differences between these couples that would cause them to accept different levels of risk.

First, the labor income of the young couple represents a larger *fraction of their current consumption* needs than true for the retired couple. The young couple is a net saver, and the retired couple is a net spender. This means that the retired couple is much more dependent on investment portfolio assets to meet consumption needs, both in terms of timing and dollar amount.

Second, the young couple has a *labor income option* that is no longer available to the retired couple. If investment returns are below expectations, the young couple can work harder to restore any decreases in wealth. In contrast, the retired couple would probably find it more difficult to supplement their retirement income by job income. Such a labor income option is potentially quite valuable and represents an intangible increase in the young couple's true wealth that might cause them to accept greater risk than otherwise.

Finally, it is conceivable that younger investors are simply more risk tolerant than older investors are.

Even though one cannot reduce investment risk by having a long investment time horizon, there are rational explanations for long-term investors to be less risk averse than short-term investors.

Forecasting Multiperiod Percentile Distributions

Although efficient frontiers are usually based on annualized numbers, many investors wish to see potential outcomes over longer time intervals. When such forecasts are made, it is best to express expected returns and standard deviations in terms of continuous compound returns. When we assume that continuous compound returns are distributed normally, the minimum future wealth level is zero and the distribution of future wealth is log normal, or skewed to the right. The following assumptions are based on Table 19-7:

$$\bar{r} = \text{Expected Yearly Continuous Return} = 5.82\%$$

$$\sigma = \text{Standard Deviation of Yearly}$$
$$\text{Continuously Compound Return} = 11.62\%$$

$$N = \text{Number of Years of Investing} = 5$$

In any year t, a random return is drawn from a distribution having a mean $\bar{r}$ and a standard deviation σ. Define this return as $\tilde{r}_t$. Given that we are using continuous normal returns, the terminal wealth from investing \$1 after N periods is equal to the number e raised to the power of the summation of the N values of $\tilde{r}_t$:

Terminal Wealth
as a Function
of Continuous Returns

$$TW_N = e^{(\tilde{r}1 + \tilde{r}2 \ldots + \tilde{r}N)}$$
$$= e^{(\Sigma \tilde{r})} \tag{19.1}$$

The important term in Equation 19.1 is Σr, the summation of continuous returns. It is important because it is also normally distributed as follows:

Distribution
of $\Sigma \tilde{r}$

$$E(\Sigma \tilde{r}) = \bar{r}N \tag{19.2a}$$
$$\sigma_N = \sigma\sqrt{N} \tag{19.2b}$$

Given our assumed value for r and σ,

$$E(\Sigma \tilde{r}) = 0.05823(5)$$
$$= 0.29115$$

$$\sigma_5 = 0.1162\sqrt{5}$$
$$= 0.25983$$

Using this data, we can calculate values of Σr for various percentiles of the cumulative normal = density function. For example:

Percentile	10th	25th	50th	75th	90th
Number of σ from Mean	−1.28	−0.67	0	0.67	1.28
$E(\Sigma r)$	0.29115	0.29115	0.29115	0.29115	0.29115
less					
Number σ	−1.28	−0.67	0	0.67	1.28
times σ	0.25983	0.25983	0.25983	0.25983	0.25983
	−0.33258	−0.17409	0	0.17409	0.33258
$\Sigma \tilde{r}$	−0.04143	0.11706	0.29115	0.46524	0.62373

Finally, each percentile Σr is converted to its associated terminal value using Equation 19.1.

Percentile	10th	25th	50th	75th	90th
Terminal Wealth $= e^{(sr)}$	0.96	1.12	1.34	1.59	1.87

These are the same terminal wealth percentile values as shown in Table 19-6.

Comments on Extrapolations. Two comments about this procedure for extrapolating long-term investment results are necessary. First, Equations 19.2a and 19.2b assume that there is no correlation between returns in one year and any previous year and that portfolio returns are serially uncorrelated. If positive serial correlation exists, future terminal wealth is more variable than with zero correlation. With positive serial correlation, good years tend to be followed by further good years and bad years tend to be followed by bad years. The serial correlation of common stocks is virtually zero. T-bill returns, however, are positively correlated.

Second, this extrapolation procedure assumes that the expected portfolio return and standard deviation are constant over the investment horizon being examined. This means that a portfolio of many asset classes is constantly *rebalanced*. The initial portfolio is not simply bought and held.

Consider, for example, a 50/50 investment in the S&P 500 Index and U.S. T-bills. If such an investment had been made at the end of 1926 and never rebalanced through 1991, the portfolio's actual average nominal return and standard deviation would have been 10.4% and 15.7%, respectively. In contrast, if the 50/50 mix had been restored at the start of each year, the average nominal return and standard deviation could have been 8.1% and 10.3%, respectively. In short, the risk of a constantly rebalanced portfolio is lower than one that is never rebalanced and the extrapolation techniques shown above assume constant rebalancing.

TACTICAL ASSET ALLOCATION

The strategic asset allocation (SAA), based as it is on the investor's expectations of *long-term* risks and returns associated with various asset classes, will be the portfolio that, on average, should be held. However, short-term investment expectations may occasionally be different from expectations about the long term. If so, the actual portfolio that is held should be different from the SAA. Such temporary changes in the portfolio's composition are commonly referred to as tactical asset allocation (TAA).

The conceptual difference between SAA and TAA is illustrated in Figure 19-6. Two efficient frontiers are shown in the figure. One is based on risks and returns expected on three asset classes over the long run. Together with the investor's risk tolerance, it is used to identify an SAA—in this case, portfolio *P*, which consists of 40% in T-bills, 10% in bonds, and 50% in stocks. The other efficient frontier is based on short-term expectations. As displayed in the figure, short-term expected returns on high-risk securities are considerably lower than long-run expectations. Thus, the optimal portfolio called for by the tactical asset

FIGURE 19-6 *SAA Versus TAA*

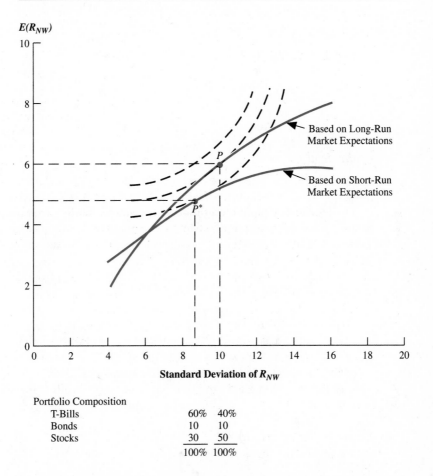

Portfolio Composition		
T-Bills	60%	40%
Bonds	10	10
Stocks	30	50
	100%	100%

allocation decision is portfolio *P**, which consists of a temporary underweighting of stocks and overweighting of T-bills.

For TAA strategies to work, one must be able to distinguish between long-run versus short-term risks and expected rewards on various asset classes. That is, one must be able to correctly *time* the purchase and sale of aggregate asset classes.

There are many ways of defining an asset class and even more ways to evaluate whether the class should be over- or underweighted relative to the SAA. In the United States, speculators have traditionally timed between stocks and T-bills (known as market timing) or long-term bonds and T-bills (interest rate timing). Recently, however, TAA decisions have been expanded to include real estate, international equities, positions in individual countries, foreign currency, and so forth.

In this section, we will explore aggregate equity market timing. The techniques discussed are based largely on fundamental analysis.

Equity Market Valuation

The decision to overweight or underweight the portfolio investment in domestic equities can be made by answering any of the following three questions:

1. Given my expectations of long-run dividends and the required rate of return on domestic equities, *is the current level of aggregate stock prices correct*?
2. Given my expectations of long-run dividends and the current level of aggregate stock prices, *is the return from investing in stocks equal to the return I require*?
3. Given my required rate of return and the current level of aggregate stock prices, *is the implied growth rate of dividends equal to my expectations of future dividend growth*?

In each case, two variables are specified and the third variable is calculated. These three questions are simply different ways to view the same issue.

To determine whether aggregate equity markets are currently priced according to long-run return and risk expectations, one has to use a stock index as a proxy of aggregate stock prices. Throughout our examples we will use the S&P 500 Index as this proxy. In truth, the S&P 500 reflects the values of large, mature U.S. corporations. It might not always capture the value of smaller firms traded on listed exchanges or in the OTC market. Nonetheless, it is a widely used index on which considerable past data are available.

The value of any financial asset (or index) should be the present value of expected future cash flows discounted at an appropriate risk-adjusted discount rate. Thus, we must answer two basic questions if we wish to assess the economic worth of the asset: (1) What do we expect future dividends to be? (2) What is an appropriate discount rate? Since we can never answer either question with absolute certainty, it is wise to use a variety of approaches.

Expected Dividend Growth. Three approaches are commonly used to estimate future dividend growth on stock indexes such as the S&P 500:

1. Historical growth
2. Sustainable internal growth
3. Long-run growth of the total economy

Historical Growth Rates. In Chapter 13 we discussed how one could estimate historical compound annual growth rates (CAGR) using log-least-squares regression. To do so, the natural log of the variable being measured is regressed against time as follows:

Log Least Squares CAGR
$$ln(DPS_t) = a + b\,(\text{Year}_t) + e_t \tag{19.3}$$

Here, DPS_t represents dividends per share in year t, the variable a represents the regression intercept, b is the CAGR estimate, and e_t is an error term in year t. Figure 19-7 and Table 19-8 show various grow rates of $ln(DPS)$ for the S&P 500 Index between 1926–1991.

FIGURE 19-7 *Growth of S&P 500 Dividends (1926–1991)*

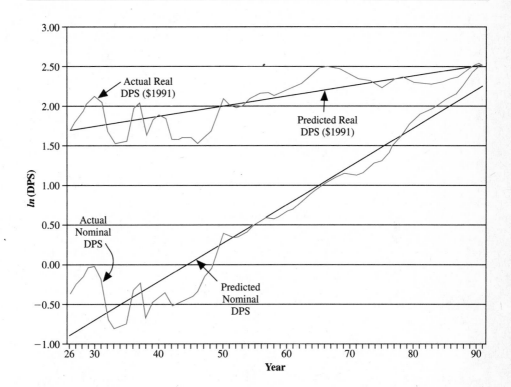

Notice in Figure 19-7 that, except for the Depression and World War II era, dividends per share have not been substantially different than predicted by log-least-squares regression equations (using the full period 1926–1991). Also notice that dividend growth has been relatively stable, particularly for nominal dividends. This provides some validity to our use of the constant dividend valuation model letter in this section.

The *R*-squares reported in Table 19-8 confirm the greater stability of nominal dividend growth. The 20-year period ended in 1991 experienced the greatest rate of nominal dividend growth, but much of this was offset by greater inflation rates.

This data suggests that: (1) a constant dividend valuation model might be a reasonable way to value the S&P 500 Index, (2) nominal dividend growth is

TABLE 19-8 *Historical Compound Annual Growth Rates S&P 500 Index 1926–1991*

	Nominal		Real	
Period	*CAGR*	*R-Squared*	*CAGR*	*R-Squared*
1926–1991	4.84%	92.8%	1.27%	63.6%
1946–1991	5.51%	97.9%	1.23%	53.7%
1971–1991	7.14%	98.9%	0.88%	43.1%

directly related to future inflation and (3) nominal growth will exceed inflation by 80 to 125 basis points.

Sustainable Internal Growth. If the return on equity (*ROE*) and dividend retention rates (*B*) are constant in the future, then internal corporate growth can sustain a growth rate in dividends (*G*) equal to:

Sustainable Internal Growth
$$G = ROE \times B \tag{19.4}$$

For example, if you believe that the S&P 500 Index will have a long-run *ROE* of, say, 12% and a dividend retention rate of 55%, this implies that future dividend growth will be 6.6%:

$$12\% \times 0.55 = 6.6\%$$

Although returns on equity and retention rates could be estimated using historical averages, there are at least two related problems in using past data. First, the past is not necessarily a good predictor of the future. Growth estimates vary widely, depending on the time span chosen. Unpredictable events such as unexpected inflation, natural disasters, and wars can have significant effects upon any one year's results. Probably more important is the implicit assumption that equity returns and retention rates are related and that growth rates for the average firm are determined by $B \times ROE$. The assumption is that corporations can increase dividend growth rates simply by retaining larger amounts of profits. Given an *ROE* of 15%, growth will be 10% if two-thirds of profits are retained and 7.5% if one-half of profits are retained. This implies that aggregate dividend growth is determined solely by management—that it is not *constrained by economic opportunities*.

Over lengthy periods of time this simply isn't true. The growth of corporate profits and dividends is constrained by the growth in aggregate economic activity. It is difficult to envision a situation in which for long periods of time dividends grow more rapidly than the GNP. As a result, a better approach to estimating profit and dividend growth may be to start with a long-run estimate of aggregate economic growth and back into likely dividend growth.

Long-Run Economic Growth. To use the long-run economic growth approach to valuation:

1. Estimate expected long-run *real* growth in GNP together with optimistic and pessimistic ranges.
2. Estimate the relationship that is likely to exist between *real* dividend growth and real GNP growth and use this to estimate dividend growth rates and ranges.
3. Estimate long-run rates of *inflation* and their impacts on nominal dividend growth rates.
4. Estimate reasonable required rates of return and ranges.
5. Estimate market values.

FIGURE 19-8 *Real GNP, EPS, and DPS*

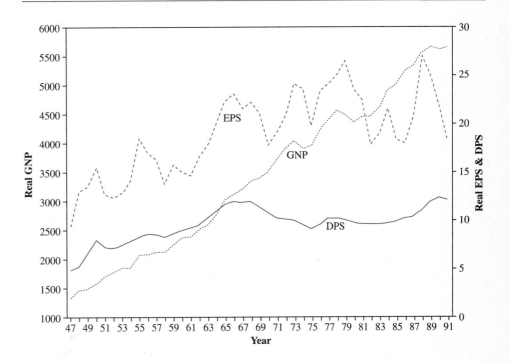

Figure 19-8 plots real levels of GNP, S&P 500 earnings per share (*EPS*), and S&P 500 dividends per share (*DPS*) from 1946 to 1991; (Values are reported in constant 1991 dollars.) During this time span, real GNP exhibited some volatility caused by various business cycles, but its long-run growth rate was reasonably stable and equal to a compound annual growth rate of 3.4%. This compares favorably with estimates made by Denison of 3.33% between 1929 and 1969 and 3.85% between 1948 and 1969. Based simply on these results, one would expect future real GNP growth to be between 3 and 4%. However, since a 3% growth versus a 4% growth can result in substantially different values for the S&P 500 Index, one should attempt to make an explicit forecast of future real growth. Table 19-9 provides just such a forecast based on one approach to determining real economic growth. Legitimate arguments could, of course, be raised about each of the forecast values, but they are designed to illustrate the types of factors that should be considered.

Selecting an Appropriate Discount Rate

The discount rate reflects the return the investor requires in order to accept the investment risks of the security. We have seen in previous chapters that the standard deviation of yearly returns on the S&P 500 depends on the time period

TABLE 19-9 *Estimates of Real Economic Growth*

	Pessimistic	Expected	Optimistic
I. Factor Inputs			
A. Employment Population growth rates will slow down and proportion of the retired population will increase.	0.95%	1.0 %	1.15%
B. Hours Hours worked will continue a slight decline as people continue to move out of the farm sector into the nonfarm sector. Slight changes will be caused by unionization, increased standard of living, smaller families, and leisure alternatives.	−0.22	−0.21	−0.20
C. Age/Sex Composition Historical negative effects were caused mainly by the movement of women into teaching areas. A reversal is forecast as they gain increased responsibility within the business sector.	0.00	0.10	0.13
D. Education Major advantages of increased worker education have probably been seen in the past 50 years. However, as better-trained women and minorities enter the work force, education will continue to play a positive role.	0.30	0.35	0.40
E. Other Use 1929–1969 average.	0.09	0.09	0.09
Total Labor	1.12%	1.33%	1.57%
F. Total Capital Major increases in capital will occur as the United States retools to meet international competition and growth in postwar houshold formations.	0.70	0.90	1.00
Total Factor Input	1.82%	2.23%	2.57%
II. Output per Unit of Input			
A. Advances in Knowledge Not only is this a difficult factor to measure, it seems to be one of the more volatile. There does not seem to be any significant slowdown in scientific knowledge, but, instead, major discoveries in organic chemistry, microcircuitry, power generation, etc.	1.00%	1.20%	1.30%
B. Improved Resource Allocation This is another difficult factor to forecast. A major pro is the development of international human and natural resources, and a major con is the depletion of scarce resources.	0.20	0.25	0.30

TABLE 19-9 *(continued)*

	Pessimistic	*Expected*	*Optimistic*
C. Economies of Scale Historical value for 1929–1969	0.35	0.35	0.35
D. Other Historical value for 1929–1969	−0.05	−0.05	−0.05
Total	1.50%	1.75%	1.90%
Total Annual Growth in GNP	3.32%	3.98%	4.47%

examined, but has generally been between 15% and 20%. The *average* return earned for bearing risk, however, is much more volatile. For example, 20-year average annual outcomes have ranged between 1.0% to 12%, and over the 1926–1991 period the S&P 500 Index had a real return about 9.2% greater than that of T-bills and T-bonds. We have also seen in Chapter 10 that there is growing empirical evidence suggesting that investor risk premiums vary as economic conditions change.

Perhaps the best strategy is to use a variety of risk premiums that appear to be reasonable in light of past returns and current conditions. In June 1992, the risk-free return on long-term bonds was 7.5%. Applying risk premiums of 4% to 7% results in discount rates ranging from 11.5% to 14.5%.

Valuation of the S&P 500 at June 1992. The value of any stock or stock index should be the present value of expected future dividends, as shown in Equation 19.5:

**Dividend
Valuation
Model**

$$P_0 = \sum_{t=1}^{D} D_t/(1 + K)^t \qquad \textbf{(19.5)}$$

D_t is our expected dividend in year t, K is the required return, and P_0 is the present value of expected future dividends (our estimate of the security's fair value).

If dividends are expected to grow at a constant annual rate of G, Equation 19.5 can be simplified as follows:

**Constant Dividend
Growth Model**

$$P_0 = \frac{D_0(1 + G)}{K - G} \qquad \textbf{(19.6)}$$

For individual stocks, the assumption of constant dividend growth is usually too naive. The dividend growth rates of individual firms go through various stages as the firm goes through various stages of its life cycle. However, for an index of large, mature firms such as the S&P 500, the assumption of constant growth is often reasonable. Thus, we use the constant growth model of Equation 19.6.

Assume that, after reviewing the various estimates of future S&P 500 dividend growth and required returns, we decide to use $G=6\%$ and $K=13\%$ as our best estimates. At June 30, 1992 the S&P 500 Index closed at about $410 and total dividends over the prior 12 months had been $12.25. This indicates that:

$$\text{Intrinsic Value of S\&P 500} = \frac{\$12.25\,(1.06)}{0.13 - 0.06} = \$185.5$$

$$\text{Expected Return on S\&P 500} = \frac{\$12.25\,(1.06)}{\$4.10} + 0.06$$

$$= 0.0317 + 0.06 = 0.0917$$

$$\text{Sustainable Growth Consistent with Existing Price} = 0.13 - 0.0317 = 0.0983$$

Clearly, either the constant growth assumption is wrong or the S&P 500 was overvalued at June 30, 1992.

Sensitivity Analysis. The estimates calculated above can be quite sensitive to input assumptions. Therefore, it is wise to consider the results of a variety of assumptions ranging from pessimistic to optimistic. An example is shown in Table 19-10. In the left column, various nominal dividend growth rates are shown. The top row shows various desired discount rates.

Entries in the matrix represent intrinsic values of the S&P 500 using Equation 19.6. Note that fair values are in excess of $410 only at low required returns and optimistic growth rates. Again, either the S&P 500 Index was overvalued in June, 1992 or the constant growth model was inappropriate.

Relative Value Measures. Two relative value measures are commonly used by practitioners. These are the price-to-earnings (P/E) and price-to-book-value (P/B) ratios. The P/E ratio is the current market price of a stock (or index) divided by last year's or next year's earnings per share. The P/B ratio is the current market

TABLE 19-10 *Sensitivity Analysis of S&P 500 Intrinsic Value*

	K Values			
G Values	*11.50%*	*12.50%*	*13.50%*	*14.50%*
0.045	195.12	172.27	154.49	140.26
0.055	227.65	196.87	173.80	155.85
0.065	273.18	229.69	198.62	175.33
0.075	342.47	275.63	231.73	200.38
0.085	455.29	344.53	278.08	233.77
0.095	682.94	459.38	347.59	280.53

$D_0 = \$12.25$.

S&P 500 ACTUAL VALUE = $410 (JUNE 30, 1992).

price of a stock (or index) divided by last year's book value per share. (Book value per share is equal to total shareholder equity divided by outstanding shares.)

Both ratios are plotted for the S&P 500 in Figure 19-9. At the end of 1991, the P/E ratio was close to its historical high. The same was true for the P/B ratio. These ratios suggested that the U.S. equity market was overvalued in 1991.

Considerable care must be taken in interpreting P/E and P/B ratios. For example, there is no reason to believe that current levels of each will necessarily return to historical averages. The value of the ratios should and does change in response to changes in market consensus estimates of K and G.

Changing Market Risk Premiums. Recall from Chapter 10 the discussion of potential stock market overreaction. When actual future dividends are discounted back to previous periods in order to calculate what stock index prices should have been if investors had been able to correctly forecast future dividends, a relatively stable series of stock prices results. This stable series of prices contrasts dramatically with the large volatility of actual prices. Actual stock prices depart substantially from a rational ex post valuation for *relatively long periods of time*. The results of one study are shown in Figure 19-10. The stable dashed line represents the ex post rational valuation of a stock index. The solid line represents the actual (detrended) index.

The cause of this apparent excess volatility is not fully understood. One possible explanation is that market participants do not price stocks (either implicitly or explicitly) using a long-term dividend valuation model. If this is true, tactical asset allocation decisions based on fundamental dividend models should provide excess returns over the long run. Alternatively, the market could be using a dividend discount approach with highly volatile estimates of G and K. Given the stable increase in past nominal dividend growth, many scholars have claimed that variability in K is the cause. According to this view, market participants are constantly changing the risk premium they require on stocks.

If stock price volatility is due to changes in the market's consensus of K, then stock prices are, strictly speaking, always efficiently priced. But even if this view of market efficiency is taken, individuals with more stable values of K will find periods of time during which stocks should be overweighted or underweighted relative to their SAA. Figure 19-10 suggests, however, that periods of over- and underweighting can last as long as a decade!

Macro- versus Micro-Efficient Markets. Some investment professionals differentiate between macro- and micro-efficiency. Macro-efficiency refers to how closely the price levels of an aggregate asset class track its intrinsic value. Shiller would argue that his study shows that the stock market is not macro-efficient for extended periods of time. Micro-efficiency refers to individual securities and requires that perfect substitutes be priced to provide the same expected returns.

It is possible that securities are efficiently priced in a micro, but not in a macro, sense. But to take advantage of any macro-inefficiencies that might exist, one must be able to identify the dates at which corrections will occur.

FIGURE 19-9 *Historical S&P 500 Relative Values*

A. Price to Earnings Ratio

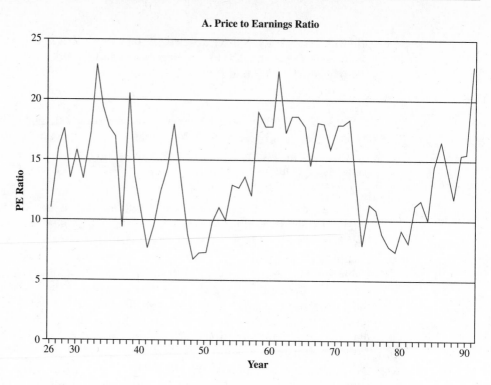

B. Price to Book Ratio

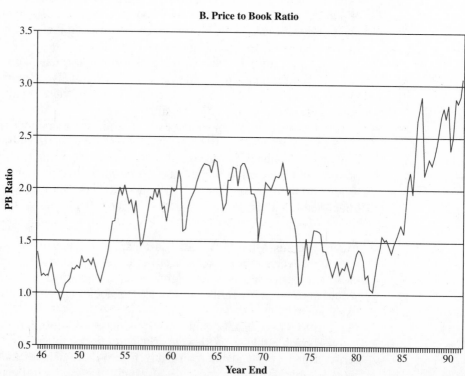

FIGURE 19-10 *Shiller's Detrended Estimates of Perfect Foresight Stock Index Versus Actual Index (DJIA)*

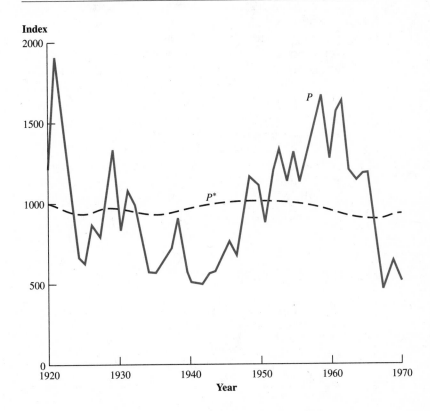

Does Tactical Allocation of Equities Work? Most rigorous studies of market timing suggest that the short-term benefits of equity timing decisions are doubtful. Over periods of approximately 10 years or less, the quarterly return series of investment managers who time are, on average, no different from those of managers who do not time. However, no studies have examined equity market timing over longer time periods. This is unfortunate, since Figure 19-10 suggests that, if equity timing is to work it will occur primarily over lengthy periods.

SUMMARY

In this chapter, we examined approaches that are used to determine a portfolo's asset allocation. We began by reviewing a recent study showing the importance of strategic asset allocation (SAA). For the 82 pension portfolios studied, more than 90% of return volatility and the major source of average returns was each portfolio's SAA.

The first step in developing an appropriate SAA is to identify an efficient frontier of the asset classes in which the investor is willing to invest. This requires that expected returns, standard deviations, and correlation coefficients be specified for each asset class. Although these estimates are difficult to make, they come easier with experience. After an efficient frontier has been developed, the statistical results for various portfolios should be recast so that they can be better understood by investors who are not comfortable with, say, standard deviation of annual returns. Typically, this involves two changes: (1) expressing returns and future payoffs in percentile form instead of expected return standard deviation form and (2) extrapolating the results to longer time horizons.

Tactical asset allocation (TAA) attempts to profit from short-term swings in relative prices of asset classes. The classic name for this is timing. People attempt to time between a wide variety of asset classes, including aggregate stocks, long-term bonds, country stock markets, and currencies. We reviewed how fundamental analysis can be used to evaluate the value of an aggregate stock index such as the S&P 500.

REVIEW PROBLEM

You have created your own index of common stock prices, which you call the EMP Index (Equity Market Portfolio Index). At present the economy is in a slump, resulting in depressed dividend levels. Dividends per share on your EMP Index over the past 10 years have been as follows:

Year	Dividends	Year	Dividends
1986	$1.39	1991	$2.45
1987	1.39	1992	2.60
1988	1.45	1993	2.65
1989	1.62	1994	2.67
1990	2.00	1995	2.68

You run a log-least-squares regression on the data and get:

$$\ln(DPS) = -181.64497 + 0.09161 \text{ (Time)} \qquad R^2 = 89.85\%$$

a. What has been the compound annual growth rate in dividends per share?

b. If you use the regression trend line, what is your expected dividend two years from now (1997)? (Assume dividend levels return to their overall trend level by then.)

c. The 1995 dividend was just $2.68. If you believe dividends will increase in 1996 and 1997 by equal dollar increments to the trend line value in part b, what is 1996's dividend expected to be?

d. Beyond 1997 you are unable to identify the impacts of any business cycles. Nonetheless, starting after 1997 you forecast growth rates equal to the historic average in part a. If you require a return of 15% on an investment in the EMP Index, what fair value would you place on the index as of the end of 1995?

e. If the EMP Index is $55.00 at the end of 1995, how would you adjust your stock/bond ratio?

Solution

a. 9.161%—the slope of the log-natural regression.
b. $3.67 = antilog [−181.64497 + 0.09161 (1997)]
c. $\dfrac{\$3.67 - \$2.68}{2} = \$0.495$ per year
   1996 dividend = $2.68 + $0.495 = $3.175
d. This requires a nonconstant dividend growth model:

$$P = \frac{D_{96}}{1 + k} + \frac{D_{97}}{(1 + K)^2} + \frac{D_{97}(1 + G)}{K - G} \frac{1}{(1 + k)^2}$$

$$= \frac{\$3.175}{1.15} + \frac{\$3.67}{1.15^2} + \frac{\$3.67(1.09161)}{0.15 - 0.09161} [1/(1.15^2)]$$

$$= \$57.42$$

e. The estimated intrinsic value of the index is slightly higher than the actual value. Thus, slightly increase the actual equity holding compared with the baseline investment portfolio.

QUESTIONS AND PROBLEMS

1. The capital asset pricing model (CAPM) and arbitrage pricing theory (APT) are two conceptual approaches to defining risk and determining how securities are priced. Discuss the implications each has on the SAA decision.
2. One approach to determining the SAA for an individual (or an organization such as a pension plan) begins by estimating an efficient frontier of expected returns and risks on various classes of securities.
   a. What inputs are needed to do this?
   b. How might you develop such inputs?
   c. Why might such "efficient portfolios" not be the best for an individual or organization such as a pension fund?
3. "Thou shalt diversify!" Explain why.
4. "Thou shalt diversify investments in marketable securities—but not totally!" Explain why.
5. Indexed equity portfolios have been available to pension funds for about 20 years. In recent years, however, specialty index funds have been created that underweight portfolio holdings in economic sectors in which the sponsoring firm does business.
   a. Explain the rationale for such specialty index funds.
   b. What problems do you see in its implementation?
6. As of year-end an equity index is selling at 1,000. To evaluate whether this is a fair value, you have developed the following data:

Equity Index Estimates	Pessimistic	Expected	Optimistic
Long-Run *ROE*	14.50%	15.00%	16.00%
Profit Retention Rate	50.00%	56.67%	60.00%
Current T-Bond *YTM*	8.00%	8.00%	8.00%
Fair Risk Premium	5.00%	5.50%	6.00%
Year 0 Earnings per Share	$100.00	$106.35	$110.00

a. Develop pessimistic, expected, and optimistic valuations of the equity index.
b. As the investment adviser for a $20.0 million pension fund, you believe that a long-run stock/bond ratio of 50/50 should be maintained. However, you are willing to alter the ratio temporarily to take advantage of perceived price imbalances. Based upon your answer to part a, would you make such an adjustment now?
7. Suppose you have made the following estimates:

	Pessimistic	Expected	Optimistic
Long-Run GNP Growth—Real			
Employment	0.9%	1.0%	1.1%
Work Hours	−0.2	−0.2	−0.2
Age/Sex Composition	0.0	0.0	0.1
Education	0.2	0.3	0.3
Other	0.0	0.0	0.0
Capital	0.6	0.7	0.8
Advances in Knowledge	0.9	1.0	1.1
Resource Allocation	0.2	0.2	0.3
Economics of Scale	0.4	0.4	0.4
Other Output	0.0	0.0	0.0
Long-Run Dividend Growth—Real			
60% of GNP Growth			
Other Information			
Long-Run Inflation per Year	8.00%	7.25%	6.50%
Current Dividends per Share on Equity Index 500	$5.70	$5.70	$5.70
Current Equity Index 500 Value	107	107	107

The required return is 15%. Would you adjust your stock/bond mix?
8. You have just completed a strategic asset allocation (SAA) study of the data below and identified the following two portfolios as efficient (all data are expressed in annualized real return terms):

	Efficient Portfolios		Expected	Standard	Correlations		
	A	B	Return	Deviation	TB	GB	SP
T-Bills	0.7667	0.0235	3.0%	2.0%	1.00		
Govt. Bonds	0.0852	0.2690	5.0%	10.0%	0.10	1.00	
S&P 500	0.1481	0.7075	8.6%	18.0%	0.00	0.50	1.00
Total							
Investment	1.0000	1.0000					

a. Calculate the expected return and standard deviation of Portfolio A and Portfolio B.
b. If an international equity class were added as a fourth asset class, what effect should this have on the efficient frontier?
c. This efficient frontier is based on real rates of return (after inflation). As such, is it appropriate for investors facing future nominal liabilities?
d. What is the difference in the efficient frontiers of individuals facing real dollar and nominal dollar liabilities?
e. Use the expected return and standard deviation of portfolio B to calculate the percentile distributions of terminal wealth of $1.00 and geometric return for the end of five years from now. (Assume $E(R)$ and σ are currently expressed as continuous returns. Also, the serial correlation of returns is zero.)

f. Mathematically, any efficient portfolio between portfolio A and portfolio B is a linear combination of them. If X is invested in A and $(1 - X)$ is invested in B, the combination is efficient. Given this, what is the composition of the efficient portfolio providing an expected return of 6%?

9. Dawon Insurance is developing an efficient frontier based on nominal dollar liabilities. The firm can lend risk-free by purchasing zero-coupon government bonds or bills. Thus, there is a linear trade-off between risk and return from the risk-free rate to a point of tangency with the efficient frontier of risky assets. Call this point P. Above point P, the firm may not short sell risk-free governments and use the proceeds to invest in risky assets. How might options and futures be used to create a linear risk-return trade-off above point P?

10. If options and futures are trading at equilibrium prices, should positions in them be considered an additional asset class?

11. The expected annual return of a portfolio is 8% and its standard deviation of annual returns is 14%. Both numbers are expressed as continuous compound returns.

   a. $1.00 is invested in this portfolio and continuously re-balanced to maintain the 8% expected return and 14% standard deviation. What is the percentile distribution of terminal wealth after 30 years?

   b. Why was it necessary to rebalance the portfolio over time?

   c. What is the percentile distribution of geometric annualized returns after 30 years?

   d. Repeat parts a and b for 1-year outcomes.

   e. The percentile distribution of the 30-year geometric returns is narrower than for the 1-year distribution. Does this prove that there is time diversification, that the longer one invests the lower the investment risk?

12. Since investment risk compounds over time, then long-term investors will invest in lower-risk portfolios than short-term investors. True or false, and why?

13. Let's assume that security markets are micro-efficient but are seriously macro-inefficient for long periods of time. What must you be able to do in order to take advantage of this macro-inefficiency?

14. One of the Trustees of the Donner College Endowment Fund is Susan Oliver, the Chief Financial Officer of a local corporation. She is now 55 years of age and plans to take early retirement. Oliver is a Donner College alumna and wants to make some lasting contribution to the college. Upon her retirement, Oliver intends to use the after-tax proceeds from exercising her incentive stock options and nearly all of her rather extensive other liquid assets to establish a charitable-remainder trust. Oliver will be the income beneficiary of the approximately $1 million trust and will also have emergency rights of limited access to the principal. Upon her death, the assets of the trust will pass to the Donner College Endowment Fund with no tax liability to Oliver's estate. She will not receive payments from her retirement pension until age 65. Oliver has asked the two investment advisors to meet with her to discuss her investment plans. Their meeting continued in a "debate" format.

Advisor 1: "The life-cycle approach to investment policy and asset allocation is best for the charitable-remainder trust. Oliver is no longer young, will have only minimal outside sources of income, and will rely on income from the trust to meet all of her spending needs. The trust's investment policy should emphasize conservatism and the production of high levels of current income. Therefore, the trust should be invested almost entirely in long-term bonds."

Advisor 2: "Oliver's stated desire to make a lasting contribution to the college implies leaving as much in the trust as possible upon her death. Therefore, the trust's goal should be to maximize capital growth. Oliver is entitled to all of its income and to some principal if needed, which should be sufficient to meet her spending needs regardless of how little income the trust might earn. The trust is able to take high risk and should invest almost entirely in small-capitalization growth stocks.''

Advisor 1 Rebuttal: ''While your approach has a chance to leave a much larger amount to the Donner College Endowment Fund, there is also the unfortunate possibility of leaving very little if stocks do poorly. With my approach, Oliver's income is secure and the trust would be able to preserve its capital.''

Evaluate the strengths and weaknesses of *each* of the *two* approaches presented above. **Recommend** and **justify** an investment policy *and* an asset allocation (which must add to 100%) that draws from the strengths of *each* approach and corrects their weaknesses.

DATAFILE ANALYSIS

1. *Historical Efficient Frontiers.* Review the instructions for the asset allocation (efficient frontier) computer package called ASSETALL. Using historical returns on a variety of asset classes found in the data sets, calculate historical average returns, standard deviations, and correlation coefficients for each. For the ASSETALL program to work without encountering mathematical difficulties, it is best if you select six or fewer asset classes. Among the asset classes include long-term U.S. Government Bonds. Use the ASSETALL package to find the historical efficient frontier. Do this twice. In the first, you should follow the directions to calculate portfolios that *do not* allow short sales. In the second, you should allow short sales to occur. Interpret the output. What do these results imply about the validity of using historical averages, standard deviations, and correlation coefficients with no modifications in attempting to find an efficient frontier associated with future security returns?

REFERENCES

The Association for Investment Management and Research has published the proceedings of various seminars on asset allocation. Two of these include:

DROMS, WILLIAM G. (Ed.), *Asset Allocation for the Individual Investor.* Homewood, IL: Dow Jones-Irwin, 1987.

JOEHNK, MICHAEL D. *Asset Allocation for Institutional Portfolios.* Homewood, IL: Dow Jones-Irwin, 1986.

Interesting papers that investigate the importance of asset allocation in determining portfolio returns include:

BRINSON, GARY P., BRIAN D. SINGER, and GILBERT L. BEEBOWER, ''Determinants of Portfolio Performance II: An Update,'' *Financial Analysts Journal,* May-June 1991.

HENSEL, CHRIS, D., DON EZRA, and JOHN ILKEW, ''The Importance of the Asset Allocation Decision,'' *Financial Analysts Journal,* July-August 1992.

Recent developments in asset allocation models are discussed in:

BEEBOWER, G.L., and A. P. VARIKOOTY, "Measuring Market Timing Strategies," *Financial Analysts Journal,* November-December 1991.

EZRA, DON D., "Asset Allocation by Surplus Optimization," *Financial Analysts Journal,* January-February 1991.

GARCIA, C. B., F. J. GOULD, and DOUGLAS C. MITCHELL, "The Historical Validity of Short Fall Estimates," *The Journal of Portfolio Management,* Summer 1992.

HAUGEN, ROBERT A., and NARDIN BAKER, "Dedicated Stock Portfolios," *The Journal of Portfolio Management,* Summer 1990.

LEIBOWITZ, MARTIN L., and STANLEY KOGÈLMAN, "Asset Allocation Under Short Fall Constraints," *The Journal of Portfolio Management,* Winter 1991.

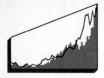

Selection of Active Managers

Once the portfolio's asset allocation has been determined, individual securities within each asset class must be chosen.

If the investor decides to invest passively in an asset class, the security-selection decision is easy—purchase shares in an index fund that emulates the returns of a particular aggregate asset class. For example, an index fund that emulates the EAFE Index could be purchased to provide the desired exposure to international equities, an index fund that emulates the S&P 500 could be purchased to provide the desired exposure to large capitalization U.S. equities, and so forth.

If investors decide to use active management, they must then decide whether they will personally select the securities to be held or will entrust such decisions to professional managers. This chapter deals with the last issue—the selection of active investment managers.

Trustees of large investment pools such as pension funds and foundations rely exclusively on professional managers. Although smaller-scale individual investors often rely on the advice of brokers as well as their own personal opinions to select individual securities, they too are relying increasingly on the services of professional managers such as open-end and closed-end investment companies. As Chapter 1 showed, more than 50% of all publicly traded securities in the United States are managed by professional investors.

We begin with an overview of the professional investment management community. The most visible part of this community to the general public is the mutual fund industry. Although mutual funds manage an important fraction of securities traded throughout the world, they represent only the visible portion of a much larger investment-management industry. Following the overview of the investment-management community, we examine two types of professionally managed portfolios available to the general public: open-end and closed-end investment companies. The chapter concludes with a discussion of the considerations to be used when selecting an active manager as well as the number of managers needed to assure reasonable diversification.

THE PROFESSIONAL INVESTMENT INDUSTRY

A Brief History of Investment Management

Investors have relied on the services of professional investment counselors for centuries. Prior to the development of active securities markets, well-to-do individuals usually obtained advice from business acquaintances and lawyers about promising ventures. Once active secondary security markets arose, investment advice increasingly came from security brokers and organizations that specialized in investment management. Usually, these investment managers were employees of a financial services firm that could provide the well-to-do client with a full range of services, including demand deposit accounts, personal loans, investment banking advice regarding the client's business, and personal advice about investment in financial assets. Prior to World War I the more important of these "banking houses" were located in Europe (particularly, the United Kingdom) and the United States. Perhaps the most powerful in the United States was The House of Morgan, which was founded by the famous financier John Pierpont Morgan.

At that time, the practice of allowing investment advisors *full discretion* over purchases and sales became common. This meant that the advisor could make security trades without first obtaining approval from the investor. Today, virtually all professional investment managers are given full discretion, allowing them to trade rapidly as prices temporarily depart from intrinsic values.[1] The only constraints currently placed on professional investment managers are legal constraints and any contractual provisions made with the investor.

Prior to the 1920s, virtually all portfolios that an advisor managed for investor clients were held separately from portfolios of other clients. The composition of each portfolio was often different and the holdings of each were physically segregated from other portfolios. This arrangement is still widely used today, and such portfolios are referred to as *separate accounts*. For example, Florida law requires that securities managed by a professional advisor to police and firefighter pension plans be physically segregated from the assets of other managed portfolios.

As security trading became popular during the 1920s, investment advisory firms began to offer their services to smaller investors through a vehicle known as a *commingled portfolio*. A few commingled portfolios had been offered during the late 1880s, but they did not become popular until the booming security markets of the 1920s. In a commingled portfolio, investors pool their funds and purchase a single investment portfolio. Each investor owns the same set of assets. Two types of commingled portfolios were initially offered to the general public: (1)

---

[1] Throughout this chapter, security brokers are not considered to be professional investment managers. Although brokers do provide advice, their principal purpose is to facilitate purchase and sale transactions.

closed-end portfolios and (2) open-end portfolios. We discuss each later in the chapter.

Over the next 60 years, two events occurred that had profound effects on the way security markets look today and the nature of the professional investment-manager community.

The Glass-Stegall Act. In late 1929, stock markets worldwide crashed. For example, in September and October of 1929 the S&P 500 Index fell by 30%. In the wake of this crash, broad new security laws were enacted in the United States in an attempt to counterbalance perceived fraudulent practices. In the United States, one of the more far-reaching legislative actions was the *Banking Act of 1933*. Named after its sponsors, the *Glass-Stegall Act* had three critical parts.

First, the act precluded commercial banks from investment banking activities. Banks such as The House of Morgan were split into two organizations—the commercial bank, Morgan Guarantee Trust, and the investment banking firm, Morgan Stanley.

This decision had dramatic implications. For example, it meant that commercial banks in the United States could not create and offer commingled portfolios in the forms of mutual funds or closed-end investment company shares *to the general public*. Banks could offer to manage separate account trust assets for individuals since this did not involve the creation and sale of a new security to the public. In addition, they could offer commingled portfolios to private investors such as pension funds and foundations since this also does not involve the creation and sale of securities to the general public. Revisions are currently before the U.S. Congress to repeal this section of the *Glass-Stegall Act*.[2]

Because U.S. banks were restricted from the creation and sale of commingled investment portfolios to the general public, other organizations grew to dominate the open and closed-end investment company industry. These include insurance firms, brokerage houses, and firms that specialize solely in investment-management services.

Second, the Glass-Stegall Act prohibited banks from paying interest on demand deposit checking accounts. When interest rates were relatively low, this had only a mild effect on the banking industry. People preferred the convenience and safety offered by their local banks to other alternatives. But as interest rates rose during the 1970s, due to increased inflation expectations, bank depositors looked elsewhere for returns to compensate for inflation losses. The "elsewhere" turned out to be a new form of open-end mutual fund, money market mutual funds. By 1989, investment in money market funds peaked at $0.42 trillion—more than a third of all assets managed by mutual funds at that time. Recent decreases in interest rates and the repeal to this provision of the Glass-Stegall Act have resulted in a decrease in assets managed by non-bank money market funds.

Finally, the Glass-Stegall Act created the Federal Deposit Insurance Corporation (FDIC), which insures demand deposits in commercial banks. Although FDIC

---

[2] Recent legislative changes in the United States now allow commercial banks to sell mutual funds and stocks to public investors.

Individual Investors' Holdings of U.S. Stocks Fall Below 50% of Total Market for the First Time

By MICHAEL SICONOLFI
Staff Reporter of THE WALL STREET JOURNAL

NEW YORK—For the first time, individual investors no longer hold a majority of all publicly traded U.S. stocks.

The percentage of stocks held by individuals fell to 49.7% in the second quarter, the Securities Industry Association said. That's down from 84.1% in 1965 and 71% in 1980, and underscores the growing dominance of institutional investors in the U.S. stock market. These big investors include insurance companies, pension funds and mutual funds.

But this doesn't mean people are fleeing from stocks. Even as individuals' direct stock holdings have fallen, their investments in stock mutual funds have soared. Mutual funds now own 8.8% of all U.S. stocks, up from 2.7% in 1980, the SIA said; the trade group estimates that individuals currently own about $280 billion in stock through their mutual fund investments.

Indeed, when mutual fund assets are counted, individuals hold 55.9% of all outstanding stock, the trade group estimated. Most mutual fund assets are held by small investors.

"Individuals are still the backbone of the stock market," said Jeffrey M. Schaefer, the trade group's research director.

For more than a decade, individuals have been net sellers of stock, despite a surging market through much of the 1980s. During the '80s, individuals sold an average of $81 billion a year more in stocks than they bought, according to the Federal Reserve. This net selling slowed to $69 billion in 1991. And for the first half of this year, individuals *bought* $1 billion more in stocks than they sold, the Fed said.

Many new investors in the U.S. stock market these days have fled low-yielding certificates of deposit and money-market funds. But this shift worries some Wall Street executives, who caution that many small investors don't realize quite how volatile stocks can be.

"As they roll over CDs with lower and lower yields, they're looking at the stock market to solve their problem," says Benjamin Edwards III, chairman of A.G. Edwards Inc., a big St. Louis-based brokerage firm. "That means going up the risk scale," Mr. Edwards says. He worries that retired investors living on fixed incomes are particularly unprepared for the stock market's periodic slumps.

For the long term, however, stocks continue to be among the best-performing financial assets, whether owned directly or through mutual funds. General stock funds tracked by Lipper Analytical Services Inc. have averaged a compound gain of 11% annually for the past 30 years, including price gains and dividends.

And people appear to have gotten this message. U.S. individual investors' holdings of stock and stock mutual funds have swollen to an average of 45% of their financial assets, up from just under 40% in 1980, the trade group said. As investors have increased their stock portfolios, they have cut back on bank deposit accounts and CDs, which now make up 37% of their financial portfolios, down from 48% in 1980, the trade group said.

At the same time, investors also have boosted their bond holdings. Since 1980, for instance, individual investors' holdings of government bonds rose to 16% of their portfolios from 11%.

"Individual investors have become much more knowledgeable about and interested in government and municipal bonds as a means of obtaining higher yields, liquidity and, to some extent, reducing tax burdens," Mr. Schaefer said.

SOURCE: *The Wall Street Journal,* November 13, 1992.

insurance and its sister insurance on deposits in savings and loans played an important role in the U.S. economy during the early 1990s, it is not central to the discussion at hand.

Institutional Investors. The second major event shaping investment markets since the 1920s has been the increased security ownership by institutions, principally pension funds. Following World War II, it became common practice for corporations to offer retirement benefits to employees as a part of their total compensation package. To assure employees that promised benefits would be paid, legal escrow accounts were set up to invest yearly employer contributions. These deposits accumulated over time together with investment earnings to the point that, in the early 1990s, pension fund assets had a claim to about one-quarter the value of all securities traded in the United States.

Investment Management in the 1990s

The use of professional investment managers currently varies across countries. Since accurate data is not available for countries other than the United States and since many countries are likely to follow the U.S. path, we will focus on investment management in the United States.

An investment portfolio can be managed by any one of three parties: (1) a professional manager other than the investor (say, a mutual fund), (2) a professional manager who owns the portfolio (say, a commercial bank) or (3) a nonprofessional manager who owns the portfolio (say, Mom and Dad). Table 20-1 provides information about each of these as of the end of 1991.

At the end of 1991, the market value of U.S. equities was $4.3 trillion. Of this amount, $2.4 trillion was managed by professional outside advisors and $0.4

TABLE 20-1 *Analysis of U.S. Security Holdings Estimates as of December 1991 ($ Trillions)*

	Equities	Money Market and Fixed	Total
Value of Outstanding Securities	$4.3	$6.3	$10.6
Managed by			
Professional External Advisors	2.4	1.8	4.2
Professional Internal Managers	0.4	3.4	3.8
Other (households)	1.5	1.1	2.6
Types of Professional External Advisors			
Commercial Banks	0.6	0.3	0.9
Insurance Companies	0.6	0.3	0.9
Investment Counselors	1.2	1.2	2.4
Tax Exempt Assets	1.2	1.1	2.3
Mutual Funds	0.3	0.4	
Indexed Assets	0.2	0.1	0.3

SOURCE: Based on data presented in *Pensions & Investments,* May 18, 1992.

trillion was managed by professional internal managers. The remaining $1.5 trillion was not managed by professional investment advisors. Sixty-five percent of total equity values in the United States were under the full discretionary control of professional managers.

Estimates are also shown in Table 20-1 of the dollar value managed by commercial banks, insurance companies, and investment counsel firms. Banks accounted for one-quarter of all professionally managed U.S. equity funds. These are not equities owned by the bank itself, but equities managed for clients of the bank. Historically, the majority of clients were individuals who set up trust accounts that the bank managed. Recently, the bulk of the equities that banks manage has shifted to tax exempt organizations such as pension funds, endowments, and foundations.

One-quarter of professionally managed assets were controlled by insurance companies. As with banks, these are not equities owned by insurance companies, but equities professionally managed for others. Although some equity money managed by insurance companies is in the form of publicly available mutual funds, the largest part of their business is with tax-exempt institutional investors, such as pensions, endowments, and foundations.

Investment counsel firms are either divisions of brokerage firms or firms that specialize solely in investment management. Similar to insurance companies, they create and offer open and closed-end investment company shares to the general public. But the majority of funds that they manage are, again, owned by tax-exempt institutional investors. Approximately one-half of all professionally managed assets are managed by investment counsel companies.

Data in Table 20-1 also provides estimates of the dollar values of:

1. *Tax-exempt assets.* These include pensions, endowments, and foundation assets. In 1991, equities of tax-exempt organizations represented more than one-quarter of all U.S. equities and one-half of all professionally managed equities.

2. *Mutual fund assets.* Mutual funds managed about 7% of the value of all U.S. equities and represented 12.5% of all professionally managed equities ($0.3 ÷ $2.4). Mutual funds are important investment vehicles for the general public. But they represent only a fraction of the total assets managed by the professional investment community.

3. *Indexed assets.* At the end of 1991, about $0.2 trillion of U.S. equities were passively managed via index funds. This represented 5% of total U.S. equity value.

Table 20-2 shows the largest 20 managers of tax-exempt portfolios. This listing is a result of a 1992 survey by the trade publication *Pensions & Investments*. The dollar value of funds managed does not include any mutual funds that the firms manage, since most owners of mutual funds are not tax exempt. The largest manager was Bankers Trust, which managed $109.8 billion in tax-exempt funds. Table 20-3 provides a breakdown of the types of portfolios that Bankers Trust managed. Of the $149.0 billion total assets managed by Bankers Trust, $109.8 billion were tax-exempt assets (nontrust accounts). The publication *Pensions & Investments* also provided the following description of the firm's investment ac-

TABLE 20-2 *Largest Twenty Tax-Exempt Managers, 1991*

Rank	Firm	$ Managed (Millions)
1	Bankers Trust	109,852
2	Wells Fargo Nikko	96,715
3	State Street Bank	61,525
4	Metropolitan Life Insurance	55,700
5	J. P. Morgan Investment	51,975
6	Prudential Asset	50 558
7	Aetna Life Insurance	44,598
8	Fidelity Investments	42,700
9	Northern Trust	35,904
10	Pacific Investment	34,971
11	Alliance Capital	34,039
12	GE Investments	33,244
13	CIGNA Investments	30,371
14	Mellon Capital	30,288
15	INVESCO MIM	26,936
16	Capital Guardian Trust	26,194
17	Equitable Capital	25,536
18	Mellon Bond Associates	24,491
19	Principal Financial Group	23,996
20	Miller, Anderson, and Sherrerd	22,363

SOURCE: *Pensions & Investments*, May 18, 1992.

tivities. Notice how closely the description follows topics discussed throughout the text.

Bankers Trust Co. is an active equity and bond, balanced, passive equity and bond, active and passive international\global equity, active and passive international\global bond, short-term, TAA, enhanced index, currency, book value bond, and options overwriting manager.

Of the assets listed above, $1.424 billion in U.S., institutional, discretionary, tax-exempt assets is managed in options overwriting, currency hedging and liquidity premium programs. All of the underlying assets are managed internally.

Its equity approach is top down and bottom up, with a focus on growth, emerging growth and low p\e stocks. Enhanced index and quantitative techniques also are used.

Its fixed-income approach uses sector and yield curve analyses, with hedged and unhedged strategies. Individual issue analysis also is applied.

The asset mix Jan 1 was 55.2% stocks; 13.6% bonds; 25.4% cash; 0.3% mortgage-backed securities; and 5.5% GICs.

The parent is Bankers Trust New York Corp.

Types of Portfolios. When an active professional manager is employed, the assets can be held in either a commingled portfolio or a separate account. As noted earlier, a commingled portfolio consists of a single portfolio owned by many parties, and a separate account consists of a portfolio owned by one party. The main advantage of owning a portion of a commingled portfolio is lower operating costs. There are significant economies of scale in portfolio management associated with accounting fees, research costs, and brokerage fees. It is also easier to get in

TABLE 20-3 *Information about Bankers Trust Investment Management, 1992*

	($ millions)
Total Assets Managed	149,008
Total Tax-Exempt Assets	109,852
Discretionary Tax-Exempt	109,852
Domestic Equity, Index	55,951
Domestic Bond, Index	3,707
International Equity, Index	1,693
International Bond, Index	139
Dedicated/Immunized Assets	6,068
Mortgage-Backed Assets	346
International Equity, Active	430
International Bond, Active	213
401(K)/457 Plan Assets	16,553
Number of Portfolio Managers	35
Size of Research Staff	19

SOURCE: *Pensions & Investments,* May 18, 1992.

or get out of a large commingled fund since securities usually do not have to be bought or sold immediately. In contrast, when one employs a manager to run a separate account, securities have to be bought and, when one fires a separate account manager, securities have to be sold.[3] This can be a time-consuming and costly task.

Some investors use separate account portfolios out of ignorance that equivalent commingled portfolios are available. But usually the separate account form is chosen because the investor wishes to constrain portfolio holdings or wants special manager attention. For example, a bank's commingled domestic equity fund would probably not be appropriate for a public pension plan that has a constraint against investing in companies that conduct business in South Africa. Consider also the following situation. Trustees of an endowment fund wish to employ an international equity manager and to meet twice each year with the manager, in order to better understand the ramifications of their foreign investment. It is doubtful that a commingled manager would be willing to meet with the trustees. As such, a separate account portfolio might have to be set up.

Benefits and Costs. There are five principal benefits to employing one or more professional investment managers:

1. *Diversification.* A small investment in a commingled fund will provide broad diversification over many securities.
2. *Cost of management.* Due to economies of scale, the costs of a managed commingled portfolio are much smaller than if one were to personally invest

---

[3] If one separate account manager is to be replaced by a second manager, it is possible that the second manager will accept the securities held by the first manager instead of cash, thereby reducing transaction costs.

the money. The costs of separate accounts are also lower than personal management since the manager has a large number of separate accounts over which fixed costs can be spread.

3. *Ease of administration.* All record keeping is maintained by the investment manager and the manager's custodian.

4. *Target desired portfolio.* If the investor has a need for a particular portfolio (say, high-growth technology stocks in Germany), the professional manager will have the data and communication network to identify such securities.

5. *Professional management.* Active managers might be able to successfully time and select securities such that they "add value" to the portfolio, that is, earn excess risk-adjusted returns.

There are two types of costs to active professional management. The first is easily measured and consists of transaction costs (brokerage fees), custodian fees, and management fees. Transaction costs depend, of course, on the turnover of the fees. Naturally, transaction costs depend on the turnover of the portfolio. If the investments are placed in a separate account, the investor can often dictate the allowable turnover. If the separate account manager believes such a constraint will hurt the portfolio's performance, then another manager can be employed. To gauge the size of transaction costs, consider a $50 stock that can be bought or sold at $0.06 per share (this is typical). If the manager holds the stock for six months and then replaces it, then a $0.24 cost should be allocated to a given year. This represents an annual 48 basis point cost. Custodian fees (ranging between 10 to 20 basis points per year) are paid to the firm that maintains physical control of portfolio assets. Finally, management fees depend on the investment strategy employed by the manager. Large commingled index funds typically will charge 25 basis points per year. Actively traded separate accounts typically have management fees between 50 to 100 basis points per year.

The second type of cost is harder to measure and applies only to taxable investors. If a taxable investor were to personally manage the portfolio, security purchases and sales could be managed in a way to minimize taxes. For example, securities with a capital gain would not be sold. Taxes would have to be paid eventually, when the portfolio is liquidated. But proper tax timing would benefit the investor by accelerating taxable losses and delaying taxable gains. In short, the investor gains the time value of money on any delayed taxes, in a benefit known as the *tax-timing option.*

When investors turn the management of their assets over to a professional manager, much (if not all) of the tax-timing option value can be lost. Separate account managers can be instructed to make trades that enhance the investor's tax situation. But this policy might conflict with the manager's desire to actively trade mispriced securities. If a commingled fund is purchased, all of the tax-timing option value is lost.

The tax-timing option value is not a concern to tax-exempt investors, but it should be considered by taxable investors.

Multiple Active Managers. Prior to the 1960s, it was common to employ a single investment manager or investment organization to run all the portfolio assets. A single firm was responsible for selecting all money market securities, bonds, and equities. In recent years, trustees of large institutional portfolios have started to employ more than one active manager within each asset class. We will discuss why and how multiple active managers are selected later in the chapter.

INVESTMENT COMPANY SHARES

Professional investment managers currently manage more than 50% of the value of U.S. equities. The largest portion of these assets are held in separate accounts and commingled portfolios owned by pension funds, endowments, and foundations—portfolios that are not available for purchase by the general public. However, insurance companies and investment counsel firms also offer commingled portfolios, known as investment company shares, that are available to the general public. In most respects, the portfolios of investment companies are similar to commingled portfolios offered to institutional investors but not available to the general public.

The services of investment management firms are made available through share offerings of two types. Shares of *open-end investment companies* are bought directly from and sold directly to the investment company. The term *open-end* reflects the fact that outstanding shares of the fund will increase or decrease as public investors purchase or redeem shares with the fund. Such open-end firms are commonly referred to as mutual funds. In contrast, shares of *closed-end investment companies* are bought and sold in secondary security markets in exactly the same manner as, say, shares of IBM. As a result, the outstanding shares of closed-end funds are fixed. In the United States, the aggregate value of assets managed by mutual funds greatly exceeds the assets managed by closed-end funds. For example, in 1991 the total value of U.S. mutual fund assets was $1.3 trillion versus a closed-end asset value of $0.06 trillion. This relationship does not hold in other countries. For example, closed-end companies remain very popular in the European community.

Shares of investment companies differ from other securities in three important respects. First, their assets represent a broadly diversified portfolio of other security issues. Thus the diversifiable risk inherent in the securities is much less than other securities. As such, investment company shares are a vehicle that individual investors can use to easily obtain broad diversification. Second, assets of an investment company represent pools of marketable securities that are managed according to specified objectives. Thus, individuals can match their unique investment objectives with those of one or more investment companies. Finally, any realized profits of the fund that are distributed to shareholders of the fund in a year are not taxable to the fund.

The fact that realized fund profits are not taxable to the fund has been crucial to the growth of the investment company industry. Although the fund investors pay personal taxes on realized fund income, investors avoid triple taxation at the fund level. To avoid such taxation, the investment company must qualify as a "regulated investment company" according to provisions of the Internal Revenue Service (IRS). Major requirements of the IRS code are shown in Table 20-4.

TABLE 20-4 *IRS Requirements to Be a Regulated Investment Company*

1. The fund must be a domestic corporation.
2. It must be registered at all times during the taxable year under the Investment Company Act of 1940 as a management company, business development company, or unit investment trust.
3. At least 90 percent of its gross income for any taxable year must be from dividends, interest, payments, with respect to securing loans and gains from sale of stock, securities, or other income (including gains from options, futures, or forward contracts) derived from investing in stock, securities, or currencies.
4. Sales of securities held for less than three months can account for no more than 30 percent of its gross income.
5. At the close of each quarter of the taxable year:
   (a) At least 50 percent of its assets must consist of cash, cash items (including receivables), government securities, securities of other regulated investment companies, and other securities limited to not more than 5 percent of its assets in securities of any one issuer and not more than 10 percent of the voting securities of that issuer.
   (b) Not more than 25 percent of its assets may be invested in any one company or in two or more controlled companies engaged in the same or a similar line of business (20 percent of voting power constitutes control).

SOURCE: CDA Wiesenberger Investment Companies, 1992.

Open-End Funds

Purchases and sales of mutual fund shares are made directly with the fund at a price known as net asset value (NAV). Consider the hypothetical balance sheet of Zodiac Mutual Fund at the close of trading on June 5, as displayed in Table 20-5.

Notice that Zodiac is an equity fund that specializes in high technology stocks. Specialization such as this becomes important when we address management selection. After the security markets have closed, each security owned by the fund is valued at its closing price and the total market value of assets is calculated. Zodiac's total asset value at the close of trading on June 5 is $101 million. To calculate the NAV per share, liabilities are subtracted and the net is divided by the number of shares outstanding *before* any new trades are processed. Zodiac's NAV on June 5 would be $10.00 per share:

$$NAV = \frac{\text{Asset Market Value} - \text{Liabilities}}{\text{Number of Shares Outstanding}}$$

$$\$10.00 = \frac{\$101.0 \text{ million} - \$1.0 \text{ million}}{10 \text{ million}}$$

(20.1)

Since the market value of assets and liabilities can be easily calculated, the true worth of each share is known with certainty!

During the business hours of June 5, Zodiac would have received numerous requests to purchase or redeem shares of the fund. These transactions will be processed in the evening *at the fund's end-of-day NAV*. For example, assume that you had wired $100,000 to the fund to purchase shares. Based on the fund's $10

TABLE 20-5 *Balance Sheet of (Hypothetical) Zodiac Mutual Fund Close of Trading June 5*

	Market Value (millions)		(millions)
Assets:		Liabilities:	
Cash Equivalents		Salaries Payable	$0.1
T-Bills	$5.0	Accruals	0.3
Repurchase Agreements	5.0	Accounts Payable	0.6
Total	$10.0		$1.0
Equities:		Equity:	
Hytek Inc.	$1.0		
Data Store Inc.	2.0	(Shares now	
.	.	outstanding	
.	.	equal 10 million)	
Robotics Inc.	4.0		
Total	$91.0		100.0
Total	$101.0		$101.0

NAV, you would receive 10,000 shares ($100,000 ÷ $10). Notice that, when trades occur at the fund's NAV, neither new shareholders nor previous shareholders are harmed. The purchase of new shares at NAV and the redemption of previous shares at NAV will have no effect on the fund's post-transaction NAV.

Information about specific mutual funds is available from a large number of sources. An example of the type of data available is shown in Figure 20-1. The fund is the well-known American Mutual Fund (AMF). The investment advisor to the fund is Capital Research and Management. Even though the assets of AMF were in excess of $4.3 billion at the end of 1991, Capital Research and Management was also the advisor to many other mutual funds and managed substantial money in commingled and separate accounts not available to the general public. The nonpublic money managed by the firm was owned mainly by pension plans, endowments, and foundations.

Return Sources. The rate of return received by owners of mutual fund shares comes from three sources: (1) receipt by the fund of interest and dividends paid on the securities owned by the fund, (2) increases or decreases in the value of securities held by the fund that the advisor *realizes for tax purposes* by selling the securities and (3) increases or decreases in the value of securities held that are *unrealized for tax purposes* because the fund does not sell the security.

For example, consider the case of AMF during the fourth quarter of 1991.[4] At

---

[4] This example is somewhat stylized, since dividend distributions were actually paid during the quarter as opposed to at quarter-end (as assumed in the text). This problem is treated correctly in the next chapter, when time-weighted returns are discussed.

FIGURE 20-1 *Sample Mutual Fund Page from Morningstar*

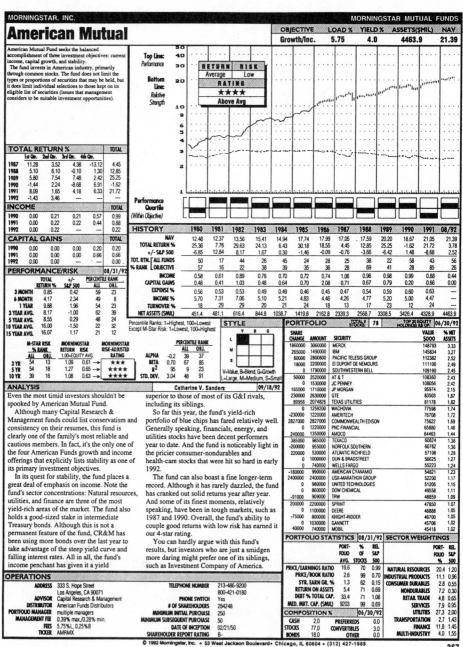

the start of the quarter, the fund's NAV was $20.83. During the quarter, dividends and interest were received on security investments held by the fund equal to $0.44 per share of the fund. If this income had been retained by AMF, it would have caused the NAV to increase by quarter-end to $21.27 ($20.83 + $0.44). In addition, the fund's advisor sold securities at a capital gain of $0.66 per fund share. This $0.66 realized capital gain would also have been reflected in the fund's NAV. Allowing for both the $0.44 income and $0.66 increase in realized security values, the firm's NAV would have been $21.93 ($20.83 + $0.44 + $0.66) by quarter-end. Finally, other securities held by the fund increased in value by $0.22 per fund share. But this value was "unrealized," since the securities providing the value increase were not sold by the advisor. The sum of these increases in value would have resulted in a NAV at quarter-end of $22.15.

To qualify as a regulated investment company under IRS regulations, and thus not be taxed at the fund level, mutual funds must distribute a large portion of dividend income, interest income, and realized capital gains. As a practical matter, virtually all mutual funds distribute 100% of all gains to shareholders of the funds. Dividend and interest income received by the fund and distributed to fund shareholders is referred to as "income dividends" to fund shareholders. In our example, the $0.44 income dividend received by AMF in the fourth quarter of 1991 can be traced to the fund data in Figure 20-1 (shown in the top left under the category "Income"). Realized capital gains that the fund distributes are referred to as "capital gain dividends" to fund shareholders. As before, the $0.66 capital gain dividend can be traced to Figure 20-1.

In summary, the change in AMF's NAV consisted of the following:

Beginning-of-Quarter NAV		$20.83
Per Share Interest and Dividends Received by Fund		0.44
Per Share Capital Gains		
Realized	$0.66	
Unrealized	0.22	
Total		0.88
NAV Prior to Dividend Payments		$22.15
Fund Dividend Distributions		
Income Dividends	−$0.44	
Capital Gain Dividends	−0.66	
Total		−$1.10
End-of-Quarter NAV		$21.05

In short, the change in NAV over time is due to unrealized capital gains or losses on securities held by the fund. In the example, the $0.22 increase in NAV ($21.05 − $20.83) was due to a $0.22 in unrealized gain in security value.

Mutual Fund Investment Objectives

Virtually all investment funds have an explicitly stated investment objective. This objective suggests the types of risk that the fund will incur, the split between current income and capital growth, industries or securities in which the fund intends to concentrate, portfolio turnover, and so forth. While these may change over long periods of time, or management may temporarily take security positions that are contrary to the stated objective, the fund's objective provides information that is helpful to potential investors.

Objectives of most funds can be categorized as follows:

1. *Aggressive growth.* Common stock funds stressing capital growth and minimal current income. Portfolio risk is above average. Portfolio turnover is usually high.
2. *Growth.* Less growth and portfolio risk than with aggressive growth funds.
3. *Growth and income.* An equal commitment to current income and capital appreciation. Such a fund may have lower portfolio turnover than growth funds. Some bonds will often be held, and portfolio risk is equal to or slightly less than that in the aggregate stock market.
4. *Balanced.* Approximately equal proportions of equity and fixed-income securities, with commensurately lower risk. The focus is more on current income than on capital appreciation.
5. *Income.* Largely high-yield, fixed-income securities. Bond funds, money market funds, and many unit trusts fall into this category.
6. *International.* Beginning in the mid-1980s, a large number of mutual funds were formed that invest in securities outside the United States. Most of these invest solely in equity securities, although international fixed income funds are becoming more common.
7. *Global.* Global funds invest in securities of both U.S. and non-U.S. organizations.

The data in Table 20-6 provides information about the asset values and number of funds seeking various investment objectives at the end of 1991. Notice that most funds specialized in either equity management or fixed income management; less than 6% of industry assets are held by funds that manage substantial portions of both equities and bonds. Also notice that within each asset class (equities or bonds) individual funds specialize even further the types of securities held. For example, within fixed income securities, some funds specialize in the management of U.S. governments, others specialize in management of Ginnie Maes (GNMA issues), some specialize in high yield (junk) bonds, and so forth. The fact that individual funds specialize in their asset holding is the basic reason why investors should employ a number of managers within each asset class, to assure broad diversification. Finally, notice that the market value of bonds managed exceeded that of managed equities. The growth of bond mutual funds is a result of massive federal debt financing as well as securitization of the mortgage markets in the late 1980s and early 1990s.

Index Funds. Most mutual fund advisors actively manage fund assets in an attempt to provide investors with excess risk-adjusted returns. While a few active managers engage in timing activities (tactical asset allocation [TAA]) most restrict their active strategies to security selection within a single asset class (plus sufficient

TABLE 20-6 *Assets and Number of U.S. Mutual Funds by Objective: End of 1991*

	Asset Value (in $ Billions)	Number of Funds
Equity Funds:		
Aggressive Growth	$ 63.3	209
Growth	105.0	395
Growth and Income	129.5	308
Income	29.3	72
International (Non-U.S.)	19.1	128
Global	17.3	65
Flexible	10.0	60
Other	4.3	39
Total	$377.8	1,276
Balanced and Mixed Income	45.8	172
Bond Funds:		
Income	27.5	139
U.S. Government	96.9	223
Ginnie Mae	36.6	54
Corporate Bond	15.5	61
High Yield Bond	26.1	95
Global	26.8	59
State and Municipal	154.1	524
Total	$383.5	1,155
Total	$807.1	2,603

SOURCE: *Mutual Fund Fact Book: Industry Trends and Statistics for 1991,* Investment Company Institute.

money market securities to meet likely share redemptions). Chapter 10 showed that active asset management might be unable to provide better performance than passive management. In fact, in an efficiently priced market, active management would have poorer performance due to larger transaction costs. We will return to this issue in the next chapter. Because of this debate, a number of mutual funds have been created that passively emulate a specific security index. These, of course, are known as *index funds.* For example, Vanguard Index Trust is a mutual fund designed to provide returns very close to those of the S&P 500 Index, and the DFA Small Company Fund is a passively managed portfolio of small capitalization U.S. stocks. Index funds are an ideal investment vehicle for people who wish broad diversification, low operating costs, and do not have the ability to select specific funds that will perform unusually well in the future.

Money Market Funds. During the 1970s, a new form of mutual fund was created because interest rates in secondary security markets were substantially higher than depository institutions could legally pay. Such funds are known as money market mutual funds. Eventually interest rate limits were lifted, allowing banks and savings and loans to compete again with money market funds. But by then, the public was familiar with trading in money market funds and a new permanent industry had emerged.

Money market funds usually invest in low-default risk instruments having a maturity of less than one year. Historically, most U.S. money market funds restricted their investments to securities domiciled in the United States. A number of funds have been developed in recent years to invest in non-U.S. money market instruments. In addition, a large number of money market funds restrict their portfolio holdings to tax-free municipal obligations of a single state.

At the end of 1991, assets of money market funds were $539 billion, representing 40% of all assets managed by mutual funds in the United States.

STIFs. A short-term investment fund (STIF) is a fund that invests in fixed income securities having a maturity between that of the typical money market fund and the typical bond fund. This usually represents a maturity range between one and three years. STIFs were created in the early 1990s in order to obtain the somewhat higher yields available in this maturity range than available on short-term money market instruments.

Benefits of Mutual Fund Ownership. In Table 20-7, information is shown about the aggregate value of the U.S. bond and equity markets together with the total assets managed by U.S. bond and U.S. equity mutual funds (not including money market assets). At the end of 1960, bond and equity funds managed 2% and 3%, respectively, of the total value in their asset class. By the end of 1991, bond funds managed 9% of all U.S. bond value and equity funds also managed 9% of all U.S. equity value. Clearly, public interest in mutual funds has increased during the last three decades, and this interest has not gone unnoticed by the mutual fund industry. For example, at the end of 1960 there were only 32 bond funds and 129

TABLE 20-7 *U.S. Bond and Equity Mutual Funds*

	1960	*1970*	*1980*	*1991*
Dollar Value of Publicly Traded Securities (in Billions):				
U.S. Bond Securities	$230	$322	$799	$4,435
U.S. Equity Securities	$345	$701	$1,380	$4,354
Total	$575	$1,023	$2,179	$8,789
U.S. Bond Mutual Funds	$5	$9	$17	$383
U.S. Equity Mutual Funds	$12	$38	$42	$377
Total	$17	$47	$59	$760
Percentage of Traded U.S. Security Value Owned by:				
Mutual Fund Holdings of U.S. Bonds	2.17%	2.80%	2.13%	8.64%
Mutual Fund Holdings of U.S. Equities	3.48%	5.42%	3.04%	8.66%
Total Mutual Fund Holdings	2.96%	4.59%	2.71%	8.65%
Total Number of Actively Traded U.S. Mutual Funds:				
U.S. Bond Mutual Funds	32	67	181	1156
U.S. Equity Mutual Funds	129	294	277	1276
Total	161	361	458	2432

equity funds. By the end of 1991, 1,155 bond funds existed and there were 1,276 equity funds.

Many of the benefits associated with investing through mutual funds were discussed earlier in the chapter when we discussed professional investment management in general. These include:

1. *Cost-effective diversification.* The ownership of one or more mutual funds can provide broad diversification within an asset class at a small initial cost and at lower annual operating costs than the investor might incur if the portfolio were personally managed. This is especially true if one decides to purchase an index fund.
2. *A targeted investment objective.* Most mutual funds have clearly defined investment objectives and constraints and restrict portfolio holdings to a well-defined type of security. Thus, investors can easily determine whether a given fund fits their personal needs.
3. *Professional management.* Although the debate over passive versus active management is unresolved, it is likely that professional managers (passive or active) can provide better risk-return performance than if the investor were to personally manage the funds. Not only are costs lower, but professional managers are less likely to make major investment blunders (such as betting too much on a single security).
4. *Liquidity.* Mutual fund shares can be redeemed rapidly with no (direct) effects on security prices.

Mutual funds also provide a range of services to their shareholders. Some of these include the following:

1. *Security custody.* The investment adviser will arrange for a bank or brokerage house to maintain physical custody of portfolio securities and ensure that all interest and dividends are received when paid by the issuing firm. This frees the shareholder from such chores. While a custody fee is charged to the fund, it will be lower than what shareholders would pay if they personally managed their own portfolios.
2. *Fund swaps.* Investment advisers often act as advisers to a variety of funds, each with a different investment objective. Holders of one fund are usually allowed to swap shares of one fund for another at reduced load charges or redemption fees.
3. *Checking accounts.* Money market funds often have arrangements with a bank that allow shareholders to write checks against their share balances. As noted earlier, each check must be written for a minimum amount. However, this provides the liquidity advantages of a checking account together with high current income on share balances.
4. *Accumulation plans.* Three forms of accumulation plans are available. The simplest involves *automatic reinvestment* of all dividend distributions in shares of the fund.

   Voluntary plans specify periodic new investments in the fund of some minimum amount. The fund mails the investor a ''gentle'' reminder just prior to the investment date. Some funds will also arrange to transfer fixed amounts from the investor's bank at prespecified dates. Investors are not legally committed to such deposits, but many seem to appreciate the discipline that such plans impose.

Contractual accumulation plans specify fixed dollar amounts to be deposited at fixed dates (usually monthly) over extended periods of time. If the contractual plan is on a load fund, a large portion of the early payments goes to cover the *total* load on all future purchases, and few new shares accumulate. While the investor is not legally obligated to make payments, early withdrawal from such a plan can leave the investor with very few shares and large brokerage fees. Contractual plans in load funds may be more of a disservice than a service.

5. *Withdrawal plans.* Some funds will arrange for the shareholder to automatically withdraw a fixed dollar amount or fixed percentage of asset value each month. This allows people with fixed cash needs and little concern about depleting capital values a guaranteed cash inflow.

Cost of Mutual Fund Ownership. There are, however, a variety of costs associated with owning mutual fund shares that investors must recognize.

The most obvious cost is referred to as the *load fee,* which is the commission paid to acquire the share. When an individual buys a load fund, a price equal to the share's net asset value plus a load is paid. Typically, commissions are not paid when the share is redeemed (thus the term *front-end load*). A typical load is stated to be 6.0%, although a few low-load mutual funds have stated loads of 3% or less. The effective load is higher than the stated load, however. For example, if you invest $10,000 in a 6.0% load fund, the broker takes a load commission of $600, and you actually acquire $9,400 in shares. While the stated load is 6.0%, the effective load is 6.4% ($600/$9,400). Shares in load funds are sold exclusively by brokers or other marketing organizations. The load represents compensation to the broker for services provided to the customer in selecting an appropriate fund and clearing the transaction. However, even when the load is averaged over both the initial purchase and the eventual sale, load charges are larger than brokerage fees on a normal stock purchase and sale.

No-load mutual funds are bought and sold at NAV without a commission. A few funds charge a redemption fee of 0.5% to cover clerical costs and discourage redemption, but usually no transaction costs are paid. No-load funds are not available from brokers (for obvious reasons) and must be bought directly from the fund itself. No-load mutual funds can be identified in the financial press by the letters N.L. listed beside the NAV quotation. In addition, investment advisors of such funds advertise extensively and have formed an industry association that provides basic fund information.

The historical performance of load funds has been no different from that of no-load funds. Recognizing this, and facing increased competition from newly created funds, load charges have declined substantially in recent years. Load fees of 8.5% are now rare. The only apparent advantage associated with load funds seems to be the availability of a broker's advice.

How costly is the load fee? Some argue that, when the load fee is spread over a lengthy investment horizon, the annualized fee is reasonable. Others counter that future wealth can be substantially higher without the load. Consider this example: Ten thousand dollars can be invested at date 0 in a no-load fund or a 6% load fund. Assume that the compound annualized return over the next 10 years is 9%. The calculations below show the outcomes from these alternatives:

	Load	*No-load*
Initial Fund Investment	($10000 − $600)	$10000
Compounded at	$(1.09)^{10}$	$(1.09)^{10}$
Year-10 Value	$22253	$23674
Compounded Annual Rate of Return	$($22253/10000)^{1/10} - 1$	
	= 8.33%	= 9.0% by definition

In terms of an annualized 10-year cost, the load fund costs 0.67% per year (9.00% − 8.33%). Notice, however, that the year-10 investment value is still 6.0% lower with the load fund.

In recent years, investment advisors have been allowed to engage in sales campaigns to attract or retain shareholders and pay for the marketing costs out of mutual fund assets. These charges occur annually and are referred to as 12b-1 fees. A typical 12b-1 fee is 25 basis points. From the perspective of the existing shareholders in the fund, these fees can be viewed as a reduction in their returns to attract new shareholders, something they pay for but receive no benefit from. Fund advisors claim that current shareholders will, in fact, benefit from lower percentage operating costs if the fee results in substantially larger assets. Evidence that this actually occurs is questionable.

There are three costs of operating the fund. First, *transactions* costs are paid to trade securities. These brokerage costs, however, are probably much lower than the investor would personally pay since the fund advisor has more power to negotiate low broker fees. It is in the interest of the advisor to negotiate low transaction costs since these costs have a negative effect on the manager's return performance. If the advisor is a division of a broker/dealer firm, the advisor is legally required to seek the best execution possible. Second, the advisor charges an annual *management fee* to manage the fund assets. The size of the fee depends on the type of assets managed (equities cost more than bonds) and the total assets managed. Management fees between 50 and 100 basis points are normal. Finally, there are *administration costs* associated with security, custody, accounting, mailing, and so forth. The *operating expense ratio* of a fund is the sum of advisory fees and administrative costs (transaction costs are not included since they are often difficult to determine in over-the-counter trades).

Information about 1991 expense ratios is shown in Table 20-8 for a number of mutual fund types. Generally, the size of a fund's expense ratio depends on the dollar value of assets managed and the type of assets managed. Due to economies of scale, expense ratios decline as the number of assets being managed increase. And bond fund costs are smaller than equivalent-size equity funds. Notice that expense ratios can be both very low and very high. For example, the 0.28%

			Equity Funds			
Percentile	Aggressive Growth	Growth	Growth and Income	Income	Small Company	World Stock
10	1.01%	0.83%	0.58%	0.67%	1.04%	0.97%
25	1.17%	0.97%	0.78%	0.79%	1.24%	1.49%
50	1.55%	1.21%	1.10%	0.98%	1.49%	1.75%
75	1.75%	1.64%	1.23%	1.38%	1.70%	2.29%
90	3.05%	2.26%	1.53%	1.88%	2.23%	2.58%
Minimum	0.83%	0.75%	0.28%	0.42%	0.64%	0.72%
Maximum	4.09%	3.50%	2.60%	2.26%	2.95%	3.47%

		Bond Funds		
Percentile	Corporation General	Corporation High Yield	Government General	Government Mortgage
10	0.67%	0.31%	0.70%	0.44%
25	0.81%	0.50%	0.80%	0.52%
50	1.00%	0.80%	1.07%	0.82%
75	1.20%	0.97%	1.44%	0.98%
90	1.50%	1.17%	1.95%	1.16%
Minimum	0.49%	0.16%	0.49%	0.25%
Maximum	1.94%	2.04%	2.24%	1.93%

SOURCE: Developed by the author using a sample of funds presented in Morningstar Mutual Fund Values.

expense ratio shown for growth and income funds is for an index fund that has very small management fees and operating costs. In contrast, one of the aggressive growth funds had an expense ratio of 4.09%. The manager of this fund would have to have very good stock selection skills to beat a passive strategy that would incur much smaller costs. In short, when selecting a mutual fund it is important to examine the fund's expense ratio.

WRAP Accounts. Facing pressure from increased public use of mutual funds, the brokerage community developed a product in the late 1980s known as a WRAP account. The broker identifies a number of investment managers (not mutual funds) who will personally manage a portion of a customer's portfolio. In consultation with the broker, the customer selects one or more managers in which to invest. The customer pays one annual fee for this service that covers the broker's compensation, fees to the advisors, and all transaction costs incurred by the advisors' trading. All costs of the program are "wrapped-up" into one fee. This fee is typically 3% per year. Although WRAP accounts might result in lower costs and greater diversification than direct security investment with the broker, the costs are much larger than if mutual funds were to be used.

In contrast to open-end funds, a closed-end fund does not stand ready to buy or sell shares in the fund. Instead, transactions in closed-end shares occur between two market participants trading in the secondary markets, just as for any other common stock. The only time a closed-end fund is directly affected by market transactions is when the shares are initially offered to the public in the primary offering. Brokerage fees identical to those of other common stocks are paid at purchase and sale.

Closed-end funds are widely used in countries such as Germany, France, and the United Kingdom. However, the United States has been dominated by open-end funds since the 1950s. For example, in 1980 the aggregate value of U.S. security assets managed by closed-end funds in the United States was only 6% of the value of U.S. equity and bond mutual funds. Recently, closed-end funds have seen a resurgence in the United States with the formation of many "country funds." Country funds invest in securities of non-U.S. countries, usually investing in equities of a single country. Country funds select a closed-end organizational form since the assets of the foreign country are often difficult to liquidate and return to the United States. Thus it might be difficult for fund managers to meet share redemption demands if the fund were open-end.

Real estate investment trusts are similar to standard closed-end investment companies except they are limited to investments in real estate-related assets and make considerable use of borrowing to finance asset holdings. There are three major types of real estate investment trusts. Mortgage trusts invest in packages of mortgages on commercial and residential property as well as in construction and development loans to real estate developers.

During the middle 1970s and late 1980s many of the loans made by mortgage trusts defaulted, resulting in insufficient cash flow to meet their own debt obligations. When their stock prices dropped precipitously, many firms elected to switch their legal status to standard real estate companies, and some went bankrupt. Equity trusts take an equity interest in commercial property, such as shopping centers, office buildings, and so forth. They, too, suffered from many of the problems associated with mortgage trusts but, on the whole, fared better. Finally, hybrid trusts represent combinations of both equity and mortgage trust assets.

Most real estate investment trusts were initially formed by large banks and insurance companies with a background in real estate lending and investment. Unfortunately, the types of assets in which they invested provided little diversification to protect against shocks within the economy, and many trusts were poorly managed. Real estate investment trusts represent a reasonable way to enter the real estate market, but because of the amount of their inherent diversifiable risk they should represent only a portion of a person's total investment portfolio.

Premiums and Discounts. The major difference between closed-end funds and mutual funds is that closed-end funds trade in secondary markets at prices *different from their net asset values* (NAVs). (When originally issued to the public in a primary offering, the public pays NAV plus a commission to purchase shares.) Some funds (such as country funds) trade at prices substantially higher than NAV—that is, at premiums. Other funds (such as U.S. equity funds) trade at prices substantially lower than NAV—that is, at discounts. And others (principally bond funds) trade at prices close to NAV. The size of discounts and premiums are illustrated in Figure 20-2. Although the existence of discounts and premiums

FIGURE 20-2 *Premiums and Discounts*

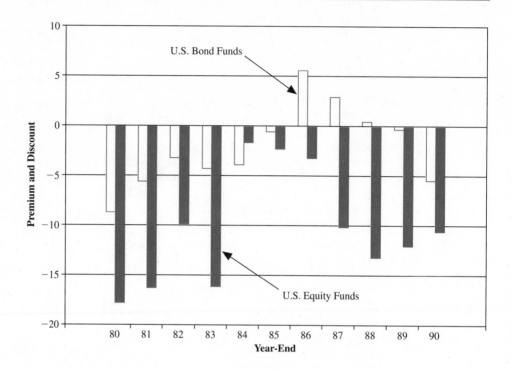

has been extensively studied, no definitive explanations have emerged. Potential explanations that have been offered include:

1. *Buying a tax liability.* Many closed-end funds hold securities purchased at prices lower than current market values. If the fund were to "realize" the gain for tax purposes by selling the securities, fund shareholders would be subject to a tax payment. For example, say you are in a 30% tax bracket and purchase a closed-end fund for $50. The fund then sells a security in which it had an unrealized appreciation of $10 per share and distributes the $10 to you as a capital gain dividend. After paying taxes, you have $7 cash-in-pocket and a share worth $40. For a price of $50, you now have wealth worth $47. Proponents of the tax-liability argument state that closed-end funds trade at discounts to reflect the potential tax loss in value.

   There are a number of problems with this explanation. For example, it does not explain the existence of premiums. Also, you can eliminate the tax liability above by selling the shares at $40 and realize a $10 offsetting loss. Finally, no statistical tie has been found between the size of a closed-end fund's unrealized appreciation and its discount.

2. *Performance.* This explanation states that premiums and discounts are caused by investor perceptions of management ability. Fund managers who are believed to be better than average will command premiums and vice versa.

While there is some evidence that this might be true, the evidence explains very little variability in discounts and has not yet been tested against country funds.

3. *Operating costs.* This explanation states that discounts reflect the present value of future operating costs. Assume that security markets are efficient such that the market values of shares owned by a fund are "correct." If costs are to be incurred in fund management, then closed-end fund shares will trade at a value lower than NAV equal to the present value of expected future operating costs.

The problems with this argument are that open-end funds are not penalized for such operating costs and closed-end fund costs are essentially the same as open-end fund costs. Also, the argument does not explain why premiums exist.

4. *Investor sentiment.* Some recent research claims that discounts change over time due to changes in demand by small, relatively uninformed investors. Larger, more informed investors who might invest in closed-end funds face a price uncertainty associated with unpredictable shifts in future small investor demand. This uncertainty is in addition to the inherent market risk of the closed-end fund security portfolio. To induce larger investors to own closed-end shares, a price inducement in the form of a discount must be offered.

Lee, Shlieffer, and Taylor offer empirical tests that they claim validate this explanation. Their evidence, however, is debatable, and the particular investor sentiment theory that they develop does not explain why premiums exist.

5. *Broker effort.* This explanation is as follows: Premiums and discounts are created by investor demand or lack of it. The level of demand is determined largely by broker advice. Since brokers receive larger commissions on mutual funds, they will push mutual funds and not push closed-end funds, which creates a tendency for a discount to exist.

Proponents of efficient markets would argue that this explanation would not hold in a rational market and that discounts or premiums from NAV arise due to a rational cause and not simply due to the commission rate schedule of brokers. This hypothesis, however, is difficult to test empirically since broker efforts cannot be accurately measured.

6. *Liquidity.* This explanation states that the market price of traded securities consists of three elements: (1) the present value of future expected cash flows to be paid by the security, plus (2) the value of an option to rebalance (sell) one's holdings in a perfectly frictionless market, less (3) the present value of future expected transaction costs associated with this security, since trading is not costless.

Consider a closed-end fund to be a bottle into which marketable securities are placed. If it is more costly to trade the bottle in secondary markets than it is to trade the individual securities in the bottle, then the closed-end fund (the bottle) will trade at a price less than the NAV of securities held. Similarly, if the bottle is less costly to trade, then a premium over NAV will be paid.

Casual evidence is consistent with this explanation. For example, closed-end funds that invest in U.S. equities are much less actively traded than the securities held by such closed-end funds. Thus a discount from NAV would

Investment Consultant Interview

Gautum Dhingra is an investment consultant with Hewitt Associates, an actuarial and investment consulting firm. In this capacity he has conducted many "manager searches" for pensions, endowments, and foundations.

Question: Gautum, what percentage of your pension clients employ active versus passive management of their U.S. equity investments?

The interest in passive management has clearly increased over the years. Most of our medium and large-sized clients (pension assets in excess of $100 million) invest a small portion of their money in passive strategies. Smaller pension funds do not use index funds to the same extent. I think this phenomenon is not unique to our clients. Greenwich Associates survey shows that 76% of large corporate pension funds (defined as those with more than $1 billion in pension assets) use indexing whereas only 15% of small funds (those with less than $50 million in pension assets) use indexing.

Question: Is this substantially different for other asset classes such as U.S. bonds, non-U.S. equities, etc.?

Equity indexing is more popular than fixed income indexing. There are several reasons for this phenomenon. One is simply the evolution of indexing. It was easier to index the key equity benchmark—S&P 500—than the fixed income indexes. Secondly, disillusionment with active management became more widespread in equities as a majority of active managers failed to beat the S&P 500 during most of the 1980s. Thirdly, the cost savings inherent in indexing (because of lower investment management fees) were much more relevant to equities. And, lastly, some people have shied away from fixed income indexing because of the trend-following characteristic of fixed income indexing. This happens because as interest rates rise, duration of the index falls, and vice-versa. This is the opposite of what a contrarian would do, and given the contrarian philosophy of a number of investment professionals, they chose not to index fixed income securities.

Within equities, large capitalization indexing (both U.S. and international) is more popular than small capitalization indexing. Once again this is partly be-

cause it was easier to index large cap stocks than small cap stocks. Other reasons include lack of a good small cap index for some time and people's belief that it is easier for a small cap manager to beat the index.

International indexing is quite popular. Most of its popularity came during the late 1980s when the international index outperformed most active managers on the strength of the Japanese market. It is yet to be seen whether the recent crash of the Japanese market will slow this trend.

Question: How do you go about a typical search for an active manager of U.S. equities? What factors are most important to your clients?

For a typical search, we first sit down with the client to discuss the objectives of the search. This discussion leads to establishing selection criteria in some or all of the following areas:

- Type of organization (e.g., bank, insurance company, independent investment counsellor)
- Type of investment vehicle (e.g., commingled fund vs. separate account)
- Investment style (e.g., growth vs. value manager)
- Risk
- Performance
- Consistency of performance
- Risk-adjusted performance
- Years of experience
- Fees
- Size
- Geographic location
- Servicing capabilities

Once selection criteria are established, we screen our investment manager database to find preliminary candidates that meet most of the criteria. Our database maintains information on a large number of professional investment managers throughout the country and is updated quarterly.

The database screening process is good at identifying candidates that have done well in the past. To identify candidates that are also likely to do well *in the future* we believe it is essential to do a thorough qualitative analysis. We do it via on-site visits to managers' offices. During our visits, we interview key investment professionals. Our goal is to find firms with the following characteristics which we believe are relevant in distinguishing superior firms from other firms:

- Experienced and knowledgeable investment professionals
- Stable professional staff
- Logical investment approach
- Strong research capabilities
- Strong incentives for superior performance
- Gradual growth in assets and a logical business plan
- Entrepreneurial decision-making process

This combination of quantitative and qualitative analysis helps us narrow the field of candidates to three or four finalist candidates. We present information about the finalists of our client. Typically, the client then asks the finalists to make presentations and makes a selection based on the presentations.

Question: How important is the manager's fee?

Investment management fees have become more important in recent years as pension fund executives are trying to find ways to improve *net* performance. Nevertheless, it is not the overriding factor. Most pension fund sponsors would select a manager that in their opinion is better even if his or her fees are higher

(e.g., by up to 30 basis points for an equity manager). As the investment management field becomes more competitive, a fee differential of 30 basis points is becoming less likely. One exception to this phenomenon is the mutual fund industry where fee differentials are still enormous.

Question: Under what conditions would a typical pension client decide to terminate a manager's service contract?

The number one reason for termination is poor performance. Most plan sponsors give their managers a reasonably long time period (three to five years) to prove themselves before discussing termination. Other reasons for termination include violation of investment guidelines by the manager, departure of key investment professionals, changes in the ownership structure, etc. Over the last few years, the following factors have also led to termination of a number of manager contracts:

- Plan termination
- Move to indexing
- Merger/acquisition leading to streamlining of manager structure

be reasonable. In addition, it is much easier for U.S. investors to acquire shares of closed-end fund country funds than to acquire the underlying securities held by the fund. In this case, a premium would be reasonable. To date, there have been no rigorous empirical tests of the liquidity explanation.

MANAGER SELECTION

The issue in this section concerns which and how many investment managers should be employed to manage portfolio assets within a given asset class. If a truly passive strategy is used, the answer is simple. For each asset class, select a passive index fund that best emulates the returns on asset class. For example, if the portfolio's passive allocation is to be:

20%	Domestic U.S. Government and Corporate Bonds
10%	Foreign Government Bonds
50%	Large Capitalization U.S. Equities
20%	Large Capitalization Non-U.S. Equities

then 20% could be invested in an index fund that tracks the Lehman Brothers Government & Corporate Bond Index, 10% invested in an index tracking the Solomon Brothers Non-U.S. Bond Index, 50% in an index tracking the S&P 500, and 20% in an index tracking the EAFE Index. If some or all of the assets are to be actively managed, the answer as to which and how many managers requires more analysis.

The manager selection procedures discussed in this section are widely used by large institutional investors who have the resources required to investigate a large pool of possible managers. In fact, the term attached to these procedures is *manager search*. But the basic techniques also apply to the selection of active managers by smaller individual investors.

Many institutional investors use a combination of passive and active strategies. Often this is accomplished by investing most of the asset class in a "core manager" and the remaining funds in managers with specialized active security selection methodologies. The core manager will invest in a broadly diversified portfolio of securities in a particular asset class, which assures that diversifiable risk within the asset class is virtually eliminated. The core manager might be allowed to trade actively, but the requirement of broad diversification will keep core portfolio returns close to those of a passive index. Noncore managers are selected to either provide excess risk-adjusted returns or to provide hedges unique to the needs of the portfolio owner. For example, if the portfolio is the pension fund of an airline company, a hedge manager portfolio might invest exclusively in equities of oil-producing firms. If airline profits are lower than expected due to increases in oil prices, this position will be at least partially offset by a larger than expected level of pension assets.

To help focus on the issues at hand, we will discuss only the selection of active managers.

How Many Managers Do You Need?

Early studies of naive diversification across U.S. equities, U.S. bonds, and global equities suggested that relatively few securities are needed to virtually eliminate the diversifiable risk. For example, in one study Evans and Archer concluded that their results "raise doubts concerning the economic justification of increasing portfolio sizes beyond 10 or more securities." If this is true, then shouldn't the employment of a single active manager who owns 30 or more securities provide sufficient diversification? The answer is no!

Individual managers tend to specialize in two possible ways: (1) the types of securities they trade and (2) the methodologies they use to select securities. The employment, for example, of a manager who owns 60 stocks provides little diversification if all 60 are related to medical technology and are selected by a particular computer scoring system. Given that managers specialize, more than one manager is usually needed to effectively reduce diversifiable risk.

In addition, the early diversification studies used a risk proxy that understates the true risk of an investment strategy. This measure is the standard deviation of the time series of portfolio returns. To intuitively see the problem, consider the

FIGURE 20-3 *Illustration of Investment Risk Using Time Series Standard Deviation*

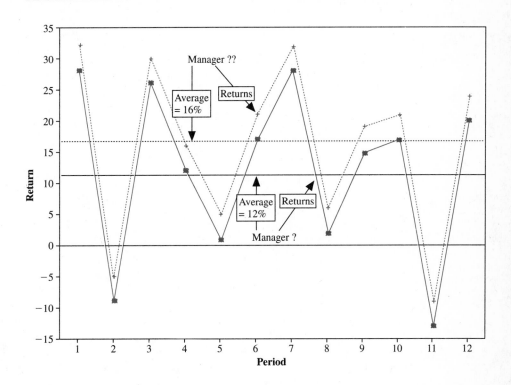

situation depicted in Figure 20-3. You are considering investing in one or both of two managers. They invest in similar types of securities and thus have a similar return series over time. The periodic returns plotted in the figure have identical time series standard deviations (TSSDs) (equal to 13.3%), and the time series returns are perfectly positively correlated. In practice, this would be unlikely. But this assumption allows us to focus on the critical point missed when risk is proxied by the TSSD. You are unsure about which manager will have which average return.

To summarize, the managers have identical TSSDs, have a time series return correlation coefficient of + 1.0, but you are unsure as to which manager will have the higher average return. Are there any benefits to diversifying across the two managers?

If one examined only how the TSSD would be affected, there would not seem to be any benefits to owning both. Any combination of the two would result in the same calculated TSSD. But the TSSD does not account for the uncertainty you have about their expected returns since the TSSD is measured around a given average return. If you are lucky and select the higher return manager then you will compound returns at 16% per period. If unlucky, you will compound returns at 12%. It is this risk that the TSSD does not capture and that can be reduced by diversifying over both managers.

A better measure of risk is the end-of-period terminal wealth standard deviation (TWSD). This TWSD is greater than TSSD due to uncertainty about average returns on the managers.

In earlier chapters, we saw that terminal wealth uncertainty can be broken into two components: nondiversifiable risk and diversifiable risk.

$$\text{Terminal Wealth Uncertainty} = \text{Non-Diversifiable Uncertainty} + \text{Diversifiable Uncertainty}$$

Non-diversifiable uncertainty, by definition, cannot be eliminated. Diversifiable risk can. Thus it makes sense to focus on how effectively diversification will reduce diversifiable risk (only part of which is captured by TSSD).

Consider the following actual experiment. A total of 170 U.S. equity mutual funds are available at the start of 1981. One dollar is randomly invested in one or more funds and reinvested each year through the end of 1990. If more than one fund is acquired, an equal investment is placed in each and rebalanced at the start of each quarter. The results of this experiment are shown in Table 20-9.

Regardless of the number of managers selected, the average terminal wealth was (approximately) $3.00. Notice also that time series standard deviation does not decline very much as the number of randomly selected managers increases. The average TSSD for one manager was 9.78% per quarter versus 9.31% for 12 managers.

But the true story is told in the last column. When one manager was selected the *average* payoff was $3.01, but not every 1-manager payoff was the same. Specifically, the standard deviation of 1-manager payoff was $1.84. Since about two-thirds of all outcomes lie within plus or minus one standard deviation from the mean, this implies that one-third of all one-manager portfolios had a payoff less than $1.17 ($3.01 − $1.84) or greater than $4.85 ($3.01 + $1.84). In contrast, if 12-manager portfolios had been used this range would have been reduced to $2.50 − $3.48. Clearly, uncertainty about future terminal wealth would have been reduced by holding multiple managers.

Even though the time series standard deviation makes it appear that manager diversification gains are small, this simply is not the case.

Optimal Number of Managers. Selecting an additional manager will usually reduce the diversifiable risk of a portfolio. Yet there are two factors that limit the

TABLE 20-9 *Random Selection of U.S. Equity Mutual Funds Investment of $1 at start of 1981*

Number of Managers	Average Terminal Wealth	Average TSSD[1]	Standard Deviation of Year-10 Payoffs
1	$3.01	9.78%	$1.84
2	$3.02	9.49%	$1.29
4	$2.99	9.45%	$0.93
8	$2.95	9.35%	$0.63
12	$2.99	9.31%	$0.49

[1] Based on the time series of quarterly returns.

number of active managers that should be employed. First, the costs of time and data analysis can be substantial. At some point, the benefits of improved diversification will be offset by the costs of identifying additional managers to hold. Second, each additional active manager selected makes the portfolio look more like a passively managed index. At some point, the portfolio owner will be paying large fees to active managers and incurring sizeable search and monitoring costs to hold what is essentially an indexed portfolio.

Which Managers Should Be Selected?

Ideally, one would like to select active managers who will have good future performance and who will improve portfolio diversification.

Future manager performance is difficult to predict. Past return performance, of course, is available and in most manager searches considerable weight is given to past relative performance. Unfortunately, as we will see in Chapter 21, past

FIGURE 20-4 *Illustrative Factor Analytic Plot December 1992*

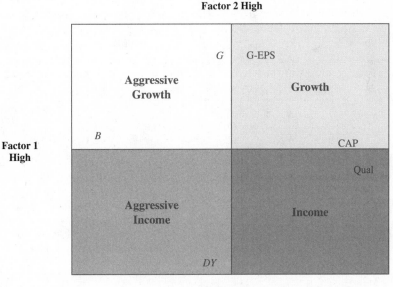

B = Beta	*G-EPS* = 5 YR EPS Growth	DY = Dividend Yield
G = Sustainable Growth	*CAP* = Market Capitalization	Qual = S&P Quality Rating

Past Is No Guarantee of Manager's Future

When selecting a portfolio manager, investors often place too much emphasis on the manager's historical return performance. There is little evidence that past manager performance is related to future performance.

Everybody loves a winner, and investors are no exception.

A winning track record is the first—and sometimes the only—thing that most investors look for when entrusting their money to a professional manager. That's true of well-heeled folk with individually managed portfolios, as well as mutual-fund investors.

But while a great track record may seem very alluring, it's just as likely to be dangerously misleading.

To start with, impressive performance numbers tell nothing about how the portfolio stacks up today. Which of yesterday's winning managers are hedging their bets by diversifying into other investments? Which are riding the same investments that did so well in the past? Those are crucial questions because it's today's investment choices—not yesterday's—that determine how a manager will do in the future.

"The predicament that you get into looking at past performance is that portfolios are dynamic. Two managers who did equally well in the past may be making diametrically opposed bets today," says Dennis Trittin, director of stock research at Frank Russell Co., a pension-consulting firm. Looking at past performance wouldn't give investors any clue that such a transformation had taken place.

Impressive performance numbers also may gloss over other important questions—in particular, whether those gains were attributable to luck or skill.

Because the "best" short-term performers often come with highly volatile track records, short-term winners often aren't very capable managers. They may just be the ones who took big risks that happened to pan out.

Conversely, short-term losers aren't necessarily bad managers. They may just be the victims of bad luck. The shorter the track record under consideration, the harder it is to know for sure who's competent and who's not.

For that reason, most pros give little weight to recent performance numbers in trying to identify superior managers. They focus instead on the strength, consistency and discipline of a manager's investment process over the very long term.

"One of the biggest traps investors fall into is to put money into the absolute top performer," says Marshall Blume, a finance professor at the University of Pennsylvania's Wharton School who also advises investors in selecting managers.

Like roulette players, big winners "become top performers by having a very undiversified portfolio, with a big bet in one area that happens to work out," he says. As soon as they hit the jackpot, however, "the odds are very low that that will repeat itself in the future."

Unfortunately, unsophisticated investors do tend to rely heavily on short-term results in judging managers and mutual funds. As a result, they often end up making bad risk-return tradeoffs.

"Individual investors appear to use the preceding year's performance ranking as the basis for their investment decisions," says William Goetzman, a finance professor at Columbia University. That observation is supported by investor surveys, as well as Mr. Goetzman's own research on how mutual-fund performance correlates with inflows of new money from investors. Such behavior means "investors end up buying volatility not return," he adds.

Extracting meaning from managers' track records becomes more confusing still, considering that even gifted managers with consistently good long-term records don't seem reliably to outperform over time.

For instance, a recent Frank Russell study tested whether an investor could predict future performance from the track records of 106 hand-picked managers monitored by the firm. It found that the winners' chances of repeating their success were "statistically indistinguishable from a proportion of 50% (the coin-flipping chance of success)."

In other words, investors have only a coin-flip chance of success that proficient managers with winning records will continue to outperform in the future. "There is no indication that there is any information on future prospects for return success contained in the manager's past performance," the study said.

There's less doubt, however, that investors should shun managers with consistently bad long-term records. When a broad mass of mutual-fund managers are held up to scrutiny, "the persistence of bad performance among losers is really striking," says Stephen Brown, a finance professor at New York University who co-authored a recent study on variations in funds' performance from 1976 to 1987.

"Really poor performance is kind of unambiguous," he says. "It's the good performance that's ambiguous."

SOURCE: Barbara Donnelley, "Past Is No Guarantee of Manager's Future," *Wall Street Journal*, 27 October 1992.

manager performance is largely unrelated to future performance. Recognizing this, many analysts give considerable weight to qualitative aspects of the investment manager's organization. This includes considerations such as:

1. Is there backup to the manager?
2. What research tools does the manager use?
3. How long has the manager been investing money according to his or her current discipline?
4. Does the investment discipline make sense?
5. Are operating costs and management fees reasonable?

Given the difficulty in predicting future performance, more attention should be paid to the diversification gains obtained from selecting alternative managers. Managers should be selected who truly differ from one another.

We noted above that investment managers will differ in two fundamental respects: (1) by the types of securities they select and (2) by the decision methodologies they use when selecting securities. The first difference is fairly easy to quantify, whereas the second is more subjective.

A common approach to differentiating between managers is to group them into various "style" categories based on the types of securities held. An example of an equity styling approach is shown in Figure 20-4. U.S. equity managers are placed into one of four groups depending on the characteristics of the equities held. Managers who own stocks with high betas, low capitalization, low quality, and low dividend yield are placed in the northwest quadrant and referred to as "aggressive growth" equity managers. Managers with exactly the opposite security characteristics are placed in the northeast quadrant and referred to as "income" equity managers.

Finally, consideration should be given to any special risks the investor faces. Earlier in the chapter, we noted that the pension fund of an airline company might overweight oil stocks to partially offset the company's risk exposure to increases in oil prices. Similarly, an employee of IBM might wish to underweight security holdings of computer stocks. In short, the investment portfolio and any managers selected should be molded to the special needs of the investor.

SUMMARY

In this chapter we examined the professional investment management industry. We saw that, as economies become more financially developed, the use of professional investment managers increases. Professional investment management is offered by commercial banks, insurance firms, and investment counsel companies. If the money being managed is physically segregated from other managed funds, it is called a separate account. If the money is pooled with investments of others into a single common fund, it is called a commingled fund.

Commingled funds that are offered to the general public in the United States must register with the Security Exchange Commission (SEC) and comply with the Investment Company Act of 1940. Investment companies which continuously offer to sell shares to the public or buy back shares from the public are called open end or mutual funds. All trades of mutual funds are at the funds' current net asset value. Investment companies which have a fixed number of outstanding shares traded in the secondary markets are referred to as closed-end funds. Shares of closed-end funds usually trade at prices which differ from net asset value. Why this happens remains a mystery.

If a passive investment strategy is used, then a single index fund will usually provide sufficient diversification. But if active investment managers are used, then multiple managers should be employed. Although any one active manager might own a large number of securities, most active managers specialize in types of securities they trade.

REVIEW PROBLEM

ABC Mutual Fund
Market Value Balance Sheet (in $ Millions)
Close of Trading, September 8

Assets:		Liabilities:	
Cash Equivalents	$15.0	Accounts payable	$1.0
Bond Investments	10.0	Salaries Payable	0.5
Common Stocks	80.0	Equity (5 million shares)	103.5
Total	$105.0	Total	$105.0

a. What is this fund's Net Asset Value (NAV)?

b. If the fund has a 6% load, how many shares could you purchase with $1,000 and what would be the true percentage cost to you?

c. If the fund were to pay income dividends based on the balance sheet above in an amount of $5 million, what would be the new NAV?

Solution

a. ($105.0 − $1.5) / 5 = $20.70

b. ($1,000 − $60) / $20.70 = 45.41 shares (fractional shares of mutual funds may be acquired)

$$\text{Effective cost} = \$60 / \$940 = 0.064 \text{ or } 6.4\%$$

c. ($100 − $1.5) / 5 = $19.70

QUESTIONS AND PROBLEMS

1. The market value of assets of a mutual fund is $1,230 million, and its liabilities are $15 million. Shares outstanding are 32 million.
   a. What is the fund's NAV?
   b. Why must this be the price at which shares in the fund will trade?
   c. All other things being equal, what would happen to the fund's NAV if security values rose by $19 million?
   d. All other things being equal, what would happen to the fund's NAV if interest is paid on bond holdings (note that the fund uses a full accural accounting)?
   e. What would happen if the fund pays an income dividend to fund shareholders equal to $0.40 per share? None of the dividend is reinvested in the fund.
   f. Assume that part e occurs, but now one-half of the dividends that shareholders receive are reinvested in new fund shares. What is the effect on the NAV?
2. List and discuss the various benefits of professional management.
3. What are the relative advantages and disadvantages of a commingled portfolio versus a separate account?
4. What are the possible costs associated with mutual fund ownership?
5. What is the "tax-timing" option?
6. What does it mean when people say that the purchase of a mutual fund's shares may involve a tax liability?
7. Why might closed-end funds trade at discounts and premiums from NAV?
8. Why might an investment advisory firm decide to use a closed-end organizational form, and not an open-end form?
9. If investors in mutual funds believed that security markets are perfectly efficient, what type of U.S. common stock mutual fund would we find being offered to the public?
10. The average U.S. equity mutual fund holds about 60 stocks at any time. Given this, why should the shares of more than one fund be held?

DATAFILE ANALYSIS

1. *U.S. Equity Mutual Fund Selection.* Review the datafile called MFEQUITY.WK1. Juan and Maria Rodrequez are both business professionals with promising careers. They are in their late 20's and just inherited $50,000, which they wish to invest in mutual funds that actively trade domestic U.S. equities. (No index funds are allowed for this exercise even though they are very reasonable alternatives to actively managed portfolios.) They intend to hold the mutual fund shares to supplement their eventual retirement income. Select and justify at least three funds that you would suggest that they acquire. (They are expected to own all three funds.)
2. *U.S. Bond Mutual Fund Selection.* Charles and Grace Dee have just entered their retirement years. They will receive social security and benefit payments from their

respective employers. In addition, they have accumulated savings of $100,000. A portion of this savings will be invested in certificates of deposit in a local bank and a number of equity mutual funds. However, $50,000 will be invested in mutual funds that invest in U.S. government and corporate bonds. Review the datafile called MFBOND.WK1. Which and how many funds would you suggest they purchase?

REFERENCES

Overview and details about mutual funds can be found in:
Mutual Fund Values, published bi-monthly by Morningstar, Inc. Chicago, IL.
Investment Companies, published annually by CDAI Wiesenberger Financial Services.

Interesting current articles about professional money managers and institutional investors are found in the trade journals:
Institutional Investor, published monthly by Institutional Investor Publications, New York.
Pensions & Investments, published bi-weekly by Crain Communications, Inc. Chicago, IL.

Interesting studies of closed-end fund discounts include:
LEE, CHARLES, ANDREI SHLEIFER, and RICHARD THALER, "Investor Sentiment and the Closed-End Fund Puzzle," *Journal of Finance*, March 1991.
MALKIEL, BURTON, "The Valuation of Closed-End Investment Company Shares," *Journal of Finance*, 1977.
THOMPSON, REX, "The Information Content of Discounts and Premiums on Closed-End Fund Shares," *Journal of Financial Economics*, 1978.

A classic study of how diversification reduces the time series standard deviation of portfolio returns is:
EVANS, J., and S. H. ARCHER, "Diversification and the Reduction of Dispersion: An Empirical Analysis," *Journal of Finance*, December 1968.

A study of diversification by equity manager style is the unpublished paper:
RADCLIFFE, ROBERT, "Equity Manager Styling." Unpublished working paper, University of Florida, 1990.

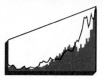

Performance Monitoring

The last step in the process of portfolio management is to monitor the portfolio over time and make any changes that appear appropriate in light of:

1. Changes in expected future asset returns and risks.
2. Changes in the financial needs of the portfolio owner.
3. Unacceptable portfolio performance.

Changes in expected asset returns and risks could require a modification of portfolio's strategic asset allocation (SAA). For example, if the risk of equity ownership increases, the portfolio commitment to equities would probably be reduced. Changes in the financial needs of the portfolio owner would probably require a change in the statement of investment policy as well as the definition of the SAA. For example, the pension plan of a corporation that is currently facing unexpected competition and declining profits may have to redefine its portfolio objectives and constraints as well as its baseline investment portfolio. Both events, however, can be handled by simply repeating the planning stage of the portfolio process, which was discussed in Chapter 18. In this chapter, we focus solely on the third reason for portfolio monitoring—to detect unacceptable performance.

The title for this chapter, Performance *Monitoring*, was carefully chosen and was used in place of the commonly used phrase, performance *measurement*. This was done because the term *measurement* has a connotation of precision to it which is simply not possible in the evaluation of investment performance. Throughout this chapter, we will encounter the problems that arise whenever we attempt to evaluate the past risk-return performance of a portfolio. For example, there are many (quite valid) ways of measuring returns, there is no truly acceptable way to measure investment risk, and all performance analyses examine relatively short historical time periods when it is usually long-term future performance that matters. We are simply unable to accurately *measure* performance.

But a number of reasonable approaches exist that allow us to *monitor* the level of historical performance compared to other investments of similar risk. Precise evaluation of portfolio performance is impossible, but broad yardsticks are available that can detect clearly superior or inferior performance. Regardless of the techniques used to monitor performance, three things should be remembered.

1. *It is the total portfolio that is most important.* If multiple managers are used, their individual performances are secondary to the performance of the aggregate portfolio. While data on individual managers have to be accumulated in order to determine aggregate portfolio performance, the actual performance analysis should proceed in a top-down fashion. The aggregate portfolio should be evaluated first, followed by an evaluation of each individual manager. As obvious as this point might seem to be, many performance services provide little or no information about aggregate portfolio performance. Instead, they concentrate solely on individual managers.

2. *Any performance analysis must examine both returns and risk.* An examination of past returns provides little information about performance unless the returns are related to the risk level incurred. Again the point is obvious but often not followed in practice. For example, some performance services compare the returns on a governmental pension fund with other government pensions. Unfortunately, such pension funds have substantially different asset holdings and risk exposure.

3. *An attempt should be made to determine why a particular performance level occurred.* If an understanding of why the performance was bad (or good) can be gained, proper steps to improve (or continue) can be taken. Knowing why performance was poor is much more important than knowing simply that performance was poor.

CALCULATING RETURNS

The basis of all performance monitoring is a sequence of accurate historical returns. In 1991, the Association for Investment Management and Research (AIMR) published a report that detailed how investment manager returns should be calculated and presented. This report is known as the *AIMR Performance Presentation Standards.* The more important standards are summarized in Table 21-1. In this section, we will review various aspects of these Standards.

Time Weighted Versus Dollar Weighted Returns

Consider a portfolio owner, Mr. A, and an investment manager, Ms. B, who manages all Mr. A's portfolio assets. There can be a difference between the rate of return earned by Ms. B on the portfolio assets entrusted to her and the rate of return Mr. A actually receives. This occurs if cash contributions or withdrawals are made to the portfolio over time.

A simple example should make the difference apparent. Assume that Mr. A has a portfolio worth $100 on January 1 and has given Ms. B full discretion over its management. By January 15, the $100 has increased to a value of $150. Seeing the marvelous return of 50%, Mr. A contributes an additional $100 to the portfolio on January 15, increasing the portfolio value to $250. Unfortunately, by month-end the portfolio is worth only $166.66.

Investment Consultant Interview

Robert Penter is an investment consultant with Hewitt Associates, a leading investment consulting firm. Hewitt Associates provides ongoing performance measurement and consulting services to more than 80 pension funds, endowments, foundations, and other institutional investors with aggregate assets exceeding $25 billion.

Question: Bob, would you summarize the types of projects you perform in servicing your clients?

We assist our clients in all aspects of managing their investment portfolios short of actually managing money. Our activities fall in three general categories: developing investment policies, selecting investment managers, and monitoring investment performance. Ongoing performance monitoring provides the framework for reevaluating investment policies and asset allocation as well as decisions regarding the retention or termination of investment managers.

Question: What are some of the specific activities that are involved in monitoring investment performance?

There are several different facets to measuring and evaluating investment performance. Obviously, calculating investment performance is a part of the task, but it truly represents only the initial step. The two key elements to monitoring investment performance are: (1) the proper definition of the performance benchmark, and (2) accurate performance attribution. In other words, clients must first determine their objectives for the portfolio in specific terms and then develop means to determine how a manager and overall portfolio have performed relative to these benchmarks and the reasons for underperformance (or outperformance).

Good performance benchmarks are: (1) reflective of the manager's investment style and risk characteristics, (2) consistent with the client's overall objectives for the portfolio and total fund, (3) readily investable, and (4) easily measurable. If the performance benchmarks are properly developed, performance attribution and evaluation is made much easier.

Question: Since much of your time is spent in assessing the performance of active equity managers, what are some of the challenges in measuring and evaluating performance?

Over and above simple (or what should be simple) issues of accurate performance calculations, there are a number of ongoing challenges in evaluating investment performance. One major problem is accurately incorporating risk in analyzing performance. While there are a number of measures of risk (e.g., standard deviation, beta, semivariance) available to be used, the utility function (i.e., investor preference) regarding risk and return differs by investor. As a consequence, measures that attempt to normalize returns by risk such as the Sharpe and Jensen ratios cannot be uniformly applied. Another challenge in evaluating performance is defining the proper time horizon over which to evaluate performance. While we generally encourage clients to consider performance over a "market cycle," market cycles are difficult to define and changes in investment managers or strategies may be warranted using performance evaluation periods that are much shorter than a full market cycle due to the degree of performance shortfall, changes in investment style, or other factors.

Question: How does performance evaluation of fixed income portfolios differ from equity portfolios?

The principles and approaches used are virtually identical across asset classes. With fixed income portfolios, the performance benchmarks typically are more easily defined, as the two key parameters are the target duration of the portfolio and the allowable exposure to different sectors of the bond market. Because these parameters frequently are based on factors specific to the client (e.g., duration linked to the duration of liabilities in a pension fund), we tend to emphasize market index based benchmarks rather than style universes or peer groups more so than for equity portfolios.

Question: Do you have any other comments regarding performance monitoring and the challenges it holds?

With increasingly sophisticated technology and analytical tools, we now can do a fairly thorough and complete job of historical performance attribution of investment portfolios. The ultimate objective for us and our clients, however, is to use this information to make some judgments as to the future results of the manager. This brings into play the art of investment consulting in helping clients assess the appropriateness of a given manager or strategy. The art includes judgments about the quality of the professional staff, the veracity of the investment disciplines and decision-making process, and the client's commitment to its objectives.

TABLE 21-1 *Summary of AIMR Performance Presentation Standards*

Requirements: To comply with AIMR Standards, managers must calculate and present historical rates of returns according to the following practices:

1. **Total returns.** Figures must include dividend and interest income plus any capital gains or losses, whether realized or not.

2. **Accrual accounting.** For periods prior to 1993, returns on fixed income securities must include accrued interest income. Accrued dividend income is optional.

3. **Time weighted returns.** Returns must be time weighted and calculated at least quarterly. For periods exceeding one quarter, returns must be calculated by a geometric linking of quarterly time weighted returns.

4. **Cash and cash equivalents.** Returns must include holdings of cash and cash equivalents. This requirement applies to returns on portfolios or a Composite of portfolios and to periods after 1992.

5. **All portfolios managed.** At least one Composite must include all portfolios over which advisor had discretionary control.

6. **Separation of model from actual portfolio.** Actual returns must be separated from presentations of returns on ''simulated'' or ''modeled'' portfolios.

7. **Market Weighted Returns.** For Composites of more than one portfolio, returns must be based on market weighting of composite portfolio returns. Equally weighted Composite returns must be supplemented with market value weighted returns.

8. ***All* portfolio results.** Newly managed portfolios must be included in a Composite after the start of the next reporting period. Terminated portfolios must be *excluded* from future Composite performance but *included* for periods during which the portfolio was managed.

9. **No restatements.** Returns must not include restatements of portfolio returns if a management firm reorganizes.

10. **No portability.** Performance is a record of the firm, not of an individual. Records of a new affiliation may not include performance results from an affiliation with a previous management firm.

11. **Unbundled costs.** Trading costs and embedded costs (such as wrap fees) which cannot be unbundled must be deducted from performance results.

12. **Ten-Year Record.** Annual returns must be for at least a ten-year period or since inception.

Recommendations: The AIMR encourages the following practices:
- Accrual accounting applied to stock investments and, for periods prior to 1993, to all investments
- Valuation on the date of a cash contribution or cash withdrawal
- Accounting based on actual trade dates, not settlement dates
- Presentation of returns as gross of any management fees or taxes
- Consistent treatment of convertible and hybrid securities
- Inclusion of additional data such as external and internal risk measures, cumulative returns for all periods, returns on an unleveraged basis, and the relative weight of taxable and non-taxable portfolios in a Composite.

Note: Summary does not consider real estate and international portfolios. Adapted from *Performance Presentation Standards,* Association for Investment Management and Research, Charlottesville, Virginia, Copyright 1993.

SOURCE: Adapted from the *Report of the Performance Presentation Standards Implementation Committee*, Association for Investment Management and Research, December 1991.

Note that Mr. A started with a $100 portfolio value to which he contributed an additional $100. However, by month-end, the portfolio's value was only $166.66. Mr. A clearly had a negative rate of return during the month.

But Ms. B can claim that her rate of return was exactly 0.0% and she would be correct. During the first half of the month, her return was 50%, ($150 − $100) ÷ $100. During the second half, her return was −33.33%, ($166.66 − $250) ÷ $250. Thus, her compounded monthly return was 0.0%:

$$(1.0 + 0.50) (1.0 - 0.3333) - 1.0 = 0.0$$

TABLE 21-2 *Data on American Mutual Fund Fourth Quarter 1991*

AMF per Share Data			NAV
Date		Dividend	After Dividend
September 30		NA	$20.91
October 4		$0.22	20.44
December 6		$0.88	19.55
December 21		NA	21.05

Assumed Investor	Dollars	After-Dividend Investment	
Transaction	Invested	Shares	Market Value
Beginning Value	NA	100	$2,091.00
Dividends	$22.00	101.07632	2,066.00
(100 × $0.22)			
Dividends	$88.95	105.6260	2,064.99
(101.07632 ×			
$0.88)			
Ending Value	NA	105.6260	2,223.43

The difference between what Mr. A earned and what Ms. B earned is clearly due to the contribution made in mid-January, just before the large negative return. Ms. B had no control over the receipt of the contribution and thus she should not be charged with the losses on it.

Time weighted returns (TWRs) *are unaffected* by any cash flows to the portfolio and represent the rate of return actually earned by the portfolio manager. Dollar weighted returns (DWRs) *are affected* by cash flows to the portfolio and represent the rate of return obtained by the portfolio owner. AIMR standards require that managers calculate and present TWR.

To illustrate the calculation of both TWRs and DWRs, consider the case of American Mutual Fund (AMF) during the fourth quarter of 1991, as shown in Table 21-2. Information is presented for both per share AMF values and a hypothetical investor who owns 100 shares at the start of the quarter and reinvests all dividends back into additional shares of AMF when paid.

The TWR calculates a return between a given date and a subsequent date at which a cash flow occurs. These periodic rates are then compounded to provide returns over longer intervals. Using the AMF data, the fourth quarter TWR would be calculated by compounding the returns in the periods 9/30–10/4, 10/4–12/6, and 12/6–12/30 as follows:

Period	**1.0 plus Return**
9/30–10/4	($20.44 + $0.22) ÷ $20.91 = 0.9880
10/4–12/6	($19.55 + $0.88) ÷ $20.44 = 0.9995
12/6–12/30	($21.05) ÷ $19.55 = 1.0767

$$\text{TWR} = (0.9880)(0.9995)(1.0767) - 1.0$$
$$= 0.0632 \text{ or } 6.32\%$$

The DWR is based on an internal rate of return calculation. It is based on the interest rate that will discount all cash flows including ending market value back to the investment's initial market value. In our illustrative AMF investor's case, the *daily* DWR is the value of R that solves the following equation:

$$\$2,091 = \frac{-\$22.00}{(1 + R)^4} + \frac{-\$88.95}{(1 + R)^{67}} + \frac{\$2,223.43}{(1 + R)^{92}}$$

The values to which $1 + R$ are raised represent the number of days from the start of the quarter to the date of the cash flow (or ending market value). Contributions to the portfolio, whether they come from reinvested dividends or new out-of-pocket cash, are treated as negative flows to the investor. Withdrawals from the portfolio would be treated as positive cash flows.

When the equation above is solved for R, it turns out to be 0.00010876. To express this as a quarterly return, it is compounded for 92 days in a quarter:

$$\text{Quarterly DWR} = (1.00010876)^{92} - 1.0$$

$$= 0.01, \text{ or } 1.0\%$$

Notice that dollar and time weighted returns will vary when cash inflows or outflows are made to the portfolio over the time period used to calculate a return.

Using DWR as a TWR Proxy. A precise time weighted return could be calculated in the example above because the portfolio's value was known immediately before and after each cash flow transaction. This will always be the case for mutual funds since they calculate net asset values at the end of each day. For most other portfolios, only month-end values are known. In such cases, a monthly dollar weighted return is calculated and used as a proxy for the true TWR. Consider the AMF data again and assume that you did not know the NAV at each dividend date. But you do know that the portfolio was worth $2,120.58 on October 30, and $2,046.80 on November 30. Other portfolio values are shown in Table 21-2. Then the October and December TWR would be approximated by an internal rate of return (DWR) calculation as follows:

October	**December**
$\$2,091.00 = \dfrac{-\$22}{(1+R)^4} + \dfrac{\$2,120.58}{(1+R)^{31}}$	$\$2,046.80 = \dfrac{-\$88.95}{(1+R)^6} + \dfrac{\$2,223.43}{(1+R)^{31}}$
$R \quad = 0.00011567$	$R \quad = 0.001309$
$\text{DWR} = (1.00011567)^{31} - 1$	$\text{DWR} = (1.001309)^{31} - 1$
$\quad = 0.00359$	$\quad = 0.041393$

Since no cash flows occurred in November, its DWR and TWR would be identical and equal to -0.0348; ($\$2,046.80 \div \$2,120.58) - 1.0$. Using the October and December DWR as the proxy for each month's TWR results in a proxied quarterly TWR of:

$$0.00876 = (1.00359) \times (1.0 - 0.0348)(1.041393) - 1.0$$

$$\text{or } 0.876\%$$

Clearly, using DWR to proxy time weighted returns can result in sizeable errors in return calculations.

MONITORING EQUITY PERFORMANCE

Performance Within Investment Style

Performance monitoring consists of a comparison of historical returns against the risks associated with such returns. A number of methods can be used to evaluate risk. Perhaps the most common approach to dealing with risk is to assign managers to various *styles* of investing and then compare one manager's returns against those of other managers having a similar style.

The investment styles used vary considerably. As an example, Figure 21-1 provides the style definitions used by Merrill Lynch, Pierce, Fenner and Smith, Inc., in their performance-evaluation service. They define seven style groups based on qualitative judgments of each manager's investment approach. Other performance-monitoring organizations use sophisticated statistical procedures to categorize managers into groups with similar characteristics and evaluate the proba-

FIGURE 21-1 *Illustrative Style Definitions*

Style Definition

1. Income: Primary purpose in security selection is to achieve a current yield significantly higher than the S&P 500.
2. Value: Primary selection motivation is to buy securities based on *known* information, and then compare this data to other historical information. Value managers, although sometimes giving some weight to earnings *projections,* rarely buy securities on this basis alone.
3. Core/Growth: These terms, although not having identical meanings, are used here synonymously. They tend to be managers who do *not* buy overly aggressive stocks but do rely heavily on earnings forecasts. This style is characterized as one devoid of extremes, not too much income and not too much risk. One might say that if you were going to place all of your retirement fund assets with one manager, this style would represent the one.
4. Timers: This management style places more emphasis on asset allocation than on stock selection. The primary decision is to own or not to own stocks, and to what extent the total portfolio should be committed.
5. Contrarians: Primarily motivated to purchase stocks that are currently out of favor with investors. These are usually stocks of companies that are cyclically out of favor while still being leaders in their industries. Some contrarians will, however, very automatically purchase stocks on the "New Low List" regardless of industry leadership or quality.
6. Rotators: Their primary emphasis is on finding industries that for some time will outperform the market as a whole. When they perceive a change in an industry's dynamics, they then rotate from the weaker industry to the stronger industry. Their selection process is a top-down, macro approach. It begins with estimates of the economy then focuses on the industries expected to perform best in this economic environment. Lastly, the industry categories are filled with the individual stocks believed to be the strongest in these industries.
7. Aggressive Growth/Small Caps: As the name suggests, these managers tend to buy stocks that have a high degree of price volatility. This style of management is bottom-up in that the primary motivation for buying a stock is inherent in the stock itself. These are the "stock pickers." There may be or may not be any similarity in the methods used by one of these "stock pickers" versus another. Some will buy based on price momentum, or earnings momentum, or, but not limited to, changes in company perceptions.

SOURCE: Courtesy of Merrill Lynch, Pierce, Fenner & Smith, Inc.

FIGURE 21-2 *Analysis of Historical Style Probabilities, Putnam Voyager*

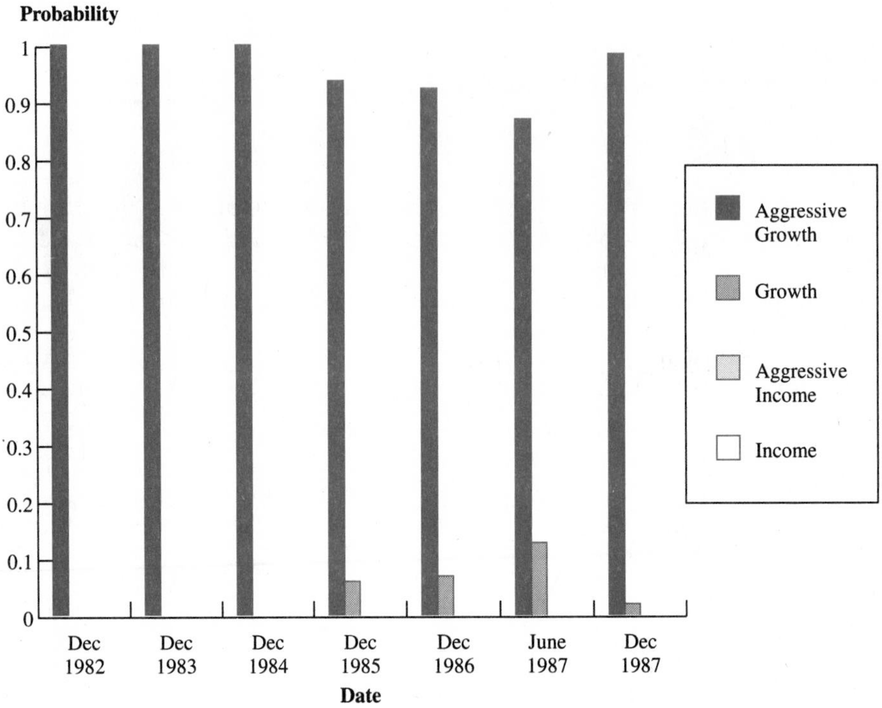

bility of a manager's belonging to one or another of various investment styles. An example of such an analysis is shown in Figure 21-2 for Putnam Voyager mutual fund. In the figure, four styles are used and a statistical procedure known as discriminant analysis is used to evaluate the probability of the fund's being in each style for various quarter-ends.

Monitoring Based on the Capital Asset Pricing Model

Comparing a manager's past returns against returns of managers with equivalent investment styles is a reasonable way to begin an evaluation of the returns earned for the risks incurred. Such comparisons, however, are often not as precise as could be desired and certainly don't address *why* a particular risk/return performance level occurred. In order to obtain more precise risk/return calculations and to examine why a specific performance level occurred, more precise estimates of risk are needed. To date, the most widely used approaches are based on the capital asset pricing model (CAPM).

Illustrative Data. To help demonstrate how the CAPM is used in evaluating investment performance, we will use the data shown in Table 21-3. This data

TABLE 21-3 *Return Performance Data*

Quarter	Raw Returns on			Excess Returns on	
	T-Bills	S&P 500	AMF	S&P 500	AMF
Q861	1.70	14.07	12.74	12.37	11.04
Q862	1.54	5.91	4.04	4.37	2.5
Q863	1.44	−6.97	−3.21	−8.41	−4.65
Q864	1.34	5.40	4.30	4.06	2.96
Q871	1.33	21.33	11.22	20	9.89
Q872	1.31	5.14	3.52	3.83	2.21
Q873	1.39	6.62	4.35	5.23	2.96
Q874	1.34	−22.63	−12.92	−23.97	−14.26
Q881	1.21	5.87	5.11	4.66	3.9
Q882	1.45	6.60	6.08	5.15	4.63
Q883	1.73	0.39	−0.11	−1.34	−1.84
Q884	1.82	3.10	1.30	1.28	−0.52
Q891	1.84	7.03	5.79	5.19	3.95
Q892	2.19	8.80	7.50	6.61	5.31
Q893	2.10	10.65	7.43	8.55	5.33
Q894	1.99	2.05	2.41	0.06	0.42
Q901	1.79	−3.02	−1.44	−4.81	−3.23
Q902	1.99	6.29	2.26	4.3	0.27
Q903	2.30	−13.78	−8.68	−16.08	−10.98
Q904	1.86	8.95	6.91	7.09	5.05
Q911	1.45	14.56	8.09	13.11	6.64
Q912	1.43	0.21	1.64	1.64	0.21
Q913	1.42	5.38	4.16	3.96	2.74
Q914	1.19	8.36	5.98	7.17	4.79
Average	1.63	4.16	3.27	2.53	1.64
Standard Deviation	0.32	8.88	5.56	8.92	5.60
Performance Measures					
Sharpe				0.2837	0.2946
Treynor				2.5308	2.6773
Jensen				0.0000	0.0896

Regression Output			
Constant	0.0896		
Std Err of Y Est	1.3074	Correlation	
R Squared	0.9500	Coefficient	0.9747
No. of Observations	24		
Degrees of Freedom	22		
X Coefficient(s)	0.6119		
Std Err of Coef.	0.0299		

represents actual rates of return on U.S. T-bills, the S&P 500 and AMF for a recent six-year period. Two return series are shown. The "raw return" series represent actual quarterly rates of return earned on each security. The excess return series are calculated by subtracting T-bill returns in any period from a security's actual raw return. Under particular interpretations of the CAPM, these excess returns reflect the return earned for bearing risk. The original version of the CAPM was a one-period model, meaning that investors invest today and liquidate at a single future date. If the investor's time horizon is three months, then the risk-free return that is available is a three-month T-bill (neglecting inflation). To examine whether an active manager is able to provide risk-adjusted returns in excess of passive combinations of the risk-free security and the market portfolio of risky securities, we could take sample drawings of the manager's excess returns and compare them with excess market portfolio returns. This interpretation of the CAPM of course is difficult to accept since it requires an extremely short investment horizon. Thus, researchers invoke multiperiod CAPM models that allow investors to make "myopic decisions."[1] That is, even though they might have a long investment horizon, investors will make investment decisions based on expected returns and risks over much shorter horizons. This is the logical justification for analyzing a series of excess returns calculated over short time intervals (say, quarterly or monthly).

The Sharpe Performance Index. Using the concepts of the capital market line, Sharpe suggested that historical performance be calculataed as "the return earned for bearing risk per unit of *total* risk." Symbolically, the Sharpe Index (referred to as S_p) is calculated as follows:

Sharpe Performance Index

$$S_p = \frac{\overline{R}_p - \overline{RF}}{\sigma_p} \tag{21.1}$$

The return for bearing risk is shown in the numerator as the average portfolio return, $\overline{R}_p$ minus the average risk-free rate $\overline{RF}$. Total risk (both diversifiable and nondiversifiable) is measured in the denominator by the standard deviation of past portfolio returns (σ_p).

Using data in Table 21-3, the Sharpe Performance Index for the S&P 500 and American Mutual Fund would be:

$$S_{\text{S\&P 500}} = (4.16 - 1.63) \div 8.88$$
$$= 0.28$$
$$S_{\text{AMF}} = (3.27 - 1.63) \div 5.56$$
$$= 0.29$$

Although the average quarterly excess return on AMF was smaller than the excess return of the S&P 500, AMF's standard deviation of quarterly return was also smaller. In terms of excess return per unit of standard deviation, AMF did slightly better than a passive investment in T-bills and the S&P 500 would have yielded. That is, during this time period, the management of AMF slightly outperformed a passive strategy.

---

[1] Such multiperiod models assume that the investment opportunity set (efficient frontiers) never changes and that the investor's utility of consumption never changes.

The Treynor Performance Index. Treynor chose to treat only the nondiversifiable market risk of an investment and developed the following performance index (referred to as T_p):

Treynor
$$T_p = \frac{\overline{R}_p - \overline{RF}}{\beta_p}$$
(21.2)
Performance Risk

The Treynor Index treats only that portion of a portfolio's (or a security's) historical risk that is important to investors as estimated by β_p and neglects any diversifiable risk. As such, it is a general performance measure that can be used regardless of any other securities an investor might own or the extent of diversification in the portfolio being evaluated. This nondiversifiable past risk is measured as β_p, the historical beta of the investment's returns. Like S_p, T_p is a relative measure and must be compared with the values of other funds as well as the aggregate market in order to determine how well an investment actually fared. Using Table 21-3 data, the Treynor measure for the S&P 500 and AMF would be:

$$T_{\text{S\&P 500}} = (4.16 - 1.63) \div 1.00$$
$$= 2.53$$
$$T_{\text{AMF}} = (3.27 - 1.63) \div 0.6119$$
$$= 2.68$$

By assumption, the beta of the market proxy is 1.0. The beta for AMF can be estimated in either of two ways: (1) by regressing the fund's raw returns against raw market proxy returns, or (2) by regressing excess fund returns against excess market proxy returns. The second approach is theoretically better and is the approach used in our example. The regression results are shown in Table 21-3 with the x-coefficient being the beta estimate.

Per unit of beta, AMF provided an excess return of 2.68% versus 2.53% for the S&P 500. Again, AMF slightly outperformed a passive strategy of investing in T-bills and the S&P 500.

Performance rankings obtained by the Sharpe and Treynor Indexes are usually very similar. When they differ, it is because some funds are not perfectly diversified. To see this, recall that beta is measured as:

$$\beta_p = (\sigma_p r_{pm}) \div \sigma_M$$

where r_{pm} is the historical correlation coefficient between the portfolio and market returns. Thus we could restate the Treynor Index as:

$$T_p = \frac{(\overline{R}_p - \overline{RF})}{\sigma_p} \left(\frac{\sigma_m}{r_{pm}}\right)$$

$$= \left(\frac{\text{Sharpe}}{\text{Index}}\right)\left(\frac{\sigma_m}{r_{pm}}\right)$$

The Treynor Index is equal to the Sharpe Index multipled by the standard deviation of market returns and divided by the correlation coefficient. If investments being evaluated are *perfectly diversified* (r_{pm} = 1.0), the Treynor Index is equal to the Sharpe Index multiplied by the market's standard deviation (a constant), and rankings obtained using either approach will be identical. If investments being evaluated *aren't perfectly diversified* (r_{pm} < 1.0), performance rankings using S_p might be different from those using T_p.

Which of the two measures is the better? This depends on the nature of the investments being evaluated. If the investments being evaluated represent *all* of an individual's security portfolio, the Sharpe measure is probably more meaningful. In this case, the total risk (both systematic and unsystematic) of the investments is the *same* as the risk being borne by the individual. However, if the investments being evaluated represent only a fraction of the individual's security portfolio, the Treynor measure might be more appropriate. In this case, only the *nondiversifiable*, systematic risks of the investments represent risk to the owner.

The Jensen Performance Index. Like Treynor, Jensen relied directly on the CAPM to develop an estimate of investment performance. However, unlike Treynor's *relative* measure of performance, Jensen's *alpha* is an absolute measure that estimates the constant periodic return that an investment was able to earn above (or below) a buy-hold strategy with equal systematic risk.

Jensen begins with the one-period security market line, which states that the expected return on an investment during period t is equal to the prevailing risk-free rate plus a risk premium (equal to the portfolio's beta multiplied by the market risk premium). That is:

SML for a Portfolio
$$E(R_{pt}) = RF_t + \beta_p[E(R_{mt}) - RF_t] \tag{21.3}$$

As long as investors aren't fooled into consistently over- or underestimating realized returns, the historical counterpart to this expectational model would be:

Market Model for a Portfolio
$$\tilde{R}_{pt} = \tilde{RF}_t + \beta_p[\tilde{R}_{mt} - \tilde{RF}_t] + \tilde{E}_{pt} \tag{21.4}$$

Each of the returns in Equation 21-4 is an actual realized return during some time interval—say, a month, a quarter, or a year. The value of β_p is the historical estimate of beta is assumed to remain constant during the time period being examined. The term ($\tilde{R}_{mt} - \tilde{RF}_t$) represents the earned risk premium on the market portfolio during period t and can, of course, be negative. Finally, the $\tilde{E}_{pt}$ term reflects portfolio returns that are unrelated to market returns. The more completely diversified a portfolio, the smaller the nonmarket-related returns in any period.

Jensen then expresses Equation 21-4 in excess-return form by subtracting RF_t from both sides. This allows him to concentrate upon returns earned solely for bearing risk and results in Equation 21-5:

Excess Return Regression in Equilibrium
$$(\tilde{R}_{pt} - \tilde{RF}_t) = \beta_p[\tilde{R}_{mt} - \tilde{RF}_t] + \tilde{E}_{pt} \tag{21.5}$$

If the CAPM is correct and speculators neither win nor lose in their efforts to find mispriced securities and call market turns, then Equation 21.5 will describe the return series on *all* security holdings. However, if some speculators consistently win and others consistently lose, portfolio returns would be better described as follows:

Jensen's Alpha $(\tilde{R}_{pt} - R\tilde{F}_t) = \alpha_p + \beta_p[\tilde{R}_{mt} - R\tilde{F}_t] + \tilde{E}_{pt}$ **(21.6)**

In this model, the portfolio alpha, α_p, represents the constant periodic return which the portfolio manager is able to earn above (or below, if negative) an unmanaged portfolio having identical market risk. Jensen suggested that statistical regression procedures could be used to estimate α_p and β_p values in Equation 21.6. If the estimated alpha values were positive and statistically significant, the fund would have outperformed a passive buy-hold strategy. If the alpha values were negative and statistically significant, the fund would have underperformed a buy-hold strategy.

When Equation 21.6 is applied to the excess returns in Table 21-3, the following results are obtained:

$$(R_{AMF,t} - RF_t) = 0.0896 + 0.6119 \, (R_{SP,t} - RF_t) \, (0.0299)$$

Standard Error of Estimates = 1.3074

R − Square   = 95.00%

These results are visually displayed in Figure 21-3.

The estimated beta for AMF is 0.6119. This could be passively duplicated by investing 61.19% of one's portfolio in the S&P 500 and the remainder in T-bill. And the excess return on such a passive portfolio would be exactly equal to 0.6119 times the excess S&P 500 return. But notice that AMF had an average quarterly return slightly greater than 0.6119 times the excess S&P 500 return. Jensen's alpha for AMF was 0.0896. Since return units in the regression were expressed in percentages, the Jensen alpha is 8.96 basis points per quarter.

Statistical Significance of Alpha. One advantage to using the approach suggested by Jensen is that we can determine whether the performance is statistically significant. This is done by calculating the following t-statistic and determining whether the *t*-statistic is significant at the desired level of confidence by consulting a "*t*-statistic table." (For a large number of observations, *t*-statistics are distributed very close to *z*-statistics. In such cases, Appendix A can be used.)

$$t = (\text{alpha} - 0) \div \sigma_a \qquad \textbf{(21.7)}$$

Here σ_a is the standard deviation of alpha and we are testing the hypothesis that alpha is zero.

The only difficulty in applying Equation 21.7 is that σ_a must be calculated. While most computer packages aimed at statistical analyses will proved σ_a estimates, common spreadsheet packages do not. If you are using a spreadsheet package, then σ_a can be calculated as:

FIGURE 21-3 *Illustration of Characteristic Line*

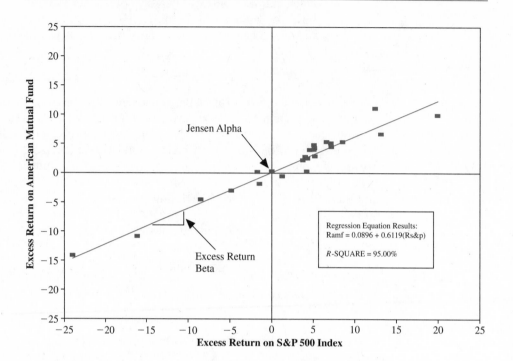

$$\sigma_a = \frac{\text{Standard Error}}{\text{of } Y \text{ Estimates}} \left[\frac{1}{n} + \frac{\overline{x}^2}{\Sigma(x_t - \overline{x})^2} \right] \tag{21.8}$$

where x_t refers to the *excess* return on the portfolio in period t, $\overline{x}$ is the average excess portfolio return and n is the number of observations.

When applied to the AMF example, the σ_a is:

$$\sigma_a = 1.3074 \, [(1 \div 24) + ((1.64)^2 \div 753)]$$

$$= 0.059$$

Thus, the *t*-statistic for AMF is 1.52 (0.0896 ÷ 0.059). At typical confidence levels, the alpha is not statistically different from zero. Although AMF supposedly beat a passive investment in T-bills and the S&P 500 according to the Sharpe, Treynor, and (calculated) Jensen alpha, this performance was *not* statistically significant.

Difficulty in Finding Statistical Significance. Due to the variability of security returns, it is difficult to find portfolios that will actually exhibit statistically significant returns that beat passive investment. This does not mean that a portfolio manager has no active management skills. It may be solely due to the lack of statistical power of the tests.

For example, let's assume that we are examining a manager whose quarterly excess returns have a standard deviation equal to that of our passive market proxy, say 9.0% per quarter. And the hypothesis that we intend to test is whether the active manager has a mean quarterly return that is different from the mean quarterly return on the passive benchmark. To obtain a z-statistic equal to 1.96 using 24 quarterly observations (as in Table 21-3), the difference in the two means would have to be 5.09%.[2]

In Figure 21-4, such required return differences are plotted against the number of quarterly return observations available. Clearly, either a large number of observations are required to claim statistical significance, or a very large return difference is needed for a small sample size. This is a simple result of the large volatility of security returns.

Problems with Capital Asset Pricing Model Performance Measures

During the years in which the Capital Asset Pricing Model (CAPM) was being developed and refined, performance measures such as those suggested by Sharpe, Treynor, and Jensen were used extensively by researchers to examine historical mutual fund performance. In more recent years, practitioners have used these approaches to evaluate investment manager performance. Yet serious questions have arisen about the validity of such CAPM-based performance statistics.

First, there is a growing belief that the CAPM is a (seriously) inadequate description of real-world security pricing. No empirical test to date has been able to show that expected and realized security returns are closely tied to beta estimates employed in the tests. This could be due to inadequate beta estimates or inadequacy of the model. A growing number of people believe it is the latter. In probably the best-known recent study, Fama and French found no relationship between future security returns and prior beta estimates. In contrast, they found the stock's price-to-earnings ratio, total market capitalization, and price-to-book value ratios are inversely related to future stock returns.

There is also a serious problem with the proxy one uses to estimate aggregate stock returns. For example, the level of Jensen's alpha can differ substantially if one uses the S&P 500 Index, the CRSP Index, the Russell 3000 Index, and so forth.

Finally, we need to recall the conclusions of Roll's critique of the CAPM discussed in Chapter 8. In short, his thought about performance monitoring goes like this. The CAPM is an equilibrium model that states that the lowest level of risk for any level of return is obtained by passive portfolios that combine holdings of risk-free securities and the risky market portfolio. No other portfolio can beat the risk-return combination of such passive positions. If one then uses a perfor-

---

[2] This uses the following equation:

$$z = (R_{\text{port}} - R_{\text{proxy}}) \div (\sigma\sqrt{(1 \div n_1) + (1 \div n_2)}) \text{ where } n_1 \text{ and } n_2 \text{ are 24.}$$

FIGURE 21-4 *Required Quarterly Return Difference*

To judge the mean quarterly returns on an actively managed portfolio to be statistically different from a passive portfolio with equal volatility, the average quarterly return difference must exceed the value on the vertical axis for a given number of quarters on the horizontal.

(Assumes 95% confidence level)

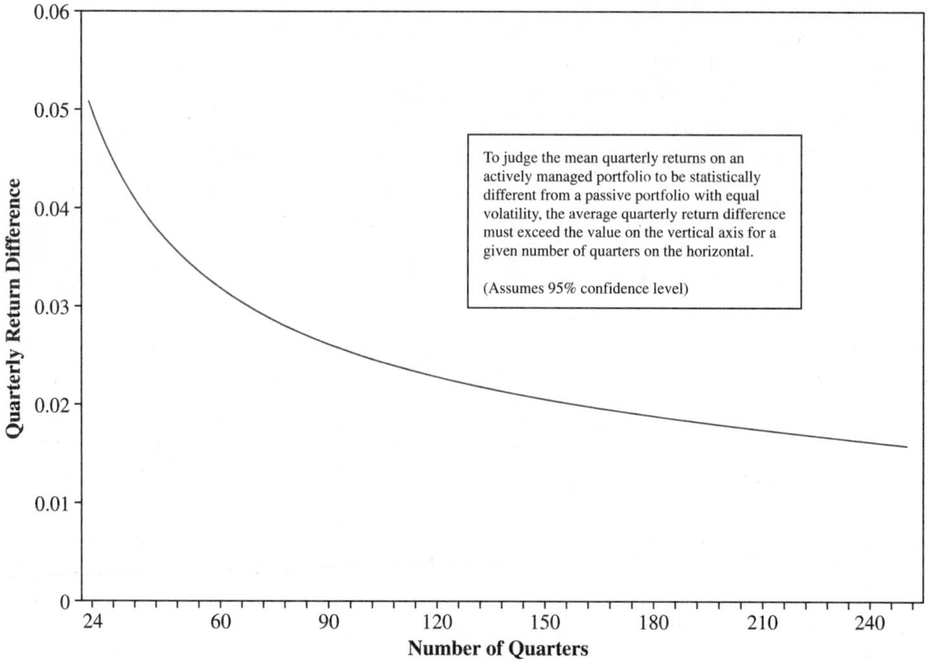

mance measure that is based on this theory and finds active managers who do, in fact, beat the passive combination, then one of two things is the case. Either the CAPM itself has been proved wrong, or the market proxy index that was used is wrong. Regardless, if a CAPM-based performance measure is used and a manager "beats" the market, then the performance measure is logically incorrect!

Nonetheless, since the procedures remain widely used, it is important that they be understood.

Analysis of Timing and Selection. The procedure that identifies a benchmark as well as timing and selection returns is based on the security market line (SML), which relates returns earned on a portfolio (or security) to its nondiversifiable risk. In Chapter 8, we defined the SML as follows:

Security Market Line
$$E(R_i) = RF + B_i[E(R_m) - RF] \qquad (21.9)$$

where:

$E(R_i)$ = the expected return on portfolio (or security) i

B_i = the beta of portfolio (security) i

$E(R_m)$ = the expected return on the market portfolio of all risky assets

Its ex post form can be written as:

Ex Post SML

$$E(R_{it}) = RF_t + B_{it}(R_{mt} - RF_t)$$

(21.10)

where:

$E(R_{it})$ = the expected return on portfolio i during period t

RF_t = the risk-free rate associated with period t

B_{it} = the estimated beta of portfolio i during period t

R_{mt} = the actual return on the market portfolio during period t

For example, during the quarter ended September 30, the return on the S&P 500 (our proxy for the market portfolio) was, say, 9.68% and the return on T-bills (our proxy for the risk-free rate) was 2.50%. Thus the relationship between the *expected* return on an investment portfolio and its estimated beta for the quarter would be:

**September 30
Ex Post SML**

$$E(R_{it}) = 2.50\% + B_{it}(9.68\% - 2.50\%)$$
$$= 2.50\% + B_{it}(7.18\%)$$

(21.11)

During that quarter Twentieth Century Growth mutual fund had an estimated beta of 0.94. Thus, the return we would have expected it to earn was 9.25%:

$$2.50\% + 0.94(7.18\%) = 9.25\%$$

If Twentieth Century Growth's *actual* return during the quarter was 5.45%, its return was 3.8% lower than we would have expected given its estimated beta. These results are shown graphically in Figure 21-5. The difference between the return that was expected *given a portfolio's current beta risk* and the actual return is referred to as the *return from stock selection*. Given the portfolio's current beta risk, Twentieth Century Growth would be expected to earn 9.25%. Since it earned only 5.45%, the difference is attributed to poor stock selection.[3]

We move now to timing and benchmark returns. Many investment managers attempt to time equity market returns by adjusting their stock/nonstock mix and by adjusting the beta level of the stocks held. Their goal, of course, is to reduce (or increase) equity holdings and betas prior to poor (or good) stock market returns.

Twentieth Century Growth appears to be no exception. Although the mutual fund made only minor commitments to nonequities, it shifted its beta level considerably. Assume that over the preceding five years, the fund had an average beta estimate of 1.30. We will refer to the fund's intended long-run beta as its *target beta* and use the historical average as a proxy for the target beta.

If the fund had been at its target beta of 1.3 during the September 30 quarter, we would have expected it to earn 11.83%:

$$2.50\% + 1.3(7.18\%) = 11.83\%$$

---

[3] Selection returns are closely related to the measure of performance suggested by Jensen—the alpha term in Equation 21.6. In fact, Jensen's alpha is the average of many periodic security-selection returns.

FIGURE 21-5 *Twentieth Century Growth, Analysis of Return*

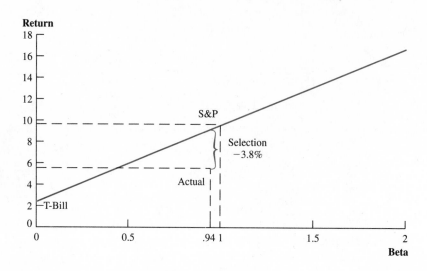

This expected return given its target beta is referred to as its *benchmark return*. However, the fund had actually reduced its estimated beta to 0.94, a level at which we would expect a 9.25% return. The difference between the return expected given its current beta and the return expected at its target beta (the benchmark return) represents the measure of *timing* return. For Twentieth Century Growth, this timing return was a negative 2.58%.

Figure 21-6 summarizes the analysis. Given the estimated target beta (b_{iT}), the benchmark return was 11.83%:

Benchmark Return
$$RF_t + b_{iT}(R_{mt} - RF_t) =$$
$$2.50\% + 1.30(9.68\% - 2.50\%) = 11.83\%$$
(21.12)

The timing return represents the difference between the current fund beta and the target beta multiplied by the excess return on the market portfolio. For Twentieth Century Growth, this was -2.58%:

Timing Return
$$(B_{it} - b_{iT})(R_{mt} - RF_t) =$$
$$(0.94 - 1.30)(9.68\% - 2.50\%) = -2.58\%$$
(21.13)

Finally, the selection return represents the difference between the actual return (R_{it}) and the return expected given the current beta estimate. For Twentieth Century Growth, this was -3.8%:

Selection Return
$$R_{it} - [RF_t + b_{it}(R_{mt} - RF_t)] =$$
$$5.45 - [2.50\% + 0.94(9.68\% - 2.50\%)] = -3.8\%$$
(21.14)

FIGURE 21-6 *Twentieth Century Growth, Analysis of Return*

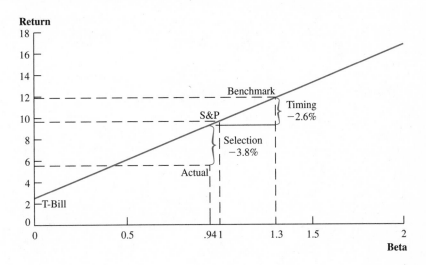

To summarize these relationships:

$$\frac{\text{Actual}}{\text{Return}} = \frac{\text{Benchmark}}{\text{Return}} + \frac{\text{Timing}}{\text{Return}} + \frac{\text{Selection}}{\text{Return}}$$

$$5.45\% = 11.83\% + (-2.58\%) + (-3.80\%)$$

Figure 21-7 shows benchmark, timing, and selection returns for a five-year period ending December 1984 for Pioneer II mutual fund.[4] A common practice is to add the timing and selection returns and refer to this as *value added* by the manager's active speculation. In the context of the CAPM, this value added represents an excess risk-adjusted return. Over the five-year period shown in the Figure, Pioneer II had an average quarterly value added of 0.45%. This translates to 1.81% on an annual basis. Note that virtually all of the value added came from stock selection and that much of this stock selection occurred in the first two quarters of 1981.

There are two advantages to a return analysis such as that in Figure 21-7. First, a more precise estimate of risk-adjusted performance can be made than is possible with a performance analysis based on style. For example, specific estimates are made of the manager's value added, and the sources are traced to speculative returns from timing or selection. In fact, it is possible to calculate the statistical significance of each. Second, the analysis shown in Figure 21-7 can be used to determine why a manager had a particular performance. For example: (1) What

---

[4] We consistently use mutual funds in illustrations since their returns are public record. The techniques are applicable to all investment managers.

FIGURE 21-7 *Pioneer II Return Analysis*

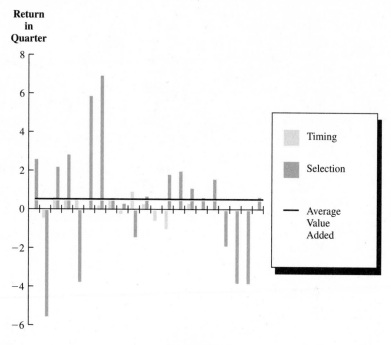

Average Quarterly Returns (Ending December 31)					
				Value Added	
Prior	*Actual Return*	*Benchmark Return*	*Total*	*Timing*	*Selection*
Quarter	2.32%	1.70%	0.62%	0.00%	0.62%
1 Year	−0.67	1.55	−2.22	−0.01	−2.21
2 Years	3.17	3.56	−0.39	0.03	−0.42
3 Years	4.06	4.26	−0.20	0.00	−0.20
4 Years	3.60	2.85	0.75	0.03	0.72
5 Years	4.30	3.85	0.45	0.09	0.36

portion was due to timing and selection? (2) Do only a few periods account for the net results? and (3) If a few periods are dominating, what was the cause, and is this likely to be reversed in the future?

Problems in Application. Calculation of these performance statistics requires access to considerable data. In particular, a realistic estimate of the manager's *current* beta is needed to determine both timing and selection returns. This can be accomplished only if the analyst knows the current portfolio holdings and has an estimate of the beta for each holding. If, for example, 30 stocks are held, the beta on each is first estimated using the market model, and the market-value-weighted average of these is used as an estimate of b_{it}. Such b_{it} values are constantly updated as stocks are sold and replaced by new stocks. Note that this procedure differs from the approach commonly used to estimate a portfolio beta that applies the market model to *total portfolio returns* over some past time interval. This second approach is certainly easier to calculate, but it cannot be used to evaluate a quarter-by-quarter portfolio beta. In fact, this approach is at best an estimate of the *average* beta position of a manager over many time periods in the past.

If a sequence of b_{it} values cannot be obtained from portfolio inventory listings, a detailed period-by-period analysis of timing and selection cannot be conducted. Some methods are discussed in the next section that allow estimates of average timing and selection abilities over a large number of periods. But these techniques do not allow for a period-by-period analysis and thus cannot investigate why timing or selection was particularly good (or bad) in a given period.

Average Estimates of Timing and Selection. Usually a sequence of past total portfolio returns is all that's available for measuring portfolio performance. In this case, two variants of the traditional characteristic line can be used to evaluate a manager's *average* timing and selection abilities.

Consider the characteristic line shown in panel A of Figure 21-8. The vertical axis is used to plot excess returns on the portfolio (portfolio returns in period t minus the risk-free rate in period t). The horizontal axis is used to plot excess returns on the market portfolio. The *traditional* characteristic line is shown as the best-fit linear relationship and is found by the following regression equation:

$$\widetilde{ER}_{it} = a_i + b_i(\widetilde{ER}_{mt}) + \tilde{e}_{it} \qquad (21.15)$$

where:

$\widetilde{ER}_{it}$ = the excess return on portfolio i in period t

$\tilde{e}_{it}$ = the residual excess return on portfolio i in period t

a_i = the constant excess return on portfolio i

b_i = the systematic risk (estimated beta) of portfolio i

As shown in panel A, the positive a_i suggests that the portfolio manager had a constant excess return. This, of course, is Jensen's alpha, which we discussed in previous chapters. In this chapter we will interpret it as the average level of *security selection* earned by the portfolio manager. But this linear characteristic line is unable to tell us anything about the timing ability of the manager—even though there appears to be some evidence of timing from the pattern of the points around the line.

Two approaches have been suggested which attempt to capture both timing and selection ability. The first approach is attributed to Treynor and Mazuy. They suggested that a quadratic regression be examined as follows:

$$\widetilde{ER}_{it} = a_i + b_i (ER_{mt}) + c(ER_{mt})^2 + \tilde{e}_{it} \qquad (21.16)$$

FIGURE 21-8 *Timing and Selection Analysis Using Characteristic Line Analysis*

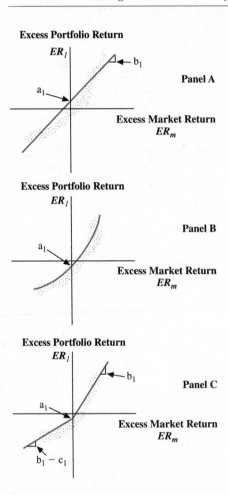

Such a quadratic curve is displayed in panel B. A positive value of c would suggest that portfolio returns are more sensitive to large positive market returns than to large negative market returns. This, of course, would be indicative of good market timing. The intercept term, a_i, would still represent an estimate of security-selection ability. Panel B suggests a positive market-timing ability and a zero (or perhaps negative) selection ability.

A second approach for examining market timing was suggested more recently by Henriksson and Merton. They suggest that two straight lines be fit to the excess returns as shown in panel C and in the regression equation below:

$$\widetilde{ER}_{it} = a_i + b_i (\widetilde{ER}_{mt}) - c_i(\tilde{Z}_t) + \tilde{e}_{it} \qquad \textbf{(21.17)}$$

The new term reflects whether the market is rising or falling and takes on the following values with the resulting regression equations:

If	Then	Implied Regression Relationship
$ER_{mt} > 0$	$Z_t = 0$	$ER_i = a_i + b_i (ER_m)$
$ER_{mt} = 0$	$Z_t = 0$	$ER_i = a_i$
$ER_{mt} < 0$	$Z_t = ER_{mt}$	$ER_i = a_i + (b_i - c_i)(ER_m)$

Clearly b_i is the slope of the characteristic line when the market is rising and $(b_i - c_i)$ is the slope when the market is falling. The value of c_i reflects the extent of market timing ability. If c_i is statistically greater (or less) than 0.0, there is evidence of positive (or negative) market-timing ability. If c_i is not statistically different from zero, no evidence of market timing is present. As before, a_i represents the average security-selection ability.

Performance Attribution. Some performance-monitoring firms attribute portfolio returns to (1) over- or underweighting of various economic sectors within the portfolio, and (2) above- or below-average returns within the sectors. The first is similar to previous measures of timing, and the second is similar to the approach used in security selection.

To illustrate, assume that the market portfolio consists of three economic sectors with the following average stock returns in each sector during the past quarter:

The Market Portfolio

Sector	Percentage of Total	Previous Quarter's Return	Product
A	20%	−10%	−2.0%
B	50%	5%	2.5%
C	30%	10%	3.0%
	100%	Average Return	3.5%

Now consider portfolio *XYZ*, which had the following weighting and returns during the same quarter:

Portfolio XYZ

Sector	Percentage of Total	Previous Quarter's Return	Product
A	10%	−10%	−1.0%
B	60%	8%	4.8%
C	30%	12%	3.6%
	100%	Average Return	7.4%

The 7.4% return of portfolio *XYZ* is explained as a function of (1) the 3.5% market return, (2) a return associated with over- or underweighting various market sectors, and (3) a return associated with performance within the market sectors.

The return associated with over- or underweighting sectors is equal to 1.5%

and is calculated below. The difference between the percentage that each sector represents of the total market and the portfolio weighting given to a sector is multiplied by the *market* return of the sector. When summed across all sectors, we have a measure of the portfolio's return that is attributable to over- or under-weighting sectors. In concept this is similar to the measures of timing that we discussed earlier:

Sector	Sector Weighting Portfolio	−	Market	=	Difference	Market Sector Return	Product
A	0.10	−	0.20	=	−0.10	−10%	1.0%
B	0.60	−	0.50	=	0.10	5%	0.5%
C	0.30	−	0.30	=	0.00	10%	0.0%
						Sector-Weighting Return	1.5%

The performance within sectors is calculated by multiplying the portfolio's percentage weight in a sector by the difference between the portfolio's return within the sector and the market's sector return. In our example, this within-sector return is 2.4%:

Sector	Portfolio Weighting	Return During Quarter Portfolio	−	Market	=	Difference	Product
A	0.10	−10%	−	(−10%)		0.0%	0.0%
B	0.60	8%	−	5%		3.0%	1.8%
C	0.30	12%	−	10%		2.0%	0.6%
	1.00			Within-Sector Return			2.4%

In sum, the portfolio's return is composed as follows:

$$\frac{\text{Portfolio}}{\text{Return}} = \frac{\text{Market}}{\text{Return}} + \frac{\text{Sector}}{\text{Weighting}} + \frac{\text{Within}}{\text{Sector}}$$
$$7.4\% = 3.5\% + 1.5\% + 2.4\%$$

As noted earlier, such an analysis results in measures similar to those used in timing and selection returns. The difficulties with the procedure are basically pragmatic: a great deal of data is needed. At the least, the analyst needs end-of-period inventory figures in order to determine sector weightings and returns. But if the analysis is to be truly accurate, the date of every security trade within a period is also needed. Only then can a correct sector-return attribution be conducted.

An illustration of return attribution as conducted by Wilshire Associates is shown in Table 21-4. Although calculation of the sector-weighting return is slightly different from that shown above, the general process and analytic intent are identical. In this case a market timer is being evaluated. Nine different sectors are used, and returns are analyzed for the prior quarter, prior year, and cumulative ten quarters. During the quarter, the manager's return was 11.06%, compared with

TABLE 21-4 *Illustration of Return Attribution*

	S&P 500		Market Timer		Variance		
Sector	A PCT of Market Value	B Rate of Return*	C PCT of Market Value	D Rate of Return	Selection	Weighting	Total
Technology	15.13	12.28	12.09	28.90	2.01	−0.07	1.94
Capital Goods	4.90	11.00	5.24	38.89	1.45	0.00	1.45
Consumer Durables	3.99	−0.07	0.00	—	—	0.41	0.41
Energy	17.47	7.93	0.00	—	—	0.38	0.38
Transportation	2.46	11.33	0.00	—	—	−0.03	−0.03
Consumer Non-Durables	27.39	10.01	46.12	9.84	−0.09	−0.01	−0.10
Materials and Services	10.57	11.12	0.00	—	—	−0.11	−0.11
Finance	6.30	16.73	0.00	—	—	−0.42	−0.42
Utilities	11.80	8.22	36.55	2.70	−2.01	−0.46	−2.47
Total	100.00	10.04	100.00	11.06	1.36	−0.35	1.01
Latest Year		43.88		62.73	11.12	7.73	18.85
Cumulative Returns Annualized**		13.90		17.06	4.93	−1.77	3.17

*Buy and hold statistics
**Calculated with 10 quarters of data

Selection = C × (D − B)/100
Weighting = (C − A) × (B − Total Index Return)/100

10.04% for the S&P 500. The excess is attributed to excess within-sector returns of 1.36% (selection) and excess sector weighting at −0.35% (timing).

MONITORING BOND PERFORMANCE

The procedures used in monitoring the performance of bond managers are often different from those applied to equity managers. This is because bonds are distinctly different securities (having fixed lives and specified promised cash flows) and because the CAPM just doesn't work well with bonds.

A large variety of techniques are used in monitoring bond performance and, of course, we can examine only a few. But a common theme runs through virtually all approaches: the critical importance of the baseline bond investment portfolio. Most monitoring systems examine bond managers' actual returns against a baseline portfolio and attempt to analyze why the two differ.

The Importance of the Baseline Bond Investment Portfolio

Most security portfolios are held in order to provide future benefits at a relatively distant date. Pension funds, for example, generally will have net cash inflows to the portfolio for 20 to 30 years before net cash withdrawals are necessary. The same is true for many individuals saving for retirement. Performance monitoring, on the other hand, focuses on relatively short time intervals. If a bond portfolio manager relies too heavily on short-term performance, long-term performance may suffer. Bond strategies that increase short-term risk/return performance often conflict with the long-term needs of the owner as specified by the baseline bond investment portfolio.

For example, consider the case of a typical defined benefit pension fund. Usually, the bond portion of such a pension is intended to provide long-run nominal cash inflows that are relatively free of risk. A reasonable baseline investment portfolio for such a situation would consist of long-term, high-grade bonds that are unlikely to be called. U.S. T-bonds with a market price low enough that the bonds are unlikely to be called (that is, a low coupon) are reasonable candidates. If such securities are held to their maturities and then reinvested in new bonds of an appropriate maturity, they should fulfill the desire for long-run, relatively riskless cash flows to the portfolio. However, over short periods of time the risk/return performance of such bonds may look quite dismal.

To see why this is true, consider Figure 21-9. In panel A the potential short-term returns are shown for three different bond strategies: (1) purchase a one-year T-bill, (2) purchase a long-term bond portfolio that is not protected against calls, and (3) purchase the baseline bond investment portfolio. The vertical axis plots actual rates of return over a given one-year period, and the horizontal axis indicates what happens to the generalized level of yields to maturity during the year in which performance is evaluated. If the yield curve does not move, the actual return on both long-term bond strategies will be about equal and somewhat greater than the T-bill return. However, note the considerable range of potential return outcomes from both long-term strategies compared with the certain return associated with T-bills. When performance is viewed from a one-year perspective, T-bills appear the least risky. In addition, the callable bond strategy appears to be somewhat less risky than the baseline bond investment portfolio.[5]

Panel B, however, examines the long-term return outcomes for various future shifts of the yield curve. Now the story is reversed. The most uncertain strategy is that of investing in T-bills, because its return is directly tied to interest-rate changes. The call-vulnerable strategy suffers low returns if rates drop as a result of the decreased rate of return at which the principal value of called bonds would be reinvested. The least risky strategy is that of the baseline bond investment portfolio. (In fact, that is exactly why the strategy *is* the baseline portfolio.) Although the reinvestment rate applied to coupon interest is unknown with the baseline portfolio, this risk is clearly less than the risk incurred with other strategies.

---

[5] If interest rates fall, bonds will be called. This would provide a call premium that is either partially or totally offset by lower reinvestment returns. If interest rates fall, the bonds subject to potential call will probably not rise as much as those unlikely to be called. This can occur simply because of differences in likely coupon rates on the two types of issues. Bonds subject to potential call will carry larger coupons and thus be less sensitive to interest-rate changes.

FIGURE 21-9 *Short-Term Versus Long-Term Bond Return and Risk*

Panel A. Return Profiles over Short-Term Horizons

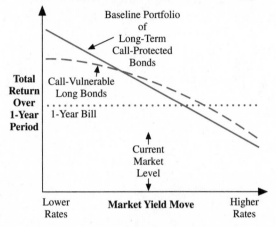

Panel B. Return Profiles over Long-Term Horizons

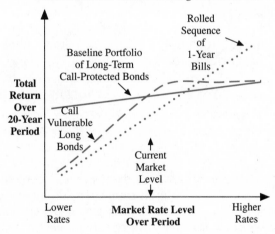

Two important conclusions should be drawn:

1. Performance monitoring over short time intervals can be misleading.
2. Performance monitoring should always include a comparison of the actual portfolio against a baseline investment portfolio.

These conclusions apply equally to equity performance and bond performance. They are simply easier to see in the context of bonds. Performance analyses should always keep the long-term objective of the portfolio in mind and be compared with a clearly defined baseline investment portfolio.

TABLE 21-5 *Illustrative Simple Bond-Performance Review*

	Rate of Return			Duration		Quality	
Prior	*Baseline Portfolio*	*Actual Portfolio*	*Excess*	*Baseline Portfolio*	*Actual Portfolio*	*Baseline Portfolio*	*Actual Portfolio*
Quarter	5.3%	5.0%	−0.3%	8.0	3.2	90	88
1 Year	15.0	15.6	0.6	8.0	4.1	90	95
2 Years	9.3	10.2	0.9	8.0	7.4	90	83
3 Years	16.2	17.9	1.7	8.0	6.9	90	74
5 Years	14.0	17.2	3.2	8.0	6.8	90	80
Standard Deviation of 5-Year Quarterly Rates of Return:	8.0%	10.3%	—				

Simple Bond Performance

Once a baseline bond investment portfolio has been identified, the performance of the actual bond portfolio can be compared against it. As an example, Table 21-5 illustrates the types of information that may be contained in a bond-performance review. Rates of return are shown for a variety of time periods for both the baseline and the actual portfolio. Clearly, long-run returns are the most important, and, in this case, the five-year returns on the actual portfolio were in excess of the baseline. However, this was accomplished by investing in shorter-duration and lower-quality bonds than called for by the baseline portfolio.

Timing and Selection

As is the case of equity portfolios, any excess returns earned from active management of a bond portfolio will result from either timing or selection activities. In practice, however, the relative emphasis given to each differs. Most equity managers place more emphasis on stock selection than on timing, whereas most bond managers place more emphasis on timing.

A number of techniques can be used to estimate timing and selection bond returns. We will examine only one. Assume that the baseline bond investment portfolio is a diversified portfolio of U.S. Treasuries with a duration of six years. Also assume that the yield curve at the start of the period for which performance is being evaluated is shown by the solid curve in Figure 21-10. At the start of the period, the yield to duration is 8.0%, as represented by point A_0. The actual portfolio, however, has a three-year duration and is invested in securities with a 2% yield spread above U.S. Treasuries. The initial actual portfolio, shown as point B_0, has a yield to duration of 9%. Apparently the bond manager expects (1) that interest rates will rise and has thus shortened the duration, and (2) that the yield

FIGURE 21-10 *Evaluation of Bond Manager Performance*

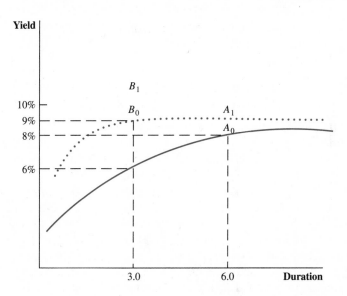

spread of 3% on lower-quality bonds will narrow and has thus overweighted such instruments.

The yield curve, say, one month later, is shown as the dotted curve, and the positions of the baseline and actual portfolios are shown by points A_1 and B_1. At the baseline portfolio's duration of six years, the yield curve has increased by 100 basis points. Thus, from Equation 12.4, the rate of return expected on the baseline bond investment portfolio would be -5.55%:

Expected Benchmark Return
$$-6.0 \left(\frac{1.09 - 1.08}{1.08} \right) = -5.55\% \qquad \textbf{(21.18)}$$

As noted, we will call this the benchmark return. The yield to duration of the actual portfolio, however, has increased from 9% to 10%. Thus, the actual return earned will be -2.75%:

Actual Return
$$-3.0 \left(\frac{1.10 - 1.09}{1.09} \right) = -2.75\% \qquad \textbf{(21.19)}$$

The difference of $+2.80\%$ between the actual and the benchmark return is due to a combination of timing and selection returns.

Let's first consider the timing return. If the bond manager had initially invested in Treasuries with a three-year duration, the yield curve would have increased from 6.0% to 9.0%. The return from this portion of the manager's strategy would have been -8.49%:

Expected Return at Actual Duration
$$-3.0 \left(\frac{1.09 - 1.06}{1.06} \right) = -8.49\% \qquad \textbf{(21.20)}$$

Since the return on the six-year-duration benchmark was -5.55%, a negative timing return of -2.94% was earned:

$$\frac{\text{Expected Return at}}{\text{Actual Duration}} - \frac{\text{Expected Return at}}{\text{Benchmark Duration}} = \frac{\text{Timing}}{\text{Return}} \qquad \textbf{(21.21)}$$

$$-8.49\% \quad - \quad (-5.55\%) \quad = -2.94\%$$

Note that the bond manager was correct in anticipating increases in interest rates but did not foresee the much larger increase in three-year-duration yields compared to the six-year-duration Treasuries. Some people who evaluate bond performance actually split this net timing return into two components: one due to parallel shifts in the yield curve and the other due to changes in the shape of the yield curve.

The selection return arises from changes in the yield spread between actual securities held and those of the benchmark portfolio at the duration selected by the manager. In our example, this yield spread fell from 3% to 1% and, thus, a positive return from selection was earned. The value of this selection return is simply an amount which balances the bond portfolio's actual return with its benchmark, timing, and selection components. In our example, the selection return would be 5.74%.

To summarize:

$$\frac{\text{Benchmark}}{\text{Return}} + \frac{\text{Timing}}{\text{Return}} + \frac{\text{Selection}}{\text{Return}} = \frac{\text{Actual}}{\text{Return}}$$

$$-5.55\% \quad + \quad (-2.94\%) \quad + \quad 5.74\% \quad = \quad -2.75\%$$

AGGREGATE PORTFOLIO PERFORMANCE

We began this chapter by stating that it is the performance of the aggregate portfolio which is most important. The performance of the individual manager is secondary. And yet all of our discussions so far have dealt with the evaluation of a single manager. The reason for this is simply that we need to know how individual equity and bond managers can be evaluated before we can accumulate their performances across the portfolio as a whole.

There are technical problems involved in actually accumulating managers' performances, but conceptually the performance of each manager is weighted by the proportion of the total portfolio managed. For example, assume there are two managers, a bond manager who invested 25% of portfolio assets at the start of the quarter being evaluated and a stock manager who was responsible for the remaining 75% of the assets. If their performances were as shown below, the benchmark total portfolio return would be 7.48%, and the manager value added from timing and selection would be -2.69% and -1.41%, respectively:

	Return	Percentage Holding	Product
Bond Manager			
Benchmark	− 5.55%	0.25	− 1.39%
Timing	− 2.94	0.25	− 0.74
Selection	5.74	0.25	1.44
Stock Manager			
Benchmark	11.83%	0.75	8.87%
Timing	− 2.60	0.75	− 1.95
Selection	− 3.80	0.75	− 2.85

Portfolio Benchmark   = − 1.39% + 8.87% =   7.48%
Portfolio Timing   = − 0.74% − 1.95% = − 2.69%
Portfolio Selection   =   1.44% − 2.85% = − 1.41%

These returns could then be compared with the actual dollar-weighted return on the portfolio in an exhibit similar to Table 21-6. Note that the actual portfolio return is stated as a dollar-weighted return since this is the true return earned by the portfolio owner. In contrast, the returns used to evaluate the individual managers' performances are time-weighted returns since these are the best measures of the managers' returns. In order for the sum of time-weighted returns to balance with the dollar-weighted return, a balancing figure is needed. This is shown in Table 21-6 as the portfolio sponsor's timing return. This is correct because the portfolio sponsor decides when contributions and withdrawals will be made to individual managers. Any difference between dollar-weighted and time-weighted returns should be charged to the portfolio owner and not to the individual managers.

EMPIRICAL EVIDENCE OF TIMING AND SELECTION

There have been few rigorous empirical studies of whether investment managers consistently earn market-timing and selection returns. The reasons are probably twofold: (1) a lack of precise estimates of beta targets and temporary beta departures from the targets, and (2) a conceptual concern with the use of CAPM-based measurement techniques. In this section, we will review two of the more recent studies of stock timing and selection.[6]

Selection

Recall that stock-selection returns represent the difference between the actual portfolio return in a given time period and the return that would be expected given the portfolio's actual beta during the period. From Equation 21.11:

---

[6] Equivalent studies of fixed-income managers have not been conducted to date.

TABLE 21-6 *Illustration of Total Portfolio Returns*

| Prior | Return* | = | Sponsor Decisions | | + | Manager Value Added | |
			Benchmark	Timing		Timing	Selection
			Analysis of Total Portfolio Returns†				
Quarter	4.13%		7.48%	0.75%		−2.69%	−1.41%
1 Year	2.62		2.30	0.60		−0.70	0.42
2 Years	20.38		20.11	0.20		−0.10	0.17
3 Years	10.06		10.00	−0.60		0.50	0.16
5 Years	15.00		15.00	−0.60		0.60	0.00

* Dollar-weighted.
† Time-weighted.

$$\text{Selection Return} = R_{it} - [RF_t + b_{it}(R_{mt} - RF_t)] \qquad (21.22)$$

In order to estimate selection returns, beta estimates for each time period (b_{it}) are necessary. In practice, such an estimate is difficult to determine. It requires that the manager hold only common stocks (no cash equivalents or bonds) and that the analyst have the end-of-period inventory listing of these stocks for all time periods for which performance is being evaluated.

Kon and Jen have suggested a statistical procedure that simplifies the data requirements.[7] They provide a way to use only total portfolio returns to derive one, two, and so forth, beta estimates. When Kon applied this "switching regression" methodology to the returns on 37 mutual funds, he concluded that 25 of the funds could be said to have used two distinct beta levels and that the remaining 12 used three beta levels. Based on such changing beta estimates, he evaluated both selection and timing returns.

Of the 37 funds examined, 25 had positive estimated selectivity, of which 5 were statistically significant at a 95% confidence level. In addition, across the total sample, there was evidence that the funds as a group exhibited an ability to generate positive selection performance.[8] Both findings are, of course, contrary to the strong-form version of efficient market theory.

Timing

Kon also evaluated the timing ability of the mutual funds. Of the 37 funds, 14 had overall timing performance estimates that were positive, but none was statis-

---

[7] See S. Kon and F. Jen, "The Investment Performance of Mutual Funds: An Empirical Investigation of Timing, Selectivity and Market Efficiency," *Journal of Business* 52 (1979): 263–289, and S. Kon, "The Market-Timing Performance of Mutual Fund Managers," *Journal of Business* 56 (1983): 323–347.

[8] Because of the lack of normality in the data, Kon expressed some concern about the true statistical significance of the results.

tically significant (at 95% confidence). He concluded that mutual fund managers should stress their skills of stock selection and not try to time the market.

Another recent study of timing, conducted by Henriksson, was based on the regression model in Equation 21.17:[9]

$$\widetilde{ER}_{it} = a_i + b_i(\widetilde{ER}_{mt}) - c_i(\tilde{Z})_t) + \tilde{e}_{it} \qquad (21.23)$$

where:

$\widetilde{ER}_{it}$ = the excess return (above the risk-free rate) on fund i during period t

$\widetilde{ER}_{mt}$ = the excess return on the market portfolio in period t

$\tilde{e}_{it}$ = residual return in period t

$\tilde{Z}_t \quad = \begin{cases} 0 \text{ if } ER_{mt} \geqq 0 \\ ER_{mt} \text{ if } ER_{mt} < 0 \end{cases}$

The parameter a_i measures net selectivity over the time period examined. The parameter b_i is the slope of the regression in rising markets, and c_i reflects the extent of market-timing ability. If c_i is statistically greater than zero, there is evidence of market timing ability.

Results of Henriksson's tests are shown in Table 21-7. Monthly returns on 116 mutual funds were used for the period February 1968 through May 1980. Looking first at the measure of timing (c_i), the study simply did not find any evidence of a consistent timing ability. Of the 116 funds over the full time interval tested, only 3 had statistically significant positive estimates of timing ability. In contrast, 9 funds had negative timing estimates that were statistically significant.

Kon also conducted a nonparametric test of the funds' timing abilities with similar results. Mutual funds did not exhibit any ability to consistently time equity market moves.

---

[9] See R. Henriksson, "Market Timing and Mutual Fund Performance: An Empirical Investigation," *Journal of Business* 54 (1984): 73–96.

TABLE 21-7 *Market-Timing Test Results*

$\widetilde{ER}_{it} = a_i + b_i(\widetilde{ER}_{mt}) + c_i(\tilde{Z}_t) + \tilde{e}_{it}$		
Period	*Feb. 1968–June 1980*	*May 1974–June 1980*
Average Estimate of		
a_i	0.0007	0.0022
b_i	0.92	0.86
c_i	−0.07	−0.08
Number of Funds with*		
$a_i > 0$	11	21
$a_i < 0$	8	5
$c_i > 0$	3	2
$c_i < 0$	9	3
* At 95% confidence.		

TABLE 21-8 *Correlation Between Past and Future Performance 190 U.S. Equity Mutual Funds, 1973–1990*

Correlation between average quarterly return:
1973–1981 vs. 1982–1990		−0.078		

Correlation for adjacent 5-year periods:

	Jensen Alpha	Sharpe	Treynor	Average Return
1973–1977 vs. 1978–1982	0.23	0.17	0.19	0.14
1978–1982 vs. 1984–1988	−0.23	−0.19	−0.20	−0.16

Is Performance Predictable?

When investors select investment managers, they commonly examine the relative past performance of a group of managers and select those with better-than-average results. But can one rely on past performance as a reasonable predictor of future performance?

Unfortunately, the correlation between past and future performance is weak. The data in Table 21-8 reports on the correlation coefficients for a variety of performance measures. The sample consisted of 190 U.S. equity mutual funds for which quarterly returns were available from March 1973 through December 1990. The first correlation coefficient shown is the correlation between average quarterly returns during the first nine years of the time period and average quarterly returns in the second nine years. The value of −0.078 suggests that past relative raw return performance is not predictive of future performance.

The other correlations shown are based on performance in one five-year period versus a subsequent five-year period. Although the correlations are somewhat different from zero, the sign of the correlation depends on the periods selected.

Numerous academic studies confirm these results. In short, there is no discernible tie between past relative performance and future performance.

SUMMARY

Investment performance should be actively monitored for two principal reasons: (1) to determine whether the objective of the baseline investment portfolio is being achieved, and (2) if the objective is not being achieved, to understand why this is the case so that proper action can be taken.

Performance of individual managers should be based on the manager's Time Weighted Return (TWR) in compliance with the Association for Investment Management and Research Standards. But the analyst should never forget that it is the aggregate portfolio that is most important and that should receive the most attention. After all calculations have been completed, the actual analysis of returns should proceed in a logical, topdown manner, starting with the aggregate portfolio, then the aggregate equity and fixed-income portfolios, and, last, the individual managers within the equity and fixed-income portfolios.

Considerable care should also be given to risk adjustments. The returns on an actual portfolio should be compared only against those on a benchmark portfolio with equivalent risk. The security market line is a widely used tool for equity performance monitoring. When it is used, the benchmark portfolio consists of an estimated beta-adjusted stock market index such as the S&P 500. When fixed-income performance is monitored, benchmarks are often specifically designed that have similar duration, call risk, and default risk to those called for in the baseline bond investment portfolio. The accuracy of a portfolio's risk-adjusted performance depends heavily on the benchmark used. Therefore, a great deal of thought should go into its determination.

Finally, an examination of why particular performance was obtained should be conducted, if possible. This usually involves the calculation of timing and selection returns.

REVIEW PROBLEM

Peter Nielson's only investment holdings for the past five years have been shares of ABC Mutual Fund. The management of ABC Mutual Fund has stated that they intend to maintain virtually a 100% equity position in stocks with prospects of above-average price growth. The purpose of this problem is to review the historical performance of ABC Mutual Fund and Mr. Nielson's investment in the fund.

a. As of November 30, 1990, Mr. Nielson owned 1,000 shares having a net asset value (NAV) of $40 per share. On December 15, he bought 120 additional shares at an NAV of $42 per share. On December 31, the fund's NAV was $39. What were the dollar- and time-weighted December returns?

b. Why do these two returns vary?

c. During the months of October and November 1990, ABC Mutual Fund had time-weighted returns of 10.0% and 0.50%. What was the total quarterly return ended December 31, 1990?

d. ABC's estimated beta during this quarter was 1.3. In the past they have had an average beta of 1.0. The return on a market portfolio proxy was 12.0% and the return on T-bills was 2.0%. Estimate the fund's benchmark return and returns from timing and selection.

Solution

a. Dollar-weighted return:

	11/31	12/15	12/31
Cash Flow	− $40,000	− $5,040	+ $43,680

15-Day IRR = − 1.61%

December Dollar-Weighted Return = $(1.0 - 0.0161)^2 - 1.0 = -3.20\%$

Time-weighted return:

	11/31	Precontribution	Postcontribution	12/31
Shares	1,000	1,000	1,120	1,120
NAV	$ 40	$ 42	$ 42	$ 39
Value	$40,000	$42,000	$47,040	$43,680
Return		5%	−7.14%	

December Time-Weighted Return $= (1.0 + 0.05)(1.0 − 0.0714) − 1.0 = −2.50\%$

b. The dollar-weighted return includes the positive or negative results for the portfolio owner due to timing of contributions and withdrawals, whereas the time-weighted return represents solely the performance of the investment manager. In this case, the dollar-weighted return is smaller since Mr. Nielson made a contribution just before ABC declined in value.

c. $(1.1)(1.005)(0.975) − 1.0 = 7.79\%$

d. Benchmark $= 2.5\% + 1.0(12.0\% − 2.5\%) = 12.0\%$
Timing $= (1.3 − 1.0)(12.0\% − 2.5\%) = 2.85\%$
Selection $= 7.79\% − [2.5\% + 1.3(12.0\% − 2.5\%)] = −7.06\%$

Benchmark	+	Timing	+	Selection	=	Actual
12.0%	+	2.85%	+	(−7.06%)	=	7.79%

QUESTIONS AND PROBLEMS

1. In the chapter, three important points were mentioned that any performance-monitoring system should include. What were these?
2. Mr. Curphey has experienced the following annual return on his portfolio during the past four years. You are asked to calculate an estimate of the average yearly return. Do so and justify your answer.

Year	1	2	3	4
Return	20%	−12%	15%	3%

3. Ms. Jane Tear invested $10,000 in a mutual fund two years ago. Since then she has regularly made an additional investment of $1,000 at each quarter-end. Today, just after her eighth and last contribution, her portfolio is worth $25,000. What was her *annualized* rate of return? The mutual fund reported an annualized return for this two-year period of 20%. Why is there a difference?
4. Mr. Morgan's only security investment is in the shares of a mutual fund called Hightech Fund. During the month of June, the following transpired:

Date	Transaction	Net Asset Value	Total Shares	Portfolio Value
May 30	Beginning-of-Month Balance	$15.00	1,000	$15,000.00
June 15	Invested an Additional $10,000	$10.00	2,000	$20,000.00
June 30	Dividends Worth $360 Received and Reinvested	$18.00	2,020	$36,360.00

   a. Calculate the time-weighted rate of return for June.
   b. Will the dollar-weighted rate of return be higher or lower than the time-weighted return in this case? Why?

5. Performance analyses are often made on the basis of investment styles. State what you believe to be the pros and cons of evaluating performance by categorizing investment managers according to their various styles.

6. Mr. Hope has just reviewed a report on the returns of an endowment fund for which he is a trustee. The report compared his endowment portfolio returns with a large number of other endowment funds. Can you suggest what critical analysis may be missing from this report?

7. Ms. A. Davis is an investment performance analyst for a major investment advisory firm. She has before her the following information about the performance of Investech Advisers for the past quarter:

$$
\begin{array}{lcr}
\text{Benchmark Return} & = & 8.5\% \\
\text{Timing Return} & = & 1.0\% \\
\text{Selection Return} & = & -1.5\% \\
\hline
\text{Actual Return} & = & 8.0\% \\
\end{array}
$$

Market Return = 8%, Risk-Free Rate = 3%

What were the actual and target betas of Investech Advisers during this quarter?

8. The performance of two mutual funds is shown below. Statistics on two of these funds are shown below. (Standard deviations of the regression parameters are shown in brackets below each estimate.)

	AMF	Putnam Investors
Average Excess Quarterly Return	2.58%	1.64%
Standard Deviation of Excess Quarterly Returns	6.96%	9.36%

$\widetilde{ER}_{AMF,t} = 0.96\% + 0.75[\widetilde{ER}_{WS,t}] + \tilde{E}_{AMF,t}$ $R^2 = 92.7\%$
    (0.31)   (0.03)

$\widetilde{ER}_{PI,t} = -0.49\% + 1.00 [\widetilde{ER}_{WS,t}] + \tilde{E}_{PI,t}$ $R^2 = 88.9\%$
    (0.51)   (0.06)

a. Calculate the Sharpe, Treynor, and Jensen performance measures for each fund.
b. Did either of these funds statistically outperform the market? (Use 95% confidence levels.)
c. Which of the funds was more diversified?
d. Which of the funds had a greater systematic risk?

9. To evaluate the historical performance of McMaster Fund, you collect the following data:

	\multicolumn{8}{c}{Percentage Return in Year}
	1	2	3	4	5	6	7	8
McMaster Fund	17.2	2.6	−33.9	−32.5	19.7	31.0	14.5	17.3
S&P 500	14.3	19.0	−14.8	−26.5	37.3	24.1	−7.2	6.6
DJIA	9.8	18.5	−13.5	−23.7	44.9	22.9	−12.9	2.8
One-Year T-Bills	7.0	6.0	7.5	8.0	8.5	8.5	9.0	8.5

a. Calculate S_p and T_p using both the DJIA and the S&P 500 as the market proxy.
b. Plot McMaster returns against the S&P 500 and visually estimate alpha.
c. Using this plot, estimate McMaster Fund's beta.

10. Suppose you have gathered quarterly data on the net returns of four funds and related them to equivalent market returns (S&P 500) and 90-day T-bill returns via the following regression model:

$$\widetilde{ER}_{pt} = a_p + b_p(\widetilde{ER}_{mt}) + \tilde{E}_{pt}$$

Fund	a_p Coefficient	a_p Std. Dev.	b_p Coefficient	b_p Std. Dev.	R^2
1	0.98%	1.00%	0.80	0.05	95%
2	2.18%	1.50%	1.30	0.15	80%
3	2.18%	0.75%	1.20	0.12	90%
4	−0.04%	0.50%	1.02	0.08	97%

a. Which funds' returns were most closely related to market returns?
b. Which fund had the most market risk?
c. Which fund had the most total risk?
d. Rank these funds in terms of the Jensen performance measure.
e. Which funds statistically outperformed or underperformed the market? (Use 95% confidence levels.)
f. Restate the alpha values in terms of their annualized equivalents.

11. The following regressions and data come from the tests of mutual fund performance discussed in the chapter.

$\widetilde{ER}_{F,t}$ =	a	+	b	×	$(\widetilde{ER}_{WS,t})$	R^2	Excess Quarterly Returns Mean	Std. Dev.
Acorn	1.40% (.74)		1.13 (0.08)			83.1%	3.82%	11.02%
Chemical	−1.31 (0.38)		0.93 (0.04)			92.7%	0.68%	8.59%
Evergreen	2.09 0.93		1.33 (0.10)			81.3%	4.93%	13.03%
Hartwell	0.44 (1.46)		1.58 (0.16)			71.3%	4.10%	13.41%
Scudder	− .61 (0.73)		0.54 (0.08)			54.2%	0.55%	6.54%

a. Assume that you now own shares of Acorn and your broker is suggesting that you sell them and buy shares of Hartwell. The broker's rationale is that the average return on Hartwell has been much better than for Acorn. Without getting into questions of consistency of performance over time, respond.
b. Which of these funds would you classify as aggressive growth? Which are low-risk funds?
c. Calculate S_p, T_p, and alpha.
d. Which funds have statistically outperformed and underperformed the market? (Use a 95% confidence level.)
e. Assume you are a believer in efficient market theory. A friend has asked which of the funds (one or more) should be bought if he wishes to obtain a market risk exposure of 1.0. What is your suggestion?

DATAFILE ANALYSIS

1. *Equity Mutual Fund Performance.* The purpose of this datafile analysis is to examine the historical performance of mutual funds that invest primarily in domestic U.S. equities. Access the MFEQUITY.WK1 data set that provides quarterly returns on U.S. stock mutual funds.

   a. Select one fund and calculate excess quarterly returns for it, for the S&P 500 and the Wilshire 5000. Use the regression option to calculate the Jensen alpha. Do this twice, once for each market proxy.

   b. Use the fund's beta calculated in part a to calculate the Treynor performance measure for the fund.

   c. For all funds in your data set as well as the three market proxies, calculate the Sharpe performance measure. What portion of the funds had performance in excess of the S&P 500? What portion of the funds had performance worse than the S&P 500?

   d. Calculate two Sharpe measures for all funds using the S&P 500 as the market proxy. The first should be based on the first one-half of the period for which returns are available. The second should be for the second one-half of the period. Plot first period performance on a vertical axis versus second period performance on the horizontal. Comment on the results.

REFERENCES

Classic studies of mutual fund performance based on the CAPM include:

JENSEN, MICHAEL, "Risk, the Pricing of Capital Assets, and the Evaluation of Investment Portfolios," *Journal of Finance*, April 1969.

SHARPE, WILLIAM F., "Mutual Fund Performance," *Journal of Business*, January 1966.

TREYNOR, JACK L., "How to Rate Management Investment Funds," *Harvard Business Review*, January–February 1965.

The Arbitrage Pricing Model (APM) has also been used to evaluate active manager performance in:

CHANG, ERIC, and WILLIAM LEWELLEN, "An Arbitrage Pricing Approach to Evaluating Mutual Fund Performance," *Journal of Financial Research*, Spring 1985.

An interesting study of the use of benchmark portfolios and the apparent success of Value Line ratings is:

COPELAND, THOMAS, and DAVID MAYERS, "The Value Line Enigma (1965–1978): A Case Study of Performance Evaluation Issues," *Journal of Financial Economics*, 10, 1982.

Studies of managers' ability to actively time movements in asset classes include:

FAMA, EUGENE, "Components of Investment Performance," *Journal of Finance*, June 1970.

HENRICKSON, RICHARD, and ROBERT MERTON, "On Market Timing and Investment Performance II, Statistical Procedures for Evaluating Forecasting Skills," *Journal of Business*, 54, 4, 1981.

KON, STANLEY, and FRANK JEN, "Estimation of Time-Varying Systematic Risk and Performance for Mutual Fund Portfolios: An Application of Switching Regression," *Journal of Finance*, May 1978.

LEE, C. F., and S. RAHMAN, "Market Timing, Selectivity and Mutual Fund Performance: An Empirical Investigation," *Journal of Business,* April, 1990.

Procedures that investment managers are expected to follow in calculating and reporting their portfolio return performance should comply with the:

Report of the Performance Presentation Standards Implementation Committee, Association for Investment Management and Research, December 1991.

Area of the Normal Distribution: Above the Distribution Mean

d1,d2 or Z-score	0	0.01	0.02	0.03	0.04	0.05	0.06	0.07	0.08	0.09
0.00	0.5000	0.5040	0.5080	0.5120	0.5160	0.5199	0.5239	0.5279	0.5319	0.5359
0.10	0.5398	0.54381	0.5478	0.5517	0.5557	0.5596	0.5636	0.5675	0.5714	0.5754
0.20	0.5793	0.58317	0.5871	0.5910	0.5948	0.5987	0.6026	0.6064	0.6103	0.6141
0.30	0.6179	0.62172	0.6255	0.6293	0.6331	0.6368	0.6406	0.6443	0.6480	0.6517
0.40	0.6554	0.65909	0.6627	0.6664	0.6700	0.6736	0.6772	0.6808	0.6844	0.6879
0.50	0.6915	0.69496	0.6985	0.7019	0.7054	0.7088	0.7122	0.7156	0.7190	0.7224
0.60	0.7257	0.72906	0.7324	0.7356	0.7389	0.7421	0.7454	0.7486	0.7517	0.7549
0.70	0.7580	0.76114	0.7642	0.7673	0.7703	0.7734	0.7764	0.7793	0.7823	0.7852
0.80	0.7881	0.79103	0.7939	0.7967	0.7995	0.8023	0.8051	0.8079	0.8106	0.8133
0.90	0.8159	0.81859	0.8212	0.8238	0.8264	0.8289	0.8315	0.8340	0.8365	0.8389
1.00	0.8414	0.84376	0.8461	0.8485	0.8508	0.8531	0.8554	0.8577	0.8599	0.8622
1.10	0.8643	0.86651	0.8687	0.8708	0.8729	0.8749	0.8770	0.8790	0.8810	0.8830
1.20	0.8849	0.88687	0.8888	0.8907	0.8925	0.8944	0.8962	0.8980	0.8997	0.9015
1.30	0.9032	0.90491	0.9066	0.9083	0.9099	0.9115	0.9131	0.9147	0.9162	0.9177
1.40	0.9193	0.92074	0.9222	0.9236	0.9251	0.9265	0.9279	0.9292	0.9306	0.9319
1.50	0.9332	0.93448	0.9357	0.9370	0.9382	0.9394	0.9406	0.9418	0.9429	0.9441
1.60	0.9452	0.94630	0.9474	0.9485	0.9495	0.9505	0.9515	0.9525	0.9535	0.9545
1.70	0.9554	0.95637	0.9573	0.9582	0.9591	0.9599	0.9608	0.9616	0.9625	0.9633
1.80	0.9641	0.96485	0.9656	0.9664	0.9671	0.9678	0.9686	0.9693	0.9699	0.9706
1.90	0.9713	0.97193	0.9726	0.9732	0.9738	0.9744	0.9750	0.9756	0.9761	0.9767
2.00	0.9772	0.97778	0.9783	0.9788	0.9793	0.9798	0.9803	0.9808	0.9812	0.9817
2.10	0.9821	0.98256	0.9830	0.9834	0.9838	0.9842	0.9846	0.9850	0.9854	0.9857
2.20	0.9861	0.98644	0.9868	0.9871	0.9874	0.9878	0.9881	0.9884	0.9887	0.9890
2.30	0.9893	0.98954	0.9898	0.9901	0.9903	0.9906	0.9909	0.9911	0.9913	0.9916
2.40	0.9918	0.99201	0.9922	0.9924	0.9926	0.9928	0.9930	0.9932	0.9934	0.9936
2.50	0.9938	0.99395	0.9941	0.9943	0.9944	0.9946	0.9948	0.9949	0.9951	0.9952
2.60	0.9953	0.99546	0.9956	0.9957	0.9958	0.9960	0.9961	0.9962	0.9963	0.9964
2.70	0.9965	0.99663	0.9967	0.9968	0.9969	0.9970	0.9971	0.9972	0.9973	0.9974
2.80	0.9974	0.99752	0.9976	0.9977	0.9977	0.9978	0.9979	0.9979	0.9980	0.9981
2.90	0.9981	0.99819	0.9982	0.9983	0.9984	0.9984	0.9985	0.9985	0.9986	0.9986
3.00	0.9986	0.99869	0.9987	0.9988	0.9988	0.9989	0.9989	0.9989	0.9990	0.9990

The data above represent the area between negative infinity and a certain number of standard deviations above the mean of a "normal" distribution. For example, if the number of standard deviations is 0.67 above the mean (or expected value), then the cumulative probablility from minus infinity to 0.67 is   0.7486

This table can be used in the Black-Scholes Option Model for positive values of "d1" or "d2".
(See Chapters 9 and 16 for a discussion of this application.)

The data can also be used to find the number of standard deviations associated with a given return percentile.
(See the Appendix to Chapter 5 for a discussion of this application.)

Area of the Normal Distribution: Below the Distribution Mean

d1, d2 or Z-score	0.00	-0.01	-0.02	-0.03	-0.04	-0.05	-0.06	-0.07	-0.08	-0.09
0.00	0.5000	0.4960	0.4920	0.4880	0.4840	0.4801	0.4761	0.4721	0.4681	0.4641
-0.10	0.4602	0.4562	0.4522	0.4483	0.4443	0.4404	0.4364	0.4325	0.4286	0.4246
-0.20	0.4207	0.4168	0.4129	0.4090	0.4052	0.4013	0.3974	0.3936	0.3897	0.3859
-0.30	0.3821	0.3783	0.3745	0.3707	0.3669	0.3632	0.3594	0.3557	0.3520	0.3483
-0.40	0.3446	0.3409	0.3373	0.3336	0.3300	0.3264	0.3228	0.3192	0.3156	0.3121
-0.50	0.3085	0.3050	0.3015	0.2981	0.2946	0.2912	0.2878	0.2844	0.2810	0.2776
-0.60	0.2743	0.2709	0.2676	0.2644	0.2611	0.2579	0.2546	0.2514	0.2483	0.2451
-0.70	0.2420	0.2389	0.2358	0.2327	0.2297	0.2266	0.2236	0.2207	0.2177	0.2148
-0.80	0.2119	0.2090	0.2061	0.2033	0.2005	0.1977	0.1949	0.1921	0.1894	0.1867
-0.90	0.1841	0.1814	0.1788	0.1762	0.1736	0.1711	0.1685	0.1660	0.1635	0.1611
-1.00	0.1586	0.1562	0.1539	0.1515	0.1492	0.1469	0.1446	0.1423	0.1401	0.1378
-1.10	0.1357	0.1335	0.1313	0.1292	0.1271	0.1251	0.1230	0.1210	0.1190	0.1170
-1.20	0.1151	0.1131	0.1112	0.1093	0.1075	0.1056	0.1038	0.1020	0.1003	0.0985
-1.30	0.0968	0.0951	0.0934	0.0917	0.0901	0.0885	0.0869	0.0853	0.0838	0.0823
-1.40	0.0807	0.0793	0.0778	0.0764	0.0749	0.0735	0.0721	0.0708	0.0694	0.0681
-1.50	0.0668	0.0655	0.0643	0.0630	0.0618	0.0606	0.0594	0.0582	0.0571	0.0559
-1.60	0.0548	0.0537	0.0526	0.0515	0.0505	0.0495	0.0485	0.0475	0.0465	0.0455
-1.70	0.0446	0.0436	0.0427	0.0418	0.0409	0.0401	0.0392	0.0384	0.0375	0.0367
-1.80	0.0359	0.0352	0.0344	0.0336	0.0329	0.0322	0.0314	0.0307	0.0301	0.0294
-1.90	0.0287	0.0281	0.0274	0.0268	0.0262	0.0256	0.0250	0.0244	0.0239	0.0233
-2.00	0.0228	0.0222	0.0217	0.0212	0.0207	0.0202	0.0197	0.0192	0.0188	0.0183
-2.10	0.0179	0.0174	0.0170	0.0166	0.0162	0.0158	0.0154	0.0150	0.0146	0.0143
-2.20	0.0139	0.0136	0.0132	0.0129	0.0126	0.0122	0.0119	0.0116	0.0113	0.0110
-2.30	0.0107	0.0105	0.0102	0.0099	0.0097	0.0094	0.0091	0.0089	0.0087	0.0084
-2.40	0.0082	0.0080	0.0078	0.0076	0.0074	0.0072	0.0070	0.0068	0.0066	0.0064
-2.50	0.0062	0.0060	0.0059	0.0057	0.0056	0.0054	0.0052	0.0051	0.0049	0.0048
-2.60	0.0047	0.0045	0.0044	0.0043	0.0042	0.0040	0.0039	0.0038	0.0037	0.0036
-2.70	0.0035	0.0034	0.0033	0.0032	0.0031	0.0030	0.0029	0.0028	0.0027	0.0026
-2.80	0.0026	0.0025	0.0024	0.0023	0.0023	0.0022	0.0021	0.0021	0.0020	0.0019
-2.90	0.0019	0.0018	0.0018	0.0017	0.0016	0.0016	0.0015	0.0015	0.0014	0.0014
-3.00	0.0014	0.0013	0.0013	0.0012	0.0012	0.0011	0.0011	0.0011	0.0010	0.0010

The data above represent the area between negative infinity and a certain number of standard deviations below the mean of a "normal" distribution. For example, if the number of standard deviations is 0.67 below the mean (or expected value), then the cumulative probablility from minus infinity to negative 0.67 is   0.2514.

This table can be used in the Black-Scholes Option Model for negative values of "d1" or "d2".
(See Chapters 9 and 16 for a discussion of this application.)

The data can also be used to find the number of standard deviations associated with a given return percentile.
(See the Appendix to Chapter 5 for a discussion of this application.)

Chapter 1

7. From Eq (1.3)

$$1{,}000 \text{ marks} = \frac{100}{(1.1)} + \frac{100}{(1.1)^2} + \frac{100}{(1.1)^3} + \frac{1{,}100}{(1.1)^4}$$

10. From Eq. (1.1)

a. $R_{Stock} = \dfrac{55{,}000 - 50{,}000 + 2{,}500}{50{,}000} = 15\%$

$R_{Bond} = \dfrac{51{,}000 - 50{,}000 + 4{,}000}{50{,}000} = 10\%$

b. Stock dividend yield $= 2{,}500 \div 50{,}000 = 5\%$
Bond current yield $= 4{,}000 \div 50{,}000 = 8\%$

c. Total return should include any price increases or decreases in addition to current yields on bonds or dividend yields on stocks.

Chapter 2

1. a. From Eq (2.1)
Buy price $= 100 - 100(0.087)(14 \div 360) = 99.6617\%$ par
Sell price $= 100 - 9(14 \div 360)\qquad = 99.65\%$ par

b. Days to maturity $= 30(\text{Jan}) + 28(\text{Feb}) + 15(\text{March}) = 73$
Buy price $= 98.2176\%$; Sell price $= 98.1507\%$

c. $r = 9.074\%$

d. Profit $= \$9{,}854{,}958 - \$9{,}821{,}758 = \$33{,}200$

2. Price of 1 BP $= \$1{,}000{,}000\,(0.0001)\,(91 \div 360) = \$25.28$

3. a. \$992,911.11

b. Bid $= 91.00$ Asked $= 91.20$

c. From Eq (2.2):
$r = [(100 - 99.291111) \div 99.29.1111](365 \div 29)$
$= 8.986\%$
From Eq (2.3):
$r' = 1.0071395^{365/29} - 1.0 = 9.367\%$

d. $r = [(99.498611 - 99.291111) \div 99.291111](365 \div 9)$
$= 8.475\%$
$r' = 1.0021^{365/9} - 1.0 = 8.835\%$

4.

(A) Discount	(B) Dollars	(C) % of Total	(A) × (C)
8.50%	$ 200	13 1/3	1.13333%
8.55	400	26 2/3	2.80000
8.56	600	40	3.42400
8.58	300	20	1.71600
	$1,500	100.00	8.55333%

Noncompetitive bidders receive the weighted average discount of 8.55 1/3%

$r = 8.864\%$ $r' = 9.163\%$

6. a. FM shares $= \$1{,}000 \div \$34.40 = 29.0698$ shares
PNH shares $= \$1{,}000 \div \$12.88 = 77.6398$ shares

b. FM load $= (\$34.40 \div \$33.37) - 1.0 = 3.09\%$
PNH load $=$ none

7. a. $(\$500 - \$10) \div 7 = \$70$ NAV

b. $\$10{,}000 \div \$70 = 142.857$ shares

8. After-tax return on:
Pref. Stock $= 9.2\% - 9.2\%\,(0.15)(0.45) = 8.58\%$
Corp. Bond $= 11.0\% - 11.0\%\,(0.45)\quad = 6.05\%$

9. a. Corporate bond $= 8\%\,(1 - 0.3) = 5.6\%$
This is better than 5% on the municipal bond.

b. $8\%\,(1 - X) = 5\%$; $X = 0.375$

12. a. 101 15/32 $= 101.468\%$ of Face Value

b. \$8 each November 30 through 2021
(assuming annual coupons)

c. outflow of \$10.2188 purchase price on June 3, 1992
inflow of \$100.0000 repayment on November 30, 2021

d. $10.2188\,(1 + R)^{29.5} = 100.00$
$R = [(9.7859)^{1/29.5} - 1] = 8.04\%$

e. Value of Principal plus Interest $= \$101.4688$
minus Value of Principal $\qquad \underline{10.2188}$
equals Value of Coupons $\qquad \$\ 91.2500$

f. Buy the coupon strip since it is undervalued. To create a risk-free arbitrage, you would also buy the stripped principal and (short) sell the actual bond. Short selling is discussed in Chapter 3.

Chapter 3

5. a.

	Per Share
Underwriter spread	$2.50
Out-of-pocket ($37,500 ÷ 50,000)	0.75
Price concession	2.00
Total	$5.25

7. b. $0.40 = \dfrac{\text{Price} \times 500 - 8{,}000}{\text{Price} \times 500}$

Price $= 26.67$

c. Assuming that the new cash is used to repay some of the loan balance: \$2,000

d. $0.4 = \dfrac{\$20(500 - N) - (\$8{,}000 - \$20N)}{\$20(500 - N)}$

$N = 250$ shares

9. a. $R_{Jennifer} = \dfrac{\$6{,}900 - \$5{,}000 + \$100}{\$5{,}000} = 40\%$

$R_{Jason} = \dfrac{100(\$69 - \$50 + \$1) - \$2{,}500(0.08)}{\$2{,}500}$

$= 72\%$

b. $R_{\text{Jennifer}} = \dfrac{\$3,900 - \$5,000 + \$100}{\$5,000} = -20\%$

$R_{\text{Jason}} = \dfrac{100(\$39 - \$50 + \$1) - \$200}{\$2,500} = -48\%$

c. The use of margin acts as "leverage" in that it magnifies any percentage profits or losses.

Chapter 5

2. a.

Year	Expected Inflation	1.0 + Geometric Average Inflation
1	4%	1.04
2	6%	$[(1.04)(1.06)]^{1/2} = 1.05$
3	8%	$[(1.04)(1.06)(1.08)]^{1/3} = 1.06$
4	5%	$[1.2501]^{1/4} = 1.0574$

From Eq (5.1)

Year	RF	Calculation
1	7.12%	$(1.03)(1.04) - 1$
2	8.15%	$(1.03)(1.05) - 1$
3	9.18%	$(1.03)(1.06) - 1$
4	8.91%	$(1.03)(1.0574) - 1$

b. From Eq (5.2)

Year	RF	Calculation
1	7.00%	$0.03 + 0.04$
2	8.00%	$0.03 + 0.05$
3	9.00%	$0.03 + 0.06$
4	8.74%	$0.03 + 0.0574$

c.

Year	Value	Calculation
1	\$93.35	$\$100 \div (1.0712)$
2	\$85.49	$\$100 \div (1.0815)^2$
3	\$76.84	$\$100 \div (1.0918)^3$
4	\$71.08	$\$100 \div (1.0891)^4$

4. Nominal return $= (100 / 90) - 1 = 11.11\%$

Real return $= (1.1111 / 1.05) - 1 = 5.82\%$
or $= 11.11\% - 5\% = 6.11\%$
(approximate Fisher Equat)

6. a. $(-20 + 30 + 5 + 15 - 4) \div 5 = 5.2\%$
b. $[(0.8)(1.3)(1.05)(1.15)(0.96)]^{1/5} - 1.0 = 3.81\%$

d.

0	1	2	3	4	5
1.0000	0.8000	1.0400	1.0920	1.2558	1.2056

e. Geometric mean from 2 through 5
$[1.2056 \div 1.04]^{1/3} - 1.0 = 5.05\%$

f.

Period	1	2	3	4	5
Return	-20	30	5	15	-4
Squared Difference From Average	635.04	615.04	0.04	96.04	85.64

Sum of Squared differences 1430.8

Variance $= 1430.8 \div (5 - 1) = 357.7$
Standard Deviation $= (357.7)^{1/2} = 18.91$

9.

	T-Bills	C-Bonds	Stocks
Expected Return	3.00%	4.60%	10.00%
Variance	1.60%	6.60%	250.00%
Std. Dev.	1.26%	2.58%	15.81%

10. (Note: The Cumulative Normal Distribution Appendix must be used in this question.)

	T-Bills	C-Bonds	S&P Stocks	EAFE
	Z-Scores $=$ (Return $-$ Average) $\div$ Std. Dev.			
Return				
-25%	-13.00	-2.96	-2.23	-1.77
-10%	-7.00	-1.66	-1.33	-1.12
0%	-3.00	-0.80	-0.72	-0.68
10%	1.00	0.06	-0.12	-0.25
20%	5.00	0.92	0.48	0.19
30%	9.00	1.78	1.08	0.62
50%	17.00	3.51	2.29	1.49
	Probability of a Return Below			
Return				
-25%	0.0	0.0015	0.0129	0.0384
-10%	0.0	0.0485	0.0918	0.1314
0%	0.0013	0.2119	0.2358	0.2483
10%	0.8413	0.5239	0.4522	0.4013
	Probability of a Return Above			
0%	0.9987	0.7881	0.7642	0.7517
10%	0.1587	0.4761	0.5478	0.5987
20%	0.0	0.1788	0.3156	0.4247
30%	0.0	0.0375	0.1401	0.2676
50%	0.0	0.0	0.0110	0.0681

11.

%-tile	0.05	0.10	0.25	0.50	0.75	0.90	0.95
Z-Score	-1.64	-1.28	-0.67	0.00	0.67	1.28	1.64
Return	-46.6%	-32.2%	-7.8%	19.0%	45.8%	70.2%	84.6%

Chapter 6

3. a.

	S&P 500	Lehman	EAFE
Average	13.76	9.60	22.20
Std. Dev.	13.30	5.39	33.60

b.

Correlations:

	S&P 500	Lehman	EAFE
S&P 500	1.00		
Lehman	0.66	1.00	
EAFE	0.44	0.36	1.00

c. Standard Deviation of an equally weighted portfolio:

$[(1/3)^2(13.30)^2 + (1/3)^2(5.39)^2 + (1/3)^2(33.60)^2 \leftarrow$ sum of variances
$+ (1/3)(1/3)(13.30)(5.39)(0.66) \quad \leftarrow$ covariance SP and Lehman
$+ (1/3)(1/3)(13.30)(33.60)(0.44) \leftarrow$ covariance SP and EAFE
$+ (1/3)(1/3)(5.39)(33.60)(0.36)]^{1/2} \leftarrow$ covariance Lehman and EAFE
$= 14.73$

Or calculate based on portfolio returns:
$\{[(34.67 - 15.19)^2 + (10.80 - 15.19)^2 + \cdots +$
$(-6.03 - 15.19)^2] \div (5 - 1)\}^{1/2} = 14.73$

   d. $(13.30 + 5.39 + 33.60) \div 3 = 17.43$
   The actual portfolio standard deviation is less because the security returns are not perfectly correlated.

4. a.

Year	Return	Year	Return
1	15.00%	6	4.62%
2	−4.55	7	12.69
3	−4.00	8	−17.14
4	34.44	9	33.18
5	16.52	10	11.79

   b. Average = 10.26
   Std. Dev. = 16.28 (using N−1 = 9 observations)

7. a. $[(0.25)(64) + (0.25)(100) + 2(0.5)(0.5)(8)(10)(0.5)]^{1/2}$
   $= 7.81\%$

   b. 5.21%

   c. From Eq (6.8)
   $X_1 = [144 - (8)(12)(0.5)] \div [64 + 144 - 2(8)(12)(0.5)]$
   $= 0.857$ (and $X_3 = 0.143$)

   d. $X_2 = 0.5454$ and $X_3 = 0.4546$

8. From Eq (6.14)

	$X_i\sigma_i^2$	covariance with A	B	C	Total Risk(i)
A	25.0	—	14.4	21.0	60.40
B	57.6	9.0	—	37.8	104.40
C	78.75	15.0	43.2	—	136.95

$\sigma_p^2 = 0.25(60.40) + 0.40(104.40) + 0.35(136.95)$
   $= 104.7925$
$\sigma_p = 10.2368$

9. a.

Bonds	Stock	E(R)	Std. Dev.	E(R) − RF ÷ Std. Dev.
1.0	0.0	5.0%	8.00%	0.1250
0.9	0.1	5.7%	7.35%	0.2311
0.8	0.2	6.4%	7.07%	0.3395
0.7	0.3	7.1%	7.18%	0.4315
0.6	0.4	7.8%	7.68%	0.4946
0.5	0.5	8.5%	8.50%	0.5294
0.4	0.6	9.2%	9.55%	0.5444
0.3	0.7	9.9%	10.77%	0.5478 optimal
0.2	0.8	10.6%	12.11%	0.5452
0.1	0.9	11.3%	13.52%	0.5398
0.0	1.0	12.0%	15.0%	0.5333

   b. If risk-free T-bills were not available, then a 100% investment in bonds would be reasonable for very risk averse investors. However, with risk-free T-bills, a 100% investment in bonds does not make sense since a higher risk return relationship is possible by combining T-bills with the optimal portfolio shown above. Notice that a 100% investment in stock will also not make sense when a risk-free security is available.

   c. Optimal risky portfolio consists of 30% in bonds and 70% in stocks.

   d. $E(R_p) = 0.04 + \sigma_p [(0.099 - 0.04) / 0.1077]$
   $= 0.04 + \sigma_p [0.5478]$

   e. For an E(R) of 6.6%:
   $0.066 = 0.04 + \sigma_p (0.5478)$
   $\sigma_p = 0.026/0.5478 = 0.0475$
   X (optimal) $= 0.0475/0.1077 = 0.4407$
   X (risk-free) $= 1.0 - 0.4407 = 0.5593$
   Invest 44.07% in the optimal combination of bonds and stocks, with the remaining 55.93% in T-bills.

   For an E(R) = 12.32%, invest 141.02% of your money in the optimal bond/stock portfolio and borrow at the risk-free rate an amount equal to 41.02% of your funds.

   For an E(R) = 7.0%, invest 50.85% in the optimal risky asset portfolio and the remaining 49.15% in the risk-free security.

   f. σ = 5.0%; X (optimal) = 46.43% and X (risk-free) = 53.57%
   σ = 20%; X (optimal) = 185.7% and borrow (short sell T-bills) equal to 85.7% of your capital

11. In a situation where you cannot identify any differences between the securities, the optimal policy is to invest an equal percentage in all (risky) securities.

Chapter 7

1. True. The only portfolios that can be *perfectly* correlated with the Market portfolio must be some combination of the Market portfolio and the risk-free security.

5. If portfolio XYZ has an expected return and standard deviation which is identical to that available from owning some combination of the risk-free security and the Market portfolio, then an investment *solely* in XYZ might make sense. If the risk-return combination of XYZ lies below the CML, then XYZ should be held only in combination with other securities (so that the combination results in holdings identical to the Market portfolio).

There are a number of ways to test whether XYZ sits on the CML. Question 1 above showed that this is the case if XYZ returns are perfectly correlated with the Market portfolio. When the correlation coefficient between XYZ and the Market portfolio is calculated, it rounds to 1.0. Thus XYZ is on the CML and would represent an optimal portfolio to hold for investors who desire its level of risk.

6. Port σ

1	7% = 0.7(10%)
2	15% = 1.5(10%)

Notice that Beta is the same thing as the percentage invested in the Market portfolio.

7. a. Port $[E(R) - RF] / \sigma$

1	0.667	
2	0.667	
3	0.875	optimal
4	0.846	
5	0.778	

b. $E(R) = 6.0\% + 4.0\% [0.875] = 9.5\%$; No

c. $16.5\% = 6.0\% + 12.0\% [0.875]$
Borrow 50% and invest 150% of IDC capital in Portfolio 3 above.

8. Security 2 has the greatest systematic risk since it has a σ equal to security 1 but a greater correlation with the Market portfolio. Security 1 has the least systematic risk, since it has a smaller σ than security 3.

9. Beta $= [40(-0.3)] / 20 = -0.6$
$E(R) = 5.0\% + (-0.6)(5.0\%) = 2.0\%$
$P_0 = (70 + 4) / 1.02 = 72.549$

10. a., b. and **c.**

Security	Beta	Next Period	E(R)
Mesa	1.6409	lower	20.4863%
An-Busch	0.3663	higher	11.5641%
Teledyne	1.3402	lower	18.3814%
XYZ	1.1488	lower	17.0416%
Index	1.0000	same	16.0000%

d. CML Equation: $E(R) = 9.0\% + \sigma_p (7.0\% / 4.3\%)$

Security	E(R) if held alone
Mesa	32.9% = 9.0% + 14.7% [1.6279]
An-Busch	19.3%
Teledyne	27.4%
XYZ	17.5%

e. Beta of Portfolio of the stocks:
$1/5(1.64) + 1/5(0.37) + 1/5(1.34) + 1/5(1.15) + 1/5(1.0)$

11. a., b. and **c.**

Security	E(R)	E(R) Given Market	Residual
i	15.5%	8.0% + 1.5(2.0%)	15% − 11%
		= 11.0%	= 4.0%
j	13.0%	10.0%	1.0%

e. $\sigma_p^2 = B_p^2 \sigma_M^2 + \sigma_e^2$
$400 = 2.25(\sigma_M^2) + 100$
$\sigma_M^2 = 133.33$ and $\sigma_M = 11.55\%$

12. a. Plan 1 is the riskiest since it consists solely of stocks

b. 7.0%

c. Pursue the low risk Plan 3. Speculative.

13. a. Fund 1 is most correlated with Market (highest R^2)

b. Fund 2 (highest Beta)

c. Fund 2 (highest Beta and Residual risk)

d. For Fund 1; $(1.0098)^4 - 1.0 = 3.98\%$

14. a.

	Campbell	Teledyne	DFA	W5000
alpha	1.65%	3.14%	0.92%	0.00%
beta	0.281	−0.116	1.125	1.00
R^2	4.44%	0.25%	75.2%	100%
σ	4.86%	8.47%	4.72%	3.64%

b. DFA is a mutual fund and owns many stocks. Thus, it has lower diversifiable risk.

c.

	Systematic Variance	Unsystematic Variance
Camp.	$(0.281)^2(3.64)^2 = 1.0462$	$(4.86)^2 - 1.0462$
Tele.	$(-0.116)^2(3.64)^2 = 0.1783$	$(4.86)^2 - 0.1783$
DFA	$(1.125)^2(3.64)^2 = 16.769$	$(4.86)^2 - 16.769$

Chapter 8

2. a. $E(R) = 0.5 + 1.0(10) + (-0.35)(3)$
$\sigma^2 = (1.0)^2(225) + (-0.35)^2(100)$
$\quad + (0.5)^2(19.4)^2 + (0.5)^2(27.5)^2$
$\quad = 520.4025$
$\sigma = 22.81$

8. a. Factors 2 and 3 are best thought of as firm, unique factors in this example. In a broadly diversified portfolio the positive and negative values net to zero.

b. Per APT the expected returns should be:

$E(R_1) = 6.0(3) = 18.0\%$
$E(R_2) = 1.5(3) = 4.5\%$

Per actual market conditions, expected returns are:

$E(R_1) = (45 / 40) - 1.0 = 12.5\%$
$E(R_2) = (10.7 / 10) - 1.0 = 7.0\%$

Stock 1 is overvalued and stock 2 is undervalued.

Transaction	$	Factor Score
Sell 1.0 Stock 1	$ 40	(6)
But 4.0 Stock 2	$(40)	6
Net	$ 0	0

Chapter 9

5. $C_0 = \$100,000 - \$90,000/1.1 + \$1,000$
$\quad = \$19,181.81$

6. Buy Nd1 units of the stock and sell 1.0 calls

7. This data can be analyzed either mathematically using the Put Call Parity Model and the Futures valuation equation or by a plot of the date T outcomes from different positions. But a short position in 1.0 call plus a short position in 1.0 put plus a long position in 1.0 future is risk-free with a positive $2 cash flow at the date of the transaction.

Cash Flows at Date

		Expiration Date T		
Position	Today	$P_S < \$100$	$P_S > \$100$	Explanation
Buy 1 future	$0	($100)	($100)	Pay contracted amt
Sell 1 call	10	—	$100	Owner exercises and you receive P_X
Buy 1 put	(8)	$100	—	You exercise put and receive P_X

8. a. We will use three possible values of the spot index to illustrate this answer.

	Position Value (in millions)		
	Spot = $200	Spot = $300	Spot = $400
Stock	$60.0	$90.0	$120.0
Dividends	3.6	3.6	3.6
T-bills	54.0	54.0	54.0
Futures profit or (loss)	33.6	3.6	(26.4)
Net	151.2	151.2	151.2

b.

	Position Value (in millions)	
	Spot = 250	Spot = 350
T-bills	$97.2	$97.2
Futures profit or (loss)	(18.6)	11.4
Net	78.6	108.6

If $90 million in stock had been purchased:

Stock	75.0	105.0
Dividends	3.6	3.6
Net	78.6	108.6

c. Sell $3,000,000 ÷ $300 = 10,000 futures contracts

9. a. In theory; C − P = Spot − PV of Exercise
= $300 − $300 ÷ 1.08
= $22.32

In the market; C − P = $26.67. So the call is overvalued relative to the put.

b. Illustrative arbitrage assuming two Spot values at Exp.:

	At Expiration		
	Today	Spot = 200	Spot = 400
Sell 1 Call	$41.67	—	($100.00)
Buy 1 Put	(15.00)	$100.00	—
Buy Stock	(300.00)	200.00	400.00
Sell T-bills	273.33	(295.20)	(295.20)
Net	$0.00	$4.80	$4.80

c. d1 = 0.4452 (say 0.45)   Nd1 = 0.6736
d2 = 0.1950 (say 0.20)   Nd2 = 0.5793

C = (300)(0.6736) − (300/e^{0.08})(0.5793)
= 41.65

d.

	Value (in mills) at T by Spot Level			
	100	200	300	400
Stock	$30	$60	$90	$120
Puts	60	30	—	—
Net	90	90	90	120

e.

	Value (in mills) at T by Spot Level			
	100	200	300	400
T-bills	$90	$90	$90	$90
Calls	—	—	—	26.798
Net	90	90	90	116.798

f. Buying puts provided the greater value since they were undervalued relative to the call. (Since part c indicates that the calls are fairly valued, the puts were undervalued— regardless of the call value.)

Chapter 11

2. a. YTM_A = 8.9975% YTM_B = 7.0038%
YTM_C = 7.0055%

b. Bond C has the lower coupon and thus the lower effective tax rate if ordinary rates are higher than capital gains rates. In that case, equilibrium would occur only when the (before tax) yield to maturity on Bond C is lower than on Bond B.

c. Bond C; it has the longest maturity and lowest coupon.

d. Bond C; lower coupon.

e. P_A = 960.17; P_B = 1,294.07; P_C = 852.43

8. $f_{Mt} = f_{1,5} = [(1.09)^6 / (1.087)^5] - 1.0 = 10.51\%$

9. a. $f_{1,6} = [(1.09)^6 / (1.08)^5] - 1.0 = 14.14\%$

b. $f_{2,6} = [(1.095)^7 / (10.8)^5]^{1/2} - 1.0 = 13.34\%$

10. $f_{15,5} = [(1.08)^{20} / (1.085)^5]^{1/15} - 1.0 = 7.83\%$

	Date		
Transaction	0	5	20
Buy 1.0 20-Year	(214,548)	—	1,000.00
Short Sell 0.3226 5-Year	214.548	(322.60)	—
Net	—	(322.68)	1,000.00

11. a.

Transaction	Date		
	0	1	2
Buy 1.0 2-Year	(873.00)		1,000.00
Sell 0.94 1-Year	873.00	(942.76)	
873 / 926 = 0.94276			
Net	—	(942.76)	1,000.00

b. Return = (1,000.00 / 942.76) − 1.0 = 6.07%

c. No. Do the opposite.

12. a. IRR = 9.3%

$$\$1,120 = \frac{\$120}{1.093} + \frac{\$120}{1.093^2} + \frac{\$120}{1.093^3}$$

$$+ \frac{\$120}{1.093^4} + \frac{\$120}{1.093^5} + \frac{\$1,120}{1.093^6}$$

b. Yes, issue bonds at 8% and save 9%.

c. For years 1–4 you earn 12% on your investment of $1.000. In years 5–10 you earn 8%. In addition, you receive $120 in call premium which earns 8% in years 5–10. Thus, your end-of-year 10 portfolio value would be:

$1,000 \ (1.12)^4(1.08)^6 = \$2,496.97$

$120 \ (1.08)^6 \quad = \quad \underline{\quad 190.42}$

Total end of Year 10 = $2,687.39

Return = $2.68739^{1/10} − 1.0 = 10.39\%$

13. a. YTM after tax on Corporate = 8%(1 − 0.3) = 5.6%
YTM after tax on Municipal = 6.0%

b. Breakeven YTM on Corporate = 6% / (1 − 0.3) = 8.5714%

c. Not if "muni's" are tax sheltered.

14. a. d1 = 2.5349 (say 2.53); d2 = 2.4694 (say 2.47)
Nd1 = 0.9943   Nd2 = 0.9932

C = 0.9943(110) − (100 / $e^{0.08}$) (0.9932) = 17.6891 mill.

b. 110 − 17.6891 = 92.3109 mill.

c. YTM = (100 / 92.3109) − 1.0 = 8.33%
Default risk premium is about 0.33%
("about" since the 8% rate is a continuous compound rate and the 8.33% is a discrete end-of-year compound rate)

d. Assuming that the higher expected return does not lead to a higher asset value, the default premium would increase (equity call value increase also) due to greater asset risk. This is the most likely event if asset prices are efficiently priced. However, if management is able to purchase undervalued assets, the firm's asset value would increase, and it is difficult to determine the net change in the default premium on deposits.

Chapter 12

1. a. $P_A = 1,000$ $P_B = 1,013.76$

b. Short sell bond B and buy equal dollar amount of bond A.

2.

Period	$	PV	%	× Period	=	Product
1	40	38.10	4.07%	× 1	=	0.0407
2	40	36.28	3.88	× 2	=	0.0776
3	40	34.55	3.69	× 3	=	0.1107
4	40	32.91	3.52	× 4	=	0.1408
5	40	31.34	3.35	× 5	=	0.1675
6	40	29.85	3.19	× 6	=	0.1914
7	40	28.43	3.04	× 7	=	0.2128
8	1,040	703.91	75.25	× 8	=	6.0200
Total		935.37	100.0			6.9615

Duration in years = 6.9615 / 2 = 3.481 years

3. −7.3[(1.11 − 1.12) / 1.12] = −6.52%

5. a. D = 0.1(1) + 0.2(3) + 0.1(5) + 0.2(7) + 0.4(12)
= 7.4 years

b. −7.4[(1.10 − 1.09) / 1.09] = −6.79%

6. First, find the purchase price:

$$\text{Price} = \sum_{t=1}^{10} \frac{90}{1.1^t} + \frac{1,000}{1.1^{10}} = 938.55$$

Next, find end of year-3 value:

End of Year Coupon	1	2	3	End of Year Value
3			90	90.000
2		90 × 1.08		97.200
1	90 × 1.08²			104.976
Price at end of year 3				1,052.060
Total value end of year 3				1,344.236

Annualized return = $(1,344.236 / 938.55)^{1/3} − 1.0$
= 12.72%

Price risk was most important here since the bond was sold prior to maturity.

7. Annualized return = $[(1.1)(1.08)(1.08)]^{1/3} − 1.0$
= 8.66%

The risk in this case is reinvestment risk. Your return was lower than 10% because reinvestment rates declined.

11. a. Required end of year 4 value:

$50 million × 1.1^4 = $73.205 million

Present worth of $73.205 million at the 11.5% immunizable rate

$73.205 / 1.115^4 = $47.3632

Maximum immediate loss and still be able to provide $73.205

($50.000 − $47.3632) = $2.6368

b. $60.0 (1.11)^3 = $82.0579

You need not immunize.

d. A portfolio of $50 million initially immunized at 11.5% would grow to $77.28 million in four years.

$50.0(1.115)^4 = $77.28

Yes, you have "added value."

Chapter 13

5. a. Annual dividend growth = ($5.00 / $2.54)^{1/10} − 1.0
= 7.00%

K = 6% + 1.5(4%) = 12%

Fair Value Price = [$5.00(1.07)] / (0.12 − 0.07)
= $107.00

b. Dividend Yield = $5.35 / $107.00 = 5.0%
Capital Appreciation = Growth rate = 7.0%

6.   G = 0.60 [(10%)(1.25)] = 0.6[12.5%] = 7.5%

K = 8% + 1.3(5%) = 14.5%

Price = [$2.50(1.075)] / (0.145 − 0.075) = $38.39

Since the stock is trading for $45, short sell it.

7. a. ROE = 4(2%)(2.0) = 16%
b. G = 16%(0.25) = 4.0%
c. K = 8% + 1.5(6%) = 17%

Fair Value Price = [$3.00(1.04)] / (0.17 − 0.04)
= $24.00

8.   Growth rate implied in today's price = 7.5%

9.   Required return implied in today's price = 12.06%

10. a. $P = \dfrac{$3.60}{1.18} + \dfrac{$4.32}{1.18^2} + \dfrac{$5.184}{1.18^3}$

$+ \dfrac{$5.184(0.95)}{0.18 − (−0.05)} \dfrac{1}{1.18^3} = 22.34

b. $P_3 = \dfrac{$5.184(0.95)}{0.18 − (−0.05)} = 21.41

$P_4 = \dfrac{$5.184(0.95)(0.95)}{0.18 − (−0.05)} = 20.34

Chapter 15

2. a. Pay $977,875 per contract or $4,889,375 for five contracts in late June.

b. At $2,000 per contract, $10,000 is initial margin.

c. At $1,500 maintenance margin per contract, you may lose up to $500 per contract. At $25 per basis point, this means discounts can rise by 20 basis points. Thus, the discount at which a maintenance margin call begins to take effect would be 9.05%.

d. Selling price at an 8.95% discount = $977,625. Your loss will be $250 per contract ($977,625 − $977,875) or 10 basis points times $25 per basis point.

e. Expected profit or loss will be zero.

f. First, find the effective 90-day yield = R_{90}.

$R_{90} = (100 ÷ 97.785) − 1.0 = 2.26%$

This is a 90-day T-bill, so the dollar duration will be:

$(90 ÷ 365) [(0.0326 − 0.0226) ÷ 1.0226] $4,889,375$
$= $11,790$

3.   Net spot price = spot price − futures profit
$95.75   = $99.75   − $4.00

4.   90-day forward rate available in the spot market is:

$1 + R_{180} = 100 ÷ 98.50 = 1.015228$

$1 + R_{90} = 100 ÷ 99.25 = 1.007557$

forward rate = (1.015228 ÷ 1.007557) − 1.0
= 0.7613%

Future's return = (100 ÷ 99) − 1.0 = 1.0101%

Arbitrage: Buy future, sell 180-day T-bill and buy 90-day T-bill. Do this in quantities so that the initial cash flow is zero and the amount received on the spot T-bills at day 90 is equal to the value of futures purchased.

5. a. 8.00%. Since they are maturing, they should sell at a price identical to spot T-bills.

b. Forward rate in spot market between day 270 and 360:

$P_{270} = 100 − 100(0.084)(270 ÷ 360) = 93.70$
$P_{360} = 91.40$

$1 + R_{270} = 100 ÷ 93.70 = 1.06724$
$1 + R_{360} = 100 ÷ 91.40 = 1.09409$

Forward$_{270−360}$ = (1.09409 ÷ 1.06724) − 1.0 = 0.02516

Price of futures due in 270 days:
$100 ÷ 1.02516 = 97.5457$

Discount on futures due in 270 days:
Dollar discount = 100 − 97.5457 = 2.4543
Discount percent quotation = 2.4543(360 ÷ 90) = 9.817%

9.

Realized Future Trading Price	=	Initial Spot	+	Initial Basis	−	Cover Basis
973.75	=	978.75	+	(1,025 − 978.75)	−	51.25

Gain or Loss:

Sell spot	973.75
Buy spot	−978.75
Loss	−5.00 per $1,000 par

or −$5.00 times 5,000 ($1,000) par bonds = −$25,000

12. $105 = $100 (3 ÷ 2)0.7

15. a. Dollar duration of portfolio addition:

$6.0[(0.11 - 0.10) \div 1.10] \$100$ million $= \$5.4545$ mill.

Dollar duration of cheapest to deliver:

$(6.5 \div 0.9) [(0.11 - 0.10) \div 1.1] \$100,000 = \$6,565.66$

Number of T-bond futures to buy:

$\$5,454,545 \div \$6,565.66 = 830.77$ contracts

18. a. Number of spot units now owned:

$\$1$ billion $\div (\$113 * 500) = 19,469$

Number of spot units desired to own:
$\$0.9$ billion $\div (\$113 * 500) = 15,929$

# contracts to *sell*	3,540

19. $F = \$400(1.0428) - \$8 = \$409.12$
Futures are overvalued.

21. a. Price of T-bill $= 100 - 100(0.08)(90 \div 360) = 98$

$1 + 90$ day T-bill Return $= 100 \div 98 = 1.02041$

$F = 300(1.02041) - 3 = 303.12$
market price is too high

b.

Today	$0	$ At Delivery
Sell 666 2/3 Futures (1)	—	$108.000 mill
Buy 666 2/3 Spot	(100 mill)	
Sell T-bills (2)	100 mill	($102.041 mill)

At Delivery		
Receive dividends (3)		1.000 mill
Buy futures and sell spot		a wash
Net	0.0	6.959 mill

(1) 100 million $\div$ (300 * 500) = 666 2/3 contracts
(2) 100 million (1.02041)   = 102.041 million
(3) (666 2/3 * 500) 3.00   =   1.000 million

c. Number of stock units held:

(250 million * 1.1) $\div$ (300 * 500) = 1,833 1/3

Number of stock units desired:

(300 million * 1.0) $\div$ (300 * 500) = 2,000.00

# contracts to *buy*	= 166 2/3

Chapter 16

1. a. through **d.**

	$40	$45	$50	$55	$60
	Expiration date cash flows				
Buy 1.0 call	0	0	0	−50	−50
Write 1.0 call	0	0	0	50	50
Buy 1.0 put	50	50	0	0	0
Write 1.0 put	−50	−50	0	0	0

	$40	$45	$50	$55	$60
	Expiration date investment values				
Buy 1.0 call	0	0	0	5	10
Write 1.0 call	0	0	0	−5	−10
Buy 1.0 put	10	5	0	0	0
Write 1.0 put	−10	−5	0	0	0

	$40	$45	$50	$55	$60
	Expiration date net profits				
Buy 1.0 call	−8	−8	−8	−3	2
Write 1.0 call	8	8	8	3	−2
Buy 1.0 put	9	4	−1	−1	−1
Write 1.0 put	−9	−4	1	1	1

3.

Sell call option	$8
Buy stock	(70)
Receive cash when exercised	65
Net cash to you	$3

4. a. $C - P = 75 - 70 \div 1.1^{4/12} = 7.19$ in theory
$C - P = 7 - 2 \qquad\qquad = 5$ in market

Thus the call is undervalued relative to the put.

b. Illustration for spot at expiration of $60 and $80:

	Today	$60	$80
Buy 1.0 Call	(7)	—	10.00
Sell 1.0 Put	2	(10.00)	—
Sell 1.0 Stock	75	(60.00)	(80.00)
Net	70	(70.00)	(70.00)
Buy T-bills	(70)	72.26	72.26
Total	0	2.26	2.26

5. a. $C = \$74 - (\$65 \div 1.1) + \$5.09 = \$20$

b.

Long Stock:	Short Stock:
Buy 1.0 call at C	Sell 1.0 call at C
Buy debt worth X $\div$ (1 + RF)	Sell debt
Sell 1.0 put at P	Buy 1.0 put at P

c.

Write Put:
Buy 1.0 call
Short sell 1.0 stock
Buy debt worth X $\div$ (1 + RF)

6.

Buy warehouse	$1.0000 mill.
Borrow 1-year debt	0.9174 (1.0 $\div$ 1.09)
Buy insurance	0.0100
Call cost	0.1926 mill.

7.

	Value at Expiration		
	High = 80	Low = 50	Range
1.0 share	$80	$50	$30
1.0 call	20	0	20

For each 1.0 call traded, trade 2/3 share of stock.

Buy 2/3 share	53.33	33.33
Write 1.0 call	(20.00)	—
Net	33.33	33.33

So: $2/3(\$60) - \$10.23 = \$33.33 \div (1 + RF)$ and RF = 11.96%

10. a.

	Call A	Call B	Call C	Call D
d1	0.70	0.25	−0.14	0.08
d2	0.40	−0.05	−0.44	−0.35
N(d1)	0.7580	0.5987	0.4443	0.5319
N(d2)	0.6554	0.4800	0.3300	0.3632
Call	16.12	10.62	6.72	11.77

$P = 0.3446[70 \div (e^{0.12*0.25})] - 0.242(80) = 4.05$

b. $P = -80 + [70 \div (e^{0.12*0.25})] + 16.12 = 4.05$

12. a. PV of Div $= [1 \div (e^{0.12*0.25})] + [1 \div (e^{0.12*0.5})] = 1.91$

Stock value to use in Call Option Model:
$= 65 - 1.91 = 63.09$

Call value $= 10.45$

14. Standard deviation of continuous returns $= 8.22\%$

15. The calls should have identical ISD values. Since call A has the smaller ISD, its price is undervalued relative to call B. Buy 1.0 call A and write 0.8 call B (0.4 / 0.5).

Chapter 17

1. a. Inflation in Canada $= 2.08\ 1/3\%$

b. 0.72—the current 6-month forward rate

c. decrease, higher expected inflation in the United States than in Canada

d. 12.11%

2. $R_{Japan} = 20\%$; $R_{US} = 5\%$

3. a. $E(I_{US}) = 5.0\%$

b. 10.29%

c. 13.6%

4. a. no

b.

Dollars	$1,000,000	
times M/$	1.4286	
Marks	1,428.571M	
times £/M	0.5000	
Pounds	714,286	
times $/£	1.9000	
Dollars	$1,357,143	

7.

	Year				
	1986	1987	1988	1989	1990
R_X	26.98%	30.77%	−2.84%	−12.66%	6.35%

8.

Local Return	Exchange Rate Return		
	14.29%	0.00%	−11.11%
−15.00%	−2.86	−15.00	−24.44
10.00%	25.71	10.00	−2.22
35.00%	54.29	35.00	20.00

10. a. $E(R_{UK}) = 23.9\%$ $E(R_F) = 15.2\%$

b. $\sigma^2_{UK} = 1.0(30^2) + 1.0(10^2) + 2(30)(10)(0.30) = 1,180$
$\sigma_{UK} = 34.35$ $\sigma_F = 36.40$

11. $E(R_p) = 15\%$ $\sigma_p = 22.22\%$

Chapter 19

6. a.

	Pess.	Expected	Opt.
G	7.25%	8.50%	9.60%
K	13.00%	13.50%	14.00%
D_0	50.00	46.08	44.00
D_1	53.63	50.00	48.22
Price	932	1,000	1,095

8. a.

	E(R)	Std. Dev.
A	4.0%	3.57%
B	7.5%	14.27%

e.

	10th	25th	50th	75th	90th
TW	$0.9671	$1.1749	$1.4450	$1.8018	$2.1890
G	−0.67%	3.28%	7.79%	12.50%	16.96%

11. a.

	30-Year Percentile Outcomes				
	10th	25th	50th	75th	90th
TW	$4.1308	$6.5945	$11.0232	$18.4260	$29.4154
G	4.84%	6.49%	8.33%	10.20%	11.93%

d.

	1-Year Percentile Outcomes				
	10th	25th	50th	75th	90th
TW	$0.9056	$0.9863	$1.0833	$1.1898	$1.2959
G	−9.44%	−1.37%	8.33%	18.98%	29.59%

Chapter 20

1. a. NAV $= (1,230 - 15) \div 32 = 37.9688$

c. NAV $= (1,230 + 19 - 15) \div 32 = 38.5625$
or increase by $19 \div 32 = 0.5938$

d. Since interest accrued is already part of the fund's asset market value, the interest receipt will have no affect on NAV.

e. $37.9688 - 0.40 = 37.5688$

f. 37.5688 (shareholder dividends are reinvested at NAV)

Chapter 21

2. Arithmetic Average Return =
$(20 - 12 + 15 + 3) \div 4 = 6.5\%$

Geometric Average Return =
$(1.2 * 0.88 * 1.15 * 1.03)^{1/4} - 1 = 5.75\%$

3.   Find R in:

$$10,000 = \sum_{t=1}^{8} \frac{-1,000}{(1 + R)^t} + \frac{25,000}{(1 + R)^8}$$

R = 5.455% per quarter
or 23.67% per year: $1.05455^4 - 1.0 = 0.2367$

The 23.67% return is a dollar weighted return. The 20% return reported by the investment manager is probably a time weighted return.

4. a.

Period	(1 + R)
May 30–June 15	$10 \div 15$ = 0.6666
June 15–June 30	$36,360 \div 20,000$ = 1.818

Full month = $(0.6666)(1.818) - 1.0 = 21.19\%$

b. Find R in:

$$15,000 = \frac{-10,000}{(1 + R)} + \frac{36,360}{(1 + R)^2}$$

$= 25.89\%$ per 15-day interval

or $1.2589^2 - 1.0 = 58.48\%$ monthly

7. $8.5\% = 3.0\% + B_T (8.0\% - 3.0\%)$; so $B_T = 1.1$
$(B_a - 1.1)(8.0\% - 3.0\%) = 1.0\%$; so $B_a = 1.3$

8. a.

	AMF	Putnam
Sharpe	$2.58 \div 6.96 = 0.3707$	$1.64 \div 9.36 =$ 0.1752
Treynor	$2.58 \div 0.75 = 3.44$	$1.64 \div 1.00 =$ 1.64
Jensen	0.96	-0.49

c. AMF was more diversified as evidenced by the larger R^2.

d. Putnam has the greater systematic (Beta) risk.

9. a.

	McMaster	SP500	DJIA
Average	-3.39	-1.28	-1.78
Beta:			
SP500	0.89	1.00	NA
DJIA	0.73	NA	1.00
Standard Deviation	24.25	21.5	22.77
Sharpe	-0.1397	-0.059	-0.078
Treynor:			
SP500	-3.80	-1.27	NA
DJIA	-4.64	NA	-1.78

These values are based on excess returns and using (N-1) in standard deviation calculations.

Page numbers followed by t and f denote tables and figures, respectively.